BLUE GUIDE GREECE

W9-BWJ-044

Cover
Temple of Athena
Pronaos in Delphi

Bronze Warrior, from Riace, Italy. Perhaps by Pheidas, and part of the Marathon monument at Delphi (c 460 BC)

BLUE GUIDE

GREECE

Robin Barber

Maps and plans by John Flower

A & C Black
London

W W Norton
New York

Fifth edition 1987

Published by A & C Black (Publishers) Limited
35 Bedford Row, London WC1R 4JH

© A & C Black (Publishers) Limited 1988

Published in the United States of America by
W W Norton & Company, Incorporated
500 Fifth Avenue, New York, NY 10110

Published simultaneously in Canada by
Penguin Books Canada Limited
2801 John Street, Markham, Ontario LR3 1B4

Printed and bound in Great Britain by
William Clowes Limited, Beccles and London

British Library Cataloguing in Publication Data

Barber, Robin
    Greece.—5th ed.—(Blue guide)
    1. Greece—Description and travel—1981–
    —Guide-books
    I. Title   II. Rossiter, Stuart   III. Series
    914.95′0476   DF716

    ISBN 0–7136–2771–9

ISBN 0–393–30372–1   USA

PREFACE

This is the first edition of *Blue Guide Greece* to appear since the death of its original compiler, Stuart Rossiter. The only possible reaction of a new editor is one of immense admiration for his achievement. The fact that his work remains the core of the book is proof of its lasting value.

The pace of development in Greece in terms of new building and road construction has probably slowed since the previous (1981) edition but the rate of archaeological and historical discovery and publication has not: indeed, with the awakening of interest in previously neglected aspects of Greece's cultural history, whole new fields have become more readily accessible to the visitor. One can only sympathise however with the heroic struggles of the members of the understaffed and under-funded Greek Archaeological Service to meet the demands that are made on them.

The main changes in this fifth edition are the incorporation of new and the revision of old archaeological information and the addition of introductory material to reflect the new areas of interest referred to above. Thrace and Macedonia have been given more attention than other regions, since they have been a focus of recent archaeological investigation and, in any case, have not previously been given the space they deserve. The extent of detailed travel information has been somewhat modified—partly because it rapidly becomes outdated and partly because access to such information, via the sources given in the text, is now infinitely easier than a few years ago.

The preparation of this new edition owes a great deal to help given by others—in particular to Ann Thomas who checked most of the Athens section, researched a new entry for the Mani and, with unfailing good humour, answered frantic transcontinental requests for the most diverse and obscure pieces of information. I am also very conscious of my debt to Karin Skawran and Peter Lock, both of whom not only wrote new introductory chapters but also brought their considerable expertise and scholarship to bear on improving the coverage of monuments within their own areas of interest. Jane Cocking wrote the chapter on Folk Art and Katherine Kafopoulos the section on the *Ethnike Pinakotheke*, an important part of Athens' cultural make-up which is often neglected by visitors.

Otherwise the number of helpers is legion. Friends and colleagues, most often both, have given generously of their time and knowledge to correct or improve aspects of the Guide, particularly entries on sites or subjects of which they have specialist knowledge. Some names, I fear, may have been omitted from the throng but my sincere gratitude goes out to: Michael Angold, Norman Ashton, Lesley Beaumont, Geoffrey Graham Bell, Elinor Bevan, John Camp, Hector Catling, Jim Coulton, Katie Dhimakopoulou-Papantoniou, Bill Dinsmoor, Archie Dunn, C.R.B. Elliot, Lisa French, Olga Hadjianastasiou, Nikolaos Hadjiioannidhis, Kerin Hope, Klaus Kilian, Ursula Knigge, Theodore Koukoulis, James McCredie, Sandy MacGillivray, Toula Markettou, Chris Mee, Stephen Miller, Veronica Mitsopoulou, Takis and Lidha Moskhou, H. Mussche, K.M. O'Neill, Jane Rabnett, the Sachini family, Hugh Sackett, M. Karamanoli-Siganidhou, Jill Carington Smith, Babette Sigalas, J. Speyer, Paula Spitaels, Stavros Stavridhis, Bill Stewart, Photini Tomaï, Charles Williams, Dyffri Williams, Hector Williams, Penny Wilson, and Susan Young.

I am grateful to Mr P. Analytis, Miss D. Katsirea and the staff of the National Tourist Organisation of Greece in London for their generous assistance; to Tom Neville and Gemma Davies of A & C Black for encouragement and much practical help; to John Flower for producing new maps and plans and revising old ones, and to Pippa Geddes for wrestling with population statistics and hotel information.

Last, but by no means least, no writer of such a book could omit to mention those numerous denizens of Greece, and in particular the Greek countryside, whose warmth, generosity, wit and wisdom make visiting their country such an enjoyable, instructive and moving experience, and the writing of this Guide the same.

CONTENTS

8   CONTENTS

MAPS AND PLANS

EXPLANATIONS

The arrangement of this guide by routes conforms in every way to the past traditions of the series without innovations.

TYPE. The main routes are described in large type. Smaller type is used for branch-routes and excursions, for historical and preliminary paragraphs, and (generally speaking) for descriptions of minor importance.

DISTANCES (placed in front of the place-name) are given cumulatively from the starting-point of the route or sub-route in kilometres and miles; on diversions from a route (placed *after* the place-name), they are specific to that place from the point of divergence from the route. Road distances have been calculated where possible from the km posts on the roads themselves, otherwise from measurement on official maps; constant realignments make it certain that these distances will vary slightly from those measured by motorists on their milometers. A Greek asked a walking distance will always give the answer as a walking *time*. Archaeologists, however, invariably use metres and the site plans are accordingly scaled in metres.

ASTERISKS indicate points of special interest or excellence.

ABBREVIATIONS. In addition to generally accepted and self-explanatory abbreviations, the following occur in the Guide:
A', B' tou Protou (i.e. 'the first'), the second, etc.
A.J.A. American Journal of Archaeology
Akr.   Akroterion (i.e. Cape)
Ay.   Ayios, Ayia, etc. (Saint or Saints)
B.C.H. Bulletin de Correspondence Hellénique
B.S.A. Annual of the British School At Athens
c   circa
C   century
dr(s)   drachmas(s)
fl.   floruit
Hdt.   Herodotus
Hesp.   Hesperia
J.H.S. Journal of Hellenic Studies
Leof.   Leoforos (Avenue)
N.T.O. see below)
Od.   Odhos (Street)
Plat.   Plateia (Square)
R.   rooms
Rest.   restaurant
Rte   route
Thuc.   Thucydides

EOT (NTO)   Ελληνικός Οργανισμός Τουρισμού (National Tourist Organisation).
KTEA (KTEL) Κοινόν Ταμειον Εισπράξεων Λεωφορειων (Joint Pool of Bus Owners).
O.T.E.   Οργανισμός Τηλεπικοινωνιών Ελλάδος (Greek Telecommunications Organisation).

THE MONUMENTS OF ANCIENT GREECE

by *Nicolas Coldstream*

A. The Monuments in their Historical Setting

The Stone Age. The earliest vestige of man in Greece—earlier than the emergence of Homo Sapiens himself—consists of a fossilised skull of Neanderthal type found near Salonika. Of the more developed food-gathering culture of Palaeolithic Greece one can now get a clear impression from three cave sites in the Louros valley, Epirus: recent excavations there have revealed occupation going back to c 40,000 BC, and a Mousterian flint industry similar to those of Balkan Europe.

The first impulses towards farming, towards the domestication of animals, and towards the foundation of settled villages came to Greece from Anatolia. The oldest farming communities in Greece—and indeed in Europe—were centred round the fertile plains of Thessaly and Macedonia. An Early Neolithic settlement at Nea Niko-midhia near Veroia (7th–6th mill. BC) shows traces of large rectangular houses, and displays several links with Anatolia in its artefacts. The later stages of Neolithic culture are best represented at Sesklo and Dimini, both near the land-locked gulf of Pagasae. At Sesklo (6th– 5th mill. BC) the lack of fortifications and the manufacture of elegant painted and burnished pottery bear witness to a peaceful and flourishing agricultural civilisation, while the importation of obsidian from the island of Melos proves the existence of trade even at this remote period. The rectangular houses, with walls built of mud brick, were founded on a stone base which remains their only visible memorial to the visitor today. At the neighbouring village of Dimini (founded c 3400 BC) concentric rings of fortification reveal a more turbulent state of affairs; in these unsettled conditions the rise of centralised authority is suggested by the building of a spacious house on the summit of the mound, whose pillared porch, leading into the main hall, foreshadows the Mycenaean megaron.

The Early Bronze Age (c 2800–2000 BC). In the ensuing centuries, while Thessaly relapsed into provincialism, the centre of civilisation moved southward with the arrival of fresh influences from Anatolia (c 2800 BC). The inhabitants learned the use of copper, and spoke a pre-Hellenic language, to which some non-Greek features in Greek place names (such as -nth-and -ss-in Corinth, Knossos) are generally attributed. Most settlements of this period lay on the eastern seaboard of the Peloponnese and of Central Greece, in the Cyclades, and in Crete. On the mainland the most impressive Early Helladic site is at Lerna in the Argolid, where the imposing House of Tiles, evidently an important seat of administrative authority, is the earliest known building of monumental proportions in the Aegean area. Even more progressive was the Early Minoan culture of Crete, perhaps owing to its proximity to the advanced civilisations of the Near East: contact had already been established with the Old Kingdom of Egypt at the very beginning of the Bronze Age. Flourishing settlements grew up in the eastern part of the island, notably at Mokhlos, where craftsmen excelled in the production of jewellery and stone vases; at Vasiliki, whose surprisingly elaborate house-plans already look forward to the later palaces; and at Fournou Korifi, where a complete village of c 2600–2200 BC has recently been unearthed. In this period the Cyclades played an active rôle in exchanges with Crete and the mainland: hence come the well-known marble idols.

The Middle and Late Bronze Age: THE PALATIAL CIVILISATIONS OF CRETE AND MYCENAE (c 2000–1100 BC). Soon after 2000 BC the unity of the Aegean world was broken for several centuries. Invaders, usually identified with the first Greeks, swept over the mainland in two waves (c 2200 and c 2000 BC) destroying the main centres of Early Helladic civilisation: meanwhile the Minoans, who suffered no such disruption, gradually extended their influence over the Cyclades.

The focus of Cretan power now moved to the centre of the island, with the foundation of the three palaces at Knossos, Phaestos, and Mallia. The similarity of their layout, and their lack of effective defences suggest the growth of a single organised kingdom, which established a 'pax Minoica' in the Aegean by the exercise of an overwhelming supremacy at sea, unchallenged until the emergence of the Greek mainland as a world power in the 16C BC.

All three palaces were frequently rebuilt after periodical destructions by earthquake, reaching their most advanced form in the 16C BC; yet their basic plan was never radically altered, consisting of a vast network of rooms grouped asymmetrically round a central court, often rising to three storeys. This plan was reproduced on a more modest scale in a fourth palace built in c 1600 BC at Kato Zakro on the east coast. On a still smaller scale are the villas of the local gentry, spaced fairly evenly throughout the centre and east of the island (Tylissos, Sklavokambos, Amnisos, Nirou Khani, Myrtos, several near Siteia and especially Gournia where the residence is surrounded by a completely excavated Minoan town). The intricacy of Minoan palaces, which in the impressionable minds of later Greek visitors gave rise to the fanciful legend of the Labyrinth, was demanded by a monarchy that was at once theocratic and bureaucratic: all the reins of authority, whether political, religious, or commercial, were held within the palace walls (although Mallia has also places of public assembly outside the palace). The spaciousness of the state apartments and the secure privacy of the domestic quarters supplied the essential needs of princely dignity. Under the same roof, the most skilful artisans plied their crafts under royal supervision. The magazines, with their ordered rows of earthenware pithoi, stored the royal reserves of oil, wine, corn, and other commodities, whose management required the use of writing: at first a system of hieroglyphs was evolved (c 2000–1660 BC), gradually superseded by a more convenient syllabic script, Linear A (c 1900–1450 BC). Neither of these scripts can yet be read. Finally the presence of small shrines and purificatory areas within the palace reminds us that the Minoan king was also High Priest: the 'Throne Room' at Knossos was perhaps an inner sanctum whither the King could retire to hold converse with his god. Outside the palaces, villas and houses cults were also practised in sanctuaries on mountain peaks and in the numinous atmosphere of caves: in later times their memory was preserved by the association of the caves on Ida and Dicte with the birth and nurture of Zeus, originally the young consort of the Minoan mother-goddess.

By the beginning of the Late Bronze Age (c 1550 BC) the Minoans had attained the summit of their power. Minoan outposts had been planted in the Cyclades (notably at Phylakopi on Melos and at Akrotiri on Thera), on Kythera (Kastri), on Rhodes (Triandha), and at Miletus: Minoan wares had been exported to the markets of Cyprus, Syria, and Egypt: after c 1500 BC, Minoan emissaries began to appear in Egyptian tomb paintings of the XVIIIth Dynasty under the name of Keftiu, bearing costly gifts of friendship to the Pharaohs. On the Greek mainland, Minoan influence was probably confined to the artistic sphere; it is first seen in the astounding wealth of gold vessels, jewellery and weapons in the shaft graves at Mycenae (c 16C BC), and continues in the rich offerings of the 15C tombs at Vapheio and in the Pylos area. The Minoan style was frequently adapted to scenes of war and hunting—subjects that were foreign to Minoan taste, but congenial to the martial temper of the mainlanders.

Some time between 1500 and 1450 BC the volcanic island of Thera erupted in a truly catastrophic manner, and devastated practically every Cretan site except Knossos. As a result, the mastery of the Aegean world steadily passed from Crete to the rising power of Mycenae—a process that was accelerated by the irretrievable wreckage of the palace at Knossos c 1380 BC, whether by human or natural agency: but even before this date some form of mainland control over the Cretan metropolis is clearly indicated by the appearance of a new script in the Knossian archives (Linear B) which has been deciphered as an early form of Greek. Likewise, by the end of the 15C BC, Mycenaean traders had taken over the Minoan overseas outposts, and after this date, the commercial initiative in the Mediterranean from Sicily to Egypt had passed into Mycenaean hands.

In the 14–13C BC Mycenae became an imperial capital, giving her name to the advanced civilisation in which she played the predominant part. Not that impressive memorials of the period are lacking in other parts of Greece: Messenia, Boeotia, Attica, and Laconia were all heavily populated, and it is to Pylos that we turn for the best preserved palace on the mainland (13C BC). The Linear B archives from there suggest that the king of each district (*wanax*) stood at the head of his own highly organised feudal system: but we also learn from the Iliad of Homer that these local rulers, in their turn, were obliged to supply contingents for foreign ventures like the Siege of Troy (a historical event of c 1250 BC) under the supreme command of Agamemnon, king of Mycenae, who was regarded as *primus inter pares*.

At Mycenae the pattern of settlement is typical of many other areas. On a low rocky eminence, fortified by a ring of massive Cyclopean masonry, dwelt the king and his court. His palace was smaller than the Cretan prototype, but more symmetrically designed. Not far below, an intricate complex of shrines ('The House with the Idols') also combines Minoan and mainland features. Outside this citadel lived the king's subjects in contiguous villages, each with its own cemetery hewn in the rock: the royal dynasty were buried in the monumental tholos (or 'beehive') tombs, one of the chief glories of the age: elsewhere only in Egypt was such veneration paid to the illustrious dead. Far beyond the limits of this lower town, the king's gaze could range over the flourishing settlements of the Argive plain (such as Prosymna, Argos, and Dendra), past the citadel at Tiryns, down to the sea at Nauplia, which, together with the little port at Asine, guarded the entrance to his kingdom from foreign invasion.

About 1200 BC the Mycenaean world found itself in mortal danger from a quite different direction. Barbarous northerners, equated in Greek tradition with the Dorians, had begun to move from their fastnesses in the Pindus mountains, destroying as they advanced. Energetic measures were taken to meet this new menace: the fortification of the Perseia spring at Mycenae, the galleries at Tiryns, and the stairway to the spring under the Acropolis at Athens, three marvels of military engineering, all belong to this date. Pylos succumbed to the first Dorian onset (c 1200 BC): Mycenae and Tiryns were devastated, and by 1150 BC, after further assaults, lay in ruins. Significantly for the future course of Greek history, Athens survived the ordeal unscathed. Many of her Ionian kinsmen took refuge on her soil before finding new homes across the Aegean on the western seaboard of Asia Minor (11–10C BC). These colonists were the vanguard of a movement which was eventually to spread Hellenic civilisation all round the shores of the Mediterranean: but in these pages we cannot follow their fortunes, being concerned exclusively with the monuments of the mother country.

The Hellenic City-State: c 1100–27 BC. The Dorian invasions destroyed once again the unity of Aegean civilisation, and ushered in a Dark Age (11–9C BC). Cut off from the outside world through the loss of their sea power, and isolated from one another by mountain barriers, the inhabitants of Greece were for a time forced to rely on the resources of their own poor soil, whose tillage became easier with the invention of iron tools. This period of poverty saw the birth of the city-state (polis) which remained the normal unit of Greek society for over a thousand years. By about 750 BC, when prosperity was beginning to return with the revival of seafaring and commerce, the political geography had become reasonably fixed: the Greek world was now divided into several hundreds of these miniature republics, each enjoying complete autonomy. Athens became an exceptionally large state by effecting the union of all Attica, but even so her territory was no larger than an average English county. In the 5C BC, when all free-born male Athenians possessed the franchise, the citizen roll numbered about 40,000, all of whom were entitled to vote in person at the meetings of the Assembly; among other cities, only a handful could muster more than 10,000. Plato fixed the number at 5040 for his ideal state: Aristotle thought that all citizens should know one another personally.

For the siting of a Hellenic city, three things were indispensable: an effective water-supply, access to arable land, and above all an easily defensible position, since relations between neighbouring states were seldom cordial. At first the acropolis served as a fortress in times of danger: later, whole cities were fortified. Athens and Thebes both grew up round typical Mycenean strongholds: in the Peloponnese, where the Dorians tended to avoid the main Mycenaean centres, the cities of Corinth and Argos were protected by yet more massive citadels. The Spartans, trusting in their military prowess, dispensed with both natural and artificial defences and chose an exposed site in the Laconian plain. In times of peace, after the disappearance of monarchical rule, the acropolis was usually set apart for the worship of the patron deity. By the end of the 6C BC, temples had been built over the ruins of the Bronze Age palaces at Athens, Mycenae, Tiryns, and Knossos: after the sack of the Athenian acropolis by the Persians in 480 BC, the cult of Athena was glorified by a series of monuments that became the wonder of Greece.

With the rise of democratic and oligarchic governments, the agora became the true centre of public life. Here, in a level square expanse at the very heart of the city, political and commercial business could be conducted; here, too, men could seek congenial company in their idle moments, enjoying the opportunities for free and leisured discussion from which Greek thought derives its originality. All round the square, buildings grew up in a more or less haphazard fashion, depending on the whim of the people and the balance of the treasury at any given time: it was not until the Hellenistic period that the agora was subjected to organised planning. The stoa, or open portico, which offered shelter from the sun and rain, became an essential component in the architecture of the agora: behind the long colonnade, where philosophers did much of their teaching, the interior could be divided into a large number of rooms suitable for shops, offices, banks, or marketstalls. By the 2C BC, the Athenian agora was virtually surrounded by stoas, of which one, that presented by Attalos II of Pergamon (mid-2C BC), has been restored as a museum. Other buildings were devoted to the smooth working of Athenian democracy: the Bouleuterion housed the Council of 500 who prepared the business of the full Assembly of citizens: in the round building known as the Tholos, a standing committee drawn from their numbers (the Prytaneis) remained on duty, in order to deal with any emergency that might arise. The Assembly, too numerous to be accommodated in the Agora, met on the Pnyx, where a bank of earth converted the rocky hill into an artificial theatre. For the same reason, public spectacles were removed from the agora at an early date: hence the construction of theatres, stadia, and gymnasia, usually sited on the outskirts of the city, and sometimes outside its walls.

The nucleus of the Greek theatre was the circular orchestra, or 'dancing-place', since drama had originally evolved from the ritual dances to the God Dionysos at country festivals. For the seating of the spectators, full advantage was taken of natural contours; the auditorium (theatron), with its tiers of stone seats, enclosed the orchestra on three sides, and, if necessary, was banked up at the ends by retaining walls (analemmata). In the 5C BC, the great age of Attic tragedy and comedy, temporary stages of wood and canvas were thought sufficient: raised stages built of stone were probably an innovation of the Hellenistic period. It was left for Roman architects to bind the stage and the auditorium into a single structure by throwing vaults over the side passages (parodoi) between the two: in the course of this transformation, both the auditorium and the orchestra assumed a semicircular shape.

The stadium and gymnasium were designed for athletic contests and athletic practice respectively. The word *stadion* originally meant a unit of distance equivalent to c 180m (200 yards), the length of the normal foot-race; where possible (as at Athens and Epidaurus) the course was sited in a long and shallow trough between two hills, and the spectators were placed on the banks either side. The familiar semicircular end (sphendone) and the idea of stone seating were borrowed from the theatre in Hellenistic times: monumental entrances (as at Delphi) were a Roman contribution. The gymnasium usually assumed the form of a large square court, surrounded by colonnades. Besides its original function as an athletic training ground, it inevitably became a social centre, like a miniature agora. The close relation between the physical and spiritual aspects of Greek education (gymnastike and mousike) becomes apparent when we recall that Plato adopted the name of the neighbouring gymnasium (Academia) in naming his own School of philosophy.

In contrast to the splendour of public buildings, private houses were modest and unpretentious. In the islands, walls were constructed entirely of rough stone; on the mainland, the usual material was mud brick, placed on a rubble foundation. A complete town of the 8C BC, with spacious square rooms, has been recently excavated at Zagora on the island of Andros. For the Archaic period (7–6C BC) the steeply terraced hill-town overlooking the harbour of Emborio on Chios offers the fullest evidence. The excavation of Olynthus has furnished the ground plan of a Classical residental suburb (c 430–348 BC) laid out with streets intersecting at right-angles, under the influence of Hippodamus of Miletus, who first designed cities on a grid system: the houses were approximately 18m square, with rooms looking out on to a small central courtyard. A greater degree of comfort is found in the mansions of the wealthy businessmen of Hellenistic Delos (mainly 2C BC) where the courtyard has acquired a handsome peristyle of marble columns, and the floors are often decorated with colourful mosaics: but not until Roman times do houses become really sumptuous.

Among the most permanent and impressive of Hellenic monuments are the walls of fortification, which frequently survive in an excellent state of preservation on sites where little else is to be seen. Full circuits became normal in the 5C BC, equipped with towers at regular intervals; with the steady improvement in siege engines, rebuilding was often necessary. Exceptionally fine are the walls of Messene, founded in 370 BC, after the liberation of Messenia from the Spartan yoke. Here the walls were built in their full height and thickness with squared stone blocks, and carefully fitted, as was customary until the Roman period, without any mortar or cement. Such walls were unusually extravagant; the usual practice was to build the parapets and the battlements in mud brick, and to fill the interior with rubble, restricting the fine masonry to the outer surfaces. The fortification of a city was regarded by Aristotle as an essential part of its adornment; and among the rich variety of masonry styles, none is more satisfying to the eye than the polygonal method of walling, which enjoyed an especial vogue before c 450 BC, before it became fashionable to lay the blocks in regular courses. At Oiniadai in Akarnania, a complete polygonal circuit (c 450 BC) survives: more accessible are the forts at Eleutherae and Aegosthena, both excellent examples of the regular isodomic style (early 4C BC). The visitor to Eleusis will find a good series of fortification and terrace walls, dating from the 8C to the 4C BC.

THE HELLENIC SANCTUARY. In addition to the temples and the shrines within the city, the countryside of ancient Greece abounded in holy places of all kinds, varying in extent from a simple enclosure with an altar to the great Panhellenic sanctuaries of Olympia and Delphi. Many such shrines give evidence of worship far back into prehistoric times, ultimately owing their sanctity to the awe-inspiring beauty and majesty of their scenery. Sometimes the surroundings reflected the attributes of the god: thus mountain peaks, were sacred to Zeus, while Poseidon was judiciously worshipped on stormy capes.

Since the offering of sacrifices played such a predominant part in the official cult of the Olympian gods, the altar was an indispensable component of even the smallest shrines; set out in the open air and surrounded by a sacred precinct (peribolos), the altar was always the main centre of public veneration. The temple was usually a later addition, whose purpose was to house the image of the god, and not to be a place of congregational worship like the Christian church—here though, an exception is provided by the famous cult of Mysteries at Eleusis, where the secret ceremonies of initiation were confined to the darkness of the Telesterion.

A sanctuary might also acquire a monumental columnar entrance (propylon) and a stoa to provide lodgings for priests, or to house stalls where pilgrims might purchase suitable votive offerings. For local shrines such as the Sanctuary of Aphaia on Aegina, or the Argive Heraion, no further buildings were necessary. By contrast, the great Panhellenic sanctuaries of Olympia and Delphi, which attracted to

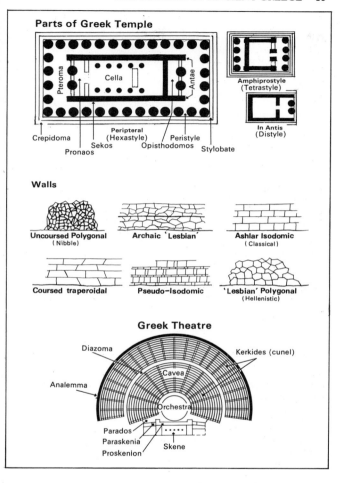

Parts of Greek Temple

Pteroma · Cella · Antae

Amphiprostyle (Tetrastyle)

In Antis (Distyle)

Crepidoma · Sekos · Pronaos · Peripteral (Hexastyle) · Opisthodomos · Peristyle · Stylobate

Walls

Uncoursed Polygonal (Nibble) · Archaic 'Lesbian' · Ashlar Isodomic (Classical)

Coursed traperoidal · Pseudo–Isodomic · 'Lesbian' Polygonal (Hellenistic)

Greek Theatre

Diazoma · Kerkides (cunel) · Cavea · Analemma · Orchestra · Parados · Paraskenia · Skene · Proskenion

their religious festivals thousands of visitors from all over the Greek world, needed many of the administrative buildings found in a large city: a bouleuterion and a prytaneion (town hall) as well as a stadium, a gymnasium, and sometimes a theatre also. Furthermore, the Greek states strove with one another not only for prizes at the quadrennial games, but also in the magnificence of their monumental dedications, which might take the form either of small votive chapels ('treasuries') or of imposing groups of sculpture. Such intense rivalry was always a powerful stimulant to the vitality of Greek art; later, when the Pax Romana put an end to the animosities between the city-states, the Hellenic spirit lost much of its creative impulse.

The Graeco-Roman Period: 27 BC–AD 330. The political independence of the Greek city-states came to an end in 27 BC, with the incorporation of the province of Achaea into the Roman Empire. Long before this date, Rome had begun to absorb the civilising influence of Greek literature, art, and thought: she now repaid her debt by maintaining unbroken peace for the next three centuries. She made little attempt to impose her own way of life on her Greek subjects: not only did Greek remain the official language of the Eastern Mediterranean, but many of the cities of old Greece were allowed to retain their local autonomy, and the responsibility for their own upkeep. In AD 160 the traveller Pausanias, whose 'Description of Greece' is a valuable source for the study of Greek monuments, found the main cities and sanctuaries in a flourishing condition, although some of the ancient sites were already desolate. Greece remained a peaceful backwater until the ruinous devastations of the Heruli (267) temporarily shattered her security.

Under Roman rule, Corinth became the administrative capital of the province of Achaea, and today her ruins offer the best impression of a spacious and thriving Graeco-Roman city. Elsewhere in the south, there is a scarcity of typically Roman monuments—of triumphal arches, imperial baths, and amphitheatres: in their stead, Greek magistrates and Greek architects preferred the simplicity of the propylon, the gymnasium, and the old-fashioned theatre, albeit in its Roman form (a characteristic example is the Odeum of Herodes Atticus at Athens). But in the north, where Hellenic culture had not penetrated so deep, there is a greater abundance of typically Roman architecture, especially in the later years of the Roman Empire: one may cite the Arch of Galerius at Salonica (c AD 300), the extensive forum of Philippi, and the purely Roman foundation of Nicopolis. A well-appointed Roman town on the island of Kos, where several mural paintings are preserved, has more in common with the sumptuous cities of Asia Minor than with the Greek mainland.

Athens, though shorn of all political power, still played the part of a university town, and remained a great artistic centre. Her sculptors took the lead in attempting to satisfy the insatiable appetite of Roman collectors. Not content with the universal practice of copying famous Classical works Athenian artists specialised in elegant pastiches of the Classical Style of the 5–4C BC: especially worthy of note are the lively Neo-Attic reliefs in the Piraeus Museum, and a fine group of Attic sarcophagi in the Salonica Museum (AD 2–3C). The more typically Roman work (idealised statues of emperors, and realistic portraits of private individuals) is best represented in the Museums of Corinth and Heraklion.

B. The Monuments in their Artistic Aspects

MINOAN AND MYCENAEAN ART

I. *Architecture*. In the absence of separate buildings reserved for religious worship, the architectural genius of the Aegean Bronze Age found its fullest expression in royal palaces and royal tombs. The conception of a building as a work of art stems from the older civilisations of Egypt and Syria, whence many of the typical features of Minoan palaces are derived: without going into excessive detail, one may cite the careful dressing of stone into large square blocks, the decorative use of stucco, the elaborate system of drainage through earthenware pipes, and, above all, the grouping of rooms round a central court. Under the fierce Cretan sun, external windows were shunned; instead, diffused light was admitted from the interior through light wells and wooden colonnades. The bright and airy effect of this device may be best appreciated in the domestic quarters at Knossos, where the functional and aesthetic aspects of Minoan architecture are brilliantly combined: it was further exploited on a truly majestic scale at the entrance to the palace at Phaistos, where a monumental flight of steps leads up to two successive porches, lit from beyond by a broad columned patio.

After the circular ossuaries of Early and Middle Minoan times in the Messara plain, the Minoans were normally buried in chambers cut into the soft local rock: the addition of masonry was evidently an honour reserved for royalty. Of the built tombs, the finest is the exceptionally well-preserved Temple Tomb at Knossos, so called because of its upper shrine, reminiscent of a medieval chantry: below, the burial chamber is preceded by a suite of rooms interrupted by an open court—clearly an imitation of a standard house plan.

After the Early Helladic House of Tiles at Lerna, the Greek mainland offers no further monumental architecture until the rise of Mycenaean civilisation. The palaces at Mycenae, Tiryns, and Pylos (14–13C BC) all owe much to Crete in the complexity of their plan, but there has been one notable modification: the central position is now occupied by a large suite of state rooms in the form of the ancestral megaron—a type of house whose history can be traced back to the Neolithic period, and which was much favoured by the first Greeks who invaded the mainland in c 2200 and c 2000 BC. Its palatial form is as follows: from a relatively small court, a pillared porch (aithousa) leads into an anteroom (prodomos) which in turn gives access to the spacious square throne room (domos) with a low central hearth, round which four wooden columns support the roof. Since all three rooms have the same breadth, and since the doors are all aligned on the same axis, the megaron introduced an element of symmetry lacking in the Minoan prototype, but prophetic of later Greek architecture.

The royal tholos tomb is the most original, and the most distinguished, of Mycenaean architectural forms. A monumental passage (dromos) led into a domed funerary chamber, whose masonry rises by corbelled courses, until the gap is closed at the apex: the chamber was then covered by a mound of earth, and the dromos filled in. Among the nine examples at Mycenae, three stages of its development may be followed. One of the earliest is the 'Tomb of Aegisthus' (early 15C BC) whose chamber is nearly all constructed of rubble, except the doorway, which is lined with rather larger masonry and crowned by a massive lintel. The enormous weight of the superstructure led the architects of the second group (of which the Lion Tomb, c 1450 BC, is typical) to leave a relieving triangle above the lintel: at the same time some attempt was made to dress the stones of the chamber. The climax of the series is represented by the superb 'Treasury of Atreus' (c 1300 BC): here the whole design is translated into handsome ashlar masonry and the façade is elaborately decorated: the portal was flanked by a tall pair of attached half-columns tapering downwards like their Minoan prototypes, a smaller pair stood at either side of the relieving triangle, which was filled in and covered with friezes of sculptured rosettes and spirals in green and stone. A close relationship exists between the structure of this façade and that of the contemporary Lion Gate, where the walling is also in ashlar technique, and the famous heraldic lions occupy the relieving triangle. Elsewhere the circuit of the citadel is mainly of Cyclopean construction, i.e. composed of roughly dressed boulders, the crevices being filled with small stones.

II. *Painting and Pottery*. Enough has survived of Minoan fresco painting to establish it as one of the major arts of the period. Since the pigments were applied when the plaster was still soft, a rapid and sure touch was essential: where his Egyptian contemporary preferred to linger lovingly over anatomical details, the Minoan artist obtained a lively effect from a few summary, impressionistic strokes. Both the subject and the style of the 'Saffron Gatherer', one of the earliest frescoes (c 17C BC), are typical of the Minoan temperament: the windswept crocus blooms reveal a delight in capturing spontaneous movement, while the representation of the monkey in a floral setting betrays a profound interest in the world of nature for its own sake, not merely as a background for human activity. Many charming frescoes in the same naturalistic manner have recently been found in the Minoan houses at Akrotiri on Thera, destroyed by earthquake in c 1500 BC. This accurate observation of nature reaches its height in the flower landscapes from Ayia Triadha (c 1600 BC) one of which shows a cat stalking a pheasant in the undergrowth. At about this time begins the series of frescoes, more monumental in size and in theme, which adorned the walls of the Knossian palace in its final form. Two of these are in painted relief: the vigorous·Charging Bull at the North Entrance, and the Priest-King, an idealisation of Minoan manhood raised to divine status. On this large scale, human figures tend to receive rather formal treatment, lacking the inner life that is so abundant in the smaller pieces as, for example, the hectic 'Toreador' scene, the delightful and individualistic 'Parisienne' and, above all, the Miniature Frescoes, where animated crowds are portrayed with astonishing economy of detail: here, as elsewhere, the sexes are effectively distinguished by the use of red paint for men, and white for women. However, formalism wins the day with the arrival of the Mycenaeans, whose taste for symmetry may be reflected in the heraldic Griffin Fresco in the throne room (late 15C BC)—a subject repeated 200 years later in the throne room at Pylos. In general the frescoes of the mainland palaces are less well preserved: typical themes are the Boar Hunt at Tiryns, a battle scene at Pylos, and the long frieze in the megaron at Mycenae showing warriors and horses preparing for battle.

Before the earliest frescoes were painted, Minoan potters had already attained a high peak of excellence in the polychrome Kamares ware, named after the cave-sanctuary high on the eastern flank of Mt Ida where it was first noted. In the best period (19–18C BC) the decoration is applied in red and white to a dark ground, and the designs strike a subtle balance between curvilinear abstract ornament and stylised plant motives. Later vases owe much of their decoration to the influence of free painting, although the potter was always guided by the shape of the vase in his choice of ornament. For this reason human figures and animals were avoided, whereas after c 1550 BC, when the decoration began to be applied in dark paint on a light ground, flowers and marine subjects could be accommodated in their most naturalistic form; the octopus became a special favourite, since its elastic shape could be adapted to suit any large surface. Such extreme naturalism was short-lived: by the late 15C BC the floral and marine motives on the Palace Style jars from the Knossos area began to assume a regular and symmetrical form. After 1400 BC, when the artistic initiative passed to the mainland, they gradually degenerate into abstract linear patterns.

III. *The Plastic Arts*. No monumental statues survive from either Crete or Mycenae, but small votive figures have a long history. A nude female figure from Lerna, gracefully natural in its pose, shows that even in Neolithic times a lump of clay could be transformed into a thing of beauty: the marble idols of the Cyclades (2500–2000 BC), more austerely stylised, belong to the same artistic milieu. The most notable Minoan contribution in this field are the two Faience Goddesses (c 1600 BC) wearing the usual flounced skirt, and the Ivory Acrobat (16C BC) leaping over a bull—a fine study in violent movement and meticulous realism, where even the veins and muscles are carefully shown: the missing hair and loincloth were almost certainly added in gold. No less exquisite is an ivory group from Mycenae, portraying two women and a child (15C BC), remarkable for its humanity and tenderness. Contemporary work in bronze was crude by comparison, although one may admire the robust expressionism of the Minoan figures of worshippers.

Minoan artists were more consistently successful in the technique of low relief, where their plastic skill could be combined with their innate pictorial talent. Their complete mastery of this medium is displayed in the two magnificent gold cups from the tholos at Vapheio (15C BC), both depicting the hunting of wild bulls: with a frame only 10cm high, full justice has been done to a tense and dramatic theme, and the majesty and ferocity of the animals has been superbly caught. Another consummate masterpiece is the Harvester Vase from Ayia Triadha (16–15C BC) carved in the soft black stone known as serpentine: in the rollicking procession of revellers returning from the harvest, sometimes marching four abreast, we meet once again the high-spirited humour that informs the Miniature Frescoes. We are also reminded of Minoan free painting by the pictorial use of precious metals in the daggers from the shaft graves of Mycenae, where gold and silver are inlaid in a background of dark niello, and minor details are incised: their free and naturalistic style makes it seem likely that they were the work of Cretan smiths, at a time when the mainland was just beginning to succumb to the spell of Minoan civilisation (c 1550 BC).

In the plastic arts both the Minoans and the mainlanders achieved their finest results when working on a small scale. Among their most valuable legacies are the sealstones and gold signet rings, which in a largely illiterate world were used as a means of identification. In the hands of Minoan craftsmen their engraving became a highly developed pictorial art: their subjects vary from intimate studies of animal and bird life to detailed representation of cult scenes, which supply us with our main source of information on the obscure topic of Minoan and Mycenaean religion.

HELLENIC ART

I. *Architecture*. The chief glory of Greek architecture is the Doric Temple. Clay models from Perachora (8C BC) and the Argive Heraion (7C BC) reveal its embryonic form, which resembled the domestic megaron of prehistoric times: a columnar porch (pronaos) led into a long hall (cella) which housed the image of the god: the roof gables were steeply pitched, and must have been thatched. In the earliest temples the roof of the pronaos was already supported by columns, arranged either between the forward continuations of the side walls (in antis) or, less commonly, in a free-standing colonnade across the front (prostyle). Behind these coluumns a single entrance gave access to the cella, and remained its only source of lighting: if necessary, the wooden beams of the ceiling were supported by one or two rows of internal columns. (The latter arrangement was eventually preferred, since a

Greek Orders of Architecture

A. Pediment
B. Entablature
C. Column
D. Crepidoma

a. Acroterion
b. Sima
c. Geison or Cornice
d. Tympanum
e. Mutules & Guttae

f. Frieze
g. Triglyphs
h. Metopes
i. Regulae & Guttae
j. Architrave or Epistyle
k_1. Capital (Doric)
k_2. Capital (Ionic) with Volutes
l. Abacus
m. Echinus

n_1 Shaft with flutes separated by sharp arrises.
n_2 Shaft with flutes separated by blunt fillets
o. Bases
p. Stylobate
q. Euthynteria
r. Stereobate

Corinthian Capital

Pergamene Capital

single row down the centre would interfere with the setting of the cult statue). Behind the rear wall of the cella, the pronaos was often duplicated by a second porch, the opisthodomos, for the sake of symmetry. Since the walls of the cella were at first built of mud brick on a timber frame, the larger temples from c 700 BC onwards were protected from the rain by a continuous veranda with an outer row of columns all round the building (peripteron).

Both the columns and the superstructure (entablature) were originally constructed of wood, and many of their characteristic features, when later translated into stone, recall the original material. Doric columns were placed directly on the upper foundations (stylobate) without any base, and tapered upwards like tree-trunks, with a pronounced convex curve (entasis): their broad and concave flutes, meeting each other at a sharp angle, might have resulted from the use of a rounded adze to shape a wooden log. Their capitals consist of two parts: a round cushion with a curved profile (echinus), supporting a square abacus. The entablature above the peripteron comprises the plain architrave, the typically Doric frieze where square metopes, sometimes bearing relief sculpture, alternate with grooved triglyphs (representing wooden beam-ends), and the projecting cornice (geison), whose two members, horizontal and sloping, frame the triangular pediments at the façades.

In the Heraion at Olympia (c 600 BC), although the columns and entablature were originally of wood, all these essential elements of the Doric order were already present: the temple had attained a monumental maturity at a time when secular building was still in its infancy. In the next two centuries its proportions were considerably improved, but the basic plan remained unaltered. Soon after, perhaps owing to the oppressive weight of the newly invented clay roof-tiles, the whole structure was translated into limestone. At first the new medium was treated with caution: the monolithic columns of the temple at Corinth (c 540 BC), the earliest in Greece that still remain standing, are extremely stout and closely bunched: their capitals are as broad as possible, so as to diminish the span of the massive architrave lintels. Further experience brought greater confidence: the columns became progressively taller, thinner, and more widely spaced, the capitals narrower and lighter: both tended to lose their curved profile. Limestone shafts were most conveniently built up in drums, and their appearance was improved by a coat of stucco: but even so they could not vie either in beauty or strength with the marble that the Athenians had begun to quarry from Mt Pentelikon, at the end of the 6C. Thereafter, beginning with her Treasury at Delphi (c 490 BC), Athens used marble for her religious buildings. Further aesthetic progress was made in the 5C with the broadening of the temple's ground plan: the cella was now furnished with increasing elaboration, and the cult statue was often flanked (as at Aegina) by a two-storied colonnade. The splendour of the façades was immeasurably enhanced by the magnificent groups of pedimental sculpture of Aegina (c 500–480 BC) and of the Temple of Zeus of Olympia (c 460 BC). After 200 years of experiment, the Doric style reaches its climax in the Parthenon, finished in 438 BC. Apart from the superlative excellence of the famous sculptured decorations, a new subtlety is introduced by the rising curves of stylobate and entablature and the inwardly slanting axis of the peripteral columns.

After the perfection of the late 5C, progress on purely Doric lines was hardly possible: but stagnation was happily averted, since mainland architects had begun to interest themselves in other styles. The Ionic order, first evolved across the Aegean in the 6C, had already found mature expression in the grandiose and ebullient temples of Artemis at Ephesus and in the Heraion of Samos, both surrounded by a double peripteron. The Ionic of Attica assumed a more restrained form, illustrated by the Erechtheion and the Temple of Nike (last quarter of 5C): apart from their well-known volute capitals, Ionic columns differ from Doric in their elaborately moulded bases, their slimmer shafts, and their deeper fluting: the architrave is divided into three shallow horizontal slabs, with a continuous frieze above, often bearing sculptured decoration. Doric and Ionic elements were often successfully married, especially by Attic architects: inside the Propylaea tall and graceful Ionic colonnades were happily combined by Mnesikles with a massive Doric exterior; his colleague Iktinos introduced Ionic sculptured friezes outside the cella of the Parthenon, and round the interior of the Temple of Apollo at Bassae (c 450–420 BC). This remote highland sanctuary also preserves the earliest known Corinthian capital: the Corinthian order (which differs from the Ionic only in the acanthus capital) was subsequently much exploited in the interiors of 4C BC buildings, reaching great heights of delicacy in the Temple of Athena Alea at Tegea and in the Tholos at Epidaurus. Its use on a gigantic scale in the double peripteron of the Temple of Olympian Zeus at Athens (174 BC–AD 138) reflects the more flamboyant taste of a later epoch: but even in Hellenistic times the Doric order was never wholly ousted, appearing in extremely attenuated form in the Temple of Isis on Delos. This is one of the few religious buildings of this period which survived to any height: in the secular field, however, the versatility of the Hellenistic architect is attested by many *stoas* (best represented by that of Attalos in Athens, c 150 BC), by the gabled façades of Macedonian built tombs, and by the ingenious octagonal water-clock in Athens, known as the 'Tower of the Winds' (c 40 BC).

II. *Sculpture*. Greek monumental sculpture began under the influence of Egypt in the 7C BC, when life-size statues of marble and limestone were first made in Crete, in the Peloponnese, and in the Cyclades. Attica entered the field with the kouros from Sounion (c 600 BC), first of a long line of nude male figures offered at tombs or dedicated at local shrines. In this great work, nearly twice life-size, we are inevitably reminded of Egyptian prototypes by the stance (left foot forward), by the rigidity of the arms, and by the stylised wig, and by the stiffness of the whole conception: but whereas the Egyptians directed their chief attention to the undulating surfaces of the skin, the sharp transitions of the early Attic statue show a determination to clarify the bone structure underneath. After this ambitious start, the kouroi from Volomandra (c 560 BC), Anavysos (c 530 BC), and Ptoon (c 510 BC), illustrate the gradual progress made by 6C sculptors in defining the anatomy of the human body at rest. With each generation, the transitions at the neck, the hips and the knee-caps are more convincingly rendered and the modelling becomes more rounded and assured. By the time of the Kritian Boy (c 480 BC) complete anatomical mastery has been attained: the body has become an organic whole, no longer the sum of its parts. The parallel series of korai (the maiden votaries of Athena dedicated on the Acropolis) reveals another facet of the archaic genius: the power to create harmonious patterns from the gay and elaborate Ionian draperies that came into fashion at the court of the Athenian tyrant Peisistratos and his sons: none, however, is more beautiful than the vivacious Peplos Kore (c 530 BC) who still wears the plainer Doric dress.

Alabastron   Phiale   Rhyton   Askos   Pyxis   Lekythos

Kylix   Kantharos   Aryballos   Skyphos

Krater   Oinochoe   Pelike   Kalpis

Lebes   Amphora   Hydria   Stamnos

Calyx-Krater   Pithos   Loutrophoros   Psykter

Pillar Stele with Sphinx (6th cent.)   Palmette Stele (with Anthemion) (5-4th. cent.)   Memorial Relief (5-4th. cent.)   Naiskos (4th. cent.)

Archaic sculptors devoted much of their thought to the decoration of temples and treasuries. Ionic friezes and Doric metopes were both adorned in relief: friezes invited continuous narrative scenes, like the Battle of the Gods and Giants on the Siphnian Treasury at Delphi (c 525 BC) while the square metopes were more suitable for detached episodes, such as the Labours of Herakles, and other single combats. In the triangular pediments, the sculptures were carved in the round and attached to the background by iron dowels: the awkward shape of the field presented a stern challenge to the artist's power of grouping his figures in an effective ensemble, and thus forced him to depart from the rigidly frontal pose of the free-standing statues. Here, too, battle scenes made good compositions. The early 'Hydra' and 'Triton' pedimental groups from the Acropolis (c 570–560 BC) show Herakles engaged with scaly monsters whose tails fit conveniently into the lower angles: more ambitiously, a later group from the Acropolis showing the Battle of Gods and Giants (c 520 BC) and the groups from Aegina (c 500–480 BC) were entirely constructed from human figures, embattled and closely entwined, either striding, falling, kneeling, crouching, or lying wounded in the corners. The Lapiths and Centaurs from the West pediment at Olympia (c 460 BC) bring this spirited tradition to a tempestuous climax.

With such valuable experience behind them, the sculptors of freestanding statues in the Early Classical period (c 480–450 BC) boldly departed from the archaic frontal stance. The Kritian Boy (c 480 BC) is allowed to relax, with the weight of the body unevenly divided; in place of the typical archaic smile, the features have assumed the noble severity also found in the Apollo at Olympia, who calmly presides over the struggle between Lapith and Centaur. Other masterpieces of this period are two bronze statues, the Delphic Charioteer (c 475 BC) and the Poseidon of Artemision (c 460 BC): the contrast between the static repose of the charioteer and the dynamic energy of the god emphasises the tremendous vitality of this versatile generation. In a century when the finest sculptors worked in bronze, it is a tragedy that no other life-size bronze originals of this time survive. For our understanding of the later 5C, the high noon of Greek sculpture and the age of Pheidias and Polykleitos, we are largely dependent on the marble copies—and art critics—of Roman times: however accurate the copies, and however discerning the critics may have been, we can only contemplate the achievement of the great masters through the eyes of a later age. We know that Pheidias superintended the building and the adornment of the Parthenon; yet few, if any, of the existing sculptures can have been chiselled by his own hand, and all would have been considered minor works in comparison with his colossal gold and ivory (chryselephantine) cult images of Athena Parthenos and of Olympian Zeus, both irretrievably lost. Nevertheless we can get some idea of the serene majesty of his style from such Parthenon marbles as still remain in Athens: from the gods and horsemen of the frieze, and from the fine and vigorous metope (Lapith and Centaur) that still remains in position at the SW corner of the Temple: although their features are still idealised, the figures are realistically posed, and their drapery falls in natural folds. In the next generation, the Nike of Paionios at Olympia (c 420 BC) and the reliefs from the Nike Balustrade at Athens (c 410 BC) illustrate a novel fashion for windswept diaphanous garments, through which the outline of the body can be clearly discerned.

In the 4C sculpture lost much of its monumental quality, and began to express the moods of individual human beings. The style of Praxiteles is well-known to us from his Hermes at Olympia (c 360 BC), while a bronze original in Athens, the Marathon Youth, may belong to his school: the softer outlines, the completely relaxed pose, the unprecedented wealth of detail in the modelling, and above all the gentle, dreamy expression of the eyes and mouth are all typical of the new spirit. His contemporary Skopas, to whose hand, or influence, the surviving heads from the Temple at Tegea are attributed, specialised in studies of violent emotion. Lysippos was renowned for the creation of a completely realistic athletic type, less heavily built than before and with a smaller head. These new proportions are embodied in the Agias at Delphi (c 320 BC); more moving, perhaps, is a work of great beauty and pathos which reflects his style: the tombstone (stele) from the Ilissos (Athens, No. 869) showing a father lamenting the death of his son, killed while hunting.

Lysippos was one of the few privileged artists who were commissioned to execute portraits of Alexander the Great, and in the Hellenistic period individualistic portraiture reached a high level of achievement. A fine early example is the brutally realistic bronze bust of the boxer Satyros from Olympia (c 330 BC): later Greek artists found a ready market among the Italian business men on Delos (c 100 BC), whose features they rendered with extreme candour. The scope of themes was vastly enlarged: foreign racial types, childhood, old age, and deformity all came within the sculptor's repertoire. The spirited Boy Jockey from Artemision (c 220 BC), who is clearly not of Hellenic stock, is a typical subject: characteristic, too, is his pose, which offers a satisfactory composition from every viewpoint. Whatever the aesthetic merit of the is work, technical virtuosity could hardly be carried further.

III. *Painting and Pottery*. The decoration of clay vases deserves an honourable place in the annals of Greek art for two reasons: first because the potter's craft preserves the only continuous artistic link between the Mycenaean and Hellenic civilisations; secondly, with the loss of almost all free painting of the finest period (6–4C BC), the art of vase-painting remains almost the sole witness to the pictorial talent of the Greeks.

After the collapse of Mycenae Athens became the chief source of ceramic ideas. In the Dark Age the decoration of pottery is severely abstract, but always relevent to the shape. On Protogeometric vases (11–10C BC) the patterns are mainly confined to neat sets of concentric circles and semicircles derived from the slovenly spirals of the latest Mycenaean: in the fully developed Geometric style (9–8C BC) the ornament becomes rectilinear in character, and the meander assumes the leading rôle. Representational art is reborn towards the end of the period (c 750 BC) when huge vases, which served as grave markers, bear stylised funerary scenes. Each region has its own local style.

The renewal of contact with the Near East ushered in an Orientalising phase (7C BC) when Greek potters borrowed the fauna and flora of Syro-Phoenician art and adapted them for their own purposes. Corinth seized the initiative in art as well as in commerce, and created a delicate miniature style ('Protocorinthian') based on animal friezes, lotus-flowers, and palmettes: when humans appear, mythical scenes may sometimes be recognised. On small vases the technique known as black-figure was first perfected: figures were first drawn in silhouette (as in Geometric times), and then elaborated with incised detail; and finally touches of colour were added in purple or white.

Other Orientalising figured styles arose in Attica ('Protoattic'), Laconia, the Cyclades, and Rhodes: all could match the vitalilty of Protocorinthian drawing, but none could excel its purity of line. In each of these regional schools, the details were at first rendered in outline, but by the end of the 7C the black-figure technique had been universally adopted under the influence of Corinth.

In Attica, where the most ambitious potters had cultivated a wild and grandiose style (best illustrated by the 'Polyphemus' amphora in Eleusis, c 660 BC) the arrival of incision imposed a salutary discipline: on a late Protoattic masterpiece, the Nessos amphora in Athens (c 610 BC), Attic grandeur is tempered by Corinthian refinement; out of this promising union grew the mature Attic Black-figure style of the 6C BC, when Athens retrieved the artistic and commercial initiative from Corinth, and eventually established a monopoly in the production of fine figured pottery. Animal friezes were now subordinated to scenes of human action, depicting the narratives of Greek mythology: the most popular themes were provided by the cycle of the Trojan war, the Labours of Herakles, and the revels of Dionysos with his attendant rout of satyrs and maenads. Black-figured drawing reached the limits of its potentialities in the work of Exekias (c 540–525 BC), who succeeded in endowing his figures with a new spiritual quality: the calyx-krater in the Agora Museum is a worthy example of his quiet and reflective manner.

The invention of the Red-figure technique (c 530 BC) allowed the painter greater freedom of expression. The colour scheme was now reversed, the figures being left in the orange tone of the clay, while the background was filled in with lustrous black; inner details could be rendered in brown or black paint, depending on the strength of the solution. By c 500 BC the finest artists were using the new technique, and had begun to lay the foundations of European representational drawing. A passionate interest in the structure of the human body led them to vary the pose of their figures: vigorous experiment with three-quarter views and foreshortened limbs introduced for the first time the illusion of a third dimension. At the same time the repertoire of themes became greatly extended, as scenes from daily life took their place beside heroic and dionysiac subjects.

Red-figured vase painting reached its highest level of achievement in the first quarter of the 5C BC, when the new medium had been fully mastered: the figures on these late archaic vases are drawn with a supple vigour that makes most subsequent work look somewhat staid and academic by contrast. With the rapid advance of sculpture and free painting after c 475 BC, the decoration of pottery was gradually reduced to a minor art, which no longer attracted artists of the front rank. A distinguished exception here is the work of the Achilles painter (c 450–430 BC) who specialised in the production of oil-flasks (lekythoi) for funerary use, decorated in subdued matt colours against a white background. His figures, isolated and statuesque, reflect the classical serenity of the Parthenon sculptures, with which they are contemporary, and enable us to visualise something of the grandeur of classical free painting. But in the 4C the figured decoration of pottery became a degenerate art, and in Attica it had died out in c 320 BC.

Tantalising glimpses of figured mural painting in the 4–3C BC are offered by the built tombs of western Macedonia. Scenes in the three royal tombs of the Great Tumulus at Vergina represent the late Classical flowering of this monumental art, already enlivened by a daring use of chiaroscuro. On the façade of the Great Tomb at Lefkadhia, the scene of Judgment in Hades, with its four statuesque figures, is a masterpiece of early Hellenistic times. Slighter work of the 3C BC may be seen on the Thessalian painted gravestones (stelai) in Volos museum.

BYZANTINE ART AND
ARCHITECTURE IN GREECE

By *Professor Karin M. Skawran*

The Byzantine monuments which are discussed here lie within the limits of the Greek state as it exists today. The limitation to Greece is arbitrary since no frontiers between this area and the rest of the Byzantine world existed. Greece today is a varied territory which comprises the mountainous end of the Balkan peninsula, a fringe of western islands, including Corfu (Kerkyra) and the numerous Aegean islands extending to Crete, Rhodes and the coast of Asiatic Turkey.

The mainland is so fragmented by mountains and inlets of the sea that, formerly, many of the settled areas were largely dependent, like the islands, on sea communications. But regional isolation, when sea travel was perilous, was offset by the impact of direct seaborne contact with the capital at Constantinople in normal times, when the Aegean also provided sea-lanes between East and West.

Athens, with only modest local resources, was particularly vulnerable and, despite its central position, did not during the Byzantine period enjoy the dominant position it does today. Salonica, on the other hand, sustained by the fertile Macedonian plains at the gateway to the Balkan hinterland, enjoyed an easy land link with the capital across the rolling hills of Thrace. Significantly it is here, at Ferai near the present Turkish frontier, that a prince of the imperial house founded the Monastery of Kosmosoteira and, not far away, on the precipitous peninsula of Mount Athos, arose the greatest of all Orthodox monastic communities. In Salonica itself, the second city of the Empire, the *Panayia ton Khalkeon*, as well as the recently uncovered 12C frescoes in Osios David, bear the strongest imprint of metropolitan influence.

Westward, the same arterial link, the *Via Egnatia*, continued more precariously through the Albanian mountains to the Adriatic coast and thence by sea to the West. Nevertheless in the Greek part of this region, centres such as Kastoria usually share a similar local character with their neighbours of the Balkan fringe.

S of Mount Olympus the settlements around the plain of Thessaly form another entity which, apart from the *Koimesis* church at Kalambaka (Church of the Dormition), preserves little from the height of the Byzantine period. Further S the central Pindus range effectively bisects the country, leaving the entire territory of Ioannina and Arta to Naupactus isolated to the W. To the E, the Boeotian plain nourished one of the richest silk industries of the Empire.

Close by, isolated by the summits of Helicon, which shut off this plain from the Gulf of Corinth, stands the great Monastery of Holy Luke (Osios Loukas). Southward of the Isthmus and the Argolid, in the adjoining territories of Thebes, Athens and Corinth (all three commercial and administrative centres of importance) was the heartland of the Greek province in Byzantine times.

Beyond the fertile plains of Argos, a tangle of mountains fills the northern Peloponnese. With their offshoots, the towering range of Taygetos and the lower mass of Parnon, these mountains leave only restricted areas for prosperous settlement: upland Arcadia; the Laconian plain that nourished Lacedaemon (the ancient Sparta), later to be abandoned for the greater security of nearby Mistra; the smiling land of Messenia, preserving in the *Zoödhokhos Piyi* at Samarina one of the most sophisticated churches in Greece, and, to the NW, the plains of Elis and Achaea, extending to the ports of Patras at the entrance to the Gulf of Corinth. Yet it is in the remoter regions that most of the surviving monuments are to be found: in eastern Laconia at Yeraki, the sea-girt stronghold of Monemvasia, and in the rugged peninsula of Mani.

Nearby Kythera always provided a stepping-stone to Crete and, like that large island, could offer a port of call for traffic from E to W, a circumstance of which some of their early frescoes remind us (in Kythera: the Cave chapel of Ay. Sophia on the N coast, near Milopotamos and Ay. Dhimitrios near Pourko; in Crete, Ay. Eftychios and the Catholicon of the Monastery of Myriokephala near Rethymnon).

The Dodecanese and Rhodes itself, the gateway to the Aegean from the E, have little to offer, with the important exception of Patmos, where the fortified Monastery of St. John the Divine boasts some of the finest frescoes of the Middle Byzantine period. The other islands off the Asiatic coast—Samos, Chios and Lesbos—marked stages on an important sea route to the capital. Chios especially, in the Nea Moni, boasts an imperial foundation and preserves other fine churches.

The Cyclades, despite their central position in the Aegean, could still be isolated, and in some cases even rendered uninhabitable, by the piracy with which the islands were often plagued. Nevertheless, in the sheltered interior of Naxos, recent exploration has brought to light some of the earliest church frescoes surviving in Greece (Ay. Artemios; the Cave church of the Nativity of the abandoned Monastery of the Kaloritissa near Sangri; Ay. Kyriaki near Apeiranthos). Santorini has an imperial foundation in the frescoed church of *Panayia tis Gonias*. In contrast few painted churches have as yet been reported from the western islands, even from the largest, Corfu (Kerkyra) (Ay. Merkourios, near the village of Ay. Markos and Ay. Nikolaos, Kato Korakiana).

The Early Christian period (4–7C). Long-lasting peace and security resulted in the building of a large number of churches and the conversion of some pagan temples into Christian churches. Over the past years, archaeologists have uncovered the remains of over 300 basilicas, either *extra muros* or within city boundaries, as at Philippi and Amphipolis (Macedonia), in Nicopolis (Epirus), Thebes (near Volos) and Corinth. In Salonica some of these early basilicas have been fully preserved. Their vast proportions and grandeur were never again equalled.

In the 5C, after the edicts by Theodosius II and Valentinianus III, all pagan temples were closed or converted into Christian churches, e.g. the Parthenon, the Erechtheion, the Theseion and many others in Athens; the workshop of Pheidias at Olympia; the Athena temple at Tegea; the Galerius Mausoleum (Rotunda) in Salonica; as well as sanctuaries on the islands of Naxos, Sikinos and Kea. Only a few buildings have been assigned to the 4C (basilica at Epidaurus) and only a few have been preserved from the end of the 6th to the middle of the 7C. It seems that this period witnessed the restoration and rebuilding of churches from the previous centuries.

During this Early Christian period the basilican type of church predominated. It is normally characterised by its longitudinal groundplan and was approached on the W through a colonnade *atrium* (outer courtyard). On its E side the *narthex* (vestibule) was entered through two doors, which in turn gave access to the *naos* (church proper) through a *trivelon* (three-arched arcade, supported by two columns). The interior of the basilica consisted of a central nave, usually wood-roofed and raised above the side aisles to incorporate a clerestory. The nave was separated from the aisles by arched colonnades. In the E it terminated in a semicircular apse which usually protruded on the exterior. There are several variants of this type with a transverse aisle at the eastern end as at Philippi, Nicopolis, the Ilissos in Athens, and Panormos in Crete. In some of these churches the transverse aisle protrudes on the N and S sides, terminating in lateral apses. This cloverleaf type of groundplan can be found in Epirus (Paramithia, Dodona) and central Greece (Klapsi).

Five-aisled basilicas with a transverse aisle are rare (Ay. Dhimitrios in Salonica and the basilicas in Epidaurus and Nicopolis); so also are basilicas with a domed centralised cross layout (Thasos, Paros). Basilicas with a central cupola developed in the 6th and 7C in Philippi (Basilica B) and in Athens, Paros and Gortyna (Crete). Variants are the octagonally planned basilica in Philippi and the inscribed-cross type of groundplan of Osios David in Salonica.

Much of the lavish decoration which characterised the interior of these basilicas consisted of sculptural decoration, particularly on the capitals, cornices and on the chancel screen (*iconostasis*), which separated the *naos* from the sanctuary, as well as on the *ambo* (lectern). The floor and the lower part of the walls were covered in marble, while the upper sections were decorated with mosaics. This is particularly evident in the basilicas of Salonica. Here one can witness the transition from the late phase of ancient art to a purely Byzantine style, for example in the dome mosaics of the Rotunda of Ay. Yioryios (5–6C). Two or three figures of saints, depicted frontally and in a strict hieratic pose, have been placed in front of elegant stage-like façades, reminiscent of Hellenistic art. The impressionistic-painterly style of these mosaics also strongly recalls the late phase of ancient art. In the Acheiropoieitos church, apart from the beautifully preserved marble floor of the nave, colourful mosaics adorn the soffits of the arches of the colonnades. The images of plant and bird life bear Christian symbolic connotations. The apse mosaic of Osios David (5–7C) and the magnificent wall mosaics of Ay. Dhimitrios, are characterised by their purely Byzantine style and can be compared with the mosaics in Ravenna.

The Period from Mid-Seventh to Mid-Ninth centuries. During this period Greece experienced dark times. The Empire was impoverished by economic crises and thrown into turmoil by the invasions of tribes from the N and by the Arabs who, from the beginning of the 7C, had invaded the country and had settled on the coasts of North Africa, Egypt and Syria. They occupied Crete in 823. Trade routes by sea were cut off and there was little building activity. Many buildings of previous periods had been destroyed by earthquakes in 521 and 551, and had fallen victim to the invaders. The Iconoclastic movement of the 8th and 9C also had devastating results, especially for painting. Most images depicting holy personnages were destroyed. Some non-figurative paintings in the remoter areas of Eurytania (Episkopi); Naxos (Ay. Artemios; Ay. Kyriaki); Mani (Ay. Prokopios) Crete and Ikaria are considered to be late survivals of the Iconoclast tradition.

The Mid-Ninth to Twelfth centuries (Middle Byzantine Period). The liberation of Crete (961) and the victory of Basil II over the Bulgars (1018) resulted in a renewed building activity during this period. The monastic movement also experienced a new height. On Mount Athos several large monasteries and churches were built.

Thebes in Boeotia, the capital of the *thema* Hellas (administrative centre and seat of the *strategos*, the civil and military governor of southern Greece) developed as an important administrative, economic and artistic centre. Its silk industry became famous, as did the orientalising style of some of its stone sculpture. The one-aisled Ay. Ioannis Theologos (872) was built by Basileos, a well-known dignitary. Another dignitary responsible for the Panayia church in Skripou on the site of Ancient Orchomenos. Important churches were erected also in Eurytania (the Episkopi church, today submerged under water and its frescoes moved to the Byzantine Museum, Athens) and the churches on Skyros (895) and in the vicinity of Salonica (Peristera, c 871).

This cultural revival lasted through the reign of the Comnenes in the 12C to the conquest of Constantinople by the Crusaders in 1204 and the foundation of the short-lived Latin Empire (1204–61).

Here and there, a few of the great wood-roofed basilicas, which had been almost universal in the early period, survived the hiatus created by the Slav migrations and Arab supremacy at sea. One of them, the *Panayia Acheiropoieitos* in Salonica, was partially redecorated in this period. Like the converted temples such as the Parthenon itself, they ensured among the builders of the much less ambitious churches of the later period a frequent preference for the three-aisled basilican form, particularly for metropolitan churches (Koimesis church, Kalambaka). These later basilicas, usually of smaller dimensions, either retained the colonnades of their prototypes, as in the *Taxiarchis Mitropoleos* at Kastoria, or, when columns were lacking, substituted arcades on masonry piers, as in *Ayioi Anargyroi* in the same town and the Basilica at Servia. In some cases columns and piers alternated, as at Kalambaka and Ay. Stephanos at Kastoria. Sometimes lack of timber imposed the substitution of masonry vaults over both nave and aisles, often without clerestory windows, so providing greater scope for painted decoration, as in Ay. Ioannis Theologos, Naxos and Ay. Pandeleimon, Crete.

For smaller churches, especially in the early phase of recovery and in more remote regions, the simplest type of chapel prevailed: a single rectangular chamber with an apse, either with a pitched roof of timber and tiles (Ay. Nikolaos Kasnitzi at Kastoria) or spanned by a masonry vault (as in St. Procopius, Mani). A variant common to both classes provided twin apses opening from the single chamber, either wood-roofed (Ay. Merkurius, Corfu) or vaulted, as in Ay. Pandeleimon, Ano Boularioi, Mani.

Even in Salonica, despite the example of the great Rotunda which was converted into a church in the 5C, church-builders were slow to adopt the system of roofing with vaults and domes, developed in Byzantium under Justinian and of which Greece preserved only one contemporary example in the great church at Paros. Ay. Sophia in Salonica, a domed square enclosed by a vaulted ambulatory which was built in the eighth century, is transitional in both form and date, for it was constructed when Greece was largely swamped by migrations.

As the recovery of the province proceeded, what was to be the classic form of the domed church in our period crystallised in the capital: the inscribed-cross domed type. This was a square hall of modest size with a small central dome carried on four piers or, ideally, columns and abutted by four radiating barrel-vaults with lower domical or cross-vaults (sometimes small domes) over the corner bays, the whole preceded by a *narthex* or vestibule at the W and screened on the E from the tripartite sanctuary. This last comprised the central *bema* with the altar flanked by the *prothesis* for the preparation of the sacrament on the N and the *diaconicon* or sacristy on the S. This architectural scheme provided, at no great distance from the worshipper, ample surfaces for figural decoration in support of the teaching of the Church, and its standardisation led to a large measure of uniformity in the arrangement of the subjects represented.

Closer ties with the capital, particularly in the 11th and 12C, were reflected in the Greek church-builders' gradual rejection of the basilica in favour of the domed and other forms. The classic type was introduced in Greece sometimes quite unchanged and with columns, not piers, as in the *Panayia ton Khalkeon*, Salonica and the *Theotokos* church, Osios Loukas. More often it was modified by adjustments to the basilica tradition. The square and strictly centralised *naos*, the church proper, was often elongated and the corner bays tended to retain the barrel-vaults which had covered the aisles of the vaulted basilicas. Frequently the *naos* and the sanctuary were telescoped so that the E vault abutting the dome covered the *bema*, its flanking corner bays became the *prothesis* and *diaconicon*, and the *iconostasis* was moved to line up with the pair of columns supporting the eastern arch of the dome, as at Episkopi, Santorini. This telescoping of *naos* and sanctuary was more usually achieved by retaining only the two western columns of the classic type and by supporting the E side of the dome on the two solid walls of the originally separate sanctuary. This simplified plan was frequently adopted for Greek churches from the late 11C and is found in many parts of the country, for instance in the church of Samarina, Messenia; Ay. Iason and Sosipatros, Corfu; it was very popular in the Mani (Ay. Stratigos, Ano Boularioi; Episkopi, Tigani).

In many of the earlier domed churches, instead of the isolated columns of the classic Constantinopolitan type, solid walls pierced by openings separate the corner bays (Episkopi, Eurytania; Metamorphosis near Koropi, Attica; Protothronos, Naxos).

In some regions and on the islands small domed churches of the most elementary inscribed-cross type are found. In these simple, one-aisled chapels the N and S cross-arms appear internally only as shallow arched recesses, as in several Naxos examples, like Ay. Kyriaki, Ay. Yioryios, and Ay. Pakhomios, all in the vicinity of Apeiranthos. The cruciform character of the superstructure is usually quite apparent from the outside, and where it is not, a dome has been set somewhat arbitrarily above the middle of a simple vaulted one-aisled chapel (Ay. Eftychios in Crete). The free-standing cross plan was also sometimes used for domed churches of modest size, as in the *Panayia Damiotissa*, Naxos. The related triconch type with lateral apses in place of the side-arms of the cross occasionally occurs, though not in any painted church of our period; the *Panayia Drosiani*, Naxos is an earlier example. The Koubelidiki in Kastoria is a 10C triconch church and contains frescoes from a later period.

Most Middle Byzantine churches in Greece of the foregoing types are of small dimensions. To meet the needs of some major monastic foundations such as Nea Moni on Chios and Osios Loukas, their founders could use a more ambitious formula, what may be called the large-dome type. In these churches the dome covers the whole span of the square *naos*, the corners of which are bridged by squinches to form the octagonal base of the large dome, as at Nea Moni, Chios and in others on the same island. In an enlargement of this type, barrel-vaulted arms extend from the four cardinal arches to an outer rectangle of which the corner spaces are filled with chapels, for instance in Ay. Sophia, Monemvasia and Ay. Nikolaos 'sta Kambia', near Orchomenos. In one case, the Catholicon of Osios Loukas, the surrounding chapels carry galleries.

From the overall architectural types we may pass to some significant component features. The *narthex* is not always present in the Greek churches. When it occurs in earlier buildings it is roofed in the simplest way with a continuous transverse barrel-vault, as in the Episkopi, Eurytania. Later, the normal arrangement in domed churches was to differentiate a central bay by roofing it at a higher level, with a vault running east–west. In the Mani the wall between the west cross-arm and the *narthex* is frequently suppressed and the west vault continues unbroken from the dome to the west wall of the *narthex*. The central bay of the *narthex* is thus included in the main body of the church, giving it the elongated proportions of a basilica, as in Ay. Stratigos, Ano Boularioi. Very rarely a gallery is added over the *narthex*: in the *Panayia ton Khalkeon*, Salonica (with domes over the outer bays), and in the much smaller church of Ay. Stephanos, Kastoria. The outer vestibule (*exonarthex*) is almost unknown. Exceptionally, the Samarina church has an elegant portico with a domed belfry flanked by bays with domical vaults. These domical vaults are used in the same church in the western corner bays; like the groined cross-vaults used in the Crypt of Osios Loukas and Ay. Varvara, below Ay. Nikolaos 'sta Kambia', they belong to the central Byzantine tradition. In Greece these forms seldom supplanted the almost universal barrel-vaults either in the cross-arms or in the corner bays.

A preference for unified surfaces and neat contours in the Greek churches contrasts with the more articulated façades favoured in the capital and followed in the *Panayia ton Khalkeon*. Occasionally, however, the form of the lateral cross-arm is repeated as a buttressing arch on the façade, for instance in the Theotokos church, Osios Loukas.

The semicircular apse and the cylindrical dome drum characterise the earlier churches in Greece and they were never altogether abandoned. The use of poor building stone imposed their retention in some remote places, as in the apse of Ay. Stratigos, Ano Boularioi, Mani; Ay. Ioannis Theologos and Ay. Kyriaki in Naxos; for it was easier to build rounded forms than polygonal ones in rubble construction. Semi-hexagonal apses and octagonal dome drums appeared earlier in major churches where brick and dressed stone were used, for instance in the Theotokos church, Osios Loukas. Such examples led to the increasing use of angular forms. In Greece from the early 11C onwards, the octagonal domes took on a special form: the horizontal cornice was suppressed and the arched cornices of each face of the octagon, for example, rising from colonnettes at the angles, form the characteristic arching eaves-line, as in Ay. Stratigos, Mani.

Differences in masonry technique characterise particular areas. Construction in brick alone, common in Constantinople, is rare in Greece outside Salonica (*Panayia ton Khalkeon* and the apse of the Catholicon of Osios Loukas). On the other hand, the use of stone alone is uncommon except in the islands, for instance in Ay. Yioryios Diassoritis and in the *Panayia Dhamiotissa*, Naxos. Mixing the two materials, the mainland builders from the second half of the 10C onwards make use of the *cloisonné* treatment in which the individual squared stones are enclosed with tile-like bricks in both vertical and horizontal joints. This basic walling system is fully developed in the Theotokos church, Osios Loukas. For a time cut bricks were used in the vertical joints to make decorative motifs, often based on Greek letters or the Arabic cufic script, as in the *Taxiarchis Mitropoleos* and *Ay. Anargyroi*, Kastoria, and the Theotokos, Osios Loukas. In the Mani brick, and with it the *cloisonné* masonry technique, makes its first appearance in Ay. Stratigos. In some Middle Byzantine churches, for instance in Ay. Iason and Sosipatros, Corfu and Ay. Sozon, Yeraki, it is common to use the *cloisonné* technique only in the upper courses, for such prominent features as the dome and the framing of windows. Usually façades were crowned with a dentil frieze, consisting of a series of bricks placed at an angle. A reaction of over-ornate brickwork led to the appearance of neat ashlar façades in the 12C, as in Ay. Nikolaos 'sta Kambia'.

Until the early 11C the arcade type of window was most frequently used in Greek churches. This type, in which the lights of a double or triple window are arched separately in brick at the same level, recalls the window arcades of the Early Christian basilicas. Its use is continued in the lower series of windows of the east end of the Catholicon of Osios Loukas. In the course of the 11C the arcade-type window was gradually replaced by the grouped type. In this the whole window is embraced in a single arch within which the individual lights are arched separately. In three-light windows of this type the central light is sometimes arched at a higher level. This grouped form of window is often flanked by blind half-arches of brick. The type appears perhaps for the first time in Greece in the dome of the Theotokos church, Osios Loukas. In the 12C it was used almost exclusively, for instance in the Evangelistria, Yeraki; but stone dressings gradually replaced those of brick, both in the window arches and elsewhere in the building. The *tympanum* of this grouped type of window was sometimes filled with designs imitating cufic lettering, but later simple geometric designs were preferred, as in the Evangelistria, Yeraki.

Glazed bowls set in mortar appeared as a type of façade ornament during the 11C and were generally used during the 12th, notably in the Mani, (Episkopi, Tigani).

Church decoration. Some description has already been given of the adornment of Pre-Iconoclastic buildings (above; Early Christian period). One of the major developments following the overthrow of the Iconoclasts was the establishment of a standard programme for the distribution of religious images in church decoration. The decoration of the interior of the domed Middle Byzantine church was conditioned by the conception of the space it enclosed as a reflection of the cosmos. It had its own heavenly sphere in the dome and a more terrestial region in the lower part of the church. In an hierarchic system the images were assigned to a higher and lower level as seemed appropriate. This cosmological-hierarchic order derives, it now seems, from the neo-Platonic writings of the Pseudodionysios Areopagita composed at the end of the 5th or the beginning of the 6C. The domed inscribed-cross type of church with its centralised plan was perfectly suited to the hierarchic arrangement required for the chosen representations, and it gave a formal unity to the spiritual conceptions which inspired this programme. Three factors determined its development: the requirement of theological instruction, the architectural forms available for decoration, and the survival in some degree of pre-Iconoclast traditions. But, above all, it was the architecture of the standard type of church which determined the elements of an ideal scheme of arrangement. In considering these we have to distinguish between mosaic churches in which the lower parts of the wall are sheathed with marble revetments, and the more humble painted churches in which these lower parts provided additional space for figural decoration, though here, in the lowest register, marble was often imitated in fresco. Although the principal Christian images *per se* had long since been standardised, the evolution of their arrangement since the Early Christian period had been crippled by a theological controversy. The Iconoclasts' ban on religious images had virtually obliterated the earlier traditions, necessitating the foundation of an almost entirely new programme in which images were in accord with the architecture they adorned, and at the same time conformed with the concepts of Greek Orthodox theology.

No complete and homogeneous church decoration from the period immediately following Iconolasm has survived in the capital, and our knowledge of the iconographic programmes of churches in Constantinople is based on some problematical reconstructions derived from contemporary descriptions and on a few surviving fragments. Photius' description of the mosaics of 864 in the Church of the Virgin of the Pharos attests the prevalence of isolated figures in a restrained and hierarchic ensemble. Christ *Pantocrator* was figured in the summit of the dome, a host of Angels in its radiating gores; the *Virgin Orans* in the apse; and elsewhere Apostles, Prophets, Bishops and Martyrs. No narrative scenes are mentioned. It appears that the first post-Iconoclastic schemes were rather simple with isolated figures arranged in an hierarchic manner, limited to the dome with its drum and pendentives, the apse and the higher vaults. It is safe to say also that these early programmes set the course for the full development of the Middle Byzantine system in which narrative scenes and other complex figural compositions found a place. Already in the time of Basil I, if not earlier, the mosaic decoration of the Church of the Holy Apostles in Constantinople embraced a full narrative cycle of the Life of Christ. Moreover, it is clear that in the central dome the figure of Christ portrayed 'as if he were the sun', was surrounded by the Apostles accompanied by the Virgin, in a representation of the Ascension. Since the Ascension prefigures the Second Coming of Christ as Supreme Judge, it does not differ theologically from the more usual bust of the *Pantocrator*, a more abstract dogmatic symbol of Christ in Glory after the Ascension.

In the 'classic' decorative programme of the Middle Byzantine period, the dome, the apse and the higher vaults are reserved for the depiction of the most sacred personages. The bust of Christ *Pantocrator* was the most favoured image for the summit of the dome. His image formed the centre, formally and spiritually, around which the rest of the images in the church were arranged in a strictly hierarchic manner. The *Pantocrator* was accompanied in the zone below by a Celestial Host, while standing Prophets were represented between the windows of the drum, and the Evangelists commonly in the pendentives. The *narthex* usually had its own heavenly zone: Christ *Pantocrator* appears above the door leading to the nave, and if there were domes, they contained the bust of the Virgin or that of Christ Emmanuel.

Almost invariably the conch of the apse was reserved for the image of the Virgin (sometimes accompanied by two worshipping Archangels), either enthroned with the Child on her lap or standing (as the *Hodēgētria*) with the Child on her arm, or alone with arms upraised as Intercessor (*Orans*).

The appropriate place for the Communion of the Apostles was near the altar, often on the wall below the conch of the apse. Likewise the Bishops, conceived as participating in the Liturgy, belong to this area and are depicted in the lowest register of the apse wall and sometimes extending along the lateral walls of the sanctuary. Deacons also belong to the same liturgical programme and occur therefore in the sanctuary, usually just outside the apse. Overtones of the Liturgy are also expressed in the themes adopted for other parts of the church.

The Ascension commonly fills the *bema* vault, while the rest of the scenes from the Life of Christ, usually limited to the twelve major episodes of the Festival Cycle, are depicted outside the sanctuary on the vaults and the upper surfaces of the walls. These narrative scenes are arranged more or less chronologically, starting with the Annunciation in the eastern part of the church and ending with the Dormition of the Virgin, usually on the west wall. Ideally the twelve scenes from the Festival Cycle are: the Annunciation, the Nativity, the Presentation, the Baptism, the Transfiguration, the Raising of Lazarus, the Entry, the Crucifixion, the *Anastasis* (Harrowing of Hell), the Ascension, the *Pentecost* and the Dormition of the Virgin. To these were sometimes added subordinate cycles illustrating Christ's Passion (the Last Supper, the Washing of the Feet, the Betrayal, the Descent from the Cross and the Incredulity of Thomas), the Infancy of Christ (his Parents, the Adoration of the Magi and the Flight into Egypt), Christ's Miracles, the Life of the Virgin or that of a favoured Saint.

There were no strict rules governing the distribution of isolated figures, although they were arranged according to the rank assigned to them by the Church. Holy Physicians, like the Deacons, were usually admitted to the sanctuary, while Holy Monks, Female Martyrs and canonised Emperors were commonly relegated to the *narthex*. Sacred Warriors and Martyrs were figured in the nave in relatively high positions where such were available, while half-figures and busts of Saints in medallions often decorated the soffits of arches.

The decoration of wood-roofed basilicas inevitably required a different distribution of the images. In the Sicilian basilica, for example, the *Pantocrator* was transferred to the conch of the apse, which automatically became the most sacred focal point of these churches, and the Virgin, together with the adoring Archangels, was moved to the next zone below. Bishops were retained in the lowest zone or zones of the apse wall, while the narrative and other cycles were distributed in two long series on the side walls of the nave.

These were the classical schemes of decoration adopted in Middle Byzantine churches, against which the programmes followed by the Greek fresco painters must be judged.

Late Byzantine art (Thirteenth to Fifteenth centuries). In 1204 Greece was conquered by the Franks and the Empire split into several political and cultural centres which largely developed independently from the capital. Fortified cities developed, such as Mistra and Moukhli in the Peloponnese and Arta in Epirus. Their newly established independence contributed towards a competitive spirit which also affected their artistic activities.

In architecture slight adjustments and changes were made to the existing basilican and domed-inscribed cross types of groundplan. Buildings from this period are characterised by their more elegant and narrow proportions and by their exterior brick and tile ornamentation. Architectural additions to the main church building resulted in their more complex appearance. The basilica, especially in Euboea and Epirus, underwent a late development. The transept was widened and raised above the other aisles, emphasising the characteristic cross-shape of the basilica during this period.

As a result of the declining economic situation of the Empire, mosaic decoration was gradually replaced by fresco painting. In the monastery church of *Porta Panayia* in Thessaly mosaic decoration has been reserved for the *iconostasis*, and in the Paregoritissa in Arta only the *Pantocrator* in the dome was executed in mosaic. Similarly, mosaics adorn the upper parts of the walls of the Apostle church in Salonica, while the rest of the church is decorated with frescoes (1310).

Despite the gradual decline of the Empire, the painting during this late phase is characterised by an exceptional vitality and a dynamic revival of classical prototypes. On the islands and in the more remote regions of Greece, however, the more conservative, linear style, witnessed in the mosaics at Osios Loukas, predominated.

During this period Salonica and the neighbouring Balkan countries developed as the important centres for monumental painting. After a period of stagnation (1330–60), painting in Constantinople gave fresh impetus to the art. Largely retrospective in character, it tended to revive the more painterly and humanist style of classical art. This style is perhaps best reflected in the fresco painting at Mistra which is characterised by its idealisation, elegance and lyrical sophistication. Crete, during the 14th and 15C, fell under the influence of the painting in Constantinople and gradually developed a distinctly Cretan school of painting which dominated Greek painting during the 16th and 17C.

POST-BYZANTINE MONUMENTS: FRANKISH, VENETIAN AND TURKISH GREECE

By *Peter Lock*

History of Frankish and Venetian Greece. Western influences on Greece go back to the 11C. Western travellers like the monk Benedict of Peterborough and the Spanish Jew Benjamin of Tudela visited the land in that century and recorded their impressions of it. But, all-too-often, the contacts were violent and were motivated by greed rather than by scholarship or tourism. The Norman conquerors of southern Italy sought to expand their dominions across the narrow Straits of Otranto and in the years 1081–84 seized Corfu and raided as far as Larissa in Thessaly. Pressure was renewed in 1146 when Thebes and Corinth were sacked and silk-workers forcibly taken from those cities and settled in Sicily.

To balance the Norman threat the Byzantine rulers resorted to the age-old policy of setting barbarian against barbarian. They signed a treaty with the Venetians in which the unique Venetian commodity, naval power, was enlisted against the common Norman foe in return for commercial advantages within the empire (1082). In turn the Venetians became dangerous and had to be restrained by the introduction of commercial rivals from the other Italian mercantile republics of Amalfi, Genoa and Pisa to whom trading concessions were granted during the course of the 12C. By 1200 the West had considerable political and commercial aspirations in the eastern Mediterranean, whilst the actions of Richard I of England in seizing Cyprus from the Byzantine authorities in April 1191 while on his way to the Third Crusade (1189–93) showed how easily lands might be gained in the East.

With the Fourth Crusade (1202–04) Greece lost what unity it had as part of the Byzantine Empire, a unity that was not to be restored until the Turkish conquests of the 1450s/70s and its incorporation in the Ottoman Empire.

After the sack of Constantinople by the Crusaders on 12 April 1204 and the establishment of the Latin Empire of Romania there, the former provinces of the Byzantine Empire were partitioned amongst the Venetians and the other Crusaders, who came mainly from France and Germany. The Republic of Venice, eager to consolidate its predominance in the carrying-trade of the Levant, acquired harbours such as Methoni and Koroni and the bulk of the Aegean islands, all strategic bases that would protect its sea-lanes to Alexandria, Alexandretta, Cyprus, and the ports of Asia Minor and the Black Sea. In many of the islands the Republic, whilst maintaining suzerainty in its own hands, was content to leave direct rule to ambitious Venetian families like the Orsini and Tocci who ruled as Dukes of Cephalonia and the Sanudi and Crispi who ruled the Cyclades as Dukes of the Archipelago. The Greek mainland wa left to Frankish barons from Flanders, France and Germany who divided up the land as it was conquered into feudal states owing vague and various allegiance to the Frankish King of Thessaloniki (to 1223), then to the Latin Emperor of Constantinople (to 1260) and thereafter to the Capetian, Aragonese and Angevin rulers of western Europe. Elements of the former Byzantine Empire survived around Nicaea and Trebizond in Asia Minor and in the Despotate of Epirus in NW Greece.

Of the various Frankish states the most important were the Duchy of Athens and Thebes (1205–1460), the Principality of Achaia (1205–1432), and the various scattered Venetian possessions with various dates from 1205 to 1715 in the Aegean and to 1797 in the Ionian islands. Late-comers were the Knights of St. John, who moved from Cyprus to Rhodes in 1310 and remained there until their expulsion by the Turks in 1522, and the Genoese, who had taken no part in the Fourth Crusade but who acquired colonies from the revived Byzantine Empire after 1261. Edward Gibbon dismissed '...the obscure and various dynasties that rose or fell on the continent or in the isles', but they are worthy of brief separate consideration to set the monuments in their political and patronage framework.

The Lordship (after 1260 the Duchy) of Athens and Thebes was granted to the Burgundian Otho de la Roche in 1205. This feudal unit retained its identity long after the passing of the Franks, forming the core of the Turkish Sanjak of Attica, Boeotia and Euboea. The splendour of the court at Thebes and the excellence of the French spoken there was much-written about by western visitors. The Frankish dynasty was overthrown in 1311 by the Catalan Company, a band of mercenaries, who, after fighting in Sicily and in Asia Minor, were employed by the Frankish Dukes and fell-out with their employer over payment. The Franks were annihilated at the Battle of the Kifisos (somewhere near the modern Levadhia railway station), a battle in many ways analogous to the Battle of Bannockburn fought in 1314.

The Catalans owed allegiance to the Crown of Aragon. Besides indulging in acts of piracy against the Venetians, they extended the territory of the Duchy to the north, incorporatng Neo-Patras, and built up Daulis (La Dablia) and Levadhia as important urban centres. In their turn the Catalans were replaced in 1381 by the Florentine banking family, the Acciaioli. The Acciaioli ruled the Duchy until 1460 and its final annexation by the Turks. The Florentines not only built the fine tower that stood by the Nike bastion on the Acropolis (demolished in 1874 and now visible only in paintings, some of which are in the Ethniki Pinakotheke, Athens) but also introduced Albanians into central Greece to re-populate the Duchy. Their descendants are still found in the area and many still speak an Albanian patois.

In the Peloponnese the Principality of Achaia with its centre at Andravidha (Andreville) was set up by two adventurers from the Champagne, William de Champlitte and Geoffrey de Villehardouin. On Champlitte's death (1209) Geoffrey assured the Principality for himself and his heirs. However, by 1278 the male line had failed and the Principality was ruled by bailes appointed by the Angevin monarchs in Naples. At this time of weakness Byzantine authority was reviving in the Peloponnese. Starting in 1262 with the regaining of Mistra, Old Maina, and Monemvasia, by 1432 the Byzantine Despotate of the Morea did in fact govern the whole of the Peloponnese with the exception of the Venetian bases at Methoni, Koroni, Argos, Lepanto and Nauplia. The Byzantine restoration was short-lived for by 1461 the Despotate had succumbed to the Turks.

The Venetians gained the islands and many coastal bases in the partition of 1204 and continued to add to those possessions throughout the period. However, the *Stato da Mar* fluctuated considerably in extent as it encountered and attempted to contain the Turkish threat. Crete, purchased in 1204, remained Venetian until 1669 despite many revolts. It was important for sugar, corn and horses. Euboea, acquired in 1209 was held until 1470. Its capital Chalkis (Negroponte) was the main base for naval patrols in the Aegean. Koroni and Methoni were important supply points on the route to Syria. They both fell to the Turks in 1500. Argos was acquired in 1388 and lost in 1463, Nauplia gained in 1388 lost 1540, regained 1686 and finally lost in 1715. This fluctuation of fortune and empire is well-reflected in Athens. Acquired in 1394, it was regained by the Acciaioli in 1402; raided in 1464, it was gained for the last time in 1687 when the forces of the Holy League, led by the Venetian Francisco Morosini and largely Venetian-inspired, captured Athens and held it for a year. This last Crusade in the Near East cost the Parthenon its roof. Despite the latter-day Crusade Venice was not strong enough to hold on to its resurrected Greek empire and in 1718 the Peloponnese together with Tinos, the last island in Venetian occupation, fell to the Turks.

Finally, the occupation of Rhodes by the Knights of St. John in the years 1310–1522 has been mentioned above. Genoese possessions on the Greek islands should also be noted. They included Chios, rich in mastic, which was held until 1566 and also Lesbos, Samos and Thasos, all of which had passed into Turkish hands by the 1470s.

Frankish and Venetian Greece was swept away by the Turkish conquest of the 15C. Its legacy to Greece might be summed up as some loan-words in the modern Greek language, a certain amount of literature such as the *Livre de la Conquête*, the *Chronicle of the Morea* and, perhaps most important of all, the *Erotokritos* of the Veneto-Cretan Vitsentzos Kornaros (1553–1617), and a very considerable body of archaeological remains in the landscape. There had been no mass conversion to Roman Catholicism, no union of the Roman and Orthodox Churches, no adoption of Gothic styles of architecture and no substantial emigration from the West to Romania. The Franks remained a tiny minority.

The Monuments of Frankish and Venetian Greece. The study of the monuments of Post-Byzantine Greece is hampered by the absence of firm historical evidence and by the lack of careful excavation of a well-stratified medieval site that might lead to a tighter dating of the pottery of the period and hence to closer dating of other sites with which it is associated. This vagueness is reflected in the tiny amount of Frankish and Venetian material displayed in museums. Examples of pottery, terracotta, and coinage may be chanced upon in museums all over Greece. However, there are small displays in the Agora and Benaki Museums in Athens, and in the museums at Chalkis, Corinth, Mistra, Nauplia and Rhodes. The Byzantine Museum in Athens, too, has some icons in its collection that reflect Frankish influence. Fragmentation is the keynote of the period, evident not only in its political history (outlined above) but also in the monuments themselves. The monuments, especially fortifications, were adopted and adapted by the successive rulers of the land, often causing an architectural confusion difficult to disentangle.

Firm documentary evidence of the fiscal and legal transactions of these Post-Byzantine regimes does not appear to have survived in any quantity and so only a very few of the buildings have even approximate dates based on documentary evidence. Thus it is known that the Castle of Chlemoutsi was constructed between 1220 and 1223 since the means by which it was financed were sufficiently high-handed to warrant Papal excommunication and so to deserve mention not only in the Papal archives but also in the *Chronicle of the Morea*. Likewise the destruction of the Benedictine monastery of Nôtre Dame at Issova by the Greeks in 1264 (and hence the dating of its construction to the first quarter of the 13C) was recorded because soon after this sacrilegious act those same Greeks were routed by a small Frankish force apparently led by Our Lady of Issova mounted on a white horse. It is, then, on the chance mention of a building in the medieval accounts of the impious and the scandalous that the architectural historian is forced to rely.

An examination of styles, of plans, and of materials can shed some light on differentiating and dating the Frankish, Venetian and Turkish monuments but this is not as straightforward as at first it might appear. With regard to Christian religious buildings, Gothic was and is a foreign style in Greece and as such it stands out as distinctive from the traditions of Byzantine architecture with its emphasis on the rounded form. There is almost no complete Gothic structure in Greece with the exceptions of the church of Nôtre Dame at Issova (Benedictine), Ayia Sophia at Andravidha (Dominican) and Ayia Maria at Zarnaka (Cistercian). At the first two churches there are both lancet and tracery windows, ogeed piscinae, diagonal ribbed-vaulting, and Gothic moulding is evident in the corbels and string courses. Not only is Zarnaka the most ruinous of the trio but the builders of the Cistercian Order were limited by their Rule as to the amount of display that they might indulge in. Nonetheless, there are the remains of foliated capitals and an intriguing keystone carved with a 'green man'—a type common in late medieval northern Europe. The masonry of these churches consists of small regular ashlar throughout although at Andravidha tile slips have been used in the joints—a typical Levantine construction technique.

More often it would appear that Gothic features were added to existing Byzantine buildings. This is particularly noticeable at the Monastery of Daphni where a 14C Cistercian porch, complete with pointed arches contrasts with the rounded, brick-decorated Byzantine openings immediately behind it. Ayia Paraskevi in Chalkis is a Byzantine basilica with added ribbed-vaulting and much Frankish foliated carving on keystones, capitals and corbels. Ayia Maria at Gastouni is another Byzantine church, this time with a Gothic doorway, whilst the Church of the *Koimesis* at Khalandritsa has a squared (i.e. Frankish) east end. Finally, Frankish tomb-chests, without effigies or other decoration but set in wall-niches with pointed arches, occasionally appear in the midst of Byzantine churches. The best examples may be seen at Ayios Yioryios, Akraifnion, Ayia Paraskevi, Chalkis, and Ayios Yioryios in the Castle of Yeraki. Existing Byzantine churches would seem, then, to have been used by the Franks. The requirements of the Latin liturgy as expressed in the church plans of Western Europe seem to have been sacrificed to convenience.

The needs of defence have seldom respected monuments in Greece and adaptation and repair by successive builders are both features of the fortifications. Poor historical documentation makes it impossible to identify exclusively Frankish, Venetian, and Turkish structures. Masonry styles are of little help since the re-use of Classical blocks, rubble masonry and a liberal use of tile slips in the joints were employed from late Roman to modern times in Greece. This makes it unwise to assume that what looks old is necessarily so.

In general the typical 13C Frankish castle is composed of baileys around a central keep with square flanking-towers in the curtain wall. This lay-out is commonly found in castles in the areas of Frankish occupation from Bodhonitsa and Levadhia to Kalamata and Old Navarino but perhaps most significantly at Chlemoutsi, the most-securely dated of early Frankish castles. This layout represents no departure from north European and Byzantine military planning of the 12th Century. However, circular flanking-towers do appear at some Frankish sites in the 13C and make a striking contrast wth Byzantine towers. Fine examples may be seen at Argos, Castel Franchi at Nauplia and at Chlemoutsi. Frankish castles are often sited on the summits of precipitous and isolated hills which not only removed the necessity for massive circuit walls but also raises questions of the reasons for and the means of their construction.

Venetian fortifications provide interesting contrasts with those of the Franks mainly with regard to siting and plan. Unlike the mountain fastnesses of the Franks Venetian forifications were sited with reference to the sea and the need to protect a harbour as the first and last resort of succour and supply. As a result they have massive landward defences with ingeniously protected gateways. They also well illustrate the adaptation of traditional medieval defences to artillery fortification with the addition of bastions, escarpments and cavaliers. These features may best be seen at Koroni, Methoni and Nauplia.

Post-Byzantine archaeology in Greece has suffered from neglect. What there is of it has tended to concentrate upon the military sites at the expense of towns, houses, rural settlement, and communications. Of these topics virtually nothing is known. Houses must have formed the great majority of buildings yet few medieval houses are known and their general typology is not worked out. Some 12C house-plans from the excavations at Athens and Corinth would indicate groups of modest rooms around a central courtyard, whilst at Mistra only the Laskaris mansion has received attention. The old city of Rhodes provides the most evocative medieval townscape. Of medieval rural settlement some attention has been given to the free-standing towers of the central Greek countryside which may, perhaps, represent the centres of Frankish fiefs, whilst abandoned village settlements still await study. The medieval road and bridge network is equally unknown (a fine Frankish bridge complete with a chapel on one of its piers survives at Karytaina). There is a great need to record these monuments and for the deliberate excavation of both medieval military and domestic sites.

The Turkokratia and its Monuments. The Turkish occupation (1460–1830) was for Greece a time of oppression and neglect. Many Turkish monuments were destroyed during and in the aftermath of the bitter War of Independence (1821–30) and there is still a disinclination to study the monuments of this period. Few Moslem monuments now survive intact except in Thrace and the old city of Rhodes where Turkish communites still exist. The atmosphere of Turkish settlements in Greece is best evoked by the towns of the north, especially Dhidhimotikhon, Kastoria, Kavalla old town, Kozani and Xanthi.

Most mosques lie in ruins or have been put to secular use after the removal of the minarets. Most notable and accessible of this latter group are the Tzisdharaki mosque in Monastiraki Square, Athens, built in 1759, the nearby Fetiche mosque at the corner of the Roman agora and the mosques in Chalkis (1470), Dhidhimotikhon, Kavalla and Nauplia. Also in Athens and in Nauplia are 18C medresses or Islamic schools. Just opposite the gateway to the Athens medresse is the so-called Tower of the Winds, which became in the 18C a tekke or headquarters for an order of dervishes. An early 19C Islamic charitable foundation is represented by the Imaret at Kavalla, an impressive grouping complete with fountains, a mosque, pointed arches and patinated copper domes. This was originally an old-people's home, built and endowed by the city's most famous son, Muhammad Ali (1769–1848) who was Ottoman governor of Egypt from 1805 to 1848, in which period this former Macedonian tobacco-merchant turned his Pashalik into a royal dynasty.

With regard to the fortifications there are few purely Turkish sites to be seen. They generally show an elaborate, even fussy plan, and construction with the needs of artillery warfare in mind. Thes best examples are at Rion (1499), New Navarino (1573) and the Karababa at Chalkis (1686). For the rest there has been adaptation and repair of existing structures often difficult to distinguish. Masonry styles are similar to those of the Franks and Venetians, and the Turks too used pointed arches occasionally distinguishable by the 'L-shaped' jointing in the soffit. Brick fan-vaulting is another pointer to Turkish workmanship. Some fine examples of this may be seen in the Castle of the Morea at Rion.

In towns the Turks seem to have occupied the defended areas like the former acropolises, leaving the Greeks in the lower towns or the suburbs. The ruined Turkish bath-houses and other buildings within the walls of the former Venetian fortress of Methoni should be contrasted with the small but lively later Greek settlements just outside the walls. The traveller George Wheler, visiting Chalkis in 1676, described how only the Turks lived within the city walls whilst 18C prints show the Parthenon being jostled by Turkish streets and houses. Acrocorinth too has the remains of Turkish bath-houses, a mosque and other buildings within its walls. Fountains were an important part of the Turkish town and examples survive at Koroni, Nauplia and Old Corinth. In the countryside 19C travellers make it clear that there were Turkish estates all over Greece, even if they were not particularly dense on the ground. Many were described as consisting of towers surrounded by mud huts. They seem to have left no trace in the archaeological record. Just what they looked like is unknown, although the travellers seem to have had no difficulty in differentiating them from Frankish towers. Bridges too, mainly of 18C date, may be found all over Greece but especially fine examples should be sought in Epirus near Zagori and Konitsa.

The artefacts of the Turkokratia and seldom displayed and less often studied. The Benaki Museum, Athens contains some Turkish material though not found in Greece. However, the various folk museums now springing up all over Greece do give some impression of the material culture of the subject population in the latter days of the Turkokratia. Nonetheless, the archaeology of Turkish Greece is still almost a virgin field.

GREEK FOLK ART

By *Jane Cocking*

The folk arts of Greece are among the most decorative and fascinating in Europe, reflecting the environment in which they are produced with beauty of style and technique. This introduction aims to answer the questions, what exactly is folk art, who made it, and for what purpose, and what can it tell travellers about the country through which they are travelling? There will follow a brief description of the main categories of folk art in Greece together with some suggestions as to where to see or purchase examples of the various crafts.

The primary feature of any item of folk art is that it is an object which can fulfil a practical purpose as well as being as decorative. Whether or not the item is actually used for that purpose is not important. A decorated wooden spoon is definitely a piece of folk art, as is an embroidered cushion or a carved distaff; even large pieces of carving on the wall of a house usually serve some architectural purpose. They are all basically functional objects which, either decorated or undecorated, were in daily use.

Greek folk art may be divided roughly into the professional and the domestic. The former comprises items made by artisans who have had some apprenticeship or training, however informal. They are often characterised by the need for specialist and often relatively costly equipment requiring financial investment. They may also involve a continuous process which necessitates an investment of time in order to be in attendance at specific moments during that process. These arts often developed a guild structure and a common craft identification and frequently became associated with specific families.

Included in the professional category are stone carving, metal work, architectural woodcarving and some forms of pottery. This last reinforces the point that objects of folk art are both decorative and functional. For example, traditional Rhodian plates painted with designs are items of folk art. They are capable of serving as plates and yet they are frequently used to decorate island homes. A plain pithos however, is also the product of the potter's workshop, but is only functional and not decorative. The pithos therefore, is an example of folk craft and not folk art.

Domestic arts are defined by their lack of specific timed processes. They may be taken up and set down as other duties allow, they are usually carried out in the home and they require little specialist equipment. As the items produced are often those that are actually used in the home, rather than being purely decorative, they are likely to need constant replacement. It is easier to produce such items oneself rather than to order them from an independent source. Such arts include basketry, weaving, embroidery and pastoral woodcarving. This last epitomises the difference between professional and domestic folk arts. Pastoral work includes all small items such as walking sticks, distaffs and spoons which can be carved and whittled intermittently. this contrasts with its professional counterpart, architectural woodcarving, which requires planning and possibly co-ordination with other workers.

In general, items of folk art are made by their users. Even professionals are usually only producing for their own community. There is no intention of exporting goods. Domestic workers are even more obviously producing for their own needs. The personal nature of the objects is highlighted by the fact that they have frequently gained significance in the family as they grew older, for sentimental and not financial reasons. For example, many pieces of embroidery found in 20C homes consist of several fragments from different items sewn together to form a whole. This is because, as embroidery began to die out, daughters who did not do as much work as their mothers divided their relative's embroideries and then, left with several small pieces, sewed them together for greater use and personal value. What had been an individual's possession had become a family heirloom.

The raw materials of folk art are usually locally produced and therefore readily available. Imported raw materials are only used to supplement local supplies and not to replace them as a matter of preference. This has two results: it underlines the idea of the actual character and appearance of folk art being dictated by local conditions, and it throws light on the position of folk art in society. It is something which is done as a matter of course and tradition which does not have great material value (for example, a blanket made from locally produced wool and dyed using natural dye stuffs gathered in the vicinity). This is completely different from an item of 'high art' which may involve the planned import of rare and costly materials.

Greek folk art also bears all the recognised hallmarks of ethnographic expression. Items are anonymous, very rarely is work actually 'signed'. This is for two main reasons. First, there is no concept of an artist conceiving an original idea and executing it for its own sake. Second, there is no reason to sign a piece of work that was either for use by the family of the creator or a member of a relatively small community where all items of a certain type were the work of one man; for example, copper objects were all made by the coppersmith. It is highly unlikely that there would be more than one specialised worker in such a field in the district.

The second hallmark is tradition. Designs and techniques changed and developed very slowly as they were passed down from generation to generation. For example, the French traveller Savary criticised the women of Kimolos for what he regarded as the ugliness of their dress. He received the reply, 'Our grandmothers were clad in the same way, we do but follow the custom'.

Finally, items of folk art are spontaneous, they are completely entrenched in the lives of the people who create and own them; they are not the result of a conscious desire to fulfil a perceived need.

Greek folk art embodies all of these general characteristics and one more of its own, regionalism. Before 1947 different parts of Greece had very different histories as they fell variously under the influence of the Ottoman Empire, Venice, Genoa and their local representatives. The folk art of the area reflects this well. It falls technically and stylistically into nine different divisions: Epirus, Macedonia, Sterea Ellas, Attica, Peloponnese, Skyros and the northern islands including Paros, the Cyclades, the Dodecanese and Crete. These divisions coincide with the historical pattern of the country as well as with other features such as dialect; for example, Paros, while geographically in the Cycladic group, has both a dialect and style of folk art which have far more in common with the Sporades with which it shares a common historical heritage.

In view of this regional differentiation it is possible to identify the origin of a piece on stylistic grounds. For example, Cycladic embroidery incorporates repeated diaper designs and tightly twisted thread while the Dodecanese is characterised by separate individual motifs and heavy flock silk.

Attribution on stylistic grounds raises the question as to whether intermarriage and travel between regions caused the actual movement of objects of folk art and the mingling of styles. Population movement did not take place as a result of historical and environmental factors and this led to certain anachronisms. For example, Robert Pashley in his 'Travels in Crete' (1837) described a girl who spent some time living in Naxos for 'protection and security during the war in Crete'. When she returned to her native village where Pashley met her she still wore the Naxian costume and worked Naxian embroidery. This, he says, annoyed her family and made her extremely conspicuous.

A further example of the transmission and mingling of designs is found in the village of Apeiranthos on Naxos today. Many of the inhabitants are the descendants of several families who migrated from Crete during the 19C and they still speak with a marked Cretan accent. The traditional textiles which are being worked there are based on Naxian techniques used together with Cretan designs.

In spite of such relatively isolated examples, a definite sense of regional identity was preserved in most places and it would require a very large-scale migration to produce a significant alteration in the style of the folk art being found in a given area worked either by immigrants or natives.

It has been mentioned before that one of the main characteristics of folk arts in general is that they are made of locally available raw materials, and in an area so clearly divided into various regions as Greece this dictates one of the most interesting features of the subject, the diversity of different categories produced in different areas. For example, metalwork is much more common in the north where silver (in the north-west) and copper (in the north-east) are more readily available than further south. Similarly, thickly wooded areas are characterised by heavy carved panelling in the vernacular architecture which is absent in stone houses of the more sparsely wooded islands. There are certain exceptions to this general rule, often in the case of relatively easily transportable light textile fibres. For example, Crete produces large amounts of woven and embroidered textiles made of wool, cotton, silk and linen. That the island definitely produced large quantities of silk, cotton and wool is shown by 19C local records and consular documents, linen however, proves to be more difficult; in the late 19th and early 20C it is known that it was imported on a large scale from the Ionian islands for semi-industrial uses and presumably some of the surplus found its way onto the home market. However, prior to this it seems quite possible that flax was produced in small subsistence quantities in areas such as the Lasithi Plain in the east and the White Mountains in the west.

Decoration is obviously an important aspect of folk art. Together with the purpose of items of folk art and the raw materials from which they were made, the designs and motifs are a reflection of the environment in which they were worked. Designs and motifs epitomise folk art in the way in which they are passed down from generation to generation by word of mouth. Nor are they passed on to specific individuals alone; they are part of a communal heritage which is available to the mass of the population in some form.

Folk art is definitely decorated and not designed. Motifs are arranged over a surface rather than the worker using an overall scheme which involves the preconceived idea of the link between the form of the object and the style in which it is decorated. This is often illustrated by the way in which designs and motifs are arranged on the item, for example, by covering the whole thing with a single repeated motif, starting at one edge and working over to the next.

Designs rarely change even when they are worked on pieces completely different in form and style. Designs on pottery from Rhodes remain basically the same whether they are worked on high necked jugs, square bottles or tiles. Similarly the same designs are used in the same area on all types of media.

The origins of the designs used in Greek folk art fall into three basic categories: those taken from personal experience, which are usual in peasant art; the more geometric designs that are repeated throughout the piece and seem to be part of a general Mediterranean heritage but are particularly common in Greece; and those which are a direct result of outside influences.

In the first group the workers were influenced by their natural surroundings, for example in depictions of flowers and birds. Human figures appear infrequently, but when they do are usually engaged in some activity, for example an Epirote wedding or Cycladic dancer. Geometric motifs fall into the simple and the complex. The simple ones are common in folk art throughout the world but the more complex ones are the result of local interpretations of basic motifs which are unlikely to be repeated elsewhere.

The third category of motifs, those which are copies of motifs indigenous in other areas, is particularly characteristic of Greek folk art. It is reasonable to assume that in the case of Greece the motifs did not emerge spontaneously, but were passed along some identifiable route of communication. The Mediterranean has always been a waterway that united peoples rather than kept them apart, and as various areas of Greece fell under a succession of foreign rulers the motifs from those cultures were absorbed into the common heritage. Examples of this process in action are the Anatolian rose spray found in Crete and in the Cyclades, the Turkish pomegranates in Epirote work and the south Italian peacocks and mermaids in the Ionian Islands and Crete. In each case the rudiments of the design are picked up either by copying imported objects or by personal teaching. However, as the new designs are worked using local raw materials they assume a slightly different appearance in each region.

To look at Greek folk art in greater detail it is necessary to examine the various crafts and their basic characteristics individually.

Pottery. One of the most common forms of folk art throughout Greece, it is particularly highly decorated with vivid red, blue and green floral designs in Epirus and the Dodecanese, quite possibly in imitation of high-quality Isnik wares. Peloponnesian material is characterised by a greenish glaze and green and yellow watery designs. Unglazed wares with incised decoration are also common throughout the area.

Textiles. Possibly the next most common form. Woven and embroidered textiles are found throughout Greece, although embroidered pieces are more often seen in the south than the north where the climate dictated heavier woollen pieces both for clothing and for home insulation. Textiles have been particularly susceptible to imported foreign designs. As a result they are often the most accurate indicators of the degree of foreign influence exerted on a given area. Classic examples are the embroidered textiles of Crete which include Byzantine double-headed eagles, Italian sirens and Turkish tulips, admirably reflecting the island's history.

Metalwork. Most metal objects tend to be easily portable or costume items. This is largely as a result of their high value and the need to be able to carry them easily if a hasty move were required. These are the most difficult items to establish a chronology for as they have been the frequent victims of melting down and reforming.

Woodwork. One of the most varied forms of folk art, woodwork decorates a wide range of pieces and more than any other form illustrates homogeneity of design throughout Greece.

Stone-carving. A less common form of folk art, stonework designs do not tend to develop but remain highly stylised or very representative of imported designs.

Wall-painting. More common in the north than the south, wall-painting is relatively rare, but where it does exist provides excellent evidence of life at the time of its painting.

Museums. There is a rapidly growing number of folk art museums throughout Greece, ranging from the large national collections to small village exhibitions. The following is a minute selection of some of the larger ones:

Benaki Museum, Athens. A vast private collection including a wide range of folk art. The collection of island embroideries is particularly fine.

Museum of Folk Art, Plaka, Athens. A beautifully displayed collection of textiles, woodwork and some metalwork. Pieces are well labelled and illustrated with photographs.

Peloponnesian Folklore Foundation. (Winner of the Small Museum of Europe Award.) An excellent display illustrating textile processing and different forms of textile techniques. The upper floor houses an extensive collection of mainland costumes.

Museum of Macedonian Folklore, Salonika. A wide collection of objects, well displayed, providing a clear insight into the way folk art represents regional history.

Folk Museum of Epirus, Ioannina. A smaller collection of Epirot objects, including some particularly beautiful costumes.

Buying Folk Art. In some areas it is possible to purchase items (pottery and textiles in particular) in the areas in which they are still being made, the most reasonable value usually being obtained from village craftsmen selling from their own premises. In the case of older items it is probably best to find dealers in the larger towns, away from the main centres of tourist activity, where it is still possible to find good pieces at relatively low prices.

GLOSSARY OF ART TERMS

AEGIS. Cuirass or shield with Gorgon's head and ring of snakes.

AGORA. Public square or market-place.

AMAZONOMACHIA. Combat of Greeks and Amazons.

AMBO (pl. *ambones*). Pulpit in a Christian basilica; two pulpits on opposite sides of a church from which the gospel and epistle were read.

ANTHEMION. Flower ornament.

APOTROPAION. A protective symbol to turn away evil.

BEMA. (*Anc.*) Rostrum; (*Byz.*) Chancel.

BRECCIA. A composite rock (pudding-stone).

CHITON. A tunic.

CHLAMYS. Light cloak worn by epheboi.

CHOROS. A hanging circle in metal or wood for the display of icons.

CHTHONIC. Dwelling in or under the ground.

CYMA (recta or reversa). A wave moulding with double curvature.

EPHEBOS. Greek youth under training (military, or university).

EPITAPHIOS. Ceremonial pall.

EROTES. Figures of Eros, god of love.

ESCHARA. Sacred hearth.

EXEDRA. Semicircular recess in a classical or Byzantine building.

GIGANTOMACHIA. Contest of Giants.

GYMNASION (in Mod Gk.). Grammar school.

HERM. Quadrangular pillar, usually adorned with a phallus, and surmounted by a bust.

HEROÖN. Shrine or chapel of a demigod or mortal.

HIMATION. An oblong cloak thrown over the left shoulder, and fastened over or under the right.

HOPLITE. Heavily armed foot-soldier.

HYPAETHRAL. Open to the sky.

ICONOSTASIS. Screen bearing icons.

KORE. Maiden; Archaic female figure.

KOUROS. Boy; Archaic male figure.

MEGARON. Hall of a Mycenaean palace or house.

NARTHEX. Vestibule of a Christian basilica.

NAUMACHIA. Mock naval combat for which the arena of an amphitheatre was flooded.

NYMPHAION. Sanctuary of the Nymphs.

ODEION. A concert hall, usually in the shape of a Greek theatre, but roofed.

OIKOS. A house.

OMPHALOS. A sacred stone, commemorating the 'centre of the earth' where Zeus' two eagles met.

OPUS ALEXANDRINUM. Mosaic design of black and red geometric figures on a white ground.

PANTOKRATOR. The Almighty.

PARECCLESIA. Chapel added to a Byzantine church.

PEPLOS. A mantle in one piece, worn draped by women.

PERIBOLOS. A preeinct, but often archaeologically the circuit round it.

PETASOS. Broad-brimmed felt hat worn by epheboi.

PHIALE. Saucer or bowl.

PINAX. Flat plate, tablet, or panel.

PODIUM. Low wall or continuous pedestal carrying a colonnade or building.

POLYANDREION. Communal tomb.

POROS. A soft, coarse, conchiferous limestone (tufa).

PROPYLON, PROPYLAEA. Entrance gate to a temenos; in plural form when there is more than one door.

PROTHESIS. (*Anc.*) Laying out of a corpse; (*Byz.*) The setting forth of the oblation, or the chamber N of the sanctuary where this is done.

PUTEAL. Ornamental well-head.

QUADRIGA. Four-horsed chariot.

SIMANTRON. Block of wood or metal bar beaten as a call to divine service.

SPHENDONE. The rounded end of a stadium.

STOA. A porch or portico not attached to a larger building.

TEMENOS. A sacred enclosure.

THEME. (*Byz.*) A province.

THOLOS. A circular building.

THYMELE. Altar set up in a theatre.

TRANSENNA. Openwork grille at the entrance to a Byzantine chapel.

TRILITHON. Gateway made up of two jambs and a lintel.

TRIREME. Greek galley rowed by 3 banks of oars.

XOANON. Wooden image or idol.

PRACTICAL INFORMATION

Introduction

This section of the Guide is designed to help prospective visitors to Greece choose the route best suited to their requirements and to enable them to travel as comfortably and effectively as possible once they arrive. The amount of advance planning needed varies enormously according to individual taste and the kind of visit intended (a package tour or cruise requires virtually no personal initiative). Accordingly we begin by suggesting various general sources of information which may be drawn on as needed. Readers should note that the 'Practical Information' includes much advice (e.g. on methods of travel within Greece, or on site and museum hours) which is vital to successful travel and is not repeated subsequently.

Sources of Information. Information about any matter to do with visiting Greece may be obtained from the NATIONAL TOURIST ORGANISATION OF GREECE (in Greek EOT) with has offices in both London (195–97 Regent Street, W1) and New York (601 Fifth Avenue), also Los Angeles (627 West Sixth Street). Regional leaflets and the regularly revised 'General Information about Greece' are available.

Useful up-to-date suggestions about places to visit and methods of travel (also current prices) can often be obtained from the travel pages of the Sunday newspapers.

Two excellent English-language monthlies (published in Athens but available in Britain, from BAS Overseas Publications Ltd, BAS House, 48–50 Sheen Lane, London SW14 8LP) are invaluable for planning travel both to and within Greece, since they contain an extremely wide range of information. They are *Greek Travel Pages* (price in Athens c £3.00, 1986) and the *Key Travel Guide* (£2.50). These publications give details of air, rail and bus travel, hotel information (not below C category) and much other useful matter (customs, shop hours, etc.). The English magazine *Time Out* is useful for cut-rate travel, including buses.

For accommodation, the detailed and comprehensive *Guide to the Greek Hotels*, published annually in mid-March by the Hellenic Chamber of Hotels (price in Athens, £3.50, 1986) gives information about hotels of all categories, with prices.

A good range of MAPS is now available, though there are sometimes inaccuracies in the designations of new or minor roads. Two good maps which cover the whole country are those produced by Hallwag and Kummerley & Frey. Others are obtainable from the British motoring organisations. The Greek equivalent (ELPA, see below) produces a useful (though rather small scale) road atlas, with a good deal of extra information, the latter requiring some knowledge of Greek. A map widely available in Athens (from kiosks and bookshops) is that published by Efstathiadhis Bros. A specialist map stockist in London is Stanford's of Long Acre.

Contoured maps at 1:200,000 (mostly compiled in the 1960s) are available for each nome (equivalent to a British county) and can be purchased from the Ethniki Statistiki Ipiresia tis Elladhos, 14 Likourgou, Athens 112 (and nowhere else). Some sheets which were revised in 1972 show ancient sites. Certain coastal areas are well covered by Greek Naval Charts which can be bought at the Hydrographic Office.

Travel to Greece

Air. This is the quickest and most convenient method of getting to Greece and can be relatively cheap. Scheduled flights are operated by British Airways (from London and, less frequently, Manchester) and Olympic Airways (London only), with several flights a day in summer, including some direct services to Salonika, Corfu, Rhodes, and Crete. The cheapest fares usually apply to trips of not more than one month's duration, where the ticket is booked well in advance and no change at all is permitted to the dates or times. As there are frequent changes in fare structures, current information should be sought from the airlines. Summer fares are usually higher than winter, and travel at weekends more expensive than on weekdays. CHARTER FLIGHTS operate from many regional airports (as well as from London) and to a considerable variety of destinations within Greece. While these are mainly intended for buyers of complete package holidays at rates which include accommodation, it is also possible to use them for travel only (with a nominal charge for accommodation). These flights are not necessarily very much cheaper than the cheapest fares on scheduled flights and may involve travelling at inconvenient times. On the other hand, they may allow direct travel from a local airport to the precise destination and, especially out of season, seats are often sold at discount prices when booked close to the departure date. Other European and American airlines also operate regular scheduled services to Athens.

In Athens, all foreign airlines use the East Terminal at Ellinikon Airport, while Olympic Airways operate from the West Terminal. It is worth remembering that, since the internal services are also based there, Olympic is the only airline whose flights from abroad do not require a change of terminal when onward air travel to another destination within Greece is intended.

Rail. Unless using a student 'Inter-rail' ticket (of limited duration), rail travel is no longer cheap and, unless the cost is further inflated by the purchase of sleepers, not very comfortable. The direct routes are from North European ports via France and Italy, or via Belgium/Holland and Germany and Austria into Yugoslavia. Couchettes or sleepers, if required, should be booked well in advance. Those who dislike the antiseptic nature of air travel may well consider taking the train to an Italian port followed by a boat crossing to Greece (see below). Timetable and other information about rail travel is available from British Rail Travel Centres (best at the larger stations).

Sea. There is no regular direct passenger line from Britain to Greece, which would in any case require a good deal of time. There are however a substantial number (less frequent out of season) of passenger/car ferry services from Adriatic ports (Brindisi, Bari, Ancona and, less frequently, Venice) to Patras (often via Corfu and/or Igoumenitsa), with onward bus connection to Athens, or direct to Piraeus through the Corinth canal. There are some services too from Marseilles and Genoa. The Brindisi–Patras route takes about 20 hours, via Corfu and

Igoumenitsa; the others correspondingly longer. Amongst the companies providing these services are Fragline (Brindisi), Adriatica (Brindisi, Venice), Ventouris (Bari), Karageorghis (Ancona), Minoan Lines (Ancona), Hellenic Mediterranean Lines (H.M.L.) (Brindisi), Libra Maritime (Brindisi) and Anco Ferries (Brindisi). Some routes continue to Turkey, Cyprus, the Levant or Egypt.

Road. The shortest overland route is c 3150km (1950 miles), via southern Germany, Austria and Yugoslavia and takes an absolute minimum of four days. For the trip to be enjoyable a more leisurely drive is preferable, perhaps following the Adriatic coast through Yugoslavia (considerably longer). Alternatively, car ferries may be used from one of the Italian ports mentioned above (the Brindisi route is the fastest, but not necessarily the most pleasant). Motorail services from a Channel port or Paris to southern France or Italy (Milan best) reduce the strain of driving. The services (including route and customs information, and bookings) provided by the AA and RAC are essential. For the Greek motoring organisation (ELPA), see below.

BUS. This is the cheapest (and least comfortable) method of getting to Greece. Vehicles travel either direct from a Channel port, or via one of the Adriatic ferries. There may or may not be night stops *en route*. The apparent economy may not be real when the cost of food and accommodation is taken into account. Travellers should be certain to choose a reliable operator. Information may be obtained from the Victoria Coach Station in London, student Travel Agencies, or newspaper advertisements (see above). The journey takes about 3–4 days.

Travelling Formalities.

Passports (British Visitors' Passports are valid) are the only travel document necessary for British nationals to travel in Greece. Application forms are available from any Post Office. Full passport requests may take some time to process and several weeks should be allowed. Those wishing to stay in Greece for longer than three months must apply, at the end of that period and not before, for a *permis de séjour*. They may be required to submit proof of financial self-sufficiency.

Customs. Normal EEC regulations on import/export of goods, alcohol, tobacco, etc. apply. Valuable items (especially electronic equipment) may be entered in the passport and re-export required (or else payment or import tax) at the end of the period of stay. This restriction always applies to private cars. Those wishing to keep a foreign-registered car in Greece for more than four months must apply for a permit from the appropriate customs department. If the owner desires, at any time, to leave the country without the vehicle, it must be sealed by the customs authorities for that period.

Currency. Only Drs 3000 in Greek currency may be imported but the amount of foreign currency, travellers' cheques, etc. is not limited. Where re-export of foreign currency of more than 500 US dollars may be desired on departure, declaration of holdings must be made on arrival. The export drachma limit is 3000.

Travel Within Greece

Sources of information. The two publications cited above (*Greek Travel Pages* and the *Key Travel Guide*) remain indispensible. Also useful is the ELPA road atlas. 'The Week in Athens', available from the National Tourist Organisation, is free and has information about entertainments in Athens and travel. The National Tourist Organisation of Greece has offices in various towns. The Athens centre is within the National Bank of Greece branch in Sintagma Square (2 Karayioryi Servias). It distributes much travel information in duplicated sheets, answers queries and can deal with hotel bookings. The 'Guide to Greek Hotels' can be purchased here. The former Tourist Police have now been replaced as a separate organisation by members of the ordinary police force who staff information desks in police stations. The central organisation in Athens has a good general telephone enquiry service (dial 171). The Greek Motoring Organisation (ELPA) has a similar enquiry service (dial 174). Foreign languages are spoken and all kinds of information provided. For enquiry services offering information about specific methods of travel only, see below.

Organised Travel. Details of the numerous cruises and coach tours of various durations may be acquired from any of the sources of information cited above.

Sea Travel plays a large part in Greek transport, most ships now conveying cars as well as passengers. Most lines are based on Piraeus but travellers in more distant parts of Greece should investigate services originating in, for example, Thessaloniki, Kavalla, Patras, Rhodes, Crete. A useful source of up-to-date and usually reliable information is the daily commercial shipping paper 'Naftemboriki (Ναυτεμπορική) which includes a complete list of the following seven days' domestic sailings from Piraeus and other main ports, also international arrivals and departures. Ability to read names in Greek is obviously necessary. Note also that π.μ. (p.m.) = English a.m. and μ.μ. (m.m.) = English p.m. Day-of-departure information about timings, which should always be checked before travelling, can be obtained in Athens from a recorded service (dial 143) or the Piraeus Port Authority (dial 108). Outside Athens, the most reliable information will be that provided by the local port authority (Limenarkhíon or Limenikós Stathmós; Λιμεναρχείον, Λιμενικός Σταθμός). A useful list of their telephone numbers is provided in the ELPA road atlas. They are the only reliable way of checking boat services in distant places, though some knowledge of Greek may be required.

BOOKING may be done in advance at travel agencies (many in central Athens, particularly the Omonia area) or, especially in smaller places, the agency (praktoríon) of the boat company concerned. It is best to choose the boat on which to travel from an independent source, as not all agencies have tickets for all boats and they naturally promote their own vessels. Be sure to choose the most direct route. Some services (especially to Rhodes) make many more stops and take much longer than others.

There are four main CLASSES: First, Second, Tourist and Third (= Deck); some vessels have a Luxe Class. Classes are officially assigned according to the quality of the available accommodation. Thus relatively few boats have all the four main classes and some do not have a First Class at all. Most boats have cabins only in the First (and Second)

Classes. No supplement is charged for cabins but there is no reduction if they are not available. To ensure a berth, it is necessary to have cabin and berth numbers entered on the ticket by the issuing agency. Vague promises that one will be available on the day are not enough. Decks of boats become very crowded and uncomfortable in the summer and, whatever the class, it is often more comfortable to travel inside. Cabins are a great benefit on night (or even long day) crossings, but can be stuffy. On long-distance ferry services, cars need to be booked well in advance. For short crossings in local waters, it is necessary only to turn up and join the queue.

Air Travel in Greece is provided by the extensive internal network of Olympic Airways. There are flights to many destinations and long distances can often be covered much more effectively by this means of travel, which is cheap by British standards. The frequency of flights obviously varies a good deal with the destination. BOOKING may be done at any office of or agent of Olympic Airways in Greece or abroad, though the fastest service is provided by those with a computer terminal. Advance booking is essential in the summer season (especially to the islands and other popular holiday areas). There is an extremely efficient and useful telephone booking system (in Athens dial 9616161; or via any office or agent). An intending traveller can be entered on the flight list simply by making a phone call. He is given a date by which the ticket must be collected and paid for (again at any

AIRPORTS

●   Airports with direct flights to Athens

○   Airports with interconnecting flights only

—   Flights between other centres
(some seasonal only)

Olympic office or agent). If the booking is not taken up in time it automatically lapses, without cost to the customer.

Railways. Greece was the last country in Europe to take up railway development (after 1881) and her railways play only a small part in the country's transport system. A line from Athens to Piraeus was constructed in 1867–69 and electrified in 1904, but the main Piraeus–Athens–Larissa line was built only in 1902–09, and did not reach Salonika until 1916. The first international express (Simplon–Orient) ran in July 1920. The former Peloponnesian Railway (SPAP) is now administratively part of the State Railway system but has a separate terminus in Athens and is of metre gauge only. The services are generally punctual but slow on account of the terrain. For the tourist the Peloponnesian Railway provides a convenient (and south of Corinth, very attractive) approach to, e.g. Argos, Patras, Olympia, Tripolis, and Kalamata. BOOKING should be done in advance to secure a seat, at stations or a network of in-town booking offices.

Road Travel. LONG DISTANCE BUSES are operated by Joint Pools of Bus Owners (Κοινόν Ταμείον Εισπράξείων Λεωφορείων; K.T.E.L.). These have been further grouped for the operation of two main Terminals, situated in the outskirts of Athens and served by city buses from central points. Each still has its own booking-office (prakoríon). Bookings (preferably in advance, and in any case before boarding the bus to ensure a numbered seat) may be made by telephone; the booking-offices are listed in the telephone directory under TAMEION, or more conveniently in one of the sources of information (above). With a booked seat it is not necessary to appear more than a few minutes before scheduled departure time when luggage is stowed.

Bearing in mind the distances involved buses keep well to schedule. The promoters have strictly-interpreted agreements about the places they serve. A bus from Kalamata may take passengers between that town (or its dependent nome) and any other place along its route to (say) Athens; it may not pick up intermediate passengers beyong Tripolis and Corinth, which, being in different nomes, are the province of other K.T.E.L. The traveller who intends to board a long-distance bus at the roadside needs some knowledge not only of schedules but of the nome boundaries, and should ascertain beforehand the appellation of the K.T.E.L. he wants (this is always prominently displayed on the front of the bus even if the destination sometimes is not). Buses are stopped, as in Britain, by a raised hand.

The State Railways (Ο.Σ.E.), also provide fast 'pullman' bus services from Athens to Larissa and Salonika, Loutraki, Mycenae and Nauplia, Patras, Zakynthos and Kefallinia, with bookings made and departure points the same as for trains.

LOCAL SERVICES. Most villages, however remote, are served by a bus based on the nearest town of any size. Small villages may be served once or twice daily or less frequently. Timings are designed to suit local markets and schools, not visitors, and the return trip may involve a night's stay. ADVICE ON BUS TRAVEL: those relying on buses as their main form of transport are most strongly urged to make the bus station or office (often, in a small place, the local café) their first port of call, immediately on arrival anywhere. A timetable of departures will often be prominently displayed and plans can be made. It is well worth postponing the compelling attractions of bed or refreshment in order to avoid missing the once-weekly bus (perhaps leaving early the following morning) to a much-desired destination.

CITY SERVICES. Buses and some trolley routes serve the capital between about 5.30 a.m. and midnight, with some all-night routes. Though frequent, they are often very crowded. Entrance is made at the front door; exit at the middle and/or rear doors. There is a flat fare over a large area of the centre of Athens and suburbs which is placed in a box by the driver, on entry. The fare is at present (1986) 30 drs but the amount is prominently displayed on the collection box. Public transport in Athens is free between 5.00 and 8.00 a.m., while supplements are charged on night services. Similar systems are operated in Salonika and other large towns.

TAXIS (metered) are numerous and cheap in the towns. Supplements are payable for journeys originating at any major public transport terminal. Outside the city boundary, a higher tariff applies. At busy times and with (or sometimes without) the permission of the original hirer, the driver may pick up other passengers going in roughly the same direction. Enquiry is made by shouting one's destination through the window. A deduction should be made for such passengers when they reach their destination, since the fare shown on the meter will be that from the original point of hire. This may not always be easy to negotiate but, at peak hours, it is probably worth ignoring the relatively small mark-up. In country areas, meters are not often found but there is a standard tariff which may or may not be publicly displayed or adhered to, and an agreement as to the fare should always be made in advance. If in doubt, enquire the price from several drivers. Travellers are advised to make good use of taxis which, judiciously employed, can enable one to see far more than might otherwise be possible in the time, where public transport is lacking, and at relatively modest cost. They can, in certain circumstances, work out cheaper than a hired car. For not-too-distant excursions, an arrangement can be made for the driver to return later, at a specified time, at a total fare less than that for two single journeys.

HIRE CARS, etc. There are numerous car hire companies in Greece (lists in the main Sources of Information and from the National Tourist Organisation). Several airports have representatives of the larger companies. Hire in Greece is relatively expensive (in 1986, about £200.00 per week for a small car, with unlimited mileage and inclusive of all taxes, in the high season). Nevertheless, the advantages to be gained in terms of extra mobility and access to remoter areas often make it an attractive option, particularly if costs can be shared. The cheapest rate is achieved by taking a full week's hire, with unlimited mileage. Three-day unlimited mileage rates are also available; otherwise the cost is calculated by adding a charge per kilometre to a modest daily rate. It is probably advantageous (though in no way essential) to arrange hire before leaving home. This is easy with international companies. Some travel firms offer inclusive 'packages' with flight, and car on arrival; others provide the option of car hire at a reduced rate. On the spot, reductions can sometimes be negotiated at quieter periods. When calculating rates from hire company leaflets, potential customers should be sure to include taxes (usually high—about 20 per cent) and any charges for additional insurance cover which may be desire. *Scooters* and *bicycles* can often be hired in tourist resorts.

MOTORING. Driving (on the right) is conducted in a competitive spirit which can be alarming to the visitor and accords Greece the dubious distinction of the highest accident rate in Europe. Nevertheless, outside the large cities, the roads are not crowded and motoring is pleasant. City traffic can always be avoided by leaving at quiet times of day. Petrol stations are plentiful on main roads but may be infrequent in remote areas. Parking is difficult in towns where there are often wide restrictions (frequently ignored). Private motorists can get road maps, information etc. from the GREEK MOTORING ORGANISATION (ELPA: EΛΠΑ). The Athens headquarters is at the Athens Tower, 2 Od. Mesogeion, and there are regional offices in all towns of any size, as well as some mobile trailers. The roadside assistance and rescue service (dial 104, in Athens) is extremely efficient and has reciprocal arrangements with other European motoring organisations. The ELPA telephone information bureau (dial 174, foreign languages spoken) has already been mentioned.

WALKING in the Greek countryside is one of the greatest pleasures to be had, partly for the natural surroundings; partly for the seemingly endless supply of friendly, helpful and hospitable people that the traveller is likely to encounter. It is virtually impossible to plan walks in any detail, since large scale maps showing footpaths are not generally available. However, since for many country people walking is the main form of travel, paths and old paved trackways (calderimia) are numerous and directions may be sought locally (for useful words, see below on finding Archaeological Sites). Directions may often be somewhat confusing (both in reality and because of language problems) and it is advisable to ask continually, if in any doubt at all. Unfamiliar hazards may be fierce dogs (who usually retreat when stones are picked up), snakes and swarming bees. Since the terrain can be rough and twisted ankles always a danger, some may prefer not to walk alone in remote areas.

Accommodation and Food

Hotels (Ξενοδοχεια: Xenodhokhía). Lists of hotels can be found in various Sources of Information (see above). The most comprehensive is the 'Guide to the Greek Hotels'. Other publications tend not to list hotels in categories below 'C'.

There are six official categories: **L** and **A–E**. Even in country districts modest but modern hotels are to be found almost everywhere. The de Luxe hotels compare favourably with their counterparts in other countries; almost all have restaurants; their rooms all have private bathrooms and air-conditioning. In all hotels of Class **A** and most of Class **B** a proportion of rooms (sometimes all) are equipped with private bath or shower. Class **C**, at present the most numerous, is the least easy to appraise. Many Greek hotels do not have restaurants. Hotels classed **D** or **E** have no public rooms and sometimes only cold water, though their standard of cleanliness and service may well be adequate for a short stay.

Charges are fixed annually by the Government. Hoteliers may not exceed the maximum permitted figure; the charge appropriate to each room, quoted with service and taxes included, is entered in a notice fixed usually to the inside of the door. Central heating or air conditioning is always extra. Considerable reductions can be obtained in November–March. In general large hotels in seaside resorts are closed in winter (except where the place is an important town, e.g. Corfu, Nauplia).

Despite the official categorisation, hotels can still vary widely. The independent traveller will realise that here as elsewhere, many hotels at popular sites and beach resorts are geared to package tours and coach groups rather than to the unexpected overnight guest. Furthermore some hotels can legally insist on demi-pension terms, thus tying the visitor to their usually unimaginative restaurants. In the provinces a universal-type basin plug and a stock of toilet paper can still prove an advantage. It is difficult to get single rooms; single occupation of a double room is usually charged at 80 per cent of double price.

Charges vary considerably, even within each category, so that a cheap B-class hotel can be less expensive than a dearer C. It is thus worth investigating establishments which seem at first sight likely to be too expensive. Provincial hotels are often considerably cheaper than those in large towns or major tourist centres. In 1986 (also applicable winter 1986/7), a twin room in a good C class hotel, with private bath, cost about £7.50–£10.00 (accommodation only). It is advisable to inspect the accommodation before making a definite agreement. Hoteliers are always willing to show rooms and respect an adverse decision.

Rooms. Where no hotel accommodation is available it is often possible, especially in holiday resorts or tourist centres, to find rooms either in specially built letting blocks ('Rooms for Rent' is an ubiquitous sign) or in private houses. The former are really modest hotels. The rooms quite often have a private bathroom and there is usually a fridge and kitchen, where food can be kept or prepared. In the islands, people often meet boats with offers of such accommodation; otherwise help may be sought from the police tourist officer or the local café.

Motels, of which there are a growing number, and seaside BUNGALOW-HOTELS have the same classification system as hotels.

Youth Hostels. The Greek Youth Hostel Association (4 Odhos Dhragatsaniou, Athens) is affiliated to the International Youth Hostels Federation. Its hostels may be used by members of any affiliated association. Accommodation is usually simple and members are obliged to keep early hours; stay is generally limited to 5 days. There are hostels in Athens, Delphi, Patras, Ioannina, Salonika, Mykonos, Corfu, and Herakleion, also smaller ones elsewhere.—In Athens are the YWCA (11 Od. Amerikis) and the YMCA (28 Od. Omirou), maximum stay 10 days, meals extra. In July and August the Polytechnic School in Athens also accommodates groups of students.

Car-Camping Sites are run by the NTOG (modest charges) at Voula, Killini, Patras (Ayia), Kamena Vourla, Thessaloniki, Asprovalta, Kavalla, Khalkidiki (Kriopiyi, Paliouri, and Kalandra), Fanarion, Alexandroupolis, and on Mt Olympos (Skotina). An up-to-date list may be obtained from the Athens Office. Elsewhere there are private camping sites.

Dining Out. In the larger centres a few restaurants and de luxe hotels achieve an international standard of cuisine. Well-prepared Greek dishes, however, are greatly to be preferred to feeble attempts at emulating alien styles. The basic ingredients are usually excellent and, since all Greeks eat out frequently, there is a wide choice of places. Travellers are well advised always to choose establishments crowded with locals, where the food will be better (and cheaper) and the atmosphere livelier.

Restaurants (Εστιατόρια: Estiatória). In Athens lunch is usually taken between 1 and 3 (earlier on Sunday) and dinner (generally the more important) between 8 and 11 p.m. (summer 9 p.m. and 1 a.m.), though hotels catering particularly for foreigners conform more nearly to Western times. Outside Athens also hours tend to be earlier.

Estiatória display at the entrance a bill of fare, showing their category (L, A–D) and the prices of each dish, both basic and with tax and service included. There are usually translations into English. Fixed-price and table d'hôte meals are rare. A service charge is added by law so that any small gratuity to the waiter (on the plate) is a recognition of personal service. The wine boy (mikrós), however, receives only what is left for him on the *table* (c 5 per cent).

The distinction between a restaurant proper and a Ταβέρνα is nowadays not clearly definable, but in general the **Tavérna** is less formal, patronised for a convivial evening rather than for luncheon, and partly at least out of doors; its fare is uncompromisingly Greek. An EXOKHIKÓN KÉNDRON (ΕΞΟΧΙΚΟΝ ΚΕΝΤΡΟΝ) ('rural centre') combines the functions of café and taverna in a country or seaside setting.—The simplest kind of meal, consisting of milk, coffee, bread, butter, honey, etc., can be had in a GALAKTOPOLEÍON, or dairy. Here in provincial towns the visitor will find the nearest equivalent to breakfast obtainable. A ZAKHAROPLASTEÍON, or pâtisserie, sells pastries and confectionery, with drinks of all sorts, though larger establishments in the cities serve light meals (generally not cheap). They increasingly resemble the French café, and for younger generations are replacing the traditional Greek kafeneion (see below).

Restaurants and taverna meals of comparable standard are considerably cheaper than in Britain. The pattern of meals is less stereotyped than in England, the sharing of portions being quite usual; it is essential to order each course separately as several dishes ordered together may arrive together. In tavernas it is usual to visit the kitchens to choose one's dishes, and in waterside tavernas it is customary to choose one's fish from the ice; this will then be weighed, the price appearing on the menu per kilo. The oily content of most Greek food is too exuberant for some tastes, and, though the local wine is a good counteragent, travellers will be well advised to take care until they become used to it. Frozen foods (still rare in Greece) must be indicated by law on the menu with the letters KAT.

Good table wines (unresinated, *arretsínoto*), both red and white, are obtainable in bottle everywhere and some of the better-known have a nation-wide distribution. Retsína, the resinated white wine characteristic particularly of Attica and the Peloponnese, has lost some of its former popularity in proportion as other wines have improved. It can always be obtained in bottle, but the traditional can or jug from the barrel is to be preferred, when available. This can still be more refreshing and less soporific in the heat of the day with an al fresco meal. Beer (of Bavarian type) is brewed in Greece and other lagers are brewed under licence or imported. The ordinary water of Athens (as generally in Greece) is safe, but mineral waters from spas such as Loutraki are readily available.

Food and Wine. The favourite Greek apéritif is *oúzo*, a strong colourless drink made from grape-stems and flavoured with aniseed; it is served with *Mezé*, snacks consisting of anything from a simple slice of cheese or tomato or an olive to pieces of smoked eel or fried octopus. As in Italy the Greek meal may begin with a foundation course of rice, such as *piláfi sáltsa*, or of pasta (*makarónia*), perhaps baked with minced meat (*pastítsio*) or with *tirópita* (cheese pie). Alternatives are soup or hors d'oeuvre, the latter being particularly good. *Taramosaláta* is a paste made from the roe of grey mullet and olive oil. *Tzatzíki* is composed of chopped cucumber in yoghourt heavily flavoured with garlic. The main course may be meat (κρέας, kréas), or fish or a dish on a vegetable base, baked (τοῦ φούρνου, too foúrnu), boiled (βραστό, vrastó), fried (τηγανιτό, tiganitó), roast (ψητό, psitó), or grilled (σχάρας, skháras). The chef's suggestions will be found under ΠΙΑΤΑ ΤΗΣ ΗΜΕΡΑΣ (piáta tis iméras; dishes of the day). *Moussaká* consists of layers of aubergines, minced beef, and cheese, with butter and spices, baked in the oven. Many foreign dishes may appear in transliteration, e.g.: Εσκαλόπ (escalope), Σνίτσελ Χολεταϊν (Schnitzel Holstein), Μπιντόκ αλα Ρούς (Bintok à la Russe), Κρέμ καραμελέ (crème caramelle), Σαλάτ ντέ φρουί (salade de fruits). Many sweets have Turkish names, and 'shish kebab' is frequently used as a synonym for *souvlákia*, pieces of meat grilled on a skewer. Also cooked in this fashion is *kokorétsi*, which consists of alternate pieces of lamb's liver, kidney, sweetbreads, and heart, wrapped in intestines. When not grilled, meat is often stewed with oil in unappetising chunks. Greek cheeses tend to monotony; the ubiquitous *féta* is better eaten—peasant-fashion—with black pepper, oil and rígani (oregano) than on its own. Sweets, however, are elaborate and varied, though more often partaken separately than as a course of a meal. Among the most popular are *baklavá*, composed of layered pastry filled with honey and nuts; *kataífi*, wheat shredded and filled with sweetened nuts; and *galaktoboúreko*, pastry filled with vanilla custard.

WINE (κρασί) in Greece is generally of good quality and has greater strength than the wines of France. Wines may be divided into two categories: resinated and unresinated. *Retsína*, flavoured with resin from pine trees, is most characteristic of the south, and to the trained palate varies as much in taste and quality as do unresinated wines. Although a great amount is bottled, retsína is better drunk young from cask. Rosé varieties (κοκκινέλλι), are locally much sought after. There is a large variety of wines, white (άσπρο, áspro), red (μαῦρο, mávro, literally 'black'), or rosé (Κόκκινο, kókkino, literally 'red'). There are good draught red wines from Nemea, Rhodes and Corfu. It is invidious to recommend bottled wines from the vast range available but some of the following may be sampled: Hymettus (red and white), Santa Elena (white), Pallíni (white), Vílitsa (white), Zítsa (white, semi-sparkling), Sámaina (white), Castel Daniélis (red), Tsántali (white, rosé), Chevalier de Rhodes (red), Náoussa (red), Robólla (white). The latter three are rather more expensive but no Greek wine is costly by British standards. The champagne of Rhodes is pleasant. The wines of the Carras estate are also good.

The MENU which follows contains a large number of the simpler dishes to be met with:

ΟΡΕΚΤΙΚΑ (orektiká), Hors d'oeuvre

Διάφορα ορεκτικά (dhiáfora orektiká), Hors d'oeuvre variés
Ταραμοσαλάτα (táramosaláta), see above
Ντολμάδες Γιαλαντζῆ (dolmádhes Yalantzí), Stuffed vine leaves served hot with egg-lemon sauce
Ντολμαδάκια (dolmadhakia), Cold stuffed vine leaves
Ελιές (elliés), Olives

ΣΟΥΠΕΣ (soúpes), Soups

Σούπα αυγολέμονο (soúpa avgholémono), Egg and lemon soup
Σούπα από χόρτα (soúpa apò hórta), Vegetable soup
Μαγειρίτσα (maghirítsa), Tripe soup generally with rice (Easter speciality)
Ψαρόσουπα (psarósoupa), Fish soup

ZΥΜΑΡΙΚΑ (Zimárika), Pasta and Rice dishes

Πιλάφι σάλτσα (piláfi sáltsa), Pilaf
Σπαγέτο σάλτσα μέ τυρί (spagéto sáltsa me tirí), Spaghetti

Μακαρόνια (makarónia), Macaroni

ΨΑΡΙΑ (psária), Fish

Στρείδια (strídhia), Oysters
Συναγρίδα (sinagrídha), Sea bream
Μπαρμπούνια (barboúnia), Red mullet
Μαρίδες (marídhes), Whitebait
Αστακός (astakós), Lobster
Γαρίδες (garídes), Scampi (Dublin Bay prawns)
Καλαμαράκια (kalamarákia), Baby squids
Κταπόδι (ktapódhi), Octopus
Λιθρίνια (lithrínia), Bass

ΛΑΔΕΡΑ (ladhērá), Vegetables or ΧΟΡΤΑ (khórta), Greens

Πατάτες τηγανιτές (patátes tiganités), Fried potatoes
Φασολάκια φρ. βουτ. (fasolákia fr. voútiro), Beans in butter
Μπιζέλια (biséllia), Peas
Ντομάτες γεμιστές ρύζι (domátes yemistés rizi), Stuffed tomatoes

ΑΥΓΑ (avgá) Eggs

Ομελέτα Ζαμπόν (Omelétta Zambón), Ham omelette
Αυγά Μπρουγέ (avgá 'brouillé'), Scrambled eggs
Αυγά ἀλὰ Ροίζ (avgá 'á la Russe'), Eggs with Russian salad

ΕΝΤΡΑΔΕΣ (entrádhes), Entrées

Αρνάκι φασολάκια (arnáki fasolákia), Lamb with beans
Μοσχάρι (moskhari), Veal
Σηκοτάκια (sikotákia), Liver
Κοτόπουλο (kotópoulo), Chicken
Χήνα (khína), Goose
Παπί (papí), Duck
Τζουτζουκάκια (tsoutsoukákia), Meat balls in tomato sauce
Κοτολέτες Χοιρινὲς (kotoléttes khirinés), Pork cutlets

ΣΧΑΡΑΣ (skháras), Grills

Σουβλάκια από φιλέτο (souvlákia apo filéto), Shish Kebab (see above)
Μπριζόλες μοσχ. (brizóles moskh.), Veal chops
Κεφτέδες σχάρας (keftédhes skháras), Grilled meat balls
Γουρουνόπουλο ψητό (gourounópoulo psitó), Roast sucking-pig
Παϊδάκια Χοιρινά (païdhákia khiriná), Pork chops

ΣΑΛΑΤΕΣ (salátes), Salads

Ντομάτα σαλάτα (domáta saláta), Tomato salad
Μαρούλι (maroúli), Lettuce
Ραδίκια (radhíkia), Radishes
Κολοκυθάκια (kolokithákia), Courgettes
Αγγουράκι (angouráki), Cucumber
Αγκινάρες (ankináres), Artichokes
Μελιτζάνες (melizánes), Aubergines (eggplants)
Πιπεριές (piperiés), Green peppers
Ρώσσικη (Russikí), Russian

ΤΥΡΙΑ (tiría), Cheeses

Φέτα (féta), Soft white cheese of goat's milk
Κασέρι (kasséri), Hard yellow cheese
Γραβιέρα (graviéra), Greek gruyère
Ροκφόρ ('Roquefort'), Blue cheeses generally

ΓΛΥΚΑ (gliká), Sweets

ΧΑΛΒΑ (ḥalvá)
Μπακλαβά (baklavá) see above
Κατάϊφι (kataifi)
Γαλακτομπούρεκο (galaktoboureko)
Ρυζόγαλο (rizógalo), Rice pudding
Γιαούρτι (yiaoúrti), Yoghourt

ΦΡΟΥΤΑ (froúta), Fruits

Μήλο (mílo), Apple
Μπανάνα (banána), Banana
Αχλάδι (akhládi), Pear
Πορτοκάλι (portokáli), Orange
Κεράσια (kerásia), Cherries
Φράουλες (fráoules), Strawberries
Δαμάσκηνα (dhamáskina), Plums
Ροδάκινα (rodhákina), Peaches
Βερύκοκα (veríkoka), Apricots
Πεπόνι (pepóni), Melon
Καρπούζι (karpoúzi), Water-melon

MISCELLANEOUS

Ψωμί (psomí), Bread
Βούτυρο (voútiro), Butter
Αλάτι (aláti), Salt
Πιπέρι (pipéri), Pepper
Μουστάρδα (moustárdha), Mustard
Λάδι (ládhi), Oil
Ξίδι (Xídhi), Vinegar
Γάλα (ghála), Milk
Ζάχαρι (zákhari), Sugar
Νερό (neró), Water
Παγωμένο (pagoméno), Iced
Παγωτό (paghotó), Ice Cream
Λεμόνι (lemóni), Lemon

The traditional Greek **Café** (ΚΑΦΕΝΕΙΟΝ) of the provinces is an austere establishment usually thronged with male patrons for whom it is both local club and political forum. Coffee (καφὲ) is always served in the 'Turkish' fashion with the grounds. It may be drunk heavily sweetened (variglikó), medium (métrio) or without sugar (skhétto). Cafe's displaying the sign ΚΑΦΕΝΕΙΟΝ-ΜΠΑΡ (Café-Bar) also serve drinks.

General Information

Prices. These change and relative values alter so frequently in accordance with fluctuations in the exchange rate that prices are rarely quoted in the following pages, though some general estimates of the relative costs in comparison with those prevailing in the UK are given. At present (1986) the exchange rate is favourable to visitors from western Europe and the USA and Greece, on the whole, seems cheap.

Season. Climatically the best months to visit Greece are April to mid-June and September–October. At more popular places the season extends from March with heavily booked hotels. In July and August beaches are crowded, and the temperature even there may be found excessive (average max. 32° C, min. 22°). During the not infrequent 'heat-waves' shade temperatures may surpass 38° in Athens and 43° in Thessaly. March and November and later often have surprisingly warm days with long hours of sunshine, but in the earlier part of the year the sea is rarely warm enough for bathing. Equally it can be rainy with chilly evenings until well into April. In winter Athens is subject to very changeable weather, bitter winds and squally rain alternating with dazzling sunny intervals, so that a heavy overcoat and sunglasses may be needed together; but snow (though commonly visible on the surrounding hills) rarely settles in the city. The Aegean islands enjoy milder winters, while the mountainous inland regions of the mainland share the general rigours of the Balkans.

Language. A knowledge of ancient Greek is a useful basis, but no substitute, for the study of modern Greek. Apart from the unfamiliarity of modern pronunciation many of the commonest words (e.g. water, wine, fish) no longer come from the same roots. Fluency in modern Greek will add greatly to the ease and pleasure of travelling, but those who know no language other than English can get along quite comfortably anywhere on the main tourist routes. A knowledge of at least the Greek alphabet is highly desirable, however, since street names, bus destination plates, etc., may otherwise be unintelligible. A smattering of Greek will often result in the traveller answering more questions than he asks, though it will certainly ensure greater contact with local people.

The Greek alphabet now as in later classical times comprises 24 letters:

A α, B β, Γ γ, Δ δ, E ε, Z ζ, H η, Θ θ, I ι, K κ, Λ λ, M μ, N ν, Ξ ξ, O o, Π π, P ρ, Σ σ ς, T τ, Y υ, Φ φ, X χ, Ψ ψ, Ω ω.

VOWELS. There are five basic vowel sounds in Greek to which even combinations written as diphthongs conform: α is pronounced very short; ε and αι as e in egg (when accented more open, as in the first e in there); η, ι, υ, ει, οι, υι have the sound of ea in eat; o, ω as the o in dot; ου as English oo in pool. The combinations αυ and ευ are pronounced av and ev when followed by loud consonants (af and ef before mute consonants).

CONSONANTS are pronounced roughly as their English equivalents with the following exceptions: β = v; γ is hard and guttural, before a and o like the English g in hag, before other vowels approaching the y in your; γγ and γκ are usually equivalent to ng; δ = th as in this; θ as th in think; before an i sound λ resembles the lli sound in million; ξ has its full value always, as in ex-king; ρ is always rolled; σ (ς) is a sibilant as in oasis; τ is pronounced half way between t and d; φ = ph or f; χ, akin to the Scottish ch, a guttural h; ψ = ps as in lips. The English sound b is represented in Greek by the double consonant μπ, d by ντ. All Greek words of two syllables or more have one accent which serves to show the stressed syllable. The classical breathing marks are still sometimes written but have no significance in speech. In the termination ον, the n sound tends to disappear in speech and the ν is often omitted in writing.

Manners and Customs. CALENDAR AND TIME: Greece abandoned the Julian calendar only in 1923 so that even 20C dates can be in Old or New Style. All moveable festivals are governed by the fixing of Easter according to the Orthodox calendar. Greece uses Eastern European Time (2 hours ahead of G.M.T.); π.μ.—a.m. and μ.μ.—p.m. When making an appointment it is advisable to confirm that it is an 'English rendezvous', i.e. one to be kept at the hour stated. The siesta hours after lunch (often late) should not be disturbed by calling or telephoning.

Attention should be paid by travellers to the more formal conventions of Greeks. The handshake at meeting and parting is de rigueur, and inquiry after the health taken seriously. The correct reply to καλῶς ὡρίσατε (kalós orísate: welcome) is καλῶς σᾶς βρήκαμε (kalós sas vríkame: glad to see you). To the inquiry τί κάνετε; (tí kánete; how do you do?) or πῶς εἴσθε; (pos íste; how are you?) the reply should be καλά, εὐχαριστῶ, καὶ σεῖς (kalá efkharistó, ke sis): well, thank you—and you?—or ἔτσι καί ἔτσι (etsi ke etsi), so-so. General greetings are

Χαίρετε (khérete; greetings, hallo) Γειά σας (yásas; hello, goodbye-lit: your health) and Στό καλό (sto kaló; keep well), both useful for greeting strangers on the road. Περαστικά (perastiká) is a useful word of comfort in time of sickness or misfortune meaning 'may things improve'. Except in the centre of Athens it is still customary to greet shopkeepers, the company in cafés, etc., with καλημέρα (kaliméra: good day) or καλησπέρα (kalispéra: good evening). Σᾶς παρακαλῶ (sas parakaló: please) is used when asking for a favour or for information, but not when ordering something which is to be paid for, when Θά ήθελα tha íthela; I should like) is more appropriate. The Greek for yes is ναί (né) or, more formally, μάλιστα (málista); for no, όχι (ókhi). Αντίο (Addío), goodbye, so long, in Greek has none of the finality of its Italian origin.

In direct contrast to English custom, personal questions showing interest in a stranger's life, politics, and money are the basis of conversation in Greece, and travellers must not be offended at being asked in the most direct way about their movements, family, occupation, salary, and politics, though they will usually find discussion of the last singularly inconclusive.

By Greek custom the bill for an evening out is invariably paid by the host; the common foreign habit of sharing out payment round the table is looked upon as mean and unconvivial, and visitors valuing their 'face' will do it discreetly elsewhere. A stranger is rarely allowed to play host to a native.

It is not good manners to fill a wine-glass, nor to drain a glass of wine poured for one, the custom being to pour it half full and keep it 'topped up'. Glasses are often touched with the toast εἰς υγείαν σᾶς, your health (generally shortened in speech to the familiar yásas or yámas, or, to a single individual, yásou); they are then raised to the light, the bouquet savoured, and the wine sipped before drinking (thus all five senses have been employed in the pleasure).

Entering a Greek house one may formally be offered preserves with coffee and water; this must never be refused. Strictly to conform to custom the water should be drunk first, the preserves eaten and the spoon placed in the glass, and the coffee drunk at leisure. Payment must, of course, never be offered for any service of hospitality. An acceptable way of reducing an obligation is by making a present to a child of the house. Equally hospitality should not be abused; those offering it nearly always have less resources than their foreign guests—even the proverbially poor student.

The 'Volta', or evening parade, universal throughout provincial Greece, has no fixed venue in Athens. Fasting is taken seriously in Lent.

Health. Climate and unfamiliar food may cause problems. Elementary precautions are obvious: avoidance of overexposure to the sun (which burns even when a sea breeze makes it seem cool), and of too much oily food. It is advisable to carry one or two patent remedies. Rice and lemon juice are good for upset stomachs. Chemists can advise on other medicines. Dog bites need immediate treatment by a doctor.

Public Holidays. Offical public holidays in Greece are: New Year's Day; 6 January (Epiphany); Kathara Dheftera ('Clean Monday'), the Orthodox Shrove Day; 25 March (Independence Day); Orthodox Good Friday, Easter Monday, 1 May; Ascension Day; 15 August (Assumption); 28 October 'Okhi' day (see below); Christmas Day; and 26 December (St. Stephen). In addition Athens celebrates the feast of her patron saint, St. Dionysios the Areopagite (3 October), and some other cities a patronal festival.

Carnival after three weeks' festivities reaches its peak on the Sunday before Clean Monday with processions and student revels. Its manifestations are strong in Patras, Naoussa, and in Athens are centred on Plaka. Procession of shrouded bier on *Good Friday* (Epitáfios); 'Christos anesti' (Christ is risen) celebration, with ceremonial lighting of the Paschal candle and release of doves, in front of churches at midnight preceding *Easter Sunday*, followed by candlelight processions and 'open house'. Roasting of Paschal lambs and cracking of Easter eggs on morning of Easter Day. These ceremonies are performed with pomp in the capital.—*Okhi Day*, commemorating the Greek 'no' (όχι) to the Italian ultimatum of 1940, is celebrated with remembrance services and military processions, especially in Salonika.

Postal Services. The main Post Offices (Ταχυδρομεία: Takhidhromía) in Athens are in Síntagma Sq. (NW corner) and Od. Eólou (just off Omonia Sq.). Present opening hours are 7 or 7.30 a.m. to 8.30 p.m., Monday to Friday; 7.30 a.m. to 2.00 or 3.00 p.m., Saturday and 9.00 a.m. to 1.30 p.m., Sunday (Sintagma office only). Minor and provincial post offices close at 2.30 p.m. and do not open at weekends. Apart from their usual services, Post Offices now change travellers' cheques. Letter boxes (ΓΡΑΜΜΑΤΟΚΙΒΩΤΙΑ) are painted yellow and may be marked ΕΣΩΤΕΡΙΚΟΥ (Inland), ΕΞΩΤΕΡΙΚΟΥ (Abroad), or ΕΠΕΙΓΟΝΤΑ (Express). Postage stamps are obtainable at some kiosks and shops as well as at post offices (10 per cent surcharge). The charge for Express letters is reasonable and usually ensures delivery in the UK two days after posting. A registered letter is ένα συστημένο γράμμα (éna sistiméno grámma). There are often considerable delays to post (especially postcards) in the summer season and internal mail is not exempt from problems. Correspondence marked 'POSTE RESTANTE' (to be called for) may be sent to any post office and collected by the addressée on proof of identity (passport preferable). A small fee may be charged. The surname of the addressee should be clearly written, and no 'Esq.' added. PARCELS are not delivered in Greece. They must be collected from the Post Office, where they are subject to handling fees, full customs charges, and often to delay. The bus companies operate an efficient parcels service from their own offices.

Telephones. The Greek telephone and telegraph services are run by a public corporation, the Οργανισμός Τηλεπικοινωνίων Ελλάδος (O.T.E.; always referred to by its acronym—'ó, té') which is quite separate from the postal authority. All large towns have a central office of the company, with call boxes and arrangements for making trunk and international calls and sending telegrams. Most villages have an O.T.E. centre, which may be a local café. If not, the hours are likely to be restricted. Major offices have a 24-hour service.

Long-distance calls can also be made from most hotels, many kiosks and any other establishment which has a meter (μετρητή; metrití) attached to the telephone. The meter records the number of units and payment is made accordingly. The availability of metered phones means that it is not usually necessary to visit an O.T.E. centre to make a long-distance call (either domestic or international). The charge per unit is fixed—lowest at O.T.E., slightly higher at kiosks and shops; highest in hotels. The cheap rate is 8 p.m. to 8 a.m. International calls are, at present charges and exchange rates, about 25 per cent higher than in the UK. There is international direct dialling. Otherwise, for Greek long-distance calls, dial 132; international 161; telegrams: domestic 155, international 165. Police 100. Time 141 (in Greek).

Local calls can be made from many kiosks, shops, etc., usually from a red phone with a coin slot taking, at present, a 5-drachma piece. There are also public coin boxes, which are frequently out of order.

Banks are open Monday to Friday (except public holidays) from 8 a.m. to 2 p.m. Some banks in the centre of Athens (especially Sintagma Square) are open for longer hours and part of the weekend. This is occasionally the case also in some holiday resorts. *Bureaux de Change* are operated by some travel agents and hotels will often change money, though it is advisable to ensure that the proper rate is being offered and that commission charges are not excessive. Post Offices may also be used (see above). Travellers' cheques are undoubtedly the easiest way of carrying funds. Major credit cards are accepted by a fair number of establishments but are often regarded with suspicion.

Shops are open in summer 8–1.30 and 5.30–8.30 on Tuesday, Thursday and Friday; 8–2.30 or 3 only on Monday, Wednesday and Saturday. In winter evening hours are 4–7.30. Some kinds of shop (e.g. dry cleaners) never open in the evening. Outside Athens, hours are more flexible. In large towns chemists take turns to offer a 24-hour service; duty chemists in Athens are listed in 'The Week in Athens', or may be discovered by dialling 173 on the telephone.

The PERIPTERO (Περίπτερον), or kiosk, developed from a French model, is a characteristic feature of Greek life. Selling newspapers, reading matter, postcards, cigarettes, chocolate, toilet articles, roll film, postage stamps, etc., kiosks are open for about 18 hours a day.

Museums and Archaeological Sites. Ancient remains of any significance are usually signposted and the sites enclosed. An admission charge is normally made, the size varying with the importance of the place concerned. Students are allowed reduced prices on production of a valid identity card. *Bona fide* foreign students of any branch of classical studies can obtain a free pass through their institutions. Opening hours of sites and museums vary in accordance with the season, the importance of the antiquities and local conditions. Museums (but not sites) are closed on Tuesdays—except for the National Archaeological Museum in Athens which closes on Monday. For smaller sites/museums, it is advisable to reckon on opening hours of 8.30–1, for absolute safety. In fact the closing time is usually about 3 p.m. and, at the more important centres, as late as 5 p.m. for museums and 7 p.m. for sites. The National Tourist Organisation in Athens provides an information sheet on opening hours, as do the travel guides. Both sites and museums are closed on 1 January, 25 March, Good Friday morning, Easter Day and Christmas Day. Hours are restricted on Christmas Eve, New Year's Eve, 2 January, 5 January, the last Saturday of Carnival, Thursday in Holy Week, Easter Tuesday. At major sites, where the number of visitors can detract considerably from one's pleasure in the tourist season, it is highly desirable to begin one's visit at opening time in the morning, before the large parties arrive. The antiquities can then be inspected at reasonable leisure and the surroundings enjoyed.

In general photography (hand cameras) is free on archaeological sites, and may be indulged freely (save where unpublished material is on display) in museums on purchase of a second ticket for the camera. ΑΠΑΓΟΡΕΥΕΤΑΙ (apagorévetai) means forbidden. Set fees (not cheap) are charged for using tripods, etc.

The Greek Antiquities Service treats its visitors' safety as their own responsibility. Travellers should, perhaps, be warned that holes are not generally fenced, nor heights guarded by railings; the very nature of archaeological remains ensures the maximum number of objects that can be tripped over. It is particularly dangerous to move about while reading or sighting a camera.

No guide-book to the whole of Greece has the space to give detailed directions how to reach every remote or minor site. These stand, unfenced and unmarked, often some way from the modern village that has taken upon itself their ancient name (proven or supposed). Assistance beyond that given in the text can usually be canvassed from the locals with the use of the following vocabulary: *yía* (towards) *ta arkhaía* ('ancient things'), *to kástro* (any fortified height), *tis anaskafés (excavations), to froúrio* (medieval castle). Country peasants rarely have any idea of periods of chronology, whereas intelligent schoolboys sometimes have a surprising knowledge of their local antiquities. Licensed guides are available in Athens, and on some major sites; casual offers of guidance are better politely declined in Athens and Piraeus, but can be disinterested and invaluable elsewhere.

Orthodox churches (usually open) may be visited at any reasonable hour; when they are closed inquiry should be made for the key. Women are not permitted to enter the sanctuary.

Antiquities. The regulations to protect Greece's heritage are strictly enforced. Importation of antiquities and works of art is free, but such articles should be declared on entry so that they can be re-exported. Except with special permission, it is forbidden to export antiquities and works of art (dated before 1830) which have been obtained in any way in Greece. If a traveller's luggage contains antiquities not covered by an export permit, the articles are liable to be confiscated and prosecution may follow. Note that the use of metal detectors is strictly forbidden in Greece and it is an offence to remove any object, however seemingly insignificant, from an archaeological site.

Equipment. Most people require sunglasses in Greece, even in winter. Suntan lotion, a sunhat, and initial caution in exposing oneself to the sun are important in the summer. A pocket compass can be useful, since many directional indications in the Guide are given by compass-points. Those travelling informally should consider taking a small camping stove for hotel-room breakfasts, etc. It is a good idea to carry washing powder, a few clothes pegs and a strong piece of string for a temporary clothes line. An electric torch is useful. Some form of mosquito repellant should be carried (though it may not be needed): small electrical devices are available from all chemists.

Diving and underwater photography are not permitted in most parts of Greece.

Newspapers. The 'Athens News' is published daily in English. Foreign newspapers are obtainable at central kiosks in Athens late on the day of publication (and the following day at other major tourist centres) at about three times the home price. 'The Athenian', a well-produced monthly magazine in English, has articles on various aspects of Greek life and culture and useful information about entertainment, restaurants and basic services in the capital. The weekly 'Athinórama' (Αθηνόραμα; Thursdays, in Greek) has comprehensive information about all forms of entertainment (including gastronomic) in Athens, for those with a knowledge of Greek.

Weights and Measures. The French metric system of weights and measures adopted in Greece in 1958, is used with the terms substantially unaltered. Thus μέτρο, χιλιόμετρο (khiliómetro), etc. Some liquids are measured by weight (κιλό etc.), not in litres. The standard unit of land measurement, the *stremma*, is equal to ¼ acre.

Note on Transliteration

Regarding Greek place-names, Col. Leake wrote 150 years ago 'It is impossible in any manner to avoid inconsistency'. Many recent writers on Greece have tried to make a virtue of 'the avoidance of pedantry', but even pedantry is preferable to chaos, and some measure of consistency must be attempted, even if doomed to incomplete success. Modern Greek is not the same language as ancient Greek, and in any case many modern places in Greece have names derived from Albanian, Turkish, or 'Frankish' roots. The most acceptable compromise is gained by using one set of rules for modern place names, and another for those of ancient times.

Names of modern localities have been transliterated in accordance with the phonetic system codified by the Permanent Committee on Geographical Names (E. Gleichen and J.H. Reynolds, *Alphabets of Foreign Languages*, P.C.G.N. for British Official Use, London 1951, pp. 52–56), used alike by NATO and by professional and archaeological journals. Though this results sometimes in visual ugliness, and for those with a knowledge of Greek increasing irritation (disguised the familiar apparently unnecessarily: thus Khlóï), it has three merits: a great measure of alphabetical consistency for indexing; easy cross- reference to most official maps and to original excavation reports; and the possibility for non-Greek-speakers of producing a recognisable approximate pronunciation. Where the result has seemed too *outré* to be borne and where there is a recognised and familiar English version (e.g. Rhodes), this has been used at least in all subsidiary references.

Ancient names have been given in the traditional English form used by classical scholars and archaeologists, preferring the purely English form where this exists (e.g. Aristotle, Homer), and the Latin form where this has become accepted everyday English usage: e.g. Boeotia, not Boiotia; Plato, not Platon. In other instances the form nearest to the ancient Greek has generally been preferred (with k for κ, rather than the misleading c), and (e.g.) Sounion rather than Sunium

This duality, though producing inconsistencies between ancient and modern (e.g. respectively ch and kh for χ), highlights the pitfall that the modern place bearing the equivalent of a Classical name is not necessarily in the location of its ancient counterpart. Where they are coincident, some reconciliation may have to be effected: it is well for Christians to remember the Beroea of St. Paul, but advisable when journeying there to think of the modern town as Vérria.

It should be pointed out that, until the recent designation of demotic Greek as opposed to katharevousa (formal Greek) as the state language, place names had often both a katharevousa and a demotic form (αι Αθῆναι, η Αθήνα for Athens). Formal versions of place names may occasionally linger on old signs. The final -v of neuter names, sometimes retained in our texts, is often omitted in practice. Neither modern form is necessarily the ancient form: thus, Thorikos, anciently ἡ Θόρικος has become ὁ Θορικός. In addition *all* place-names, like other nouns, decline; this often produces a change of stress as well as of inflexion. Some places have their more familiar spoken form in the accusative (given, where thought desirable, in the text), though they appear on maps in the nominative; places ending in -on often drop the 'n' in speech, sometimes the whole syllable. Street names are in the genitive when called after a person, e.g. Ermou (of Hermes), also in the genitive when leading to a place, e.g. Patission (to Patissia). As in English, a church may be spoken of by the name of its saint in the nominative or genitive. In the vexing instance where the Greek name is in itself a transliteration from Roman characters, each example has been treated on its apparent merits. Thus Βερανζέρου (which in Greek pronunciation bears little resemblance to the Fr. *Béranger*) has been rendered Veranzérou; Βύρωνος similarly has been rendered Víronos by sound since Lord Byron properly appears in Greek literary criticism as Μπάυρον Names of modern Greeks have been rendered where possible as their owners transliterated them or as arbitrary custom has demanded.

No consistency can be attempted in the language or spelling of hotel names, since they are often chosen quite arbitrarily themselves. What is displayed on the building is likely not to correspond with the name listed in the hotel guide—only experience can help in the realisation that (e.g.) Ilios, Helios, and Soleil designate the same hotel (Ηλιος), or that Mont Blanc and Lefkon Oros are one and the same.

In this book, at its first mention, a place-name is given also in lower case Greek, where the difference from English may make this an aid to reading maps and road signs. On main roads signposts are printed in Greek and Roman characters (but inevitably not in a consistent transliteration). In the Guide, accents have been put on transliterated place names at their main entry, since they show pronunciation stress. For the sake of economy they have sometimes been omitted elsewhere, though an attempt has been made to accent words which travellers may need to use for asking directions; the names in the index are fully accented. Ancient names, if accented, have been given their modern stress, where this may be a help in asking directions. Breathings are not normally given. Accents on initial vowels are not given, in accordance with modern practice.

Some Books about Greece

Prehistory
*Sinclair Hood, *The home of the heroes* (Thames and Hudson, 1967); *The arts in prehistoric Greece* (Pelican History of Art, 1978).

Ancient History
*A.R. Burn, *A traveller's history of Greece: the Pelican history of Greece* (Pelican, 13th rev. ed., 1982).

Art and Architecture
*C.M. Robertson, *A shorter history of Greek art* (Cambridge University Press, 1981). *A.W. Lawrence, *Greek architecture* (Pelican History of Art, 1968). *D.E. Strong, *Roman art* (Pelican History of Art, 1976). *F. Sear, *Roman architecture* (Batsford, 1982). *D. Talbot Rice, *Art of the Byzantine era* (Thames and Hudson, 1963). *R. Krautheimer, *Early Christian and Byzantine architecture* (Pelican History of Art, 1975).

History
W. Miller, *The Latins in the Levant* (J. Murray, 1908). J. Campbell and P. Sherrard, *A history of modern Greece* (Cambridge University Press, 1968).

Other
R. and M. Clogg, *Greece* (Oxford World Bibliographies, 1980), gives bibliographical information on a wide variety of Greek topics, ancient and modern. R. Clogg (ed.), *Greece in the 1980s* (Macmillan, 1983), aspects of life in contemporary Greece. K. Andrews, *Athens* (Methuen Cities of the World Series, 1967), not easy to obtain but one of the best books ever written about Greece: a sensitive and finely written appreciation of Athens and its people. Osbert Lancaster, *Classical landscape with figures* (John Murray, 1975), rather dated, but witty and penetrating about the country and its inhabitants. *Dilys Powell, *An affair of the heart* (M. Haag, 1983), a sentimental but understanding book about Greek village life as observed by the author during her husband's excavations at Perakhora in the 1930s. A. Huxley and W. Taylor, *Flowers of Greece and the Aegean* (Chatto and Windus, 1977). *British School at Athens/Society for the Promotion of Hellenic Studies *Archaeological Reports*, an annual, and somewhat technical, survey of recent discoveries in Greece and its ancient colonies. Enquiries to the Secretary, Hellenic Society, 31–4 Gordon Square, London WC1H 0PY.

* = Obtainable in paperback, though some such works on art and architecture are not particularly cheap.

I ATHENS

ATHENS (η Aθήνα), the capital of the Hellenic Republic (Elliniki Dhimokratia), is situated in lat. 37° 58' N and long. 23° 43' E, 6·5km from the sea. The city, which now occupies the greater part of the Attic plain, is surrounded by an amphitheatre of mountains, nowhere far distant, and to the E, in Hymettos, barely 8km from the centre. At the 1981 census Greater Athens (Periféria Protevoússis), comprising 37 demes and 19 communes partly in the nome of Attiki and partly in that of Piraeus, numbered 3,027,331 inhabitants; of these the city proper, or deme of Athens, accounted for 885,737 and Piraeus for 196,389, while the remainder was distributed between their modern residential and industrial suburbs extending in every direction. Athens has thus engulfed the subordinate and almost isolated group of lesser hills, which more nearly defined the limits of the ancient city.

The northernmost of these hills, which are in reality fragments of the Anchesmos or Tourkovouni range, is Strephis. Immediately S rises the conical rock of Lykabettos, still called by its classical name. This remarkable hill is to Athens what Vesuvius is to Naples or Arthur's Seat to Edinburgh. From its summit the city is seen as on a map. To the SW of Lykabettos are five more hills, all of which were included in ancient Athens. Of these, the nearest is the Acropolis or citadel of Athens, rising abruptly to 156m, a little more than half the height of Lykabettos. To the W of the Acropolis are the Areopagus, the Pnyx, and the Hill of the Nymphs; and to the SW is the Mouseion.

Athens, although one of the most easterly cities of Europe and in spite of nearly 400 years of Turkish rule, is almost entirely western in appearance. A creation of the 19C and 20C, it was planned by the Bavarian architects of King Otho, who laid out a new street plan round the large village that then occupied the N slope of the Acropolis. Though its approaches are ugly and gimcrack, the centre with squares planted with exotic trees is by no means unattractive; in recent years a number of fine neoclassical buildings have been restored; the best of the new buildings achieve a style appropriate to the strong light by successful use of deep balconies and white marble; while the splendour of its ancient monuments grouped about the dominating Acropolis, gives to Athens a distinction enduring time and change.

'Odhós' (Street) is often omitted in addresses; the practice has been followed here, except where the omission might cause confusion; then, for brevity, it has generally been abbreviated to 'Od.'

Airport at *Ellinikó*, 9·5km SE on the coast, for both international and internal flights (two terminals, separately approached). Bus between East and West terminals. Direct bus from East Airport (**18**, yellow) to Leof. Amalías, frequent 6 a.m. to midnight; also **121** to Leof. Olgas. Direct bus of Olympic Airways from West Airport to Leof. Amalias; also **122** to Leof. Olgas; see further, suburban services, below. To Piraeus (Dhimotiko Theatro): from East Airport **19**, yellow, also **101**; from West Airport **107** or **109**, the latter starting from Voula. Yellow buses are express.

Arrival by Sea at Piraeus (see Rte 12); Athens may be reached in 25 minutes by the Electric Railway, by bus, or taxi (approx. 10 x bus fare).

Railway Stations. *Lárissa* (2, *1*), in the NW of the city, for the standard-gauge line to Thebes, Larissa, Salonika, and Idhoméni (connecting via Gevgelija and Belgrade with the European trunk lines).— *Peloponnísou* (2, *1*), adjoining Larissa to the SW, for the metre-gauge line to Corinth and the Peloponnese. Booking offices at stations or, in town, Karólou 1, Sína 6 (Panepistemíou), Filellínon 17. Access by bus **405** from Leof. Alexándras, trolley **1** from Leof. Amalías or Panepistemiou for *Larissa Station*; bus **047** from Od. Menándrou (Omonia) for *Peloponnísou*.—*Omonoia* (3, *3* underground), Omonoia Sq., for the Greek Electric Railway (Ελληνικοι Ηλέκτρικοι Σιδηρόδρομοι) to Piraeus and Kifisia (see below).

Hotels. Athens has numerous hotels in every class (see Practical Information). Several of the higher class hotels are located in the area of Sindagma Sq., more modest round Omonoia.

For hotels in the hills and near the sea, see Rtes 13 and 15.

FLATS (apartments), rated as A or B class hotels, may be rented by the week.

YOUTH HOSTELS. 1 Ay. Meletíou (170 beds; open always); 2 Alexandras (220 beds; July–Sept only); 20 Ioulianoú (82 beds); 5 Kipsélis (180 beds); 4 Patis-síon. For general information, apply to *Greek Association of Youth Hostels*, Dhra-gatsaníou 4.—YMCA, 28 Omírou; YWCA, 13 Ameríkis.

Restaurants (lunch usually between 12.30 and 3; dinner between 8.30 and 12). International food and décor (not cheap) at L class hotels. Otherwise, for up-to-date guidance consult current periodicals, e.g. *The Athenian, Athinorama* (see Practical Information).

Tavernas (some open evenings only, 8.30 or 9 to 1 p.m.) offer excellent food and entertainment of a characteristically Greek kind. They are crowded and convi-vial; a table once occupied is often kept for the evening. The menu may be in Greek only, but it is not unusual to choose dishes at the kitchen. Tavernas are ubiquitous. Many in Plaka cater for tourists; a more local atmosphere may be sought e.g. behind the Hilton or on the slopes of Lykabettus. In summer Athe-nians tend to dine farther out in Attica.

Zakharoplastéia, properly speaking, are confectioners. In general now they have the function of a superior type of café or tea-room, serving also alcoholic drinks, and the largest also substantial cold dishes. Among the best known are *Zonar's*, 9 Venizélou and *Floca*, 4 Koraï.

Cafés (Kafenéia) are numerous, serving coffee, soft, and a limited range of alco-holic drinks. Those in or near the main squares and avenues cater for tourists.

Post Office (3, 5; all services, including cables) 100 Aiólou (corner of Omónia Sq.), open Monday–Friday 7.30–8 p.m. Saturday 7.30–2 p.m.; branch offices: Sindag-ma, at Othonos/Níkis; Omonoia Sq. (underground); also in Patriárkhou Ioakhím, etc.—O.T.E. CENTRES: 85 Patissíon, (open 24 hrs); also 15 Stadhíou; 53 Sólonos; 7 Kratínou (these 7 or 8 a.m. to 10 p.m. or midnight).—**Police Office** (Aliens Dept.), 173 Alexándras.—TOURIST POLICE. There is a Tourist Police depart-ment in every police station and an excellent telephone service is provided (tel. 171; English spoken).

Information Bureaux. *National Tourist Office*, 2 Karayeóryi Servías; 4 Stadhiou; in booking hall of Omonoia Underground Stn; and at the Airport; publishes (weekly, free) 'The Week in Athens' in English and French. *Royal National Foundation*, 9 Filellinon.

Travel Agents. *Trans Hellenic*, 36 Voúlis; *Alfa*, 12 Vas. Sofías; *Ghiolman and Hellas*, 7 and 14 Filellinon; *American Express*, 2 Ermoú; *Wagons-lits/Cook*, 2 Kar. Servias; *Hermes en Grece* and *C.H.A.T.* 4 Stadhíou; and many others. The *Periyitiki Leskhi*, 12 Polytekhniou, organises excursions to many places difficult of access by public transport.

Shipping Offices, mostly in Piraeus (Rte 12), except *Hellenic Mediterranean Lines* at 28 Amalías, *Strintzis Lines*, 48 Amalías.

Airline Offices. *British Airways*, 10 Othonos (Sindagma); *Olympic Airways*, 6 Othonos (all bookings); 96 Singroú (coach terminal); *TWA*, 8 Xenofóndos; *PAN AM*, 4 Othonos; *Air France* and *Lufthansa*, 4 Karayeoryi Servias; *Qantas* 5 Mitropóleos.

Taxicabs (ranks in main squares), equipped with taximeters, when disengaged exhibit the sign ΕΛΕΥΘΕΡΟΝ. At busy times the sign may be left illuminated when the taxi has been engaged and other passengers taken on; if they are going in the same direction as the original hirer. Charges are modest. Tip by rounding up to the nearest 10 drs; a little more if a long journey. Surcharges operate from a public transport terminal, during night hours and at holiday periods.

Electric Railway. Frequent metropolitan service from *Kifissia* via *Omonoia* to *Piraeus* in 40 min. Principal intermediate halts (S of Omonoia): *Monastírion* (2, 8), *Thissíon* (2, 8), *Kallithéa*, New *Pháleron*; N of Omonoia: *Victória* and *Patíssia*.

City and Suburban Buses (KTEL 1–6 of Athens, plus yellow trolleys) —Owing to the one-way traffic system, outward routes through the city seldom coincide with the return journey; between the Omonia area and Sindagma Sq., traffic goes N by Leof. Venizelou (Panepistemiou), S by either Stadhiou or Akadhimias. As an approximate guide (see maps for destinations and departure points), the first digit of the bus number indicates its general destination, as follows: 0, Central Athens; 1, coastal suburbs S towards Vouliagmeni; 2, S suburbs on slopes of Hymettos; 3 and 4, SE and E to central and eastern Attica; 5, Kifissia and N suburbs; 6 and 7, NW and 8, W towards Dhafni; 9, SW to Piraeus. (For other routes in the vicinity of Athens, see below.)

On nearly all city buses passengers enter by the front door, place their fare (flat rate, change required, 30 drs in 1986) in a box by the driver, and pass along the bus.

Among the most useful routes are:

(a) *Within the city.* **2/11/12** (trolleys). *Pangrati*–Sindagma–*Patissia* (Museum); **022.** *Marasleion*–Gennadhion Library–*Plat. Kaningos;* **023.** *Votanikos*–Assomaton–Monastiraki–*Sindagma;* **040** (green bus). *Piraeus*–*Sindagma* (Od. Filellinon); **049.** *Piraeus* (Dhimotiko Theatro)–*Omonia* (Od. Athinas); **051.** *Od. Veranzerou*–Akadhimia Platonos (Plato's Academy); **230.** *Od. Ippokratous*–Akadhimias–Akropolis–*Thission.*

(b) *Suburban and Attica.* **115.** *Leof. Olgas*–*Varkiza;* **118.** *Olgas*–*Vouliagmeni;* **121.** *Olgas*–Ay. Nikolaos–*Glifadha;* **122.** *Olgas*–*Ano Voula;* **224.** *University*–*Kaisariani;* **421.** *Od. Vasileos Irakleiou*–Museum–*Palaia Pendeli;* **503.** *Kaningos*–*Varibobi;* **538/589.** *Kaningos*–*Kifissia;* **603.** *National Library*–*Psikhiko.* From Piraeus, **109.** *Piraeus*–Glifadha–*Voula.*

To *Sounion, Lavrion, Porto Rafti, Marathon, Kalamos, Rafina, Oropos,* and places in E Attica, from Od. Mavromatéon and Mavromateon/Leof. Alexándras. (To central and SE Attica, also from Thissíon.)

To *Megara* from Thissíon.

To *Eleusis* from Plat. Koumoundoúrou.

Long-distance Bus Stations. Services to the *Peloponnese, Macedonia, Epirus,* and the *Ionian Is.* from 100 Kifissoú (reached in 15 min. by bus 051 from Menandrou (Omonia), near Ayiou Konstandinou booking office).

Services to *Euboea, Central Greece,* and *Thessaly* from 260 Liossíon (reached by bus 024 from Leof. Amalias).

BOOKING is possible by 'phone, provided tickets are collected by a specified time in advance of travel. Advance booking is essential at busy periods, if you wish to travel on a specific service. In any case tickets must be bought before boarding the bus to ensure a numbered seat.

RAILWAY PULLMAN BUSES to *Loutraki, Corinth, Patras,* etc. from Peloponnese Stn; and to *Salonika, Edhessa,* and *Alexandroupolis* from Larissa Stn (booking office at 18 Ayíou Konstandínou).

Car Hire (self-drive). *Hertz,* 12 Singroú; *Avis,* 48 Amalías; *Hellascars,* 7 Stadhiou; *Budget,* 90 Singroú; etc. List available from N.T.O.G.

Embassies, Legations, and Consulates. *British,* 1 Ploutarkhou (4, 8); *United States,* Leof. Vas. Sofias (5, 6) and (visas) 9 Leof. Venizelou; *Australia,* 15 Mesogeíon; *Canada,* 4 Yennadhíou; *Yugoslavia,* (visas) 25 Evrou (late mornings only).

English Church, *St Paul's* (7, 5), Odhos Filellinon, Rev. J. Findlow, services on Sun at 8, 9 and 10 a.m.; special times on Saints' days. AMERICAN CHURCH (4, 5; *St Andrew's*), 66 Sina; ROMAN CATHOLIC CHURCH (4, 7; *St Denis*), Leof. Venizélou.

Banks. Head Offices: *Bank of Greece,* 21 Venizélou; *National Bank of Greece,* 86 Aiólou; *Commercial Bank of Greece,* 11 Sofokléous; *Ionian and Popular Bank of Greece,* Pesmazóglou/Venizélou, etc. Normal hours, 8 a.m.–2 p.m.—Of many branches with exchange facilities, several near Sindagma Sq. are open additional hours: *National,* 2 Karayeoryi Servias (Monday–Friday 2–9 p.m., Saturday and Sunday, 8 a.m.–8p.m.); *Ionian and Popular,* 2 Mitropóleos (Monday–Friday 2–5.30 p.m., Saturday 9 a.m.–12.30 p.m.); *Commercial,* 11 Venizélou (Monday–Saturday 2–3.30 p.m., Sunday 9 a.m.–12 p.m.).

Learned Institutions. *British School at Athens,* 52 Souedías; *British Council,* 17 Kolonaki Sq., with good library; *American School of Classical Studies,* and *Gennadhion Library,* 54 and 61 Souedias; *American Library at Hellenic–American Union,* 22 Massalías; *Greek Archaeological Society,* 20 Venizélou; *Direction of Antiquities Services,* Old Palace; *École Française d'Archéologie,* 6 Dhidhotou; *Institut Français d'Athènes,* 29 Sína; *Deutsches Archäologisches Institut,* 1 Fidhíou; *National Library* see Rte 10; *Municipal Library,* Odhos Kleisthénous; *Parliament Library,* Parliament Building; *Benakios Library,* 2 Anthímou Gazí; *Royal Research Institute* (Byzantine and Modern Greek studies), 4 Leof. Vas. Sofías; *College of Music,* 35 Piraios; *Foreign Press Service,* 3 Zalokósta.

Clubs. Sofias/Mesogeion; *Hellenic Alpine Club*, Plat Kapnikaréas; *Greek Youth Hostels Assocn.*, 4 Dhragatsaníou.

Booksellers. *Eleftheroudhakis*, 4 Níkis; *Kaufmann*, 28 Stadhíou, also 11 Voukourestiou; *Compendium*, 28 Nikis (new and secondhand); Foliá tou Vivlíou (in arcade), 25/29 Panepistimíou; second-hand shops at lower end of Ippokratous.

Theatres. WINTER SEASON (October–May): *Ethnikon* (National Theatre Company), Ay. Konstandínou; *Olympia* (Liriki Skini), 59 Leof. Akadhimias, opera and operetta; *Arts* (Tekhnis), Odós Stadhíou; *Rex*, Leof. Venizélou, plays, concerts, and films; *Akropol*, Ippokrátous; *Elsa Verghi*, 1 Voukourestiou; *Kava*, Leof. Venizélou; *Athinon*, 10 Voukourestíou; *Dhionissia*, 10 Ameríkis; *Moussouri*, Plat. Ay. Yeoryíou Karítsi; *Bourneli*, 37 Patissíon. SUMMER SEASON (June–September) in the Odeion of Herodes Atticus; *Samartzi*, Kаrólou; *Poria*, 69 Trítis Septemvriou.—CONCERTS. Athens State Orchestra (Monday) in winter at Rex, in summer at the Odeion; light orchestral music in winter at Kentrikon (Monday); recitals at Parnassos Hall (Od. Chr. Ladá).—SON ET LUMIÈRE, lighting of the Acropolis viewed from the Pnyx.

Cinemas are numerous and cheap. The principal houses (many with films in English) are in Stadhíou and Venizélou.

Baths (Loutrá), 26 Veranzerou, and (sea water) at 100 Andromákhis, Kallithéa.—PUBLIC LAVATORIES can be found, inadequately marked, in most main squares.

Sport. TENNIS at *Athens Tennis Club*, Leof. Olgas; *Panellinios*, Odhos Mavromatéon. SWIMMING, open-air pool Leof. Olgas. Indoor pool, 277 Patission. GOLF at Varibobi; also at Glifadha. SAILING (Wednesday and Saturday afternnon and Sunday) in Phaleron Bay. RACECOURSE at Phaleron. MOTOR RACING, *Acropolis Rally* (late May) for touring cars starts and ends in Athens; *Autumn Rally* in November.

Festivals. *Athens Festival of Music and Drama*, June–August; *Blessing of the Waters* at Epiphany (6 January) in Plateia Dhexameni after procession from St. Dionysios the Areopagite just to the St; *Feast of St. Dionysios* (3 October); *Anniversary of 1944 Liberation* (12 October), hoisting of National Flag on Acropolis; *Easter* candlelight procession on Lykabettos (other general celebrations, see prefatory pages).—WINE FESTIVAL at Daphni (Rte 16) in September.

Ancient History. The slopes of the Acropolis have been occupied since Neolithic times. As the early migrations had least effect in Attica, there may be some truth in the classical Athenian claim to be autochthonous. Athens first attained the status of a town in the Middle Helladic period, when the worship of Athena was established on the Acropolis in addition to that of Poseidon Erechtheus; this bears out the traditional date assigned to Kekrops (1581 BC), mythical founder of the royal line. The fabled union (synoecism) of several cities into one state under Theseus (1300 BC) is doubtful, but an Achaean–Ionian kingdom of Mycenaean type does seem to have been based on Athens.

The Dorian invasions are followed by an obscure period, characterised by Geometric pottery, during which the Phoenician alphabet was adopted (? late 9C) to express Greek in writing. Athens begins to emerge for the first time as an artistic centre of Greece; this probably coincides with a historical unification of Attica under Athens (8C BC). The 7C is marked by the vigorous 'Protoattic' style of pottery, though sculpture is comparatively little developed. An attempt by Kylon in 632 BC to seize power was thwarted; the archon Megakles and the whole Alkmaeonid family in perpetuity were banished for allowing the murder of Kylon while in sanctuary, which led to an unsuccessful war with Megara, his father-in-law's city. At the beginning of the 6C, when the 'Archaic' style of sculpture was already passing from the Cyclades to Athens, Solon reorganised Athenian agriculture and encouraged commerce with more distant parts. He reformed the currency with the state-owned silver mines of Laurion. He inspired the conquest of Salamis from Megara soon after 570 BC by Peisistratos, whose triumph enabled him later to seize power. After ten years' exile in Macedonia Peisistratos defeated his opponents at Pallene c 545. By the acquisition of the Thracian Chersonese and the colonising of the Hellespont, he and his sons laid the foundations of the Athenian empire. His edition of Homer made Athens the literary centre of Greece, while he instituted the Great Dionysia of the City, the festival from which Attic drama was born. He began the architectural embellishment of the city, and in his reform of the Panathenaic festival (566 BC) he gave it a prestige equal to that of the gatherings at Olympia and Delphi. Under Peisistratid autocracy Athenian mature black-figure pottery ousted its Corinthian rival by its masterful technique and art, with an export to Syria and Spain. The reign of Hippias, elder son of Peisistratos, became oppressive after the murder of his brother Hipparchos during the conspiracy of Harmodios and Aristogeiton (514 BC). His overthrow was engineered by the Alkmaeonids with the assistance of Kleomenes, king of Sparta. Liberty was thus regained only at the expense of joining the Peloponnesian League, and Hippias retired to plot at the court of Darius, king of Persia. The Athenians aided Plataea against Thebes, and in 506 defeated Chalkis; an expedition against them the same year by Kleomenes failed.

When Aristagoras of Miletus, originator of the Ionian revolt against Darius, appealed for help in 498 BC only Athens and Eretria responded. Twenty Athenian ships took part in the burning of Sardis. In revenge Darius dispatched a huge army and fleet, accompanied by the aged Hippias, to sack Eretria. Marching on Athens, the Persian army was met at Marathon (August or September 490) by 9000 Athenians and 1000 Plataeans under Miltiades and decisively defeated. An unsuccessful war against Aegina, at this time supreme at sea, helped to wake Athens to her maritime danger before the Persian storm again broke in 480, when Xerxes came to avenge his father's defeat. The heroism of the Spartans under Leonidas at Thermopylae retarded but did not stop his advance. The Athenians abandoned their city and, guided by Themistocles, trusted themselves to their ships. The Acropolis was sacked, but the power of the Persians was broken in the naval battle of Salamis (20 September 480). At Plataea (479) the remnant of the Persian force was defeated on land. With heightened prestige, Athens, led by Kimon and Aristides, assumed the leadership of the naval Confederacy of Delos (478 BC) and the Persian danger was finally extinguished at the battle of the Eurymedon in 468. In Aeschylus (fl. 499–458), who fought against the Persians, Greek drama first reaches maturity in Athens.

Members of the Delian League at first contributed ships to a common fleet, an arrangement commuted later to a money tribute to Athens, after which the treasury of the league was moved (454 BC) from Delos to the Athenian acropolis. Under Pericles the Athenians put much of the profit towards the aggrandisement of their city, and having defeated Aegina and Corinth, abandoned an unprofitable rivalry with Sparta and Thebes for commercial expansion at sea, signing a thirty years' truce in 445. The Periclean vision of a pan-Hellenic congress was nullified by Sparta's refusal to co-operate. The circle of Pericles included some of the greatest names in Athenian arts and letters. Stimulated by Zeno and Anaxagoras, he extended his patronage to the visiting Herodotus; inspired Thucydides; encouraged Attic drama, which attained in his day its completest development in the art of Sophocles (495–406 BC); and gave free scope to the genius of Pheidias in the design of the Parthenon. In the foundation of Aegean cleruchies Pericles anticipated the Roman colonial system.

The Peloponnesian War (431–404 BC) was the inevitable outcome of rivalry between Sparta and Athens. With the death of Pericles in 429, the now fully-developed democracy lost its only capable leader. The ill-fated Sicilian Expedition (415–414 BC), urged on by Alcibiades, was the prelude to the disaster of Aegospotami in 405. The humiliating conditions of peace forced on Athens in 404 included the destruction of her enceinte. For a brief time even democracy was eclipsed in the *coup d'état* of the Thirty Tyrants, until Thrasyboulos restored the constitution in 403, marring its record by the execution of Socrates (399). The comedies of Aristophanes (fl. 427–387) span these troubled times.

The recovery of Athens was swift. Against Sparta Konon won his great victory at Cnidos in 394 BC; and assisted by Thebes Athens re-established her naval hegemony with the Second Maritime League, organised in 378. Art and literature declined but little, and philosophy and oratory reached their apotheosis in the 4C. It was the age of Plato (428–347), Xenophon (c 430–354), and Isocrates (436–338). A new danger now arose in the person of Philip of Macedon, who conquered Amphipolis in 357, Potidaea in 356, and Methone in 353. Spurred on by the oratory of Demosthenes (383–322), Athens took up the role of champion of Greek liberty, but was finally vanquished at Chaeronea in 338.

The subject city was treated with favour by Alexander the Great, whose Macedonian tutor, Aristotle, taught in the Lyceum. An unsuccessful bid for independence on Alexander's death (323 BC) led to the imposition by the usurper Kassander of a collaborating governor, Demetrios of Phaleron (318–307). A brief liberation by Demetrios Poliorketes, claimant to the Macedonian throne, ⸱⸱⸱⸱ followed by a period of alternate freedom and subjection to Macedonia; aft defeat by Antigonus Gonatas in the Chremonidean War (266–263), Athens s fered a garrison until 229, although her democratic institutions were respecteɑ. Supremacy in science had now passed to Alexandria, but Athens still led in philosophy; in Menander (342–291) comedy reached a new peak. The fall of Perseus in 168 BC substituted the Roman for the Macedonian rule, but the city of Athens continued to flourish, retaining many privileges when the province of Achaia was formed out of S Greece after 146. Having espoused the cause of Mithridates in 86 BC, it was captured by Sulla, when its fortifications were razed, its treasures looted, and its privileges curtailed. It nevertheless received a free pardon from Julius Caesar for siding with Pompey and from Antony and Augustus after supporting Brutus, who removed here after the Ides of March. Athens continued to be the fashionable seat of learning in the ancient world, attracting the sons of rich Romans, including Cicero and Horace.

St. Paul preached 'in the midst of Mars' hill' (Acts, xvii, 22) in AD 54. Hadrian (120–128), under whom Plutarch was procurator of Achaia, frequently lived in the city and adorned it with imperial buildings. His example was followed by Herodes Atticus in the time of the Antonines, when the city was visited by Pausanias; and Athens remained the centre of Greek education until the Edict of Justinian in AD 529 closed the schools of philosophy.

Later History. The agora suffered in the first Gothic (Herulian) raid of 267, but Alaric's capture of the city in 396 seems to have caused little damage to its monuments. In the reign of Justinian, or earlier, many temples were consecrated to Christian use and modified. Under Byzantine rule Athens dwindled to an unimportant small town. It was sacked c 580 by the Slavs. Constans II wintered in the city in 662 on his way to Sicily, and Theodore of Tarsus studied here before becoming Archbishop of Canterbury (669–690). Basil II, the Bulgar-slayer, celebrated his victories of 1018 in the Parthenon.

After the fall of Constantinople in 1204, the Greek provinces N of the Isthmus of Corinth fell to the share of Boniface III, Marquis of Montferrat, with the title of King of Thessalonica. Boniface granted Attica and Boeotia to Otho de la Roche, a Burgundian knight, with the title of Grand Seigneur (Megas Kyr; i.e. Μέγας Κύριος) of Athens and Thebes. A century of pacific and prosperous 'Frankish' rule brought some amelioration to the condition of the Athenians but no part in affairs; trading privileges were granted to Genoese and Venetian merchants. Matthew Paris records a visit as a student by Master John of Basingstoke (died 1252). In 1258 Guy I accepted the title of duke from St. Louis of France; the magnificence of the Athenian court of this period is noted by the Catalan chronicler Ramon Muntaner. On the death of Guy II in 1308, the duchy passed to his cousin Walter de Brienne. Walter's designs on Byzantine territories leagued the rulers of Constantinople, Neopatras, and Epirus against him, and he called to his aid the Catalan Company. Being unable later to rid himself of them, he precipitated the disastrous battle of Kopais, where in 1311 the Catalans totally destroyed the power and nobility of Frankish Greece.

The Grand Company now assumed sovereignty of Athens and Thebes, but placed Roger Deslau, one of the two noble survivors of Duke Walter's army, at their head. After pursuing a career of conquest in N Greece, they approached Frederick of Aragon, king of Sicily in 1326, with the result that his second son Manfred became duke and for sixty years the Duchy of Athens and Neopatras (as it was now styled) was misgoverned from Sicily by avaricious General Commissioners. In 1386 the Siculo-Catalans fell foul of Nerio Acciaioli, governor of Corinth, a member of that family which was 'plebian in Florence, potent in Naples, and sovereign in Greece' (Gibbon). Nerio seized Athens, Thebes and Levadia, and in 1394 received the title of duke from Ladislas, king of Naples. Captured by a band of Navarrese troops, he bought his ransom by rifling all the churches in his dominions.

Under his son Antony, Athens, protected by Venice, enjoyed forty years' peace, but Antony's weak cousin and successor, Nerio II (1435–53) held his duchy as a vassal of the Sultan. During his reign Athens was twice visited by Ciriaco de' Pizzicoli (better known as Cyriacus of Ancona), the antiquary. Demetrius Chalcondyles (1424–1511), the Renaissance scholar who published the editio princeps of Homer, was an Athenian. When Nerio's widow and Pietro Almerio, the Venetian governor of Nauplia and her new husband, seized the dukedom, the Athenians complained to the Sultan, who replaced Almerio by Franco Acciaioli, a nephew of Nerio. Franco banished his aunt, the ex-duchess, to Megara and had her murdered there, whereupon Pietro complained to the Porte. Mehmed II ordered Omar, son of Turahan, to seize the Acropolis, and annexed Attica to the Ottoman Empire in 1456. A guide book written by the so-called Vienna Anonymous, describes Athens in 1456–60. A Venetian raid in 1464 achieved nothing but the plunder of the city.

Nearly 400 years of Turkish rule followed, a peculiar result of which was the rehabilitation of the Orthodox Church, so long dispossessed by Rome. Athens was visited in 1672 by Père Babin, a French Capuchin, who drew the earliest extant plan, and in 1675 by Francis Vernon, who sent back to the Royal Society the first English account of the city. The same year Lord Winchilsea, then ambassador to the Porte, secured some architectural fragments. In 1676 came Spon and Wheler. In 1687 occurred the siege by Francesco Morosini, during which the Parthenon was shattered. Thenceforward until 1821, the condition of Athens under the Turks is picturesquely described by Gibbon, who accuses the Athenians of his day of 'walking with supine indifference among the glorious ruins of antiquity'. The worst period of tyranny was experienced under Hadji Ali Haseki in 1775–95. After the appearance of Stuart and Revett's 'Antiquities of Athens' (1762), based on a visit of 1750, travellers to Athens became more numerous.

VEDUTA DEL CAST. D'ACROPOLIS DALLA PARTE DI TRAMONTANA.

Athens, Acropolis. Venetian bombardment and explosion of the Parthenon in 1687. Engraving

In 1821, soon after the outbreak in Patras of the War of Independence, the Greek general Odysseus seized Athens and the Acropolis. In 1826–27 the Acropolis, besieged by Reshid Pasha, was bravely defended by the klepht Gouras and after his death by the French general Fabvier. Vain attempts to raise the siege were made by Karaïskakis and after his death in 1827 by Admiral Cochrane and General Church. On 27 May 1827, the Acropolis was taken by the Turks and held until 12 April 1833. In 1834 Athens became the capital of liberated Greece.

During the First World War the city was occupied by British and French troops after some opposition by Royalist troops of the pro-German government. The population was greatly increased by the exchange of Greek and Turkish nationals in 1923. On 27 April 1941, German forces entered the capital unopposed after a campaign lasting three weeks, and Athens remained in their hands until October 1944. In December 1944 open Communist revolution broke out in the Theseion area after a demonstration had been fired on by police earlier the same morning in Sindagma Sq. After bitter street fighting British troops, with reinforcements, landed at Phaleron, eventually restored order and at a conference called by Churchill on Christmas Day an armistice was arranged whereby Archbishop Dhamaskinos became regent.

Topography. PREHISTORIC ATHENS. In Early Helladic times groups of settlers had lived within reach of the fortress, and Late Helladic chamber tombs have been found in the N and W slopes of the Areopagus hill and in the area which later became the agora. The Mycenaean royal city centred on the fortress of the Acropolis, where a 'Cyclopean' wall enclosed the palace complex, Homer's 'strong house of Erechtheus', but settlements and shrines extended S to the Ilissos. At an early date part of the S and W slopes of the Acropolis were enclosed by the Pelasgikon wall, but evidence of Sub-Mycenaean and Protogeometric graves shows a gradual spread of occupation towards the NW, where the Kerameikos became the chief necropolis.

THE ARCHAIC CITY. Peisistratid palatial occupation and the siting of a new temple perhaps in 566 BC for the Panathenaic festival must have lessened the living space on the Acropolis. The Pnyx and Mouseion hills were already occupied by houses in the 6C, and even before the Peisistratids the popular Kerameikos quarter was becoming the centre of Athenian life. It was the meeting-place of the assembly, the altar of the Twelve Gods was set up there, and the archons had their offices in the vicinity. By the end of the 6C the population seems to have resided wholly in the lower city. No archaeological evidence has been found to suggest that any wall was built to replace the Pelasgikon which was slighted under or after the Peisistratids. Since the water supply was now brought by aqueduct and a group of temples existed near the Kallirrhoë spring and the Ilissos, a 7–6C wall now seems unlikely.

CLASSICAL ATHENS. The Acropolis and much of the town outside was laid waste by the Persians in 480. After the battle of Plataea, Themistocles, who had begun to fortify Piraeus as early as 493, began a city wall on a course which endured until the time of Hadrian. Thucydides (1, 93) records its hasty erection with whatever material was at hand. No general plan of the sort adopted in Piraeus was ever made for Athens, and the narrow crooked streets remained. Kimon finished the circuit; and the two Long Walls, connecting Athens with Piraeus, were completed under Pericles. Of the fifteen city gates located, the names of ten are known but not certainly identified. In 450 Kallikrates completed the Phaleric Wall. Much of the monumental greatness of Athens dates from the third quarter of the 5C. The Academy, embellished by Kimon, became a favourite Athenian promenade. In 404 the walls were demolished at the Spartan command, and the Long Walls never rose again. Konon rebuilt the enceinte in 393, and Lycurgus (338–326) completed, rebuilt or embellished much of the city, modifying the Pnyx for the Assembly's use. The walls were shortened about this time by the erection of the Diateichisma, and the city flourished with gradual modifications until the Roman sack of 86 BC.

IMPERIAL ATHENS. Archaeologists have disagreed whether Hadrian extended the enceinte, but the discovery in 1959 near the Olympieion of a gate which confirms the E course of the Themistoclean wall suggests that Hadrianopolis was indeed an extension to the E and not merely the aggrandisement of an older quarter. Here were gymnasia, thermae, and the usual manifestations of Roman rule. Under Augustus a new market had been built E of the Agora; Hadrian added a huge library in the same area. He also built a new reservoir on Lykabettos. A generation or so later Herodes Atticus founded his Odeion and reseated the decaying Stadium in marble. After the Herulians had destroyed most of Athens in 267, the Athenians lost confidence in the Roman army and withdrew behind the post-Herulian ('Valerian') wall enclosing the N slope of the Acropolis.

LATER TOPOGRAPHY. Christian Athens remained round the Acropolis where the Frankish dukes had their palace in the Propylaia. The Turks fortified the S slope of the Acropolis, Serpentzes turning the Odeion of Herodes Atticus into a redoubt. The later Turkish town was lightly walled by Haseki in 1778–80, using in the N the ruins of the ancient circuit. The modern city owes its basic inner plan to the Bavarian architects of King Otho and its unplanned suburban development to its rapid growth in 1923.

1   From Síndagma Square to the Acrópolis and the Agorá

BUS 230: by this route hurried tourists may quickly reach the Acropolis by road while seeing some of the more obvious sights of Athens on the way. For the traveller on foot whose immediate object is the Acropolis it is more rewarding to approach it from the N side by plunging directly into the narrow streets of Plaka (Rte 6); the shortest way is by Odhós Apollónos and Odhós Adhrianoú, whence Odhós Mnesikleous leads to the path under the awe-inspiring cliff crowned by the Erechtheion.

Those on foot who wish to combine the S slope with the Acropolis itself may avoid the noisiest streets by taking Odhós Níkis and Odhós Kidathenaíon to the Monument of Lysikrates. The buildings on the S slope will, however, be better appreciated after being seen from the Acropolis wall whence their plan is more clearly apparent. This may prove sufficient for the casual visitor.—For the direct approach to the Agora, see Rte 4.

The centre of the visitors' quarter is **Síndagma Square** (3, 8; Πλατεία του Συντάγματος, or *Constitution Sq.*), a busy open space closed on the E by the palace from whose balcony in 1843 the constitution was proclaimed. The square itself, to the W and below the level of Amalia Avenue, bustles with the life of its hotels, cafés, and air terminals. The gardens are planted with orange trees, oleanders, and cypresses. The figures in bronze beside its walks are copies, presented by Lord Bute, of antique originals in the museum at Naples. The ancient *Stele* in the NW corner marked a boundary of the Garden of the Muses (see below). The *Hôtel Grande Bretagne*, enlarged (1958) and refaced in marble, began in 1842–43 as a private house built by Theophilus von Hansen. It was the headquarters of the French School in 1856–74, and of the Greek, German, and British forces in turn during the Second World War. During Christmas eve, 1944, while Churchill was visiting strife-torn Athens, an attempt to blow up the hotel from the sewers was just foiled. Above Amalia Avenue, a paved hollow square, framed by trees, fronts the palace, in the retaining wall of which is placed a *Memorial to the Unknown Soldier* (its removal elsewhere is mooted at intervals).

The bas-relief, depicting a dying Greek, was modelled on a figure from the Temple of Aphaía at Aegina now in the Munich collection; the adjacent texts are from Pericles' funeral oration. On the walls bronze shields celebrate Greek victories since 1821. The guard, drawn in turn from the armed services, is changed on Sunday mornings (11.00), and the square is used as a saluting base for national processions. From it a ceremonial marble staircase (1928) leads up to the ex-Royal palace (visitors ascend by the side roads).
    Excavations during rebuilding round the square in 1957–61 brought to light 119 graves dating from Classical times when the area, which lay along the Themistoclean wall between the Acharnai and Diocharous gates, was a necropolis.
    The *Lykeion*, or Lyceum, dedicated to Apollo, lay beyond the Diocharous gate at the foot of Lykabettos. Its grounds served as a parade-ground for the ephebes; before the time of Solon, the Polemarch had his offices here. Later Aristotle expounded his philosophy here; his disciples were dubbed 'Peripatetics' from their habit of walking as they discoursed. The trees of the Lyceum were cut down by Sulla to make siege-engines. The *Garden of the Muses*, or Mouseion, was given c 320 BC by Demetrios of Phaleron to Theophrastos, Aristotle's heir and successor at the Lyceum, who left it to the school.

The old **Royal Palace** (3, 8; *Pálaion Anáktoron*), since 1935 the seat of the GREEK PARLIAMENT (Βουλή; *Voulí*), is well situated on rising ground E of the square. Designed by Bavarian court architects, it was built in 1836–42, King Ludwig of Bavaria laying the first stone. It is in the early plain classicising style and the original interior decoration was in the Pompeian manner. The W front has a Doric portico of Pentelic marble. The interior was damaged by fire in 1910 and transformed in 1935.

After the senate was abolished in 1862, apart from an unsuccessful attempt in 1927–35 to revive the Upper House, Parliament consisted of one House only. During the military dictatorship of 1967–74 its functions were in abeyance.

LEOFÓROS VASILÍSSIS AMALÍAS (Queen Amalía Av.), a handsome boulevard where many suburban buses terminate, leads S alongside the *National Garden (Ethnikós Kípos; open daily to sunset). Designed by Queen Amalia for the palace and still referred to as the *Royal Gardens*, this is a favourite Athenian retreat from the summer sun. Its subtropical trees are irrigated by a channel that succeeds the aqueduct of

Peisistratos; peacocks and waterfowl frequent its serpentine walks and ornamental ponds; and nightingales sing here in the spring. There is a *Botanical Museum* housed in a charming small pavilion (1857) with an imaginative display of all the trees, shrubs and plants in the garden.

In the garden are busts of the poets Solomos and Valaorites, of Count John Capodistrias, and of Eynard, the Swiss philhellene. Farther N, behind the palace, are some remains of *Roman Baths* with large geometric mosaics, and traces survive of Hadrian's city wall.

Farther along (right), the **Russian Church** (*St. Nicodemus*, properly *Sotíra Likodhímou*; 7, 4) overlooks a small square. The church, the largest remaining medieval building in Athens, was founded shortly before 1031 by Stefan Likodemou (died 1045). Its monastic buildings, ruined by earthquake in 1701, were pulled down in 1780 to provide material for Hadji Ali Haseki's wall. Damaged by shell-fire in 1827, the church remained derelict until restored by the Russian government in 1852–56. The external walls have a terracotta frieze, and the wide dome rests on squinches. The detached belfry is a 19C addition; the great bell was a gift of Tsar Alexander II.

Under the church and square are remains of a Roman bath (2C AD); excavations in 1961 suggested its early adaptation as a place of Christian worship. An inscription of the 1C BC, still near the church where it was found, comes from the Gymnasium of the Lyceum (comp. above), with which this bath is probably to be associated.

Just beyond is the **English Church** (*St.Paul's*; 7, 5), designed by C.R. Cockerell in an undistinguished Gothic style in 1840–43. Within on the N side are a British funerary memorial of 1685, removed here from the Theseion, and a painted window to Sir Richard Church with an inscription by Gladstone. The E window commemorates the victims of the 'Dilessi murders' (1870). At Amalias 36 is the *Jewish Museum* (still in course of arrangement), founded in 1977 to illustrate the heritage of the Jewish community in Greece whose origins go back to the 3C BC. On the opposite side of the avenue open the *Zappeion Gardens*, the S continuation of the National Garden. To the left of the entrance is a charming marble Pan by Yeoryios Demetriades and in the central avenue a figure of Varvakis, founder of the high school. The **Záppeion** (7, 6), founded by the cousins Zappas as a national exhibition hall, was built by Theophilus von Hansen in 1874–88 and renovated in 1959–60. The semicircular exterior has a handsome porticoed façade and encloses a circular colonnade surrounding an open court. In front are statues of the founders; beyond is a popular café with an open-air stage (evening cabaret).

The S side of the Zappeion Gardens is bounded by Leofóros Olgas (see Rte 7) which meets Amalia Avenue in a large open triangle, one of the busiest traffic centres in Athens. On the corner (left) stands a sentimental 19C group of Byron and Hellas, by Chapu and Falguière. On the far side is the **Arch of Hadrian** (7, 5), an isolated gateway in Pentelic marble erected by Hadrian c AD 132 to mark the limit of the ancient city and the beginning of Novae Athenae or Hadrianopolis (Rte 7). The façades, otherwise identical, bear differing inscriptions on the frieze: that on the NW side towards the Acropolis reads 'This is Athens, the ancient city of Theseus'; that on the SE side towards the Olympieion records 'This is the city of Hadrian and not of Theseus'. The gate is some way W of the line of the Themistoclean Wall; it was incorporated in the 18C Turkish enceinte.

The gate is 18m high, 12·5m wide, and 2·3m thick, with an archway 6m across. The piers of the arch were adorned with Corinthian columns, the bases and consoles of which can be traced. Above the archway is an attic consisting of a portico of four Corinthian columns with three bays, the middle one having a pediment.—Behind is the *Olympieion* (Rte 7).

Odhós Lissikrátous leads W into Plaka (see Rte 6), passing the church of *Ayía Aikateríni*. The ancient columns that front the palm-shaded garden were probably reused as an earlier church façade in the 6C. At the end of this street ran the STREET OF THE TRIPODS.

It was the custom of the victorious choregi to dedicate to Dionysos the tripods which they had gained in dramatic contests. These tripods were erected either in the precincts of the Theatre or on shrines or columns in a street specially appropriated to them, which led in a semicircle round the E of the hill from the Prytaneion to the Theatre. The tripods were placed over the works of art, the kettle or cauldron forming a sort of roof. Pausanias singles out for mention the Satyr of Praxiteles, no longer extant (torso of a copy in the Louvre), but ignores the monument of Lysikrates. Such other foundations as were located in 1921 and 1955 (to the number of seven) have been left *in situ* and covered again.

The well-preserved ***Choregic Monument of Lysikrates** is renowned not only for its graceful detail, but as being the earliest building known in which the Corinthian capital is used externally. A square base of Piraeus stone 4m high, with a cornice of Eleusinian marble, bears three circular steps of Hymettos marble. On this base six monolithic Corinthian columns are arranged in a circle to support an entablature crowned by a marble dome, wrought with great delicacy from a single block; from the centre of the roof rises an elaborate finial of acanthus-leaf carving, the support for the tripod itself. An inscription on the architrave informs us that 'Lysikrates of Kikyna, son of Lysitheides, was choregos; the tribe of Akamantis won the victory with a chorus of boys; Theon played the flute; Lysiades of Athens trained the chorus; Evainetos was archon' (334 BC). Round the frieze is represented the story of Dionysos and the Tyrrhenian pirates, whom he turned into dolphins. The whole of the superstructure is in Pentelic marble, except the curved panels (of Hymettian marble), engaged between the columns, that form the central drum. Of these only the three showing a frieze of tripods are original.

The inside of the drum was never intended to·be seen for the capitals are unfinished within and there is no provision for light. However, the missing panels were removed during the period (1669–1821) when the monument was incorporated in the library of a French Capuchin convent. It was then known as the 'Lantern of Demosthenes' from a belief that the orator prepared his speeches in it. Byron, one of many English guests at the convent, is said to have used it as a study; he wrote part of 'Childe Harold' here in 1810–11. On the occupation of Athens by Omer Vrioni the convent was accidentally burned down; the monument was freed and later properly restored in 1892 with French funds. Recent excavations in the immediate vicinity of the monument have uncovered a further section of the Street of the Tripods and the foundations of other choregic monuments. Later finds include Roman burials and the remains of an Early Christian basilica. To Monastiraki and the N side of the Acropolis, see Rte 6.

The Street of the Tripods curved down to the main Propylaia of the Sanctuary of Dionysos (see below). Inside the curve, just E of the theatre, stood the **Odeion of Pericles**, built originally before 446 BC, burnt during the sack of Athens in 86 BC by Aristion, a general of Mithridates, who feared that Sulla might use the timbers of the roof for siege engines, and rebuilt in marble on the former plan by Ariobarzanes II, king of Cappadocia (65–52 BC). Its side has only recently been expropriated from beneath a jumble of poor houses, but investigations by the Greek Archaeological Society in 1914–31 proved it to be rectangular in plan, not circular as had been assumed from classical references to its being modelled on the tent of Xerxes. It was a large hall with interior columns arranged in nine rows of ten, somewhat similar in plan to the Telesterion at Eleusis, and had a pyramidal roof with a lantern. The scene of the musical contests of the Panathenaic Festival, it had the reputation of being the best concert-hall in the Greek world; and rehearsals of the tragedies presented in the Theatre of Dionysos at the Great Dionysiac Festival were held in it.

We continue by the broad Odhós Dhionissíou Areopayítou (named after St. Paul's convert, Dionysius the Areopagite) to an entrance to the **Excavations on the S slope of the Acropolis** (6, 6; there is also a gate above giving access to the Acropolis). Immediately within the gate we cross the line of the wall that once bounded the TEMENOS OF DIONYSOS ELEUTHERIOS. Traces of the wall survive to the E, but the main entrance to the precinct from the Street of the Tripods (see above) has not been excavated.

The worship of Dionysos Eleutherios was introduced into Athens in the 6C BC from the then Boeotian city of Eleutherai. The festival of the Great Dionysia of the City, instituted by Peisistratos, which eclipsed the old festival of the Wine-press (Lenaia) held in the marshes, was characterized by the competing choruses of satyrs, clad in goatskins, who danced round the altar of the god and sang their 'goat songs'. These dithyrambic contests were the forerunners of Attic tragedy.

We pass the breccia foundations of a small 4C *Temple* consisting of pronaos and cella, built to re-house the chryselephantine statue of Dionysos by Alkamenes, seen by Pausanias; the great base on which it was placed remains. Nearer the theatre are scantier remnants of an *Older Temple* dating from the 6C. To the SE are foundations representing either the great altar or the base of a large votive dedication.

The **Theatre of Dionysos** was rebuilt in stone by Lycurgus in 342–326 BC to replace an earlier structure in which the masterpieces of Aeschylus, Sophocles, Euripides, and Aristophanes were first performed. Extensive modifications in Hellenistic and Roman times involved the re-use of old material so that the existing remains present a puzzling conglomeration of the work of 750 years.

History. Archaeologists differ about the dating of much of the structure and historians of the Greek drama have reached no certain conclusions about the superstructure or internal layout of the skene before Roman times. The clearest exposition of the many problems can be found in *A. W. Pickard-Cambridge*: The Theatre of Dionysos in Athens (O.U.P., 1946) and may be supplemented by the reports of further investigations in 1951 and 1963. A meticulous survey was started in 1979. The results, which may modify presently held theories, are intended as a preliminary to restorations.

It is probable that a circular *Orchestra*, or dancing ground, with a central altar, existed here in the 6C BC (though traces of a terrace-wall are all that survive from this period) and that by the beginning of the 5C spectators occupied wooden stands. Following an accident (c 500–470 BC) to a stand either here or in the agora, an earthen auditorium (*theatron*) was constructed. Here, against a background of wood and canvas, the great dramas of the Golden Age were performed. About the time of Pericles the auditorium assumed nearly its present shape, when supporting walls were built to the E and W; the seats were still probably of wood. The orchestra was moved a little to the N but remained circular, and a long foundation wall served both to retain the extended terrace and to support a wooden stage set. Immediately behind and slightly below this was built a stoa, connected to the orchestral area by a flight of steps and having an open colonnade on its S side.

A reconstruction in the 4C was probably finished c 330 BC by Lycurgus, when the theatron was rebuilt in stone in much the form it has today, and a permanent skene in stone, flanked by columned paraskenia, replaced the movable wooden sets. Plays continued to be acted at orchestral level but in Hellenistic times, when attention had passed irrevocably from ritual dancing to dramatic acting, a raised stage was added, supported by a stone proskenion. At the same time the paraskenia were taken back and the parodoi (side entrances) widened to give easier access to the auditorium.

The skene and stage were again rebuilt, possibly by T. Claudius Novius c AD 61. At some time the Roman stage was further extended over the parodoi to meet the auditorium, and a marble barrier erected round the orchestra to protect the audience from gladiatorial exhibitions. At a later period (?3C AD) the Bema of Phædrus was added in front of the Roman proskenion. Still later the reliefs on the bema were truncated and cemented over when the orchestra was turned into a watertight basin for the performance of naumachiæ.

Even in classical times the theatre was used for other purposes than drama. The presentation of crowns to distinguished citizens, the release of orphans from state control on their reaching man's estate, and other ceremonies served as curtain-raisers to the play. The golden crowns presented by independent foreign states and the tribute of subject states were displayed in the theatre. Annual cock-fights, instituted after the Persian wars, took place here. The Assembly, occasionally in the 4C (Thuc. VIII, 93) and regularly after the 3C, met here instead of in the Pnyx. Demetrios Poliorketes after making himself master of Athens (292 BC) here overawed the Assembly with a military display.

The AUDITORIUM retains roughly the form it assumed under Lycurgus when, on the W side, the outer wall of poros was added to the earlier buttressed wall of breccia. At the same time the supporting wall on the E, irregular in contour due to the proximity of the Odeion (see above), was extended to the rock above. Concentric tiers of seats, radiating fanwise from the orchestra, are separated into 13 wedges (kerkides; *Lat.* cunei) by narrow stairways. Some 25 tiers survive in part.

It is generally assumed that there were 64 tiers of stone seats divided by a postulated gangway (*diazoma*) into two sections of 32 rows each. Above this the *Peripatos* (comp. below) formed a second diazoma. An upper section of 14 more rows of seats, hewn from the rock, may have been a later addition; the higher remains are fragmentary. The seating capacity can hardly have exceeded 17,000, far short of Plato's estimate of 30,000 (Symposium).

The seats, made (except for the front row) of Piraeus limestone, are shaped so that one row of spectators did not incommode the next row: each person sat on the flat section in front (probably on a cushion), placing his feet in the trough hollowed behind the seat below. The front row consisted of 67 *Thrones* in Pentelic marble. Sixty remain in the theatre, of which 14 were found in place; the remainder have been restored with some certainty to their original positions. Each bears the name of the priest of dignitary for whom it was reserved; since some of the original inscriptions were replaced with later inscriptions, the thrones have been called replicas of the 1C BC. However, the style of the relief sculpture and both the design and workmanship of the thrones indicate that the entire front row dates from the time of Lykurgos. Distinguished by its more elaborate shape and fine sculpture is the *Throne of the Priest of Dionysos Eleutherios*, placed in the centre, exactly opposite the thymele, or altar of the god, which stood in the middle of the orchestra.

The throne is a beautifully carved armchair with lion's-claw feet. On the back, delicately worked in low relief, is a representation of two satyrs, supporting on their shoulders a yoke whence hangs a branch of grapes. In front is inscribed the name of the owner; above the inscription is a remarkable relief of two kneeling male figures in Persian costume, each of whom grasps a gryphon by the throat with one hand, lifting with the other a scimitar. On each arm is a beautiful figure in low relief of a winged boy conducting a cock-fight. The Throne of Hadrian occupied the large plinth just behind. The area in front of the seats drains into a channel surrounding the orchestra.—Statues of Roman emperors, tragic and comic poets, orators, statesmen, and philanthropists were numerous; the base of one of Menander, by Kephisodotos and Timarchos (sons of Praxiteles), stands at the NW corner of the skene.

The ORCHESTRA preserves today none of its classical appearance. The existing area, in the form of a slightly extended semicircle, represents the orchestra of the Roman rebuilding under Nero. The surface was then paved in marble slabs with a central rhombus made of smaller coloured pieces. Slabs also cover the Lycurgan drainage channel. Both these and the marble barrier protecting the auditorium are pierced with drainage holes, which were later stopped up (and the water channel blocked) when the theatre was used for mock sea-fights.

The so-called *Bema of Phædrus* stands in a mutilated condition for about half its length. This presumably represents the final front of the Roman stage. It takes its name from the dedicatory inscription on the slab that surmounts the uppermost of the four stone steps in the centre. The date of the inscription is doubtful; Phædrus is otherwise unknown; and the stone is not in its original place. The reliefs have been dated to the 2C AD, and almost certainly came from somewhere near by. They portray scenes in the life of Dionysos, the last (westernmost) relief showing the God installed in his theatre on a gorgeous throne with the Acropolis and Parthenon in the background. The well-preserved crouching sileni were forced into place afterwards. When found in 1862 the figures were still plastered with cement from the waterproofing (see above).

Behind lie the foundations of earlier stage buildings. We may trace the Hellenistic proskenion, flanked by paraskenia, some truncated columns of which survive, and, farther back, the outline of the long stoa of Periclean date; but the remains between are too confused by late masonry, designed merely as support for the Roman skene, to aid any imaginative reconstruction in the mind of a layman, and admit of widely diverging interpretation by experts.

Above the theatre opens the **Panayía Chrysospiliótissa**, or *Chapel of Our Lady of the Cavern*. On the walls are faded Byzantine paintings. Within, every evening, a solitary lamp is lit. Round the mouth of the cave the rock face is cut vertically to form a scarp known as the *Katatomé*. The entrance was masked, until Turkish gunfire destroyed it in 1827, by the *Choregic Monument of Thrasyllos*, erected in 320 BC by Thrasyllos, who dedicated the cavern to Dionysos. The monument took the form of a Doric portico raised on two steps. Three marble pilasters supported an architrave bearing the dedication, above which was a frieze adorned with eleven wreaths carved in relief; the tripod stood above the cornice. Fifty years later, when president of the Games (agonothetes), Thrasykles, son of Thrasyllos, added two further dedications commemorating similar victories of his own in choregic contests. The inscriptions may still be seen. A seated figure of Dionysos found above the monument, and now in the British Museum, was a Roman addition.—The two Corinthian *Columns* above the cavern also supported votive tripods; the cuttings for their feet in the triangular capitals may be seen from the top of the wall of Kimon. To the right is a *Sundial* in Pentelic marble, noted in the 15C Vienna Anonymous.

To the W of the theatre the ancient remains extend along the slope in two terraces. The upper terrace is supported by a massive retaining wall buttressed by a continuous row of arches (some 40 of which now provide from the road the most conspicuous feature of the area), over which ran the PERIPATOS, the main highway, nearly 5m wide, round the Acropolis. Steps descend to it from the upper part of the theatre. If we ascend from the orchestra, we see (left) the rectangular foundations of the *Choregic Monument of Nikias*, erected in 319 BC in the form of a pro-style hexastyle and demolished soon after AD 267 to provide material for fortifications. The stones were used in the Beulé Gate, where part of the inscription from the architrave may still be seen (comp. Rte 2); the full text read: 'Nikias, son of Nikodemos of

Xypete, dedicated this monument after a victory as choregos with boys of the tribe of Kekropis; Pantaleon of Sikyon played the flute; the *"Elpenor"* of Timotheos was the song; Neaichmos was archon.'

Above the peripatos and to the W of the theatre extends the **Asklepieíon**, or *Sanctuary of Asklepios in the City*, dedicated in 418 BC by Telemachos of Acharnai on a site already sacred to a water-god. The 5C sanctuary occupied the W portion of the terrace; in the 4C a new precinct was built to the E, extending to the theatre wall. Each contained a sacred spring, a temple and an altar, and an abaton or stoa. The most conspicuous remains within the temenos are, however, the walls of a large Byzantine *Church* of the 5C or 6C, where, probably under the patronage of SS Cosmas and Damian, the cure continued under the Christian ægis.

The worship of Asklepios, which spread from Epidauros, was introduced into Athens on the occasion of the plague of 429 BC. The 'cure' followed a ritual, during which patients washed in the sacred spring, offered sacrifices at an altar, and then retired to the stoa where the mysterious process of incubation (ἐγκοίμησις) was assisted by incense from the altars. This and religious excitement produced dreams, through the medium of which Asklepios was supposed to effect his cure. Many ex-voto tablets to Asklepios and Hygieia have been found showing the portion of the anatomy treated. These were affixed to a wall or inlaid in the columns; larger votive stelai, some showing the god visiting sick patients in their sleep, were fixed to the stoa steps (examples in the National Museum).

To the E, somewhat obscured by the Byzantine walls, can be traced the foundations of the later *Abaton*, consisting of a colonnade with 17 Doric columns and two interior galleries separated by another colonnade. The long plinth of Hymettian marble, the back wall to the E and the intermediate row of bases are all that remain *in situ*, but the stoa probably had two floors, the upper one being the *Enkoimeterion*, or dormitory of the sick. A narrow passage leads from the N gallery into a circular spring house hewn in the rock. The wonder-working nature of the sacred spring continues, and the ancient spring house is now a chapel which is kept locked.

At the W end of the stoa, probably under a baldachin roof, was the so-called *Bothros*, perhaps a sacrificial pit where blood was poured to chthonic divinities, but more likely the dwelling of the sacred snakes. In front of the stoa are the foundations of a small *Temple* in antis. In the W part of the temenos, which is bounded by the Pelasgikon wall, are the foundations of the smaller 5C *Stoa*. The *Old Spring* was contained in a fine 5C rectangular cistern of polygonal masonry, transformed by the Turks. Just to the S is another huge *Cistern*, probably of Byzantine date.

To the W of the Asklepieion the sanctuaries enumerated by Pausanias have disappeared beneath the Turkish fortifications. A path follows the general direction of the peripatos through confused remains round the top of the Odeion (see below) to the entrance to the Acropolis.

The arches of the peripatos road were formerly concealed by the so-called **Stoa of Eumenes**, which began c 9m from the Theatre of Dionysos and extended for 163m. At its W end it communicated with the Odeion by two doors. The impressive socle of its back wall is in Hymettian marble. The outer Doric colonnade had 64 columns.

This is assumed to be the colonnade built by Eumenes II, King of Pergamon (197–159 BC), who is recorded by Vitruvius (V, 9, 1) as having built a stoa near the theatre to serve as a shelter and promenade. In Roman times it was connected with the much later Odeion of Herodes Atticus and remained in use until the 3C when it was destroyed and the materials used in the Valerian wall. Column drums can be seen at No. 30 Veïkou. The Turks incorporated the remnants in their lower enceinte (Wall of Serpentzes) in 1687.

To the W of the stoa is the **Odeíon of Heródes Atticus**, built in honour of Regilla, wife of Herodes, who died in AD 160. It has the typical form of a Roman theatre with a seating capacity of 5000–6000, and was one of the last great public buildings erected in Athens.

The sudden rise to wealth of Julius Atticus, father of Herodes, is wittily related by Gibbon. Julius, who had accidentally found a vast treasure buried in an old house, anticipated the officiousness of informers by reporting his find to the emperor. On being told by Nerva to have no qualms about using—or abusing—fortune's gift, Julius devoted large sums to public works and to educating his son. Herodes, after a distinguished public career, including the consulship at Rome, retired to Athens and continued the munificence of his father, paying for projects in Troas, Delphi, and Corinth, as well as for the stadium and this Odeion in Athens. The Turks converted the Odeion into a redoubt, without, however, injuring its plan. The interior was excavated in 1857–58, when evidence showed that it had been destroyed by a fire. A large quantity of murex shells found at the same time suggest that the Byzantine Greeks had a factory there for Tyrian purple. The theatre is the scene of orchestral and operatic performances during the Athens Festival.

The massive *Façade* stands everywhere to the second storey and in places to the third, though the portico that stood in front has disappeared (mosaic excavated and re-covered). Entrance is made to either side through vestibules (traces of mosaics) leading to the parodoi. The stage wall is pierced by three doors and has eight niches for statues. Above are windows. Three steps of the E stair connecting the stage with the orchestra remain. The steeply-rising *Auditorium*, supported by a thick circular limestone wall, was roofed with cedar. It consists of a cavea, c 78m across, divided by a diazoma, below which are five wedges of seats and ten above. The seating was entirely restored in Pentelic marble in 1950–61, and the *Orchestra* repaved in blue and white slabs.

To the S of the Odeion, on either side of the modern entrance stairway, are remains (of various dates) including a *Sanctuary of the Nymphs*, excavated by the Greek Archaeological Service in 1955–59 and identified by its boundary stone. Loutrophoroi found date from the mid-7C; these were vessels used for the bridal bath and offered here afterwards as dedications.

Just beyond the Odeion is a busy junction. To the right a drive (no motor vehicles) mounts to the entrance of the Acropolis. Ahead a panoramic avenue circles Mouseion Hill to the Philopappos monument (see Rte 3). Between them Leoforos Apostólou Pávlou continues (c 1km) to the W entrance of the Agora (Rte 5).

2   The Acropolis

The Athenian **Acropolis** stands alone in its unique combination of grandeur, beauty, and historical associations. This rocky height, traditionally connected with the Pelasgi, was the original city (πόλις) and the abode of the early kings and their courts. It possessed also an irresistible attraction for the tyrants, Kylon making an abortive, and Peisistratos a successful, attempt to establish it as a fortified residence. After the fall of the Peisistratids, however, the Athenians lived entirely in the Lower City and resigned the Acropolis to their gods. It was sacked by the Persians in 480 BC. New walls built by Kimon and

Pericles were followed by the great era of construction under Pericles, who was responsible for the array of buildings which, despite the vicissitudes of time, remain an inspiration to the world. It is particularly beautiful in the setting sun and by the light of the full moon.

The *Acropolis* is a rock of coarse semi-crystalline limestone and red schist, of very irregular form, measuring c 320m by 128m. Its summit (156m), to the NE of the Parthenon, is 91m above the general level of the city. From the summit two ridges run towards the W, the more important of them ending in the bastion of the Temple of Athena Nike, to the SW. The only accessible slope follows the depression between these two ridges. Elsewhere the hill is precipitous or even overhanging, with inaccessible clefts and caverns in the rock. The sheer descent on the S side, however, is largely artificial.

History. Natural springs have attracted man to the slopes of the Acropolis since Neolithic times (c 5000 BC) and the site was inhabited continuously throughout the Helladic periods. Towards the end of the Bronze Age (Late Helladic IIIB) the Mycenaean settlement was strengthened with a 'Cyclopean' rampart (sometimes loosely called the Pelasgic Wall), consisting of two facing walls of large undressed stones in more or less regular courses, with a core of rubble. It was filled in with clay and its thickness varied from 4·5m to 6·7m. The surviving fragments show that the wall followed a sinuous course adapted to the contour of the rocky height. A well-preserved section (4·3m) runs from the Propylaea to the S circuit wall. To the N the wall overhung the escarpment of the Long Rocks and is now mostly obscured by later walls; to the S and E it kept nearer to the ridge than the later wall of Kimon. The bastion on which the Temple of Athena Nike stands has Mycenaean foundations and probably defended a principal W entrance akin to the Lion Gate at Mycenae. A postern gate to the NE, approached by narrow steps hewn in a natural cleft, which provided the entrance in Early and Middle Helladic times, was abandoned about this time. Farther W a secret reservoir, deep underground, was reached by eight flights of stairs, accessible only from the top of the Acropolis, thus securing an unassailable water supply for the Acropolis in time of siege. Explorations, made with great difficulty in 1937–38, showed that the reservoir dated from the latter half of the 13C BC and was in use for c 25 years only. Its existence was quite unknown in Classical times, when the lower flights were buried and the uppermost two flights of stairs were used to provide a secret exit from the Acropolis to the N slope. The principal Mycenaean building was the Royal Palace, Homer's 'strong house of Erechtheus', which stood somewhere on the N side probably in the region of the Old Temple of Athena. The Tomb of Kekrops, founder of the dynasty, was presumably just to the W. A few remains of Mycenaean dwellings exist on the N side, and tombs below.

At some later date a lower wall was constructed on the W slope to form a precinct similar to that at Tiryns. This wall was known as the Pelasgikon or Pelargikon, perhaps because it was built by the Attic Pelasgi (Hdt. VI, 137), perhaps from the storks which used to nest on the battlements. It was known later as the 'Enneapylon' (nine gates), but no trace of it remains and its course can only be inferred from literary references. Though this was dismantled after the fall of the Peisistratids in 510 BC the area enclosed by it remained unoccupied in obedience to the oracle of Delphi until refugees crowded it at the time of the Peloponnesian War.

Little is known of the Acropolis in the five centuries between the Mycenaean and Archaic periods, though continuity of the cults of Erechtheus, Kekrops, etc., suggests uninterrupted occupation. The original wall, the Kekropion, and the great altar of Athena seem to have survived until the Persian War. A Geometric temple to Athena is assumed to have stood on the same site as the Peisistratid Temple of Athena which replaced it c 529 BC. Numerous fragments of architecture and of pedimental sculpture belonging to a sizable poros limestone temple of the mid-6C BC have been found on the S side of the Acropolis between the Parthenon and the S wall. This temple has, rightly or wrongly, been identified with the *Hekatompedon* (or 'hundred-footer') to which ancient inscriptions refer. Because the inscriptions clearly name the Parthenon cella 'Hekatompedon' and use the same name for a pre-Parthenon building on the Acropolis, and because the architectural and sculptural remains were found in the immediate vicinity of the Parthenon, many archaeologists equate these remains with the Hekatompedon and consider it a predecessor of the Parthenon built on the Parthenon site; others consider that this material belongs to the building whose foundations were identified by Dörpfeld between the Parthenon and the Erechtheion (comp.

below, *Old Temple of Athena*). Pedimental sculpture and other members of four small Archaic buildings have been found on the Acropolis; the better preserved fragments are displayed in the museum.

The victory of Marathon (490 BC) and the opening of new marble quarries on Mt Pentelikon stimulated a scheme, presumably stemming from Aristides, for an ambitious new temple (usually referred to as the Older or Pre-Parthenon). The surface area of the Acropolis was enlarged by building terraces with retaining walls filled in with debris from the demolished Hekatompedon. The new foundations in poros had been completed and work started on the columns when the Persian sack of 480/79 BC reduced the Acropolis to calcined ruins.

Essential cleaning up and patching up were undertaken directly after the battle of Plataea. The gateway was repaired and part of the cella of the Old Temple of Athena may have been restored as a Treasury. In accordance with an oath taken before Plataea, the sanctuaries were left in ruins as reminders of Persian impiety. The Persians had demolished enough of the fortification wall of the 13C BC to render it useless, and when the Acropolis north wall was rebuilt the Athenians created a perpetual reminder of Persian barbarism by incorporating remains of both the Old Temple of Athena and of the Older Parthenon near the top of the wall where they can be seen to this day. On the S side more terrace walls were undertaken and filled in with debris to extend the area of the Acropolis still further. The spoils of the Battle of the Eurymedon (468 BC) eventually enabled Kimon to undertake a more ambitious plan whereby a massive S wall was started. This was completed under Pericles and established the bastion, c 18m high, that still exists.

The decision to rebuilt the Acropolis on a monumental scale was taken by Pericles about the time the peace treaty was signed with the Persians at Susa (448 BC). The Parthenon was finished in 438 BC and the Propylaia immediately begun. The Temple of Athena Nike followed and the Erechtheion. The latter was not finished until 395, and the final demolition of the restored Opisthodomos of the Old Athena Temple in 353 marks the end of the old order. From the time of Pericles until the death of Augustus (AD 14) the general appearance of the Acropolis underwent little change. Votive offerings in the form of shields were added to the Parthenon by Alexander the Great, and Antiochus Epiphanes added a gilded Gorgoneion to the S wall of the Acropolis. The siege of Sulla in 86 BC affected only the buildings of the S slope.

Claudius began the embellishment of the entrance c AD 52 with a monumental staircase (a typical manifestation of Roman grandeur), and Hadrian enriched many shrines. The building of the 'Beulé' Gate in the 3C marked the beginning of the second fortified period presaging damage and deterioration, and the Edict of Theodosius II in AD 429 dealt the final blow to pagan worship. Justinian converted the temples to Orthodox Christian churches, restored the military character of the citadel, and provided for the water supply of the garrison. The bronze Athena Promachos of Pheidias was removed to Constantinople before 900 to adorn the Hippodrome.

In 1204 the Acropolis was taken by the Marquess of Montferrat. At the end of the same year it was occupied and plundered by Otho de la Roche. In 1387 Nerio Acciaioli captured the citadel after a long siege. On Nerio's death, the succession was disputed; his son Antony occupied the Acropolis in 1403 after a 17-months siege. During his reign the Propylaia were converted into a Florentine palace. In 1458 Franco, last duke of Athens, surrendered the Acropolis after a two-years defence, to Omar, Attica having been annexed to Turkey in 1456.

To meet the threat of the extended use of cannon, the defences of the Acropolis were remodelled. In 1640 or 1656 a powder magazine in the Propylaia was struck by lightning, causing its first serious injury. After 1684 the Temple of Athena Nike was removed to make way for a new battery. On 21 September 1687, the Venetian army under Morosini landed at Piraeus, and on the 23rd two batteries opened fire on the works before the Propylaia. After an explosion in the Parthenon, a fire raged on the Acropolis for 48 hours. On 3 October the Turks capitulated, but in April 1688 they reoccupied the citadel and for the next century its ruins were obscured by a maze of little streets. In 1822 the Turkish garrison surrendered to the Greek insurgents; but in June 1827 the Acropolis was recovered after 11 months desultory siege by Reshid Pasha. The Turks now retained possession until after the end of the war when, in 1833, they were succeeded by a Bavarian garrison, which did not quit till 30 March 1835.

In 1801 Lord Elgin, then British Ambassador to the Porte, obtained permission in a firman to fix scaffolding, to excavate, to make casts and drawings, and to take away pieces of stone with inscriptions or figures. Whatever may be the opinion of his action, it should be appreciated that at the time fragments were being reduced to lime in the lime-kilns on the Acropolis; the sculptures which Elgin took away were at least spared the further ravages of time and of successive wars. A campaign by the Greek Government to have the sculptures returned to Greece is winning increasing support in Britain.

Excavations. Demolition of Turkish and Frankish structures began immediately in 1833, not without dissentient voices, one of the regents as early as 1835 opining that 'the archaeologists would destroy all the picturesque additions of the middle ages in their zeal to lay bare and restore the ancient monuments'; as indeed they have. Restoration and rearrangement of existing fragments continued to 1853, when Beulé uncovered the gate that bears his name. Burnouf discovered the Klepsydra spring in 1874 and Schliemann demolished the Frankish Tower in 1875. In 1876–85 the Greek Archaeological Society subsidised excavations by Kavvadias and Kawerau, when the surface of the Acropolis was investigated in many places to bedrock. Restorations and examinations of buildings in detail have gone on almost continuously ever since, with a mass of published reports.

By 1976 continuing damage to the Acropolis had reached unacceptable levels. There were three main causes: internal deterioration of the marble through the use of iron clamps and supports in 19C restoration works; external chemical changes wrought in the surfaces by sulphurous pollution from central heating and vehicle exhausts; and wear to surfaces by visitors' feet. Legislation has already reduced oil pollution. Motor vehicles are no longer permitted on the approaches. Severe restrictions are in force as to where visitors may walk: when new paths have been laid, a channelled round may have to be enforced. The former moonlight openings have ceased. Entry to all buildings is forbidden, except to parts of the Propylaia that are floored. A programme has been started to replace all iron by titanium, to remove much of the remaining original sculpture to controlled museum atmospheres, and replace it with copies (some supplied from British Museum casts of an earlier era). Work on the Erechtheion is expected to be complete soon, but for many years visitors will certainly encounter scaffolding and restricted areas.

At a later date it is planned to remove the present museum from the Acropolis to a new site below the Theatre of Dionysos. A design competition to incorporate an existing scheduled 19C building was inaugurated in 1980.

To explore the Acropolis thoroughly is thus almost impossible at present. A superficial tour may be made in 1½–2 hours by taking a route from the Beulé Gate through the Propylaia, circling the Parthenon, and visiting the Museum; thence via the Belvedere and the Erechtheion back to the Beulé Gate. Though visitors will not be able to see everything described hereunder, it is hoped that the text in its present complete form will best serve the changing situation.

Approaches. A paved road, through gardens planned by Queen Amalia, leads up from Odhos Dhionissíou Areopayítou (Rte 1). Paths lead from the Agora round the Areopagus, and round the N slope from Plaka (see Rte 6).—**Admission**. Tickets are taken at the Beulé Gate. Museum closed Tuesday. Refreshments are available below the entrance in summer; food may not be taken on to the Acropolis. There are lavatories in the grove below the ticket office, and by the NW corner of the Museum.

A. The Entrance

In Classical times the Panathenaic Way ended in a ramp going straight up from the level of the tourist post office to the gateway of the Propylaia with an inclination of one in four. On the modern approach we cross first the line of a medieval wall, then the Turkish wall of Serpentzes that ran N from the retaining wall of the theatre of Herodes Atticus. The ceremonial entrance by which we enter is known as the **Beulé Gate** after the French archaeologist who discovered it in 1852. A marble wall between two unequal pylons (the N one restored) is pierced by a trilithon gateway aligned with the central opening of the Propylaia. This had a defensive purpose and was paid for, c AD 280, by F. Septimus Marcellinus. The gate was built of stones from the destroyed Choregic Monument of Nikias. The name of Pantaleon of

Sikyon the flute-player, may be clearly read above the lintel; the remainder of the inscription is higher up. The inner face of the gate incorporates a grey slab carved with two victor's wreaths.

Within the gate parts of many levels exposed show that the way up was frequently modified. A few courses of polygonal walling lower down on the axis of the Propylaia are all that remains of the N retaining wall for the late-Archaic ramp of the Panathenaic way; in Pericles' day the ramp was widened to the full width of the central section of the Propylaia; by the time of Pausanias all save a central path for sacrificial animals had been concealed beneath a broad MARBLE STAIRCASE, some 73m long, erected within the Propylaia wings in AD 52 by Claudius and completed in its lower courses much later.

At the foot of the steps, just to the left of the Beulé Gate, are four fragments of an architrave, with doves, fillets, and an inscription, belonging to the *Shrine of Aphrodite Pandemos*, which stood below the SW corner of the hill (confirmed by excavations in 1960).

Half-way up the staircase is a natural landing from which a terrace opens to the N. Partly blocking this is the so-called *Monument of Agrippa*, identified by inscriptions on its face and on the landing below it. The colossal plinth, 8·8m high, has a shaft of Hymettos marble set off by a base moulding and cornice in poros (the foundation steps of conglomerate were not intended to be seen). It bore a quadriga. A partially effaced inscription on the W side under the Agrippa inscription records the original dedication, probably in 178 BC, to celebrate a Pergamene chariot victory in the Panathenaic Games. Cuttings in the top show that two chariot groups occupied the plinth at different dates. What happened to the original group depicting Eumenes II is not known. Later, according to Plutarch and Dio Cassius the plinth bore statues of Antony and Cleopatra, which were blown down in 31 BC. The group to Marcus Agrippa was raised after his third consulship in 27 BC.

Behind the monument a terrace of the Periclean period extends below the N wing of the Propylaia. The mound on it consists of marble fragments, many inscribed, dating from the Turkish period. The terrace affords an excellent *View of the Agora and Temple of Hephaistos; the course of the Panathenaic Way along the Wall of Valerian can be traced towards the Klepsydra spring which lies below the bastion. Thither descends the late stairway (inaccessible) that begins from the terrace; emerging from the bastion beneath our feet by a Byzantine doorway, the steps follow a gully and enter a late-Roman well-house.

Klepsydra cannot be visited but can best be understood from this point. The spring, originally called *Empedo*, attracted Neolithic settlers and was early the centre of a cult of Nymphs. It issued from a small natural cave. Within this, c 460, a well-house with a deep *Draw-Basin* was built, and adjoining it a substantial structure, of which the paved floor and a wall survive. Part of the roof of the well-house fell in the 1C BC, though the well was still usable in 37 BC when Mark Antony set out for Parthia taking (in obedience to an oracle) a bottle of water from Klepsydra. In the reign of Claudius a further fall ruined the building without rendering the water inaccessible. In Roman times a vaulted *Well-House* was built over the fallen roof of the original cave with a shaft driven to water level, and the whole sealed with concrete. The new structure was linked for the first time by a stair to the bastion above and was henceforth accessible only from the acropolis, though the overflow later fed a 6C cistern. At the time the new well-house was built, the court seems to have been abandoned, and later was covered by the Wall of Valerian. The Roman well-house received frescoes during its medieval transformation into a *Church of the Holy Apostles*, perhaps of the same period as the Byzantine door (see above). By 1822 all lay beneath a deposit of earth, though the spring itself bubbled up and served a Turkish fountain lower down the hill. After the Turks on the Acropolis had capitulated in 1822 for lack of water, the Greeks, searching for a water supply, found Klepsydra and repaired it, and in 1826 Gen. Odysseus Androutsos enclosed it in a bastion (demolished 1888). Its water served the Greek garrison throughout the siege of 1827. Excavations by Kavvadias in 1897 uncovered the paved court, but the American investigations of 1936–40 form the basis of modern study.—The remainder of the N slope is described in Rte 6.

From this point to the Propylaía we mount the modern zigzag ramp that resembles the Mycenaean and medieval approaches rather than the classical ramp.

The * *Propylaía, a monumental gateway, was designed by Mnesikles to replace an earlier entrance, its axis aligned to that of the Parthenon. It provides the only certain example before Hellenistic times of designing one building in direct relationship to another. The exact nature of the original plan is a matter of some dispute. Built in 437–432 BC, it was left incomplete at the beginning of the Peloponnesian War and the work was never resumed. Except for the foundations, and for certain decorative features in black Eleusinian stone, the construction is wholly of Pentelic marble. Discreet restorations have minimised the ravages of later history and a great part of the building still stands.

History. The Greeks gave the name of Propylon ('gate-building') to the entrance of a sanctuary, palace, or agora. The plural form Propylaia was reserved for more elaborate entrances. Earlier propylaia, probably to be ascribed to Peisistratos, but shown by the re-use of material from the Hekatompedon to date in their later form from 488–480 BC, were aligned differently from the existing structure. The Propylaia of Pericles (the existing edifice), begun upon the completion of the Parthenon, was hampered by political and religious agitation. It is possible that the original plan of Mnesikles was curtailed on the S in deference to the prejudices of the priests of the adjoining sanctuaries. The enormous cost was defrayed by grants from the Treasurers of Athena and Hephaistos, from the sale of old building material, from the rent of houses, and from private subscriptions, as well as by contributions from the Hellenotamiai, but Pericles was accused of squandering the funds of the Delian League on the embellishment of the Acropolis.

The Propylaia remained almost intact down to the 13C, being then used as the Byzantine episcopal palace. The dukes of Athens raised the N wing and used it as their chancery. Nerio Acciaioli made the propylaia his palace and erected the so-called Frankish Tower, 27·5m high, on the S side. The Turks covered the centre vestibule with a cupola and turned it into a magazine, the Aga making it his official residence. In the 17C it was struck by lightning and the magazine exploded with the result that the architraves of the E portico fell and were broken and two Ionic columns collapsed. The W facade and the celebrated ceiling were demolished in the Venetian bombardment of 1687. Later on a Turkish bastion was erected between the Bastion of Athena Nike and the S wing. Some columns were used to make lime. The building suffered again in the siege of 1827. In 1836 Pittakis removed the Frankish and Turkish additions, except the Tower, which was not taken down until 1875 (at the expense of Schliemann). Reconstruction of the central hall was undertaken in 1909–17 and the wings were restored after the Second World War.

The Propylaia comprise a central hall containing the portal and two wings flanking the approach. The CENTRAL HALL forms a rectangle 23·7m long and 18·2m wide, with side walls having antae at each end and Doric hexastyle porticoes facing E and W. It is divided two-thirds of the way through by the portal itself, to the W of which is a vestibule screened by an entrance portico. This *West Portico*, 19·8m wide, rests on four high steps, except in the middle, where the steps give place to a continuous ramp (transverse cuts for foothold visible at Roman level). Six sharp-fluted Doric columns are spaced to correspond with the five gateways of the portal. The two end columns stand to their full height (nearly 8·8m) and retain their capitals and portions of their architrave; other parts lie beneath the N colonnade.

Behind is the *Vestibule*, 13·7m deep, whose coffered ceiling of marble, 12m high and painted and gilt, earned the praise of Pausanias. The panels were supported on beams of 5·5m span, each weighing 11 tons, that rested on two rows of blunt-fluted Ionic columns flanking the central carriage way. The beams were reinforced with iron bars set in their upper face. The six Ionic columns were two-thirds of the diameter of the Doric columns, and about 10 diameters (10·2m) high. One of the beautiful Ionic capitals has been restored to position, with a section of the coffered ceiling. Traces of the paint and star decoration can be seen on a well-preserved panel standing below. The *Portal* stands on a platform at the higher level of the E portico, and consists of five gateways, graded in size from the centre outwards. The paved ramp continues through the largest gateway in the centre, while the four side gateways are approached from the vestibule by flights of five steps, the topmost of black Eleusinian marble. The entrances had massive wooden gates. Three transverse steps are cut in the rock below the portal but these relics of an earlier entrance are now concealed by wooden planking.

The *East Portico* corresponds to that at the W, having six Doric columns of the same size and arrangement, but reduced in height by nearly a foot; it stands on a simple stylobate. The depth (5·8m) of the portico allowed the ceiling to be supported on beams laid parallel with the axis of the Propylaia, so that no inner colonnade was necessary. Each of the porticoes was surmounted by an entablature of triglyphs and unsculptured metopes supporting a pediment, but though pedimental sculpture was planned it was never started.

The N and S wings had Doric porticoes of three columns in antis, facing each other and at right angles to the W portico of the central hall; but whereas the N portico screens an important chamber, that to the S was left with nothing behind it. The wings had hip roofs. The NORTH WING is in a very perfect state. The architrave still has its plain frieze of triglyphs and metopes. The walls of the room at the back still stand; entered by a door and lighted by two windows in the partition wall, this room is called the *Pinakotheke* (picture gallery) from the pictures, many possibly by Polygnotos, that Pausanias saw there. The door and windows are not centred in the wall; scholars have attempted to explain this strange asymmetry with four mutually incompatible theories of varying degrees of implausibility. The rough surface of the walls suggests that the pictures were easel paintings. The joist-sockets of the storey added by the dukes of Athens are still visible.

The SOUTH WING appears from the outside to be the counterpart of the N Wing, but there is no chamber behind the portico, and the area of the portico itself is much smaller. The back wall stops opposite the third column, the W anta being a sham. At the SE corner the wall is slightly chamfered, so as not to interfere with the surviving section of the *Mycenaean Wall*, which bounded the Temenos of Artemis Brauronia. It has been suggested that the peculiar shape of this wing means that Mnesikles only temporarily abandoned his design, hoping to overcome the opposition of the priests to its completion. However, the corner is chamfered to ground level and later continuation would have been very difficult.—Above the S wing later stood the Tower of the Franks.

Mnesikles intended to add two E halls on the N and S sides of the central hall, which would have occupied the entire W end of the acropolis and given the

Propylaia the same length exactly as the Parthenon. The existence of a cornice running round the two walls designed to form inner walls of the N hall on the S and W, and of other structural features (comp. below), proves that the NE hall was actually started; the SE hall, planned as the exact counterpart of its fellow, was abandoned at an early stage, though an anta exists at what would have been its NE corner. Both halls would have measured about 21m by 12m, much more spacious than the Pinakotheke.

The L-shaped foundations between the Mycenaean wall and the S wall of the S wing (which overlies them) represent a corner of the exedra that flanked the older Propylaia, forming a grandstand for the Panathenaic procession. Here may have stood the well-known 'Hekatompedon Inscription', cut in 485 BC on the reverse of an earlier metope, which enumerated prohibitions to visitors to the Acropolis.—The small trapezoidal enclosure to the S was a precinct of the Graces, associated probably with the worship of Hekate of the Tower, whose triple image by Alkamenes was located hereabouts by Pausanias.

The charming little ***Temple of Athéna Níke** (not accessible to visitors), called inaccurately 'of Nike Apteros' (wingless Victory), reached from the S wing of the Propylaia, stands on a precipitous platform, 8m high, projecting towards the W. The bastion originated as a Mycenaean outwork. In Peisistratid times it was consecrated to the worship of Athena Nike, being furnished with an altar and sanctuary, lost in the sack of 480 BC. In 449 a new *naiskos* (miniature temple) was decreed, with Kallikrates as architect, to celebrate the peace with Persia, and the following year the bastion was faced with poros. The present temple was built in 427–424. A theory that the Temple itself (rather than the naiskos) is referred to in the 449 decree, but not built until later, is now less persuasive.

The Temple of Athena Nike was thrown down by the Turks in 1686 in order to use the bastion as an artillery position, the pieces being used in the construction of another gun emplacement above the Beulé Gate. With the help of Stuart and Revett's drawings of a temple by the river Ilissos, designed by Kallikrates who may also have been responsible for the Nike temple, it was reconstructed piece by piece in 1836–42 by Ross, Schaubart, and Hansen, but again dismantled and rebuilt in 1936–40 in order to strengthen the bastion which had become unsafe.

The temple, built entirely of Pentelic marble, stands with its W front along the W edge of the bastion on a stylobate of three steps measuring 5·5m by 3·5m. It consists of an almost square cella with an Ionic portico of four columns at either end. The fluted shafts are monolithic and the capitals closely resemble those of the Propylaia. A *Frieze*, 46cm broad, round the whole exterior of the building, is adorned with sculptures in high relief. It originally consisted of 14 slabs, four of which are in the British Museum (replaced by casts in cement). The genuine slabs, whose correct positions are uncertain, are badly weathered. Divinities (headless) occupy the E front. Athena may be distinguished by her shield; next to her appears to be Zeus. At the S corner are Peitho, Aphrodite, and Eros. Of the 22 figures which can be made out, 16 are female. The other sides bear scenes from the Battle of Plataea (479 BC); on the W front Athenians are fighting Boeotians and on the flanks Persians.

The cella housed a marble statue, reproduction of an archaic Xoanon or wooden statue, probably destroyed by the Persians. The goddess held in the right hand a pomegranate, emblem of fertility, which indicated her pacific side, and in her left hand the helmet of the Athena of War. Her correct name was Athena Nike or Athena, bringer of victory. In Greek art the goddess Nike (Victory) was represented as a winged female; common tradition, confusing the two goddesses, supposed the statue of Athena Nike to be a wingless 'Victory' (Nike apteros). The story (retailed by Pausanias) grew up that the Athenians had deprived the Victory of wings to prevent her flying away.

The numbers in circles refer to routes in the text.

Key page
to
Map numbers

0	100	200	300	400 yards
0	100	200	300	400 metres

The *Pyrgos*, or platform, on which the temple stands was paved with marble and surrounded by a marble parapet, sculptured in high relief and surmounted by a bronze screen. The grooves into which the slabs were bedded are still visible on the edge of the platform. Many fragments have been recovered and are now in the museum. The reliefs, which date from c 410 BC, represented a band of Winged Victories attendant upon Athena, and include the famous Victory adjusting her sandal.

At the top of the small flight of steps that gave access to this temple is a block of Hymettian marble with marks of an equestrian statue and a Greek inscription of c 457 BC, recording that it was dedicated by the cavalry and executed by Lykios of Eleutherai, son of Myron. The block appears to have been turned upside down and used for a statue of Germanicus when he visited Athens in AD 18. A second inscription (below the block) records this event.

If the air is clear, the platform commands a magnificent view (best at sunset) of Phaleron Bay, Piraeus, Salamis, Acro-Corinth and the mountains beyond it, Aegina, the E tongue of Argolis, with Idhra behind it, and the coast-line to the left towards Sounion. In the foreground the contour of the Pnyx is clearly seen.—This is the spot where, according to legend Aegeus kept watch for the return of his son Theseus from his expedition against the Minotaur. Theseus, who had promised to hoist a white sail if he was successful instead of his usual black sail, forgot; Aegeus seeing the black sail, thought his son was dead and threw himself over the rock.

B. Walk Inside the Walls

Few visitors can resist walking straight from the Propylaia to the Parthenon; but they are strongly recommended to make a circuit of the Acropolis before approaching the Parthenon a second time. In Classical times the focus of attention was on the great statue of Athena while the direct approach to the Parthenon was channelled through a propylon; from the Propylaia all but the pediment of the Parthenon was hidden by intervening buildings.

Turning to the left beyond the Propylaia, we pass (left) the anta or pilaster of the projected N hall (comp. above). On the open ground to the left stood the chapel of the Frankish dukes, removed in 1860. From here we may observe the beautifully regular but unfinished masonry of the Pinakotheke and the projection at the NW corner which is another indication of the unbuilt N hall. Walking E we cross an ancient drain, and farther on pass large *Cisterns*, probably built by Justinian c AD 530. We now bear towards the Acropolis wall, and at its next angle observe a flight of steps of Classical date descending from S to N. This may represent a *Secret Staircase* used annually by the Arrephoroi.

The Arrephoroi were two (or four) girls of noble birth between the ages of seven and eleven, chosen by the King-Archon to perform an obscure service in honour of Athena. Their duties (in addition to the weaving and the carrying of the Peplos) apparently consisted in carrying down by an underground passage to the Sanctuary of Aphrodite in the Gardens (not located) a burden whose contents are unknown. This they exchanged for another mysterious burden, which they brought back.

A platform above the steps affords a fine view towards Piraeus, with the Areopagus in the foreground and the 'Theseion' below. A few metres E a Turkish staircase, probably on an earlier course, descends from W to E, turns abruptly under the wall, and enters a cavern. Investigations were started here in 1937 in an attempt to find further evidence of the Arrephoroi; though unsuccessful in this, they unexpectedly uncovered traces (not now accessible) of a secret *Mycenaean Stairway*, hewn in the rock, partly in a natural cleft, partly underground, constructed in wood and stone in eight flights to a depth of 33·5m and leading to a natural spring.

The outer face of the acropolis wall at this point is composed of blocks from the entablature of the Old Temple of Athena: architraves, triglyphs, metopes, and cornices. A row of them is seen directly to the right as we stand at the wall behind the Turkish staircase.

We now pass between a Byzantine cistern, which abuts on the Acropolis wall, and the Erechtheion. Built into the wall on the left are two of the unfinished drums intended for the columns of the Older Parthenon. Farther on are four others in a row. A flight of marble steps leads up to a platform, from which we can view a large section of the N wall, exposed when the korai, etc., were extracted from the fill. Here unfinished marble column drums and stylobate blocks from the Older Parthenon (490–480) are built into the wall. In the next deep excavation are the remains of the stairway in a rock gully which led down from the *Mycenaean Postern*. Beyond the far side of the chasm a few steps farther E we see poros drums and capitals (reddened by fire) from the Old Temple of Athena, and, to the left of the path farther on, other poros remains from the Old Temple of Athena including an inverted Doric capital with four rings above the fluting.

At the extreme end of the enclosure is the *Belvedere* (*View). By the steps are beautiful fragments of many periods. In the NE corner, behind the museum, a capacious Turkish storage jar stands on a well-preserved curving stretch of the Pelasgic wall.

Returning towards the Parthenon, we notice (right) a large platform in the natural rock, which may have been the *Precinct of Zeus Poleios*. Immediately in front of the Parthenon, the architectural remains of the circular *Monopteros of Rome and Augustus* have been assembled on and around foundations which are still awaiting investigation. The conical roof was supported on nine Ionic columns. The inscribed architrave was recorded by Cyriacus of Ancona.

In front of the museum the parapet above the Wall of Kimon overlooks the Theatre of Dionysos (*View over the Olympieion and Stadium to Hymettos). Hereabouts Attalos I, king of Pergamon, erected four groups of sculpture (probably in bronze), representing the Gigantomachia, the Amazonomachia, the Battle of Marathon, and his own victory (in 230 BC) over the Gauls of Asia Minor. Plutarch relates that the statue of Dionysos from the Gigantomachia was blown by a high wind into the theatre below. Marble copies exist in various European museums.

Walking W along the massive *Wall of Kimon* (restored), we pass a triangular enclosure, where a cross wall of the Ergasterion is visible, and come near the SW corner of the Parthenon, to two deep pits revealing earlier walls.

The W front of the Parthenon is approached by a flight of nine steps cut in the rock, continued upwards by seven more in poros of which fragments survive. These served as a decorative retaining wall for the Parthenon W terrace and later were used for votive offerings, as is shown by some 38 rock cuttings where the various stelai were fixed. Before the steps at the W end stood the bull set up by the Council of the Areopagus. Below them was the Periclean *Entrance Court*, conjectured as part of Mnesikles' commission to tidy the Acropolis; rock cuttings suggest that it was entered on the N by a propylon. The court was closed on the S side by the *Chalkotheke*, or magazine of bronzes, dating from c 450 BC. The foundations show it to have been not quite oblong (c 41m by 14m), the E wall being slightly askew. It was later embellished with a N portico which encroached upon the steps leading to the Parthenon.

On the inner N wall are laid five fragments of a long base with inscriptions, from which it appears that they once bore statues by Sthennis and Leochares (350 BC). Roman inscriptions on the S face show that the bases were afterwards appropriated by Drusus, Tiberius, Augustus, Germanicus, and Trajan. Other pedestals, some detailed by Pausanias, lie hereabouts, and the area is further confused by modern ceiling blocks prepared to protect that part of the Parthenon frieze remaining *in situ* beneath the W peristyle.

To the W of the Chalkotheke and the Court lay the **Sanctuary of Artemis Brauronia**, the bear goddess, which took the form of a stoa with two projecting wings. Votive offerings, including a well-carved little Bear, have been found on the site (see Aristophanes, 'Lysistrata', 646), and inscriptions record the storage of others. Within the precinct, of which the foundations of the N and W walls (4C BC) can be easily traced, is the pedestal of a colossal bronze figure of the Trojan Horse by Strongylion. Its two marble blocks, c 1·8m long, bearing an inscription, were discovered in 1840; they lie nearly on a line with the E portico of the Propylaia.

The remnant of Mycenaean wall bounded the sanctuary on the W. Behind and below this, in the angle of the Propylaia, foundations remain of one corner of the pre-Periclean propylaia. By the corner column of Mnesikles' propylaia is the round *Pedestal* of a statue to Athena Hygieia, with clear traces of her feet and spear.

Plutarch ('Pericles', 13) tells that during the building of the Propylaia one of the workmen 'the quickest and handiest of them all' fell and was badly hurt, Pericles was told by Athena in a dream how to cure him, and in gratitude set up a bronze image of the goddess in her attribute of health-giver. Pliny adds the information that the remedy was the plant parthenion (feverfew), a pleasant punning conceit. Just E of the pedestal is an *Altar* to Hygieia, which Plutarch records as older than the statue.

In front of the Propylaia the surface of the rock is carefully roughened by transverse grooves, to afford foothold in the ascent to the Parthenon—a rise of c 12m. The numerous rectangular cuttings were occupied by pedestals of statues. On the right are rock-hewn steps ascending to the Sanctuary of Brauronian Artemis. The Sacred Way passed through the entrance court (see above), and along the N side of the Parthenon, to end at its E front.

Some 40 paces in front of the Propylaia are some foundations of poros on which stood the colossal bronze *Statue of Athena Promachos* by Pheidias. Blocks of the capping course of its pedestal, with huge egg-and-dart moulding, lie a little to the W. The statue, which Demosthenes calls 'the great bronze Athena' was finished c 458 BC as a trophy of Athenian valour in the Persian wars. Details of its form are safely known from the medieval description of Niketas Choniates as well as from contemporary medals. The goddess was represented standing with her right arm leaning on her spear, and holding in her left a shield, with figures in relief (battle of the Lapiths and Centaurs) designed by Parrhasios and wrought by Mys. In later times the epithet Promachos (Champion) was given the statue, to distinguish it from the statues of Virgin Athena in the Parthenon and of Athena Polias in the Erechtheion. It was c 9m high; the spear blade and helmet crest were visible to sailors coming from Sounion as they rounded Cape Zoster. The statue, removed to Constantinople at an uncertain date, was destroyed in a riot in 1203, because the superstitious people believed that her apparently beckoning hand (already lacking the spear) had summoned the invading Crusaders out of the W.

Farther E, opposite the seventh N column of the Parthenon and protected by a grating, is a rock-carved dedication to Fruit-bearing Earth (Ge Karpophoros). Here stood a personification, rising apparently from the ground, of Earth, praying for rain to Zeus.

C. The Parthenon

The * ***PARTHENON**, or *Temple of Athena Parthenos*, represents the culmination of the Doric, indeed of the Classical, style of architecture; as a monument it has no equal. The temple was designed to provide a new home for Athena, her fine new cult statue and the continually increasing treasure. It was erected in 447–438 BC as the cardinal feature of Pericles' plan. The loftiest building on the Acropolis, it is situated on its highest part, midway between E and W. Under the order of Pheidias as 'surveyor-general' were the architects Iktinos and Kallikrates, who built the Southern Long Wall. The most celebrated sculptors in Athens, rivals or pupils of Pheidias, such as Agorakritos and Alkamenes, worked on the pediments, the frieze, and the metopes. Pheidias supervised, if he did not actually design, the whole of the sculptures, reserving entirely to himself the creation of the chryselephantine statue of Athena. The result is a peerless blend of architecture and sculpture. The Parthenon was regarded, indeed, principally as an artistic masterpiece and as the state treasury, and never replaced the Old Athena Temple or the Erechtheion in the veneration of the Athenians as the holy place sanctified by tradition.

The name Parthenon (Παρθενών), meaning the virgin's apartment, originally applied to one room in the temple. Its first recorded application to the whole building appears in the speeches of Demosthenes. Before this the temple seems to have inherited the sobriquet 'Hekatompedon' from its predecessors on the site. The statue of Athena Polias became popularly though unofficially known as Athena Parthenos.

Except for the roof (which was of wood) the Parthenon is built entirely of Pentelic marble. The whole of the stylobate survives, together with the columns of the peristyle and of the end porticoes, though some are incomplete and some restored. The entablature at the E and W ends, most of the W pediment, fragments of the E pediment, and considerable portions of the walls of the W portico and cella still stand.

History. At least four temples were built successively on the Parthenon site. Rooftiles of the late 7C have been attributed to the first archaic temple here. The second temple may have been the **Hekatompedon**, though fragments attributed to it could belong with the Dörpfeld foundation (comp. below). Enough architecture remains to show that the Hekatompedon was a peripteral temple of the mid 6C BC which might be restored as 30m long. The interested visitor may get an idea of Hekatompedon architecture by looking at a restoration of the entablature set up behind the museum, outside, at the N corner. He may then pass round the museum to the S wall of the Acropolis and stand by the low fence, looking into the area between the S side of the museum and the S wall of the Acropolis. There can be seen the mighty grey poros capitals of the Hekatompedon and, behind them, fragments of the columns and other architecture stacked in an oblong.

The scheme to replace the poros Hekatompedon, mooted perhaps after the fall of the Tyrants, seems to have matured under Aristeides after the victory of Marathon, just as new marble quarries were opened on Pentelikon. Remains of the earlier building were used to build up a new terrace on the W and S (comp. above). A massive limestone stereobate 76·8m by 31·4m, was bedded on the rock, from which it rises in places by 22 courses of masonry. The marble stylobate, the lower drums of still unfluted columns (6 × 16), and the first course of the wall of the **Pre-Parthenon** were already *in situ* when in 480 the Persians did their work of destruction. Marks of fire are still visible under the later stylobate (to the W near the N angle), as well as on the column-drums built into the acropolis N wall. Kimon enlarged the terrace on the S when he built his wall. 'The chief interest of this temple is that it initiated marble construction in Attica on a large scale, introduced the use of Ionic elements and the application of delicate refinements in upward curvature and column inclinations, and even contributed much of the material and many of the dimensions for the present Parthenon' (Dinsmoor).

Pericles proposed the erection of a new temple in Pentelic marble with a different columnar arrangement and somewhat wider and shorter than the existing base. It was brought more to the N and W so that the old foundations project 4·3m on the E and 1·7m on the S, while extra foundation courses were necessary on the N. Work on the **Parthenon** started in 447; in 438, at the Great Panathenaic Festival, the statue of Athena was dedicated in the cella; in 435 the opisthodomos was opened to receive the treasure, and in 434 the first inventories were made; the sculpture was complete by 432. Structurally the Parthenon remained virtually intact for 2000 years. New embellishments were added from time to time, such as the shields of gilded bronze presented by Alexander. In 305 BC, Demetrios Poliorketes desecrated the temple by turning the W portion into a residence for himself and his seraglio. In 298 he returned to besiege Lachares, who fled with the golden ornaments of the temple and the precious casing of the statue. The Parthenon was respected by the Romans, except that the statue had disappeared by the 5C AD. There are grounds for believing that the cult statue of Athena Parthenos was still in place until that time, when the Panathenaic festival was still being celebrated.

In the 6C AD the Parthenon was turned into a church. Under Justinian the edifice was dedicated at first to Saint Sophia (Holy Wisdom), then to the Virgin Mother of God (Theotokos), and became the metropolitan church of Athens. The entrance was made at the W end; the opisthodomos became the Byzantine pronaos and the Parthenon proper the narthex. The wall between the Parthenon proper and the cella was pierced with three doorways, two of which gave access to side staircases leading to the womens' galleries, which were erected over a colonnade, probably of Hellenistic date and from a building in the city of Athens but inserted into the Parthenon in the 4C AD. The walls were covered with frescoes and the ceiling replaced by a barrel-vaulted roof. The pronaos was converted into an apse to receive the altar. Vaults for the interment of the bishops were discovered under the floor in 1910. As the cathedral of the Frankish dukes, it followed the Latin rite in 1208–1458. It was later converted into a mosque, and a Byzantine bell-tower at the SW angle of the opisthodomos was converted into a minaret.

Jacques Carrey, a painter in the suite of the Marquis de Nointel, made (in 1674) above 400 drawings (now invaluable) of subsequently destroyed sculptures, and Spon and Wheler (in 1676) were the last travellers to see the Parthenon intact before the disaster of 1687. Carrey's drawings are preserved in the Bibliothèque Nationale in Paris. They include the pediment groups, a large portion of the frieze, and many of the metopes. On 26 September 1687, at 7 pm, a mortar placed by Morosini on the Mouseion Hill was fired by a German lieutenant at the Parthenon, which the Turks were using as a powder magazine. The resulting explosion carried away practically the whole of the cella and its frieze, eight columns on the N side, and six on the S, together with their entablature; and the temple was cut into two ruinous halves. Morosini added to the damage, on gaining possession of the Acropolis, by attempting to remove from the W pediment the horses and chariot of Athena: the group fell during the process of removal and was smashed.

By 1766 a small mosque had been built within the ruins. With the revival of antiquarian interest, the Parthenon suffered further damage. The Comte de Choiseul-Gouffier removed to France in 1787 one detached piece of the frieze. His example was followed in 1801 by Lord Elgin, who secured an official permit 'to remove some blocks of stone with inscriptions and figures'. The artist Lusieri superintended the work of removing the greater part of the frieze, 15 of the metopes from the S side, the figures from the pediments, etc. In 1816 these 'Elgin Marbles' were placed in the British Museum.

Restoration started in 1834–44. After the earthquake of 1894, Balanos replaced a few pieces of architrave and capitals on the W façade. In 1921–30, in the face of considerable opposition, he reconstructed the N peristyle. The new columns were made of Piraeic stone with a covering of concrete; this harmonises well with the ancient marble yet distinguishes the true from the false. Five missing capitals have, however, been replaced in Pentelic marble. The roofing of the W portico with copies in Pentelic marble of the original ceiling blocks was planned to protect the remaining section of the cella frieze, which today contrasts sadly with Elgin's casts. Many blocks were made and lie below the W façade; their erection awaits results of tests to determine whether the structure will now stand their weight.

*Athens. Parthenon. Four drawings by J. Carrey (1674).
From top to bottom: sculptures in W pediment (left);
sculptures in E pediment (left); sculptures in W pediment
(right); sculptures in E pediment (right)*

Exterior. The foundations are best studied on the S side, where the steps of the earlier temple may still be distinguished beneath the three marble steps that form the *Crepidoma* of the present temple. The Doric *Peristyle* consists of 46 columns (8 by 17), an octastyle arrangement matched only by the earlier Temple G at Selinus in Sicily. The columns, which have a base diameter of 1·9m, rise to a height of 10·4m. Each column is formed of 10–12 drums of varying height and has 20 shallow flutings.

A peculiarity of all Greek buildings of the best period, specially remarkable in the Parthenon, is the use of optical refinements executed with great mathematical precision. These include varying the breadth of the intercolumniation throughout the building, thickening the corner columns, and grading the spacing of the triglyphs. Lines that appear horizontal are in fact curved, and lines that appear vertical are slightly inclined. If we stand at one corner and look along the upper step, we notice a perceptible rise in the centre giving to the whole pavement a convex character. The rise is less than 7·6cm in 30·8m on the fronts, and 2·6cm in 69·5m on the flanks: the latter giving a radius of curvature of c 5·5km. The rising curve is imparted to the entablature. The axes of the columns lean inwards to the extent of nearly 6·4cm in their height. The inclination can be detected by measuring the lowest drum of a corner-column, which will be found shorter on the inside than on the outside. The columns themselves have a convex entasis, or swelling, designed to correct the optical illusion by which straight tapered shafts appear concave.

The deep *Architrave* was adorned at a later date with gilded bronze shields, fourteen on the E front and eight on the W, between which were inscribed in bronze letters the names of the dedicators; the shields may have been presented by Alexander the Great in 334 BC after the battle of the Granicus. An inscription on the E front, relating to some honour conferred on the Emperor Nero by the Athenian people has been deciphered by means of the marks left by the nails. On the N and S sides were bronze nails or pegs for hanging festoons on days of festival. The *Frieze* above was decorated with triglyphs and metopes. The *Cornice* consisted of a slab overlapping the frieze, the projecting ledge of which supported the sculptures of the pediments. On its under side were mutules with guttæ. The upper part was surmounted by a beautiful hawksbeak moulding. The apex of the pediment, 18m above the stylobate, was crowned with an immense anthemion, or leaf ornament as acroterion, of which a few fragments have been recovered. The wooden roof had tiles of Pentelic marble, from which the rainwater ran off without any gutter. At each of the four corners was a lion's head, purely ornamental since the mouth was not pierced, and the eaves were surmounted by palmette antefixes.

Details were brought into relief by polychrome decoration. Many mouldings retain traces of ornaments beautifully drawn; in some of the most protected parts the pigment itself remains. Strong colour seems to have been confined to the parts that were in shade. The intense whiteness of the columns, architraves, and broader surfaces was probably modified by some ochreous colour to such an extent only as to anticipate the rich golden hue produced by time on Pentelic marble. The channels of the triglyphs, or possibly the triglyphs themselves, were painted dark blue, as were also the six guttæ below them. The ceilings were adorned with deep blue panels and gilt stars.—In the British Museum is a coloured reconstruction of the NW corner of the Parthenon.

SCULPTURES. *Eastern Pediment*. We know from Pausanias (I, 24, 25) that the subject was the birth of Athena, but there is little left on the pediment, which was ruined when the Byzantine apse was built. Of the various fragments found, some are in the Acropolis Museum, more in the British Museum; a puteal in Madrid is believed to have been copied from the central group. (For recent discussion of the composition in detail, see A.J.A. 1967.)

The *Western Pediment* represented the contest of Athena and Poseidon for the possession of Attica. These sculptures, practically intact when Jacques Carrey made his drawings, were those destroyed by the clumsy avarice of Morosini.

The *Metopes* were originally 92 in number: 14 at either end and 32 on each side. Of these, 41 remain *in situ*, but with rare exceptions they are so battered as to be unintelligible. Their artistic value appears to have been very uneven. Fifteen are in the British Museum and one is in the Louvre. The remaining 35 are, with the exception of some fragments (in the Acropolis Museum, and in the Vatican Museum), entirely destroyed (the greater number in the explosion of 1687) and they are only imperfectly known from Carrey's drawings. The metopes in the British Museum and the Louvre are all from the S side, and illustrate the contest of the Lapiths and Centaurs at the marriage feast of Peirithoös. Those of the E front remain in position; they represent a Gigantomachia. The subject of the metopes of the W front appears to be an Amazonomachia. All the metopes appear to have been deliberately chiselled off in the (?) 6–8C.

The **Interior** has been closed to visitors to protect the structure. Within the peripteral colonnade the ambulatory, 4·3m wide on the flanks and nearly 4·9m at the ends, is equipped with drainage channels. The ceiling was formed of coffered panels of marble, those at the ends supported by marble beams; four of these remain *in situ* at the W end, where restoration is in progress.

The SEKOS, or temple proper, stands on a socle raised two steps above the stylobate. Unlike the usual Doric temple of three chambers, it was divided by a blank partition wall into two halls, each with a portico of six Doric columns. The ends of the walls forming the sides terminate in antæ facing the portico columns. The Pronaos, or E portico, opened into the Cella and there were probably also windows between the two, while the Opisthodomos, facing W, fronted the Parthenon proper. Frieze, see below.

The CELLA or *Hekatompedos Naos* is presumed to have inherited its alternative name from an earlier building; its interior measurements are somewhat less than 100 Attic feet. An inner colonnade, formed (like those at Aegina and Paestum) of two storeys separated by an architrave and carried round three sides, supported beams for the roof and ceiling. Some of the circular marks left by the original column-bases are still visible, but the more obvious remains are from slenderer columns of Hellenistic date reused after a fire. Bronze barriers between the 23 lower columns formed an ambulatory from which privileged visitors (among them Pausanias) could view the great chryselephantine *Statue of Athena Polias*, by Pheidias. Its site is clearly located by an oblong space where the marble floor is economically replaced by plain Piraeic stone; it was placed in position in 432 BC.

Literary references, combined with extant reproductions, provide an accurate account of the work. The statue was of gold plate over an inner wooden frame and stood, with the pedestal, 11·9m high. The face, hands, and feet were of ivory (Plato, Hippias Major). The pupils of the eyes were of precious stones. The goddess stood upright, clad in a dress that reached to her feet; on her breast was the head of Medusa wrought in ivory; in her right hand she held a crowned Victory about four cubits high, and in the other a spear. Her helmet was surmounted by a sphinx, with griffins in relief on either side, representing the winged beasts that fought with the one-eyed Arimaspi for gold (comp. Hdt. III, 116). On her sandals was wrought the battle of the Centaurs and Lapiths. At her feet stood a shield, on the outside of which was represented in relief the battle of the Amazons with the Athenians: in this scene Pheidias introduced figures of himself and Pericles that got him into trouble with pious Athenians (Plutarch, Pericles). On the inside was a representation of the Gigantomachia. Near the base of the spear was a serpent, perhaps Erichthonios. On the pedestal was wrought in relief the birth of Pandora. The dress and other ornaments, all of solid gold and weighing some 40 or 50 talents, were so contrived that the whole could be temporarily removed, in case of national emergency, without injuring the statue (Thuc. II, 13). The whole work was presumably designed to glow softly in subdued light from the doorway and limited windows. It became known as the *Athena Parthenos*.

The W wall was originally blank. Three doorways were made in it and all the interior columns were removed when the building was con-verted into a church. Beyond this wall lay the PARTHENON proper, a chamber of the same width as the cella but only 13·1m long, of which three walls still stand. Here four presumably Ionic columns (traces on four square slabs larger than the rest) supported the roof.

Many archaeologists have argued that Parthenon means the 'chamber of the maidens' (i.e. of the priestesses of Athena). This is borne out by a recent discovery at Brauron. If it means the 'chamber of the maiden' (Athena herself), the fact that her statue was not placed there needs explanation.

The *Opisthodomos* corresponded to the pronaos in all its details, save that the columns were c 5cm thicker; they are probably fashioned from drums cut for the Pre-Parthenon. There are conspicuous traces here on the columns and antæ of the grating which separated the opistho-domos from the ambulatory. A relic of the days when the Parthenon was a mosque is the base of the minaret, below the level of the marble pavement at the SW corner, where a rough staircase mounts to the pediment. Some interesting relics are still visible from the time when the opisthodomos served as cathedral narthex: on the left pillar, Byzantine Greek inscriptions; to the right of the doorway, fragmentary wall-paintings. Between the second and third pillars from the N of the W peristyle a chequer-board is incised in the pavement.

It is believed that the opisthodomos served as treasury of the Delian League in succession to *the* 'Opisthodomos', part of the Old Temple of Athena.

Right round the outer walls of the sekos, just below the cornice and 11·9m above the stylobate, ran a continuous Ionic **Frieze**. Although much of its sculptural detail was destroyed by the explosion in 1687 and above 13·7m are altogether unrecorded, yet the existing 53·6m in Athens, together with 75·3m in the British Museum, out of a total length of 159·5m suffice with Carrey's drawings to give a tolerably adequate idea of the whole. Its uniform height is ·99m and its relief nowhere exceeds 5·7cm. It has generally been taken to represent the procession of celebrants at the Great Panathenaic Festival, though an attempt has recently been made, by equating the number of figures with the number of dead at Marathon, to proclaim the frieze a record of a specific heroising ceremony.

The *Greater Panathenaia*, traditionally founded by Erichthonios (see below) and renewed by Theseus, was refounded in the archonship of Hippokleides (566/565) and turned into a ceremony of the first rank by Peisistratos. It occurred on every fourth anniversary of the goddess's birthday, in the month of Hekatom-baion (August). Athletic, musical, and equestrian contests were held and the victors received Panathenaic prize amphorae filled with tax-free olive oil from the sacred olive trees. The main feature was the Procession, in which the new embroidered saffron peplos woven to drape an early wooden Xoanon of Athena Polias was borne in state through the streets of Athens on a ship on wheels. The ship was manned by priests and priestesses wearing golden crowns and garlands of flowers (see Philostratus, Vit. Soph. II 1, 7). The chief citizens of Athens, the envoys from the allied states, and even resident aliens had a fixed part to play in the ceremony. The citizens were on this occasion allowed to bear arms without exciting suspicion—at any rate in the time of Hippias (Thuc. VI, 56). The peplos may have been woven by, and was certainly carried (at some part of the procession) by the Arrephoroi, the maids in waiting on Athena. The route of the procession was from the Pompeion in the Kerameikos to the Eleusinion then past the Pelargikon to the Python, where the ship was moored. It is probable that the procession halted outside the Parthenon or its predecessor and that the victors in the Panathenaic games there received their prize amphorae. The proceedings ended with a sacrifice on the Great Altar and in the depositing of the robe (at any rate latterly) in the Erechtheion.

The entire WEST FRIEZE, with the exception of three figures, remains *in situ*, and in surprisingly good state: the Athenian knights are seen putting on their sandals and cloaks, bridling their horses, mounting, and moving off under the marshals. Viewed from outside the W front of the building, it gives an excellent idea of the way in which the frieze was intended to be seen between the columns of the peristyle.

Somewhat less than one-third of the N frieze and five slabs of the S frieze are in the Acropolis Museum (see below). The remainder is in London, together with all the extant remains of the E frieze (except for three slabs and sundry fragments in the Acropolis Museum, and eight slabs in the Louvre).

D. The Erechtheion

Looking towards the Erechtheion from the N colonnade of the Parthenon we see the foundations of a temple, published by Dörpfeld in 1886 and ever since its discovery 'the subject of endless controversy as to its identity, its date, its relation to its neighbours, and how long it continued in use' (Ida Thallon Hill). It is now generally called the **Old Temple of Athena** and is believed by Dinsmoor to be of Peisistratid date (529 BC is suggested by astronomical calculations from its orientation). Two column bases (once attributed to the Mycenaean megaron) are now ascribed to a Geometric predecessor but are not *in situ*. The temple is the only pre-Persian building in Athens of which complete foundations are extant; to it are ascribed Archaic sculptures (independently dated stylistically to c 525 BC), now in the museum. The building, amphidistyle (or perhaps prostyle) in antis with a peristyle of 12 columns by 6, was partially destroyed in the Persian sack and poros and marble remains of it were built into the N wall and used as fill for later terraces. The rear part of it seems to have survived to be rebuilt as a treasury; it may have been the 'Opisthodomos' referred to in the Kallias Decree (439 or 434) and the 'Megaron facing W' which Herodotus describes with smoke-blackened walls; it was dismantled (says Demosthenes) in 353 BC.

The *Erechtheion, one of the most original specimens of Greek architecture, stands near the N edge of the rock, about midway between the E and W ends. Designed to succeed the Old Temple as the joint shrine of Athena and Poseidon-Erechtheus, it was finished after 395 BC and owes its curious plan to the sacrosanct nature of the associated sanctuaries that preceded it. Like the Parthenon, it became generally known by a name that originally applied only to one of its parts.

The **Legendary History** of the contest between Poseidon and Athena for possession of the Acropolis in the reign of Kekrops occurs in many ancient authors (comp. Hdt. VIII, 55; Apollodorus, Lib. III, xiv). Poseidon produced a 'sea' called Erechtheïs and Athena an olive-tree. Athena was judged the winner but was reconciled with Poseidon and henceforth they were worshipped together. Another myth tells of Erichthonios, born to Hephaistos and Earth, who was placed by his foster-mother Athena in a chest and committed to Pandrosos, daughter of Kekrops. Erichthonios, who had serpent attributes, grew up to expel Amphictyon and become king of Athens; to him is attributed the setting up of the xoanon to Athena and the institution of the Panathenaia. His grandson Erechtheus also became king of Athens. These myths and their dramatis personæ are indissolubly confused, but the sacred tokens (μαρτύρια) venerated in Classical times— Athena's olive tree and the mark of Poseidon's trident—probably date at least from pre-Homeric times. At some time Poseidon and Erechtheus became identified with one another.

As historical fact we can say that the N side of the Acropolis became the centre of a group of cults, based on the worship of Athena and Poseidon-Erechtheus, all with elements in common and stemming probably from late Helladic times, since they grew up round the Mycenaean megaron. The tokens survived in Roman times and Dionysios of Halicarnassos locates the olive-tree in the *Pandroseion*. Pausanias speaks of Poseidon's well of sea-water within the Erechtheion. The *Kekropion*, or Tomb of Kekrops, was near by, and sacred snakes dwelt in the precinct. No archaeological evidence has been found to suggest a combined temple earlier than the Erechtheion as we know it today.

History. The *Erechtheion* formed part of the programme of Pericles. The construction was delayed by the Peloponnesian War, but the evidence of inscription proves that it was nearly ready in 409 BC and probably complete three years later. It was damaged by fire in 406 (Xenophon, Hellenica, I, 6, 1) and was not rebuilt until 395 or even later. Another fire caused damage in Augustan times, and the reconstruction incorporated some new features. The building was converted into a church about the 6C AD, and the greater part of the interior destroyed in the successive alterations. The Turks, in 1463, turned it into a harem for the wives of the Commandant of the Acropolis. It suffered from the acquisitiveness of Lord Elgin in 1801 and was damaged during the various sieges of the War of Independence. In 1838 Pittakis cleared some of the wall of rubbish; in 1842–4 Paccard restored the Portico of the Caryatids. A violent storm on 26 October 1852 blew down the upper part of the W façade with its engaged columns. In 1903–09 the exterior was virtually rebuilt by M. Balanos. In 1980 much of it was dismantled or covered in scaffolding.

Curiosities. The temple must have been profoundly interesting to visitors. In addition to the tokens (see above) and the ancient xoanon and its lamp (see below), here also were a wooden Hermes, said to be an offering of Kekrops, a folding chair made by Daedalus, and some Persian spoils from Plataea, including the corselet of Masistius (of gold links) and the sword of Mardonius.

The Erechtheion is unique not only in plan but also in elevation since the foundations of its S and E walls stand nearly 2·7m above those on the N and W. No attempt was made to correct the various levels of the terrain on which it stands, and the exterior is manifestly that of a single building in spite of incorporating existing features at these differing levels. When seen from the E it has the appearance of an Ionic prostyle temple with a hexastyle portico; behind the façade it is in fact a plain rectangle with a projecting porch on either flank.

The EASTERN PORTICO had six Ionic columns, on a stylobate of three marble steps, supporting a pediment without sculpture. Five columns with their architrave are standing; the sixth (at the N corner) was carried off by Lord Elgin. They are 6·7m high, including bases and capitals, and 0·8m in diameter at the base. The back wall of the portico, which had a central doorway and two windows, was pulled down to make way for the Byzantine apse. The S anta survives, while that to the N, reconstructed in 1909, lacks the capital (in the British Museum).

The INTERIOR is a tangle of late substructures, which have destroyed even the foundations of the Classical building. The modern traveller can only stand at the porches and use his imagination.

The description of Pausanias is unusually ambiguous, and even after considering beddings in the rock together with the original building specifications and progress reports, which survive on marble, archaeologists differ widely on their reconstruction of the classical interior. Previous views of the internal arrange-

ment were challenged c 1970 by John Travlos, but his views have been questioned in their turn. Some of the argument centres on the route of the profane dog
(Philochoros, Fr. 146).

The EASTERN CELLA was at a higher level and separated by a cross-
wall from the rest. It is not clear whether this or the WESTERN CELLA
was the main cult chamber. In one of them were located three altars: of
Poseidon-Erechtheus, of Hephaistos, and of the hero Boutes; also the
thrones of their priests (the inscribed thrones of Boutes and Hephaistos are now outside). On the wall, says Pausanias, were portraits
of the Boutad family from whom the priests of the cult were drawn. In
the other cella was the highly venerated *Statue of Athena Polias*, in
olive-wood. This was presumably removed to safety at Salamis in 480
BC and housed in a temporary building on the site after Plataea.

The goddess seems to have been represented as standing and armed
(Aristophanes, 'Birds', 826–31). She held a round shield on which was the gorgon's head (Euripides, 'Electra', 1254–57). The sacred Peplos, renewed every
four years at the Panathenaic Festival, was woven to adorn her shrine. The so-
called Dresden statue of Athena is supposed to be a copy of this wooden image. In
front of the statue burnt the golden lamp made by the ingenious Kallimachos
with an asbestos wick that needed oil only once a year, and a brazen palm-tree to
serve as chimney. The lamp was tended by elderly widows; during the siege of
Athens by Sulla in 86 BC it was allowed by Aristion to go out (Plutarch, 'Sulla',
13).
    An enlarged cistern, cut deep into the rock in medieval or Turkish times, has
destroyed most of the evidence which might have allowed a positive identification beneath the ante-chamber of the Erechtheïs 'sea' (see above). The visible
fragments of brick vault are medieval; the 'sea' or well was presumably covered
with marble tiles and seen through a puteal. When the S wind blew the well gave
forth the sound of waves.

To reach the North Porch we descend a modern staircase, replacing an
ancient flight. The court enclosed between the stair and the building
was paved and probably served a ritual purpose. The **NORTH
PORCH** formed a lateral pronaos to the Erechtheion proper, hence its
Greek description (πρόστασις η πρὸς του θυρώματος). Formed of an
elegant Ionic colonnade of four columns in front and one at each side,
with its architrave, its frieze in dark blue Eleusinian marble, its panelled ceiling; and its richly decorated N door, this porch is one of the
masterpieces of Attic art. The superstructure was restored from fragments that date from a Roman reconstruction. The porch protected the
marks left perhaps by a thunderbolt, which are seen through a gap in
the tiles as three holes in the rocky bottom of a crypt. A corresponding
opening in the roof over this pit was purposely left on the analogy of
leaving open to the sky places struck by lightning. By the gap stood
the *Altar of the Thyechoös*, a priest important enough to have a place
reserved in the theatre. He offered sacrifices of honey-cakes to Zeus
Hypatos. An opening leads from the crypt into the basement of the
temple. Here perhaps within the adyton surrounding the Tomb of
Erechtheus dwelt the serpent guardian of the house (comp. Hdt. VIII,
41, and Plutarch, 'Themistocles' 10), for whom the honey-cakes served as food. The *North Doorway* is celebrated for the magnificent
moulding of its Ionic decoration, though much of it consists of exact
copies of Augustan date replacing the originals destroyed in a fire; the
pierced centres of the rosettes are omitted. The inner linings are
Byzantine additions.
    From the N porch, which projects some way beyond the W façade of
the building, a smaller opening leads down two steps into an outer
court of the temple, no longer enclosed. This was the **Pandroseíon**, or
Temenos of Pandrosos, a precinct of uncertain boundaries containing

a small temple. Here grew the *Sacred Olive of Athena*. Herodotus tells how it sprouted again after being burnt down by the Persians; the existing tree was planted on 22 February 1917, on Washington's birthday, by Bert Hodge Hill, near a fine ancient copper water-pipe which he excavated, and which he conjectured had been installed to supply water to something of especial importance. More to the S was a further precinct, the **Kekrópion**. The foundations of the Erechtheion were modified at the SW corner to avoid disturbing an earlier structure, the presumed *Tomb of Kekrops*, which was spanned by a single huge block, c 4·5m long and 1·5m deep.

Above rises the WEST FAÇADE of the temple, restored in 1904 (after being blown down in 1852) to the form it acquired in the 1C BC. It consists of a high basement, upon which were set engaged columns joined by a low solid wall with a parapet. The upper part of the intercolumniation was closed with wooden grilles, except above the Kekropion where it was left open, presumably for some important cult purpose. The original column-bases remain but everything above was renewed after the fire in Roman times to the existing design with three windows; even then, however, the S opening was left open. The S block of the entablature is a copy; the original, removed in 1805, has been recovered defaced by Turkish inscriptions. It lies on the ground in front of the W façade.

ERECHTHEION

0   20 metres

Poseidon   Zeus

N

Athena

after Dinsmoor and others

The SOUTHERN PORTICO, or *Porch of the Caryatids*, consists of a solid marble wall, rising 1·8m above the peristyle of the Old Temple on which it is founded, surmounted by six statues of maidens (*korai*), rather over life-size, popularly known as Caryatids. The figures stand four in front and two behind, their long Ionic tunics draped like column flutings about their outer legs, on which their weight is thrown. They support an entablature which has capitals of a special decorative form and no frieze. At the close of the War of Independence only three of the caryatids remained in place, all much damaged; the second figure from the W, removed by Lord Elgin, was later replaced by a cast. All surviving originals have been removed to the museum and the porch will be rebuilt with casts having a titanium core. The porch was entered through the E wall of the podium by narrow steps which seem unlikely to have served the needs of the public. The floor has disappeared, but the flat coffered ceiling is nearly entire. A portal gave access by an awkward descending L-shaped stair to the W cella.

The idea of using statues in lieu of columns seems to have been borrowed from the Treasuries of the Knidians and Siphnians at Delphi. Vitruvius states that the sculptors took as models the girls of Karyai, in Laconia: whence the name Caryatids. Prof. Dinsmoor suggests that here the figures represent the Arrephoroi, bearing Athena's burdens on their heads.

The temple was given structural unity by its balancing pediments and by the emphatic nature of the *Frieze*, which, save where the roof of the N portico interrupted it, extended right round the building above the architrave. Unique in design, it consisted of coarse-grained Pentelic marble figures, cut in high relief and attached by bronze clamps to a ground of dark Eleusinian stone. Two large blocks of the background are still *in situ* above the columns of the E front; part of the frieze above the N porch also remains. The holes for fitting the sculptured figures are plainly visible. Of these only 112 small fragments have been recovered, mostly in bad condition; they are in the Acropolis Museum. The theme of the work is not known.

It must be remembered that here, as in the Parthenon, to the beauty of form was added the attraction of colour. The capitals of the columns were enriched with gilt bronze ornaments, and inlaid with coloured glass 'gems'. The panelled ceilings of the porticoes were painted blue and had gilt bronze stars.

E. The Acropolis Museum

The *Acropolis Museum, founded in 1878 and reconstructed since the Second World War, was reopened in sections in 1956–61. It occupies the SE corner of the Acropolis and is sunk below the surface level of the rock in order not to interfere with the skyline. Started as the repository of finds collected haphazard on the citadel, it was greatly enriched by the systematic excavations of Kavvadias in 1885–90, when the whole of the rock was laid bare. With the exception of the bronzes and the vases (now in the National Museum), it contains all the portable objects discovered since 1834 on the Acropolis. As an education in the development of Attic sculpture, the collection is unique. The arrangement is roughly chronological.

Admission weekdays; closed Tuesday. Small charge for photography; cameras must otherwise be left in the vestibule. Concise Guide in English (1965). Students are referred to the 'Catalogue of the Acropolis Museum', 2 vols; (Cambridge), Vol. I (1912) by Guy Dickins and Vol. II (1912) by Stanley Casson, and to 'Archaic Marble Sculpture from the Acropolis' (1939) by Humfry Payne and G.M. Young.

Outside the entrance (right) is 1347. Colossal marble owl.
    VESTIBULE. 1338. Panel of a pedestal dedicated by Atarbos to com-

memorate a victory with his chorus in a Pyrrhic dance, which the youths are executing (late 4C); 1326. Quadrilateral base, with relief of an apobates (a soldier who leaps on and off a chariot at full speed); 2281. Male head; 1331. Youthful head (4C), possibly Alexander the Great; 1358. Statue of a woman and child (late 5C; much mutilated), perhaps the Prokne and Itys mentioned by Pausanias as being dedicated by Alkamenes.

We turn left. The first three rooms contain **Pedimental Sculpture**, in poros limestone or in imported island marble, from destroyed 6C buildings on the Acropolis. Much shows traces of the bright paint then favoured for accentuating the design and movement of the figures. ROOM I. 552, 554. Fragments of a leopard, in Hymettian marble, perhaps from the metopes of the Hekatompedon; 4572 is notable for its painting; 1. Pediment of a small building (c 570 BC; the oldest known relief from the Acropolis); it shows Herakles and the Hydra, with Iolaos driving his car; on the left is the crab sent by Hera to hamper the hero. 4. Lioness rending a small bull, one of the earliest groups; flanked by serpents (comp. below), it may have formed part of the centre of the W pediment of the Hekatompedon. 122. Lion's head in Hymettian marble; 701. Archaic head of a running Gorgon, perhaps the acroterion above the E pediment of the Hekatompedon.

ROOM II. In the doorway, 56. Owl; 41. Serpent's head. Within, 36, 35. Left and right portions of a pediment: 1. Herakles and Triton (the head came to light in 1938); right Typhon, a blue-bearded monster with three human heads and bodies ending in a serpent's tail (traces of vivid colouring). It has been suggested that the lions in the next room should be restored between these two to form the E pediment of the Hekatompedon. 2, 37, 40. Serpents from a pediment (comp. above). 9. Right half of an early pediment representing the Introduction of Herakles to Olympos; Iris presents him to Zeus who has Hera or Athena beside him. 624. *Moschophoros, a man bearing a calf on his shoulders, in Hymettian marble (c 570 BC), one of the earliest examples of native art in marble, still employing techniques suitable to working in limestone; an inscription on the base bears the name Rhombos. Triglyphs and cornice fragments. In a glass case, terracotta figurines found S of the Acropolis in 1955–59. 52. The 'Olive-tree' Pediment, with its remarkable representation of a building: the masonry, roof-tiles, and other architectural details are lovingly rendered. On the left a single olive-tree stands within a walled precinct. Although the figures allow various interpretations, the temptation to recognise Athena's token, the Acropolis olive-tree, is hard to resist. 593. Kore, wearing chiton and Doric peplos (mid-6C); this is one of the earliest of these figures (see below). 575. Small quadriga (fragmentary) in Hymettian marble.

ROOM III. 3. Part of a colossal group of two lions attacking a bull, a remarkable 6C work which may have been the centre-piece of the E end of the Hekatompedon (comp. above).

Here also are two primitive korai (677, 619) executed in Naxian marble in the shape of the xoanon; one very stiff, once thought to be of Samian workmanship; the other headless. 618. Lower part of an enthroned female figure (note the modelling of the feet); 620, another, clumsily executed.

In ROOM IV are displayed the majority of the **Korai**, or maidens, perhaps the chief treasure (because unique as a group) of the museum. These female statues were dedicated as votive offerings to Athena in the course of the 6C BC in the precinct of one of her temples. Ruined in the sack of 480 and later scrupulously buried, they were discovered during excavations in 1882–86 mainly to the E of the Parthenon or NW of the Erechtheion. All the statues are clothed and painted, and each kore held an offering in one hand. Under the Peisistratids the Doric dress gradually gave way to the Ionic; we see in the statues the simple symmetry and contour of the woollen Doric peplos and chiton being replaced by the linen Ionic chiton worn with the himation. The new chiton, both thinner and more voluminous, posed new problems in modelling the body, the contour of which was more emphasised in some places by the thinner nature of the material and more covered in others by the increased drapery. The manner of wearing the himation gave a marked diagonal emphasis of line. Parallel to the sartorial changes we notice the developing naturalism of the features, including the losing of the archaic 'smile'. This development was once taken as the ascendancy of 'Attic' art over Ionic or island styles; but it seems likely to have been a development common to sculpture in general, more characteristic of a period than of a region. The korai are arranged with other works of their period, but the exact chronology of this period of Attic art and the importance of outside influences ('Ionic' or 'Samian') on it are still the subject of scholarly controversy.

The room divides into three sections. In the first: 1340. Head of a horse in Pentelic marble (? from a 5C votive relief); 581. Worshippers bringing a sacrificial sow to Athena. Grouped together are four works assigned to the same artist, probably called *Phaidimos*: 679. The Peplos Kore (c 530 BC), so called from the girded Dorian peplos she wears over her chiton; it is famous alike for the facial expression and the preservation of the ancient colour. *590. Horseman (c 560 BC); the head is a good cast of the 'Rampin Head' in the Louvre first recognised by Humfry Payne in 1936 as belonging to this figure. This and the second statue (700 below) may be a memorial to Hippias and Hipparchos, the horse-racing sons of Peisistratos. *143. Hound. 69. Lion head, a spout from a cornice. 606. Horseman in Persian or Scythian dress, dedicated by someone with N interests (? Miltiades), c 520 BC.

702. Relief of Hermes, the three Graces, and a boy; 1343. Fragmentary relief of a bearded man, wearing the exomis (singlet); 669. Kore; the hair, the set of the eyes, and the modelling of the ears recall mid-6C styles, but the drapery shows important innovations; this is thought to be the earliest example of the chiton and himation pattern which became standard (? c 540).

In the second section: 700. Equestrian statue carved in one piece (pre-Persian); of the rider nothing survives above the hips. 665. Kouros (mid-6C), damaged by fire; the muscles are modelled with greater accuracy than usual at this period. 145. Small torso of a warrior, also marked by fire. 594. Kore (headless) of Ionian workmanship; an epiblema (shawl) is thrown over the himation and colours are freely used. 694. Nike, c 480 BC. 675. Kore, preserved with much original colour, having the high forehead and features characteristic of Chiot art; 673. Kore, probably by a Chiot artist; 190. Lamp in island marble decorated with four human and four animal heads.

The third part of the room is grouped about a fine selection of korai of the last quarter of the 6C BC. 682. The hair and dress afford a striking example of late-Peisistratid elaboration (c 525); the figure is still heavy and stiff. 1342. Chariot relief (comp. 1343, above). Korai: 684. The face is intellectual, the eyes straight, the mouth firm; 674. Shoulders finely modelled; although the head is too large, the face is most delicately rendered (near the end of the 6C); 670. Clad in simple chiton, with features showing a considerable advance in naturalism. 625. Seated Athena (headless), found at the N foot of the Acropolis, conjecturally identified with that by *Endoios*, seen by Pausanias. The goddess wears the Ionic chiton and appears, from the position of the right foot, to have just sat down—an early example of such mobility. The aegis on her breast was coloured. Korai: 633, 685, and 595 all repay attention; *671. A severe beauty; 696. The 'Polos' kore; note the headdress and the simplicity of the hair.

ROOM V. Pedimental figures of the Gigantomachia from the Old Temple of Athena (c 525 BC). These are particularly striking from behind, though presumably never designed to be so seen: 631. Athena, attacking with lance, and aegis snake, newly restored; two terminal kneeling giants. Here also are *681. 'Kore of Antenor', the largest of the Korai, with unusual vertical emphasis of the drapery, and (left) a base which may or may not belong to it; the base bears the dedication of Nearchos, the donor, and of the sculptor *Antenor* (both Attic work in island marble c 525 BC). 1360. Kore, damaged by fire, but beautiful and elegant.

At the entrance to the alcove, 683 (left), a curious Kore, disproportionate and heavy; 597 (right). Youth riding a hippalektryon. 6476 A and B, two terracotta Korai. In the alcove, seven cases of choice pottery and terracottas, mostly from excavations of 1955–59 in the Sanctuary of the Nymphs, and archaic *Marble fragments from the Acropolis. Particularly interesting, in addition, are the original cedarwood blocks from the centre holes of column drums.

ROOM VI is devoted to works of the 'severe' style, a stage in the emergence of the Classical style from the Archaic. Most characteristic is *698. The Kritian Boy (c 480 BC); the weight is at last correctly posed and the body liberated from archaic stiffness; the confident modelling and bodily proportions of the early classical style is already felt; it is now proven beyond doubt that head and body belong together. 695. Relief, 'Mourning Athena'; *689. Head of a Kouros, delicately modelled; 697. Forequarters of a horse, in a more developed style than No. 700 (above); 692. Torso of a young boy; 699. Male head (Pheidian school?); 599. Male torso; 688. Kore; 302. Torso; 67. Pinax with painting of a warrior running; 690. Nike.

In ROOM VII are arranged the mutilated fragments from the **Parthenon Pediments**: their probable relative positions can be seen from the plaster models constructed in 1896–1904 from the then available evidence: Pausanias' description, the Madrid 'puteal', Carrey's drawings, portions in the British Museum, etc. The composition of the W pediment is tolerably certain; that of the E end considerably less so, since the central 12·2m was destroyed in the Christian alterations; most of the figures still extant in Carrey's day are in London (comp. 'Blue Guide London').—WEST PEDIMENT. The subject is the contest of Athena and Poseidon. 882. Head of a horse from Athena's team; 1081. Head from Poseidon's team, with hoofs, etc.; 885. Part of torso of Poseidon fitted to a cast of another piece in London; 1735. Seated goddess; 888. Oreithyia (?); 887. Torso and leg from the statue of Ilissos.—EAST PEDIMENT. The birth of Athena. 1202. Two fragments of Hera's robe.

Also in this room are 705. Metope, Centaur carrying off a Lapith woman; 727, 720. Centaurs' heads, from the S metopes of the Parthenon; 1309. Head of a young girl.

In ROOM VIII, admirably lit and mounted at eye level, is all the detached part of the * *Parthenon Frieze** that remains in Athens. Many of the slabs were blown clear in the explosion and buried, thus escaping Lord Elgin. The slabs have been arranged in correct order; their original positions are indicated on a wall diagram. The subject is the

Panathenaic procession.

Since the frieze is displayed on an inside instead of an outside wall for which it was designed the relative positions are reversed: the sculptures from the N side of the Parthenon are on the S wall and vice versa. They lead up to the three remaining slabs of the East Frieze on the E wall. West frieze (*in situ*), see above.

We start at the W door of the room and proceed along the long S wall. Here are 13 slabs out of the 42 which composed the *North Frieze*. The beginning of the procession on this side (corner slab and the following 12 pieces) is all in London. *862, 861, 863 (adjoining slabs) portray horses and riders, very spirited; one is turning and apparently being exhorted by a marshal to close up. The next three (872, 859, gap, 871) form a group from the chariot procession (just over half-way along the cella); one chariot has an apobates; an official directs. 874. Youth leading horses. Two adjoining slabs (865, 876) depict thallophoroi (bearers of olive branches), and another (875), from farther along, lyre-players. The remaining three slabs are from the head of the procession (alternate slabs are missing): *864. Four epheboi carrying hydriai; the expressions and drapery are exquisite; 860. Four men with rams; 857. Youths leading sacrificial heifers.—The *South Frieze* fragments, five in number, begin opposite by the anta on the N wall. 866–69. Four slabs from near the W end, depicting horses and riders; 873. Magistrates and two women. On the adjacent wall to the left of the door follow three slabs (797, 877, *856) from the right side of the *East Frieze* of the Parthenon: nearly all the remaining slabs, which show the ceremony of the peplos, are in London. The third, well-preserved, shows three of the twelve gods attending the Theoxenia, probably Poseidon, Apollo, and Artemis.

In the SW corner of the room are displayed the surviving thirteen slabs of the parapet that extended round three sides of the Temple of Athena Nike. This parapet was executed in high relief by a number of artists between 421 and 407 BC; the scenes represent winged *VICTORIES at their various tasks, among them the well-known Victory adjusting her sandal.—On the upper part of the central anta are placed fragments of the ERECHTHEION FRIEZE. The marble statues, attached to a background of blue Eleusinian marble, were commissioned at 60 drachmas apiece from a number of sculptors, whose names are known from the building ⸮records of 408 BC. 1075. Presentation of Erichthonios.

In ROOM IX have been placed the surviving Caryatids from the Erechtheion porch; these will be seen through a transparent screen behind which they will have a sterile atmosphere. Also here (but possibly to be moved) are later sculptures, mostly fragmentary. 1339. 'Lenormant' relief of a trireme (c 400 BC), with two finials and a colossal head; 1333. Relief of Athena receiving Hera, symbolising Samos, with the text of a treaty between Athens and Samos (405 BC), defaced under the Thirty Tyrants, and re-engraved two years later when Samos also had meanwhile suffered a change of government.

3 The Areópagus, Mouseíon, Pnyx, and Hill of the Nymphs

The WEST SLOPE OF THE ACROPOLIS, now covered by ornamental groves, has never been systematically explored, though Dörpfeld unearthed a street and part of the quarter flanking it (see below) in the valley to the W where Leoforos Apostolou Pavlou now runs. This he took to be the Panathenaic Way; but the agora excavations (Rte 5) have conclusively proved that the processional approach from the Agora to the Acropolis passed to the E of the Areopagus. The saddle that links the Areopagus spur to the Acropolis, where now extends the car park, may have been the site of the earliest agora of the Archaic period.

A flight of rock-hewn steps mounts to the **Areópagus** (6, 5; 115m), the low hill that gave name to a council of nobles which became at once the senate and the supreme judicial court; with the rise of democracy, it gradually lost its powers.

History. The name, commonly derived (comp. Euripides, 'Elektra', 1258) from the tradition that Ares was tried here by the other Gods for the murder of Halirrhothios, more likely signifies the Hill of Curses (arai). Here Aeschylus placed the camp of the Amazons ('Eumenides', 681–706). The Persians encamped on the hill when they besieged the Acropolis in 480 BC (Hdt. VIII, 52). The 7C council of elders, composed entirely of the Eupatridai became known as the *Council of the Areopagus* (η Βουλὴ η εξ Αρείου πάγου) to distinguish it from later councils. Its original and most important function was the conduct of criminal justice, particularly in cases of murder and manslaughter; but in the aristocratic days it became the governing body of the state. The archons were ex-officio members, or, according to Plutarch (Pericles), became members on quitting office. The Assembly of the people was at this time merely the recording machine for the decisions of the Areopagus. Solon transferred its powers of administration and legislation to the Assembly; but he made the Areopagus the protector of the constitution and the guardian of the laws, with control over the magistrates and the censorship of morals. Under Ephialtes (c 461 BC) censorship and control over the magistrates were transferred to the people, and the jurisdiction of the Areopagus limited once again to cases of homicide. Aeschylus, in the Eumenides, 458 BC, described the trial of Orestes on the Areopagus for the murder of his mother Klytemnestra, and the institution of the Court of the Areopagus—the implication being that this was its proper function and that the restriction of its powers thereto was strictly correct.

In the 4C BC the Areopagus dealt also with crimes of treason and corruption, notable cases being the trials of the deserters after Chaeronea in 338, of Demosthenes in 324, and of the courtesan Phryne. It was in existence during the Empire. In AD 51 St. Paul (Acts xvii, 22–34) delivered 'in the midst of Mars' Hill' the sermon on the Unknown God, which converted the senator Dionysius (St. Dionysius the Areopagite, patron saint of Athens).

On the artificially levelled summit of the hill are remains of beddings in the rock for the walls of a small edifice, probably connected with the formalities of the tribunal. Bishop Wordsworth started the tradition that these were rock-hewn seats. 'The unwrought stones', says Pausanias (I, 28, 5) 'on which the accused and accusers stand are named eespectively the Stone of Injury (υβρις) and the Stone of Ruthlessness' (αναιδεία; comp. Euripides, 'Iphigenia in Tauris', 961).

Looking down from the summit we trace the ruins of the 16C church of *St. Dionysios the Areopagite* (see above), which stood (as did its predecessors) on a level platform beneath the N side of the hill. This is believed by Prof. E. Vanderpool to be the site of the court's sessions. Lower down the N slope four ruined *Mycenaean Chamber-tombs* (explored in 1939 and 1947; see Agora Museum) yielded gold rosettes, ivory toilet boxes, swords, etc., suggesting royal burials of the second quarter of the 14C BC. Tradition places the **Cave of the Furies** beneath the NE brow of the hill. A spring here was locally credited with medicinal virtues in recent times. Like the Theseion, the precinct of the cave was a recognised sanctuary for murderers and fugitive slaves. Kylon's fellow-conspirators were killed within it in abuse of the right of sanctuary. Persons acquitted by the court of the Areopagus were wont to sacrifice at the cave. Within the enclosure stood the Tomb of Oedipus, the possession of which was long regarded as essential to the safety of Athens. The closing scene of the 'Eumenides' of Aeschylus is placed in the cave.

The Areopagus also affords the most illuminating general view of the Agora. A path descends the E side of the Areopagus past the Cave of the Furies (see above) to join the road bordering the S gate of the Agora excavations.

From the Areopagus we descend the Acropolis approach road to Leoforos Dhionissiou Areopayitou. To the SW, by the Dionysos Restaurant, paths mount the tree-clad slopes of the **Mouseíon** (148m), a hill which throughout history has played a strategic role in the fortunes of Athens. A Greco-Roman tradition derives its name from Musæus, the poet-disciple of Orpheus; it was more likely the *Hill of the Muses* who, in their character of Oreades, may have had a shrine here.

The Themistoclean Wall climbed its gentle E slope, followed the top of its sheer S face (visible traces), and joined the Southern Long Wall near its W extremity. The later Diateichisma (see below) ran NW from the summit. In 294 BC, Demetrios Poliorketes built a fort to command the Piraeus road; it changed hands four times in the ensuing struggles. From the hill Morosini bombarded the Acropolis in 1687. At the end of Novemebr 1916, Greek royalist forces occupied the ground here, and on 1 December fired on Allied troops. It was again a scene of activity during the coup of 21 April 1967.

On the summit stands the **Monument of Philopáppos**, built in AD 114–116 by the Athenians in honour of C. Julius Antiochus Philopappus, a prince of Commagene (Northern Syria), who had a distinguished career both as an Athenian citizen and as a Roman consul and prætor. The monument, of Pentelic marble, consisted of a rectangular tomb with a slightly concave façade 12·2m high. Intact in 1436 when Cyriacus of Ancona saw it, it later became ruinous. The *Façade*, which faces the Acropolis, is decorated with a frieze showing Philopappus as consul (AD 109) driving in his chariot. Above are four Corinthian pilasters which frame three niches. The central niche contains the statue of Philopappus as an Athenian citizen of the Deme of Besa; the left one his grandfather Antiochus IV Epiphanes, last king of Commagene (dethroned by Vespasian); the right one, according to Cyriacus of Ancona, held the statue of Seleukos I Nikator, the Macedonian founder of the dynasty. On the left central pilaster is inscribed in Latin the deceased's cursus honorum at Rome; on the right, in Greek, were his princely titles.—The tomb, traces of which are visible, lay behind the façade.

The *View from the monument, especially at sunset (often windy), is particularly fine, embracing the Parthenon, Hymettus, the Attic Plain with its encircling mountains, and the Saronic Gulf.

A paved path descending directly towards the Observatory (a little W of N) along the ridge of the hill follows the **Diateíchisma**, the lower courses of which are visible for most of the way. Built to shorten the city's fortifications after the slighting of the Long Walls had made Themistocles' original line untenable, this cross wall was formerly attributed to Kleon on the evidence of Aristophanes ('Knights', 817–8), but is now securely dated on evidence from excavation to the end of the 4C BC. To it was joined the *Fort of Poliorketes* (comp. above), of which the remains of a tower 10m square, can be seen c 70m N of the Philopappus monument; the foundations of another may be traced at a lower level to the NE.

The region enclosed by the two diateichismata formed the ancient quarters of *Koile* and *Melite*. It is occupied by a very large number of **Ancient Dwellings**, once thought to represent the region of the Pelasgic *Kranaa*; but archaeological evidence does not support any great antiquity. They belong for the most part to the 5C BC. This quarter, then entirely within the city walls, became over-populated at the time of the Peloponnesian War, when the Athenians flocked from the country into the city (Thuc. II, 14); but it was deserted before the end of the 3C BC. In the Roman era these old dwellings and cisterns were used as tombs. They lie thick on the ground on both flanks of the hills. The ruins include rooms, niches, terraces, flights of steps, and cisterns. Often two or three walls of the buildings were formed by excavation in the rock. Nearly sixty cisterns, large pear-shaped excavations, may be observed; they vary in depth from 4m to 6m. Seven rock-hewn seats, in an elevated spot c 137m W of the wall, may possibly represent an ancient court of justice. In the bottom of the valley are extensive traces (cart-ruts) of an ancient road that led SW from the Ayios Dhimitrios gate (see below).

The path follows the wall down to the modern drive that serves the Philopappos Theatre on the SW flank of Mouseion hill. Here on the foundations of the N tower of the *'Dipylon above the Gates'* (S tower excavated in 1936 and filled in again) stands the little chapel of *Ayios Dhimítrios Loumbardhiáris*. The name (from loumbardha or canon) is derived from a miracle attributed to the saint in which a Turkish canon, located on the Acropolis, was struck by lightning at the moment it was about to open fire on his congregation. The chapel has some surviving Byzantine frescoes. The restoration of the building and attractive refurbishment of the surrounding area (including pleasant outdoor cafeteria) is the work (1951–57) of the leading architect Dhimitrios Pikionis, his students and local artists. The gate (comp. above), wrongly identified from a late 4C inscription, is not a dipylon. The so-called *Tomb of Kimon*, which served in later times as the tomb of a certain Zosimianos, is really a rock-dwelling of the 5C BC. In the cliff-face, a little to the S, is the equally misnamed PRISON OF SOCRATES, another such dwelling having no proven connection whatever with the philosopher. It consists of three rooms, one with a sloping ceiling, and a bottle-shaped cistern once independent of the rest.

Above Ayios Dhimitrios rises the *Hill of the Pnyx* (109m), in Classical times popularly called 'The Rocks' (αι Πέτραι). On its NE slope, 27·5m from the top, is the site of the **Pnyx**, approached by a path (right) past Ay. Dhimítrios, the meeting-place of the Assembly, or Ecclesia (Εκκλησία), firmly identified by the discovery in the 19C of its boundary stone (inscribed ΟΡΟΣ ΠΥΚΝΟΣ) and scientifically investigated by Kourouniotes and Homer Thompson between 1930 and 1936. With the establishment of democracy under Kleisthenes the Assembly changed its venue from the Agora to the Pnyx, where its deliberations could not be overlooked; they were thus held, significantly perhaps, above instead of below the Areopagus. Here the great statesmen of the 5C and early 4C, among them Aristides, Themistocles, Pericles and Demosthenes, held their audience.

The word *Pnyx* (η Πνύξ, gen. Πυκνός) means the place where people were tightly packed (πυκνός, compact, dense, crowded). The 'tight-packing' must have had special reference to the single entrance, as there was room inside for four or five times the number of legislators. The Assembly was presided over by the Prytaneis (see the Agora). The citizens, 5000 of whom were needed to form a quorum,

Athens, Pnyx. Hypothetical reconstruction with Panathenaic stadium, c 329 BC

were hustled towards the Pnyx by Scythian archers who held across the Agora and neighbouring streets cords daubed with wet red paint in order to hurry up the laggards, and to prevent any citizen from 'cutting' a meeting. There was only one entrance. Here the arrivals were scrutinised so that no unauthorised person should slip in. No person not a citizen was allowed to attend without special authority. Citizens marked with the red paint forfeited their allowance.

Athens, Pnyx. Reconstruction of Classical houses

Three periods of construction have been confirmed. In the first, c 500 BC, the seating faced N and the bema S towards the sea, a natural adaptation of the configuration of the ground. Under the Thirty Tyrants (403 BC) the arrangements were reversed so that the bema faced to landward because, according to Plutarch

('Themistocles', 19, 4), they thought oligarchy less distasteful to farmers than to mariners. The retaining wall of this period, uncovered in 1930–31, was of poor masonry and carelessly constructed. Most of the extant remains date from the last period; this was first thought to be of Hadrianic date but is now attributed to a comprehensive plan of Lycurgus for the embellishment of the site (comp. below). The buildings planned to accompany the new auditorium were left unfinished and the Assembly seems to have migrated to the Theatre of Dionysos.

The Pnyx is a huge artificial terrace in the form of a semicircle, the ends of which joined a perpendicular wall of rock, a man-made scarp forming the base-line. The semicircle, 198·5m round, is formed by a colossal *Retaining Wall*, 1·8m thick, built of trapezoidal blocks quarried in the fashioning of the scarp. The blocks, one of which is 4m long and 1·8m high, are remarkably well jointed without the use of mortar. About one-third of the wall, now diminished to a height of 4·5m, remains, at the central part of the arc. Its object was to keep in place the gigantic embankment of earth which was built to convert the natural downward slope of the ground into an upward slope, so that the area had the form of a crude theatre. The ravages of time and the mutilation of the retaining wall have restored the natural slope of the earth, which still, however, lies in places 1·8m above the top of what is left of the wall. The single entrance to the Pnyx of the third period was by a flight of steps on the N side of the wall. The remains of a second and concentric wall exist ten yards within the outer wall below present ground level; this belongs to the second period.

The *Auditorium* presumably had a shallow slope like a scallop-shell, but there is no material evidence for seating of any kind or even for a floor other than of earth.

The perpendicular wall of rock that forms a base-line of 118·8m is hewn in two sections which make an obtuse angle (158°) at the centre, where it is highest (4·6m). At the angle is a three-stepped platform, 0·9m high, 9·4m wide, and projecting 6·4m from the wall, which formed the *Bema* or tribune, from which the orators spoke. The sockets of the balustrade that surrounded it are still visible. It is crowned by a cube of rock 1·8m high and 3m sq. with a flight of five steps at either side. Round its base was a ledge for votive or legislative tablets.

In the wall of rock, 12m to the left of the Bema, is a large niche, surrounded by over 50 smaller ones. Twelve marble tablets, found by Lord Aberdeen in 1803 in the ground below them, are now in the British Museum, and others have been recovered since. Most of them are ex-votos dedicated by women to Zeus Hypsistos and date from Roman times.

Above the Bema is a broad terrace levelled from the rock. In the centre, in line with the tribune, is a bedding probably for a monumental *Altar*, flanked by rock-cut benches, perhaps the seats of the prytaneis. Farther back another bedding in the rock may mark the site of the *Heliotropion*, or sundial, erected by the astronomer Meton in 433 BC. At a higher level are beddings for foundations of two large stoas. The *West Stoa* measures 148m by 18m, and would have had 54 columns. The *East Stoa*, 21·5m by 6m, was begun on a different alignment and in its second form accords with the placing of a smaller central building, perhaps a *Propylon*. These three structures are dated to the third quarter of the 4C BC and have been conjectured to represent a scheme of Lycurgus, c 330–326 BC, for the comfort of the Assembly. A recent reappraisal (A.J.A. 1985) of the site has however suggested that the 'stoas' actually form part of the Lycurgan Panathenaic stadium, of which no archaeological indication has ever been found on the site of the later stadium (comp. below). In this case, the two rectangular foundations were not for stoas but for earth embankments on which the spectators would have stood to watch contests taking place on the levelled terrace immediately in front.

Soon after these buildings were begun, a decision was taken to carry the Diateichisma (see above) through the site. The wall did not survive long at this point, being replaced by a parallel wall of white poros with towers, traces of which can be seen to the S and W. This probably strengthened a weak point in the circuit at the time the Long Walls and the outer diateichisma were finally abandoned as a defensive line (c 200 BC).

To the N of the Pnyx, rises the so-called **Hill of the Nymphs** (104m), a modern name borrowed from the dedication to the Nymphs carved on a rock inside the Observatory garden. The slopes of the hill are covered with ancient foundations, in the midst of which stands the little church of *Ayia Marina* and its multi-domed modern successor. On the rock below the church, is a 6C inscription written from right to left, which marks the limit of the Precinct of Zeus (Όρος Διός). On the summit of the hill stands the conspicuous *Observatory* (Asteroskopíon), founded by Baron Sinas in 1842, which is open to visitors on the last Friday of the month. A second building, with a large telescope, was added in 1905, and a seismological station in 1957.

Behind the observatory a path leads towards a radio station. To the right (c 70m) is the 'Little Pnyx', a small rock-cut assembly place. Traces of the *Northern Long Wall* may be seen close by. A long depression to the W, partly filled up, is generally identified with the *Barathron*, the ancient Athenian place of execution.

Returning past the observatory and descending to Leofóros Apostólou Pávlou (comp. below), we face two gates: to the left an entrance to the *Agora* excavations (Rte 5); to the right access to a tract of ground excavated by Dörpfeld in 1892–97. His contentions that he had discovered here the Temple of Dionysos in the Marshes and the true Enneakrounos were based on topographical suppositions about the location of the Agora which have since been conclusively disproved. DÖRPFELD'S EXCAVATIONS are now largely overgrown, and their identification, though interesting to the scholar, need not delay the ordinary visitor.

An ANCIENT ROAD, c 4m wide, equipped with a gutter and bordered by walls of polygonal masonry, is laid bare for some 228·5m. It was possibly the principal street of the deme of Melite. To the right stood a *Lesche* (club) identified from inscriptions. Farther on is a private house with a record of two mortgages (for 1000 and 210 drachmæ respectively) inscribed on its outer wall in letters of the 4C BC. On the other side of the ancient road is an early triangular precinct, not the Dionysion in Limnai, but very possibly the *Heroön of Herakles Alexikakos*. The site, which is 1·8m below the level of the road, is covered with later buildings which have no connection with it. In the S corner is a small *Temple*. In the middle of the adjoining courtyard are the foundations, in poros, of a square base which may have supported the statue of Herakles by Agelades (Scholiast to Aristophanes, Frogs 501). In the NW corner is a building formerly identified by Dörpfeld with the *Lenaion*, i.e. the building which enclosed the Sacred Wine Press (Λήναιον). The remains of a wine press were found here. Overlying the Greek remains and extending a little to the E are the foundations of a Roman basilica, identified from the long inscription (2C AD) on a column, which relates to the religious guild of the Iobacchoi, as their clubhouse or *Baccheion*. Farther on, on the same side of the road, are the ruins of the *Amyneion*, a small shrine to the hero Amynos, the assistant of Asklepios, of which Sophocles held the priesthood. Inside are a temple and a well which was fed by a conduit from the main fountain.

Opposite are remains of the great WATER SYSTEM OF PEISISTRATOS, which Dörpfeld asserted were those of the Enneakrounos. These are partly beneath the modern avenue and partly on its far side. At the foot of the Pnyx is a small square chamber hewn out of the rock, with a niche from which water still occasionally flows. It feeds a smaller round basin, also rock-hewn, a few feet lower down. This primitive supply, later covered by a Roman well- house, was identified by Dörpfeld with the Fountain of Kallirrhoë (comp. Rte 7). In the time of Solon, the yield was supplemented by cutting connecting channels from neighbouring water-courses on the Acropolis and Mouseion hills. A much more important undertaking, attributed to Peisistratos, was the construction of an *Aqueduct* nearly 5km long, which led from the valley of the Ilissos under the present National Garden to the foot of the W slopes of the Acropolis. It ended in a large square *Cistern*, hewn like the others from the rock, from which pipes lead to a spacious *Square*, where stones belonging to a fountain base have been found.

The ancient road goes on some way farther S and SE along the line of the aqueduct, and then bends NE towards the Acropolis. A footpath from the Amyneion leads through the pine-trees to the foot of the Areopagus where we started.

Leoforos Apostolou Pavlou continues NW past public gardens to *Ayios Athanásios*, whence a footbridge leads to the entrance gate of the Kerameikos (Rte 4).

4   From Síndagma Square to the Agorá and the Kerameikós

Bus No. 026 from Amalias, via Mitropoleos, returning via Ermou.

From Sindagma Square the long ODHOS ERMOÚ (Hermes St.), lined at first with fashion and textile shops, runs straight W for nearly 1·5km, dividing the old city in two; as it descends it changes character, being devoted to the furnishing and building trades. In a large square to the S stands the **Cathedral** (7, 3), built in 1840–55 out of the material of 72 demolished churches and from the designs of four architects. The resultant incongruity is not, therefore, surprising. Since 1864 the Metropolitan Archbishop of Athens has been the chief dignitary of the independent Greek Orthodox Church. To the left of the W entrance is the tomb of the Patriarch Gregory, transferred from Odessa in 1871, fifty years after his execution at Constantinople. To the S stands the **Small Metropolis**, or old cathedral, known also as *Panayia Gorgoepikoös* and *Ayios Eleftherios*. In its present form it dates from the 12C, though legend attributes its foundation to the Empress Irene c 787. Its external dimensions are only 12·2m by 7·6m; the cupola is under 12m. The walls of the church are artfully constructed entirely of ancient architectural blocks and reliefs, some inscribed, and of reliefs from an earlier church or churches of the 6–7C. On the W side above the arch over the door is a calendar of the Attic state festivals (? 2C AD). Each festival is represented by symbolic figures or objects in relief; signs of the zodiac indicate the time sequence. One of the Maltese crosses added by the Christians has blotted out the sole known representation of the Panathenaic ship; its wheels are visible to the right of the second cross from the left.

Outside the S wall lies a block of grey marble 2·1m long and ·6m wide, known as the Stone of Cana, with a late Greek inscription recording its use at the Marriage Feast of Cana of Galilee. It was discovered at Elatea, in Phocis.—Behind the Apse: inscriptions and tablets, archaic relief with dancing figures.—N side: ancient votive tablets.

The modernised church of *St Andrew* at the top of Odhos Filotheis to the S is now the chapel of the archbishop's palace.

About 450m W of Sindagma Square Odhos Ermou divides to form a little square round the tiny church called *Kapnikarea* (7, 3). The origin of its name is doubtful, as is the inevitable attribution of its foundation to the Empress Irene. The existing cruciform structure, of stone with the usual courses of brick, cannot be older than the 11C; the porch, the exo-narthex and the parecclesion (or N chapel) were added in the 13C. Saved from demolition in 1834 by Ludwig of Bavaria, the building was carefully restored by the University and is its official church. The dome is supported by four columns with Roman capitals.

We cross Odhos Aiolou (Rte 8), overshadowed at its S end by the towering rock of the Acropolis, then skirt the N side of Monastiráki Square (Rte 6). To the right lies the district of PSIRI, less appealing than Plaka though still maintaining its irregular street plan. In Odhós Ayías Théklas No. 11 was the scene of Byron's ten-week stay on his first arrival in Athens in 1809; he later immortalised the 13-year-old daughter of the house, Teresa Makris, as the Maid of Athens. Farther N, on the corner of Evripídhou and Menándrou streets, is the chapel of *Ayios Ioannis stin Kolona*, built round an unfluted Roman column with a Corinthian capital which projects through the roof. The column, probably from a gymnasium dedicated to Apollo, has reputedly the power of curing fevers.

Off the S side of Odhos Ermou lies the little Plateia Avisinias with the *'Flea Market'* (Sunday mornings). The antiquities (especially coins) are not always what they seem. Metal-workers practice their traditional craft in Odhos Ifestou, to the E. Odhos Astingos, its W continuation, is named after Frank Abney Hastings, the English philhellene who was mortally wounded at Aitoliko. Near by, Ayios Filippos stands above the railway cutting near the N entrance to the *Agora* (see Rte 5). This may be conveniently visited on the return.

The church of the *Asomaton* (6, 3), freed in 1960 of its 19C additions, closes the N side of the square fronting Thission Station. Beyond this, Odhos Ermou continues alongside the excavations of the Kerameikos. In the street flanking their E end is a *Synagogue* with a marble 'classical' façade.—On the far side of the railway some traces of the city walls can be seen to the W of the church of *Ayios Athanasios* (6, 3); the church and adjacent cottages utilise ancient rock-cut foundations.

The **Kerameikós** (6, 1) includes the ruins of the Dipylon and Sacred Gates and excavations made outside the walls in the ancient *Cemetery of the Kerameikos*. Here roads from Piraeus, Eleusis, and Boeotia converged upon that from the Academy, so that by this way most ancient travellers entered the city. The brook Eridanos flows from E to W across the area, which is frequently waterlogged; frogs abound and tortoises may be seen. The place Kerameikos is said by Pausanias (I, 3, 1) to take its name from the hero Keramos, a supposed son of Dionysos and Ariadne.

Cemeteries existed in the Kerameikos district at least from the 12C BC. By the 7C a line seems to have been drawn between the Inner Kerameikos, a quarter of potters and smiths, and the *Outer Kerameikos*, but it was the building of the city wall that conclusively separated the two. Few burials later than this are found in the inner area, as thenceforward it became usual (just as later in Rome) to bury the dead outside the enceinte along roads leading from the city gates. The importance of the W entrance to the city was enhanced by the Dionysiac and Eleusinian processions which passed through it and by that of the Panathenaia which set out from it. In consequence the Academy Road outside the Gate of Thria (later the Dipylon) had perhaps already by the 6C become the Demosion Sema, the **Cemetery** *par excellence*, reserved for state tombs and cenotaphs of individuals or polyandreia for groups of Athenian battle heroes. Here were the graves of Pericles, Thrasyboulos, Konon, Zeno, Harmodios and Aristogeiton, and other worthies. Thucydides tells how 'when the remains have been laid in the earth, some man of known ability and high reputation, chosen by the city, delivers a suitable oration over them'. From a platform here Pericles delivered the famous

KERAMEIKOS

0   75 metres

N

Propylon

Dipylon

Pompeion

Spartan
Polyandreion

Boundary of Stones

Bath

Sacred Gate

Eridanos Aquaduct

SACRED WAY

Ayia Triada

Pythagoras

Triнopatreion

Thersandros
& Similos

Burial Mound

STREET OF TOMBS

Temenos of Hekate

MUSEUM

ERMOU

P I R A I O S

oration (Thuc. II, 35–46) on those who died in the first year of the Peloponnesian War. The remainder of the ground was available to all classes, including slaves.

Many tomb monuments removed in the 19C are in the National Archaeological Museum. The Greek Archaeological Society began excavations in 1863, continuing at intervals until 1913. In 1913–41 the German Archaeological Institute conducted excavations directed by A. Brückner and K. Kübler. In 1956 the Greek government requested the Institute to resume responsibility for the Kerameikos site and further intensive work began under the direction of D. Öhly. New excavations have been initiated; the old areas have been reinvestigated, conserved and landscaped; the museum, built with funds donated by Gustav Oberlaender (1867–1936), a German-American silk-stocking manufacturer, has been renovated and expanded. The Academy Road, whose course lies largely beneath modern houses, has not been properly explored, though many casual finds are in the National Archaeological Museum. The sector that has been cleared lies S of the main Kerameikos and consists of an extension to the SW made at the beginning of the 4C BC. Most of its tombs were destroyed for material to repair the city walls after the battle of Chaeronea (338 BC), but those remaining were covered by successive layers of earth and later tombs to a depth of 6–9m and so were untouched by the extensive siege work of Sulla in 86 BC.

Half-right inside the entrance on top of a mound is a plan of orientation with a view over the whole site. From it can be clearly identified the Wall of Themistocles with its later outwork and sectional moats. Of the wall the bottom course of masonry only is Themistoclean. On top of this in blue 'acropolis' stone are two courses of Konon's wall, then, in creamy limestone, two courses of a Demosthenian renewal, further courses attributable to Lycurgus, and, to the right, in long and short work, masonry of the period of Justinian.

A path descends to give a closer view of the double **City Walls**, which here occupy a frontage of c 183m, interrupted by the Dipylon and the Sacred Gate. The inner line of wall was built by Themistocles in 479 and rebuilt by Konon in 394. It is only 2–2·4m thick and consists of one course of poros blocks (truly Themistoclean) and two rows of well jointed polygonal blocks of blue limestone (Kononian), interspersed with hastily reused marbles, with a core of rubble. The upper part was of unbaked bricks. The outer breastwork, with moat, was of later date, and may have been contemporary with the Dipylon. It is 4·3m thick and has facings of regularly cut blocks of conglomerate, with an earthen core. To the SW of the Sacred Gate both are fairly well preserved, the 'Themistoclean' wall with its later superstructures being 4m high in places and the outer wall still higher. Plutarch's contention that Sulla, before he stormed Athens in 86 BC razed the whole section of the wall between the Sacred and the Piraeic Gates indicates that earlier socles were by this time below ground level.

The **Sacred Gate** (Ἱερὰ Πύλη) spanned both the Sacred Way to Eleusis and the Eridanos brook. In the Themistoclean period an inner gate was constructed 18m inside the circuit wall. The road was protected on the S by a high wall which joined the enceinte in a massive tower, and a matching tower was added to the E exit of the gate in the 4C BC. The water, which presumably bore the sewage from the Agora area, was conveyed in a vaulted channel.

A well-preserved section of the WALL OF KONON, in rusticated polygonal masonry on the Themistoclean line, runs NE between the Dipylon and the Sacred Gate. About 2·5m short of the gate is a *Boundary Stone*, inscribed perpendicularly ΟΡΟΣ ΚΕΡΑΜΕΙΚΟΥ; this is one of several found at different points of the Kerameikos boundary. The space between the two gates was occupied by the **Pompeíon**, a place of preparation for processions (πομπαί), which served as a storehouse for the heavy vehicles and other paraphernalia used in the Panathenaic festival. It was adorned with painted portraits of the comic poets and a bronze statue of Socrates by Lysippus, and in emergency served as a centre for distributing corn. The Greek edifice of the 4C BC consisted of a court surrounded by a colonnade of six columns by thirteen, known to have been a haunt of Diogenes. The orthostats in Hymettian marble of the E wall and of part of the S wall still stand. Off the N and W sides project six small dining-rooms. A simple *Propylon* in the E corner, which gave access from the city, preserves its plan complete. Prominent are the metal clamps joining the marble blocks, wheelruts, and the holes for door fittings.

The classical Pompeion was destroyed in Sulla's siege, evidence of which survive in the shape of stone balls from his catapults. A new building occupying the same area was erected on massive concrete foundations in the time of Antoninus Pius. This was basilican in form, divided by two rows of 11 pilasters, and its most prominent remaining features are the buttresses of its S wall. It was destroyed in turn during the Herulian raid of 267. The plans of both can be best appreciated from an artificial terrace in the SE corner of the excavated area.

The **Dípylon** (Δίπυλον, double gateway), was the main gate of the city. Not only was it larger than any of the others, but it received the greatest volume of traffic. A broad thoroughfare known as the Dromos (now built over), bordered with gymnasia and porticoes, ascended direct to the Agora (comp. Rte 5). Outwards, an important avenue led to the Academy, with a branch road to the *Hamaxitos*, the busy old road to Piraeus. This last intersected the *Sacred Way*, which led from the Sacred Gate (see below) to Eleusis, whence high roads ran W to Megara and N to Boeotia.

History. The Dipylon was built at the end of the 4C BC, on the exact plan of its predecessor, the Themistoclean gate of 479 BC, known as the Thriasian Gate (comp. Plutarch, 'Pericles', 30) which was so-called because it led to Thria, a deme near Eleusis. Known also as the Keramic Gate, it provided the favourite, though not the most direct, way to or from the Piraeus, as it avoided the hills and led straight into the heart of the city. In 200 BC Philip V of Macedon, furiously attacking Athens for siding with Pergamon and Rome against him, penetrated into the court and extricated himself with some difficulty (Livy XXXI, 24).

The Dipylon gateway was strategically placed at the end of a deep court c 13·5m long and 7m broad, open on the W and protected by flanking towers. A considerable portion of the SW tower is preserved. This is nearly 7·5m sq. and is built of large blocks of conglomerate cased with limestone, very well worked. The *Court* was flanked by thick ramparts. The two gates are separated by a central pier, behind which is a square base supporting a round marble altar dedicated to Zeus Herkeios, Hermes, and Akamas (eponymous hero of the tribe of Akamantis). To the E of the entrance was a classical fountain-house behind which are preserved the first few of the steps leading up to the NE tower. The *Outer Gate*, added to the defences in the 1C BC, was set back c 8m from the city wall and was divided vertically by a stone pier c 11m wide; the openings on either side were 3·5m wide. The marble base of a monument stands outside the pier.

The Apotheke or dig-house lies beyond (no adm.).

The **Kerameikos Cemetery** lay outside the Dipylon and extended alongside the two principal adjoining roads. Part of the area is being slowly cleared. At present the ACADEMY ROAD offers little on the spot to justify its fame. Opposite the late *Sarcophagus of Philotera*, to the left of the road are scanty remains of a *Bath-house* of the 5C BC, the earliest of its kind yet discovered. Also to the left of the road is a *Polyandreion* which was found to contain the skeletons of 13 Spartan officers who fell fighting in the civil war in 403. Two of the bodies in the central chamber were named on an inscribed marble slab as Chairon and Thibrachos (mentioned by Xenophon); the third was probably the Olympic victor Lakrates. Here and to the NW of the church are two original *Boundary Stones*. Where the road disappears below the modern Odhos Piraios, is an elaborate grave monument formerly known as the Tomb of Chabrias, of c 350 BC, half excavated.

Literary evidence, casual finds, and excavations at intervals to the N augment our knowledge of the road. Identified post holes are believed to come from the wooden stands erected for spectators of the annual torch races in honour of the dead. Inscriptions have been found from the polyandreia of the battles of Potidaea, the Hellespont, and Corinth. About 185m NW of the Dipylon lay the *Peribolos of Artemis Kalliste*, identified with walls discovered at No. 11 Odhos Plataion, where votive reliefs came to light in 1922. For the *Academy of Plato* (c 1km NW of the Dipylon), see below.

Retracing our steps, keeping the church on our right, we cross the excavations where c 8000 ostraka (discarded from the Agora in ancient times) came to light in 1966, cross over the Eridanos and reach the *Tritopatreion* in the angle of the SACRED WAY (ΙΕΡΑ ΟΔΟΣ) and the so-called Street of the Tombs. Beyond the excavated area the present-day Ierá Odhós follows the line of the ancient Sacred Way all the way to Eleusis. The Tritopatreis were perhaps deities connected with ancestor worship and three boundary stones warn of their sacred precinct.

Opposite, on the S side, stand the stelai of Pythagoras, consul (proxenos) of Athens at Selymbria in Thrace (early 5C BC) placed on a stepped pyramid of interesting geometrical proportions, and of the Corcyraean envoys, Thersandros and Simylos, who came to Athens at the outbreak of the Peloponnesian War (Thucydides, I, xxii); their tomb furniture in the museum indicates a 5C grave, though the monu-

Athens, Kerameikos. Funeral plot with grave stelai, etc.

ment was refurbished in the early 4C and the lettering of the stele is of that date.

Behind these ambassadorial stelai rises an enormous *Grave Mound* which was erected for two foreign dignitaries (ambassadors?) in the third quarter of the 6C BC. Opposite them, on the N side of the sacred way and beyond the Eridanos, there is a further large grave mound which was partly surrounded by a wall in the 4C. Its origin dates to the 7C BC and it may have belonged to the old Attic clan of the Kerykoi. It was the burial place of the herald Anthemokritos, of the same clan, who was murdered in Megara shortly before the beginning of the Peloponnesian War and whose grave is often mentioned by ancient writers (e.g. Pausanias, I, 36, 3). Adjoining it to the W are several grave tumuli, including one with the 'stele of the myrtles' and a large mound of the second half of the 5C BC.

The **Street of the Tombs** is a planned funerary avenue unique in Greece if we except the usage at the Hieron of Epidauros. It was begun c 394 BC. The street, 8m wide, has been excavated for 91·5m. On either side of the street the cemetery was divided into plots reserved for wealthy citizens (both Athenian citizens and metics). About 20 of these plots have been discovered, divided into distinct terraces (especially on the S side).

All types of funerary monument common in the 4C are represented: the plain *stele* with palmette anthemion; more elaborate *stelai* with reliefs enclosed in a frame, culminating in the *naïskos*, or *œdicula*, where the sculptural frame achieves architectural proportions; the *column* surmounted by a device or animal; and the great marble *lekythoi* (with one handle) and *loutrophoroi* (with two handles; used for unmarried persons), which enjoyed special favour in the 4C. In 317 BC Demetrios of Phaleron limited memorials to a plain *trapeza* (slab) or a *kioniskos* (or cippus; a small undecorated column). A few wells here and there provided the necessary water for the funeral rites.

To the left stands the **Memorial of Dexíleos**, the 20-year-old son of Lysanias of Thorikos, who was one of the 'five knights' killed in action at Corinth in 394 BC. On a massive conglomerate base stands a crescent of poros on which the inscribed monument was set off by two sirens. The marble relief (case *in situ*) represents the young man in the act of despatching a prostrate adversary. The lance, horse, trappings, and bridle were of bronze. The tall stele crowned with a palmette commemorates Lysias and a smaller one (behind) Melitta, brother and sister of Dexileos; a trapeza tombstone bears the names of Lysanios, another brother, and his family.

The adjacent plot of the brothers Agathon and Sosikrates of Herakleia contains the *Ædicula of Korallion*, wife of Agathon, as well as the tall *Stele of Agathon and Sosikrates.*—The *Monument of Dionysios of Kollytos* is an ædicula without relief backed by a pillar stele, which supports a conspicuously fine bull, in Pentelic marble.—In the plot of *Lysimachos of Acharnai*, with retaining walls of excellent polygonal masonry, are a Molossian Dog in Hymettian marble and a pudgy Roman sepulchral relief representing a funeral feast on the banks of the Styx, with Charon in attendance. The temenos of Nikostrates and Kephisodoros occupies the angle of a lateral road mounting to the *Temenos of Artemis Soteira*, a precinct long attributed to the worship of Hekate.

Returning along the NORTH SIDE of the Street of Tombs we see first the concession of Eubios of Potamos, with the *Stele of Euphrosyne* (c 386), sister of Eubios, and the *Monument of Bion* (his nephew) in the form of a Doric column surmounted by a loutrophoros. The plot of *Koroibos of Melite* contains his own stele, the *Loutrophoros of*

Kleidemos, his grandson, and a facsimile of the ædicula of Hegeso, his wife. Beyond are the stelai of *Samakion* and *Menes* (on horseback). Farther over the *Ædicula of Eukoline*, a little girl with her dog; and the *Ædicula of Aristion*, a boy with a pet bird and a slave holding a strigil; below is a mourning siren, supported by kneeling figures. On the side of the mound on which stood the church of Ayia Triada can be seen the small *trapezai* of *Hipparete*, granddaughter of Alcibiades, and of *Phanokles of Leukenoe* and *Philokrates of Kydathenaion.*

In the LATERAL WAY, to the S, are the graves of two actors, *Makareus* and *Hieronymos.* The plot of Demetria and Pamphile includes the fine *Ædicula of Pamphile* represented as a seated figure beside her sister Demetria, who is standing. Beyond is the reservation of the family of *Philoxenos of Messenia* with a statue of his wife and three trapezai, one for himself and two for his sons; also tombstones of slaves.

The **Oberlaender Museum**. ROOM I. SCULPTURE recovered from the Themistoclean Wall: *Dexileos Monument (comp. above); P 1130 *Stele of Ampharete holding her infant grandchild, with beautifully executed drapery (5C BC). I 190, Base of a grave monument (c 515 BC) for the Carian Tymnes, son of Skylax, with three lines in Greek and one in Carian; Skylax may be the famous Carian captain, the earliest explorer of the Indus region and of the coasts of the Indian Ocean and Red Sea. P 105, Sphinx (c 550 BC), acroterion of a grave stele. P 1001, Base (c 560 BC) with four horsemen in relief on the front, found in S tower of Diplyon, perhaps the base for the famous Discophoros relief in the National Museum. P 1051, Horse and rider (c 520 BC); P 1052, Seated man, grave monument of c 530 BC, both found in the Themistoclean Wall. P 1054, Boxer stele (c 550 BC): head of boxer with cauliflower ear and thongs of glove tied round his wrist. P 1169, Stele of Eupheros (5C BC), grave relief of youth with strigil. P 1132, Grave stele of warrior with staff and sword (c 570–560 BC).

ROOM II contains terracotta figures and choice *Vases of all kinds of the Sub-Mycenaean, Protogeometric, Geometric and Protoattic periods (11–7C), part of a most important collection, from which the definitive dating of the period has been largely deduced. Among these are the earliest pictorial representation (a horse: the 'Ur-Pferd') on a pot since Mycenaean times, and a bronze bowl of Phoenician workmanship (late-9C BC), 'the earliest confidently dated Near Eastern art object found in Greece' (Akurgal).

ROOMS III AND IV. Grave groups of the Archaic, Classical, and Hellenistic periods, containing black-figured and red-figured pottery of well-known painters (Amasis, Kleophrades), terracotta figurines including 'four exquisite figures attached to a base' (Higgins). Ostraka, from a find of about 18,000, naming Themistocles and other famous citizens.

The Academy, made famous by Plato's school of philosophy, was a sacred wood c 2 stadia in diameter, situated at the end of an avenue (comp. above) 6 stadia from the Dipylon. Pious walkers wishing to follow as nearly as possible the avenue's course should take Odhos Plataion or the parallel Odhos Salaminos (2, 5) and their extensions from the NW side of the Kerameikos (2·5km). The church of Ayios Yeóryios on the corner of Palamidhíou, two-thirds of the way along, stands on the ancient road, which has been located at many points. *Ayios Trífon*, standing in Kolokínthou off the N side of the main Corinth road, marks the S corner of the **Academy of Plato**, whose position was confirmed in 1966 by the discovery *in situ* of a boundary-stone dated to c 500 BC. The area is more easily reached by bus No. 051 from Odhos Veranzerou via Kolonos.

The hill of *Kolonos Hippios* (56m), the refuge of Oedipus, the flowers of which are celebrated by Sophocles' chorus (Oed. Col., 688–719), lies to the E of Odhós Lenormán, enveloped by the city. On its bare top, above the trees, tombstones commemorate Charles Lenormant (1802–59) and Karl Ottfried Müller (1797–1840), two archaeologists who died in Athens.

The ACADEMY, more correctly the *Hekademeia*, was traditionally founded by Hekademos, who told the Dioscuri where their sister Helen was hidden; hence, in gratitude to Hekademos, the Lacedaemonians always spared it when they invaded Attica (Plutarch, 'Theseus', 32). Twelve sacred olive-trees, supposed to be offshoots of Athena's tree on the Acropolis, grew here. In the 6C BC Hipparchos built a wall round the Academy (perhaps that which has been located), and excavations have shown that the Kephissos was diverted at about this time. Kimon converted the place 'from a bare, dry, and dusty spot into a well-watered grove, with shady walks and racecourses' (Plutarch, 'Kimon', 13). It was a gymnasium in the time of Aristophanes ('Clouds' 1002). Plato taught here from c 388 BC, while dwelling between the Academy and the hill of Kolonos; he was buried on his estate. Sulla cut down the Academy trees to make siege engines in 86 BC, but the damage was immediately made good since Cicero, who visited Athens in 79 BC, here sets the scene of one of his philosophical dialogues. Funeral games in honour of the dead buried in the Kerameikos were held in the Academy, where also was an Altar of Prometheus, the goal of torch-races from Athens. Excavations, begun in 1929–40 by the Greek architect P. Aristophron, were continued by members of the Greek Archaeological Society. There are now two main areas of excavation some 230m apart.

Standing   Foundations   Traces or supposed

'Cyclopean' wall

Pre-Persian (Myc & Archaic.)

Classical

Roman

Medieval & Modern additions

ACROPOLIS

0   50 metres

chtheion

Temple
thena

Belvedere

Temple of
Rome and Augustus

rthenon

Museum

Choregic Monts

Asklepieion

Theatre of
Dionysos

Mont. of
Nikias

Roman Bath

The entrance to one is in Odhos Thenaias near the bus terminus. Here the W wall of the *Peribolos* (? the Ιππάρχου Τειχίον) has been laid bare for about 137m. During the clearance of debris inside the wall many schoolboys' slates came to light, bearing inscriptions (with the names of Demosthenes and Sophocles) of the late-5C or early-4C BC. The most surprising discoveries, however, have been of pre-Classical date and outside the wall. An early Helladic dwelling may indeed be the *House of Hekademos*, since a short distance to the S is a large *Heroön* of the Geometric period (8–7C), extraordinarily preserved since it is built entirely of mud brick, with seven rooms and an eschara nearly 1·5m in diameter, which served presumably for his cult. Unearthed in 1956, this is now protected by a metal roof. Many fine vases have been found in the area, which is honeycombed with graves from pre-Mycenaean times and later cremation burials. A large circular *Well*, of excellent masonry, inscribed round the mouth, has been reconstructed here.

In a second enclosure, to the SE near Ay. Trifon, are the excavated remains of a *Gymnasium* of the 5C AD.

5 The 'Theseíon' and the Agorá

Approaches. There are three entrances to the Agora: at the SW corner from Leof. Apostólou Pávlou (Thission terminus of bus No. 230, comp. Rte 1); from the N side by bridge over the railway from Od. Adrianoú (comp. Rte 4); from the S side near the Church of the Holy Apostles (comp. Rte 3).—An excellent 'Guide to the Excavation', published in English by the American School, is available (3rd edn 1976).

The upper gallery of the Stoa of Attalos has six plans showing the topography of ancient Athens and five stages in the development of the Agora; these are augmented by a model reproducing the agora at its greatest extent (2C AD). Having got his bearings, the visitor can begin with either the Theseion or the square itself, reserving the museum till later. Lavatories and iced water are available in the Stoa of Attalos (railway end).

ARCHAEOLOGICAL NOTE. The approximate location of the Agora had been demonstrated as early as 1859–62, from the identification of the Stoa of Attalos by the Greek Archaeological Society and the interpretation of ancient texts. Haphazard digs were made by Greeks and Germans between 1859 and 1897 where remains showed above the surface, and when the Athens–Piraeus railway was extended through a cutting in 1890–91. In 1931–40 the American School of Classical Studies, with the financial backing of John D. Rockefeller, Jr, undertook systematic excavations under Prof. T. Leslie Shear. They have been continued in 1946–67 under Prof. Homer Thompson and since 1968 under T. Leslie Shear, Jr. The area between the railway and the Acropolis and the Areopagus was declared an archaeological zone by law; some 350 dilapidated 19C houses were expropriated and demolished and 300,000 tons of accumulated deposit sifted and removed until the whole area had been excavated to classical, and parts of it to prehistoric, levels. Of the area investigated about two-thirds is now open to the public, the enclosure including the Agora, the buildings bounding its W, S, and E sides, and the hill of Kolonos Agoraios to the W. Excavations started in 1970 in a further expropriated zone beyond the railway revealed the *Stoa Basileios*, in 1980 the *Stoa Poikile*.

The so-called '**Theseíon**' (Agora Pl. 5) that crowns the low knoll of *Kolonos Agoraios* is now identified with the *Temple of Hephaistos and Athena* noted by Pausanias, although the misnomer, applied as early as the Vienna Anonymous MS, is not likely to be easily displaced from popular usage. The * ***Hephaisteíon**, as it should rightly be called, is the most complete example remaining of a Doric hexastyle temple. Archaeological and stylistic grounds alike support the foundation date of 449 BC suggested by Prof. Dinsmoor. It thus opens the great period of reconstruction following the Persian peace.

The temple was mistaken in the Middle Ages, on the evidence of its metopes, for the heroön erected by Kimon c 475 BC to receive the bones of Theseus recovered from Skyros. Excavation has shown that the Hephaisteion stands appropriately amid foundries and metalworkers' shops; sherds have fixed its dates within narrow limits; and its position is unequivocally located by Pausanias. The true Theseion, which ancient sources locate on the Acropolis N slope, has not yet been found.

The temple, adapted to Christian use probably in the 7C with the addition of an apse, was further modified c 1300, when it became the *Church of Ay. Yeoryios*, by the construction of a concrete interior vault. A later apse survived till 1835, though in Turkish times the liturgy was celebrated here only once a year, hence its late nickname ἀκαμάτης (the idler). The last services held in it were a Te Deum to celebrate King Otho's arrival in the newly founded capital on 13 Dec 1834, and a centenary Te Deum in 1934. The surroundings of the building were explored in 1936–37 and the cella and peristyle excavated in 1939.

The temple consists of a cella, with pronaos and opisthodomos, both distyle in antis, surrounded by a peristyle of 34 columns (6 by 13). Except for the lowest step of poros it is built entirely of marble, the structure in Pentelic, the sculptured members in Parian. The EXTERIOR lacks only the roof and, save for the sculpture, is excellently preserved. The columns are slighter than those of the Parthenon, though the entablature is heavier; the same optical refinements are incorporated. The pronaos (to the E) is arranged unusually with the antae in line with the third columns of the peristyle; the E pteroma is given special emphasis by the sculptural arrangement. The ten *Metopes* of the E front depict nine of the twelve Labours of Herakles: those omitted are the Augean Stables, the Stymphalian Birds, and the Cretan Bull. The metopes above the E pteroma, four on each flank, show eight exploits of Theseus; the remainder are blank.

The subject of the W pediment may have been a Centauromachia. That of the E pediment is not known; in the lower colonnade of the Stoa of Attalos are displayed fragments attributed to this pediment and conjecturally restored as the Apotheosis of Herakles.

INTERIOR. The EAST PTEROMA is still covered by its coffered ceiling. Its importance is emphasised within as without by its sculpture, here an Ionic *Frieze* of heroic combat which extends beyond the antae to bridge the ambulatory and return above the columns of the peristyle. Since the E wall was removed and the columns of the *Pronaos* re-erected in 1936–37, the CELLA, with its barrel vault, strikes an uneasy balance between its pagan origin and its dedication to St George. Its proportions were altered during construction, probably under the influence of Iktinos, and a surface treated to take plaster begun inside, presumably in preparation for frescoes, was never completed. The composition of the interior colonnade is still a matter of scholarly controversy. The walls bear sepulchral slabs dating from 896 to 1103, parts of a 'Stone Chronicle' listing events in 1555–1800, graffiti of British visitors (1675), and memorials to others who died in Greece in the 17–19C, when the building seems to have been used as a Protestant cemetery. That of George Watson (d 1810) bears a defaced Latin epitaph by Byron. The marble floor was ruined in the Middle Ages when graves were dug through it. Two blocks of Eleusinian limestone, which bore the cult statues by Alkamenes erected c 420, were recovered from the E wall in 1936 and restored to position; the clay moulds, perhaps used to cast the statues themselves, came to light

ACADEMY

ELEUSIS

Outer Kerameikos

V

IV

III

Inner
Kerameikos

Panathenaic Way

II

'Theseion'

Agora

Libr
Ha

Roman
Agora
Eleusinion

I

Hill of the
Nymphs

Areopagus

Diogene

Themistocles
(early 5th cent. BC)

XV

Pnyx

AD 267
Valerian

AD 267, 260

Acro

Diateichisma
(before 306 BC)

XIV

South Long Wall

Mon. of Herodes

Mouseion

XIII

ANCIENT ATHENS

0 _____ 500 metres

I	Demian Gate
II	Peiraic Gate
III	Sacred Gate
IV	Dipylon Gate
V	Eriai Gate
VI	Acharnian Gate
VII	N.E. Gate
VIII	Diochares Gate
IX	Hippades Gate
X	Diomeian Gate
XI	Itonian Gate
XII	Halade Gate
XIII	South Gate
XIV	Dipylon above the Gates
XV	Melitides Gate

VII

Garden of Theophrastos

VIII

Lyceum

Hadrian (2nd cent. AD)

Gymnasium

Arch of Hadrian

IX

Olympieion

X

Stadium

Tomb of Herodes

ILISSOS

XI

Metroon in Agrai

Artemis Agrotera

Temple of Tyche

Poseidon Helikonios

Kynosarges Gymnasium

Classical ■
Roman ▨

after J. Travlos 1970

9m from the temple.

In the 3C BC–1C AD a formal garden, planted in sunken flower-pots, bordered
the S, W, and N sides of the temple. It has been replanted as far as knowledge
permits with plants known to have been there in antiquity (e.g. pomegranate and
myrtle).—To the N are scanty remains of a large Hellenistic building conjectured
to be the *State Arsenal*.

The **'AGORÁ** (Ἀγορὰ = assembly), or *Kerameikos Agora*, was the ass-
embly-place *par excellence* where the citizens of Athens met daily in
the open air for all purposes of community life. In early days the scene
of athletic displays and dramatic competitions, it became the recognised venue for the transaction of business or the discussion of philosophy. In its small compass traders rubbed shoulders with administrators in the shadow of buildings and an ever-increasing number of
monuments bearing witness to their past achievements. St. Paul disputed in the Agora daily with those who met with him (Acts xvii, 17).

Athens, Agora. Reconstruction of area in 2C AD

History. The site, which has been occupied since the Protogeometric period,
developed slowly in the 6C BC as the main square of the city, probably in succession to a site nearer the entrance to the Acropolis. The earliest Council house
is known to date from the time of Solon, and the Peisistratid tyrants laid on a
water supply. A great drain was built in the time of Kleisthenes, whose constitutional reforms necessitated much reconstruction, most of it swept away in the
Persian sack of 480 BC. The new agora seems to have been well in hand before
Pericles' time, since Kimon is known to have embellished it with plane trees. A
large addition made by Lycurgus to the E side of the square was removed in the
time of Attalos, king of Pergamon (159–138 BC), when the agora was replanned
in the more formal style in vogue in Asia Minor. Stoas bounded it on the E and S.
The agora seems to have survived Sulla's sack in 86 BC and, with the addition to
the centre in the reign of Augustus of an Odeion and a temple, retained its

identity with minor changes until the Herulian raid of AD 267 laid it waste. For the next century and a half the site outside the new fortification, the mis-named Valerian wall, which was largely built of stones from the shattered agora. When the old outer walls were re-established in the 5C part of the site was occupied by a large gymnasium which went out of use in the 6C (possibly to be identified with the University closed down in 529). Abandoned until the 10C, the area was covered by successive dwellings throughout Byzantine, Frankish, and Turkish times, its only public monument of this period being the little church that survives.

Ancient Institutions. The people of Attica belonged to four phylae (tribes), or clans, whose identity survived the union under Athens, while their territory comprised three districts known as the Plain (Pediake), the Coast (Paralia), and the Hill (Diakria). The population was early divided also into three classes, *Eupatridai*, or nobles; *Georgoi* and *Agroikoi*, or farmers (of hill and plain); and *Demiourgoi*, or artisans, all of whom were ipso facto equal members of the *Ekklesia*, or Assembly. The arabic land held by free men was immemorially inalienable from their family or clan. A fourth class of freemen without civic rights, known as *Hektemoroi*, included agricultural labourers. At an early date, possibly about the time of the Dorian invasion, the kings of Athens had been overthrown by the Medontid family, who held the hereditary office of *Archon* (regent) for life. Power gradually passed to the *Areopagus*, or Council of Nobles, who supervised the three executive archons elected by the Assembly: the *Basileus*, the *Polemarch*, and the *Eponymos*, whose functions were, broadly speaking, respectively religious, military, and civil. The Archon Eponymos was chief magistrate and nominal head of the polis, or city-state, and after these offices were restricted in 683 BC to yearly tenure gave his name to the year. On relinquishing office Archons automatically became life members of the Areo-pagus. Later their number was increased to nine by the addition of six recording judges (*Thesmothetai*). The aristocracy monopolised political office though after Kylon's unsuccessful attempt to usurp power and the consequent war with Me-gara, popular discontent extorted Draco's legal code in 621 BC. The harsh law of property that allowed a debtor's person to be taken in pledge still reduced many peasants to slavery, but a Court of Appeal of 51 judges (*Ephetai*) was instituted to deal with cases of bloodshed.

Athens, Agora. Reconstruction of Classical prison

after J. Travlos with permission of the American School of Classical Studies, Athens.

THE AGORA

0 ————————— 50metres

N

3

4

RAILWAY

Altar of Ares

Tyrannicides

7

'Giants'

Gymnasium

Odeion

Rotunda

Bema

Donor's Mont.

Stoa

of

Attalos

8

12

Gate

dle

Stoa

11

Gymnasium

Drain

East Stoa

Tower

Mill

Library of Pantainos

Valerian Wall

South Stoa

15

1st South Stoa

Nymphaion

Fountain House

Mint.

Towards the end of the century new classes (the *Timocracy*) were emerging, founded on wealth gained in commerce or agriculture, and a new division of the people, based on landed property qualification, was made. The highest class was now the *Pentakosiomedimnoi* (those whose income was equivalent to 500 medimni of corn); next came the *Hippeis* or Knights (300–500 medimni) from whose ranks came wartime cavalry; and below them the *Zeugitai* or Yeomen (those with a pair of oxen) who in war became Hoplites, or infantrymen. The fourth estate of peasants and artisans (*Thetes*) were excluded from the Assembly but paid no taxes. In war they became oarsmen and marines.

Solon, who became Archon Eponymos in 594 BC, promulgated the Seisachtheia, cancelling all debts involving the person of the debtor. He retained the classes of the Timocracy, limited election to archonship to the highest class, but enfranchised the Thetes. He increased the judicial dignity of the Areopagus while transferring its deliberative functions to the Assembly, and created a new Council of Four Hundred (*Boule*), upon which devolved in effect the transaction of the business of the Assembly. The Thetes were excluded from the Boule. Popular tribunals (*Heliaia* or Heliasts) were enrolled by lot so that justice should be impartial to rich and poor alike. Magistrates were made answerable at the end of their term of office to the Heliaia. Despite Solon's reforms party strife between the clans (including the returned Alkmaeonids) caused thirty years of anarchy, which ended in the constitutional tyranny of the polemarch Peisistratos. Under his benevolent dictatorship the reforms of democracy were preserved, and Herodotus (1, 59) acknowledges that he 'administered the state according to the established usage and his arrangements were wise and salutary'.

After the overthrow of his more despotic son, Hippias, the Alkmaeonid Kleisthenes (c 508 BC) reorganised the tribes. Finding Attica composed of c 170 *Demes* or parishes, he altered their traditional division into three *Districts*: the City (Αστυ), the Coast (Παραλία), and the Inland (Μεσογεία), and to stamp out their old regional rivalries, he regrouped the inhabitants. In each of the Districts the Demes were divided into ten *Trittyes*; three trittyes, one from each district, went to form a new tribe, named after a hero, thus forming ten new *Tribes* independent of old clannish loyalties. The old Council of 400 became a *Council of 500* composed of 50 deputies from each tribe, elected annually by lot. The deputies of each tribe held office in rotation for about five weeks in the year as *Prytaneis*, or Presidents. They chose one of their number by lot as *Epistates* (Chief President), who with nine *Proedroi* as assistants, and a *Grammateús* (secretary), not of their body, formed the *Prytaneia*, or Presidential Committee. The Prytaneis presided also over the meetings of the Ekklesia, which was the ultimate authority without whose sanction no bill could be passed into law. By the institution of *Ostracism*, a ten years' banishment without loss of rights (used between 487 and 417) the duty of guarding the state against the plots of potential tyrants was transferred from the Areopagus to the sovereign people. Philochoros tells how in such cases 'the Agora was fenced with boards, ten entrances being left, through which the citizens entered by tribes to cast their votes; the nine archons and the Boule presided'. The classes of the Timocracy were retained; below the rank of citizen were the Metics (Μέτοικοι), or resident aliens, and slaves.

In 487 BC the power of the nine archons was reduced by the institution of their election by lot. Before this date the Polemarch had acted as Commander-in-Chief, assisted by the ten military generals; henceforward the *Ten Generals* (Strategoi), elected every year óne for each tribe, became not only the supreme commanders of the army and navy (one or more being named by the Assembly to lead each expedition), but were also the dominant magistrates in the political field. Pericles was elected general every year from 443 till his death in 429 and to this fact he owed his unique position. To Pericles and his elder contemporary Ephialtes is due the completion of Athenian democracy. Nearly all the powers of the Areopagus were transferred to the Assembly. The archonship, no longer confined to the two higher classes, became a paid office, having little political power and pay was also introduced for the Council and the Jurymen. By the time of the Peloponnesian War all property ceased to be entailed.

We descend a path towards the SW corner of the excavated area. Near the junction of the two branches of the great drain (see below) stands the **Hóros** (Pl. 10), or *Boundary Stone*, inscribed in Attic characters of the 5C BC with the legend 'I am the boundary stone of the Agora'. This was necessary because the square was a sacred precinct from which certain classes of convicted persons were barred; citizens entering it performed a purificatory rite. At a higher level immediately to the S is the stump of a marble pedestal of the 1C AD, which probably supported a *Perirrhanterion* or holy-water stoup.

The boundary stone is set against a contemporary wall belonging to a row of dwellings or shops. The discovery here of hobnails and of a black glazed cup dating to the third quarter of the 5C BC and bearing the name of its owner, Simon, makes it likely that here really was the *Shop of the Cobbler Simon*, where, according to Diogenes Lærtius, Socrates spent much of his time.

The WEST SIDE of the agora was flanked by a group of public buildings. The circular foundations of the **Thólos** (Pl. 5), discovered in 1934 much farther N than had been expected, provided the first certain fixed point for the topography of the Agora. Built c 465 BC, this is the 'Prytanikon', also known from its roof as the *Skias*, or parasol, where, as Aristotle records, the fifty Prytaneis dined daily at the public expense and offered sacrifice before their deliberations. Here their chairman (epistates) and the third of his colleagues who were on duty also slept (Aristotle, 'Constitution of Athens', 44) and the building became the effective headquarters of Athenian government. A set of standard weights and measures were kept here; they are now in the museum.

A porch was added to the original rotunda at the time of Augustus. The six columns that supported the roof (three stumps *in situ*) were cut down during the reign of Hadrian when a single-span roof was substituted. At the same time the floor of mosaic chips (1C AD), part of which remains uncovered, was overlaid by marble slabs. The original clay floor is 45cm below the surface, and, save for a few blocks of poros, the visible outer wall is a restoration. Fragments remain to the N of a small room that served as a kitchen.

The foundations of the **New Bouleutérion** (Pl. 5), or Council House, lie to the NW on a platform cut back into the hill of Kolonos. Here the Boule met under the Prytaneis to prepare legislation for the Assembly. The building apparently replaced its predecessor at the end of the 5C BC. A formal S Portico was added by Lycurgus, together with an Ionic *Propylon* facing the agora, the two being connected by a passage along the S front of the old Bouleuterion. The *Old Bouleuterion*, a square building erected for the Council of 500 soon after its inception by Kleisthenes, replaced a still earlier edifice of the time of Solon. When the council moved to its new chamber, the old building was used to store official documents. Parallel with its N side was a small archaic *Temple* which was destroyed by the Persians. This is presumed to have been dedicated to the Mother of the Gods, since her worship seems to have survived on this spot until, in the late 2C BC, a **Metróön** (Pl. 6), consisting of four rooms with a colonnade fronting the square, was built on the site. This had the dual function of *Sanctuary* of the Mother of the Gods (2nd room from the S) and *Repository of State Archives*, which seems, like the library at Pergamon, to have had quarters (N end) for a superintendent. The mosaic pavement in the third room from the S dates from a transformation in the 5C AD.

In front of the Metroön is a row of foundations for monuments. At its NE corner are monument bases carelessly made up in Christian times of reused material. Here has been re-erected a headless *Statue of Hadrian* (AD 117–138) found in the great drain. It is identified by the decoration of the corselet, which bears a crowned Athena standing upon the wolf suckling Romulus and Remus, a symbol of the captive taking the captor captive. The statue is probably contemporary with the emperor.

The *Great Drain of Kleisthenes*, aligned with the Old Bouleuterion, and beautifully constructed of polygonal blocks of limestone, channelled the waters from the hills on the SW towards the Eridanos brook to the

ANCIENT ATHENS (Centre)

0 — 100 metres

Hadrian's Library

Stoa of Attalos

Stoa Poikile

▶ Agora ◀

'Theseion'

◀—N—

Acropolis

Wall of Valerian

THEORIAS

Areopagus

Dörpfeld's excavations

LEOF: APOSTOLOU PAVLOU

after J. Travlos with permission of the American School of Classical Studies, Athens.

N. The two branches that flow into it near the boundary stone were dug in the 4C BC or later. Beyond the drain, remains of a fenced enclosure round a long base locate the *Monument (or Peribolos) of the Eponymous Heroes*. The 4C base, on which stood statues of the ten legendary heroes chosen for Kleisthenes by the Delphic oracle as 'founders' of his ten tribes, was several times extended after 307 BC as additional 'tribes' were created. It bore also two tripods. The sides of the plinth were used as a notice-board for official announcements and for proposed new legislation (comp. Demosthenes, XXIV, 23).

A little to the E again is an *Altar* (? *Zeus Agoraios*), of 4C workmanship, known by the identifying letters of its parts to have been moved in the mid-1C, presumably from the Pnyx, where a cutting of exactly similar size has been located.

*Athens, Agora. Monument of the Eponymous Heroes.
Reconstruction*

The gap below the Hephaisteion was never completely closed by buildings. Before the Metroön was built, four rows of stone slabs, of which blocks remain, extended N from the Bouleuterion, serving perhaps as a *synedrion* (meeting-place). In early Imperial times a grandiose stairway was erected as an approach to the Hephaisteion.

Beyond the gap stood the *Temple of Apollo Patroös* (Pl. 6), a small structure, tetrastyle in antis, of c 330 BC, with conglomerate foundations and walls in the late polygonal style. The two Omphaloi may have stood beneath its porch. The statue of Apollo by Euphranor, that stood within, is probably that found in 1907 and now in the Stoa of Attalos.

Apollo 'Patroös', that is the father of Ion, was specially worshipped by the Athenians who counted themselves of Ionian descent. He was patron deity of state administration; before him magistrates were sworn and citizens registered. A 6C temple on the site was destroyed by the Persians and apparently left derelict in accordance with the Plataean oath for more than a century.

Adjoining are the remains of a slightly earlier cella, identified from the inscription on the altar with the *Temple of Zeus Phratrios and Athena Phratria*, the deities of the ancestral religious brotherhoods, or phratries. The foundations at the E end supported a porch added to the 4C cella in the mid-2C BC.

To the N the poros foundations of the **Stoa of Zeus Eleuthérios** extend to the railway, the cutting of which destroyed the N wing. The portico, which had two projecting wings, was built by unknown architects c 430 BC to honour Zeus as saviour of the Athenians from the Persians. Externally of the Doric order, with marble acroteria on the gables of the wings (flying Nike in the museum), the building had Ionic columns within. It was decorated, according to Pausanias, with paintings by Euphranor. Under its colonnade citizens transacted their private business. Socrates is known to have discussed philosophy here with his friends. An annexe was added behind in the 1C AD.

The piled marble fragments in front mark the site of superposed altars of the 6C and (?) 3C BC.

The whole of the NORTH SIDE OF THE AGORA, lying beyond the railway, is to be laid bare, but will only gradually become accessible to the public. At its NW angle the *Dromos* (comp. Rte 4), or Panathenaic Way, entered from the Dipylon. The street between the gate and the Agora was lined with porticoes fronted by bronze statues of the famous. Here we may imagine the popular and crowded markets of the day, the money-changers, barbers' shops, and bustle of the most commercial part of the city (comp. Lysias, XXIV, 20; Theophrastos, 'Characters'). Here also lay the *House of Pulytion*, where Alcibiades played the hierophant in the parody of the Eleusinian mysteries (Plut., 'Alcibiades' XIX) before the mutilation of the herms (see below). Between the Pompeion and the Stoa of Zeus lay the *Sanctuary of Demeter, Kore, and Iakchos* with statues of them by Praxiteles (Pausanius, I, 2, 4); a damaged monumental base, signed by Praxiteles, found built into a wall N of the railway, is in the museum.

The 1970 excavations immediately uncovered the **Stoa Basiléios**, or Royal Portico, where the Archon Basileus held his court. A clear cut identification is provided by the text of Pausanias (I, 3, 1), and the claim to have recognised in the expected spot the 'Lithos'—'*the* Stone' par excellence—on which the archons took their oath of office. A surprisingly small building, with a colonnaded façade of eight Doric columns, it can be dated c 500 BC, perhaps rebuilt on the original lines after the Persian sack of 480 BC. It survived with alterations until AD 400. Two porches were added in the late-5C probably expressly to house the revised statutes of Solon and of Draco. Here occasionally the Council of the Areopagus met—perhaps even when it heard St. Paul. A number of sockets for herms may be seen at the N end, and many herm fragments have been recovered. A base *in situ* records prizewinners in the Epilenaia, a drama festival possibly held in front of the Royal Stoa. To the E stood a small crossroads shrine of the 5C. Also in the area was the *Leokoreion* near which, while marshalling the Panathenaic procession Hipparchos was assassinated in 514 BC by Harmodios and Aristogeiton.

Of the two large groups commemorating the Tyrannicides, only a fragment from an inscribed base has been recovered. The earlier group by Antenor (c 505 BC) was carried off by the Persians. A replacement was fashioned by Kritias and Nesiotes in 476 BC, and after the original had been returned from Persepolis by Alexander the Great, both groups stood together in the *Orchestra of the Agora*.

This early open circle designed for ritual dancing was thus closely related both to the Royal Stoa and the assassination spot, but its exact location is uncertain.

Between the Stoa Basileios and the Stoa Poikile (see below) stood a row of *Herms*, celebrating with epigrams Kimon's great victories over the Persians. On the eve of the Sicilian expedition (415 BC) the Athenians were profoundly shocked by the wholesale mutilation of these figures (Thuc. VI, 27–61), and they believed that the outrage was a prelude to an attempt on the constitution. Alcibiades was charged with being the ringleader, recalled from Sicily, and (in his absence) sentenced to death. About 40 fragments listing his personal possessions, confiscated by the state and sold at public auction, have been recovered from the Eleusinion. An inscription naming a 'Stoa of the Herms' was unearthed in 1962.

Excavations (visible from street) in 1980–82, beneath a demolished building on the N side of Od. Adhrianoú, uncovered the W end of the **Stóa Poíkile**, or painted portico, founded c 460 BC by Peisianax (Kimon's brother-in-law), after whom it was sometimes called. Here Zeno taught his disciples, who thus acquire the name Stoics. The building was decorated with battle scenes (Marathon, Troy, etc.), painted by the leading artists of the 5C BC, including Polygnotos, Mikon, and Panainos, brother of Pheidias. Their work was probably executed on wooden plaques; some blocks fitted with iron spikes (now in the museum) are believed to be from the wall against which they were fixed. The paintings, seen by Pausanias, had disappeared before AD 402. In this stoa were also displayed bronze shields captured from the Spartans at Sphakteria in 425 BC, a fine example of which is displayed in the museum.

The stoa (12·4m deep) is in the Doric order, with Ionic columns in the interior. To the W, partially over the steps of the building, are massive square piers, probably the supports of the gate on which Pausanias saw a trophy set up by the Athenian cavalry to celebrate a victory over the Macedonian Pleistarchos in 303/2 BC.

Further W lie the remains of a handsome altar of island marble, built c 500 BC and repaired in the second half of the 5C. From Pausanias' account, it should be part of the sanctuary of *Aphrodite Ourania*.

Immediately E of the Altar of Zeus is a late-Roman building, a rectangular structure of unknown purpose on massive concrete foundations. Its NE angle lies over the **Períbolos of the Twelve Gods** (Pl. 3), much of which is obscured by the·railway, but which has been investigated and firmly identified by an inscription found *in situ*. The *Altar*, was set up by Peisistratos the Younger in 521 BC within a fenced enclosure. Situated in the open section of the Agora bordering the Panathenaic Way, it was the 'London Stone' of Athens whence road distances were measured. A recognised place of sanctuary, it may possibly be the '*Altar of Pity*' seen by Pausanias.

The Twelve were not synonymous with the twelve Olympian gods but represent a local Athenian grouping.—Remains of a 6C Eschara, or ground altar, to the S may mark the *Altar of Aiakos*, mentioned by Herodotus (V, 89).

The site of the TEMPLE OF ARES (Pl. 6) has been marked in gravel. Some architectural fragments have been arranged at its W extremity and foundation blocks are visible at the E end. These bear Roman masons' marks showing that the temple, which markedly resembled the Hephaisteion and is ascribed to the same architect, was removed to this site in the Augustan period possibly from Acharnai. Foundations of a large altar can be seen to the E.

To the S the construction known to 19C archaeologists as the '*Stoa of the Giants*' marks the N limit of two huge interrelated structures, the

Agrippeíon (Pl. 7), or *Odeion of Agrippa*, and a much later *Gymnasium*.

The site may perhaps be equated with the *Perischoinisma*, where some public functions (ostracism, etc.) continued until c 15 BC, when an *Odeion*, or concert-hall, was endowed by M. Vipsanius Agrippa, son-in-law of the Emperor Augustus, on the site. Shortly after Pausanias saw it in this form, its roof collapsed, but in the reign of Antoninus Pius (c AD 150) it was rebuilt on a smaller scale, probably as a lecture-hall. This was consumed by fire in the Herulian sack of 267 and much of the masonry used in the 'Valerian' wall. About AD 400 a vast *Gymnasium* rose on the site extending well to the S; this was perhaps the principal seat of the university until its closure in 529.

The ODEION, which was roofed by a single span c 24·5m wide, was surrounded on three sides by a two-storeyed portico and entered from the stoa to the S. Traces can be seen of the lower storey. Of the *Auditorium*, which seated c 1000 people, only a few marble seats are preserved, together with some of the polychrome paving of the *Orchestra* floor. The remains of the *Skene* have been buttressed with modern walling. The position of the façade of the Antonine rebuilding is marked by two seated figures (?philosophers) which formed part of its sculptural ornament. The '*Giants*', two of which are in fact Tritons, were reused in the façade of the 5C GYMNASIUM. Copied from figures on the Parthenon pediments, they also belonged originally to the second Odeion, where (being then six in number) they supported the architrave of the remodelled N façade. The great *Rectangular Court*, behind the gymnasium's façade, can be traced by its rough wall.

To the S, reached by a rectangular lobby and a semicircular corridor, is a *Square Court*, with a *Bath-House* on the W, and on the E a third *Small Court*, surrounded by well-preserved rooms, which may have served as the administrative offices of the university. The whole of this S complex lies athwart earlier stoas (see below) now believed to have fulfilled the same function.

We cross the PANATHENAIC WAY, here marked by its stone water channel and lined with bases of unidentified monuments. The processional road crossed diagonally in front of the Stoa of Attalos, where it had a gravel surface, passed in front of the Library of Pantainos (see below), where in later times it was paved, and climbed the slope of the Acropolis on a ramp.

The E side of the agora is closed by the *Stoa of Attalos (Pl. 12), dedicated as the **Agora Museum** by King Paul in 1956. Erected by Attalos II, king of Pergamon (159–138 BC), as the inscription (recovered in 1861) on the architrave records, it was used for promenades, for watching the Panathenaic Procession and events in the Agora, and for retail trade, and is mentioned by Athenaeus alone of classical writers. Pausanias ignores it. The stoa was sacked in AD 267, but the ruins were incorporated in the Valerian wall so that the N end survived throughout the ages to roof height, and sufficient of its plan and members were recovered to make an accurate restoration possible. The building was reconstructed on its old foundations in 1953–56 with materials from the same sources as those originally used, the expense being defrayed by private donors in the United States. The façade is of Pentelic marble, the remainder of creamy limestone from an ancient quarry in Piraeus.

Excavations beneath the foundations uncovered graves of the Mycenaean and Protogeometric periods and later wells. The earliest building on the site (late 5C BC), consisting of an irregular court surrounded by small rooms, was found to contain bronze voting discs for jurors. It is conjectured to have been the *Parabyston*, or Court of the Eleven, a petty sessions court for offenders taken in flagrante delicto. This was superseded as part of the Lycurgan improvements by an edifice c 59·5m sq., which probably served the same function. The Stoa of Attalos survived in part from late-Roman to Turkish times incorporated in a rampart, its rooms being filled with rubble. An oblong tower was built at the N end, another in the middle of the building. At the SW corner stood a gate, the N tower of which was converted into the chapel of *Panayia Pyrgiotissa* (Our Lady of the Tower), now demolished.

The stoa, a two-storeyed building 116·4m long and 20m wide, has a colonnade of 45 columns, Doric below, double Ionic above, closed by a low balustrade. Within, the portico is divided lengthwise into two aisles by a row of 22 columns, Ionic on the ground floor, Pergamene above. Twenty-one rectangular chambers designed as shops opened from the back of the portico on each floor; each had a door opening on to the inner aisle and a loophole in the back wall. The arrangement has been modified in the reconstruction. The exterior staircase at the N end has been restored as originally planned; below it an exedra with a marble bench is entered through an arched opening (the earliest known use of a visible arch in an Athenian building). The S end follows the alterations that were made at the end of the 1C AD (comp. below). In front of the centre of the stoa are a *Bema* and the base of the *Donor's Monument*, more than 100 blocks of which have been recovered from the dismantled Valerian wall. It resembled the monument of Agrippa on the Acropolis and bore, about the level of the second storey of the stoa, a bronze quadriga. It was later re-dedicated to the Emperor Tiberius. Other statues stood against the terrace wall to the N.

The ancient design has been somewhat modified internally to house c 180,000 finds from the Agora excavations; the vast majority of these form study collections (available to specialists on application) on the upper floor and in the basement, where there is a unique library of 7,500 documents on stone.

The GROUND FLOOR contains a selection of the most notable pieces of the collection. Beneath the portico is displayed **Marble *Sculpture**. AT THE S END: S 2154, Apollo Citharoedos (350–325 BC), conjecturally the cult statue of Apollo Patroös by Euphranor. I 4165, Base for statues of Demeter and Kore; note signature of Praxiteles; the monument was dedicated by Kleiokrateia, daughter of Polyeuktos the Teithrasian (the 41st oration of Demosthenes concerns a lawsuit about Polyeuktos's estate).—ALONG THE WALL: S 2038–39 & I 6628, The Iliad and Odyssey personified and inscribed base for the first, group of the 2C AD, signed by Jason the Athenian on one of the long lower lappets of the Iliad's cuirass. Odeion stage front restored (model). S 1882, Aphrodite (c 420 BC). S 182, 'Nereid' acroterion (c 400 BC). I 7154, Cave of Pan relief, inscribed (c 320 BC). S 429, Acroterion group of Hephaisteion (c 415 BC), flanked by fragments attrib. to the E pediment of the temple. S 1232, Torso of Athena (5C BC). I 7167, Rider relief (early 4C BC), commemorating victory won by the tribe Leontis in the anthippasia, the cavalry contest of the Panathenaic Games. S 676, 679, 870, 1072, Reliefs from the Ares temple frieze (c 420 BC). S 654, Torso of Athena (second half 5C BC).—AT THE N END: S 657, Portrait statue of a magistrate (end 5C AD). This elaborate but lifeless piece may be compared with S 312, the Nike acroterion from the SE corner of the Stoa of Zeus Eleutherios (c 400 BC), a vivid flamboyant figure with drapery billowing in the wind.—ALONG THE INNER COLONNADE: IG 112 3781, Base of a statue of Karneades, founder of the new Athenian Academy, under whom the dedicators of the statue, the future Attalos II and Ariarathes V, king of Cappadocia, studied as princes. S 270, Roman copy of portrait of Herodotus. S 1654 Nymph with water jar, copy of a famous 5C statue of Aphrodite. S 2354, Head of goddess, faithful replica of a classical original, extraordinarily close to the Nike of Paionios. S 2094, Head of goddess (c 430 BC), by an Attic sculptor of the first rank. *I 6524, Stele inscribed with a law of 336 BC against tyranny (the relief represents Democracy crowning the Demos of Athens).

The *EXHIBITION GALLERY, occupying the length of ten shops, is arranged chronologically and demonstrates the almost unbroken occupation of the site from Neolithic to Turkish times. Representative pottery of all periods is attractively displayed. Case 1. Neolithic vases found in wells on the N slope of the Acropolis, the earliest evidence of habitation (note the red polished jar of the 4th millennium BC). Objects from royal chamber-tombs of the 14C BC on the N slope of the Areopagus: Case 4 (right) Mycenaean bronze sword; Case 5 (left), BI 511, Ivory *Toilet-box carved with griffins bringing down stags. Burials of various periods, urn, grave, and pithos. Cases 13–18. Pottery of the Geometric period from burials and sacrificial pyres (model chariot, child's boots, etc.). Contents of the grave of a rich Athenian lady of c 850 BC. Case 23 (right) Earthen mould for casting a bronze statue of Apollo (6C BC). Heads of Herms. On the right are three inscriptions: I 2729. Rules of the library of Pantainos; I 4809. Dues owed to Athens in 421 BC by the tributary cities of the Hellespont; I 4120. List of 6C Eponymous Archons, including the names of Hippias, Kleisthenes, and Miltiades for successive years (525–523 BC). I 3872. Fragment of a base belonging to the second group of Tyrannicides. *P 1231. Kneeling boy, terracotta oil flask in the form of an athlete binding his hair with the victor's fillet (540–530 BC). To the left (Cases 26–28) standard weights and measures; objects from a court of justice: Bronze voting discs (comp. above); klepsydra, or water clock, in terracotta (5C BC), designed to measure the time allowed for pleadings (comp. Aristotle, 'Constitution of Athens'); I 3967. Part of a kleroterion for selection by lot using numbered balls.

There follow cases (30–32) of choice black-and red-figured *Vases, attributed to particular vase-painters and potters: P 12628. Alabastron, by *Amasis* (mid-6C); P 24114, P 24110. Two cups assigned to *Epiktetos*. Cups: P 1272. Youth jumping using halteres; P 1273. Youth reclining: P 1274. Youth playing the game of cottabus. P 23165, P 24102, P 24116, P 24115. Four cups attributed to *Chairas* (c 500 BC); P 24113. Kylix signed by *Gorgos* (c 510 BC; possibly providing the real name of the Berlin Painter?), depicting Achilles and Memnon the Ethiopian in combat; P 24131. Kylix by *Epiktetos*; Calyx-krater (by *Exekias*, c 530 BC), the earliest known example of this form, found in a well on the N slope of the Acropolis; the paintings show the introduction of Herakles to Olympos and Greeks and Trojans fighting for the body of Patroclus.

*B 30, Bronze Nike head of 430 BC. The head was originally plated with sheets of gold over silver, which must have been hammered on to the modelled surface of the bronze. Edges of the sheets were bent down in the channels and securely keyed by a packing of solid gold. This may still be seen behind each ear and at the back of the neck.

To the left, B 262. Huge bronze shield, captured by the Athenians from the Spartans at Sphakteria (Pylos), 425 BC, crudely inscribed ΑΘΗΝΑΙΟΙ ΑΠΟ ΛΑΚΕΔΑΙΜΟΝΙΩΝ ΕΚ ΠΥΛΟ. Child's commode (or 'potty') in terracotta (early 6C BC). Case 38 contains Ostraka (sherds used in secret ballots by citizens recommending banishment) of 487–417 BC with the names of Aristides the Just, Themistocles, Kimon, and Pericles as candidates for ostracism. Case 39. Household grills and ovens in terracotta. Case 42. A few of the 75,000 coins (mainly 6C BC to 6C AD) found in the Agora, including four in gold (Persian Daric, 465–425 BC; Alexander the Great, 336–323 BC; Silvestro Valiero, 1694–1700; and Napoleon III, 1854). BI 236. Statuette in ivory, reconstituted from fragments; this is a replica (2C AD) of the Apollo Lykeios of Praxiteles. Among the sculptural fragments to the left is (S 922) a miniature copy of the cult image of the Mother of the Gods by Agorakritos.

The far end of the museum is devoted to Hellenistic pottery, Roman terracottas, including a toy animal on wheels, lamps from the 7C BC illustrating a return after 14 centuries of evolution to the crude design of the original, Roman portrait busts; Byzantine and Venetian ceramics (portrait of a Doge). *S 221. Young Satyr in marble, a copy of the 2C AD of a Hellenistic prototype. Mosaic pavement from a house of the 5C AD.

The *Rotunda*, or Monopteros, in front of the N part of the Stoa may have been an ornamental fountain. The green marble columns probably supported a brick dome.

To the S of the Stoa of Attalos, the misnamed **'Valerian' Wall** (Pl, p. 103) is a Roman fortification built with stone from buildings partially destroyed in the Herulian sack of AD 267 (when the Emperor Valerian was already dead). An inscription attributes it to Claudius Illyrius. The large tower at the N end of the standing curtain was one of two forming a gate. The wall, which has now been largely dismantled in order to recover the precious earlier inscriptions incorporated in it, followed the line of the façade of the destroyed **Library of Pantainos**, erected before AD 102 at the expense of Titus Flavius Pantainos, who dedicated it to Athena Polias and the Emperor Trajan (inscription from the lintel of the main door exposed). A portico of nine Ionic columns faced the road (graffiti suggest youthful readers) and gave on to rooms grouped round a peristyle; the principle rooms lay to the E.

Between the library and the stoa a street led E towards the Roman market through an *Arch* provided with a small fountain. The construction of this right-of-way necessitated modifications to the S end of the Stoa of Attalos.—Remains of a *Water-Mill* of the 5–6C AD and of its well-built conduit can be traced on the outer side of the Valerian wall.

At the SE corner of the Agora a temple was erected in Augustan times from materials brought from a Doric building at Thorikos. Its hexastyle porch was cleared in 1959.

Beyond the fenced enclosure the *Panathenaic Way* continues upward, showing well-preserved paving of the 2C AD. The site of the *Eleusinion*, about half-way up on the E side, has been identified by the discovery of reliefs, inscriptions, and cult pottery (kernoi) relating to the worship of Demeter and Kore.

Near the SE gate is the pretty **Church of the Holy Apostles** (Pl. 16), stripped in 1954–57 of 19C additions and restored by the American School to its form of c 1020. Within the narthex are 17C wall-paintings from the demolished church of St Spiridon. Of the four Roman columns that supported the dome, one of the originals remains; the other three are copies.

Beneath and to the E of the church are the remains of a *Nymphaion*, a fountain-house with a semicircular outer wall, similar to that at Olympia built by Herodes Atticus. Its construction necessitated the demolition of the N half of a building dated to c 400 BC, identified with the *Argyrokopeion*, the mint of Athens, whence may have come the famous 'Owls' that became the accepted coinage of the Eastern Mediterranean for 200 years, though only bronze coins have so far been found. To the N, bordering the modern road (which retains a course from the Bronze Age), are remains of a *Fountain-House* (the Enneakrounos of Pausanias), probably erected by Peisistratos. This road ran along the back of the *First South Stoa*, which, from the 5C to the 2C BC, dominated the S side of the Agora, probably as administrative offices. At its W end the ground plan has been recovered of a large structure which survived, with alterations, from the mid-6C BC to the sack of Sulla. This is tentatively identified as the *Heliaia*. In the 4C BC the building had a *Water Clock* attached to its N side, which probably told the time by means of a float on a column of water. Another *Fountain-House* stands to the SW.

In the 2C BC the S side of the Agora was entirely remodelled. This was achieved by constructing the MIDDLE STOA (Pl. 11) a portico open on both sides and divided lengthwise by a screen wall. Over 137m long, it was the largest edifice of the Agora, extending from the Panathenaic Way to the Tholos, in front of which it was raised on a high podium. The red conglomerate foundations are best seen at the W end (where the floor level is indicated) and members of the poros colonnade, which had unfluted Doric columns, will be noted at the NE corner. The N terrace of the stoa provided access to the Odeion (comp. above). In Hadrian's time a small annex of the Metroön was built against the podium opposite the Tholos. The *East Stoa* and *Second South Stoa* completed the Hellenistic project, much of which has been obscured by the Roman gymnasium.

To the W of the Middle Stoa near the Tholos are scanty remains of a large building of the 5C BC, perhaps the *Strategeion*, headquarters of the Ten Generals.

Athens, Agora. Reconstruction of dining room in South Stoa

6   Pláka

The name **Pláka** seems to be of recent origin and is unsatisfactorily derived either from the Albanian *pliaka* (old), or from a *plaque* said to have marked the crossing of its principal streets (see below). The area it describes has no official boundaries but may be said to comprise that part of the old town extending between Odhos Ermou and the N and NE slopes of the Acropolis, corresponding to the ancient deme of KYDATHENAION and including four small districts once known as *Rizokastro, Brizaki, Alikokou*, and *Anaphiotika*. In Turkish times much of this area was called *Gorgopikos* after the little cathedral. Its narrow undulating lanes have no pattern but follow the configuration of the terrain, rising in steps in the higher sector. The principal streets are Adhrianoú and Kidathenaíon, which still follow Turkish (perhaps ancient) courses. The houses, several of which have been excellently restored, date for the most part from the mid-19C and despite popular occupation often proclaim their patrician origin. Many of them are occupied by tavernas. The best time for sightseeing is in the morning.

Plateia Monastirakiou, or **Monastiráki Square** (6, *4*), opens from the S side of Odhos Ermou (Rte 4); from the Agora it may be quickly reached by following Odhos Adhrianou (right; see below) from the N exit. Here is Monastirion Stn, where the Piraeus railway is still underground. In the square stands the church of the *Pantanassa*, or Great Monastery, commonly called MONASTIRAKI because of its smallness. An aisled basilica of the 10C, with an elliptical cupola, it was badly restored in 1911.

At the SE corner, dominating the square, is the former **Mosque of Tzistarakis**, built in 1759 by the Voivode Tzistarakis, when a column of the Olympieion was sacrificed in its construction. An open loggia, approached by steps, precedes a plain square building surmounted by a heavy octagon; its minaret was razed after 1821. Used for years as a prison, it became a museum in 1918. It was reopened in 1958 under the directorship of Mme P. Zora as the *Museum of Greek Popular Art* (at present closed for restoration).

The narrow Odhos Pandróssou, which runs E towards the cathedral, masking the N wall of Hadrian's Library, is the principal relic of the Turkish *Bazar*, now occupied by antique dealers and shoemakers; the Albanian tsarouchia (scarlet boots with turned-up toes) are exposed for sale. Ifestou, the other way, runs to the original Flea Market (see Rte 4).

Beyond stands the chief surviving portion of the so-called *Stoa of Hadrian*, a vast façade of the Library of Hadrian (see below). The marble W wall had at the centre a simple propylon, standing forward of antæ and approached by six steps, the only entrance so far discovered. The left portion survives as far as the jamb of the doorway; the mosaic to the left adorned the little chapel of *Ayios Asomatos sta Skalia* that adjoined the porch until the late 19C. The porch was flanked on either side by seven unfluted columns of Karystos marble standing slightly forward of the wall and supporting on Corinthian capitals an architrave which returns over each column. The finely preserved section N of the porch remains.—Odhos Areos, lined with booths of workers in old rubber and basketry, continues towards the Acropolis.

A few paces to the left is the *Taxiarkhón* (6, *4*), or Church of the Archangels, rebuilt after a fire in 1832, which houses a much venerated ikon, the Panayia Grigorousa. Excavations in Odhos Poikilis (right) show the Roman way from the new market (see below) to the Agora; a house in this street, described by Chateaubriand as 'a splendid museum', after his reception here by Fauvel, the French consul, in 1806, is now ruinous.

To the left stands the *Gate of Athena Archegetis*, the main entrance to the Roman market (see below), set a little S of centre in the W wall. It consists of an outer Doric portico with four columns supporting an entablature and pediment, most of which is still in position. This stood just forward of the main wall, its antæ forming the ends of two side walls which were carried back to the inner colonnade of the market to form a vestibule. Within this a double porch of two columns between antae formed the gate proper.

A worn inscription on the architrave records the dedication of the building to Athena Archegetis, and states that its erection was due to the generosity of Julius Caesar and of Augustus during the archonship of Nikias. On the central acroterion, as is known from the inscription (lost) that it bore, stood a statue of Lucius

Caesar, son of Agrippa and Augustus's daughter Julia, who was adopted by Augustus in 17 BC and died in AD 2. The gateway was doubtless erected between these dates. On the N jamb of the doorway is engraved the celebrated edict of Hadrian regulating the sale of oil and the excise duty thereon.

The site of the Roman agora, which is entered from the NE corner, was partially excavated in the 19C. Just within the gate (right) are the foundations of a large *Public Latrine* of the 1C AD. The *Tower of the Winds* (6, 4), properly the *Horologion of Andronikos Kyrrhestes*, stands beyond, just outside the market enclosure. Built in the 2 or 1C BC by the astronomer Andronikos of Kyrrhos (authorities disagree whether this is the Syrian or the Macedonian town), it served the triple purpose of sundial, water-clock, and weather-vane. The tower, which stands on a base of three steps, takes the form of a marble octagon with a pyramidal roof of marble slabs held together by a round keystone. Each face accurately marks a cardinal point and is adorned with a relief representing the wind blowing from that direction. On the NE and NW faces were porches of two fluted Corinthian columns with peculiarly simple and graceful capitals. Fragments of the NW entablature have been reassembled close by. The tower, according to Vitruvius (I, 6, 4), was originally surmounted by a revolving bronze Triton holding a wand, which pointed out the face corresponding to the prevailing wind.

The eight figures are represented as winged and floating almost horizontally through the air. Beginning at the N side and proceeding clockwise: N, Boreas, in a thick sleeved mantle, with folds blustering in the air, and high-laced buskins, blows a twisted shell; NE, Kaikias empties a shield full of hailstones; E, Apeliotes exhibits flowers and fruit; SE, Euros, with his right arm muffled in his mantle, threatens a hurricane; S, Notos, emptying an urn, is producing a shower; SW, Lips, driving before him the stern ornament of a ship, promises a rapid voyage; W, Zephyros showers into the air a lapful of flowers; NW, Skiron bears a bronze vessel of charcoal in his hands, with which he dries up rivers.—Beneath the figures of the winds are traced the lines of eight sundials.

Attached to the S face is a reservoir in the form of a semicircular turret, from which water could be released in a slow steady stream to run the clock works. Through the doors in the porches can be seen the ancient pavement of white marble, scored with circular channels for a parapet and other channels so far unexplained. At present miscellaneous finds from all over Athens are stored here, obscuring some of the detail of the interior.

In Turkish times the tower was occupied as a Tekke by dervishes.—The arches of Hymettian marble on a massive base to the S form the façade of a building dedicated to Athena Archegetis and the Divi Augusti in the 1C AD. The function of the building, formerly wrongly identified as the Agoranomion (office of the Magistrates of the Market), is not known.

At a lower level to the W extends the **Roman Market**, the S half of which is revealed. This was a large rectangle c 111m by 96m, bounded by a poros wall (early 1C BC), within which, on the S side at least, a (probably Doric) colonnade flanked central blocks of rooms. Later (? under Hadrian) an Ionic *Peristyle* was added within, having unfluted columns of Hymettian marble with bases, capitals, and epistyle of Pentelic. The central area was bordered by a deep drainage gully and later paved in marble (in places still *in situ*). To reach this we descend the five steps of the *South-East Propylon*, which, though smaller and later, has a similar plan to the W gate (see above). It is neither on the central axis of the market, nor at right angles to the wall. Its lower portion is well preserved, though the columns are all broken off 2·4—

3m from the pavement. It is flanked by a row of shops, of which five have been explored, when inscriptions were found on the floor or on columns giving the names of the shopkeepers.

The mosque, now used as an archaeological workshop, that occupies the corner of the site, dates from the late-15C and is probably the *Fetihie Cami*, or Victory Mosque, built to celebrate the Turkish conquest. From time to time visiting Sheikhs perform their devotions here.

On the corner of Odhós Aiolou all that remains of the *Medresse*, or seminary, is a ruined gate bearing a Turkish inscription that records its foundation by Mehmet Fakri in 1721. Here, a century later, the cadi Haci Khalil dissuaded the Turks from a general massacre of male Greeks in Attica. A few paces along this street is the **Library of Hadrian** (6, *4*), closed to the public. The E wall is buttressed by six Corinthian pilasters and originally presented an unbroken face to the street; the ancient entrance was in the marble W façade (comp. above). The building consisted of a huge rectangular wall of poros, c 122m by 82m, portions of which survive on three sides, which enclosed a cloistered court adorned with a 'hundred splendid columns' (Pausanias) of Phrygian marble (long since vanished). In the N and S walks three recesses opened in the outer walls, the central one rectangular, the side ones semicircular. On the E side the main block of five rooms was ranged along the cloister. The central chamber, which was entered through a porch of four cólumns, housed the *Library* proper, in the E wall is a large central niche with four smaller ones on each side, which held the bookshelves—an arrangement similar to that of the library of Pergamon. The rooms on each side were probably (like those in the contemporary library at Alexandria) workrooms and repositories for archives.

The interior of the quadrangle was doubtless laid out as a garden, with a long central reservoir or pool. About AD 410 a square building, either a lecture hall or a church, quatrefoil in plan, was erected by the governor Herculius over the E end of the pool. Its NE angle stands to c 2·7m and some mosaic fragments of the exedræ survive. This building was replaced in the 6C, by a basilica which, under the Byzantines, became the *Megáli Panayía*, or church of Great St. Mary, and survived in a later modification until 1885.—Much of the market site was occupied by a bazar, through which passed Odhos Adhrianou, divided since the excavations into two parts.

We cross the pleasant squáre opposite, and from Odhós Adhrianoú climb the picturesque Odhós Mnesikléous to the little 14C church of the Transfiguration (Μεταμόρφωσις του Σωτηρος), known as *Sotiraki*. This stands just beneath the Acropolis but below the level of the ancient *Peripatos*, which here divided the official precincts of the lower slope from the primitive sanctuaries above.

Close by is the **Kanellópoulos Museum** (closed Tuesday), opened in 1976. The 19C mansion has been tastefully restored and the interior arranged functionally to display the eclectic family *Collection of antiquities of all periods. It is especially rich in bronzes, jewellery and everyday objects. The ground floor and basement have a variety of Byzantine and Late Antique material. On the ground floor: vases, bronzes, crosses and jewellery. In the basement: ikons, bread stamps, jewellery, liturgical accoutrements, silver bowls, crosses, furniture, etc., as well as huge blocks of an Archaic wall. On ground floor landing: embroideries, etc. On first floor: prehistoric (including Mycenaean) and Geometric vases and bronzes; Near-eastern and Cypriot objects. On top floor: Archaic and Classical vases and major and minor sculpture.

Odhós Theorías, a modern road, runs (right) to the entrance of the Acropolis.

The daunting **North Slope of the Acropolis** (no adm.), occupied in Neolithic times and known in antiquity as the LONG ROCKS, repays inspection from this level. Here were worshipped the primitive deities of vegetation and fertility cults which survived from the remotest times into the Classical period. A decree of 415 BC, forbidding the erection of altars within the Pelargikon area, may represent an attempt to restrict these rites. Later writers pointedly ignore or mock these survivals of popular belief. The area was investigated by the Greek Archaeological Society and the American School in 1931–39, when a mass of black-figured pottery was discovered, together with many objects apparently thrown down from the Acropolis; these included the Erechtheion accounts, the Opisthodomos inventory, the accounts for the Athena Promachos statue, about 200 ostraka inscribed with Themistocles' name, and a calyx-krater of Exekias.

At the W end, above Klepsydra (comp. Rte 2) are four *Caves*. The first is little more than a niche with rock-cut seats. In the second (B), somewhat larger, have been found a number of tablets (of Roman date) dedicated to Apollo Hypoakraios by archons taking the oath of office. The third (Γ), which is separated from the second only by a spur, has been suggested as the place where the Pythiasts watched for the flash of lightning from Mt Parnes before starting the procession to Delphi. The narrow tunnel-like cave (Z), above which later stood a chapel of St Athanasios, is identified with the *Cave of Pan*. Herodotus (VI, 105) tells how the worship of Pan was revived after his appearance to Pheidippides in 490 BC. This cave is referred to by Euripides ('Ion' 938) and Aristophanes ('Lysistrata' 911). Farther E cult reliefs with phallic and fertility emblems were discovered as well as fragments of a frieze of Erotes which may have decorated the temenos wall. On a large boulder is inscribed a boundary mark of the Peripatos. The huge *Cave* in the E face of the Acropolis rock has not been fully explored though much pottery came to light here in 1936.

Just to the N of the Sotiraki, No. 5 in Odhós Thólou, is the *Old University*, a building dating from the Venetian occupation, used as public offices by the Turks, and rebuilt with a third storey by Cleanthes in 1830; here the university functioned in 1837–41. It has recently been excellently restored and will become a *Museum of the University*, with accommodation also for seminars and educational programmes. *Ayioi Anárgyroi* (6, 6), a little farther E, is by tradition associated with the Athenian orphan who became the Empress Irene (752–803), reigning alone in Byzantium after the death in 797 of Leo IV, her husband. The Sarandapichos family, to which she belonged, is said to have come from this district. The church, remodelled in the 17C, serves the monastery Metokhi tou Panayiou Tafou, a dependency of the Holy Sepulchre at Jerusalem. The Byzantine chapel of *Ayios Nikólaos Rangavás* (7, 5) stands at the corner of Odhós Pritaníou. The site of the Prytaneion itself (the official centre of the city where the sacred flame was kept burning) has not yet been found. Some slight remains to the N of Od. Kirístou are tentatively identified with the Diogeneum. Overlooking this street, at the corner of Odhós Fléssa, are the rooms in which Caroline, Princess of Wales, was entertained in 1816.

We descend to ODHÓS ADHRIANOÚ. No. 96, built under the Turks by the Benizelos archons, is perhaps the oldest surviving house in Athens. The family name survives in Odhos Benizelou, which descends hence to the Cathedral (Rte 4). We follow Adhrianou, where, in a house built c 1780, lived George Finlay (1799–1875), the historian. The *Demotic School* at the corner of Odhos Flessa occupies the site of the 'Mosque of the Column', which became for Morosini's Lutheran gunners (for a short time in 1687) the first Protestant Church in Greece. The *Hill Memorial School*, at the corner of Thoukidídhou and Nikodímou streets, to the NE, was founded in 1831 by John Henry Hill (d. 1882), an American missionary. We may continue to the Monument of

Lysikrates (Rte 1) or turn left into Odhos Kidathenaíon, where, at No. 27 (garden) Ludwig of Bavaria stayed in 1835. Many of the neighbouring houses date from this period.

At No. 17 has been installed the **Museum of Greek Folk Art** (closed Monday; free). The collection of embroidery, ranging from Coptic cloths of the 2C AD to local fabrics of the Greek islands, is outstanding. Two magnificent *epitaphioi* (processional palls) date from the 17C. Displayed are gold and silver ware from Asia Minor, ikons, and jewellery of barbaric splendour which emphasises the affinity of Greek medieval art with the Balkans and Near East.

From the little shaded *Plateia* (cafés; 7, 5) we may descend NE towards Sindagma Square.

7   From the Arch of Hadrian to the Benáki Museum

Immediately behind the Arch of Hadrian (Rte 1) extends the archaeological park (entrance in Leof. Vasilissis Olgas) surrounding the Temple of Olympian Zeus. To the left are the remains of a *House* of the 4C BC; a cast marks the site where a fine relief (now in the National Museum) was discovered. A second *House* of the same period, with traces of a pebble mosaic floor, is partly overlaid by **Roman Thermae** of AD 124–131, of excellent construction, having four public halls with mosaic floors and the usual three bath chambers off the S side. It apparently survived into the 7C AD.

Farther on, excavations at a lower level have revealed part of the *Themistoclean Wall* (c 479 BC), incorporating drums from the Peisistratid Olympieion, with the *Hippades Gate*, a defensive ditch added in the late 4C BC, and a stretch of ancient road. The ground plan of the *Basilica at the Olympieion*, or St. Nicholas of the Columns, a church built of classical fragments in the late 5C, was recovered in 1949 between the baths and the peribolos.

The SANCTUARY OF OLYMPIAN ZEUS occupies an artificial terrace supported by a *Peribolos* of square Piraeic stones buttressed at regular intervals. Except near the propylon and at the SE corner, where the buttresses and arched drains date largely from the time of Hadrian, this retaining wall is mostly a work of restoration. It measures 205m by 129m, making a perimeter (as indicated by Pausanias) of 4 stadia. The ground plan of its principal entrance, a Doric *Propylon*, has been clarified by restoration.

In the centre stand the majestic remains of the **Olympieíon**, or *Temple of Olympian Zeus*, the largest temple in Greece. It took 700 years to complete, 'a great victory of time', as Philostratus happily describes it. Livy says 'it is the only temple on earth of a size adequate to the greatness of the god', though it was in fact exceeded in extent by temples to other gods at Agrigento and Selinus in Sicily, and at Ephesus and Miletus in Asia Minor.

History. Scanty remains of a small shrine have been discovered with vaults beneath having an exit through a subterranean passage to the Ilissos. This may account for the tradition that a temple was founded here by Deukalion over the chasm through which the waters receded after the flood. Pausanias relates that in commemoration of this event an annual sacrifice of flour mixed with honey was thrown into the cleft. Peisistratos seems to have been the first to undertake the construction of a temple on a grand scale, possibly, as Aristotle suggests

('Politics'), to keep the people too busy to indulge in plots. Work ceased before the stylobate was complete when Hippias went into exile and much of the masonry was used in the Themistoclean wall (comp. above). In 174 BC Antiochus Ephiphanes, king of Syria, resumed building to a new design by Cossutius, a Roman architect, who substituted the Corinthian for the Doric order. Work was again interrupted at the entablature stage and put back further in 86 BC, when Sulla carried off some of the shafts and capitals to Rome for the Capitoline Temple. The honour of its completion was reserved for Hadrian who dedicated the temple on his second visit to Athens c AD 130 and set up a chryselephantine statue of the god within the cella (a copy of that by Pheidias at Olympia), as well as a colossal statue of himself. Cyriacus of Ancona (c 1450) noted 21 standing columns with their architraves. In 1760 the Turkish governor converted one to lime for the construction of a new mosque; the great storm of 26 October 1852 overthrew another.

The **Temple** stands on a stylobate (107·8m by 41m) of three steps, the lower two of poros from the original foundation, the upper one of marble (partially restored in 1960–61). The foundations, which were laid by Peisistratos, exhibit the same curvilinear features as those of the Parthenon. Dipteral octastyle in arrangement with an extra row of columns at each end, the temple had 20 columns at each side, making 104 in all. Of these 13 survive in a group with part of the architrave at the SE, and two farther W. They are of Pentelic marble with 16 blunt flutings. The fallen column, which was blown down in 1852, shows clearly the construction of base, 16 column drums, and capital in two sections. Its base diameter is 1·7m, and height 17m. The capitals are beautifully carved. The original height of the front is estimated at 27·4m. The stones comprising the architrave weigh up to 23 tons; in the middle ages a stylite lived on the architrave that still covers the two W columns of the SE group. The remains are not sufficient to determine the plan of the cella, though Vitruvius records it as hypæthral. The ruin is popularly known as *Kolónnes* (columns); the columns are floodlit in summer.

We leave Leoforos Singroú (Rte 12) on our right and take Odhós Athanassíou Diákou to (5 minutes) the *Kallirrhoi Bridge* over the seasonal Ilissos. An older bridge, surviving beneath, is well seen from Kallirrhoi (see below).

The **Ilissos** (Ἰλισός) flows from two sources on the slopes of Hymettos, one at Kaisariani, the other at St. John Theologos. The united branches, diminished since Classical times and now either underground or canalized, flow on the S side of the city and, passing to the S of the Mouseion, descend to the Bay of Phaleron.
   The district extending outside the S wall of the city along the river bank was anciently known as KEPOI, the Gardens. To the SW of the Olympieion lay the *Pythion 'on the Wall'*. Two large fragments (now in the National Museum), found on the right bank of the Ilissos, have been certainly identified with the Altar of Apollo Pythios by their inscription, a dedication to Peisistratos the Younger, which is quoted in full by Thucydides (VI, 54). Further finds in 1965–68 below Od. Iosifton Rogon may locate the site.
   Beyond the river lay the district known as DIOMEIA. Downstream, c 275m below the bridge, is the presumed site (excavated by the British School in 1896–97 and recent rescue excavations) of the *Gymnasium of Kynosarges*. An inscription naming Kynosarges has been found near the church of Ay. Pandeleimon.

Just above the bridge somewhat artificially contrived is the *Kallirrhoi*, a shallow fall where the Ilissos flows over a ridge of rock. The traditional name, which dates back at least to Byzantine times, recalls that of the ancient **Kallirrhóë Spring** (8, 5), but the locality has drastically altered since Classical times. In 1896 floods swept away remains of ancient masonry and even altered the contour of the rock. The course of the river has now been irretrievably interfered with and its waters have largely vanished underground. On the S bank, beyond the modern chapel of Ayía Fotíni, a much eroded figure of Pan adorns a right-angled chamber hewn out of the rock.

Extending towards the Olympieion is the 'ILISSOS AREA' excavated by Threpsiades in 1956–67 during the covering of the Ilissos and the construction of the Arditós highway. The area is traversed by a section of the Valerian Wall, for the building of which most of the ancient structures were quarried. The gate here may be that of Aigeus (comp. Plutarch, 'Theseus', xii). Foundations remain of a temple of late date (mostly under the road) and, between this and the Olympieion te-menos wall, of three buildings of some importance amid a confusion of ruins. These are from E to W: the *Precinct of Kronos and Rhea*, with prominent foundations of a Doric temple ascribed to the 2C AD; a much larger Doric temple of the 5C BC, which had a peristyle of 13 columns by 6, perhaps to be identified with the *Temple of Apollo Delphinios*; and a civic structure in archaic polygonal masonry belie-ved to be the *Law court of the Delphinion*.

From the S end of the bridge Odhós Anapáfseos mounts to the main gate of the *Próto Nekrotafíon Athinón*, the principal Cemetery of Athens. Here, in sump-tuous tombs, generally in Classical styles and decorated by the best sculptors of the day, are buried many celebrated Greeks of the 19C and 20C. Among heroes of the War of Independence are the generalissimo, Sir Richard Church (1784–1873), and Kolokotronis (1770–1843), as well as Makriyannis and Androutsos. Writers include Rangavis (1810–92), Panayiotis Soutsos (1800–68) and the states-man-historian Trikoupis (died 1896). Averoff (see below), Singros (died 1899), and Antoine Benaki, benefactors of the city, lie here. *The Mausoleum of Heinrich Schliemann* (1822–90), the archaeologist, is decorated with Trojan scenes in bas-relief, while the *Tomb of Adolf Furtwängler* (1853–1907) bears a marble copy of a sphinx he unearthed at Aegina.

On the S side of the Arditós highway, near Od. D. Koutoula, are the remains of the terrace wall of a temple, known to antiquaries as the *Temple by the Ilissos*, which was discovered and drawn by Stuart and Revett in 1751–55 but destroyed in 1778 by the Turks. It appears to have been constructed before the Temple of Athena Nike from the same specifications of Kallikrates, and may be the Temple of Artemis Agrotera. It became an orthodox church but was abandoned after a Roman mass had been said there in 1674.

To avoid the noisier Arditós highway we may return by footpath to LEOFÓROS VASILÍSSIS OLGAS (*7, 6*), an attractive avenue that skirts the S side of the Zappeion Gardens (Rte 1). To the right, between the avenues, are the *Tennis Club*, the *Olympic Swimming Pool* (ΟΛΥΜΠΙΑΚΟΝ ΚΟΛΥΜΒΗΤΗΡΙΟΝ), and the *Ethnikos Athletic Club*. The athletic track occupies the site (once an island in the river) where stood the '*Basilica by the Ilissos*' (mosaics in Byz. Mus). The countryside hereabouts was lyrically described by Plato at the begin-ning of the 'Phædrus'. The two highways join below the hill of *Arditós*.

On the hill, the former **Ardettos**, or *Helikon*, where the Heliasts came to take their oath, are some scanty foundations (no adm.) assigned to the *Temple of Fortune*, erected by Herodes Atticus. On the opposite height beyond the Stadium some ruins (no adm.) are presumed (from an inscription *in situ* in archaistic letters to the 'Marathonian Hero') to be the *Tomb of Herodes*, who died at Marathon but was given a public funeral at Athens.

The **Stadium** (Στάδιον; 8, 5) occupies a natural valley between these two low hills, which is closed at the S end by an artificial embankment to form the semicircular sphendone. Faithfully restored in 1896–1906 by Anastasios Metaxas, it has the normal plan of a Greek stadium and corresponds to the description of Pausanias, who saw the gleaming Pentelic marble of the first restoration as we see the pristine whiteness of the second. The Plateia tou Stadhiou bears a statue of Averoff (1867–1930), the benefactor who financed the work.

History. Lycurgus constructed the stadium in its original form in 330 BC to provide for the contests of the Panthenaic Festival. On the occasion of Hadrian's presidency a thousand wild beasts were baited in the arena. The stadium was reseated in marble by Herodes Atticus for the Games of AD 144. In the course of centuries' use as a quarry, the marble all but disappeared. Ernst Ziller cleared the site in 1869–70 at first at his own expense, later with the support of George I of the Hellenes. In 1895, for the forthcoming revival of the Olympic Games, Yeoryios Averoff, a wealthy Greek of Alexandria, emulating Herodes, undertook to restore the marble. The sphendone was provided with seats in time for the first modern Games of 1896, and the work was completed for the extra 'Olympic' Games, held out of series as a 10th anniversary celebration in 1906 and visited by Edward VII.

The *Arena*, in the form of an elongated horseshoe, measures 204m by 33m. As restored it comprises a modern running track with provision in the centre for athletic and gymnastic contests. On the E side a tunnel, c 3m high, admits competitors and officials from the changing rooms.

In ancient times the course was a straight track measuring one stade of 600 Greek feet, whence the name stadion. The Greek foot varied slightly from place to place, but the Athenian track seems to have measured c 185m. It was divided down the centre by a row of pillars, of which four, in the form of double hermae, have been recovered. The finishing point was in front of the sphendone, which was surmounted by a Doric stoa to provide shelter for the top corridor. A Corinthian propylon (restored, but since removed) formed a ceremonial entrance at the open end.

The course is enclosed by a low marble parapet, behind which a paved promenade 2·7m wide, follows the circuit. Rainwater is channelled through gratings in the pavement into an arched drain of brick. A wall, 1·6m high, forms the substructure of the first tier of the *Auditorium*, thus affording the spectators a clear view over the parapet. The side tiers are slightly curved to give better visibility. Twenty-nine narrow flights of steps (12 on each side and 5 in the sphendone) lead from the promenade to the seats. These are arranged in 47 tiers, divided into two blocks by a *diazoma*, or gangway, behind the 24th row. The seats are of the same simple pattern as those in the Theatre of Dionysos. The seating capacity is 60,000. A block on the S side and the front row of the sphendone provide more comfortable accommodation for honoured patrons and royal occasions.

Across the square, at the SE entrance to the Zappeion Gardens, stand a bronze statue of a discus thrower (1927) and a huge equestrian figure, also in bronze, of Karaïskakis, by Michael Tombros (1966).

Leoforos Konstantinou continues NE to meet Leoforos Vasilissis Sofias (see Rte 10). An important Dark Age cemetery was found here during the construction of new barracks in 1975.

Opposite the stadium Odhós Iródhou Attikoú runs between the E side of the National Garden and the modest former **Palace** (8, 3), residence of the king after the restoration of 1935 and more recently of the president. The picturesque Evzones have their barracks at the top of the street, which emerges into Leoforos Vasilissis Sofias (Rte 10).

Just opposite in the avenue is the ***Benáki Museum** (8, 3; open mornings only; closed Tuesday), containing the fruits of 35 years eclectic collecting by Antoine Benaki. In 1931, having arranged his collection in the family town house, Benaki endowed the museum and presented it to the state. Later gifts have been accepted.

Entry is through the garden and by the door facing Vas. Sophias. The GROUND FLOOR presents a roughly chronological display of the ancient and medieval arts. We turn left where the first hall is devoted to ancient Greece. Among many notable items: two gold cups of the Bronze Age (c 3000 BC) from N Euboea; a Mycenaean gold cup with hounds in relief. Bronze Age finds from Chalcidice and Thessaly; good collection of fibulae; bronze figure of Herakles from the Ptoion in Boeotia (490–480 BC) and Macedonian helmets from Dodona. Jewellery from the Bronze Age to the Hellenistic periods. Outstanding are: gold head of a bull (6C BC) and a diadem and accompanying ornaments of the 3C BC found in Thessaly.

The front section of the next hall contains Greco-Roman and Coptic cloths and embroidery (3C–8C AD) from Christian Egypt; in this room also are displayed examples of Persian, Byzantine and Coptic workmanship, mostly objects of daily use, from which the Arabic style evolved. 227 (on the wall) Greco-Roman portrait (2C or 3C AD) in watercolour on canvas. The remaining room, towards the back, contains icons and on the end wall two works of the Cretan painter Dom. Theotokopoulos, better known as *El Greco*. On the right is his earliest known work, The Adoration of the Magi (c 1560); on the left, The Evangelist Luke. The two rooms to the right contain ecclesiastical furniture (17–19C) brought back from Asia Minor and Thrace by refugees in 1922, and icons.

The back section of the farthest gallery is arranged as a Moslem reception hall with original 17C mosaic, etc. from Cairo, and ceramic decorations, including so-called 'Rhodian' ware (16C) which in fact comes from Nicaea in Asia Minor. Ranged against the wall are funerary monuments of the 10–11C bearing Cufic inscriptions. Among objects of fine workmanship are a box in copper and silver from Mosul (1220), and two astrolabes, one of ivory signed and dated 1341, one of brass, signed by Ahmad ibn al-Sarrâj (1328) who was well-known for his treatises on astronomical instruments. In a case containing glass vessels from Egypt (8–12C) is a lamp enamelled and gilded, made for the Mausoleum of Sultan Kuckuk (died 1341), and a goblet. The walls are hung with Brusa velvets and various pieces of Turkish armour and bronze helmets. Before we ascend the stairs on the left a wall case contains a carved wooden door (9) from Baghdad.

We ascend to the FIRST FLOOR where there is a reconstruction of the interior of a period room from Rhodes containing a magnificent silk embroidered marriage bed canopy (late 17–18C). The hall on the left has three sections devoted to the historical relics of 19C Greece, in particular the War of Independence (1821–27). Among objects with British associations may be mentioned: rifles made in London for Eastern potentates; a case containing memorabilia of Byron including his portable writing desk. On the wall is an oil painting of Byron in Suliot dress. In Room XVI is a ring inscribed 'Long live Alfred, King of Greece', recalling the offer of the throne (rejected) to Queen Victoria's second son. Room XVII has a collection of coins of the Ionian Isles under British rule (1815–64).

Room XX is devoted to Chinese ceramics arranged by dynasty. This collection will eventually be housed in a neo-classical building in Palaion Faliron presented by Mrs Verra Kouloura. The farthest hall contains embroidery of the Greek islands. This art flourished in the 17–18C, but is now almost extinct.

The BASEMENT rooms are devoted to a unique display of Greek regional *Costume and popular art including the bonnet of Theresa Makri, Byron's Maid of Athens.

On the SECOND FLOOR there is a pleasant cafeteria with a wide terrace and a view to the wooded hill of Ardettos.

8 From Monastiráki to the National Museum

From Monastiraki (Rte 6) ODHÓS ATHINÁS strikes N straight to Omonoia Square. Crowds throng the vegetable and meat markets that line its southern half and extend into the narrow turnings on either side. We take the narrower ODHÓS AIÓLOU, a popular shopping street, parallel to the E where excavations in 1961–62 disclosed tombs of c 500 BC. On the right is *Ayia Irini* with a colourful market of nurserymen on the N side.

About 450m farther on, beyond Odhós Sofokléous, opens the PLATEÍA DHIMARKHEÍOU (formerly KOTZIA), which, since the demolition in 1937 of the Municipal Theatre, extends to Odhós Athinás. To the left stands a mansion by Ziller which for many years housed the main post office. The severe *Dhimarkhion*, or Town Hall, in Athinás to the W, faces the *National Bank of Greece* (Ethnikí Trápeza tis Elládhos). In an adjacent vacant plot the discovery of extensive remains of the ancient city wall has held up rebuilding. The square has recently been completely cleared in advance of redevelopment allowing extensive archaeological investigation of an area which lies just outside the Acharnian Gate of the ancient city. Finds have ranged in date from the Geometric to Roman periods and include burials, roads and, most impressive, a series of potters' establishments, better preserved than any known to date. The finds have not yet been fully reported in print. Odhos Aiolou continues N, crosses Stadium St. (Rte 10), and passing E of Omonoia Sq. becomes Odhos Patission (see below).

Odhos Athinas leads directly to **Omónoia Square** (3, 3; Πλατεῖα της Ομονίας), the busy centre of commercial Athens, where eight important roads converge. Its name (Concord Sq.) commemorates the reconciliation of two warring 19C political factions. Its fountain is ringed by undistinguished buildings. Escalators lead down to the main station of the Piraeus–Athens–Kifissia Railway (E.H.Σ.), where shops, cafés, a bank, and an information office of the National Tourist Organisation surround the concourse.

Immediately to the left the broad ODHÓS PIRAÓS begins its straight course to the port of Athens. Many treasures, now in the National Museum, have been found during building operations along its route; but nothing of interest survives above the surface, and the depressing street has been largely superseded as a highway by the boulevards to the S.

To the W, Odhós Ayíou Konstandínou, lined with electrical and record shops, descends to the large modern church of *Ayios Konstandinos*, in front of which is the booking-office for bus services to the Peloponnese. Opposite stands the *National Theatre*.

Larissa Station of the Greek State Railways and the Peloponnisos Station lie c 1km NW.

Odhos Patissíon (comp. above), alternatively named Odhos Ikosiokhto Oktovriou, an uninteresting modern thoroughfare, passes to the W of PLATEÍA KÁNNINGOS (3, 3), with a busy local bus terminus, where stands a *Statue of Canning* by Chantrey (1834), erected here in 1931 to honour the British minister's services to Greek independence. The plinth, marked by shrapnel, also celebrates a descendant who fell in Greece in 1941. The street continues N to the **Polytekhneíon** (Εθνικόν Μετσόβιον Πολυτεχνεῖον), designed by Kaftandzoglou and built of Pentelic marble in 1862–80. Two side pavilions in Doric style

form propylæa to the main block, where an Ionic upper storey is superimposed on the lower Doric. Here the *School of Fine Arts* and the
Polytechnic School jointly constitute an institution having university
status and teaching the practical and artistic subjects not recognised
by the Panepistimion. In 1973 student occupation of the Polytechnic
buildings, brutally ended by the police, was the focus of opposition to
the military regime, which fell the following year.

We pass the **National Archaeological Museum** (see below), with its
shady garden (café), beyond which (c 1km from Omonoia) we reach
the Plateia Areos at the SW corner of the **Pedhíon Areos** (3, 2; 'Champ
de Mars'). Before the main entrance to this pleasant park stands an
equestrian *Statue of Constantine I*. An avenue to the N of this (running
E–W) is flanked by busts of heroes and martyrs of the Revolution of
1821.

On the S side of the park, facing Leoforos Alexandras, is a *War Memorial* (1952)
in Pentelic marble erected 'to the memory of soldiers of Britain, Australia, and
New Zealand, who fought for the liberty of Greece'. Three cenotaphs (each with
a bowl for a sacred flame) bear the arms of the three Commonwealth countries;
behind, a Greek lion sits on a plinth of steps before a column bearing a statue of
Athena. Her left arm holds a shield, the right arm is lacking since the spear it held
was struck by lightning. In the park, near the chapel of Ayios Kharalambos is a
Monument to the 'Sacred Battalion' (Ieros Lokhos), an irregular brigade of students commanded by A. Ypsilanti, which was unnecessarily sacrificed in 1821 in
a skirmish at Dragashan in Rumania.—At the NE end of the park stands the
EVELPIDHON, formerly the military academy and now housing the main law
courts. The fine building, now restored, was designed by Ziller and erected at
expense of Averoff in 1889–94. In front stands a bronze *Statue of a Youth* (1940),
by Athanasios Apartis, cast in Paris and since damaged by bullets.

9   The National Archaeological Museum

Approaches. Trolley-bus/bus No. 2, 12 or 3 from Sindagma Sq. to the museum
which is in Odhós Patissíon (Rte 8), 450m N of Omonoia Sq., and a short walk from
Plateía Kánningos. No direct service from the Acropolis.

Admission. Closed Monday. A printed catalogue to the Sculpture (1968) and
good illustrated souvenir volumes are available in English; guide to the Prehistoric collections, at present only in French and German.

Cafés. In gardens outside Museum and, within, off the central ATRIUM (see
plan and Room 20, below)—not cheap.

The **‘‘NATIONAL ARCHAEOLOGICAL MUSEUM** (3, 2; Eθνικόν
Αρχαιολογικόν Μουσείον) contains an outstanding collection of
masterpieces from excavations throughout Greece. All periods of
pagan antiquity are included but new finds are now brought here only
where no regional museum has a prior claim; Cretan antiquities, for
example, are retained in Herakleion and barely represented in
Athens. The museum, erected in 1866–89, and extended to the E with
a large new wing in 1925–39, forms a vast rectangle round an inner
cross. The façade comprises an Ionic portico flanked by open galleries
with plain square pilasters; the wings at either end are marked by
plain pediments.

Arrangement. The first collection of antiquities formed in Athens was exhibited
at the Theseion, which received sculptures transferred from Aegina in 1834. Both
the Tower of the Winds and the Library of Hadrian served as repositories for
occasional finds. The systematic excavations undertaken by the Greek Archaeological Society and the explorations of the British, French, German, and American Schools at Athens led to the construction of the present building. For safety
during the Second World War the collections were scattered. After the war the

museum was entirely redecorated, alterations were made to the structure, and a whole new wing was available. For the first time the collections are being arranged as a whole; some rooms will inevitably be found closed, but the final arrangement, which is basically chronological, is predicated by the room numbering. Direct access is not normally allowed from the Prehistoric central halls to the outer galleries. From the entrance hall the visitor proceeds by the N wing to the central gallery, then usually visits whatever is accessible in the new wing. After making the round of the upper floor (pottery galleries open mornings only), he will eventually regain the entrance by the S wing. Here and there private bequests and donations, or finds from a particular excavation preserved complete, break the sequence. The splendid display, started by the late Dr Christos Karousos (Director 1942–64) and Mrs Semni Karousos, and continued by subsequent directors, is still inadequately labelled even in Greek.

We cross the vestibule and enter the **Hall of Mycenaean Antiquities** (R. 4). In this great room are grouped the results of excavations at Mycenae and at other Mycenaean sites from 1876 to the present day. Chief among the splendid treasures are the contents of the six shaft graves from the Grave Circle A at Mycenae, five excavated by Schliemann and the sixth by Stamatakis; these are now rivalled in fame by objects from Vaphio and in archaeological importance by more recent finds from elsewhere.

The cases are numbered in sequence round the room without regard to content; we follow the logical progression of the room, giving case numbers only for easy identification. Every case merits detailed study; only the outstanding or unique objects are indicated below. The numbers of the objects themselves correspond with the catalogue raisonné of G. Karo, 'Die Schacht-Gräber von Mykenai' (Munich, 1930).

Within the doors (right and left), two cases of miscellaneous finds from chamber tombs excavated in 1886–87 and 1892–99 outside the Acropolis of Mycenae. CASE 26 (right) contains an ivory head (T 27) wearing a helmet of boar's tusks (comp. below).—CASE 1 (left): Seal-rings; jewellery; 2947. Small bull in gold; sword-blades and hilts. In the next case (CASE 2) similar finds from Wace's excavations of 1921–23: outstanding are the bone objects, especially T 518; seal-stones. Helmet of boar's tusk pieces.—In CASE 25, on the right, begins the material from GRAVE CIRCLE A. Contents of *1st Shaft Grave* (three women; 1550–1500 BC) and of *2nd Shaft Grave* (one man; 1580–1550 BC): Gold diadem and cup, arms, fine vases. To left and right of the room are displayed four of the stelai from the grave circle, carved with hunting scenes (of the 17 stelai found, 11 were so decorated).

There follows a group of five cases containing the most valuable objects from the 3rd, 4th and 5th Shaft Graves. In the centre: CASE 27 (*4th Grave*, the richest: three men and two women; 1580–1550 BC). Three bronze * *Dagger blades inlaid in gold, silver, and niello with hunting scenes: 394, 395. Lions hunting and being hunted; 765. River scene (? the Nile) with cheetahs retrieving duck. 253, 254, 259. Three portrait masks in gold leaf; 252. Breastplate (plain). *Gold cups of varied designs (note No. 427 behind); * *481. Silver rhyton with gold foil rim and handle and repoussé decoration depicting the siege of a maritime town. *412. Gold libation cup with two handles reaching to the foot of the stem and ornamented with falcons (not doves); it recalled to Schliemann Nestor's cup in Homer (Il. XI, 632–5). * *Bull's head in silver with gold horns and a gold rosette; Seal rings; 555–70. Symbolic knots moulded in pottery; leg bones with gold ornaments attached.—CASE 24 (right; same grave): Gold diadems and cups; 388. Base silver rhyton in the form of a stag or reindeer (possibly of Hittite workmanship); 273. Lion-head rhyton in gold; headbands and (263) bracelet in gold; three gold pins, one (245) with a spirited reproduction of a goat; golden ornaments in the form of an octopus; three models of temple fronts, in gold, each having an altar surmounted by horns of consecration; on the two corners are doves with outstretched wings. Clasps and buttons; sword-blades and daggers.—Beyond, CASE 23 contains objects from the *3rd Grave* (three women and two children; see also Cases 10 & 11): Gold *** *Diadems** and discs; these may have been affixed to wooden coffins, long since vanished, but more likely were used for personal adornment. Recumbent lions in gold repoussé; pair of scales in gold leaf; three gold seals engraved with a lion fight and a single combat; 116–8. Engraved gems; Gold pin, portraying a goddess of Minoan type, with thick silver shaft.—To the left of the room CASES 3 & 4 are devoted to the *5th Grave* (three men; 1580–1500 BC); *Gold mask of a man, bearded and moustached. Schliemann claimed, having removed this mask, to 'have gazed upon the face of Agamemnon'; breastplate adorned in spirals; swords (one with chased gold hilt); *656. Cup with repoussé lions; *629. Large gold cup; hexagonal wooden box overlaid with gold panels (in a remarkable state of preservation); 829, 854. Vases (in alabaster) of great elegance; sword pommel of alabaster; *Daggers and swords with blades inlaid with gold and silver or patterned with volutes of gold; 828. Ostrich egg adorned with dolphins in alabaster; 812. Sycamore box.

Two low CASES (28 and 29) placed back to back in the centre contain gold objects from the 3rd grave, notably the sheets that covered the bodies of two royal infants; small jugs, boxes, and ornaments; below, Huge bronze bowl.—Lesser objects from the 4th and 6th shaft graves are displayed in CASE 22 (right): 389. Elaborate vase with three handles of Cretan alabaster; 552. Decorated ostrich egg; metal shield of Minoan type (in miniature; c 30 cm high); ceramic vases of fine shape with interesting decoration. Beyond, in CASE 21, are miscellaneous finds from the Acropolis of Mycenae, including elaborately shaped pottery figurines and (2665, 2666) painted plaques; 4573. Blue monkey with cartouche.—On the opposite side of the room (CASES 5 and 6) is a selection of the finds from GRAVE CIRCLE B (1650–1550 BC) discovered in 1952–55. These are similar in scope to the foregoing; note, however, the rock-crystal duck vase, the cruder mask, and the differences in the sword-hilt.

Against a blue wall (right) are displayed a female head in limestone, perhaps from a sphinx (13C BC); a painted decorated plaque; and a stele originally incised, later covered with plaster and painted. There follow two cases of miscellaneous finds of Late Helladic date (1500–1200 BC) from Mycenae: CASE 30 (centre): Four gold vases with dogs' heads on the handles and a gold cup; two large rings or seals, one very elaborate; 991. Small recumbent lion of gold; *Group of two women and a child in ivory; inlaid handles; vases, and alabaster pommels most accurately shaped.—CASE 7 (left): Bronze mirror with an ivory handle; small carved plaques in ivory; bronze pins.—The low central CASE 31 contains ivory *Panels from furniture boxes, etc., and inscribed clay tablets from the House of Shields at Mycenae; below is a vase of unusual shape. On the opposite wall, CASE 20 has pottery, figurines, bronze weapons and jewellery from the important 12C cemetery at Perati in East Attica. Next to it stands the 'Warrior Vase' found by Schliemann. This is a large vase (c 1200 BC) painted dark red on light yellow. On one side is a line of six armed soldiers marching in single file away from a woman who bids them farewell. On the handles are modelled animal heads. Beyond the vase are two restored pillars from the 'Treasury of Atreus'. Other pieces of the pillars are similarly restored in the British Museum.

The remainder of the room is devoted to other Mycenaean sites. On the left side of the Hall, CASE 8. Finds excavated at Pylos before the site museum was founded. Two daggers, one (* *8340) in a wonderful state of preservation with repoussé gold hilt and inlaid blade; bronze mirror with ivory handle; ivory comb, seals, and ornaments. The low CASE 9, adjacent, contains some of the many calcined clay tablets with inscriptions in Cretan Linear B script.—Mounted on a partition wall are fragments of wall-paintings from the old (1350 BC) and later 1300-1200 BC) palace at Tiryns. Beyond (left), two CASES (10 and 11) of objects from Prosymna are placed either side of a table of large jars (that with the octopuses on the left has many Minoan parallels at Heraklion): the smaller pottery in the cases (from chamber-tombs and Middle Helladic graves) is particularly varied and graceful.

In the centre of the room, in CASE 32, are the famous * *Gold cups (15C BC; subject of countless reproductions) from the beehive tomb at Vaphio dug up in 1889: 1758. Capture of wild bulls with nets; 1759. Trapping bulls with a decoy cow and other finds from the same site: engraved gems; shallow silver cup with gilded rim and bowl. To the right (CASE 19) are miscellaneous objects from Mycenaean sites in Attica including Athens, Brauron, Markopoulo, Salamis, and an interesting vase in the form of a boot from Voula.

CASE 12 (left: *Spata*). Ivory comb, tablets, and boar's-tusk (restored).—CASE 18 (right). Objects found in the tholos tomb at *Menidhi*: musical instruments in ivory, including a lyre (restored), cylindrical box with sheep carved in relief on its sides and lid; glass ornaments; engraved gems; stirrup vases.—The last centre CASE (33) is devoted to gold and silver cups, swords, etc. from *Midea* (Argolis), while the remaining five cases contain objects from *Nauplia* (13), *Mycenae* (14; three wall *Paintings), *Tiryns* (15), *Skopelos* (16), and (17) a selection of vase fragments from Mycenae chosen for their unusual representations of animal and human figures. CASE 15 includes the 'Tiryns Treasure', the loot of a tomb robber who had buried it, found in 1915 in a house of the lower town; the objects date from 1500–1100 BC: 6208, a huge seal-ring, is especially notable. Against the end wall (left) are recently discovered frescoes of the 13C BC from the cult centre at Mycenae: Goddess (?); figure-of-eight shields; (right) fragment of carved stone decoration from the Treasury of Atreus at Mycenae.

To the left and right of the Mycenaean Hall are long narrow rooms devoted to earlier antiquities. In that to the left (R. 5), objects of **Neolithic and Helladic** cultures from Thessaly (Dimini and Sesklo), Orchomenos, Attica (Ayios Kosmas, Rafina, Nea Makri) and Poliokhni on Lemnos, the latter having ceramic affinities with Troy. A case of objects from Troy itself was presented by Sophie Schliemann. To the right (R. 6), Cycladic objects from the islands: particularly important are finds from Phylakopi (Melos) with characteristic painted pottery showing Cretan influence, and the well-known Flying-fish fresco; vases from Syros; *Statuettes of male figures playing musical instruments, in Parian marble (2400–2200 BC), from Keros; and the contents of tombs found intact on Naxos.

We return to the vestibule and enter the NORTH WING, where seven rooms contain **Archaic Sculpture**. Free-standing sculpture of the 7–6C BC has two principal types: the *Kouros* or youth, represented nude with one leg forward of the other, and the *Kore* or maiden, portrayed draped. The form may derive from the Xoanon, or ancient wooden statue, the stiff position of the arms, held tightly to the body, being dictated in wood-carving by the available shape of the timber. But many of the conventions show marked affinities with Egyptian and Phoenician models.

ROOM 7. In the centre, 804. Huge sepulchral amphora in ripe Geometric style (c 760 BC) found in the Kerameikos area (the like became known from the provenance as 'Dipylon vases'): on it are represented the prothesis (laying-out) and lamentation over the dead. In glass cases behind, 770–79. Geometric pottery and four ivory statuettes from the same grave, one from a Syrian model. 57. Statue of a goddess (?; c 630 BC) found at Ayioryitika near Tripolis. 1. Statue of Artemis found at Delos, the work of a Naxian sculptor (c 630 BC); the inscription on the left side records its dedication by Nikandre of Naxos. 2869. Part of a limestone relief in the 'Dædalic' style, possibly a metope of a temple (Mycenae; c 650–630 BC), one of the oldest monumental stone reliefs of continental Greece. 56. Grave monument of Kitylos and Dermis, set up by Amphalkes; work of a Boeotian sculptor (mid-6C BC), found at Tanagra. In the doorway, 16513. Archaic bronze flautist from Samos (cast solid).—ROOM 8. Kouros figures and fragments. Dominating the room, 2720. Colossal *Kouros* from the earlier Temple of Poseidon at Sounion (c 600 BC), newly restored. 3645. Torso of another. 71. Torso of an Athenian youth (590–580 BC) from Kerameikos. 3372. The 'Dipylon Head' from a Kouros funeral monument in the Kerameikos, remarkable Attic work of c 610 BC. The hand (3965) in the wall case is from the same work. 353. The 'Piraeus Amphora', funerary vase of 630–620 BC (chariot scenes). 15. Head of a kouros from Sanctuary of Ptoan Apollo, of crude Boeotian technique (c 580 BC).

Off R. 8 open three small rooms continuing sculpture of the 6C, with exceptional recent finds. ROOM 9. *1558. Kouros from Melos; 22. Kore; 21. Winged Nike, both from Delos; 10. Kouros from Sanctuary of Apollo at Ptoön; 73. Torso of Kore (Aegina, 570 BC); *4889. Myrrhinous Kore (c 590 BC), found in 1972 with a kouros (see below). The lead ring found with it fitted a known base inscribed Phrasikleia and signed by Aristion of Paros.—ROOM 10, beyond. 28. Sphinx (Spata, c 570); 76. Sphinx (Piraeus, c 540 BC); *38. Fragment of grave stele of a discophoros, of great vitality, executed in Parian marble by an Attic sculptor c 560 BC. (Kerameikos); *4890. Myrrhinous Kouros (comp. above). 2687, 2891. Tall stele and crowning sphinx from the Kerameikos; the stele, typical of the 6C style, was hastily chipped back for use in the Themistoclean Wall (the two parts may not belong together).— In Room 10A are *1906. Kouros from Volomandra (Kalivia), a charming Attic work of c 550 BC; 14. Unfinished kouros from Naxos showing tool marks; 18232. Bronze vessel with sculptured handles; 4871. Head of Kouros.

Return to ROOM 11. In the centre, 3686. Kouros from Keos, local work of 530 BC. Round this are grouped marble sculptures and steles: 8. Kouros from Thera; 3728. Well-preserved Herm from Siphnos (c 520 BC); 1673. Part of pediment, perhaps from the precinct of Pythian Apollo; the other half is in the Metropolitan Museum (N.Y.); 27. Head of a woman with red hair and earrings, from Eleusis; 30. Grave stele of Lyseas erected by his father Semon (c 500 BC) found at Velanideza in 1838: the faded painting is reproduced in the adjacent copy; 26, 25. Ex-voto Korai figures from Eleusis, remarkable for their drapery. 31. Lower part of a stele of a horseman with well-preserved painted decoration, found in Aeolus St. (c 500 BC). *29. Funeral stele in Pentelic marble representing the warrior Aristion and signed by Aristokles (Velanideza); this is a typical stele of the period, narrow and crowned with a palmette, bearing a formalised relief of the dead person in a characteristic attitude; the full-length figure retains traces of colour. 3072. Mask of Dionysos; *3071. Grave stele of a hoplite found in Stamata (c 525 BC); 13. Kouros found at Megara (c 540 BC); 93. Marble discus dedicated to Aeneas 'the wise and excellent physician' (c 550 BC); 81. Base of a grave monument (c 550 BC) found in Vourva; only the feet of the statue of Phaidimos' daughter survive above the inscription. 41. Crowning member of a grave stele showing the squire of the deceased youth on horseback, carved in very low relief.

We enter ROOM 13, a long hall in which the most striking work stands at the far end before a screen: *3851, the *Anávyssos Kouros*, found in 1936; the middle step of the base, found near by in 1938, has the inscription 'Stop and lament at the tomb of the dead Kroisos whom furious Ares slew when he was fighting in the forefront'. Though in archaic posture, its mobility and modelling suggest a date of c 520 BC. Other Kouroi in the room, 12, 20, both from the Sanctuary of Apollo at Ptoön in Boeotia (end of 6C BC); 9. A coarse work from Orchomenos; *3938. Sepulchral statue unearthed near Keratea during the German occupation and smuggled to Athens; it represents the young Aristodikos (Attic work of c 500 BC); *16365. Bronze statuette of Apollo from Sparta (end of 6C BC). Other fragments include: 32. Sepulchral stele of two youths, Agathon and Aristokrates, from Thespiai (500 BC); 1926. Pair of stone halteres (jumping weights) of archaic type from Corinth; 89, 2823, 2826. Slabs decorated with reliefs, probably from a tomb, cut back for use in the Themistoclean wall in 478 BC. At the far end (right and behind the screen) are two celebrated bases with reliefs on three sides, found in 1922 in a section of the wall of Themistocles: *3477. In front, six nude epheboi playing a ball game with curved sticks, strongly resembling modern hockey; left and right sides, chariot scenes (c 490 BC). *3476. In front, nude epheboi practising wrestling, jumping, and throwing the javelin; left side, six epheboi playing a ball game; right side, four clothed epheboi starting a fight between a dog and a cat (c 510 BC). To the left of the far door, 796. Acroterion of stele (Cycladic, c 440 BC). To the right of door: 36. Fragment of a relief, notable for the finely executed detail of its drapery (Attic, c 500 BC).

ROOM 12 leads off towards the front of the building. SCULPTURE FROM THE TEMPLE OF APHAIA AT AEGINA. 1933–38. Warriors' heads from the first version (c 500 BC) of the E pediment; for some reason unknown the figures were later replaced by new ones (now in Munich) and the heads buried. 1959. Relief of a running hoplite (end of 6C BC) found near the 'Theseion'; 1605. 'The Daphni Torso'; 3711. Seated marble figure, draped; 782. Palmette from a stele of c 500 BC; 3687. 'Kouros of the Ilissos' (early 5C).

5C Sculpture. ROOM 14 is devoted to funerary stelai or GRAVE MONUMENTS of provincial origin. The period here represented, during which the sculptured stele developed from a single figure to a group composition, is almost entirely lacking in Attica, probably due to a decree of Kleisthenes (c 509) prohibiting unnecessary expenditure on grave monuments. In the centre: *3990. Fragment of votive medallion of Parian marble, unique in form, found at Melos in 1937; the expressive relief may represent Aphrodite, and is dated stylistically to 460 BC 11761. Bronze Warrior, damaged but fine.

Round the walls (left to right): 734. Stele of Ekkedamos, found at Larissa (local work of c 440); 39. Stele, signed by Alxenor of Naxos, found at Orchomenos (Boeotia); 739. Stele of Amphotto, found at Pyri, near Thebes, work of a Boeotian artist c 440 BC; 735. Stele found at Vonitsa (c 460); 3344. Votive relief of a boy victor crowning himself (Cape Sounion, c 470); 741. Stele of a youth wearing the petasos and holding a hare, 733. Stele of Polyxena (both local Thessalian work); 4478–9. Ionic capitals from Sounion.

The principal masterpiece of ROOM 15 stands in the centre. * *15161. *Poseidon*, a powerful bronze of heroic proportions salvaged from the sea off Cape Artemision in 1928. This is an original work of c 450 BC possibly by the sculptor Kalamis; the god held, and is poised to hurl, a trident. It is surrounded by 5C marbles. Within the door (left) is the famous *Relief from Eleusis* (126) representing Triptolemos receiving

the ears of corn from Demeter, while Kore crowns him with a garland
This grand work in very low relief and somewhat hieratic style be
longs to the period (c 440 BC) immediately preceding the highes
development of Greek sculpture.

To the left, 742. Grave relief of a youth from Thespiai (Boeotia), work of a loca
artist influenced by Ionic prototypes (c 440 BC; the inscription shows re-use ii
Roman times when the hair was probably restyled); 54. Base with sculpture
reliefs; 1732. Hebe (mutilated) found near the Temple of Ares in the Agora
probably the central acroterion of the temple. On the other side of the room are
various heads; 1825. Stele of a boy; 1385. Relief (fragmentary) of an idealise
youth standing behind his horse; 828. Thespian stele (c 440); the hero, witl
chlamys flying, rides a galloping horse.

Beyond the great bronze, 332. Head of Hermes, from Piraeus, perhap
by Euphron (440 BC). To the left, 1664. Roman copies of statues o
Theseus and the Minotaur. At the far end of the gallery, 248. Roma
copy in marble of another bronze youth of the school of Kalamis (foun
in the Olympieion in 1888); 45. The *'Omphalos' Apollo*, misname
from the base (46, in the corner) found with it in the theatre of Dio
nysos; it is a copy (2C AD) of an original bronze by Kalamis.

We enter (ROOM 16) the HALL OF CLASSICAL GRAVE MONUMENT
where are displayed examples of Attic work of the late 5C when Kleis
thenes' decree had lapsed.

Attic grave reliefs, starting again c 440 BC, continue all the provincial develop
ments. Four main types may be distinguished: narrow stelai, sometimes in th
form of a pilaster crowned by palmettes or the like, with a rectangular 'picture' ii
low relief, often with the addition of rosettes; monuments in the form of a vas
ornamented in low relief; broad stelai with sculptured family groups, terminatin
in a cornice or pediment; lastly the great naïskos monuments (*or ædicula*) of th
4C (comp. below) with increased emphasis on the temple-like character of th
architectural frame.

Opposite the doorway stands (4485) the wonderful *Myrrhin*
Lekythos, found in Sindagma Sq. and acquired in 1960 from the Vou
ros mansion; Hermes Psychopompos leads Myrrhine to the river c
Acheron while her living relatives look on (c 420 BC). Also in th
centre are: 14498. Red-figured Pelike by the painter Polion (420–41
BC), found on the Sacred Way near the Botanic Garden; it contained
cremation burial. 3709. Stele from the Kerameikos, unusual in havin
reliefs (lion and lioness) on both sides. 4502. Marble *Base on whic*
stood a lekythos or loutrophoros; the reliefs show Hermes Psychopom
pos, the dead maiden receiving apples picked by a youth (? Elysia
Fields), and a bearded priest with a knife (found in Athens). *715
Tombstone of Pentelic marble (c 430 BC, perhaps by Agorakritos), i
high relief and surmounted by a superb frieze of palmettes and lilies
the youth bids farewell while his small grieving slave leans sadly on
pillar bearing a (?) cat below a birdcage.

Round the walls: 711. Stele of a woman seated in a high-backed chair, in a sever
style probably not Attic (found at Piraeus); 766. Stele of Aristylla, erected by he
parents (Piraeus c 440 BC); 716. Later stele from Piraeus, notable for the expres
sions of grief of the mourners; painted stelai, with names incised but no relie
714. Early naïskos from Piraeus (c 390 BC); 1858. Upper part of a stele in low relie
showing the profile of a young girl; 910. Similar: 3845. Stele of Mnesagora an
her little brother Nicochares, erected by their parents (found at Anagyrous, Vari
713. Stele of Lysander; Chairestrate (? the boy's mother), standing, offers him
bird. 37. Fragment of a striking life-sized figure from Kythnos, by an islan
sculptor; 880. Two old men shake hands, while a little girl offers her hand to
(Piraeus c 435 BC); 712. Attic stele of the family of Iphistiadai, with facing lions o
the fronton.

ROOM 17 displays CLASSICAL VOTIVE SCULPTURE, selected examples of the work of practised sculptors of the 5C. In the centre, *1783. Double relief found near New Phaleron station; on one side the local hero Echelos carrying off his bride Iasile in a chariot, with Hermes in the role of nymphagogos (best man); on the other, Artemis with gods and nymphs; 1500. Offering to Dionysos by actors holding masks (from Piraeus); 254. Attic marble statue of a young athlete from Eleusis (4C BC; probably after an original by Polykleitos). 176. Young girl, from Piraeus. Round the walls: 199. Statuette of a young man found at Rhamnous, dedicated by Lysikleides, son of Epandrides; 203–214. Fragments of sculptures from the base of the statue of Nemesis at Rhamnous, by Agorakritos of Paros, pupil of Pheidias (430–420 BC). Architectural sculpture from the Heraion at Argos is displayed on two sides of the room: fragmentary metopes, cornice with lion's head spouts, and reliefs of cuckoos, Hera's bird; 1571. Head of Hera, by Argive sculptor of Polykleitan school. 226. Stele of a priestess of Apollo found at Mantinea, possibly the famous Diotima of the Symposium of Plato (c 410 BC); 2756. *Relief dedicated by Xenokrateia, showing her leading the little Xeniades to the river-god Kephissos who greets him; to the left and right are Apollo and Acheloös (c 400 BC, from the same sanctuary as 1783); 1391. Relief of an apobates, from the Amphiaraion.

ROOM 20 leads off from R. 17 (turn right; to the left is ROOM 19). Votive reliefs: 1394. Ephebos with horses, showing influence of the Parthenon frieze (430–420 BC); 1329, dedicated to Pan and the Nymphs, from the S side of the Acropolis; 3572. Persephone seated with Demeter standing (c 430 BC). 309. Funeral banquet; 223. Small torso of Apollo (copy of 2C BC). The remainder of the room is devoted to copies deriving from works of *Pheidias* (and his school), notably the Athena Parthenos; 1612. Torso of Apollo, Roman copy of a lost original by Pheidias; 200–202. Statuettes from Eleusis, copies of figures from the W pediment of the Parthenon. At the far end, 129. The *Varvakeion Athena*, so called because discovered near the School of that name in 1880. This statuette is a reduced copy dating from the 2C or 3C AD (at one-twelfth of the original) of the great chryselephantine statue of Pheidias though in itself it is disappointing and the workmanship, careful enough in its way, lacks inspiration. Nearly all the features of the original seem to be reproduced; Athena's right hand (in which she holds the winged victory) is here, however, resting on a pillar of no known order, possibly following a late addition made (after damage ?) to Pheidias' work. 4491. Part of a colossal head of Athena, from the workshop of Agorakritos; 177. Head of a goddess, copy of another chryselephantine statue of the 5C (found in the Herodes theatre); 128. The *Lenormant Athena*, an unfinished copy in miniature from the Roman period of Pheidias' statue; 3718. Athena of the Pnyx; copy (2C AD) of the head of a colossal statue in the style of the master.

R. 19. 3854. Relief of youths (in the Pyrrhic dance); 1811. Aphrodite, copy (1C AD) of a bronze original, perhaps by Kallimachos; 3949. Copy of the cult statue of Nemesis at Rhamnous by Agorakritos (Roman; found in Athens, 1934); 3569. Head of Aphrodite, a contemporary replica in miniature of an Attic bronze, c 420 BC; 3043. Acroterion (c 410 BC); 4531. Choregic relief with masks (5C BC) from Dhionisos.

Steps lead down from R. 20 to the charming ATRIUM, with a mosaic of Medusa in the centre. The surrounding colonnade shelters moving 4C grave stelai of children and Roman sarcophagi, as well as much-eroded marble statuary recovered from the sea off Antikythera (comp. below).

At the far end, a pleasant café.

In ROOM 18 are displayed LATE-5C AND EARLY-4C SEPULCHRAL

MONUMENTS. *3624. *Stele of Hegeso*, c 400 BC, from the Keramei-kos cemetery, a masterpiece perhaps by Kallimachos himself; Hegeso seated examines a necklace (originally painted in) from a trinket-box held by her maid. 3472. Funeral stele of Theano, wife of Ktesileos of Erythrai (Athens; late 5C BC). Two marble lekythoi (835. Rider and hoplites; the background, perhaps an addition, is delicately sketched in but unfinished; 2584). Round the walls. 765. Stele of Mika and Dion from the Kerameikos; 2744, 754. Parts of the War Memorial erected by the city of Athens in honour of hoplites and cavalry who fell near Corinth and at Koroneia in 394 BC, found NE of the Dipylon; the list includes the name of Dexileos. 902. Stele of Tynnias, from Piraeus; 831. Stele of Phrasikleia; 3790. Stele of a young mother, from Psyk-hiko; Case of Attic white-ground lekythoi of the same period; 723. Stele of Polyxene; *717. Stele from the Kerameikos; a young girl bids farewell to her parents; 752. Stele of Demokleides, son of Demetrios, a hoplite list in a naval battle; 718. Grave relief of Ameinokleia from Piraeus (360–350 BC); 724. Stele of Phainarete; 13789. Bronze funeral kalpis (ash jar; 5C); 1822. Funeral stele of a woman, by a Peloponne-sian Sculptor (420–410 BC) found near Omonoia Square.

ROOM 21 (Central Hall). In the centre, *15177. *Horse and Jockey of Artemision*, a lively masterpiece in bronze of the 2C BC, found with the statue of Poseidon, and pieced together from many fragments. The jockey is winning a race at full gallop; note, on the horse's right hind leg below the rump, brand markings of ownership. *1826. *Diadoumenos*: a good copy of c 100 BC of a lost bronze original by Polykleitos, found at Delos. The support with the false attributes of Apollo is an addition of the copyist. 3622. The 'Matron of Hercula-neum', copy of a Greek work attributed to Lysippos; the best known copy of this work was found at Herculaneum. 218. Hermes of Andros, found at Palaiopolis (Andros); copy in Parian marble of an Attic ori-ginal of the school of Praxiteles. 720. Sepulchral relief of Melite from Piraeus (mid-4C BC); 2308. Epikranion; 3964. Stele of Pausimache (Attic, c 370 BC); *3708. Base of a grave stele (early 4C BC) with reliefs of a rider fighting a hoplite, found near the Academy of Plato.

Since rearrangement is still proceeding in the New Wing, it is better to see next the rooms that are open there (and at least the Thera frescoes on the upper floor, see below) before continuing to Room 22, even though this breaks the intended sequence.

Beyond the colonnade, ROOM 34, connecting the old museum with the new wing, is arranged to suggest an open-air sanctuary. In the centre, 1495. Altar dedicated by the Boule near the Agora to Aphrodite Hege-mone and the Graces. Grouped round it are reliefs of differing prove-nance and quality. To the left: 303. Triple Hekate, Goddess of the crossroads (late Roman) found at Epidauros; 252. Pan holding the syrinx, from Sparta; another example of the same subject (3534) stands farther on; 4465, 4466. Attic reliefs (4C BC) dedicated to the nymphs, found in the Cave of the Nymphs, Mt Pentelikon; 1778. Attic relief dedicated to Zeus Meilichios (3C BC), found near the Ilissos. At the end of the room, to either side, 2756, 1783. Two limestone bases (end of 5C BC) bearing the inscriptions of the dedicators surmounted by casts of the votive reliefs now in the Classical gallery (see below). Returning along the other side, 227. Torso: copy of the 1C BC from the same original as the Aphrodite of Arles now in the Louvre. 1451–52. Reliefs (4C BC). Erotes carrying incense-burners, from the sanctuary of Aphrodite and Eros on the N slope of the Acropolis.

We enter (left) the NEW WING, where the arrangement is still unfin-

Upper Floor rooms indicated by Roman numerals

NATIONAL ARCHAEOLOGICAL MUSEUM

ished. ROOM 36. The **Karapános Collection**, the fruits of excavations by K. Karapános in 1875–77 at Dodona and elsewhere, with later finds from the same sites. The original collection, presented to the State in 1902, is particularly rich in small bronze objects, of which we note the most outstanding. On a pedestal in front of the door: 27, 16547. Bronze horseman; the horse was recovered in 1956. *First Case* (right): Bronze strips with inscriptions of decrees, treaties, manumissions, etc., and Leaden strips with questions asked of the Oracle at Dodona and answers similarly inscribed; the strips were varnished with some preservative. Cheek-shields. The *Second Case* contains votive figures dedicated to the god of the oracle: 22. Satyr; 31. Zeus hurling a thunderbolt; 54. Ram; on the shelf below, 70. Hand holding a dove; 166. Cheek-piece of an ancient bronze helmet, of exquisite hammered work probably Corinthian (early 4C BC); bottom shelf, Helmet. On a pedestal, 25. Woman playing the double flute. In the *Third Case* (right) are delightful animal figures, and (557) Bronze frying-pan. In a *Wall Case*, beyond: Archaic terracotta figures of Artemis from Corfù.—The

First Case (left) contains 24. Statuette of a runner, c 530 BC; 36. Horseman. In the *Third Case* is a finely wrought statue of a warrior (550 BC). Beside, on a pedestal, a fine 5C statuette of Zeus hurling his thunderbolt. Farther on, mounted on a reconstruction in wood, bronze wheelhubs and decoration of a Roman state chariot. At the end of the room, 965. Attic gravestone, slave handing open jewel-box to her lady (330 BC).

ROOM 37 is the first of the BRONZE ROOMS to be opened. To left, case with finds and reconstructions demonstrating ancient casting etc. techniques. The other cases have a fine range of votive offerings from various parts of Greece: Boeotia (including the Ptoon sanctuary), Macedonia, Thessaly and the North, Crete (the Idaean cave).

Rooms 38–43 are at present closed. The bronze statues from Piraeus, formerly on display here are now in the Piraeus Museum (comp. below).

First Floor, see below.

We now return to the central hall and continue in the SOUTH WING. ROOM 22. SCULPTURES FROM EPIDAUROS. The display has been remounted since all the fragments formerly at Epidauros were brought together here by Mr. N. Yalouris. Figures from the W pediment of the Temple of Asklepios at Epidauros (c 380 BC), probably by Timotheus; the positions of the three acroteria are shown; one depicts Penthesilea, queen of the Amazons. The fragments from the E pediment, which represented the capture of Troy, include the Nike (or Eros) of the central acrotcrion. 173. Relief panel showing Asklepios.—RR. 23–24. 4C FUNERARY MONUMENTS, notably (in R. 23) *869, 'Stele of the Ilissos', commemorating a young hunter; his father stands at the right, a little slave sits at his master's feet (c 340 BC; possibly by Skopas); *870. Grave relief of two women, Attic work of the mid-4C BC; (in R. 24) 823, 824. Scythian archers, probably from the monument of an officer (Kerameikos; ? from the tomb of Lysimachides of Acharnai); 1488. Stele with bilingual inscription in Greek and Phoenician and an unusual theme; 3716. Seated woman (note the drapery; 380 BC); 2574. Monument of Alexos of Sounion (c 320 BC).

Rooms 25–27 are at present closed.

ROOM 28 is devoted to late Classical sculpture. LAST FUNERARY MONUMENTS OF ATTICA comprise the first group: 738. Monument of Aristonautes (c 310 BC), a realistic armed figure depicted in full relief in a deep naiskos; 803, 804. Pair of marble lions from the Kerameikos; *4464. Large relief of a small negro trying to control a spirited horse (c 300 BC) found near Larissa station (Athens) in 1948; 1005. The latest known Attic tomb-relief before the prohibition of 307 BC, found in the Kerameikos (the drapery is astonishing). In the centre of the room: 13396. **Ephebos of Antikythera (c 340 BC), found in 1900 at the bottom of the sea; this is possibly the Paris of the sculptor *Euphranor*. The eyes are inlaid and the lashes fashioned from bronze plate. The famous bronze is surrounded by originals and later marble copies of works of the same period. 178–80. Boar's and warriors' heads from the Temple of Athena Alea at Tegea (? W Pediment), by *Skopas* (c 340 BC), almost the only surviving certain work of one of the greatest Greek sculptors. The expression of emotion contrasts with the 5C calm and foreshadows the agonies of the Hellenistic school of Pergamon. 182 (? also by Skopas). Head of Ariadne. 323. Head of Asklepios. *3602. Hygieia from Tegea (by Skopas ?).

ROOM 29, FIRST HELLENISTIC SCULPTURE ROOM. Centre (right), 247. Fighting Gaul, from Delos (c 200 BC); (left), 231. Statue of Themis, goddess of Justice, from Rhamnous (by Chairestratos; early 3C BC); to the left, 239. Young Satyr (Lamia; 3C BC); 215–217. Three reliefs found at Mantineia. representing the musical contest of Apollo and Marsyas, perhaps the bases of a group of Leto and her Children, executed by Praxiteles and noted by Pausanias; 245. Dionysos embracing a Satyr (unfinished; late 4C); 327. Head of Demosthenes, found in

1849 in the Royal Garden, a late copy of a bronze by Polyeuktos; Heads of a colossal group by Damophon from Lykosoura (p. 309).

ROOM 30. *13400. Portrait head of a philosopher, found in the sea off Antikythera (3C BC) and other fragments from the statue; 2772. Statuette of Ianiskos playing with a goose (3C BC), found at Lilaia. *6439. Portrait of a boxer from Olympia, uncompromisingly naturalistic; possibly the head of a bronze statue of the athlete Satyros by the Athenian sculptor Silanion (c 340 BC); the lips are inlaid. *3266. Portrait head from a statue, from the Stoa of Attalos (c 150 BC); 3556. Ariarathes V (c 120 BC); 235. Poseidon of Melos (of Parian marble; c 140 BC); *14612. Head from Delos, a lifelike portrait of a man torn by doubts, of c 100 BC; *351. Portrait of a (?) Thracian priest, a fine Attic work of the end of the Hellenistic period (1C BC); 3485. 'The little refugee', a child holding a dog (brought from Asia Minor in 1922); 232. Aristonoe, a priestess of Nemesis, dedicated by her son Hierokles at Rhamnous; 3335. Aphrodite defending her honour from Pan (the so-called 'Slipper Slapper'—well-preserved but inartistic), from the House of the Poseidoniastai at Delos, c 100 BC; 1829. Artemis, also from Delos; 457. Head of a youth (late 1C BC); 259, 260. Two relief slabs from the Theatre of Dionysos, depicting (?) Horai, with wind-blown drapery.— R. 31 has a miscellaneous collection of sculpture, including a large sarcophagus.

In R. 32 is displayed the *** *Hélène Stathátos Collection**, presented in 1957, consisting of objects of all periods from the Bronze Age to Byzantine times from Thessaly, Chalcidia, and Macedonia, and a most precious array of ancient *Jewellery and gold ornament. Unique are a breast ornament in gold of the 3C BC from Thessaly, consisting of a medallion of Aphrodite in relief surrounded by a network of fine chain; and a naïskos (c 300 BC) in gold, set with precious stones, depicting Dionysos and a Satyr. No finds similar to these have ever been recorded in any scientific excavation. Unique also (Case 6), St. 332 the red-figured ceramic in the shape of an egg. Among small bronzes are (St. 328) an Archaic kriophoros and (St. 316) a graceful doe; and a fine bronze helmet of Illyrian type, with a gold funeral mask, which perhaps belong together. In ROOM 33 a display of sculpture of the Roman period is in preparation.

The FIRST FLOOR, approached from the central hall (comp. above), is devoted to **Pottery**, mainly of post-Mycenaean date with a few typical earlier pieces; in general earlier pottery is displayed on the ground floor with other contemporary objects. Classical vase-painting is represented by a daunting array of examples, of all shapes and great mythological interest, and of high average quality; if few rank with the greatest masterpieces now in the major museums of Europe and America, they have the special advantage of being entirely free of foreign admixture. The collection, which is beautifully displayed in chronological sequence, is unique for the *** *Early Vases**.

VESTIBULE. Typical pithos, with plain bands in relief, of the Minoan period in Crete, found at Knossos (1878) before systematic excavations were undertaken there; other large storage jars; case of a votive relief (from the Acropolis), depicting a potter offering two cups to Athena Ergane, goddess of industry; case of prehistoric pottery from various places and periods.

Off the centre of the vestibule has been mounted a temporary exhibition of recent finds from **Akrotiri on Thira** (Rte 73); these are eventually to be accommodated on the island. The first room contains an extensive display of Cycladic and imported Minoan pottery of the early Late Bronze Age (16C BC). Especially attractive are some of the pictorial scenes (vegetation, dolphins, birds). Also stone vessels and bronze objects (sickles, scale balances etc.). The second room has the spectacular **Frescoes**: swallows and lilies in a rocky landscape; monkeys; antelopes and boxing childrren (perhaps juxtaposed to compare rites of passages in the human and animal kingdoms); fisherman with catch; priestess; *ikrion* (stern cabin from ship)—the motif visible on the 'ship fresco', part of a frieze c 6m long showing a maritime procession from one coastal town to another (perhaps in celebration of the Annual Resumption of Navigation after the close winter season); from the same room (in the 'West House') and the same fresco series are a sub-tropical landscape and a battle by a town, with warriors on the shore. The state of preservation of these paintings is unique in the Aegean Bronze Age. They are clearly based on Cretan models for both technique and subject but there are also local Cycladic (and possibly Mycenaean) features. Their full significance for our understanding of the representational art of this period is only beginning to be properly appreciated.

We leave the Akrotiri exhibition and turn left into the vase rooms.

ROOM I. Characteristic pottery of the **Bronze Age** (3rd–2nd millennium BC), showing the first attempts at painting in the Aegean, together with Mycenaean idols; note the lily and papyrus motives derived from Cretan models and ultimately from Egypt. **Protogeometric and Geometric Pottery** (10–7C).

In the upheaval following the Mycenaean downfall, as pottery deteriorated into 'sub-Mycenaean', designs grew more stylised and perfunctory and were reduced to geometric patterns. About 1025 BC, a new pottery style developed. This *Protogeometric* style, though it involved no change of actual technique and though it made use of the previous shapes and decorative motives, was important because it was the first sign of a new spirit, creative instead of decadent (comp. the works of V.R. Desborough). The style is common to the whole of Greece (disseminated, perhaps by Attic seamen?), but Attic invention soon becomes dominant and Athens emerges for the first time as the artistic centre of the Greek world. At the beginning of the period vase-painters use simple decorative motives, circles, and semicircles drawn in dark glaze on the light surface of the clay. Later, in the full *Geometric* style, which brings in new vase types with broad bases, potters begin to cover the greater part of the surface with black glaze; the decoration, at first restricted to zones filled with circles and linear patterns arranged in panels, later covers the whole vase in horizontal bands. In the 8C the human figure begins to take a prominent place in vase decoration, chiefly on large sepulchral amphorae and kraters. Scenes generally show the prothesis (laying out of the dead), the ekphora (funeral procession), and funeral games, especially chariot racing. This period coincides with the historical unification of Attica under Athens. The leading artist of the age is the so-called 'Dipylon Painter' of the Kerameikos.

To the left of the room, typical examples, standing alone, add emphasis to the general exposition. Against the wall (right): progression of 10–9C (Protogeometric) vases, at first with simple geometric motives; we see the first appearance of the meander (218) and of the swastika; designs cover larger areas and show increased mastery of technique; more elaborately decorated pottery. In the centre, 216. Amphora. To the left, Geometric vases of the 9–8C. To the right, freestanding, are two Amphorae from the Kerameikos, with overall geometric decoration, one with serpents in relief on the handles; in the large case at right angles to them; 169, 186, 201–202. Fine examples of the Geometric style (8C), including a bronze tripod that supported a kalpis (cremation urn); beyond, a case with many figured fragments. In a case on the left wall: vases from excavations (1935) on Mt Hymettos; 192. Oinochoë with a graffito in primitive Greek characters of the

8C, reading 'He who dances better than the other dancers will receive this'. 17935 (beyond). Painted Geometric amphora with chariot race and helmeted warriors. Case: contemporary bronze and terracotta figurines, and pyxides. Further case of mature Geometric pottery (8C). Between the pillars, *803. Large late-Geometric amphora of the 'Dipylon' type from the Kerameikos, with typical scenes of prothesis and ekphora (c 750 BC).

In the long vestibule to the next room, various large works in the Ripe Geometric style: 810. Vase in the form of a bowl (frieze of men and four-horse chariot) on an ornamental stand with four bands of painting; 894. Tall amphora with two friezes: chariots, with warriors, and procession of warriors.

ROOMS II AND III are mainly devoted to **7C Ceramics** of the style known generally as *Orientalising* and in its regional application as *Protoattic*.

By the end of the 8C Geometric art becomes perfunctory. The old precision of drawing is neglected but often for the sake of giving the whole composition movement and pictorial coherence. In the 7C Greek colonists penetrated the Black Sea and ranged to Sicily and beyond, making close contacts with both Egyptian and Phoenician culture. Greek potters come under the rejuvenating influence of oriental motives. Linear patterns are replaced by lotus and palmette ornaments, trees, birds, animals (often in hieratic stance), chimaeras, gorgons, sphinxes, etc. (comp. the grave monuments of Archaic sculpture). Mythological subjects are increasingly depicted: at first Centaurs and monsters, later heroic myths distortedly reflecting a memory of the great Mycenaean days, transmitted in Homeric poetry.

Along the right wall: Empedocleous Bequest (Geometric). Early 7C vases showing the beginning of oriental influences. 313. *Analatos Hydria*, having mixed decoration, Geometric on the neck, Orientalising on the shoulder, with a choral scene on the body. Amphora painted with scene of a warrior's departure, perhaps Hector and Andromache. In the centre: a case of Late Geometric then, on its own, a fine crater by the Hirschfeld Painter. Case of regional Geometric pottery. To right, case of Corinthian aryballoi showing (right to left) the evolution of the shape. In the centre, 220. Huge amphora from Thebes; metopes depict a bird of prey and Artemis as mistress of the brute creation. Returning along the left wall: contents of a tomb from Pyri, near Thebes; Boeotian figurines; 13257. Priest-king seated on a throne. 228. Boeotian stamnos with horse and lion metopes. 15424. Protoattic krater of the earliest Orientalising style from Phaleron (early 7C). Case of Boeotian and Euboean pottery: note *14481. Clay cart in the form of a horse on wheels carrying six amphoræ (Euboea; ? 9C). To the left as we pass into the next room, 238. Attic louterion from Thebes; the centaurs have human forelegs, an early conception. 14497. The *Kynosarges Amphora*.

ROOM III. Four cases in the left-hand corner contain 7C ware from Crete (12509 shows Egyptian influence); from Naxos, Santorin, and Rhodes (12717. Oinochoë decorated with lotus flowers and realistic gazelles); from other Aegean islands; and from Cyprus (17376. Chariot with three figures in pottery). In front are four fine amphorae from Melos, *911. Two Muses (?) in chariot, accompanied by Apollo and Artemis; on neck, combat of Ajax and Odysseus over the arms of Achilles. *354. On neck, meeting of Hermes and Iole; on body, Herakles mounting chariot in which Iole is accompanied by Eurytos and Antiope, her father and mother; the colouring is rich and the ornamentation elaborate.—We pass into the main body of the room. To the left, Tanagra vases. To the right, Ripe Protoattic pottery: on the middle stand, three kraters from a tomb at Anagyrous, near Vari, probably all by the same painter (c 620 BC) and clearly occupying a position midway between the Orientalising and Black-figure styles; 16384. Prometheus bound and Herakles shooting the eagle. Opposite stands 221. *The Siren Amphora* (c 630 BC) with black figures on a yellow-grey ground. In the last case to the left: 16391. Amphora, a good example of several showing Chimaera and Bellerophon. At the end of the room, *1002. *The Nessos Amphora*, still archaic but with many of the techniques brought to perfection in black-and red-figure work; on the neck, the struggle of Herakles with the Centaur, Nessos; below, the three Gorgons (Medusa has already been beheaded by Perseus); from the Kerameikos (c 600 BC).

ROOM IV. Three cases inside the door (right) contain miscellaneous finds from the *Heraion of Argos*, both pottery and bronzes, covering many centuries. The large amphora in front comes from a cemetery near the Academy of Plato (c 570 BC). A group of cases opposite the door contains examples of the **Early Black-Figured Style**, several signed by the painter *Sophilos* (590–580 BC): 15499. Fragmentary Lebes, representing the funeral games of Patroklos, found near Pharsala; another, similarly signed, Marriage of Thetis and Peleus; others from the Acropolis by the 'Gorgon painter'. 12587. Krater, by *Sophilos*, Herakles and Nereus; in both style and subject it recalls the poros pediment from the Acropolis; 991. Loutrophoros from Vourva, by the same; on stand, 1036. Amphora, a late work by *Sophilos* found in the Tumulus at Marathon.

The *Black-Figure* technique, which is first clearly distinguished in Protocorinthian pottery, neglects outline drawing in favour of silhouette. The design is laid on the reddish clay with some addition of incised lines. Later the black is improved to the brilliant Attic glaze, and white (for women's flesh) and dark red paint are added. Decorated patterns are reduced until only the body of the vase has importance, usually adorned with paired subjects on opposing sides.

Continuing clockwise round the room: Vases and terracotta figurines from graves in Boeotia (early 6C). Pottery (of Corinthian workmanship; 7C and 6C from the Heraion at Perachora (comp. below).

In the last case (left), ivories from the Temple of Artemis Orthia at Sparta (late 8C or early 7C BC) of material imported from Syria or Phoenicia; lead figurines of the same provenance. On the end wall, terracotta metopes from the archaic Temple of Apollo at Thermon in Aetolia, with painted decoration by Corinthian artists (c 630 BC); above, antefixes from the same temple. On the right wall, two cases of Protocorinthian pottery: notable are 295. Bombyle (for pouring a drop at a time) and vases showing Bacchic or Dionysiac scenes; 664 has the earliest known representation of Dionysos (last quarter of the 7C). Model temples in terracotta (8C Geometric) from the Heraion at Perachora. Bronzes and model Archaic house (7C) from the Heraion of Argos. In the centre group of cases: Bronzes from the Sanctuary of Athena of the Brazen House, and Ivories from the Temple of Artemis Orthia, both at Sparta. Portions of tempera painting on wood from Corinth (520–500 BC).

In ROOM V we are able to compare and contrast works of the mid-6C BC from Attica, the Islands, and Asia Minor.

In the course of this century **Attic Black-Figured Vases** win all the markets from Corinth. New shapes (e.g. the kylix) are invented; old shapes are refined as pottery is increasingly demanded for practical household use by the aristocratic society of the Peisistratid period and for export all over the expanding Greek world. A characteristic of technique is the use of incision; mythological scenes are treated with increasing naturalness and humanity; scenes from everyday life become more usual. Known artists of the period include Kleitias (570–560), Phrynos, Nearchos, Lydos, Exekias (540–530), and the 'Amasis Painter'.

Of shapes there was a variety for different uses. To name the most important: at a 6C or 5C banquet wine was mixed in the *krater*, ladled out with the *kyathos*, distributed in the *oinochoë* or *olpe*, and drunk out of a *kylix*, *kantharos*, *kotyle*, *skyphos*, or *rhyton*. A *psykter* served for refrigeration. The *stamnos* and *amphora* were used for storing wine or oil, libations were poured with a *phiale*, scents or oils were carried in a *lekythos*, *alabastron*, or *aryballos*, water in a *hydria*. A *loutrophoros* was used for lustral waters at weddings and funerals.

Inside the door (left), vases, many with scenes from the myth of Herakles; *404. Lekythos (Rape of Helen), found at Tanagra, by the '*Amasis Painter*', c 530 BC; 567. Another with satyr watching a maiden. Beyond is displayed a terracotta model (7C) of a funeral chariot from the Anagyrous necropolis: mourning women surround the bier; the small figure on the pall may represent the spirit of the dead; a rider escorts the procession. On a stand, Attic black-figured lebes, Greeks and Trojans fighting (560 BC). In a case including early-6C Corinthian ware, 559. Amphora foreshadowing the Panathenaic type with fluteplayer and jockey; 521. Olpe, Akamos in chariot; the horses' names are inscribed.

The centre case and the remaining three cases on the left contain Athenian vases of thematic interest: In the centre, 445 (kylix). Epheboi with instructors; 493 (lekythos). Sacrifice scene; 1054 (kylix). Monkey on a horse's neck; 1055. Aryballos with inscription 'Kealtes painted (it), Mnesikleides gave (it) to Phokis' (c 550 BC). In the second, fragments found on the Acropolis including pieces by major painters (Kleitias, Lydos, Nearchos (a fine piece with Achilles and horses), the Amasis Painter. In the fourth, 2410–7. Plaques (pinax) by *Exekias*, part of a frieze from an erection over a tomb. Two Ionian sarcophagi and pottery from Klazomenai (near Smyrna; late and early 6C). Etruscan vases in terracotta or bronze. Finds from the islands, notably 3886. Funeral stele with low relief of a man holding a lance, with inscriptions written in Greek characters but in an unknown language, from Lemnos.

ROOM VI. On the left, Lekythoi with mythological scenes: 488. Death of Aktaion; others depict Theseus and the Minotaur, Thetis and Peleus, etc. In the next case, excellent Attic examples of the *Black-figured style (some, unusually, on a white ground); 1134. Dionysos, (Apollo and Hermes; 1124. Theseus slaying the Marathonian bull (?); 550. Peleus bringing the young Achilles to Cheiron. 1045. Oinochoë made by *Xenokles* and painted by *Kleisophos*, Bacchanalian scene (found in the Theatre of Dionysos).

The black-figured ware continues on the right side of the room. In the first case, amid other lekythoi on a yellow ground: 1129. Satyrs torturing Lamia, legendary queen of Libya, realistically violent; 1125. The chariot of Amphiaraos is swallowed up by the earth (490 BC). On a stand, 19312. *Panathenaic Amphora* (prize given at the Games, which remained by tradition in black-figure to the end), with boxing scenes, etc. Further case with material from Acropolis, including that of named painters.

Black-figured decoration reaches its peak c 500 BC and gives way to **Red-Figured Pottery**, in which the decoration is left in the ground colour and the background filled with black (a technique already started by 520). Detail is rendered in thin glazed lines. As complete mastery of draughtmanship is attained, figures lose the archaic stiffness and the art reaches perfection in the time of Pericles. Accessory colours, sparingly used in the 5C, are increasingly added in the 4C. Contemporaneously from c 460 develops white-ground ware (comp. below), with designs at first in black glaze, later in matt polychromy.

The free-standing *Calyx-Krater (Theseus and the Minotaur; by *Syriskos*, c 480 BC), in the centre of the room, begins the display of

RED-FIGURED VASES. The case beyond (left) shows early examples: 15002. Alabastron signed by *Pasiades*; 1409. Kylix signed by *Pamphaios*; 1628. Kylix (helmeted hoplite), signed by *Phintias*. On the opposite side of the room, wall-case, Vases found on the Acropolis, mostly dedicated to Athena by the artists themselves (e.g. pyxis by *Makron*). At end (left), case of Attic RF lekythoi.

ROOM VII contains red-figured vases of mature style, to the left mainly of black ground, to the right on white. On pedestal, 9683. Pelike, Herakles killing the attendants of the Egyptian king Busiris, by the *'Pan' Painter* (470 BC). Vase, by *Polygnotos*, representing the poetess Sappho and her pupils. Here, continued in ROOM VIII, begins the unrivalled collection of ***White Lekythoi**, sepulchral vases from Athens and Eretria, with polychrome designs on a white ground.

The commonest subjects are: Offerings at the Tomb; Prothesis, or Lying-in-State; Burial in the Tomb; and Descent into Hades. In the last the deceased is conducted by Hermes to the Styx, where Charon awaits him with his boat. The purest style coincides with the rebuilding of the Acropolis (450–430), after which follows a period of freer design with the addition of red and purple lines. The gems are by the *'Achilles Painter'*, a contemporary of Pheidias, and by contemporaries of *Parrhasios* (420–400). The custom of placing white lekythoi on the funeral stele or in the grave stops at the beginning of the 4C. The references in the 'Ecclesiazusae' of Aristophanes (392 BC) are contemporary with the 'Triglyph Painter' whose work ends the series.

In ROOM VIII, against the end wall is a long new case with examples of two specialised shapes, the *chous* and the *nuptial lebes*, the former used at festivals of Dionysos, the latter in marriage ceremonies.

In ROOM IX are displayed a selection of red-figured vases of various provenance (5C–3C), some of them chosen more for the fascinating themes depicted (Dionysiac, Kabeiroi, etc.) than for fineness of execution. At the far end are a group of mixed red and white figured calyx-kraters; black-figured Panathenaic amphorae (comp. above; Athena on one side; a scene of the contest for which the vase was a prize, on the other), by the door, the 'Niinnion Pinax' from Eleusis.

The unrivalled ***Numismatic Collection** in the S wing begins with Mycenaean bronze talents in a form recalling the double-axe (comp. Il. xxiii, 852); hoard of iron spits (used as currency) and a weighing standard found in the Heraion of Argos in 1894, perhaps those dedicated by Pheidon of Argos (according to Herakleides of Pontus) when he introduced his coinage there after the Lydian model. Among c 400,000 coins (only a few poorly displayed) all the principal types are represented: incuse in electrum with a heraldic design (7C BC); in gold and silver, bearing a religious motive (gods, etc.) from the mid-6C; the famous Classical 'Owls' of Athens; tetradrachms of Philip of Macedon and Alexander the Great with inscriptions; and a fine range of later portrait types.

The **Epigraphic Collection** (entered through a courtyard from Odhos Tositsa), a classical library in stone, comprises some of the most important historical records found in excavations, including decrees, laws, building records, inventories, treaties, etc. Among them are the *Troezen Stele*, with a text of Themistocles' decree of 480, ordering the evacuation of Athens and the naval preparations which led to the battle of Salamis.

10   From Omónoia Square to Ambelókipoi

The whole of this route, which comprises the most important thoroughfares of Athens, is followed by trolley-bus No. 3.

From Omonoia Square (Rte 8) as far as Sindagma Square a choice of two routes is offered by Stadium St and University St, which run parallel in a SE direction. Both are one-way streets, the former in the direction we are describing.

ODHÓS STADHÍOU (in 1945–55 renamed Churchill St), one side of the triangle of streets laid out by Kleanthes and Schaubert in 1834, takes name from its alignment with the stadium (nowadays hidden by the trees of the National Garden). It is a busy street, commercial at the N end, with fashionable hotels and cafés farther S. Half-way along it, opposite the wide Odhós Koraí (left), which affords a sight of the University (see below), the large PLATEÍA KLAFTHMÓNOS opens to the right. During rebuilding operations in this square in 1960–61 a large section of the classical *City Wall* was discovered, part of which is visible in an office building on the NW side. At the W corner is the cruciform **Ayii Theódori** (3, 7), the most attractive Byzantine church in Athens. Founded in 1049 or 1065 (inscription in W wall), it was entirely rebuilt in stone with brick courses and Cufic decoration in the 12C, as an inscription above the W door records. The belfry is a later addition. The humble two-storeyed building with the balcony on the SE side of the square was *King Otho's Palace* and is now a *Museum of the City of Athens* in the 19C (open Monday, Wednesday, Friday mornings). Off the S corner of the square is the fashionable modern church of *Ayios Yeoryios*, with the hall of the Parnassos Literary Society opposite.

In the triangular Plateía Kolokotrónis, farther on, stands an equestrian *Statue of Kolokotronis*, a copy of that in Nauplia by L. Sokhos; the reliefs on the plinth repay examination. Behind is the PALAIA VOULI, a building designed by Boulanger in 1858 to house the National Assembly and finished (with modifications due to the suppression of the Upper House) in 1874. On its steps Theodoros Deliyannis, three times Prime Minister, was assassinated in 1905. In ten rooms on the ground floor is arranged the **National Historical Museum** (closed Monday). The display, which is chronological, includes the ceremonial sword of the Emperor Leo V (813–20); helmets (14–16C) found in the castle at Khalkis; and a painting on wood of the Battle of Lépanto, probably by a Kephalonian eye-witness. Among the extensive collection of portraits, arms, and relics of the War of 1821–28 are objects recovered from Navarino Bay and Byron's helmet and sword; *David d'Angers*, Girl weeping for the death of Botzaris; and a splendid series of small watercolours of the first five years of Otto's reign by Ludwig Kölnberger. The study of King George I is preserved and royal portraits, photographs, etc. of campaigning monarchs. Temporary exhibitions occupy the upper galleries round the *Chamber*.

Shortly beyond, the street bends to enter the lower side of *Sindagma Square* (Rte 1). Continuation, see below.

If we take the alternative LEOFÓROS ELEFTHERÍOU VENIZÉLOU, formerly and still popularly called *Panepistimíou* (University St.), we pass (right) the site of the *Arsakeion* (now demolished), built for a girls' school and training college, founded in 1836 by Apostolos Arsaki (see Rte 15), and until recently used as law courts. The classical building by Kaftandzoglou (1848) is now being restored and will eventually house the Supreme Court. Farther on an important group of buildings is fronted by formal gardens.

In the centre stands the **University** (Πανεπιστήμιον; 3, 6), built in 1839–42 by the Danish architect Christian Hansen. It is the least disturbing of the neo-Greek buildings, the polychrome decoration having been used with discretion. The handsome Ionic portico is of Pentelic marble; its upper part is frescoed with groups of ancient Greek authors. In front stands a statue of Gladstone, to the left and right of the steps are Capodistrias and the philologist Koraï, and before the façade the poet Rhigas and the patriarch Gregory.

The University is modelled on the German system and is governed by a Council (Σύγκλητος) and by a Rector (Πρύτανις), elected annually from among the professors. It comprises five faculties (Σχολάι) of theology, law, medicine, philosophy, and science, each under its Curator (Κοσμήτωρ). The teaching staff of 1289 consists of Professors (Καθηγηταί), ordinary and extraordinary (Τακτικοί and Εκτακοι), and of Lecturers (Υφηγηταί). The Students (Φοιτηταί; 44,438) mostly read law or medicine. Other faculties are provided by the Polytechnic Institute.— Connected with the university are scientific museums (at 33 Akadimias); laboratories and scientific institutes at Goudhi; a Library (see below); a Botanic Garden, a herbarium at Haïdhari, near Dhafni, several hospitals and clinics, and the Observatory.

To the left is the **National Library** (3, 6), planned by Th. von Hansen and built of Pentelic marble in 1887–91 at the expense of P. Vallianos of Kephalonia, whose statue stands in front. The classical style is used with sufficient freedom for the building to look more than a pastiche. Adm. free daily, except holidays, 9–1 & 5–8.

In 1903 the contents of the National Library and the University Library were brought together in this building. It contains c 500,000 printed books and 3500 MSS. The 700 MSS from Thessalian convents include two 10C or 11C Gospels, richly illuminated.

On the far side of the University is the **Hellenic Academy** (3, 6), built in 1859, at the expense of Baron Sinas, to the designs of Th. von Hansen. A pastiche in the style of the Erechtheion, it is entirely faced with Pentelic marble, and is adorned with Ionic columns and sculptured pediments. The façade is painted and gilt after the manner of the buildings of classical antiquity, but the effect is 'academic' in every sense of the word.

The colossal figures of Athena and Apollo, which occupy two lofty and unhappy Ionic columns in front, are by the Greek sculptor Drosos, who was responsible also for the figures in the pediment as well as for the seated statues of Plato and Socrates on each side of the entrance and for the statue of Baron Sinas in the hall.

Just beyond are the *Eye Hospital* (Οφθαλμοιατρείον), designed in a Byzantine style (1847–51) by Th. von Hansen, and the *Roman Catholic Church*, a large Italianate basilica (1870) to a design by Klentze, dedicated to 'St Denis', the composite Western version of the Areopagite. Both buildings were completed by Kaftandzoglou; they face the dignified *Bank of Greece*. Beyond the *Archaeological Society* (founded 1837), *Schliemann's House* (left) may be identified by the inscription on the loggia (Iliou Melathron: Palace of Troy); its pleasing Renaissance style (by Ziller; 1878) was castigated by the neo-Greek Kaftandzoglou as 'an incurable leprosy'. From 1928 until recently it has housed the Areopagos, or Supreme Court of Appeal, an institution reconstituted in 1834. It has now been restored and will shortly become the *Numismatic Museum*.

At the NE corner of Sindagma Square we turn left alongside Parliament House into the aristocratic LEOFÓROS VASILÍSSIS SOFÍAS, lined on the N with embassies and ministries. Hymettos rises ahead. From the left enters Leofóros Akadhimías (once briefly renamed after Roosevelt), a busy avenue that starts at Canning Sq. (Rte 8) and runs parallel to Venizelou. At No. 50, immediately behind the University, is the *Theatre Museum*, with collections illustrating the ancient and modern Greek stage. Here are sets for various plays, the reconstructed dressing-room of Katina Paxinou, and a library.

We pass the **Benaki Museum** (Rte 7). To the left the fashionable district of Kolonaki (see below) rises on the S slope of Lykabettos.

The ***Byzantine Museum** (4, 8; closed Monday) occupies the *Villa Ilissia*, built in a Florentine style in 1848 by Stamatis Kleanthes for the eccentric Sophie de Marbois, duchesse de Plaisance (1785–1854). Here the circle she received included David d'Angers, Edmond About, and Théophile Gautier. The museum was installed in 1930.

We cross a large COURT, in the centre of which is a Phiale, a reproduction of a fountain represented in one of the Daphni mosaics. The mosaic before it is of the 4C, and the font came from the church of the Apostoloi in the Agora. The sculptural fragments to the right are from basilicas of the 5–7C, while those to the left came from 9–15C churches. Below the arcades of the wings are (right) mosaics (Heron killing a snake) from the Basilica by the Ilissos (5C), and (left) window panels from houses in Tinos and other Cycladic islands. The Right Wing contains a display of ikons arranged regionally and chronologically, a great help to appreciation of the main collection.

VESTIBULE. Characteristic examples of early Christian sculpture of the 4–6C: columns, capitals, etc. The doorway in the centre is from the Church of Ay. Dhimitrios in Salonika. Below, Bust of a Priestess (?; 4C) bearing the inscription IZBAPΔIA. To either side, inscribed fragments of a cornice from the Acropolis. Sculptured remains of tombs.— We turn right. ROOM II reproduces a 5–6C **Basilica** in the form of a rectangle divided into nave and aisles by two rows of columns. The nave ends in an apse separated from the *Naos* by transennae and a central free-standing arch. Round the apse is the *Synthronon* (sedilia) with the *Cathedra* (priest's throne) in the centre. Below the marble Altar (*Hiera trapeza*, a square table, with a central circular depression, borne on four columns) is a reliquary in the form of a model sarcophagus sunk into a cruciform depression. To the right of the nave are a plaster copy of an *Ambo* from Salonica and a prothesis table in marble (4C) with sculptured reliefs of animals in a Hellenistic tradition. Round the walls are placed fragments of SCULPTURE from this and other churches. Right Aisle: 72. Christ the Good Shepherd in the guise of a boy (4C; from Old Corinth); 95. Relief of the Nativity, with charming animals; 113. Carved wooden cross. Beneath the arcade: 27. Prothesis table in marble, with reliefs of hunting scenes and Hellenistic heads (4C). Left Aisle: 93. Orpheus surrounded by wild animals; 35. Griffins; epigraphs.

From this aisle opens ROOM III, devoted entirely to **Sculpture** of the main Byzantine period (9–15C). Against the left (W) wall are three marble ikons of the Virgin: in the centre, 148. Virgin as fountain of life, a stiff and formal creation of the 10C or 11C; to either side, 147. Virgin 'Hodegetria' (13–14C), and 149. Virgin 'Orans' (11–12C), each surmounted by a marble arch (152, 154) with representations of the Descent into Hell (from 13C Franco-Byzantine tombs). Round the lower part of the walls are relief slabs of the 9–12C (from iconostases), showing typical Byzantine motifs influenced strongly by the Orient: 159. Lion devouring a gazelle. Above those on the N wall are reliefs with mythological subjects, probably used in secular decoration: 176. Hercules and the Erymanthian boar; 177. Gerene, queen of the Pygmies; 178. Centaur playing a lyre. In the centre of the E wall, 150. Marble plaque with a painting on wax of three apostles, from Moni Vlatadon (Salonika). This is framed in (155) a great arch, surmounted by (251) a slab bearing scenes of the Nativity, both of which formed part of the entrance of a Franco-Byzantine church. Flanking them are two capitals, one (217) bearing monograms referring to Irene, the Athenian empress of Constantinople (AD 797–802). The S wall is devoted to reliefs of the Frankish period: 250. St. John the Baptist, from Zante;

heads of Venetian doges from Corfu.

ROOM IV reproduces a cruciform **Church**, with a cupola, of 11C Byzantine type. The plan is square with the dome supported on two columns and two pilasters. Between the latter a marble screen (*templon*) separates the nave from the sanctuary. This templon consists of a sculptured architrave (copy of that from the Erechtheion) resting on pillars with capitals, and the lower part is filled in with sculptured panels. In the centre under the dome is a slab with a sculptured eagle (*to omphalion*). The sanctuary floor is decorated in *opus Alexandrinum*. The carvings (of finer workmanship than those in R. III) came from Athenian churches. Above the W door, fresco of the Virgin and Child (15C). The impression is of simple dignity, good taste, and harmony of proportion.

Hence we enter ROOM V, a reproduction of a **Post-Byzantine church** in a plain square building (of mosque type) with a flat ceiling. The decoration, mostly 18C, is rococo with marked Turkish influence. The *Iconostasis* is of wood, sculptured and gilded, and panelled with painted ikons; it was reconstructed from pieces from Kephalonia and Ithaca. The bishop's *Throne* was brought by refugees from Asia Minor in 1923. The *Epitaphios*, from Kimolos, was used in the procession of the Dormition of the Virgin. From the ceiling hangs the *Choros*, a huge circle of sculptured wooden plaques. Round the walls frescoes from destroyed churches in Atalanta, Delphi, and Athens (Ay. Filothei).

The EAST WING of the museum houses a special exhibition of restored Early Christian and Byzantine frescoes and ikons. Amongst these are fragments from an Early Christian tomb at Thessaloniki (4–5C) and from the Roman Agora (6C); three layers of frescoes from the Episkopi church in Evrytania (9–13C); frescoes from the Old Metropolis in Verroia (12–13C), the Dhrosoiani on Naxos (9–15C), Khios, Kithira, Crete, etc.

FIRST FLOOR (reached from the portico). The *Vestibule* and the next two rooms contain **Ikons**, the sacred images of the Orthodox religion. Scenes and figures are treated without any concern for natural realism in a formal and hieratic manner. The artist is as far as possible subordinated to an established tradition of representation in an attempt to materialize a spiritual vision of the basic truths of the Christian faith. Thus the ikon itself is believed to embody an inspired truth which can exalt the worshipper. ROOM II (right) contains the oldest and finest panel paintings, including a number of works of the 14–15C dating from the Palaeologian 'renaissance', as well as three large frescoes.

198. St. George (15C) from Asia Minor; 191. Virgin and Child (14C); 157. Double sided: Crucifixion (12C, with 13C additions), backed by Virgin and Child (15C); 100. Mystical Virgin, holding Christ in both hands; 134. Illustration of the hymn, 'For Thee rejoices' surrounded by Passion scenes (Cappadocian; 16C); 89. St. George (13C), a painted bas-relief in wood from Kastoria; 176. St. Anthony, expressive; 177. Theotokos Hodegetria; *169. Double sided, Crucifixion, fine work of the Palaeologian period; 246. Crucifixion, showing Florentine influence; 145 (mosaic). Theotokos Glykophilousa (14C) from Trilia (Tirilye) on the Sea of Marmara; 2162. Archangel Michael, of the Classical school of Constantinople (14C); 85. St. Marina, combining simple composition and spiritual feeling; Chrysobulon of the Emp. Andronikos II conferring privileges on the diocese of Monemvasia (1301); 188. Christ Pantokrator; 185. Wisdom of God, from Salonika. Case by door: Evangile and Cross of Alexis Comnenus of Trebisond. In the centre cases: Liturgical rotuli, bibles, and documents.

ROOM III. Frescoes from vanished churches.—In ROOM IV (MINOR ARTS) are exhibited objects in metal, wood, and ivory, also pottery from the excavation of the basilica of Ay. Dhimitrios at Salonika.—ROOM V. Vestments arranged to show their chronological development, including Coptic work of 5–7C; croziers; *685. Epitaphios of Salonika, magnificent embroidery of the 14C, made, perhaps, in Constantinople.

Adjacent is the imposing **War Museum** (adm. free; closed Monday), erected during the military dictatorship to demonstrate the prowess of Greek arms through the ages. The early galleries are cleverly embellished with reproductions from many Greek museums of sculptured battle scenes, armour, and armaments, as well as helmets and other excavated artefacts and graphic battle plans.—HALL A. Mycenaean to Classical periods.—HALL B. Campaigns of Alexander the Great, with explanatory maps.—HALL Γ. Byzantine wars.—HALL Δ. 'Tourkokratia' (Turkish Occupation) with good prints.—HALL E. The 'Epanastasis' or uprising of 1821–28.—HALL Z. The period 1828–1908 is well documented by contemporary maps.—HALL H. Balkan wars.—HALL Θ. First World War. •1912–13.—HALL I 1919–22; Italian War of 1940; and German occupation of 1941.

Greek arms (Middle East, Italy, etc) in the Second World War occupies Galleries of the MEZZANINE FLOOR. Uniforms are displayed in the BASEMENT. On the GROUND FLOOR; Turkish weapons; early firearms, and 19C dress armour.—Outside are a tank and seven aircraft, including a restored Farman biplane of 1912 and a 'Spitfire', heavy artillery and missiles.

Beyond the next cross-roads (left) a small public garden fronts the *Evanghelismós Hospital*, founded in 1881. A new wing with 483 beds was built in 1983, a gift of John Diamantis. Behind are grouped the *Marasleion*, which combines the function of secondary school and teachers' training college, and the British and American Schools (5, 5).

The **British School of Archaeology** (opened in 1886), though founded primarily to promote the study of Greek archaeology, includes within its province 'research into the language, literature, history, religion, or art of Greece in ancient, mediaeval or modern times'. The results of its studies are published in the 'Annual of the British School at Athens'. The school is celebrated for excavations at Knossos, Perachora, and Mycenae. The *Penrose Library* (c 30,000 vols) is reserved for members of the school, but applications for reader's tickets (fee per session) from students with a suitable letter of introduction will be considered by the Assistant Director. The **American School of Classical Studies** (1882), adjoining, has similar aims and publishes its findings both in its journal 'Hesperia' and in the 'American Journal of Archaeology'. Its most spectacular recent work has been on the Athenian agora, at Corinth, and at Isthmia. The excellent GENNADEION LIBRARY, donated to the school by a former Greek minister in London, is housed, a little higher up the S slope of Lykabettos, in a tasteful building with a central portico of eight columns in antis and two wings. It was erected by the Carnegie Foundation and opened in 1926.—Close by, to the SE, is the formerly monastic *Moní Petráki*, founded by a 17C doctor and now, much restored, given over to a theological seminary. The church (14C) has frescoes of 1719 by George Markos of Argos.

The conspicuous *Hilton Hotel* (5, 7), with a huge incised carving by John Moralis, stands at the important junction of Leoforos Vasilissis Sofias with Leoforos Konstandinou.

On the corner of the latter street, opposite the Hilton Hotel, is the **Ethnikí Pinakothéke** (National Picture Gallery) and **Aléxandros Soútzos Museum** (closed Monday). This museum is devoted to 19 and 20C Greek painting and sculpture. It is not a museum of contemporary Greek art.

There are two important collections of contemporary Greek art in the Athens area: the *Vorrés Museum* in Paiania (tel. 664–2639) and the *Pierídhes Museum* in Glifadha (tel. 865–3890). Because of restricted opening hours, it is advisable to check by 'phone before visiting.

It was established in 1954 by the consolidation of the former National

Gallery, founded in 1900, and the Alexandhros Soutzos legacy, bequeathed to the Greek nation in 1886 for the founding of a museum of painting. It was the donor's wish that the museum be named after his father, Alexandhros Soutzos. Also bequeathed were the Soutzos numismatic and art collections. This endowment lay unexploited until 1954. Construction finally started in 1964 and the museum was inaugurated in 1976

The permanent collection consists primarily of 19 and 20C Greek art, although there are European acquisitions, for instance, a considerable collection of prints and engravings by Dürer, Goya and Manet (not on public view). Certain rooms, such as the entrance hall, the main mezzanine (off to the left of the entrance) and the lower floor, are devoted to temporary exhibitions. The Pinakotheke programme includes concerts, musical recitals, dance performances, etc.

From the high-ceilinged hall, visitors pass across an enclosed ramp, where a series of paintings donated by 20C French masters, including Picasso, Albert Marquet, Utrillo and Picabia, are hung. These were gifts to the Greek people, commemorating their liberation from the german occupation. A sculpture by *Réné Magritte*, The Therapist (1967), is also exhibited here. The ramp leads to the main wing.

The first floor is devoted to 20C painting. The section opposite the stairs is the *N. Khatzikyriakos-Ghikas Room*. This artist was born in Athens in 1906, and is considered to be the main exponent of the Cubist style in Greece. The exhibit represents a good retrospective of his work, which dates from 1927 (Open Door) to the present. Oddly, Khatzikyriakos-Ghikas passed through a surrealistic stage (Barracks; 1927) prior to his Cubism. His most fecund and significant years were the 1950s, as seen in Athenian Balcony (1955) and Sunflower and Trellis (1956).

Across the room from the Ghikas room is the section comprising Greek painting from 1900 to c 1950, a period characterised by a pluralism of expression. In contrast to the 19C, when most Greek artists culled their inspiration from the Munich School, the 20C art scene in Greece had essentially three sources: the Byzantine and Classical heritage, the folk and popular tradition, and the contemporary European mainstream.

Some of the more significant artists of this period are: *Alekos Kontoglou* (?1898–1965), who came to Greece from Asia Minor in 1922. He was one of the first artists in Greece to draw directly on his Byzantine heritage. Much of his early painting of secular themes was executed in the Byzantine manner (see the wall paintings at his home in Kypriadi; 1927). In his later work he concentrated primarily on ecclesiastical decoration and hagiography. *Constantinos Maleas* (1879–1928) and *Spiros Papaloukas* (1892–1957) demonstrated the initial influences of Parisian art in Greece. This can be seen particularly in their treatment of light and of the flat surfaces of colour, as, for instance, in Maleas's *Monemvasia*. George *Bouzianis* (1885–1959), the leading exponent of Expressionism in Greece, studied in Paris and subsequently in Munich. Curiously, his palette differs from that of the German Expressionists—his is dark and sombre. *Yannis Tsarouchis* (1910–) was influenced both by the popular tradition and by modern trends which he combined to create original paintings with a vital local character (see, for instance, his *Cafeneion 'To Neon'*; 1935). In his early work *Yannis Moralis* (1916–) drew on Classical prototypes for the human figure (see *Mourning*). His later, more abstract work again shows Classical derivation in the innate balance and equilibrium of composition. *Nikos Engonopoulos* (1910–86), also a poet, was the most important representative of Surrealism in Greece (see *Theatre*). His bold bright colours produce a more joyous version of Surrealism. *Alexos Kontouplos* (1905–75) is important as the painter who introduced abstract art to Greece after 1950. However, his later paintings were never entirely abstract—some recognisable form or image was usually included. *Yannis Spyropoulos* (1912–), Greece's foremost abstract artists, won international acclaim after being awarded the Unesco prize at the 1960 Venice Biennale. His predominantly dark and heavily textured paintings are flat, without spatial depth, and have well-structured and tectonic compositions.

Visitors wishing to see the collection in chronological order should start at the far end of Floor 2 and make their way back towards the entrance.

The mezzanine between the first and second floors has a small collection of works by the self-taught primitive painter *Theophilos* (1878–1934), now widely and highly acclaimed. Of interest is the manner in which this artist interprets religious, popular and mythological themes. His naive and detailed style is replete with narrative.

The rooms to the right on the second floor are devoted to Greek 19C painting. The last room in this section has a heterogeneous collection of post-Byzantine icons of the Cretan-Italian and Ionian schools, and *El Greco's* Concert of Angels (detail), St. Francis of Assisi, and a Crucifixion. Also exhibited is *Eugène Delacroix's* small but exquisite painting, A Greek Warrior (1856).

The 19C section can be divided roughly into two groups: the Greek mainstream and genre, comprised mainly of historical, seascape and portrait painting. THE GREEK MAINSTREAM: the most important painters are N. Lytras (1832–1904), N. Gyzis (1842–1901) and G. Iakovides (1853–1932). The first two, educated in Germany, reflect a style of painting influenced directly by the Munich school. Gyzis, in particular, emulates the German Romantic movement in choice of subject, sobre palette and, often, a turbulent brushstroke (Destruction at Psara; 1878). Lytras excelled when painting scenes and characters from the café, the street, and family life. His work is altogether lighted and less anguished than that of Gyzis. Iakovides paints in the tradition of Lytras but with more impressionistic results in both colour and execution (Children's Concert; 1900).

GENRE. *Historical*: T. Vryzakis (1814–78) is the main interpreter of this epic style, depicting scenes from the Greek War of Independence. Of particular interest to English visitors is the painting of Lord Byron at Messolongi (1861). *Seascapes*: the chief exponents in the latter part of the 19C were C. Volanakis (1837–1907), I. Altamouras (1852–78) and V. Khatzis (1870–1915), who are represented by an ample collection of interesting and often lovely seascapes and admirably executed naval battles. *Portraits*: late 18C portraits in the collection are by N. Koutouzes (1741–1813) and N. Kantounis (1767–1834), both from the Ionian island of Zante. Other portraitists represented are E. Economou (1823–1887) and N. Kounellakis (1828–69). These indifferent and somewhat dour depictions show the influence of Italian painting, via the Ionian school, in both manner and mood.

On the same floor, to the left of the ramp, is the *C. Parthenis Room*, which holds a comprehensive retrospective exhibit of this Alexandria-born artist (1878–1967) who, in effect, bridged Greek 19 and 20C painting. His influence on Greek painting has been considerable: he established the Impressionist style and introduced Art Nouveau elements. He painted many themes—religious, mythological, and landscape. His later painting, influenced by Byzantine art, has a spiritual and idealistic character (Musicians; 1930–35).

19 and 20C Sculpture. To visit the sculpture section, return to the main entrance and take the stairs down through the main mezzanine to the lower floor. These lead to the sculpture garden and sculpture hall. The Garden, devoted to 20C sculpture, is the most attractive section of the exhibit. Amongst and otherwise all-Greek collection is *Rodin's* beautiful bronze, The Prodigal Son (1889). Noteworthy are

Zalonga, by G. Zongolopoulos (1903–), Acrocorinth (1965) by K. Loukopoulos (1908–), and the abstract constructivist sculptures by Philolaos (1923–) and K. Koulentianos (1918–). (The two last live and work in Paris.) The recently opened Sculpture Hall is a long, narrow, elegant building, very much like a classical Greek stoa, with a glass façade allowing the visitor to see the exhibits from the garden, and *vice versa*. On entering the building, the left-hand sectioin houses the 19C collection—including work by Y. Halepas (1851–1937)—while the right-hand section holds the 20C material. Probably the most important 19C sculptors are P. Prosalentis (1784–1837), who worked chiefly in marble (particularly lovely is his Plato; 1815), D. Philippotis (1834–1920), and T. Vroutos (1843–1909), who also worked in marble. While Prosalentis preferred realistic themes taken from daily life, Philippotis and Vroutos drew on subjects from mythology (e.g. Echo; 1887). Vroutos' work is executed in the tradition of classical sculpture except perhaps when he indulged in sculptural acrobatics and produced precariously balanced works like The Spirit of Copernicus (1877).

Y. Halepas is considered to be one of Greece's most important and creative sculptors. Among his commissions were several tombstones, of which the best known is The Sleeping Maiden in the Athens First Cemetery. At the Pinakotheke the collection of small clay works such as Secret (1925) and Aphrodite (1931), in which the subject consists of a head or bust combined with a small figurine, reveal a strange co-existence of clumsiness and vitality—in effect, a schizophrenic co-existence. (The sculptor was mentally disturbed and spent several periods in hospital.) The small clay works by Halepas have an implicit inner tension which imbues them with a forceful presence.

Most noteworthy amongst the 20C sculptors in the sculpture gallery are: M. Tombros (1889–1974), who worked in marble and bronze; M. Lelakis (1907–), whose interesting wooden abstract forms are labyrinthine and free (Rhythm; 1959–74); C. Kapralos (1909–) (Horse's Head); A. Apartis (1889–1972); A. Apergis (1909–86), and K. Andreou (1917–) who, like the Greek-Parisians mentioned above, makes abstract constructivist sculpture from welded metal sheets.

Nearly 1km farther out, on the left, are the site of the *Hall of the Friends of Music*, begun in 1976, and the *United States Embassy*, an imposing building in marble and glass attractively landscaped, by Walter Gropius and H. Morse Payne Jr. (1960–61). The road continues to *Ambelokipoi*, where it meets Leoforos Alexandhras, a dual highway from Pedhion Areos (Rte 8). A little farther on below the 'Athens Tower' the road to Marathon and the Mesogeion divides from Kifissia Avenue (Rte 17B).

11 Lykabettos

The ascent of Lykabettos, which takes c 45 minutes from Sindagma Square, is best made in the early morning or late afternoon when the superb view is clearest. For funicular railway from top of Od. Ploutarchou comp. below.

Lykabettos (Λυκαβηττός; in modern Greek parlance *Likavittós*; 4, 4) is the highest (277m) of the hills of Athens, and the S termination of the Anchesmos range. Although perhaps the most conspicuous feature of the Athenian landscape, it gets its only classical reference in the

'Clouds' of Aristophanes. Formerly the NE surburban limit of the city, it is now an island in a sea of houses. The slopes are wooded, thanks to the Philodhasiko Society of Greece, and many pleasant approaches by shady but sometimes steep paths may be made from the S side.

According to legend, Lykabettos was a rock which Athena was carrying to Athens to form a bulwark for her citadel; in her surprise at hearing that, in defiance of her injunction, Aglauros and Herse had looked into the chest containing Erechtheus, she dropped it.

The N slopes are readily accessible from any of the turnings leading S from Odos Asklipiou (Bus 023) and afford the gentler ascent. In Odos Dhidhótou (named after Ambroise Firmin Didot, the French publisher and philhellene) is the **École Française d'Athènes**, the oldest archaeological school in Greece, founded in 1846 and removed to this site in 1874. Edmond About was a student in 1851–53. The French School has explored sites in Asia Minor as well as in Greece where it is perhaps most celebrated for its work at Delphi and Delos. Its journal 'Bulletin de Correspondence Hellénique' is one of the first archaeological importance. Just behind rises *Skhisti Petra*, a curiously shaped rock (called by the Germans *Frog's Mouth*) easily climbed in a few minutes from its S side. Behind it ascends a road built to serve a *Wireless Station* of the Royal Hellenic Air Force which occupied the W slopes of Lykabettos until 1961. In 1941 this was the Operations Centre of the Greek Air Force and formed King George's last H.Q. on the mainland before he retired to Crete in the face of the German advance. Here also are sited the ceremonial cannon used for royal salutes.

A Cable Railway, in a tunnel, c 200m long, was opened in 1965 from the top of Ploutárkhou, and a Tourist Pavilion (Refreshments) has been hewn from the rock just below the summit.

Visitors are better advised to make on foot the steep approach from the SW. From the Benáki Museum (Rte 7) the short Odhós Koubári leads to the PLATEÍA KOLONÁKI, centre of the most fashionable district of Athens. On the right is the *British Council*, with an excellent library with lending facilities for residents only.

From the SE corner of the square, at Od. Neofítou Doúka 4, reached via Od. Kapsáli, is the **Goulandrís Museum**, opened in 1986 by Mrs Dolly Goulandris, in memory of her husband. The museum has fine objects of ancient art from prehistoric to Roman times and is particularly rich in marble figurines and other material of the Cycladic Early Bronze Age. The displays are modern and the museum shop is well stocked. From the NE corner of the plateia a short ascent leads to the *Dhexamení*, or reservoir of the old Town Aqueduct, a Roman work begun by Hadrian and completed by Antoninus Pius. It was recommissioned in 1840, restored in 1869, and again in 1929, when the ancient aqueduct leading from Tatoi was brought up to date. It is now ancillary to the reservoir on Tourkovouni, served by the Marathon pipeline. Here at Epiphany takes place the ceremony of the Blessing of the Waters. From the top of Odhos Loukianou a zigzag path, passing near the chapel of *St. Isidore* (16C), mounts to the little 19C chapel of *Ayios Yeoryios* on the summit, which commands a magnificent *Panorama of Athens and Attica. The Acropolis is however more effectively seen from the steps (café) on the way up, when its matchless marble ruins stand out against the sea.

12   New Pháleron and Piraeus

Approaches from Athens. BY RAIL, by the Piraeus Electric Railway (E.H.Σ.) from *Omonoia*, 11km in 20 minutes. Trains every 7 minutes; intermediate stations: *Monastírion* (2, 8), *Thissíon* (2, 8), *Petrálona*, *Kallithéa*, *Moskháton*, *Néon Fáliron*.—The State Railway lines do not carry local passengers.

BY ROAD. The shortest route to Piraeus (9km) is by the old Odhós Piraiós, followed by bus No. 049 (from Omonoia Sq.), which traverses the dreary industrial suburbs of Petrálona and Réndis. The ΕΗΣ bus (No. 040 from Sindagma Sq.) takes Leofóros Singroú, then diverges via *Kallithéa* to reach Phaleron Bay at Tzitzifiés. Leofóros Ilissoú follows the course of the Ilissos and to link the Stadium with Kallithéa.—The pleasantest route (11km) is by Leoforos Singrou and Phaleron Bay, described below.

From the Olympieion (Rte 7), two of whose columns dominate the head of the road, LEOFÓROS ANDRÉAS SINGROÚ (7, 7), an imposing dual highway named after the philanthropist Singros (1830–99) runs straight to the coast. We soon pass the *Fix Brewery* (now derelict), scene of sharp fighting in 1944, then cross the Ilissos and its boulevard (Rte 7) by a viaduct with good retrospective views of Philopappos Hill and the Acropolis.—2·5km *Ayios Sostis* (left), a church built by Queen Olga as a thank-offering after an abortive attempt on the life of George I in 1897. Running between Kallithea and the large refugee suburb of *Nea Smirni* (New Smyrna), and passing (left) the *Ledra Marriot* and *Athens Chandris Hotels* and the *Planetarium*, the avenue reaches Phaleron Bay at (6km) the *Racecourse*. We turn right along the shore, now recovering from former squalour and pollution by the main sewer outfall from Athens and with much land recently reclaimed from the sea.—7km *Tzitzifiés* (Hotels, C) is noted for tavernas with bouzouki music.

PHALERON BAY, a shallow and exposed roadstead, stretches from the peninsula of Munychia on the W to the headland of Old Phaleron (Rte 13) on the E. Here until the beginning of the 5C BC the Athenians beached their triremes, and the gently sloping sands were traditionally held to be the departure place of Theseus for Crete and of the Athenian contingent to Troy. In 1929–39 flying-boats of Imperial Airways en route to India and Australia called at a station opposite the racecourse; an earlier seaplane service of Società Aero-Espresso Italiana from Brindisi to Istanbul had called since 1926. Warships of the Greek Navy or of visiting fleets may often be seen anchored offshore.

8km **Néon Fáliron**, or *New Phaleron* (*Hotels* C, and others), founded in 1875 as a seaside resort. It lies along the low sandy shore, anciently marshy and called *Halipedon*, on either bank of the Kifissos, the position of which is now marked only by a street name. The *Anglo-French Cemetery*, behind the Karaïskakis Stadium, N of the railway station, contains monuments to sailors who died in Piraeus in 1855–59. The area is now dominated by the vast (126m × 28m) and impressive boat-shaped *Stadium of Peace and Friendship*, completed in 1985. Set in 3·25 hectares of land, with tennis courts, marina, etc., the building comprises an indoor stadium with a seating capacity of 16,000, concert and recreation halls and facilities for all indoor sport. New flyovers are being constructed to alleviate traffic congestion in the area.—From New Phaleron we may follow the railway and Odhos Skilitsi to meet the old Athens–Piraeus road (Pl. 8) or, by Odhos Tzavela and Plat. Ippodamias, reach the central harbour of (11km) *Piraeus*.

PIRAEUS (Πειραιεύς), in modern parlance *Piraiévs*, is now, as in classical times, the port of Athens. The town (196,389 inhab.), which owes its rebirth to the choice of Athens as capital in 1834, is with its suburbs the third largest in Greece (476,304). It is the seat of a bishop and an important naval and commercial shipping base. Piraeus proper occupies a rocky spur-shaped promontory or double peninsula, joined to the mainland at the NE by a stretch of low ground. The SW part of the peninsula, called *Akti*, is joined to the E part by an isthmus which separates the Great Harbour (*Kantharos*) from the circular Pashali-mani (anciently *Zea*). Farther E, below the hill of Kastella (*Munychia*) is the still smaller harbour of Tourkolimano. The spine of the peninsula divides the modern town into the more fashionable quarter to the S, and E, well supplied with restaurants and places of amusement, and a commercial sector surrounding the main harbour. Beyond this the mainland extensions, including *Dhrapetsona* and *Nikaia* form the most important manufacturing centre in Greece, with more than a hundred factories, cotton mills, distilleries, soap works, and metal foundries.

The modern town follows the rectangular plan of its ancient predecessor, of which visible remains are scanty and, save to the professional archaeologist, unrewarding. The visitor is better employed in a tour of the harbours, where the interest is equally divided between the seafaring bustle of a busy Mediterranean port, the considerable remains of ancient installations, and the varied views of the Saronic Gulf from the indented coastline. On summer evenings Piraeus is agreeably cooler than Athens.

Arrival by Sea. Customs and passport formalities generally on board; from Greek ports no formalities. On departure for abroad, passports are examined at 53 Akti Miaoulis and baggage at the Custom House on the quay. Taxicabs plying to addresses in Athens are entitled to double fare.

Steamer Quays. Akti Poseidhónos (Pl. 3) to Aegina, Poros, Idhra, and Spetsai; **Plateia Karaïskákis** (Pl. 3) to most other Greek destinations; **Aktí Miaoúlis** (E end; Pl. 7) to Italy, Turkey, and other ports beyond Greek frontiers; (W end) for ocean liners.—**Pashalimáni** (Pl. 11) for hydroplanes to Idhra and Spetsai.

Railway Stations. ΕΗΣ (Pl. 3), for Athens and Kifissia; ΕΠΑΠ (Pl. 3), for Corinth and the Peloponnesus; ΟΣΕ (Pl. 2) for Salonika.

The Piraeus Kouros, c 500 BC

Restaurants along waterfront at Tourkolimano (seafood, some expensive), also on Akti Themistokleous.

Post Office (Pl. 7), Odhos Fílonos.—TOURIST POLICE at corner of Aktí Miaoúlis and Filellinon.

Buses. From Electric Rly Stn; 20 (circular) to *Kastella* and *Tourkolimano*; also to *New Phaleron, Custom House*. From Plateía Koraḯ (Pl. 7); **040** (green) to *Athens* (Filellínon); 904/905 (circular) to *Akte*. From Leofóros Ethnikís Antistáseos (Pl. 7) to *Athens* (Omonia; **049**), *Glifadha* (**149**) and suburbs. From Plateía Karaïskáki (Pl. 3) to Piraeus suburbs.

Shipping Offices. *Adriatica, Greek Line, Turkish Maritime Lines*, all TANPY bldg, 19 Aktí Miaoúlis; *Kavounides*, 33 Aktí Miaoúlis; *Karageorgis*, 10 Aktí Kondíli; *Epirotiki*, 87 Aktí Miaoúlis; *Hellenic Mediterranean Lines*, Electric Stn Bldg.; *American Export Lines*, 33 Aktí Miaoúlis; *Mediterranean Sun Lines*, 5 Sakhtoúri; *Libra Maritime*, 65 Aktí Miaoúlis.

Steamer Services (quays see above). Argossaronikos to *Aegina* (2–3 times per hour), continuing (many times daily) to *Methana* and *Poros*, and (3–4 times daily) to *Idhra, Ermioni*, and *Spetsai*; twice weekly to *Leonidhion*. Also to Aegina by hydroplane (hourly). Aegean services daily (usually except Sunday) to *Siros, Tinos, Mykonos* (1–3 times), *Samos, Chios, Mytilene, Kos, Rhodes* (1–3 times), and *Crete*. From 2 to 5 times weekly to many other Aegean islands, the *Ionian Is., Brindisi, Venice, Istanbul*, etc.—HYDROPLANES, from Zea to *Poros, Idhra, Spetsai, Leonidhion, Monemvasia*, etc.

Car Hire. *Hertz*, 9–11 Ay. Nikólaos, facing Custom House (Pl. 6).

Festival. *Blessing of the Waters* at Epiphany (6 January).

History. *Piraeus*, originally an island, was still isolated in archaic times by the marshes of Halipedon. While Corinth and Aegina remained the principal maritime powers the Athenians kept their triremes on the beach at Phaleron Bay, which was in full view of the city while Piraeus was not. Hippias began to fortify Munychia c 510 BC. When Themistocles created an Athenian fleet of 200 ships, he chose Piraeus as its base, beginning in 493 BC the ambitious scheme of fortification which was to include the whole of the double peninsula and the approaches from Athens. By the outbreak of the Peloponnesian War (431 BC), the three Long Walls (see below) were complete. At its close the Phaleric Wall had fallen into decay, and the conditions of peace offered by Lysander after the defeat of Athens at Aegospotami (405) included the destruction of the remaining Long Walls as well as of the walls of both cities. The population of Piraeus at the zenith of Athenian power consisted largely of Metics (μέτοικοι), or resident aliens, who controlled much of its manufacture and trade, and introduced strange cults, giving the city its cosmopolitan and radical character. Thrasyboulos sought the support of the citizens of Piraeus in 403, launching his *coup d'état* against the Thirty from Munychia. Munychia became the chief seat of the Macedonian garrison which controlled Athens in 322–229 save for brief intervals (liberation by Demetrios Poliorketes, 307–294). By 200 BC, when Philip V of Macedon again attacked Athens, the Long Walls had been abandoned, though Piraeus itself (its walls repaired by Eurykleides and Mikion, c 306–298) was flourishing as a commercial centre, and the Roman garrison used it as a base. In 86 BC Sulla ravaged the city, destroying the arsenal and the docks; but though Strabo dismisses it as an unimportant village, it seems to have revived early in the Imperial era, and could still serve as a base for Constantine's fleet in AD 322. After Alaric's raid in 396 it lost all importance. In 1040 Harald Hardrada, the Viking, in the service of the Byzantine emperor, disembarked at Piraeus to suppress an Athenian insurrection. In medieval times the town was known as *Porto Leone* (comp. below) and by the Turks as Aslan-liman. When, in 1834, Athens became the capital of Greece hardly a house stood in Piraeus. Resettled by islanders with the trading instincts of the ancient metics, it grew rapidly through the 19C, playing a large part in the revival of Athens. The population which did not exceed 4000 in 1840, rose from 11,000 in 1870 to 75,000 in 1907. The refugee settlement of 1922 increased it threefold. In 1854–59 Piraeus was occupied by an Anglo-French fleet to prevent Greek nationalists embarrassing Turkey, an allied power in the Crimean War. In the Second World War the port was put out of action and 11 ships sunk on the first night of the German air attack (6 April 1941) when the moored 'Clan Fraser' carrying 200 tons of TNT, and two other ammunition ships, blew up. Fully restored, it provides a port of call for most steamship lines operating in the E Mediterranean and is the focus of Greek services to the islands.—The opening scene of Plato's *Republic* is laid in Piraeus, at the house of the aged Kephalos.

Defences of Ancient Piraeus. The LONG WALLS, sometimes called the 'Legs' (τα σκέλη), formed part of the original fortification scheme of Themistocles. The *First* or *Northern Long Wall* (7km long) ran from Athens to Piraeus, the *Second* or *Phaleric Long Wall* (6·5km long) from Athens to the E end of Phaleron Bay. The walls were completed c 456 BC. (Thuc. I, 108). A *Third* or *Southern Long Wall*, parallel with the first and of the same length, was built by Kallikrates under the direction of Pericles to guard against the possibility of a surprise landing in Phaleron Bay. The Northern and Southern Long Walls, starting from two points in the outer wall of the Piraeus, converged to within 183m of each other and then ran parallel to the region of Pnyx hill (comp. Rte 3). Between them ran a road. A second road, probably the 'carriage-road' (άμαξιτός) mentioned by Xenophon (Hellenica II, 4, 10), ran outside the Northern Long Wall. The direct modern road (Odhos Piraios, above) follows the Northern Long Wall for much of its course, the Electric Railway the Southern Long Wall. Sections of both can be seen between the Karaïskakis Stadium and Odhos Piraios (left) and in front of the Klostoufant-ourgou School.

The Themistoclean *City Wall* guarded all three harbours; fortified entrances to each, forming part of the circuit, were probably closed by chains. The W half of Akte was excluded from the defences which crossed the peninsula from NW to SE. On the landward quarter they followed the solid land behind the Halai marsh, and on the side nearest Athens the contour of the ground, making a circuit of 60 stadia (Thucydides II, 13). The rebuilding of the walls is commonly credited to Konon (Xenophon, Hell. IV, 8), though an inscription has shown that this was started before his victory at Knidos and the work was probably finished only after 346 (Demosthenes XIX, 125). The defences were shortened on the N side by carrying the wall across the Choma (see below) to Eëtioneia, but the circuit was extended round the whole of Akte.

Asklepios treats a patient. Relief sculpture from Piraeus

Under Pericles the *City* itself was laid out by Hippodamos of Miletus on a chess-board plan with a spacious agora at the centre. Special attention was paid to the needs of the fleet, no less than 1000 talents being spent on the construction of *Ship-sheds* and dry docks. Demosthenes considered the ship-sheds of Piraeus worthy of mention in company with the Parthenon and the Propylaea. In 330–322 BC they numbered 372, of which 196 were in Zea, 82 in Munychia, and 94 in Kantharos. This corresponds roughly with the strength of the Athenian navy under Lycurgus (c 400 ships), who completed the work by the construction in the Harbour of Zea of a NAVAL ARSENAL or SKEUOTHEKE (σκευοθήκη), designed by the architect *Philo* in 346–329 BC.

Odhós Skilítsi and Odhós Ippodamías (comp. above) converge at the PLATEÍA IPPÓDAMOS, with a busy hardware market, whence roads lead W to the Electric Railway Station and SW to the main harbour.

Just off Skilitsi, c 90m E of Plat. Ippodamos, are the remains of the *Asty Gate*, where the Hamaxitos, or 'carriage-road' (see above), entered the city. Its Themistoclean round towers were later rebuilt on a square plan. Many neighbouring buildings incorporate classical masonry from the Long Walls. A little to the E are foundations of a second gate and of a sanctuary. Near the Merchant Navy School in Odhós Evanghelistrías, and in Odhós Kódhrou, further sections of the defences can be traced.

At the heart of maritime Piraeus at the E angle of the **Great Harbour** stands the *Dhimarkhion* (Pl. 7), or Town Hall, in front of which is a clock, a local landmark ('to roloi'). Immediately in front along Akti Poseidhonos moor the small steamers that ply to ports in the Saronic Gulf. To the SW along AKTÍ MIAOÚLIS extend the liner berths (adm. restricted) with the *Passenger Terminal* and *Custom House* (Pl. 6). Here and in PLATEÍA KARAÏSKÁKIS (Pl. 3), to the N beyond the lively Bazar, are situated the offices of shipping companies. From the open quay alongside the square and the mole to the W depart ships plying to the Peloponnese and the Greek islands, as well as those making calls at Greek ports before continuing to Italy.

The modern harbour corresponds very nearly to the ancient KANTHAROS ('goblet'), which was divided, then as now, between naval and commercial shipping. To the navy was reserved the shore of Eëtioneia (see below) and the N shore of Akti beyond the custom house (then a temple site); these locations are still favoured by warships. The *Emporion*, or commercial quay, coincided with the modern berths along Akti Miaoulis and Plat. Karaïskakis (comp. above). A jetty, called the *Diazeugma*, divided it into two, roughly where the Passenger Terminal now stands. Five stoas lined the quay, traces of one of which have been found c 140m from the quay SE of the custom house; other vestiges of the Emporion are visible in the foundations of the church of *Ayia Triadha* (Pl. 7). The short S mole projecting from Plat. Karaïskakis corresponds to the ancient *Choma*, the point of assembly where, on the eve of naval expeditions, the trierarchs had to report to the Council of 500 (when the first three to arrive were rewarded). The Trierarchy, instituted by Themistocles, was a form of taxation whereby the state provided the bare hulls of new warships, while the duty of fitting the galley, launching it and training the oarsmen, fell by rotation on the richest citizens. The Trierarch sailed with his ship and was responsible for its repair during his term of office.—The ancient harbour was guarded after 337 BC by two moles, extending respectively from the S end of Eëtioneia (still surviving in part) and from the N shore of Akte, leaving an entrance, 50m wide, guarded by towers or lighthouses. Nowadays an *Outer Harbour*, beyond this, formed by the construction of two breakwaters in 1902, shelters naval stores and yards, coal wharves, and a dry dock (comp. below).

NORTH-WESTERN QUARTER. Such vestiges of classical buildings as remain on the peninsula of Eëtioneia are scattered among factories, railway sidings, and somewhat rough popular quarters. Enthusiastic antiquaries may take Akti Kalimasíou from Plat. Karaïskakis (taxi advisable, but driver will need guidance; tram or bus to Larissa Stn) and, leaving on the right of the *Stations* of the Piraeus Electric Railway and S.P.A.P., follow the dreary Akti Kondili behind the wharves that line the inner harbour, or *Limin Alon*. Anciently a miry lagoon called the *Halai* or *Kophos Limen* (κωφὸς λιμήν; 'silent harbour'), this is a relic of the marshes that once surrounded Piraeus. The ancient fortifications may at first have run to shoreward of it; later they crossed its entrance. Beyond *Larissa Station* of the State Railway extends the peninsula of **Eëtioneia** (Ηετιώνεια), called by Thucydides 'the mole of Piraeus'. This peninsula was included in the Themistoclean circuit, which enclosed also the inlet of Krommydaron. Theramenes in 411 BC gave Eëtioneia separate fortifications but tore them down later owing to a change of policy (comp. Thuc. VIII, 92). The 4C walls enclosed only the peninsula. Railway sidings cross the road (traces, 3–3·6m thick, of the *Wall of Konon*) to enter the modern quays which have obliterated the ancient shipbuilding yards (νεώρια) and slipways (νεώσοικοι). Beyond the rails (right), at the entrance to Odhós Monímon Dhexamenón, is a little hill (16m) on which are the remains of the 4C *Aphrodision*, a sanctuary dedicated to Aphrodite Euploia, goddess of navigation. This was closely ringed by Konon's wall, of which the *Aphrodision Gate* (excavated by the French School in 1887) can be traced just to the NW; its towers are more than 9m in diameter. The *Inlet of Krommydaron*, now the Monimai Dexamenai (dry docks), yielded five marble altars in 1866, one with a Phoenician inscription. To the W are some vestiges of the *Themistoclean Wall*, slighter than that of Konon. Beyond, in the suburb of *Dhrapetsona*, an obelisk in the Anastaseos cemetery commemorates French naval dead of the First World War.

From the Town Hall Leofóros Yeoryíou tou Prótou leads shortly to the *Tinan Gardens*, laid out in 1854 by a French admiral. Opposite stands the CATHEDRAL (Pl. 7; *Ayia Triadha*), gutted in 1944 and rebuilt in 1958–62 in its former style. On the corner of Odhos Filonos in July 1959 workmen digging a drain suddenly uncovered a bronze hand; careful excavation brought to light the unique collection of statuary now in the National museum. It is believed that this formed part of Sulla's loot, stored away in 86 BC in a commercial stoa for shipment to Rome and overlooked. Farther on in Plateía Koraï is the *Municipal Theatre*. The broad Leofóros Iróön Polytekhníou (Ηρώων Πολυτεχνείου) leads SW along the spine of the peninsula, passing between pleasant gardens; streets at right angles lead (right) to Akti Miaoulis and (left) to Pashalimani (see below).

At No. 38 Odhós Filellínon (Pl. 6) is the newly refurbished **Archaeological Museum**, with interesting material, excellently displayed. We enter up steps from the street. (The rooms are unnumbered.) In the VESTIBULE, a statue of Hermes of the 2C AD. Through the vestibule, we enter a HALL with fine *Neoclassical reliefs of Amazonomachies from Kifissia, c AD 200. Lion stele from Moschato, 400 BC. A gallery to the right (as we entered the hall) contains funerary urns and stelai, also Roman sculpture, including Heads of the Emperors Claudius (1163) and Trajan (276). Beyond the main hall, the last room downstairs contains a massive funerary monument from Kallithea with relief (Amazonomachy, Zoomachy) and free-standing commemorative sculptures, c 400 BC.

Returning to the main hall, we ascend the stairs to the UPPER FLOOR. To the left, off the vestibule, a large gallery has funerary stelai of the 5 and 4C BC, also an East Greek archaic kore of cylindrical shape (c 580 BC). Beyond the vestibule, we find, in the small HALL, Roman herms. Through the hall, we approach the superb **'Piraeus Kouros'**, the oldest known hollow-cast bronze statue of large scale, found with the clay filling and iron supports preserved inside. It was almost certainly a cult statue of Apollo, who held a bow in one hand. It may be from a NE Peloponnesian workshop of c 530–520 BC (? Kanachos of Sikyon). The room to the right is not yet open; that to the left contains other fine bronzes from the same cache as the Piraeus kouros (found in the course of drain construction in 1959): *Athena, her helmet decorated with griffins and owls, 350–300 BC; *Artemis, with quiver on her shoulder; smaller statue of same deity; bronze mask.

Next to the museum are the scanty remains of the **Theatre of Zea**, a Hellenistic edifice of the 2C BC which (unusually) was not altered in the Roman period. The rock-hewn cavea was divided by 14 flights of steps. The orchestra, better preserved, is surrounded by a covered channel.

We reach **Pashalimáni** (Pl. 11), the ancient harbour of ZEA, a landlocked basin connected with the sea by a channel c 200m by 100m, lined on either side by the ancient walls, which terminate at the inner end of the channel in two short moles. The port was occupied by 196 *Ship-sheds*, spread fanwise round the bay; many traces of these may be seen, particularly in the basement of a block of flats on the E side. On the W side the construction of an outer yacht basin, incorporating the bay to the W, has modified the shore line and narrowed the entrance to Zea.

PIRAEUS

0   500yards

0   500metres

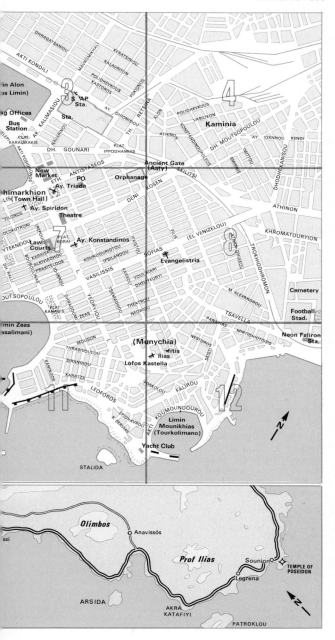

Excavations in 1885 revealed the plan of the Ship-sheds. The flat beach round the basin was enclosed by a wall, c 15m from the water's edge, which formed the back wall of the sheds. These, with an average breadth of 6·4m extended at right angles to it; each was separated from its neighbour by plain columns of Piraeic limestone, which supported the roofs (probably of wood). Between the columns the rock was hollowed out to form slipways which descended some way into the water (model in the Naval Museum).

The YACHT BASIN is generally crowded with large sea-going craft. Behind the reclaimed shoreline below Aktí Themistokleous a new **Naval Museum of Greece** (ΝΑΥΤΙΚΟΝ ΜΟΥΣΕΙΟΝ ΤΗΣ ΕΛΛΑΔΟΣ) faces a formal garden in which are displayed guns, conning towers, torpedo tubes, etc. The main door is to the right, but entrance more normally to the left. Opposite the main entrance the building incorporates part of the Themistoclean wall; to the right, carvings and models of ancient ships, including a fine trireme; representations of the Battle of Salamis in the Peloponnesian War. Returning, the order is chronological with Byzantine battles and Lepanto explained by drawings and plans. Among interesting documents is a letter from Nelson dated from New York in 1782. In the War of Independence emphasis is placed on the careers of admirals Miaoulis, Kanaris, etc. and the Battle of Navarino. Later Greek naval exploits (e.g. the 'Averof' and 'Elli') are celebrated, and the course of Greek naval warfare to the present day shown by relics salvaged from the sea, pictures, uniforms, flags, and ship models.

In the other direction the landing-stage for liberty-boats of visiting fleets continues the harbour's tradition as the *Stratiotiki Limen* (Military Port). Here the shaded PLATEIA KANARIS (Pl. 7) is a favourite promenade. Hereabouts was situated the SKEUOTHEKE, or *Arsenal of Philo*, of which the architect's complete specification was discovered in 1882 (model in the Naval Museum); no trace of the building remains.

The promontory to the SE ends in a salient of the fortification where was a series of wells (Φρέατοι). Here was possibly *Phreattys*, where sat the criminal court that tried those charged with homicide committed abroad. The judges sat on the shore while the accused pleaded from a boat in order not to pollute the land.

On the neck of the peninsula is the site of the *Asklepieion*, or Sanctuary of Asklepios Munychios, from which bas-reliefs were recovered in 1886.

The cliff to the E of the salient is the alleged site of the SERANGEION (σήραγξ, a hollow rock). Here have been found the remains of *Baths* hollowed out of the rock and paved with mosaic: the main bath, with three apses, is connected with the sea by a passage through the rock 11·8m long; to the E is the cloak room with 18 compartments for the bathers' clothes. The place is now a restaurant.

The road to New Phaleron here quits the shore and passes below *Kastella*, the terraced quarter occupying the slopes of the hill that rises to the left. Ancient quarries have been discovered in the area. The HILL OF MUNYCHIA (85m; 10 minutes walk), the Acropolis of Piraeus, commands all three harbours and
*Views of Phaleron Bay and the Saronic Gulf. In 403 BC Thrasyboulus made it the base of his operations against the Thirty Tyrants, then in possession of Athens. Here in 1827 Karaïskakis was killed during an abortive campaign led by Sir Richard Church, designed to relieve the Greek garrison of the Athenian acropolis. Gen. Thos. Gordon held Munychia from February until May, but the defeat of an attempted attack on Athens made from Phaleron Bay put an end to the expedition and the siege. The modern chapel of *Ayios Elias*, near the summit marks the site not of the Temple of Artemis Munychia but of *Bendis*, a celebrated sanctuary. About 90m W is the upper entrance to a flight of 165 steps, known as the *Cavern of Arethusa*, which leads to the stuccoed subterranean galleries that

held the water supply of the citadel (65·5m deep). On the W slope of the hill (discovered in 1880, but now covered up) was the ancient *Theatre of Dionysos* referred to by Thucydides (VIII, 93).—From Munychia, Leoforos Yeoryiou tou Protou (comp. above) descends to the main harbour. Half-way down stands a charming marble group of Mother and Child (1959).

We keep to the cliffs above the popular bathing beach which faces the rocky islet of *Stalidha*, then descend past the *Yacht Club of Greece* (Ναυτικός Ομιλος Ελλάδος). During its construction in 1935 large un-worked blocks belonging to the fortress of Hippias were unearthed and inscribed sherds from (?) the *Temple of Artemis Munychia*. The picturesque yacht basin of *Tourkolímano** (Pl. 12), gay with coloured sails and lined with restaurants, retains the form it had as the ancient PORT OF MUNYCHIA. This also was protected by two long moles, each ending in a lighthouse tower, leaving an entrance between them only 36·5m wide. The *N. Mole* affords a good example of ancient marine fortification and bears lower courses of a massive structure of unknown purpose. The harbour had slips for 82 triremes, of which some foundations can be seen under water to the N and S. The build-ings themselves, apparently of wood, have long since vanished and traces only of the surrounding wall exist. The name Tourkolimano seems unlikely to survive a chauvinist campaign to change it to *Mikrolimano*.

The return to either Pashalimani or the Great Harbour can be accomplished by bus No. 904/905 (circular route).

The rocky and usually deserted S coast of the **Akte Peninsula** affords a delightful *Walk, especially in the late afternoon when Salamis and the islands of the Saronic Gulf are thrown into relief by the setting sun, which falls full on Hymettos and the coast to the E.

The tour is best made in an anticlockwise direction; the uninteresting popular quarter on the N side of the peninsula may be avoided by taking bus No. 904/905 (circular route from Plat. Koraï) to the point S of the Naval School where it emerges on the shore. Thence Pashalimani can be reached on foot in 1 hour.

The W extremity of the peninsula, once a royal park, is now a restricted naval area whose points of interest can be seen only from offshore. On the most nor-therly point, the ancient promontory of *Alkimos* (Pl. 1), once stood the great *Marble Lion* (probably from Delos) that was inscribed in runes by Harald Har-drada and gave to Piraeus its alternative names of *Porto Leone* and *Porto Draco*. The lion was removed to Venice by Morosini in 1687. About 275m W of Alkimos are some graves of English soldiers and a *Monument to Andreas Miaoulis* (1769–1835), the admiral. Behind are quarries whence comes the bluish-grey Piraeic stone, and farther on, to seaward of the lighthouse, a rock-hewn grave traditio-nally known as the Tomb of Themistocles and a poros *Column*, re-erected in 1952, that marked the S entrance to the harbour.

Leofóros Iróon Polytekhníou is continued to the W by Leofóros Kiriá-kou to the *Naval School* (Pl. 5), whence Akti Themistokleous follows the indented S shore of the peninsula. The **Wall of Konon** is visible in its lower courses for most of the way. Built of local stone (c 394–391 BC) just beyond the reach of the waves and often of blocks cut from the rocks above which it is built, it is closely followed by the road, which is sometimes supported by it. The curtain, 3–3·5m thick, is reinforced at intervals of 46–55m by square *Towers*. The bases of many of these now support little wayside tavernas. A short section of the *Wall of Themistocles* survives to the SE of the *Signal Station* (56m) that crowns the highest point of the peninsula. Beyond the *Villa Skouloudis* (Pl. 10), now the Institute of Hydrology, polygonal masonry at the base of Konon's wall shows where the earlier wall was at first carried some way to the SW of the point where it turned across the peninsula.

II ATTICA

The name of **ATTICA** (Αττική; Attikí), the region which surrounds
Athens, is probably derived from the word άκτη (akte), 'promontory' or
'peninsula', literally 'the place where the waves break'. It became an
entity with the amalgamation of the old Mycenaean centres during the
late-Geometric period. Geographically the region forms a roughly
triangular peninsula terminating in Cape Sounion; its base, c 50km
wide, is the almost continuous mountain barrier that runs from the bay
of Aigosthena, in the W, to the channel of Euboea, in the E. This
consists of the ranges of Pateras, Kithairon, and Parnes and the coastal
hills of Mavrovouni. The ancient boundary between Attica and
Boeotia lay along this barrier, with disputed areas around the three
passes: the Megarid, Eleutherai, and Diakria. Possession of Salamis
and the Megarid secured the W approaches, which are effectively cut
off from the Peloponnese by the great Yerania range. Athens itself,
protected by the inner ring of Aigaleos, Pentelikon, and Hymettos, but
connected by easy roads with the plains beyond, is the natural centre
of the region. Many of the Attic mountains, in the time of Pausanias
crowned by images of the gods, are now surmounted by ugly radar
stations, which inhibit access to their summits.

Modern Attica became a separate administrative entity in 1899 when it was detached from Boeotia. The boundaries have been altered several times since. There are now two nomes: Attiki and Piraios. Attiki consists of two eparchies: Attica proper and the Megarid. Piraios has five: Piraeus itself (which, however, includes Salamis and Spetsai); Aegina, Idhra; Kithira; and Troezenia. Greater Athens, comprising part of the eparchy of Attica and part of the eparchy of Piraeus, enjoys special administrative status within its territory.

Among features of interest are the coastal resorts SE of Athens; the hill resorts to the N; Mt Hymettos; the monasteries of Kaisariani and Daphni; the Mesogeia with the remains of Brauron; and Sounion. Archaeologically rewarding in addition are Eleusis and Aegina, the new discoveries in the plain of Marathon, and farther away the Amphiaraion at Oropos, and Rhamnous. New roads are fast being built and old ones improved, and with a car it is possible to combine two or three places in one day. Bus services are steadily becoming more extensive and frequent to outlying places, though they radiate from central Athens and are little help to those in seaside hotels. In the season there are coach excursions to the main sites. Walkers will find much of Attica within their reach, though expanding towns, military zones, and spreading villa development are ever-increasing obstacles. The countryside is carpeted with flowers in spring, when also the crisp air and clear Attic light are best enjoyed. Dogs are less troublesome than in more distant parts of Greece, but it is still quite easy to get lost on Parnes.

Rtes 13–16 are in the nature of excursions which can be made by public transport leaving every few minutes from Central Athens; they can be accomplished at any time of day without advance planning. The later routes demand a little organisation, but except for that to the more distant islands of Rte 23, they can each be made in a single day from Athens. In Rte 19, 20, and 22 the old roads out to the N are described, in order to indicate what remains of historical interest, every day more hidden in suburbia; a speedier arrival can be gained at the expense of intermediate interest by using the Athens–Salonika Highway.

13 The Attic Coast to Vouliagméni

ROAD, dual carriageway, 25km (15½ miles). BUSES (Prefix 1) every few minutes from Sindagma Sq. to Edhém; from the Academy, Omonoia Sq., Leof. Olgas, etc. (meeting at the Olympieion) to Glifádha and Vouliagméni, see under Athens. The distances below are measured from Sindagma Sq.

The WEST COAST OF ATTICA, in classical times a flourishing region with many demes, degenerated into insignificance at an early date, and for centuries lay neglected and difficult of access. The discovery of medicinal springs near Glifádha and Vouliagméni after the First World War led to the foundation of bathing resorts, and in recent years the coast has been developed as the summer playground of Attica. The hinterland, a bare stony tract, is little developed beyond the airport, and still studded with ancient graves, but the coast is very crowded in July–August.

From the Olympieion to (6km) the *Racecourse*, see Rte 12. We turn left. The rocky headland that closes Phaleron Bay to the E, once identified with Cape Kolias (see below), is more likely the site of ancient Phaleron itself, which is usually placed near the Chapel of St George. At the bus-stop called Trocadero below the road is the *Marine Biological Institute*.

The ancient deme of *Phaleron*, which was the original port of Athens, was connected with the capital by the Phaleric Long Wall. Scanty remains of this have
been found on the hill, and the foundations of a mole have been detected in the
sea. In the neighbouring plain were defeated the Spartans who had been tricked
by the exiled Alkmaeonids into invading Peisistratid Athens.

7km Palaión Fáliron (Παλαιόν Φάληρον: Hotels B, C; Restaurants), or
Old Pháleron, a pleasant seaside resort (53,273 inhab.) with a water-
sports stadium and swimming pool, extends E along the shore, here
broken into tiny creeks. The *Pumping Station* of the Ulen Company of
the shore supplies salt water for the Athens fire brigade. We cross the
stream of Pikrodaphne. The *Edem Restaurant*, on a small headland, is
the terminus of the Edem bus. To the left in the *Phaleron War
Cemetery*, stands the Athens memorial, dedicated in May 1961, to
2800 British dead of 1939–45, who have no known grave in Greece or
Yugoslavia.—9·5km **Kalamáki** (Hotels A, B, C), with a small yacht
basin and good tavernas, affords views of Hymettos.—11km *Alimós*
(Hotel B) corresponds to the ancient *Halimous*, birthplace of Thucydides (471–c 400 BC), whom Macaulay called 'the greatest historian
that ever lived'. The clay in this area was highly valued by Athenian
potters.—13km. A turning (left), signs to Mesogeíon Av. and Olympic
Stadium, skirts the airport and joins a major new bypass of Athens
which leads through the S suburbs on the foothills of Mt Hymettos, to
debouch in Od. Mesogeíon, on the NE side of the city (Rte 17B). Trees
partly hide a wireless station, beyond which extends the promontory
of **Ayios Kosmás**, named after a 19C chapel, whose conventual buildings are now a taverna. The headland probably represents the ancient
Kolias Akra, where many wrecked Persian ships were washed ashore
after the Battle of Salamis.

Excavations by Prof. G. Mylonas in 1930–31 revealed no evidence of ships but
proved that the coast has sunk since Classical times. On the E side of the headland and in the sea below were found remains of two separate occupations, one
Early Helladic, the other Late Helladic. Stone walls of houses may be seen. The
necropolis along the E shore, which provided many finds, belongs to the Early
Bronze Age. The graves show affinities with Cycladic types, suggesting that this
was a trading-post to which mariners from the Cyclades brought Melian obsidian. It came to a violent end c 1900 BC. In Mycenaean times the site was a
fortified village, which was abandoned in the 12C BC. The Classical sanctuary of
Aphrodite seen by Pausanias may lie beneath the chapel.

To the right of the road is the *National Athletic Centre*; to the left
extends *Athens Airport*, named after (12km) *Ellenikó*. The terminal
building, begun in 1961, was one of Eero Saarinen's last works.
    17km **Glifádha** (Γλυφάδα; Hotels L, A, B, C, D, Restaurants), a flou-
rishing seaside resort (44,018 inhab.) with sandy beaches and an 18-
hole golf course, owes its foundation in 1920 to the discovery of medicinal springs. Prospective visitors should be aware that the flight path
to the airport lies over the town. Near the Antonopoulos Hotel are the
ruins of an Early Christian basilica said to commemorate St Paul's
supposed first landing in S Greece at this spot. We join the old road
from Athens.

The old inland road, a trifle shorter, passes S of the Olympieion, crosses the Ilissos
near the Kallirrhoë (8, 5) and turns S. Beyond (3km) *Ayios Dhimitríos*, a pleasant
modern church, Mt. Hymettos, previously hidden by suburbs, is well seen to the
left.—5m *Trákhones* (the ancient deme Euonymon) has a theatre of the mid-4C
BC.
    Before the airport (right) the new bypass (comp. above) leads off to the left. The
airport itself can be seen and there is a turning to the West Terminal (Olympic
Airways). Farther on is an entrance to the Greek and U.S. Air Force bases, followed immediately by the access road to the East Terminal (foreign airlines).

After the airport the main road continues to Vari, while a right fork serves Glifadha, where we may join the coast by Astir Beach.—At the S end of Hymettos lay ancient *Aixone*, where the Thesmophoria, celebrated by women in the Temple of Demeter, provided Aristophanes with the theme for a play; Aixone has been identified with Glifadha.

From Glifadha, 1km beyond Astir Beach, opposite Tiffany's 'discotheque', a road bears left round a hospital and, after passing through an area of suburban development, ascends *Mt Krevati* (290m) to an air traffic control building (6·5km; 'No Entry' notice). About 550m before the notice, a saddle leads right to a hill (c 10 minutes) on the S slope of which, not far below the top and overlooking the Bay of Varkiza (Rte 17), is the remarkable stalactite GROTTO OF PAN, APOLLO, AND THE NYMPHS, with its crude sculptures. The mouth is difficult to find and the descent into the cave needs care. A wall of rock divides the grotto into two chambers. The large chamber, in which is a spring of clear water, contains the curious *Relief of Archidamos*, by whom the grotto appears to have been decorated. The figure holds a hammer and chisel, with which it is working at some indefinite object cut in the rock. Likewise cut in the rock are a primitive altar of Apollo Hersos, a headless seated goddess, and a much defaced head of a lion. The cave was excavated by the American School in 1903, when votive reliefs representing Hermes and the Nymphs, Pan playing the syrinx, etc., of the 4–3C BC were found as well as coins and deposits proving occupation from c 600 to 150 BC and in the 4C AD. At the S foot of the hill, below the cave, a classical farmhouse was explored by the British School in 1966: only the outline is now visible. This is the so-called 'Vari house'. Also at Vari is now the MILITARY ACADEMY, or *Officer Cadets' School*, the Sandhurst of Greece. In addition to military leaders, it trained naval cadets until 1846 and civil engineers in 1870–87. Founded at Nauplia in 1828 by Capodistrias, the academy was transferred first to Aegina, then in 1837 to Piraeus. In 1894 it moved to the *Evelpidhon* building (now lawcourts) in central Athens. It has been in its present location since 1981. Cadets wear a dark blue uniform, with yellow collar and bands and white gloves. Roads lead from the village of *Vari* to the coast at Voula and at Varkiza.

Vari. Reconstruction of the Classical farmhouse

On the promontory of *Alikí* (right) late-Mycenaean chamber-tombs have been explored.—At (19km) **Voúla** (Hotels A, B, C, D; Restaurants), a garden city (10,539 inhab.) of summer villas, the beach

ENVIRONS OF
ATHENS

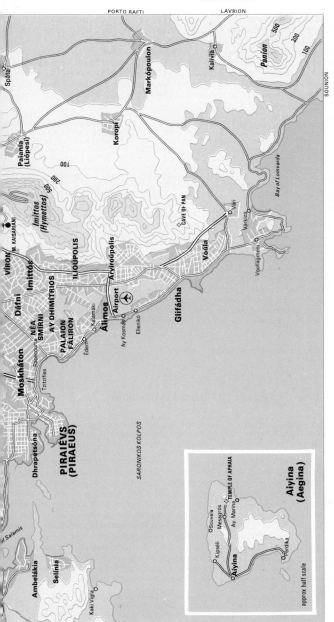

and camping site are controlled by the N.T.O.G. In Ano Voula, to the E and to be identified with the ancient deme of Halae Aixonidae, a variety of ancient buildings have been excavated, including farm and country houses. The little church of *Ayios Nikólaos ton Palon* stands just beyond the junction of the Vari road (comp. above), beyond which the main road passes behind (22·5km) *Kavoúri* (Hotels A, B, C), crossing the peninsula of *Kaminia* to Vouliagméni. Two wine-trading galleys (of the 4C BC) were found in 1960 lying in five fathoms off the islet of *Katramonisi*.

The three-tongued promontory, which forms the seaward end of the Hymettos range, was famous in antiquity as CAPE ZOSTER ('girdle'), strictly the name of the central tongue (now *Cape Lombárdha*). Here Leto unloosed her girdle before the birth of Apollo and Artemis (see Paus. I, 31, 1). The 6C *Sanctuary of Apollo Zoster*, unearthed in 1925–26, has been absorbed by a hotel garden; the attendant building of the same period, later enlarged, discovered in 1936, may be the priests' house or a pilgrims' hostel. Herodotus (VIII, 107) tells us that, after the battle of Salamis, the Persians mistook the rocks of the headland for Greek ships. The uninhabited island of *Fleves* (the ancient *Phabra*) lies 1·5km off the cape.

25km **Vouliagméni** (Βουλιαγμένη; Hotels L, A, B, C; inc. luxury flats; Restaurants), the most fashionable seaside resort in Attica (2743 inhab.; no hotels below class B), has a large yacht marina. It takes its name from a picturesque *Lake* (bathing establishment) of warm, green water enclosed by the sheer limestone rocks of the E cape of Kaminia. Its brackish, sulphurous waters are beneficial in cases of rheumatism, neuritis, arthritis, and skin diseases. The overflow from the lake runs underground to the sea and bubbles up from the sea bottom, raising its temperature for some distance. The fine sandy beaches (open all year) enclosed by the three headlands have been efficiently equipped by the N.T.O.G. in the international style with good restaurants.

From Vouliagméni to *Sounion*, see Rte 17.

14   Kaisariani and Hymettos

ROAD, 15·5km via Kaisariani, to the Prohibited Area, c 3km before the summit of Hymettos. BUS (No. 224/234 from the University) in 20 minutes to the suburb, whence the monastery is 30 minutes on foot.

Hymettos (Υμηττός, in modern Greek *Imittós*), famous for its sunset glow, its honey, and its marble, is the range of hills, 16km long, that shuts in the Attic plain on the SE, almost reaching the sea at Cape Zoster. It is divided by the Pirnari Glen into the *Great Hymettos* (Μεγάλος Υμηττός; 1027m) and the *Lesser* or *Waterless Hymettos* (Ανυδρος Υμηττός), of which the highest point is *Mavro Vouni* (804m). The W slopes reach almost to Athens, the *Kakorrhevma Gorge* extending from below the summit to Zoödhókhos Piyí and Pankráti; the abrupter W side dominates Liópesi. The mountain is almost treeless and the aromatic plants and shrubs which produced the best food for bees are less widespread than in classical times, though terebinth, juniper, thyme, sage, mint, lavender, etc., are still to be found.

The Hymettian bee has migrated to Pentelikon and Tourkovouni. The violet colour which now, as in antiquity, suffuses the mountain at sunset is peculiar to Hymettos (comp. the 'purpureos colles' of Ovid, below). Hymettian marble (so-called Kará marble) was anciently quarried on the W side of the mountain, close to the Kakorrhevma Gorge and approximately on the site of the ruined *Convent of Karyaes.*—Near the Convent of St John the Hunter (Rte 17B), at the N end of the ridge, are some modern quarries.

From a little E of the Hilton Hotel (5, 8) a shrinking pine copse marks the defile of the Ilissos between the suburbs of Zográfou and Kaisarianí. Leoforos Vasileos Alexandrou to the S of the wood is the main approach road to the suburb of *Kaisariani.*—5·5km **ᐧMoni Kaisarianís** (341m), an 11C monastery, is closely confined at the end of the ravine amid the welcome shade of cypress, pine, and plane trees. Here since pagan times shrines have marked the source of the Ilissos.

On the brow of the hill just above the monastery is a famous fountain, known in ancient times as *Kyllou Pera;* its waters were supposed to cure sterility. A temple of Aphrodite was adjacent and the spot was made famous by Ovid in the well-known lines of the Ars Amatoria (III, 987) describing the sad legend of Cephalus and Procris. The spring supplied Athens with drinking water before the construction of the Marathon Dam. It feeds a fountain on the outside E wall of the monastery where the water gushes from a ram's head (cast; the original is now in the Acropolis Museum). Fragments built into the walls belong to an earlier Christian basilica, probably of the 5C.

The present structure is first mentioned in the 12C. It has been conjectured that the name derives from Caesarea, whence perhaps came its original ikon. In 1458 when the Sultan Mehmed II visited newly conquered Athens, the Abbot of Kaisarianí was chosen to deliver up to him the keys of the city, in recognition of which the convent was exempted from taxation by the Turks. Until 1716 it was independent of the Metropolitan and had a school and a celebrated library (moved to Athens and destroyed in the War of 1821). It was noted also for its honey. Deserted in the 18C, it is now a national monument. During the Second World War the secluded ravine was used by the Germans for the execution of hostages. The monastery was restored in 1956–57; the church is still a goal of pilgrimage on Ascension Day.

The CONVENTUAL BUILDINGS (entered from the far side), grouped round a pretty court, include a *Mill* and *Bakery,* and a *Bath-House,* now restored after use as an oil-press. The *Refectory* has a finely moulded Roman lintel over the door and a domed kitchen. The *Church,* built of stone with brick courses, takes the form of a Greek cross. The dome is supported on Roman columns. The parecclesion (dedicated to *St. Anthony*) was added in the 16C, the narthex in the 17C, and the belfry in the 19C. The frescoes, save for those by Ioannis Ipatos (Peloponnesian, 1682) in the narthex, are in a 17–18C Cretan style. A tomb in the crypt was explored in 1950.

The road crosses a bridge over a gully, then swings left to a saddle below an outcrop of rock that affords a sudden view of the whole of Athens. It then climbs to (9km) the pretty *Moní Asteríou* (548m), another 11C monastery, restored in 1961. Hence a path descends in c 1·5km to *Ayios Ioánnis Theológos,* another Byzantine church above the suburb of Goudí (Rte 17B).—We reach (10km) *Mávra Vrákhia* (646m) a col 3km N of the summit. The col is marred by a radar station, but now that the summit is prohibited, affords the best vantage point on Hymettos, with a wide view over the Mesogeia and to the plain of Marathon. The road climbs S but the view, though more extensive toward the W, looking across Salamis to the Peloponnese, does not include the E.—At 15km are Stop signs, with a place for turning.

The summit (1027m) was crowned in Classical times with a statue of Zeus. Vestiges of an altar were found in 1939, and a cave has yielded Geometric pottery.

15 Kifissiá and Pentelikon

A. From Athens to Kifissiá and Ekáli

ROAD. 14km (9 miles). Bus 525, 538/539 from Plat. Kánningos every few minutes to Kifissiá; 513 (Ayios Stéphanos) and others from same terminal, to Ekáli. The nearer suburbs are served by many local routes.

RAILWAY, 16km, by Piraeus Electric Railway (E.H.Σ.) from Omonoia Square.

Leoforos Vasilissis Sofias (Rte 10) from Sindagma Sq. and Leoforos Alexandras from Omonoia Square meet at *Ambelókipoi*, 2km from Sindagma Square. We take the left fork and follow LEOFÓROS KIFISSÍAS. To the left rises *Tourkovoúni* (338m), the ancient *Anchesmos*, with a reservoir and purification plant of Athens Waterworks. On the E slope is (6km) **Psikhikó** (Ψυχικό), a garden suburb. Here at Benaki Hall is *Athens College*, a boarding school for boys on an American pattern, founded in 1925; its 225 Greek boys, nearly half from overseas, are taught bilingually in Greek and English. Next to it is the *Arsakeion*, a progressive girls' school removed c 1930 from a site near the University.—6·5km. Turning (right) to Nea Pendeli, see below.—8km. *Filothéi* (Φιλοθέη), a model suburb erected by the National Bank of Greece in 1930–35, with film studios, is favoured by foreign residents. Roads lead W to Nea Ionia and E to Ayia Paraskevi (Rte 17B).—9km. There is a turning (right) for the *Olympic Stadium*. Completed in 1982, the stadium, which is set in 250 acres, seats 80,000 spectators. It has an indoor sports hall, training fields, tennis courts, an Olympic training centre and accommodation for 320 competitors. For visitors without cars, access is either by the electric railway from central Athens (Omonoia, etc.) to the new station of Eirene (next after Herakleion) or by any Kifissia bus (and 500m walk).—The main highway passes to the right of (12km) **Amaroúsion** (Hotel D), or *Maroússi*, the ancient *Athmonia*, which derives its name from a temple of Artemis Amarousia. It is celebrated for its bright glazed pottery. Off the old road, *Anávryta College*, a boarding school started in 1947 by Jocelyn Winthrop Young after the model of Gordonstoun, occupies the former Singros estate.

In the main square is a bust, by Tombros (1961), of Spiros Louis, the local shepherd who won the first modern marathon race at the Olympic Games of 1896.

14·5km **KIFISSIÁ** (Κηφισιά; 268m) is an attractive and popular 'garden city' (31,876 inhab.) on the SW slopes of Pentelikon. The summer temperature averages 10° lower than in the city, and the shade of its pine trees affords a welcome relief from the glare of Athens. Menander was a native of Kifissia, and here Herodes Atticus had a villa, a visit to which inspired Aulus Gellius to write his rambling 'Noctes Atticae'. Now, as in Roman times, the town is a favourite retreat of the Athenians in summer. It is the seat of the Metropolitan of Attica and Megaris.

The suburb has many *hotels*, mostly in the higher categories, and mainly in the Kefalári area. There are also excellent zakharoplasteia and numerous *restaurants*. Kifissia and the Northern suburbs generally are pleasant places to eat, especially in summer, when there are also direct buses to bathing resorts. In Kifissia also is the *Goulandris Natural History Museum*, at Od. Levídhou 12.

In December 1944 Tatoi aerodrome (occupied by the R.A.F. in October) was evacuated in face of the ELAS rising and British air headquarters set up in the Pentelikon and Cecil hotels in Kifissia, already cut off from Athens. ELAS attacked on 18 December and forced the garrison to capitulate. On the 20th the survivors (c 600 officers and men) were subjected to begin a forced march, in company with civilian hostages, largely on foot through Central Greece. R.A.F. aircraft tracked their progress through Thebes, Levadhia, Lamia, and Larissa to Trikkala, dropping supplies wherever possible. At Lazarina (Rte 47C) in the Pindos on 23 January an exchange of prisoners was effected and the airmen repatriated from Volos.

The road enters Plateia Platanou. On the left gardens descend to the station; the road to Kefalari forks right. On this corner (right) a shelter covers four *Roman Sarcophagi*, with reliefs, perhaps from the family vault of Herodes (busts of Herodes and of Polydeukion, his pupil and cousin, were found in 1961 in a garden near the church of Panayia tis Xidhou, a short way N of the Plateia. Subsequent discoveries, 1972–74, have revealed more sculpture and a probable bath building. All may be from the villa of Herodes Atticus; comp. above). *Kefalári*, a district of villas, gardens, and hotels, takes its name from a small and usually dried up stream, which, after rain, is a source of the Kifissos. The place is fast expanding into the foothills of Pentelikon, and it is possible to walk to Moni Pendeli and the ridge of the mountain.

From the N end of Kifissia a road branches to the left towards Tatoi and Dhekelia (comp. Rte 20).

The main road continues NE to *Kastrí* (Hotel C), above which (right) an ancient fort crowns the NW spur of Pentelikon, and (20km) **Ekáli** (Hotel C), a pleasant summer resort amid pine woods, which has adopted the name of an ancient deme situated farther NE.

Immediately N of Ekali a road diverges (right) to (3km) **Dhiónisos** (Hotel C), ancient *Ikaria*, where Dionysos is alleged to have been entertained by Ikarios, and the grateful god of wine instructed his host in the cultivation of the grape.— At 5km a turning to the left leads (550m) to the Sanctuary of Dionysos (left) discovered by the American School in 1888.—At 10·5km *Ayios Petros* (café), fine view over Marathon Bay.—The road descends to Nea Makri (Rte 21).
  Beyond (1km) the Dionysos turn, another road leads (right) in 2km to Stamáta where, on the hill of *Mygdhaléza* (2km to the N) an Early Christian basilica and associated buildings were excavated in 1977. The complex, probably built in the 5C AD, incorporated Classical masonry and inscriptions and may be on the site of the ancient deme of Hekale. Bus 507 to Stamata leaves from Plateia Kaningos.

B. From Athens to Moní Pendéli

ROAD, 16km (10 miles). Bus 415 from Od. Vasiléos Iraklíou (behind National Archaeological Museum).

From Athens to (6km) *Psikhikó*, see above. Shortly beyond we take the right fork to (10km) **Khalándri** (Χαλάνδρι; Hotels B, C) on the road to the N), a pleasant suburb occupying the site of *Phyla*, birthplace of Euripides (480–406 BC). The ancient orgies of the 'Great Goddess' (probably Mother-Earth) at Phyla antedated the mysteries at Eleusis. About 1km S the chapel of *Panayia Marmariotissa* covers the remains of a Roman tomb.—At 14·5km, near a rustic villa (now a taverna) built by the Duchesse de Plaisance, we are joined by a by-road from Amarousion (4km, via *Melissia*, with film studios).

16km *Moní Pendéli*, a monastery founded in 1578 and now one of the richest in Greece, is shaded by a cluster of lofty white poplars. The buildings are modern, but the chapel contains 17C paintings. The road curves round the monastery grounds and ends at a large open space (bus terminus; Hotel D, tavernas); in the centre is the chapel of *Ayia Triadha*, near which traces of terraces mark the site of *Palaia Pendeli*, the ancient deme of Penteli. A little to the S of the convent (on a by-road towards Stavrós) stands the *Palace of Rodhodhafnis*, built in a Gothic style for the Duchesse de Plaisance by Kleanthes. Here she died (1854) and is buried. It was restored in 1961 as a royal residence, and is now the setting for concerts on some evenings in the summer.

PENTELIKÓN (Τὸ Πεντελικόν; modern Pendéli), the mountainous range enclosing the Attic plain on the NE, extends for 7km from NW to SE. Its ancient name was *Brilessos* (Βριλησσός), but by Classical times it had come to be called Pentelikon after the township of Pentele where the famous marble quarries lay. The principal summit (*Kokkinarás*; 1110m), to the NW, is, like that of Hymettos, inaccessible since it was crowned by an ugly radar station. *Vayati* (1007m), the secondary summit, ½km SE, can still be attained on foot, as can the little platform between them, the site of the statue of Athena mentioned by Pausanias.

The area beyond the monastery is largely blocked by quarrying, a military hospital, and villa development. However it is still possible to find a way through to the slopes of Pentelikon and the ANCIENT QUARRIES, which lie SE of the summit.

No less than 25 of them can be made out, one above the other, at a height of 700–1000m. Their exploitation, though begun c 570 BC, was unimportant before the 5C BC, and became general in Pericles' day. The crystalline rock of Pentelikon yielded the fine white marble which was used for the most important buildings and even in sculpture. It superseded Hymettian marble and poros for architectural purposes, though it never quite ousted Parian marble, which is easier to chisel, for sculpture. The rich golden tint that age gives to Pentelic marble alone is due to the presence of iron oxide. The stone yielded by the modern quarries at Dhionisos, on the N slope of Pentelikon, is less white.

We come first to an ancient *Paved Way*, down which the cut blocks were transported on wooden sledges. The holes on either side held bollards round which steadying ropes were wound. The *Quarry of Spilia* (700m) was worked out by the ancients. In the NW corner opens a large *Stalactite Grotto* containing twin chapels. The S unit contains some relief decoration with crosses, angels, eagles and an inscription, indicating that it probably was a place of worship in the pre-Iconoclastic period. To the N a domed chapel of the abbreviated cross type was subsequently added. The S chapel retains frescoes from c 1225, including a representation of the *Melismos* in the apse and a portrait of Michael Choniates, bishop of Athens between 1182 and 1204. The N chapel also retains fresco decoration. Remains of walls and inscriptions at the entrance mark a monastery of Byzantine date that survived the Frankish period.—From the grotto the climb to the ridge takes c 75 minutes.

The *View, one of the most extensive in Attica, is remarkable for its vast expanse of water, visible in all directions save on the NW. To the N rises the pyramidal Dhirfis, while on the E lie Euboea, Andros, and Tinos. The Plain of Marathon is partly hidden by an intervening spur. To the SE the sea is studded with innumerable islands; across the valley to the S the ridge of Hymettos runs down to the sea; on the SW Athens spreads itself over the plain. Far to the S are the mountains of Milos, 150km distant.

16 From Athens to Elévsis

ROAD, 22km (14 miles), by the Ierá Odhós to *Elévsis*, via (11km)
Dhafni. Buses: No. 864, every 15 minutes, from Plateia
Koumoundhourou (Eleftherias) (2, 6) for Dhafni (20 minutes) and
beyond to Elevsis (45 minutes); No. 026 from Sindagma Sq., etc. to
Plateia Koumoundhourou and Votanikós; buses also from Piraeus.

The first 5 or 6km are heavily industrialised and tedious to the pedestrian.
   The faster but unrewarding LEOFÓROS ATHINÓN (taken by all long-
distance buses), which forms the initial section of the highway to Corinth, runs
almost parallel, c 1km to the N. It is reached from Omonoia Sq. by Ayíou Konstandínou and Akhilléos streets (2, 5) and, after crossing Kifissoú by a new flyover
near the Peloponnesian bus station, it joins the Sacred Way just beyond the
conspicuous mental hospital at Dhafni.—Beyond Asprópirgos we must take the
old road (right); the Corinth highway now by-passes Elevsis.

By RAIL TO ELÉVSIS (S.P.A.P.), 27km in 35–45 minutes. The line strikes N
through haphazard suburban settlements to (10km) *Ano Liósia*, where it curves
SW. Beyond a large army transport depot it threads a low defile, passing through
a gap in the DEMA (το Δέμα; 'the Link'), or *Aigaleos-Parnes Wall*, a westward-
facing rampart that follows an undulating course for 4·5km along the watershed.
The S two-thirds are built in various styles of masonry (comp. B.S.A., vol. 52, 1957)
in 53 short sections separated by 50 sally-ports and two gateways. Farther N the
wall is crude and continuous. Two signal (?) towers command the wall, which is
apparently military and may date from the Lycurgan period. A *House*, of the late
5C BC, disposed round a court, was excavated in 1960 just N of the railway.—The
uninhabited valley between the Aigaleos ridge and the foothills of Parnes is
dotted with beehives. Emerging into the Thriasian Plain (see below) at (23km)
Asprópirgos, with a huge oil refinery, the line joins the road on the outskirts of
(27km) *Elevsis*.

From Omonoia Square (3, 3) Odhos Piraiós leads to (1km) the Kerameikos (Rte 4). The Ierá Odhós preserves both the name and very
largely the original course of the SACRED WAY (Ἱερα Ὸδος) traversed
by initiates from Athens to Eleusis, though nowadays few indications
remain of the tombs and shrines described at length by Pausanias.
From the Kerameikos the narrow road threads the noisy industrial
area of *Votanikós*. We pass (2km; left) the *Botanic Gardens* (Βοτανικός
Κήπος), with its tall poplars, and the Agricultural School of Athens
University. A little farther on, *Plato's Olive-tree* (so called) is one of
very few survivors from the famous grove that once bordered the
Kifissos from Kolonos to the sea.—3km *Ayios Savas* (right), a medieval
church near the conspicuous naval signal station, stands on the site of
a Temple of Demeter supposed to commemorate the spot where she
rewarded the hospitality of Phytalos by giving him the first fig-tree.
Classical and Byzantine marbles are visible in the walls. Farther on, a
by-road to the right passes the *Hydrographic Office* of the Greek
navy, and joins Leoforos Athinon. We cross Leoforos Kifissou, the extension to Piraeus of the National Highway, with the canalised
Kifissos some way W of its ancient bed. The country opens out amid
sparse olives as we approach the comparatively low ridge of *Aigaleos*
(Αιγάλεως), the W horn of the natural amphitheatre that surrounds
Athens. On the right is the conical hill of *Profitis Ilias* (189m), surmounted by a chapel. From this point the traveller from the W gets the
first sudden view of Athens, especially striking at sunset. The new
highway (see above) joins the ancient road at *Dhafni*.
   The **Monastery of Daphni** (or *Dhafní*; camping site), surrounded by
a high battlemented wall, stands to the S of the junction. Both church
and walls incorporate ancient materials from a *Sanctuary of Apollo*, on
the same site, mentioned by Pausanias but destroyed c AD 395. The
convent owes its name to the laurels (δάφναι) sacred to Apollo, which

once flourished in the neighbourhood.

History. The monastery, founded in the 5C or 6C, was dedicated to the Virgin Mary. It was rebuilt at the end of the 11C, but sacked by Crusaders in 1205. In 1211 Otho de la Roche gave it to the Cistercians, who held it until 1458. Two Dukes of Athens, Otho himself and Walter de Brienne, were buried here. The convent was reoccupied in the 16C by Orthodox monks until its abandonment in the War of Independence. Restorations were made in 1893 after the building had been used in turn as barracks and lunatic asylum. The structure was strengthened in 1920, and a more elaborate restoration was undertaken after the Second World War.

The fortified enceinte and a few foundations inside near the NE corner survive from its earliest Christian period. Of the 11C monastic buildings only some foundations of the great *Refectory* can be seen on the N side. The pretty *Cloister* (restored), S of the church, dates from the Cistercian period, with the addition of 16C cells. Round it are displayed sculptural fragments, Classical and Byzantine, but the two sarcophagi, ornamented with fleurs-de-lys and Latin crosses, are doubtfully those of the Frankish dukes.

The *CHURCH is a fine example of Byzantine architecture of c 1080, with an added exo-narthex, which was restored in 1961 to the later form given it by the Cistercians. The pointed arches and crenellations contrast not unpleasingly with the reused classical pillars. The truncated W tower on the N side bore a Gothic belfry. The three-light windows of the church are separated by mullions and surrounded by three orders of brickwork. The lights are closed by perforated alabaster slabs. The drum of the dome has round engaged buttresses between each of its sixteen windows. We enter from the cloister by the S door. The interior is noted for its *Mosaics, which, though fragmentary in comparison with their original extent, have no rivals in S Greece; indeed none nearer than Salonika save for those of Osios Loukas in Phocis. Most complete are those on the S side of the narthex, portraying the Presentation of the Virgin and the Prayer of Joachim and Anna. On the vault of the dome is a celebrated representation, uncompromisingly stern, of Christos Pantokrator, on a gold ground. The frieze, round the drum below, depicts saints and prophets. Finely preserved on the pendentives are the Annunciation, Nativity, Baptism, and Transfiguration. On the W side of the N choros, the Entry into Jerusalem shows interesting perspective effects (note the little boys' foreshortened feet). In the bema, or sanctuary, though the Virgin above the apse is fragmentary and the vault is empty, the flanking Archangels are well-preserved. Of the frescoes that once adorned the lower walls of the church, four are still comparatively clear.—The *Crypt* has recently been cleared.

WINE FESTIVAL (Sept–Oct, daily in the evening; sometimes rather rowdy) in grounds and pine woods. Entrance fee covers *ad lib.* tasting of 60 or more wines, folk dancing, etc.

Beyond Dhafni the highway has been straightened and nearly trebled in width by blasting away the rock, so that the now intermittent traces of the Sacred Way must be sought first to the left then to the right. A mile beyond the monastery (right) are the scanty foundations of a *Temple of Aphrodite*.

In the face of the wall of rock behind are several niches for votive statuettes with mutilated inscriptions below them. Remains are visible also of 'the wall of unwrought stones that is worth seeing' (Pausanias, I, 37, 7). This wall, which was outside the precinct of Aphrodite, at its SE corner, was built of rude blocks of stone and was nearly 30ft thick; it may have been part of an ancient fort. The

Plan labels:

John Baptist — Virgin and Child — Nicholas
Silvester — Michael — Gabriel — Eleutherios — Aberkios
Stephen — Laurence — Euplos

Aaron — Gregory of Agrigentum

Nat. of Virgin
Crucifixion
Andronikas
Tarachos
Probos
Entry into Jerusalem
Lazarus

Annunciation — David — Isaiah — Solomon — Nativity
Moses — Elijah
Jeremiah — Elisha
Ezekiel — PANTOKRATOR — Jonah
Zachariah — Habakkuk
Joel — Zephaniah
Micah — Malachi — Christ's Baptism
Daniel

3 Magi
Resurrection
Samonas
Gourias
Abibos
Thomas

Zachariah — Transfiguration
Akindymos — Elipidiphoros — Anempodismos
Bakchos

Pigasios — Orestes — Auxentios — Eugenios — Eustratios

Assumption of Virgin — Mardarios — Sergios

Gregory Thaumaturgos

Last Supper — Presentation of the Virgin

Washing of the Feet — Judas's Betrayal — Prayer of Joachim and Anna — Benediction

DAPHNI

0   3 metres

Sacred Way, laid bare here during the excavation of the temple in 1891–92, ran between the temple and the wall.

We descend towards the Bay of Eleusis, landlocked by the island of Salamis and horribly industrialised. At 14·5km the road reaches the shore, and turns abruptly to the right (N).

To the left a road leads in 1·5km to **Skaramángas** (Hotels C), with the *Hellenic Shipyards*, founded in 1956 by Stavros Niarkhos, on the site of naval yards destroyed during the Second World War and taken over by the State in 1985. The first ship to be built here, a 25,000-ton tanker, was launched in 1960. The graving dock, opened in 1970, can accommodate vessels up to 250,000 d.w. tons, and is the largest in the Mediterranean. At the *Naval Training Headquarters* conscripts of the Royal Hellenic Navy receive instruction.—A coastal road continues round the Skaramangas Hills (270m; a spur of Aigaleos) to *Pérama* (8km; see Rte 18), the starting-point of the ferry to Salamis.

The modern road along the *Paralía Aspropírgou* or Asprópirgos shore, which for a long time occupied the ancient causeway of the Sacred Way, has been widened by land reclamation. On the right are the *Limni Koumoundhourou*, now salt marshes and ponds but anciently the *Rheitoi* streams, which formed the fish preserves of the Eleusinian priesthood, and marked the boundary between Athens and Eleusis. We are now skirting the Thriasian Plain, so called from the ancient deme of Thria.

The *Thriasian Plain*, extending for c 14·5km along the Eleusinian Gulf, is usually identified with the Rarian or Rharian Plain, in Greek myth supposedly the first to be sown and the first to bear crops; here Demeter made the ground lie fallow while her daughter remained in the underworld. The plain is now one of the most highly industrialised areas in Greece; its oil tanks, chimneys, and the installation of cargo quays combine with the heavy motor traffic to make the last four miles of the Sacred Way the least romantic road in Greece. Salamis is usually obscured by dust and sulphur fumes.

18km. The *Government Nautical College* (0·5km left) trains captains of the merchant navy.—18·5km. Turning (right) to Asprópirgos (1·5km; see above).—At 21km we fork right (signposted 'No toll road') from (and pass under)·the main highway. To the left of the old road, c 200m beyond a group of cypresses, by a well ('Kalo Pigadhi'), are four complete arches of a *Roman Bridge*, which carried the Sacred Way across the Eleusinian Kifissos. The bridge, 5·5m wide and c 46m long, built of poros, probably dates from AD 124 when Hadrian was initiated into the Eleusinian mysteries. A hundred feet of the Sacred Way have been uncovered to the W. At the entrance to Elevsis is the desecrated chapel of *Ayios Zakharias*, where the famous relief of Demeter and Kore was found.

22km (14 miles) **ELEVSI'S** (Ἐλευσίς, usually Elefsína; Hotels C), an expanding industrial town (20,320 inhab.) with cement, petrochemical, and steel works, is occupied also with shipbuilding and the manufacture of soap and olive oil. The ancient city of **Eleusis**, birthplace of Aeschylus (525–456 BC) and home of the Sanctuary of Demeter and of the Eleusinian Mysteries, was situated on the E slopes of a low rocky hill (63m) which runs parallel and close to the shore. The *Sacred Way*, of which large sections (paved and with kerbs) have been traced, led direct to the sanctuary. It lies left of the modern road at the entrance to the town, but the modern approach to the site is signposted from the centre. The extensive excavations of the sanctuary, which had a continuous history from Mycenaean to Roman times, are of the greatest interest to antiquaries, but their appreciation is demanding to the lay imagination.

History. The legendary foundation of a city at Eleusis by Eleusis, a son of Ogygos of Thebes, before the 15C is substantiated in date at least by existing remains of houses (Middle Helladic II), dated to the 18–17C BC. Tradition tells of wars between the Athenians and Eleusinians in heroic times, resulting in the deaths of Erechtheus and of Immarados, son of Eumolpos. Eumolpos was reputed to be the first celebrant of the mysteries of Eleusis. The introduction of the cult of Demeter is ascribed by the Parian Chronicle to the reign of Erechtheus (c 1409 BC) and by Apollodoros to that of Pandion, son of Erichthonios (c 1462–1423). The first shrine on the sanctuary site is dated by sherds to the Late Helladic II period, though there is nothing concrete to connect it with Demeter. The 'Homeric' Hymn to Demeter (late 7C BC) gives the orthodox version of the institution of the mysteries by Demeter herself (comp. below). The city seems to have been a rival of Athens until it came under firm Athenian sway about the time of Solon. Henceforward its cult grew and the sanctuary was constantly enlarged. Its reputation became panhellenic and initiation was opened to non-Athenian Greeks. Peisistratos rebuilt it, enclosing it with a strong wall and doubling its area; but his work fell victim to the Persian invasion. Kimon initiated the reconstruction which was completed under Pericles. His telesterion was to survive with modifications to the end. Eleusis suffered heavily under the Thirty Tyrants, who here established a fortified base against Thrasyboulos, massacring those who opposed them. The sanctuary was extended again in the 4C BC. The town remained a stronghold throughout the Macedonian period. Under the *pax Romana* the sanctuary was adorned with a new gate. The Imperial transformation of Eleusis probably began under Hadrian. In AD 170 the sanctuary was sacked by the Sarmatians, but was immediately restored at the expense of Marcus Aurelius. At his initiation in 176 the Emperor was allowed to enter the anaktoron, the only lay person so honoured in the whole history of Eleusis. The Emperor Julian was initiated, completing his sanctification (according to Gibbon) in Gaul; Valerian (253–60) reorganised the defences of the site in the face of threats from Barbarian tribes (Goths and Herulians); Valentinian permitted the continuance of the Mysteries, but Theodosius' decrees and Alaric's sack were jointly responsible (c 395) for their end. The town was abandoned after the Byzantine era and not reoccupied till the 18C.

The Homeric *Hymn to Demeter* sets down the anciently accepted mystique of the cult's divine foundation. While gathering flowers, Persephone (Kore, or the Maiden), Demeter's daughter, was carried off by Hades (Pluto) to the nether regions. Demeter, during her quest for Persephone, came to Eleusis, where she was found resting, disguised as an old woman, by Metaneira, consort of King Keleos. After her first disastrous attempt to reward the king's hospitality by immortalising her son Demophon, Demeter revealed her identity and commanded Keleos to build a megaron in her honour. To this she retired, vowing that she would neither return to Olympos nor allow crops to grow on earth until Kore was delivered up. Finally Zeus commanded Pluto to return Persephone, but because she had eaten pomegranate seeds while in the underworld she was bound to return there for part of every year. Before leaving Eleusis, Demeter broke the famine and gave to Triptolemos, second son of Keleos, seeds of wheat and a winged chariot, in which he rode over the earth, teaching mankind the use of the plough and the blessings of agriculture.

Candidates for initiation were first admitted to the *Lesser Eleusinia* which were held in the month of Anthesterion (February–March) at Agrai, in Athens, on the banks of the Ilissos. Being accepted as Mystai (initiates), they were allowed to attend the GREATER ELEUSINIA, which took place in Boëdromion (September), and lasted nine days, beginning and ending in Athens. For them a truce was declared throughout Hellas. During the seventh night the qualified Mystai became Epoptai. These annual celebrations (*teletai*) consisted of a public secular display and a secret religious rite. The former, the responsibility of the Archon Basileus and his staff, took the form mainly of a *Procession* (*pompe*) from Athens to Eleusis. The religious rite was entirely in the hands of the Hierophant and priesthood of Eleusis, hereditary offices of the Eumolpids and the Kerykes. The most important officials included the Dadouchos (torchbearer) and the Hierokeryx (herald). The procession, which took place on the fifth day, was headed by a statue of Iacchos, god associated with the cult, and bore with it the Hiera, or sacred objects, in baskets (*kistai*). During the Peloponnesian War, when no truce was declared, the procession was reduced; for some years after the Spartan occupation of Dekelia the pompe went by sea. In 336 BC the news of the destruction of Thebes by Alexander the Great caused the only recorded instance of the procession's cancellation after it had set out.

The fundamental substance of the **Mysteries**, the character of the sacred objects displayed, and the nature of the revelation experienced were never divulged. Alcibiades was condemned to death in absentia for parodying part of the mysteries (though later reprieved); Aeschylus was almost lynched on suspicion of revealing their substance on the stage. It is thought probable that a pageant (dromena) was performed representing the action of the Hymn of Demeter. Initiation carried with it no further obligation, but seems to have afforded spiritual pleasure. Cicero derived great comfort from the experience.

Eleusis attracted the attention of western travellers from Wheler (1676) onwards. E.D. Clarke bore away a statue to Cambridge in 1801. The Propylaea were laid bare in 1812 by the Society of the Dilettanti. Systematic excavations, started by the Greek Archaeological Society in 1882, were greatly extended by Konstantinos Kourouniotes in 1917–45, especially after the Rockefeller Institution had provided a grant in 1930. Both the earlier work and that done since the war by G.E. Mylonas, Prof. Orlandos, and John Travlos are admirably summarised in Mylonas: 'Eleusis and the Eleusinian Mysteries' (1962).

A good idea of the layout and complexity of the excavations can be gained from the terrace in front of the prominent 19C chapel. Visitors who are pressed for time can then confine themselves to the forecourt, the two propylaea, the Telesterion, the SE walls, and the Museum. A full exploration of the remains takes all day and necessitates a certain amount of scrambling. Care should be taken on the Acropolis, where there are unfenced cisterns.

The EXCAVATIONS lie at the foot and on the E slopes of the Acropolis and comprise the greater part of the **Sanctuary of Deméter and Kóre** and its dependencies. This was protected on three sides by the main city wall and separated from the city on the fourth side by a dividing wall. As we pass the entrance gate the *Sacred Way* changes from a modern to an ancient paved road, which ends on the **Great Forecourt** before the city walls. This spacious square formed part of the new monumental entrance planned probably in the reign of Antoninus Pius. Here the mystai gathered in order to perform the necessary acts of purification before entering the sanctuary. From the square the Great Propylaea led directly to the sanctuary; to left and right triumphal arches led towards the main gate of the town and to the visitors' quarter of baths, hotels, and recreation centres.

Numerous marble blocks on the square came from the buildings that defined its limits. To the left are the remains of a *Fountain*. Beyond it stood a *Triumphal Arch*, one of two (comp. above) faithfully copied from the Arch of Hadrian at Athens. The foundations remain; its gable has been reassembled in front; and its inscription (replaced near by) reads 'All the Greeks to the Goddesses and the Emperor'. Close to the NE corner of the Great Propylaea is the sacred well that passed throughout classical times for the **Kallíchoron**, or *Well of the Fair Dances*. The well-head, beautifully fashioned in polygonal masonry with clamps, probably dates from the time of Peisistratos. Mylonas has suggested that this is, in fact, the *Parthenion*, or Well of the Maidens, mentioned in the Hymn as the place where Demeter sat to rest. The name Kallichoron may have been transferred to it from the well near the Telesterion after the importance of the Parthenion had been centred on the 'Mirthless Stone' on which she sat (comp. below).

In the centre of the court are the scanty remains of the *Temple of Artemis Propylaia and of Poseidon*, amphiprostyle in form and constructed in marble. It must have been quite new when described by Pausanias. The *Altar* to the E presumably dedicated to Artemis, that to the N probably to Poseidon, while at the NW corner is an *Eschara*, constructed in Roman tiles, on remains proving that the sacred nature of the spot goes back to the 6C BC. The rectangular area that interrupts the pavement beyond the eschara has been identified with the *Temenos of the Hero Dolichos*; beneath the houses outside the enclosure are extensive remains conjectured to be of a *Pompeion*.

The **Great Propylaéa**, built in Pentelic marble on a concrete core by Marcus Aurelius or his predecessor, is a close copy of the Propylaea at Athens, both in plan and dimensions. It is approached by six marble steps and faces NE. Reassembled on the pavement in front are two of the six Doric *Columns* of the façade and the *Pediment* with its central medallion bust of (?) Marcus Aurelius. Parts of the entablature are assembled to the right of the steps. The bases of the six Ionic columns that flanked the central passage are in situ. The transverse wall was pierced by five doorways: the threshold of the small one to the left shows the greatest wear. At some time of danger (? under Valerian) the Doric colonnade was closed by a thick wall; the single door that then gave entrance has left a roller groove in the pavement. Crosses scored on the pavement probably derive from Christian fears of pagan spirits.

The gateway covers a corner tower of the Peisistratid enceinte. To the W this remained the city's fortification in later times; to the E a later wall enclosed a Classical extension to the city, while the Peisistratid circuit continued to serve as the peribolos of the sanctuary. Between the two walls are numerous small buildings dating mainly from the time of Kimon. The area between the two propylaea seems to have been a level forecourt in Roman times.

The **Lesser Propylaéa**, which face N and form the entrance to the innermost court, were vowed to the Goddesses by Cicero's friend Appius Claudius Pulcher in his consulship (54 BC) and completed after his death by two nephews. The structure consisted of two parallel walls, each 15m long, with Ionic attached columns, which enclosed a passage 10m wide. This is divided into three at its inner end by two short inner walls (parastadia) parallel to the exterior walls. Forward of the doors, whose supporting rollers have left prominent grooves, extended antae; the bases in front of them supported two Corinthian columns. The inner façade had caryatids instead of columns. Portions of the inscribed architrave and frieze are recomposed at the side. The frieze is composed of triglyphs and metopes, both carved with emblems of the cult.

We now enter the inner **Precinct of Demeter**, for two thousand years an area forbidden to the uninitiated on penalty of death. To the right is the *Plutonion*, a triangular precinct of the 4C BC, enclosing a cavern sacred to Pluto. A shrine was built at its mouth in the Peisistratid era; the surviving foundations are of a temple completed in 328 BC (a dated inscription has been found referring to the purchase of its wooden doors). Following the *Processional Road*, we come next to a rock-cut *Stepped Platform* (Pl. A) which adjoined a small building, perhaps a *Treasury* (Pl. B). The platform may have served as a stand from which the start of a sacred pageant was watched; Mylonas suggests that the 'Mirthless Stone' (Agelastos Petra) may be identified with the worked piece of rock that here projects above the pavement of the Roman sacred way. The levelled terrace beyond the treasury supported a *Temple* (Pl. C) possibly dedicated to Sabina, wife of Hadrian, on whom the Greeks had conferred the title of New Demeter. Between this and the treasury is a *Thesauros* (offertory box) hewn from a boulder. We ascend to the large square platform on which stood the Hall of the Mysteries.

The first shrine decreed by Demeter 'beneath the citadel and its sheer wall upon a rising hillock above the Kallichoron' occupied a limited site on ground which sloped steeply away. As each enlargement of the sanctuary was undertaken, it became necessary to extend the artificial terrace on which it stood. In consequence each shrine in turn escaped complete destruction by being buried under the next. The result is an archaeological palimpsest of rare completeness but, to the layman, of baffling complexity.

The great **Telestérion**, or TEMPLE OF DEMETER, the Hall of Initiation and the Mysteries, is an almost square chamber 53m by 52m, partly cut out of the rock of the Acropolis and partly built on a terrace. The existing remains appear to be those of the Periclean rebuilding (with the addition of the Portico of Philo), as finally remodelled by Marcus Aurelius. On each of the four sides were eight tiers of seats, partly hewn from the rock and partly built up; these were interrupted at six points only, where two doors on each of the disengaged sides afforded entrance. The hall accommodated 3000. Six rows of seven columns each supported the (? wooden) roof; they were in two tiers separated by an epistyle (possibly with a frieze). The bases of most remain; one of them has as its top course a reused block of the 1C AD, showing the extent of the Roman restoration. In the centre, on a site it had occupied from the first, was the *Anaktoron*, or holy of holies, a small rectangular room roofed somehow by Xenokles with an Opaion, or lantern, of which no vestige has survived. By the side of the anaktoron stood the throne of the Hierophant. Externally the solid walls, broken only by doorways, must have enhanced the air of mystery. Later the SE front was adorned along its whole length by the PORTICO OF PHILO, whose pavement and massive supporting wall (18 courses of masonry) form one of the most prominent features of the site. It was completed, according to Vitruvius, in the reign of Demetrios of Phaleron. The huge prostoön had a colonnade of twelve Doric columns by two, which were left unfluted. An ancient *Well* cut into the rock below may be the original Kallichoron (comp. above).

Excavations have revealed traces of at least six earlier structures on the same site. The *Mycenaean Megaron*, traceable in the remains of two walls in the NE half of the hall, was a chamber c 17m square. This was replaced by a Geometric edifice, a Solonian telesterion, and again by the *Telesterion of Peisistratos*, which occupied the NE corner of the final structure. This hall had five rows of five columns each, with a portico on the NE front, and was destroyed by the Persians. Kimon incorporated the ruins into a rectangular hall, designed round the old Anaktoron, and having seven rows of three columns each. It was apparently not finished. Pericles probably instigated a grander design by which the building again became square, doubling that of Kimon. This was first entrusted to Iktinos, whose plan to support the roof on only 20 columns (foundations visible) had to be abandoned for technical reasons. The design was replaced by another by Koroibos, which was completed after his death by Metagenes and Xenokles. Lycurgus may have ordered the Portico of Philo. The L-shaped foundations that extend beyond the E and S corners show that earlier plans for building a peristyle were started. After the Sarmatian sack, the Romans restored the interior with somewhat makeshift columns and extended the NW side another six feet into the rock.

From the Portico of Philo the *Court* of the sanctuary, a level artificial terrace, extended to the E and S. This had been built up and enlarged with each successive reconstruction, generally using the fortification wall of the previous sanctuary as a retaining wall for the new. The greater part of the late-Classical fill has been removed to show the successive stages, making apparent the steepness of the natural contour. Sections of the *Wall of Peisistratos* are roofed with corrugated iron to preserve their upper part constructed in unbaked bricks. A stretch immediately below the centre of the Portico of Philo shows where Kimon filled the Persian breach in the mud-brick wall with limestone masonry in alternately large and small courses (pseudo-isodomic), based directly on the Peisistratean socle. The inner face is rough and evidently retained a fill of earth. Within this wall parts of an Archaic polygonal terrace wall may be seen. Beyond the Peisistratean corner-tower are the remains of a Kimonian *Gate*. This was later blocked by the Periclean *Siroi*, where the first-fruit offerings were stored; five of its piers are very prominent.

The S side of the court was bounded in the 5C by the *Periclean Wall*, the function of which was minimised in the following century when the sanctuary was extended to the new *South Wall* of Lycurgus. Against the inside face of this are some remains identified with successive rebuildings in Hellenistic and late-Roman times of a

Bouleuterion, or chamber of the city council. Outside the Lycurgan *South Gate* is a trapezoidal precinct surrounded by a wall (see below). Within this wall are the foundations of a *Hiera Oikia*, a Geometric house sacred to the memory of a hero; the building was destroyed early in the 7C, but remained a scene of religious rites into the Archaic period. Beyond are some vestiges of a *Mithraeum*. From outside the extreme S corner of the precinct we get an instructive panorama of contrasted types of ancient wall building.

Looking towards the museum we see the perfectly fitted polygonal masonry (6C) of the peribolos of the Sacred House. To the right is the '*Lycurgan*' *Wall* (? 370–360 BC), one of the best preserved examples of ancient fortification, with both a square and a round *Tower*. On four slightly receding courses in pecked Eleusinian stone are set tooled courses in yellow poros; this is probably a conscious matching of the Periclean style. Beyond the corner the wall is masked by ruined Hadrianic cisterns. Farther on, the *Periclean East Wall*, like the Lycurgan, has a separate socle, here rusticated, while the upper part shows traces of bevelling.

On either side of the Telesterion a flight of steps was hewn in Roman times to give access to a wide *Terrace*, 6m above the hall floor. We mount the S steps to the **Museum**, which houses the important but relatively few works of art found in the ruins. Outside the entrance are a Roman sarcophagus (c AD 190) in marble with a well-carved representation of the Kalydonian boar-hunt (the lid does not belong to it); two representations in white marble of torches, c 2·5m high; a capital from the Lesser Propylaea; and a fine head of a horse.—ROOM I (to the right). Copy of the 'Niinnion Tablet', a red-figured votive pinax now in the Athens museum; the figures are believed to be performing rites from the Mysteries, the only known representation. Reconstruction of one corner of the geison of the Peisistratid telesterion; Archaic kouros (c 540 BC). Running girl from a pediment of c 485 BC. In the centre, huge Protoattic *Amphora (7C BC), depicting Odysseus blinding Polyphemos and Perseus slaying Medusa. Dedication reliefs: marble stele, Demeter seated with (probably) Hekate (c 475 BC); stele (411 BC) depicting a fight between Athenian cavalry and Spartan hoplites. Decree of 421 BC concerning the construction of a bridge over the Rheitoi (comp. above), with relief.

ROOM II (entrance-hall) contains a cast of the most famous Eleusinian Relief, now in the Athens museum. Facing the door is a *Statue of Demeter (headless and armless), perhaps by Agorakritos of Paros, pupil of Pheidias (420 BC); behind is the fragmentary Relief of Lakratides (1C BC), showing Triptolemos setting out in his chariot; the statue of Persephone is of Roman date. Relief: Demeter on the 'Mirthless Stone' approached by votaries.—ROOM III. Heads and statues, including Asklepios, dedicated by Epikrates (320 BC), found in a field.—ROOM IV displays a model of the site at two stages of its development (Peisistratid and Roman). Roman statuary; *Antinoos, represented as a youthful Dionysos standing by the Delphic omphalos; Tiberius as pontifex maximus; small and delicate Herakles.

ROOM V. Caryatid in the form of a kistephore (basket-carrier) from the inner parastade of the Lesser Propylaea (its fellow is in the Fitzwilliam Museum, Cambridge); green stole, in a good state of preservation, from a burial of the 5C BC (the only linen cloth surviving from the Classical era); Amphora of c 610 BC from Megara by the Chimaera painter; inhumation burials, including that of a boy in a larnax (terracotta coffin); decree reliefs.—ROOM VI. Vases of all periods from 1900 BC to AD 450, including a plain Mycenaean vase with a Linear B inscription (? an unidentified Cretan place-name) which recurs on the Knossos tablets; kernoi, the characteristic sacred vessels of the cult.

	Mycenean
	Geometric
	Early Archaic
	Peisistratid
	Kimon
	Pericles
	Lycurgus
	Hellenistic
	Roman
	Modern

Classical

D

Panayia

C

B **A** **Plutonion**

Lesser Propylaea

Greater Propylaea

Eschara

Temple of Artemis

Well

Sacred Way

Baths

Siroi

ELEUSIS

0   30 metres

The tourist may well conclude his visit with the museum. The student of antiquities should continue to visit the Mycenaean complex beyond, the Acropolis, and the sectors of the town adjoining the forecourt.

Beyond the museum are some remains of a settlement of Middle Helladic date (18–17 C BC). Many Late Helladic vestiges have been discovered on the ACROPOLIS, from which there is a pleasant view towards Salamis. On the plateau beyond are Hellenistic remains. The Frankish tower that formerly crowned the W height fell victim to the quarrying activities of the cement factory. At the E point of the acropolis a *Chapel* (Panayia) with a detached belfry occupies part of a platform on which, in Roman times, stood a *Temple* (Pl. D), probably dedicated to Faustina, wife of Antoninus Pius. We descend thence to the Lesser Propylaea. To the NW are some ruins of a Roman house conjectured to have belonged to the Kerykes, one of the hereditary priestly families. Farther off is the *Asty Gate* of the Peisistratid enceinte; its plan, uncovered by Travlos in 1960, is well preserved; still further W lay the *Megarian Gate*. The wall is not preserved but part of the ancient road from *Eleusis* to *Megara* has been traced from there. The *Roman Quarter* to the E of the Great Forecourt is interesting for its bathing establishments with piped water and a great drain running brick vaults and manholes at regular intervals.—In the town, near the church of Ayios Yeoryios, another *Roman Bath*, partially excavated in 1959, proved to be one of the largest discovered in Greece (time of Hadrian).

17   From Athens to Soúnion

The excursion to Sounion, seldom omitted by any visitor to Athens, is generally made by the coast road. The old inland road, less obviously attractive, nevertheless abounds with interest, especially for the unhurried visitor who can make diversions at will. Much of the E coast of Attica, c 8km from the road and easily accessible from it by track or footpath, is yet largely unspoilt, though a coastal road from Lavrion to Marathon, already approved, will ensure its rapid spoliation.

A. By the Coast Road

ROAD, 70km (43½ miles). Buses from Odhós Mavromatéon c hourly take passengers for destinations beyond Varkiza. Half-day excursions by coach (C.H.A.T., etc.). Buses (No. 145 etc.) for Várkiza depart from Leofóros Olgas.

To (25km) **Vouliagméni**, see Rte 13. The road continues 'en corniche' winding along a rocky *Coast, though the pine-clad slopes, once renowned for game, are fast being interspersed with hotels and bungalows.—31km *Várkiza* (Hotels A, B, C), with camping sites, a sandy beach (N.T.O.G.), a marina, and water-sports. The place gave name to the Agreement of 1945, whereby the organisations ELAS and EAM were demobilised and disarmed, bringing the first Communist rising to an end.

A little farther on a road leads inland to *Vari* (1·5km), a village amid pines (comp. Rte 13).

35km. The *Bay of Lomvardha* may represent the harbour of the Attic deme of *Lamptrai*, sited due N on the slope of Hymettos. Churches mark the seaward ends of roads from Koropi (Rte 17B).—42km *Lagonísi* (Hotels L, B) is a bungalow resort. Mt Panion, to the NE, is lost behind the Attic *Olimbos* (Olympus; 486m), a pyramidal hill which we skirt. Beyond (46km) *Saronis* (usually Saronídha; Hotel B) are the large Eden Beach and Alexander Beach hotels.—The little island of

Arsidha lies close to the coast off the Bay of *Anávissos* (Hotels A, B, C). A by-road leads left to the hamlet (1·5km), where the celebrated kouros was found and an important Geometric cemetery has been excavated, then passes between Olimbos and Panion to Kalívia (16km).—Off (60km) *Cape Katafiyi*, which affords a fine panorama of the Saronic Gulf, lies the uninhabited *Gaïdourónisi*, Known to Strabo as *Patroklou Charax*, the palisade of Patroclus. Remains may be seen of the 3C fortifications built here by Patroclus, admiral of Ptolemy II, who commanded the Egyptian fleet sent to help the Athenians against Antigonus Gonatas in the Chremonidean War.—64·5km *Legrená* (Hotels B).

70km (43½ miles) **Cape Soúnion**, known also as *Cape Kolónes* (Κάβο Κολώνες), is a precipitous rocky headland rising 60m from the sea. The low isthmus which joins it to the mainland separates the sandy and exposed *Bay of Soúnion* (Hotels A, B, C), a developing resort, from the rocky but sheltered haven to the E, which provides a welcome refuge for mariners unable to weather the cape. On the highest point of the headland, at its end, are the columns of the ruined Temple of Poseidon (see below), which give the headland its alternative name. The visitor wishing to share Byron's experience of 'Sunium's marbled steep, Where nothing save the waves and I may hear our mutual murmurs sweep' should visit the site out of season and in the morning. On Sundays and towards sunset it is overrun by coach trippers.

The township of *Soúnion* (Σούνιον; Lat. *Sunium*), whose wealth was proverbial in classical times, stood at the head of the bay of the same name, where regattas were held in honour of Poseidon. After the battle of Salamis the Athenians here dedicated a captured Phoenician ship (one of three; Hdt. VIII, 121). Some years before, the Aeginetans had seized the sacred Athenian *Theoris*, the ship that conveyed the sacred envoys (Θεωροι) to Delos, while it lay at Sounion (Hdt. VI, 87). The town was a port of call of the corn ships from Euboea to Piraeus. The Athenians fortified it during the Peloponnesian War and, in 413 BC (Thuc. VIII, 14), the entire headland was enclosed, the promontory forming the citadel. The inhabitants were noted for harbouring runaway slaves whom they often enfranchised without question. On one occasion a strong gang of slaves seized the fortress and devastated the neighbourhood. Terence mentions Sunium as a haunt of pirates. It was a favourite resort of the corsairs, one of whom, Jaffer Bey, is supposed to have destroyed some of the columns of the temple. One of three of the crew who escaped the foundering of a Levantine trader here was the second mate and poet, William Falconer, who immortalised the incident in 'The Shipwreck' (1762).

The remains of the W half of the promontory now form an archaeological precinct. The Temple of Poseidon was measured by Revett in 1765 and by the Dilettanti Society in 1812. Byron carved his name on a pillar. The site was excavated by Dörpfeld in 1884 and by the Greek Archaeological Society in 1899–1915. In 1906 two colossal kouroi were found in the debris to the E of the temple. Since 1958 some columns have been re-erected.

The whole Acropolis was enclosed by a double *Fortification Wall*, c 500m long and strengthened at intervals by square towers. It formed a semicircle from the Bay of Sounion on the NW, where some remains are well preserved, to the S cliff edge. Its SE angle enclosed the TEMENOS OF POSEIDON, a precinct supported on the N and W by a terrace wall. This was entered on the N side by Doric *Propylaea*, built of poros and marble in the 5C, the axis of which is aligned with the E front of the temple.

A square room to the W of the gate, separated it from a *Stoa*, which extended along the peribolos wall. Its foundations have collapsed in the far corner, but five bases remain of six interior columns that divided it lengthwise. A second stoa, running N–S, abuts on the first at the W.

The ***Temple of Poseidon**, near the edge of the cliff, forms a conspicuous landmark from the sea. From a distance it presents a dazzlingly
white appearance that proves illusory at closer view: the columns are
of grey-veined marble quarried at *Agrileza* (5km N by an ancient
road), where bases of columns of the same dimension can still be seen.
The attribution to Poseidon was confirmed by an inscription. On stylistic grounds Prof. Dinsmoor ascribes the design of the temple to the
architect of the Hephaisteion at Athens, placing it c 444 BC. It stands
on the foundations of an earlier edifice in poros stone, founded shortly
before 490 BC and unfinished at the time of the Persian invasion. The
Doric peristyle had 34 columns (6 by 13), that stood on a stylobate
measuring 31·1m by 13·4m. Nine columns remain on the S side and six
(four re-erected in 1958–59) on the N side, with their architraves. The
columns are unusual in having only sixteen instead of the normal
twenty flutes. The sculptural arrangement also departed from the normal custom, an Ionic frieze (see below) lining all four sides of the front
pteroma (comp. the Hephaisteion), and the external metopes being
left blank (perhaps because of the exposed nature of the site); the
pediments, which were sculptured, had a raking cornice with a pitch
of 12½° instead of the more usual 15°.

Sounion. Restored view of the Sanctuary of Athena

The INTERIOR had the usual arrangement of pronaos, cella, and opisthodomos. Both pronaos and opisthodomos were distyle in antis. There survive only the N anta of the pronaos, with its adjacent column, and the S anta, which was reconstructed in 1908.

Thirteen slabs of the frieze, in Parian marble, stand to the E of the approach path. The sculpture, much corroded, is believed to illustrate a contest of Lapiths and Centaurs, the Gigantomachia, and exploits of Theseus (comp. the *Hephaisteion*).
  The *View from the temple over the sea is most striking. To the E lies Makronisos. About 11km S lies the rocky island of Ay. Yeoryios, the ancient *Belbina*. The nearest islands to the SE are *Keos*, *Kithnos*, and *Seriphos*, to the S of which, on a clear day, even *Melos* can be made out. To the W is *Aegina*, in the centre of the Saronic Gulf, with the E coast of the Peloponnese behind it.

Beyond the Tourist Pavilion on a low hill commanding the isthmus on the N, are the remains of a small *Temple of Athena Sounias*, noted by Vitruvius for the irregularity of its plan with an Ionic colonnade along the E and S sides of the structure of c 450 BC. The cella was 5·9m by 3·8m, with four columns in the middle arranged in a square. The cult statue stood at the back. A little to the N are the remains of a small Doric temple, distyle prostyle, probably dedicated to the hero Phrontis.

B. Via the Mesógeia

ROAD, 64·5km (40 miles). 12km *Stavrós.*—18km *Liópesi.*—24km
Koropí.—30km **Markópoulo**.—40km *Keratéa.*—55km **Lávrion**.—
64·5km **Soúnion**. Buses from Od. Mavromateon every hour (more
frequently on Sundays and holidays) to *Lavrion* (in 1½ hours
(taking passengers for Keratea and beyond only); usually continuing
after an interval to *Soúnion*); also to *Markópoulo* and *Pórto Ráfti*. To
Liópesi (Paiania; Nos. 125, 310) and to *Koropí* (Nos 307, 308), every
20 minutes from Theseion.

From the centre of the city to (2·5km) *Ambelókipoi*, see Rte 11.—We
take the right fork. The N foothills of Hymettos appear intermittently
above the suburban development. In trees (right) stands the *Police
College*. The S bypass (Rte 13) joins Mesogeion by an underpass.—At
(4km) *Goudhí* the University of Athens has its Ilissia precinct. Above
stands Ay. Ioannis Theologos (Rte 14).—At (6·5km) *Kholargós*, which
bears the name of the native deme of Pericles (c 490–429 BC), we pass
(left) the huge administrative H.Q. of the Greek army. Mt Pentelikon
rises behind.—6m. *Ayía Paraskeví*. The Nuclear Research Centre
(which includes amongst its activities the analysis of archaeological
artefacts), designed by a British company and opened in 1961 by King
Paul, bears the name of Democritus, the first scientist to propound an
atomic theory. A by-road leads (right; 2km) to *Moní Ayios Ioánnis
Kynigós*, the monastery of St. John the Hunter (view); its 12C church
has a strangely supported dome and a 17C narthex (festival, 26
July).—At (12km) *Stavrós*, by a radio-telephone station, we round the
N spur of Hymettos, leave the Marathon road (flyover), and turn S into
the Mesogeia.

The *Mesogeia* (τα, anciently η Μεσόγεια, 'the inland'), which lies between
Hymettos and the Petalion Gulf, is watered by two seasonal rivers: the Valanaris
entering the sea S of Rafina and the Erasinos near Vráona. Its red clay is the most
fertile soil in Attica, producing good wine, much of which is flavoured with pine
resin to produce the retsina favoured by Athenians. Anciently Brauron was of
importance; the modern capital is Koropí. Many of the attractive little churches
have frescoes by Yeoryios Markos and his school.

18km **Liópesi** (*Kanakis Taverna* in a lemon-grove at the N end),
officially *Paianía*, a straggling village (7,278 inhab.) in pleasantly wooded country, has readopted the name of the birthplace of Demosthenes (c 384–322 BC), identified with some remains to the E. Here is
the *Vorrés Museum*, a seven-acre complex which combines modern
with traditional architecture and gardens. The buildings contain traditional artefacts, prints and pictures relating to modern Greek history
and (in a specially designed gallery) a collection of modern painting
and sculpture. To the S of the village is the church of *Ayios Nikoláos
Chalídhou* which has unusual decoration in the dome (12C). A by-road
(signposted) leads to the *Koutouki Cave* (open daily).—**Koropí**, the
liveliest village (11,214 inhab.) in the Mesogeia, is surrounded by
vineyards; the retsina vats are prominent. By-roads lead (right) to the
coast. SE of the village is the church of *Metamórphosis Sotíras*, decorated with late 10C/early 11C frescoes. Interesting is the dome
decoration which includes the Pantocrator, the symbols of the
Evangelists, Seraphim and Cherubim.—30km (18½ miles)
Markópoulo, a busy and prosperous centre (6,116 inhab.) is noted for
its bread. By its conspicuous *Church*, the interior of which is enlivened
with encaustic illustrations of the lives of various saints, diverges the
road to Brauron and Pórto Ráfti.

FROM MARKÓPOULO TO PÓRTO RÁFTI, 8km by good road (through bus from Athens). 2·5km. By-road to Vraona (see below). About 5km S rises *Mt Miranda* (613m). Between our road and the mountain near a medieval watch-tower, lay the ancient deme of *Myrrhinous*, where Artemis Kolainis, the Bird Goddess, was worshipped. Inscriptions to Artemis were found on the site in 1960–61, after the Greek Archaeological Service had explored 26 tombs, mostly of the 8C BC, uncovered a section of prehistoric road, and confirmed the existence of a Shrine of Pythian Apollo. From this area in 1972 came also a superb kouros and kore now in Athens Museum.—6km. Track (right) to Prasiai (Hotels A, C, D, E), see below.

6·5km. **Pórto Ráfti** has one of the best natural harbours in Greece, of which little use is made. The beautiful bay is unequally divided by the narrow rocky spit of *Ayios Nikólaos* (Tavernas), off which lies the islet of *Prasonisi*. It is protected on the seaward side by the islets of *Ráfti* and *Raftopoula*. On Ráfti is a colossal seated marble statue of the Roman period, popularly known as the 'tailor' (ράφτης), whence the modern name of the harbour. The statue, which is female, is conjectured to represent Oikoumene and to have served as a beacon-light. Helladic and Byzantine sherds have been noted on the steep slopes of both islets. From the beach, the last in Attica to remain in Allied hands, 6000 New Zealand troops were evacuated in April 1941. Scholars locate ancient *Prasiai* on the S slopes of the bay, where 22 Mycenaean tombs were found in 1894–95.

From **Prasiai** the annual Theoria, or sacred embassy, set out to Delos in the ship believed to be that in which Theseus returned triumphant from Knossos. Here Erysichthon, an envoy of Delos, who died on his return journey, was buried, and here came the mysterious first-fruits of the Hyperboreans on their way from central Europe to Delos.

The bay is closed on the S by the peninsular headland of *Koroni*, anciently *Koroneia*. Its Acropolis and an unbroken Long Wall with nine towers within the isthmus formed a *Fortress*. Excavated in 1960 by the American School, this is proved by coins of Ptolemy II Philadelphus to be an Egyptian encampment of the Chremonidean War (? 265–261 BC). In this war the Athenians threw in their lot with Egypt and Sparta in an unsuccessful bid to free themselves from Macedonian domination.—On the N the bay is dominated by the precipitous *Perati* (307m), with unexplored caves. The road continues beneath the hill past two tavernas at *Ayios Spiridhón* (the bus terminus, 2km from Ayios Nikolaos; Hotel C), 10 minutes beyond which, above the banks of a stream, has been discovered a huge *Necropolis* of chamber tombs (Late Helladic III c). One can continue round the shoreward side of Perati (taverna) to Brauron (c 8km; see below).

From Ay. Spiridon a boat may be hired for the visit to Ráfti (see above; rocky disembarkation and stiff climb).

THE BY-ROAD TO VRAÓNA (Brauron), 6km from Markópoulo, diverges from the Pórto Ráfti road (comp. above). A square *Tower* (left; c 1km from the road), beyond the fork, is of Frankish date. Farther on (left) are the interesting remains of an Early Christian *Basilica*.

The name Vraóna (Βραώνα) is a medieval corruption of Βραύρων, but the ancient name is being readopted as Vravróna.

Brauron (Hotel A, on the shore), one of the twelve ancient communities antedating the Attic confederation, is situated in the broad and marshy valley of the subterranean Erasínos c 1·5km from the sea. The district apparently comprised the townships of *Halai Araphenides* (now Loutsa, a little to the N) and *Philiadai*. Peisistratos had estates in the neighbourhood. The attractive SANCTUARY OF ARTEMIS BRAURONIA lies at the foot of a low hill, just below the little late-Byzantine chapel of *Ayios Yeoryios*. Beyond the chapel a small *Shrine* marked the entrance to a cavern, the roof of which fell in the 5C BC. This seems to have been venerated in Archaic times as the *Tomb of Iphigeneia*. Other tombs probably belong to priestesses of Artemis.

Tradition relates that Iphigeneia brought to Brauron the image of Artemis which she and Orestes stole from Tauris (Euripides, 'Iphigeneia in Tauris', 1446–67). In one version she is virtually identified with the goddess and performs the ritual sacrifice of her brother; in another she herself dies at Brauron. A wooden image was taken by the Persians from Brauron to Susa. In Classical times the savage rites had been moderated, and Artemis was worshipped in her function as protectress of childbirth. The Brauronia was a ceremony held every four years, in which Attic girls between the ages of five and ten, clad in saffron robes, performed rites which included a dance where they were dressed as bears (comp. Aristophanes, 'Lysistrata', 645.) The connection between bears, childbirth, and Artemis recalls the legend of Callisto, but the purpose of the ritual remains mysterious. In the late 4C BC the site suffered from inundations and by the time of Claudius it was deserted, for Pomponius Mela (De situ Orbis, II, 3) exclaims that Thorikos and Brauron, formerly cities, are now but names. Excavations, carried out with difficulty in the waterlogged valley by the Greek Archaeological Society under John Papadhimitriou in 1946–52 and in 1956–63, show occupation since Middle Helladic times (earliest on hill above).

At a lower level, discovered in 1958, are the remains of a Doric *Temple* of the 5C BC, measuring c 20m by 10m, the foundations of which stand on rock-hewn steps (? the 'holy stairs' of Euripides). Here were discovered dedicatory reliefs in coloured terracotta, bronze mirrors, and votive jewellery. Adjoining the temple is a huge Π-shaped *Stoa*, built before 416 BC, in which have been found inscriptions recording it to be the 'parthenon' of the arktoi, or 'bears'. It had nine dining-rooms. Part of the colonnade and entablature was re-erected in 1962. Just to the W is a remarkable stone **Bridge* of the same period.

The large well-arranged site MUSEUM (round the next bend of the road) displays marble statues and heads of little girls and of boys, and beautiful 4C marble reliefs. These are numerous dedicatory offerings from the sanctuary—vases, figurines, mirrors, jewellery, etc. Models reconstruct the appearance of the site. Here also are Geometric finds from Anavyssos and splendid L.H. IIIc **Pottery* from Perati.

The main road by-passes (34km) **Kalívia** (2,577 inhab.), with attractive churches. In the village is the church of *Ayios Petros*, which has a portrait of Michaelis Choniates, bishop of Athens. The halo shows that the picture was executed after his death and the frescoes must therefore date to after 1220. About 1·5km SW, on a by-road to Anávissos (16km; Rte 17A), is the pretty *Taxiarkhis*, a deserted monastic church. At the 36th km. post a track leads (left) to *Ayios Yeoryios*, a Byzantine church with reused Ionic capitals. The countryside becomes more hilly. To the left rises Mt Mirenda (see above), to the right the double crest of *Paneion* (651m), known locally as Keratovouni (the horned mountain). Its steep E summit dominates (40km) **Keratéa** (Hotel A), a prosperous village (5,600 inhab.), with orchards, vineyards, and good water, where Chateaubriand suffered from sunstroke. Here a track descends to the *Convent of the Palaioimerologitai* (Adherents of the Old Calendar), 8km E, above the exposed beach of Kakí Thálassa.— The little mining hamlet of (50km) *Plaka* lies below the top of the next ridge (168m), from which we look down towards the *Bay of Thorikos*, reached by a zigzag descent.

Dominating the bay (1·5km NE of the road), is the conical hill of *Velatouri*, the acropolis of ancient **Thorikos**. Towards the sea is the promontory of Ayios Nikolaos, which divides Portomandhri, to the S, from Frankolimani, a smaller bay to the N, protected by Cape Vrisaki. This deep refuge is halfway between Piraeus and Rhamnous.

The mines of Thorikos are now known to have been exploited in the third millennium BC. In the Mycenaean period legend (its king, Kephalos, married Prokris, daughter of Erechtheus) suggests dynastic ties with Athens. Thorikos was fortified in 412 BC as a defensive outpost of the Laurion mines (comp. Xenophon Hell. i. 2, 1). It was deserted after the Classical period but there are signs of renewed settlement in late antiquity (4–6C AD).

The most significant remains lie at the S foot of the hill. There is a stretch of fortification wall, with one *Tower* standing to a height of c 3·5m. Higher up is the *Theatre*, unique in its irregular plan, which clumsily follows the contour of a natural declivity. The first orchestra was laid out with a retaining wall in the Archaic period. In the mid 5C the theatre had 21 rows of seats; a century later it was extended to provide room for a further 12 rows, some of which may have had temporary seats. At that point the theatre would have accommodated about 6000 spectators. The *Cavea* forms an irregular ellipse and is divided by two stairways, almost parallel, into three sections, the central one nearly rectangular, those at either end sharply curved. The seats are roughly hewn. The lower rows were approached from below; the upper via two ramps set against the marble retaining wall of the structure. The W ramp is pierced by a corbelled passage. The narrow W parodos is bounded by a small *Temple of Dionysos* in antis, which faces across the rectangular orchestra towards a large *Altar*.

On the top of the hill, Mycenaean and earlier remains have been excavated by the Greek Archaeological Society in 1890 and 1893; and recently by the Belgian Mission. On the NE side of the hill are Mycenaean chamber and tholos tombs. There is an unusual oblong tomb and, nearby, a Middle Helladic tumulus in some respects resembling those found at Marathon. The maritime fortress of 412 BC occupies the isthmus between the two harbours to the W of the church. A good deal of excavation has been undertaken in the area to the NW of the theatre, where 5C houses were converted into workshops for processing the metal ores mined close by in the late 5C or early 4C.

A hoard of 4–3C tetradrachms was found in 1969.—The remains of a peripteral Doric *Temple of Demeter and Kore* of unusual design, with 7 columns on the fronts and 14 at the sides, unearthed in 1812 c 1km W of the theatre, have been covered again. Much of its materials were transported to Athens in Augustan times and re-erected in the SE corner of the Agora.

About 5km offshore lies the island of *Makrónisos*, anciently called *Helena*, from a tradition that Helen rested here on her flight with Paris. Used after the civil war of 1946 as a detention centre, it is now uninhabited save by shepherds in summer. Traces of prehistoric settlement have been located recently.

54km (34 miles) **Lávrion** (Λαύριον), known in the 19C as *Ergasteria* because of its workshops, is a scattered industrial town of 8921 inhab., which owes its existence to the neighbouring mines and its name to the ancient district of *Laurion*. Its chimneys, placed on the surrounding hills to render the fumes less unpleasant, are conspicuous from afar. To the possession of the silver mines of Laurion the Athenians owed, in great measure, their commercial and political greatness; the Athenian silver coinage ('Laureot owls') had prestige all over the world.

The mines were exploited in prehistoric times; Aeschylus alludes in the 'Persae' (235) to the Θησαυρός χθόνος. The decision of the Athenians in 483 BC to finance the building of a fleet with the surplus yield of the mines laid the foundations of their naval supremacy, and by the time of Pericles the industry had reached the peak of its prosperity. As a result of the incursion of the Spartans in 413, the mines were closed. Though they were reopened c 355 thanks to Xenophon's treatise on mines as a neglected source of revenue and lasted another four centuries, they were never again as important. Pausanias refers to them in the past tense and for centuries they lay neglected. Modern exploitation, very largely the result of French initiative, is in the hands of three companies; one French (reconstituted after disputes about government royalties in 1873), one Greek (1860), and one American. The modern mines are concerned principally with the extraction of cadmium and manganese, and, to a less degree, with reworking the ancient slag-heaps for lead. The synthetic textile mills are important.

The best preserved ANCIENT MINES are situated in the Berzeko valley, which runs S from *Kamáriza*, about 5km to the W. A car can be taken as far as the church of Ayia Triádha near a huge ruined 19C installation above the valley.

The mines anciently belonged to the State, which granted them on perpetual leases to contractors. They were worked by slave labour. Over 2000 ancient shafts have been found, some perpendicular (18–122m deep) and some sloping. The roofs of the galleries (24–46m deep) were supported either by artificial piers or by natural ore-bearing pillars left in the rock. The removal of these pillars, which was dangerous, was punishable by death. Ventilation shafts carried off the bad air. Some miners' lamps and other relics have been found. In various places chains of huge *Cisterns* and ore-washeries and furnaces are to be seen. One in the Agriléza valley was excavated by the British School in 1977–78.

From Lavrion a caïque service plies to the island of *Kea* daily in summer (pm); sometimes continuing to Kíthnos.

The road continues S at some distance from the sea. On the W are moderate wooded hills. Above the coast (Hotel B) are dotted many summer villas of the Athenians. The columns of the Temple of Poseidon are seen on the skyline as we join the coast road at the approach to (64·5km) *Soúnion*.

18 Sálamis

The crescent-shaped island of **Sálamis** (ΣΑΛΑΜΙΣ; often Salamína; 93 sq. km) lies in the N of the Saronic Gulf close inshore. Its NW coast is less than 1km from the coast of Megaris, and its NE coast is separated from the mainland of Attica by the Strait of Salamis, scene of the famous battle. The island thus gives to the Bay of Eleusis the character of a lagoon. Salamis with 20,407 inhab., mainly of Albanian descent forms part of the eparchy of Piraeus. Its soil is dry and rocky and though a few vineyards and corn fields are found in the plains, the climate is unhealthy. The highest point is *Mavrovouni* (404m). According to Strabo the ancient capital originally lay on the S coast opposite Aegina; this was moved before Classical times to the E coast; the modern capital is on the W side of the island at the head of the Bay of Koulouris. Salamis is famous for its battle and important as a naval base, but it is of run-down appearance and archaeological remains are meagre. Military establishments impede a close study of the scene of the battle, the best general view of which is still obtained from Xerxes' vantage-point behind Perama.

History. In Mycenaean times *Salamis* seems to have had dynastic connection with both Aegina and Cyprus. The Homeric catalogue records a contribution of twelve ships led by Telamonian Ajax. In the 7C the island was disputed between Athens and Megara. It was annexed to Athens as a cleruchy by Solon, the Athenians going so far as to forge an extra line of Homer in support of their claim. In 480 BC the Athenians evacuated Athens and, with Salamis as base, entrusted themselves to their 'wooden walls'. After 318 BC Salamis surrendered to the Macedonian Cassander, but in 229 BC it was recovered for Athens by Aratos, when the Salaminians were expelled in favour of new colonists.

Approaches. FROM ATHENS in 35 minutes by frequent bus Nos. 841, 842 from Plateía Koumoundhourou (Eleftherías) (or from Piraeus by frequent bus, No. 843) to Pérama on the S coast of the Skaramangas peninsula. The road traverses the sprawling industrial town of *Níkaia* (90,368 inhab.), which extends NW of Piraeus to the Aigaleos hills, and passes below the supposed vantage-point from which Xerxes watched the Battle of Salamis.—15km **Pérama** has shipyards where trawlers, tugs, and coastal steamers are built. The buses terminate at the quay, whence ferries (c ½ hourly) cross the Strait of Salamis to the island; to *Paloúkia* (cars taken), via the N side of the island of Ayios Yeoryios, for the town of *Salamís* (2km; bus every 10 minutes); to *Kamateró*; and to a landing-stage E of Ambelakia for Selénia. The crossings take c 15 minutes. Buses serve all main points on the island.

FROM PIRAEUS by sea (no cars) every ½ hour.

FROM MEGARA, via Megálo Péfko (Rte 24) and a by-road to a landing-stage (also called *Pérama*), whence a ferry plies to the NW tip of the island.

The STRAIT OF SALAMIS, which averages less than than 3km in width, forms roughly an S-bend with an island at each turn. From Piraeus the N–S channel is divided into two arms by the island of *Lipsoukoutáli*, where there are naval installations and a monument to the 'unknown Sailor'; it then turns W between the Skaramangas peninsula and the long E promontory of Salamis known as Kynosoura ('the dog's tail'). Beyond the narrowest point (1100m), which lies between the Kamateró peninsula (site of classical Salamis) and the cape S of Pérama, the strait bends N and NE. The widening corner N of Kamateró is divided into two channels by the islet of *Ayios Yeoryios*, used as a quarantine station. In the narrow confines of this strait the Persian defeat was mainly decided.

The **Battle of Salamis** was fought about 22 September 480 BC. The tactics of the battle and the fundamental identification of the island of Psyttáleia (Ψυττάλεια) are still the subject of scholarly disagreement. Most commentators identify Psyttáleia with Lipsokoutali, a view excellently argued by A.R. Burn ('Persia and the Greeks', 1962) and by Paul W. Wallace (A.J.A., 1969). N.G.L. Hammond (J.H.S., 1956) identified Psyttáleia with Ayios Yeoryios and Lipsokoutali with Atalante. This may be thought to accord better with the accounts of Herodotus (VIII, 70–94) and of Aeschylus who fought in the battle and describes it in the 'Persae' performed eight years later. The general strategy of the battle is not in doubt though Athenian tradition seems as usual to have exaggerated the disparity between the opposing forces.

Salamis was a key point in Themistocles' plan of defence against the Persians and in the event a decisive one. While all Athenian women and children were evacuated to Troezen, Salamis was to receive the old men and exiles (who were ordered to return). An attempt to stem the Persian advance was to be made with half the allied fleet at Artemision while the remaining Athenian triremes with the reserves of the fleets of Sparta, Corinth, and Aegina were to lie off Salamis. Before the action the Persians were in Phaleron Bay. The news that they had despatched an army by land towards the Isthmus alarmed the Peloponnesians who had to be persuaded against retiring on Corinth. Xerxes' first plan to bottle the Athenians in the Skaramangas strait or force them into open water to the E by building a pontoon boom across the strait itself was foiled by Cretan archers. Themistocles, hoping to force an immediate battle in the narrows, where he would have the advantage, organised a leak of information to Xerxes that the Peloponnesians intended to retreat. Under cover of darkness the Persians put into operation a new plan to encircle the supposedly disunited Greeks; Psyttaleia was occupied; a squadron of 200 Egyptian ships was despatched to block the W strait between Salamis and Megara; and the remaining ships were drawn up in a line right across the E exit. The Persian plan seems to have been to surprise the Greeks, while they were still drawn up on the beaches at dawn, and capture their base. Xerxes himself set up a silver throne on Aigaleos, 'the rocky brow that looks o'er sea-born Salamis', whence he could watch the battle. Aristides, the exiled rival of Themistocles, who succeeded in slipping through to the Greek fleet from Aegina, was the first to bring the news of the investment. His statement was confirmed by a Tenean deserter. The forewarned Greeks, who now had no alternative but to fight, embarked before dawn, retired apparently in flight before the advancing enemy and formed up in hiding behind a promontory. When they emerged in battle order the advantage of surprise was with them. With their more maneuverable ships, lower in the water, they made deadly use of the technique of ramming. As Themistocles had foreseen, the Persians became hopelessly confused, Artemisia, queen of Halicarnassos, being noticed to sink one of her allies' ships. 'Their multitude became their ruin' (Aeschylus). The Corinthian contingent (70 ships) under Adeimantos was later said by Athenian gossip to have taken no part in the battle, perhaps because executing a feint withdrawal or shadowing the Egyptian squadron.

At the critical moment a force under Aristides captured Psyttaleia, making the victory complete. The fleet of Aegina is said to have distinguished itself most, and next the Athenians. Although the battle did not become such a legend to the Athenians as Marathon, it is much more entitled to rank as one of the 'decisive battles' of the world. To the Persians Marathon was merely the defeat of a punitive expedition, Salamis the overthrow of a royal scheme of conquest.

To the N of *Paloúkia* the *Arsenal*, the most important naval station in Greece, extends round the Bay of Arapi, cutting off access to the NE part of the island. From Paloukia roads lead S to *Abalákia*, crossing the base of the *Kamateró* peninsula on which stood classical Salamis (few traces) and to *Selínia*, a villa resort; and W to **Sálamis**, or *Kouloúri*, the chief town (20,437 inhab.) of the island, at the head of a deep bay on the W coast. Much of the bay is a rash of bungalows. In the bay, since the laying up in 1959 of ships from Far Eastern waters, the Japanese pearl oyster has been found: attempts to cultivate it are being made at *Megalo Pefko*.—A road skirts the bay to the straggling village of *Aiándheion*; at the entrance to the village roads lead E to *Kakí Vígla*, a hamlet on the coast, and S (rough) over the mountain to (6·5km) *Ag. Nikólaos* and then down to the coast.

Beyond Salamis the road traverses the island's NW peninsula.— 8km. The *Moni Faneroméni*, or Convent of the Apparition of the Virgin (Φανερωμένης), has a remarkable fresco of the Last Judgment. It is crowded with pilgrims on 4 September and there are traditional processions in Passion week. Nea Peramos (Rte 24) is seen across Vasiliká Bay.—The road ends at (10km) the landing-stage of the Megaris ferry (see above).

To the S of the road, overlooking St. George's Bay just below the ridge, is a long fortification-wall, identified in 1960 by the American School with the fort of *Boudoron*, built by the Athenians in the 5C to keep watch over Megara, and ravaged in 429 BC by the Peloponnesian fleet.

19 Mount Párnes

Mount Párnes, in Greek *Párnis Oros* (Πάρνης Ορος), the rugged mountain range to the NW of Athens, forms the central part of the massif dividing Attica from Boeotia. It is limited at the E end by the Diakria, or 'Upland', the lowest exit from the Attic plains, and on the W by the pass between Mt Pastra, its W extension, and Kithairon. Parnes thus extends some 40km from E to W. Its wildness is well appreciated from the air. Though the disfigurement of radar has come to its summits, it remains sparsely populated, scored by ravines, and, except where its slopes are clothed in forests of pine or oak, exposed to the elements. Wolves and bears, seen in Roman times, are no longer found, but sheepdogs may be encountered. The mountain is crossed by only one road suitable for wheeled traffic (via Dhekelia; see Rte 20), though the ancient route to Thebes by way of Phyle and Pyli is still practicable on foot. Walkers intending to make expeditions should take provisions and a compass; prudent travellers will also take a tent, since to the W of Phyle there is no hotel nearer than Thebes, and, except on the two approaches described below, public transport can be reached only on the Salonika highway or at Avlon Station to the N, or on the Thebes road to the S. The SE slopes have been made easily accessible since 1960 and are being developed for winter sports. The W forts (Panakton, etc.) are more readily visited from the Thebes road (Rte 41).

By car the two routes below may be combined without returning to Athens by using the link road through Akhárnai to Ano Liósia.

A. To Ayía Trías and the Summit

ROAD to *Grand Hotel Parnes*, 35km (22 miles); bus No. 714 to Ayía Trías (twice daily) from Od. Sourmelí. 736 (Sundays only; hourly, 09.00–21.00) to terminus (thence by telepherique) from Od. Sourmelí (Plateía Váthis, below Archaeological Museum; 2, 4). ('Parnis' is signposted via Odhós Akharnón and the National Highway, quitted after 10km to join the road described below c 1·5km N of Akharnai.)

From Plateía Váthis, NW of Omonoia Sq., Odhós Liossíon (*Railway Museum* at No. 301; open occasionally in evening) passes under the National Highway at (5·5km) *Tris Yéfires* ('Three Bridges'), in the natural 'gap' where the road and two railways cross the Kefissos.—At (6km) *Ayioi Anáryiroi* the Filí road diverges left (see below). We bear right and after c 2km pass a knoll (left) marked by some medieval remains; this is possibly the hill occupied by the Peloponnesian army under King Archidamos in 431 BC, when it ravaged the Athenian Plain. The frustrated Acharnians, prevented by Pericles from defending their lands, were later prominent in opposing the peace party in their desire for revenge (comp. Aristophanes).—12km **Akhárnai** (Αχαρναι, Hotels C, D), or *Menídi*, in modern as in ancient times is a large deme surrounded by vineyards. Its classical inhabitants engaged in charcoal-burning on Parnes. Here in 1932 was found a marble stele of the 4C engraved with the 'Oath of Plataia'. Menidhi Tomb, see below. The road climbs gradually at first, then in steep turns, offering wider and wider views over the plain of Attica. At (33km) *Ayía Trías*, a little mountain resort amid pine woods, the bus terminates. The road divides: to the right on a spur with a superb *Panorama is (2·5km farther) the Grand Hotel Mont Parnes (L; cable-car, casino, swimming pool, tennis courts, cinema, etc.); to the left we may reach (3km) the *Refuge* of the Greek Alpine Club (1165m) and the entrance to the radar station (no adm.) that crowns (7km) *Karábola* (1413m), the summit of Parnes.

Within a few yards of the top a sacrificial pyre, explored in 1959–60, yielded pottery and 3000 knives of the period 1000–600 BC. This discovery probably locates one of the two altars to Zeus mentioned by Pausanias.

From the left fork (see above) a track branches (left) towards the W, then divides. Bearing right, a winding descent may be followed towards the gorge which runs SW to the Moní Klistón (see below). At a conspicuous pine tree, a path leads SW into the gorge to a spring gushing from a column. Immediately below (easy scramble) is the *Cave of Pan* which forms the locale of Menander's

'Dyskolos'. Across the gorge (SW) rises the wooded spur of *Kalamara*, a hump with sheer sides anciently called *Harma* because, when seen from Athens, it resembled a chariot. The Pythiasts watched for lightning to play on its summit as a signal for the departure of the sacred mission to Delphi. A covering of cloud is today taken as a sign of rain.

B. To Phýle

ROAD. 31km (19½ miles) through the village of Filí (bus No. 737 from Plat. Váthis (Od. Sourmelí); 2, 4) and on to Moní Klistón and the fortress of Phýle.

To (8km) *Ayioi Anáryiroi*, see above. We bear left in company with the Peloponnese railway, beyond which can be seen a castellated mansion (Pirgos tis Vasilissis), once a model farm of Queen Amalia. Its wine ('Tour la Reine') is celebrated, but the house is now a school for officers of the Boy Scout movement.—12km. *Ano Liósia* (railway station; see Rte 16) stands in the gap between Aigaleos and Parnes. We ascend through a defile to (18·5km) *Filí* (Φύλη), a village (formerly Khasiá) in a hollow, which has readopted the ancient name. The road enters the gorge of *Potámi Goúras* and then climbs to (22·5km) **Moní Klistón**, correctly Panayia ton Kleiston (Our Lady of the Gorges), an old convent with a 14C church rebuilt in the 17C. There is a school and a terrace with a fine view down into the gorge. A fountain in the court bears the date 1677.

For **Phýle** we ignore the turning to Moni Kleiston and continue upwards to (31km) the fortress which lies (left) on a prominent flat-topped hill. It can also be reached on foot (c 2 hours) by leaving the main road (left) at the entrance to the gorge and, after c 15 minutes, ascending to the right up a ravine; but the route is difficult to find.

The fortress (649m) crowns a precipitous triangular platform extending forward from a summit some 5m higher. It dominated alternative defiles of the ancient direct route from Thebes to Athens (of strategic value only for a comparatively small force) and looks out over the whole Athenian plain. It apparently replaced an earlier fort (see below) in the 4C BC; it was garrisoned by Kassander and subsequently dismantled and ceded to the Athenians by Demetrios Poliorketes.

The main entrance is on the E side. The enclosure has a pentagonal plan. To the W and SW the defences have crumbled, but elsewhere the well-preserved walls stand to the sixth course of squared blocks. Of five towers, four were square and one round. Like Eleutherai and Rhamnous, the fort had no water supply within the walls; in the neighbourhood and also near a spring, 20 minutes NE, are vestiges of houses.

A track continues along an ancient course to the Plateau of Skourta, in which stand *Pili* (24km from Filí) and *Pánakton* (Rte 41). From Pilí the Skhimatari–Thebes road (Rte 44) can be joined at various points.

About 1·5km to the NE of Kastro is another summit, on which are considerable remains of polygonal masonry. These are presumed to mark the post which Thrasyboulos captured in 403 BC after his expulsion from Athens by the 30 Tyrants and defended with 70 men against 3000. Hence he proceeded to the capture of Piraeus.

20   From Athens to Tatóï and Skála Oropóu

ROAD, 50km (31 miles). Local buses (No. 505, etc. from Kanningos) to Tatóï and Varibóbi; buses to Skála Oropoú (twice daily), and for Euboea via the ferry, start from Od. Mavromateon, but follow the Kifissia road (Rte 15), joining this route at Malakássa. (Skála Oropoú can be reached more directly by the National Highway and a new road diverging at 34km).

We quit central Athens by the Patissia road (Rte 8), passing the National Archaeological Museum.—5km **Patíssia** (Πατήσια) is a favourite suburban resort of the Athenians. It is said to derive its name (*padishah*, Sultan) from the fact that under the Turks the land was crown property.—6km *Alissídha*.

Above *Perissos*, 2·5km NE, on the NW slope of Tourkovouni, is the *Omorphi Ekklesia*, or 'beautiful church', dedicated to St. George in the 12C. It has mural paintings by a Salonican artist of the 14C, when the S chapel was added; the narthex is more recent.

We cross the Piraeus Electric Railway, then traverse (7km) *Néa Filadhélfia*, a planned refugee suburb. The road divides by a football stadium.

The left fork leads to Akharnai (5km; Rte 19), crossing in turn the old Lavrion railway, the National Highway, and the Kifissos. In *Likótripa* (2·5km), up the hill beyond the cemetery, to the right of the road, is the tumulus covering the so-called *Menidhi Tomb*, a Mycenaean tholos tomb dug by the German School in 1879. Its yield is in the National Museum.

We continue NE. On the hill of Nemesis (left of road) was the Mycenaean settlement to which the Menidi tomb belonged.—Beyond (10·5km) *Koukouváounes*, we cross the National Highway, then the Kifissos.—Near (14·5km) *Dhekélia Station*, on the State Railway, is *Tatóï Airfield*, a Hellenic Air Force base and flying school.—19km. *Varibóbi* (Βαρυμπόμπη; Hotels L, B, C) where we join a road from Kifissia, is noted for its golf course. About 1·5km NW are the ruins of the so-called *Tomb of Sophocles*. We ascend towards the pass.

24km Tatóï, known also by its ancient name of *Dekelia*, is beautifully situated amidst oak-woods in the entrance to the pass of Klidhí ('key'). To the right the former *Summer Palace* stands in a fine park, a good example of scientific afforestation on uncongenial soil. Local antiquities from the royal estate were gathered together into a small museum by George I; this was destroyed by fire in 1916 but its surviving objects, together with later finds from the area, have been described by the Princesses Sophia and Irene (1959–60). At Tatóï were born George II (1890) and King Alexander (1893). The *Mausoleum* of George I and Alexander (d. 1920) stands on the hill called *Palaiokastro* above the village (left), where are also the ruins of a Spartan fortress constructed in 413 BC. George II and King Paul are also buried at Tatóï.

Ancient *Dekelia* (Δηεκέλεια) guarded the easternmost of the three passes over Parnes, the vital route by which food from Euboea reached Athens. By this pass Mardonius retreated into Boeotia before the battle of Plataia. On the advice of the renegade Alcibiades, the Spartans captured the pass in 413 BC and built a fortress (see above), initiating the blockade by land which, after the naval victory of Lysander at Aegospotami, led to the surrender of Athens.—*Hadrian's Aqueduct*, lengthened and restored by the Ulen company, runs S from Tatóï to a reservoir below Lykabettos.

The defile passes between the two hills of *Strongyle* (right) and

Katsimidhi (850m). On the latter are vestiges of an Athenian fort, built
in the 4C to guard the pass. The wooded uplands resound to the
clonking of sheep bells.—Beyond (32km) *Ayios Merkourios*, a chapel
with a spring, the steep zigzag descent commands a superb *View
across the Euripos to Euboea. In the foreground are the railway and
the highway to the north (Rte 44B), which we cross at (37km)
Malakássa. The road winds through upland scrub, then descends in
more wooded country, with good views of the Strait of Euboea, to
(50km) **Skála Oropós** (Hotels C; Tavernas), or more correctly *Skála
Oropoú* (Σκάλα Ωρωπού), on the site of the ancient Oropos. From its
shallow bay a ferry provides the shortest connection between Athens
and Euboea. From the beach King Constantine I embarked in 1917 for
Messina on his way to exile in Switzerland.

Ancient *Oropos* was important to Athens as the nearest accessible place of embarkation affording a short sea passage to Euboea. To it came ships bringing vital
corn supplies and cattle for the capital. According to Dikaiarchos, the Oropians
were rapacious and ill-mannered; their customs officers were especially notorious. The town fell alternately under Thebes and Athens, with intervals of independence. Diodoros records that in 402 BC the Thebans moved the Oropians 7
stades inland, presumably from Skala to the site of modern Oropós.
   The modern village of *Oropós*, 5km inland to the SW, has a 17C church. Lignite
mines are worked in the neighbourhood.
   Road from Skala to the *Amphiaraion*, see Rte 22. Car Ferry (frequent) to *Eretria*
(comp. Rte 42).

21   From Athens to Marathón. Rhámnous

ROAD to Marathon, 42km (26 miles). 12km *Stavrós.*—*27km. Turning
for Rafína* (3km right).—30km. Turning for *Ayios Andréas* (2km
right).—38km. *Marathon Tomb.*—42km. *Marathón.*—*47km Káto
Soúli.*—51·5km. Turning (right) to *Ayía Marína* (2·5km).—58km
Rhámnous.

BUS to *Marathon* from Od. Mavromateon (frequently) in c 1 hour,
continuing (regularly) to *Grammatikó* (comp. below) or to *Kato Souli*
(½ hour more); also several times daily to Ayia Marina (best for
Rhamnous; ferry to Nea Stíra, Rte 42); also to *Rafína* and to *Spáta*.

From Athens to *Stavrós*, see Rte 17B. We leave the Mesogeion road to
our right, cross the old Lavrion railway, and pass a modern church
surrounded by cypresses and a cemetery. *Gargetos*, birthplace of Epi-
curus (341–270 BC) lay hereabouts.—15km *Pallíni*, formerly Kharvati
and now marked by a radio station, has readopted the name of classical *Pallene*, which had a noted temple of Athena. It was associated
with the legendary victory of the Heraklids over Eurystheus and with
Theseus' defeat of the Pallantids. Here c 545 BC Peisistratos, returning
from exile in Macedonia, defeated an Athenian force to make himself
finally master of Athens. The local white wine is noted.

Spáta, a large village, c 6·5km SE, in a wine-producing district, has enriched the
National Museum with Mycenaean finds from chamber-tombs excavated by
Stamatakis in 1877. It has been designated the site of a second airport for Athens.
Beyond Spáta, on the coast, is the frequented beach of *Loútsa* (Hotel D;
Tavernas), identified by an inscription as *Halai Araphenides*. Here in 1956 re-

mains were discovered of a Dionysion and a temple of Artemis Tauropolos and (1975–76) a possible *propylon* (originally 5C BC) to the sanctuary.

We pass (right) a tomb of partisans executed in 1942.—22km *Pikérmi* (Hotel C; Restaurants) is noted for the discovery of fossil remains of the neo-Tertiary period, brought to light by the action of a local torrent; the finds, which include the dinotherium, largest fossil known, are now in the natural history museum of Athens University. The 16C nunnery of Ayia Filothei is now a private house. We now pass through a district rich in vineyards and olive-groves, and the scenery is most attractive. The summit of Pentelikon, which we have been skirting, is hidden behind an intervening spur. Along the road here in April 1941 British troops abandoned their transport before embarking.—Near (24km) *Drasesa Bridge*, where the road crosses the Megalo Rhevma, some English tourists, including Lord Muncaster, were captured by brigands in 1870. The scandal attending the subsequent murder of four of them at Dilessi in Boeotia caused energetic steps to be taken to suppress brigandage.—27km. Turning (right) for Rafína.

Rafína (Hotels C, D, E), site of the ancient deme of *Araphen*, is 3km away on the sea (bathing). Its small harbour is connected by steamer with Karystos (Euboea) and with Andros and Tinos. A heavy swell hampered evacuation here in 1941. On the height of *Askitarió* (2km S) are the remains of an Early Helladic town (explored in 1955).

On the wooded SE slope of Pentelikon, sharp left opposite the junction for Rafina, stands the conspicuous sanatorium of the *Moni Dáou Pendéli*. The convent, founded in the 10C, was refounded in 1963 after being deserted since 1690. A huge dome, borne on six columns, crowns the church, which shows many Eastern features. The 13C narthex dates from its Frankish period which ended in 1456. The woods are scored by fire lanes. Here, in a *German Military Cemetery* approved in 1962, have been concentrated the German dead of the campaign in Greece (1941–44).

The road approaches within a mile of the shore to cross the ridge where *Xilokeratiá* (268m), the last spur of Pentelikon descends to the sea. As we descend behind the attractive shore of *Máti* (Hotels A, B), the whole Bay of Marathon is seen across the woods that back *Ayios Andréas* (2km right), a popular bathing place with tavernas.—32km **Néa Mákri** (Hotels B, C, E), frequented for bathing, stands at the seaward end of a road that follows the N slope of Pentelikon from Ekali (Rte 15A). It has an extensive Neolithic settlement and may be the site of *Probalinthos*, whose name betrays a prehistoric origin. The road passes between *Mt Agriliki* and the small marsh of *Brexisa* (comp. below) into the Plain of Marathon.

The PLAIN OF MARATHON claims attention both because of the battle and because of archaeological discoveries, particularly those made in 1969–70. Geographically the plain, 10km long and 2·5–5km wide, extends in crescent form round the Bay of Marathon from the *Kynosura Promontory* (with an unidentified acropolis) in the N to Cape Kavo on the S. On the landward side it is shut in by the stony mountains that 'look on Marathon', making up for their moderate height by rising abruptly from the plain. *Stavrokoráki* (310m), the northernmost of these, is separated from *Kotróni* (235m) by the torrent bed of the *Kharadra*, which descends from the Marathon Lake past the modern village of Marathon to the sea. Geologists suggest that in the plain it would have been a negligible obstacle in Classical times. Between Kotroni and *Aforismós* (573m) runs the *Valley of Avlona*. The valley is joined at the village of VRANÁ (possibly the ancient Marathon) by the Rapentosa Gorge. This defile runs NNE from the hamlet of Rapentosa between Aforismos and *Agrilíki* (556m), the mountain forming the southern barrier of the plain. Agriliki has rubble walls that may date from the Mycenaean period.

In the N of the plain the *Great Marsh* (Μεγάλος Βάλτος; nowadays criss-crossed by drainage canals) stretches from Stavrokoraki to the base of the Kynosura Promontory, where it ends in the small saltwater lake of *Drakonéra*. The *Little Marsh* (*Brexisa*) at the S end is probably a post-Classical formation; it is now partially drained and occupied by a United States forces radio station and the Golden Coast Hotel (B).

Battle of Marathon. After the easy destruction of Eretria the Persians crossed to Attica. Datis, their general, was probably influenced in his choice of the Bay of Marathon by Hippias, whose father had landed here successfully fifty years before. Meanwhile the Athenians, after despatching Pheidippides post haste for Spartan aid, marched to Marathon and encamped in the Sanctuary of Herakles, a strong position astride the mountain track from Athens and commanding the only road. The Persian numbers, not stated by Herodotus and grossly exaggerated by later Athenian tradition, are now thought not to have exceeded two divisions of infantry (? 24,000 men) and a small force of cavalry. The Athenians received unexpected aid from Plataia, which sent its whole available force, perhaps 1000 strong to join the 8000–9000 men of Athens. The command was vested in the Polemarch, Kallimachos, whose staff of ten generals included Miltiades (the traditional architect of the victory), and perhaps Themistocles and Aristides.

Four days passed, the Persians being unwilling to attack the strong Athenian position, the Athenians loth to leave it without the expected Spartan reinforcements. Believing he had failed to lure the Athenian army down into the plain, Datis re-embarked his cavalry to move on Athens by sea, sending a land force forward to cover the operation. Seeing them within striking distance, probably soon after dawn on 12 September 490 BC, Miltiades gave the word for action. He had left his centre weak and strengthened his wings to the utmost: the right wing, the place of honour, was led by Kallimachos; on the left wing were the Plataians. The Greek hoplites advanced rapidly across the mile of No Man's Land before the surprised Persians could get their archers properly into action, aided possibly by tree cover (Prof. Burn has pointed out the similarity of tactics used at Bannockburn). The Athenian wings were successful, while their weak centre was pierced by the Persians. The wings then enveloped the Persian centre which broke. In the ensuing rout the Persians fled to their ships. Many of them were caught in the Great Marsh. They lost 6400 men, while the Athenian dead numbered only 192, including Kallimachos. All were buried on the spot. A runner is said to have been sent to Athens, where he died of exhaustion after announcing the victory.

The Persian fleet, having lost only seven ships, put out to sea in an attempt to surprise Athens; but Miltiades, by a rapid march, reached Athens first, and the Persians sailed back to Asia. The battle proved that the long-dreaded Persians were vulnerable and was 'the victory of which the Athenians were proudest'. The Spartan army arrived in time to view the battlefield on the following day. Of the many legends that accrued to Marathon perhaps the best known are those of the ghostly assistance of Theseus and of Pan. The impressive silence of the plain is said to resound at night to the clash of arms and the neigh of steeds (though it is almost certain that no cavalry took part). Unsolved mysteries connected with the battle include the flashing of a shield on Pentelikon (Hdt. VI, 115). The most detailed modern appraisals are by Burn (Persia and the Greeks) and in 'Journal of Hellenic Studies' (vol. 52, 1932), but these and even Kendrick Pritchett's Studies in Ancient Topography II (1969) need to be considered in the light of continuing finds.

THE ARCHAEOLOGICAL SITES. As we enter the plain, there is first a road (right) across the Brexisa Marsh to the Golden Coast hotel (comp. above), just to the S of which, on an island of solid ground are vestiges of Roman masonry, commonly supposed to be the family mausoleum of Herodes Atticus (AD 101–177, a native of Marathon), and earlier remains have been located in the area. A little farther along, a second road (right) is signposted 'Marathon Tomb' (350m; large car park; café). This **Sorós**, 10m high and c 180m round, marks the graves of the 192 Athenians who fell in the battle. The top of the mound commands a view of the battlefield. At the foot is a marble bas-relief, copied from the 'Warrior of Marathon'. The 'tombstones with the names of the fallen arranged according to tribes', which Pausanias (I, 32, 3) tells us were set over the Sorós, have disappeared.

Contrary to usual practice, the fallen at Marathon were buried where they fell in token of their signal valour. Excavations undertaken in 1890 confirmed the ancient tradition attaching to the Sorós: ashes and calcined bones, as well as small black-figured lekythoi of the early 5C, were discovered. Obsidian arrowheads found on the surface by Schliemann six years earlier, which led him to attribute a much earlier date to the mound, may have been used by the Ethiopian archers (Hdt. VII, 69). No graves have been located of the slaves, who are said to have fought for the first time at Marathon. It is probable that Pausanias was right that the Persian dead were merely flung into an open trench.

The Soros road continues to the shore (Hotels A, C; cafés) where a road leads N along the beach for c 1km to the site of *Plasí*, a slight rise 100m inland, excavated in 1969–70. Here are an Archaic peribolos of polygonal stones, possibly belonging to a shrine, and, near by, a M.H. settlement. This may be the site of the ancient deme.

We return to the main road, where c 1·5km farther on a road forks back to the hamlet of Vrana (3km; signs to Mouseion Marathona). About 100m down this road (right), largely covered by a hangar is the *Tsépi Vraná* site, a large E.H. cemetery containing carefully arranged and well-built cist graves. Vases found, as well as the graves themselves, are of Cycladic type. Between here and Vrana extends NW the Avlona valley, where (2·5km) a huge walled enclosure is known from an inscription on the ruined gateway to have belonged to Herodes Atticus. At the entrance to Vrana is (left) a large tumulus, excavated in 1969–70 and probably the TOMB OF THE PLATAIANS who fell at Marathon, which Pausanias records as a separate memorial. The identification is not certain. The mound, constructed entirely of stones, contains two circles of pit graves; skeletons found were mostly of young men, and the pottery in the graves is contemporary with that in the Athenian Soros.—At the far end of Vrana, under a large shelter, are groups of grave circles consisting of paved slabs, each circle containing stone tombs of M.H.–L.H. date. The skeleton of a Przewalski-type horse occupies a separate tomb but this is probably a later intrusion. Another circle stands in the open.

The **Museum** has five rooms. We turn right. Room A, Neolithic pottery from the Cave of Pan (comp. below). Room B, case 5, finds from the Early Cycladic cemetery (Tsepi); case 6, from Middle Helladic tumuli (Vrana); case 8, from Geometric graves. Room Γ, vases etc. from the Tombs of the Athenians (case 13) and Plataians (case 10); bronze cinerary urn; boundary stones and inscribed stelai. Room Δ, Classical grave stelai and furnishings; rare bronze mirror with wooden covers; objects from various cemeteries; Panathenaic amphorae. Room E, Hellenistic and Roman finds, including an inscription concerning Herodes Atticus, and an Egyptianising 'kouros' of 2C AD.

About 1km SE of the museum, the small chapel of *Ayios Dhimítrios* stands alone just above the foot of Agriliki; close are the remains of an open-air precinct, c 140m square, identified in 1954 by Prof. Sotiriades with the celebrated sanctuary of Herakles (comp. above).—On the

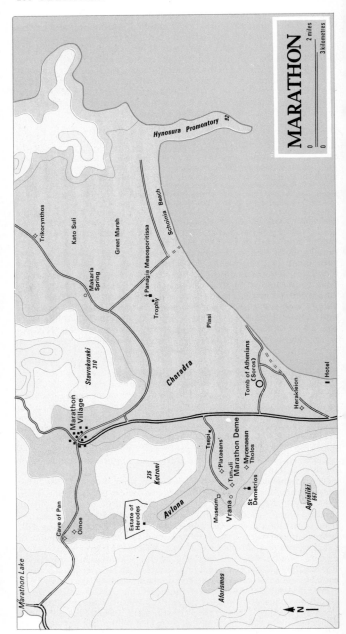

plain, 1km from the chapel, in a small grove of low trees, is a Tholos Tomb (Mycenean II; locked): it yielded a gold cup, and the complete skeletons of two horses were buried beneath the dromos. Also in the vicinity of the church are the foundations of the funerary peribolos of Gyles of Probalinthos and his family.

The main road continues N past the Rhamnous turn.—42km **Marathón** (commonly Marathóna), a sprawling agricultural village. At the entrance is a marble platform with flag poles, the starting-point for annual marathon races.

FROM MARATHON TO KAPANDRITI, 20km (12½ miles), occasional buses to Grammatikó. Beyond Marathon the road climbs via (5km) *Ano Soúli* to (8km) *Grammatikó.*—*14km. Varnávas,* on the slope of Mavrovouni.—20km *Kapandríti,* see Rte 22.

A road leads W from Marathon to (8km) Marathon Lake (Rte 22), passing below the site of ancient *Oinoe.* Here in 1957 Papadimtriou discovered the *Cave of Pan and the Nymphs* of Marathon, described by Pausanias and identified by an inscription of 60 BC found in situ. The cave (no adm.) seems to have been a place of cult from Neolithic times to the end of the Bronze Age, after which it was deserted until the 5C BC. Herodotus tells of the resurgence of the worship of Pan following his aid to Pheidippides before the Battle of Marathon.

From the entrance to the village an asphalt road diverges E, following the foot of the hills. At 46km a road diverges (right) to *Skhoiniá,* the narrow strip of solid ground between the marsh and the sea chosen as the venue of the Boy Scouts' 11th World Jamboree in 1963. It is being developed as a bungalow resort.—47km *Káto Soúli,* where (left) are vestiges of the walls (3C AD) of ancient *Trikorythos.* We cross a lonely upland valley with barren hills on either side.—51·5km Fork; to the right lies the little seaside hamlet of *Ayía Marína* (regular ferries to Néa Stíra; Rte 42B). We bear left, rise gradually, and join the path from Gramattiko (see below) within sight of (58km) *Rhamnous.*

Rhámnous (commonly Rhamnoúnda), uninhabited save for the phylax and a few shepherds, is one of the least spoilt sites in Attica, worth visiting more for its romantic isolation and the beauty of its setting than for its archaeological interest.

The headland was famous as early as the 6C BC for the worship of Nemesis. Its small cove provided shelter on an otherwise inhospitable coast for ships about to pass the dangerous narrows of Ayia Marina. Later a fortress was built to watch over navigation in the Euripos. This achieved importance in 412 BC after the Athenian loss of Dhekelia, when Rhamnous became the port of entry for food from Euboea, since it offered the only route wholly on Attic soil that did not involve passing the narrows. The name of the city was derived from the prickly shrub (ράμνος) which still grows in the neighbourhood. In more recent times it was known as *Ovriokastro,* a corruption of Εβραιόν κάστρον (Jews' Castle). It was the birthplace of the orator Antiphon (b. 480 BC), whose school of rhetoric was attended by Thucydides.—The sanctuary was first described by the Dilettanti Society in 1817; partially excavated by Staïs in 1890–94; and re-examined by Orlandos in 1922–23 (B.C.H., 1924). The fortress was described by J. Pouilloux in 1945. Since 1975 extensive reinvestigation has been directed by V. Petrakos (author of *Rhamnous; a concise guide,* Athens, 1983).

Nemesis was the compensating goddess, measuring out happiness and misery. She took especial care of the presumptuous, punishing 'hubris', the crime of considering oneself master of one's destiny. She was known also by the surnames of 'Adrastia' ('inescapable') and of Rhamnousia, from her sanctuary at Rhamnous. Associated with the worship of Nemesis was Themis, the goddess who personified law, equity, and custom.

At the head of a glen is an artificial platform, 45m wide, constructed, in the 5C BC, of large blocks of local marble laid horizontally. Nine courses are exposed at the NE corner. The sacred precinct thus formed contains the remains of two temples, an altar, a stoa and a small fountain house. Although none of the visible remains are earlier than the 5C, both votive offerings and rooftiles of the early 6C show that there was ritual activity from that time.

The smaller TEMPLE (of Themis?) was built on a virgin site in the early 5C. It measures 10·7m by 6·5m and consists merely of a cella in antis with a Doric portico of two columns. The walls which stand to c 1·8m are built of large polygonal blocks of white marble. Two marble seats dedicated to Themis and Nemesis and three statues from the cella with inscribed pedestals (found in 1890) are in Athens. The building continued in use (as a treasury/storeroom) into the 4C AD.

The first TEMPLE OF NEMESIS, nearer the sea, was constructed at the end of the 6C BC in poros limestone as a Doric building, distyle in antis. This temple was probably destroyed by the Persians and replaced by that whose remains are still visible. This successor is a Doric peripteral building with six columns by twelve, the last of four sometimes ascribed to the so-called 'Theseum architect'. According to Dinsmoor, it was probably begun on the Festival Day of the Nemesieia (Boedromion 5; i.e. 30 September) 436 BC, and it is known by an inscription to have been rededicated to the Empress Livia, probably by Claudius in AD 45. The interior had the usual arrangement of cella, pronaos and opisthodomos in antis. The unfinished fluting on the remaining drums of six columns (S side) suggests that the building was never completed.

Fragments both of the cult statue of Nemesis (including a colossal head, now in the British Museum) and of its base have been found. The statue (c 421 BC) was in Parian marble and the work of Agorakritos. Pausanias believed it to have been made from the very marble brought by the Persians for use as a victory monument and incorrectly attributed it to Pheidias. The base had carved decoration on three sides, showing Leda introducing Helen to her real mother, Nemesis.

Still within the precinct are, to the E of the temple, the foundations of an altar; to the N the remains of a stoa of the 5C (34m long) which originally had wooden columns in its façade. In front of the stoa was a small fountain house, with a two-columned porch. Opposite the precinct, on the other side of the road, are the foundations of a large Hellenistic structure.

Both N and S (beyond the car park) of the sanctuary runs the sacred way. Beside it can be seen funerary enclosures with sculptured stelai and inscriptions commemorating the dead.

Descending the rocky glen N towards the sea (*access not permitted at present*) we reach in 10 minutes an isolated hill girdled with the picturesque but overgrown enceinte (c 1km in circuit) of the ANCIENT TOWN. The lower part of the South Gateway is well preserved, as are short portions (3·7m high in places) of the walls, in ashlar masonry of grey limestone. Nine towers of the fortress can be made out. Within are some remains of a small *Temple*, a *Gymnasium*, and an inner citadel. A small sanctuary of Amphiaraos lies outside, to the NW.

A rocky mule path to the SW leads shortly to a bad road which, partly utilising an abandoned mineral railway, comes up from Grammatikó (1½ hours on foot).

22 From Athens to Marathon Lake, Kálamos, and the Amphiáraion

ROAD to the *Amphiaraion*, 49km (30½ miles); to *Marathon Lake*,
31km (20¾ miles). Buses to *Kalamós* (45km; for the Amphiaraion)
from Odhos Mavromatéon; to *Marathon Lake* (infrequent) from Plat.
Kánningos.

From central Athens to (20km) *Ekáli*, see Rte 15. We continue N
passing the road to Dhiónisos (Rte 15), to (22·5km) *Drosiá* (Dhionysos,
Hotel C, D), another upland resort. At *Stamáta* (2km right; and see Rte
15A) some ruins may be identified with ancient *Hekale* where Theseus instituted a festival to Zeus in memory of the priestess who sheltered him on his way to fight the Bull of Marathon. *Plotheia* was also
hereabouts.—At (24km) *Ayios Stéfanos* a road (right) leads in 9km to
Marathon Lake (Tourist Pavilion) and on to Marathon (Rte 21).

Marathon Lake (in Gk. *Límni Marathónos*) is an irregular sheet of water (c 243
hectares) formed by impounding the Charadhra and Varnava torrents. It supplies
the needs of Greater Athens, though since the Second World War its capacity has
had to be augmented by artificial inflows from Parnes and the Boeotian lakes.
The *Dam*, built by the Ulen company of New York in 1925–31, at the SE end of the
lake, consists of a curved concrete wall 285m long, 47m wide at the base, and 4m
wide at the top. It is claimed to be the only dam in the world faced with marble. A
roadway runs across it. It rises 54m above the river bed to an elevation of 227m
above sea-level. At the downstream side is a marble replica of the Athenian
Treasury at Delphi, which serves as an entrance to the inspection galleries.

At Ayios Stefanos we can, after 1km, join the Athens–Salonika highway, leaving it again at the Kapandriti exit. Alternatively we can take
the Marathon Lake turning, then bear left almost immediately at Ayios
Stefanos, rounding the station (*Oion*) on our left and crossing the
line, to continue by the old road running parallel with the highway.
Seen to the left is modern *Kioúrka*, formerly *Aphidnai*; to the right, at
the N end of Marathon Lake, beyond the new works which control the
entry of waters piped from N Parnes, is a hill (Kotroni) with some
ancient walls to be identified either with classical Aphidna or with
Oion.

Theseus hid Helen at Aphidna after carrying her off from Sparta. Her where-
abouts were divulged by the inhabitants of Dekelia to her brothers, Castor and
Pollux, who laid siege to Aphidna and rescued her. Aphidna was the home of
Kallimachos, polemarch at Marathon.

After (36km) *Kapandríti*, where we join a road from Grammatikó (Rte
21), the pleasant road winds over tree-clothed hills to (45km)
Kálamos, the small centre (329m) of a well-watered and wooded
region above the Gulf of Euboea.

The road continues to (5km farther) *Ayioi Apóstoloi* (Hotels B, C; restaurants),
originally a fishing village, now a seaside resort.

From Kalamos a road descends in loops to the *Amphiarion* (4km) in
the Mavrodhilisi ravine. On foot the site can be reached in 25 minutes
by the old path (difficult not to lose), shaded by pines, which crosses
the road several times. The road must be followed for the last 100m as
the entrance lies beyond the bridge that crosses the stream. Approach
by the road is less uncertain and not unpleasant.

The ***Amphiaraion**, or *Sanctuary of Amphiaraos*, founded in honour
of the healing god, was at once an oracle and a spa. It occupies a
sheltered and sunny situation, well suited to a resort of invalids, on the

left bank of a wooded glen, watered by a mountain torrent. In spring anemones carpet the site.

The sanctuary commemorated the elevation to divinity of Amphiaraos, the great seer and warrior of Argos, who fought as one of the seven against Thebes. On the defeat of this expedition he fled, pursued by Periklymenos, but the earth opened and swallowed him up, together with his chariot, near Thebes. His cult was adopted by the Oropians and concentrated here near a spring famed for its healing properties. Mardonius came to consult the oracle before the battle of Plataia. Whoever wished to consult the god sacrificed a ram and lay down for the night, wrapped in its skin, in the portico allotted for the purpose, and there awaited the revelations to be made to him in his dreams. The process of incubation (εγκοίμησις) was very similar to that practised in the Asklepieion. The cure did not, however, wholly depend on these miraculous communications, for there were medical baths in the precinct. After his cure, the patient had to throw gold or silver coins into the sacred spring.—The excavations (1927–30) of the Greek Archaeological Service were interrupted by the death of Leonardos, the excavator. Restorations have been effected since 1960.

Descending the path parallel to the stream, we see (right) the little *Temple of Amphiaraos*, a Doric building of the 4C, with a pronaos and a cella divided into three by parallel colonnades. The foundations, partly eroded by the stream, have been restored. The base of the cult statue is still in position. The back wall was joined by a porch (door marks in the threshold) to the priests' lodging. Ten yards from the temple is the *Altar*, on which the ram was sacrificed; and below the altar the *Sacred Spring*, into which the coins were thrown. Its waters were drunk from shells, many of which have come to light. Above the altar is a terrace with a line of over 30 inscribed *Pedestals* of statues, mostly Roman. On a line with these are the remains of a long bench. In front is the *Museum* (rarely open; enquire at entrance to site), containing numerous inscriptions, a curious early Herm, torsos, and, in the back court, reassembled architectural members of the temple and stoa. Beyond are the remains of the *Enkoimeterion*, a long stoa, erected c 387 BC, having 41 Doric columns on the façade and divided internally into two long galleries by 17 Ionic columns. It had a small room at either end, possibly reserved for women patients. Along the walls ran marble benches, resting on claw feet, on which the patients submitted to the process of incubation. Behind the stoa is a small THEATRE, having a circular orchestra and seating for 300 spectators.

Five marble *Thrones* with scroll ornaments are preserved. The *Proskenion* (restored) has 8 Doric columns surmounted by an epistyle with a dedicatory inscription. Beyond the stoa were the *Baths*. On the opposite bank of the stream are some confused remains of the accommodation provided for patients and part of a *Klepsydra*, or water-clock, its bronze plug mechanism visible.

A new road continues to *Skala Oropou* (Rte 20), c 6·5km NW.

23 From Piraeus to Spétsai

Motor Vessels of the Argossaronikos Lines from Piraeus (opposite the Dhimarkhíon) ply to *Spétsai* in 4–5 hours, calling at *Aégina* (1¾ hours). *Méthana* (2 hours), *Póros* (2½ hours), *Hydra* (3¾ hours), and *Ermióni* (4¾ hours). Not every boat calls at every port. In summer 4–5 times daily to Hydra and Spetsai; 10–12 times to Poros; several times per hour to Aegina (gap between mid-morning and early afternoon). Extra services at weekends. Also (by launch) to Ayía Marína (Aegina) direct.

EXPRESS SERVICE ('*Flying Dolphin*' Hydroplanes) from Piraeus (Pashalimani; Pl. 11), twice daily to *Poros* (1 hr), *Hydra* (1½ hr), and *Ermioni* (1¾ hr); 4 times to *Hydra*, *Spetsai* (1¾ hr), and *Porto Khéli* (2 hrs); daily to all these ports continuing to *Nauplia* (4 hrs); also service continuing to *Monemvasia* (3¾ hr; see Rte 32), or to *Kithira* (5 hrs) and *Neapolis* (5¾ hrs).—From the main port 10 times daily to *Aégina* in 35 minutes. Bookings may be made at Wagons-Lit Cook at 2 Karageorghi Servias (Sindagma).

BY CAR. Only residents with a special permit may have cars on Spetsai. However the island can be reached by driving to Kósta on the Argolic peninsula (where cars may be left by the landing-stage) and taking the ferry.

To explore the islands and the Argolic peninsula, five or six days are necessary. From Poros (via Galatá), Ermioni (via Kranídhi), or Spetsai (via Kheli) it is possible to reach *Nauplia* by bus.

Within the day a round cruise (without landing) may be made to Spetsai, or a superficial visit may be made to any one island; organised day trips (C.H.A.T., etc.) briefly visit Aégina, Póros, and Hydra.

A. From Piraeus to Aégina

The steamer passes down the centre of the *Great Harbour* of Piraeus with liner berths to the left and commercial wharves to the right. The prominent square building on the Akte peninsula is the Hadjikiriakou Orphanage. We pass between the remains of the ancient moles; from the *Outer Harbour* the W landmarks of the Akte peninsula (comp. Rte 12) are clearly visible. The channel opens out into the **Saronic Gulf** (*Saronikós Kólpos*), the skyline of which, on a clear day, seems filled with mountains. The long islet of *Lipsokoutali*, with naval installations, is usually taken to be the ancient *Psyttaleia*, though some recent theories about the Battle of Salamis have thrown doubt on this (comp. Rte 18). To the W rise the scrubby hills of *Salamis*, backed by the higher peaks beyond Megara. Astern the scars of Pentelikon are prominent and the Attic coastline is visible as far as Vouliagmeni and the islet of Fleves. As we draw level with the lighthouse on the S point of Salamis, we see the sugar-loaf of Acrocorinth backed by the frequently snowy cap of Killini filling the W end of the Saronic Gulf. Ahead rises Aegina; the temple of Aphaia can just be made out high up on the left. The steamer passes E of *Eleousa* and heads towards the low Akr. Plakakia, the NW cape of Aegina (lighthouse). Away to starboard appear the five *Dhiaporioi Nisoi*, the ancient Isles of Pelops. We turn S into the Strait of Metopi, the shallow channel that separates Aegina from *Angistrion*. The jagged peaks of Methana rise ahead to the right of Moni. A solitary column (see below) marks the promontory guarding (27km) the port of Aegina.

AEGINA or AIYINA (Αιγινα; the stress is on the first syllable), a triangular island of 86 sq. km occupies the centre of the Saronic Gulf, being almost equidistant from Attica and from Argolis. With Angistrion and the small attendant islets to the W it forms nowadays an eparchy (11,893 inhab.) of the nome of Piraios. The island is difficult of approach on account of the sunken rocks and reefs that surround it. It relies for its water on wells. Much of the W part consists of a plain which, though stony, is well cultivated with pistachio nuts and, farther S, with citrus fruits. The interior of the island is mountainous, pine-clad to the NE, and affords pleasing landscapes, while at the S corner rises the magnificent conical mountain, *Oros* (531m), the finest natural feature of the island. The climate is delightful and the island is fast developing as a holiday area. The local industries include sponge-fishing and pottery. The two-handled porous water-jars (kanátia), common in Athens, are made here. In addition to pistachio nuts, olives, vines, almonds, and figs are cultivated.

History. Notwithstanding its small size, the key position of Aegina in the Saronic Gulf ensured the early importance of the island. The name probably derives from a divinity (Hellenised as Aigáios) imported from Anatolia by Early Helladic invaders speaking a Lycian dialect, but Neolithic finds make it certain that the island was occupied as early as the end of the 4th millennium BC. About 2000 BC the inhabitants were supplanted by a Bronze Age people, probably of Indo-European race, speaking an Aeolian or Arcadian dialect and worshipping Poseidon. Their culture was brought to an end, c 1400, by an Achaean invasion and a period of Mycenaean occupation. Later legend tells of its only hero-king, Aiakos, son of Zeus and Aegina, who afterwards became one of the three judges of the Underworld. His sons Peleus and Telamon had to flee for the murder of their half-brother Phokos; Telamon afterwards became king of Salamis. A Dorian invasion brought the Thessalian cult of Zeus Hellanios. Aphaia seems to have been a variant of the Mother-Goddess from Crete, perhaps imported during the early Iron Age.

Perhaps abandoned for two centuries before 950 BC, the island was recolonised probably from Epidauros (Herod, VIII, 46). Its infertile soil combined with its geographical situation spurred the inhabitants to maritime enterprise. At the end of the 8C it enjoyed parity with fellow members of the Kalaurian League, and was apparently no longer subject to Argos. By the 7C the Aeginetan marine held first place in the Hellenic world. The island was noted for pottery and especially for the quality of its bronze-founding. The system of coinage introduced in Argos by Pheidon (c 656 BC) was probably borrowed from Aegina (rather than the other way about); indeed coinage very likely first reached Europe by way of the island. Its silver coins became the standard in most of the Dorian states, and in the 6C Aegina was a major centre of Greek art. Aeginetan merchants set up a temple to Zeus at the founding of Naukratis on the Nile; one, Sostratos, according to Herodotus (IV, 152) had also sailed to Spain. Their harbour was crowded with merchant ships (Thuc., V, 53) and the Aeginetan navy grew to a formidable size, exciting the jealousy of Athens. Solon's laws prohibiting the export of corn from Attica were probably directed mainly against Aegina, which henceforward, whatever its alliance, was always anti-Athenian. Aristotle calls it 'the eyesore of Piraeus' ('Rhet.', III, 10, 7); Herodotus (V, 82) adduces a mythical feud, and may be historically unreliable about the war between Athens and Aegina (? 488–481) in which the Athenians were worsted.

At Salamis (480 BC) the Aeginetans atoned for any previous homage to Persia by distinguishing themselves above all other Greeks, and the battle marked the zenith of their power. As a member of the Spartan League, Aegina was protected from attack until the reversal of Kimon's policy, when the Aeginetans were quickly defeated by the Athenians in two naval battles. In 457 BC the city was humiliated after a siege (Thuc., I, 108). At the beginning of the Peloponnesian War the Athenians expelled the inhabitants and established a cleruchy. The scattered remnants were allowed to return in 404 from their exile in Thyrea (where the Spartans had accommodated them), but Aegina never rallied from this blow. It passed with the rest of Greece to Macedon and afterwards to Attalos of Pergamon. In Byzantine times it constituted a joint bishopric with Keos. Paul of Aegina, celebrated for a treatise on medicine and surgery was born here in the 7C AD. Saracen raids caused the inhabitants to shift the capital inland (comp. below) where it remained until the 19C. After 1204 the island was a personal fief of Venetian and Catalan families until, in 1451 it passed to Venice. Captured and laid waste in 1537 by Khair-ed-Din (Barbarossa), it was repopulated with Albanians. Morosini recaptured it for Venice in 1654, and it became one of the last Venetian strongholds in the E, being ceded to Turkey in 1718. In 1826–28 the city was the temporary capital of partly liberated Greece, and here the first modern Greek coins were minted. Many of the present inhabitants are descended from families who came at this time from the Peloponnese, or from refugees who fled here from Chios and Psara.

The modern town of **Aíyina** (6,333 inhab.; Hotels B, C, D; Restaurants on the quay), near the NW corner of the island, occupies part of the site of the ancient city, which extended much farther to the N. It still preserves buildings erected during the presidency of Capodistrias, to whose memory a statue stands in the main square. From the sea the most conspicuous features are two churches: Ayios Nikólaos, and the Cathedral on the quay. The modern HARBOUR, oval in shape and crowded with picturesque caïques, corresponds with the ancient *Commercial Harbour*. Its moles were rebuilt by Capodistrias on the ancient foundations. The S mole marked the S limit of the ancient city, forming an extension of its walls. The N mole bears a tiny white chapel of typical Aegean design. Beyond the N mole remains of rectangular quays of the ancient *Military Harbour* (Κρύπτος Λίμην) can be seen beneath the surface of a smooth sea.

It was protected on the N by a low promontory (Kolonna; 10 minutes from the quay), which formed the citadel, fortified from Neolithic to Christian times. In the Classical period at least it was within the enceinte which was continued seaward from farther N by a breakwater. The MUSEUM is to the right on entry to the archaeological site. It contains a selection of Neolithic and Bronze Age pottery (the latter both local and imported, found at the Kolonna site); later vases including the fine Orientalising Ram Jug (Odysseus and companions escaping from the Cyclops); sculpture including a 5C sphinx, a Herakles from the Temple of Apollo, funerary stelai; stone anchors; inscriptions from the Temple of Aphaia. Beyond the Museum are the main EXCAVATIONS, greatly extended W and S of the temple since 1969, with the discovery of the substantial remains of an Early–Late Helladic fortified settlement, whose remains now dominate the area. Of the *Temple of Apollo* (formerly attributed to Aphrodite), all that remains are a lone column, without its capital, from the opisthodomos, and some scanty poros foundations of polygonal masonry. The temple (Doric, 6 columns by 12), built c 520–500 BC, was superseded by a late-Roman fortress, fragments of which survive on the seaward side; the area was quarried during the rebuilding of the harbour.

German excavations by G. Welter in 1924 beneath the temple showed remains of a building about a century earlier, below which again were late-Mycenaean houses.

To the SE a square edifice of Archaic date is possibly the *Aiakeion*. To the NW of the temple a circular structure is thought to accord with Pausanias' description of the *Tomb of Phokos*. On the extremity of the cape near the water, some scanty Pergamene remains are perhaps those of *Attaleion*.

The Quay has a Tourist Information Office (open only in the season). At its S end is the *Panayitsa* (1806), cathedral of the Metropolitan of Idhra, Spetsai, and Aegina. Inland from the quay is the Post Office.

Beyond the Post Office, we reach Odhos Ayiou Nikolaou which leads past the medieval *Markelon Tower* to *Ayios Nikolaos*, a modern church. Behind this are some remains of an Early Christian basilica. A street running N leads shortly to *Kanaris's House*, once occupied by the hero of Chios. Many of the local houses are given over to the processing of sponges.—In the S part of the town (Od. Aféas) is the former *Orphanage*, built by Capodistrias for children orphaned by the War of Independence and, since 1854, used successively as barracks and prison and now a Folk Museum. Below the courtyard is an ancient catacomb. Farther on (5 minutes) is the *Faneroméni* (18C), with the remains of a basilica over a crypt. On the coast road, opposite the cemetery is the *House of Trikoupis*, where both Charilaos Trikoupis (1832–96), the statesman, and Spyridion, his historian father, lived for a short period.—To the left of the road to the temple (see below), about ¾ hr from the town, is the *Omorfi Ekklesia*, a church of 1282 built of antique materials and dedicated to SS.Theodore. Its frescoes (somewhat later) are well preserved.

BUSES and taxis to the Temple of Aphaia and elsewhere, from beyond the W end of the quay.

THE PRINCIPAL EXCURSION is to the Temple of Aphaia (by Ayía Marína bus). The road runs through pistachio plantations, and vineyards dotted with olive and fig trees.—6·5km **Palaiokhóra** (left), capital of the island from the 9C until 1826. It was rebuilt twice after destruction by Barbarossa (1537) and by the Venetians (1654). Covering the bare hillside are the ruins of more than twenty churches and monasteries (contact phylax for access), survivors from the 13C and later, some with stone ikonostases and tolerably preserved frescoes. A ruined castle crowns the summit. Below this ghost town is a monastery containing the embalmed body of Ay. Nektários (Anastasios Kefalas; 1846–1920), Metropolitan of Pentapolis and the first saint to be canonised (1961) by the Orthodox Church in modern times.—8km *Mésagros*. From this village a road (unpaved) leads to the N coast and then through *Souvalá* (Hotel C, D), a pleasant fishing village with radio-active springs, back (paved) to Aiyina.—At 10·5km the road bears right and climbs.

12km. The *Temple of Aphaía* stands on a pine-clad hill commanding a splendid view over the Saronic Gulf. Erected at the end of the 6C or in the early years of the 5C on the site of two earlier temples, it has been called 'the most perfectly developed of the late Archaic temples in European Hellas'. The appearance of its shattered peristyle was enhanced in 1956–60 by the re-erection of fallen columns and the restoration to position of their entablature, though lightning caused damage to the SW corner in 1969.

The temple was explored in 1811, when its sculptures were borne off to Munich (comp. below). Bavarian excavations undertaken in 1901–03 by Furtwängler in order to complete these groups proved the dedication to Aphaia, the Aeginetan equivalent of the Cretan goddess Britomartis. The shrine had previously been attributed first to Zeus Panhellenios and later to Athena. Numerous fragments were recovered (D. Öhly) in 1969 and subsequent years of the earlier Archaic temple's polychrome stonework.

We pass through the *Outer Peribolos Wall*. To the right are some remains of the living quarters of the priests; three stucco baths served for purification rites. The artificial *Terrace* on which the temple stands is approached by a *Propylon* of the 5C, having an unusual arrangement of pilasters on the façade. To the E are the foundations of the latest *Altar*, from the base of which a *Ramp* rises to the *Stereobate* of three steps on which the temple stands.

TEMPLE OF APHAIA

0 _____ 20 metres

after Welter and others

The TEMPLE is now roped off to preserve the remaining traces of the red stucco which originally covered the floors of the pronaos and cella. It is Doric peripteral hexastyle, having twelve columns on the flanks. It was built in local limestone which was coated with a thin layer of stucco and painted. Of the original 32 columns, 24 now stand. They are 3 Doric feet in diameter at the base and axially spaced at 8 feet. The corner columns are thickened for optical effect. All the shafts are monolithic, save for three adjacent columns on the N flank which are built up of drums, presumably for the purpose of leaving a gap until the last moment to facilitate the erection of the interior. The architrave is extensively preserved and the whole entablature has been restored at the W end of the N side by the replacement of the triglyphs, metopes, and cornice. The sekos is divided into a cella with pronaos and opisthodomos in antis. Two columns survive of the *Pronaos*, which once housed figureheads of Samian triremes captured at Kydonia. Marks can be seen on the columns where the entrance was closed off with a high grille.

The *Cella*, the walls of which have been partly rebuilt, was divided internally by two colonnades of five columns each; above an epistyle a second row of smaller superposed columns carried a flat ceiling. Seven of the interior columns have been restored to place with three of the upper shafts; their taper is continuous throughout. At a later date aisle floors were put in at triforium level, approached presumably by wooden stairs. The position of the cult statue (fragment of the acrolithic arm in the National Archaeological Museum in Athens) is shown by marks in the floor where a railing stood round it.—The doorway from the opisthodomos is not central and was pierced after a solid cross-wall was started.

The pedimental sculptures were of Parian marble. Seventeen statues found by Cockerell and von Hallerstein in 1811 were acquired by Ludwig I of Bavaria and, after restoration by Thorvaldsen in Rome, sent to Munich, where they remain. The scenes represented two combats before Troy in the presence of Athena. Parts of a third and a fourth group (now in Athens and Aegina museums) have since come to light; these are believed to have been deliberately removed but the reason is unknown.

At the NE corner of the terrace is a cistern which caught rainwater from the roof; it connects with a 'cave' which was built as a cistern for the Archaic temple.

To the W of the Temple is the excavation house where it is hoped in due course to open an architectural museum with finds from recent excavations, in particular the (painted) façade of the archaic temple.

Beyond the temple the road descends to **Ayía Marína** (Hotels B, C, D, most closed in winter), a resort on an attractive bay, used by cruise ships to disembark passengers for Aphaia and served in summer by launches from Piraeus. The road is being extended S to join the W coast at Perdhika.

FROM AIYINA TO O'ROS (3 hours). We take the Perdhika road (bus), which leaves the town by the S quay and skirts the shore, and follow it as far as (6km) *Marathon*. Hence a path runs inland to *Pakheiá Rákhi*. From here there is a road (unfinished) to *Anitsaíon*. 1·5km along the road, a track (right) leads to the church of *Taxiárchis*, on the site of substantial Hellenistic remains. These include a great stepped road (visible from the modern road below) which leads to a rectangular *Terrace* supported by stepped polygonal retaining walls. Thence a staircase, 7m wide, gives onto a second area with a hypostyle structure. There are two connected cisterns higher up.

From the chapel an arduous path ascends the N slope of the pyramid to the summit. *Oros* (The Mountain), known also as *Ayios Ilias* and to the ancients as *Panhellenion*, is a conspicuous landmark (531m) from all over the Saronic Gulf. The gathering of clouds on its peak is a sure sign of rain, a phenomenon noted in antiquity. Near the summit was a settlement (13C BC) whose people may have introduced the cult of Zeus Hellanios (the rainbearer) from Thessaly and which came to the violent end suffered by so many Mycenaean sites. It was reoccupied in the Geometric period. The Oros commands a splendid *View; nearly the whole island is visible, rising apparently from the midst of a vast lake encircled by an almost continuous coastline.—The return may be made by descending to *Anitsaion* and following the road through *Pórtes* to *Ayia Marina* on the coast. Below Portes, a track (left) leads to the *Panayia Khrisoleóntissa*, an isolated monastery of 1600 whose church, enlarged in 1806, has a remarkable ikonostasis.

From Marathon the road continues to (9km) *Perdhika* (Hotels B, D), whence a track leads to the S point of the island. Here stands the monastery of *Ayia Triádha*, built by Ay. Nektarios (comp. above). The islet of *Moní*, offshore from Perdhika, is being developed for holiday use with a camp site and Tourist Pavilion. That of *Angístri*, pleasant for bathing, can be reached by excursion launches in 20 minutes from Aegina town (summer only).

B. From Aégina to Póros

Quitting Aégina, the boat heads S to pass through the Vathy Strait. To port (E) the islet of *Moní* (comp. above) has a prominent lighthouse; to starboard (W) the tree-clad *Angístri* hides *Kyra*. We pass beyond Moni and the conspicuous Mt Oros, when the SE coast of Attica becomes visible to the E all the way to Sounion. About 6km S of Aegina is *Petrokáravon*, a dangerous isolated rock, used for target practice. We pass close below the terraced hillsides of MÉTHANA, a peninsula connected by an isthmus less than 300m across with the mainland of the Peloponnese. The name, properly ἡ Μεθάνα, was corrupted as early as Pausanias to Τα Μέθανα.

The interior consists of the bare ridges of *Mt Khelóna* (742m), an extinct volcano.

Strabo gives an imaginative or derivative account of the seismic disturbance that gave birth to the mountain, which Pausanias places in the reign of Antigonus Gonatas. The peninsula, which was by confusion called *Methone* even in early texts of Thucydides (as Strabo mentions), was fortified by the Athenians as early as 425 BC in the Peloponnesian War. The fortifications, traces of which are visible, were strengthened during the Ptolemaic occupation (3C BC).

The little port of (44km) **Méthana** (988 inhab.; Hotels B, C, D, E) has the usual attractions of a watering-place. The warm sulphur springs, used in the cure of rheumatic and allied affections, give name to *Vromolímni* ('stinking shore'), the village on the hillside above. *Nisaki*, a rocky islet connected by a causeway with the waterfront, is charmingly planted with pines and oleanders. Both here and on the Thrioni plateau above Vromolimni are traces of antique wall.

A bus (occasional) follows a coastal road to Galatás, passing close to Troezen.

A pretty walk leads via (40 minutes) *Stenón* on the isthmus to the W slope of the peninsula where, below the village of *Megalokhóri*, are (2½ hours) the remains of the acropolis of ancient *Methána*. The *View from *Kaiméni Khóra* ('the burnt village'; 45 minutes farther) is delightful: across the Bay of Methana the majestic Mt Ortholithi (1114m) and Mt Arachnaion (887m) rise sheer from the water. Above the village is an ancient tower. The tiny chapel of the *Panayia Krasáta*, on the W point of the peninsula, was erected by a wine merchant saved from shipwreck; wine is said to have been used to mix the mortar.

The steamer threads the narrow right-angled strait dividing Poros from Troezenia and in 2½ hours from Piraeus reaches the town and port of (51·5km) *Poros*.

PÓROS, an island about 10km long from E to W, is separated from the mainland by a strait (350m across at its narrowest) crossed by a ferry. The name (πόρος) means both strait and ferry. The island was anciently known as *Kalauria*, and was the headquarters of the Kalaurian League. The interior is occupied by low rocky hills wooded with pines. The scenery and climate are delightful and the island is a favourite summer resort of the Athenians.

History. The *Kalaurian League* was a historically shadowy maritime confederation, formed c 7C BC under the aegis of Poseidon. Its members included Athens, Aegina, Epidauros, Troezen, Hermione, Nauplia, and Prasiai (in Attica), together with Boeotian Orchomenos. Under the Turks Poros was practically independent. Here in 1828 were held the conferences of the British, French, and Russian plenipotentiaries entrusted with the task of settling the basis of the Greek kingdom (*Protocol of Poros*). In 1831 the independent islanders, under the leadership of Hydra, took up an attitude of open hostility to the arbitrary government of Capodistrias and established a 'Constitutional Committee'. The national fleet of Greece, including the frigate *Hellas* (flagship) and the steamship *Karteria*, lay in Poros harbour. Capodistrias gave orders for this to be made ready for sea, but Admiral Miaoulis, acting under the orders of the Hydriot government, seized the fleet and the arsenal. On 13 August 1831, Miaoulis, rather than hand over the fleet to the Russian Admiral Ricord, blew up the flagship *Hellas* and the corvette *Hydra*.

The town of **Poros** (3,605 inhab.; Hotels, B, C) lies on the strait, opposite the village of Galatá on the Peloponnesian coast. The small volcanic peninsula on which it is built was once the island of *Sphaeria*, named after Sphaeros, the charioteer of Pelops. A low isthmus and bridge now joins it to the island. The first naval arsenal of independent Greece was established here in 1830 and survived until 1877, when it was closed in favour of Salamis. The buildings now house the *Boys' Naval Training School* (Κέντρον Εκπαιδεύσεως Ναυτοπαίδων) the Greek Dartmouth. On the shore stands an obelisk to the memory of Frank Abney Hastings, buried in Poros. The boys' training ship, the former cruiser *Averoff*, celebrated for its exploits at Cape Helles in

1912, is the most prominent feature of the bay. The anniversary of the battle (6 December) is marked by parades. There is a small archaeological and historical museum with material from the island and adjacent mainland (chiefly Troizen).

The view across the strait, with its busy small boats, is delightful: Galata (see below) is backed by a long range of green hills. To the left are the *Lemonodhásos*, a picturesque spot where lemon groves grow amidst water-mills. The conspicuous fort above was built by forced labour during the German occupation.

From the quay the short road continues beyond the Naval School (see above), crosses the causeway, and follows the coast to the E, passing (2·5km) several summer seaside hotels.—4km. The *Monastery of Zoödókhos Piyí* is beautifully situated in a verdant glen above the Sirene Hotel (B), where there is a beach and tavernas (bus).—Before the monastery a new road encircling the heights to the E mounts through the pinewoods to the plateau of *Palátia*, where the ruins of the SANCTUARY OF POSEIDON are picturesquely situated in a saddle between the highest hills of the island, c 550m above the sea (*View). The ancient city of *Kalauria* was situated near by, and the sanctuary was the headquarters of the Kalaurian League. Excavations in 1894 by the Swedish archaeologists Wide and Kjellberg showed that the entire precinct was built in the 6C BC on the site of a sanctuary that dates back to Mycenaean times. The scanty remains of the *Temple of Poseidon* show it to have been a Doric peripteral hexastyle (6 by 12 columns), built of bluish limestone. Here Demosthenes, seeking sanctuary in 322 BC, was cornered by Antipater's emissaries and took poison. The inhabitants buried him with honour in the precinct and Pausanias saw his grave. To the SW of the temple four *Stoas* formed a quadrangular precinct.

FROM POROS TO TROEZÉN (AND NAUPLIA). FERRY in 5 minutes to **Galatás** (Hotels B, C, D) on the mainland; thence ROAD (level walking but little shade) and by-road to (9km) *Dhamalá* (Troezén).

Buses twice daily to *Dhamala*, several other services pass (6·5km) *Ayios Yeoryios* on their way to Methana, Lesia, etc., making it possible with a little planning to ride most of the way in both directions. An alternative is to take a small boat to (1 hour) Kelenderis, the ancient mole of Dhamala in the Bay of Vidhi, and to walk thence to Dhamala in 40 minutes.—Daily buses continue beyond Ayios Yeoryios, via (22km) *Driópi*, and (41km) *Trakheiá*, to (60km) *Ligourió* (Rte 29), passing close to the Hieron of Epidauros, and thence to (85km) *Nauplia*.

The road runs W, soon quitting the coast and passing through orange and lemon groves. At 4km a rough mule path (left), though shorter, affords little saving in time or effort. Near the first cottage of (6·5km) *Ayios Yeoryios* a by-road ascends to (9km) *Dhamalá* (Refreshments), a village lying below the N shope of Mt *Aderes* (719m), the ancient *Phorbantion*. It occupies part of the site of **Troezén** (Τροιζήν), the ancient capital of the small and fertile territory of Troezenia. To the S between the deep ravines of Ayios Athanasios (E) and the Yefirion (W) rises an isolated hill (313m; view), on which a Frankish tower marks the site of the acropolis. The principal ancient ruins, however, lie to the W of the village.

Troezén appears early in legend as the birthplace of Theseus. Here also Poseidon caused the horses of Hippolytos, his son, to take fright and drag their master to death. Orestes was purified at Troezén after his matricide. In 480 BC when the Persians occupied Athens, the Troezenians gave hospitality to Athenian refugees. Here was found the famous stele detailing Themistocles' plan of evacuation. The Athenians captured the city in 457–446. In the Peloponnesian War the Troezenians sided with Sparta. Their city was a member of the Kalaurian League. The Franks here established a barony and a bishopric. At *Dhamala*, in March 1827, was held the Third Greek National Assembly, at which Capodistrias, the Corfiot foreign minister of Russia, was elected President of Greece. In May 1827, was published the *Constitution of Troezen*, usually known as the charter of the liberties of Greece, though it was put into immediate abeyance at the time. This was the third of the 'constitutions', the others being those of Epidauros (1821) and of Astros (1823).

The proverbial expression 'a bishop of Damala', signifying one whose cupidity has made him overreach himself, springs from the story commemorated in local song of a medieval bishop surprised by a Barbary corsair and sold into slavery while trying to catch fish bigger than some which had been presented to him.

The scanty but scattered remains, exposed by the French School in 1890 and 1899 and re-examined by the German Institute in 1932, lie near three ruined Byzantine chapels incorporating ancient fragments. They have been variously identified without certainty and are best found with local aid. We come first to the so-called *Theseus Stone*, then (10 minutes) to the remains of the city walls with a fine *Tower*, 13m square and 10m high, having a postern and a staircase. The lower half is ancient, the upper medieval. Hence we may follow a path along the course of an ancient aqueduct to the gorge of Yefiraion, spanned by the picturesque single-arched *Devil's Bridge* (Yéfira tou Diavólou).

Of the other remains the most interesting (15 minutes W of the tower) is an edifice, c 30m square, consisting of a colonnaded court surrounded by rooms and, on the W side, a hall with benches and a channelled floor. This has been identified by Welter as an enkoimeterion and the building may therefore be an *Asklepieion*. Beyond this, the deserted *Palaia Episkopi*, or bishop's palace, is perhaps the site of the *Temple of Aphrodite Kataskopia* ('Peeping Aphrodite'). Pausanias records such a temple built on the spot where the amorous Phaedra used to watch Hippolytos at his manly exercises; their graves were in its precinct.

C.   Hydra (Ídhra)

From Poros the steamer heads SE. The Strait of Poros is guarded at the E end by the tiny island of *Boúrdzi*, where there are conspicuous remains of a medieval fortress. We round *Cape Skilli*, the ancient Skyllaeon, off which lie the rocky Tselevínia. Ahead extends Idhra, separated from the Argolic peninsula by the sea of Ermione (Ermionis Thalassa).

HYDRA or **ÍDHRA** (as it is pronounced), the ancient *Hydrea*, is a long narrow island, with inhospitable shores, largely barren of vegetation and short of water. Everywhere mountainous, it rises to 590m in Mt Klimakion. The island, with the islet of Dhokós, constitutes an eparchy of the nome of Piraios, most of its 2,732 inhabitants are concentrated in its only town. There are no motor vehicles. Since its discovery as a location for film-making, the island has aspired to become a fashionable artists' colony and retreat of intellectuals and has attracted also a less orthodox fringe of idlers.

Hydrea anciently belonged to the inhabitants of Hermione, who sold it to Samian exiles. They gave it in trust to the Troezenians whilst they went on to Crete. During the centuries of Turkish rule, enterprising refugees from Albania and the Peloponnese settled in Hydra to escape the exactions of the Turkish governors. The Hydriots became practically self-governing, paying no taxes but supplying sailors for the Turkish fleet. Their mercantile marine flourished, carrying corn to France through the British blockade of the French Revolutionary wars, and by 1821 the island had a population of 40,000 and a fleet of 150 merchantmen. After a month's vacillation in 1821, they threw themselves heart and soul into the War of Independence, merchant families, notably that of Koundhouriotis, converting their trading vessels at their own expense into men-of-war. Among the many Hydriot naval commanders of the war were Tombazis, Tsamadhos, Voulgaris, and Miaoulis, the commander-in-chief. Among their famous descendants are Admiral Paul Koundhouriotis (1855–1935), hero of the war of 1912, later regent and president of Greece, and Demetrios Voulgaris (1802–77), prime minister in 1855. The islanders, however, never recovered from their patriotic efforts in the War of Independence and the commercial centre moved to Syra. The inhabitants now live by fishing for sponges off the North African coast, and increasingly by tourism.

72km. The town of **Ídhra** (2,563 inhab.; Hotels A, B, C, D; accommodation always difficult; rooms must often be sought in private houses), which is hidden until the last moment from those approaching by sea, rises in an amphitheatre on the slopes of the steep hills that enclose its deep natural harbour. It takes character from the imposing mansions, built in the late 18C for the great Hydriot families by Venetian and Genoese architects. They are unusual in Greek island architecture for their individuality, their size, and their sloping tiled roofs. Many retain their ancient doors of cypress and are gaily colour washed. The *Houses of George Koundhouriotis* and *Lazaros Koundhouriotis*, both with relics of the war of 1821–28, are shown on application, by courtesy of family descendants. A Merchant Navy Training School occupies the *House of Tsamadhos*; adjacent is a small *Museum* of Hydriot archives. *The House of Tombazis* shelters an international hostel for artists run by the Athens School of Fine Arts. The 17C conventual *Church of the Dormition of the Virgin* (Koimísis Theotókou) has a notable screen; the monastic cells are occupied as municipal offices. Narrow lanes succeeded by paths lead upward past *Ayios Ioánnis*, a church with 18C frescoes, to (1 hour) the twin convents of *Ayia Efpraxía* (nuns) and *Profítis Ilías* (monks) just below the summit (595m) dominating the town.

To the E of the town a coast path leads in 40 minutes via the village of *Mandhráki* (Hotel A, closed in winter), with a deserted naval boatyard, to the dying monastery of *Ayia Triádha* (1704). At the E end of the island (2 hours more) is the more flourishing *Monastery of Zourvas* (43 monks).—To the W of the town a mule path follows the N shore to (¾ hour) *Kamíni*, where on Good Friday the epitaphios is borne in procession into the sea. The path continues to (½ hour) *Vlíkhos*. A few poor and stony beaches break the rocky inaccessibility of the coast (bathers will do better to hire a boat). A medieval bridge and some offshore islets provide points of interest on the way to (1½ hours) *Mólo*. At (2½ hours) *Episkopí*, on a plateau, scanty Byzantine remains have been found.

D. From Hydra to Spétsai

From Hydra some boats turn along the N coast of the island and pass directly through the Petassi Strait, which separates it from Dhokos (see below), to Spetsai (96km). Others cross first to (88·5km) **Ermióni** (Hotels B, D, E), c 19km W on the mainland where *Petrothálassa*, *Plépi*, and *Saládhi* on the neighbouring coast have huge holiday hotels. The little town (2,104 inhab.) stands at the base of a spit of land, which separates the two excellent natural anchorages that gave to *Hermione* its ancient importance. At the end of the promontory (good bathing) are some foundations of a *Temple of Poseidon*. A mosaic exposed near the school belonged to a complex of Early Christian buildings dependent upon a *Basilica* of the 6C.

A chasm in the neighbourhood was supposed in ancient times to be a short cut to Hades, avoiding the Styx. The frugal Hermionians accordingly put no passage-money in the mouths of their dead.

Buses connect Ermioni with *Galatás* and with *Kranídhi*.

From Ermioni the steamer passes between the sparsely populated island of *Dhokos* and the promontory of *Mouzaki* which protects Ermioni on the S. To the S of Dhokos lies the island of *Trikeri*. Rounding

Cape Milianos (*Kolyergia*; remains of a temple and a tomb), we drop anchor at Spetsai, capital of the island of the same name.

SPÉTSAI, a small oval island 6·5km long with 3,655 inhab., comes directly under the eparchy of Piraios. The central ridge of the attractive and healthy island rises gently to 291m. Spetsai, the ancient *Pityoussa*, or pine-tree island, was the first of the archipelago to revolt from the Turks in April 1821, and her sailors distinguished themselves in the war by their ferocity. The anniversary of the naval engagement of 8 September 1822, when Spetsiot brigs and fireships repelled a superior Ottoman force, is celebrated by a regatta.

The clean and tastefully built town of **Spetsai** (Hotels A, B, C, D, E) is a fashionable resort, favoured by the Athenians in summer. Transport is provided by carriage or donkey. The DAPIA, or fortified point, just by the jetty, is a historic small square where the main cannon battery was deployed. Cannon still decorate its walls. It now forms the modern *Plateia*, with many cafés. Here the rising of 1821 was planned. The Port Offices on the right occupy the Chancellery of the time. The family mansion of Hadzi-Yiannis Mexis, the first Archon of Spetsai, houses a *Museum* of relics of the war, including a casket containing the bones of Bouboulina, local heroine of the struggle. The house in which she lived is behind the Dapia. The four churches of the town are not without interest. The bishop's seat, once in the church of the *Assumption*, is now in *Ayios Nikolaos*: during the revolution the church was monastic, and Napoleon's brother Paul occupied one of its cells. Outside the town is the *Anarghyrios and Korghialenios School of Spetsai*, founded in 1927; the blue blazers of its pupils, emblazoned A.K.S.S., proclaim the English inspiration of this Greek 'public school'.

To the E of the town the old harbour of *Limáni* is closed by a promontory, on which stands the little chapel of *Panayía Armádhas*, built to commemorate a naval victory over the Turks in 1822. Farther on is the nunnery of *Ayioi Péndes*. The beach of *Ayía Paraskeví*, on the S side of the island, is the scene on 26 July of a panegyric.—*Spetsopoúla*, a small island off the SE coast of Spetsai, belongs to Stavros Niarkhos, the shipowner.

FERRY AND MOTOR BOATS to Kósta and Portokhéli on the Peloponnesian coast, whence buses to Kranidi and Nauplia. In summer boats also to Nauplia; excursions to Monemvasia; tour of the island by boat in 2½ hours.

24 From Athens to Corinth

The ATHENS–CORINTH TOLL HIGHWAY replaces much of the former road following the general course of the railway. The realigned road holds a straighter and more level course avoiding level-crossings (a notorious hazard before); but with the dangers have also gone the charming proximity to the sea. The narrow bends of the Kaki Skala (see below) no longer need to be negotiated. We describe the old road.

ROAD, 81km (50½ miles) 23km **Elevsís**. Fork left beyond the town.—42km **Mégara**.—63km *Ayioi Theódhoroi*.—75km **Corinth Canal**.—81km **Corinth**.

BUSES frequently from 100 Od. Kifissoú.

RAILWAY (S.P.A.P.) 91km (56½ miles). 11 trains daily in c 2 hours.

From Athens to (23km) *Elevsís*, see Rte 16. Beyond the town we bear left from the Thebes road (Rte 41), pass large ammunition factories, and gain the shore. The *Trikérato*, the jagged SE end of the Pateras range (known in ancient times as Kerata, 'Horns') formed the ancient boundary between Attica and Megaris. It ends in a small cape, below which are the Eleusis Shipyards. The road crosses the cape and continues en corniche with fine views across the landlocked bay to Salamis.—29km *Loutrópirgos* (Hotels C, D) is a pleasant resort with villas.—At (31km) *Megálo Pévko* (Hotel C) are the Piraïki-Patraïki textile works.—35km. *Néa Péramos* (4,129 inhab.) founded as a refugee settlement, has artillery and commando schools. The road now crosses the fertile *Plain of Megaris*, planted with vines and olives. We pass the road to the Salamis ferry, signposted 'Perama'.—42km *Mégara* can be by-passed, but its twin hills are seen to the right.

Mégara, chief town of the eparchy of Megaris, with 17,719 inhab., rises on the S slopes of two moderate hills, *Karia* (E, 270m) and *Alkathoos* (W, 287m). These heights, the twin citadels of the ancient city, are connected by a long and narrow main street which runs W from the Plateia (bus station). Of the many buildings described by Pausanias (I, 39–44), only the *Fountain of Theagenes*, in the dip between the hills, survives. It was cleared in 1958; the large reservoir had a roof supported on columns. Numerous traces of Megara's past have been discovered in rescue excavations—including a section of the 4C city wall, with towers, near the Athens–Corinth road—but little is visible. Many ancient blocks are built into chapels and houses, which are still constructed of the white mussel-stone mentioned by Pausanias. There is an archaeological collection in the High School (Yimnásion).

At the crowded fair, held on Easter Tuesday on the open space W of the town, the beauty of the inhabitants and of their gay costumes is more striking than their monotonous traditional dance ('trata': seinenet).

History. Though the Homeric catalogue treats Attica and Megaris as a whole, in the Geometric period *Megara* was independent. Her woollen industry prospered and she planted colonies as far W as Megara Hyblaea (728 BC) and as far E as Selymbria, Chalcedon, and Byzantium, founded according to tradition by Byzas c 685. About 640 BC Theagenes, a popular leader, made himself tyrant. Rivalry with Athens for possession of Salamis led to strife with Kylon, his son-in-law, and the island fell c 570 to Peisistratos. Possibly about the same time Perachora was finally lost to Corinth. The invasion of Megaris by Mardonius marked the W limit of the Persian advance; 3000 Megarians fought at Plataia. In 461, menaced by Corinth, Megara formed a short-lived alliance with the Athenians, who built Long Walls to protect her access to her port, Nisaea. She soon reversed her policy, encroached on sacred Eleusinian land, and murdered an Athenian envoy. Pericles' decree of 432, excluding Megarians from Attic markets and harbours, was one of the prime causes of the Peloponnesian War. During the war the Athenians invaded Megaris twice yearly until in 427 Nikias seized Minoa, then an island connected to the mainland by a causeway, and established a close blockade not a mile from the city. Though the acropolis of Nisaea and the long walls fell in 424, the city itself was never taken. It has never been of much importance since, Pausanias remarking of the Megarians that 'they were the only Greek people whom even the Emperor Hadrian could not make to thrive'. Their fortifications nevertheless survived to be repaired in the 5C AD.—Megara was the birthplace of Theognis (c 570–485), the elegiac poet, and of the sophist Euklides (450–380), a disciple of Socrates, who founded the Megarian School of philosophy.

The well, still in use, 15 minutes N of the town, is doubtless the *Fountain of the Sithnidian Nymphs*.—The chapel of *Ayios Nikólaos*, at the seaward end of Odhos Pakhi, marks the site of the ancient harbour of *Nisaea*. *Palaiókastro*, bearing a Venetian tower to the W, may represent the acropolis of Nisaea; the hill of *Ayios Yeóryios* (chapel), to the E, with ancient walls, is probably *Minoa*, though some authorities have sought to place this farther E beyond the modern harbour of *Pákhi*.

A road crosses the isthmus to (16km) *Alepokhóri* on the Bay of Aigósthena. At 2·5km a turning to the left leads to the monastery of **Ayios Hierótheos** (3·5km after a further left fork), where the church of the *Panayía Kyparissiótissa* (one-aisled) has recently-cleaned frescoes in the dome. At Alepochori there are impressive remains of *Pagai*, a fort held by the Athenians in 459–445 BC. The track hence to Aigósthena (Rte 41) provides a strenuous but rewarding walk.—From Megara a road across Yeraneia to Loutraki was constructed during the German occupation. This follows the line of an ancient road (visible in places) but is itself now derelict. From the saddle between the gulfs there is a magnificent *View.

Beyond Megara the YERANIA MOUNTAINS (Γεράνεια Ορ; 1370m), the forest-clad range which stretches from the Gulf of Alkionídhon to the Saronic Gulf, form a natural barrier between Central Greece and the Peloponnese. The road at first runs high above the sea, affording a *Panorama of the Saronic Gulf. From the *Malouris Petra* (near the 48th km post) Ino leapt into the sea with Melikertes. We descend almost to sea-level by the KAKÍ SKÁLA (Κακή Σκάλα; 'Evil Staircase'), a narrow tortuous pass under the vertical cliffs. Above tower the *Skironidhes Petrai* or Skironian Rocks.

In antiquity the road occupied a ledge high up the cliff. The Megarians attributed its construction to their polemarch, Skiros, one of the first settlers in Salamis. The Athenians told of Skiron, a robber who, after despoiling travellers, kicked them into the sea to be eaten by a turtle; he met a like fate at the hand of Theseus. Hadrian made the road passable for chariots, but the route was as dangerous as ever in the 19C. It could always be blocked in time of emergency. The Peloponnesians obstructed it on receiving news of Thermopylae; a section was blown up in the War of Independence.

We enter a little plain that ranges the sandy coast (good bathing).—63km *Ayioi Theódhoroi* (Hotels A, B, C, D) is noted for its crystallised fruits. The district of *Mulki* occupies the site of *Krommyon* (fl. 8C–3C BC), where Theseus slew the wild sow. Out in the gulf lies *Evraiónisi*, an islet fortified by the Franks.—We now cross the Plain of Sousaki, marred by oil refineries but with good views of the Peloponnesian mountains ahead: prominent in the foreground, the jagged N face of the Onia Mountains and the sugar-loaf of Acrocorinth; in the distance the great cone of Killini. The ISTHMUS OF CORINTH, a low, flat, and barren tract of limestone, less than 100m at its highest point, connects the Peloponnese with the rest of Greece. It is 16km long and barely 6·5km wide at its narrowest point.—73km *Kalamáki*, a little port (ferry to Isthmia; Rte 25C), on the site of ancient *Schoinous*, lies 1km to the left at the entrance to the Corinth Canal. Soon after the turn we join the main highway just beyond the toll point, pass the turning to Loutraki and Perachora (Rte 25F), and cross the *Corinth Canal on a bridge only 33m long but over 60m above the water. The bridge was doubled in 1974 by the addition to the E of a similar structure supplied by a Stockport company. The railway bridge is close on our right.

The ancients used to drag small ships across the Isthmus by the Diolkos (comp. Rte 25D), but the idea of piercing a canal dates at least from the time of Periander, and was periodically revived by Greek and Roman rulers. Caligula had the isthmus surveyed and Nero actually started operations in AD 67, using 6000 Jewish prisoners sent by Vespasian from Judaea. The work was stopped by the insurrection of Vindex in Gaul. Its traces, investigated by the French School (B.C.H., 1884), were obliterated by the building of the modern Canal in 1882–93.

This is nearly 6·5km long, 25m wide, and 8m deep. It is protected at each end by breakwaters, those at the W end 240m long, serving to enclose the port of *Poseidonia*. The central portion of the canal runs in a cutting through the rock, 87m deep. It is quite straight and there are no locks. A current of 1–3 knots necessitates a cautious passage. The canal can accommodate comparatively large vessels, and shortens the distance from Piraeus to Brindisi by c 320 km.— German parachutists captured the bridges over the canal on 26 April 1941, thus severing communications between the retiring British forces.

As we breast a low rise the Bay of Corinth comes into view with the W end of the canal, Loutraki, and the heights of Perachora. We fork right for Corinth and Argos, avoiding the Patras Highway, and enter (81km) **Corinth** (Rte 25). Those bound direct for Ancient Corinth can avoid the modern town by continuing on the Highway for a further 5km and taking a signposted turn before the next toll-point.

III THE PELOPONNESE

The **PELOPONNESE**, or *Pelopónnisos*, forms the S extremity of the Balkan peninsula. Joined to the mainland of Greece by an insignificant isthmus, it was known to the ancients as the Island of Pelops (ή Πελοπόννησος); its medieval name, THE MOREA, was probably derived not from a fanciful resemblance to the leaf of the mulberry-tree (μόρον), which it does not resemble in the least, but from the fact that the mulberry flourished in the country. The modern division into the seven nomes of Argolis (E), Corinthia (NE), Achaea (N), Elis (NW), Messenia (SW), Laconia (SE), and Arcadia (inland, N centre) roughly corresponds to the ancient regional division. The largest towns are Patras and Kalamata. The scenery of the Peloponnese is of the rarest grandeur and beauty, and its archaeological interest is unsurpassed.

The N coast, ending in *Cape Drepanon*, opposite Naupaktos, is separated from the mainland of Greece proper by the long narrow gulf of Corinth, and is comparatively free from indentations. To the S the peninsula sends out the three long tongues of land, separated by the Messenian and Laconian Gulfs, which give it its characteristic shape. These end (from W to E) in *Cape Gallo* (the ancient Akrítas), fringed by the Oenoussae Islands: in *Cape Matapan* (Taínaron), the southernmost point of continental Greece: and in *Cape Maléa*, off which lie the islands of Elaphonisi, Kythera, and Antikythera. A fourth but less obtrusive tongue, fringed with islands and ending in *Cape Skilli* (Skyllaion), stretches SE between the Gulf of Nauplia and the Saronic Gulf. Off the NW coast lie the Ionian islands of Zante and Kephalonia. The greatest length of the peninsula is 212km (from Cape Dhrepanon to Cape Matapan); its greatest width is 216km, but road distances tend to be longer both in miles and hours than this might indicate, owing to the terrain.

An irregular series of mountains, encircling Arcadia, forms the backbone of the country, with articulations almost reaching to the sea in all directions. The highest peaks of this central group are *Zereia* (the ancient Kyllene; 2378m), *Aroania* or Chelmós (2355m), and *Olonos* or Erymanthos (2224m). These form a natural barrier across the peninsula from E to W. To the N of Erymanthos *Mt Voïdià* or Panakhaïkon (1929m) rises above Patras. Two important chains run S from the Arcadian group. The long range of *Taiyetos*, with *Ayios Ilias*, the highest mountain in the Peloponnese (2408m) separates the Messenian Plain from the Laconian Valley and ends in Cape Matapan. The parallel chain of *Parnon* (1940m), continuing the E mountain wall of Arcadia (culminating in *Artemision*, 1772m), closes the Laconian Valley on the E, reaches to Cape Malea, and reappears in the hills of Kythera.

Practically the only low-lying portions are the Isthmus and shores of the Bay of Corinth; the coastal district of Achaia and Elis from Patras to Pirgos, with the vale of Olympia; and the plains or valleys of Messenia, Laconia, and Argos, at the head respectively of the Gulfs of Korone, Laconia, and Nauplia. A feature of Arcadia is the bleak Plain of Tripolis, lying 610m above the sea. The vale of Olympia is watered by the *Alpheios*, the longest and most famous river in the peninsula; the Messenian Plain by the *Pirnatsa* or Pamisos, the most copious stream; the Valley of Laconia by the *Eurotas*; and the Argolic Plain by the seasonal *Panitsa* or Inachos. The *Elean Peneios* flows into the Channel of Zante. The whole of the N coast is seared by small torrents, generally dry but occasionally sweeping the road into the sea. A feature of the plateaux of the interior is the number of *Katavóthrai* (καταβόθραι), swallow-holes into which the rivers disappear underground; they are common in Arcadia. The only natural lakes are *Pheneos* and *Stymphalos*, both shallow almost to the point of being seasonal, but there are hydroelectric reservoirs behind the Peneios and Ladon dams.

Communications in the main are excellent and it is possible to make a tour of the most famous sites with ease and comfort, either by public transport or by organised coach tour. The 4–5 day tours (from Athens) allow the hurried traveller to see more than would be possible in the time except by private car; even those less pressed, who are satisfied to see the popular highlights of archaeological discovery, may favour this means of transport, arranging longer halts with continuation by a later tour. The Argolid is readily accessible by train as also is Olympia (via Patras): the Arkadian route between Corinth and Kalamata is particularly attractive. Intending visitors to the SW may profitably fly direct to Kalamata. The traveller who wishes to gain more than a superficial acquaintance with antiquities will be greatly rewarded by a more leisurely tour, taking in the remoter areas with their characteristic modes of life, where a few hours' hard travelling brings incommensurate rewards.

History. The Peloponnese was inhabited in Early Helladic times (3rd millennium

BC), but neither archaeology nor tradition gives any certain answer its peoples came or what language they may have spoken. From them perhaps come the non-Hellenic place-names ending in ινθος-, -σσος, and -ηνη (e.g. Corinth, Mycenae). They were probably of Asiatic origin. Their implements were of copper and later of bronze; their hand-turned pottery had elongated spouts (the so-called sauce-boat is characteristic) and were painted with brown glaze. Their existence is probably mirrored in the legendary Pelasgoi of Herodotus. Remains of typical sites can be seen at Zygouries and Lerna.

At the beginning of the 2nd millennium opens the period called Middle Helladic. A violent upheaval marks the arrival of new racial groups, of Indo-European stock (perhaps from N of the Black Sea), presumably the first Greek-speaking people, since their culture develops without a break into the Mycenaean civilisation now known to have written records in Greek. They were a warrior race, who brought with them a wheel-made grey monochrome pottery ('Minyan') and developed another ware with matt-painted decoration; the latter may represent an assimilation from the earlier race whose culture they absorbed. Their houses were small, but those of the chiefs had a characteristic horseshoe plan, with a hearth in the centre of the largest room and an open porch; the scheme is the prototype of the later megaron. The race understood fortification and developed sculptural carving. Their dead were buried (originally without or with few offerings) in a squatting position in cist graves. Their traditions survive in the hero legends of Perseus, Herakles, etc. Middle Helladic remains have been excavated at Lerna, Asine, and Mycenae. The contents of Grave Circle B, now in Athens, give a good idea of the art of the end of this period of development (c 1550 BC). Thereafter the mainland becomes influenced by Middle Minoan civilisation, though developing Cretan ideas in an individual way.

A very rapid development marks the Late Helladic period; a widespread civilisation evolves, which Homer knew as Achaean and we call Mycenaean because both archaeology and tradition confirm that it reached its apotheosis at Mycenae. The other main centres of the Peloponnese were at Argos and Pylos. No danger seems to have threatened from abroad, quite the reverse if the references to marauders from Ahhiyawa (found on the Hittite tablets) indeed refer to the activities of the Achaeans in Asia Minor.

A fresh wave of Greek-speaking people from the N, the so-called Dorian Invasion, brought widespread destruction to the Peloponnese. Classical historians attributed this break to the return of the Herakleidai, descendants of an earlier Mycenaean dynasty (which included Herakles) exiled by the Pelopid rulers of Mycenae before the Trojan War. This was a political upheaval of a very violent kind which put back civilisation several centuries, but cultural and racial continuity was evidently not affected for Attica seems not to have been occupied by the Dorians and is neither less nor more Greek than the Peloponnese. Arcadia is fabled never to have been subordinated to either Achaeans or Dorians. The dispossessed Achaeans supposedly resettled in the N in the area which perpetuates their name to the present day.

The recovery of the Peloponnese is associated with the change from the Bronze to the Iron Age, and the slow development of new techniques and more sophisticated arts. ARGOS at first took pride of place, which it held for a long but not very noteworthy history.

The early recorded history of the Peloponnese deals with the rise of SPARTA (comp. Rte 31). From 337 BC when the Synedrion of Corinth confirmed Philip of Macedon as leader of the Greek world, the historical centre of the Peloponnese becomes CORINTH (comp. Rte 25). After the sack of Corinth in 146 BC, the peninsula formed part of the Roman senatorial province of *Achaea*; this was temporarily joined in AD 15—44 to Macedonia.

The Peloponnese was ravaged in AD 267 and 395 by the Goths and by Alaric. Placed by the Constantinian reorganisation in the diocese of Macedonia, the province enjoyed (alone of Eastern provinces) proconsular rule. Ecclesiastically it remained subject to Rome (under the Metropolitan of Thessalonica), sending only one bishop (of Corinth) to Ephesus (431). By 457 the Peloponnese had a number of bishops and Corinth had become a metropolitan see. In 540 the Huns penetrated to the gates and Justinian refortified the Isthmus; the W shores were attacked by Totila's Ostrogoths in 549; but in the Peloponnese the ancient era survived into the 6C. Widespread earthquakes devastated the peninsula in 522 and 551.

Avar and Slav incursions submerged the Peloponnese c 587, bringing two centuries of barbarism. Plague wrought havoc in 746—47. In 805 the MOREA (as it was now called) became a Byzantine 'theme', and under the Orthodox church slowly refined and assimilated the Slav elements, although predominantly Slav pockets survived in the Taiyetos region far into Frankish times and the Mani remained aloof as ever. New menaces soon arose in the Saracen corsairs, beaten off in 881, and the Bulgars, who penetrated the Morea in 924–27 and in 996. In general the 11C was a period of reconstruction and prosperity, during which Venetians merchants began to acquire the trading privileges that they developed throughout the 12C.

A year after the fall of Constantinople in 1204 *William de Champlitte* landed in the western Peloponnese. Assisted by *Geoffrey de Villehardouin*, he conquered the Morea and divided it up into 12 fiefs among various barons of France, Flanders and Burgundy. Geoffrey de Villehardouin, who became in 1210 Prince of Morea (or Prince of Achaea), governed the country with moderation. In 1261 Michael III Palaeologus regained Monemvasia, the Maina, and Mistra, where he installed a Byzantine 'Despot'. The house of Villehardouin lasted till 1301, when Isabella Villehardouin married Philip of Savoy. Philip became Prince of Morea, sharing his sovereignty with the Marshal of St Omer. In 1318 the principality passed to the Angevin House of Naples, which held it insecurely till 1383. The Venetians occupied Methone, Argos, Nauplia, and Navarino; and Nerio Acciaioli established himself in Corinth, Argolis, and Achaea.

The Byzantine Palaeologi gradually won back the Peloponnese by means of matrimonial and other alliances. In 1453 two rival despots, Demetrius Palaeologus at Mistra, and his brother Thomas at Patras, simultaneously appealed to Turkey for help against the Albanians, who were devastating the country. The Turkish general *Turakhan*, after assisting, proceeded to conquer the two brothers. In 1458 Mehmed II ordered the invasion of the Morea under *Omar*, son of Turakhan. In 1460 the conquest was completed. The Venetian coastal settlements were abandoned in 1573. *Francesco Morosini* reconquered the peninsula in 1685–87, and in 1699 it was ceded to Venice by the Treaty of Carlowitz. In 1715 *Ali Pasha* retook it for Ahmed III, and the Treaty of Passarowitz gave it back to Turkey. In 1770 an insurrection led by Orloff was repressed.

In 1821 the War of Independence was begun in the Peloponnese by the action of *Germanos*, Archbishop of Patras. The same year *Peter Mavromichales*, Bey of the Maina, took the field, his example being followed by *Kolokotronis*, a celebrated klepht of the Morea, and by other chieftains. Tripolis fell in October 1821. In 1822 Kolokotronis defeated Dramali in the defile of Dervenaki and took Corinth; in 1823 Nauplia fell. The Greeks suffered a set-back in 1825, when *Ibrahim Pasha* invaded the Morea with an Egyptian army; but some months after the battle of *Navarino* (1827) the French landed in the Gulf of Korone, under Gen. Maison, and Ibrahim fled. The Turks evacuated the country in October 1828, and the French withdrew soon afterwards. In 1831 an insurrection of the Mainotes, who resented sinking their independence even in liberated Greece, was suppressed by Bavarian troops. In the Second World War the evacuation of British troops was effected at Nauplia, Monemvasia, and Kalamata; a notable naval engagement was fought off Cape Matapan; and Kalavryta suffered one of the more atrocious reprisals of the war.

25   Corinth and its Environs

A. Corinth

CORINTH (Κόρινθος; Hotels, B, C, D, E), or *New Corinth*, capital of the nome of Korinthia and seat of a bishop, is a modern town of 22,658 inhab., situated on the Bay of Corinth. 2·5km W of the Corinth Canal. It dates only from the destruction of Old Corinth by earthquake in 1858. The new town was wrecked in its turn in 1928 and rebuilt on antiseismic principles. It seems to turn its back on the sea and offers little to the visitor; sea-bathing is best sought to the W of the town. OLD CORINTH (Hotel A; rooms), or *Arkhaía Kórinthos*, now a mere village, occupies part of the site of the ancient city. Its little square, with a fountain, lies 5·5km to the SW of New Corinth (frequent bus) or may be reached in minutes from the main Patras highway.

The **Ancient City** lay below the N slopes of the mountain of *Acrocorinth* (575m), its almost impregnable citadel. Its commanding position between two seas early made it a centre of commercial intercourse between Europe and Asia: cautious traders preferred the safe portage of the isthmus to the dangerous voyage round the Peloponnese. In addition, the renowned *Isthmian Games*, which were held every other year in the neighbourhood, further increased its importance. In its most flourishing period Corinth is said to have had a population of 300,000; the number of slaves is put by Athenaeus as high as 460,000. Two important harbours belonged to it: *Lechaion*, on the Bay of Corinth, united to the city by means of Long Walls, and *Kenchreai*, on the Saronic Gulf—hence the epithet 'bimaris' Corinthus. In addition, there was the less important port of *Schoinous*.

The ancient inhabitants, whose worship of Aphrodite was characteristic, were notorious, in an age of licence, for their vices. The Greek proverb, latinised by Horace 'Non cuivis homini contingit adire Corinthum', is usually taken to mean that not everyone could afford to go and join in this reckless profligacy. On this uncongenial soil St Paul founded a church during his eighteen months sojourn in the city. Peculiarly apposite, therefore, is his reminder to the Corinthian citizens that 'evil communications corrupt good manners' (I Cor. 15, 33). The First Epistle gives a vivid picture of the internal troubles of the early Church.

Corinth has given its name to an architectural order (the Corinthian capital having been invented according to Vitruvius by Kallimachos in the 4C BC; but see Olympia), and in modern times, to the currant (Κορινθιακή σταφίς), which was first cultivated in the neighbourhood. In England the 'Corinthian' of the early 19C was a sporting gentleman riding his own horse or sailing his own yacht; today the adjective survives as the name of a yacht club.

History. The name *Korinthos* is of pre-Greek origin and the vicinity of Corinth has been occupied with interruptions since the 5th millennium. The longest break seems to have followed a disaster contemporary with the destruction of the House of the Tiles at Lerna (Rte 30; Early Helladic II). The Homeric city of *Ephyra* ('The Lookout'), home of Medea, Sisyphus, and Bellerophon, is probably to be located at Korakou nearer the coast; Mycenaean settlements in Corinthia were subordinate to the Argolid. The site of classical Corinth was refounded by the Dorians. Towards the end of the 8C the historical last king of a semi-mythical line gives place to the oligarchy of the Bacchiadai, under whom Corinth became a mercantile power. Overpopulation may have occasioned the foundation of colonies at Corcyra and Syracuse (c 734), but Corinthian prowess at sea is attested by the tradition that Ameinokles of Corinth built ships for Samos in 704, by the finding of typical Protocorinthian pottery (aryballoi, alabastra, skyphoi) all over the Mediterranean, and by the naval battle of 664 against her revolting colony Corcyra (at which, according to Thucydides, the trireme was introduced into Greek waters). In the mid-7C the Bacchiads were overthrown by Kypselos, who devoted thirty years to the development of trade and industry.

Under his son Periander, one of the Seven Sages, who reigned for 44 years (629–585), the city reached a level of prosperity that it maintained under Psammetichos, his nephew, and the moderate oligarchy of merchants who overthrew him. New colonies were founded on the Ambracian Gulf, Leukas was occupied, and Corcyra reconquered. The Isthmian Games were founded or reorganised. Trade in bronzes and vases expanded to Egypt and Mesopotamia, to the Black Sea and to Spain. The Corinthians are credited with the invention of the pediment and its decoration.

During the Persian War the city served as Greek headquarters and her forces were represented in the major battles. The increasing commerce of Athens robbed Corinth of her foreign markets. She failed to prevent Athens from annexing Megara (457 BC) and for the remainder of the 5C found herself, not always happily, in the Spartan camp. The war in 434 BC between Corinth and Corcyra was a cause of the Peloponnesian War, in which Corinth supported the Syracuafter J. Travlos

with permission of the American School of Classical Studies, Athens.

CORINTH
Central Area

0 —————————————— 75 metres

Exit only

rth Market

Baths of Eurykles

Greek Bath

LECHAION ROAD

North Building

Basilica

Peribolos of Apollo

A

Temple of Apollo

Peirene

Northwest Stoa

Propylaia

Julian Basilica

B

Captives facade

Starting line

Northwest shops

Sacred spring

Greek Grandstand

Agora/Forum

D

Babbius Monument

Central Shops

Southeast Building

J

K

H

Bema

G

Central shops

South Stoa

Greek Terrace

F

KENCHREAI

New excavation

Bouleuterion

South Basilica

sans against the Sicilian expedition. After the death of Lysander she joined Thebes, Athens, and Argos against her former ally, but fared badly in the ensuing Corinthian War (395–387). At Corinth, after 362, Xenophon wrote the 'Hellenica'. In 346 Timophanes seized power only to be killed by his brother Timoleon, who was later to achieve fame as the saviour of Sicily from the Carthaginians.

Corinth shared in the defeat of Chaironeia (338 BC) and received a Macedonian garrison. At the Synedrion of Corinth, the following year, the Greek world ratified the leadership of Philip of Macedon, and after his assassination, of Alexander, in the campaign against Persia. The city flourished under a century of Macedonian rule. To this period belongs the Corinthian painter Euphranor, who practised in Athens c 336 BC. The Cynic philosopher Diogenes (412–323) ended his days in Corinth as tutor to the sons of Xeniades. Aratos expelled the Macedonian garrison in 224 BC and united Corinth to the resuscitated Achaean League. In 146, after the defeat of the League by the Romans, the defences of Corinth were mercilessly razed to the ground by Mummius and his ten legates. It lay desolate until, in 44 BC, Julius Caesar planted on its site a colony of veterans, the *Colonia Laus Julia Corinthiensis*, which soon achieved splendour and importance as the capital of the province of Achaia. The luxury and dissipation of Corinth again became a byword. St Paul spent 18 months in Corinth in the proconsulship of Gallio (c AD 51–52), plying his trade of tentmaker in company with Aquila and Priscilla (Acts, XVIII, 3). Gallio refused to be judge of complaints about Paul, laid before him by the local Jews. Nero's proclamation of Greek independence at Isthmia was rescinded by Vespasian, but Corinth, embellished by Hadrian (with an aqueduct from Lake Stymphalos) and by Herodes Atticus, became the finest city in Greece.

Though it survived the ravages of the Herulians in 267 and of Alaric in 395, Corinth suffered from disastrous earthquakes in 522 and 551, and its decline set in. After a final period of prosperity in the 11C, it was sacked by the Normans in 1147 and the rest of its history is one of successive captures. Its masters included Villehardouin (1212), the Acciaioli (1358), the Palaeologi (1430), the Turks (1458), the Knights of Malta (1612), and the Venetians (1687). In 1715 it was retaken by the Turks: the siege of Corinth is the one described by Byron. The victory of Kolokotronis over Dramali to the S opened the way to Corinth, which fell into Greek hands after a short siege; Dramali himself died here and the remnant of the Turks was evacuated by sea.

The Defeat of Dramali. Engraving

ANCIENT CORINTH lay on a rocky plateau (60m) between its citadel and the sea. Its area was very extensive. The Long Walls started at the top of Acrocorinth, included the city, and ended at the port of Lechaion (see below). The actual length of the city walls does not, however, tally with the measurements of Strabo (viii, 6, 21–22). The principal excavation area lies close to the village cross-roads.

The inspection of the excavations and museum requires at least half a day; with a car it is possible to combine Corinth, Acrocorinth, Lechaion, Isthmia, and the Diolkos in one day's visit, but the unhurried traveller would be well advised to devote two or three days to the region and should on no account omit the visit to Perachora.

The entrance to the archaeological site and museum is from the car park above the Odeion. There is an exit from the Lechaion Road (where this description terminates) which leads into the modern village close to the square. The *Odeion*, *Theatre*, and *Asklepieion* do not lie within the fenced archaeological site and may be visited either before or after. They are closer to the entrance and are therefore here described first.

Across the road from the site entrance is the **Odeion**, a Roman construction cut largely from the rock, resembling in plan that at Pompeii. It held c 3000 spectators. Built towards the end of the 1C AD, it was reconstructed (c 175) by Herodes Atticus; the interior was totally destroyed by fire and after AD 225 was again restored as an arena or beast-pit by cutting away the lowest rows of seats. Even after a further destruction in 375 by earthquake, the building was patched up to serve until Alaric's holocaust. Adjacent to the N is the **Theatre**, with a similar but even longer history. Founded in the 5C BC, it ended by presenting naumachiae. Here the multitude acclaimed Aratos of Sikyon after his nocturnal capture of Acrocorinth (243 BC). The *Cavea* of the Greek period is well preserved because the Romans filled it in with earth to produce a steeper rake before rebuilding the seating; the central portion has been excavated. When it was dug out in 1925–29 wall-paintings of gladiatorial scenes were found on the late-Roman barrier round the arena; they have since perished. An inscription, scratched in the plaster, was also found recording the story of Androcles and the lion. In the *Orchestra* several levels of pavement can be distinguished.

To the E of the stage buildings is a paved square. An inscription on a paving block records that Erastus laid the pavement at his own expense in return for the aedileship. This is probably the Erastus known to St Paul (Romans, xvi, 23).

About 500m N of the theatre are the remains of the **Asklepieion**, which stood at the edge of the bluff just within the city wall (cars may get close by taking the road which runs immediately below the Xenia Hotel). Rock cuttings show that a small prostyle tetrastyle Doric *Temple* of the 4C BC stood in the centre of a colonnaded court. Except on the N side the spaces within the colonnades are too narrow to have been an ambulatory and probably sheltered the dedications of the cured. Many ex-votos are now in the museum. Near the entrance to the precinct is a stone offertory box in which copper coins were found. Behind and below the W wall of the sanctuary lies the health centre itself, arranged round a lower court. Off the E side of its peristyle are three rooms, of which that to the S preserves its stone benches; they were probably dining rooms. Over them was a great hall, which closed the W end of the upper court. The S and W walks of the peristyle are given access to draw-basins of the FOUNTAIN OF LERNA, fed by four large reservoirs which extend S into the rock.—Another copious supply of water, c 180m E, is known as the *Baths of Aphrodite*. Here a

Turkish staircase and some fortifications date from the late 17C (These sites are all individually fenced by barbed wire; however a reasonable view can still be obtained.)

A road leads W between the Odeion and the Theatre to the site of a *Roman Villa* (2km), discovered in 1925 and protected by a shelter (key at the Museum). Some of the mosaics from its five rooms have been removed to the museum. More important are the excavations (15 minutes on foot farther SW) in the KERAMEI-KOS, or *Potters' Quarter*, on the W edge of the plateau. Remains of workshops and storerooms of the 7–4C lie inside the Archaic city wall (? 7C). Through them run the massive foundations of the Classical *Fortifications*. The later wall with remnants of towers and gates may be traced to the gates of Acrocorinth (see below).

We return to the car park and the entrance to the main site. Beyond the ticket office the path leads to the Museum.

En route, we see (left) a cubic mass of rock, in which are hewn the four large reservoirs that formed the *Fountain of Glauke*, a construction similar to the Peirene fountain (see above). Pausanias (II, 3, 6) attributes its name to Glauke, Jason's second wife, who is supposed to have flung herself into it to obtain relief from the poisoned robe sent her as a wedding-present by Medea. Roman alterations, the decay of the roof in medieval times, and the earthquake of 1928 have all but obliterated its porticoed façade and three drawbasins. The reservoir, which was fed by a small conduit from the base of Acro-corinth, had a storage capacity of c 64,000 litres (14,000 gallons).—Adjoining the fountain to the E is a colonnaded precinct, the entrance to which faced the Sikyon road. Within the court stood a somewhat earlier temple (C), perhaps the *Temple of Hera Akra*, though not (needless to say) that on whose altar the citizens of Corinth slew the children of Medea

The **Museum**, endowed in 1931 by Ada Small Moore in memory of her father, a Philhellene of Chicago, was extended in 1950.

In the ENTRANCE COURT: Part of a dolphin from the Fountain of Poseidon.— VESTIBULE. Restored mosaic. Two griffins attacking a horse (c 400 BC, one of the earliest known Greek pebble mosaics); Head of Herodes Atticus.

To the right opens the GREEK GALLERY, arranged to show the rise of Corinth from a small settlement to an important manufacturing city-state. (By the door is a case of finds from the Sanctuary of Demeter and Kore, recently excavated, including a large terracotta figure). Archaic period; Sphinx of limestone (6C BC); inscribed stone from the sacred spring reading in archaic Corinthian letters 'Sanctuary boundary; do not come down. Fine 8 drachmai'; forepart of a horse (? part of a metope from the Temple of Apollo); small altars, Doric capital, etc. from the Potters' quarter.

The cases contain vases of local manufacture showing the progression of style from Protogeometric (case 8), through Geometric (9–11), to Protocorinthian (cases 12–13; 725–625 BC), known throughout the Mediterranean; the aryballos occurs frequently (fine example showing two warriors fighting). Cases 13–15. *Corinthian Pottery (624–550 BC) is at its best in the first 25 years.

Head of a fallen Amazon from a fragmentary terracotta group painted Sphinx; bronze helmet of Corinthian type; Sarcophagus of the 5C BC containing the bones and grave furniture of a youth. Cases 22–24. Black-figured ware (550–450 BC) in imitation of the Attic style which was capturing all the markets compared with vases imported from Attica (kylix signed by Neandros). The black glaze did not adhere firmly to the local Corinthian clay. Case 25. Decorated terracotta altars and relief plaque with gorgon. Cases 26–28. Corinthian and imported Attic red-figured pottery (500–350 BC); Attic and Corinthian black-glaze pottery; Hellenistic vases; pottery from other sites

Cases 29 and 21. Late Classical and Hellenistic terracottas. In centre cases: figurines and moulds; lamps and other items.

Across the vestibule is the ROMAN AND POST-CLASSICAL GALLERY. Statues from the Julian Basilica, representing members of the Gens Julia, including Augustus as Pontifex Maximus (c AD 13); head of Nero. In Case 46, marble statuette of Aphrodite (copy of the cult statue of the Akrokorinthos shrine in the Roman period); also Byzantine and Roman glass. Three mosaics (2C AD) from a villa outside the NW wall. Roman copies of classical heads from the theatre, probably the Sappho of Silanion and the Doryphoros of Polykleitos; also of an Artemis of the 5C, and of a Tyche. Fragment of a large relief of dancing Maenads (neo-Attic, 1C AD). Head of Dionysos (after Praxiteles). Colossal figures from the 'Captives' Façade'. Fragmentary sarcophagus of Hadrian's day with reliefs of the departure of the Seven against Thebes and the death of Opheltes. Roman copy of an athlete (after Myron or Kalamis).

Heads of Antoninus Pius (33), Caracalla (34) as a youth of eighteen, 35. Woman with her hair in braids. *43. Head, a rare example of its period (4C AD). 44–46. Marble statues of emperors or governors (6C AD), the third recut from an earlier work. Sgraffito and incised pottery of the 12C and 'Protomajolica' ware (finds so far paralleled only at Athlit in the Holy Land). Case 52. Byzantine pottery; wooden lute of 10C.

In the CLOISTER. Frieze reliefs from the Theatre (Hadrianic rebuilding), representing the Labours of Herakles and an Amazonomachia; the goddess Roma, on a base with other statues from Temple E Byzantine decorative carvings; inscription reading Συναγώγη Εβραίων (Jewish synagogue; 3C AD or later), and a Head of Coptic type, perhaps of Egyptian sandstone and imported in the 4C or 5C AD. In the NW corner of the courtyard is a base inscribed to Regilla (probably the wife of Herodes Atticus).—The *Asklepieion Room* (opened on request) contains finds from the Asklepieion, the site of which (to the N; comp. below) may be seen from the window. They include typical ex-votos, Early Christian gravestones, and a cache of silver and weapons of the early 19C.

Immediately to the right, as we leave the museum we pass the foundations of *Temple E*, an early Imperial building of imposing proportions, possibly the Capitoleum or the Temple of Octavia. Parts of the entablature are displayed on the platform.

Opposite Temple E the path leads directly to the excavation. Before the gate (left) is a display of architectural fragments including column capital types (Doric, Ionic, Corinthian, from left to right along the back wall).

We descend steps to the site whence it is best first to make for the **Temple of Apollo**, prominent on a knoll to the left, one of the oldest temples in Greece and the most conspicuous monument on the site. The temple, of the Doric order, had a peristyle of 38 columns (6 by 15). Seven adjacent columns remain standing, five on the W front and two more on the S side; the five that form the corner support part of their architrave. Four further columns lie where they fell; foundations remain of four others removed by the Turkish owner in 1830. The shafts are monoliths, c 7m high and 1·8m in diameter at the base, hewn of rough limestone. The lower side of the fallen columns shows the well-preserved Greek stucco and the thicker plaster of a Roman restoration. They have 20 flutes. Their flat archaic capitals are characteristic of the mid-6C BC.

The naos had two unequal chambers separated by a wall, with a distyle portico in antis at either end. Two rows of interior columns supported the roof. The foundations of a statue base have been found in the W chamber, near the partition-wall.

In the SW corner of the Pronaos was found a rectangular strong-box lined with waterproof cement.—The precinct of the temple has been cleared, exposing slight remnants of an earlier temple (7C).

Below to the N, partly obscured by the modern road, lie the remains of the *North Market*, a rectangular peristyle surrounded by shops. Some mosaic pavements survive. The market was rebuilt and used in Byzantine times. At an earlier date a Greek *Bath-house* stood on the site. Extending to the W was the long *North Stoa*; some of its coloured terracotta antefixes are in the museum. The gold necklace and hoard of 51 gold staters of Philip and Alexander the Great found here are at the National Archaeological Museum at Athens.

To the S, there is a good overall view of the so-called **Agora**, more accurately the FORUM, since what we see is a Roman market-place. Its vast extent (c 210m by 90m) was determined by the existence of the South Stoa (comp. below). The Greek and Hellenistic agora is now being sought elsewhere since no earlier buildings of importance have been found below the area between the temple hill and the South Stoa. This seems to have been occupied by a race-course and various cult places. In a radical Roman replanning the former declivity was transformed into two unequal but more or less level terraces, the upper portion being c 4m higher at the centre. The divisions between the two was marked at first by a terrace wall; later, shops were erected in front of this.

The WEST SIDE of the Forum was bounded by a row of shops, fronted by a colonnade (an inscription on the entablature relates to a repair after an earthquake in AD 375), through the middle of which we entered the site; this is now seen to the right. Set forward of the shops were six **Roman Temples** and a monument, all now so ruined as to mean little to the layman.

From excavation and the description of Pausanias these have been identified from S to N as a *Temple of Venus Fortuna* (Pl. F); the *Pantheon* (Pl. G); two *Temples*, erected by Commodus, perhaps to *Hercules* (Pl. H) and to *Poseidon* (Pl. J), the latter replacing the Poseidon fountain seen by Pausanias; the *Babbius Monument*, a rotunda on eight Corinthian columns, of which some members are set up at the side of its square concrete base; the *Temple (?) of Clarian Apollo* (Pl. K); and a *Temple of Hermes* (Pl. D). These identifications have recently been disputed (*Hesperia* 44 (1975) 25–9).

The SOUTH SIDE of the forum (the administrative centre of the Roman province of Achaea) is closed by the **South Stoa**, the largest classical secular building in Greece, dating originally from the 4C BC. It had already been reconstructed before 146 BC. Facing the forum was a double colonnade with 71 Doric columns in front and 34 Ionic columns in the middle. Some columns have been collected and restored to position. The rear of the building was transformed in Imperial times.

In its original form it was divided into a row of 33 shops, each giving on to another room behind. All but two of the front compartments had a well, supplied from the Peirene system. From the number of drinking cups recovered from the wells, it is conjectured that the 'shops' served chiefly as places of refreshment and the wells as refrigerators. A second floor, reached by stairs at either end, probably served as night quarters, and the stoa is believed to have been a huge hostelry built to house delegates to the Panhellenic Union which Philip of Macedon convened at Corinth. The building was restored in Julian times, but in the 1C AD most of the rear half was demolished to make way for administrative buildings; the colonnades remained. The Greek form is best observed at the W end, where at one point Greek walls stand to a height of 2·75m; a section of the roof has been reconstructed from tiles found in the wells.

From the NW corner of the stoa a Roman foundation wall extends at right angles to the building; on it stand archaic columns, taken possibly from the Temple of Apollo, across the top of which a water channel supplied a basin.

The Roman administrative buildings begin near the W end of the stoa where a square hall may be the *Duovirs' Office*; this was later encroached on by a *Bath-house* (well-preserved hypocaust). Towards the centre of the stoa, two shops retained their function in the Roman reconstruction; finds from here included a well-preserved head of Serapis in gilded marble, a base inscribed with the full name of the Roman colony, and the remains of a cash box with coins showing the place to have been destroyed by fire c AD 267, perhaps in a Herulian raid. Next are the BOULEUTERION, or council chamber. Its curved stone benches have been replaced in position. Through the centre of the stoa a paved *Road* led S towards Kenchreai. To the E (under cover) is a beautiful marble fountain. The next section of the stoa was turned into a forecourt, through which, by a marble stairway and porch, access was given to the *South Basilica*. This was similar to the Julian Basilica (comp. below) and, like it, once adorned with Imperial statues. We come to the presumed *Office of the Roman Governor*, with an antechamber, floors of marble veneer, and (in the antechamber) the base of a statue inscribed to a procurator of the Emperor Trajan.—The third hall in from the E end of the stoa was probably the *Office of the Agonothetes*, who directed the Games at Isthmia. Here (beneath a shed) are preserved a mosaic of a victorious athlete standing before the goddess of good fortune (Eutychia), and the restored roof section (comp. above). Two further mosaics of Dionysiac scenes are preserved farther S under another shelter.

In front (c 3m) of the South Stoa we cross the line of a low terrace wall below the level of the Roman pavement. Cuttings suggest that this supported over 100 monuments, all probably carried off to Rome during the century following the sack in 146 BC. Pausanias mentions marble or bronze statues (reproductions perhaps) of Zeus, Athena, Aphrodite, Ephesian Artemis, Apollo, and Hermes, as well as gilded wooden statues of Dionysos with faces painted red. During the period of ruin a cart road passed diagonally across the forum (traces at the E end of the wall).

The Upper Forum was the administrative centre of the Roman province of Achaea. The *South-East Building* (right) had a marble Ionic colonnade. It was rebuilt three times and may have been the Tabularium, or archive respository of the Roman colony. In front stands a prominent *Circular Pedestal* with a truncated shaft.

The EAST END of the Forum is closed by the **Julian Basilica**. The well-preserved remains are of a crypto-porticus which formed the base of a Corinthian basilica of the Augustan period. Four imperial portrait statues were found here.

In front of the basilica the Roman pavement has been removed to expose an earlier Greek one. It is as well to keep in mind this difference in levels as otherwise the relationship of Greek to Roman buildings is hard to understand.

Parallel to the building and partly underlying its projecting entrance porch is the starting-line of a *Race Course*, preserved in its entire length of 18m and having places for sixteen contestants. An earlier starting-line with a different orientation lies beneath it. To the S is a curved retaining wall which may have supported a judges' grandstand. These remains may be connected with the Hellotia, a Corinthian festival mentioned in the 13th Olympian Ode of Pindar.

From the Circular Pedestal, whose function is unknown, a line of buildings extended W, dividing the lower from the upper forum. Its central feature was the **Bema**, a monumental rostra upon which Roman officials appeared before the public. Since later a Christian church was built above its ruins, this may be the place where Gallio, the Roman governor, refused to act upon Jewish accusations against the Apostle Paul. To right and left of the rostra extended rows of *Shops*, replaced in Christian times by a flight of steps running the whole length of the forum. In the centre of the lower forum are the foundations of an *Altar* and of an elevated *Grandstand*.

NORTH SIDE. Almost opposite the bema, towards the centre of the north side, where the Lechaion Road enters the Agora, stood the *Captives' Façade*, an elaborate two-storey structure of Parian marble. The lower storey consisted of Corinthian columns; the upper storey had at least four Atlantes of barbarian captives (portions in the Museum). This constituted the final screen of the Basilica flanking the Lechaion road (comp. below), from which it was separated by an open court.

Adjoining is the *Triglyph Wall*, a low terrace wall decorated with a triglyph frieze, originally painted. It bore tripods and statues, and a surviving base of dark Eleusinian limestone has the signature of Lysippos. Of the two openings for stairways which divide the wall into three sections, one leads down to the *Sacred Spring* (closed by a grating; key with the custodian). The spring, which had two bronze lion's head spouts (5C BC—one now on display in the E room of the Museum), was originally in the open air, but was transformed into an underground chamber when the surrounding ground level was raised. It apparently ran dry and was unknown to the Romans, being covered by a later basin fed by a conduit. On the terrace to the N of the Triglyph Wall, and connected with it by an elaborate tunnel, was a small *Oracular Shrine*. The tunnel, entered by a secret door disguised

Corinth. Restored view of the ancient city in the Roman period

as a metope between the triglyphs, probably housed the 'oracle'—a priest who pronounced through a small hole below the floor of the shrine. The whole of this area was sacred and public access was forbidden; a minatory inscription has been found on its boundary (comp. above, Museum).

To the W stood the colonnade of the 15 *North-West Shops* (3C AD). The large central shop, with its stone vault intact, forms the most conspicuous ruin of the Forum; the concrete vaults of the others have fallen. Behind, the *North-West Stoa*, in poros, over 90m long, earlier formed the N boundary of the Forum. The front had Doric columns and the interior Ionic. The front stylobate is well-preserved and many columns are still in position (3C BC).

Returning past the Captives' Façade, we pass through the PROPYLAIA, the gateway to the Agora (which we use as an exit). Originally a long shallow building, in poros, with a large central arch and two smaller ones on each side, the portal was replaced in the 1C AD by a typical Roman triumphal arch in marble, surmounted in the time of Pausanias by two gilt bronze chariots bearing Helios and his son Phaethon. Little remains beyond the foundations of the later arch and a portion of the façade of the earlier one. From the road the approach to the Propylaia is by a flight of three steps, a landing and a larger staircase.

The **Lechaion Road** led into the city from its N port (comp. below). An impressive monument to Roman town planning, 12m wide, paved and drained in the 1C AD, it remained in use for centuries. Steps at its steepest part seem to have precluded use by wheeled traffic.

To the right, at the foot of the steps which descend from the Propylaia, is the *Fountain of Peirene, the lower one of that name, the upper fountain being on Acrocorinth, a natural spring of immemorial antiquity, which has been so much elaborated and remodelled that it looks like an artificial fountain. The water is stored in four long reservoirs fed by a transverse supply tunnel. The reservoirs are hidden by a fountain-house, having a six-arched façade, 'with chambers made like grottoes, from which the water flows into a basin in the open air' (Paus. II, 3, 3). This basin measures 9m by 6m and is sunk below the level of the court of the fountain.

Peirene 'was a woman who was turned into a spring of water by the tears she shed in bewailing her son Kenchrias, whom Artemis had unwittingly killed' (Paus, II, 3, 2). The fountain-house has undergone several modifications. In front of the reservoirs are three deep draw-basins, immediately behind the six chambers of the arcade. Before the arcade was built, the front wall of the basins formed a parapet over which the water was originally drawn in jars. Then the clear space in front of the draw-basins was divided into the existing six chambers. Later (3C BC) Ionic columns were erected on the old parapet of the draw-basins, which ceased to be accessible. When Corinth was rebuilt by the Romans the old façade was masked by a new two-storey poros façade—the present series of stone arches. Their engaged Doric columns supported an architrave and a second storey of engaged Ionic columns. This arrangement was continued at right angles to the façade and made to enclose a court 15m square. At the same time the open-air fountain was built in the courtyard. Towards the end of the 1C AD the walls of the court were lined with marble. In the 2C AD the court was remodelled (probably by Herodes Atticus) to the form which exists today with massive vaulted apses on three sides. About the same time the arched openings of the façade were narrowed so as to allow of blind arches between each of them, giving 11 arches instead of six. The front walls of the chambers were reinforced and the side walls decorated with paintings of fish swimming in dark blue water (best preserved in Chamber 4). Finally, in early Byzantine times a row of columns was built across the façade, and alterations were made to the court. An iron pipe now taps the fountain for the villagers' use.—Corinth was known in verse and to the Delphic oracle as 'the city of Peirene'. Euripides mentions its 'august waters' ('Medea', 68).

Immediately to the N is the PERIBOLOS OF APOLLO, an open court 32m by 23·5m, surrounded by a marble Ionic colonnade, 5m wide, upon a stylobate of Acrocorinthian limestone. Some columns have been re-erected and parts of the epistyle assembled. The heavy foundations in the centre may have supported the bronze statue of Apollo mentioned by Pausanias. A dyeing works occupied the NE quarter in the 5C BC. Below runs the overflow of Peirene, which served the quarter as a main sewer. On the W side, by the Lechaion road, are the foundations of a small Greek *Temple* (Pl. A) of the 4C BC; this was soon replaced by an open shrine in which a covered statue faced its altar across a pebble pavement.

Off the S side of the Peribolos is an *Apse*, which has been cut into by the E apse of the Peirene court. At an earlier level are scanty remains of a Doric hexastyle *Stoa* and, near the foot of the steps ascending to the Peirene court, some basins from the earliest water system of the Tyrants.

Also on the E side of the road and extending below the village are some remains of a great bath of the Imperial era, perhaps the *Baths of Eurykles* praised by Pausanias as the finest in the city. To the S, is a with permission of the American School of Classical Studies, Athens.

Public Latrine with some seats in situ.

The W side of the road is largely occupied by a terrace on which are the foundations in poros of a *basilica* of the 1C BC, 64m by 23m, possibly a judgement hall. This was later rebuilt in marble on a larger scale and with a façade on the agora (comp. above). The basilica terrace was supported at the E by the rear wall of a colonnade which masks 16 small shops. A flight of steps leads through one of the S shops to the extensive though indistinct remains of a *Greek Market* of the 5C BC, which lies deep underneath the basilica.

We return to the road and ascend to the exit from the site, leaving to the left the remains of a square *Roman market*, with colonnades and shops (later replaced by a semicircular court) which is still partly concealed under the modern road.

To the E of the village are some vestiges of an *Amphitheatre* of the 3C AD, of the *Isthmian Gate*, and of the Early Christian *Basilica of Kranneion*, with a martyrium, that existed in various forms from the 5C to Frankish times. This lay just within the *Kenchreai Gate*, whence sections of city wall can be traced.

To the S of the village, just below the road to Acrocorinth and on its lower slopes, can be seen a **Sanctuary of Demeter**, excavated since 1968 by the American School. The sanctuary dates back to the 7C BC, and among the finds has been a marble head of the 2C from a cult statue of the goddess.

B. Acrocorith

APPROACH. A motor road mounts from the Museum to the gate, where there is a Tourist Pavilion. On foot the visit requires at least 3 hours. From the Museum a track leads due S to a cluster of houses below the *Fountain of Hadji Mustapha*; thence a path winds up to the right round the W face of the mountain to (1 hour) the outer gate.

* **Acrocorinth** (Ακροκόρινθος), the Acropolis of Corinth, the limestone mountain (575m) which rises precipitously to the S of ancient Corinth, is among the strongest natural fortresses in Europe. The citadel was the goal of all who aspired to the domination of the Peloponnese and it changed hands many times. The summit is enclosed by a wall not less than 2·5km in circumference and the only approach is defended by a triple line of fortification. To this construction Byzantines, Franks, Venetians, and Turks contributed; but their walls and towers stand mainly on ancient foundations.

In the Frankish invasion Acrocorinth was besieged by William de Champlitte for 3 years (1205–08); its defender, Leo Sgouros, flung himself to his death in 1208, but the citadel continued to resist Geoffrey de Villehardouin and Otho de la Roche until 1210, when Theodore Angelos fled to Argos with the church treasure of Corinth.

We cross a dry moat, once spanned by a drawbridge, to the first of the three gateways which are connected by ramps. The *Outer Gate* is largely Turkish, while the *Middle Gate* is a Venetian rebuilding of a Frankish structure; vestiges of ancient walls can be seen. The *Inner Gate* is flanked by massive square towers, that to the right little altered since the 4C BC. The gateway incorporates reused Byzantine columns and had a portcullis worked from an upper room. Students of military architecture will not miss the well-preserved *Fortifications* to the N or the Frankish *Inner Keep* to the right above the gates. Visitors pressed for time may prefer to take the path across more gently rising ground amid an overgrown jumble of ruined Turkish houses, Byzantine chapels, and brick-vaulted cisterns, to the S circuit wall of the citadel. Here, near ruined Turkish barracks at the SE corner, is the UPPER PEIRENE SPRING. The subterranean well-house is covered by a vaulted roof of Hellenistic date (protected above by modern concrete). A stairway leads down to a pedimented entrance screen and continues below water level. The water, which is clear and cold (but *not* safe for drinking), is 3·5m–4·5m deep and has never been known to retreat beyond the screen. The higher of the two summits of Acrocorinth, due N of Peirene, bore in turn a *Temple of Aphrodite*, a small basilican church, a watch tower, a cloistered mosque, and a paved Venetian belvedere. The worship of Aphrodite, the Syrian Astarte, was accompanied by religious prostitution, and the temple is said to have been served by a thousand sacred courtesans. Little remains now but the *View, one of the finest in Greece. It was described by Strabo and extends on a clear day from Aegina and the Parthenon in the E almost to Navpaktos in the W, embracing most of the Saronic Gulf and the whole of the Gulf of Corinth.

The N horizon is bounded, from E to W, by Salamis, the hills of Megara, Kithairon, and Yeraneia. The Perachora peninsula is prominent in the foreground, then the distant peaks of Helikon, Parnassos, Ghiona, and the mountains of Aetolia. On the S side of the Gulf, Killini blocks a more distant prospect to the W; farther SW the sharp point of Artemision is conspicuous; to the S Mycenae is hidden amid the ranges of Argolis. The tiny Frankish castle of *Pendeskoúphi* (Mont-Escorée: bare mountain) boldly crowns the nearest precipitous height of Kastraki.

C. Isthmia and Kénchreai

ROAD, diverging (right) from the main road to Athens c halfway between New Corinth and the Canal bridge; coming from Athens the *second* turning (left) after the canal.—7km *Isthmia*.—12km *Kénchreai*.

The *Ancient Road* ran E from the agora to Examilia, where it divided, the left branch making directly for Isthmia while the right branch led to Kénchreai.

From New Corinth we follow the Athens road, join the main highway, then fork right for *Kriás Vrísi*, passing considerable traces of the **Isthmian Wall**, which extends for c 9·5km across the narrowest part of the Isthmus. The fortification which follows a natural line of low cliffs, can be traced for practically its whole length. The best preserved section is that immediately E of the Isthmian Sanctuary (see below), where the wall is 7m high and 2·5m thick. Most of the visible remains date only from the time of Justinian though a wall is recorded by Herodotus.

We pass through the village to the Isthmian Sanctuary which stands (left) on a natural terrace between the village and the Isthmian wall.

The **Sanctuary of Poseidon at Isthmia**, one of the four Panhellenic sanctuaries celebrated in the Odes of Pindar, was famous for its games. Like those of Olympia, Nemea, and Delphi, the games appear originally to have honoured the funeral of a particular hero.

Tradition tells of Melikertes, the Phoenician Melkarth, son of Athamos and Ino. When his mother leapt with him into the sea from the Molurian Rock (Rte 24), the drowned boy was landed on the Isthmus by a dolphin. Corinth was undergoing a famine and an oracle declared that this would stop only when the Corinthians gave the boy fitting burial and honoured him with funeral games. His name was changed to Palaimon and the Isthmian Games instituted in his honour. The oracle later declared that, to prevent the famine returning, the games must be perpetual.

It would appear, disregarding legend, which ascribes their foundation to Poseidon, the Sun, or Sisyphos, and Attic tradition, which gives the honour to Theseus, that the games were instituted about the time of Periander, the date of the first Isthmiad usually being given as 582 BC. They were held in the 2nd and 4th year of each Olympiad. Their organisation was in the hands of Corinth until its destruction in 146 BC, when it passed to Sikyon; the venue of the games may even have been transferred. They reverted to Corinth after the refoundation of the city by Julius Caesar. The Athenians originally had the place of honour while the Eleans were excluded. In 288 BC the Romans were allowed to compete. The athletic contests were second only to those at Olympia, which they resembled.

At the games of 336 BC Alexander the Great was nominated leader of the Greeks against Persia; at the games of 196 BC Flaminius declared the independence of Greece; and here in AD 67 the second proclamation of independence was made by Nero. Scientific excavation of the site was begun in 1952 by the University of Chicago under Oscar Broneer.

By the road, at the top of a rise, stands the MUSEUM, so well supplied with explanatory plans and photographs that it is best visited first. The first section is devoted to Isthmia itself: panathenaic amphorae; athletic equipment including halteres (jumping weights); two perirrhanteria (restored); tiles and paintings from the archaic temple (7 by 19 columns). Beyond are finds from Kenchreai, notably panels in opus sectile (glass mosaic) depicting a harbour town (these were found packed in crates and may have been imported from Egypt; they were damaged in an ancient earthquake); wooden doors; sculptured ivory plaques with male seated figures.

The site entrance, just beyond the museum, leads directly to the square foundation in opus incertum of the Roman *Palaimonion*. The temple had a circular open colonnade of eight columns, which is depicted on local coinage of the Antonine period. It is built over an early underground water-conduit, which tradition evidently took to be the tomb of Palaimon. Alongside, beneath the *South Stoa*, has been laid bare the open end of the *Older Stadium* (perhaps abandoned in 390 BC). The triangular pavement, scored with radiating grooves, is part of a *Starting Gate* for sixteen runners of the kind alluded to by Aristophanes (Knights 1159). A starter, standing in the pit, operated traps (balbides) hinged to wooden posts, by means of cords which ran in the grooves under bronze staples.

On level ground immediately to the N are the remains of the TEMPLE OF POSEIDON, a 5C Doric edifice which had a peristyle of 6 columns by 13. In the words of its excavator, 'the casual visitor will marvel chiefly, perhaps, at the thoroughness of its destruction' (O. Broneer). A 7C BC Archaic temple on the same site, particularly important for its early use of dressed stone, had been totally destroyed by fire. Another mysterious fire in 394 BC damaged the later building (Xen. 'Hell.', IV, v, 4), which was afterwards re-roofed. A colossal statue, unearthed in 1952, formed part of a cult group of Poseidon and Amphitrite.

ISTHMIA

The sanctuary became derelict after the sack of Corinth and traces of a wagon road can be seen passing across its altar. Reorganisation was undertaken by Tiberius. In the 2C AD the *Temenos* was extended and the temple area surrounded by stoas, the cost of which was defrayed by the high priest, P. Licinius Priscus.

The *Theatre* was situated in an artificial hollow, now a ploughed field, midway between the precinct and the Isthmian Wall. Virtually nothing remains of the building originally constructed in the early 4C BC and several times modified. Its roof tiles are stamped with the name of Poseidon or with a dolphin and trident. Here Nero delivered his speech of liberation.

At present visible only from the fence are the remains of a huge Roman *Baths*, in which excavations since 1975 have uncovered the Great Hall with a superb mosaic floor, an elaborate hypocaust, and traces of an earlier pool.

On the opposite side of the road, in an obvious gully to the SE of the Sanctuary is the *Later Stadium*, larger than the first and orientated at roughly right angles to it. It was in use from c 390 until 146 BC. The starting line at the open end was discovered in 1960. On the slope beyond the stadium are traces of a *Cyclopean Wall* of the end of the Mycenaean period. This may have been merely the retaining wall of a road.

A prominent feature of the area is a BYZANTINE FORTRESS, constructed of materials pillaged from the sanctuary by Victorinus, a general of Justinian. This irregular enclosure abutting the Peloponnesian side of the wall was taken by early excavators to be the peribolos of the Sanctuary itself. Its identity was established by a British examination in 1933; and full excavation has been undertaken by the University of California since 1967. The South Gate and two adjacent towers have been cleared, and the junctions of the fortress with the Isthmian Wall investigated.

The road continues past by-roads (left) to the modern hamlet called *Isthmia* (Hotels A, B) at the E end of the canal. This is served by a minor road direct from the canal bridge. Round a headland (5km farther on) lies **Kenchreai**. Here the ancient S port of Corinth, on the Saronic Gulf, started yielding its secrets to underwater searches and the excavator's spade in 1963 (Indiana University and University of Chicago, under Robert Scranton). The S harbour mole can be seen clearly, extending into the sea. It has a system of warehouses (1–5C AD), also partly visible but continuing under the modern road. At the shoreward end of the mole are the remains of a Christian church with some mosaics (covered) and a Sanctuary of Isis (now mostly underwater). From the latter came the remarkable panels in glass *opus sectile* (now in the Isthmia Museum) with Nilotic and architectural panoramas, as well as large full length portraits of Homer, Plato and others. These items were sealed in the sanctuary after an earthquake c AD 375, along with wooden furniture, a pulley block, bone and ivory decoration, etc.

The N mole can be seen a few minutes' walk away at the other side of the harbour. Near it are the remains of a substantial Roman brick building of the 2C AD, possibly the Sanctuary of Aphrodite mentioned by Pausanias. On the hill behind is an extensive Roman necropolis, including a monumental Early Roman mausoleum.

To the N of the road are remains of a number of Roman structures excavated in a rescue operation by the Greek Archaeological Service in 1976. Insubstantial traces of the pre-Roman city can be discerned on the low hills further to the N. St. Paul commends to the Romans (16, 1) one Phoebe of Kenchreai who may have been the bearer of the epistle itself. Remarkable panels in glass opus sectile depicting architectural panoramas have been recovered from the Isis sanctuary and are now in Isthmia museum.

Beyond Kenchreai a fine new road providing a direct approach to Epidauros passes below *Stanotópi*, the E spur of Mt Oneion, with remains of a fort of the 4–3C BC.—At (13km from Corinth) *Loutrón Elénis* (Hotels B, C) a hot sea spring (Helen's Bath), known to Pausanias, is still in use. The road passes through sparsely populated wooded country with views down to the sea. Before *Néa Epídhavros* (32km) is skirted lies the *Moni Taxiarchon Agnoundas*. At 39km the better of two roads to Palaiá Epídhavros branches left.—49km *Ligourió, see Rte 29.*

D. The Diolkos

Near the W end of the Corinth Canal excavations in 1956–62 uncovered a long stretch of the **Diolkos**, the paved slipway across which ships were winched in ancient times from Poseidonia on one gulf to Schoinous on the other.

A well-preserved section (?6C BC), including traces of the dock at the entrance, can be seen (left) by the car ferry linking Corinth with Loutraki.

E. Lechaion

The site lies to the right of the Corinth–Patras road, c 4km W of Corinth beyond the prehistoric (E.H.) hill site of *Korakou* excavated by the American School in 1916. We turn right just beyond the turning (left) for Ancient Corinth.

Lechaion, the ancient N port of Corinth, can be identified by its artificial harbour, which, though silted up, clearly retains its outline. Here in 396 Stilichon disembarked his punitive expedition against the Gothic invaders of the Peloponnese. Excavations between the harbour and the sea since 1956 have uncovered the complete ground plan of a vast *Basilica*, c 186m by 46m, built in the reign of Marcian (450–457) and extended under Justin I some seventy years later. It may have been dedicated to St Leonidas and the Virgins, who were martyred by drowning off Corinth by Decius. The church was ruined in the earthquake of 551, after which the *Baptistery*, to the N of the narthex, served for worship for two or three centuries. Much of the marble pavement survives and some exquisite capitals; fragments of coloured glass have been recovered.

F. Loutraki and Perachora

ROAD, 33km (20½ miles), asphalted to Vouliagméni and practicable for motors to within 400m of the *Heraion*.—BUSES frequently to Loutráki, every two hours from Loutraki to Perakhora village, continuing occasionally in high summer to Vouliagmení. Walkers from Loutraki who are willing to swim a few yards can follow a delightful cliff path (3 hours) direct to the Heraion, keeping seaward of the lake.

From Athens by bus or by train, to Loutraki; occasional weekend excursions to the Heraion by the Periyitiki Leskhe of Athens (see Practical Information).

From Corinth we take the Athens road, cross the Canal, and beyond the bridge turn left to (9·5km) **Loutráki** (Λουτράκι; Hotels A, B, C, D), one of the principal watering-places in Greece, situated at the E end of the Bay of Corinth and sheltered by the towering Yerania Mountains Like its ancient predecessor *Therma*, the town (6,823 inhab.) takes name from the hot springs that issue from the mountainside only a few yards from the sea. Their saline waters (30–31°C.) are used both internally and externally in cases of dyspepsia, arthritis, and liver complaints. The sea-front is attractively laid out with eucalyptus and exotic shrubs.

A long steep climb to the NW rises above (12km) *Village Pallas*, a chalet hotel on the shore, with splendid views over the Bay of Corinth. We pass below a monastery and reach a small plain about 305m above the sea, dominated to the N by a sheer crag.—22·5km *Perakhóra* (Hotel D) is the local village centre (1,425 inhab.). From the little museum (at present closed because of recent earthquake damage), a road leads W through olives, then descends a valley to the Fishing Club (spring) at the NE corner of *Lake Vouliagméni*, the ancient *Eschatiotis*, separated from the sea by a narrow spit through which a channel was cut c 1880. Skirting the N shore of the lake, we come to a group of tavernas, to the right of which, fed by a catch-pit, is a well-preserved *Cistern* (? 4C BC) still in use. Larger cisterns near by, with staircases descending 30m into the ground, are more difficult of access. Ancient **Perachora** occupied the greater part of the narrowing *Peninsula to the W. This was anciently called *Peraion* or Πέρα Χώρα, 'the country beyond the sea' (as seen from Corinth), and commands, as even Acrocorinth does not, the entire Gulf. All round jagged rocks tumble towards the sea, save where a valley descends to the sheltered cove which attracted the mariners of the ancient world. The *View extends to the heights behind Naupaktos, 105km away, where a bend in the straits gives to the gulf the appearance of a huge lake ringed by mountains. Predominant to the N are Helikon and Parnassos; to the S, Killini.

History. Only slight traces of occupation have been found from the Middle Helladic and Mycenaean periods, at which time, according to Plutarch, Perachora belonged to Megara. In the Geometric period, presumably under Argive influence, a Heraion was founded, but the site flourished as a Corinthian town mainly in the Archaic and Classical periods when Corinth, as an independent city state, dared not allow it to fall into other hands. In the Corinthian War of 391–390 BC Agesilaos of Sparta captured the place; Xenophon, who served on the Spartan side, describes the brief campaign (Hell., iv, 5). Save for shepherds, the site has been deserted since Roman times, but its remains have suffered from stone robbers from the opposite coast. Perachora was excavated in 1930–33 by Humfry Payne and the British School.

The road (unpaved) terminates on a plateau (parking space). A high-level path leads thence E to the lighthouse, where polygonal walling suggests the existence of a fortified acropolis.

A lower path leads to the pretty harbour where are the remains of a sanctuary of *Hera Akraia*. The site was excavated by the British School in 1930–33 (the venture charmingly described by Dilys Powell in 'An affair of the heart'): numerous votive offerings were probably the dedications of passing mariners. Only foundations remain: a section of the earliest temple (apsidal, Geometric period), and nearby the narrow rectangular temple which succeeded it in the 6C. There may have been an intermediate building of which nothing has survived. Associated with the temple is a fine triglyph altar, whose decoration is a Doric frieze. To the W of the temples was an enclosed area (so-called 'agora') which had a stoa in the 5C. E of the temples, an L-shaped Doric stoa was constructed in the 4C BC.

The small chapel of Ay. Ioannis, originally overlying the apsidal temple and moved in 1933 is visible to the E up the valley. A path leads by the church to a prominent oval water cistern of Hellenistic date and, immediately to the S of this, the remains of ritual dining-rooms, such as are regularly associated with Greek sanctuaries. The path continues upwards to the temenos of *Hera Limenia*, a walled enclosure within which is a rectangular Temple or Treasury of the mid 8C BC. Here were found numerous votive offerings (many now displayed in Athens). Immediately to the W of the temenos was a sacred pool, now dry, into which offerings were thrown, possibly prior to consultation of the oracle which is said by Strabo to have existed at the site.

About 300m E of the temenos a circular structure, 28m in diameter, has been excavated since 1982. The edifice, belonging to the Classical period, was waterproofed, doorless and has a floor which slopes inward towards the centre—features which suggest that it was a water collection tank. It is almost certainly the monument mentioned by Xenophon (Hellenica, IV, 5. 6) as the place where King Agesilaos of Sparta sat reviewing his war booty in 392 BC.

Bathers from the cove should not venture beyond its mouth (danger of currents and sharks).

26 From Corinth to Mycenae, Argos, and Nauplia

ROAD, 60km (37¾ miles). 18km *Khiliomódhion*.—29km. By-road for **Neméa**.—39km. By-road for **Mycenae**.—48km. **Argos**.—54km **Tiryns**.—60km **Nauplia**. The former level crossings are being replaced by bridges and the road improved. This route is served by the Athens–Nauplia BUSES, and as far as Argos by other Athens–Peloponnese services; from Corinth to Nauplia in 1½ hours, every 90 minutes; frequent local service between Argos and Nauplia.

RAILWAY, S.P.A.P. 5 times daily to *Argos*, 53km (33 miles), in c 1 hour; through trains from Athens. To *Mycenae*, 43km (27 miles) in c 50 minutes.

This route traverses the nome of **Argolis**, the easternmost of the divisions of the Peloponnese. Bordered on the N by Korinthia and on the W by the mountains of Arcadia, it consists of the Argolic plain (see below) and a mountainous peninsula, the fourth and least conspicuous tongue of the Peloponnese, which separates the Gulf of Nauplia (the ancient Argolic Gulf) from the Saronic Gulf. The modern province corresponds roughly to the ancient **Argolid** shorn of the islands off its E coast (Poros, Hydra, and Spetsai), which nowadays fall under the administration of Attica. The modern capital is Nauplia which provides the most comfortable and convenient centre for exploration. The region is of the highest archaeological importance, including within its borders Mycenae, Tiryns, Argos, and Epidauros as well as many other important (though less visited) sites, both Classical and Mycenaean.

From modern Corinth the Argos road runs SW through vineyards. On our right rises Acrocorinth. Both road and railway climb the wooded valley between the *Oneia* hills (563m; left) and *Mt Skiona* (700m).—13km *Athikia Station*; in the village, 4km SE, was found the Apollo of Tenea, an archaic kouros, now in Munich.—At (18km) *Khiliomódhion*

(1,634 inhab.) a bad road branches left to the *Pass of Ayiónori* (8km) with a medieval castle repaired by Morosini. By this road Dramali succeeded in fighting his way out of the plain of Argolis, at the cost of a further 1000 men, two days after his defeat at Dhervenaki (see below). The scanty remains of *Tenea* lie near this road at Klénia 1·5km S of Khiliomódhi.

The inhabitants of Tenea claimed to be Trojans brought captive by the Greeks from Tenedos, Oedipus, who had been exposed as a child by his father, was here brought up by the shepherd Polybos. The town sent out most of the colonists of Syracuse. It sided with Rome in 146 BC and so escaped the destruction of Corinth. A man from Asia, contemplating a move to Corinth, asked the oracle's advice, and received the unexpected reply, 'Blest is Corinth, but Tenea for me'.

The road passes N of (25km) *Ayios Vasílios*. Above the village (1·5km left) are the remains of a medieval castle; and a little to the E, off the road to Klénia (comp. above; signposted), the low hill of *Zygouries*, an Early Helladic settlement excavated in 1921–22 by the American School.—To the NW is seen the truncated top of *Mt Fokas*, the ancient *Apesas* (872m). We now enter the territory of *Kleonai* the ruins of which lie 3km NW.

'Well-built' *Kleonai* (Iliad, II, 570) was 80 furlongs from Corinth on the prehistoric road over the hills to Argos. Its site (well-fortified, as Strabo remarks) occupies an isolated hill overlooking the valley of the Longos. Off a by-road (right) a track, initially signposted, leads in the general direction. Ploughed-out blocks and washed-down sherds cover a wide cultivated area, but interpreting what may be found is a matter for experts.

The road becomes increasingly shut in by hills as it reaches its summit-level (392m) near (30km) *Neméa-Dhervenákia Station*. Before the station a new section of the projected Corinth–Tripolis trunk road diverges, shortly to join the older route to Nemea (comp. below). Immediately after we cross the track, a branch road doubles back (left) to (c 1·5km) a chapel in a grove beside a spring. Above stands a colossal statue of Kolokotronis, victor in the battle of 1822 (comp. below).

At 31km a road diverges (right) to modern *Neméa* (9·5km), formerly *Ayios Yeoryios*, situated at the S end of Trikaranon (727m). Here (2·5km S) is the monastery of Vrákhos (1633). The site of ancient **Nemea** is at *Heráklion*, a village only 4km along this road. It lies on a lonely little plateau (364m), 4km long and 1km wide, watered by the river Nemea (or Koutsommati), which flows into the Gulf of Corinth. The valley of Nemea is celebrated for its red wine. Like Olympia, Nemea was a sacred precinct and not a city, though Strabo speaks of the village of Bembina as being close by. Near here Herakles slew the Nemean lion. In the cypress grove surrounding the Temple of Zeus (now partially replanted in ancient pits) were celebrated biennially the NEMEAN GAMES, one of the four great Panhellenic festivals.

According to one legend of Roman date the Games were instituted by Herakles after he had slain the Nemean lion, but in classical times the foundation myth involved the death of the infant prince Opheltes in whose honour the Argive Adrastus and the Seven Against Thebes held the first games. The festival was managed by the people of Kleonai from the time of their historical foundation in 573 BC until the late 5C when the games appear to have been moved to Argos. Returned to Nemea in c 330 BC, the games remained under Argive control and were removed again to Argos in the 3C probably never to return to Nemea. Excavation has suggested there was no occupation between Mycenaean times and the 8C, and little activity until the 6C.

The French School studied the temple in 1884 and 1912; the site was partly excavated by the American School in 1924–27, and again in 1964. Large-scale excavation commenced in 1974 and continues today.

The STADIUM can be seen to the left of the approach road just after the first sight of the temple is obtained. (Take left fork shortly after beginning descent into valley). Of embanked earth, it occupies a partly natural hollow. The starting line is in situ and a stone water channel surrounds the course. Foundations of a judges' stand and distance markers are visible. The *Entrance Tunnel* (c 320 BC) has graffiti (boys' names) written by admirers.

0 metres 50

N

↑ Naiskos

Altar

Temple of Zeus

River Nemea

Cypress grove

Oikoi

Byzantine Church

Bath

Xenon

Heroon

Road

Houses

Houses

Pathway

to Museum

NEMEA
Sanctuary of Zeus

We continue down the main road to the outskirts of the village, where a lane (right) leads to the archaeological zone. The *Museum* (car park), opened in 1984, has models of the site, finds, architectural elements (in the court) and a display of early travellers' views and accounts of Nemea.

Leaving the museum, we turn right and pass through the site to begin our visit with the central structure.

The TEMPLE OF NEMEAN ZEUS, a Doric peripteral hexastyle (6 columns by 13), was built between 340 and 320 BC of locally quarried stone, on the site of an earlier sanctuary. Its columns are unusually slender; three remain standing, one from the peristyle and two from the pronaos which still support their architrave. The drums of many other columns lie in order as they have fallen as the result of deliberate destruction at various times from the 4C AD to the 13C. The roof had already fallen before Pausanias saw it. Other column drums are now lined around the site, having been studied and inventoried for a possible reconstruction of the temple which has begun on the crepidoma of the N side. The lowest course of the cella is sufficiently well preserved to show that it had a pronaos in antis but no opisthodomos. Within the cella fourteen columns enclosed the central space, while to the W, between the colonnade and the wall, and below the floor level, is an *Adyton*, or secret inner chamber, approached by a flight of crude steps.—Parallel to the façade are the foundations of a long narrow *Altar* of unusual type.

To the SE of the temple stood a row of nine *Oikoi*, or treasuries, seen by their foundations to be about twice the size of those at Olympia and dating to the early 5C.

Parallel and farther to the SW is a *Bath House* of the late 4C, the bathing chamber of which was protected by a shelter in 1925 but still is often waterlogged. Beyond (left), extends a rectangular edifice of the late 4C whose central wall re-used a pedestal (now in the museum) bearing a dedicatory inscription of Aristis, son of Pheidon of Kleonai, who four times won the pankration in the Nemean Games in the mid 6C. The building, which had at least five separate entrances from a roadway to the S, is believed to have been a *Xenon* (or hostel). Overlying its middle section is a large ˙Christian Basilica (6C AD) constructed in great blocks from the temple, and refloored in terracòtta in the 12C. The screen and sanctuary floor are of limestone blocks from a monument of the 4C BC. The apse and narthex can be traced, and on the N side, a baptistry with a large font. The mound which covered these remains had earlier been conjectured to cover the 'Tomb of Opheltes'. The latter has now been identified with an enclosure W of the Bath House. It consists of a large five-sided compound of the early 3C which lies over a curvilinear predecessor of the 6C, and surrounded a series of altars.

S of the Xenon stretches the terracotta aqueduct which carried water to the Bath House are visible, and farther S a line of large houses, perhaps for the priests.

The entrance to the site as a whole lies farther S and is marked by the new museum (opened May 1984; comp. above) which includes also finds from neighbòuring areas.

On the hill of Tsoungiza, immediately W of the Sanctuary of Zeus, a settlement from all periods of the Bronze Age has been identified and is currently being excavated. Deep man-made pits on the slopes of this hill have produced large quantities of Early Neolithic pottery.

FROM NEMEA TO TRIPOLIS. Road, asphalt except for two very short stretches between *Skotini* and *Kandhíla*. The road leaves modern *Nemea* (no signs; ask for road to *Psári*) and crosses the plain of Phliasia (305m), passing (3·5km, right) the site of *Phlious* (commonly Phlioúnda) which is marked by a small chapel (Panhyía Rakhiótissa) on a ridge, round which are scattered the somewhat indeterminate remains, re-examined in 1970 and 1972 by the American School. They include a theatre and a square colonnaded court, between the Chapel and the road. After *Galatás* (11km) the road climbs, with retrospective views, to the pleasant village of *Psári* (25km). Just beyond *Psári* a by-road leads in 7km to *Kiónia* and Lake Stymphalos (Rte 38). The road continues amid mountain scenery, by-passing *Skotini* (46km), then descending to *Kandhíla* (62km) and the plain of Orchomenos. A sign (facing traffic from Tripolis only) points to *Ancient Orchomenos*.

Turning off the road, we take the left of two tracks (narrow, roughly graded) and climb in 2km to the hamlet of *Kalpáki* which lies at the SE foot of the acropolis, on the site of the lower city. The track proceeds through the village, climbs the mountainside (keep right) and becomes a footpath leading to the main site.

Arcadian Orchomenos occupied a strategic position on the midland route between N and S Peloponnese. Homer calls it 'rich in sheep' (πολύμηλος; Iliad II, 605). Herodotus tells us that 120 Orchomenion soldiers fought at Thermopylae and 600 at Plataia. Just before the first battle of Mantinea (418 BC) the Athenians and Argives besieged and took the city.—The scattered remains excavated in

1913 by the Fr. School (boy as guide helpful) include the foundations of two *Temples* (Apollo and Aphrodite, and, higher up, Artemis Mesopolitis), a stoa of the agora, cisterns, and a small *Theatre*, but the site (save for its situation) is not very interesting. The Acropolis (936m) stands 245m above the plain on an almost isolated hill dividing the plain into two halves. On the E a narrow defile connecting the divided plain is commanded from either side by ruined Venetian watch-towers. The *View is extensive. To the SW across the plain towers Mainalon, while farther SE we look into the Plain of Mantinea. The fields, under waving corn, present the appearance of a patchwork quilt whose colours change with the passage of clouds. To the N loom the high peaks round Mt Feneos.

Near Orchomenos is the church of *Áyios Nikólaos 'sta Kámbia'*, with a frescoed crypt of *Ayía Varvára* beneath. Together they reproduce at a small scale the architecture of Osios Loukas, of which this monastery was a dependency. The crypt is of the inscribed-domed cross plan with ten groin-vaulted bays with barrel-vaulted extensions E and W. The frescoes in the crypt are assigned to the 12C.

The Argos road turns S into the *Pass of Dhervenaki* (Δερβενάκια), the ancient 'Pass of the Tretós', between the twin summits of *Mt Tretós*, the 'perforated' mountain (τρητος), so called because it is honeycombed with caves. Road and railway descend the rocky defile. Near by, on 6 August 1822, Kolokotronis caught the army of Dramali, which was retreating from the plain of Argolis. The Turks left 4000 men dead on the field, and though a few cavalry fought their way through to Corinth, Dramali and the remainder retreated to try an alternative route (comp. above). From the S outlet of the pass we look into the plain of Argos.

The view is generally limited by haze. To the left the bare summits of *Márta*, (811m), *Ayios Ilias* (750m), and *Zára* (600m) overshadow the acropolis of Mycenae. On the right Argos sprawls below its mountain citadel while the E Arcadian mountains rise behind, *Artemision* reaching 1772m, and *Ktenia* 1599m. In the centre, beyond the ruins of Tiryns, the battlemented acropolis of Acronauplia rises for a moment above the blue line of the Argolic Gulf.

Near (38·5km) *Fíkhtia* are the remains of two ancient watchtowers. Just beyond (left) are the turning for **Mycenae** (4km; Rte 27) and *Mycenae Station*. The road runs down the middle of the Argolic Plain.

The ARGOLIC PLAIN takes the form of a triangle which extends from a base of c 19km on the Argolic Gulf to an apex at Mt Tretos; to the E and W it is hedged in by barren mountains. The plain is watered by the capricious *Panítsa* (the ancient *Inachos*), the *Xerias* (Charadros), and other seasonal streams, their dryness being anciently attributed to the anger of Poseidon because Inachos allotted the country to Hera. Hence Argos is 'very thirsty' in Homer (πολυ-δίψιον Αργος). Close to the sea, however, the land is marshy, and between the marshes and the upper part of the plain is the fertile tract of land which was famed for the horses bred in its pastures (Αργος ιππόβοτον, Iliad, II, 287; 'aptum equis', Horace, Odes, I, 7, 9).

43·5km *Koutsopódhi* lies amid olive-groves, vineyards, and cotton and tobacco fields. We cross the Panítsa and the wide bed of the Xerias.

48km (30 miles) **ARGOS** (Αργος; Hotels C), the seat of an eparch, is a prosperous but unexciting town of 20,700 inhab. situated in the centre of the Argolic plain just W of the Xerias and 8km from the sea. Local industries include cattle breeding and tobacco growing. The modern town occupies the site of the ancient city, at the foot of its two citadels ('duas arces habent Argi', *Livy*). The ancient importance of Argos is reflected in the fact that in Homer 'Argive', like 'Danaan' and 'Achaean', is a synonym for 'Greek'. Argos is generally ignored by tourists, but if the antiquities are of somewhat specialised interest, the museum is a model of modern display.

History. *Argos*, which traditionally traced its foundation to Pelasgians from another Argos in the north, was occupied from the early Bronze Age. Hither the mythical Danaos fled from his brother Aegyptos. Adrastus of Argos, who led the Seven against Thebes to restore his son-in-law Polyneices to his throne, was the sole survivor of that disastrous expedition. Diomedes, successor of Adrastus and next to Achilles the bravest hero in the Greek army, led the Argive contingent in the Trojan War.

After the Dorian invasions had superseded the power of Mycenae, Argos aspired to the predominant position in the Peloponnese for over four centuries. Her last great king, Pheidon, led an army to the banks of the Alpheios and restored the Olympic Games to Pisa. He was the first to introduce coinage and a new scale of weights and measures into continental Greece. His defeat of the Lacedaemonians at Hysiae (c 668 BC) marked an early round in the long struggle with Sparta for the E seaboard of Laconia. In 550 Sparta defeated Argos and annexed Argive Thryeatis. An attempt to retrieve this loss was crushed c 494 BC at Sepeia, near Tiryns, when Kleomenes I routed an Argive army. The defence of Argos by the poetess Telesilla is probably legendary. The city took no part in the Persian Wars and resented the participation of Mycenae and Tiryns. A renewal of the struggle against Sparta enabled her to destroy her former dependencies in 468 BC. Ten years later we find Argos in alliance with Athens and adopting democratic government. During the Peloponnesian War, in 420, Athens, Argos, Elis, and Mantinea formed a league, but the defeat of the allies in 418 by the Lacedaemonians at the First Battle of Mantinea, and an oligarchic rising in Argos effectively put that city out of the war.

Argos was an ally of Corinth in the Corinthian War (395–386). She helped to defeat the Spartans at the Second Battle of Mantinea (362 BC). Pyrrhus attacked Argos in 272 BC; he was killed in the abortive street-fighting after being felled by a tile thrown by an old woman from a rooftop. In 229 BC Argos temporarily joined the Achaean League, and after 146 BC was included in the Roman province of Achaia.

The city became a bishopric in the 5C and was elevated to the rank of metropolis in 1088. It withstood the Franks for seven years before surrendering in 1212;

thenceforward its history is bound up with that of Nauplia. The Turks ravaged in 1397. In the War of Independence the seizure of the Larissa by Demetric Ypsilantis caused the retreat of Dramali (comp. above). At Argos Ypsilantis 'National Convention' of 1821 met before its removal to Epidauros, and here in 1829 Capodistrias convened the Fourth National Assembly which concentrated power in his hands. The city was sacked by Ibrahim Pasha in 1825 and occupied by the French in 1832 after a fight with armed bands had caused the last bloodshed of the war.

The Argive school of sculpture was famous. Its most renowned member was *Polykleitos* (fl. 452–412). It was commonly held that while Pheidias made the noblest statues of gods, Polykleitos was unsurpassed for his statues of men.

Since the modern town covers much of the area of the ancient city, visible remains are scanty. Systematic explorations outside the town were made in 1902–30 by the Dutch archaeologist, Wilhelm Vollgraff. Since 1952 further excavations have been made on these sites by the French School and new investigations made to the S of the town.

In the PLATEIA stands *Ayios Petros* (1859), the church of St. Peter, patron saint of Argos. Within, the modern woodwork is carved in a traditional style.

To the SW is the **Museum** (FOYER, Mosaic; large Geometric vases, giant burial pithos. GROUND FLOOR GALLERY. Middle Helladic, Mycenaean, and Geometric pottery and bronze objects from tombs. Bronze *Helmet and cuirass of the late Geometric period. Krateutai (fire-dogs) in the shape of triremes (bronze); spits; pottery fragment showing Odysseus and Polyphemos (7C BC); Red-figured vase by Hermonax showing Theseus and the Minotaur; terracotta figures playing blind man's buff; lyre (6C BC; restored) made of the shell of a tortoise and ibex horns.—Upstairs: Roman sculpture including statues from the Baths; mosaic floor.—Descending we come to the LERNA ROOM with important pottery finds of Lerna I–VII, excavated by John Caskey since 1952; they extend in time from Early Neolithic through all phases of Helladic to Mycenaean. Terracotta statuette (c 4500 BC); seal impressions. Early Helladic ceremonial hearth (restored).—On the TERRACE outside are large well-preserved mosaics of the 5C AD (Seasons; Months; Bacchus; Hunting scenes).

Beyond the museum extends the animated open *Market*. Hence Odhos Tsókri, the old *Bazaar*, provides the shortest approach to the *Aspis* (see below).

We take the Tripolis road to (1km; left) the **Agora**. The archaeological site is divided by the main road at the point where it turns S towards Tripolis. To the E of the road is a large excavated area, somewhat unrewarding to the visitor. Nearest the road are the lower courses of a substantial building, probably a *bouleuterion* of the Roman period. Immediately to the S of this building lie the remains of public buildings on the W side of the Roman *agora*. The stylobate of the colonnade (and the brick structures within it) can be traced well to the E. South of the stoa are remains of a *bath complex* with mosaic floors etc. Opposite the N face of the stoa, to the NE of the bouleuterion, is a square structure of the 4C AD of brick within a stone surround, possibly an *exedra*. Immediately beside the corner of this (towards the main road) are two *starting blocks* from a racecourse which must have been laid out in the agora area (comp. Athens, Corinth): its date is uncertain. To the NE again, in a deep trench, are the poros foundations of a building of the 5C BC, which was later rebuilt as a *Roman temple* (base of cult statue visible). Continuing on the same line, we come to the untidy remains of a *nymphaeum*, identified as such by the inscriptions on the surviving architrave block. At the NW corner of the excavated area can be seen the massive *drainage channels* for the area which were roofed with brick vaults in the Roman period. The pre-Roman history of the site is still obscure. Opposite the stoa are the remains of a square *Nymphaeum* of the 2C AD. The 18 temples recorded by Pausanias were probably destroyed by the Goths in 395, for all the excavated buildings were repaired about this period. Many buildings were altered in the Roman period.

To the W of the main road, the entrance path lies above the original approach road (the visible paving is Hellenistic; that of earlier periods recovered below) to the theatre. To the S of the ancient road are the impressive remains of a Roman *bath building* of the 1–2C AD, remodelled after the Gothic incursions. The apse of the W end is preserved to roof height. The layout can best be seen from the hillside to the S of the theatre. The frigidarium was equipped with three plunge-baths and the establishment had three *Calidaria* with marble-faced baths. In the *Crypt* below the apsidal reception hall are three sarcophagi. Many architectural fragments and sections of mosaic floor (much now covered over) testify to the original splendour of the building. Sections of the hypocaust heating system can be seen.

Hewn in the side of the hill above is the **Theatre**, which accommodated c 20,000 spectators and is thus rivalled in size on the Greek mainland only by those at Dodona and Megalopolis. It dates from the end of the 4C BC or a little later, but was twice remodelled in Roman times.

In the S parodos is a small relief of the Dioscuri. The *Orchestra*, 25·5m in diamater, was paved in blue and white marble in the 4C AD when it was turned into a waterproof basin for the staging of naval contests. The late Roman modifications to the stage have been removed to reveal the foundations of the Greek *Skene*, largely destroyed in the 2C during the Imperial reconstruction. The wings of the *Cavea*, which were built on artificial banking, have disappeared, but 81 rows of seats remain in the rock-hewn centre section. Two (later three) diazomata and seven flights of steps, not placed regularly, divided the seating. The surviving seats of honour in the front row include an imperial *Throne* probably of the time of Gratian. In the theatre two national conventions met in the War of Independence (comp. above).

To the S are some remains of the *Aqueduct* that brought water for the naumachiae. Fragments of 4C walling here probably upheld a road leading to the theatre. Farther on a **Roman Odeion** of the 1C AD (later restored) covers vestiges of a second *Theatre* antedating the larger one farther N. Fourteen curved rows remain of the Roman seating. The straight banks of the Greek structure, originally of some 35 rows, probably constituted the meeting-place of the Argive assembly. To the S of the Odeion are remnants of an *Aphrodision* which survived from the Archaic period to c AD 405.—From the modern reservoir above the theatres a toilsome zigzag path (better used for the descent) leads up in 45 minutes to the *Kastro* (see below), a fortress crowning the ancient Larissa.

Skirting the base of the Larissa we approach the *Deíras*, the ridge joining the Larissa to the Aspis; the ancient road from Argos to Mantinea passed through a gate on this ridge. The convent of *Panayía tou Vrákhou* (Virgin of the Rock; left, above) stands on the site of a *Temple of Hera Akraía*. The rounded hill of *Ayios Ilías* which rises to the NE of the ridge is the ancient ASPIS ('Shield'), the original citadel of Argos, which lost its importance when the Larissa was founded. At its SW foot Vollgraff discovered a *Mycenaean Necropolis*, which was more fully explored in 1955–59. Twenty-six chamber tombs and six shaft graves have come to light as well as a Middle Helladic building of the early 2nd millennium. About 140m NW the SANCTUARY OF APOLLO AND ATHENA forms a long rectangle divided into four terraces.

On the W is a *Great Court* with a stone altar, and bases of tripods and statues. Thence a rock-hewn staircase of 10 steps, 27·5m wide, leads to the central terrace, which contained the *Temple of Pythian Apollo* or *Apollo Deiradiotes* (Apollo of the Ridge) and the *Manteion* or oracle, a rectangular building of unbaked bricks on a stone foundation. A large Byzantine church was built on this spot. To the E, on a lower terrace was a *Round Temple* or Tholos, and on an upper terrace was the *Temple of Athena Oxyderkes* (Sharp-eyed Athena), supposedly dedicated by Diomedes 'because once when he was fighting at Ilium the goddess lifted the darkness from his eyes' (comp. 'Iliad', V, 127). Here also was a large cistern.—The *Stadium* lay farther N outside the wall.

The summit of the Aspis (100m) is crowned by the little chapel of *Ay. Ilías*. Here the Argives had a small ACROPOLIS, built over the remains of an Early Bronze Age Settlement (c 2000 BC), discovered by Vollgraff.

The polygonal 6C walls of the Hellenic fortress describe an oval round the chapel. They were everywhere built on the remains of the prehistoric enceinte, except in the NE where they formed a triangular salient with two square towers and four posterns. Within the walls, against the E wall and round the chapel, are two groups of *Pre-Mycenaean Dwellings*, in ashlar bonded with clay. To the S and W a group of Macedonian buildings surrounds an Archaic temple. A conspicuous hexagonal *Tower* marks the junction of the Acropolis and City walls.

From the Deiras a road runs W before climbing steeply to the summit of the **Lárissa** (276m) the principal citadel of Argos. The ancient citadel was formed of two concentric enceintes, an outer wall of Hellenic masonry (5C) having been added to the polygonal work of the 6C which protected the Archaic acropolis. Sections of antique masonry can be traced in the medieval *KASTRO, which was built largely on the old foundations by the Byzantines and Franks and enlarged by the Venetians and Turks. The 5C wall survives on the NW of the outer enceinte, while the polygonal wall is best seen on the NE side of the *Keep*. This fine medieval structure incorporates fragments from a *Temple of Zeus Larisaos* and a *Temple of Athena*, the poros foundations of which were excavated in the court by Vollgraff. Traces of Mycenaean wall and a votive deposit of the 8C BC were also found.

The view embraces the whole Argolid and the Gulf of Nauplia. Far to the E rises Arachnaion. Immediately to the W is *Mt Lykone*, crowned by the remains of a small temple of Artemis Orthia; behind rises Artemision. To the N the flat summit of Mt Fokas is conspicuous.
   The descent may be made by one of two paths, neither distinct and both steep. The more westerly passes close to some vestiges of the *Town Walls*, while that to the E passes a rock-cut relief of a horseman and a snake to reach a rectangular *Terrace* supported by a polygonal wall. At its NE corner is a relief of seated divinities. Vollgraff identified the place with the *Kriterion*, or Judgement Place, where Hypermnestra was condemned by her father Danaos for refusing to kill her husband; at a later date it supported a fountain.

From Argos to the *Heraion*, see Rte 28; to *Lerna* and *Tripolis*, see Rte 30.—BUSES every ½ hour to *Nauplia*; many times daily to *Corinth* and *Athens*, to *Tripolis* and *Kalamata*, etc.; also once or twice daily to *Mycenae*, to *Sparta*, and *Yithion*, etc.

Road and goods line continue across a fertile plain which supplies the markets of Athens with vegetables.—53km. Turning (left) for Khónika, (Argive Heraion), Dhendrá and Mycenae (Rtes 27, 28).—54km **Tiryns**.

The massive walls of the ancient city (Rte 28B) are seen to the left.—
60km (37¾ miles) **Nauplia**, see Rte 28A.

27   Mycenae

Approaches. ROAD. From Corinth or Nauplia to *Fíkthia* (Rte 26) or
from Nauplia via Tiryns and Khónika (Rte 26). From Fikthia a good
by-road mounts to the Lion Gate. Daily COACH TOURS from
Athens (less frequent in winter). Several BUSES per day (not after
early afternoon) from Argos and Nauplia.

RAILWAY to *Mycenae Station*, see Rte 26. Thence, on foot (4km), as
below.

From Fikhthia or the near-by railway station of Mycenae the road leads E to (2km)
Mikínes (formerly Kharváti). 2km further on is the archaeological site, where a
huge car-park just below the Lion Gate allows the hasty visitor to approach with
the minimum of exertion. Since the citadel has been fenced it is more difficult to
appreciate the skilful siting of the fortress and the magnitude of Mycenaean
conception as a whole. However, out of tourist hours, a better sense of the human
scale in comparison with the rugged and difficult terrain can still be obtained by
approaching on foot.
    A by-road (asphalt, but rough in places) leads from Mikínes to Khónika (for the
Argive Heraion) and Tiryns (Rte 28C).

MYCENAE (Μυκηναι), in modern pronunciation *Mikínai*, a city
known to archaeology as the centre of the great Helladic civilisation
and to tradition as the capital of Agamemnon, lies 15km from the sea,
half-hidden in a mountain glen or recess (μυχὸς), between *Mt Ayios
Ilías* (750m) on the N and *Mt Zára* (600m) on the S. Its position commands the landfall in the Gulf of Nauplia and controls the natural
roads N through the mountains to Corinth and the Isthmus. The city,
which Homer calls 'rich in gold' (πολύχρυσος) and 'well-built'
(ἐϋκτίμενον πτολίεθρον) and 'broad-streeted' was proverbial in classical times for its wealth. At its zenith Mycenae consisted of a fortified
administrative centre with inhabited settlements outside the walls.
The Acropolis, the residence of its kings (who enclosed within its walls
the tombs of some of their predecessors), stands on an almost isolated
hill skirted by two deep ravines which fork from the mouth of the glen,
the *Kokoretsa* running W and the *Khávos* SW. From the NW corner of
the Acropolis a long narrow ridge runs S parallel to the Khávos. In the
slopes of this ridge are the tholos or beehive tombs which Pausanias
mistook for treasuries, and, in part overlaying these, the less important
ruins of Hellenic buildings from the 3C BC.

Excavations. The earliest systematic excavations, which uncovered the first

enceinte - temenos
or enclosed area - not religious

circle of shaft graves, were initiated in 1874–76 by Heinrich Schliemann, who was succeeded by Stamatakis. In 1886–1902 digging was continued by the Greek Archaeological Society under Tsountas. Extensive excavations in 1920–23 by the British School at Athens under Prof. Alan Wace showed that some of the interim conclusions reached by Evans and Myres about the chronology of Mycenae were ill-founded. Wace resumed excavations in 1950–55; in 1951 work of restoration and preservation was begun on behalf of the Greek government. Since 1952, when Grave Circle B was excavated, the Greek Archaeological Society has been actively engaged at Mycenae, with extensive investigations undertaken by Prof. G.E. Mylonas. Lord Wm. Taylour directed British excavations after Wace's death, first in collaboration with J. Papadhimitriou, then under the general direction of Mylonas.

History. Archaeological evidence shows that the site was first occupied by man in the 6th millennium BC and preserved an unremarkable Neolithic and Early Helladic culture to c 2000 BC. In Middle Helladic times only the summit of the hill, an area slightly larger than that now occupied by the ruins of the palace, was fortified. Scattered settlements existed on the lower slopes, and a large cemetery consisting of groups of cist tombs extended to the W in the nearest rock soft enough to be dug. In the middle of this area, in the period called Late Helladic I (c 1600 BC), six large shaft graves were dug for a ruling family; a further 14 shaft graves, forming another group farther from the citadel, are slightly earlier.

The earliest of the tholos tombs seems to date from the following century, and this type of interment continues to 1300 BC, showing a progressive structural development culminating in architecture of a high order. Nine such tombs have been discovered at Mycenae; they are of persons of a royal or ruling class and bear the same relationship to the contemporary chamber tombs as the shaft graves do to the cist tombs. Soon after 1350 BC a Cyclopean enceinte was constructed, and the Palace and most of the buildings within replanned on a more lavish scale. This first circuit was extended c 1250 BC to include Grave Circle A within the fortification and, at the same time, the Lion Gate replaced an earlier and differently aligned entrance system. The walls of this new 'West enceinte' cut through the original cemetery of the area. This, the period of greatest prosperity, was interrupted by a violent earthquake, which was followed by only partial rebuilding. Fifty years later (c 1200 BC) the site was devastated by fire: at about the same time the final element of the fortification system was built—the North-east extension, which protected the site's water supply. At or after the end of the 12C a further fire destruction occurred, after which the citadel was abandoned until the early Iron Age, though the walls remained virtually intact. Then a small township developed which sent contingents to fight at Thermopylae and Plataea; this fell to the jealousy of Argos in 468 BC and the site was again left waste. Later the walls were repaired and a Hellenistic town spread over the W ridge. The importance of Mycenae, however, begins c 1650 BC and ceases c 1100–1050 BC with the fall of the civilisation to which it gives name.

Mycenaean Civilisation. Towards the end of the Middle Helladic period a sudden stimulus apparently influences the previously unremarkable mainland culture. There appears at Mycenae (already a dominant centre) evidence in the shaft-graves of a sophisticated and dynamic aristocracy with very considerable wealth. The technique and artistry is highly accomplished. A generation earlier Helladic dead were much less lavishly provided. The theory that Minoan conquerors or colonists were responsible is untenable, the form of burial, the use of gold, and the warlike accoutrements alike being foreign to Minoan custom. Helladic building styles continue unchanged by Cretan influence. A later theory that the riches of these graves were loot from Minoan Crete brought back when Helladic warriors destroyed the Old Palaces must be discarded, since wider exploration has shown that the Cretan sites were more likely ruined in some natural calamity. There is no evidence of gold on this scale in Crete whereas contemporary documents in Egypt record that there it was 'like dust beneath the feet'. The Egyptian pharaohs of the XVIII dynasty paid their commanders in gold. At the time of the shaft-graves (c 1600 BC onwards) the Egyptians were seeking aid from overseas in their struggle against the Hyksos. It is possible that the heavily-armed Achaean warriors fought as mercenaries on the Nile, when they brought back to Mycenae the Egyptian belief in life after death, the fashion for golden death-masks, and provision of elaborate grave-goods (comp. the representations of cheetah, and the ostrich eggs, among the finds). Legend attributes an Egyptian origin to the hero Danaos.

Petsas' house
House of the Wine Merchant
Kato Phournos tomb
Grave circle B
Lion tomb
Citadel
House of shields
West House
House of Oil Merchant
House of Sphinxes
Tomb of the Genii
Cyclopean tomb
Epano Phournos tomb
Mycenaean Houses
Panayia
Tomb
Treasury of Atreus
Epano Pegadi
House of lead
Kato Pegadi
Ayios Yeoryios
Tourist Hotel
Agamemnoneion
Causeway
MYCENAE VILLAGE

1 Tomb of Aegisthus
2 Tomb of Klytemnestra
3 Hellenistic terrace walls
4 Hellenistic lower town walls
5 Hellenistic theatre
6 Perseia Fountain House
7 Prehistoric Cemetery

MYCENAE

0   200 metres

Nevertheless, in Late Helladic I (early 16C BC), Mycenaean culture does assume in addition many Minoan characteristics in its pottery, jewellery, representation of bulls, and the symbols of the double-axe, the sacred pillar and horns of consecration, associated with a cult of the Mother Goddess. Relations led to dynastic marriages; this would account for the presence in female tombs on the mainland of engraved gold seal-rings of a type exactly paralleled in Crete. For whatever reason, Mycenaean craftsmen learned from Minoan masters new techniques.

The following period (L.H. II; 15C BC) sees the expansion of Mycenaean civilisation all over mainland Greece, with considerable trade farther afield. It is uncertain whether or not Knossos itself fell c 1375 either to mainland aggression or dynastic inheritance (comp. Rte 78A). The graves of this period have mostly been plundered and the architecture obscured by later rebuilding so that less of it is known than of the periods before and after. It is characterised by the earlier tholos tombs and represented artistically by the splendid contents of three such tombs found intact at Vaphio, Midea, and Pylos. The presence of amethyst and amber beads proves that trading relations already existed with Egypt and the Baltic. The vases are better made, their drawing magnificent. The large 'palace-style' vases as well as the beehive tombs typify the insolent exuberance of the age.

The full tide of Mycenaean influence (L.H. III) is reached in the 14C. The glory of the latest era was its architecture, so that its remains are more substantial. Houses have basements for storage and several rooms. Royal dwellings, with more than one storey and frescoed walls, have become palaces indeed. Accounts are kept in writing, though so far no evidence has come to light of literary composition. The cities are linked by roads and chariots are used.

The ruler of Mycenae seems to have been the overlord of a loose federation of vast extent. Immediately subordinate strongholds in the Argolid included Tiryns, Midea and Asine. The whole of the Peloponnese was under the dominion of Mycenae. Her cultural influence extended to Attica, Aegina, Boeotia, Euboea, Thessaly, the Ionian Islands (except perhaps Corcyra), Aetolia, Phokis, and the islands of the Aegean. Even Crete which had largely inspired the civilisation of Mycenae was now subordinated to the younger nation. The principal gates of mainland citadels, which previously faced the hinterland, are rebuilt to face the coast as Mycenaean interests of trade or conquest reach out to the confines of the Mediterranean. There was a vigorous export and import trade with Cyprus and the Levant and on to Egypt. The S Sporades appear to have had settlers. Mycenaean objects have been found in Macedonia, in the Troad, and on the W coast of Anatolia. Ugarit on the Syrian coast had a Mycenaean trading post.

The almost total eclipse of Mycenaean civilisation over the whole area has not yet been adequately explained (comp. V.R. d'A. Desborough, 'The Greek Dark Ages', 1972). A surge of defensive building in the later 13C, in particular the ensuring of a secret water-supply at Mycenae, Tiryns, and Athens, suggests an external threat. Many important Mycenaean sites suffered destruction towards the end of the 13C. The majority of smaller settlements are abandoned at this time, except in Achaea, the Ionian Islands, the E. Aegean, and Cyprus, where they increase (presumably reflecting an influx of refugees). Before 1100 BC there had been a second wave of disasters throughout the region which effectively ended a whole way of life. The 'Dorian Invasions' of Classical historians, internal risings, famine, pestilence, change of climate, seismic disaster, have all been suggested as the reason, none of them by itself accounting for all the conflicting archaeological evidence. What is indisputable is that the continuity of civic life was disrupted and material progress set back for four centuries.

Homer, Mycenae, and the Trojan War. The visitor to Mycenae can hardly avoid the attempt to fit the Homeric stories into the archaeological setting. The historical trustworthiness of Homer was first questioned by Herodotus and the consistency of the texts by Zoilus of Amphipolis. Quite apart from questions of authorship, date of composition, or unity of the transmitted text, 'there remain many anachronisms in language and in social customs and inconsistencies in the narrative of the poems (whether internal, as between the "Catalogue of Ships" and the rest of the *Iliad*, or external, as between the *Iliad* and the *Odyssey*, or between Homeric and actual geography, as in the description of Ithaca), which have to be accounted for' (A Companion to Homer). Recent finds in Mycenaean archaeology, however, have proved the persistence of Mycenaean traditions in Homer in matters of armament, social and burial customs, and religion, of which evidence had wholly vanished by Classical times. The deciphering of Linear B tablets found on Mycenaean sites has thrown new light on some of the problems. Finds at Troy show that the site was destroyed twice during the period of

Mycenaean hegemony in the Aegean but there is still no conclusive proof that the Mycenaeans were responsible.

A copy exists of a letter from a Hittite ruler to the king of Ahhiyawa (? Achaea) about events in Lycia; the Homeric letter from the king of Argos to the king of Lycia (*Iliad*, VI, 168–69) may be part of the same correspondence. Myrtilos, the charioteer of Oinomaos, bears a name suggesting that he was a Hittite expert from whom the Greeks learned the art of the chariot. The Attarssyas with a hundred chariots who harried the Hittites in the 13C were perhaps a member of the house of Atreus. Hittite documents record Mycenaean activity in Asia Minor amounting to a large-scale expedition. Whether or not this is to be connected with any of the archaeological evidence for destructions at Troy, it implies a fleet and a single leader. The Catalogue of Ships in *Iliad* II reproduces the basic form of Mycenaean lists found in Linear B tablets, and is taken by some scholars to be a quoted document from the Bronze Age. Aulis, where the ships assembled, has a Mycenaean cemetery. It seems, therefore, that a historical 13C Mycenaean king who led a large expedition to Asia Minor, contributed largely to Homer's Agamemnon.

It is probable, however, that the story of the siege of a maritime town, defended by people whose background is known, belongs to Mycenaean tradition as early as the 16C BC (comp. the siege rhyton, Athens Mus.). This is confirmed by the discovery on tablets found at Pylos, Knossos and Mycenae, of many names that are given in the 'Iliad' to Trojan warriors. This traditional story was elaborated for generations in the different Mycenaean kingdoms, gathering later exploits, with changes of locale and dramatis personae, and sometimes of fashion and armament; it could have then been given a new eastern setting when Troy was attacked by an expedition led by a king of Mycenae.

Chronological problems are also raised by the *Odyssey*, the action of which is set after the Trojan War. The correspondence between objects (e.g. Nestor's cup; 'the wrought mixing bowl of solid silver doubled with gold about the rim' given by Menelaus to Telemachus; etc.) described by Homer and those discovered in Mycenaean excavations is often exact, though the Homeric object may be more typical of a period before the Trojan War or placed in juxtaposition with an anachronistic object. However, the ascribed provenance of Achaean riches accords with archaeological probability, as when Menelaus mentions his adventures in Egypt and claims to have 'seen Ethiopians in their native haunts'; Polybus of Egyptian Thebes had given him ten talents in gold. It seems that events from several periods of Mycenaean adventure may be telescoped in the *Odyssey* into one ancestral epic; the Egyptian expedition, the Trojan War, and the voyages of colonists to the W Mediterranean. The series of treacheries, improper marriages, and acts of revenge that characterise the Homeric dynasty of Mycenae, and supplied the basis for the embroideries of Classical drama, may actually have happened in the 16C BC (comp. below).

From Mikínes the motor-road up to (2km) the Acropolis of Mycenae runs below an older track which follows some remains of a Turkish aqueduct and overlooks the ravine of the Khávos, or Chaos. The prehistoric road from Mycenae to Prosymna traversed this ravine by a *Bridge* and causeway, the ruins of which may still be seen. The ancient road lies below and to the E of the modern just below the chapel of *Ayios Yeoryios*, in the cemetery of which is buried Humfry Payne (1902–36), excavator of Perachora.

To the left is the tourist-pavilion, whence the old track follows the ridge back to the village, passing the *Kato Pigádhi*, the ancient lower well of the city, 'modernised' in 1940 and still in use. An upper well, *Epáno Pigádi*, lies 500m farther N between the late-Helladic cemetery of Kalkani and the Panayia Tomb.

The modern road continues to skirt the Atreus Ridge, cutting through a large chamber tomb. Farther on a massive wall of undressed stone supports a wide paved terrace built of packed boulders fronting the so-called *Treasury of Atreus, or *Tomb of Agamemnon*. An architectural masterpiece, as well as being the largest and best-preserved of the tholos tombs, this is also one of the latest, being dated from the fineness of its construction to c 1350 BC. The connection with Atreus (the father of Agamemnon) is speculative.

Mycenae. Isometric view of the Treasury of Atreus

The THOLOS or BEEHIVE TOMBS, which have given their name to the later dynasty that flourished at Mycenae, are characteristic of the period known as Late Helladic II to IIIA at Mycenae but are found over a longer period elsewhere. Over 100 have been found in widely separated parts of Greece. They are usually composed of two parts, the *Dromos*, or approach, an unroofed passage cut horizontally into the hill, and the *Tholos*, which formed the actual tomb. This was of masonry, built into a circular excavation in the hill, and rising in a cone like a beehive to about the same height as the diameter of the floor. The top of the cone projected above the slope of the hillside and was covered with earth. Occasionally, as in the 'Treasury of Atreus', an additional chamber, rectangular in shape, opened from the tholos; the exact function of this is not certain.

At Mycenae nine such tombs have been discovered, all outside the fortifications. Unlike the shaft-graves on the acropolis they had all been plundered, with the result that less is known about their contents. Architecturally the tholos tombs at Mycenae fall into three groups, showing a progressive structural development, marked in particular by the increased use of dressed stone and the placing of a relieving triangle above the lintel. They may be dated between c 1520 and 1300 BC and the Treasury of Atreus is the finest example of the third group.

By the time of Pausanias the original purpose of these structures had been forgotten and they were taken for underground treasuries. The discovery of six skeletons in the tomb at Menidhi placed the question of their purpose beyond all doubt.

The tomb is built into the E slope of the ridge. From the artificial *Terrace* (see above), we pass through vestiges of the *Enclosing Wall* that barred the entrance. The *Dromos* is 35m long and 6m wide; its walls, which naturally rise as we penetrate the hillside, are built of great squared blocks of breccia laid in horizontal courses and water-proofed behind with a lining of clay. At the end of the approach is a *Doorway* nearly 5·5m high tapering slightly towards the top. The lintel is formed of two large slabs of stone, of which the inner one is 8m long, 5m wide, and 1m thick, with an estimated weight of 120,000kg. Above, the stone courses are built up obliquely to form a triangle thus lightening the weight borne by the lintel. On either side of the door-way, on a square stepped base (still in position), stood an engaged half-column of dark green limestone. Parts of the shafts and of the carved capitals have been found; a few of these are in Athens Museum, but the greater part is in the British Museum. Above, smaller columns flanked the facing of ornamental coloured bands that masked the 'relieving triangle'; some rosso antico fragments of this façade are also in London. They derive probably from quarries at Kyprianon near Cape Matapan (see B.S.A. 1968). The entrance passage is 5m deep; in the middle a stone threshold shows the pivot holes on which the double doors were swung. The bronze nails that held the door-frame and fixed the wood or bronze covering of the threshold are still in place.

The *Tholos* is a circular domed chamber, 13m high and 14·5m in diameter, formed by well-fitting blocks of breccia in 33 concentric courses, joined without mortar and gradually diminishing in height. The blocks vary from 1·25m–2·15m in length. Each course overlaps the one immediately below it (corbelling), the topmost course being closed by a single block which, unlike the keystone of an arch, could be removed without endangering the stability of the structure. The overlaps have been cut away, so that the interior presents a smooth unbroken surface curved both horizontally and vertically. The floor is of the natural rock. From the third course upwards are rows of holes in regular order, some of them with their original bronze nails; these were bored to receive <u>bronze rosettes</u> as at Orchomenos. The outside of the dome was wedged with smaller stones.

A much smaller doorway, 2·8m high and 1·3m wide, similarly surmounted by a triangular opening, leads from the N side of the beehive chamber into a *Rock-Hewn Chamber*, 8·25m square and 5·8m high. The walls may have been lined and decorated with sculptured slabs as at Orchomenos. In the centre is a circular depression.

On the thyme-covered ridge to the W (view) are remains of a settlement of late-Helladic date. The walls are known since the excavations of 1955 to be terrace walls of outlying villas ('House of Lead', 'Lisa's House', etc.), not fortifications; earlier theories of a fortified prehistoric 'lower town' have been abandoned. Just below the conspicuous *Panayia Chapel* is the *Panayia Tomb*, another tholos chamber (of the second group), discovered by Tsountas in 1887; it lacks its upper part. A hundred metres farther N is a tholos of the first group, known as the *Epano Phournos Tomb*.

To the N of the *Treasury of Atreus* are the remains of houses belonging to the Mycenaean settlement outside the citadel.

We round a corner beyond the Treasury of Atreus and traverse an area of confused Hellenistic ruins surrounded by a wall, the course of which can still be traced. Farther on (right) are the excavated foundations of several **Houses**, probably the residences of wealthy merchants of the 13C BC; all were destroyed by fire. The names given them by the British excavators derive from the objects discovered in them. They are built of rubble packed with clay, which supported a timber frame filled in with brick.

In the *House of Sphinxes* were found ivory plaques depicting sphinxes and nine Linear B tablets which had fallen from an upper room. The *House of the Oil Merchant*, adjoining to the N, contained (N room) eleven large pithoi and an installation for warming them. Thirty-eight written tablets came to light amid the burnt ruins. Across a narrow lane, the *House of Shields* yielded carved ivories, many in the shape of the figure-of-eight shield.—The *West House*, which adjoins the House of the Oil Merchant, has been excavated by N. Verdelis.

At the N end of the ridge the road turns E towards the citadel. On the left is the level *Car Park*; in the angle of the road (right) lies **Grave Circle B**, discovered by accident in 1951 and excavated in 1952–54 by the late John Papadhimitriou.

Though archaeologically one of the most important of recent discoveries at Mycenae the circle affords little of interest to the view. The enclosure, bounded by a wall similar to that of the larger grave circle on the acropolis (see below) and containing 25 graves, 15 of them shaft graves, lay partly beneath the road, while the section to the E had been overlapped by the vault of the Tomb of Klytemnestra. The bodies had been buried over a period of years with objects of ivory, gold, bronze, and rock crystal, though less sumptuously than the burials of Grave Circle A. The burials are thought to date from c 1650 BC and may represent a rival royal faction to the kings of the larger circle since their resting-place was of sufficient sanctity not to be looted. Grave Rho, now roofed, is a built tomb, inserted into the cemetery later, in the 15C BC.

In the dip below (right; footpath) are two tholos tombs. That known as the **Tomb of Klytemnestra** was partially excavated by Mrs Schliemann in 1876 and more fully explored by the Greek Archaeological Society in 1891–92. It is of the normal type without a side-chamber, and is built on the same principle as the Treasury of Atreus, though a little smaller. From the more refined workmanship it is considered to be the latest of the tholos tombs (c 1300 BC). The upper 18 courses of its dome, destroyed probably by Veli Pasha, were restored in 1951. The *Dromos* (65m long) contained a circular depression which seems to have been a woman's grave, as gold trinkets and bronze mirrors were found in it. The *Doorway* is recessed and was flanked by fluted half-columns. Here we can see clearly how the ornamental façade that covered the relieving triangle was supported. Above the dromos vestiges of a small *Theatre* of the Hellenistic period show that by then the existence of the tholos was already forgotten. Only one semicircle of seats can be clearly descried.—The so-called **Tomb of Aegisthus**, farther E, was excavated by the British School in 1922. This is on the same plan, but both the manner of its construction with rubble walls and the pottery found within were used to date the tomb with the first group (c 1470 BC), though an earlier (Middle Helladic) date has since been proposed; the collapse of the tholos was due to the weakness of the material and it had been looted before the Hellenistic period.

On the other side of the modern road, in the N slope of the ridge, is the *Lion Tomb*, a tholos of the second group. Its dome has collapsed. Over to the left is *Petsas' House*, where a store of over 600 unused pots, ranged in sizes, was unearthed.

The road now reaches the *Acropolis, built on a triangular hill (278m) of which the N side is c 320m long and the others c 180m long. The enceinte as we see it today, with the Lion Gate, the palace, and most of the houses within, represents the result of architectural developments

N

CITADEL
(Mycenae)

0   50 metres

Sally Port

Cistern

Drain

Cisterns

Postern Gate

House of Columns

Artisans' Quarters

Temple

Palace

16   17
15
18
6
5
10
11
4
8
9
12   14
13

Guardhouse ?

Lion Gate

Granary

Ramp

Cemetery

Grave Circle A

House of the Warrior Vase

South House

Cult Centre

Hellenistic (above Mycenaean) Houses

Ravine

after Wace-Williams, with permission.

over a period from c 1350–c 1200 BC. The *Walls* are preserved for their whole extent, except for a gap in the middle of the precipitous S slope, which had no need to be fortified. They follow the contours of the rocks and in general vary in height between 4·5m and 10·5m, reaching 17m in the middle of the SW side. Their general thickness varies from 3m to 7m but in places on the N and SE sides they are as much as 10–14m wide. There were two gates and a sally-port.

Three different styles of construction may be distinguished. The 'cyclopean' walls are of huge blocks of dark limestone, shaped only roughly if at all. This masonry takes name from the tradition that the original walls, like those of Tiryns, were built by the Cyclopes. The two gateways, with their towers and approach walls, are in squared blocks of breccia, hammer-dressed and in regular courses like the later tholos tombs. This gives extra strength and dignity to the entrances to the city. The so-called Polygonal Towers are built of finely-jointed polygonal blocks of breccia; these and the short sections of wall repaired with similar but curved blocks date from the reoccupation of the 3C BC.

The famous *Lion Gate stands at the NW angle of the Acropolis. It is reached by an approach 14·5m long and 9m wide, formed on the left (NE) side by a salient of the fortification wall and on the right (SW) side by a tower or bastion projecting from the wall. This tower commanded the right or unshielded side of anyone that approached. The gateway, unlike the entrances to the tholos tombs, has monolithic gateposts (3·2m high) sloping inwards to give an opening that narrows from 3·1m at the bottom to 2·9m at the top. Across these, and probably mortised to them, is placed a massive lintel, 4·5m long, 1·9m thick, and 1m high in the centre, diminishing in height towards the sides. In the lintel and threshold are pivot-holes for double doors, and sockets in the side posts show where a wooden bar held them closed. The pavement is scored to give foothold and rutted on either side for chariot-wheels.

Above the lintel a triangular slab of grey limestone, 3·7m wide at the base, 3·1m high, and 0·6m thick, fills the relieving triangle. Carved in relief on it is a pillar supported by two lions (more properly, perhaps, lionesses), which rest their front paws on the two joined altars that constitute its base. Their heads have disappeared. The pillar, which tapers downwards, supports an abacus, and probably has a religious significance. A seal found at Mycenae depicts a similar device, perhaps the badge of the city or of its royal house; in this representation a dove rests on top of the pillar.

Within the gate (right) is the *Granary*, so-called because pithoi of carbonised wheat were found during its excavation. The building, which was of two storeys, may rather have been a guard-house.

From the gate the main route climbed by a ramp to the Palace, at first in a SE direction, then N following the line of the wall. Its surface was dug away in Schliemann's excavations, but the massive embanking walls of the ramp remain. The terrace-wall to the N, designed to support the higher ground above, is a modern reconstruction.

To the right is **Grave Circle A**, the ROYAL CEMETERY, a circular enclosure 27m in diameter, formed by a double ring of dressed slabs 0·9m–1·5m high and 0·9m apart. The space between the two concentric rings appears to have been filled originally with rubble; the top was covered with horizontal slabs, of which one is in place, showing the mortise-and-tenon joints. The entrance, formed by a well-made opening in the circle, 3·7m wide and lined with slabs, is opposite the Lion Gate. In the centre, all at the same level, were found 10 sepulchral stelai and a small round altar. The stelai, now in the National Museum at Athens, are adorned with crude sculptures in low relief, most of them representing men in chariots fighting or hunting. These are contemporary with the circle and with it represent the final stage of the royal shrine.

Within this enclosure are six SHAFT GRAVES, hewn perpendicularly in the rock at a depth of 7·5m. They vary considerably in size, but all were floored with pebbles and lined with rubble masonry; they appear to have been covered with slabs, which had collapsed beneath the weight of the soil above. In the tombs were found 19 skeletons; the bodies had been interred in the contracted attitude, not burnt. The burial furnishings, which constitute one of the richest archaeological discoveries ever made, are splendidly displayed in Athens.

Archaeologists date these tombs to the end of the late Middle Helladic and early Late Helladic periods, and postulate a 16C royal house, which they call the 'Shaft Grave dynasty'. The cemetery, of which the graves form part, lay outside the early citadel; when the later enceinte was planned the common graves were treated with scant respect and even looted, while this royal group was incorporated within the walls and replanned as a monument. The circle was renewed and the entrance moved from the W to the N. The stelai were lifted and replaced, and an altar installed in the centre.

This is presumably the prehistoric Frogmore pointed out to Pausanias as the graves of Agamemnon and his companions; the local peasants added, following a tradition that goes back to Homer, that the murderers Klytemnestra and Aegisthus were buried outside the walls as they were considered unworthy of burial within. It was Schliemann's unshakeable belief that what he had found was in fact the grave of 'all those who on their return from Ilium were murdered by Aegisthus after a banquet which he gave them'. The belief was fortified by the contents of Grave III, in which were the skeletons of two infants wrapped in sheets of gold together with the remains of three women. Schliemann inferred that these were Cassandra with her two attendants and the twins that she had borne to Agamemnon. For a short time it seemed that Homer might after all be shown to be documentary history.

The grave circle is however undoubtedly centuries earlier than any possible date for the siege of Troy. If the discovery of a second grave circle has confirmed the probability that two rival royal factions did exist in Mycenae, it has strengthened the evidence that any feud between them took place long before the Trojan War. Just as Homer describes customs (e.g. cremation) which are quite foreign to Mycenae at any period, so he seems also to have fused more than one period of Mycenaean events into one anachronistic saga. Malory's treatment of the Arthurian legends may be compared. The traveller who here feels himself cheated of the tomb of the legendary hero of Troy may console himself that he has below him the last resting-place of a great king who certainly existed at an age still more remote.

The characteristic shape of the inlaid daggers found here and at other Mycenaean sites is curiously echoed in the dagger-shaped marks cut in the trilithons of Stonehenge, the construction of which has elements in common with the final arrangement of the Mycenaean monument; no satisfactory theory yet accounts for what are perhaps coincidences.

To the S of the royal cemetery several groups of buildings have been uncovered; the remains represent only their basement level, drained and strongly built in stone to support a brick and timber floor above. They were constructed over the Middle Helladic cemetery in the 13C BC. The first group consists of the *Ramp House*, the *House of the Warrior Vase*, named after the famous vase found here by Schliemann, and the *South House*.

Further S is *Tsountas' House*, so-called from its first clearance by the Greek archaeologist in 1886. Further work here in 1950 and in 1970–72 shows the complex to consist of an elaborate shrine, with a separate house on the lower two terraces to the W. Work on the intervening area, the only unexcavated part of the Citadel with any depth of deposit, began in 1953 and was completed by a Helleno-British team under Professor Mylonas and Lord William Taylour. The area includes a large handsome hall with a covered passage leading to it and, on the lower terraces, two roughly built shrines which contained unusual clay idols and coiled snakes, a unique fresco and fine ivories (mostly displayed in the Nauplia Museum). This section is now known as the **Cult Centre**. Further S still is another area of well-built and well-arranged basements.

From the ramp a modern path follows the contour of the hill to the domestic entrance of the **Palace**. Two guard rooms (Pl. 1, 2) precede a cobbled court, where the column bases of the *Propylon* are seen. An *Inner Gate* (4) gave access to a long corridor (6) and to the state quarters, the official entrance to which was, however, on the S side. These centre round the *Great Court* (8). In Mycenaean times a *Grand Staircase* (9) led the visitor viâ an *Anteroom* (11) to a room (10) whose use is uncertain. It may have been a throne room, a guest suite or a control post and archive room. From the E side of the Great Court a *Porch* (12) and *Vestibule* (13) lead into the MEGARON (14), a room 12·7m by 11·8m, in the centre of which was the sacred *Hearth*. Four wooden pillars supported a roof; the bases are still visible. The rooms to the N are believed to represent the private apartments; a small one (17) with a red stuccoed bath is pointed out as the place of Agamemnon's murder. The topmost point is overlaid by scanty remains of a *Temple* rebuilt in Hellenistic times with material from an earlier structure of the Archaic period. The view comprehends the Argolid with the Larissa of Argos prominent.

E of the Palace on the lower terraces are important buildings, now considered to form an E wing of the Palace. The first is the artisans' quarters, an open corridor with workshops opening off on either side. Below, in the SE angle of the citadel, lies the so-called *House of Columns* which has close similarities to the palace of Odysseus as described in the Odyssey. Beyond are two groups of storerooms. Farther E is the heavily fortified late extension of the acropolis with a sally-port and a *Secret Cistern*, of the kind now known at both Athens and Tiryns, approached by a passage through the wall and descending stairs. A little to the W is a *Postern Gate* of the same epoch as the Lion Gate.

28 Nauplia, Tiryns, and the Argive Heraíon

Quite apart from its own charm, Nauplia is the best centre for excursions in the Argolid. It is possible by hiring a car there to make a superficial tour of Tiryns, Argos, Mycenae, and the Heraíon in one day. Visitors who are not pressed for time are recommended to take three days, devoting one to Nauplia and its surroundings, and dividing two between Tiryns, the Heraíon, Mycenae and Argos, reserving a fourth for the visit to Epidauros (Rte 29).

A. Nauplia

NAUPLIA (Ναύπλιον, pron. Návplion), called by the Venetians *Nápoli di Romanía*, is the chief town (10,609 inhab. Hotels L, A, B, C, D) of an eparchy and the capital of the nome of Argolis. Its delightful situation near the head of the Argolic Gulf and its splendid examples of late-medieval military architecture make it one of the most attractive towns in Greece. Originally walled, the quiet city huddles along the N slopes of a small rocky peninsula, crowned by the citadel of Its-Kale (85m), towards which narrow streets, lined with old houses attractively bal-conied and shuttered, rise from the quay. On the SE the conspicuous fortress of Palamidi (215m) dominates the peninsula.

Facing away from the open sea, Nauplia provides the safest harbour on the coast of Argolis, with some trade in tobacco, currants, and cotton. Though the seat of a bishop and a military station, the town has lost the importance it once had as the temporary capital of Greece, and is frequented mainly as a holiday resort.

Restaurants. On quay; in Plateía Iatroú; in and behind Plateía Sindágmatos. CAFÉS in same areas.

Tourist Police. Plateía Ethnosineléfseos 6 (in police station on left at the top of Od. Avérof).

Buses. From Plat. Nikitára (various positions in SW corner) to *Tiryns* and *Argos* (frequent); to *Corinth* and *Athens* (frequent); to *Toló* (for *Asine*) (frequent, less so in winter); to *Ligourió*, *Asklepieíon*, *Palaiá Epidhavros*, *Néa Epídhavros* (several); to *Kranidhi* (for *Ermióni* and *Spétses* and *Galatá* (for *Póros*) (several)).

Bathing. Below the Xenia Hotel (to the S).

History. Palaeolithic remains have recently been found on Akronavplion, and a Neolithic cave site in the area. In Mycenaean times *Nauplia* may have been, as its name suggests, the naval station of Argos. The legend later grew of a mythical founder Nauplios, son of Poseidon by Amymone, daughter of Danaos. A descendant of Nauplios, Palamedes, is said to have invented lighthouses, the art of navigation, measures and scales, and the games of dice and knucklebones, in addition to introducing the letters Y, Φ, X and Ψ into the alphabet of Cadmus (historically anachronistic). He was slain by his fellow-Greeks in the Trojan War on a false charge of treachery for playing a trick on Odysseus. About 625 BC Nauplia, previously a member of the maritime League of Kalauria, fell to Argos. The Nauplians fled to Messenia, where the Lacedaemonians gave them Methone. The town was again deserted in the time of Pausanias, who saw only walls, a sanctuary of Poseidon, the harbour, and the Spring of Kanathos.

Nauplia is mentioned as a trading-post in 11C Venetian annals. After the fall of Constantinople (1204), it remained for a time in Byzantine hands, the governor Leon Sgouros vainly trying to make it the nucleus of a Greek kingdom. In 1210 the town was taken by Geoffrey de Villehardouin, who gave it, with Argos, to Otho de la Roche. It remained an appanage of the Dukes of Athens, but on the fall of Athens to the Catalans in 1311 remained loyal to the Brienne family. In 1388 Nauplia was bought from Marie d'Enghien by the Venetians, whose first task was to recover it from the hands of Theodore Palaeologos of Mistra. It repelled Turkish sieges in 1470, in 1500 when Bayezid II attacked it in person, and for 14 months in 1538–39, but in 1540 it became the Turkish capital of the Morea. Count Königsmark, Morosini's lieutenant, recovered it for Venice in 1686, and until the Turks recaptured it in 1715 it became capital of the kingdom and seat of the Bp. of Corinth. Morosini died within sight of its walls in 1694. After its recapture Ahmed III visited Nauplia in person. As a consequence of a temporary occupation of Nauplia by the Russians in 1770, the capital was removed to Tripolis.

During the War of Independence Nauplia was the most important fortress in the Morea, its two strongholds being regarded as impregnable. The Greeks besieged it for over a year in 1821–22; a few months after the rout of Dramali they seized Palamidi, and the town capitulated. Later the two citadels were for a time in the hands of rival Greek chieftains, who indulged their passion for civil war at the expense of the luckless inhabitants, until Adm. Codrington and Sir Richard

NAUPLIA

EPIDAUROUS & TOLO

Tourist Police

ARGOS & CORINTH

AVERÓF

Football
Ground

BOUBOULINAS

MERARKHÍAS

SIDIRÁS

MARTIOU

LEOFÓROS 25

Palamídi

Station (Goods)

OTE

Statue

PO

Grímani Bastion

PLAT.
NIKITARÁ

WC

KTEL

Steps

High
School

AMALIAS

KTEL

Mus. of
Folk Art

LEOF. KONSTANDINOU

PO

Toron

Dhimarkhíon

VASIL.

AY.
Spyridon

Cath. Church

Library

PLAT.
AGHIAS (KTEL)

KAPODISTRIOU

PAPANIKOLAOU

Custom
House

BOUBOULINAS

PLAT.
SINDAGMATOS

Bank

Clock
Tower

WC

PLAT.
IATROU
Mon.

STAIKOU

Museum

Vouleftikó

Dolfin
Bastion

ITS KALE

AKTÍ MIAOULI

West Mole
(Porporella)

N

ARGOLIKÓS KÓLPOS

300 yards

300 metres

Church intervened. The town escaped destruction and hither in 1828 Capodistrias, the regent, moved his provisional seat of government from Aegina. In 1831, Capodistrias was assassinated in the church of St. Spiridion. Otho, first king of Greece, disembarked at Nauplia in 1833 after the ratification of his election in 1832 at Pronoia, remaining here till the government was removed to Athens in 1834. The insurrection of the garrison here helped to bring about his abdication in 1862.

Arrival of King Otho at Nauplia, 1833

At Nauplia on 26 April 1941 the British evacuation of 6685 men and 150 nurses was made chaotic in the darkness and many men were lost when the transport 'Ulster Prince' ran aground, blocking the harbour entrance. 'Hyacinth', trying to free her, fouled the tow wire in her screw, and 'Slamat' was sunk by dive bombers. Two destroyers (HMS 'Diamond' and 'Wryneck') were also lost.

The railway station and bus terminus are at the N foot of Palamidi, where three squares divide the suburb of Pronoia from the town. In the E square stands a vigorous equestrian *Statue of Theodore Kolokotronis* by Lazaros Sochos (1901), and in the central Plateia Dikasterion a marble figure of Capodistrias. We enter the old town by the Plateia Trion Navarkhon, where the *High School*, the first to be founded in liberated Greece, faces the building (now the Institut Français) in which it was installed by King Otho in 1833. In the centre stands a *Monument to Demetrios Ypsilantis*. Behind the High School, with an entrance in Od. Vasiléos Alexándrou, is the new *Museum of the Peloponnesian Folklore Foundation*, winner of the European Museum of the Year award in 1981 for its fine displays. The foundation was set up in 1974 under the directorship of Mrs I. Papantoniou and based on her extensive collection of Greek folk art. It now comprises a research centre and library in Athens and the Museum in Nauplia. The foundation sponsors projects in all areas of folklore and folk art studies and publishes the periodical *Ethnográfika*. The **Museum** (closed in February) occupies an attractively restored Neo-classical house. The ground floor is devoted to a display of the techniques involved in the production of folk textiles in Greece, beginning with an historical introduction to the subject. All the processes from raw fibre to the finished item are illustrated. Of special interest are the looms, the more unusual types of weaving (e.g. tablet and band weaving) and the display in the final case of the inner room which shows highly decorated folk art items re-used as ecclesiastical vestments. The upper storey is now open and contains the Museum's collection of folk costumes and other memorabilia. There is a small museum shop.

Close by, in Leof. Amalías, is the restored building of the first *Military Academy* of Greece (1828).

Odhos Vasiléos Konstandínou, the narrow main street, thronged during the evening volta, leads from the main square (comp. above) to PLATEÍA SINDÁGMATOS, the centre of the town. In the SW corner is the ex-Mosque of *Vouleftikó* (now being restored), in which the first Greek parliament met in 1827–34. It is said that this building, the medresse behind it (now the museum store), and the second mosque in the square (now a cinema) were erected by one family in expiation of a crime.

The *Archaeological Museum* occupies the upper floors of a dignified Venetian building of 1713, once a naval depot. FIRST FLOOR. Unique and virtually complete *Suit of Mycenaean Armour found in a tomb at Dhendhra in 1960. Neolithic pottery from the Franchthi Cave. Early to Late Helladic pottery from sites in the Argolid (including Grave Circle B at Mycenae), that of LH I–II showing marked Minoan influences in shape and decoration; stele from Grave Circle B with incised figure of a horseman; terracotta idols mainly from the Citadel House shrine at Mycenae (various types of figures, snakes) plus the 'Lord of Asine'; fragments of frescoes from Tiryns and Mycenae; Mycenaean lamp from Midea; sherd inscribed in Linear B.—SECOND FLOOR. Sub-Mycenaean *Helmet from Tiryns; finds of the Geometric period and later; Votive discs (7C BC) with painted scenes; grotesque masks (8C) from Tiryns and Asine; the 'Tiryns Inscription'; sole inscription found at this site until the surprising discoveries of December 1962; figurines and votive objects; Panathenaic amphorae; blackglazed krater (4C); Hellenistic terracotta bath.

The QUAY commands a fine view across the bay to the mountains of Argolis. In the Plateía Iatroú in front of the *Custom-House* is the *Monument to the French*, a marble obelisk erected in 1903 in memory òf General Fabvier, Admiral de Rigny, and others, who fell in the War of Independence. Akti Miaouli, a wide promenade on the site of the old town walls (demolished 1929–30), leads to the *West Mole*, built on the foundations of the 'porporella', or underwater stone barrier, that once protected the entrance to the harbour. It also ringed the islet of **Boúrdzi** (450m offshore), on which stands the *Castel Pasqualigo*, erected by the Bergamasque architect Ant. Gambello in 1471, and many times modified. It was used in the 19C as a retreat of the execrated public executioner. From the W mole a path follows the *Bastion of the Five Brothers* (Πενταδέλφια), the only surviving part of the circuit wall begun in 1502, to the W extremity of the peninsula. Here, high up, can be seen a postern gate and a few steps of the way up cut by Morosini's galley-slaves in 1686. We follow the S side of the peninsula towards the little bay of *Arvanitia* in the neck of the isthmus, now arranged as a bathing place (adm. charge). Above tower the crags of ITS KALÉ (Turk. Üç Kalè), the 'three castles' (Greek, Frankish, Venetian) that constituted **Akronávplion**.

A fortress has existed on the site since ancient times. The original walls of polygonal masonry (still visible from below on the N side) have served as a foundation for each successive rebuilding. The decaying walls were partly restored by the Venetians in 1394–1409 and the lower *Castello del Torrione*, designed by Gambello (see above), added c 1477–80. This now supports the Xenia Hotel. After the erection of the town wall in 1502 the upper castle was allowed to fall into disrepair until 1701–04 when Dolfin strengthened its entrances. Within, the former untidy but historic ruins have given way to hotels and tourist installations, but good views can be had from the panoramic road. From the far end long flights of steps within the *Baluardo Dolfin* descend to the *Porta Sagredo* of 1713, above the main square. On the S side of Akronavplion, traces of Palaeolithic occupation were found in 1973.

In the lower town Odhós Kapodhistríou has surviving Turkish fountains. On its N side is the charming Venetian portal of the church of *Ay. Spiridón*, built in 1702, outside which Count John Capodistrias was assassinated in 1831 by George and Constantine Mavromichales; the mark of the bullet fired by Constantine is still shown near the entrance. A little higher up the slope, the *Metamórphosis* (Transfiguration), a Venetian conventual church returned by King Otho to the Roman rite after it had served the Turks as a mosque, contains a curious register of Philhellenes.

The **Fortress of Palamidi** (Παλαμήδειον; 215m) stands on the summit of a lofty and almost inaccessible rock commanding the whole of the Argolid with a *View of the surrounding mountains. On foot it is reached by a dizzy climb of some thousand steps requiring fortitude even in cool weather; best in the morning. A tourist road has been engineered on the S side (comp. below). The name preserves the legend of Palamedes, but the difficult terrain seems to have inhibited building here until the governorship of Agost. Sagredo, when, to a design of Anti. Giaxich, a Dalmatian engineer (wounded at Argos, 1695), the fortress was built by Lasalle in 1711–14. The *Caponier*, or covered way, was erected a little earlier to provide a protected retreat from the hill to the city. The complex fortification, entered by a series of gates bearing the Lion of St. Mark, consists of outworks and ramparts connecting three independent fortresses, in ascending order named *San Girardo* (the patron saint of the Sagredo), *San Nicolò*, and *Sant'-Agostino* (after the podestà).

Palamidi, inadequately garrisoned, fell after eight days' siege in 1715. The poet Manthos of Ioannina, who was present, slanderously attributed its fall to the betrayal of its plans by Lasalle. More recently the forts were renamed after Greek heroes and Fort Miltiades (S. Nicolò) served as a convict prison. Kolokotronis was here incarcerated.

The new road up the SE slope of Palamidi passes close to a Mycenaean cemetery of rock-hewn chamber-tombs.

THE PRINCIPAL LOCAL EXCURSION is to Tolón (9·5km; bus). We take the Epidauros road. After 250m a sign points (right) to the *Bavarian Lion*. This was carved in the rock by order of Ludwig I of Bavaria to commemorate his soldiers who died in a epidemic at Tiryns in 1833–34. In this suburb of *Prónoia* in 1832 the National Assembly ratified the election of Prince Otho to the throne of Greece.—1km. Turning (right) to the *Ayía Moní*, or nunnery of Zoödókhos Piyí, founded by Leo, Bishop of Argos; its elegant church dates from 1149. The curious fountain (1836) in the garden, decorated with reliefs and fed by an ancient conduit, is reputed to occupy the site of the Kanathos, a spring in which Hera annually renewed her virginity.—At 3·5km, beyond the hamlet of *Areia*, we leave the Epidauros road, turning right.—At 6·5km a tarmac road forks left, passes *Dhrépanon* (Hotel C) at the head of a long marshy inlet, then skirts the coast to *Iria* (27km), whose scattered remains attest a Mycenaean origin and classical history; this road continues (part unpaved) to join Rte 29.—We keep right, pass through the village of modern *Asíni*, then, ignoring a turn to Dhrépanon (left), arrive at the rocky headland (Kastráki) on which stand the ruins of **Asíne**. A path leads past a small chapel.

Asine was occupied from the Early Helladic period; later by migrants from N Greece, Dryopians according to Strabo. The inhabitants sided with the Spartans in their invasion of Argos after the First Messenian War, and afterwards fled to Messenia, settling at Korone (Rte 34). The place was deserted until the 2C BC when it again became a fortified township.—The Swedish excavations of 1922–30 were the idea of Crown Prince (later King) Gustav Adolf, who himself took part. The results were published in English (Stockholm, 1938). Excavations were resumed in 1970.

The *Lower Town* retains imposing portions of Hellenistic ramparts on the N side, with a gate and section of paved road. Within were found widespread traces of Early Helladic occupation, foundations of many houses of the Middle Helladic and Late Helladic periods, and of Roman baths, as well as Venetian additions to the fortifications (Morosini landed at Tolo in 1686). Geometric and Hellenistic remains survive on the *Acropolis*. On the S point are some inscriptions left on a gun position by Italian soldiers in 1942. The wild flowers are varied. A Middle Helladic and Mycenaean necropolis was explored on Mt Barbouna.

Beyond the site, the road turns W, skirting the sandy shore at the foot of Mt Barbouna (91m) to (9·5km) *Toló* (Hotels B, C, D), a summer resort with camp-sites. The bay is protected by islets. A better beach extends E of the site.

Among other places accessible by local bus is *Ayios Adhrianós*, 5km NE, where in 1962 a site was located on a hill-top to the NW (remains of Cyclopean walls; chapel on temple foundations above a cave), perhaps to be identified with ancient *Lessa* (though this is claimed for each of three other forts on the Ligourio road).

B. Tiryns

Tiryns is 4km from Nauplia on the level road to Argos (Rte 26). After 1·5km appear on the right the two limestone hills of *Ayios Ilias* (111m and 213m), each crowned by a chapel; these hills were used as quarries by the builders of Tiryns. Farther on we reach the penal *Agricultural College* founded by Capodistrias. In 1926 in a field belonging to the college was discovered the so-called 'Treasure of Tiryns'. The ruins lie just beyond to the E of the road.

The citadel of ****TIRYNS** (ΤΙΡΥΝΣ) occupies the summit of a low rocky height known inevitably as Palaiókastro (27m), the lowest and most westerly of a series of isolated knolls rising like islands from the level plain. It is separated from the sea (now c 1·5km distant) by reclaimed marshland. The fortress-palace is enclosed by the famous walls the finest specimens known of the military architecture of the Mycenaeans. Homer speaks of 'wall-girt Tiryns' (Τίρυνθα τειχόεσσαν; Iliad, ii, 559); Pindar admires the 'Cyclopean doorways' (κυκλωπία πρόθυρα; Frag. 642); and Pausanias compares the walls of Tiryns with the pyramids of Egypt. The palace within is more elaborate than those at Mycenae and Pylos. The unfortified city lay in the surrounding plain.

History. *Tiryns* was inhabited before the Bronze Age; the earliest people may have been lake-dwellers in the marsh. In one legend Tiryns is the birthplace of Herakles and the base of operations for his labours (Apollodoros, II, iv, 12). It was fortified early in Mycenaean times and rebuilt in its present form during the 13C BC. Despite its size and wealth, Tiryns seems always to have been secondary to Argos or Mycenae. Though it continued to be inhabited through Geometric times and sent a contingent to Plataia in 479, the place never again had any importance. It was destroyed by Argos in 468 BC. It became a fortress in the Hellenistic period and the strength of the walls proved an attraction in the Byzantine era when a church was built in the great forecourt. The site was explored by Schliemann and Dörpfeld in 1884–86. Considerable reconstruction of fallen walls was effected in 1962–64; the long-delayed discovery of the water-supply in 1962 by the late N. Verdelis has led to further investigation of the lower enceinte. This has continued in recent years by the German Archaeological Institute.

The fortress is most impressive from below. The summit on which it stands has the form of a waisted oblong 299m long and from 20m to 34m wide, descending from S to N in three terraces. The whole of the area is enclosed by the *WALLS, nearly 700m in circuit, which are built of two kinds of limestone, red and grey, in irregular blocks of different sizes, laid as far as possible in horizontal courses. The stones, the largest of which are estimated to weigh over 14,000kg, are partially hammer-dressed; smaller stones bonded with clay mortar fill the interstices. Round the lower citadel the walls are 7m–8m thick; round the irregular upper citadel, where their line is broken by towers, salients, and re-entrant angles, they vary in thickness from 5km–11m, in places containing galleries and chambers. They stand to about half their original estimated height of 20m.

The main entrance was in the middle of the E wall. A smaller entrance opened in the great semicircular bastion that projects on the W side, and there were three posterns in the lower citadel.

Admission is by a new gate from the by-road (E) to the steep and ruinous *Ramp* (Pl. 1), c 5m wide, which formed an approach impracticable for chariots. Its disposition exposed the visitor's right or unshielded side to the defenders as at Mycenae and necessitated at the top a sharp turn. The MAIN ENTRANCE (Pl. 2) opened in the outer wall, here 7·5m thick. The original opening of c 5m has been reduced to 2·5m by later masonry; there is no trace of a gate. We are now in a long passage running N and S between the inner and outer walls. To the right, passing a square niche below an arch (probably a guard post), it leads down to the lower citadel (see below). 50m to the left is the *Outer Gateway* (Pl. 3), similar in dimension to the Lion Gate at Mycenae. In the monolithic threshold may be seen the holes for the pivots of folding doors, and in the rebated gateposts are bolt holes, 15cm in diameter, allowing a cross-bar to be shot home into the wall. The right gatepost is intact, the left one is broken, and the lintel has disappeared. Beyond, the passage widens to form a *Barbican* (Pl. 4), narrowing again to a point where an *Inner Gate* (Pl. 5) probably guarded the oblong *Courtyard* (Pl. 6). Here, to the left, in the thickness of the outer wall, is the first of the two series of *GALLERIES AND CHAMBERS for which the fortress is specially renowned. The *E. Gallery*, fronted by a colonnade, had a corbelled vault and communicated by six doors with six vaulted *Chambers* (Pl. 7), each 3·4m square.

Opposite opens the GREAT PROPYLAIA (Pl. 8), a double porch divided by a wall, in which was a single doorway. Between antae within and without stood wooden columns, the stone bases of which are still in position. The gateway supersedes an earlier one. From the inner porch a narrow passage leads off direct to the smaller megaron (comp. below).

We enter the *Forecourt* (Pl. 9) of the palace, from which remains of a Byzantine church have been removed; it is bounded on three sides by the fortress walls and the complex of *Casemates built into them. We descend by a covered staircase, with a right-angled bend in the middle, to the vaulted *S Gallery* (20m long, 5m high, and 1·5m wide) at a level 7m below that of the court. The sides narrow to a loophole in the E wall by which it was lit. Five doorways open from the gallery into rectangular vaulted *Chambers* (Pl. 10).—On the SW side a rectangular *Tower* (Pl. 11), with a frontage of 19m, enclosed two cisterns.

The **Royal Palace** is reached from the N side of the forecourt by the *Smaller Propylaia* (Pl. 12). The earliest palace complex probably dates to the 14C BC. It was rebuilt after a destruction in c 1250 BC and redesigned after devastation by fire in c 1200 BC. The walls of the palace stand to a height of only 0·5m–1m; above this limestone base they were of sun-dried brick, the whole being then covered by stucco and decorated with frescoes. The huge stone thresholds of the doors remain in situ; the floors are of concrete made of lime and pebbles. In the colonnaded court (Pl. 13) is a round sacrificial altar. A *Porch* (Pl. 14; aithousa), with two columns and elaborate benches, gives access by triple doors to an ante-chamber, and thence through a door (closed in antiquity only by a curtain) to the MEGARON (Pl. 15), or *Great Hall*. In the centre is a circular clay hearth, 3·4m in diameter. The roof was supported by four wooden columns, set on stone bases, which had an open lantern to give light and let out the smoke. The base of the throne is well preserved and the painted floor intact in places. The walls were frescoed with scenes of a boar hunt and a life-size frieze of women. Reached from the ante-chamber is the *Bathroom* (Pl. 16), with a floor composed of one huge limestone monolith 4m by 3m.

The apartments described above are duplicated on a smaller scale behind and to the E (outer court, Pl. 17; inner court, Pl. 18; smaller megaron, Pl. 19; and ancillary buildings), representing, perhaps, the women's quarters. Behind is a large open court separated by the massive inner wall from the LOWER ENCEINTE. In the Early Helladic period, a massive round building, c 28m in diameter, occupied the hilltop. It is now concealed beneath the megaron and court. The Lower Enceinte has been intensively investigated by the German Archaeological Institute (Prof. K. Kilian) in recent years. The area was occupied as early as Neolithic times and substantial remains of Early Helladic buildings have been discovered. The massive fortifications, however, were only built in the later 13C. About 1200 BC there was a catastrophic destruction, probably by earthquake, after which the layout of the buildings was completely changed. The most interesting discoveries (not yet accessible) are of a cult room of 12C date, with a predecessor on the same site, and associated ritual equipment, including large numbers of terracotta figures of various types. There is also much evidence of industrial activity, including metal working.

From a square tower to the W of the rear court a well-preserved *Secret Stair* (Pl. 20) winds down within a massive bastion to an inconspicuous corbelled *Postern Gate* (Pl. 21). We pass out of the fortress, turn right, and skirt the outer walls. At the NW angle of the lower enceinte two secret passages lead steeply downward through the walls from inside to two *Underground Cisterns* fed by springs. There are comparable arrangements at Mycenae and on the Acropolis at Athens, but the Tiryns passages were discovered by accident only in 1962. Stones covering the cisterns were found (only, unfortunately, after some had been moved) to bear Archaic inscriptions shallowly cut in boustrophedon c 600 BC.

C. The Argiv

Approaches. Asphalt road from Argos t̶
church (restored 1963), thence (partly pav̶
Ayía Triádha, see below. BUS from Narphai ̶
The view is clearest in the evening.

The **Heraíon of Argos**, or *Sanctuary of Hera*, ̶ 311
lary goddess of the Argolid, was common to Argos
imposing complex of ruins, usually ignored by the p̶
veller, the sanctuary occupies a spur (Palaiókastro; 128m̶
SW and commands a fine view over the plain to Argos.

The site was discovered in 1831 by the Philhellene, General Thomas Gor̶
who dug here in 1836; its excavation in 1892–95 constituted the first major wo̶
of the American School (under Charles Waldstein). Further work was accomplished by Carl Blegen in 1925–28; and a chance discovery led to a short but
profitable investigation in 1949 by P. Amandry and J. Caskey (Hesperia XXI).
The summit of the hill was first occupied in Early Helladic times. Pausanias refers
to the area by the name *Prosymna* and in the surrounding slopes Blegen dug
many tombs extending in date from Neolithic to Late Mycenaean. At the Argive
Heraíon Agamemnon is fabled to have been chosen leader of the Trojan expedition. Hither from Argos Kleobis and Biton drew the chariot of their mother in the
story told by Solon to Croesus (Herod I, 31). The old temple was burnt down in
423 BC by the carelessness of the aged priestess Chryseis.

The Archaic and Classical sanctuary is built on three terraces, above
which is the Helladic settlement. A path, to the right, leads to the
UPPER TERRACE, supported by a massive retaining wall in conglomerate, which has all the appearances of Mycenaean workmanship
but is believed to date from the Late Geometric period. The surface of
the terrace is paved and remains to this day almost perfectly level. On
it may be seen traces of the stylobate of the **Old Temple**, perhaps the
earliest peripteral building of the Peloponnese, dated to the first half of
the 7C. In the Doric style (6 by 14 columns), its upper structure may
have been of wood and unburnt brick.

In the centre of the MIDDLE TERRACE stands the poros stereobate of
the **New Temple**, erected c 420–410 BC by Eupolemos of Argos. This
was a Doric peripteral building (6 by 12 columns) in which was set up a
chryselephantine statue of Hera by Polykleitos, said to have deserved
comparison with the Olympian Zeus of Pheidias. Pausanias claims to
have seen here also the ancient xoanon in pearwood removed by the
Argives from Tiryns in 468 BC, a bejewelled golden peacock dedicated by Hadrian, and a purple robe offered by Nero.

The buildings bounding this terrace have many unexplained features. Below the wall that supports the upper terrace is the *North Stoa*,
believed (on the evidence of surviving capitals which are not known
with certainty to belong to it) to date from the 6C BC or even earlier.
The foundations are of limestone and the blocks forming the rear wall
are well squared. In the centre are statue bases and at the W end a
basin, lined with cement, is connected to an elaborate water-supply
system. The *North-East Building*, dating from the end of the 7C, was
altered at a later date. The *East Building* is a mid-5C rectangular
structure in poros with a portico and a triple row of interior columns.
The *West Building*, one of the earliest examples known of a peristyle
court (late 6C), has three rooms leading off its N side; it may have been
a banqueting place. To the NW are further foundations, possibly
belonging to a late monumental entrance. Farther W are a large
Roman bathing establishment and a palaestra.

, at the third level below the retaining wall of the , shows the finest workmanship of any building on the site, and is dated to the mid-5C. It is now suggested that the flights of steps, formerly postulated as leading up to the S stoa and past it on the E side to the temple, are in fact Archaic retaining walls of stepped construction (analemma).

The site guard will show a well-preserved tholos tomb c 200m below the main site.
   The Middle Helladic and Late Helladic cemeteries of *Prosymna*, explored by Blegen, are in the hillsides to the NW at approximately the same contour height as the upper terrace.

From Khonika a road continues NE to (9km) *Berbatí* (which has readopted the name Prosimni; but comp. above). Here in 1936–37 the Swedish Institute explored a cemetery of Mycenaean chamber-tombs and a settlement of Early Helladic II date.
   Another road runs SE from Khonika to (5·5km) *Merbaka*, officially *Ayía Triás*, where it meets a better road from Argos (7km). The village, which has an attractive 12C church, is said to derive its name from William of Meerbeke, Latin Archbishop of Corinth (fl. c 1280), who translated various Greek medical classics. Turning E for a further 5km we may reach **Dhendrá** (on foot a more direct track from Khonika avoids Merbaka). Here (on a slope NW of the village) the Swedish Institute dug an unrobbed tholos tomb in 1926–27 (L.H. IIIA; finds in Athens) and, in 1937–39, richly furnished Mycenaean chamber-tombs surrounding it (gold cups, remains of wooden coffin, etc.). Another tomb dug in 1960 yielded the Mycenaean ceremonial armour now in Nauplia museum. The cemetery belongs to the Middle–Late Helladic settlement of *Midéa*, the acropolis of which stands 30 minutes E of Dhendrá (to the right of the road to Midhia village, from which the ascent is easier); it preserves its cyclopean enceinte (late 13C BC). Excavations were resumed in 1983.

29   From Nauplia to Epidauros and the Argolic Peninsula

ROAD, 30km, (19 miles) to *Epidauros*; 94km, (59 miles) to *Kósta*, for Spetsai. Buses, see Rte 28. The Epidauros sanctuary is called locally Ierón Ligouríou and is not at either New or Old Epidauros (comp. below).

On leaving Nauplia we enter the valley separating the slopes of Palamidi, on the S, from the bare waterless range of *Arakhnaíon*, to the N. Its highest point rises to 1199m but its most striking peak is the less lofty Mt Arna (1079m) above Ligourio. The view is much better on the return journey when the serried ranges of the Peloponnese rise ahead. Just after the 14km stone, 50m before a modern bridge at a sharp corner, we see above the road (left) the corbelled arch of a massive *Cyclopean Bridge*, perhaps of the 5C BC but probably of Mycenaean origin. A little farther on (left) rises *Kazárma*, a small but precipitous hill (280m) with some remains of a citadel of the 5C with walls standing to 6m in polygonal masonry. A second fortress of the same period stands conspicuously above the road at (16km) *Kastráki* (left; 430m).— 27km. The decayed church of *Ayía Marína*, to the left, is built on the site of an Ionic temple of Athena. Near by are the scanty remains of a pyramidal structure of the 4C BC, believed to be a guard-house capable of accommodating a patrol in emergency.—27km **Ligourió** (Λιγουριό; Hotels D), with 2018 inhab.; has several Byzantine churches, of which the most interesting (on our road, beyond the centre) incorporates small fragments from the Tholos in the Sanctuary (see below).

From Ligourió a road continues NE through a defile, then divides. The left branch joins the new road from the Corinth Canal (Rte 25C) just short of *Néa Epídhavros* (13km; Epidauros C), where the first 'National Assembly' met on 20 December 1821 to declare the independence of Greece ('Constitution of Epidauros'). Above the town (1381 inhab.) are ruins of the Frankish castle of Nicholas de Guise, Constable of the Morea.—The right branch leads to *Palaiá Epídhavros* (9km; Hotels C), with a little harbour. The ancient city of *Epidauros* stood on the headland to the S of the harbour. Cyclopean walls still stand and a group of Mycenaean chamber tombs was excavated in 1888. There have been sporadic discoveries of remains of Archaic–Roman date.

Submerged buildings have been identified and a *Theatre of Dionysos excavated in 1972 having 10 kerkides and 18 rows of seats (late 4C BC), many inscribed with names of citizens who endowed the seating.

We bear right in Ligourió and 2·5km farther on left for the Sanctuary of Epidauros. The right branch continues through the peninsula (see below).

30km (19 miles) The **Hieron of Epidauros** (Ierón Ligouríou), or *Sanctuary of Asklepios*, is situated in a broad and lonely valley between Mt Velanídhia, the ancient *Titthion* (858m), on the NE, and Mt Kharáni, the ancient *Kynortion*, on the SE. The place was at once a religious centre and a fashionable spa. In addition to the temples and colonnades devoted to the cult of Asklepios (or Æsculapius) and the cure of his disciples, there were dwellings for the priest-physicians, hospitals for the sick, sanatoria for the convalescent, and hotels and places of amusement for the healthy. In Roman times were added baths, fed by reservoirs which collected water from the local springs.

In extent the Sanctuary compares with Delphi or Olympia, but apart from the Theatre the ruins themselves are interesting only to the specialist, though the pine-clad setting remains charming despite the artificial landscaping and paraphernalia of the festival. The road passes between the Stadium and the fenced part of the site (entrance gate, left; car park, right), then enters the main gate. Within are (right) a *Tourist Pavilion* (Refreshments) and the *Xenia Hotel* (B), and (left) the Museum. The road and paths continue to the Theatre where we start the visit.

History. The worship of Apollo at the Epidaurian sanctuary seems to go back into the mists of time, that of Asklepios being grafted on not earlier than the Archaic period. It superseded that of Apollo by the 4C, by which time Epidauros had become established as the 'birthplace' of Asklepios. The cult seems to have originated in Homeric times in Thessaly, possibly at Trikke, and to have been carried S viâ Phokis and Boeotia, but first attained prominence at Epidauros in the 6–5C spreading thence to Athens. Kos (Rte 75) always claimed a Trikkan origin for it. Some of the medical as opposed to magical expertise of Asklepios may have filtered through Asia Minor and Kos from Egypt. The Ptolemaic Greeks identified with their own hero-god Asklepios Imhotep (lived c 2780 BC), the Egyptian genius and deified physician, around whose tomb at Sakkara the first healing sanctuary grew up. The fame of the sanctuary at Epidauros reached a peak in the 4C BC when, perhaps, magic and faith were giving place to more scientific treatment.

The Hieron belonged to the city of Epidauros (comp. above) and was in charge of an annually elected Priest of Asklepios, assisted by recorders, choristers, police, and other officials. Recovered patients gave costly offerings and votive inscriptions. Every four years, nine days after the Isthmian Games, an athletic and dramatic festival known as the *Asklepieia* was celebrated.

Livy and Ovid both tell how Rome, ravaged by an epidemic in 293 BC, sent for the sacred serpent from Epidauros. the sanctuary was despoiled by Sulla in 86 BC and the loot distributed among his soldiers.

The excavations, begun in 1881, became the life's work of P. Kavvadias. The French School also excavated just after the Second World War, J. Papadimitriou in 1948–51 and V. Lambrinoudhakis in recent years.

The ***Theatre**, the best-preserved of all Greek theatres and one of the best-preserved Classical buildings in Greece, dates from the 4C BC and seems to have escaped alteration until its judicious restoration in recent years. It is now celebrated as the centre of an annual summer festival of drama. Its acoustics are unusually perfect, the slightest whisper or rustle of paper from the orchestra being clearly audible from any of its 14,000 seats. The *Cavea*, c 114m across, faces N. It has 55 rows of seats, 34 below the diazoma and 21 above. The lower block is divided into 12 wedges by 13 staircases; the upper block has 23 staircases. The seats of honour were of red, the ordinary seats of white limestone. The two flanks of the theatre were supported by poros retaining walls, recently restored. The *Orchestra* is a complete circle 20m in diameter, the circumference of which is marked by a ring of limestone flags. The floor is of beaten earth. In the centre is the round base of the *Thymele*, or altar. Between the circle and the front row of seats is a semicircular paved depression, 2·1m wide, placed to collect rainwater. Access to the theatre is by two *Parodoi*, passing through double doorways (restored) having pilasters embellished with Corinthian capitals. The foundations of the *Stage* can be seen when they are not covered by temporary wooden scenery.

Above the theatre, but now not easily accessible owing to the fences, is (15 minutes) the *Sanctuary of Apollo Maleatas*, in which excavations have continued since 1974.

The **Museum** may conveniently be visited before the excavations. To right and left of the entrance are two Corinthian columns from the interior colonnade of the Tholos and two Ionic columns from the Abaton.—ROOM I. Inscriptions recording miraculous cures; Roman statuary; surgical instruments; building stele with accounts for the Tholos and Temple of Asklepios.—ROOM II. Sculpture (mostly casts) from pediments; reconstruction of the entablature of the Propylaia.—ROOM III. Reconstructions: part of the Temple of Asklepios (380–375). Pavement of the Tholos, a curious building of which two different conjectural versions are illustrated by drawings; it was built c 360 BC possibly by Polykleitos the Younger. Corinthian capital, section of circular wall, ornate ceiling, and decorated doorway, all from the same building and finally a reconstruction of its entablature.

The **Excavations** lie to the NW. We come first to the remains of a vast square building, probably the *Katagogion*, a hotel to be compared with the Leonidaion at Olympia. It had four cloistered courts from each of which opened 18 rooms. The polygonal walls stand to a height of 0·6m and most of the threshold blocks are in place.—To the W are the ruined Greek *Baths*.—The GYMNASIUM, (usually so-called but more probably a ceremonial BANQUETING HALL), a huge colonnaded court, with exedrae and other rooms off it, survives only in one course of the outer walls. The two rooms at the SE and SW corners have off-centre doorways for the convenient insertion of dining couches and the large E hall preserves traces of stone couch-supports with dowel holes in their upper surfaces. The Romans built an *Odeion* in the court, of which considerable portions of the brick-built auditorium and stage buildings survive. The whole base of the *Great Propylaia* of the Gymnasium, at the NW corner, is preserved with its pavement and ramp, though its Doric colonnade has vanished.—The indeterminate ruins to the NE are of the *Palaestra*, or *Stoa of Kotys*, a building originally of

EPIDAUROS
0 ————————— 100 metres

unburnt brick that collapsed and was rebuilt (along with other parts of the sanctuary) by a Roman senator Antoninus, probably the Emperor Antoninus Pius.

The most important group of buildings in the Hieron now opens out to E and W; this was the area that the Byzantines surrounded with walls and converted into a rectangular fortress. At the SE corner, immediately N of the palaestra, is the little Greek *Temple of Themis*, with an unidentified Roman building beyond. Turning to the W, we come to the foundations of the *Temple of Artemis*, a Doric prostyle building with six columns on the front (4C BC). Almost adjoining on the N is a large rectangular building which may have been the original *Abaton*, where patients slept expecting the visitation of the god and a cure by miraculous dreams. It was replaced in the 4C by another building (see below) and this site altered in Roman times. Various inscribed bases may be seen to the N, which probably bordered the sacred grove.

The **Temple of Asklepios** is approached by a paved road and ramp. The temple was a Doric peripteral hexastyle, with 6 columns by 11, about 24m long, and dating from c 420 BC. Nothing, however, remains but foundations and the fragments in the museum.

A stele found in 1885 supplies many details of the method and cost of construction. The work was supervised by the architect *Theodotes* and the temple took 4 years and 8½ months to build. The sculptor *Timotheos* supplied the models for the pedimental sculptures, which were executed by other artists. The doors were of ivory and the cult statue in gold and ivory was by *Thrasymedes of Paros*. According to Pausanias Asklepios was represented seated on a throne, grasping a staff in one hand, and holding the other over the head of the serpent; a dog crouched by his side. Two marble reliefs, possibly copies of the statue, were found (now in Athens).

To the S of the temple is the *Great Altar of Asklepios*, and farther S, crossed by the line of the Byzantine wall, are the foundations of a small building which may be the *Epidoteion*, or sanctuary of the bountiful healers.

The most interesting building after the Theatre is the **Tholos**, or *Rotunda* (reconstruction project in progress), built c 360–320 BC by the same Polykleitos, a more florid and elaborate construction than the corresponding buildings at Delphi and Olympia. Nothing is left but the foundations, but a very good idea of the appearance of the building may be obtained from the partial reconstructions, drawings, and plans in the museum (comp. above). The foundations consist of six concentric walls, in conglomerate, with an extreme diameter of 22m.

The Rotunda stood on a stylobate of three steps. The three outer foundation walls supported an outer peristyle of 26 Doric columns, in poros, stuccoed and painted; the main circular wall of the building with a large portal flanked on either side by a window; and an interior colonnade of 14 marble columns with beautiful Corinthian capitals. The three inner foundation walls form a miniature labyrinth, the purpose of which, as indeed of the whole building, is obscure. A sacred well or a snake pit are among possibilities. Above the labyrinth rested a spiralling chequered pavement in black and white marble. The ceiling was coffered, carved, and painted. Lion's head gargoyles were regularly placed at the edge of the roof, on the apex of which was a carved floral acroterion.

To the N of the tholos and forming the N side of the area enclosed by the Byzantines, is a line of two adjacent stoas, each 10m deep, now reduced to their foundations. Their combined length was nearly 71m; the W colonnade was built, owing to the slope of the ground, in two storeys, so that its upper floor continued the level of the single storey of the E colonnade. The two together comprised the **Abaton**, or *Enkoimeterion*, the place of incubation. One or two of the benches which lined the walls and joined the columns still survive. A staircase of 14 steps led up to the second storey. In the E colonnade were found tablets (now in the museum) inscribed with accounts of miraculous cures. In the SE corner is an ancient *Well*, 17m deep; in the SW corner an underground passage. The well was sunk in the 6C BC and incorporated in the 4C building more, apparently, in piety than for practical use.

Turning N we leave over on our right a large Roman *Thermal Establishment* fed by water from Mt Kynortion and reach the main *Propylaea of the Sanctuary* with part of the *Sacred Way* from the town of Epidauros. The limestone pavement and the ramps leading to the great gate are in good condition. To the S among the trees are some not very clear remnants of a huge basilican *church* with double aisles and a large atrium. Skirting the boundary fence, to the W, we pass a small *Temple of Aphrodite* and a huge *Cistern* of Hellenic date.

We may leave by the NW gate and cross the road to the **Stadium**, arranged in a natural declivity during the 5C BC, with seats partly hewn from the rock and partly built up in masonry. The starting and finishing lines survive, c 180m apart, and the construction, without sphendone and with an inclined entrance tunnel, has some resemblance to its counterpart at Olympia. A stone water channel with basins at intervals surrounds the track.

TO KOSTA (for Spetsai), asphalt road. The right branch at (28km) the Epidauros turn (comp. above) runs S and E.—Beyond (43km) *Trakheiá* an unpaved road branches (left) to Méthana and Galatás (comp. Rte 23B); while c 1·5km farther on a by-road (right; at first unpaved) leads back to Nauplia via Íria (see Rte 28A). We continue S, cross the scrub-covered W flank of Mt Dhídhima (1074m), and from a saddle (488m) have a *View across the Argolic Gulf.—64km *Dhídhima*, which with its mountain preserves an ancient name, lies below in the centre of its circular plain.—76km. A road leads (right) to *Koiládha* (4km), an active fishing and boat-building village. In the *Fránchthi Cave*, on the N side of the bay, has been discovered a stratigraphical sequence going back to the Palaeolithic period (8th millennium BC), including, at the bottom of the Mesolithic deposit, the earliest complete skeleton found in Greece. This is a key site for the study of the Early and Middle Neolithic in Europe.—80km (50 miles) **Kranídhi** (Hotels C) is the market centre (3794 inhab.) of the peninsula. Hither the Greek senate removed in 1823 following their rupture with the executive. The chapel of the *Ay. Triádha* (Holy Trinity) has frescoes by John of Athens, dated to AD 1244. These include the Ascension and the Hospitality of Abraham. Ermioni (Rte 23D) lies 8km E.—We continue through fine stone-pines to 87km **Portokhéli** (Hotels A, B, C, D), on the N side of an inlet. The remains on the S side of the harbour have been equated with *Halieis*, settled by refugees from Tiryns after 479 BC. Here, from 1962–68 and subsequently, the American School of Classical Studies explored the ancient site which is now partly under-water. The fortification system is visible on the acropolis and its continuation has been traced beneath the sea. The lower town was laid out, in the 4C BC, on a grid plan with typical small courtyard houses; the higher zone is earlier in date and unplanned. The agora and an industrial quarter have been identified. To the SE of the town were found graves of the 6C–4C BC, one group covered by a tumulus.

Many huge summer hotel complexes have been built on the adjacent coasts; there is a ferry to Spetsai (40 minutes).

We turn left round the E side of the bay, and reach (93km) **Kósta**

(Hotels B), also undergoing holiday development. Ferry to Spetsai (several times daily in 15 minutes); also (more expensive) constant motor boats.

30 From Argos to Trípolis

ROAD, 61km (38 miles), one of the best in the Peloponnese, with good mountain scenery.—10km **Lérna**.—29km (18 miles) *Akhladhókambos*.—61km **Trípolis**. Buses from the square (originating from Athens; regularly in 4 hours).

RAILWAY, 69km (43 miles), 5 trains daily in 1½ hours, all starting from Athens (add 2½–3 hours; comp. Rtes 24, 26).

Leaving Argos by the avenue that passes the theatre (see Rte 26), the road turns S, skirting the hills that hem the Argolic plain.—5km. Byroad (right) to *Kefalári* (2·5km W), a shaded village at the foot of the precipitous Mt Khaon, where the Kephalari, the ancient *Erasinos*, issues from the rocks. The ancients thought that the waters came underground from Lake Stymphalos (51km NW; Rte 38). The spring (Kefalóvrisi) forms a pool, above which open two caverns, dedicated to Pan and Dionysos. The larger resembles an acute Gothic arch and extends c 60m into the mountain; the smaller one has been converted into the chapel of the Panayia Kefalarítissa. The ancient festival of *tyrbe* (disorder) is recalled by the modern festival on 18 April. Nearby, above prehistoric remains, is a fine large basilican church of the 6C, probably dedicated to St. Paul.

At *Kókla* (c 3km further) in 1981–82 were excavated some unplundered tombs of an important Mycenaean cemetery of LH I–II date. Nine chamber tombs and five pit graves were located, but the most important was a tholos tomb with a plastered and painted doorway and rich finds which included gold and silver vessels.
    About 2km SW (take a left turn just before Kefalári, signposted Ellinikó) on a hillock (left) stands the ruined PYRAMID OF KENKREAI, the more complete of the two pyramids in the Argolid. The interesting structure is of hard local limestone, laid roughly in courses, having both squared and polygonal blocks. A corbelled arch, at the SE corner, gives access by a blind corridor to an inner rectangular room. The pyramid was excavated in 1901 by Wiegand who concluded that it was not, as Pausanias believed the polyandrion of the Argives who fell at Hysiae. Louis Lord re-examined it (Hesperia 1938) and takes it to be a late-4C BC guard house used by patrols.

To the right Mt *Ktenias*, the ancient *Kreopolon*, rises to 1599m; Mt *Pontinos*, its easternmost spur, closes the Argolic Plain, extending to within 300m of the sea. On its summit rise the ruins of a Frankish castle, occupying the site of a house of Hippomedon and a temple of Athena Saïtis.

The vigorous defence of the narrow gap below on 25 June 1825 by Demetrios Ypsilanti with 227 men against a much larger force of Egyptians checked the advance of Ibrahim Pasha on Nauplia after his capture of Tripolis. From the shore here in 1941 Gen. Maitland Wilson, C.-in-C. Greece, departed by flying-boat to reorganise the continuing struggle in Crete. The Germans added three forts to defend the gap.

10·5km (6½ miles) *Míloi* (Μύλοι, the mills) lies between Mt Pontinos and the sea, on the site of ancient **Lérna**. Here in a sacred grove of plane-trees were celebrated the Lernaean mysteries in honour of Demeter, and here Herakles slew the Hydra. At the S end of the village, to seaward of the road on a mound fortified by the Germans in

1943, stands the conspicuous concrete shelter protecting the EXCAVATIONS made by the American School under John Caskey in 1952–58. The site was occupied from the 4th millennium BC to the close of the Mycenaean age, and is one of the most important in Greece for remains of the Early Helladic period. The *Fortifications* are virtually unique for their period. The HOUSE OF THE TILES, so-called from the extensive remains of its rectangular terracotta roof tiles, is the most elaborate E.H. building yet found. A palace, or administrative centre, it is 25m long and 12m wide and had two storeys. It was destroyed by fire at the end of E.H. II, so helping to preserve its mud-brick walls. The E.H. III level yielded pottery from Troy, whereas the Middle Helladic settlement, which here seems to follow without any violent upheaval, has pottery imports from near Niš (Balkan) as well as from Crete and the Cyclades. Two Mycenaean royal shaft graves (robbed in antiquity) cut through the house of the Tiles. Geometric graves have been found to the SW of the site.

We leave on our left a road to Astros (20km S).

Ástros (Hotel D), an agricultural centre (2459 inhab.), grows olives and fruit, being especially noted for peaches. It belongs to Kynouria, an eparchy of Arcadia. Here in 1823 was held the Second National Assembly called by various Klepht leaders of the insurrection to revise the constitution of 1821. The *Moní Loukoús* (4km away) has a church of 1100. *Parálion Ástros* (Hotel D) is pleasantly situated on the sea, 5km to the E. A good road continues via *Áyios Andréas* and *Tíros* along the precipitous coast to *Leonídhion* (Rte 32; 80km from Argos) and thence via *Kosmás* (a further 30km) to *Yeráki* (Rte 32; 50km from Leonídhion).

The road turns W, climbing *Merovítsa*, the S spur of Mt Ktenias, by steep, but well-engineered and protected, hairpin bends, which afford splendid retrospective *Views of the Argolic Gulf. The railway runs farther S in the red gorge of Kivéri, into which we cross by (21km) a saddle c 610m high (*View; café c 3km farther on). The valley opens out as we descend by sharp hairpin bends (springs).

At 18km (left) there is a turning to (30km) *Akhladókambos* (Αχλαδόκαμπος; 520m), a village (843 inhab.) on the hillside, with its railway station (273m) in the fertile valley below. The place takes name from the wild pear (αχλαδιά) which once grew on the mountain slopes.

On a ridge nearer the railway are the ruins of *Hysiai*, where the Argives defeated the Lacedaimonians in 669–668 BC. The town lay on the frontier between Argos and Tegea, and was destroyed by the Lacedaimonians in 417 BC. Its acropolis is marked by good polygonal walling.

We cross the railway twice on level ground, then ascend towards the head of the valley; the vegetation becomes scrubby and alpine. On a hill near the road summit (780m) are the ruins of *Moúkhli*, a Byzantine fortress used by the Franks and destroyed in 1460.—We enter Arcadia.

At (50km) *Ayioryítika* (Αγιωργίτικα) we rejoin the railway after its tortuous detour (far to the S) round *Parthenion* (1215m), now on our left. On Parthenion's slope a sanctuary once marked the spot where Pan promised the runner Pheidippides that he would aid the Athenians at Marathon.—52km *Stenón*, watered by the Sarandapotamos, lies amid rolling cornfields of the Plain of Tripolis.

The PLAIN OF TRIPOLIS, a monotonous plateau enclosed by an amphitheatre of barren mountains, really consists of two adjoining level tracts, the *Plain of Tegea* in the S and the *Plain of Mantinea* in the N. About 30km long from N to S and with an extreme width of 16km, it averages 655m above sea-level and suffers extremes of temperature with violent hail and thunderstorms in summer. Vines, wheat, and barley are grown, but, apart from the mulberry, the plateau is now almost treeless. There are several marshes, but few rivers or streams; such as exist mostly disappear into swallow-holes (katavothrae). The plain was famous in antiquity for the three Arcadian cities of Mantinea, Tegea, and Pallantion.

61km (38 miles) **TRÍPOLIS** (Τρίπολις; Hotels A, B, C, D), the capital (21,337 inhab.) and only large town of the nome of Arcadia, is the chief centre of communications in the Peloponnese. It lies in a bleak situation at the S foot of Mt Apáno Krépa (1559m), a peak of the Mainalon range. A modern manufacturing town, with hollow-ware and carpet factories, tanneries, and a flourishing wine production, it is also the seat of a bishop.

History. Tripolis was founded, under the name of *Droboglitza* or *Hydropolitza* about the 14C to take the place of the three derelict cities of the plain (comp. above) and the eparchy to which it belongs still keeps the name of Mantineia. Later it was called *Tripolitza* (in Turkish *Tarabolussa*) and became in 1770 the fortified capital of the Pasha of the Morea. It was taken in 1821 by Kolokotronis, when the Turkish population was massacred, and retaken in 1824 by Ibrahim Pasha, who completely destroyed it in the retreat of 1828. It revived after 1834.

The most attractive features of the town are the three squares, with animated cafés beneath their trees, and the saddlery and harness shops in the streets joining them. Some of the shops and cafés in the sidestreets have not lost their traditional style.

Buses of KTEL 6 Arkadias go from Plat. Ay. Konstandínou to (8km) *Aléa* (no refreshments), formerly Piali, the site of ancient Tegea. **Tegéa**, one of the oldest and most important cities in Arcadia, occupied a large area and its few remains are scattered.

The largest city in the plain, Tegea waged a long war with Sparta until beaten into submission c 560 BC as a vassal-state. The Tegeans sent 500 men to Thermopylae and 1500 to Plataia, and after the Persian wars tried unsuccessfully to throw off the yoke of Sparta with Argive aid. In the Peloponnesian War the Tegeans sided with Sparta. In 370 BC, after the battle of Leuktra, Tegea joined the Arcadian League, and at the second battle of Mantinea (362 BC) she fought on the side of Thebes against Sparta. In 222 BC Tegea became an unwilling member of the Achaean League. Still a flourishing city in the time of Strabo and in the time of Pausanias, Tegea was destroyed by Alaric in the 5C AD. It was refounded by the Byzantines, and under the name of *Nikli* it became one of the most important cities in the Morea. In 1209 Geoffrey de Villehardouin here established a barony.—Tegea was the birthplace of *Atalanta*, the fleetest runner of the age and the heroine of the Calydonian boar-hunt.

The site was excavated by the French School in 1889–90, 1902, and 1910 and by the Greek Archaeological Service in 1965.

In the village the bus stops outside a well-arranged little MUSEUM, reconstructed in 1967, containing finds from the site. *Central Room.* Marble thrones from the theatre; Hellenistic female statues.—*Room to left.* Sculpture from the Temple of Athena Alea, from the workshop of Skopas: Head of Telephos or Herakles; two torsos of Nike Apteros (not Atalanta); torsos of Heroes from the pediments; architectonic decoration from the temple.—*Room to right.* Six herms conjoined; Head of Herakles. Relief from a sarcophagus, depicting Achilles and the corpse of Hector. Reliefs: Lion, lioness; funeral feast.—*Inner Room,* beyond, in cases: Geometric bronzes from Asea, Classical vases, terracotta and Bronze statuettes; fragment of Daedalic relief; terracotta votives and plaques; Geometric and Archaic bronzes, both in the round and repoussé; funeral stelai; Early Helladic pots.

In 3 minutes we reach (near the church of Ayios Nikolaos) the TEMPLE OF ATHENA ALEA, excavated in 1889 and 1902. It was one of the most famous sanctuaries in Greece; here two kings of Sparta, Leotychides and Pausanias, took refuge, as well as Chryseis, the careless priestess of the Argive Heraion. An Archaic temple was burnt down in 395 BC and the rebuilding entrusted to Skopas of Paros. The new Temple had a Doric peristyle of 6 columns by 14, and an internal colonnade of Corinthian half-columns, with Ionic above. The substructure is virtually complete; many fragments of fallen column survive. The pediments were decorated with sculpture (? by Skopas), fragments of which survive in the local museum and in the National Museum at Athens. The E pediment represented the Hunt of the Calydonian Boar, with figures of Meleager, Theseus, Atalanta, and Ankaios. The W pediment depicted the Fight of Telephos and Achilles on the banks of the Kaikos in Mysia.

We continue to *Palaiá Episkopí* (20 minutes), where a huge church of 1888 replaces the Byzantine basilica of Nikli (fragments are rebuilt into the walls, and ancient mosaic ikons are venerated); a hotel has been provided for pilgrims. Under the triple apse is the semicircular retaining wall of the *Theatre*, rebuilt in marble by Antiochus IV Epiphanes (175–164 BC). In the great park to the W are fragments of the *Agora*. To the NE stands part of the medieval wall.—A long avenue leads directly to the main Tripolis–Sparta road at *Kerasítsa* (see below), where we may regain the bus.

The marble for the Tegea temple sculptures came from *Dholianá*, c 10km SE as the crow flies. A village bus from Tripolis (not daily) plies to *Vérvena*, a roundabout climb of c 30km, where the phylax may be found. Thence it is 40 minutes on foot to the Quarry, where a ruined 6C Temple of Artemis commands a *View over Arcadia.

FROM TRIPOLIS TO MANTINEA, 14km. The Kapsia road runs NNE across the plain. To the left is the long range of Maenalos with the village of *Merkovoúni* on the hillside. The cornfields give place to vineyards producing a celebrated non-resinated red wine. We approach the narrow gap (1·5km wide) between projecting spurs of Maenalos and Mt Ktenias that marked the ancient frontier between Tegea and Mantinea. On a shoulder of (6km) *Mýtika* (left) are the ruins of a square watchtower of polygonal masonry doubtfully identified as the *Skopí* ('look-out') from which the dying Epaminondas watched the

Second Battle of Mantinea. This district, once covered by an oak wood, was called *Pelagos* ('the sea'), thus satisfying the oracle's prediction that Epaminondas should beware of the sea. Here were fought several great battles (comp. below).

A by-road descends into the *Plain of Mantinea*, where are grown the marella cherries used in the manufacture of 'Vissinádha', a popular soft drink. The road passes through the **Ruins of Mantinéa**, marked by an eccentric church (1972), a Minoan-Classical-Byzantine folly dedicated to Ay. Photeini.

Mantinéa, anciently perhaps more correctly Mantíneia (629m), one of the most important Arcadian city-states, was the inveterate rival of Tegea, and its whole history is coloured by this mutual antagonism based probably on disputes over water-supply. The earliest settlement was 1km N on the hill of *Gortsoúli*, known to the ancients as *Ptolis*. Its existence from Geometric to Classical times was confirmed by excavation in 1962. In the Peloponnesian War the Mantineans were generally allies of Athens, the Tegeans being on the side of Sparta. After the Peace of Nikias in 421 BC Mantinea joined Athens, Argos, and Elis in the quadruple alliance that led up to the *First Battle of Mantinea* (418 BC), described by Thuc. 5. 64–74.

In 385 BC King Agesipolis, at the head of the Lacedaemonian army, besieged and took Mantinea after undermining the mud-brick fortification walls with the help of the dammed-up waters of the Ophis. He razed most of the city to the ground and dispersed the population. After the battle of Leuktra the Mantineans, with the help of Thebes, returned to their city, and built the extensive fortifications whose ruins we see today. They rearranged the course of the Ophis so that it became a protection instead of a danger. The foundation in 370 BC of the Arcadian League was due to the efforts of *Lykomedes*, a native of Mantinea, but six years later the Mantineans themselves seceded from it and openly joined the Spartans.

At the *Second Battle of Mantinea* (362 BC) Tegea, hitherto the age-long ally of Sparta, fought on the side of Thebes, while Mantinea shared in the defeat of her former enemy, Sparta (Xen. Hell., 7, 5, 18–27). Epaminondas was mortally wounded in the moment of triumph and the battle marked the end of the fourth and last Theban invasion of the Peloponnese. Joining the Achaean League the following century the Mantineans fought against Agis IV and helped to defeat Kleomenes III at Sellasia. Revolting against Macedonian dominance of the Achaean League, the city was captured in 222 BC by Antigonos Doson, who changed its name to *Antigoneia*, a name it kept until Hadrian's time. In 208 BC occurred another 'Battle of Mantinea', in which the Achaeans under Philopoemen defeated the Lacedaemonians, Philopoemen killing the tyrant Machanidas with his own hand (see Polybius, 11.11). An excellent exegesis of the three battles is in Pritchett, *Studies in Ancient Greek Topography* II.

The WALLS of Mantinea, though no longer standing to any height, are among the best examples of Greek period fortification. They are contemporary with the walls of Messene (c 370 BC), and may have been built by the same Theban architects. The circuit is almost entire, elliptical in form, with a perimeter of nearly 4km. The walls, encircled by the diverted *Ophis*, are built of large square or polygonal blocks; up to four courses are still standing. The curtain wall was 4m thick. There were over 120 square towers, placed about 26m apart, and 10 gates, defended in various ways.

Within the walls are the remains of the *Theatre*, of Roman date, and, immediately to the E, of the *Agora* and *Council House*.

A cemetery (late Classical to Roman) belonging to the site was excavated at Mília, to the W, in 1979.

FROM TRIPOLIS TO VITÍNA VIA ALONÍSTAINA, 36km (23 miles). The unpaved road quits Tripolis to the W, passing (5km) within 1km of *Selimna*, where the Russo-Greek forces gathered in the 1770 insurrection. We continue NW below the sullen slopes of Mainalon.—15km *Daviá*. A local 'Palaiókastro' marks the site of ancient *Mainalos*, with a medieval fortress. A temple with painted terracotta sculpture and architectural decoration was found here in 1972. The road divides (left, see Rte 36); the right branch continues round Mainalon to

(27km) *Alonístaina*, a pretty mountain village founded c 1300 amid wooded crags.—37km *Vítina*, see Rte 36).

31 From Trípolis to Sparta, Mistrá

ROAD to Sparta, 63km (39 miles) with views of wild grandeur, and thence to *Mistrá*, 6km farther.—BUSES from Athens, viâ Trípolis, to Sparta, about 8 times daily; from Sparta to Mistrá, see below.

A straight road runs across the plain of Tegea.—5km *Ayios Sóstis*, on the old road to the left, occupies the acropolis of Tegea; the main ruins (Rte 30) of the ancient city lie to the left at (8km) *Kerasítsa*. The road climbs into rocky hills with views back to the marshy *Lake Taka*, drained by swallow-holes.—14km *Manthiréa* (780m; formerly Kamári) has adopted the new name from Manthyrea, one of the nine original townships of Tegea.—19km Petrol Station (Restaurant; 854m). We cross an intermittently cultivated upland plain, then descend S to the *Kleisoura Pass*, the long defile that provides the best approach to Laconia, though we have already entered the modern nome. At the S end is a *Memorial* to 118 Spartans of the resistance movement who were killed by the Germans on 26 November 1943. We climb out of the defile to (42km) the summit (831m) of the pass crowned by a modern defence post. The road descends a ridge with *Views of the Taiyetos and Parnon ranges.

At 49km the site of ancient *Sellasia* appears (right) on a hill now crowned by a chapel of Ayios Konstandinos. At the BATTLE OF SELLASIA in 221 BC Antigonos Doson routed the Spartan forces of Kleomenes III. The young Philipoemen of Megalopolis distinguished himself in the allied Achaian force.—The twisting descent reaches (59km) *Kladhás*, where the tributary Oenous is crossed. Shortly after, a long iron bridge carries the road across the Eurotas into (63km) Sparta.

SPARTA (224m; Hotels B, C, D), in Greek **Spárti** (Σπάρτη), the capital of Laconia, seat of the Metropolitan of Sparta and Monemvasia, and the agricultural centre (11,911 inhab.) of the Eurotas valley, dates only from 1834. Laid out with broad streets on the Diktynnaion Hill (comp. below), the town enjoys a striking situation at the foot of Taiyetos and is protected on the E by the more distant Parnon. Cool breezes blow, especially in the early evening when the sun disappears behind the mountains. The olive and orange groves which produce its main livelihood are nowhere far distant; and if its buildings lack architectural merit, they are not so high as to spoil the spectacular mountain views.

ANCIENT SPARTA, or *Lakedaimon*, occupied a vast triangular area on the right bank of the Eurotas including six low hills: the *Kolona*, the *Acropolis*, the *Hill of Argive Hera*, the *Issorion*, the *Diktynnaion*, and the *Hill of Armed Aphrodite*. During the period of its greatness the city remained unwalled, since the natural strength of its position and the bravery of its soldiers were considered sufficient protection. The inhabitants dwelt in a group of five scattered townships, separated by gardens and plantations. Sparta had few of the magnificent public buildings that adorned other Greek cities and its scanty remains—as Thucydides foretold—reflect little of its ancient renown.

Buses from street opp. Hotel Menelaíon to *Trípolis* and *Athens*; from the same street to *Yithion* and *Monemvasia*; from the square to *Mistra*; to *Yeraki*; and to other Laconian villages.

History and Institutions. Though some traces of L.H. IIIB occupation have been found on the acropolis, Homeric *Sparta* seems to have been elsewhere, perhaps at *Therapnai* near the Menelaion, while *Kouphovouno*, to the SW, was occupied from Neolithic times. The only site so far discovered to be comparable in extent to Mycenae or Pylos is at *Amyklai*. *Lakedaimon* was a Dorian foundation and developed in its later history those traditions and customs least suited to urban progress. These fossilised into a constitution which by classical times was unique among city states. Tradition ascribes it to the reforms of Lycurgus (for whom many dates have been argued in the 9C–7C), but its developed form may not be earlier than the end of the 7C BC. The inhabitants of Lakedaimonia were divided into three classes; Spartans, or more correctly Spartiates, Perioikoi, and Helots, of whom only Spartiates had citizen rights.

The government of the state was composed of the five *Ephors*, the *Gerousia*, or council or elders, the two *Kings*, and the *Apella*, or assembly of citizens over 30 years old. The Gerousia consisted of 28 citizens over 60 years old and the two kings. They prepared necessary legislation and put it to the assembly. The ephors were elected annually and while in office were the most powerful men in Sparta, although final decisions of war and peace were in the hands of the Gerousia and the Apella. The kings were under the control of the ephors and the only power they retained was command of the army in the field. All citizens could attend the assembly, but its power was limited to accepting or rejecting proposals put to it by the Gerousia.

Our knowledge of Spartan 'caste' system is limited to its evolved state by the Classical period. The *Spartiates*, whose numbers may never have exceeded 10,000, were the rulers of Lakedaimonia. Each was given an estate of public land which was cultivated by slaves, leaving the Spartiate to spend his whole life in military and public service. From birth he was subject to stern discipline. Weak or deformed children were left to die on Taiyetos. Stronger children remained with their mothers until their seventh birthday. Their education in camps was supervised by young soldiers and discipline enforced by pack leaders; drill exercises and brutal competitive games figured largely. At twenty the Spartiate entered the army proper (perhaps after a period in the *Krypteia*, or secret police, which was at intervals let loose upon the Helots). He was expected to marry but continued to live in barracks and to eat in a mess on prescribed rations supplied from his own estate. He became a full soldier-citizen at the age of thirty.

Perioikoi, or 'dwellers around', lived in a number of villages in Laconia and neighbouring Messenia. They had no citizen rights but were free-men. Their only duty to the state was to serve, when called upon, as hoplites. The *Helots* were serfs and completely under the control of the Spartiates, whom they always greatly outnumbered. They consisted of the descendants of former inhabitants of Laconia and of surviving Messenians who were enslaved. They were obliged to cultivate the Spartiate's estates and to deliver the required produce from them.

Though the system itself had all the characteristics least acceptable to the 'democratic' ideal, either ancient or modern, the Spartan regime seems to develop its ruthlessly illiberal and wholly militaristic nature only about the time of the Persian wars. From the Geometric period to the 6C Spartan arts flourish; pottery, sculpture in bronze, and essential architecture, though never opulent, keep pace with those of other cities. The music and dancing of her festivals are famed. In the 7C poetry flourishes with the native Kinaithon, Terpander of Lesbos, and Tyrtaios. By the 5C every setback—the numerical inadequacy of the ruling caste, the earthquake of 464 BC, the chronic Messenian discontent—is countered only by greater austerity. This policy was superficially successful while the war machine functioned and the quality of Spartan troops made up for their dwindling numbers, but did nothing in the long run to stave off the inevitable effects of depopulation and an outmoded economy.

Spartan expansion began near the end of the 8C with the attack on the fertile territory of Messenia. This conquest was later followed by a long revolt of Messenians (685–668). After the region had been subdued Sparta began to increase her power in the Peloponnese. A long war with Tegea (c 600–560) showed that expansion was possible only by dominating vassal allies not by annexation. By the end of the century Tegea and Thyreatis were subdued and the *Peloponnesian League* instituted with Sparta at its head. Argos, the only neighbouring state that could hope to defy Sparta, was decisively defeated at Sepeia c 494.

Sparta took no part in repelling the first Persian expedition, but in 480–479 added to her prestige by the exploit of Leonidas at Thermopylae and the victory of Plataia under Pausanias. The later intrigues of Pausanias in Byzantium and the campaign of Leotychides in Thessaly, both opposed by Athens, showed Sparta that better policy lay in maintaining strength in the Peloponnese; control of the Aegean was left to Athens. In 464 the Helots revolted and only outside aid saved the state from destruction. The imperialism of Athens in the second half of the 5C forced the Greeks to turn to Sparta as their champion.

The Peloponnesian War ended with the defeat of Athens, leaving Sparta the most powerful state not only of the mainland, but also in the Aegean, where she waged an unsuccessful war with Persia. The Greeks were already finding Sparta a worse master than Athens and in 395 she was attacked by a coalition led by Athens, Thebes, Corinth, and Argos. Although Sparta triumphed on land (at Corinth), her fleet was defeated at Knidos in 394 and all hopes of an overseas empire were abandoned. With the peace of 386, Sparta kept her position by forcing the Persian terms on the rest of the cities. A powerful new enemy soon arose in Thebes; Theban hoplites, using new tactics, at Leuktra in Boeotia (371 BC) broke for ever the legend of Spartan invincibility. Epaminondas of Thebes invaded Laconia and reached the outskirts of Sparta itself. To keep Sparta powerless Messenia was revived as an independent state, the Arcadian League was formed, and a chain of fortresses was founded encircling Sparta's N frontier.

The Achaian League and the Macedonians continued the campaign against Sparta. In 295 BC Demetrios Poliorketes all but captured the city, and in 272 Pyrrhus could easily have taken it after defeating the Spartans in the field. Kleomenes III abolished the ephorate and ruled as a tyrant in a vain attempt to restore Spartan hegemony, but was utterly defeated at Sellasia. Sparta became a dependency of Macedon, regaining momentary independence only under the tyrants Machanidas (207 BC) and Nabis (195–192). After Nabis' assassination Philopoemen forced Sparta to join the Achaian League, razed the city walls, and repealed the laws of Lycurgus.

Under the Romans Laconia had a period of prosperity in the 2C AD as a province of Achaia and under Septimius Severus was even allowed to revert to a Lycurgan regime. The city was destroyed in AD 396 by Alaric and when the Slavs invaded in the 9C the population migrated to the Mani. The Byzantines refounded a town under the name *Lakedaimonia*, but by 1248 it had lost all importance to Mistra and disappears from history until 1834. Excavations were undertaken by the British School in 1906–10 and 1925–29.

The course of the CITY WALLS has been traced for most of the 10km circuit. The walls of Sparta were a feature of her decline. The first defences were made in 307–295 BC and supplemented when Pyrrhus threatened the city in 272. By 218 walls and gates existed. These were strengthened by Nabis against Flaminius, pulled down by the Achaians in 188 and rebuilt by Appius Claudius Pulcher in 184 BC.

Sparta centres upon a large flagged and arcaded PLATEIA, scene of the evening volta (unexpectedly elegant). To the E is the **Museum**, containing Laconian sculpture and votive offerings from the sanctuaries.

VESTIBULE. Stelai and inscriptions once bearing inlaid votive sickles of iron, dedicated to Artemis Orthia by boy-victors in ordeal contests; 218. Stele retaining its sickle.—ROOM 1 (right). Archaic reliefs and statuary. 1. Stele representing (?) Helen and Menelaus; terracottas from Amyklai.—ROOM 2 (beyond). Votive reliefs dedicated to the Dioscuri, notably those of the Archaic period; mixed Doric and Ionic capitals from Amyklai.—ROOM 3. 326. Statue of Artemis; *Leonidas in marble, upper part of a superb warrior statue, perhaps the memorial raised to Leonidas on his reburial at Sparta (it inspired the modern memorial at Thermopylae); 1030. Stele of Anaxivios (c 550 BC); 440. Stele of Damonon, victor in chariot races, with a long mutilated inscription recording the circumstances of its dedication (5C BC); small 5C grave relief from Yeraki; male torso. In cases: Mycenaean pottery from the Menelaion, Epidauros Limera, and elsewhere; also Neolithic from Alepotrypa (Mani); votive lamps and plaques, orientalising pottery (black on yellow).

ROOM 4 (left of vestibule). Masks in terracotta, lead votive figurines and limestone reliefs from the Sanctuary of Artemis Orthia; kraters and amphorae showing Spartiate warriors in combat; statuary representing Herakles; Archaic bronze *Figurines.—ROOM 5 (beyond). Archaising and later sculpture: Head of Artemis; Hermes; torso of Asklepios; Dioscuri; wild boar in steatite; 307. Fragmentary relief from a sarcophagus; 717. Triglyph and two metopes from the acropolis. Clay votive model of a Roman galley found in the sea.

SPARTA

| 0 | 400 yards |
| 0 | 400 metres |

TRIPOLIS

Moussga

Altar of Lycurgus

Heroon

Moundouna

Eurotas

Aqueduct

Athena Chalkioikos

Church

Olive Grove

Targaris Garden

Sanctuary of Artemis Orthia

Acropolis Lakedaimonia

N. Gate

Theatre

Church

Rotunda

Byzantine Wall

Kolona

Temple

S Gate

Portico

Agora

Tombs

Football Stadium

Mont

School

TRIAKOSION

THERMOPILON

Psychiko

Leonidaion

STADHIOU

TRIPOLEOS

KALAMATA

LEONIDHOU

KTEL Mistra

KTEL

LIKOURGOU

Dhimarkhion

PO

OTE

Os Nikonos

DAFNOU

Xenia

Museum

PAL.EVANGHELISTRIAS

MISTRA

Cathedral

Nomarkhia

PALAIOLOGOU

WC

MENELAOU

MONEMVASIAS

School

OTHONOS-AMALIAS

GYTHEION

Extent of Ancient City

Witti

N

*Mosaics survive from Roman villas in the town; the phylax will show these on request. The best known portray Orpheus, Zeus with Europa, and Alcibiades.

The ruins of **Ancient Sparta** lie N and NE of the modern town. We take Odhos Stadhíou at the top of which stands a modern memorial to Leonidas. His tomb lay near the theatre, where the broken statue believed to represent him was found. To the left of the sports stadium a track leads through olive-groves to the S gate of the ACROPOLIS, the highest of the low hills of Sparta (20m above the plain). Its walls were built between AD 267 and 386 and completed on the E side after the Slav invasion in the 8C. Here was the centre of Byzantine Lakedaimonia. The contour of the summit has been altered by a modern reservoir and the view is obscured by trees. Immediately inside the gate is a brick-built Roman portico of the 1C AD. Following the left path along the crest of the hill past two ruined 11C churches, we reach (below; left) the THEATRE built in the side of the hill in the 2C or 1C BC. Next to the theatre at Megalopolis it is the largest in Greece, but much of its masonry went into late fortifications or was quarried for Mistra. The stage buildings have been excavated and the cavea can be measured

seating area

by the existing retaining walls. The theatre, which was used for public meetings as well as theatrical performances, had a movable stage building which was pushed into position on wheels. The grooves of the tracks can be made out. The E parodos wall has more than 30 inscribed blocks, bearing lists of magistrates of the 2C AD. Numerous discoveries in emergency excavations beneath the modern town have attested to its prosperity in the Roman period when it had a regular plan and many fine houses with mosaics, etc.

Sparta, Theatre. Top: Plans of tracks for moving stage.
Bottom: Restoration of mobile stage building

The terrace to the N yielded in 1907 remains from the *Temple of Athena Chalkioikos*, a building, lined with bronze plates, legendarily associated with Aristomenes' defiant gesture at the beginning of the first Messenian revolt, when he came by night to hang up a shield with an insulting dedication; and later with the vindictive and sacrilegious treatment accorded to King Pausanias when he sought sanctuary here. Today nothing can be seen.

From the bend in Odhos Tripóleos a path descends to the **Sanctuary of Artemis Orthia**, scene of the endurance tests by flogging that featured in the upbringing of Spartan boys. The sanctuary existed in the 10C BC, and in Archaic times comprised a walled enclosure with an *Altar* on the E side and a small *Temple* on the W. In the 2C AD the whole complex was rebuilt and a Roman theatre built to accommodate spectators. There seem in earlier days to have been other contests of milder sort; singing, oratory, and probably not very gentle games for boys of 10 and upward. Farther N along the Eurotas are a *Heroön* and a huge stone altar.

Excursions may be made to the sites of the Menelaion (5km) and the Amyklaion (8km). For the first, we cross the Eurotas, turn right on the Yeraki road, and at 4·5km take a path to the left (20 minute walk), bearing right at the chapel of *Ayios Ilias*. On a hill of conspicuously red earth are three platforms on which stood the

Menelaion, or Shrine of Menelaus and Helen, whose identification, originally based on the records of Pausanias, has recently been confirmed by the discovery of dedications inscribed to both. Its ruined masonry is imposing and the view superb. Just below the summit to the NE are Mycenaean remains uncovered in 1910 and since 1973. These consist of a 'Mansion' of which three structural phases have been distinguished; the first on the lower terrace only, the second and third involving additional elements on the terrace immediately above. The arrangement of rooms in all phases closely resembles that of the developed Mycenaean palaces (comp. below, Palace of Nestor at Pylos), though on a more modest scale. Mansion 1, dated to the 15C BC, is one of the earliest of such complexes so far known. The site was destroyed by fire in c 1200 BC. There are other Mycenaean remains in the vicinity, suggesting that the site covered a large area.—From the centre of Sparta the Yithion road leads to modern Amiklai, where we turn left at a sign 'Amyklyon' to *Ayía Kiriakí*, a chapel on the site of the *Amyklaion*, excavated by the German School in 1925. The sanctuary surrounded the Tomb of Hyakinthos, which was crowned by an archaic statue of Apollo seated on a chryselephantine throne. Here took place the great festival of the Hyakinthia in July. The place is firmly identified by an inscription, but the remains are not illuminating. The site however seems to have had continuous occupation since Mycenaean times (and Hyakinthos is a pre-Greek deity). The church of *Ayía Paraskeví*, to the S, may occupy the site of the *Sanctuary of Zeus-Agamemnon and Alexandra-Kassandra*, from which a huge Archaic votive deposit with hero-reliefs was unearthed close by in 1956.—**Amyklai**, the ancient capital of the Mycenaeans in Laconia, probably lay nearby at *Palaiopíryi*, the largest Late Helladic settlement yet discovered in Laconia, and close to the Vaphio tomb (guide necessary). Palaiopiryi has not been excavated.

THE EXCURSION TO MISTRA (8km W) should on no account be missed. Buses, though not infrequent, are irregular with a long mid-morning interval. The road runs W to the foot of Mt Taíyetos, crossing a luxuriant region, thick with orange, fig, and mulberry trees. The eroded mountain sides are scored with langadhes (deep gorges), each with its torrent. The gorge of *Paróri*, the gloomiest and most forbidding ravine, has been identified with the *Apothetai* where the Spartiates used to expose their weakly children. It may also be the *Kaiadas*, or criminal pit, from which Aristomenes made a miraculous escape. To the N of Parori is the Gorge of Mistra, at the entrance to which is a hill with the ruins of the medieval city. We pass through modern Mistrá.

**MISTRÁ (Μυστράς), a purely medieval town in its ruin, has been likened to a Byzantine Pompeii, though it has a nearer parallel in Les Baux in Provence. Churches, monasteries, palaces, and houses line the narrow winding streets. The situation alone would make it an enchanting spot, but within its walls are preserved some of the finest examples of 14–15C Byzantine architecture in Greece, and the numerous wall-paintings are among the most characteristic of their kind. Unfortunately they had already reached an advanced stage of decay before reconstruction of the churches provided so much more for the visitor to enjoy (even if its authenticity is sometimes doubtful). An impregnable fortress crowns the summit.

History. On the hill of *Mezythra*, 5km from medieval Lakedaimonia, William de Villehardouin built a fortress in 1249 to protect the town from the marauding Slavs of Taíyetos. Mezythra was corrupted by the Franks to *Mistra*, which in the French dialect of the time meant 'mistress'. Villehardouin, taken prisoner in 1259 at Pelagonia by Michael Palaiologos, was forced after three years captivity to surrender Mistra, together with Monemvasia and Maina, by way or ransom. The Greeks, using Mistra as a base, drove the Franks into Elis, but were completely defeated in 1265 in the defile of Makriplagi near Gardiki and William returned to Laconia. The inhabitants of Lakedaimonia had meanwhile settled on the hill of Mistra under the protection of the fortress.

After 50 years of strife the Greeks reconquered the greater part of the Morea. Monemvasia gave way in importance to Mistra and here from 1349 the peninsula was governed by a Despot, either a son or brother of the emperor (often his heir presumptive). The despots were successively Manuel Cantacuzene (1349–80);

Matthew, his brother (1380–83); and Demetrios (1383–84). Here after his abdication in 1354 John VI Cantacuzene lived with his sons as the monk Ioasaph Christodulos (died 1383). The Cantacuzenes were followed by the Palaiologi; Theodore I Palaiologos (1384–1407), who became a monk and was succeeded by his nephew, Theodore II (1407–43); Constantine Dragatses (1443–48) who succeeded to the Imperial throne to be the last Emperor of Byzantium; and Demetrios (1448–60), whose unedifying squabbles with his brothers gave the Turks their opportunity. In 1400–42 Mistra was the home of the philosopher Gemistos Plethon, the rediscoverer of Plato. Card. Bessarion (1389–1472), the illustrious scholar of Trebizond, attended his lectures in 1423.

Mistra passed to the Turks in 1460, though it was temporarily invested in 1464 by Sigismondo Malatesta of Rimini, then in the service of Venice. From 1687 to 1715 the city was in the hands of the Venetians when it reached its second peak of prosperity. It attained a population of 42,000, whose main industry was silkworm culture. On the return of the Turks the town rapidly declined. It was burnt in 1770 by Albanian troops after the Mainotes had captured it for Orloff, and again in 1825 by Ibrahim's soldiers. After the refounding of Sparta in 1834 Mistra was virtually abandoned. The French School saved the site from complete ruin in 1896–1910, but it served as a battlefield in 1944 between various partisan forces. The last 30 families were moved by the Greek Archaeological Service in 1952, and wholesale reconstruction has since been undertaken by Prof. A. Orlandos.

The ruins rise on the N and E side of the hill. They are in three parts. The *Kastro* occupies the summit; below to the N is the walled *Upper Town* (Khora), the houses of which cluster around the Despot's palace; below again extends the *Lower Town* (Katokhora), added somewhat later, which includes the cathedral. The parapets and upper sections of defence walls are generally Turkish refurbishings. A modern motor road ascends the hill to a point above Ayia Sophia (car park), providing the easiest approach to the Kastro. It is best to enquire below whether this entrance is open. The bus stops at the main gate. About 150m farther on is the *Byzantion Hotel* (B).

We enter by a restored gate into the LOWER TOWN and turn right.

The CATHEDRAL, or *Metropolitan Church of Ayios Dhimitrios* (Metrópolis), built (or perhaps rebuilt) in 1309 by the Metropolitan Nikephoros Moschopoulos, stands in a spacious court in which are an antique sarcophagus and a fountain dated 1802. The basilica was altered in the 15C when the upper part was replaced by five domes after the model of the Aphentiko. As a result the paintings in the nave have been cut in two. The arcade of the marble ikonostasis has remarkable fretwork carving; the cornice above was added in the 15C. The 17C walnut throne is richly carved. In the floor is a two-headed marble eagle that possibly commemorates the coronation here of the Emp. Constantine XII (comp. above). The paintings are ascribed to ten different artists in three periods. Those in the *N Aisle* (Portraits of saints, Torture and burial of St. Demetrios, Sufferers from dropsy and leprosy), are shown by their symmetry and repose to be the earliest works. *S Aisle*, Prophets, Life of the Virgin, Miracles of Christ, more realistic (14C). *Narthex*, also 14C but by a different hand, Last Judgement.

Adjoining the Cathedral is the **Museum**, formed by Gabriel Millet (died 1954), who did so much to save Mistra from further ruin. It contains decorative fragments, mostly from the churches. Marble relief of Christ; fragments of a lintel with the monogram and arms of Isabella de Lusignan.—Little survives of the *Episcopal Palace*, part of which gave place to monastic cells in 1754.

Above and to the left stands the 14C *Evangelistria*, a simple mortuary chapel (two ossuaries) with good sculptural detail (notably ikonostasis). We diverge (right) from the main street for the **Vrontókhion**, a great monastic complex, cultural centre, and burial-place of the Despots. It has two churches, both built by the Archimandrite Pachomios, the first *Ayii Theodori* (c 1296) being the last in date of the churches in Greece built with a central octagon (comp. Daphni, on a larger scale). It was restored in 1932. Farther on is the attractive

APHENTIKÓ, or *Panayia Hodegetria*, dating from 1310 but much restored since it was largely pulled down in 1863. It was the earliest church at Mistra built to a composite plan, a fusion of the basilica and the cross church with domes, an idea revived from earlier practice. It has four small cupolas and a central dome (rebuilt), with a beautiful bell-

The INTERIOR is remarkable for its proportions, its purity of line, and the carved ornamentation. The marble facings have disappeared. In a side chapel on the N side of the narthex is the tomb of Theodore II, with (above) frescoed portraits of him in the robes of despot (Aphentis) and the habit of a monk. Here also the tomb of Pachomios. In the corresponding S chapel the walls bear copies of chrysobuls detailing the foundation, properties, and privileges of the monastery. The *Frescoes, in bold colour, include the Miracles of Christ (narthex); Group of

Martyrs (in NW chapel); and a panel of St. Gregory, the illuminator of Armenia (in the apse).—The ruined *Cells* and the *Refectory* can be identified.

Beyond the Evangelistria the road passes under a machicolated Gothic archway and higher up divides: the left branch leads to the Pantanassa, which we visit on the descent. By the right branch we enter the UPPER TOWN by the *Monemvasia Gate*, pass below a tall 15C house with arcades and machicolations, skirt a small *Mosque*, and reach the square in front of the Despot's palace.

The **Palace of the Despots** (*Anaktora*), a rare example of a civic Byzantine building, is an extensive ruin dating from various periods. The wing nearest to the mosque may have been erected under the

Franks (13C) and had two successive additions under the Cantacuzenes. The Palaiologi added in the 14C the fourth building in the
line and in 1400–60 the immense vaulted audience-hall at right angles; its façade was painted and its flamboyant windows are framed in
porós mouldings and covered with stucco. The hall was heated by
eight chimney-pieces. Behind the palace are other official buildings
which extend to the massive *Nauplia Gate*, protected by an external
redoubt.

Visitors who are pressed for time should here turn back and make directly for the
Pantanassa and Perivleptos.

To the W of the palace, beyond a small *Turkish Bath* is the church of
AYIA SOPHÍA, built in 1350 by Manuel Cantacuzene as the katholikon
of the Zoödhotos monastery. It was used as the palace chapel and here
are buried Theodora Tocco, wife of Constantine (died 1429) and
Cleopa Malatesta, wife of Theodore II (died 1433). There survive remains of the ikonostasis, of the pavement, and of the refectory and
cells. The paintings were preserved by Turkish whitewash. A fine
view is obtained from the porch.

Hence we continue to ascend, passing under a small aqueduct, to
the **Kastro**, built in 1249 by William de Villehardouin and repaired and
refortified along existing lines by the Turks, so that the plan remains
Frankish even though much of the masonry is later. The *Keep* (564m)
commands a magnificent *View, well demonstrating its strategic
importance.

On the descent we may pass Ayia Sophia and make our way through ruined
houses (right) to the so-called *Little Palace*, a spacious Byzantine house of early
date, then go down steps to *Ayios Nikolaos*, a curious building of the Turkish
period with a modern roof.

The **Pantánassa**, the most beautiful of the churches of Mistra, was built
in 1365 by Manuel Cantacuzene and enlarged in 1428 by John
Frangopoulos, protostrator (minister) of Constantine Palaiologos. It
now belongs to a nunnery. In plan the church resembles the Aphentiko, but the proportions are more slender. It is orientated N–S. A
broad flight of steps leads to a picturesque loggia commanding a fine
view over the Eurotas valley. Over the narthex is a gallery reached by
an external staircase and opening into the Gothic tower (splendid
*View). The side galleries are continued over the aisles as far as the
apses.

The paintings in the body of the church are late, with the exception of the fine
portrait of Manuel Chatsikis (1445) in the narthex. Those in the galleries are more
decorative. Under the W gallery will be observed a happy combination of architectural lines and painted ornament (fine Head of Prophet on the NW
pendentive); in the NW cupola is a vigorous Patriarch. Note also Palm Sunday,
with children playing; Annunciation; and Presentation in the Temple.

We descend a path on the open flank of the hill to the Monastery of the
PERÍVLEPTOS, named on a plaque over its entrance (1714). The *Church*
(latter half of the 14C) in stone and brick, with pentagonal apses and
an octagonal dome, has the pure style of three centuries earlier. Below
the E end is an unusual little chapel with a tiled pavement. To the S of
the church is a square battlemented tower, richly ornamented on its E
face. The *Frescoes give a good idea of the iconography of a 14C
Byzantine church. The dome has retained its Pantokrator. Above the
side entrance, Dormition of the Virgin; in the Prothesis chapel to the
left, Divine Liturgy, celebrated by Christ and the angels; in the Bema,

Ascension; in the vaulting of the S transept, Nativity; In the W nave, Transfiguration (observe the silhouette of Christ); in the S aisle, Childhood of the Virgin.

Returning towards the main gate we pass (right) the 18C *House of Krevatas*, a vast mass of ruins. The chapel of *Ayios Ioannis* lies outside the walls near the *Marmara Fountain*.

FROM SPARTA TO YERÁKI, 40km (25 miles), asphalt and gently undulating through cultivated country; bus. We take the Tripolis road and beyond the bridge turn right. Soon after there is an unpaved turning (left) to *Khrísafa* (Χρύσαφα; 20km), where the churches of the Chrysaphiótissa (1290) and Ayii Pándes (1367) both have wall paintings. Ayios Dhimítrios dates from 1641, and the Moní Prodhrómou from 1625.—We continue along the left bank of the Eurotas. At *Skoúra* we turn E. 2km N of Skoura, at *Melathriá*, on the hill of *Profítis Ilías*, is a cemetery of Mycenaean chamber tombs.—Beyond (24km) *Goritsá* we get a distant view towards Yeraki across a wide valley.—40km **Yeráki** (Γεράκι), a large village (1638 inhab.), almost unknown to tourists, occupies the site of ancient *Geronthrai*. Its imposing acropolis (591m) has walls in the cyclopean style, best preserved on the N and E. They were investigated in 1905 by the British School and certainly date from Mycenaean times; they may even have Middle Helladic origins. A small *Museum* contains local finds.

About ½ hour SE by bad road (4-wheel drive advisable) on a long detached ridge of Parnon stands medieval *Geraki*, one of the original 12 Frankish baronies, with remains of fifteen small medieval churches. It is best to contact the phylax in the village (enquire at cafés in main square) for directions and to open the churches which are nearly all locked. The KASTRO, at the N end of the ridge (easy path in 20 minutes to summit), was built by Jehan de Nivelet in 1254. It commands fine views of Parnon and Taiyetos. *Ayios Yeóryios*, the basilican castle chapel (13C), has a florid Gothic shrine recalling South Italian work. The W door of the *Zoödókhos Piyí* (1431), and the shrine in *Ayía Paraskeví*, both lower down the slope, show rude incised and sculptured decoration in a local Gothic idiom. During cleaning in 1964, frescoes of the late 12C were found in the *Evangelistria*; particularly interesting are those in the dome. *Ayios Sózon* has frescoes of the same period. *Ayios Athanásios* has been over-restored (dome rebuilt). The church at the extreme S end of the ridge has a mural painting representing Joshua attacking a city of the Amorites.

FROM SPARTA TO KALAMATA, 60 km (37½ miles) over the *LANGADHA PASS. (Occasional buses). The road is steep with hairpin bends and affords marvellous views of the Taiyetos and into Messenia on the W. The road is asphalt but the safety of the crossing depends on weather conditions.—5km. Superb view of Mistra (left). At 7km we start to climb, and at (9km) *Trípi* (Hotel D) enter the Langadha Gorge. To the right is one of the places claimed as that where the Spartans exposed weakly children. After 16km we pass into Messenia amid fir forests. There are superb views of the Taiyetos peaks, often snow-capped.—24km Hotel (B). At the summit (1524m), a little farther on, is a Tourist Pavilion.—35km *Artemísia*. We descend a gorge but, at 48km, climb a steep zigzag to a col, from the top of which fine view down to Kalamata. The road enters Kalamata by the Frourion; for the centre we keep the river on our right.

32   Southern Laconia

The predominantly mountainous region·S of Sparta is seldom visited by foreign tourists and little more by the Greeks themselves. The area is however now more accessible with mainly asphalted roads, between Sparta and Monemvasia and from Leonidhion, across Mt Parnon, to Yeraki. Nevertheless, in the Taíyetos and Parnon ranges the mule is still often the only means of transport; haste is impossible, accommodation limited and often primitive. The unhurried visitor who is willing to travel light will, however, be rewarded by superb scenery and unexpected traces of the past. Byzantinists will not willingly miss seeing Monemvasia, best approached by sea. Yithion is a quiet and pleasant enough seaside town. Like Cornwall, southern Laconia is ethnically several invasions behind the rest of the country. The Maniots claim never to have been conquered by Slav or Turk, the Tzakonians to have survived from remoter times still; but claims by either to be indigenous are exaggerated or at best unproven. Certainly both peoples display characteristics of their own and are very resistant to change.

A. From Piraeus by Sea

STEAMER weekly to *Monemvasía* in 6–8¾ hours, continuing either to Kíthira and Andikíthira direct, or via Neápolis and Kithira to *Yíthion* (in 22¾ hours) as described below.
HYDROPLANE ('Flying Dolphin') daily in summer (3½ hours to Monemvasia) as far as Neapolis, sometimes to Kasteli, in western Crete.

Quitting Piraeus harbour the ship steams due S for Cape Skillaion, passing E of Aegina and between Hydra and the mainland of Argolis (comp. Rte 23). We leave Trikkeri and Spetsopoula to starboard, then head W across the open sea.

4 hours *Skála* is the landfall for **Leonídhion** (Λεονίδι), the chief town (3,557 inhab. Hotels C, D) of Kynouria, an Arcadian eparchy which is separated from the hinterland by the abrupt ranges of Mt Parnon, a long and sparsely populated range rising to 1936m, without low passes. Wolves still have their habitat here. A large wooded tract was designated as a game reserve in 1961.

FROM LEONIDHION TO YERAKI VIA KOSMAS, 50km (31 miles), asphalt except for 16km between Kosmás and Yeráki, which is adequate. In Leonidhion the road (signs to Sparti) turns inland past a memorial to the dead of a battle (1949) in the civil war, climbs to pass below the *Moní Elónas* and crosses Parnon (spectacular scenery) to Kosmas and Yeraki (50km, Rte 31).

6½ hours *Kiparíssi* (Κυπαρίσσι; Hotels C), a charming village, occupies an olive-planted plateau above its picturesque little harbour (*Paralía*) at one of the few points where the forbidding Laconian coast does not rise sheer from the sea.—We follow the rugged and lonely seaboard. The white *Evanghelístria Monastery* is backed by a hill crowned with three round fortress towers.—7¾ hours. *Limín Iérakos*, known also as Kastrí or Yéraka, the harbour of *Iérax*, a mountain village, is enchantingly situated in a narrow fjord. Dominating the entrance from the N, on a flat rock, is an extensive and unexplored acropolis of (?) Mycenaean date (*Zarax*).

8¾ hours **MONEMVASÍA** (Μονεμβασία; Hotels A, B, C, D), aptly described as the Gibraltar of Greece, owes its name to the single entrance (μονὴ ἐμβασις) by which it is reached from the landward side. Called by our old writers *Malmsey*, by the Venetians *Napoli di Malvasia*, and by the French *Malvoisie*, it was once famous for its export of wine. Situated at the seaward end of a forbidding rocky promontory, the decayed Byzantine town (*G.H.*), melancholy and evocative (especially by night) now shelters only 52 of the 631 inhab., the majority of whom live in *Yéfira* (Hotels B, C, E), the mainland settlement. The two are linked by a succession of causeway, bridge (renewed 1889), and roadway round the S side of the rock. The ship anchors in the bay and landing is made near the causeway.

History. The promontory was anciently called *Minoa*, a name that suggests but by no means proves Cretan influence. After the Slav invasion it became a refuge for the Greeks of Laconia and, under the name of *Monemvasia*, it developed into an important fortress and flourishing port. In 1147 it repulsed an attack by the Normans of Sicily and thereafter was nearly always the last outpost of the Morea to fall to succeeding waves of conquerors. In 1249 William de Villehardouin took it after a siege of three years, but he had to give it up in 1262, with Mistra and the Maina, to Michael Palaiologos, in payment of his ransom. It became the tenth see in the empire, the commercial capital of the Byzantine Morea, and enjoyed special exemptions and trading privileges. The town later came into the hands of the Pope (1460–64), of the Venetians (1464–1540 and 1690–1715), and of the Turks (1540–1690 and 1715–1821). In 1564 the Turks repelled an attack of the Knights of Malta. Monemvasia was the scene in April 1821 of a particularly odious massacre of the surrendered Turkish garrison. Hence in 1941 c 4000 men of the 6th N.Z. brigade were successfully evacuated.—Malmsey, or Vin de Malvoisie, was originally the name of the celebrated red and white wines shipped from Monemvasia, though produced in Tinos and other Aegean islands.

The end of the approach road (20 minutes) is barred by the impressive W wall with towers and bastions, which descends directly from the castle to the sea. A tiny gate admits pedestrians and their donkeys. Within, the houses are piled upon one another and intersected by steep, narrow, and intricate streets. In the LOWER TOWN four churches survive of an original forty. The CATHEDRAL of the diocese, the largest medieval church in Laconia, dedicated to *Elkómenos Chrístos* (Christ in chains), dates from the reign of Andronikos II, who in 1293 elevated the see to metropolitan rank. The portal was rebuilt of Byzantine fragments in 1697. Massive piers with pointed arches support the heavy barrel-vaulted nave and aisles. Opposite, *Ayios Pávlos*, built in 956 and transformed by the Turks, serves as a *Museum* of marble fragments, including a Frankish tombstone of 1245 and a 16C font. Just above stands the decayed *Myrtidiótissa*, and farther on, nearer the sea, the 16C *Panayía Chrysaphítissa*, attractively restored and whitewashed.

We wind up a fortified zigzag to the KASTRO, or *Goulá*, entered by a tunnel that still retains iron-bound gates. The ruins, extensive but indeterminate, have been fenced round. On the edge of a vertiginous cliff (*View of wild grandeur at sunset) stands **Ayia Sophia**, a splendid Byzantine church founded by Andronikos II, on a plan similar to that at Daphni, well restored in 1958. The exo-narthex is a Venetian addition. The five doorways have sculptured marble lintels. Four frescoed medallions survive in the squinches, above which a 16-sided drum of impressive proportions supports the dome. The church also contains fragments of frescoes assigned to the early 13C; in the sanctuary, the Ancient of Days (vault), hierarchs; in medallions in the drum of the dome, busts of saints; in the narthex, above the entrance to the nave, Christ Pantokrator between worshipping angels.

On the cliffs, 5km N of the town, *Palaiá Monemvasía* occupies the site of *Epidauros Limera*, a colony from Epidauros and one of the free-Laconian cities. The walls of the acropolis are traceable all round; in some places they retain more than half their original height. The town was divided into three by cross walls.

FROM MONEMVASIA TO SPARTA. ROAD, 95km (59 miles) asphalt. Regular buses to *Molaoi* and Sparta in c 6 hours; by changing at Tarapsa, it is possible to reach Yithion in c 7 hours and even the Mani the same day; through bus occasionally to Athens.

From Monemvasia a bad road runs N along the sandy shore of *Ayía Kiriakí*, turning inland short of Epidauros Limera (comp. above) into a stony valley of scrub.—At 12km we are joined by a road from Velies and Neapolis (41km).—17km *Sikéa* (1084 inhab.) stands (left) on a hill above the road. We cross a plain cultivated with olives, leaving on the left a turning for Papadhianika and Plitra.—22km **Moláoi** (Inns), a well-watered market town (2416 inhab.) below a ravine on the E slope of an isolated hill (914m), preserves remnants of a fortress and of a Byzantine church.

Among low stony hills we pass below the *Monastíri tis Kanganiás* (1km left) and leave (35km) a turning for *Apidéa* (8km right), which preserves a 14C church and traces of the walls of ancient *Kome*.—45km *Vlakhióti* (Βλαχιώτης; Hotel D), a depressing village (1925 inhab.), is connected by road with Yeraki (17km). Among rice and cotton fields (3km left) lie vestiges of *Helos*, by tradition the first town to be enslaved by the Spartans, providing an etymology for the word 'Helot'. Many traces of prehistoric occupation have also been noted near *Astéri*, to the S. We pass the old church of Paniyiristra and cross the Eurotas.—47km *Skála* (Hotels D) is the modern market (2790 inhab.), of the plain.—62km *Krokeaí* (1585 inhab; Hotel D) was famed in antiquity for its stone quarries (Lapis Lacedaemonius). The ancient town lay to the SE of its modern counterpart and the quarries beyond.—At (72km) *Kháni Tárapsa* we join the main Sparta–Yithion road (Rte 32B).—95km **Sparta**, see Rte 31.

The steamer next passes Cape Kamíli, a low narrow promontory, beyond which rises *Cape Maléa*, the S extremity of Laconia. The cape, the 'Formidatum Maleae caput' of Statius, was dreaded by mariners.—Doubling the cape, we come to (11 hours) *Neápolis* (Hotels B, D), a small town (2107 inhab.) on the Voiátic Gulf. This and the peninsula take name from the free-Laconian town of *Boiai*, some remains of which can be seen near the shore to the S. A museum is destined to house finds from the Pavlopetri site (M.H.–L.H.), to the N, investigated by Cambridge University in 1967–68, mostly underwater. The gulf is closed on the W opposite Pavlopetri by *Elafónisos*, anciently a promontory named Onugnathos (ass's jaw) and now separated from the mainland by a strait c 400m wide. After calling at (11¾ hours) its little port, the steamer heads S to Kithira.

Kíthira (Κυθηρα), or *Kythera*, known to the Venetians as *Cerigo*, and historically one of the Ionian Islands (comp. Rte 56), has more recently been administered as an eparchy of Piraios. It is connected with Athens by air (7 times weekly in May–Oct). With Andikithira (see below) it has 3469 inhabitants. Kithira, 32km long by 19km broad, is separated from Elafonisos by a channel 8km wide. The surface of the island is rocky but the hills do not exceed 503m. It is mostly uncultivated, but some parts produce corn, wine, and olive-oil. The honey is much esteemed.

History. In remote antiquity *Kythera* is said to have been called *Porphyrousa* from its abundant murex. The Phoenicians may have developed its purple industry and introduced the worship of Syrian Aphrodite, but in the first half of the 2nd millennium BC it was a Minoan colony. In the Iliad Amphidamas and Lykophron are native to Kythera. In the Peloponnesian War the island guarded the S seaboard of Lakedaimonia until subdued by Athens in 424. It became a Venetian possession in the late 13C, having previously been under Byzantine rule. After the Fourth Crusade it suffered from pirate raids, the inhabitants being sold into slavery by Barbarossa in 1537. In 1715–18 it passed into Turkish hands but from 1719–97 was again controlled by Venice, thereafter sharing the fortunes of the Ionian islands (comp. Rte 56) until 1864. The Greek island, at first linked with Laconia, is now administered by Attica. Its population has halved in the last century and its economy is now tied to migrants in Australia. Some 850 British troops got away via Kithira in 1941 after the mainland was completely in German hands.

Its two weekly steamers from Piraeus call first at *Ayía Pelayía* (11–13 hours) in the NE, then at Kapsáli at the S end of the island.

13–15 hours *Kapsáli* is joined by road (3km) with **Khóra**, or *Kithira*, the chief place (268 inhab.), which stands on a narrow ridge 500m long, terminating at the SE end in a precipitous rock crowned by a medieval *Kastro* with a museum. There is a small Hotel and a few rooms are available locally. Visitors should be aware that accommodation can be extremely difficult to find in season.

Of interest to the visitor are the stalactite caverns and the Minoan colony site of Kastri, near *Avlémonas* (24km from Chora; summer camping site at Palaiópolis) on the wide E bay. It was occupied as a trading post c 2000–1450 BC; the British School excavation here in 1964 also showed Neolithic, Roman and Early Byzantine occupation. Palaiokastro, farther inland, is believed to be the site of ancient Kythera. Here the church of Ayios Kosmas incorporates Doric capitals traditionally associated with a sanctuary of Aphrodite.

Also on the E coast, some 9km from the village of *Pótamos* (bad road) is the deserted Byzantine settlement of *Palaiochóra* (30km from Chora).

On the W coast, near *Milopótamos* and a few hundred metres W of the village, is an early 16C castle. Near the same village (c 2·5km S, to the right of the road to Chora) is a cave which has been transformed into a simple one-aisled chapel dedicated to *Ayía Sophía* and her daughters the Saints *Elpis*, *Pistis* and *Agape* (Hope, Faith and Charity). The well-preserved frescoes which decorate the stone iconostasis are 11–early 12C.

To the N (c 6km) of Chora, in the village of *Livádhi*, is a church of *Áyios Andréas*, of domed-inscribed cross type with an irregular three-naved basilican appearance. Fragments of frescoes from three periods (9C, 11C and early 13C) have been distinguished.

About 37km to the SE of Kithira and nearly half-way to Crete is the little island of ANDIKITHIRA (Αντικύθηρα), or *Cerigotto* (14 hours from Piraeus, twice weekly), known as *Lious* to its 115 inhabitants. Like Crete it has undergone upheavals in recent times: along the entire coastline runs a dark band, rising to a height of c 3m above the present sea-level, and exhibiting furrows formed by a dozen successive sea levels. The chief place is the hamlet of *Potamos*, 1·5km NE of which, on the headland of Palaiokastro, are the walls (5–3C BC) of *Aigilia*, chief place of classical Antikythera.

In the channel between Kithira and Andikithira are the remains of a wreck of the 1C BC which has yielded bronzes and marbles now in the National Museum.

B. From Sparta to Yíthion and the Máni (Alika)

ROAD, 101/123km (63/76 miles), asphalt throughout, excellent to Yíthion (bus several times daily) and Areopolis (bus 3 times daily). 24km *Khâni Tárapsa*.—46km **Yíthion**.—73km **Areópolis**. Thence alternative routes to *Alika*: 2km S of Areopolis, a turn (left) leads to the E coast to join the main S road at Alika (1 bus daily) via (85km) *Kótronas*.—109km *Láyia*.—123km **Álika**. The W coast road continues from Areopolis to (79km) *Pírgos Dhiroú*.—97km *Yeroliména*.—101km **Álika**.

Sparta, see Rte 31. The road runs S through orange groves, crossing one tributary of the Eurotas after another. We pass, before and after (5·5km) *Sklavokhóri*, the hills of Ayia Kiriaki and Palaiopiryi, both to the left, from whose ruins the village has readopted the name of Amyklai (comp. Rte 31).—8km. Turning (right) for the climbers' refuge inaugurated in 1962 at *Ayía Varvára* (c 27km) on Taiyetos. From the refuge (1399m) the summit of *Taíyetos* (2400m; *Profitis Ilias*) may be climbed.

We continue through olive groves and mulberry plantations.—14km Turning to *Xirokámbi* (3km; right) where the torrent is spanned by a single-arched bridge in polygonal masonry of the Hellenistic era.

The road ascends the low Vardhounokhoria Hills, which extend E, from the Taiyetos. We pass (right) the village of Tarapsa, just before

(24·5km) *Khâni Tárapsa* (Refreshments), where the road divides. The left branch forms the main road to Monemvasia (Rte 32A). Our road continues to ascend through wooded country. From the summit (300m) there are fine views of the Helos Plain and the Laconic Gulf. On the descent we pass (35·5km) the ruins of *Aegeiai*, which had a temple to Poseidon by a lake. We thread a wooded defile.

45km (28 miles) **Yíthion** (Γύθειον; Hotels A, B, C, D), or *Gytheion*, the ancient and modern port of Sparta, is the second largest town (4054 inhab.) in Laconia and the seat of an eparchy. Olives, oil, and valonia are its chief exports. It has a pleasant promenade and is connected by steamer with Piraeus (comp. Rte 32A).

The inhabitants of *Gytheion* claimed Herakles and Apollo as joint founders; classical tradition speaks of Minyan colonists and Phoenician traders in purple-dye. The town became the naval arsenal and port of Sparta, and was sacked by the Athenian admiral Tolmides in 455 BC. Epaminondas besieged it in vain. Nabis rebuilt and fortified it. Gytheion was the most important city of the free-Laconian League.

The modern town behind the waterfront is largely on reclaimed land. The ANCIENT CITY was situated on low hills, now nearly 1km from the shore. The diminutive *Theatre* was excavated in 1891. Above the town is a ruined *Castle*. The *Museum* contains a few local antiquities. The island of MARATHONISI, the ancient *Kranaë*, is a low rocky islet (connected by causeway) crowned by a folly (Pírgo tón Grigorákidhon). Here were probably the most ancient settlements.

The remainder of this route lies through the highland region known as the **Mani** (Μάνη), or *Maina*, comprising the last 30m of the Taïyetos range as far as Cape Matapan. The area is known locally as *Kakavoúlia* or *Kakóvouna*. The mountains are treeless and almost barren, though olives thrive and the ground is laboriously cultivated wherever a terrace can be contrived. The population is distributed in small villages, often perched on apparently inaccessible mountain ledges. The Outer Mani is described in Rte 32C. Inner or Deep Mani lies beyond Areopolis.

It was extensively settled in the Neolithic period and there is some archaeological evidence of activity in Mycenaean times, through to the 9C BC. Urban settlements are known to have existed since Homeric times when Messe, Las and Oitilo contributed ships to the expedition against Troy. The Dorians established small city states which later became satellites of Sparta. In the decline of Sparta they organised their towns into the Confederation of Free Laconians, whose independence was recognised by Augustus while the rest of the Peloponnese was subject to Rome. Their descendants acquired the name of Maniotes and continued in the same independent spirit. They clung to paganism until the reign of Basil I (867–86). Many elaborate churches were built dating in the 10–12C, providing evidence of new prosperity. The Frankish invaders of the mid 13C built or restored fortresses. With the restoration of Byzantine rule the area acquired new importance. Reinforced by refugees during the Slav invasions, they lived in clans commanded by chieftains and did not welcome strangers. Blood feuds were common and families built towers of refuge. The Turks failed to subdue the area, recognising its principal chieftain as 'Bey of the Maina' owing nominal allegiance to the Porte. The Maniotes eagerly joined the Orloff rising and in the War of Independence when the family of Mavromichales produced one of its most famous generals (Petrobey). In 1834, however, the Maniotes strongly resented merging their independence in the new kingdom and were with difficulty subdued.

Beyond Yithion the road at first runs SW along the coast affording views across the Laconic Gulf to Kythera.—After *Mavrovoúni*, by the 5th km stone from Yithion, there rises (right) a prominent sandy hill (Skina) with Mycenaean chamber tombs. We cross the fertile and marshy plain of Passava and then turn inland through woodland. On many of the hills stand medieval towers.—53km. The road passes below a hill surmounted by the ruined Frankish CASTLE OF PASSAVA, built in 1254, and incorporating fragments of ancient Greek masonry.

The fine enceinte is best reached by a short climb from the W. This was probably the site of Classical *Las*, but no Mycenaean remains have so far come to light to justify identification with Laas of the Iliad.— Beyond (56km) *Karioúpolis*, we pass through a picturesque defile to emerge high above *Liménion*, the harbour of Areopolis, and join the road from Oitilo on the bare grey slopes of Profitis Ilias (813m).— 77km (44 miles) **Areópolis** (Αρεόπολις; Hotel C), a constricted village (900 inhab.) of tower houses, is the chief centre of the Mani. The church (*Taxiárkhis*), dating from 1798, has primitive reliefs of martial saints.

The landscape S of Areopolis is dominated by the Kakavoulia and Sangias (1218m) which rises between Pirgos Dhirou and Kotronas on the E coast. It is dotted with tower-houses and primitive barrel-vaulted chapels (probably 9C); the domed Byzantine churches date mainly from the 11C and 12C. At 75km a turn (left) leads to the E coast.—79km *Pírgos Dhiroú* has a small tourist pavilion, whence a road leads (in 4km) to the Bay of **Diros** (Refreshments; bathing). Here two spectacular *Caverns, Vlykádha* (or Glifádha; adm. daily, incl. boat on underground lake) and *Alepótrypa* ('fox-hole'; closed temporarily) were opened to the public in 1963; both have stalactites and stalagmites and are lit by electricity. Detailed study of the Neolithic burials found has been undertaken since 1970. At *Glézou* (80km, left), the church of the *Taxiárkhis* dates from the 11C (façade rebuilt). At 87km a turn to the left at *Bríki* is the best approach to *Vamvárka*, where the church of *Áyios Theódhoros* is dated by an inscription to 1075. At 88km, a road (right) leads to (1km) *Erimos*, with the domed cruciform church of *Ayía Varvára* (1150), which is distinguished by its fine proportions and masonry. *Mézapos*, possibly the site of Homeric Messe, lies on the coast. On the promontory of Tigáni, (W) of the same bay, stands the CASTLE OF MAINA, the Frankish fortress erected by William II de Ville-hardouin in 1248. An earlier wall with three towers on this promontory may be Mycenaean. A considerable portion of the ramparts remain. There are the ruins of one of the largest (22m by 15m) and possibly the earliest Christian basilicas (5–6C). To reach it turn right at 91km to *Stavrí* and the conical hill of Ay. Kiriakí. (45 minute walk). On this road a right turn past the hamlet of *Ay. Yeóryios* leads to the 12C church of *Episkopí*, once the seat of the Bishopric of Maina. It stands on a hillside with a view across the Bay of Mésapos to the peninsula of *Tigáni*. The fine frescoes are mainly 12C, with a Last Judgement in the narthex. It has been restored.—92km *Koíta*, now almost depopulated, was reported by Leake to have almost 100 families and 22 towers. Above Koíta the decayed church of *Ay. Asómatoi* has a carved marble iconostasis.—96km (left) in *Káto Boularioí* is the Anemodhoura tower, one of the earliest towers (possibly 1600). It is built of huge dry stones tapering to the top. There is also the well-preserved late 18C tower of the Mantoúvalos family. Just above Ano Boularioí is the cruciform 11C church of *Ay. Stratigós*, the dome of which is supported by Roman Ionic columns. It contains an almost complete cycle of frescoes (mainly 12C).—97km *Yeroliména* (Hotel E), a small fishing village no longer on the steamer route. At (101km) *Alika* there are two inscribed stelai in the square. One is the dedication to Gaius Julius Laco by the Union of Free Laconians, the other to an 'excellent citizen' named Tanagros from his own 'City of the Tainarians'. Here the road divides; the S road continuing to Portokayio (comp. below) and the left fork to the E coast.

FROM ALIKA TO PORTOKAYIO, 12km (7½ miles). The road continues S.—At 2km, on the coast, is *Kipárissos*, ancient Kaenipolis, one of the most important cities in the Messenian Gulf in the 1C AD and later. There are extensive remains round the two bays of *Almirós* and *Psaroliméni* and up to the village of Alika. On a headland, the *Hill of Metamórphosis*, stands a ruined 19C tower surrounded by fragments of marble, possibly the site of Pausanias' Megaron of Demeter. By the beach the church of *Ay. Paraskeví* incorporates ancient marble and pieces of columns possibly from the Temple of Aphrodite mentioned by Pausanias. Behind the church is a massive inscribed stele in honour of the Emperor Gordian. In the olive groves SE are the ruins of the basilica of *Ay. Pétros* (early 6C), incorporating ancient material. The jambs of the W door are two inscribed stelai, to the Empress Julia Domna and to a generous citizen Lysicrates.

The road follows the coast before climbing steeply inland to 5km Váthia, a village of tower-houses standing on a hill. The National Tourist Organisation is restoring some of the tower-houses. We continue to climb with spectacular views N up the coast to *Cavo Grosso* before rounding a headland to a dramatic road cut into the cliff with a precipitous drop to a long narrow plateau high above the sea (view S to Cape Matapan, ancient Tainaron).—At 10km a turn (left) leads 1·5km through a small gorge full of cypress and citrus to the 16C Turkish castle of Portokáyio, perched high on a cliff edge overlooking the almost circular bay of *Portokáyio*, the name of which is a corruption of the Venetian 'Quaglio' (quails). The road curves E towards the isthmus. Below (right) between two sandy inlets, is *Porto Marmári*, ancient Achilleion. On the highest point of the isthmus (left) is the prominent tower of Khárakes. The road descends steeply to (12km) the small sandy beach of *Portokáyio*, ancient Psamathoús. Tainaron can be reached on foot (1 hour) from the highest point of the road before it descends to Portokáyio. A path (right) meets a rough road under construction from Porto Marmári. Keeping Vathí Bay on the left, walk on a descending path along a scarp, take the right fork and continue S to the shoulder of the promontory of *Livádhi*, which forms the bottom end of *Vathí Bay*. Over the low saddle is the hamlet of *Kokkinóyia* and, below, the *Bay of Asómatos*. The chapel of *Asómatos* on the headland occupies the site of the famous *Temple of Poseidon* (5C BC), part of the extended shrine of Poseidon Tainarios where the Free Laconians had their religious headquarters. The large blocks on the N wall formed part of the ancient temple. On a pebbly beach (left) is the cave of the Oracle of Poseidon mentioned by Pausanias. There is evidence of a religious complex attached to the oracle which was still in use during the late Roman period. In the bay (right) there are numerous cisterns which give it its name of *Pórto Khísternes*. In the next small bay to the S there is a pebble mosaic. The track continues (½ hour) to the lighthouse at the tip of *Cape Matapan*. Cape Matapan has much the same latitude as Gibraltar and is thus the second most southerly place on the European mainland. Off Cape Matapan, on 28 March 1941, four Italian ships were sunk or damaged by a British contingent under Admiral Cunningham.

We continue left towards the E coast through a valley skirting the southern tip of the Kakavoúlia and cross the watershed (view of the Laconian Gulf) to (115km) *Láyia* (bus to Sparta daily), 400m above sea level. Now depopulated, it was once the main town of SE Mani. There are some fine towers.—At 118km (500m before the village of *Dhimarístika*) the main road cuts across an ancient road from the harbour of Kiprianós to the marble quarries of rosso antico (Tainarion marble) highly prized in antiquity and used (*inter alia*) in the decoration of the Treasury of Atreus at Mycenae. The quarries were exploited by an Italian company before the First World War. The road loops down through scattered towered settlements (view N to the great promontory of Stavrí) to (125km) the small harbour of *Kokkála* (beach, pensions).—At 128·5km there is a turn (left) to *Nímfi* (500m) whence a steep path up the Kournós ravine leads to the Monastery of the *Panayia* and the ancient shrine of *Kiónia* (500m beyond). Below the Monastery is a circular cistern incorporating ancient material. The cistern has a constant water supply from a spring above the Monastery. Water was supplied to the sanctuary and settlement of Kiónia. Situated on a high plateau 480m above sea level are the foundations of two Doric temples built in local grey limestone. The larger (peripteral) temple dates from the second half of the 2C BC, the smaller (in antis) from the Augustan period. There are extensive remains, of a settlement with cisterns, a cemetery with rock-cut reliefs and a fortified acropolis. Magnificent views E to Cape Malea and SE to Kíthira.

(1½ hours) The road continues with the grey, barren Kakavoúlia rising steeply to the W, punctuated by sombre ravines and towered villages. Across a small coastal plain with olives and cypress the high towers of *Flomokhóri* (138km) are visible.—At 139km we turn right to the delightful small fishing village of (3km) *Kótronas*, ancient Teuthróne with a sandy beach (Hotel; rooms). On the small peninsula of *Skopá* to the SW are the remains of a Byzantine fortress. To the E, on the high point of Stavrí Peninsula, are remnants of fortifications associated with Spartan defences during the Corinthian War. The road climbs to (140km) *Loukadhiká*, with its once-fortified citadel, and turns W through a pass with oaks and cypress opening onto the cultivated plain of (144km) *Pírrichos* which still bears its ancient name. According to Pausanias the city derived its name either from Pyrrus, the son of Achilles, or from the god Pyrrichos who was one of the Kouretes. Beyond, the road descends through a valley, affording a view of the Bay of Dhiros, to join—at 149km—the Areópolis—Yeroliména road, 2km S of (151km) **Areópolis**.

C. From Kalamáta to Areópolis

ROAD, 76km (47½ miles), asphalt. No road in Greece offers more spectacular coastal scenery. The greater part of this route lies in Messinian territory. BUS daily to Areópolis.

Kalamáta, see Rte 34. We quit the town by the E suburb of *Yiannitsánika*.—7km *Almirón* (Hotel B), villa resort of Kalamáta, and *Káto Sélitsa*, where Mount Kalafi rises steeply from the sea, both form part of the commune of Vérga. The narrow gap was blocked by a wall, the '*Mandhra tis Verghas*', in 1826 and the Mani successfully defended against Ibrahim's ravaging army. The road now climbs inland with many turns (* Views first over Cape Kitries to the Messenian Gulf, then inland to the Taïyetos). *Avía*, on the shore (Hotel C), may be the *Híre* of the Iliad.—The road passes below *Sotiriánika*, whose castle is conspicuous from Kalamata but seen only in retrospect from the road. A concrete arch over the wild wooded *Kóskaras Defile* replaces an old packhorse bridge, best seen from the steep hairpin bends on the far side.

20km (12½ miles) **Kámbos** (471 inhab.), with a conspicuous church, a tholos tomb (dug in 1888), and vestiges of an ancient temple, is dominated by the CASTLE OF ZARNATA, a huge Frankish enceinte (before 1427) with a Turkish keep built by Achmet Kiuprili in 1670. It was captured by stratagem in 1685 by Morosini. The kastro rests on polygonal foundations, perhaps of *Gerenia*. The S wall was torn down during the disturbances of 1943–49 and further damage done by earthquake in 1947. The Byzantine church of *Zoödókhos Piyí* has a carved wooden templon. Farther on, the square battlemented *Tower of Koumoundhouráki* crowns a second height.

Beyond the next summit, the descent affords a tremendous * View right down the Mani: Kardhamili in its little plain of olives is seen below as from the air. Venitiko I., off Cape Akritas, is clearly descried across the Gulf.—36km (22½ miles) **Kardhamíli** (Καρδαμύλη; Hotel D), a seaside village of 277 inhab., perpetuates the name of *Kardamyle*, one of the seven cities that Agamemnon offered to Achilles to appease his wrath. It was transferred by Augustus from Messenia to Laconia. The medieval *Castle* has an 18C church and ancient foundations. The acropolis has rock-cuttings of probably Mycenaean date. Offshore is a fortified islet.

The road, hewn from the rock, clings perilously to the coast. It passes below *Proásteion*, where the church of Ayioi Theodoroi has 13C paintings.—41km *Stoúpa* or *Lévktron*. Ancient Leuktra, a free Laconian city, may have occupied the curious table-top hill below the village. The acropolis became Castle Beaufort in the middle ages.— 46km *Selínitsa* (Hotel), or *Áyios Nikólaos*, by the seaside, has a prominent war memorial. At *Áyios Dhimítrios*, to the S, is a stalactite cave. Beyond *Rínglia* the road crosses a ravine and climbs continuously. *Plátsa* and the succeeding villages have little Byzantine churches and arcaded foundations incorporating ancient fragments. The isolated church of *Áyios Dhimítrios*, on a spur above Platsa, commands a superb view to the N. *Koutifári* is proposed as the site of ancient Thalamai.—The tower-houses of (56km) *Langádha* rise in terraces. *Trakhíla*, with a cave, is seen on the coast below. We pass into Laconia. Areopolis appears across the Limenion Gulf and the wilder ranges of Inner Mani rise ahead.—70km **Oítilo** (Οιτυλο), or *Vitylo*, a village making a potent unresinated wine, was the capital of the Mani before Areopolis. Its name survives unchanged from Homeric times. Here Napoleon I put in on his way to Egypt. The village is divided by the Ravine of Milolangadho, the boundary between Outer and Inner Mani, from *Kelfá*, where stands the huge walled frontier-post, erected by the Turks in the 17C to control the Maniotes. The road continues with superb views via *Limenion* to (76km) *Areópolis*.

33 From Tripolis to Kalamáta

ROAD, 95km (59 miles), bus in 2¾ hours).—34km *Megalópolis.*— 95km *Kalamáta.*

RAILWAY, 123km in 2¾ hours. To *Biláli*, junction for Megalopolis, in 1 hour; to *Zevgolatió*, junction for Kiparissía, in 2 hours.

Quitting the central square the Kalamata road runs SW.—4·5km. Byroad to *Valtétsi* (6·5km) where in 1821 Khurshid Pasha's Turks, marching to the relief of Tripolis, were defeated by Kolokotronis.—6km *Makrí* crossroads (village 1km right); to the left (c 3km), at the foot of *Mt Krávari*, the ancient Boreion (1143m) are the insignificant ruins of *Pallantion*, confined to foundations of three unsophisticated temples of Archaic and later date and traces of the city walls. The site is being reinvestigated. The approach is by confusing tracks across fields, only the first few hundred metres being motorable.

According to legend, 60 years before the Trojan War, King Evander, the son of Hermes by an Arcadian nymph, founded from *Pallantion* a colony by the river Tiber. The name of the Palatine hill reflects his native town, and Pallantion was accordingly regarded as the mother-city of Rome itself. When Megalopolis was founded, Pallantion dwindled to a village, but Antoninus Pius, in memory of Evander, restored its civic status and privileges. It was explored by the Italian School in 1940. Just SE of the ruins are the remains of an embankment, of rammed earth encased with stone, that served both as a dyke against the waters of *Táka Marsh* and as a frontier barrier against Tegea.

The road now climbs the *Pass of Kaloyerikos* (810m; fine retrospect of the Plain of Tripolis), and descends into the dreary plain of Asea. The high range of Taïyetos is seen to the S.—16·5km *Aséa* station (654m) lies 3km below its village, near the springs that form the source of the Alpheios.

An isolated hill below the modern village, c 1km beyond the ruined khan of Frankovrísi, is the acropolis of ASEA, shown by Swedish excavations in 1936–38 to have had a continuous existence from Neolithic to Middle Helladic times and to have been reoccupied in the Hellenistic period. The remains have been covered again.

Beyond Aséa the railway draws away to the S to pass, after *Marmariá*, below the site of the ancient *Oresthasion* on the long ridge that runs N from *Mt Tsemperon* (1252m). The line traverses the hills by a gorge, then descends by wide loops through Leondári (see below) to Bilali, junction for the Megalopolis branch.—The road surmounts the ridge (view) and descends in zigzags to the plain.

THE PLAIN OF MEGALOPOLIS, the great W plain of Arcadia, is about 30km long from N to S and 16km wide. With an average altitude of 427m, it enjoys a much more temperate climate than the Plain of Tripolis. It is pleasantly wooded and well watered by the Alpheios, while the outlines of the encircling mountains make a fine background.

34km (21¾ miles) **Megalópolis** (Μεγαλόπολις; 427m; Hotels D) comprises a modern small town (4735 inhab.) and, about 1km N, the widespread but unrewarding ruins of the 'Great City', at once the chief town of the surrounding district and the capital of the federated states of Arcadia. The city straddles the *Hellison*, one of the seven tributaries of the Alpheios, the federal capital (*Oresteia*) occupying the nearer bank while the municipal city lies across the river. The view and atmosphere are marred by the large power station which dominates the vicinity.

History. When the Pan-Arcadian League was formed after Leuktra, Arcadia lacked a capital city. Mutual jealousies precluded the choice of any existing city, and a new site was selected. Its position was determined by Epaminondas of Thebes in accordance with his concept of a strategic barrier to contain the Spartans, the other bastions of which were to be Messene, Mantineia, and Argos. The 'Great City' (ἡ Μεγάλη Πόλις) as it was called by the Greeks (Megalopolis being a Roman corruption), was built in 371–368 BC, and populated by wholesale transplantation from 40 local villages and smaller migrations from Tegea, Mantineia, etc. The League had a federal Council of 50 members and an Assembly called the Ten Thousand, which met in the Thersilion at Megalopolis: the executive power was held by a Strategos who had an army of 500 Eparitoi at his command. The confederation soon broke up; Mantineia withdrew in 364 after the League had tampered with the sacred treasuries at Olympia, and in 362 half the Arcadians fought with the Spartans against Thebes. The inhabitants of Megalopolis had to be prevented from returning to their former homes by Pammenes' Theban soldiers. Spartan attempts to reduce the city were foiled in 353 with Theban aid and again in 331 when Megalopolis sided with Macedon. Having joined the Achaean League in 234, the city again suffered Spartan attack; saved once by a hurricane, it was sacked in 223 BC by Kleomenes III. Two-thirds of the population escaped to Messenia under the leadership of Philopoemen (253–183 BC), almost the only great man produced by Arcadia, returning two years later after Kleomenes' defeat at Sellasia. Strabo quotes an unknown comic poet to the effect that 'the Great City was a great desert', and Pausanias found it 'mostly in ruins', though under the later emperors it was the seat of a bishop. It finally disappeared in the Slav invasion.—Besides Philopoemen, the only native of note is Polybius (204–122 BC), the historian.

Megalopolis was excavated by the British School in 1890–93; ploughing has since wrought havoc with much of the site, which is principally interesting for the theatre. This is reached from the Andritsaina road, which passes through the ancient city, by taking a track to the left just before we reach the bridge over the river.

The THEATRE, which is built up against the N side of a hillock, 100m from the river, was the largest in Greece. It dates, in its original form, from the 4C BC, but is later than the Thersilion. The *Cavea* is divided by 10 stairways and two diazomata, to make 59 rows of seats for c 21,000 spectators. The lowest tiers are well preserved. The *Orchestra* is 30m in diameter. The place of the W parodos is taken by a *Skenotheke*, or property room. The portico of the Thersilion seems to have served also as a permanent skene for the theatre. The stone *Stage*, adorned by 14 marble columns between antae, is a Roman addition.

The *Thersilion* is perhaps the most elaborate example known of the square hall. Measuring 52·5m by 66·5m, it had five concentric rows of columns, set parallel to the outside walls and arranged on radials from a tribune offset from centre. The bases of the columns remaining in situ show that the wooden floor sloped down towards the tribune, above which the roof line was probably broken by a lantern. Facing the theatre and originally separated from the hall only by piers (later by a continuous wall with doorways), was a Doric prostyle portico having 14 columns beneath a single pediment. The building was destroyed in 222 BC and not rebuilt.

Beyond the river the *Sanctuary of Zeus Soter* and the *Stoa of Philip*, demarcating the Agora, are now barely identifiable. Sections of the town wall have been found.—For the continuation of the road to Andritsaina, see Rte 35.

A tarmac road runs S via (5km Biláli (comp. above).—11km **Leondári** (Λεοντάρι), a medieval village, 1·5km SW of its station, occupies a commanding position on the top of the hill (578m) forming the N end of the Taïyetos range and overlooking a narrow pass separating Arcadia from Messenia. The Frankish *Castle* is in ruins. Here Thomas Palaiologos was defeated by the Turks in 1460; the inhabitants fled to Gardhiki only to be massacred there. The little two-domed Church of the *Apostoloi* (14C) was converted into a mosque. Near it is the smaller 12C church of *Ayios Athanasios*.—About 2·5km NW of Leondári, on the left bank of the Xerillas, are the scanty vestiges of *Veligostí* (Βελιγόστη), in the Byzantine age an important place. It is reached from the bridle-path that leads in 1¾ hours between the Samara Hills and Mt Ellenitsa to Paradhísia (see below).—Beyond Leondári tracks lead S to the scattered villages (Dhirrákhi, etc.) on the W slopes of Taïyetos.

Perhaps the most interesting excursion from Megalopolis (after that to Bassae; Rte 35) is to the finely situated site of **Lykósoura** (14km). We take the Kalamáta road (see below) and just beyond the Alpheios branch right on road which is asphalted as far as the second village (*Apidhítsa*), where we again branch right, and at 11km left. The museum is visible on a saddle to the left; immediately below, a rough track forks left. The site is fenced; key from hamlet below. The *Museum* contains inscriptions and much of the colossal cult statues by Damophon (casts of heads, which are in Athens). The site is more interesting below the museum. There are considerable remains of a prostyle *Temple* with a side door on the S of the cella (comp. Bassae). In front is a *Stoa*, and in the hillside (S) a stepped retaining wall.

Beyond Lykosoura tracks continue via *Líkaion* and *Kastanokhórion* to Ano Kariá (25km) whence one hour on foot will bring us to the Sanctuary of Pan (1195m) on the S side of *Mt Lykaion* (comp. Rte 35). Tracks go on W from Ano Kariá to *Figalía*.

From Megalopolis the Kalamáta road runs SW, crossing (36km) the Alpheios; just beyond the bridge (right) is the by-road to Lykosoura (comp. above).—47km *Paradhísia* guards the approach to the *Makriplayi Pass* (600m), the main route of communication between Arcadia and Messenia. *Kháni Vídhi* marks the summit of the pass. Here a by-road diverges (left) to *Kheirádhes* (3km) whence a path continues in one hour to *'Kókkala'* on a W spur of Taïyetos. Here the ruined old fortress on ancient foundations (? *Ampheia*) is the Byzantine and Frankish *Castle of Gardhiki*, near which William de Villehardouin and Ancelin de Toucy, marching from Kalamáta in 1265 beat the forces of the Great Domestic of the Eastern Empire.—The road winds down with views across the tree-covered Plain of Stenyklaros (Rte 34C); Mt

Ithome appears behind Meligalá to the SW.—At the foot of the descent, turnings (right) first to Kiparissia and then to Ancient Ithome (Rte 34C), as the road runs straight across the plain through thick olive groves.—The copious springs near (74km) *Ayios Flóros* were considered by the ancients as the source of the Pamisos proper before it joined the Mavrozoumenos.

82km *Palaiókastro* (1km E of the road) is the site of classical THOURIA, a city destroyed in 464 BC by the Spartans and rebuilt by Epaminondas. It was given by Augustus to Laconia to punish the Messenians for siding with Antony. The classical remains are at the N end of a long ridge in which many Mycenaean tombs have been found: this may be the place known to Homer as *Anthea*. Modern *Thouría* is 3km farther along the road.

At 90km we join the road from Messini (Rte 34) and enter (95km) **Kalamáta** (see below).

34 Messenia

Messenia (mod. Messinía), one of the six ancient countries of the Peloponnese and one of its seven modern nomes, is bounded on the N by Elis and Arcadia, on the E by Laconia, and on the S and W by the Ionian Sea. The region consists mainly of the SW peninsula of the Peloponnese, occupied by the triangular mass of high ground that culminates in Aigaleon. To the E of this range lies the fertile Messenian Plain watered by the Pamisos, the most considerable river in the S Peloponnese: to the N and NE are secondary plains; and the natural boundaries lie along Xerovouni and Taïyetos. The capital and principal trading port is Kalamáta.

In the Homeric age Messenia belonged to the Neleid princes of Pylos, of whom the most famous was Nestor, while the E part was included in the joint kingdoms of Agamemnon and Menelaus. In the Dorian invasion Messenia was assigned to Kresphontes. The original inhabitants absorbed their conquerors and their prosperity excited the envy of Sparta. In the *First Messenian War* (? 743–724 BC) the Spartans conquered the country, and, notwithstanding the devotion of Aristodemos, the Messenian king, captured the fortress of Ithome, reducing the inhabitants to the condition of Helots. A rebellion known as the *Second Messenian War* (or First Messenian Revolt; ? 685–668 BC) was with great difficulty suppressed, when the fort of Eira was captured. The hero of this was Aristomenes, 'the first and greatest glory of the Messenian name'. Many of the Messenians emigrated to Sicily, where, in 493 BC, their descendant Anaxilas of Rhegium captured Zancle and renamed it Messana (now Messina). *The Third Messenian War* (or Second Messenian Revolt) in 464–455 BC had far-reaching consequences. The Athenians, who had sent an expeditionary force to help the Lacedaemonians, were rudely dismissed. After the fall of Ithome they therefore befriended the exiled Messenians, settling them in Naupaktos. It was these Messenians who in 425 BC aided the Athenians at the siege of Sphakteria. After the battle of Leuktra in 371 BC, Epaminondas repatriated the Messenians and founded for them the city of Messene. They remained independent till the Roman conquest in 146 BC.

The ancient topography has been the subject of intensive study by the University of Minnesota Messenia Expedition since 1958 and is now published.

A. From Kalamáta to Pýlos

ROAD, 51km (31½ miles), asphalted. BUS several times daily in
1½ hours, some continuing to Khóra and Kiparissía.

KALAMÁTA (Καλαμάτα; Hotels B, C, D, E) a manufacturing town and
port (41,911 inhab.) amid groves of citrus fruit trees is the best base for
expeditions in Messenia. The capital of the nome of Messenia, it is the
focus of local communication and has air, rail, and coach services from
Athens. The centre stands a long mile from its harbour, once the principal outlet for exports from the Peloponnese. Kalamáta olives have a
high reputation and figs are dried, processed and packed. Kalamáta
claims to be the first Greek city to have revolted against the Turks in
1821. In 1941 it was forced to surrender after the Royal Navy had put to
sea to meet an Italian threat and 7000 allied troops fell into enemy
hands.

On 14 September 1986 a severe earthquake caused loss of life and
serious damage to Kalamáta and nearby villages. The description that
follows takes no account of this tragic event.

Airport at Tríodhos (16km NW), with daily service to Athens.

Railway to *Athens* 5 times daily (incl. overnight) in c 7½ hours; to *Kiparissia*,
Pirgos, and *Patras*, etc.—CAR PARK in Plat. Venizélou, near Station.

Post Office, Iatropoúlou 4.

Buses of KTEL 4 Messenias (Od. Artémidhos 96) to *Athens*, via Tripolis and
Corinth; also to *Koroni*; to *Pylos*, *Khora*, and *Kiparissia*—all several times daily; to
Kardamyle, *Oitilo*, etc.

The centre is the PLATEÍA VASILÉOS YEORYÍOU B', the tree-lined broadening of Odhos Aristoménous, the long main street. *Ayioi Apostoloi*,
farther N, has a Byzantine core of 1317. Odhós Ipapandís, lined with
exotic trees, leads N to the cathedral church of *Tis Ipapandí* (1859).
Steps mount to the **Kastro**, erected by Geoffrey I Villehardouin in 1208
on the acropolis of ancient *Pharai*. Some remnants of walls dating back
to Mycenaean times have been traced. The castle consists of an outer
enceinte, an inner redoubt, and a keep.

A Byzantine double enceinte had already fallen into disuse before 1204, and in
1208 its church was encased within the walls of the new keep. The castle was
held by the Villehardouins for nearly a century and here William (1218–78) was
born and died. It was captured by the Slavs in 1293 but won back, and passed by
marriage to Guy II, Duke of Athens in 1300. Florentines and Angevins held it in
turn until it passed to the Palaiologoi in 1425. The Venetians held it during the
first Turko-Venetian war (1463–79) and sacked it in a raid in 1659. The Turks
blew up part of it in 1685 and the Venetians continued its demolition.

Two fine old houses of the Benaki and Kyriakou families, near the
church of Ayios Ioannis, house an *Archaeological Museum* containing
a good Roman mosaic, Byzantine icons, and relics of the War of Independence; also the Swedish finds from Malthi.

At *Akovítika*, a hamlet 3km due W of Kalamáta, S of the railway, an E.H. megaron
was unearthed in 1969, representing perhaps a stage of development between
that of Troy II and the House of Tiles at Lerna, but larger than either.

From Kalamáta to the *Mani*, see Rte 32; to *Sparta*, see Rte 31.

We take the Tripolis road and after 5km bear left. Beside the branch
railway, the road, passing a military air base, crosses the fertile
marshes of the Markaria plain and the Pamisos to (8·5km) **Messíni**
(Μεσσήνη; Inn), principal town (6565 inhab.) of its eparchy. A centre of
rice production, locally called *Nísi* it should not be confused with the
ancient city (Rte 34C) whose name it has adopted. From its vast square

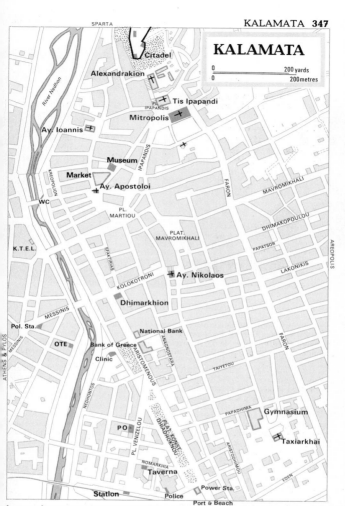

buses ply to many Messenian villages.—Olives and figs alternate with vines and fruit-trees. San Agostino Beach Hotel (B) lies to the S of (14km) *Análipsis*.—Near (19km) *Rizómilos* investigations by the University of Minnesota on an eroded hill-top (Nikhória) have shown occupation throughout the Bronze Age and later.

A branch road (left) approaches the Messenian Gulf, with views to the mountains of the Mani.—At (6km) *Petalídhi*, a small port (1113 inhab.) on the W shore of the Gulf of Kalamáta, on 30 August 1828, General Maison landed 14,000 French troops, causing Ibrahim Pasha's immediate evacuation of the Morea. Just behind the town rises the acropolis (some remains) of ancient *Aepeia*, renamed by Epimelides (c 370 BC) after Koroneia, his native town in Boeotia, whence the later corruption *Korone*. Its inhabitants migrated farther S in the middle ages (comp. below) and the town was repopulated in the 19C by Maniots. The whole coast to modern Koroni comes into view, while to the W rise the pretty cypress-dotted foothills of Mt *Likódhimon* (957m). The road runs above the sea.—At *Longá*,

Kalamáta. Benaki family house ('arkhontikó')

1·5km W of (18km) *Ayios Andréas* remains of four successive temples mark the site of a temple of Apollo Korythos.

29km **Koróni** (Hotels B, D, E), a picturesque medieval town (1376 inhab.) stands on a promontory at the foot of a Venetian castle. The antique remains (breakwater, cisterns, walls, etc.) are of *Asine*, a colony planted by perioikoi from Argive Asine. The derelict site was reoccupied in the middle ages by the inhabitants of Korone (now Petalidi, see above), whence its modern name. This was corrupted by Frankish conquerors into *Coron*. In 1206 after a year's tenure the Franks had to cede it to the Venetians. Coron was attacked from the sea in 1428 by the Turks. In 1500, the inhabitants, demoralised by the news from Methone (comp. below), mutinied and gave in to the Turks only to be banished to Kefalonia. Andrea Doria captured Coron in 1532 for the Holy Roman Empire but, being beseiged in turn by Khair-ed-din Barbarossa, was taken off with the inhabitants in a squadron of Sicilian ships, leaving the empty town to the Turks. It fell in 1685 to Morosini who massacred its 1500 defenders. Its final period (1718–1828) under Turkish rule was ended by General Maison.

The principal points of interest in the *Castle* are the reused classical masonry in the outer curtain; the Gothic Entrance Gate; the great talus of the E scarp moulded to the rocky bluff; the SE and SW artillery bastions, probably Turkish work; and the Byzantine wall of reused fragments which divides the inner from the outer court.

A partly surfaced road leaves the Messini road at *Kharakopió* (5km, left) and crosses the S part of the promontory, via *Finikoúndha* to Methoni.

Messenia ends (11km SW) in *Cape Gallo*, the ancient *Akritas*, off which lies the rocky uninhabited islet of *Venetiko* or *Theganousa*. Methoni lies 32km NW.

To the W of Rizómilos the road is crossed by torrents and may be difficult after rain. It closely follows the course of a prehistoric road explored in 1962 and suggested to be that taken by the Homeric heroes between Sparta and Pylos. Beyond (31km) *Kazárma* oak woods clothe the hill slopes.—At (36km) *Soulmári* there is a turning (right) for *Kremmídhia* (3km further) where a complex of small tholos tombs and pithos burials of the M and LH periods has recently been excavated.—At 39km, the road summit (488m) affords a view over Navarino Bay; to the right begins the Venetian aqueduct which feeds a Turkish fountain at Pylos.—We join (48km) the Kiparissia road (see below).

50·5km **PYLOS** (Πύλος; Hotels B, C, D), pronounced Pílos, known locally as *Neókastro*, and more familiar to foreigners as **Navaríno**, is the chief town (2107 inhab.) of the eparchy of Pylia. The clean and attractive little town, built with arcaded streets by the French in 1829, rises from the S shore of Navarino Bay at the foot of a promontory (N end of *Mt St Nicholas*, 484m) on which a castle guards the S entrance to the bay. It is the pleasantest centre from which to explore Southern Messenia.

History. This site was not occupied in antiquity. In 1572 the Turks built on Mt St Nicholas a fortress which was called Neokastro to distinguish it from the Palaiokastro to the N of the bay (see below). The name of *Navarino*, locally obsolete, is probably a Venetian corruption of *Ton Avarinon* (Castle 'of the Avars'), originally given by the Byzantines to the old castle and carried over to the new castle during the Venetian occupation of 1686–1718. In 1825 Ibrahim Pasha made it the centre of his operations in Messenia, which he utterly devastated. The intervention of the powers in 1827, the consequent battle of Navarino (see below), and the imminent arrival of French troops brought about Ibrahim's evacuation of the Morea in September 1828. The town dates from General Maison's occupation and has attracted to itself the classical name of *Pylos*, causing still further confusion (comp. below).

The PLATEIA TRION NAVARKHON, planted with planes and limes, has a memorial (1927) to Admirals Codrington, de Rigny, and von Heyden, who commanded respectively the British, French, and Russians at Navarino. The *Museum* contains mementoes of the battle, contents of Hellenistic tombs at Yialova, and Mycenaean finds from Koukounara (9·5km NE; 1958–59). 16ᵗʰ–12ᵗʰ C

The Turko-Venetian fortress of NEOKASTRO to the SW is reached in ten minutes by the shore or from the Methoni road, along which are remains of its Turkish aqueduct. The fortress consists of a large crenellated enceinte, enclosing a citadel with six bastions, an attractive domed mosque converted into a church, and a small hotel. The outer bastion, to the SW, with a platform above the sea, affords the best view of the enceinte as a whole and commands the whole bay. The citadel was rebuilt in 1829 by the French and was in use as a prison until recent years; it now shelters Boy Scout headquarters.

BUSES to *Methóni, Kalamáta, Gargalianoí*, etc.

NAVARINO BAY forms a magnificent natural harbour, 5·5km long (N–S) and 3km wide, with a depth of 12–30 fathoms (22–55m). Its W side is formed by Sphakteria (see below). The only practicable entrance, on the S, is 1190m wide and divided into unequal channels by the islet of *Pylos* and the *Tsichli-Baba Rocks*. On the islet are a lighthouse and the *French Monument*, erected in 1890 when the remains were transferred here from the mainland cemetery of fallen from Navarino and from the Morea Expedition of 1828–30. In the centre of the harbour a low rock called Khelonaki ('small tortoise') is crowned by the *Memorial to the British Sailors*.

BATTLE OF NAVARINO. The Treaty of London (6 July 1827) provided that Great Britain, France, and Russia should guarantee the autonomy of Greece, under the suzerainty of Turkey, without breaking off friendly relations with the Porte. Their fleets were, without open hostilities or bloodshed, to intimidate Ibrahim Pasha into withdrawing the Turkish and Egyptian fleets from the Morea. A wide discretion was left to the senior admiral (Codrington). The allies called for an armistice; the Greeks promptly accepted but the Turks rejected the demand. On 20 October the allied fleet of 26 sail (11 British, 7 French, 8 Russian), mounting 1270 guns, entered the Bay of Navarino, which sheltered the Turko-Egyptian fleet, numbering 82 warships, 2438 guns, and 16,000 men. After an ultimatum to Ibrahim Pasha demanding his withdrawal from the Morea, a few shots fired by the Turks brought about a general action. At nightfall the Ottoman fleet, reduced to 29 ships, had lost 6000 men. The allies lost 174 killed and 475 wounded, but not a single ship. The news of this unexpected victory was received in England with mixed feelings (being referred to in the King's speech of 1828 as 'an untoward event'), in Russia with ill-concealed satisfaction, and in France with frank delight. Prince Metternich denounced the action as 'an unparalleled outrage'.

The uninhabited island of SPHAKTERIA, or *Sfayiá*, which all but closes the bay on the W, is 4·5km long and 450–900m wide. The uneven interior of the island is covered with thickets. On the harbour side the cliffs, 30–90m high, are precipitous. The highest point, Ay. Ilias (168m), near the N end, is partly surrounded by a ruined cyclopean wall—the 'ancient wall made of rough stones' (Thuc. iv, 31), where the Spartans made their last stand (see below). In favourable weather we may cross in a small boat from Pylos to the S end of Sphakteria and cruise up its E coast. At the S end of the island is the *Tomb of Capt. Mallet*, a French officer killed in the War of Independence. Farther N is the *Grotto of Tsamadhas*, named after a Greek officer; beside it is the *Monument of Santorre di Santa Rosa* (1783–1824), the Tuscan philhellene. Below the clear waters farther N the wrecks of Turkish ships can sometimes be seen. We land in the *Bay of Panagoula* in the middle of the E coast. Here, near a chapel, is the *Monument to the Russian Sailors* with an additional inscription of 1960.

A path ascends in ten minutes to a plateau with two brackish wells. Here for 72 days in the summer of 425 BC 420 occupying Spartans held out against an Athenian force under Demosthenes and Kleon. When the 292 survivors eventually surrendered, the myth that Spartans always fought to the death was broken. Thucydides describes the affair in great topographical detail which can easily be related to the terrain.—Sphakteria was long famous as a nest of pirates and it is said to be the scene of Byron's 'Corsair'.

Passing the *Tortori Rocks*, at the NE end of Sphakteria, we cross the practically useless Sikia channel, which is only a few feet deep. We land (by prior arrangement with boatman) at the foot of the KORYPHASION PROMONTORY, near the remains of an ancient breakwater called *Porte de Junch* (des joncs: 'rushes') by the Franks and 'Zonchio' by the Venetians. A path leads up to the acropolis of 'OLD PYLOS', surmounted by a Venetian Castle. It seems probable that also here was the harbour town of the prehistoric Palace of Nestor (comp. below).

Strabo records that some of the inhabitants of Messenian Pylos 'at the foot of Mt Aigaleos' (comp. below) moved to this site, which the Spartans called *Koryphasia* (Thuc. IV, 3) from κορυφή ('summit'). Its occupation by the Athenians in 425 BC was the first act in the drama of Sphakteria.

From the 6C to the 9C AD Pylos was the home of a colony of Slavs and Avars: hence its name *Avarinos* or *Navarinon* (comp. above). In 1278 Nicholas II of St Omer built a castle here. In 1353 the Genoese captured a fleet under its walls. In 1381 it was occupied by Gascon and Navarrese adventurers; to the latter is sometimes attributed the origin of the name of Navarino. The castle was purchased by the Venetians in 1423 and fell to the Turks in 1501. After it had been bombarded by Don John of Austria in 1572 it was superseded by the Neokastro and known as *Palaiokastro*. Its capture in 1686 by Morosini and Königsmark ended its utility.

The spacious CASTLE (interior barely accessible because of undergrowth; circuit of walls possible, with care), reached in half an hour by the path from Porte de Junch, is fairly well preserved. Its crenellated walls and square towers rest partly on 4C foundations. The area enclosed is about 180m by 90m. There are outer and inner courts. Fragments of ancient walls, both polygonal and cyclopean, may be traced near the middle of the S wall, on the NE side, and on the W side of the castle. There are also ancient cisterns and staircases hewn in the rock.—Below, to the N, is Voïdhokoiliá (good bathing) probable site of the Mycenaean harbour.

A steep path leads down from the castle to the mouth of the so-called Grotto of Nestor, on the N slope of Koryphasion. The arched entrance is c 9m wide and 3·5m high. The cave itself is 18m long, and 12m wide and 12m high. Clinging to the walls are stalactites having the shapes of animals and of hanging hides, whence the legend that Neleus and Nestor here kept their cows. The grotto is identified with the cavern of the Homeric Hymn to Hermes in which Hermes hid the cattle stolen by him from Apollo and hung up the hides of the two beasts that he had killed. Sherds attest its intensive use in the Mycenaean age and Neolithic material has also been found.

On the promontory opposite to the N reached by walking round Voïdhokoilia Bay, is one of the earliest tholos tombs in Mainland Greece. Recent researches have shown that it was inserted into a Middle Helladic tumulus. An Early Helladic settlement preceded the tumulus and Neolithic finds have also been made. Votive offerings of the Classical and Hellenistic periods show that a later cult grew up centred on the tholos.

A rough and largely overgrown path descends the N side of Koryphasion in 45 minutes to the Pylos–Kiparissia road (see below).

The area can also be reached on foot from the villages of Petrochóri or Romanós, both accessible by car (left turn 12km N of Pylos on the Kiparissia road).

A road, engineered in 1828–29 by the French army, runs S to (12km) **Methóni** (Μεθώνη; Hotels B, C, D, E), a small fortress town of 1248 inhab., situated on a promontory opposite the island of Sapienza. The harbour is almost sanded up but the imposing fortifications still testify to its medieval importance.

History. Methoni or Mothone, originally called Pedasos, was said to be one of the seven cities which Agamemnon promised to Achilles. In Homer it has the epithet ἀμπελόεσσα (rich in vines). It received a colony of 'perioikoi' from Nauplia about the time of the Second Messenian War. In 431 BC an Athenian attack was foiled by the bravery of Brasidas the Spartan. The descendants of the Argive immigrants remained here even after the restoration of the Messenians by Epaminondas. Marcus Agrippa's capture of the site in 31 BC cut off Mark Antony's supplies from Egypt. Trajan granted independence to the city. Having become a haunt of pirates, it was razed in 1125 by the Venetians, and after a period of desolation firmly assigned to Venice in 1204. Until 1206, however, Geoffrey de Villehardouin and William de Champlitte used it as a base, establishing a bishopric here. The Venetians fortified it as their main port of call on the way to the Holy Land, to which it sent an annual convoy of pilgrims. The town, known as Modon, was noted for its wine and bacon, and had a flourishing silk industry, but although it was a naval station and shared with its neighbour Coron the description 'Oculi capitales communis', its public buildings were never lavish. The Venetian navy, totally defeated at the Battle of Sapienza in 1354 by the Genoese under Andrea Doria, took their revenge in 1403 off Modon, defeating a Genoese fleet commanded by the French marshal, Boucicault. Here on neutral ground in 1366 Count Amadeus VI of Savoy arbitrated in the struggle between Marie de Bourbon and Angelo Acciaioli, Archbishop of Patras. In 1500, after resisting a month's bombardment, Methoni fell to Sultan Bayezid II when the defenders prematurely deserted the walls to welcome a relieving force sent from Corfú. An attack by the Knights of Malta in 1551 was unsuccessful, and save for a second brief Venetian period in 1686–1715, following Morosini's conquest, the town remained in Turkish hands until 1828. Chateaubriand made landfall here in 1806, and here Ibrahim Pasha disembarked his army in 1825.—The story of the captive told in 'Don Quixote' may reflect Cervantes' own experience here as a Turkish prisoner.

The Venetian *Fortress-town occupies a promontory washed on three sides by the sea, except where the sand has built up. Its strongest fortifications on the landward side are separated from the mainland by a great ditch. We cross this on an attractive bridge, rebuilt by the

French in 1828, to a Venetian monumental gateway of c 1700. Within
a covered way leads through a second *Gate* to a third, opening into the
area occupied by the medieval town (pulled down by the French when
they built the modern area on the mainland). A granite *Column* with a
weathered inscription probably commemorates Rector Fr. Bembo
(1494). Little remains except a *Turkish Bath*, the ruin of the Latin
Cathedral, and cisterns. The *Curtain Wall* shows masonry of all periods from Classical (exposed when a section was dynamited in 1943)
to 19C. The CITADEL contains many subtleties of Venetian defence,
including casemates and underground passages for counter-mining.
Numerous lions of St. Mark, escutcheons, and dated inscriptions survive. At the S end of the enceinte an imposing *Sea Gate* (restored) and
causeway lead to the little islet where the remnant of the Venetian
force was massacred in 1500 (fortifications Turkish).

Offshore lie the *Oinoussai Islands*, a group consisting of *Sapienza* (comp. above)
and *Schiza* or *Cabrera*, with the tiny islet of *Ayía Mariani* between them. The
storms here are very dangerous. The bay between the islands and the mainland
was anciently called *Port Phoenikos*.

B. From Pylos to Kiparissía

ROAD, 65km (40½ miles), asphalt usually in poor state. 21km
Khóra.—34km *Gargalianoí*.—48km *Filiatrá*.—65km *Kiparissía*.
Buses several times daily.

From Pylos the road skirts Navarino Bay. The hamlet of *Zoúnchio*
derives its names from the Venetian version of the Porte de Junch (see
above). At (5km) *Yíalova* are shipyards and large warehouses where
currants, valonia, etc. are stored while awaiting shipment. A large port
with an oil refinery is planned. We skirt the drained *Lagoon of Osman-
Aga*, which extended to the foot of Koryphasion; traces of ancient
occupation have shown the lagoon to have been a post-Classical formation. Turns (left) to *Petrochóri* (comp. above) and *Romanós* (14km
from Pylos; bathing).—12km Modern *Korifásion*.

The road passes immediately below (17km) the low but abrupt hill
of *Epano Englianos* (excavation roof prominent) on which stand the
remains of the *Palace of Nestor, explored in 1939 and excavated
since 1952 by Carl Blegen (excellent illustrated guide-book, to which
the numbering of our plan conforms). The site, which had been occupied in the Middle Bronze Age, seems to have been reserved in c
1300–c 1200 BC for a royal palace, which was destroyed by fire at the
end of Mycenaean IIIB. The Iliad preserves a tradition of a Neleid
dynasty at Messenian Pylos, of whom Nestor ruled for three generations. In the 'Catalogue of Ships' he is credited with the second largest
fleet (90 ships against Agamemnon's 100); the palace of Englianos
compares in size and richness with that of Mycenae and has dependent tholos burials.

Linear B tablets (the first to be found on the mainland) were unearthed in the
room to the left of the entrance within two hours of the first day's digging in 1939,
the day Italy invaded Albania. They were stored in a bank vault in Athens
throughout the war.

The perimeter seems not to have been fortified in the palace period.
The PALACE consisted of two-storied buildings in three main blocks,
whose construction somewhat resembled that of Tudor half-timbered
buildings, having wooden columns, roofs and ceilings, with the result
that the superstructure disappeared during the fire depositing only

baseboards.

non-inflammable objects from the upper floor. The exterior walls were faced in squared blocks of limestone; the inner walls were of rubble, faced with plaster and decorated with frescoes, and had wooden wainscots. Most of the walls stand to c 1m above floor level giving a clear ground plan. The upper storey had brick walls between the wooden beams.

The MAIN BUILDING was approached across an open court paved in stucco. Jutting out (right) beyond the entrance stood a *Guard Tower* (Pl. 57). The simple *Propylon* (Pl. 1, 2) had one column in each façade with a single door in the cross-wall between. The stone bases of the columns survive and show that the wooden pillars had 64 flutes. A *Sentry-box* (left) guarded the palace door and also two small rooms (Pl. 7, 8) beside the gateway, where nearly 100 clay tablets inscribed in Linear B script were found. Here perhaps was the tax collector's office. A large interior *Court* (Pl. 3), open to the sky, gives access to various sectors of the palace. To the left are a *Pantry* (Pl. 9), its wine jars and cups lying in ruin, and a *Waiting-Room* (Pl. 10) with a stuccoed bench.

A wide *Portico* (Pl. 4), distyle in antis, opened into a *Vestibule* (Pl. 5) and thence by another door into the PRESENCE CHAMBER (Pl. 6), or Megaron proper, 12·8m long by 11·3m wide. In the centre a great ceremonial hearth of stuccoed clay forms a circle 4m across and raised 20cm above the floor. Round this four great columns, each with 32 flutes, supported a galleried upper storey, probably having a lantern above to let light in and smoke out. The floor was divided into patterned squares, all abstract in design save for one which bore an octopus. This is directly in front of a depression in the floor against the right-hand wall where almost certainly stood a throne. Beside it in the floor is a hollow from which a channel leads to another hollow, 1·8m away. These may have been used in some libation ceremony perfor-

NESTOR'S PALACE

0   20 metres

Ionian Sea

Tholos Tomb

Voidhokoilía
Bay

Cave of Nestor

Koryphasión
Promontory

Navarino Castle
(Old Pylos)

Sikía Channel

to Gargalianoí
○ Koryphasion

○ Romanós
Petrokhóri

■ Navarino Castle
(Old Pylos)

SPHAKTERIA

SPHAKTERIA

**ENVIRONS OF
PYLOS**

○ Pylos
Neókastro

to Kalamáta

0 metres   500

Inset
kms
miles

N

med from the throne. The chamber must be imagined as painted or frescoed, the wall behind the throne being adorned with reclining griffins and lions.

Corridors either side of the Megaron served suites of service rooms and gave access to staircases leading to the upper floor. Five small rooms (Pl. 18–22) filled with thousands of cups and pots of more than 20 types must have formed as much a central depot for issue or sale as the palace pantry. Behind the megaron are magazines (Pl. 23, 24, 27) with larger pithoi fixed in stucco. Tablets were found in *Storage* one room detailing their contents as olive-oil. Particularly evocative is the *Bathroom* (Pl. 43) with its fixed terracotta tub (larnax) still in situ, together with its pithoi for water and its pouring vessels (kylikes).

On the SE side of the court a colonnade (which supported a balcony) gives access to a duplicate but smaller set of apartments (Pl. 45–53) surrounding what appears to be the *Queen's Megaron* (Pl. 46). The suite includes a small room (Pl. 53) with a drain hole, either another bathroom or a lavatory.

The SOUTH-WESTERN BUILDING is conjectured to be an earlier and less sophisticated palace, perhaps turned into a dower house when the new palace was completed. Despite differences in plan (the arrangement is not axial and the storerooms open one from another instead of from corridors) it is a self-contained unit with most of the features of the later construction (megaron, Pl. 65, etc.). Much of its stonework has been robbed through the ages, though parts of the supporting ashlar wall survive.

The NORTH-EAST BUILDING may represent the palace *Workshops*, yet it seems to have had an altar in the court. The functions of various workrooms have been divined from fragments found in them and tablet lists; they included a chariot repair-shop and an armoury. Vestiges of an elaborate water-supply system are visible.—Farther to the N is the WINE MAGAZINE, a separate edifice, in which a large room contains 35 or more great jars. Clay sealings were found marked in Linear B with the character interpreted as 'wine' and indications of its source (or vintage?).

Outside the NE gate of the Citadel (100m) is a *Tholos Tomb*, excavated by Lord William Taylour in 1953 and restored in 1957 by the Greek Archaeological Service. It is rough in construction compared with those at Mycenae.—Three other tholoi, S of the palace, excavated in 1912, 1926, and 1939, have been filled in.

The richest finds from Pylos are in the National Museum at Athens; various frescoes, etc., in a small museum at Khora (see below).

Near *Papoúlia*, c 10km E of the Palace of Nestor, is a Middle Helladic burial complex, consisting of pithoi inserted into a stone-built mound.

21km *Khóra* (Hotels B, E) formerly *Ligoúdhista*, has an excellent Museum, opened in 1966, containing Mycenaean antiquities from Messenia, including the Palace of Nestor. The three halls contain objects from tholos and chamber tombs, including swords, and gold cups from one of the Peristeria tholoi; *Frescoes from the palace; Linear B tablets; pottery from the palace 'pantries'. The town (3086 inhab.) lies at the SW foot of *Kondovounia*, the ancient AIGALEON, a mountain range which forms the backbone of the peninsula and rises in Ayía Varvára to 1219m. We turn NW into its foothills. 34km *Gargalianoí* (296m; Hotels A, D, E) with 5371 inhab., has a monument to Agras the Macedonian guerilla, who was born here.—48km *Filiatrá* (Hotel D), a well-planned and prosperous town (4931 inhab.) amid currant fields and orchards of citrus fruit. All these towns have been rebuilt since the earthquake of 1886, but their populations are falling by migration to the cities.

Ayía Kiriakí, its little port (4km SW), had more important days as *Erane*, as is shown by remains of basilica and baths (5C AD) and coins from its Frankish mint.

A poor road climbs SE to *Khristianó* (10km), the *Christianoupolis* of the Byzantines and seat of an archbishop in the 12C. It lost importance in the 14C and the bishopric was transferred in 1837 to Kiparissía. The 12C cathedral of Ayia Sotira, wrecked in 1886, has been restored.

65km **Kiparissía** (Κυπαρισσία; Hotels C), the chief town (4013 inhab.) of the eparchy of Messenian Triphylia and the seat of the Bishop of Triphylia and Christianoupolis, was called *Arkadiá* in the middle ages. The town, with pleasant broad streets, has expanded from the foot of the acropolis down to its small harbour and beaches, which are backed by groves of trees. The acropolis is a craggy rock 152m high connected with Mt Psykhro (1116m), the NE end of the Aigaleon range. Vestiges of Hellenic masonry survive in the ruinous Byzantine and Frankish *Castle* (*View, including Zante, Kephalonia and the Strophades), which reintroduced the round tower to Greece.

The ancient city of *Kyparissiai* was founded by Epaminondas as the port of Messene. During the Slav invasions it became a refuge of the Arcadians, whence its medieval name. It was taken after a 7-day siege by William de Champlitte in 1205. In 1391–1430 it was held by the Genoese Zaccaria. The town was destroyed by Ibrahim Pasha in 1825 and on its rebuilding resumed the ancient name.

C. From Kalamáta to Kiparissía

ROAD, 72km (44½ miles), asphalted.—21km Turning (left) for ancient **Messene** (Ithome).—31km *Meligalá*.—35km *Zevgolatió*.—72km *Kiparissía*.

RAILWAY, 67km (41½ miles), in 1¾–3¾ hours viâ *Zevgolatió* and *Kaloneró* where a change is sometimes necessary. To *Válira*, 21km, for Mavromati, in ½ hour.

The route traverses the LOWER MESSENIAN PLAIN, known to the ancients as *Makaria* ('Happy Land'), and described by Euripides in a lost play, quoted by Strabo, as a 'land of fair fruitage and watered by innumerable streams, abounding in pasturage for cattle and sheep, being neither very wintry in the blasts of winter, nor yet made too hot by the chariot of Helios'. Curtius observes: 'High hedges of cactus divide the well-tilled fields; the great aloe stands in thick clumps, lemons and oranges flourish plentifully, the date itself ripens under the Messenian sun, and the superabundance of oil and wine is exported from Kalamáta'. Today, in addition, bananas are successfully grown.—The shorter road, on the E slope of the valley (25km to Meligalá), is described in Rte 33.

From Kalamàta to (8·5km) *Messíni*, see Rte 34A. On the outskirts of Messini we fork right, then turn N up the valley of the Pamisos.—At (16km) *Tríodhos* roads lead right to the airport, left to (4km) **Androúsa** (Ανδρούσα; 726 inhab.) the medieval *Druges*, once a bishopric of Frankish Messenia. It is well situated on an elevated terrace overlooking the plain. To the N of the imposing Frankish *Castle* on the other side of a ravine, is the small Byzantine church of *Áyios Yeóryios*.

Half-an-hour farther W, in a peaceful valley, lies *Ellinoklisiá*, with an elegant church (Samarina), supposedly founded in the 14C by Andronikos II Palaiologos. Its dedication to Zoödókhos Piyí (Source of Life) comes from a spring beneath the church. Built in horizontal layers of brick and stone, it has three apses and a dome supported by ancient marble columns. The narthex supports a square belfry. Within, the mosaic borders, part of the iconostasis, and a mural painting merit a glance. Some column drums nearby show that an earlier building occupied the site.

21km *Khánia Lábaina*. A by-road (signposted *Ithomi*) ascends (left) in 10km to **Mavromáti** (bus from Kalamata), the pretty well-watered village (419m) that occupies part of the site of ancient Messene. At the far end of the village is a sign to 'Archaeological Site' (footpath).

From the railway the best approach on foot is from Válira station (comp. Below), whence we ascend W for (1¾ hours) the MONASTERY OF VOURKANO (383m), which has long been visible half-way up the N slope of Mt Eva. The convent is an off-shoot of an older foundation on the summit of Ithome (see below) and accords hospitality. On the 15C entrance gate is displayed the escutcheon of the Knights of St. John. The conventual buildings, which date only from 1712, are disposed round a cloistered court, with an earlier *Church* in the centre. The beautiful situation commands a view of S Messenia and of the Arcadian mountains.—In 20 minutes from the monastery we ascend to the saddle between Mts Eva and Ithome and reach the Laconian Gate (see below).

Messene dates from 369 BC, when Epaminondas restored the Messenians to their country and encouraged them to build a capital. The city was built in a hollow between three hills, Eva on the SE, Psoriari on the W, and *Ithome* on the N, the acropolis being on the last named which was included in the circuit. The well-preserved *Fortifications are an outstanding example of 4C military architecture.

History. *Messene*, with Megalopolis, Mantineia and Argos, completed the strategic barrier against Sparta organised by Epaminondas after the battle of Leuktra. Diodorus says that the city was built in 85 days. In 214 BC Messene was besieged by a Macedonian general, Demetrios of Pharos, who was killed under its walls; in 202 an attack by the Spartan tyrant Nabis was frustrated by Philopoemen. After the demagogue, Dinokrates, had incited the Messenians to revolt against the Achaean League, Philopoemen attacked the rebels, but was taken prisoner by them, thrown into a dungeon in Messene, and forced to take poison. He was avenged by Lykortas, the father of Polybius, who succeeded him.—The sculptor Damophon was a native.

The path crosses walls of still-buried buildings. On the right is the analemma wall of the *Theatre* (overgrown), pierced, like that at Thorikos, with corbelled archways. Lower down we reach the Hellenistic AGORA or, more probably, SANCTUARY OF ASKLEPIOS, c 69m square, surrounded by a colonnade which had Ionic bases and Corinthian capitals with a winged nike rising from their acanthus leaves. The *Propylaia* occupy the middle of the E side, between, to the N, a small *Theatre* (restored) and, to the S, the *Synedrion*, a small council

meeting-place.—In the NE corner is an oikos. The remainder of the N
side is divided into two equal terraces identified by an inscription as
the *Sebasteion*, an area set aside for the worship of the Roman emperors. Its two parts were each reached by a stair and divided by a
monumental staircase leading to an upper terrace. Here was found a
stone 'standard' for the size of tiles.—Down the W side are a *Temple of
Artemis Orthia*, divided by columns, with three other buildings forming part of the same architectural scheme.—Off the S side is a square
edifice having an inner court, perhaps the Prytaneion.—In the centre
of the agora are foundations of a peripteral temple (6 by 12 columns)
dedicated to Asklepios and Hygieia.

A little to the SW are some remains of the *Stadium* (overgrown)
beyond which we approach the line of the walls, here almost disappeared. We may follow their traces W and then N, or return to the road
and follow it past the *Museum* (not open) to the *Arcadian Gate*, which
forms, with the adjoining section of the city wall and the tower to the E,
the best-preserved part of the fortifications.

The gateway, through which a road still runs, consists of an outer and an inner
entrance, separated by a circular court. The *Outer Entrance* was flanked by
square towers, 10m apart, the foundations alone of which survive. The gateway is
nearly 5m wide. The open *Court*, 19m in diameter, is remarkable for the perfection of its masonry, laid without mortar on a base of two more massive courses. On
either side, near the outer gate, is a niche for statues of the protecting gods, one
doubtless the Hermes noted by Pausanias. Under the right niche a worn inscription describes the restorations of Q. Plotius Euphemion. The *Inner Gate* has an
enormous monolithic doorpost, now half fallen. A short section of *Paved Road*
with chariot ruts is visible. Outside the gate is the stepped base of a large
monument.

The main road continues W within the walls towards a line of towers
standing to their original height.

The circuit of the *WALLS, c 9km long, follows the line of the ridge descending
from Ithome and was continuous except at various inaccessible points. This vast
enceinte, planned to enclose cornfields, doubtless served also as a refuge for the
surrounding population in time of danger. The battlemented *Curtain* consists of
an outer and inner facing of unmortared squared blocks, with a rubble core; it is
2–2·5m thick and averaged 4·5m high. The steepness of the escarpment precluded the approach of siege engines. The curtain was flanked at irregular intervals (30–90m) by projecting battlemented *Towers*, of which there were at least
thirty. These were square or, at the salient angles, semicircular. Seven are still
partly extant. They had two storeys, the lower with four loopholes, the upper with
six small windows. Four of the *Gates*, have been distinguished.

From the village a path, now difficult of access, ascends Ithome past
the *Aqueduct* which fed the destroyed Fountain of Klepsydra. Higher
up is a small terrace on which are the remains of an Ionic temple
(perhaps of *Artemis Laphria*) discovered in 1844. The ascent (1½
hours from the village) is now best made by taking the track from
Mavromati to the Laconian Gate (comp. below) and following the path
from there. The summit of **Ithóme** (Ἰθώμη: 'step'; 802m) is really a
ridge running SE to NW. Mentioned by Homer, Ithome figured as a
refuge in the First and Third Messenian Wars. On the summit stands
the small *Monastery of Vourkano*, dating from the 16C, and the
mother-convent of the later monastery below (comp. above). It was
finally abandoned in 1950 and its ikon removed from the ruined Katholikon. A paved threshing floor may have been the scene of the
festival of the Ithomaea, which survives to this day in an annual festival of the Panayia. The convent occupies the site of an *Altar-sanc-
tuary of Zeus Ithomatas* where human sacrifice was occasionally offered. To the S are two large cisterns. The *View embraces most of

Messenia.—We may descend again to the *Laconian Gate*.

Outside the Arcadian Gate a poor road bears left via *Zerbísia* and *Neokhóri Ithómis* to Meligalá (see below).—From Mavromati a track leads S to *Samári*, where the church of Zoödókhos Piyí has 12C frescoes.

Returning to the main road, we cross the Pamisos.—24km *Válira*.—At 28km we pass (right) a short link (2km) to the Kalamata-Tripolis road.—31km **Meligalá** (Μελιγαλά; Hotel E), with a prominent clock-tower, is the largest town (1431 inhab.) in the Upper Messenian Plain, or *Plain of Stenyklaros*, the home of the Dorian dynasty of Kres-phontes. The site of the royal city is unknown. This beautiful and fertile valley, watered by many streams, enjoys a more temperate climate than is suggested by its vegetation, which includes figs, olives, oranges, mulberries, cactus, and date palms.

About 1·5km SW is the triple **Mavrozoúmenos Bridge**, built over the confluence of two rivers. The W arm spans the *Upper Mavrozoumenos*, the E arm the *Amphitos*. The N arm forms a causeway over the apex of land between them which is liable to be flooded. The bridge has seven arches (span 5·2m, height above water 4m) and one rectangular opening 2·2m high by 1·2m wide. The piers are ancient, probably contemporary with Messene; the arches mainly Turkish. English travellers may be reminded of the 14C triangular bridge at Crowland in Lincolnshire. The river below the bridge is called the *Pamisos*.

Beyond the railway junction of *Zevgolatió* we meet the road from Megalopolis and turn W. The road, which is being realigned, crosses the *Soulima Plain*, a broad corridor through which flows the Upper Mavrozoumenos.—44km *Vasilikó* has a small Museum containing objects from Malthí and a Roman mosaic found near Korone. On the *Malthí Ridge* between Vasilikó and the hamlet of Kókla (left) is the site doubtfully identified with the Homeric *Dorion* where Thamyris lost his eyesight. Excavations in 1927–36 by the Swedish archaeologist Natan Valmin disclosed a largely M.H. existence. Two small tholos tombs and a sanctuary containing a bronze double-axe were brought to light.—52km *Káto Kopanáki*, on the watershed between the Arkhadéïka (Aëtos) and the W tributaries of the Pamisos, lies 5km N of Aëtós, a village on the N slope of *Mt Sekhi* (1391m) where there are cyclopean ruins and remains of a 14C Venetian fort.—63km Turning (right; across the railway) for *Sidhirókastro*, a village in the hills to the NE. On a hill behind it is the 13C castle from which it takes name.

At (65km) *Kaló Neró* we join the coastal road (comp. below) and turn left.—72km **Kiparissía**, see Rte 34B.

D. From Kiparissía to Pírgos

ROAD, 63km (39 miles).

RAILWAY, 63km, several times daily in 1½–5 hours; to *Kaïáfa*, 33km, in 50 minutes (only the slowest trains stop at *Samikó*).

Heading N from Kiparissía, there is a turn (3km, right; indifferent road) to *Mírou*.

At *Peristeriá*, 1·5km N of Mírou, important Mycenaean tholos tombs with rich finds (in Khora Museum) were found in 1960–65 and further recent work has revealed additional burials as well as evidence of a Mycenaean settlement.

At (6·5km) *Kaló Neró* we meet the main road from the E. Thence the road and railway follow the sandy shore.—16km The *Nédha* river forms the boundary between Messinia and Elis (comp. Rte 40).—20km *Thólon*. A minor road (bus) serves *Lépreo* (8km), on the heights above which are well-preserved walls of ancient *Lepreon*, where, in the SE part of the site, can be seen architectural fragments from and the foundations of a *Temple of Demeter* of the 4C BC.—20km *Káto Figalía* (or Zoúrtsa; 14km), whence bridle-paths wind in 8½ hours to ancient Phigaleia (Rte 35).—25km **Kakóvatos** is well-known to archaeologists for the site (15 minutes to the NE at 'Marmara') identified by Prof. Dörpfeld, following Strabo, as Triphylian Pylos, a place confused until the discoveries at Englianos with the Pylos of Nestor. Three tholos tombs and traces of a palace or sanctuary (L.H. I or II) were excavated in 1909–10, and the position of the lower town was identified in 1961.

Beyond (28km) *Zakháro* (Hotel C; 2783 inhab.) we pass between the sea and the LAGOON OF KAÏÁFA, which is 5km long and contains valuable fisheries. On the lake-island of Ayía Aikateríni (cross by causeway right at 32km) are the sulphur *Baths of Kaïáfa* (Λουτρό Καιάφα; Hotel, May–October with annexes).

The waters come from springs in two large sulphurous caverns, the *Cave of the Anigrian Nymphs* and the *Cave of Yeranion* to which the ancients resorted for the cure of skin diseases. The first feeds the baths, the second is used for drinking. Local tradition ascribes the name of the lagoon to Caiaphas, High Priest of Judah who bathed here after having been shipwrecked. The offensive pungency of the sulphur-laden waters is attributed to him.

The road rounds the W spur of *Mt Kaïáfa* (744m). On the N slope of the mountain, immediately above the road and best seen from the N, stands (38km) ancient **Samikón**. To visit the site, turn right on to a dirt road by sign for *Káto Samikón*. The imposing enceinte in developed polygonal masonry of c 450 BC stands in places to 12 courses. Within is a less well preserved and earlier defensive wall to be dated before the 6C BC. The site has been inhabited since Early Helladic times and a Mycenaean burial mound has yielded much pottery. The place was taken by Philip V of Macedon in 219 BC.

We pass inland of the shallow lagoon of *Agoulínitsa*, itself separated from the sea by a belt of dunes with pines. Roads (right) lead to Kréstena (whence to Bassae, see Rte 35) and on over the Alpheios Dam to Olympia (13km; Rte 36).—50km *Epitálion* (1815 inhab.), formerly Agoulínitsa but now probably correctly recording an ancient site, straggles on the hillside, surrounded by cornfields and vineyards. The hill of Ay. Yeoryios has produced L.H. III remains of (?) Homeric *Thryon*. Hence the road runs straight across the alluvial plain, crossing the Alpheios on a bridge 400m long that serves also as an irrigation sluice. The railway curves NE to cross the river higher up by a long iron bridge and join the branch from Olympia.—63km *Pírgos*, see Rte 40.

35 From Megalópolis to Andrítsaina (Bassae) and Pírgos

ROAD, 110km (68½ miles) affording spectacular scenery. 20km **Karítaina**.—45km **Andrítsaina**, turning for **Bassae** (14·5km).—60km *Kréstena*.—110km **Pírgos**. BUS daily from Megalopolis to Andritsaina; twice daily from Andritsaina to Krestena; more frequently Krestena to Pirgos. Taxis in Megalopolis for Bassae.

Megalópolis, see Rte 33. The road runs through the ancient remains crossing the Helisson.

A minor road leads (right) in 15km, via *Trílofos* to Likókhia, near which a late Archaic and Classical sanctuary of *Artemis* (perhaps that of Artemis Kalliste, mentioned by Pausanias) was excavated in 1972 and 1975).

We follow the Alpheios at varying distances from its right bank.— 11km *Katsímbali*. Here a track diverges (left) across the river to *Kiparissía*, between which and *Mavriá*, just to the N, are some remains of *Trapezous*.—We see ahead (20km) *Karítaina* (winding ascent for 3km) above the junction with the road from Dhimitsána.

Karítaina (Καρύταινα; Hotels), a picturesque medieval town, is spectacularly perched on an isolated hill at the NW corner of the Plain of Megalopolis above the right bank of the Karitaina (as the Alpheios is called at this point).

Karítaina, Frankish bridge

Karítaina occupies the site of ancient *Brenthe*, a deserted city which became a refuge for the people of Gortys when they were driven out by the Slavs. The name is, in fact, a corruption of Gortyna. In 1209 the Franks made Karytaina the capital of a barony of 22 fiefs. The castle was built by Hugh de Bruyères in 1254. His son Geoffrey I de Bruyères (died. 1272) was the 'Sire de Caritaine' and the pattern of Peloponnesian chivalry. The castle passed by sale in 1320 to Andronikos II Palaiologos. In the War of Independence, Kolokotronis used the castle as a stronghold from which he defied Ibrahim Pasha.

The churches of the *Panayía* (11C), with a Frankish belfry, and of *Áyios Nikólaos* (frescoes; key from hotel), merit a visit. A precipitous path climbs in 10 minutes to the *CASTLE (583m) which occupies the summit of a high rock, extremely steep and in places overhanging the river side. The triangular enceinte, adapted for defence by artillery as well as musketry, is a notable example of feudal fortification. In the central court is a large vaulted hall and on the W the remains of a gallery with large windows and of numerous cisterns (care needed). The *View is superb.

From Karitaina a bad road leads N via Ipsoúnda (19km; Rte 36) to Dhimitsána. The road winds high in the accidented mountain range on the E side of the gorge down which the clear, green Lousios (or Gortynios) flows to its confluence with the Alpheios. About 10km along this road is *Ellinikó*. Before this village a mule-path diverges (left) to *Atzíkholo* (1½ hours) on the right (W) bank of the Lousios where the fine acropolis of **Gortys** occupies the oblong summit of a precipitous height. On all sides except the E, which falls sheer to the river, are remains of walls and towers in trapezoidal masonry of the Macedonian epoch. These were explored in detail by the French School (BCH 1947–48). A smaller walled enclosure borders the ravine at the SE corner. Beyond are some foundations of a sanctuary of Asklepios with a Doric temple (explored 1950–52). To the N of the acropolis (30 minutes) near the little chapel of Ayios Andreas are the more interesting remains of a second *Asklepieion* with a thermal establishment (? 4C BC), excavated in 1954. Important remains of houses of the same period have also been found. Gortys still gives name to a modern eparchy of Arcadia.

Near by in 1955 were explored three strong-points commanding the ancient route from Megalopolis to Elis: above the village of *Vlakhoráfti*, to the W, on the highest point (942m) of the W chain overlooking the gorge; at *Palaiókastro*, at the W end of this chain, overlooking the Alpheios (ancient *Bouphagion*); and (smaller but probably of the Archaic period) at Elliniko (see above).

The Andritsaina road crosses the river on a new bridge affording a good view of the *Medieval Bridge*, renovated (as an inscription once recorded) in 1439 by Manuel Raoul Melikes, a member of a noble Turkish family serving the Palaiologi at Mistra.—27km *Strongiló*. We climb high along the N slopes of the barren Mt Lykaion with views into the Gorge of the Alpheios.

Mt Lykaion (1407m) was the centre of a primitive cult of Zeus involving rainmaking, human sacrifice, werewolves, and athletic games. Within its precinct neither man nor beast cast a shadow. The sacrificial pyre and precinct were excavated in 1903. The site of the hippodrome can be distinguished. Lykosoura, on the S flank, see Rte 33.

45km (28 miles) **Andritsaína** (Ανδρίτσαινα; Hotels B, D, E) an attractive ramshackle town (863 inhab.) of wooden houses, was shaken by earthquakes in 1965. It is beautifully situated on elevated ground (765m) facing NW and watered by a mountain stream. In the square stands a monument to Panayotis Anagnostopoulos, one of the Philike Etairia who was educated at the local school. The town has an excellent *Library* founded with a bequest in 1840.

A road (14·5km; taxi; bus daily, not returning), well-engineered but often in bad condition, and not for those nervous of unprotected drops, ascends to the remote Temple of Bassae. The 2½-hour walk through the valleys is rewarding. Continuation to the coast, see below.

The celebrated *TEMPLE OF APOLLO EPIKOURIOS at **Bassae** is situated at 1131m on a narrow rocky terrace of *Mt Kotilion* (now Paliavlakhítsa), whose summit rises above it to the NE. The mountain is scored with ravines (βάσσαι; vássai) from which the place takes its general name; the temple site is called locally 'the columns' (στοὺς στύλους). The temple, which owes its fine preservation to its inaccessibility, is built of a cold grey local limestonę that contributes to, rather than lightens, the melancholy bleakness of the landscape. The immediate surroundings are softened a little by a few oak trees and wild flowers. The only other building is a house belonging to the phylax.

The temple is attributed by Pausanias to Iktinos. Its style makes it almost certainly an earlier work than the Parthenon, and so designed c 450–447 BC, though the execution may not have been finished before 425 BC. The locality was rediscovered in 1765 by Joachim Bocher, a French architect employed by the Venetians in Zante. It was visited in 1805–06 by Leake, Dodwell, and Wm Gell. In 1811–12 the party of British and German antiquaries who had previously stripped the Aegina temple, explored the ruins and removed the sculptures. The 23 marble slabs of the cella frieze were bought by the British Government for £19,000 for the British Museum. In 1902–06 the Greek Archaeological Society replaced some fallen column fragments and restored the cella walls. Additional fragments of the frieze were unearthed in 1961. The foundations have been shown to incorporate reused blocks from an Archaic predecessor which occupied the area immediately to the S and whose outline can be discerned.

The temple (at present swathed in wooden splints for conservation and eventually to be roofed) is a Doric peripteral hexastyle, 38·3m long and 14·6m wide, longer, therefore, by about one fifth and fractionally wider than the Hephaisteion in Athens. The orientation is unusual, being N and S. The *Peristyle*, 6 columns by 15, on a stylobate of three steps, is complete save for the SE corner column. Most of the architrave blocks are in position, but nothing of the pediments or the roof. The pediments were prepared for sculptured groups which Dinsmoor concludes were taken off in ancient times to Rome: the roof-tiles were of Parian marble. The colonnade had a coffered ceiling of different patterns.

The **Interior** has the conventional pronaos, cella, and opisthodomos, but the arrangement is unusual. The *Pronaos*, 5·5m long, had two columns between antae. It was decorated with a metope frieze, now in a very fragmentary state. A metal barrier, with gates, shut it off from the colonnade. A door led into the cella. The *Opisthodomos*, 4·1m long, was similarly distyle in antis, open to the colonnade, but cut off by a wall from the cella.

The **Cella**, 16·8m long and 7m wide was in two parts. The N section, 12·2m long, was adorned on either side with a series of 5 semi-columns engaged in buttresses that projected from the side wall, the first four pairs at right angles and the fifth pair (at the S end) diagonally inward. The semi-columns are most unusually located not opposite the peristyle columns but between the intercolumniations. The first four pairs had bell-shaped bases, resting on a step, 10cm high, and volutes on three faces of the Ionic capitals. The fifth pair had Corinthian capitals, with between them, a single Corinthian column, in marble, with 20 flutes. Its capital, now lost, is recorded as having acanthus decoration, and thus formed the earliest example of the Corinthian order yet known to us. The height of the interior colonnade (6·3m) is greater by a foot than that of the peristyle. It supported an Ionic entablature having a frieze, 102ft long, richly carved in island marble and representing the battles between Greeks and Amazons, and between Lapiths and Centaurs.

The inner *Adyton*, occupying the remaining 4·6m of the cella, is also of unusual design, having a door on the left (E side). This fact prompted speculation as to whether the cult statue stood against its W wall, and whether the plan follows that of an earlier sanctuary on the site. It seems clear, however, that the god stood in a more usual position in the cella. Pausanias records that the figure of Apollo in bronze was transferred in 369 BC to the agora at Megalopolis and replaced by an acrolithic statue.

TO PHIGALEIA AND THE GORGE OF THE NEDHA. From Bassae a road, graded and adequate but unsurfaced before Káto Figália, descends S and W via (8km) *Dhragóni* to (11km) *Perivólia*, where remains of a Doric temple were found in 1972. Here a track winds S towards Áno Figalía, passing the site of ancient

Phigaleia (1 hour; Hotel E), an Arcadian city on the borders of Elis and Messenia, which had a reputation for wizardry, witchcraft, and drunkenness. The ruins of its walls and towers occupy a high and uneven plateau with precipitous sides, surrounded by mountains. On the S the Neda flows far below. The road continues to (14km) *Petrálona*, from which an occasional bus goes down via (18·5km) *Káto Figália* and *Lépreon* (comp. Rte 34D) to (31km) Figália station on the coast.— Alternatively, for those on foot, a difficult but rewarding walk may be made (preferably with a guide from Áno Figália) following the track into the spectacular GORGE OF THE NEDHA to *Aspro Neró*, a superb *Waterfall. Ancient ship-sheds were discovered lower down the river in 1972.

Beyond Andritsaína the road, asphalt but subject to landslides and subsidence, commands tremendous views across the Alpheios valley towards the N heights of the Peloponnese. All along this road, which must duplicate the course of an ancient way from Olympia towards Sparta, are remains of classical places, for the most part unexcavated, seldom visited, and not certainly identified (comp. E. Meyer: 'Neue Peloponnesische Wanderungen', Berne, 1957).—We pass through *Míloi* (or Makhalas)—most villages in Arcadia have a Slav or Albanian name and a readopted Greek one—and come to (51km) *Keramídhi* (Kaléntzi).

A little farther on a track leads (right) to *Alífira*, near which, at *Kastro tis Dhrosítsas*, A.K. Orlandos excavated in 1932–35 (and published in 1968) the acropolis of ancient *Alipheira*, uncovering foundations of a Doric temple of Athena (6 by 15 columns), founded in the mid-6C, and of a sanctuary of Asklepios (late 4C). A funerary shrine was also located on the course of the ancient road N to Heraia.—Near *Vrestón*, to the S of our road, a large unidentified site was located in 1955.

60km (37¾ miles) **Zákha** (Ζάχα), officially *Kallithéa*, a village of 872 inhab. through which the road all but disappears, stands at 550m barely 4km S of the confluence of the Ladon with the Alpheios (Rte 36). We turn SW to *Barakítika*, whence a track goes off (right) to *Bitzibárdi* (or Tripití) with a Gothic monastery of Notre Dame d'Issova, built by the Franks and burnt by the Byzantines in 1264 (see Traquair in *Journal of the Royal Institute of British Architects* 31 (1923–24)).

69km *Platána*. Above the village to the S are the walls of ancient **Typaneai**, of splendidly preserved regular isodomic masonry (? 3C BC). Their perimeter encloses a narrow ridge, 594m long, rising at its W end to 599m. Within are remains of an antique *Theatre*, cisterns, and two Christian churches. About 1km farther E are some medieval ruins (Paliakumba) of *Cumba*, a Frankish castle held in 1364 by Marie de Bourbon, widow of Robert of Taranto.—79km *Gréka*. We pass below a hill (right) called *Kástro Múndriza*, identified with ancient *Hypana*, and leave on our right a track leading towards another site, perhaps that of Homeric *Aipion*.

91km (56½ miles) **Kréstena** (Hotels E) is a large village (3539 inhab.) served by bus from Pirgos. A good road leads via Makrísia and over (8km) the Alpheios barrage to Olympia (14·5km). *Makrísia* is the site of ancient Skillus. Here the stylobate of a Doric temple has been said by Yalouris (1954) to be that of Athena Skillountia mentioned by Strabo, rather than that known to have been erected at the cost of the exiled Xenophon on his estate here c 444–434 BC. Recent work by I. Triandi has clarified the character of the temple (peripteral, internal colonnade) and revealed another substantial building, as well as a fortification wall and tower; also fragments of pedimental sculptures.

1·5km before Olympia, the road passes through *Flóka*, to the NW of which, at *Panoúkla*, an extensive Roman bath complex of the 3C AD was discovered in 1972.

The road soon joins the Kiparissía–Pírgos road. Hence to (110km) *Pírgos*, see Rte 34.

36 From Trípolis to Olympia and Pírgos

ROAD, 156km (96½ miles). A well-engineered modern road with fair surface and spectacular mountain scenery, the central section narrow and difficult driving; a few buses daily in 4 hours:—10·5km Turning for *Mantinea* (see Rte 30).—26km *Levídhi.*—35km Turning for Kalávryta and Patras (Rte 39).—46km **Vitína.**—60km *Karkaloú,* turning for (13km) **Dhimitsána.**—72km **Langádhia.**—86km *Stavrodhrómi.*—132km **Olympia.**—153km **Pírgos.**

RAILWAY from Olympia to Pyrgos, 4–5 times daily in 30 minutes.

From Tripolis to (11km) the Mantinea turn, see Rte 30. The road follows the W side of the plain of Mantinea close beneath the foothills of Mainalon, whose triangular summit appears at first to block the broad valley ahead.—Beyond (14·5km) *Kápsas* (581 inhab.) we thread a defile to the small diamond-shaped *Plain of Alkimedon*, immediately below the towering *Mt Ostrakina* (1981m), topmost peak of *Mainalon*. A mule track (left) skirts its S side to Alonístaina (11km; Rte 30). Farther on, a defile (right) affords a glimpse of (22·5km) *Simiádhes* at the N end of the Plain of Mantinea.—From the top of the next long rise we descry, crowning the next hills the campanile of (26km) *Levídhi* (Hotel D; 1442 inhab.), native town of Alex. Papanastasiou (1879–1936), republican statesman and prime minister in 1924. A chapel of the Panayía on a low hill to the E is supposed to mark the site of the sanctuary of Artemis-Hymnia, common to the peoples of Mantinea and Orchomenos. Just beyond the town the road commands a wide view across the plain of Orchomenos (magnificently backed by the Chelmos range), into which a by-road drops abruptly towards *Kandhíla* and Arkadian *Orchomenós* (5km; Rte 26).

32km *Vlakhérna* (1000m). *Khotoússa*, in the valley to the N (45 minutes), stands close to the scanty remains of Hellenistic and Roman *Caphyae.*—At 34·5km the road to Patras (Rte 39) drops away in a valley (right) as we climb round the N end of the Mainalon range; the village of *Kamenítsa* is seen far below.—46km (28½ miles) **Vitína** (Βύτινα; Hotels B, C; camping), an attractive summer resort (857 inhab.), stands in a cool and healthy upland situation (1040m) amid fir-clad slopes. It has a School of Forestry and a tradition of woodcarving. The town was Kolokotronis' supply-base.—Our road twists through sharp outcrops of rock.—50km. On a hill to the S are the scanty remains of *Methydrion*, a town sacrificed in the building of Megalopolis.—53km Turning (unpaved) to Magouliyiá (4km right) and Valtesiníkón (13km).

Magouliyiá, birthplace of Theodore Kolokotronis, the klepht hero of the War of Independence, was a summer residence of the Villehardouin—hence the ruined Frankish fortress (Argyrókastro). *Valtesiníkon* lies just E of the site of ancient *Glanitsa*, where the French School found a late-Archaic bronze head in 1939.— Tracks go on through the mountains and across the Ladon to Dhafní (Rte 39).

Approaching (60km) *Karkaloú* we descend through pine-woods, with the pleasantly situated Xenia Motel (B), passing a campsite (left) with a memorial bust in bronze of Dhimitri Mitropoulos (1896–1960), the conductor, by Apartis. Some polygonal walls (? *Theisoa*) survive near the village.

From Karkaloú a tarmac road diverges on the left to (8km) **Dhimitsána** (Δημητσάνα; Hotel C), an attractive village (612 inhab.) in a magnificent situation above the Lousios, on the site of ancient *Teuthis*. An example of cyclopean wall forming part of a modern house may be seen just below the more westerly of the two main churches. Some classical walls also survive, but medieval building predominates. Dhimitsána became a centre of Greek learning after 1764, when its school was founded, and hence of opposition to the Turks; the Patriarch Gregory V and Germanos, Archbishop of Patras, were both pupils. It became a centre of activity of the Philike Etairia, and an arsenal for the War of Independence with 14 powder factories. The Museum, Archives, and Library are worth a visit. The *Moní Filosófou* was founded in 963 but not on its present site, 2·5km SE, below Zigovisti.

The road continues (unpaved, rough) to (18km) **Ipsoúnda** (Ηψούντα; Hotel C), a beautiful mountain village (1076m) formerly known as *Stemnítsa*, grandly situated against the side of Mt Klinítsa (1548m). The Kastro incorporates several little churches: *Ayíou Nikoláou* was repaired in 1589; the *Panayía Baféro* dates probably from 1640. The monastery of *Áy. Ioánnou tou Prodhrómou*, founded by Manuel Comnenos in 1167, lies 4km W in the Lousios gorge (precipitous path from Dhimitsána road).

Beyond Ipsoúnda the road forks, the right branch (very bad) for Karítaina and Megalópolis; the left (bad) for (62km) *Trípolis* via Daviá (Rte 30).

Threading rocky gorges in an increasingly barren landscape to a summit of nearly 1220m, clothed in ferns, we cross the infant Lousios.— 72km (44¾ miles) **Langádhia** (Λαγκάδια; Hotel C), native town (821 inhab.) of the Deliyianni family, appears ahead tumbling vertically down an outcrop of rock above the valley. By a series of sharp downward curves we approach its centre, where a little Plateia (café) forms a superb *Belvedere.

The long descent continues as the tortuous road follows a vertiginous shelf of rock a thousand feet above the gorge.—Beyond (79km) *Lefkokhóri* it crosses a side valley and, surmounting a ridge, reaches the upland village of (86km) *Stavrodhrómi*.

Here a by-road (right) leads to *Trópaia* (4km; Hotel E), a mountain village. About 1·5km E of Trópaia are three towers of the Frankish castle of the barony of Akova, and two hours W some remains of classical *Thelpousa*, another site investigated by the French School in 1939, which had a huge 4C agora.—In Trópaia the road (now unpaved) hairpins right and continues to (10·5km) the *Ladon Dam (Frágma Ládhonos; Φράγμα Λάδωνος), 100·5m long and c 53m high, which has formed a lake, ringed by pine trees, in the upper valley. The waters are fed to hydro-electric works, near the village of Spáthari (comp. below) to the W, by a tunnel, 8km long, through a mountain.

The mountains give place to rolling hills as we descend to the broad valley of the *Ladon*, most copious of the seven important tributaries of the Alpheios until its reduction by damming (see above).—96km Turning (right; 6km) to the hydro-electric station. We cross the river and descend the right bank.—Beyond (97km) *Bertsia*, with its charming wooded stream, the road climbs a ridge commanding the confluence of the Ladon and the Alpheios, where Pausanias' 'Isle of Crows' is seen. On the way up we pass a by-road which returns to the left bank of the Ladon to *Loutrá Iraías*, S of which, near Ay. Ioannis on the bank of the Alpheios, some remains of ancient *Heraia* were identified by the Greek Archaeological Service in 1931.—A sharp hill and (113km) the *Yéfira Koklamá*, a concrete bridge, takes us across the Erímanthos and into Elis (comp. Rte 40).—119km *Vasiláki* (400m) occupies the summit of the ridge of Sauros, a highwayman killed by Herakles. Hence we descend amid lush vegetation to the wide bed of the Alpheios.—124km *Mouriá*.

The ALPHEIOS or *Alfios*, the largest river in the Peloponnese, rises in south-east Arcadia, close to the source of the Eurotas and flows through Arcadia and Elis, past Olympia, into the Ionian Sea. Pausanias describes it as 'a broad and noble stream, fed by seven important rivers'. These are the Helisson, Brentheates, Gortynios, Bouphagos, Ladon, Erymanthos, and Kladeos. The Peloponnesians regard the Ladon as the main stream, calling the Alpheios proper the Karytaina above the confluence. In the early part of its course this runs underground. According to legend the river-god Alpheios fell in love with the nymph Arethusa. Spurning his advances she fled to Ortygia, an island off Syracuse in Sicily, and was there changed into a fountain, whereupon Alpheios flowed under the sea to join her. Shelley, celebrating the legend, calls the river a 'brackish, Dorian stream'. It was the favourite river of Zeus, and on its banks first grew the wild olive, a garland of which was the reward of victors in the Olympic Games.

129km *Miráka* (on a by-road; right) is 15 minutes S of the site of ancient *Pisa*.—Approaching (132km) **Olympía** (Ολυμπία; pron. Olimbía) we see (right) the spacious International Olympic Academy, inaugurated in 1961 with the object of maintaining and promoting the Olympic spirit. Annual summer courses are held. Immediately after this (right) is a stele enclosing the heart of Pierre de Coubertin (1862–1937), who revived the games. We pass between Mt Kronon and the excavations (left; see Rte 37), cross the Kladeos, and turn into the village, 1063 inhabitants.

Railway Station, 500m W of the village.

Youth hostel.

Buses to Athens via Pirgos and Patras.

At 137km *Plátanos* we join the road from Kalávrita (Rte 39). Most of the villages stand on low hills between successive small tributaries of the Alpheios, and are surrounded by orchards. *Broúma*, on the right beyond (139km) *Kreboúki* (officially Pelópion), occupies the site of *Herakleia*, which once had curative springs.— 146km The *Eripeus*, now called Lestenítza, was the scene of the myth of Poseidon and Tyro.—153km (95 miles) **Pírgos**, see Rte 40.

37   Olympia

Approaches and hotels, etc., see above.

OLYMPIA, in Greek *Olimbía* (Ολυμπία; 43m) is situated in the quietly beautiful valley of the Alpheios in the territory of Pisatis, at its confluence with the Kladeos. The setting, in great contrast with most Greek sites, is pastoral, green, and lush, the ruins being plentifully shaded by evergreen oaks, Aleppo pines, planes, and poplars, as well as by olive-trees. The Kladeos bounds the site on the W and the Alpheios on the S, while to the N rises the conical Mt Kronos (123m). Olympia was not a city, but a sacred precinct occupied exclusively by temples, dwellings for the priests and officials, and public buildings in connection with the Games, and it became a sanctuary in which were concentrated many of the choicest treasures of Greek art. In the midst was the enclosure known as the *Altis*, dedicated to Zeus, in whose honour were held the quadrennial festival and the games. The best view of the site is from Mt Dhroúva above the SPAP hotel, which is also a good area for walks for those who wish to escape the now somewhat garish village.

The fame of Olympia rests upon the Olympic Games. Whatever may have been their origin, they remained until they were degraded by specialisation and professionalism a great national festival influencing the character and fortunes of the entire Hellenic race. A striking feature of the festival was the proclamation of the *Ekecheiria*, or Olympic Truce; still more surprising was its almost universal observance, a fact sufficient witness in itself to the high prestige of the Olympic festival. During the week of the celebrations the competitors, while not forgetting that they were Athenians, Spartans, Milesians, Syracusans, or whatever, remembered that they were Greeks, and they regarded an Olympic victory as the highest possible honour. The simple reward of a crown of wild olive not only immortalised the victor and his family, but redounded to the glory of his native city.

The Greeks came to use the Olympiads, or periods of four years between festivals, as the basis of their chronology. The Games were held regularly in peace and in war for over 1000 years from 776 BC until their suppression in AD 393. From the first Olympiad to the time of Hadrian the embellishment of Olympia never ceased. The vitality of the festivals is reflected in the architecture and works of art that have survived.

History. Excavations since 1959 have shown that *Olympia* was already flourishing in Mycenaean times. The legendary foundation of the Games and the elaborated later traditions may be found recorded by Pausanias (Bk V). Homer does not mention them and the official era of the Olympiads started in 776 BC. The conduct of the games seems at first to have been disputed between Pisa and Elis and ancient authorities differ widely as to the date when the Eleans finally prevailed (between 572 and 471 BC).

Despite the vicissitudes of fortune and of war, the Olympic Games were held with the utmost regularity, the wealth of the various sanctuaries steadily accumulated, and the prestige of Olympia increased until it reached its zenith in the 5C BC. The Olympic Truce was strictly observed, with one or two exceptions. In 420 BC the Lacedaemonians were excluded from the festival on the ground of truce-breaking (Thuc. V, 49). In 364 BC, during the invasion of the Pisans and Arcadians, a battle was fought in the Altis in the presence of the crowd that had come to watch the games.

After the age of Hadrian Olympia ceased to have much religious or political significance, but was visited for sentimental reasons or out of curiosity. The games were, however, kept up until AD 393, when the edict of Theodosius I, prohibiting all pagan festivals, put an end to them. In 426 Theodosius II ordered the destruction of the temples and the Altis was burnt. Soon afterwards the ruins were quarried to transform the Workshop of Pheidias into a Christian church and to build a fortification against the Vandals. In 522 and 551 the ruins were devastated anew by earthquakes, the Temple of Zeus being partially buried, while a landslip from Mt Kronos destroyed the buildings at its foot. A new settlement was swept away when the Kladeos overflowed and buried all the buildings on the W side of the precinct deep in sand and mud. Further landslips on Mt Kronos occurred and the Alpheios, changing its bed, carried away the Hippodrome and part of the Stadium, thus completing the ruin of Olympia, which for centuries remained an uninhabited waste covered with a layer of debris 3–3·75m deep.

The first modern traveller to visit Olympia was Dr Chandler, in 1766, though as early as 1713 Montfaucon had suggested excavation. In 1768 Winkelmann planned a restoration of Olympia. In 1811 Stanhope had a plan made of the site. A French expedition of 1829 partially excavated the Temple of Zeus. In 1852 Prof. E. Curtius revived the plan of Winkelmann for the excavation of Olympia and interested the German royal family in the project. At last, in 1874, a convention with Greece was reached, whereby the German government was permitted to carry out excavations. Their work covers three periods: 1875–81, 1936–41, and since 1952. Everything of importance has been housed in the Museum, except for some bronzes (now in the National Museum in Athens). The temples of Zeus and Hera have suffered from exposure since they were uncovered.

ADMINISTRATION. The Altis was reserved for the gods, the dwellings of the priests and officials being outside. The supreme governing body was the *Olympian Senate*, elected from the Elean aristocracy, which met in the Bouleuterion. The senate had control of the revenue and the Olympian officials were responsible to it. The magistrates and priests, Eleans of good family, were elected for the period of each Olympiad. They lived in the Prytaneion. Though each sanctuary had its own staff, a superior hierarchy looked after the administration as a whole and regulated the service of the temples. At its head were three *Theokoloi*, or High Priests, who lived in the Theokoleion and dined at the Prytaneion. Next were three *Spondophoroi*, heralds whose duty it was to travel abroad and proclaim the date of the festival and of the Olympic Truce. Finally the two (later four) hereditary *Soothsayers* interpreted the Oracle. In addition there was a host of minor officials such as the *Kathemerothytes*, or priest of the day, the *Exegetes* (who doubled the role of master of ceremonies with that of cicerone to visitors), the *Epimeletes*, or keeper of the Sanctuary, three *Epispondorchestai*, or dancers, a flute-player, an architect, a doctor, a chef for the Prytaneion, a wood-cutter (who provided the wood for the altars), etc.

THE QUADRENNIAL FESTIVALS. The most important of all the festivals at Olympia was the *Festival of Zeus*, accompanied by the Olympic Games. It took place at the time of the second (or possibly first) full moon following the summer solstice, i.e. in August or September. A sacred truce fortified by severe sanctions, universally suspended hostilities during the week of the festival, forbade armed forces to enter the confines of Elis, and proclaimed the inviolability of visitors. The special representatives of the various cities and states were publicly entertained, being housed in buildings adjoining the Altis and fed at the Prytaneion. The *Theoroi* or special ambassadors from foreign states, were sent at their national expense. The crowd of humbler pilgrims were accommodated in tents, or like the competitors slept in blankets on the ground.

THE OLYMPIC OR OLYMPIAN GAMES. The direction of the games (ἀγωνοθεσία) was, with certain interruptions, in the hands of the Eleans. Only men and boys who spoke Greek as their mother-tongue were originally allowed to compete; barbarians were admitted as spectators, but slaves were entirely excluded. No married woman might be present, or even cross the Alpheios while the games were going on, under penalty of being hurled from the Typaeon Rock. Later Romans were admitted.

Ten months before the date of the games the Elean magistrates chose a body of 10 *Hellanodikai*, or umpires, who supervised training and discipline as well as the actual contests. The competitors had to train for the whole ten months, the last month being spent at Elis (comp. below). A ceremonial procession to Olympia took place just before the festival began. They took the oath at the bouleuterion on the Altar of Zeus Horkeios, swearing that they would loyally observe all the regulations of the games, and involving not only their family but their native town in the penalties consequent on any infraction.

The Eleans kept registers of the winners of the foot-race, the oldest event, after the successive winners of which each Olympiad was named; Plutarch, however, questions both their antiquity and authenticity. To the foot-race were added at intervals other competitive events, most notably the Pentathlon (in which jumping, wrestling, and throwing both spear and discus were combined with running), boxing, chariot-racing and horse racing (the 'hippic' as opposed to gymnastic contests at which tyrants and nobles competed, employing professional charioteers and jockeys), and the Pankration (a form of all-in wrestling). An Athenian took the prize for the first time in 696, and in 688 the inaugural boxing contest was won by a man from Smyrna, the first overseas city to claim an Olympic victor. Southern Italy records its first victory in 672. The Spartans were frequent winners. Events for boys were inaugurated in 632 BC.

The athletic fare was varied by the presence of historians, orators, and sophists, who read their works aloud to the assembled spectators. Herodotus here read extracts from his history. Themistocles attended the 76th Olympiad in celebration of the Persian defeat. The 211th Olympiad was postponed two years to AD 69 to allow Nero to compete and win special musical contests and a chariot-race. The records were later expunged.

After each event a herald announced the victor's name and handed him a palm. On the last day the successful competitors (Olympionikai) were each given a garland of wild olive and entertained in the Prytaneion. A victor had the right of

OLYMPIA

0 ⎯⎯⎯⎯⎯⎯⎯⎯⎯⎯ 50 metres

Treasuries

1 2 3 4 5 6 7 8 9 10 11

12

Spring

Metroon

Stadium

Altar of
Zeus

Hippodàmeion

Echo-hall

Zeus

Racecourse

Gate

House of Nero

Altar of Oaths

Odeion

Gate to Racecourse (?)

South Hall

erecting a statue in the Altis, which might represent his own features if he had won three events. By the time of the older Pliny the statues had accumulated to the number of 3000. On returning home, the victor was publicly entertained and a lyric composition was recited in his honour. Fourteen of Pindar's odes celebrate olympionikai.

In 1896 a quadrennial international athletic festival, taking the name of the *Olympic Games*, had its inception at the Stadium in Athens, when a Greek won the 'marathon'. The Games are held successively in different countries. There is no modern ekecheiria and the First World War prevented their celebration in 1916, as did the Second in 1940 and 1944. It will not be forgotten that King Constantine II of the Hellenes (when Crown Prince) won a gold medal at the 1960 Games, held in Italy.

To reach the ancient site from the village we take the Tripolis road, pass the museum on a hill (right), cross the Kladeos, and see (right) the entrance to the **Excavations** (best guide, available at site, A. Mallwitz, *Olympia und seine Bauten*, repr. 1981, [in German]). We visit first the large buildings that lie outside the Altis to the W.

On the right, immediately beyond the entrance, some remains parallel to the path mark the *Xystos*, or covered running track (an Olympic stade long), which formed the E wing of the **Gymnasion**, a large quadrangle extending to the Kladeos. Its propylon (? 1C BC) consisted of a Corinthian portico raised on three steps. Some capitals survive. Adjacent on the S is the **Palaestra**, often called a 'wrestling school' but in fact a place for meetings and social intercourse, as well as for athletic practice of various kinds. It corresponds closely with Vitruvius' description of such a building. An open court, 41m square, is surrounded by a Doric colonnade with 19 columns on each side. Behind the colonnade, on three sides, were rooms of various sizes, entered through Ionic porches or through plain doorways. Some of them retain ancient stone benches set against the wall. On the S side the colonnade was divided into two long corridors by an inner row of 15 Ionic columns. The main entrances were at the E and W ends of the S side, through porches of two Corinthian columns in antis. The capitals are of unusual design, having parallels in Pompeii and Asia Minor rather than in Greece. The style generally suggests a date in the 3C BC.

A water channel, entering the Palaestra at its NE corner, ran round its four sides. In the N part of the court is a pavement of grooved and plain tiles, 25m by 5·5m; its object is unknown. From the central room in the N colonnade a plain doorway gave access to the Gymnasium.

To the S lies the THEOKOLEION, the official residence of the priests. The ruins belong to three periods. The original Greek structure (c 350 BC) consisted of eight rooms round a central court and covered an area 18m square. The foundations and pavement are well preserved. In the court is an ancient well lined with blocks of sandstone. Later three rooms were added on the E side and a large garden court, with cloisters and rooms, was constructed. The Romans took down the E half of the extended Greek building and enlarged the garden court. A colonnade was built round it, having 8 columns on each side.

To the W is a small round *Heroön*, c 8m in diameter, enclosed within a square. The lower blocks of the circular wall are well preserved; the upper courses were probably of mud brick. Within was found an altar of earth and ashes, coated with stucco.

Adjacent on the S side is a Classical building, the sandstone walls of which are still standing to a height of 1·8m with later brickwork above. In its later form it was a *Byzantine Church* divided by columns into nave and aisles within an apse on the E and a narthex on the W. Near the E end is a ruined ambo (left) with two flights of three steps, and, beyond it, a perforated marble screen of Byzantine workmanship. The original building was none other than the **Workshop of Pheidias**, described by Pausanias. This has been confirmed archaeologically by the discovery of tools and terracotta moulds used in the manufacture of the great chryselephantine statue of Zeus, and finally in 1958 by a cup bearing Pheidias' name. The building has the same measurements as the cella of the temple and a similar orientation; it probably also had similar internal structure, being divided into two compartments having galleries supported on columns.

A long narrow building, to the S, divided by crosswalls into small rooms, is believed to have sheltered his working technicians.

Olympia. Workshop of Pheidias. Model

To the W (not accessible) remains of Roman baths overlie *Baths* of the Archaic period, near the bank of the Kladeos, together with part of a swimming pool of the 5C BC. This was 23m long and 1·5m deep. In the same area (S) was a Roman guesthouse.

Farther S, built at a slightly different angle, is the **Leonidaion**, erected by Leonidas the son of Leontas of Naxos in the 4C BC, possibly as a hostel for distinguished visitors, and adapted in the 2C AD as a residence for the Roman governor of Achaia. It stands at the crossing of the roads from Arcadia and Elis outside the processional entrance to the Altis. As originally built it had an open court, 30m square, surrounded by Doric colonnades of 12 columns per side, off which rooms opened on all four sides. The principal rooms were on the W side. Outside ran a continuous colonnade of 138 Ionic columns, the bases of which are almost all in situ, together with many of the capitals. Their bases and capitals were of sandstone, the shafts of shell-limestone; the whole was covered with stucco. In Roman times the rooms were remodelled, and an ornamental garden with elaborate ponds was laid out in the middle of the court. Many fragments of the colonnades were found built into the Byzantine Wall (comp. below) and these, especially those from the terracotta cornice, show great richness of decoration.

The Altis, or SACRED PRECINCT OF ZEUS, acquired its name from a corruption of the Greek word αλσος meaning 'Sacred Grove'. On the N it was bounded by Mt Kronos and on the other three sides by walls, the

lines of which can still be traced. On the W side are remains of two
parallel walls, the inner one Greek and the outer one Roman. The S
wall is Roman. The original S wall, now called the South Terrace Wall,
was more to the N, the Altis having been enlarged about the time of
Nero. The Greek walls seem to have been merely low stone parapets
and the precinct was probably not fully enclosed by high boundary
walls until the Roman period. Within were the Temple of Zeus, the
Heraion and the small Metroön, besides the Pelopion, or shrine of
Pelops, and innumerable altars to Zeus and other divinities. Much of
the remaining space was taken up by statues of Olympic victors.

Entering the precinct by the *Processional Entrance*, a small triple
opening with an external porch of 4 columns, we see on the right a row
of large oblong pedestals, mostly belonging to equestrian statues. On
the left are two pedestals bearing respectively the names of
Philonides, courier of Alexander the Great (Paus. VI, 16, 8) and of
Sophocles, the sculptor. Turning to the right we pass on the right a
wilderness of scattered remains recovered from the Byzantine Wall,
but originally forming part of the Leonidaion, Bouleuterion, and many
other buildings. Passing between the remains of two unknown Greek
buildings with several small partitions, we reach the Bouleuterion.

The BOULEUTERION, or *Council House*, seat of the Olympic Senate,
consists of a square hall flanked N and S by larger wings of practically
equal size and plan. The building was originally quite outside the
Altis. On its southward extension, the new S wall of the precinct was in
line with the northernmost wall of the Bouleuterion, which was provided with a special gateway of its own. Each wing consisted of an
oblong hall with a central row of 7 Doric (?) columns on separate
foundations and a cross-wall cutting off its apse. Each apse was divided into two by a central wall. A triglyph frieze appears to have
decorated the exteriors of the wings, whose appearance was further
enhanced by the two-stepped basements on which they were raised.
On the E side each wing ended in a screen of three Doric columns in
antis. A spacious Ionic portico ran along the whole length of the E
façade, forming the only means of communication between the three
parts of the building. This portico had 27 columns on its front and 3 on
each side of the narrow sides; only three drums are in situ. The N and S
wings are of the Archaic period; the central hall and the E colonnade
were constructed between 373 and 364 BC.

The *Central Hall*, which is much later than the wings and may be
contemporary with the Ionic Colonnade (3C BC), appears to have had
columns on its E side and blank walls without doors on the other three.
A foundation in the middle may have supported the *Statue of Zeus
Horkeios*, beside which competitors, their relatives, and their trainers
swore that they would be guilty of no foul play in the games. At an
earlier date this would have been open to the sky. Of the *N Wing*, the
oldest part of the building (6C BC), very little except foundations is
left. The *S Wing* (5C) is the best preserved. The drums of the columns
of the Doric porch are still standing; the outer walls are one or two
courses high; and some drums of the seven interior columns are in situ.
The S Wing differs from the N Wing in that its long walls are not
straight but form with the apse an elliptical shape recalling ancient
structures at Sparta and Thermon: it has been conjectured that it was
rebuilt on old foundations.—In front of the connecting portico is an
irregular colonnaded court of Roman date, usually called the
Trapezium Court.

To the E of the Bouleuterion, recent work (inaccessible) has identified a system of ditches which probably represent temporary defences erected by the Arcadians in the course of the battle fought in the sanctuary during the 104th Olympiad (comp. above). In this area have also been found a Roman *odeion* and the foundations of a gate, which may have been a minor entrance to the *hippodrome* (comp. below).

To the S of the Bouleuterion is the *Southern Stoa*, over 78m long, built of tufa and raised on three limestone steps. Gardiner conjecturally identifies this colonnade with the *Proedria* and assigns it to the 3C BC. It was closed on the N by a wall, with a narrow passage-way at either end. The other sides were open and had Doric columns. Within it was divided longitudinally (probably in Roman times) by a central row of sandstone Corinthian columns. The Byzantines used the stoa as the S wall of their fort.

To the S of the Leonidaion and between it and the Proedria extended the *Agora*, where temporary booths were set up during the festival. This area (inaccessible) is being investigated.

The ***Temple of Zeus**, dedicated to the sovereign god of Olympia, is the most important temple in the Altis and one of the largest in mainland Greece. It was built from the spoils of Pisa, after its sack by the Eleans c 470 BC, and completed before 456, when an inscribed block (quoted by Pausanias and since found) was let into the E gable to support a gold shield dedicated by the Spartans in commemoration of their victory at Tanagra. The architect was Libon of Elis. After an earthquake c 175 BC both façades were dismantled and rebuilt and three of the W pedimental statues replaced. In the early 6C AD the edifice was completely shattered by earthquakes.

Olympia, Temple of Zeus. Restored view of cult statue in cella

The building, which is a Doric peripteral hexastyle, stands on a crepidoma of three unequal steps, itself borne on a massive platform. The foundations, which are of shell-limestone with inter-spaces filled with earth, are complete. They were sunk 90cm deep in the soil and rose 3·1m above its natural level. An embankment was raised all round, giving the appearance of an artificial hillock. Access was by a ramp at the E end. The *stylobate* is made of huge stone blocks averaging 2·6m in width. Its length, measured on the top step, seems to have

ly 200 Olympic feet. There is no evidence of optical curva-
as distinguishes the Parthenon, though it has now been
ed that the columns had *entasis*.

EXTERIOR. The *Peristyle* had 6 columns at either end and 13 at the
sides; these also were made of shell-limestone, but were covered with
fine white stucco to give the appearance of marble. Their height was
twice the axial spacing. Each of them had the usual 20 flutes and three
incised rings round the neck. The echinus of the capitals was similar in
outline to those of the Temple of Aphaia on Aegina. Apart from one or
two drums in their original positions, none of the columns is standing.
On the S side they lie as they were thrown by the earthquake of the 6C.

Fragments of the entablature lie around. Above the architrave a frieze of triglyphs and plain metopes ran all round the peristyle; 21 gilded shields dedicated
by Mummius in 142 BC to commemorate his destruction of Corinth were placed
on the 10 metopes of the E front and on the adjacent metopes on the S side. The
marks of attachment can still be seen.

The two pediments were filled with sculptured groups in Parian marble: on the *E Pediment* the preparations for the chariot race between
Pelops and Oinomaos; on the *W Pediment* the battle of the Lapiths and
Centaurs at the wedding of Peirithoös. Pausanias attributed these to
Alkamenes and Paionios. The surviving sculptures are in the Museum
(see below). At the apex of the E, Pediment was the gold shield dedicated by the Spartans (comp, above), crowned sometime later by a gilt
bronze Victory, by Paionios. The corner-acroteria were in the form of
gilded bronze tripods.

The roof was of marble tiles, many of which are preserved in the Pelopion. The
earliest tiles are of Parian marble, the later ones (replacements of the Augustan
era) of Pentelic. There was a continuous marble sima interrupted by 102 lion's-
head water-spouts, of which 39 survive (some are crude later replacements).
Traces of colour found on the architectural members show that parts at any rate of
the temple were painted.

The wide ambulatory surrounding the sekos was occupied by bronze statues
and votive offerings. The ceiling was of wood. The pavement was of large blocks
of conglomerate covered with river pebbles embedded in mortar. This was replaced in Roman times by a mosaic pavement, traces of which remain.

INTERIOR. The sekos had the usual arrangement of Pronaos, Cella, and
Opisthodomos. It was raised one step above the stylobate. The Pronaos and Opisthodomos each ended in a portico of two Doric columns
between antae, surmounted (unusually) by a Doric entablature consisting of an architrave and triglyph frieze. The 12 Parian marble metopes were decorated with sculptures depicting the Labours of Herakles, six at each end. Some were carried off by the French expedition of
1829 and are now in the Louvre; the rest are in the museum.

The *Pronaos* was closed by three folding bronze doors. On the floor
are the remains of the earliest known Greek mosaic (now covered)
representing a Triton with a boy seated on his tail. Pausanias noticed
here the statue of Iphitos being crowned by Ekecheiria
(personification of the Olympic truce). Traces of various bases here
indicate the former presence of other statues he mentions. A great
door, about 4·9m wide, led into the cella.

The CELLA was 28·7m long and 13·3m wide. It was divided down the
middle by two-tiered colonnades of 7 Doric columns to form a nave c
6·7m wide. This colonnade supported the wooden ceiling and the
arrangement of galleries above the aisles from which the public were
allowed to view the image of Zeus. The only light came from the
doorway.

Olympia. Reconstruction of the Sanctuary of Zeus in c 350 BC

The *Nave* was divided laterally into four sections. The first, in the nature of a vestibule (open to the public) extended to the second column. On either side, by the first column, was a wooden staircase leading to the galleries. The next two sections were forbidden to the public. The second, closed by a barrier, extended to the base of the statue, and had side screens formed of slabs of conglomerate to divide it from the aisles. A square, the full width of the nave, was paved with black Eleusinian limestone, bordered with a kerb of Pentelic marble, to form a receptacle for the sacred oil used for the anointing of the statue. This probably served two purposes both practical: those of mirroring light from the doorway and providing oil for the wooden core in order to prevent swelling in the damp climate which might have split the ivory. The third section, from the 5th to beyond the 7th column, is entirely occupied by the base of the statue of Zeus. The fourth section is merely a passage 1·7m wide connecting the two aisles behind the statue.

The similarity in both proportion and decoration with that of the Parthenon makes it certain that the interior arrangement was designed by Pheidias himself. If Pausanias is correct that Pheidias took as model for one of the throne figures the youth Pantarkes, who was victor in the boys' wrestling in 436 BC, the work at Olympia would seem to have been done in 436–432 after the Athena Polias was finished. This has been recently claimed as confirmed by a study of the moulds for the gold drapery, though C.H. Morgan places the Zeus before the Athena (Hesperia, 1952).

The chryselephantine STATUE OF ZEUS, the masterpiece of Pheidias, was accounted one of the Seven Wonders of the ancient world.

Apart from one or two Hadrianic coins of Elis, no authenticated copies of the statue exist, and Pausanias alone of ancient writers describes it in detail, and even he devotes more attention to the throne than to the figure. It is believed to have been about 7 times life-size or c 12m high. Pausanias, noting that the measurements had been recorded, says that they did not do justice to the impression made by the image on the spectator. Strabo, on the other hand, tells us that the artist is thought to have missed true proportion as the seated god almost touched the roof, giving the impression that if he rose he would knock the roof off. The ancients on the whole, however, concur in praising the extraordinary majesty and beauty of the statue. Cicero (Orator, II, 8) says that Pheidias made the image, not after any living model, but after that ideal beauty seen with the inward eye alone.

The *Pedestal*, 90cm high, and decorated with gold reliefs of various divinities, was of blue-black Eleusinian stone, fragments of which have been discovered. Zeus was represented seated on a *Throne* made of ebony and ivory overlaid with gold and precious stones. The four legs of the throne were adorned with carvings and strutted with stretchers which bore golden reliefs of combatants. Some of the great weight was taken by four pillars underneath, hidden by screens on which were paintings by Panainos, and by the footstool which had golden lions and a relief of Theseus fighting the Amazons. The *Figure of Zeus* held in his right hand a chryselephantine *Victory* and in his left a sceptre with an eagle. The undraped parts of the statue—head, feet, hands, and torso—were of ivory. The *Robe* was decorated with figures of animals and lilies.

The care of the statue devolved upon the descendants of Pheidias, who were called the 'Burnishers'. By the 2C BC, however, the ivory had cracked and had to be repaired by Damophon of Messene. In the time of Julius Caesar it was struck by lightning. The Emperor Caligula wanted to remove it to Rome and to replace the head of Zeus with his own, but every time his agents came near the statue it burst into a loud peal of laughter. It is believed that after the reign of Theodosius II the statue was carried off to Constantinople, where it perished in a fire in AD 475.

In 167 BC Antiochus IV Epiphanes, King of Syria, dedicated (?) behind the statue, 'A woollen curtain, a product of the gay Assyrian looms and dyed with Phoenician purple' (Paus. V, 12, 4). There are grounds for believing this to have been the veil of the temple at Jerusalem which Antiochus carried off (II Macc. VI, 2).

The *Opisthodomos* had no direct communication with the cella. It was reached from the W peristyle and does not appear to have been enclosed by gratings. It had a long stone bench where people used to meet and talk.

In front of the entrance ramp to the temple are some interesting pedestals of statues detailed by Pausanias. The statues were built into the Byzantine Wall (comp. below).

It was the custom to erect in front of the E façade of the temple the statues of the Olympionikai and the chariots dedicated by them. The latter included the *Chariot of Gelo*, by Glaukias of Aegina, and the *Chariot of Hiero*, by Kalamis and Onatas of Aegina. Near the large rectangular bases of the semicircular base of a group of *Nine Heroes of the Trojan War* dedicated by the Achaean cities and made by Onatas of Aegina; they are represented as drawing lots for the honour of the duel with Hector. Opposite, on a round base, stood *Nestor shaking the lots in his helmet*. Close by is the restored triangular base of the famous *Nike of Paionios*, dedicated by the Dorian Messenians. Adjacent were statues of famous Olympionikai: *Telemachos the Elean* (end of 4C); *Dorieus*, and other Rhodian athletes. Rather more to the W are the base of *Diagoras of Rhodes*, his son *Praxiteles*, a Mantinean athlete (484–461 BC), and the cylindrical plinth of a *Statue of Zeus*, dedicated by the Lacedaemonians in the 6C after the second Messenian revolt. Near the NE corner of the ramp are three semicircular moulded plinths which bore statues of the *Elean Women* (1C BC). Adjacent are the pedestals of the *Eretrian Bull*, by Philesios (5C BC) with an inscription on its E margin (fragments in the museum); and the historian *Polybius* (146 BC). These bases and others transferred to the new museum were within the trapezoidal area enclosed by the 6C *Byzantine Wall*, which had as its N and S limits the Temple of Zeus and the S Stoa. The wall, made of ancient blocks from many buildings in the Altis, was demolished by the excavators and the fragments recovered.

Moving SE we reach a heap of grey limestone blocks belonging to a pedestal that supported an equestrian group of *Mummius and the Ten Legates*. Close by on the E are remains of a Roman *Triumphal Arch*, erected for Nero's visit. It was largely built of older materials, including the pedestals of statues, destroyed lest the memory of their prowess should overshadow that of the megalomaniac emperor.

In the SE corner of the Altis are foundations of the *South-East building*. It had four compartments and was faced on all sides but the E by a 4C Doric colonnade having 19 columns along the front and 8 at each side. It was paved with small pebbles embedded in plaster. The most recent suggestion concerning its function is that it may have been the shrine of *Hestia*, mentioned by Xenophon. It was demolished to make way for the *House of Nero*, hurriedly built for the emperor's visit, the peristyle of which lies farther E. This house has been identified by the discovery of a lead water-pipe inscribed NER. AVG. The Doric columns of the Greek building were broken up into small pieces to form the opus incertum of the walls. Later a large Roman edifice was constructed immediately E of Nero's house, which was partially sacrificed to the new building. This contained over 30 rooms, one octagonal, and explorations in 1963–64 showed it to have been *Baths*.

Farther E lay the *Hippodrome*, long since washed completely away by the Alpheios. Here was installed the 'hippaphesis' an ingenious starting gate invented by Cleoitas in the 6C BC and described by Pausanias. To the S of the House of Nero, in 1963 was uncovered the *Altar of Artemis*.

The greater part of the E side of the Altis is occupied by the foundations of the *Echo Colonnade* or *Stoa Poikile*. The former name is due to its sevenfold echo, the latter to the paintings with which it was decorated. Most of the remains are from the time of Alexander the Great when the stoa was rebuilt, those farther E from the earlier version of the 5C BC. Previous to this the stadium extended into the Altis.

In front of the Stoa Poikile are numerous statue bases including a long plinth bearing two Ionic columns, which supported statues of Ptolemy II Philadelphos and Arsinoe, his queen.

We reach the vaulted entrance to the **Stadium**, completely explored in 1958–62 by the German Institute and restored to the form it took in the 4C BC. The artificial banks never had permanent seats, but could accommodate c 40,000 people. The track originally extended NE from near the Pelopion and was not separated from the Altis until the 5C when the Stoa Poikile was constructed. The embankments were several times enlarged and the German excavators found many older weather-worn votive offerings (helmets, shields, etc.) which had been buried during the alterations as sacred objects not to be profaned by re-use. The starting and finishing lines are *in situ*, 600 Olympic feet apart. The stone kerb round the track and the water-supply opening at intervals into basins are visible; the paved area for judges on the S side has been uncovered.

Immediately outside the entrance is a row of twelve pedestals which supported the *Zanes*, bronze images of Zeus erected out of the fines imposed on athletes in the 98th and 112th Olympiads for cheating.

A flight of ancient steps ascends to the **Treasuries** which are arranged roughly in line on a terrace overlooking the Altis at the foot of Mt Kronos, the soil of which is kept back by a substantial retaining wall. These take the form of a small temple, consisting of a single chamber and a distyle portico in antis facing S. They were erected by various cities, all but two outside Greece proper, for the reception of sacrificial vessels used by the theoroi, and possibly for storing weapons and gear used in the games. Little remains but the foundations. The description of Pausanias is not without its difficulties and the proper identification of many of them is not certain. They seem to have been added roughly chronologically from E to W.

The oldest and largest, built c 600 BC and modernised about a century later, belonged to *Gela* (12). Though constructed of shell-limestone, those parts of the masonry which were most exposed to the weather, e.g. the pediment cornices, were encased in painted terracotta plaques and tiles—a survival from the days when buildings were made of wood. The terracottas were made in Gela and the building was presumably designed by Sicilian architects.

Though little more than the foundations of the Treasury of *Megara* (11) remain in situ, many fragments were recovered from the S Byzantine wall. It was erected between those of Gela and Metapontum c 570 BC as is shown by the fact that all ornamentation (fluting, mutules, etc.) was omitted where it could not be seen. The pediment may not have received its sculpture until c 510.—Adjacent are foundations of the *Metapontum* treasury (10), slightly earlier in date. That of *Selinus* (9) is next, squashed in later between existing buildings, then (8) a structure which was probably not a treasury but the *Altar of Gaia*. The next three treasuries, which are very ruinous, are assigned to *Kyrene* (7), to which two sculptured fragments of African limestone probably belong; *Sybaris* (6) which must date before 510 BC when that city was destroyed; and *Byzantium* (5).

The architectural remains of the next building (4) belong to the 6C BC suggesting that it is more likely that of *Epidamnos* than (as usually attributed) of *Syracuse*. The Syracusan treasury, which contains the spoils of the victory at Himera (480 BC) may have been farther along (2), but both this building and that tentatively assigned to *Samos* (3) seem to have been obliterated in Roman times. The Treasury of *Sikyon* (1), by contrast, has well preserved foundations. Many blocks of the superstructure in Sikyonian stone with identifying inscription have been recovered, and the building has been partially reconstructed. They date from c 480 BC. A Sikyonian treasury was dedicated by Myron to celebrate his chariot victory in the 33rd Olympiad, when the two huge bronze shrines also dedicated necessitated a special strengthening of the floor. This must have concerned an earlier building but the existing floor is also strengthened.

Immediately beyond is an *Altar to Herakles* (whether the Idaean Herakles or the famous Herakles Pausanias could not say) and, N of it, an ancient *Shrine* with a pronaos facing S.

Descending the terrace steps we immediately reach the METROÖN, a small peripteral hexastyle Doric temple of the 4C BC, dedicated to the Mother of the Gods. It measured only 20·5m by 10·5m. The remains include most of the foundations and a portion of stylobate with the drum of one column and a fragment of another. In Roman times the worship of Cybele gave place to that of Augustus and Rome, and the excavators discovered in the foundations a statue of Claudius and another of Titus.

To the W of the Metroön six prehistoric houses were uncovered by Dörpfeld, traces of two of which may be seen in front of the EXEDRA OF HERODES ATTICUS. This was the termination of a much-needed supply of pure drinking water brought to Olympia between 157 and 160 by an aqueduct c 3km long. The water was stored in a large semicircular tank from which it flowed through lion's-head spouts into an oblong basin in front. The upper tank was paved with marble and backed by an apse supported by eight buttresses which rose to a half-cupola. The inner side had 15 niches which held statues of the family of Herodes and of their imperial patrons. At each end of the lower tank a small circular Corinthian temple enclosed a statue. A large marble bull bore an inscription recording that Herodes dedicated the reservoir to Zeus in the name of his wife Regilla, who was a priestess of Demeter.

Olympia. Exedra of Herodes Atticus

The **Heraion**, the oldest but the best preserved building at Olympia, is situated near the NW corner of the Altis. It was originally a joint temple of Zeus and Hera but after the grander temple of Zeus was built was reserved to the goddess alone. The worship of Hera, which played little part in the history of Olympia, may be introduced by Pheidon of Argos who supposedly usurped control of the festival. The temple is not earlier than the beginning of the 7C, and was originally built of wood, which was gradually replaced by stone. Even in the time of Pausanias columns of wood survived.

The temple, raised on a single step, was a Doric peripteral hexastyle with 16 columns at the sides. Thirty-four of the columns survive in part; two of them were re-erected in 1905 and another in 1970. They vary in diameter, in the height of the drums (while three are monolithic), and in the number and depth of the flutings, while the 18 surviving capitals show by the outlines of their echinus that they belong to every period from the foundation to Roman times. As no trace has been found of the entablature, it is believed to have been of wood. The roof was covered with terracotta tiles.

INTERIOR. The division into three chambers was conventional, though the interior details are unusual. Both Pronaos and Opistho-domos were distyle in antis. The walls of the sekos were nearly 1·2m thick; the four courses forming the inner face are well preserved to a height of 90cm. The upper part was of mud brick with wooden door-posts. The *Cella*, long in proportion to its breadth, was lighted only by the door. Four internal cross-walls, recalling the structure of the much later temple at Bassae, served to buttress the outside walls and to support the cross-beams of the roof. At a later date the cella was divided longitudinally by two rows of Doric columns, every second one being engaged with the corresponding buttress. There was a flat wooden ceiling.

Pausanias tells how, during the repair of the roof, the body of a hoplite was found between the ceiling and the roof. The soldier had apparently fought in the war of 401–399 BC between Elis and Sparta, during which a battle had swept over the Altis. Wounded, he had crawled to shelter only to die, remaining undiscovered for 500 years.

At the W end of the cella stands the pedestal of the archaic group of Zeus and Hera. The head of Hera has been recovered. Of all the other treasures and statues known to have been in the Heraion only the Hermes of Praxiteles has been found. It was lying in front of its pedestal between the second and third columns from the E on the N side. Six bases in the Pronaos bore statues of noble Elean women. The opisthodomos is known to have held the cedar-wood *Chest of Kypselos*; the *Disk of Iphitos*, on which was inscribed the Olympic truce; and the gold and ivory *Table of Kolotes*, on which the victor's crowns were displayed.

To the S of the Heraion is the site of the PELOPION, a grove containing a small eminence and an altar to Pelops, the principal Olympian hero, enclosed by a pentagonal wall. A Doric propylon at its SW end, of which foundations remain, appears to date from the 5C BC and to have replaced an older entrance. Immense quantities of archaic bronzes and terracottas were recovered in the enclosure as well as roof-tiles from the Temple of Zeus.

Somewhere to the E must have stood the *Altar of Olympian Zeus*, the most sacred spot in the Altis, where a daily blood sacrifice was made. A heap of stone marks the supposed spot.

As we turn towards the exit we pass, in the NW corner of the Altis, the foundations of the **Philippieion**, a circular monument begun by Philip of Macedon after the battle of Chaironeia (338 BC) and probably finished by Alexander the Great. Two concentric colonnades stood on a stylobate of three steps, the outer peristyle having 18 Ionic columns, the cella having 12 engaged columns with Corinthian capitals. The roof had marble tiles and a bronze poppy on the top which held together the rafters. Within was a group of five chryselephantine statues, by Leochares, representing Philip, his mother and father, his wife Olympias, and their son Alexander. Excellently carved fragments of their bases have been recovered.

Beyond stood the PRYTANEION, the official residence of the magistrates, in which Olympic victors were feasted. The remains are scanty. The building, which dates in some form from very early Greek times, was remodelled more than once in Roman times. The later Greek Prytaneion was a square of 33m with an entrance on the S side and a vestibule leading into a central chamber, 6·7m square. On both sides of the central chamber were open courts. In Roman times a banqueting hall was added to the W.

As we quit the enclosure there are (right) remains of Roman baths.

Across the road a drive leads to the ****Museum**, opened in 1972. Finds formerly in the old museum and many more previously in store are arranged chronologically.

In the ENTRANCE HALL, model of the Sacred Altis (a gift of the city of Essen), and another of the central area made to Dörpfeld's specifications and given in 1931 in memory of Kaiser Wilhelm II. Statue bases of Olympic victors: Kallias of Athens, by *Mikon*; Euthymos of Lokri Epizephyrii, by *Pythagoras*. Straight ahead is the CENTRAL HALL (comp. below).

To the left is GALLERY 1. Neolithic to Geometric, including grave goods from sub-Mycenaean chamber-tombs; Mycenaean boars' tusk helmet; *Tripods and handles of cauldrons adorned with bronze figures (Telchines); small Geometric votive offerings including miniature tripods and bronze and terracotta figures; in the centre, large Geometric horse in solid bronze.—GALLERY 2. Geometric and early Archaic bronzes and terracottas; orientalising bronze plaques, griffins, etc; *Armour and weapons, many richly fashioned, displayed according to type and development: shields and corselets on the wall, cases of greaves, lances, and helmets below; one finely decorated Archaic cuirass recently recovered after being stolen in the First World War; shield bosses; sphyrelaton (sheet bronze hammered over wooden core) sphinx; restored terracotta pedimental acroterion and antefixes from the Heraion; colossal limestone head of Hera, probably from the cult statue of the same building.

GALLERY 3. Statuettes and tripods; sculptures and simas from various Treasuries, including the pedimental statuary of the Megarian and a section of polychrome sima from the Gela Treasury; Archaic figures from a perrhiranterion; battering ram; fine vases.—In GALLERY 4 the Classical period is introduced by the arresting and vigorous group of *Zeus carrying off Ganymede*, a late Archaic work executed in terracotta; warrior from a similar group; Persian *Helmet taken by the Athenians at Marathon and dedicated to Zeus; the *Helmet of Miltiades, victor at Marathon; small *Bronzes and pottery; tools; objects from the Workshop of Pheidias, including terracotta moulds for forming section of drapery for the cult statue. Access to CENTRAL HALL.—GALLERY 5. Large-and small-scale sculpture (not all from Olympia) in stone and terracotta, Classical and later; minor dedications in bronze and terracotta; pottery; 3C BC statue base with foot of bronze figure still in place; bronze head of a boy (plus reconstructed version) from the stadium.

GALLERY 6. The *Hermes of Praxiteles, a work found in the Temple of Hera in 1877 in the place where it was noted by Pausanias. Its attribution to Praxiteles rests on his summary description; he seems to have considered the work worth no more than the briefest remark. After a period of the greatest artistic adulation, it is no longer necessary to award it uncritical praise. It remains, however, one of the best-preserved Classical statues that have survived to modern times, preserved by the fallen clay of which the upper walls of the temple had been built. The statue is of Parian marble, its original polish scarcely marked by the passage of time, though not quite entire.

Hermes, the messenger of the gods, was charged by Zeus to take his infant son Dionysos out of the reach of the jealous Hera, and to bring him to the nymphs of Mount Nysa, to whose care was entrusted the rearing and education of the child. Hermes is represented as resting on his journey. He stands in an attitude of easy grace, the left knee slightly bent, leaning his left arm on the trunk of a tree. In his left hand was doubtless the caduceus (missing). His cloak is carelessly thrown across his arm and falls in simple graceful folds over the tree trunk. On his left arm sits the ill-proportioned infant Dionysos, reaching up towards an object (a bunch of grapes?) which Hermes holds in his right hand. The form of Hermes, which is entirely nude, presents an ideal combination of grace and strength, not without some danger of the charge of preciosity. The head is slightly turned towards the child. The hair is in short crisp locks, indicated rather than sculptured in detail. Both behind and before can be traced the groove of a metal wreath. Traces of paint have been detected on the hair, lips, and sandal. The date of this masterpiece is usually put between 363 and 343 BC though some authorities consider it a Roman copy.

GALLERY 7. Roman sculpture, especially pieces from the Exedra of Herodes Atticus (restored drawing showing sculptures in position), including marble bull (inscribed), fine figure of Antinous (?). Several members of the imperial family.—GALLERY 8. Objects directly concerned with the Olympic Games; part of starting block of earlier stadium; dedications of victors; base of statue (by Lysippos) of the Athenian Poulydamas; bronze discus; jumping weights (halteres); inscriptions; minor dedications.

The huge CENTRAL HALL contains the pedimental sculptures of the Temple of Zeus, together with the metopes and some fragments of the cornice, with lion's-head water spouts. The standard work on the sculptures was published by B. Ashmole and N. Yialouris in 1967. In the course of their recent transfer to this new gallery, about 300 fragments have been added and some rearrangement of the figures made. Since no description of the rearrangement has yet been published, the following account may be inaccurate in some details, especially the positions of the central figures in the West Pediment.

The EAST PEDIMENT, attributed by Pausanias to Paionios, represents the start of the chariot-race between Oinomaos and Pelops. All the figures are sculptured in the round except the three inner horses of each team, which are in moderate relief. Not a vestige of either chariot has been found, but the marks of attachment are seen on the horses. The figures, none of which is complete, are 1½ times lifesize and sculptured in the severe style, consistent with a date in the mid-5C.

Oinomaos, King of Pisa, warned by an oracle that he would be killed by a son-in-law, was unwilling to give his daughter Hippodameia in marriage. Aspirants to her hand were challenged to a chariot-race from Olympia to Isthmia and given a start with Hippodameia while Oinomaos sacrificed a ram. By the fleet footedness of his horses Oinomaos overtook his potential sons-in-law, spearing them in the back. He had thus disposed of 13 suitors when Pelops appeared as claimant. He bribed the charioteer Myrtilos to tamper with the axle-pins of his master's chariot so that Oinomaos was killed when his chariot crashed. Pelops thus won both his bride and her father's kingdom. The unedifying story of cheating and treachery (generally accepted as the root cause of the curse of the Atrides) seems to have provided one legendary version of the founding of the Olympic Games. Alternative versions have omitted Myrtilos' part and attributed Pelops' victory to his magical steeds (a present from Poseidon) and Oinomaos' death to hubris punished by Zeus. The pediment seems to omit Myrtilos and this may have been the Elean version of the story.—NOTE: the terms 'right' and 'left' used below are from the spectator's point of view.

The centre of the composition is the colossal figure of Zeus; to the left (according to the latest of a long series of suggested reconstructions) stand Oinomaos and his wife, Sterope; to the right Pelops and Hippodameia. Zeus, who is invisible to the contestants, is looking toward Pelops in token of his good will. The identification of Sterope and Hippodameia and their consequent placing left or right made by Yalouris has been questioned by Kardhara (comp. A.J.A. 1970). On each side of the women is a four-horse chariot, that of Pelops attended by a boy, that of Oinomaos by a girl. Behind the team of Pelops is his charioteer (? Killas), a seer, and the personified Alpheios. Behind that of Oinomaos, a seer, a boy, and the personified Kladeos.

The WEST PEDIMENT, executed according to Pausanias by Alkamenes, illustrates the fight between the Lapiths and Centaurs at the marriage-feast of Peirithoös. Again none of the figures is complete though the Apollo is almost perfect.

Peirithoös, King of the Lapiths in Thessaly and a reputed son of Zeus, invited his friend Theseus and the Centaurs to his wedding. The Centaurs had too much to drink and assaulted the women and boys present, one of the Centaurs, Eurytion attempting to carry off the bride. Peirithoös, assisted by Theseus, defended the attacked, slew many of the Centaurs, and routed the rest.

The central figure is *Apollo, calmly towering above the tumult, who has come to the assistance of the Lapiths. On the right Hippodameia is in Eurytion's clutches; Peirithoös stands ready to strike with his sword. Beyond, a boy is being picked up by a Centaur. Next comes a Lapith woman, her garment torn, trying to tear herself free from a Centaur who has already been transfixed by the sword of a kneeling Lapith. They are watched from the corner by a crouching and a recumbent woman. The left hand side is similar, but even less well preserved. The boy throttling the Centaur is being savagely bitten in the arm and shows his pain in a furrowed brow.

The sculptures are all of Parian marble with the exception of the two old women in the W pediment, the young woman in its left hand corner, and the arm of the other young woman, which are of Pentelic marble and are thought to be antique restorations. From traces of colour discovered it is clear that all the figures were painted.

On the end walls are the sculptured *METOPES from the cella frieze, illustrating the *Twelve Labours of Herakles*. Each slab measured 1·6m by 1·5m, the figures being slightly under lifesize. The metopes were originally painted, the brush completing the details of hair, clothes, etc, which the chisel has merely indicated. In delicacy of execution they may be thought superior to the pedimental figures, especially in the moulding of the features.

Visitors should be aware that the important late 5C VICTORY (NIKE) OF PAIONIOS is at present undergoing conservation and is not on display.

In a new building in the village is the *Museum of the Olympic Games*, which includes a collection of commemorative stamps.

38 From Corinth to Patras

ROAD, 135km (84 miles), mostly near the shore along the Gulf of Corinth.—21km *Kiáto*, for *Síkyon* (5km).—34km *Xilókastron*.—90km *Dhiakoftó*.—94km **Aíyion**.—127km **Ríon** (car-ferry to *Andírrion*, for NW Greece).—135km **Pátras**.—TOLL HIGHWAY, parallel to (and generally inland of) the old road needing great care in bad weather. BUSES (starting from Athens) frequently (2¾ hours journey; 3½ hours from Athens).

RAILWAY, 130km (81 miles), 6 good trains daily in 2¾–3 hours, all starting from Athens, whence 1¾–2 hours should be added. To *Xilokastron*, 34km (21 miles) in c 40 minutes; to *Dhiakofto*, 77km (48 miles) junction for *Kalávryta*, in 1½–1¾ hours; to *Aiyion*, 91km (56½ miles) in 1¾–2 hours. The railway is seldom out of sight of the road.

This route follows the S shore of the GULF OF CORINTH (*Korinthiakós Kólpos*), which extends for nearly 130km from Aigosthena in the E to the 'Little Dardanelles' in the W. It varies in width between 2 and 30km, being widest in the centre and narrowest at the W. The E end of the gulf is divided by the peninsula of Perachora into the Gulf of Alkionídhon and the Bay of Corinth, with the entrance to the Corinth Canal. The N and S sides are in remarkable contrast. The alluvial coast of Achaia, with its innumerable torrents and its currant vineyards fringing the shore, runs WNW almost in a straight line from Corinth to Cape Dhrepanon. The rugged and abrupt coast of Phokis, Lokris, and Aitolia, chiefly forest and pasture and sparsely inhabited, is broken by the Bay of Aspra Spítia (Andíkiron Kólpos) and the Bay of Salona (Krissaíos Kólpos), in addition to several minor indentations. The encircling mountains are among the highest in Greece so that the gulf resembles a large inland lake. The fine scenery recalls that of the Italian lakes, and the storms that spring up are as sudden as those in the Alps.

Corinth, see Rte 25. The road runs W along the coast. Across the Bay of

Corinth is seen the long low promontory of Perachora; farther E,
behind Loutraki, rises the great mass of Yeraneia. After 3km we pass
the site of *Lechaion* (Rte 25E); on the left towers Acrocorinth.—10km
Periyiáli, the first of many villages strung along the road, is situated
amidst currant-vines and fruit trees in the fertile coastal plain of
CORINTHIA, now completely recovered from the earthquake of 1928.
In world production of currants, Greece is second only to the United
States. Corinthian lemons are of the green variety, which are artificially turned yellow after picking to satisfy foreign demand.—We
cross the Lóngos (or Rakhiani) near (11km) *Assos*, a village surrounded by cypress groves; hereabouts was fought the Spartan victory
'near the Nemea River' in 394 BC. Behind, the flat top of *Mt Fokas*
(873m; the ancient *Apesas*) is prominent.—At (14km) *Vrakháti* (Hotel
D), a centre for sultanas on the Nemea, is the Kokkoni Holiday Village.
Near *Zevgolatió*, 1·5km left, are some remains of a late Roman bath
explored in 1954.—Beyond (18km) *Véllo*, where fruit juices are extracted, we cross the Peloponnesian *Asopos*, said by classical tradition
to be an extension of the Maeander flowing beneath the sea from near
Miletus. The flutes of the presumptuous Marsyas were thrown up on
its bank.

21km **Kiáto** (Hotels B, C) or *Sikionia*, with a prominent modern
church, is a flourishing port (8232 inhab.) exporting raisins. Hence the
excursion by boat to Perachora (Rte 25F) may be made. Near the
railway station are some remains of an early Byzantine basilica. The
modern village of *Vasilikó* (c 5km SW; bus) has readopted the official
name of Sikyon, the later site of which it occupies.

Síkyon (Σίκυων), reputedly one of the oldest of Greek cities, was the
capital of Sikyonia, a small district, anciently (as now) renowned for its
almonds and olive-oil. In the Classical period the city was a centre of
Greek art. Its school of bronze sculpture was made famous by Aristokles, Kanachos, Polykleitos, and Lysippos. Its academy of painting,
established by Eupompos, produced Pausias and Pamphilos, the
master of Apelles, and endured to Hellenistic times. Sikyonian dress,
and in particular Sikyonian shoes, had a wide reputation. Both the
ancient city, which lay in the plain, and the later one founded by
Demetrios Poliorketes on the acropolis, lay close to the Asopos.

History. Sikyon ('Cucumber Town' from σικύα, a cucumber) was originally
named *Aigialeia*, probably from the Aigialaean ('coast-dwelling') Ionians who
founded the city, and later called *Mekone*. The traditional list of its heroic kings
includes the Argive Adrastus, the only survivor of the 'seven against Thebes'.
The Homeric catalogue makes him commander of the Sikyonian contingent to
Troy, and Homer gives to *Sikyon* the epithet ευρύχορος (wide open). After the
Dorian invasions it became subject to Argos. About 660 BC Orthagoras, a popular
tyrant, established a dynasty lasting a century, during which the city rose to
prosperity. Its metal work and pottery were of a high standard and a school of
sculpture was founded from Crete. Boutades of Sikyon is credited with inventing
the relief. Kleisthenes, greatest of the dynasty and grandfather of the Athenian
legislator, joined the Amphictyonic League in the Sacred War (c 590 BC). His
destruction of the city of Krisa freed Delphi. After reorganising the Pythian
Games there, he instituted similar games at Sikyon, abolishing the worship of the
Argive hero Adrastus. His successor Aeschines was expelled by the Lacedaemonians c 556, and Sikyon lost its political independence in the Peloponnesian
League. It remained a centre of art and industry (comp. above), and its coinage
was in widespread use in the 5–3C.

The Sikyonians were loyal allies of Sparta during the Persian invasions, in the
Peloponnesian War, and after, on more than one occasion providing a fleet. The
city was conquered in 368 BC by the Theban Epaminondas, but shortly afterwards a Sikyonian citizen called Euphron achieved a brief local notoriety by
seizing the government. In 303 BC Demetrios Poliorketes razed the ancient city

in the plain and built a new one, temporarily called *Demetrias* in his honour on the ruins of the old acropolis. In 251 BC Aratos, son of Kleinias, united the city to the Achaean League, later becoming its leader. During the eclipse of Corinth after 146, Sikyon took over control of the Isthmian Games, but after the refounding of Corinth, gradually declined. Fulvia, wife of Mark Antony, died in exile here in 40 BC.

The 'new' city of 303 BC is admirably situated 3km from the sea on an extensive triangular plateau between the gorges of the Asopos and the smaller Helison. Defended on all sides by precipitous cliffs, the plateau is divided by a rocky slope into a lower terrace, the acropolis of the old city, and an upper terrace, forming the apex of the triangle, which became the acropolis of the new. The city walls ran round the edge of the plateau and are least ruined on the W side. Excavations by the Greek Archaeological Society under Prof. Orlandos have uncovered only a small part of the city, which seems to have been laid out on a rectangular plan.

The modern village stands on the lower level of the plateau. We cross the presumed site of the Agora to (10 minutes) the large Roman *Baths*, built in brick in the 2–3C and restored as a MUSEUM for the site. In three rooms are displayed Mosaics (? 4C BC); bronze mirror; painted terracotta frieze; pieces of sculpture; and pottery models of hedgehogs.

To the left are the foundations of an archaic *Temple*, reconstructed in the Hellenistic epoch; this may be the Temple of Apollo mentioned by Pausanias as being rebuilt by Pythokles. The S end of the agora was closed by a Hellenistic *Stoa* and the *Bouleuterion*, an almost square hypostyle hall, the ceiling of which was supported by 16 Ionic columns. At a late date it was adapted to other uses. Near it are extensive remains of the GYMNASIUM OF KLEINIAS, built on two levels; on either side of the central stairway linking them is a fountain. The **Theatre**, one of the largest of continental Greece, occupies a natural depression in the slope dividing the upper and lower terraces. It was excavated by the American School in 1889–91 and tidied up in 1951. The building dates from the beginning of the 3C BC. It is known from Polybius that the Achaean League met here in 168 BC. The *Cavea* is c 120m across. The lower diazoma could be reached by two vaulted passages as well as by 16 staircases from the parodoi. The fifty-odd tiers of seats, mostly hollowed out of the rock, were divided into 15 wedges, each of which forms one twenty-fifth part of a circle. The front seats have backs, armrests, and sculptured feet. The *Orchestra*, of stamped earth, surrounded by a drain, had a diameter of c 20m. Foundation walls of the stage buildings show that they were twice altered in Roman times. They had as façade a Doric portico of 13 columns in antis.—In a ravine to the W of the theatre are the remains of the *Stadium*. The straight end had a wall of polygonal masonry, still partly standing. On the upper terrace are scanty ruins of the new *Acropolis*. The dividing slope is honeycombed with subterranean *Aqueducts*. The classical cemetery area was located in 1976 belòw the track from Vasilikó to Traganá. The *View, especially lovely at sunrise and sunset, embraces Helikon, Kithairon, and Parnassos, with a verdant foreground contrasting with the blue of the Gulf.

The old city in the plain and its harbour have left little to mark their sites. The modern road follows the ancient alignment and road-construction in 1966 located a necropolis and mosaics of the old city.

FROM KIATO TO THE STYMPHALIAN LAKE, KASTANIA AND PHENEOS.
Road, 68km (42¾ miles), asphalt, via Soúli (13km), to Goúra (bus), more interesting for the landscape than for the remains of antiquity. Skirting the N side of
Mt Botsika (1300m), we turn SW between it and Kyllíni.—35km *Kefalári* (432
inhab.) nestles below the secondary E summit of Kyllíni (see below; the ascent
from this side, in 12 hours, is difficult). At (39km) *Kaliáni* diverges a sound asphalt
road to *Nemea* (32km; comp. Rte 26).—Just beyond (41km) the village of
Stimfália (Hotel E; tavernas), to the left of the road, are the conspicuous remains
of the Frankish Gothic church of the Cistercian abbey of Zaraka and its gate
tower. Ancient architectural members were extensively used in the construction
of the church and these probably came from the nearby Temple of Artemis,
mentioned by Pausanias but no longer visible. Some of the medieval architectural carving, especially of the capitals, is very fine and in a completely western
style.

About 500m to the S is the low acropolis of ancient *Stymphalos*, clearly marked
by the foundations of the city wall. Crowned by a tower, it overlooks the lake
below. To the E and N of the acropolis the Canadian Archaeological Institute has
recently discovered (by electrical resistivity and proton magnetometer survey)
evidence of a town, carefully laid out to an orthogonal plan in the 4C BC. The
house blocks are long and narrow and the streets 6m wide. On the N side, by the
lake, are the remains of a curious round structure and a spring house (cleared by
A. Orlandos in the 1920s) which still functions. A small temple and altar to
Athena Polias lie on a terrace just to the E of the acropolis. Also by the lakeside
are the well-preserved remains of massive polygonal walls supporting a road,
whose wheel ruts (1·5m apart) are visible in places.

At the E end of the lake are remains of a Roman aqueduct, probably built by
Hadrian to take the abundant local spring waters to Corinth. It can be traced
across the valley to the modern irrigation tunnel beneath the pass to Nemea.

Several kms to the W of Stymphalos are the foundations of a monumental
circular tomb (18m across) and a rectangular building nearby, which may have
been a farmhouse.

The road climbs steeply from the W end of the valley to (52km) *Kastaniá* (Hotel
C, at 1302m above the village), a mountain resort (902m) on the S slope of Kyllíni
below the saddle that separates Stymphalos from Pheneos. It is a good area for
walking and for botanists. We descend to the E side of the *Pedhías Feneoú*, in
ancient times a shallow lake or marsh, nowadays more often dry.—From
(59·5km) *Mesinón* a path crosses the valley to *Kalívia*, passing the site of *Pheneos*,
with remnants of a small Temple of Asklepios and the colossal head and feet of a
broken statue. A small museum contains a Classical female statue. The church of
Ayios Yeoryios, to the NW, has frescoes. The road continues between Feneos and
Kalivia to (68km) *Goúra*; the modern village of *Feneos* lies on the W side of the
valley, midway between the summits of Kyllíni and Chelmos. Here a monument
was erected in 1960 to nationalist victims of a communist massacre in 1944. Track
across the N slopes of Kyllíni (4 hours) to Trikkala (see below).

On the N slopes of Aroánia (Chelmos; 2354m), in a lugubrious and eroded
valley, is the 'Source of the Styx' (4 hours W of Feneos). Make for *Vounariánika*,
from which the waterfall is visible and the footpath apparent. Hence Kalavrita
(Rte 39) may be reached in a further 6½ hours (guide advisable), or, via *Sólos*,
the descent may be made to the coast (see below).

30km *Melíssi* (Hotels, C, D) with a Mycenaean tomb (500m S).—34km
(21 miles) **Xilókastro** (Χυλόκαστρο; Hotels, A, B, C, D, E) is a popular
seaside resort (4937 inhab.), agreeably situated amid luxuriant gardens at the mouth of the Sithas valley. It probably occupies the site of
ancient *Aristonautai*, a seaport of Pellene, where the Argonauts put in.
Along the sandy E shore towards Sikia is a pinewood, called *Pefkías*,
with a campsite. A *Museum* devoted to the memory of Angelos Sikelianos (1884–1951), the poet, has been established in a villa he once
owned. To the SW on the mountainside stands *Zemenó*, (8km), where
a wine festival is held in September.

TO TRÍKKALA (34km) and MT KILLÍNI. Just W of Xilokastro a road climbs into he Sithas valley.—12km *Pellíni*. The insignificant ruins of ancient *Pellene*, on the op of the mountain separating the valleys of the Sithas and the Forissa, com-nand an excellent view.—34km **Ano Tríkkala** (1067m; Hotels C, D), a winter-sporting resort, stands on the N slope of *Mt Zíria*, the ancient *Kyllene*, second iighest mountain in the Peloponnese (2377m). Climbers should obtain keys of he refuges from the Greek Alpine Club in Athens. An easy path climbs in 2½ iours to *Refuge A* (1646m; 50 beds; water), and (30 minutes more) to *Refuge B* 1737m; 20 beds), whence the W summit may be reached. The Gymnos summit 2134m), to the E overlooks Kefalari on the Kastaniá road (comp. above).

The mountains come closer to the coast. Parnassos may be seen 50km iway across the gulf. Above (40km) *Kamári*, birthplace of Panayiotis Tsaldaris, opposer of Venizelos, who brought back the monarchy in 1935, rises the pyramidal *Koryphe* (732m) with a nunnery on its sum-nit. We cross the Forissa torrent.—48km *Likoporiá* (Hotel C). The conspicuous Cape Avgó, between Petséïka and (52km) *Stómion*, con-ends with Koryphe the site of *Donussa*.—56km *Dhervéni* (Hotel D), a small town (1171 inhab.) with a long narrow street, has a sandy beach. We enter the nome of Achaia.

Achaia, or Achaea, the mountainous NW division of the Peloponnese, marches on the S with inland Arcadia and maritime Elis. Its capital is Patras. In the Myce-naean period the name of the province connoted almost the whole of the Pelo-ponnese. In classical times its meaning was restricted to the N coastal area. When the Romans conquered the Achaean League they gave the name to the whole peninsula.

The ACHAEAN LEAGUE was a confederation for mutual defence and protec-tion of the coastal cities of Achaia, which met until 373 BC at Helike. It was refounded in 280 BC on an anti-Macedonian basis and admitted non-Achaeans. Aratos of Sikyon united Sikyon, Corinth, and other cities to the League, became its general in 245 BC, and made it the chief political power in Greece. The admission of Megalopolis antagonised Sparta and during the Cleomenic War Aratos allied the League with Antigonus Doson. The League went over to Rome in 198 BC under the leadership of Philopoemen (252–183 BC) the last great man of free Greece. It lost all power in 146 BC. The 'twelve cities' of the League were Aigai, Aigeria, Aigion, Boura, Dyme, Kerynea, Olenos, Patrai, Pellene, Pharai, Rhypes, and Tritaia.

59km *Mávra Lithária*. Aigaí (6·5km inland) and (62km) *Aígeira* (Hotel D) perpetuate the names of two of the Achaean twelve cities.

The site of Classical *Aigeira* (excavated by the Austrian Archaeological Institute, 915, 1926, 1972–) is reached by turning under the railway just beyond Mávra Lithária and taking the inland road (unsurfaced but adequate) towards *Aígai*. After c 3km there is a stopping place with a water fountain to the right. The antiquities lie to the left (theatre, etc.) and right (acropolis) of the road. The Hellenistic *Theatre*, remodelled in the Roman period, is the most impressive monument. Beyond it are a group of *naïskoi* arranged in a semi-circle, in one of which was found a head by the sculptor Eukleides. A large building (Hellenistic/Roman) lies to the W. This is probably the bath building of the Gymnasium, as troughs and channels for water control have been found.

Remains on the two main terraces of the acropolis (sharp climb) are less tangi-ble. Mycenaean buildings and pottery have been discovered, and a Hellenistic/Roman square with shops. Architectural fragments and foundations of the 7C BC may be from a Temple of Artemis-Iphigeneia mentioned by Pausanias.

The city was called *Hyperesia* by Homer (Iliad II, 573). Its inhabitants are said to have frustrated a Sikyonian invasion by collecting goats (αιγες) after dark and tying torches to their horns, thus misleading the enemy into believing reinforce-ments had arrived: hence the later name of the city.

From (65km) *Akráta Station*, below its village, tracks climb to *Sólos* (6 hours) providing a possible approach to the Styx (comp. above); its waters feed the *Krathis* which we shortly cross. For some miles the mountains now reach to the sea and the road runs higher with views ahead and across the Gulf of Corinth. To the right some striking olive groves and cypresses.

81km (50¾ miles) **Dhiakoftó** (Διακοπτό; Hotels C, D), in a plain noted for its cherries, is the railway junction for Kalávrita and has a frequent bus connection with Patras. The excursion by train at least as far as Zakhloroú should on no account be missed.

The **Kalávrita Railway** was engineered in 1885–95 by an Italian company in the fantastic, sombre * *Gorge down which the Vouraïkós, or Kerynites, tumbles its boulder-strewn course. The replacement of the original steam rolling-stock by diesel railcars from 1960–62 has ended the former discomfort and for period enthusiasts much of the romance; but nothing detracts from the awe-inspiring scenery or from the achievement of the engineers. Sometimes pushing, sometimes pulling, the little locomotives (of 75cm gauge) proceed partly by adhesion (max. gradient 1 in 28), partly by rack-and-pinion (Abt system gradient 1 in 7), rising 700m in 22·5km. The line crosses the water several times on bridges and runs in tunnels or on overhung ledges. The sites of ancient *Bura* and *Keryneia* occupy hilltops to E and W of the entrance to the gorge. Just below Zakhloroú, where the gorge is only a few feet wide an original tunnel on the E side suffered a partial collapse and after the Second World War a new tunnel was hewn in the solid cliff on the W and a new bridge constructed.

12·5km *Zakhloroú* (Hotel D, on the picturesque station). A steep zigzag ascent (mules available; *View towards Kalávrita up the cypress and fir-clad valley) leads E in 45 minutes to the **Moni Megaspéleion** (Ιερά Μονή του Μεγάλου Σπηλαίου), or monastery of the great cavern, built against a vertical and almost smooth cliff. After a disastrous fire in 1934, when a powder magazine (said to date from the War of Independence) exploded, the monastery was courageously rebuilt in an uncompromising 20C style. It has a hostel of 50 beds.

Visitors are shown round by a monk (adm. fee). The *Church* has ancient ikons. There is a miraculous ikon of the Mother of God, supposedly found in the great cavern by the shepherdess Euphrosyne in AD 362, and attributed to St Luke. The painting is on waxed wood. A museum of sacred relics illustrate the history of the convent.—Seraphim, carved in wood (c 1700); note two epitaphioi from Asia Minor, one of Russian workmanship; gospels on vellum (9–11C), with Byzantine enamel-work covers; reliquaries containing the left hand of the martyr Charalambos in the attitude of blessing; the heads of the monks Symeon and Theodore, founders of the monastery; hands of the SS. Theodore; crosses, etc. There is also a 17C wooden iconostasis.

Beyond Zakhloroú the valley gradually broadens.—22km (14 miles) *Kalávrita*, see Rte 39.

Beyond Dhiakoftó the railway continues near the shore while the road runs farther inland amid olive and cypress groves. The villages become more closely placed.

At 83km a minor road (left) runs inland to *Mamoúsia*, where a Hellenistic funerary building (*peribolos*) was excavated in 1975 and 1981. The façade is decorated with Ionic pilasters and there is a frieze with shields in relief. The structure was reused in the Roman period.

87km *Elíki* (Hotel B) recalls the name of the Classical *Helike* drowned by a tidal wave in the earthquake of 373 BC. The sanctuary of Helikonian Poseidon was the early meeting-place of the Achaean League. It stood 2·5km inland. Following a similar seismic disturbance in 1963, underwater investigation was undertaken in 1966, without conspicuous success.—Immediately before we cross the rapid Selinous, or Vostitsa, amid vineyards of currants, a road diverges (left) for *Ftéri*, or Ptéri (Πτέρη; 20km; Hotels C, E) a summer hill-resort with a growing local reputation and fine views which have earned it the sobriquet of the 'Balcony of God'.—*Valimítika* (Hotel C) lies E on the shore.

94km **Aíyion** (Αἴγιον; Hotels B, C, E), the chief town (20,824 inhab.) of the eparchy of Aigialeia and the seat of a bishop, is a small commercial port. Called *Vostitsa* in the middle ages, it gave name to the finest currants grown in Greece. Currants and olive-oil are exported and there are large paper-mills. It has a ferry to Ay. Nikolaos (Eratini).

History. According to legend *Aigion* took its name from a Local goat (αιξ) which suckled the infant Zeus. The city is mentioned in the Homeric Catalogue and sherds attest local occupation from Neolithic to Geometric times. The Achaean League met here in the Homarion and for a time it was the chief city of Achaia. The name *Vostitsa* is of Slav origin. After the division of the Morea in 1209 it was given by Geoffrey de Villehardouin to Hugh de Lille de Charpigny as the barony of La Vostice. After a period under the Acciaioli, it surrendered to the Turks in 1458 and except for a Venetian interlude in 1463–70 remained Turkish until 1821. It was partly destroyed by earthquakes in 1819 and 1888.

The town is built on a cliff 30m high above a narrow strip of shore and has several fountains. The Panayía Tripití stands in an attractive nursery garden. The main square is Ayía Lávra and the attractive smaller *Plateia Psila Alonia* commands a fine view of the Gulf of Corinth. To the W of the cathedral (*Mitrópolis*), between Od. Mitropóleos and Andreiopoúlou, a fine mosaic floor depicting the Good Shepherd was found in 1973–74. It may be from the narthex of an Early Christian basilica of c AD 500.

A pleasant excursion may be made up the Selinous valley to see two monasteries, the Taxiárkhis beyond the river on the right bank, whither it was removed in the 17C from an earlier site, 1 hour farther on, at *Paliomonástiro*.—From the valley a road branches (right) to mount the foothills of Panakhaïkón (1925m), where at *Dháfnai* (12km) are two refuges of the Greek Alpine Club.

The coastal plain is well-watered by torrents descending from Panakhaïkon, and bamboo is grown.—97km *Rodhodháfni*.—105km *Selianítika* (Hotels C)—108km *Lambíri* (Hotel C), with a Club Mediterranée holiday camp, lies on the semicircular harbour of *Erineos*, founded by earthquake refugees from Boura; here an indecisive battle was fought between the Corinthian and Athenian fleets in 415 BC.—117km *Psathópirgos* (Ψαθόπυργος, 'thatched tower'; Motel B) lies in the midst of very fine scenery resembling the Italian Riviera, with the additional advantage of a lovely coastline across the Gulf. The mountains, thickly clothed with firs, plane-trees, arbutus, oleander, and a variety of flowering shrubs, run down to the coast, while the road and railway pass immediately above the sea, crossing a number of torrents.—120km *Arakhovítika* (Hotel B). To the right is Cape Dhrépanon, the northernmost point of the Peloponnese.—At (127km) *Ayios Yeóryios* is the turning for **Ríon** (3km; Hotels A, C, E;

ELPA Car Camp) whence a car ferry plies at frequent intervals (day
and night) to Andírrion (20 minutes; Rte 55) on the N shore of the Gulf.

The *Castle of the Morea* (no adm.), or 'Kastelli', on the shore, was built by Bayazid
II in 1499 before his campaign in the Morea. Parts of its aqueduct still exist by the
roadside. Here took place the last stand of the Turks in October 1828 when
Ibrahim Pasha's troops held out for three weeks against a combined Anglo-
French force under Marshal Maison. Its use as a prison and the presence of oil
storage tanks near by make a diversion hardly worth-while though the moated
fortress is impressive from the sea.

135km (84 miles) **PÁTRAS** (Πάτρας; Hotels A, B, C, D, E), the largest
town (141,529 inhab.) in the Peloponnese and the third largest in
Greece, is the capital of the nome of Achaia, and the seat of a bishop
(the historic archiepiscopal see having been degraded in 1899). The
ancient city lay some distance inland from its port, to which it was
connected by Long Walls. The high status of Patras (a *colonia*, comp
below) in Greece under the Roman empire has left correspondingly
exotic traces, though relatively little is visible today because of the
extensive urban development of recent years. Myriad rescue excavations have uncovered public buildings and private houses, often with
mosaic floors and fine objects. Streets have been traced and evidence
of agricultural activity (wine presses, etc.) discovered. Numerous graves and funerary monuments lined the roads outside the city. Patras is
celebrated in Greek national annals as the see of Archbishop Germanos, who raised the standard of the Cross at Kalavryta in 1821, and
important geographically as the W gateway to Greece. The modern
city was rebuilt on a grid plan with broad arcaded streets by Capodistrias after the Turks had burned the medieval town in 1821. Manufactures include cotton textiles and motor-tyres; among other products
shipped from the busy port are currants, olive-oil, valonia, hides, and
wine.

Restaurants. On the quay.—Tavernas in the upper town.

Post Office. Zaïmi/Maízonos. O.T.E., Leof. Goúnari.—TOURIST POLICE, on the
quay directly opposite Railway Station. N.T.O.G., in port.

Bookseller. *Papakhrístou*, 16 Ay. Nikoláou.

Buses to the suburbs (including *Rion*) from Kolokotróni/Kanári.—MAIN
K.T.E.L. TERMINAL prominent on quay, to E of and opposite Railway Station. To
ATHENS (frequent), also railway buses from the station; to *Aiyion* and *Dhiakoftó*
(frequent); to *Pirgos* (regular); to *Vardha* (frequent); to *Kalavrita* (regular); to
Tripolis (daily; once via Kalavrita, once via Tripotama); to *Mesolonghi* and
Agrinion (regular); to *Navpaktos* (regular); also (daily) to *Levkas*; to *Arta* and
Ioannina; to *Thessaloniki*; to *Kalamata*.

Steamers to the Ionian Islands. (*Zante*; *Argostoli*; *Sami*; *Paxoi*; *Ithaka*; and
Corfu); also to *Brindisi* (car ferry), to *Ancona* (car ferry), and to *Venice*.

Festivals. *Carnival* in February (10 days before Lent); *Classical Theatre Season* in
Summer; *Procession* of St. Andrew, 30 November.

Swimming at Itiés, 4km SW.—*Hellenic Alpine Club*, Pantanássis 29.

History. *Pátrai* was a substantial though not conspicuous member of the Achaean
League. The idea of building her long walls came from Alcibiades (Thuc. V, 52).
During an invasion of the Gauls the Patraians were the only Achaeans to cross
into Phokis to help the Aitolians and they suffered accordingly. After the battle of
Actium Augustus settled many of his veterans in the depopulated city which he
refounded as the *Colonia Augusta Aroë Patrensis*. Hadrian is dubbed 'Restitutor
Achaiae' on coins of Patrai.
   St. Andrew, the first disciple, preached at Patrai and is said to have been
martyred there. The town sent a bishop to the Council of Alexandria in 457 but
not to earlier councils. Invading Slavs, assisted by a Saracen fleet, besieged
Patras in 805 when the supposed intervention of St. Andrew confirmed his veneration as the city's patron saint. The archbishop was raised to metropolitan rank

about this time. In 1205 Patras became a Frankish barony and the seat of a Latin archbishop who soon ruled an almost autonomous principality. Carlo Zeno got his early military experience as a canon of Patras when it was besieged by Marie de Bourbon. In 1408 Patras was sold by its archbishop to Venice, and in 1426 the Pope appointed Pandolfo Malatesta in an attempt to hold it against the brothers Palaiologos. Constantine, however, took it in 1429 and his brother Thomas held it until 1460 when it passed to Mehmed II. It remained the commercial capital of Greece despite the political changes. Here in 1809 Byron first set foot on Greek soil. Both in the abortive rising of 1770 and in 1821 Patras claims to be the first town to have taken up arms. The Turks, however, aware of the intention of Archbishop Germanos to march on Patras from Kalavryta, occupied the citadel whence the town was bombarded and set on fire. It was not freed till 1828.

Natives of Patras are Kostis Palamas (1859–1943), the national poet; Stylianos Gonatas (1876–1966), revolutionary Prime Minister in 1922–24; and Jean Moreas (1856–1910), the French poet (born Papadiamantopoulos).

The QUAY, with the *Railway Station* and an information bureau opposite (Tourist Police), is generally animated. The long mole ending in a lighthouse is a favourite promenade. A little to the E, beyond the busy commercial arcades of Odhos Ay. Andreou, is PLATEÍA OLGAS. Here the **Museum** is at present closed for reconstruction. A temporary display is expected to be available before the end of 1987.

Odhós Maízonos leads SW past the Roman Catholic Church to Od. Ayíou Nikoláou which we mount to the top, continuing up a broad flight of steps (view) to the **Kastro** built on the site of the ancient *Acropolis*. This area of Patras (upper town) should not be missed. It has a pleasant and relaxed atmosphere which is lacking nearer the quay. The *Lower Ward* of the Kastro has round and polygonal towers and is planted with flowering shrubs. The N curtain wall, of early Byzantine date, incorporates Classical drums and blocks; similar elements occur in a flanking tower of the S curtain, but all periods of Byzantine–Turkish–Venetian rebuilding up to the 17C are represented. The well-preserved *Keep* (no admission) has square towers but is equally indeterminate in date. The view embraces Zante and Cephalonia, the mountains of the Roumeli coast above Navpaktos, and, to the S, the peaks of Erymanthos.

From opposite the E gate of the castle a narrow paved road, skirting below the radio station in the park, passes (15 minute walk) through two sections of a *Roman Aqueduct*, the first well-preserved, the second (ruinous) standing in places to 30m above the valley.

To the SW of the Kastro is the **Odeion**, a characteristic Roman theatre of the Imperial epoch, which, when discovered in 1889, had 25 rows of seats (in 4 wedges) nearly entire, made of brick and faced with marble. Much of the marble was later removed by enterprising local builders and the theatre was extensively restored in 1960 and is now used for dramatic productions. The cavea faces S; the orchestra is 9·6m in diameter. On the lower side of Plateía Ikosipénde Martíou are the remains of a substantial Roman building, which excavations in the street below (Iféstou) have suggested may be a hippodrome or amphitheatre (vaulted structure visible in Iféstou). We may then take Od. Sisini, passing other Roman remains, to the PLATEÍA PSILÁ ALÓNIA. From this irregular space, planted with palms, a vigorous bronze of Archbishop Germanos raising the standard dominates the city. A substantial Roman terrace wall, typical of those needed to support buildings in this sloping area of Patras can be seen in Od. Dhiákou, immediately below the Plateia.

Odhós Tríon Navárkhon descends to the W towards the huge ugly church of *Ayios Andreas*, not yet completed in reinforced concrete by G. Nomikos. Here is venerated a gold *Reliquary containing the head

of St. Andrew, returned by Pope Paul VI from St. Peter's, Rome, in 1964, where it had been since Thomas Palaiologos fled with it in 1460.

The church is supposed to be on the site of the Apostle's crucifixion, but is more likely over a Temple of Demeter. An earlier Byzantine Church suffered in the fire of 1821. An inscription from the Kastro commemorates the restoration of a church by Archbishop Malatesta in 1426; the composer Dufay is recorded to have written music in the same year for a consecration of his cathedral.—According to a much older tradition the relics of St. Andrew had already been removed in the 4C, when St. Regulus, or Rule, Bishop of Patras, fled with the body to Scotland and was wrecked off Muckcross, in Fife, where he founded St. Andrews.

We may return via Od. Korinthou or Od. Maizonos, passing the not very distinguished public buildings of Patras to PLATEIA YEORYIOU TOU PROTOU, the central square of the city, with the *Theatre*, and thence to the quay.

EXCURSIONS may be made to the Akhaia-Klauss wine vaults (8km), founded 1861, where parties are given conducted tours (7–2, 4–7). The buildings occupy a Mycenaean site round which many chamber-tombs have been located.

Climbers wishing to ascend *Mt Panakhaïkon* (1927m) should contact the Hellenic Alpine Club in Patras. From *Romanós* (6·5km from Patras) it is three hours on foot to *Psarthi Refuge A* (1494m; 50 beds; water; ski-lift), then 45 minutes to *Prassondi Refuge B* (1798m).

39 From Trípolis to Pátras

A. Via Kalávrita

ROAD, 175km (109 miles) magnificently scenic, the middle section unsurfaced, the remainder largely reconstructed since 1961, but needing care in the Erymanthos Mts. Bus daily (early morning) in c 6 hours (including ½ hour in Kalávrita); additional morning bus from Kalávrita to Patras. 58km *Káto Klitoría*.—90km Turning for **Kalávrita** (3km right).—153km *Khalandrítsa*.—160km Turning for Pirgos.—175km **Pátras**.

Tripolis, see Rte 30; thence to (35km) *Vlakhérna*, see Rte 36. 1km farther on, at the N end of Mt Mainalon, we quit the Olympia road and turn right to make a long descent into the wooded and marshy valley of the lesser (S) affluent of the Ladon.—42km *Panayítsa*.—We pass below (45km) *Dára*, where Photakos (1798–1878) lived in exile and wrote his history of the war of 1821. The narrow road enters Arcadia and runs close to the rushing stream, threading a defile to join the wide valley of the Ladon below the village of *Sellá*. We turn upstream (N), crossing (50km) the *Aroanios Bridge* (Yéfira tou Aroaníou) to the W bank, and leaving on the left the Tripótama road (Rte 39B).

58km **Káto Klitoría** (Hotel E), locally known as *Mazéïka*, a market village (1015 inhab.) at the junction of two valleys, lies at the SW foot of the Aroania Mts (comp. Rte 38). On a near-by hill (Palaiópolis) are imposing walls of ancient *Kleitor*. The view opens to the W as we pass (64km) *Áno Klitoría*.—72·5km *Kastélli* lies below us (left) under iron-bearing hills. The mountain views become immense as we climb in increasingly rough country to (74km) *Afkhéna tou Khelmoú* (the 'Aroania neck'; 1049m), a saddle where diverges a bad road to Tripótama (27·5km; see below).

We descend in loops to (76·5km) *Priólithos* (799m) at the head of the long and pretty valley of the Vouraïkos which gradually broadens. We pass below Ayia Lavra (see below) and reach the Pátras–Kalávrita road, 3km W of Kalávrita.—92km (57 miles) **Kalávrita** (Καλάβρυτα; Hotels B, C, D), chief town (1802 inhab.) of an eparchy and seat of a bishop, is situated at 756m on the Vouraïkos at the foot of Mt Velia. Cool mountain springs and the freshness of the air make it especially attractive in summer.

Kalávrita is the successor to ancient *Kynaithes*, whose inhabitants were distinguished for their independence, wildness, and irreverence. The town was destroyed by the Aetolians in 220 BC but revived under Hadrian. After 1205 the fief of *Kalovrate* fell to Otto de Tournai, and in 1301 passed to the barons of Chalandritsa. In modern Greek history it disputes with Kalamata the claim to be the first town liberated in the War of Independence (comp. below). It twice fell into Ibrahim Pasha's hands, in 1826 and 1827. On 13 December 1943 German occupying troops here massacred 1436 males over the age of 15 and burnt the town. On the E side of the town, there is a chapel and memorial garden on the site of the massacre (signed 'sacrifice of 1943'). Since 1962 the German Federal government has re-endowed Kalavritan schools.

The clock on the *Metropolitan Church* stands at 2.34, the hour of the massacre of 1943. Some antique remains may be seen between Ay. Aikaterini and Ay. Yeoryiou and round the Kalavritiní spring, to the SW of the town, identified with the classical *Alyssos*. About 1 hour E of the town on a rocky height stand the ruins of '*Tremola*', or the *Kástro tis Oriás*. The first name derives from Humbert de la Trémouille, the second from the beautiful Katherine Palaiologos, daughter of a Chalandritsa baron, who is said to have committed suicide rather than fall into Turkish hands in 1463.

Taxis may be hired for the excursion to (7km) *Ayía Lávra*, the celebrated monastery where Germanos, Archbishop of Patras, raised the standard of revolt on 21 March 1821. A hermitage, started in 961, developed into a monastery many times destroyed and rebuilt. The present edifice, begun in 1839, has suffered by earthquake and fire and in 1943, but, again rebuilt, retains the *Church of the Dormition* from before the sack by Ibrahim in 1826. A little *Museum* contains historical relics and medieval MSS.

From Kalávrita, an indifferent road (partly surfaced, improvement in progress) leads SE to (12km) *Áno Loússoi*, (13km) *Káto Loússoi*, (19km) *Kastría* and (27km) *Káto Kleitoriá* (comp. above). At *Káto Loússoi*, there is a turning (right) for *Sigoúni*, by which may be reached (in 4km; one bus daily in each direction to/from Kalávrita) the remains of ancient Lousoi. A good but unsurfaced track leads in loops up the hillside. A few hundred metres from the main road are the recent excavations (Austrian Archaeological Institute) which have uncovered a Hellenistic house with peristyle, bathroom and farming equipment. The area was reconstructed in the Roman period and there are also signs of pre-Hellenistic occupation. Higher up the track (left), on a bluff above the valley, lies a Hellenistic Sanctuary of Artemis (Austrian Institute 1898–99 and renewed excavation). The temple, by the roadside, is of unusual design; the pronaos, cella (with base for cult statue) and opisthodomos being flanked on either side by porticoes which replace the usual colonnade. Below are remains of a semicircular bouleuterion, with propylaea, and of a fountain house. The latter was supplied by an aqueduct whose line has been partly traced higher up the valley.

From Kalávrita to *Megaspíleion* and *Dhiakoftó* (Athens), see Rte 38.

The Patras road heads W across the valley to enter the winding gap between *Panakhaïkón*, to the N, and *Erímanthos*, to the S, whose jagged peaks are well seen from (107km) *Flámboura*.—113km *Boúmbouka* retains a Turkish appearance. The road climbs to nearly 1067m before descending to (122km) *Káto Vlasía* under the N face of Erímanthos. About 3km W of the road is the site of ancient *Leontion* with a theatre (4C BC) excavated by N. Yialouris in 1958. New engineering has removed many loops of the road, which climbs steadily up the N side of a wild gorge. The dizzy ledge runs along the S outliers of Panakhaïkón. 135km *Plátanos* and *Kálanos* are superbly sited facing

*Vistas of epic grandeur extending W to the sea.—Beyond (135km)
Kalanístra (*View) the road reaches a further summit (721m) with a
magnificent retrospective panorama. A by-road diverges (right) to
Dheméstikha (8km) with vineyards producing well-known wines bottled by Akhaia-Klauss near Patras.—146km *Katarráktis* lies in an enclosed valley above which extensive Mycenaean settlements (and,
more surprisingly, traces of Middle Helladic occupation) were located in
1957 in the region of ancient *Pharai*.—153km *Khalandrítsa* (963
inhab.), once a Frankish barony and preserving a fine partly-ruined
church, looks over the coastal plain towards Zante. A Mycenaean
settlement has been located at Ay. Antonios and a tholos tomb at
Troumbe, both near by.—We join the road described in Rte 39B.—
175km (109 miles) **Patras**, see Rte 38.

B. Via Tripótama

ROAD, 179km (112 miles), since its improvement the main link
between Arcadia and Achaia.—50km *Aroánios Bridge*.—83km (52
miles) *Tripótama* (Psophis).—179km **Patras**.—BUS, once daily in
either direction; also once daily Athens–Patras–Tripótama–Dháfni,
whence uncertain connections to Pirgos and Kalávrita.

From Tripolis to (50km) the *Aroanios Bridge*, see Rte 39A. Here a new
road diverges W and, beyond (55·5km) *Kalívia*, quits the Ladon valley.
At 68km a bad road ascends to the S to *Dháfni* (5km), a deme of 1287
inhab. in a delightful situation, with a monastery (Evanghelistrias) of
the late 17C and many medieval churches. We cross a saddle and join
the Seiraíos (Versiótiko). To the left the Afrodísion range divides
Achaia from Arcadia.—83km **Tripótama** (550m), a small village,
stands at the confluence of the Seiraíos and the Aroánios (Livartsinó)
with the Erímanthos (Nousaïtiko), where the common frontiers of
Achaia, Arcadia and Elis meet. Here are extensive but scanty remains
of ancient *Psophis*, destroyed by Philip V of Macedon in 219 BC. The
situation, hemmed in by mountains, is subject to extremes of heat and
violent winds. The sanctuary of Aphrodite Erykina was identified in
1967–69 at Ayios Petros near by. These and subsequent excavations
have revealed an extensive complex (temples, stoa, fountain, stadium,
etc.). A sacred road connects the site with Psophis. Finds are of the 7C
and later. Hephaestos was also worshipped here and the sanctuary
included metalworking installations.

Joining a road from Kalávrita (comp. above), we cross the Eriman-
thos into Elis, rising high above its right bank on the slopes of Mt
Lámbeia.—97km *Lámbeia* (Hotel E), a well-watered spot with plane-
trees, lies below the Ano Moní Dhívris. As Dhivri, it was the headquarters of the Peloponnesian communist rebels in 1948.

About 5km beyond Lambeia a road diverges (left) across the extensive plateau of
PHOLÓIS, the watershed between the Alpheios and the Pineios, which ancient
legend peopled with Centaurs. Some remains near Koúmanis, off the road (right)
at 8km, have been identified with Classical *Lasion*.—22km *Lála* (Hotel D) was of
some importance in Turkish times. The road makes a long winding descent to
(39km) *Plátanos* (Rte 36), 3km W of Olympia on the Pirgos road.

The main road descends gradually by twists and turns above a series
of ravines, passing into the basin of the Pineios.—At (125km) *Ayía
Triádha*, formerly Boukovína, we turn N, crossing the Pineios into
Achaia, and run through uplands between Mts Skóllis (W) and

Erímanthos.—144km By-road to *Kaléntzi* (8km right; Hotel B, April–
October), a pleasant mountain base (975m), from which the Ionian
Islands can be seen and the second summit of Erímanthos (2128m)
climbed. Here was born George Papandreou (1888–1968), prime
minister in 1961–65.—At 164km the Kalávrita road (Rte 39A) comes in
on the right. We pass below *Kallithéa*, with a Late Helladic III cemetery, then descend to the olive-groves in the coastal plain.—179km
(112 miles) **Patras**, see Rte 38.

40   From Pátras to Pírgos

ROAD, 96km (60 miles) in flat fertile country.—23km *Káto Akhaía.*—
62km *Lekhainá*, for *Killíni* and *Chlemoútsi.*—66km *Andrávidha.*—
72·5km *Gastoúni*, for *Loútra Killíni.*—84·5km *Amalías* (E of the
road).—96km **Pírgos**. Frequent buses.

RAILWAY, 100km in c 2 hours following the road closely all the
way.

The greater part of this route is in **Elis**, a territory bordered on the N by Achaia, on
the E by Arcadia, on the S (for a very short distance) by Messenia, and on the W by
the Ionian Sea. The Channel of Zante separates it from that island, and Kephalonia lies off its N seaboard. Elis faces W towards Europe, is remote from the
Aegean, and cut off from the rest of the Peloponnese by a mountain barrier
intersected by easily guarded ravines.

In antiquity the region was divided into three parts: *Hollow Elis*, or Elis proper,
in the N, watered by the Elean Peneios; *Pisatis*, the country of Pisa, on the
Alpheios, in the centre (including Olympia; comp. Rtes 36, 37); and *Triphylia*,
between the Alpheios and the Neda, in the S. Famous for the grove of Altis and
the Temple of Zeus at Olympia and for the Olympic Games, Elis was regarded as
a holy land and its neutrality respected from high antiquity until the Peloponnesian War. The country was noted for its horses and especially suited to the growth
of fine flax.

Its place-names attest later occupation from the N and W by Avars, Slavs, and
Albanians. The coastal plain became an important centre of the Frankish occupation and has always supported horses, sheep, goats and cattle. The cultivation of
the currant-vine since 1850 has greatly increased its prosperity and importance,
though only since the Second World War has it ceased to be malarial.

The road leaves Patras by an unattractive stretch of shore, backed by
untidy factories and workshops, though (5km) *Itiés* is the best known
beach of Patras.—8km *Paralía Proastíou* (Hotels B). The coast now
commands a view across the Gulf of Patras. The plain produces
lemons   and   currants.—12km   *Vraknéïka.*—Beyond   (13km)
Tsoukaléïka a by-road ascends inland. After 3·5km it divides, the left
branch ascending to *Mazaráki* (12km), where a large Protogeometric
and Geometric votive deposit belonging to the sanctuary of a female
deity was excavated in 1973 and 1982. The right branch leads to Ano
Soudhenéïka (12km) whence a poor track continues (3 hours) to
Sandaméri a village deriving name from a Frankish Château de Saint-
Omer.—We cross the Pirros and enter (23km) **Káto Akhaïa** (4936
inhab.; Hotel D), the site of ancient *Dyme*. The Chronicle of the Morea
is probably incorrect in locating here the landing of Guillaume de
Champlitte in 1205.

Here a branch road goes off (right) to *Araxos* (13km), the airfield of Patras, near
the marshy lagoons of the NW promontory of the Peloponnese. Above the fish-
hatcheries rises the 'Kastro tis Kalogrias', a hill with an enceinte of cyclopean
walls that stand in places to 9m. This is the **Teichos Dymaion** of Polybius. Excavations of the Greek Archaeological Service in 1962–65 have shown occupation in
Early, Middle, and Late Helladic times. Most important is that the site has yielded

Mycenaean IIIC finds showing reoccupation after a destruction c 1200 BC and before a final catastrophic eclipse in the 11C. There are impressive walls and good views—but beware of snakes.

As we turn S from the town green foothills rise ahead with the long stark arête of *Skóllis* (1015m), above Sandaméri, farther left.—35km *Lápas*. We enter the nome of Elis (comp. above).—43km *Néa Manoládha*.—47km *Várdha* lies 2km E of *Manoládha*, an estate formerly held by the Crown Prince, scene in 1316 of a battle between Louis of Burgundy and Ferdinand of Majorca in which the latter was slain. It has a 12C church and is noted for water-melons and yoghourt. Beyond Manoládha the by-road continues to *Loutrá Kounoupéli* (10km; sandy beach) in an area troubled by mosquitoes.—62km *Lekhainá*, a market town of 2937 inhab., is the birthplace of Andrea Karkavitsa (1866–1923), the novelist.—64·5km Turning (right) for Killini, Chlemoutsi, and Loutra Killini (see below) on the extreme W projection of the Peloponnese.

The road joins a by-road direct from Lekhaina at (4km) *Mirsíni* and runs W to (8km) *Neokhóri*, where it divides. To the right is (16km) **Killíni** (Κυλλήνη; Hotels A, C), ferry-boat station for Zante (three times daily in 1½ hours, more frequent in summer; also, less often, to *Kefallinía*; comp. Rte 56). As *Glarentza* (or Clarence) it was the chief port of Frankish Morea.

Ancient *Kyllene* was the port of Elis, a trading point with Magna Graecia, and in the Peloponnesian War served as a Spartan naval station. Here Alcibiades landed after his fugitive journey from Thurii. Kyllene was captured by Sulpicius in 208 BC. In the middle ages *Clarence* became the residence of the Villehardouin princes of Achaia, and their Angevin successors here developed the court life described in the Chronicles of the Morea. 'Chiarenza' became the port of transit for Venetian and Genoese galleys from Brindisi or Taranto. In 1428 it passed to Constantine Palaiologos, who systematically destroyed it as soon as he held the last Frankish outpost (Patras).

Scattered foundations of the medieval city remain on the low plateau NW of the modern village with a large ruined church similar to that at Andravidha. A medieval castle was dynamited during the German occupation. Earlier remains may be traced near the 12C Byzantine *Moní ton Vlakhernón* (30 minutes to the E), completed by the Franks.

The conspicuous *Castle of Chlemoútsi** on the lone height to the S known to the ancients as *Cape Chelonatas* (from its resemblance when seen from seaward to a tortoise-shell) is reached from Neokhori (comp. above) by taking the Loutrá Killínis road to *Kástro* (8km). The site can also be approached direct from Killíni itself via the coast road, with a turn inland (6km) to Kástro. Above the village towers the crenellated enceinte of the best-preserved Frankish monument in the Morea.

Chlemoútsi was built in 1220–23 with revenues confiscated from the Latin clergy by Geoffrey I Villehardouin, who called it *Clairmont*. The Venetians later dubbed it *Castel Tornese* perhaps after the coins (tournois) minted in Glarentza. The castle was held by Ferdinand of Majorca in 1314–16. It fell in 1427 to Constantine Palaiologos, who used it as a base for his campaign against Patras. The Turks refortified it after 1460.—Some traces of Middle Helladic occupation of the hill have been recognised in the castle foundations. On the lower E slopes of this hill palaeolithic implements came to light in 1960.

The original recessed *Entrance Gate* has been obscured by the Turkish addition built flush with the curtain into the outer passage. Within to the left is a well-preserved 13C construction, but most of the buildings that backed the *Curtain Wall* have disappeared; their fireplaces only remain. The breach made by Ibrahim Pasha's guns in 1825 can be seen near the SW angle. The *Keep*, a huge irregular hexagon, consists of a series of vast vaulted galleries arranged round a court. These were divided into two stories either by an intermediate vault (as in the N and NW) or by wooden floors (S and SW). The massive barrel-vaults, in fine ashlar masonry, were strengthened by reinforcing arches; though those have mostly fallen much of the vault has held. The double-arched windows are interesting. The *View commands the Zante channel and the whole plain of Elis.

Beyond *Kástro*, we turn left onto the coast road to *Loutrá Killínis* (6km; Hotel C, D; comp. below).

66km **Andravídha** (Ανδράβιδα), an uninteresting market-town of 3335 inhab., replaces *Andreville*, once the flourishing capital of the Frankish principate of the Morea and seat of a catholic bishop. Of his cathedral church of *Ayia Sophia*, two Gothic bays of the E end with the apse and E aisle chapels survive in a ruinous state. Of the Templars' church of St. James, where the Villehardouin princes were buried, no vestige remains.—70km *Kavásila* is the railway junction for Killini and Loutra Killini. We cross the Pinios, less copious since its harnessing (comp. below).—72·5km *Gastoúni* (Inns), the livestock market (4751 inhab.) of the plain, takes name from the Frankish fief of Gastogne and under the Turkish occupation was the chief town of Elis.

Here a road diverges W to *Vartholomió*, another large village (3236 inhab.), where it meets a road from Lekhaina (comp. above), continuing to **Loutrá Killínis** (16km; Hotels C, D), a thermal establishment amid pine woods, near the excellent sandy Olympic Beach (holiday camp and extensive tourist development). By the *Baths* are remains of their Roman predecessors.

In the opposite direction from Gastouni (occasional buses; others from Amaliádha) a good road leads NE via *Boukhióti* (officially Avgeíon) to (12km) **Ancient Elis**, excavated by the Austrian School in 1910–14 and conjointly with the Greek Archaeological Service since 1960. The bus stops by a small museum, which has a plan of the excavated remains. These are scattered and, with the exception of the theatre, largely overgrown and invisible. From the 5C the site was of considerable importance, not only as the main city of Elis, but also because of its dominant role in the organisation of the Olympic Games (comp. above). Athletes trained here under supervision for one month before the start of the games and facilities for them (palaistrai, gymnasia) and the officials (Hellanodikaion; Stoa of the Hellanodikai) were provided. All these buildings have been identified in the vicinity of the agora, where is also the South or 'Corcyraean' stoa, mentioned by Pausanias, although his explanation of its name which requires a foundation date in the 5C cannot be reconciled with the archaeological evidence for one in the 2 or 1C BC. A path leads to the *Theatre*, a Hellenistic reconstruction of a Classical edifice, again altered in Roman times. There are remains of parodoi, foundations in poor limestone of the paraskenion, and portions of the analemma. The cavea was banked, probably with radials in stone, but did not have stone seats. Stone 'tickets' were found. An Early Helladic tomb came to light and nine slab-covered graves attributed to the transitional period between sub-Mycenaean and protogeometric. The boundaries of the city have been fixed and two cemeteries explored. The *Acropolis* was on the hill locally called Kaloskopi, a name which gave rise to the erroneous placing here of Beauregard, a lost Frankish castle.—About 5km farther up the river near *Kéndron* is the huge Pinios irrigation dam, built in 1961–62 by American engineers, forming a large lake. In a series of international 'salvage digs' in the area, the flat-topped hill of Armátova, in the angle of the confluence of the Ladon and Peneios, just NW of *Agrapidhokhóri*, upheld its claim to be the site of *Elean Pylos*.

78km *Savália*. The main road avoids **Amaliádha** (6km E; Hotels C), a modern market town with 14,698 inhab., served by both the railway and the buses. To the right extends the sandy *Paralía tis Kouroútas* (car camping; tavernas, etc.) frequented by Elians in summer.—At

(88km) *Khanákia* a by-road runs (right) to *Skafídhia* (5km; Hotels A, E), with a Byzantine monastery. We leave on our right Ayios Ioannis (see below) and enter (97km) **Pírgos** (Πύργος; Hotels C, D, E), a busy market town (21,958 inhab.), occupied with the currant trade (Stafidhikó Institoúto, etc.)

A branch railway and road run W.—5km *Ayios Ioánnis* occupies the site of ancient *Letrinoi* which gives to Pirgos its official deme-name.—11km Turning (right) to *Ayios Andréas* (Pheia; see below).—13km **Katákolo** (Hotel D) is a small port founded for the currant trade in 1857. It is used by cruise ships as a base for the visit to Olympia. *Fía*, on the bay of Ayios Andreas, is a hamlet with a good beach. Ancient *Pheia*, once the main port of Elis, was partially engulfed by the earthquake that overthrew the Temple of Zeus at Olympia in the 6C AD. Its low acropolis (Pondikokastro) became the *Beauvoir* of the Villehardouin, and its archaeological traces extend from Neolithic to Hellenistic. The walls can be traced underwater, where the remains were explored by N. Yalouris and John Hall in 1957–60.

To.*Olympia*, see Rte 36; *Samikon* and *Kakovatos*, see Rte 34.

IV CENTRAL GREECE

CENTRAL GREECE (*Steréa Ellás* in modern parlance) denotes an administrative grouping comprising seven nomes that extend from Attica to Akarnanía. Of these only Viotía (Boeotia), Évvia (Euboea), Fokís (Phocis), and part of Fthiótis come in this section. In antiquity **Boeotia** (Βοιωτία; in modern Greek Viotía) was a district, lying between the Euboean Straits and the Gulf of Corinth, bounded on the N by Opuntian Locris, and on the S by Attica and Megaris. The low-lying interior is nearly surrounded by mountains. On the S is the barrier of Parnes and Kithairon. On the W are Helikon and Parnassos, and on the N the Opuntian mountains. The highest summit in Boeotia is Helikon, which rises to 1750m. Near the E coast are more isolated heights, between which the Asopos plain reaches to the sea. The Asopos, rising near Plataiai, flows past Tanagra, and falls into the Euboean Channel N of Oropos. Its plain is adjoined on the N by the plain of Thebes, beyond which extend the Boeotian Lakes. The Copaïs, once the largest lake in Greece, is now a fertile plain growing cereals and cotton and grazing pedigree cattle. The Boeotian Kephissos, the other notable river, finds its outlets in swallow-holes. Between Helikon and the coastal ridge to the S is the plain of Thisbe.

Boeotia had a flourishing existence in prehistoric times with Mycenaean centres at 'Minyan' Orchomenos, at Gla, and at 'Cadmeian' Thebes. The history of the region is summarised with the descriptions of these places. With two sea coasts and good harbours Boeotia was well placed for maritime trade. All land routes between northern and southern Greece pass through it. The soil was fertile. Despite these natural advantages the Boeotians never (save for nine short years under Epaminondas) took the leadership in Greek affairs, because, in the opinion of Strabo, 'they belittled the value of learning and of sociability, and cared alone for the military virtues'. They had in antiquity a reputation for slow-witted illiteracy and boorish manners, but a certain astuteness is evidenced by their policy towards the Euripos.

Among the many battles fought in Boeotia, three were of vital importance: Plataea, in 479 BC, which secured the independence of Greece at the end of the Persian wars; Leuktra, in 371, which ended the long-suffered hegemony of Sparta and gave Thebes her nine-years' period of leadership over the rest of Greece; and Chaironeia, in 338, at which city-state democracy was virtually extinguished by the victory of Philip of Macedon.

On account of its Classical interest and sparse modern habitation, Boeotia was one of the earliest regions to attract the archaeologist's spade; it has since been neglected, but is again coming into its own in the study of the Bronze Age. Some of the sites explored by earlier generations, especially those of battles, are only rewarding to dedicated antiquaries, though many of them still enjoy that romantic isolation fast being lost elsewhere. Aigosthena, Gla, and the Museum at Thebes should on no account be missed. Orchomenos is impressive. Places of natural beauty include the valley of the Muses on Mt Helikon and the N coast of the Gulf of Corinth, the latter accessible with difficulty, but offering a number of impressive fortified sites to the energetic walker. The most populous centres are Thebes and Levadhia, in both of which fair accommodation and good food can be found. Levadhia is the administrative capital of the modern nome. A rash of factories has begun to disfigure the E plains.

Phocis is a small territory famous for containing the city and oracle of Delphi. In antiquity it was bounded on the N by Epiknemidian Locris and Opuntian Locris, on the E by Boeotia, on the W by Ozolian Locris and Doris, and on the S by two inlets of the Gulf of Corinth, the Krisaean Gulf (Bay of Itea) and the Antikyran Gulf (Bay of Aspra Spitia). At one time its territory extended across Greece to the port of Daphnous, on the Atalante Channel. The interior is unproductive and mountainous, culminating in Parnassos (2457m). None of the 22 Phocian cities was very populous.

41 From Athens to Thebes. Central Boeotia

ROAD, 74km (46 miles) undulating and sinuous over Mt Kithairon.— To (22·5km) *Elévsis*, see Rte 16. We by-pass the town and fork right.—27km *Mándhra*.—51·5km. Turning for *Aigósthena*.—53km **Eleútherai**.—61km *Erithrai*.—74km **Thebes**.—BUSES from Liossíon Terminal frequently in 1½ hours, also, several times daily, to *Villiá* and *Aigósthena*.

The RAILWAY, 100km (62 miles) to *Thebes* (8 times daily in 1½–2 hours) runs very close to the Lamia highway described in Rte 44B.

From Athens to the Elevsis turn, see Rte 16. We continue by the main Corinth highway, but at 24km branch right and by-pass *Mándhra* (7972 inhab.) at the base of the stony hills that shut in the plain of Eleusis on the W. The road ascends to (36km) *Ayios Sotír*, the church of the Saviour, the silver-painted dome of which marks the summit of the first ridge. We traverse the mouth of the valley of Palaiokhori (small Byzantine church), the road undulating across several ridges.—42km Restaurant on a col. We descend. An ancient watch-tower marks the entrance to (47·5km) modern *Oinói*.

To find the scanty ruins uncertainly identified with ancient *Oinoe*, an important Athenian border fortress, we take the by-road (right; now signposted to the Kithairon waterworks tunnel) towards Pánakton. They lie right of the road after c 3km, just before a turning (left) to *Osios Melétios* (3km N), a monastery with an 11C Byzantine church.—At (10km) *Pánakton*, a medieval tower on a conical hill commanding the cultivated plateau at the W end of Parnes marks another fortress, taken by treachery by the Boeotians in 421 BC and returned to the Athenians by Demetrios Poliorketes. The identification of both places leaves many historical problems unexplained (comp. J.H.S. 1926). Some scholars would exchange the identities of Panakton and Eleutherai (comp. below). The road goes on to (13km) *Píli*, a remote village connected by mule-path with Filí (Rte 19B).

5km Turning (left for Aigosthena.

This road runs W and bypasses (4km) *Villiá* (Βιλιά; Hotels B, C, tavernas), a chicken-farming village of 1739 inhabitants. Avoiding a military road which goes off right up Kithairon, we continue and at (12km) *Ayios Vasíleos* cross the line of an ancient road, explored by N.G.L. Hammond (B.S.A. v. 49, 1954) and claimed by him to be the main highway from Boeotia to the Peloponnese. Near Vathikhória, to the SW, are the remains of seven guard-towers of Classical date, two of which stand to almost their original height.—Our road descends (*View) to the sheltered bay of Aigosthena (22km; Hotel (summer) C; tavernas), the most E arm of the Gulf of Corinth, known before it readopted the ancient name as *Porto Yermano*. It is thickly planted with olives and shut in to the N by Kithairon and to the S by Pateras. **Aigósthena** (Αιγόσθενα) belonged to Megara; it was never of great importance, but its *Fortifications are among the most perfect in Greece. The walls enclosed a rectangle c 550m by 180m. The E wall, partly of polygonal masonry, with four square towers in regular ashlar courses, is the best preserved. The tower at the SE angle, considered one of the best examples of Greek defensive architecture of the 4C BC, rises over 10m above the top of the wall. Joistholes for wooden floors can be seen in the middle towers. Within the enceinte two little churches locate the remains of late-Byzantine monastic cells; lower down is a larger basilica with floor mosaics. Long Walls descend to the sea.—The Lacedaemonians retreated to Aigosthena after their defeat at Leuktra in 371 BC.

52km *Kháni Káza* lies just within the entrance to the *Pass of Gyphtokástro* between Vordositi (956m), the E outlier of Kithairon, and the W spur (930m) of Mt Pástra. It is still argued whether this or the pass farther W crossed by a military road represents the ancient *Pass of Dryoskephalai*. At the entrance on the right of the road rises a steep and rocky knoll crowned by the *Fortress known as **Eleutherai** (commonly Yiftókastro), though the identification is questionable (comp. above). Eleutherai, originally Boeotian, went over to Athens in the 6C BC. The defences, in excellent masonry of the 4C BC, are nearly entire on the N side. Eight rectangular towers, 35m–45m apart, are connected by walls about 3·5m high. Several of the towers cover sally-ports in the adjoining curtain. Each tower had a door giving on to the court and three small openings in the upper storey.

In the fields opposite the Aigosthena fork (and well seen from the E wall of Eleutherai) is the substructure of a temple dating from c 300 BC, perhaps that of Dionysos mentioned by Pausanias. Farther E two Early Christian basilicas have been located.

To the W the heights of *Mt Kithairon* rise to 1410m. The mountain, where Oedipus was exposed and where Pentheus was torn to pieces by the Bacchantes, became the frontier between Attica and Boeotia when the Eleutherians cast in their lot with Athens. Its pine-woods are celebrated for their game. At (57km) the summit of the pass, the great

Boeotian plain lies at our feet, though Thebe[...]
diate hillock. In the middle distance the two [...]
by Mt Ptoön, while farther W rise the summ[...]
sus, and on the NE horizon the pyramidal D[...]
curves down to (61km) *Kriekoúki*, officially [...]
days an enclave of Attica, with 3550 inhabi[...]

At the far end of the town a road leads W to (5km) [...]
village, on both sides of the road, are the widespr[...]
There is a plan of the battle. The ruined enceinte showing some stretches of
excellent 4C ashlar masonry and other, less well-preserved, pieces of polygonal
work encompasses foundations of a small temple, and of the *Katagogeon*, or
hotel, erected for its visitors after the destruction of the town in 426 BC, neither
now visible.

Plataea, a small Boeotian town, near the border with Attica, early turned to
Athens in an attempt to maintain its independence of Thebes. In 490 BC the
Plataeans achieved fame by sending their entire army of 1000 men to support the
Athenians at Marathon. During the invasion of Xerxes, they remained staunch to
the Athenian cause and their city was destroyed by the Persians and Thebans. A
period of peace when Plataea was guaranteed from attack followed the battle of
479 (see below). A Theban attempt in 431 to invest the rebuilt city was foiled, but
in 427 after a two years' siege Plataea was razed to the ground by the Spartans
and its people slain. Rebuilt after the Peace of Antalcidas (387), it was again
destroyed in 373 by the Thebans. After the battle of Chaironeia, Philip, in fulfilment of his policy of humiliating Thebes, refounded the town, but its subsequent
history demonstrable archaeologically and to Byzantine times is of no importance.

The *Battle of Plataea* is described in detail by Herodotus (IX, 19). In 479, after
sacking Athens, Mardonius retired by way of Tanagra to Boeotia, where the
terrain was better suited to his cavalry. He encamped before the Asopos near
Plataea, facing the foothills of Kithairon over whose passes armies from Attica or
the Peloponnese must come. The forces of the Greek league, commanded by the
Spartan Pausanias, with Aristides' Athenians on the left wing, took up their first
position along the foothills. They were outnumbered three to one and lacked a
cavalry arm. For three weeks the opposing generals manoeuvred for favourable
positions. The Greeks suffered constant harrying by the Persian cavalry, though
a picked force of 300 Athenians succeeded in killing Masistius, the Persian cavalry commander. A Greek attempt to outflank the enemy and cut them off from
Thebes miscarried; in the subsequent retreat the Greek forces became split into
three. Mardonius attacked the Spartans, whose fighting qualities proved superior, and the Persian general was slain. The Athenians fought a pitched battle
with the Boeotians, annihilating the Theban Sacred Band. When the Persian
camp was stormed, no quarter was given. The battle clinched the defeat of the
Persian campaign, and though its outcome was decided more by the quality of
the men than the tactics of their generals, the three weeks' campaign was a
notable achievement of Greek unity in the spirit of the oath taken by the League.
In honour of the dead the member states instituted a pan-Hellenic festival to
Zeus Eleutherios (the Liberator), which survived many centuries.

We cross the tiny Asopos and enter the nome of Boeotia.—74km (46
miles) *Thebes*.

THEBES (Θῆβαι; Hotels B, C), in modern parlance *Thívai*, a town
(18,712 inhab.) with an extreme climate, has twice been rebuilt after
destructive earthquakes in 1853 and 1893. The modern centre is confined to the brow of the ancient acropolis, or *Kadmeía*, a plateau 800m
long and 400m wide, situated 60m above the surrounding plain. The
Kadmeia is bounded on either side by rocky gullies, too often filled
with rubbish; in recent years haphazard building has spilled into these, further obliterating the scanty pointers to the ancient topography.
Beyond, sprawling suburbs occupy part of the area once included in
the classical city, which had a circuit of 6·5–8km.

As the birthplace or home of Dionysos, Herakles, Teiresias, and the
Labdacidae in the legendary period, and of Pindar, Epaminondas, and
Pelopidas in historical times, the 'seven-gated city' is inextricably
bound up with Greek myth, literature, and history. The city of Kadmos

invention of the Greek alphabet. The historical city strove
.ress of Boeotia and, for a very short period in the 4C BC led
.ole of Greece.

.th the exception of the Palace excavations and the contents of the
.ne museum, there are hardly any visible remains sufficiently important to excite the interest or awaken the enthusiasm of the visitor.
Classical scholars may derive satisfaction from topographical detec-
tion of the sites of the monuments, streams and fountains that figured
so vividly in Greek tragedy and in Greek history.

History. *Thebes* is called Ogygian by many classical poets from the tradition that
the land was first inhabited by the Ectenians, whose king was Ogygos. The
traditional foundation of the city by Kadmos (or Cadmus; trad. date 1313 BC) and
the sowing of the dragon's teeth begin a saga of tragedy and bloodshed paralleled at Mycenae. Among the Labdacidae, descendants of Kadmos, was Laios
who married Jocasta. Thus Thebes was the scene of the tragic destiny of Oedipus, who slew his own father and became by Jocasta the father of Eteocles,
Polyneices, Antigone, and Ismene. Rivalry between Eteocles and Polyneices
brought about the intervention of the Argives under Adrastos (father-in-law of
Polyneices) and the disastrous war of the Seven against Thebes (trad. date 1213
BC). In the reign of Laodamos, son of Eteocles, the Epigonoi (sons of the Seven)
took Thebes and razed it to the ground (trad. date 1198 BC).

From the earliest times Thebes is represented as a flourishing city, with seven
gates. Sixty years after the fall of Troy Thebes is said to have defeated Orchomenos and to have become the capital of a loose federation, later known as the
BOEOTIAN LEAGUE. This federation of the greater cities of Boeotia was governed (in the 4C BC, at any rate) by eleven magistrates called *Boeotarchs*, Thebes
supplying two, whereas the other members were allowed only one each. Thebes
was a member of the Amphictyonic League.

An inveterate opponent of Athens, Thebes was naturally inclined to favour
Athenian enemies. She medised in the Persian Wars. The Spartans are said to
have forced some Thebans to help them at Thermopylae, but they deserted at the
first opportunity. The fortified city of Thebes was the base of Mardonius before
the battle of Plataea (479 BC) and his Theban allies shared in his defeat. Shortly
before the battle of Tanagra in 457 the Lacedaemonians marched into Boeotia
and re-established Thebes at the head of the Boeotian League. At the beginning
of the Peloponnesian War Thebes attacked Plataea (431); as an ally of Sparta she
helped to bring about the downfall of Athens. In 394, however, she joined a
confederacy against Sparta. The seizure of the Kadmeia by the Lacedaemonian
Phoebidas in 382 in defiance of the Peace of Antalcidas and its recovery in 379 by
the Theban exiles under Pelopidas precipitated war. The battle of Leuktra (371),
won by the genius of Epaminondas and the devotion of the Sacred Band, gave
Thebes for a brief period of nine years the hegemony in Greece. By restoring
Messenia, helping to found Megalopolis, and organising the Arcadian League,
Epaminondas completed the humiliation of Sparta. After his untimely death at
Mantinea in 362 the Theban supremacy, which depended entirely on himself,
disappeared, and the subsequent history of Thebes is a record of disasters.

Joining her traditional enemy Athens against Philip at the instigation of
Demosthenes, Thebes shared in the defeat of Chaironeia in 338, and a revolt
shortly after Philip's death was ruthlessly suppressed by Alexander the Great in
336. The city was completely destroyed, with the exception of the temples and
Pindar's house; 6000 inhabitants were killed and 30,000 enslaved. In 316 Cassander rebuilt Thebes, but in 290 it was taken by Demetrios Poliorketes. The
Thebans sided with Mithridates in his war with Rome, but eventually went over
to Sulla. In spite of this the city was finally dismembered in 86 by Sulla, who gave
half its territory to the Delphians, by way of compensation for plundering the
oracle. Strabo (IX) found Thebes hardly the size of a respectable village. In the
time of Pausanias (IX, 7, 6) only the Kadmeia was inhabited. In AD 248 and again
in 396 it was taken by the Goths, being spared (by Alaric) on the second occasion.

Thebes enjoyed a second period of renown in the Middle Ages. From
the 9C it was the seat of the Strategos of Byzantine Hellas. In 1040 it
surrendered to the Bulgarians after fierce resistance. In 1146 it was
sacked by the Normans of Sicily led by their great admiral, George of
Antioch. The city was now famous for its silk manufactures, and it was
from Thebes that King Roger introduced silk culture into Sicily,

THEBES

- - - 15th century Palace
● remains
- - - 14th century Palace
□ remains
△ other Mycenean finds

| 0 | | 200 yards |
| 0 | | 200 metres |

Station

Taverna ■

Ay Paraskevi ✚

✚ Ay Athanasios

PIRI

Ampheion ▲
Pyramid

✈ Ay. Theodhoroi

Gate
Museum

Fountain of Oedipus

Extent of Kadmeia

Ay. Yeoryios ✚

Gate

KEVITOSOU

PINDAROU

Mikro Kastelli

School

CHIM

EPAMINONDHOU

VOURDHOUMBA

Market Place

Gate

Painted Tomb

Megalo Kastelli

△

ANTIGONIS

Law Courts

METAXA

KADMOU

PINDAROU

KLEOPA

Town Hall

ELEKTRAS

EPAMINONDHOU

IDHIPODHOS

DHIRKIS

ANTIGONIS

Gate

Extent of Mycenean Palace

△

Gate

■ Ay. Dhimitrios

PANAG DHIRAKOU

Cathedral

Electra Gate

SAIMBOU ALLAN

Gate

Ismenion

AYIAS TRIADHOS

Piniotissa (Dirke)

KHALKIS

CHRYSSORHOAS

LEVADHIA

N ↑

✚ Ay. Loukas
Cemetery

⚓ Ay. Níkolaos

ATHENS

whence it reached Lucca a century later, and eventually spread to the rest of Europe. The silks of Thebes, which were worn by the Byzantine emperors, were ultimately supplanted by those of Sicily, and with the decline of the silk trade the prosperity of Thebes departed. In 1205 it was taken by Boniface III of Montferrat, who granted it to Otho de la Roche. Under his house Thebes was the capital of the Duchy of Athens. Half the city subsequently passed by marriage to the family of St-Omer. Under the Turks Thebes degenerated into a wretched village, overshadowed by Levadia, which was made the seat of the pasha.

The plateau is covered by a grid of parallel streets; the main thorough-fare comprises the S half of Odhós Epaminóndhas, a short section of Odhós Antigónis, at right angles, and the N half of Odhós Pindhárou. Beneath the modern streets lie two superposed Mycenaean palaces, the extent and positions of which have been tentatively plotted. The **Kadmeion** proper, or *Palace of Kadmos*, was succeeded by a *New Palace*.

The site was identified and partly dug by Keramopoulos in 1906–29; spectacular finds have been made since 1963 by Greek archaeologists mainly during rescue digs on building sites. The archaeological evidence, reappraised, shows that above many earlier levels, the Kadmeion is placed diagonally to the present grid, while the New Palace is set on the N–S alignment that the town has followed ever since. The megaron complex excavated by Keramopoulos on Od. Pindhárou, behind the present market place, was identified by him as the 'House of Kadmos'. Other archaeologists are of the opinion that this has not yet been located and may lie beneath the modern *Plateia*. Annexes of both palaces, including comparable jewellers' workshops, have been explored. The Kadmeion was destroyed by fire about the beginning of L.H. IIIA2 (c 1375–50); the New Palace, designed for a new orientation and with foundations down to bedrock, was begun immediately but destroyed in its turn at the end of L.H. IIIB1 (c 1250–40). Linear B tablets found at 28 Pelopidhou were in the context of the earlier palace.—Classical masonry, which overlies parts of the two Mycenaean palaces at the junction of Pindharou and Antigonis, and continues under those streets, is identified with the peribolos wall of the *Sanctuary of Demeter Thesmophoros* (which Pausanias placed with the House of Kadmos).

The principal excavations are located on the plan. Not much comprehensible is likely to be visible to the visitor, though the two orientations are obvious in Pindharou, where Keramopoulos' original excavations which produced the stirrup jars with linear B inscriptions are a little N of a more recent dig where the cylinder seals (comp. below) were found.

The *Museum (excellent handbook available in English), at the N end of Pindhárou, stands within the enceinte of the Frankish castle of Nicholas II de St Omer, largely destroyed in 1311 by the Catalans, below its surviving 13C *Tower*. The pleasant garden and courtyard are strewn with inscriptions of varying dates, sculptural remains including fine Byzantine reliefs, Turkish tombstones, architectural fragments and Early Christian mosaics (Seasons). There are five rooms. In the first are a few important inscriptions from different parts of Boeotia, including a stele of the general Xenokrates, a colleague of Epaminondas at Leuktra, Nero's proclamation at the Isthmian games in AD 67, and a list of dedications at the Heraion of Khorsiai illustrating an important stage in the development of the alphabet. In the second are displayed Archaic *Kouroi from the Ptoïon; 5 and 4C funerary stelai from Akraiphnion, Thebes and Thespiai; Daedalic bust (mid-7C BC) from Tanagra; marble torsos and reliefs; Geometric stone tripods from Plataea. Third room in cases, *Pottery, prehistoric from Eutresis and Litharés and Thebes, Mycenaean from Moustapháthos and Thebes (including stirrup jars painted with Linear B characters); 30 *Cylinder seals of lapis lazuli, 14 with cuneiform inscriptions, nearly all from the East (a few are Cypriot, 15–13C BC), the greater number being of the Kassite-Babylonian period of the 14C BC, seemingly confirming the traditional connection of Thebes with Phoenicia; bronze plates and shoulder pieces from a Mycenaean corselet; granulated jewellery; carved legs (of a throne or its canopy ?), the largest pieces of worked ivory so far found in Greece; Linear B tablets; fragments of a fresco from the Old Kadmeion, showing a procession of women bearing gifts; Archaic, Classical and Hellenistic *Vases and *Terracottas found at the Rhitsona cemetery (including rider and Priapic figure). Fourth room, sepulchral stelai painted and incised, representing Boeotian warriors killed at (?) Delion in 425 BC (note the shields adorned with representations of Pegasus, the Chimaera etc.); inscriptions and statues of priestesses from Aulis. Fifth room, Mycenaean painted *Larnakes and other finds (pottery, terracottas, bronzes, etc.) from a large cemetery near Tanagra.

On Kastelli hill, just outside the E gate, a large frescoed chamber-tomb, approached by two long parallel dromoi, was discovered in 1971.

Other surviving vestiges of ancient Thebes may be sought in clockwise direction beginning from the museum. The Levadhia road descends below the museum through the site of the *Borean Gate*. On the left is a pleasant park on the hillock of the *Ampheion* where recent excavations have revealed a large grave mound of Early Helladic or early Middle Helladic date. We turn right and cross the bed of the Strophia or 'Hollow Road', N of which extended the *Agora* and, out towards the Railway Station, the *Theatre*. Following the Khalkis road away from the *Proetidian Gate* (where vestiges of the polygonal Roman wall, found in 1915, are partly visible by the road side), we cross the bed of the Ayios Ioannis (ancient *Ismenos*) by a bridge. On the right of this bridge once gushed the spring of Ayios Theodoros, the ancient *Fountain of Oedipus*, where Oedipus washed off his father's blood (small pleasant park). Following the course of the supposed Isme-nos to the S, we pass on our right the wooded hill of *Kastellia* partly occupied by an old People's Home and the Grammar School. Chamber tomb, see above; Christian catacombs are also in evidence. We soon reach to our right the Isme-nian Hill, sacred to Apollo, where in 1910 was discovered the *Ismenion* (4C BC), the temple where was celebrated the festival of the Daphnophories (laurel-bearers). The foundations are best preserved on the W. There are Mycenaean tombs underneath. At the side of the hill in the cemetery chapel of St. Luke are fragments of a large marble sarcophagus (3C AD), locally venerated as that of the Evangelist, though its three inscriptions refer to the family of a Roman official called Zosimus. The old Athens road returns towards the Kadmeia by the line of the 'Hollow Road' and ends at the *Electra Gate*, the circular foundations of whose two flanking towers in ashlar masonry may be seen on either side of Odhos Amphíon. Near the gate was the extensive Sanctuary of Herakles, now probably occupied by the church of *Ayios Nikólaos* (Byzantine lintel in the interior). Cross-ing the main Athens road, we reach the medieval *Aqueduct* (Kamáres) which brought water from the sources on Mt Kithairon to the Kadmeia. The Athens road enters the town through the probable site of the *Onka Gate*. To the SE is the *Kolonáki* hill with an extensive cemetery of Mycenaean chamber tombs. To the NW of the centre is a *Necropolis* of the 8C BC. The stream that flows along the W foot of the Kadmeia is the *Dirce*.

Excursions from Thebes

TO LEUKTRA, 18km (11 miles). We take the Athens road and after a mile turn right.—12km *Melissokhórion* (Báltsia).—18km *Parapoúngia*, officially Lévktra, is a group of three hamlets on a hill. At the *Battle of Leuktra* in 371 BC the Boeotians under Epaminondas defeated a larger force of Spartans in battle. This was the final blow to the legend of Spartan invincibility and for a short time gave Thebes the hegemony over all Greece. Visible up a valley to the right as we approach Leuktra and signposted at the track is the *Tropaion* (locally 'Mármara'), a monumental trophy erected by the Thebans after the victory and now restored. A circular plinth of triglyphs has a domeshaped roof of nine stone shields sculptured in relief; it probably supported a warrior figure in bronze.—A dirt road (passable by car in summer) goes on from the village down the right bank of the *Livadhóstra* to its mouth on the Gulf of Corinth. Here are some ashlar walls of *Kreusis*, the port of Thespiai, which was occupied by the Spartan Kleombrotos before the battle of Leuktra, and probably saw his retreating embarkation for Aigosthena.

Just under 3km NE of Leuktra are the foundations of massive walls in polygonal masonry, forming an enclosure 500m square, doubtless the Homeric Eutresis. About 300m SE at the foot of the ridge is the *Arkopódhi Fountain*, at the junction of the ancient ways from Thebes to Thisbe and Thespiai to Plataiai. To the E of the fountain the American School excavated in 1924–27 a series of Early Helladic, Middle Helladic, and Mycenaean *Houses*. In 1958 they found traces of Neolithic occupation, including steatopygous clay figurines.

TO THESPIAI AND THISBE, 37km (23 miles), asphalted. We take the Levadhia road, and after 5km diverge left (signposted 'Paralia Beach') up the cultivated Kanavári valley.—17km The twin villages of *Leondári* and *Thespiaí* (Erimókastro) rise to the right. Below, near the road, are scanty vestiges of ancient **Thespiaí**, excavated by the French School in 1888–91, when they demolished what was left of the walls to recover more than 350 inscriptions. The Thespians honoured Love above all the gods, and here the courtesan Phryne made her home. Her famous marble statue of Love by Praxiteles was still at Thespiaí in the time of Cicero. It was carried off to Rome by Caligula and then (after having been restored to Thespiaí by Claudius) by Nero.

20km Fork. Ahead the shorter road (unpaved) avoids the villages but it is better to bear left through *Ellopía* and (27km) *Xironomí*.

On a disused road running S from Xironomí to Alikí (comp. below) over the W shoulder of Mavrovouni are a fine watch-tower and foundations of two fortresses, one a large enclosure dating to the Spartan invasions of Boeotia in the early 4C BC, and the other small of late Roman date.

36km *Dhómvrena* (officially Koríni), was resettled here after a reprisal destruction in the Second World War. Immediately S of Kakósi (modern *Thísvi*), its twin village to the NW, on a low plateau stand the extensive remains of ancient **Thisbe** (Θίσβη), still, as Homer says, 'the haunt of doves'. A fine length of wall with seven towers of good Classical masonry defends the S slope. On a hill to the NW of modern Thísvi are early polygonal walls.

A rough road leads SW from Dhómvrena, crossing the plain by the ancient dyke dividing it into two halves for alternate annual drainage and irrigation. It passes cliffs and an isolated shore to (6·5km) *Ayios Ioánnis* on the Bay of Dhómvrena. A difficult path round the bay leads E to *Alikí*, dominated by Mt Korombili, on which stand the 4C fortifications of an acropolis identified with the *Siphai* of

Thucydides and *Tipha* of Pausanias; other ancient remains are by the shore.

The asphalt road continues beyond Thisvi to (6·5km) *Khóstia* (or *Pródhromos*), then descends through rocky outcrops and olive groves to *Paralía*, a hamlet on the Bay of Saranda. A hill site with 4C BC walls on the left of the road, 4km from Khóstia, may be *Korsiai*. Recent excavations here (Canadian Archaeological Institute 1980–) have shown that this site was occupied (not continuously) from Neolithic to Roman times. Some of the walling is Archaic/Early Classical; most is 4C.

TO THE VALLEY OF THE MUSES AND MT HELIKON. To Thespiaí, see above. We quit the Dhómvrena road and take a poor road W to (24km) *Palaiopanayía*, the farthest point attainable by motor. Here it is advisable to take a guide. On foot or mule-back we rise gently to the NW and come in ½ hour to *Palaiópirgos*, a medieval tower possibly on the site of *Keressos*. The tower has a fireplace, proving that it was lived in. On the slopes to the S and SE of the tower are the remains of a late medieval Turkish village, including a small church. We cross the stream of *Episkopi* and see on our right a hill still crowned by the ancient Hellenic tower (Pirgáki) which Pausanias recorded as all that survived of *Askra*, a site more plausibly located by a recent survey on the saddle of land between Keressos and the tower. Here was the farm of Hesiod, who called it 'a cursed town, bad in winter, unbearable in summer, pleasant at no time'.—1¾ hours We cross the Permessos and reach the **Valley of the Muses**. Here on the site of the chapel of Ayia Triádha (now removed) are the remains taken in 1888–89 to be a temple of the Muses, but reappraised in 1954 as a monumental altar. A little higher up is the *Theatre* (late 3C BC) in which were held the contests of the Mouseia. The cavea may be clearly distinguished.

The whole of the upper valley of the Permessos, with its groves and springs, was dedicated to the Muses. Their sanctuary and *Mouseion*, stood in a sacred grove. The district is now sadly disafforested and the scanty trees that survive scarcely enable the visitor to recapture the charm and mystery of this region; its religious significance appears, however, to have lasted well into the Christian era, for ruined chapels are seen on all sides.

The cult of the *Muses* came originally from Pieria at the foot of Mt Olympos. It was inhabited by Thracian shepherds who worshipped the goddesses of the mountains and springs. They came south and founded Askra. In Boeotia Mt Helikon and the fountains of Aganippe and Hippocrene were sacred to the Muses, and in Phocis Parnassos and the Kastalian fountain. Libations of water, milk, and honey were the usual offerings.

The *Mouseia*, or Musean Games, were held every four years and comprised musical and poetic contests, to which were later added dramatic contests. The prize was a wreath of myrtle. In addition there were *Erotica*, or games in honour of Love, which included athletic sports as well as musical competitions. The sanctuary became a fount of poetic inspiration. It was adorned with statues of the Muses by Kephisodotos, Strongylion, and Olympiosthenes; of Dionysos by Lysippus and by Myron; and of the great lyric poets. The sanctuary was despoiled by Constantine the Great.

From the Valley of the Muses to Hippocrene takes about 5 hours there and back. The route is comparatively easy and most of the distance can be ridden. The fountain is on Mt Zagora, an E summit of **Mt Helikon**, which comprises a whole range extending W to the Bay of Aspra Spitia. Its highest point is separated from Mt Zagora by the Pass of Koukoura, and called *Palaiovouni* (1750m). From Ayia Triadha we make for a side valley which opens at the foot of the Marandhali, an eastern outlier of Zagora. We cross a stream; on the right bank near the chapel of Ayios Nikolaos (476m) and a ruined monastery is a grove with a scanty spring. This may be the *Aganippe Fountain*. After a climb of 2½ hours we reach a glade (1360m) near the top of the N slope. Here, concealed near the W angle under rocks and arbutus trees, is seen the mouth of an ancient well, now known as *Krio Pigádhi* ('Cold Water'). This was the HIPPOCRENE ('Fountain of the Horse') which, so tradition tells us, gushed forth from the spot where Pegasus struck his hoofs when he landed from the skies. Here we are a ½ hour below the summit of Mt Zagora (1530m). From Krío Pigádhi we may descend by the N slope of the mountain (on foot) direct to Ayia Triádha in 45 minutes.

To *Akraifnion* and the *Ptoion*, to *Khalkis* and *Aulis*, to *Anthedon*, and to *Larimna*, see Rte 44B.

42 Euboea

EUBOEA (Ευβοία), in modern Greek *Évvia*, next to Crete the largest Greek island, extends NW to SE for over 150km almost parallel to the mainland of Greece (Locris, Boeotia, Attica), from which it is separated by a strait virtually landlocked at either end. Midway along the W coast the strait contracts to a narrow channel called the Euripos. Here from the 5C BC a succession of bridges has joined Euboea to Boeotia. The E coast is virtually inaccessible by reason of its abrupt and hostile cliffs; it has one port, at Kími. The other ports are nearly all on the gentler W coast, chief of these being Khalkis on the Euripos and Karystos, near the S tip of the island. In antiquity the two principal cities were on the W coast: Chalkis, looking towards Boeotia, survives as the modern capital; Eretria, though still the ferry terminal from Attica, is a seaside village with no continuous past.

The centre of Euboea is largely occupied by an irregular mountain range, geographically the SE continuation of Ossa and Pelion, and broken by valleys. The highest point is Mt Dhírfis (1745m). In the N half the mountains are clothed with forests of chestnuts, pines and planes. In the exuberantly fertile plains are grown corn in large quantities, as well as vines, figs, and olives. The most famous of these is the Lelantine Plain between Khalkis and Eretria. The mineral wealth is considerable, lignite and magnesite being exported. The marble and asbestos of Karystos were renowned in antiquity; here was the source of the cipollino extensively used for building in Rome in the Imperial era and later.

Euboea is one of the most delightful regions in Greece. Until recently indifferent roads and the paucity of excavated remains have deterred foreign visitors from its shores, but its equable climate, the wonderful vegetation and the enchanting views, as well as the comparatively undeveloped coastline, are attracting increasing numbers of Athenian motorists, especially at weekends.

History. Euboea was peopled in remote antiquity by colonists from Thessaly who settled in the N (Ellopians), in the W (Abantes) and in the S (Dryopes). According to tradition the early settlers were joined by Ionians from Attica, Aeolians from Phthiotis, and Dorians from the Peloponnesus. The island, also called *Makris* because of its length, was divided between seven independent city-states, of which the most important were Eretria and Chalkis, rivals for the possession of the fertile Lelantine Plain. These two rich and powerful merchant cities founded colonies on the coasts of Thrace, Italy and Sicily, as well as in the islands of the Aegean. After the expulsion of the Peisistratids Chalkis joined Boeotia against Athens. In consequence, in 506 BC, the Athenians crossed the strait, defeated the Chalcidians and divided their land between 5000 cleruchs. Eretria had assisted in the Ionic revolt against Persia some ten years before the first great Persian invasion of Greece. The Persians, in retaliation, took the city by storm in 490, burned it, and enslaved the inhabitants. Although later rebuilt, Eretria never fully recovered her former power. After the Persian wars the whole of Euboea became subject to Athens. In 446 Euboea revolted, but was reconquered by Pericles. In 411 a second revolt, inspired by the defeat of the Athenian fleet at the hands of the Lacedaemonians, and coming at a time when Athens was weakened by the Sicilian disasters and internal faction, was more successful. The same year the inhabitants of Chalkis, with the cooperation of Boeotia, built a bridge over the Euripos and thereby hampered the maritime trade of Athens (see below). In 378 the Athenians induced most of the Euboean cities to join their new maritime league; but, after the battle of Leuktra (371), the island passed under the suzerainty of Thebes. In 358 it was liberated by Chares, who restored it to the protection of Athens. It was incorporated in Macedonia after the battle of Chaironeia (338). In 194 it was taken from Philip V of Macedon by the Romans, who restored its cities to nominal independence. The island later came under the sway of Byzantium.

In AD 1209 Euboea was divided into the three baronies of Chalkis, Karystos and Oreos, which owed allegiance to the king of Salonika. The Venetians held the ports and numerous minor Frankish nobles occupied the interior, which they adorned with their castles. By 1366 the Venetians were masters of almost the whole of Euboea. It was they who gave to the island the name of *Negroponte* ('Black Bridge'), which apparently referred to the bridge over the Euripos (see below). The name is a twofold corruption of Euripos. This had already been corrupted to Egripo, and Egripo was turned by the Venetians into Negroponte. Under the Venetians Negroponte ranked as a kingdom, and its standard was one of the three hoisted in St. Mark's Square. After the expulsion of the Venetians from Constantinople by the Genoese, Negroponte became the centre of their influence in Romania. In 1470 the island was conquered by the Turks and came under the immediate government of the Capitan Pasha, high admiral of the Ottoman Empire. In 1830, after the War of Independence, Euboea passed to Greece. By special decree, a certain number of Moslems were permitted to remain in the island.

A. Khalkís and Northern Euboea

Approaches from Athens. To *Khalkís*, BY ROAD, 81km (50½ miles), bus every half-hour in 1½ hours, comp. Rte 44. BY RAILWAY, 83km (51 miles), 19 times daily in c 1½ hours.—*Loutrá Aidipsoú* is most easily reached by ferry viâ *Arkitsa* (Rte 44); buses 3 times daily.

KHALKÍS (Χαλκίς, commonly Khalkídha; Hotels A, B, C, D, E), attractively situated on the Euripos at its narrowest, is the capital (44,867 inhab.) of the nome of Euboea and the seat of an archbishop. The town carries on an important trade in butter, livestock, and agricultural implements. Its industries include distilleries. It is the centre of bus communications of the island.

Ancient *Chalkis*, of which few vestiges remain, was famous for its manufactures in bronze, exporting arms, vases, and votive tripods; it was the mother-city of many early colonies. The archaic site lay E of the present town, harbouring on the bay of Ayios Stéfanos, with an acropolis farther E on the lower height of *Vathrovouniá*. Here polygonal walling probably dates from 377 BC. In the 4C the city spread over the low hill on which the modern city stands; this may be the classical *Kanethos*.

History. According to the ancients the name of Chalkis (from *chalkos*, bronze) reflected the importance of its chief industry, though modern scholarship has suggested an alternative derivation from *chalke*, the limpet shell yielding purple dye (murex). The site of the Mycenaean city of the great-hearted Abantes (Il. II, 540) remains unknown, but the present site was occupied in late-Geometric times. The situation of the city, with two harbours on the Euripos, outlet of a rich island, made for its early development into a commercial and colonising centre. It was on the trade route between Thessaly (horses and corn), Thrace and Macedonia (gold of Thasos, timber, corn) and Attica and central Greece. In the 8C BC Chalkis colonised the Northern Sporades and so many cities (32 in all) in the Macedonian peninsula between the Thermaic and Strymonic gulfs that the whole peninsula was called *Chalkidike*. Later its settlers established themselves in Sicily; Naxos, Messana (now Messina); and in Italy: Rhegion (Reggio) and Cumae.

Chalkis fought many wars with Eretria for possession of the Lelantine Plain, and in the 7C emerged victorious. Its last king Amphidamas, a contemporary of Hesiod, was killed in one of these wars, and the government passed to the aristocracy, who were themselves overthrown when the Athenians overwhelmed the Chalcidians in 506 BC. Chalkis sent 20 ships in 480 to the Greek fleet and its soldiers took part in the battle of Plataea. Its subsequent history is largely that of Euboea. In 1210 it was seized by the Venetians, who fortified it with walls and made it the capital of the kingdom of Negroponte. When the Turks acquired Euboea in 1470, Chalkis became the headquarters of the Capitan Pasha. Morosini attacked it in 1688 but had to call off his siege after 4000 of his troops and Königsmark, their commander, had died of malaria.

The mainland approach to the Euripos is guarded by **Karabába**, a Turkish fortress of 1686; scanty rock-cuttings suggest an ancient fortress on this site, supposedly a Macedonian fort built c 334 BC. The walls afford a wonderful *View of the strait and of the whole town. In the mainland suburb below are (left) the town beach and (right) the *Railway Station* and an information office. The unusual *Bridge* that carries the road over the Euripos opens by a double action; the carriageway descends just sufficiently to allow each half-span to roll on rails under its own approaches.

The **Euripos** is notorious for its alternating currents, which change direction 6 or 7 times a day and on occasion as often as 14 times in 24 hours. The current flows from N to S for about 3 hours at a rate which may exceed 6 knots. It then suddenly subsides; then, after a few minutes of quiescence, it begins to flow in the opposite direction. The passage of the channel with the current is dangerous and the bridge is opened only when the direction is favourable. A red ball indicates a N–S current; a white ball a S–N current. The phenomenon is alluded to by Aeschylus (Agam. 190), as well as by Livy, Cicero, Pliny and Strabo. The cause is complex and still not fully understood. According to a popular tradition, Aristotle, in despair at his failure to solve the problem, flung himself into the Euripos.

Khalkis. Mosque (A.M. Chenavard, 1850)

The Euripos was first spanned in 411 BC. In 334 the Chalcidians included the Boeotian fort of Kanethos within the city boundaries. Under Justinian the fixed wooden bridge was replaced by a movable structure. The Turks replaced this with another fixed wooden bridge. In 1856 a wooden swing bridge was erected; in 1896 a Belgian company enlarged the channel, demolished the Venetian fort that had guarded the approach, and built an iron swing bridge. This gave place in 1962 to the existing structure.

The bridge leads to the older part of the town ('Kastro'), S of Leofóros Venizélou. Immediately to the left, across the bridge, is an interesting modern metal sculpture, after the Nike of Samothrace, by Carmelo

Mendola, given by Chalkis' Sicilian twin-town, Giardini. A *Mosque*, with ancient columns and a truncated polygonal minaret, is used as a store (no admission) for medieval antiquities. In front is a handsome marble *Fountain*. A road from the SW corner of the square, by which the mosque stands, leads S to the church of **Ayía Paraskeví**, a basilica with pointed arches, above which runs a second row of large arches, incomplete and without a gallery. The columns are chiefly of cipollino and Hymettian marble, and the capitals are much varied. It was converted by the Crusaders in the 14C into a Gothic cathedral. Note the fine carved boss in the S choir aisle vault. Near the old Venetian *Governor's Palace*, now a prison, is the arcaded *Turkish Aqueduct*, which supplied Khalkis with water from two springs on Mt Dírfis, 25km away. At Od. Balalaíou 43 is the sole survivor of many *Venetian city towers* which once existed in Chalkis (Negroponte). Unlike other medieval towers in Euboea, it has a ground floor entry. There is a *Folklore Museum* (open Tuesday and Thursday evenings, Sunday morning) in Od. Skalkóta, E of Ayia Paraskevi.

Khalkis, Ayia Paraskevi. Variant column capitals

From the broad ESPLANADE, Leofóros Venizélou leads past the Law Courts to the **Archaeological Museum** (at present closed for repairs following earthquake damage; 1987), which contains Mycenaean pottery from local tombs and marble sculpture from Chalkis, Eretria, and Karystos. *4. Theseus carrying off Antiope, a fine Archaic group from the pediment of the temple of Apollo Daphnephoros at Eretria; 5. Archaic headless statue of Athena; 3. Male torso; 7. Youth killing a sacrificial animal; 6. Relief of Dionysos with the kantharos; 30. Antinous as Bacchus; 33. Seated woman (4C); three horses from a pedimental quadriga.

AN EXCURSION may be made (viâ Nea Artaki, see below) to (33km) **Steni** (Hotels C), the pleasant village below the cone of **Mt Dhírfis** that provides the best starting-point for climbing the highest mountain in Euboea (1745m). The ancient name *Dirphys* gave the goddess Hera her name 'Dirphya'. Many species of plant are purely local.

THE ASCENT has been simplified by a new road. We continue beyond the village. In 1km, beyond springs and a large car park, the asphalt ends. An earth road now climbs in zigzags but may be driven in dry weather to a fork just above the tree-line, where a branch (left) leads in 1km to the *Fountain of Liri Refuge* (36 beds; keys from Alpine Club, Khalkis); or it may be quitted 1·25km before the fork, where a signed path, with painted marks, leads left to the refuge. A few yards before this path a good, but not motorable, track bears left to a col between the refuge and the summit-ridge, and on the track from the Refuge to the summit (c 1½ hours), which is clearly marked in red all the way. The *View is magnificent.

FROM KHALKIS TO LOUTRA AIDIPSOU, 153km (94½ miles), asphalt. The road runs N, skirting the shore.—At 6km, the promontory of *Mánika* has important remains of an Early Helladic settlement and cemetery, at present being further investigated. 8km *Artáki* (Hotels B, C). To Steni Dhírfios, see above.—From (15km) *Psakhná* (Ψαχνά), a small town (5320 inhab.) with a chapel containing frescoes dated AD 1245, can be visited *Kastrí*, one hour N, a hill surmounted by a Venetian castle. At *Triádha* (6·5km) are the house in which was born Nikolaos Kriezoti, the local hero of 1821, and some excavated remains of an Early Christian basilica.—We climb the outlying E spur of *Kandhílion* (1222m), the ancient *Makistos*, a long range that now cuts us off from the Euboic Gulf; fine retrospective view to Khalkis and the Euripos.

From the summit (over 600m; café), the road descends in bold curves through the *Kleisoura*, a succession of wooded ravines amid scenery of the greatest beauty; there is a magnificent *View across the forests to the islands of Skopelos and Skiathos. We enter a grand defile, in which is the church of Ayios Yeoryios. This gradually opens into a beautiful wide valley, where plane-trees shade a limpid stream.

51·5km *Prokópion* (Inn), renamed after 1923 by refugees from Prokopion (Urgüp) in Turkey, has a chapel enshrining the relics of St. John the Russian, a Tsarist soldier who died in 1730 as a Turkish slave at Urgüp. He was canonised by the Russian church in 1962 (pilgrimage, 27 May). The place is better known by its former name of **Akhmetága** for the estate of the Noel-Baker family and for their *North Euboean Foundation* which runs a health centre, a veterinary service, and a model farm. The by-road E traverses fine wooded country to a disappointing shore.—56km *Mandoúdhi* (1km right of the road) has magnesite quarries, a brick factory, and a little harbour at *Kimási* on the E coast (4km).—59·5km *Kírinthos*, where some ramparts of the 6C BC are taken for the site of Kerinthos.—At (66km) *Strofiliá* the road forks; the left branch crosses the hills to **Límni** (17km; Hotels C, E), a beautiful fishing village of 2392 inhab., served by coasting steamers of the Khalkis–Volos line. Its sands and pine-woods make it beloved of artists. An early Christian basilica came to light in 1960 but little to demonstrate the site of Classical *Aigai*. The hills above are quarried for magnesite. There is a good beach, backed by shady olives, 2·5km N on the Roviés road.

From Limni the *Moní Galatáki*, to the SE beyond *Katoúnia*, may be reached by boat in 1 hour or by road (9km).—*Roviés*, c 13km NW of Limni, was anciently *Orobia*. Hence it is 40 minutes walk to the Byzantine monastery of Gerónda, with fine frescoes.

Beyond Strofiliá the right branch continues along the E slopes of Mt Xiron.—At 70km there is a turning (right) to *Angáli*, where the remains of ancient Trychas have been tentatively identified. After (75km) *Ayía Ánna* we continue climbing, with a view back along the cliffs to the E coast. We follow a pine-clad ridge (412m), devastated by fire in 1979, to (85km) *Pappádhes*, then wind down high above a precipitous valley with views of Skopelos and Skiathos.—97km *Vasiliká*.—Just before (109·5km) *Agriovótanon* a track leads in 2km to **Cape Artemision**. In the straits below in July 480 BC took place the first encounter of the Greek fleet with the Persian fleet, based on Trikeri, the peninsula opposite. Neither side could claim the advantage. Near here in 1928 was found the famous bronze Poseidon, now in the National Museum. The countryside is dotted with beehives.

129km *Istiaía* (Hotel D), or *Xerokhóri*, with 4017 inhab. the chief town of an eparchy, is beautifully situated in an amphitheatre of hills overlooking the northern plain. This is the only habitat of storks in Euboea. A gravel road runs NW to the bathing beach of *Kamatádhika* (6km).— 134km *Oreoí* (Hotel D), with 1162 inhab., has a small harbour with remains of an ancient mole. Near the village square is a fine Hellenistic bull found in the sea in 1965. The *Kastro* is a Venetian fort built on the foundations of a Hellenic enceinte and reusing earlier material. Finds go back to the Mycenaean period. In the valley between the Kastro and the village are the foundations of a marble temple.

History. The Euboean city of *Histiaia* or *Hestiaia*, colonised by Ellopians of Thessaly, was called by Homer *polystaphylos* ('rich in vines'). It was conquered in 447–446 BC by Tolmides and Pericles. The Athenians, having expelled the inhabitants, founded a colony of 2000 cleruchs at *Oreos*, to the W of the deserted city. After the Peloponnesian War Oreos was subdued by the Lacedaemonians and the cleruchs driven out. The Histiaeans were recalled to their former city, thenceforward known by either name (comp. Strabo X). From now on it was ruled by tyrants until the Macedonian invasion. In 207 it was surprised by Attalos II of Pergamon and the Romans; in 200 it was taken by the Roman fleet under Apustius.—According to Livy, Oreos had two citadels separated by a valley; hence the modern plural *Oreoi*. The maritime acropolis, which dominated the port, was attacked by the Romans; the inland acropolis, now *Oreos Apanos*, was simultaneously attacked by Attalos.

The road now crosses the wooded spurs of *Mt Teléthrion* (1352m).— 142km Approach road (right) to the car ferry (regularly) from *Ayiókambos* to *Glífa* in Thessaly.—152km **Loutrá Aidhipsoú** (Λουτρά Αιδηψού; Hotels A, B, C, D, E), mostly May–October only) is a frequented spa well known to the ancients and patronised by Sulla. The sulphur-impregnated springs, with a temperature of 21–71°C, rise near the sea at Cape Therma (hydropathic) at the S end of the town, in powerful little jets, exhaling steam and leaving alkaline deposits. The ancients believed that they were connected with Thermopylae (Rte 44B). The waters enjoy a high reputation for the cure of stiff joints, gout, rheumatism, sciatica and other related ailments. Near the spring of Ayii Anaryiroi are the ruins of Roman baths.

Car ferry to Arkitsa (Rte 44B; regularly in 45 minutes); buses to Athens in 3½ hours. Caique daily in summer to Khalkis.

A road runs W from Aidhipsos to Líchas (24km) on the W point of the island, passing *Yiáltra* and *Gregolímano* (Hotel A).—A new road along the steep coast to the E is in construction to Rovies (see above).

B. From Khalkís to Kími and Káristos

ROAD to Kími, 93km (58 miles), asphalt; bus. 23km **Erétria**.—46km *Alivéri*.—54km *Lépoura*, turning for **Káristos** (127km from Khalkís).—93km **Kími**.

FROM ATHENS the shortest and quickest approach to *Erétria* is by the car-ferry (½ hour) from Skála Oropoú (50km from Athens; Rte 20); through buses to *Kími*.—By public transport *Káristos* is perhaps best reached via Rafína (Rte 21) by boat in 2 hours; or via the Ayía Marína to Néa Stíra ferry (Rte 21).

The road threads the industrial outskirts of Khalkis. On the left rises Vathrovouniá (see above). We cross the LELANTINE PLAIN, the object in the 8–7C BC of deadly rivalry between Chalkis and Eretria. In the Hymn to Apollo it is noted as famous for its vineyards, and it is so still.—Beyond (6·5km) *Néa Lámpsakos*, turning (left) to *Mítikas* and *Fílla* (6·5km). Between the villages is a hill with two towers. Above Fílla, on the hill of Kastélli conspicuous even from the mainland, a castle (view) stands on an ancient enceinte. A cemetery of the 6C AD has been found.—10·5km *Vasilikó* also has a tower. The three towers above, with a fourth at *Ayia Triádha*, are Venetian and sited in combination with the castle to protect the S part of the Lelantine plain. The Vasilikó tower was occupied by the Turks in 1470 during their siege of Negroponte.

A by-road descends in 2km to *Lefkandí* (Hotel C; tavernas), a fast developing coastal resort. The flat headland ('Xeropolis') to the S, was explored in 1965–66 and 1969–70 by the British School and found to be a high occupation mound (no visible remains) with three associated cemeteries. The place seems to have barely survived beyond the Geometric period, but had been occupied from the Early, through the Middle, and Late Helladic periods, and yielded unusually informative layers of L.H. IIIC to Protogeometric from which light is being thrown upon the disappearance of Mycenaean civilisation and the Dark Ages which followed. Lefkandí has been suggested as the site of *Old Eretria*, the city Homer linked with Chalkis in the Catalogue of Ships.

About 200m N of Lefkandí village, on Toumba hill, an important Dark Age cemetery has been investigated, as well as the largest building of that period (c 1000 BC) so far known in Greece. The structure was about 10m wide and 45m long, with an apsidal end. It was built of mud brick on a high (1·5m) stone socle. There was a peristyle of wooden columns. In the main chamber was a double grave, one compartment containing the cremated remains of a warrior, wrapped in a fine cloth and placed in a bronze urn, together with the body of a woman with rich accoutrements; the other four horses. The building was abandoned and deliberately filled in in the same generation as it was constructed.

23km **Erétria**, with 2501 inhab., was founded as *Néa Psará* in 1824 by refugees from the island of Psara. The new town overlies much of the ancient city, the ruins of which are the most considerable in Euboea. *Malakonta Beach*, to the W, has been developed as a holiday resort with large bungalow hotels.

History. *Eretria*, next to Chalkis the most important city in Euboea, was one of the chief maritime states of Greece and is included in the Homeric catalogue. Traces of Mycenaean and Protogeometric occupation have been found on the acropolis, and more recently an early Geometric amphoriskos of the mid-9C has come to light. Eretria contributed five ships to the support of Miletus in the revolt from Persia (500 BC), a gesture which drew upon it the wrath of the Persians ten years later, when they razed the city to the ground and enslaved the inhabitants. Nevertheless Eretria made a partial recovery, sending contingents to Salamis in 480 and to Plataea in 479. In 377 it joined the Second Athenian Confederacy. In 198 it was plundered by the Romans. After destruction in 87 BC in the Mithridatic wars, the city was never in antiquity rebuilt.—A school of philosophy was founded at Eretria in 320 BC. The ceramics of Eretria, including painted vases and sepulchral lekythoi, rank with the finest; many are exhibited in the National Museum in Athens.

The Swiss Archaeological Mission (now the Swiss School) started a systematic exploration in 1964. Subsequent excavations have been conducted by both Swiss and Greek archaeologists. On foot a full round of the visible ruins requires at least

ERETRIA

0   200 metres

Theatre

West Gate

Temple

Palace

Thesmophorion

Gymnasium

Sanctuary (Artemis Olympia)

Site of Stadium

Museum

LEOF ISIDOS

TIMOKRATOUS

HEGELOUCHOU

ARCHAIOU THEATROU

ARISTOTELONTOS

APOSTOU

KANARI

MENEDEMOU

ANTIOCHOU THEIODOTOU

DAPHNEPHOROS

Temple of Apollo

MANTIDOROU

APOLLONOS

Fountain

EUNOMOU

KALLIKRATOU

EPHESIOU

Agora

Tholos

GLAUKIPPOU DIONYSIOU

Baths

ARTEMIDOS

NIKODEMOU

Palaestra

Isaion

Ancient Walls

ARISTONIKOU

ERATONYMOU

LEOF AMARYSIAS

APST

APOLLONOU

VARVAKI

three hours, but the Museum and lower sites can be cursorily seen more quickly.

On the NW outskirts of the village the **Museum** contains vessels of bronze, and pottery from the temple of Apollo (sculpture at Khalkis) from graves outside the city walls and from the city itself through its various phases of occupation from Geometric to Roman times; grave stelai; a loutrophoros supported by griffins; an early Ionic capital; and boustrophedon inscriptions. On display also is a selection of pottery and jewellery from the Early Iron Age cemeteries of Lefkandí (including the fine terracotta centaur of the 10C); also material from Xeropolis.—Turning towards the acropolis we come first to a large area of recent excavation within the W fortifications of the city. These comprised a broad moat and a wall. The *West Gate* had a barbican which extended across the moat on a corbelled arch. The masonry on a tightly interlocking trapezoidal system is impressive. Extensive remains of a 4C peristyle *house*, with a Hellenistic extension, cover an abandoned Heroön of the 7–6C. A well-preserved clay bath remains *in situ*. To the NE are foundations of a *Temple of Dionysos*.

Beyond rises the **Theatre**, excavated by the American School in 1890–95. It retains its seven lower rows of seats, much defaced; the upper tiers, which were exposed to view, have nearly all been carried away, block by block, to build the modern village. A semicircular drainage channel 2m wide runs in front of the lowest row. From the orchestra steps descend through a square opening into an underground vaulted passage, leading to the hyposkenion; it was used for the sudden appearance and disappearance of a 'deus ex machina'. The lofty stage is raised on seven or eight courses of masonry. Under its centre is another vaulted passage, probably constituting the public entrance to the orchestra.

Farther E at the foot of the acropolis is a *Gymnasium*, excavated in 1895 (fenced). Near its W end was found an inscribed stele set up in honour of a gymnasiarch benefactor. Near the same spot is the pedestal of a statue bearing an inscription within a votive wreath to one who had encouraged boys in athletics. At the E end is an extensive series of water conduits which supplied the bathing troughs.

On a hill 10 minutes W of the theatre a tumulus encloses a *Macedonian Tomb* (key from Museum). The Dromos, on the N, leads to a square vaulted chamber, containing two funeral couches in marble, with their pillows and draperies, and two thrones and a table, all picked out in colours.

Above the theatre we climb in 20 minutes to the **Acropolis**, with its ashlar walls and towers. It commands a fine *View to the SW; on the left and in front, part of Attica, with Pentelikon and Parnes; on the right, Kithairon, with Parnassos in the distance; immediately below, the Lelantine Plain.

On the descent are remains of a *Thesmophoreion* and a Sanctuary of a female deity, perhaps Artemis Olympia. Traversing the town we see bare foundations of the **Temple of Apollo Daphnephoros**, unearthed in 1900 by the Greeks and restudied by the Swiss in 1964, when remains of the Geometric period were found below it, together with potters' workshops near by. Superimposed are the stylobates of a Doric peripteral temple of 6 by 14 columns, having a cella in three equal parts, erected c 530–520 BC; and an Ionic peripteral edifice of c 670–650, which probably had 6 by 19 columns in wood.

To the E are some remains of an *Isaion* excavated in 1915 by the Archaeological Society, and beyond them ruins of a *Palaestra*. Close to the sea a mosaic marks an ancient bath site.

31·5km *Amárinthos* (3228 inhab.; Hotels B, C, D) has a sandy beach and (on a hill to the E) two little Byzantine churches. The hills come nearly to the shore.—46km **Alivéri** (Inn), with 4864 inhab., is situated on a hill, the site of ancient *Tamynai*, where the Athenians under Phokion defeated Kallias of Chalkis in 354 BC. A mineral railway descends from an important lignite mine in the hills to *Káravos*, its little port. Here was probably the landing-place of an ancient ferry. On a knoll above the E shore of the bay rises a square medieval fortress, with a door 6m above the ground; it is a good specimen of the structures common on this coast. At Aliveri taxis may be hired for the visit to Dystos.—52km *Veloúsia* (officially *Vélos*). To the NW is a castle and to the S a square tower.—At (54km) *Lépoura* the road divides.

The visit to ancient **Dystos** is best made by taking the Káristos road through *Kriezá* (3km); after a further 5km (ignore signs to modern *Distos*) the site can be seen (1km right; access difficult). The ruins stand on an isolated, overgrown, and snake-infested hill overlooking the E shore of a marshy lake encircled by swallow-holes. The walls of the 5C city, of polygonal construction, 3m high and 2m thick, with 11 towers, describe a semicircle eastward from the W cliff. The main entrance on the E, between two towers, leads to the Agora. On the slopes of the hill, especially on the N, are terraces with remains of *Houses*, almost the only examples surviving from the 5C BC. They had an entrance passage, an inner court, a living room, two bedrooms, and possibly an upper storey. On top of the hill, to the W, is the *Acropolis*, the N part of which became a Venetian fortress (*View from the shattered tower).

TO KARISTOS. From Lépoura the right branch continues SE.—57km *Kriezá*.—Near the hamlet of (71km) *Zárakes* we pass ruined windmills and some foundations, possibly of *Zaretra*, a place captured by Phokion in 350 BC.—Between 77km) *Almiropótamos* and *Polipótamos* a rocky ridge along the narrowest part of the island affords sea views on both sides. Just beyond the Mesokhória turn a Turkish stone road can be seen below (left).—97·5km *Stíra* has a pleasant little square. A Venetian castle crowns probably the acropolis of Homeric *Styra*. *Néa Stíra* (Hotels C), 4km SW, is a seaside resort, connected by ferry with Rafína and Ayía Marína (Rte 21). The island of Stíra, offshore, lies almost opposite Rhamnous.—The road winds round the S end of the *Kliosi Ridge*, on a low spur of which is a small terrace surmounted by three buildings of great antiquity called locally the *Dragon's Houses*. The landscape is reminiscent of Dartmoor with tors'.—118km Turning (right) via Kakagióni, to *Marmári* (Hotels C), another seaside resort with ancient cipollino quarries.

127km **Káristos** (Κάρυστος; Hotels B, C), an attractive town of 4081 inhab., founded after the War of Independence near the site of ancient *Karystos*, is the seat of a bishop and of an eparch, and a pleasant summer resort on a broad bay facing S. From Attica it is more easily visited by steamer departing from Rafina. The ancient city was famous for its cipollino marble and for asbestos.

At the SE end of the esplanade a medieval tower incorporates ancient blocks. From it a road leads inland to *Míli* (3km), a hamlet (cafés) in a lush ravine. From the little plateia the left fork climbs to Graviá and by a fine stone bridge across a ravine to *Castel Rosso* (view), a fine Venetian fort so called from the reddish colour of its stone, probably the ancient acropolis of Karystos. In the ancient quarries are half-worked columns.

The ASCENT OF MT OKHI can be made from Míli in c 3 hours, by a path difficult to follow) round the S side to the Refuge (1000m) above a chestnut wood. Easier to find is a mule-path to a col (1 hour; goatherds' huts) below the W summit; this can also be reached from *Melissón* (guide necessary) via the Gorge of Kallianou, through magnificent country. Thence the approach is up a ridge round the N side. The summit consists of a line of tors, of which the W (Profitis Ilias) is the highest (1405m). Below the tors farther E, on the S side, is a primitive building similar to those at Stira, called the *House of the Dragon*. It may have been a watch-house of the 6C BC.

About 5 hours NE of Karystos is Kafirévs (Cabo Doro), the ancient *Kaphareus* where Nauplios, father of Palamedes, is said to have lighted torches to mislead the Greeks on their return from Troy, in revenge for the murder of his son on a false charge of treachery.—About four hours SE of Karystos, near the extreme S point of Euboea, is the site of *Geraistos*, where triglyphs and an inscription have been found from the celebrated sanctuary of Poseidon. The coast facing E between these two points is probably the 'Hollows' (τά κοίλα) of Herodotus 8. 13, where in 480 a Persian squadron came to grief in a storm.

From Lépoura the Kími road runs N in a wooded valley between Dhirfis and the hills of the E coast.—64km *Khania Bouzi*, by two little streams.—65km *Avlonári* (1km right) stands on the road to *Okhthoniá* (540m), a summer resort, which appears (right; 7km) massed on its hill beneath a pretty church and a Venetian tower (762m), built on Roman foundations. The road now enters the attractive valley of the Oxylithos, guarded on all sides by the picturesque Frankish towers so common in Euboea, and sown every km or so with hamlets and chapels.—73km *Monódhri*. We climb with many bends to (77km) *Dirrévmata*.—80km *Konístrais* has a long main street on a ridge amid rolling olive-clad hills. The road undulates and winds amid lush greenery and small hillside villages.—At (88·5km) *Kalimeriánoi* a new road descends directly to the shore, while the old road threads a pass.

93km **Kími** (Κύμη; Hotels C, D, E), locally called Koumi, is a cheerful town (2770 inhab.), which owes its prosperity to its vineyards and orchards, and to the lignite mines to the W. It stands at 262m on a ridge overlooking the island of Skyros. It is celebrated for figs and honey and for its bold sailors; in 1821 it put to sea a fleet of 55 merchant ships which earned it a bombardment from the Turks. *Paralía Kímis* (Hotel D), its small port with a merchant navy school, lies 4km away. Its harbour was repaired after 1945 by one Robert Nesbit, as a plaque records.

In the vineyards round Kími are many graves of the 4–3C BC. A passable road leads NE to the Monastery of the *Sótiros* (1643) which may occupy the site of ancient *Kyme Phyrkontis*. Another road runs N from Kími to springs and a café whence a track climbs round the summit of *Mt Ortári* (756m) to *Cape Kalám* (splendid cliff scenery from either).

At *Ano Potamiá* (6km to the S, reached via the coast road) are the remains of ancient *Oechalia*, with buildings and an enceinte wall of the 4 and 3C.

43 The Northern Sporades

Grouped near the Thessalian coast are Skiathos, Skopelos, Alonissos and numerous smaller islands; these together comprise the eparchy of Skopelos, part of the nome of Magnesia. Some way to the E is Skyros, the largest of all; with its attendant islets, it forms part of the eparchy of Karistia in the nome of Euboea. The whole group is given the geographical designation of **Northern Sporades**, though the islands have very marked individual characteristics. The usual approaches to the islands are given below; these are only part of a complex net of services round the N Aegean by four ships. Most inter-island journeys can be made most days, the least easy being from Skyros to Skopelos.

A. Skýros

APPROACHES. FROM ATHENS by bus to Kími in Euboea (comp. Rte 42), thence by steamer; daily in c 10 hours, through booking from Athens.

SKYROS (Σκύρος; Skíros; pop. 2757) is the most easterly as well as the largest of the Northern Sporades, with a length of c 27km and an area of 205 sq. km. It is divided into two nearly equal parts by a low-lying isthmus with a natural harbour sheltered by islets in Kolpos Kalamítsas on the SW, and the exposed little haven of Akhíli on the NE. On the S coast is another natural harbour, Trís Boúkes. The fertile N half of the island contains the capital *Skyros* and rises in Mt Olympos to 400m. The mountains of the rugged S half culminate in Kokhílas (782m) and are covered with forests of oaks, pines, and beeches. Here also are marble quarries, put into production again in 1961 after not having been worked for some years. The Skyrian variegated marble was famed in antiquity. Crayfish are caught in large quantities off the coast. Skyros abounds in water, which affords pasture to a few oxen and to numerous sheep and goats, descendants of the goats that were highly prized in Strabo's time. Wheat, oranges, lemons, honey and wine are among the exports.

Legend and History. Achilles, disguised as a girl, was sent by his mother Thetis to the court of Lykomedes, king of Skyros, to prevent his going to the Trojan War. Her precaution was in vain; for Ulysses lured him to Troy, where he was killed before it fell. Neoptolemos or Pyrrhos, son of Achilles, was brought up in Skyros and thence taken by Ulysses to the Trojan War (Sophocles, *Phil.* 239). It was in Skyros that Lykomedes treacherously killed Theseus, king of Athens, who had sought asylum with him.—In 476 BC Kimon conquered the island, enslaved the inhabitants, and planted Athenian settlers (Thucydides I, 98). Kimon discovered the bones of Theseus in the island; he had them taken to Athens and enshrined in the Theseion. In 322 BC the Macedonians took Skyros from the Athenians. In 196 the Romans forced Philip V of Macedon to restore the island to the Athenians.

Linariá (Inns), the landing-place, with good fishing, is on the W coast. About 11km away (bus), on the NE coast, is the capital **Skyros** (Hotels B, E), situating facing inland on a high terrace at the foot of a precipitious hill, on which is the ruined *Kastro*. The hilltop was the acropolis of the ancient city which Homer calls αιπύς ('steep'). This may have been Plutarch's 'high cliff' from which Lykomedes pushed Theseus to his death. Remains of ancient walls may be traced in the foundations of the Venetian enceinte; over the gate is a lion of St. Mark; within is a decaying convent (St. George the Arab), founded in 962, once famous for its miracles. The town has steep narrow and winding streets, and is noted for its little white cubic houses with flat black roofs, furnished with low tables and elaborately carved chairs, ancient and modern embroidery and island pottery. A small *Museum* (9–11) in the Town Hall contains medieval church furniture. Overlooking the sea, on a conspicuous bastion, is an inappropriate *Memorial to Rupert Brooke* in the form of a bronze 'statue of an ideal poet' (1931), by M. Tombros.

Rupert Brooke (1887–1915) was buried on the W slope of Mt Kokhílas (or Konchylia), in an olive grove about 1·5km from the shore, during the night of 23 April 1915, having died of septicaemia the same afternoon in the French hospital ship Duguay Trouin. The expeditionary force, of which he was a member, sailed from Skyros at dawn for the Dardanelles. The visit to the grave, restored by the Royal Navy in 1961, is best made by motor-boat from Linariá to *Trís Boúkes*.

B. Skíathos and Skópelos

APPROACHES FROM ATHENS (apply Alkyon Agency, 98
Akadhimías). Daily by coach to Ayios Konstandínos (Rte 44), whence
by steamer to Skíathos, Glóssa, Skópelos, and (less frequently)
Alónnisos.—FROM VOLOS: weekdays to Skiathos and Glossa,
continuing most days to Skopelos and Alonnisos.—Occasional
caiques also operate locally.

Skiathos has a direct air service from Athens in 45 minutes.

SKÍATHOS (Σκίαθος), nearest of the Northern Sporades to the
Thessalian coast, resembles Mt Pelion in its beautiful scenery and
thick forests. It is particularly famed for its excellent sandy beaches
with exclusive summer hotels. The island has an area of 78 sq. km and
a friendly population of 4129, all but a handful living in the one town
many are occupied in fishing. The fertile but ill-cultivated land yields
grape-vines, olives, fruit-trees, and cereals.

At Skíathos in 480 BC three Greek guardships of the Artemision fleet were
surprised by a Sidonian squadron of Xerxes' fleet (providing Herodotus with one
of his most realistic details); Pytheas of Aegina, wounded and captured, was
spared for his valour and later rescued at Salamis. Skiathos became a subject
ally of Athens. It was devastated by Philip V of Macedon in 220 BC. The island
was the home of the novelists Alexander Papadhiamandis (1851–1911) and Alexander Moraitidhis (1851–1929).

Skíathos (Hotels B, C, D, E, F/A), the only town, lies in a declivity on
the SE coast, with densely wooded hills rising behind it. This is the site
of the ancient city but was deserted in the middle ages (comp. below)
The picturesque pine-clad islet of *Boúrtzi* (Tourist Pavilion), adorned
below the Gymnasion with ancient cannon, is reached by causeway
and affords a fine view of the harbour. In the upper town is the
Cathedral of the Trion Ierarkhon.

A road runs SW along the shore, passing above (3km) the pleasant
beaches of *Akhladiás* (Hotels A, F/A), then crosses the peninsula of
Kalamáki, a large headland with the Nostos villa hotel. Beyond are the
two superb bays (also served by motor-boats in summer) of (7km)
Platánia and (10·5km) *Koukounariés* (Hotels A, B, E), said with some
justification to have the finest beach in Greece.

In 1538–1829 the inhabitants removed to an almost inaccessible
position on the most northerly tip of the island. The *Kastro*, as their
deserted town is called, is 3 hours distant from Skiathos Town. It is
built, on a rocky peninsula formerly connected to the rest of the island
by a drawbridge. Of its ruinous buildings, the *Church of Christ* is the
best preserved, with a wooden screen of 1695 and some of its frescoes
more or less intact. Once of great importance but now inhabited by
only one or two monks, are the *Convent of the Annunciation*, with a
fine Byzantine church containing frescoes and a library of MSS, and
the *Convent of St. Charalambos*, to which the novelist Alexander
Moraitidhis retired shortly before his death.

SKOPELOS (Σκόπελος), the ancient *Peparethos*, separated from Skíathos by the Skopelos Channel, grows grape-vines, olives, almonds
pears, and other fruit. A well-watered island of 122 sq. km , it is more
intensively cultivated than Skiathos. Its 2728 inhabitants are more
scattered, less seafaring, and more conservative. Local costume may
be seen on feast days and pottery is made.

Ancient Peparethos had become *Skopelos* by Ptolemaic times. In the Byzantine
era it was used as a place of exile. In Frankish times it was taken by the Brothers

Ghizi and attached to the duchy of Naxos. In 1538 Barbarossa slaughtered the entire population.

The capital, **Khóra Skopélou** (2668 inhab.; Hotels A, B, C, D, E, F/A) rises imposingly on slopes above a roadstead exposed to the blasts of the Meltemi. The houses have characteristic blue slate roofs quartered by white ridge tiles. Blindingly white in the sun are the many little churches, said to number 123, some of which, notably the *Panayitsa*, stand high on the steep W scarp of the town. Their ikons and screens (17–18C) are of good local workmanship, notably those in the church of *Khristó*, which has a gilded 'choros' or corona lucis. Pleasant black ware is produced by a local potter. Beyond his workshop, E of the town, on the shore are vestiges of a Classical building (Asklepieion ?), fast being eroded by the sea. Farther on is *Moní Episkopí*, former seat of the bishopric of Skopelos, suppressed in the last century. Fragments remain of the church of 1078, possibly on the spot where Reginus, first bishop and patron saint of Skopelos, was martyred in 362.

A road (buses daily in 45 minutes) crosses the island to *Agnónda*, a sheltered harbour on the S coast where the boats call if the Meltemi blows (in which case a special bus connects). It passes the Bay of Stafilos (Hotel B), said to take name from Staphylos, a Minoan general. A tomb dug here in 1927 was claimed as his. *Glóssa* 1171 inhab (Hotel C), above the W coast facing Skiathos, and *Klíma*, a smaller village to the E, are reached from their little port (Kalamáki) at which the steamers call. Glossa has Venetian remains.

A narrow channel, partly occupied by two islets, separates Skopelos from *Khelidhrómi*, the ancient *Ikos*, known also as *Liadhrómia* and officially as **Alónnisos** (Αλόννησος; 1554 inhab.). It is a hilly wooded island culminating in Mt Kouvoúli (494m). Its main village is *Alónnisos*, or Liadromia, well situated on a hill at the SW corner of the island above *Patitíri* (Hotels B, C, E), its little harbour. The other village, *Vótsi*, lies just to the E.

There are several rocky islets to the E and NE of Alónnisos, uninhabited save for a few shepherds and their flocks. They include *Pelagonesi*, *Gioura*, *Piperi* ('Peppercorn', so called from its shape), and *Psathoura*, the northernmost of the group, where an extensive ancient city lies submerged. Some authorities consider that Psathoura not modern Alónnisos was the ancient *Halonnesos*, the ownership of which was a bone of contention between Philip of Macedon and the Athenians; one of the surviving orations of Demosthenes is on this subject. A Byzantine wreck off Pelagonesi was examined in 1970. Cargo raised was mainly glazed sgraffito pottery (mid 12C).

44   From Athens to Lamía

A. Via Levádhia

ROAD, 212km (131½ miles). To (74km) **Thebes**, see Rte 41.— 119km (74 miles) **Levádhia**.—125km *Orchomenós* turn.—132km *Chairóneia*.—180km *Brállos*. Steep pass.—212km **Lamía**.—BUSES daily by this route; more frequently to *Levadhia*, and from Levadhia to Lamia.

RAILWAY, via Thebes (comp. Rte 44A), beyond which it follows closely the general course of this road.

From Athens to (74km) *Thebes*, see Rte 41. We quit Thebes by a short curving descent, then pass after 5km a road (left; comp. Rte 41) to Thespiai and Thisbe.—At 80·5km, just beyond a bridge over a torrent bed, a just motorable track (left) leads across fields in c 1·5km to a fold in the hills in which is the **Kabeírion**, a sanctuary explored in 1887 and more fully excavated in 1956–69.

The E end of a *Temple*, showing four architectural styles, forms the skene of a large *Theatre*, twice rebuilt. A central *Altar*, the focus of both temple and theatre, shows that the spectacle was a sacred rite. Three circular buildings and two water basins with pipe connections are of cult significance. Three halls form an open square at the periphery of the sacred area. Various walls show occupation from Roman to Archaic times. The site is notable for the amusing Kabeiran pottery produced at or near it, and apparently exclusively intended for use there.

The road runs across the Teneric Plain. To our N *Mt Fagas* (567m), or *Sphingion*, the reputed haunt of the Sphinx, rises above the *Varikó* marsh.—From (91km) the low ridge of Kazarma, which separates the Theban from the Copaic plain, Parnassos may be seen in the distance ahead. On the ridge stood *Onchestos*, at one time seat of the Amphictyonic League and, in Macedonian times, of the Boeotian Confederation; the Poseidonion and Bouleuterion were identified in 1972. A medieval watch-tower and grotto lie just off the road (left). The grotto produced material from the Old to Middle Stone Age. The road now follows the margin of the drained **Lake Kopáïs**.

Lake Kopáïs (Copais, Κωπάϊς) is named after the ancient city of Kopai. It was the largest lake in Greece, measuring 24km by 13km; Strabo says that it had a circuit of 380 stadia (68km). For most of the year it was a reedy swamp, while large tracts dried up completely in summer. In the rainy season the surrounding basin used to be frequently inundated and it is doubtless to some flood of exceptional severity that the tradition of the Ogygian deluge is due. The eels of Copais were very large and succulent, and the reeds which fringed its shores were the raw materials of the Greek flute.

The natural outlets of the lake (all on the E and NE) were swallow-holes (katavothrae). These were not, however, sufficient to cope with a sudden inrush of water, and from a very early age attempts were made to increase the natural out-flow. On the dry bed of the lake traces of prehistoric dikes and canals, attributed to the Minyans, have been found; they channelled the waters to various katavothrae with such success that the whole basin was reclaimed. Strabo repeats the tradition that it was dry cultivated ground in the days when it belonged to Orchomenos. Herakles is said, out of emnity to the Orchomenians, to have blocked up the katavothrae; Strabo explains that the chasms were affected by earthquakes. After the destruction of the Minyan drainage works and throughout the historic period the Copaic basin remained a lake.

Attempts were made, however, in historical times to supplement the katavothrae by means of tunnels. Two artificial emissaries have been discovered. The more extensive work is the tunnel towards Larimna. This may have been the work of Krates, engineer to Alexander the Great. The other appears to have anticipated the modern tunnel from Copais to Likéri. Neither of the ancient tunnels was completed. A further attempt to control the inflowing rivers was undertaken in the reign of the Emp. Hadrian. In 1887 Scottish engineers took over from a French company works started twenty years earlier. A dam was built, two canals were cut from W to E, and the *Melas*, the main affluent, was diverted and canalised. The *Great Central Canal* is 25km long, 23m wide, and 1·8–8·2m deep. The *Outer Canal* (32km long), to the S collects the waters of the affluents from the S side. The water of the Melas flows down the 'Great Katavothra'. The water of the Outer Canal and the winter overflow is drained through a tunnel into Lake Iliki, and thence to the sea. After reclamation, completed in 1931, the ground was divided between pasture and the cultivation of cereals and cotton. The area under cultivation by the British Lake Kopais Company steadily increased to 180 sq. km by 1952, when the Greek government acquired the estate by expropriation.

At the *Battle of Lake Kopais*, in 1311, the Catalan Grand Company practically annihilated the chivalry of Frankish Greece. The battle was fought near Orchomenos (Skripou), comp. below.

82·5km *Alíartos*. Some scanty remains of ancient *Haliartos*, excavated by the British School in 1926, can be seen on a rocky hill (right), now known as Palaiókastro or *Mazi*. This was one of several fortified places that commanded the road from Orchomenos to Thebes, the only natural highway through Central Greece. Part of the Classical fortification wall of the town was found in 1976 near the main road. Medieval fortification is represented by the *Moúkhli Tower* which overlooks a modern canning factory, immediately S of the modern town.

At *Seínti*, 3km E of Aliartos, beside the main road, a 4C building complex (stoa and shops?) may be part of an agora.

To the S behind (97·5km) *Pétra* rises a jagged row of hills. At *Solinári* (left) is a site tentatively identified with the Temple of Tilphoussios where the seer Teiresias died.—107km Crossroads. To the left is modern Koroneia, but off the next turning (left; to *Ayios Yeóryios*), in a valley 4km S, are some remains (theatre, temple foundations, walls) of ancient *Koroneia*, where in 447 BC the Athenians suffered the defeat that lost them control of Boeotia. The Spartans under Agesilaus failed to consolidate a victory here in 394. We turn N for a short distance with the railway, then quit it to turn W into the plain of Levadhia.

119km (74 miles) **Levádhia** (Λεβάδεια; Hotels B, C, D) is a busy town of 17,769 inhab., the capital of the nome of Boeotia, and the seat of a bishop. It is pleasantly situated at the mouth of the gorge of the Erkina (ancient Herkyna) between Mt Lafistios on the E and Mt Ayios Ilias on the W. A Frankish castle once protected and still dominates the town. Levadhia is a prosperous industrial centre making gay coloured textiles. The railway station lies 7km NE of the centre.

History. The earliest settlement on the Herkyna was *Mideia*, known to Homer (Il. ii, 507), the citadel of which was possibly on a hill, now called Tripolithári, which rises c 2km N of the modern town, at the point where the gorge opens into the plain. During the classical period *Lebadeia*, built at the foot of Tripolithari, was not of much account. It was sacked by Lysander and later by Archelaus. Pausanias found it 'equal in style and splendour to the most flourishing cities in Greece'; its fame and prosperity were chiefly due to the oracle of Trophonios, which was the only one functioning in Boeotia in the time of Plutarch. Having a certain strategic importance *Levadia* prospered in the Middle Ages. It was the birthplace of St. Nicholas Peregrinus (1075–94), a demented youth who, dying in Trani (Apulia), was canonised by the Roman church. In the 13C it passed to the dukes of Athens. In 1311–81 it was the third city of the Catalan duchy of Athens and Neopatras, its military capital, and the seat of a bishop. It withstood a siege by Walter II de Brienne in 1335, but fell by treason to the Navarrese in 1381. The town passed to Nerio Acciaioli in 1385 and Bayezid captured it in 1394. Levadhia gained importance under the Turks and at the War of Independence was still the second city of the Greek mainland.

The most conspicuous feature of the town is the 18C *Clock Tower*. By the riverside are fulling and spinning mills. We make for the S end of the town where a picturesque *Turkish Bridge* spans the Herkyna just below the *Springs of Trophonios* (Restaurant; tavernas; swimming pool).

The *Oracle of Trophonios* was renowned as far back as the 6C BC. Among those who consulted it were Croesus, Mardonius, and the traveller Pausanias, who gives from personal experience a detailed account of the ritual (see Paus. IX, 39, 5–14).

The visit to the gorge and springs of the Herkyna and to the Kastro and summit of Mt Ay. Ilias (the last two on opposite sides of the river) takes about 2 hours. The river, whose ultimate source is on Mt Lafistios, is mainly fed by the group of springs which gush from the foot of the cliff which bears the Kastro. On the left bank the *Cold Spring* (Kria), whose waters are collected in a reservoir, appears to correspond to the *Spring of Memory* (Mnemosyne). Above the spring are votive niches cut in the rock, one of them a chamber 4m square and 3m high, with benches, a favourite retreat of the Turkish governor. Below, to the left a narrow passage 9m long leads to another spring in the heart of the cliff; this may be the *Spring of Forgetfulness* (Lethe). On the right bank, opposite, under a clump of plane-trees, is another group of springs. Higher up the gorge is an extensive *View, including the Chapel of Jerusalem of the Grotto. At the top of the gorge is a lonely mountain valley.

The sanctuary and oracle of Trophonios were situated on Mt Ayios Ilias. The *Temple of Trophonios*, which was surrounded by a sacred grove, may be sought in the *Chapel of the Panayía*, on the left bank of the Herkyna, where ancient inscriptions referring to Trophonios have been found and some ancient blocks have been built into the chapel walls; or on an artificial terrace, now occupied by the Chapel of SS. Anna and Constantine just below the Kastro.

Fifteen minutes above the springs we reach the medieval **Kastro**, a ruined fortress used by the Catalans in the 14C and partly built of ancient blocks. Its custody was entrusted to the most important Siculo-Catalan families and it held the precious relic of the head of St. George. It was severely damaged by earthquake in 1894 but is impressive in its ruin. Half-an-hour's climb from the springs brings us to the summit of *Ayios Ilias* (402m) where a chapel covers the remains of the unfinished Temple of Zeus seen by Pausanias. To the SW are remains of a circular subterranean construction identified with the *Oracle of Trophonios*, at a late stage (3C AD) of its existence.

FROM LEVADHIA TO ORCHOMENOS, 11km (7 miles). We quit Levadhia by the Lamia road (comp. below), turning off after 5·5km to the right and passing cotton ginneries. The Frankish tower of *Thourion* is visible on a hill c 1km to the NW. The Battle of Lake Copais is thought to have been fought in the immediate vicinity and the Duke of Athens to have surveyed the battlefield from this tower prior to the engagement.—11km *Orchomenós*, a town of 5369 inhab., combining the former hamlets of Petromagoula and Skrípou, lies at the foot of a desolate rocky ridge, known in antiquity as *Akontion* ('Javelin') and today as *Dhourdhouvana*. The *Church* of the former convent of the Dormition (Koimisis tis Theotokou), admirably restored since its fabric was split by an earthquake in 1895, was built in 874. Designed in a Bulgar tradition of Byzantine building, it is the unique example of its type in Greece, though similar in plan to Ayia Sophia at Ohrid. The single squat cupola rests on solid walls, but the proportions are good. The whole building consists of column-drums from a Temple (of the Graces) and blocks from the theatre. The interior, architecturally unadorned, is frescoed but cluttered by the usual ornate and tasteless furniture.

Ancient **ORCHOMENOS**, occupying a strong position at the E end of Akontion, was, as the capital of the Minyans, one of the richest and most important centres of Mycenaean times. Homer compared its treasures with those of Egyptian Thebes. It appears to have been inhabited almost continuously from the Neolithic period to the time of Alexander the Great.

History. The Minyans came from the Thessalian seaboard (or, according to more fanciful theories, direct from Egypt) to Orchomenos and made it their capital. They drained Lake Kopaïs and built a series of fortresses of which the most

ORCHOMENOS

Lake Kopais

Church of Dormition
on site of Temple of Graces

Mycenaean megaron

Treasury of Minyas

Orchomenos
(Mediaeval Skripou)

to Chaironeia
Thebes
Levadhia & Delphi

Theatre

Classical Temple

Sacred spring

Classical City

Prehistoric remains

147m

168m

River Melas

Classical Temple

Line of classical wall

208m

280m

Gate

Cross
Wall

Hellenistic City
& Fortifications

Postern Gate

305m

River Kephisos

Gate

348m Tower

Rockcut Stairs

N

0 metres 100 200 300

remarkable is Gla. Their dominion extended across Boeotia, and Thebes itself came, for a time, under their sway. Minyan Ware, so-called because Schliemann first discovered it at Orchomenos, is a 'fine wheel-make ware of well refined, grey clay with a very smooth polished surface which is curiously soapy to the touch'. Its origin is a mystery, its period Middle Helladic and it comes also in yellow and other colours.

About 600 BC Orchomenos joined the Boeotian League, but did not put its emblem on her coinage until 387 BC. If she became a member of the Kalaurian League it was in virtue of her authority over the Boeotian coast towns. She took the side of the invader in the Persian Wars. Orchomenos joined Sparta against Thebes in 395 and 394 BC, and was saved after Leuktra (371) only by the good offices of Epaminondas. In 364 Thebes seized the pretext of a conspiracy to destroy her venerable rival during Epaminondas' absence. Eleven years later the Phocians rebuilt Orchomenos, but it was again destroyed by the Thebans in 349. Under Philip of Macedon and Alexander the Great it was again rebuilt. In 87 Sulla defeated Archelaus, the general of Mithridates, under its walls. The Graces, or Charites, were first worshipped at Orchomenos.

Immediately W of the church, excavations since 1970 have revealed a *Mycenaean palace* built c 1350 and destroyed 1200 BC, with extensive remains of fresco decoration. Across the road are impressive remains of a *Theatre* of the 4C BC. About 150m SW of the church, in a walled enclosure, is the so-called *Treasury of Minyas* (adm. restricted), a Mycenaean tholos tomb recalling the Treasury of Atreus at Mycenae. It was excavated by Schliemann in 1880–86. The stone revetments of the *Dromos* were robbed in 1862 and the roof of the *Tholos* has fallen in, but the gateway still has its threshold and lintel of dark grey Levadhia marble and eight courses stand of the tholos itself. The most remarkable features were the bronze rosettes, which decorated the walls, and the *Thalamos*, or inner sepulchral chamber hewn out of the rock. In its ceiling are slabs of green schist, carved with spirals interwoven with fan-shaped leaves, and surrounded with a border of rosettes. In the middle of the tholos are remains of a marble pedestal belonging to a funerary monument of the Macedonian period, once erroneously taken for the tomb of Hesiod, which was in the agora.

The *City Walls* of the Archaic period ran along the N and S sides of the ridge forming a long triangle, whose apex was the acropolis. Within these walls the excavations of Furtwängler and Bulle in 1903–05 laid bare a series of superimposed settlements.

To the W and E of the Treasury of Minyas are the remains of a NEOLITHIC CITY (? 6000–3400 BC), consisting of beehive huts built of unburnt brick on bases of masonry. Above this was a second city of Early Helladic date (3000–2000), characterised by deep circular ashpits, 6–8m diameter. Above this again appear the apsidal house and rectangular megaron common in Thessaly and Elis (2000–1750) and yielding the so-called Minyan ware (see above) of Middle Helladic date.

Near the cemetery are the substructions (21m x 85) of an *Archaic Temple*, of the 9C or 8C BC, resting, as at Tiryns and at Mycenae, on a much older settlement. This was a part of the MIDDLE HELLADIC CITY of 1700–1450 BC. About 350m W of the Cemetery, on an intermediate terrace, are the remains of a *Temple of Asklepios*, measuring 22m × 11·5m. Thence we reach the upper terraces, on which was built the *Macedonian City*.

An ancient staircase mounts to the *Acropolis* (308m), in size hardly more than a square keep. The cliffs on the E and N formed a natural defence; on the S and W the site was protected by massive walls, dating from the 4C BC and among the finest extant examples of ancient Greek fortification. The view is extensive including the entire Copaic plain.

From Levadhia to *Arakhova* and *Delphi*, and to *Osios Loukas*, see Rte

45.

The Lamia road turns N out of Levadhia and rounds the easterly foothills of the Parnassos range to enter the broad valley of the Boeotian
Kefissos.—125km Turning (right) for *Orchomenos* (comp. above). We
now cross the battlefield of Chaironeia at the entrance (left) of the
defile of Kérata.—132km *Kápraina* has readopted the old name Khai-
rónia. Ancient **Chairóneia** (Χαιρωνειχ) cannot be missed since the
*Lion stands at the roadside. It guarded the *Polyandrion*, or common
tomb, in which the Thebans buried the members of the Sacred Band
killed in the battle of Chaironeia. This remarkable but not very realistic sculpture, which was discovered by a party of English visitors in
1818 almost buried in the ground, was smashed during the War of
Independence by the brigand patriot Odysseus Androutsos under the
impression that it contained treasure. In 1902–04 the Greek Archaeological Society restored it and replaced it on its ancient plinth. It is built
up of three hollow sections of bluish-grey Boeotian marble, and is
represented seated on its haunches; its height is 5·5m, or, including
the plinth, 8·5m. The ossuary which it adorned was a rectangular
enclosure surrounded by a peribolos wall; inside it were found 254
skeletons and various objects now in Athens.

Adjacent is a *Museum* containing Neolithic and Protogeometric ware from Chaironeia; Neolithic, E.H., and M.H. vessels
from Elateia; black-figure vases from Abai; finds from Exarkhos
and Ayia Marina (comp. below) and Mycenaean remains from Orchomenos, including a fragment of fresco from the palace; vases, terracottas, and arms from the Tumulus of the Macedonians.

The BATTLE OF CHAIRONEIA was the outcome of the sabre-rattling policy of
Demosthenes, who, by rousing anti-Macedonian feeling in the Athenians and
concluding an alliance with Boeotia, provoked Philip of Macedon to attack
Southern Greece. After capturing Amphissa, Philip entered Boeotian territory at
the head of 30,000 foot and 20000 horse. He found the allied army, perhaps
slightly inferior in numbers, barring his way in the plain to the E of Chaironeia.
The Athenians, attacking on the left wing, gained an initial advantage. The
Macedonian cavalry, led by the 18-year old Alexander, overwhelmed the Theban sacred band, who fought on to the death. The Athenians (among them
Demosthenes himself), taken in the rear, fled. Philip buried the Macedonian
dead in a great tumulus (to be seen near the railway); he burned the Athenian
corpses and sent the ashes to Athens. The Thebans were permitted to bury their
dead in a common tomb (comp. above). The result of the battle was the unques-
tioned supremacy of Macedon, crystallised the following year at the Synedrion of
Corinth. After the battle Philip treated Thebes with the utmost severity, but was
unexpectedly lenient towards Athens.—In the same plain Sulla won his great
victory over Archelaus in 86 BC.

The ancient city, whose chief industry was the distillation of unguents from the
lily, rose, narcissus, and iris, was the birthplace of Plutarch (AD 46–?127), who
kept a school here, holding a priesthood for life from AD 95 at Delphi. The
Acropolis (270m) occupies two summits separated by a saddle. There are remains
of Hellenic walls and fragments of earlier walls in polygonal and Cyclopean
work. At the N foot of the hill is a little *Theatre*.

We pass a by-road (left) to Ayios Vlásios, a name disguising St. Blaize,
above which (left) stand *Walls of the acropolis of ancient *Panopeos*,
the reputed home of Epeios, who built the Trojan Horse. We cross the
railway near (137·5km) *Dhávlia* Station. The village lies 7km W; and
30 minutes S of the village, in a wooded situation on an abrupt E spur
of Parnassos, the ruins of ancient *Daulis*. Road and railway pass out of
Boeotia into Lokris through the *Pass of Belessi*, anciently Pass of Para-
potamoi, down which Philip marched to Chaironeia in 338 BC.—At
141km the road divides by a cotton-mill.

The right branch runs NE to *Atalándi* (28km; Rte 44B). At 7km we leave on our left an asphalted by-road to modern *Elatía* (6·5km), formerly Drakhmani, with a small museum and (3km farther N by a dry-weather track) a Neolithic settlement mound. An (uncorrected) Carbon 14 dating of c 5520 BC was obtained for monochrome pottery and of c 5080 for the earliest painted pottery. The road crosses a ridge between *Mt Khlomón* (right; 1081m) and Mt Varvás, the E spur of Kallídhromon with a fine view of Parnassos. At (13·5km) *Kalapódhi*, near the church of Ay. Apostoloi, German excavators have uncovered in the last few years, beneath Byzantine material, the remains of a *Sanctuary of Artemis Elaphebolia and Apollo*. The most substantial remains are those of three temples, two Archaic and one Classical but there were earlier structures on the site and the numerous offerings from votive deposits suggest continuous cult activity here from the Mycenaean period. A road (left) leads to *Zéli*, from which in 40 minutes may be reached the ruins of *Elateia*, the capital of ancient Phokis and the city of Onomarchos, a noted general in the Sacred War of 357–346 BC. Philip made Elateia his base for the invasion of Greece. The consternation which seized the Athenians on learning of its capture by Philip in 339 BC is described in a famous passage of Demosthenes. In 198 it was taken by the Roman general Flaminius. It was unsuccessfully besieged in 86–85 BC by Taxilas, a general of Mithridates, and c AD 176 by the róbber horde of the Costobocs (from Hungary). On a hill called *Kástro Lazoú* (fine view) are the ruins of a Temple of Athena Kranaia, excavated by the French School in 1886. The temple, which was served by boy-priests, was in the Doric order with 6 columns by 13.—To the E of Kalopódhi a bridle path leads round Mt Khlomon in 8km to *Exarkhos*, passing the remains of *Abai* and *Hyamopolis*.

The main road bears left. The long range of Kallídhromon appears ahead.—At (150km) *Kifissokhóri* a by-road runs SW to *Velitsa* (6·5km), a tobacco-growing village (1121 inhab.), officially called *Tithorea* after the near-by ancient remains of that city. Its walls, 3m thick, and towers are noteworthy. *Ayía Marína*, to the S has a Neolithic settlement. We traverse a defile between Parnassós and Kallídhromon.—164km **Amfíklia** (Αμφίκλεια), or Dadí, with 3496 inhab., the most considerable town in W Lokris, is piled up the hill in terraces, as was its ancient predecessor to the W. The acropolis of the ancient site is marked by a Frankish tower, now in the middle of the cemetery. We cross the river and the railway to (169km) *Lílaia* Station. The citadel of *Lílaia*, with walls and towers standing to a great height, occupies the precipitous edge of a remote slope of Parnassós, 6·5km SW beyond *Polídhroso*. Beside the Classical walls, at the top of the slope, is a very large Frankish tower (13·3m × 7·6m).—We start to climb through increasingly grand scenery.

At (180km) **Brállos** (Μπράλλος; restaurant) a turning for Amfissa, important as connecting Lamia via the Rion ferry with Patras, drops across the valley to enter at *Graviá* a defile on the opposite side (comp. Rte 45). Just below Gravia (3km S of Brallos station) is *Bralo British Military Cemetery* with the graves of 95 allied soldiers who died (mostly of influenza) in the 49th Stationary Hospital, transferred here in 1917. Brallos was the N end of the overland supply route from Itea for the Macedonian front.—Road and railway now start their arduous passage of the *Pass of Fournataki*, the col connecting Mt Oiti on the W with Mt Kallídhromon.

The railway threads two long tunnels, between which a long iron viaduct crosses the *Asopos*. Farther on another viaduct traverses the *Gorgopotamos*. Both these bridges were blown up in 1942–43 by British parachutists aided by Greek partisans, exploits which cut for six months a German supply route to North Africa. The Gorgopotamos Bridge was again blown by the retreating Germans and the present bridge was built by US army engineers in 1948. The anniversary of the allied exploit is usually celebrated every November; at the commemoration in 1964 an old mine exploded killing 13 people and injuring 51 others.

On the steep ascent the road passes (187km) *Elevtherokhóri*, starting-point for (1½ hours) the refuge-hut on Kallídhromon (organised from Lamia). Just beyond the summit (619m) is (190km) the *Khani Karnásou* (Rfmts), overlooking the great plain of Lamia. The descent is one of the steepest and most tortuous in Greece. The region is steeped in legends of Herakles. Some ruins above the gorge of the Asopos (left) are taken to be *Trachis*, his last residence, whence, suffering torments from the poisoned shirt of Nessus, he ascended to his self-immolation on Mt Oite. During the Persian invasion of 480 BC the Persians had their camp at Trachis and from here the Anopaia path, betrayed to them by Ephialtes, led to the rear of the Greek position at Thermopylae.—From the foot of the pass the road drives straight across the plain and the Spercheios to (212km) **Lamia** (Rte 47).

B. Via Kamména Voúrla

ROAD, ETHNIKI ODHOS 1, 214km (133 miles), toll highway.— 38km *Malakássa*.—61km (38 miles) Turning for *Khalkís* (20km).— 85km (53 miles) Turning for **Thebes** (6km).—110km *Kástro* (**Gla**).— 170km **Kamména Voúrla**.—194km **Thermopýlae**.— 214km **Lamía**.— BUSES 10 times daily in 3½ hours.

RAILWAY, 219km (136 miles), through carriages 7 times daily in 3½–4¾/A hours. The line closely follows the highway nearly to *Thebes* (90km, comp. below); thence it takes the course of the old road, via *Livádhia*, described in Rte 44A, leaving the main Salonika line at *Lianokládhi* (6·5km W of Lamía).

To reach the National Highway we may leave central Athens by Patission (Rte 20), by Liossíon (Rte 19B), or (best) by Akharnón, between the two, to merge beyond *Patissia* with the approach from Piraeus.— At 20km we pass under the railway. A turning (signposted Ay. Stéfanos) branches (right) for Marathon Lake, which, near the 25km post, comes briefly into view.—We cross the railway; here the highway follows a course parallel to the old Kalamos road (Rte 22).—Near (29km) *Polidhéndhri* (Hotel A), road (right) to the Amphiaraion (Rte 22). To the left rises *Béletsi* (841m), the NE extremity of Parnes. Road and railway pass through the narrow gap between Béletsi and *Mavrinóra* in the district known in ancient times as the Diakria.

We by-pass *Malakássa*, standing at the foot of the Dhekelia pass, with (38km) the road (right) to Skala Oropos and the ferry to Euboea. We traverse the gentle rolling country that extends from Parnes to the S Euboean Gulf.—47km *Avlón*, with pop. 5124, lies 2km left on the railway. We enter Boeotia and cross the Asopos.—Beyond (53km) *Staniátes*, which has readopted the ancient name *Oinófita*, TOLL GATE. The battle of Oenophyta resulted in a victory for the Athenians in 457 BC.—59km Turning for *Dílessi*, a little coastal village made notorious by the murders of 1870. It probably occupies the site of ancient *Delion*; the Athenian defeat of 425 BC is to be placed c 5km to the S near 'Palaiokhani'.—The road crosses the Khalkis branch line just beyond its junction and the main railway at *Oinói* (1·5km left).— 61km *Skhimatárion* (left) in a spreading industrial zone has a small and badly lit Museum containing steali, figurines, and inscriptions from Tanagra.

Ancient *Tanagra* occupied a nearly circular hill rising from the N bank of the Asopos, c 5km S of Skhimatarion and a similar distance from modern Tanagra. The most prominent feature of the plain today is an airfield of the Hellenic Air Force, for which reason identity documents should be carried. Tanagra was the scene of a Spartan victory over the Athenians and Argives in 457 BC and (?) birthplace of the poetess Corinna, who defeated Pindar in a musical contest at Thebes. The ruins, not easy of access, include an enceinte of c 385 BC and a visible but still buried theatre. The place owes its fame to the terracotta figurines discovered in the extensive necropolis in 1874. A further series of chamber tombs by modern Tanagra excavated since 1969 has yielded Mycenaean larnakes and associated terracotta plaques of most unusual design. A clay larnax can be dated to L.H. IIIB but shows two scenes of Prothesis together with a chariot scene and one of bull-leaping, the first association of two typically Geometric motifs with a Minoan motif in a Mycenaean mainland context.

TO KHALKIS (81km from Athens). A new road diverges N to (7km) *Vathý* (Hotel C), with shipyards, a huge radio station, and a station on the Khalkis branch line. The coast roads to the E are to be avoided. To reach ancient **Aulis** (commonly *Avlídha*), famed in the Homeric epic as the place where Agamemnon sacrificed Iphigeneia, we take an older and poorer road from Vathy (*not* the main coastal highway). The long narrow *Temple of Artemis* was discovered during the building of the road in 1941. Its identification is certain from the inscription of a statue base. The site was excavated by Threpsiades in 1956–61. The cella dates from the 5C but was restored in Roman times; it originally had a porch with two columns in antis, which was rebuilt with four columns in Hellenistic times. To the S of the temple are some remains of *Potters' Establishments*, with a kiln, and a third building, perhaps a hotel. Beyond a cement works we join the old road (see below) and cross the Euripos (Toll).—20km **Khalkis**, see Rte 42A

In the mainland outskirts of Khalkis a road runs N to *Khaliá* (4km), renamed *Dhrosiá*, whence a passable dirt road continues round the coast past the site of (?) *Salganeus* (large mound with E.H. traces) to *Anthedon* (11km), excavated by the American School. Here are some well-preserved remains of a quay, now thought to be of Byzantine date, and of two moles (partly submerged). The line of the city walls can be traced round the acropolis, a low hill close to the shore to the E, and around the lower town to the SW.

At 70km (43½ miles) diverges the old road to Khalkis (19km).

This road diverges NE. At the approach to (5km) *Rhítsona*, now a mere hamlet after its destruction as a reprisal during the German occupation, is the site of ancient *Mykalessos*, mentioned by Homer and bearing a pre-Greek name. Its existence ended in 414 BC when a body of Theban mercenaries hired by Athens fell upon the place on their way home and slew every living creature, including the animals and a school of boys just gathered for their morning lesson. The road crosses a tortuous pass (view) between Messapion and *Mt Galatsidheza*, then runs in the flat plain through the industrial mainland development to Khalkis.

We continue very straight with the low grey *Messapion Oros* on our right, rising at its N end to 1021m. The railway diverges towards Thebes. At 85km (53 miles) the flyover junction, **Thebes** (4km) is well seen to the left. On the W side of *Lithárés*, the next hill to the right, near the lake shore, excavations in 1971–72 uncovered a large E.H. habitation comparable with Zygouries. The N side of Mt Fagas crowds in on the left as we approach the **Boeotian Lakes**, reduced to two since the draining of Kopaïs. The road skirts the rocky SW shore of Lake Iliki (Motel; Restaurant), an irregular sheet of water ringed by low steep hills.

Lake Likéri, renamed *Ilikí* (Υλική), occupies a deep depression 50m below the level of the Kopaic plain. After the lake received the waters of Kopaïs its level rose to 80m and the lake spread, submerging a ruined city (? *Hyle*) on the W shore. In 1958, however, a new aqueduct was opened to supply water from Iliki to Marathon Lake. Iliki is 8km long and, at its widest, N–S point 3·6km broad. The ridge of *Mouriki* (83m), pierced by a canal, separates Iliki from *Lake Paralimni* (Παραλίμνη), which extends to the NE towards the sea. Oval in shape, 8km long and 1·5km broad, it is enclosed by Mt Ptoon, to the N and W, and Messapion, on the E. The ridge (95m) which separates it from the sea, is pierced by a tunnel which carries off its superfluous waters to the Euboean Channel near Anthedon. Both ridges are seared by ancient cuttings. A recession of Paralimni exposed two sets of remains investigated in 1965–66 and identified with the *Isos* of Strabo at the NE end and with the early site of Hyle at the SW end.

At 100km, to either side of the main road, over 600 tombs have been excavated in a large cemetery of the Archaic to Hellenistic periods.

102km (64 miles) *Akraífnion* (1301 inhab.; 1·5km right), formerly *Kardhítsa*, has readopted a variant name of the ancient ruined city occupying the ridge of Kriaria, 10 minutes SE of the village beyond a ravine. Here was found the inscription relating to Nero's proclamation of Greek freedom, now in Thebes museum. Vestiges of fortifications (4C BC) may be traced. The church of Ayios Yeóryios high above the village bears an inscription of 1311 naming Antoine le Flamenc, one of the survivors of the Battle of Kopaïs. The village is the starting-point for the Ptoion.

From Akraifnion we take the road towards Kokkinó and at its first bend continue straight ahead on a motorable track which soon divides. The right branch crosses the valley in 10 minutes towards a quarry, to the left of which on the flat hill of *Kastráki* is an ESPLANADE dedicated to the HERO PTOIOS. Two altars, two buildings, and the bases of 28 tripods suggest that the cult flourished during the two periods when Akraiphion enjoyed relative autonomy (c 550–480 and 456–446). Above are remains of a 4C *Temple* to an Earth goddess, mother of the hero. —The left track keeps to the N side of the valley (view back over the esplanade) and leads in ¾ hour to the ravine of *Perdhikovrísi* on the slope of Mt Ptoön (725m). Here, below the main summit, was the *Ptoion*, or *Sanctuary of Ptoan Apollo*, seat of an infallible oracle. The ruins were cleaned up in 1963–64 by the French School, but had already suffered greatly from the depredations of men and goats since their excavation in 1885. These yielded statues, bronzes, vases, and inscriptions, now divided between the museums of Athens and Thebes.

The site occupies three terraces below a spring. We pass to the W of the disused chapel of Ayia Paraskevi and come to the *Lower Terrace*, on which are the ruins of a large CISTERN, with seven compartments, which collected the waters of the upper spring and fed them by a conduit to an ablutionary building just below. Above the cistern extends the *Middle Terrace* mainly occupied by two long parallel stoas. The *Upper Terrace* bears a few courses of the foundations of a TEMPLE of the Doric order that had 6 columns by 13. It was rebuilt in the 3C BC over the ruins of a 7C edifice. A little higher up is a CAVERN, perhaps the abode of the oracle. The modern *Fountain* on the path above has taken the place of the ancient one at the foot of the sanctuary. From the S end of the site, fine view over the Lakes.

The main track mounts in 30 minutes to the *Convent of Pelayía*, visible on its plateau (546m).

The Kokkino road can be used as an approach to Larimna. The first col affords a fine view down to Gla (see below), which on foot can be reached from the Ptoion in 1 hour.

We cross the channelled effluents of Lake Copais, which extends to the left. On a clear day Mt Parnassos is seen ahead. The road sweeps right.—110km *Kástro*, formerly *Topólia*, rises on a hill to the left, which was once an island; here vestiges of polygonal walling and inscribed stones in the church mark the site of *Kopai*, the city mentioned in the 'Catalogue of Ships' which gave name to the 'Copaic'. To the right, on a low eminence also an island in antiquity, is the Mycenaean stronghold of ***Gla**, a remarkable fortress many times larger than Mycenae or Tiryns, whose very identification is uncertain. The approach road, signposted *Lárimna*, (passable for motors; 25-minute walk) leaves the highway immediately before a large petrol station and before the Kastro exit, and makes a complete circuit of the fortress. The site was partially explored by the French School in 1883. The four gates of the city were cleared in 1956–60 by the Greek Archaeological Service under Threpsiades and work has been continued since 1979 by Prof. Sp. Iakovidhis. They were damaged by fire when the city fell. The FORTIFICATIONS, 2·8km in length, run along the edge of a precipitous low cliff. The South or *Royal Gate* had double bronze-faced doors. Hence a road led directly to the vast walled '*Agora*', a space enclosed by long parallel buildings, probably storerooms. The best-preserved ruins are of a *Palace* on the highest eminence (72m above the plain) against the N wall. Usually described as a 'palace' since it appears to contain a megaron, storerooms, etc., the complex lacks the Classic Mycenaean palace form and its precise function remains problematic.

We continue N and climb through scrub-covered hills.—119km Turning for *Lárimna*.

A poor road descends via (1·5km) *Martínon* to (8km) **Lárimna** (Hotel D), a friendly village on an inlet of the N Euboean Gulf. On the farther shore of the inlet are the extensive works of the only nickel mine in Europe lying W of the 'Iron Curtain'. The village, built largely on ancient foundations, fronts two small bays. In the bay to the W (taverna; bathing) are considerable remains of the port installations of the 4C BC, when *Larymna* had the most easterly harbour of Locris. Two piers forming the harbour mouth (once guarded by a chain) can be seen underwater with the line of a long protective mole; the quay, of ashlar masonry, was guarded by towers.—At *Ayios Ioánnis Theólogos*, on the coast farther W (approach road at top of hill before Próskinas, see below), are the ruins of *Halai* comprising harbour and acropolis excavated by the Americans in the 1910's.

We descend through cultivated country (132km Toll Gate) to the Gulf of Atalandi. The little port of (141·5km) *Skála* is connected by steamer with Khalkis. It serves *Atalándi* (Hotel D), 5km to the W, the chief town of the eparchy of Lokris with 5456 inhabitants, connected also with the main road from Thebes to Lamia. It brews a popular German beer under licence.—145·5km *Livanátai*. On a spur to the W is a military satellite station.—Our road now runs in the cultivated strip between the hills of Lokris and the narrowing North Euboean Gulf (or Atalandi Channel).—150km *Arkitsa* (1km right; Hotels B, C, D) has a car-ferry service 7 times daily to Loutra Aidhipsou in Euboea.—154·5km *Ayios Nikólaos* (Hotel D) is on the shore. The landscape becomes grander as the *Knimís Mts* (937m) crowd in towards the sea.

Beyond the olive groves of Cape Kálamos is (166·5km) **Ayios Konstandínos** (Hotels A, C, D), a pleasant developing resort on a little bay near the site of *Daphnous*. Steamer services to the Northern Sporades, see Rte 43. On our right is the *Dhiavlos Knimidhos*, the narrow channel blocked with islets that separates the W tip of Euboea from Cape Knimís.

175km (109½ miles) **Kaména Voúrla** (Hotels A, B, C, D) is a fashionable thermal resort ringed by olive trees; its salt radioactive waters are recommended to sufferers from rheumatism and arthritis.—182km *Kainoúrion*. The site of ancient *Thronion* is on a hill to the left. For a brief moment distant Parnassos can be glimpsed again behind the foothills of Kallidhromon. We cross several broad torrents.—187km Modern *Skárfia*, with an earth satellite station, lies to the right; the site of ancient Skarpheia is on a hill (left) just before we by-pass (190km) *Mólos*.—194km *Ayía Triás* (2·5km right) lies in the flat alluvial marsh that borders the Maliakos Kolpos; across the gulf are seen the distant slopes of Mt Othrys.—At 199.5km a good gravel road winds back E to Mendhenítsa (9·5km).

Mendenitsa, the site of ancient *Pharygai*, is occupied by the *Castle of Bodonitsa*,

seat of the Frankish marquisate of the Pallavicini in 1205–1410. It survived the
Catalan invasion by placing itself under Venetian protection in 1335, but fell to
the Turks after a siege. The fortress has a double enceinte, the lower enclosure on
ancient foundations; the upper part, better preserved, is approached by a
barbican.

We approach the famous PASS OF THERMOPYLAE (Στενά τῶν
Θερμοπυλῶν) between the steep N side of Kallídromon and the sea.
The pass will always be remembered for the devotion of Leonidas and
his Spartans during the Persian invasion of 480 BC. The defile, which
is just under 6·5km long, ran between precipitous mountains and the
sea. It was extremely narrow at both ends, but widened in the middle,
where were the hot springs that gave the pass its name. It was in
antiquity, for a force of any size, the only practical means of communication on land between Thessaly and S Greece. To understand the
ancient topography, we must imagine the sea on our right hand.
Today the silt brought down by the Spercheios has advanced the
coast-line by nearly 5km, though the plain is still marshy. The modern
road coincides with the ancient road for most of the way, except at the
critical narrows where it runs N of the old course; here we must visualise the road nearer to the cliffs with the sea extending to within a few
metres of their foot.

History. By the time Xerxes was bridging the Hellespont for his invasion forces,
the confederacy gathered at the Isthmus of Corinth was planning a combined
forward defence of Greece. The Pass of Tempe, in N Thessaly, was considered
but found impracticable because it could be turned. The next point of defence
was Thermopylae, which it was decided to hold. Like Xerxes' invasion, the defence was to be a combined operation on land and sea. While the small Greek
army occupied Thermopylae, the Greek fleet lay off *Artemision* (Euboea) to
prevent the Persian fleet sailing down the Euboean Gulf in support of their army.
Meanwhile the Persian army had reached Trachis and the Persian fleet the coast
of Magnesia, at which point the weather came to the aid of the Greek naval
forces.

The Greek army was under the command of Leonidas, king of Sparta. He
repaired the Wall of the Phocians and took up his main position behind it, in the
centre of the pass. The total Greek force was about 7300 men. The Persians are
credited by modern historians with 300,000 men, though Herodotus adduces a
grand total of more than 5¾ million. The Persians made several unsuccessful
and costly assaults on the improvised fortifications of the Greeks. Xerxes had
almost given up hope of forcing a passage when the Malian Ephialtes indicated a
means of turning the Greek position by a mountain path called the *Anopaia*.
Leonidas had posted the 1000 Phocians along it so that there could be no surprise
from that quarter. However, Xerxes determined to use the path. Led by Ephialtes, Hydarnes, commander of the Persian 'Immortals', set out in the evening with
2000 men and marched through the night. The next morning they routed the
Phocians and reached the E end of the pass, where they took the defenders in the
rear.

Leonidas, foreseeing that he would be crushed between two attacks, had already ordered the withdrawal of the main force, retaining only his 300 Spartans,
the 700 Thespians, and the 400 Thebans, who 'were kept back as hostages, very
much against their will' since the Thebans were suspected of medising; they
deserted in a body to the Persians as soon as opportunity offered. The course of
the desperate battle, the death of Leonidas, and the famous 'last stand' of the
Spartans on the hillock of Kolonis is told in detail by Herodotus (Bk VII), and
visitors wishing to traverse the ground in detail cannot do better than follow his
vivid and dramatic account.

All save two of the 300 Spartans were killed. One atoned for his survival by his
valour at Plataia; the other hanged himself on his return to Sparta. The dead were
buried where they fell and later commemorated by monuments bearing two
celebrated epigrams. On the hillock a stone lion, which survived to the time of
Tiberius, was erected to Leonidas. Forty years after the battle his body was taken
to Sparta.

Thermopylae was seized by Leosthenes in the Lamian War. The tactics of
Xerxes were copied by all who wished to force the Pass of Thermopylae. In 279
Brennus, at the head of his Gauls, finding himself checked by the troops of

Kallipos, used the Anopaia path to turn the Greek position; but this time the Greeks were able to escape to their ships. In 191 Antiochus III,King of Syria, with 10,000 men, tried to deny the pass to the 40,000 legionaries of the Roman consul Manlius Acilius Glabrio and his legate M. Porcius Cato. Antiochus raised a double wall, with trenches, across the defile, and built forts on the slopes of Mt Kallídromos. Cato succeeded in carrying the forts and in taking the position in the rear, while Glabrio made a frontal attack. Antiochus escaped with only 500 men.

In AD 395 Alaric entered the pass without opposition. In the 6C 'the straits of Thermopylae, which seemed to protect, but which had so often betrayed, the safety of Greece, were diligently strengthened by the labours of Justinian' (Gibbon, *Decline and Fall*). In 1204 Boniface of Montferrat came through unopposed. Retreating British troops began to take up position here in 1941, but evacuation was ordered before the Germans reached the area.

201km **Thermopylae** (Hotels C, D), or *Thermopíles*. Here in 1955 King Paul inaugurated the *Memorial* to Leonidas and the Three Hundred, a white marble monument, surmounted by a striking bronze figure of Leonidas. The base bears reliefs of scenes from the battle and records the famous epigrams. It was erected at American expense. On the opposite side of the road is the *Grave Mound*. On the left, just beyond, are hot springs, with a hot waterfall, a frequented hydropathic establishment and a restaurant. The waters (43°C), which are abundant, are impregnated with carbonic acid, lime, salt, and sulphur, and are said to be efficacious in the cure of sciatica, stiff joints, and glandular complaints. At the W exit to the defile a hill is probably the site of *Anthela* where the meetings of the Amphictyonic League were held in autumn (in spring they met at Delphi).

We cross the Spercheios. The *Alamánas Bridge* here was heroically defended on 5 May 1821 by Athanasios Diakos and the Bp of Salona, with 700 Greeks, agains a superior force led by Omer Vrioni and Mehmet Pasha (monument with mosaic). To the left the solemn mass of Mt Oiti is well seen, and, farther behind us, the zigzag descent from Kallidromon of the road from Amfissa and Livadhia (Rte 44A). Looking up the Specheios valley we see the imposing mass of Mt Timfristos.

215km (133½ miles) **Lamia**, see Rte 47. The National Highway turns E, the Lamia by-pass continues straight on; we turn left entering the city from the E side.

45   From (Athens) Levádhia to Delphi and Amfissa

ROAD, 189km (117½ miles). To *Thebes*, see Rte 41, thence to (119km) *Levádhia*, see Rte 44A.—141km (88 miles) Turning for **Osios Loukás** (14km).—156km (97 miles) *Arákhova*.—166km (103 miles) **Delphí** (Rte 46).—189km **Amfissa**. Extensive widening and realignment has been effected.

From Athens to (74km) **Thebes**, see Rte 41; thence to (119km) **Levadhia**, see Rte 44A. The road continues W, winding up the N side of the narrowing valley. The scenery becomes increasingly grand as Parnassos dominates the whole region, though its summit is often hidden in cloud or capped with snow. Korakólithos is now avoided by a tunnel. The road descends before climbing through a defile.—At (141·5km) *Schíste*, or *'Tríodhos'* (424m), the meeting-place in antiquity of three roads, from Daulis, Delphi, and Ambrossos, Sophocles laid the scene of Oedipus' murder of his father (Oedipus Tyrranus). Lying in a setting of lonely grandeur between the heights of Bardana and Kastri, it is still a parting of the ways, where diverge roads important alike to industry and tourism.

The branch road leads S in an open valley to **Dhístomo** (Δίστομο; 4km; Hotels D), scene of a Nazi reprisal massacre on 10 June 1944, when 218 villagers were killed (plaques on church façade). In commemoration a community in Atlantic City adopted the name Distomo. The little town occupies the site of *Ambrossos*, few traces of which are visible. Parts of the wall and Classical and Hellenistic graves

OSIOS LOUKAS

Crypt
at smaller scale

0   5 metres

have been located. Most travellers will here turn left to Osios Loukás (comp. below). Ahead the road zigzags down a further 10km to *Áspra Spítia*, on the Bay of Andíkira, a hideous dormitory town built by Aluminium of Greece, whose works were erected in 1962–65 at Ayios Theodhoros on the E side of the bay. Here the Roman and Byzantine remains of *Medeon* were excavated by the French School and Greek Archaeological Service in 1962–63 before they were built over. A huge Mycenaean acropolis was also explored and 250 tombs dug. At the W end of the bay, 2·5km farther on, is *Andíkira* on the site of the ancient Phocian town of *Antikyra*. Continuation to *Itéa*, see Rte 55C.

Osios Loukás, the *Monastery of St. Luke Stíris*, lies 8km E of Dhístomo by an asphalt road which passes through *Stíris* and then through almond groves. The monastery, one of the most interesting ecclesiastical groups in Greece, stands on the brow of a peaked hill facing S and commanding wonderful views of Helikon and the surrounding country. Though there are still monks, the place is more ancient monument than retreat, and is equipped with a small Hotel and Restaurant (B; frequently closed).

The monastery is dedicated not to the Evangelist, but to a local beatified hermit, the Blessed Luke (Ósios Loukás) of Stíri. His family fled from Aegina on its invasion by the Saracens and Luke was born in 'Kastorion' (probably Kastri, i.e. Delphi). After many adventures the hermit came to Stíri, where in 953 he died. Already between 941 and 944 a church had been founded, dedicated to St. Barbara, but tradition attributes the foundation of the monastery to Romanos II in 961 in recognition of the fulfilment of Luke's prophecy that Crete should be liberated by an emperor named Romanos. Both the existing churches have suffered from earthquakes, and their latest restoration in 1958–60 has reversed former ideas of their chronological sequence. The mosaics are incomplete and parts have been reset, but they remain important and beautiful.

From the flagged terrace we see the rebuilt *Trapeza*, or Refectory, above which rises the S flank of the *Katholikon set off by the flowing line of its dome. Dedicated to St. Luke and dating from c 1020, it is comparable with the church at Daphni (Rte 16) and with it coupled by Krautheimer as 'probably the most beautiful representatives of the Greek-cross-octagon plan'. The foundation walls are of stone with stone and brick above. Columns of cipollino, Hymettian marble, and bigio antico divide the windows, each of which is surmounted by a large impost bearing a Greek cross. The lower parts of the windows are filled with sculptured marble. An inscription in the outer wall records the dedication by Xenocrates and Eumaridas of a *Fountain*; the slab probably came from ancient Stiris.

INTERIOR. The W door opens into a *Narthex*, which has a vaulted ceiling and is decorated with *Mosaics on a gold ground. Upon the arches are depicted the Apostles; in the lunettes, the Washing of Feet, the Crucifixion, and the Resurrection. On the ceiling are medallions of the Baptist, the Virgin with angels, and saints. On the pavement are slabs of verde antico.

The central domed *Nave* is approached through a vestibule, which, with the two transepts and the Bema, form in plan the arms of the cross enclosed within the external rectangle of the walls. The angles are filled in by twelve groin-vaulted or domed bays, surmounted by a second storey of equal height to form a *Matroneum*; this is frescoed (interesting graffiti of medieval ships) and carried over the transepts by open galleries. The piers have polychrome marble revetments. The *Bema* and its flanking chapels are each closed off by a templon, that in the centre forming the ikonostasis, those to left and right open colonnades. There are ikons by Mikhail Damaskinos (16C).

The interplay of light and shade produced by the multiplicity of arches gives an air of solemn mystery, enhanced by reflected light from gold MOSAICS. Those in the dome were damaged in 1659 by earthquake and replaced by paintings. The mosaics are most complete in the vestibule and its aisles, and in the N transept (though these are medallions with busts of saints only). On the squinches supporting the dome mosaics of the Nativity, Presentation and Baptism. In the *Apse*, mosaics of the Virgin and Child; above, in the vault, Descent of the Holy Ghost. The Katholikon also retains frescoes from the early 11C in the NE, NW and SW chapels, and in the gallery above the narthex.

The *Crypt*, once taken to be the original church of St. Barbara since it contains St. Luke's tomb, is supported by square bevelled columns with imposts. It is lavishly decorated with 11C frescoes illustrating the Passion of Christ. The groin vaults are divided into panels containing busts of saints and monks in medallions. Beneath is a rock-cut refuge with its own water supply.

The smaller church of the **Theotókos** forms part of the N transept of the Katholikon. The discovery of the fresco of Joshua as a Holy Warrior (end of 10C/early 11C) on the outer face of the N wall of the narthex, now seen in the interior of the later Katholikon, has recently proved it be the earlier of the two churches; it had previously been assigned to c 1040, but may be the church of Romanos' foundation. The exterior has elaborate cloisonné masonry decorated with courses of deep dog-tooth brickwork and a cufic frieze. The *Drum*, architecturally clumsy, has marble panels worked in great sculptural detail, recalling Islamic work. The church is preceded by an *Exonarthex* (16C), having a triple portico surmounted by a loggia. The interior beyond the narthex is a plain cross-in-square, the dome being borne on four large granite columns with Byzantine capitals and imposts. The two columns in the narthex have Corinthian capitals. The floor mosaic is notable.

The Delphi road passes through the *Stenopos Zemenous*, the upper ravine of the Platania, between the precipices of Parnassos and the bare slopes of Xerovoúni (1554m).—146·5km *Khan of Ziméno* (700m), with a spring at the foot of a large oriental plane tree.—We reach the *Khan of St. Athanasius*, with a chapel by a spring, at the head of the pass (766m). At a bend in the road, which winds steeply upwards, there is a good view of Arákhova, perched on a rocky spur of Parnassos above the gorge of the Pleistos. We thread a short tunnel.

157km (97 miles) **Arákhova** (Αράχωβα; 942m; Hotels B, D), a town of 2793 inhab., is noted for its rugs, wines and embroideries, and for the copious streams of water running down its narrow streets. The houses rise in terraces on the mountain spur; at the top is the church of *St. George*. The town may occupy the site of a small classical place called *Petrites*, which succeeded the two prehistoric towns of *Anemoreia* and *Kyparissos*. Vestiges of these may be seen below and above the Katoptirio rock. Arákhova is the best starting-point for the climb of *Parnassos*.

Parnassos is a complex mountain mass, with two main peaks: hence Ovid's *biceps Parnassus*. The higher summit is called *Lyakoura* or *Lykeri* ('Wolf Mountain', anciently *Lykorea*; 2457m) and the lower *Gerontovrachos* ('Old Man's Rock'; 2435m). To the Greeks Parnassos was sacred to Dionysos and the Maenads; it was the Latin poets who made it, with the Castalian Fountain, the home of Apollo and the Muses. During the flood, Deucalion's ship rested on the top of Parnassos.

The Ski Centre at *Fterólakkas* (c 1500m; car park) is reached by road (c 26km) from Arakhova via (9km) *Kalívia* (Hotel B). The centre is open for skiing in December–April (Restaurant), when chair-lifts operate in two stages to c 180m where there are ski slopes (ski-lifts). Higher slopes with lifts and a restaurant at *Kelaria* were planned for 1980. The lower centre functions as an excursion resort in summer. July and August are the only practicable months for climbing to the summit when the paths are free of snow. Due to recent changes in road and accommodation facilities, it is desirable to seek up-to-date information as to the most suitable approach. With a car and guide (or precise directions) it is possible to drive to within 45 minutes' walk of the summit via the access roads to the skiing installations. The traditional method of making the proper climb is to spend a night at the Hellenic Alpine Club refuge (*Katafíyion Sarantári*; 1890m, 28 beds); a robust vehicle can get to within 15-minutes' walk of the refuge. The guide lives in Arákhova, where contact should be made through the Alpine Club (preferably from Athens as the Arákhova guide can be hard to find). Only food need to taken to the Refuge. The climb is usually made before dawn and takes about 5 hours there and back, though fell-walkers would do it in less. It is practicable for a fit climber, who does not mind the heat, to do the whole expedition in the day from Kalivia, ignoring the refuge.

The * View at sunrise, before the mists gather, exceeds in grandeur and interest almost every other prospect in the world. Little by little the map of Greece unfolds. To the NW are Timphristos and Pindos; to the N, beyond Kallidromon, are Oite, Othrys, Pelion, Ossa and Olympos. To the NE we see the Atlante Channel and the island of Euboea, with the Gulfs of Lamia and Volo, and the Northern Sporades beyond. In the far distance the grey mass of Mount Athos rises from the sea. To the SE are Helikon, Attica and the Cyclades; to the S the Gulf of Corinth, with its isthmus; beyond, the Peloponnesian mountains; Kyllene, Maenalon, Aroania, Erymanthos, and Panachaikon, with Taiyetos in the background. To the W, beyond the vale of Amphissa, the view is masked by the mountains of Locris and Doris, two of which, Kiona (2500m) and Vardousi (2495m) are higher than Parnassos.

The road now descends gradually, skirting the cliffs of Parnassos on the right and keeping high above the Pleistos, whose ravine is hidden by vineyards. Egyptian vultures may be seen. We pass through one of the ancient cemeteries of Delphi. To the left of the road (1200m before the Castalia spring) are the remains of a square tower, probably of the 4–3C BC and one of a chain controlling the Livadhia–Delphi road. It was subsequently used as a burial place in the Roman period. On the right are the Phaedriades, the precipices that shut in Delphi on the W. We now pass through the centre of **Ancient Delphi** (Rte 46). On the left is Marmaria, with the Sanctuary of Athena. The road bears right and then makes a sharp bend to the left at the Castalian Fountain. To the S is the Papadhia Glen, through which the overflow from the spring flows into the Pleistos. Passing on the right the Pythian Sanctuary and the Museum, we sweep round to the right to enter the modern village.

166km (103 miles) **DELPHI** (Δελφοί; Hotels A, B, C, D), in modern Greek *Dhelfí*, at one time called *New Kastri*, is a modern village (2426 inhab.) built since 1892, about 1km W of the former village, *Kastri*, which stood on the ruins of ancient Delphi. By a special convention with the Greek Government in April 1891, the French School obtained a ten-years' lease of the ancient site, bought out the inhabitants, and arranged for their transplantation to the new village, which was supplied with water by means of an aqueduct from the Fountain of Kassotis. In Delphi is an annexe of the School of Fine Arts in Athens, where artists of all nationalities may stay, and here in 1965 was founded an International Cultural Centre sponsored by the Council of Europe.

From Delphi the road descends steeply with many acute bends.—175.5km Khrissó (now just off the road) is the modern equivalent of *Krisa* without the importance of the ancient town. Krisa gave its name to the Krisaean Gulf (Krissaíos Kolpos), on which Itéa stands, and to the plain that extends for c 18km from the head of the bay to Amfissa. The plain, which is divided into two parts by the intrusion above Itéa from W and from E of two mountain spurs, is exceptionally fertile in the N section (the Krisaean Plain proper as opposed to the Kirrhaean Plain), where grows the largest plantation of olives in Greece.—At 178·5km the road divides; to the left the Navpaktos road descends in

4m through the olives to *Itéa* (see Rte 55C), our road drives straight for Amfissa.

189km **Amfissa** (Αμφισσα; 180m; Hotels C, D), the chief town (7156 inhab.) of the eparchy of Parnassidhos and the seat of a bishop, is better remembered by its medieval name of *Salona*. It is well situated at the NW end of the Krisaean Plain on the first slopes of the Locrian mountains. In antiquity *Amphissa* was the capital of Ozolian Locris. The ruined Frankish **Castle**, or FROURION (1205), has three enceintes, partly built on the walls of the ancient *Acropolis*. Antique survivals include the remains of walls of Classical quadrangular and Hellenistic polygonal masonry, some reused, and of two towers. A Roman building on the E slopes was investigated in 1973. It had a large apsidal room with niches in its well-preserved walls. That and another room had fine mosaic floors. There are also a cistern of which the lower part is ancient and the upper part medieval, two ruined churches, and a circular keep. At the S foot of the castle are a fine arcaded Turkish fountain and the 12C church of the *Sotiros*. Mosaic floors from Roman buildings have been found in various parts of the town. On a site to the N of the cathedral is a baptistery of the late 4C BC, with marble facings and fine mosaics.

Amphissa was denounced by Aeschines in 339 BC for violating the Krisaean Plain. The Amphictyonic League appealed to Philip of Macedon, who, making good use of the opportunity, invaded Greece and destroyed Amphissa. The city was rebuilt and furnished 400 hoplites in the war against Brennus in 279 BC. Destroyed again, by the Bulgars in the Middle Ages, it was rebuilt by the Franks, who renamed it *Salona*. The Picard Autremencourt barons of Salona were feudatories of the kings of Salonika. In 1311 the Catalan Roger Deslaurs took the title of count, which passed in 1335 to Alfonso Frederichs of Aragon. In 1394 Salona fell to the Turks.

FROM AMFISSA TO LAMIA, 73km (bus), magnificent asphalt road with sharp winding ascent and descent of the *Pass of Graviá* (870m), between Gkiona and Parnassos, celebrated for its heroic defence in 1821 by Odysseus Androutsos with 180 Greeks, against 3000 Turks.—33km *Graviá*, and thence via (41km) Brallos to Lamia, see Rte 44A.

To *Návpaktos* and *Mesolongi*, see Rte 55.

46 Delphi

Approaches and hotels, see Rte 45. A hurried visit to the site can be made in 3 hours; a reasonably thorough exploration requires at least twice as long. The hilly terrain is tiring though there are good paths. Changes of temperature are frequent and often violent; even in high summer a light woollen garment or wind-cheater is an advisable precaution.

* *DELPHI (Δελφοί; Dhelfí), transformed by the excavators' skill since it disappointed Byron and Barry, is by common consent the most spectacularly beautiful ancient site in Greece and the one which, even to the uninitiated, most vividly evokes the Classical past. In antiquity Delphi was regarded as the centre of the world (ὀμφαλὸς γῆς) and to this and to its oracle the place owed its prestige, which extended far beyond the Greek world. The sacred precinct enjoys a superb situation below the S slopes of Parnassos within the angle formed by the twin *Phaedriades* ('Shining Rocks', so called because they reflect the light), which constitute a tremendous precipice 250–300m high. The W rock is called *Rhodini* ('Roseate'), anciently Nauplia; from the E rock, *Phleboukos* ('Flamboyant', anciently Hyampeia) the Delphians

used to hurl those found guilty of sacrilege. The cleft between the two rocks, hollowed out by cascades from the upper plateau is continued on the S by a line of ravines, by which the waters flow into the Pleistos. To the W the rocky spur at Mt Ay. Ilias (700m) completes the theatre-like setting. On the S Delphi is bounded by the ravine of the river Pleistos, in which the pipeline from Lidhoriki is conspicuous; beyond rises the barrier of Mt Kirphys. The site is in a seismic area. On several occasions earthquakes and storms have caused the fall of great fragments of rock from Parnassos and serious landslips endangering the safety of the monuments. The *View down the sacred plain to Itéa, with its myriad olive-trees, is not the least of the delights which make Delphi the goal of countless excursions every day of the year.

History. The natural features of the site, in the 'centre of the world', with its springs, exhalations and crevasses, in a theatre of forbidding precipices, have helped to give Delphi its mysterious and sacred character. In the beginning it was sacred to Mother Earth and Poseidon, and was called *Pytho*, the name by which it is known in Homer (Iliad IX, 405; Odyssey VII, 80). It had an oracle where the Pythia officiated near the cave of the serpent Python, son of Mother Earth. At an early date Delphi was colonised by settlers from *Lykorea*, which was situated on the plateau above it, but it was in the territory of *Krisa* and was therefore partially subject to that city.

The importation into Krisa from Crete of the cult of Apollo Delphinios, an island deity worshipped in the form of a dolphin, led to the introduction of his cult at Pytho, which then changed its name to *Delphoi*. Henceforward the holy place became the Sanctuary of Pythian Apollo. Later other gods were associated with the sanctuary; these included Dionysos and Athena Pronoia. The Pythian Games, one of the four great national Greek festivals, were instituted in honour of Apollo, Artemis and Leto, and at first were held every eight years (see below). The fame of the oracle, whose efficacy was fostered by its priestly administrators, spread all over the ancient world, and the festival attracted competitors and visitors from far and wide.

After the Dorian Invasion (c 1100 BC) the sanctuary beccame a centre of an association called the *Amphictyonic League*. This was by false etymology supposed to have been founded by Amphictyon, but really only means the league of the dwellers round a particular locality. The league was composed of twelve tribes, each of which contained various city-states, large and small, all of which had equal status within it, whatever their importance outside. Both Athens and Sparta belonged to the league, but they had in theory no more authority in it than some insignificant states that happened to be members. This rudimentary United Nations included Thessalians, Dorians, Ionians and Achaeans.

The city of Krisa levied dues on all pilgrims to Delphi, many of whom had to disembark at its port of Kirrha. Early in the 6C the pilgrims complained of extortionate charges, and the Delphians appealed to the Amphictyonic League. The league, urged on, it is said, by Athens, declared war against the Krisaeans. The ensuing conflict was known as the *First Sacred War* (c 595–586 BC). Invaluable assistance was given by Kleisthenes of Sikyon, and Krisa, with its port Kirrha, was destroyed. Its territory was confiscated. The Amphictyonic League took the Temple of Apollo at Delphi under its wing, and the state of Delphi was made autonomous. The Krisaean Plain was dedicated to the god and no one was allowed to till it or use it for grazing on pain of excommunication. About this time the Pythian Games were reorganised and, from 582 BC, like the Olympic Games, were held every four years (see below). Kleisthenes won the first chariot race. He later instituted Pythian Games at Sikyon. Now followed a period of great prosperity. In this century the Treasuries of Corinth, Sikyon and Klazomenai were dedicated. Croesus, last king of Lydia (560–546 BC), was a great benefactor of the sanctuary—to no avail in his case. Amasis, king of Egypt, was another. These world-wide benefactions show that, while Olympia may be regarded as an expression of Greek nationalism, the prestige of Delphi rested on its international character. In 548 BC the temple was destroyed by fire. The contract to rebuild was let to the exiled Athenian Alkmaeonidae, who gained a reputation for munificence by facing the new temple with Parian marble instead of the common stone prescribed in the specifications (Hdt. V, 62).

In the Persian Wars the oracle was inclined to medise. Nevertheless, in 480 BC, Xerxes sent a detachment to plunder the temple. The soldiers had reached the Sanctuary of Athena Pronoia when thunder was heard and two huge crags rolled down and crushed many of them to death (Hdt. VIII, 35–39; comp. below). After the Persian defeats, trophies, statues, and new treasuries were set up in celebration. Delphi now became involved, despite the prudence of its administrators, in the rivalries of the leading Greek states. The oracle lost much of its prestige because of charges of partiality and corruption; but offerings continued to arrive from the conflicting states and from foreign rulers such as the tyrants of Syracuse.

In 448 BC occurred the *Second Sacred War*, in which the Lacedaemonians wrested the temple from the Phocians and handed it over to the Delphians. As soon as they had withdrawn the Athenians recovered the temple and handed it back to the Phocians. The Delphians soon got it back and their possession of it was confirmed in the Peace of Nicias (421 BC). In 373 the temple was again destroyed, this time by an earthquake, and it was again rebuilt, by international cooperation. In 356 the Phocians, who had, on the accusation of Thebes, been fined by the Amphictyonic League for having cultivated a portion of the Krisaean Plain, retaliated by seizing Delphi with all its treasures. This precipitated the *Third Sacred War*, during which Phocis temporarily became one of the leading powers in Greece. In 346, when the conflict had been determined by the intervention of Philip of Macedon, the temple was restored to the custody of the Amphictyonic League. In the same year Philip, who had replaced Phocis in the league, was elected president of the Pythian Games. The *Fourth Sacred War* broke out in 339. This time it was the Amphissans who were accused of cultivating the Krisaean Plain. The Amphictyons appealed to Philip, who invaded Greece in 338, won the battle of Chaironeia, and destroyed the city of Amphissa.

The Aetolians succeeded the Macedonians as masters of Delphi. In 279 BC Brennus and his Gauls advanced to the attack of Delphi by the same route as the Persians in 480. They were repulsed in the same supernatural manner. Their retreat was disastrous. Some years later their discomfiture was celebrated in the festival of the *Soteria*, organised by the Aetolians. In 189 the Aetolians were driven out by the Romans. Under Roman sway the oracle lost former prestige, as the Romans did not take its utterances very seriously. The precinct was plundered by Sulla in 86 BC; by the way of compensation, he gave the Delphians half the territory of dismembered Thebes.

In the imperial era the fortunes of the oracle depended on the whim of the ruler for the time being. Augustus reorganised the Amphictyonic League. Nero seized over 500 bronze statues in a fit of rage at the oracle's condemnation of his matricide. Domitian effected some restoration. Pliny counted more than 3000 statues and Pausanias found Delphi still rich in works of art. It was restored by Hadrian and the Antonines to much of its former splendour. Constantine carried off several of its treasures to adorn his new capital. The oracle was consulted by Julian, but was finally abolished by Theodosius about AD 385. Long before its extinction its authority, impaired by its strong Doric prejudices, had sadly diminished. Towards the end its utterances were almost entirely concerned with private and domestic matters such as marriages, loans, voyages and sales.— Cyriac of Ancona copied inscriptions here in March 1436, after which the site appears to have been ignored until rediscovered by Wheler and Spon in 1676. Flaubert records finding in 1851 Byron's name on a column of the now-destroyed Panayia.

The Oracle. The Delphic oracle was the most famous in Greece. Those who wished to consult it first sacrificed a sheep, goat, boar or other animal, after which (if the omens were favourable) they went into the room adjoining the *Adyton*. There they awaited their turn, which was determined by lot, unless they had received from the Delphians the *Promanteia*, or prior right of consultation. No women were admitted. They handed in questions written on leaden tablets, many of which have been discovered. The *Pythia*, or priestess who delivered the oracle, was a peasant woman over 50 years old. At the height of the oracle's fame there were three of them. After purifying herself in the Castalian Fountain and drinking of the water of the Kassotis, and munching a laurel leaf, she took her seat upon the tripod, which was placed over the chasm in the Adyton. Intoxicated by the exhalations from the chasm, she uttered incoherent sounds, which were interpreted in hexameter verse by a poet in waiting. The interpretation, which was always obscure and frequently equivocal, was handed over to the enquirer, who not seldom returned more mystified than he had come. Even Croesus, the great benefactor of Delphi, was cruelly misled by the oracle on the eve of his war with Persia. All the same, according to Strabo, 'of all oracles in the world it had the reputation of being the most truthful'.

Festivals. The PYTHIAN GAMES were instituted to commemorate Apollo's slaying of the serpent Python. At first they were held every eight years. Originally they were little more than a religious ceremony taking the form of a hymn in honour of Apollo. After the Amphictyonic League had taken over the control of the temple in the early 6C (see above), the games were reorganised and held every four years. The first Pythiad of the new regime was in 582 BC. The festival began with sacrifices and a sacred play about the fight of Apollo and the serpent. There followed, in the theatre, musical contests of cithara, flute and song, and hymns of praise in honour of Apollo; later tragedies and comedies were added. Then came athletic competitions in the stadium, and finally chariot races in the Krisaean Plain, the prize for which was a laurel wreath. The Greek states sent *Theoriae*, or sacred embassies, to the games, who were loaded with gifts to the god. The Athenians also sent on occasions not connected with the games a special embassy or *Pythiad* for the purpose of holding a separate festival, whic'ı included athletic games and plays. After the repulse of the Gauls in 278 BC a special festival called the *Soteria* was held under the aegis of the Aetolians (see above). In the imperial era the interval between the games reverted to eight years.

Excavations. The French architect Laurent examined the site in 1838. He was followed in 1840 by Ottfried Müller, who succumbed to a fever contracted here, and E. Curtius. In 1860–61 Foucart and others did some preliminary work. In 1892 an exhaustive survey was begun by the French School, under the leadership of Th. Homolle. The work went on at high pressure until 1903. Since then it has slowed down but not ceased. The figures on the plan correspond with those of the French excavation reports.

Following Pausanias (X, 8, 6 ff.), we begin our visit with the attractive spot called **Marmaria**, nearly 1·5km to the E of the Sanctuary. We descend to it from the Arakhova road by a pathway. Marmaria was the **Sanctuary of Athena**, whom the Delphians worshipped as *Athena Pronaia* (Guardian of the Temple), or, by a play upon words, as *Athena Pronoia* (Providence). Some of the finest sculptures found here are in the Museum. The precinct is roughly rectangular, with the entrance on the E.

An upper terrace N of the gate supported the small *Precinct of Phylakos*; one of its two buildings was the *Heroön of Phylakos*, who, with Autonoos, routed the Persians in 480 BC. The other may have been dedicated to the saviours of Delphi at the time of the onset of the Gauls in 279 BC. An inscription on the retaining wall locates the *Altars of Athena Hygieia* and of *Eileithyia*.

We pass through the gateway, noticing the huge lintel on the ground, into the oldest part of the sanctuary, dedicated to *Athena Hygieia* and *Zosteria*, where the excavations of 1922 revealed the existence of a Mycenaean settlement (finds in the Museum). We immediately come upon the remains of the OLD TEMPLE OF ATHENA PRONOIA. This was a Doric peripteral hexastyle in tufa, built at the beginning of the 5C BC on the site of a still older edifice (7C) from which capitals survive. The temple was damaged in 480 BC by the fall of rocks that routed the Persians and its ruin was completed by the earthquake of 373. Fifteen columns and the stylobate had been brought to light when in 1905 another landslip demolished all but three of the columns.

The centre of the precinct is occupied by three buildings. A *Doric Treasury* (490–460 BC), of marble, stood on a lime-stone foundation. The Aeolian *Treasury of Massalia*, in antis, built c 530 BC in Parian marble, was of remarkably fine workmanship, recalling the Treasury of the Siphnians. The third building, a Pentelic marble *Tholos, or Rotunda, of the early 4C, was one of the finest in Delphi. Its dedication and purpose are unknown. It has a circular peristyle of 20 slender Doric columns on a platform of three steps. Three columns with their entablature were re-erected in 1938; the cornice and metopes have been restored in replica from the best surviving fragments. The entr-

ance to the circular cella was on the S. The paved interior was decorated with Corinthian half-columns. To the W of the Tholos c 360 BC
rose the NEW TEMPLE OF ATHENA PRONOIA, a severe prostyle edifice
having a portico of six columns of the Doric order. Beyond this temple,
and partly built over by it, is an earlier rectangular building (5C),
probably a priest's dwelling.

To the NW of Marmaria are the remains of the **Gymnasium**, originally dating from the 4C BC, but rebuilt by the Romans. The slope of
the ground necessitated its arrangement on different levels. On the
upper level was the *Xystos*, or covered colonnade, where the athletes
practised in bad weather, with a parallel track in the open air. The
lower terrace was occupied by the *Palaestra*. This is divided into the
Palaestra proper, a court 12m square surrounded by a colonnade on all
four sides, and the *Baths*, comprising a circular (cold) bath 9m in diameter and 1·8m deep, and, in the retaining wall at the back, a series of
douche baths.—The hot baths, N of the court, are a Roman addition. A
column hereabouts bears the names of Byron and Hobhouse.

We return to the road. A short way farther up, on a sharp bend,
opens the ravine separating the two Phaedriades. Here is the celebrated **Castalian Fountain** (538m). By this spring Apollo planted a
cutting of the laurel he had brought from Tempe (see Rte 57). The base
of a statue of Ge, the goddess of Earth, shows that the spring was an
early place of cult-worship.

In this spring all who came to Delphi for any religious object whatever had to
purify themselves. The bathing of the hair seems to have been the principal part
of the ceremony and is one attributed to the god himself. Murderers, however,
bathed the whole body. The fancy which ascribed poetic inspiration to the waters
of the Castalian fountain was an invention of the Roman poets. The fountain as
we see it today is of Roman or Hellenistic date.

The spring was ornamented with a façade of seven marble pilasters. The four
niches seen therein doubtless were for votive offerings; in the largest of them is a
column drum once used as the altar of a Byzantine chapel. The water was col-
ected in a long narrow reservoir (9m × 1m) which fed seven jets (holes still
visible). These jets fell into a rectangular court, 9m × 3m, reached by rock-hewn
steps. The overflow from the fountain joins the water of the gorge dividing the
Phaedriades, which plunges into a deep rocky glen, to join the Pleistos flowing in
the Delphic valley far below. An Archaic square fountain house, discovered in
1957, lies nearer the road.

A wide, paved path leads to the main entrance of the PYTHIAN SANC-
TUARY AND MUSEUM. (Lavatories at top of first flight of entrance
steps.)

The **PYTHIAN SANCTUARY**, or *Temenos of Apollo*, like the much
more extensive Altis at Olympia, was an enclosure containing many
monuments besides the temple. This sacred precinct was situated on
the rising ground above the town. It was surrounded by the usual
Peribolos, or enclosure wall, with several gates. Its shape is that of an
irregular quadrangle or trapezium, and it measures about 183m ×
128m. The S wall is built of squared blocks and dates from the 5C BC;
the N and N walls, which are polygonal, from the 6C; while the splendid E wall was rebuilt in the 4C on the old foundations by the architect
Agathon. The steepness of the slope necessitated terraces, running E–
W, and the provision of a separate platform for each building. The
terraces, some having a gate on either side, were intersected by the
Sacred Way, which wound up from the main entrance, at the SE, to the
NW corner.

From the main entrance modern steps lead to a paved rectangular
Square, which was enclosed by Roman porticoes and doubtless used
as a market-place for the sale of religious objects. Four steps lead up to

the *Main Gate*, 3·7m wide, through which we enter the **Sacred Way**. This is 3·7–4·9m wide, and was paved in the Roman period with slabs taken from near-by buildings. Some of this makeshift pavement is intact. The Sacred Way was adorned on either side with the votive monuments that are a feature of the precinct.

Immediately within the gate, to the right, stood the *Bull of Corcyra* (Pl. 1). The base, which we see, supported a bronze bull by Theopompos of Aegina, dedicated c 480 BC from the proceeds of a catch of tunny. Next, beyond a flight of steps, are the *Offerings of the Arcadians* (Pl. 2). The line of bases supported nine bronze statues of Apollo, Victory, and Arcadian heroes. They were erected to commemorate a successful invasion of Laconia in 369 BC and placed, out of bravado, facing the Lacedaemonian monument, insult being added to injury by employing the ageing sculptor Antiphanes (comp. below). The *Base* (Pl. 3), beyond, bore a statue of Philopoemen. The grandiose *Monument of the Admirals*, dedicated by the Spartan Lysander in 403 BC after he had crushed the Athenians at Aegospotami, held 37 bronze statues of gods and Spartiate admirals, made by nine Peloponnesian sculptors including Antiphanes of Argos. The inscriptions from the statues of Lysander and Arakos, in verse composed by Ion of Samos, have been recovered.

Until 1963 it was commonly accepted that the large rectangular exedra (Pl. 4) behind the Arcadian bases was Lysander's monument though there have been attempts recently to place it on the S side of the Sacred Way (Pl. 6).—On the S side also was the *Offering of Marathon*, dedicated by the Athenians 30 years after the battle in honour of Miltiades. The long base supported 16 statues, the original ones of Pheidias, according to Pausanias. One theory assigns the *Riace Bronzes* (two Classical Greek bronze masterpieces, recovered from the sea off southern Italy and now in the museum in Reggio Calabria) to this monument.

We pass between two semicircular exedrae, both dedicated by the Argives, that to the left erected in honour of the *Epigones* (Pl. 8) the successors of the Seven Champions, likewise out of the spoils of Oinoe. To the right the *Kings of Argos* monument (Pl. 9) was added at the foundation of Messene, and its position near to the Spartan offering would not have gone unnoticed. This exedra was to bear 20 statues of the early kings and heroes of Argos. Ten statues only were finished, filling the W quadrant; their bases have been restored to place.—The adjacent square niche is covered with personal decrees.

To the left four plinths survive, three of them with inscriptions, from the *Offerings of the Tarentines* (Pl. 10). the statues were by Ageladas of Argos. Beyond is the first of the many TREASURIES we shall encounter. These served much the same purpose as those at Olympia; in them were stored smaller votive offerings, vessels, etc., and here important documents were recorded. The TREASURY OF THE SIKYONIANS (Pl. III), a Doric edifice in antis, was built about the beginning of the 5C in place of those raised by Kleisthenes after the First Sacred War. In the foundations were used remains of two older buildings, a tholos of 13 columns (c 580 BC) and a rectangular monopteros of 14 columns surmounted by a roof, perhaps designed to shelter the chariot of Kleisthenes; to this belong the metopes in the museum.

Opposite, to the right, behind unidentifiable bases, are some confused foundations of an unidentified Aeolian treasury. Another destroyed *Treasury* (Pl. V) was perhaps that of the Megarians.

The TREASURY OF THE SIPHNIANS (Pl. IV) the massive foundations of which we now pass, was built in 526–525 BC with a tithe of the profits

Parnassos

Fortifications of Philemos

Stadium

Sacred Precinct

Castalia

0   400 yards
0   400 metres

N

Museum

Tombs

Pits

Synedrion

Papadia Ravine

Gymnasium

Marmaria

Temple of Athena Pronaea

Extent of the Ancient Town

Temple of Athena Eegane

Ancient Delphi

Lesche of Knidos

45

44

Theatre

XIX   XVIII

Dionysion

43

41   40   39

XVII

38 Stoa of Attalos

42

33

35

34   36

30   29

XXXI   37

XXX

32

31

27   28

Temple of Apollo

26

XXI   XX

24

XIX

25

XXIII

Asklepieion

18

23

XV   XVI

XVII

16

XVIII

17

19

XXIV

Prytaneion

X

IX

XI

XXVI

20

22

XIV

VIII

12

XXV

21

XIII

VII

V

XII

Aiolian Treasury

Treasury of Kyrene

VI

IV

III

King of Argos

9

Theban Treasury

Sikyonian Treasury

10

Sacred Way

8

7   3   2

4

1

Epigones

5

6

DELPHI
Temenos of Apollo

0   30 metres

ROAD

Entrance

N

from the gold-mines of Siphnos and was intended to surpass in opulence the existing treasuries at Delphi. It was an Ionic temple in antis, with two columns in the form of Caryatids between the antae. Fragments of the Caryatids were found on the site (now in the museum). The treasury faced W. A sculptured frieze of Parian marble ran round the four sides (also in the museum).

We have reached the so-called CROSSROADS OF THE TREASURIES. A branch-road, 27m long runs to a W gate. On its S side was the *Treasury of the Thebans* (Pl. VI) built after Leuktra. At the corner some vestiges may mark the *Treasury of the Boeotians* (Pl. VII). Behind the Treasury of the Athenians (comp. below) are unimportant remains of three further treasuries; that of the Potidaians (Pl. VIII), an older Athenian treasury (?; Pl. IX), and that of the Etruscans (Pl. X).

The Sacred Way, now at an altitude of 550m, describes a semicircle and ascends to the NE. Prominent on the left is the *Treasury of the Athenians* (Pl. XI), built just after 490 BC with a tithe of the spoils of Marathon. The French School, aided by a large grant from the municipality of Athens, re-erected the building in 1904–06. The scattered stones were put back in their proper places (more than four-fifths of them having been found), though the foundations had to be readjusted and the columns supplied. This Doric building is distyle *in antis*, and measures 10m × 6m. It stands on a terrace ending in a triangular buttress and reached by a staircase from the Sacred Way. The triglyph frieze depicted the exploits of Herakles and of Theseus; the originals are in the Museum, the sculptures *in situ* being casts in arbitrary positions.

The walls are covered with more than 150 inscriptions. Many of them, decorated with crowns, refer to the Athenian Pythaid, or special embassy; others include honorific decrees in favour of the Athenians, decrees of the Amphictyons about Dionysiac artists, and two *Hymns to Apollo*, with the musical notation in Greek letters above the text.—On the S the terrace ended in a triangular space on which were displayed the trophies of Marathon with the dedication 'The Athenians dedicate to Apollo the spoils of the Medes after the battle of Marathon'. The inscription is a 3C copy of the damaged original.

Just across the Sacred Way must be located the *Treasury of the Syracusans* (Pl. 12), which (true to form) was erected here after the Athenian expedition had come to grief. This part of the sanctuary was dug into by a Christian cemetery, but some surviving foundation blocks mark the spot. Adjacent are the foundations of the *Treasury of the Knidians* (Pl. XXV), built in Parian marble before the capture of Knidos in 544 BC by the Persians, and probably used on occasions for ritual dining. A lateral road leads E to the *Treasury of Cyrene* (Pl. XIII), probably of mid-4C date.

The *Bouleuterion* (Pl. XXVI), seat of the Delphic senate, was a plain rectangular building. Higher up is the SANCTUARY OF EARTH or of GE-THEMIS (Pl. 16), part of which was destroyed to make way for the great retaining wall. This is a circle of rocks surrounding a natural cleft in the ground, and is the site (or one of them) of the primitive oracle of Ge-Themis, guarded by the serpent Python. One of the rocks, supported by modern masonry, was the *Rock of the Sibyl* (Pl. 17) on which, according to ancient local tradition, the sibyl Herophile prophesied. Another rock supported a statue of Leto; on a third was the *Monument of the Naxians* (Pl. 18) dedicated c 570 BC. This was an Ionic column with 44 flutings, over 9m high, surmounted by a sphinx (now in the museum). The lower part of the column is in situ. An inscription of 322 BC on the base renews to the Naxians the right of Promanteia.

A little higher up the Sacred Way crosses the *Threshing Floor* (Halos), a circular place 15m in diameter, surrounded by seats. Here was presented every seventh year the Septerion, a morality play cele-

brating the death of Python. To the N was the STOA OF THE
ATHENIANS (Pl. 23), dedicated after the end of the Persian Wars. A
three-stepped limestone basement supported a colonnade, 30m long
and 4m deep, consisting of 8 Ionic columns in Parian marble, set 4m
apart. The architrave was of wood, as well as the roof, which leaned
against the wall of the temple terrace. On the top step of the basement
is an Archaic inscription recording the Athenian dedication of cables
(from the pontoon bridge thrown by Xerxes across the Hellespont) and
figureheads (from Persian ships).

Beneath the Byzantine paving in front of the portico was found a deposit of ivory,
gold, and bronze votive objects, which had been damaged in a fire in the mid-5C
and deliberately buried.—A lane branches off to the right to a small gate in the
peribolos wall. On the right (S) of this lane is the *Treasury of Corinth* (Pl. XXIV),
ascribed by Herodotus to Kypselos. It was not only the oldest but the richest of the
buildings of this kind, thanks to the generosity of the kings of Lydia. Opposite (N)
are the remains of two destroyed treasuries (Pl. XV, XVI) and of the *Prytaneion*
(Pl. XIV).—Outside the gate, to the N, are Roman baths, with mosaics.

The Sacred Way now describes another curve (to the N; 561m), below
and to the right of the remarkable POLYGONAL WALL, which supports
the platform on which stands the Temple of Apollo. It is built in irregular interlocking blocks with curved joints, a style unique to Delphi,
having the double practical and aesthetic advantages of strength in
seismic shocks without appearing to be a rigid barrier across the
sanctuary.

The wall, site of the first excavations at Delphi, follows the irregularities of the
ground. Its height varies from 1·8 to 3·7m, and its total length from E to W is c 82m.
The dressed face of the wall was covered in the 2C BC–1C AD with inscriptions of
every kind, more than 800 having been found. Along the base the rough-hewn
blocks project in their natural condition. The blocks of the upper courses were
joined by double T-clamps run with lead.—Towards the SE end the inscriptions
are particularly numerous. Records, public and private, important and trivial, are
all mixed together; they relate above all to the emancipation of slaves, and
constitute an invaluable record of Delphic families and events.

The SACRED WAY, here about 6m wide and well paved, climbs steeply.
On the right is the site of the TRIPOD OF PLATAIA (Pl. 27). The circular
pedestal has been re-erected. This offering was dedicated by the
Greeks from the spoils of Plataea (Paus. X, 13, 9). On the stone base
was a gilt bronze pedestal about 5·5m high, consisting of 3 intertwined
serpents, on which were engraved the names of the 31 city-states
contributing to the victory. This was carried off by Constantine the
Great and still reposes in a mutilated state in the ancient Hippodrome,
at Istanbul. The three serpent heads supported a golden tripod, which
was seized by the Phocians after 356 BC.

At the top of the slope we come to the so-called Crossroads of the
Tripods, where stand the bases of long vanished votive offerings. The
most remarkable were the *Tripods of Gelon and Hiero* (Pl. 36), tyrants
of Syracuse, and of their brothers. The offering which commemorated
Gelon's victory at Himera over the Carthaginians in 481 BC, comprised four monuments supporting golden tripods and Victories,
weighing 50 talents in all. They were some of the earliest objects to be
looted when in 353 BC the Phocians needed funds for the Sacred War.
The *Stele*, in front, adorned with a bull, bears an honorific decree in
favour of a citizen of Kleitor in Arcadia. The base adjoining that of the
tripods on the left is that of the *Acanthus Column* with the dancing
girls, now in the museum.

Before entering the temple terrace, we may visit a group of buildings to the E. On our right, adjacent to the Plataian Tripod, is the rectangular plinth of a *Chariot of Helios* (Pl. 28), dedicated by the Rhodians. A detailed examination (see B.C.H. 1963) of the cuttings into which the hooves of the quadriga fitted has suggested that the missing horses may be those now adorning St. Mark's cathedral, Venice, though these have been derived by other authorities from a similar group made for Alexander the Great and set up at Corinth in 336 BC. On the left are a ruined Treasury (Acanthians ?), and two enormous bases, which bore statues of *Eumenes* (Pl. 29) and *Attalos* (Pl. 30) of Pergamon. Above, extending across the temenos wall, are the ruins of the *Stoa of Attalos* (Pl. 38).

The Sacred Way turns W and becomes the upper walk of the temple precinct (573m). In front of the entrance to the E is the *Great Altar of Apollo* (Pl. 31) a rectangular structure with steps in black and white marble, dedicated by the Chians in gratitude for their deliverance from the Persians. It presumably kept the orientation of its predecessor, which is slightly oblique to the present temple but accorded with that of the temple burnt in 548 BC. The altar was piously re-erected in 1920 at the expense of the inhabitants of Chios but restored more accurately in 1960.

Between the altar and its temple extends an esplanade bearing bases of other monuments. By the altar stood a golden statue of Eumenes II (Pl. 32). A big square plinth (Pl. 35) bore perhaps the Apollo Sitalcus; there follow the dual column-bases (Pl. 34) of the offering of Aristaineta and the base of the Palm-tree of Eurymedon, dedicated by the Athenians after their victory of 468 BC. Behind is the restored *Monument of Prusias II* (Pl. 33), king of Bithynia (182–149), which bore an equestrian statue of that devious monarch.

The **Temple of Apollo**, reduced before the restorations of 1939–41 to its bare foundations, rests on its N side on the living rock, and on the S side on a huge substructure of irregular courses nearly 61m long and 3–4·6m high. The foundations consist of two concentric rectangles, the outer supporting the peristyle and the inner the sekos. The stylobate, on three steps of fine bluish local limestone, has been partially restored and many of the pavement blocks returned to place. One complete column of the 4C façade and portions of the others have been re-erected so that the building, even in its ruin, once again dominates the sanctuary as it should. A stone ramp leads up to the entrance of the temple on the E.

History. Discounting the legendary constructions of laurel, beeswax, and bronze, of which Pausanias gives the traditional account but for which there is no archaeological evidence, the existing building had two predecessors. An edifice of the 7C was burnt in 548 BC, and replaced by a larger temple, started perhaps in 536, but completed in 513–505 by the Alkmeonids, who were in exile from Athens. Of this archaic temple, which was admired by Aeschylus, Pindar, and Euripides, fragments, including some of the pedimental sculptures by Antenor, have been found (now in the museum). It was ruined in 373 BC. The existing temple was built in 366–c 329 by Xenodoros and Agathon on the old foundations. It was fired in 88 BC by Thracian invaders, and restored by Domitian after the further ravages of Sulla. The robbing of the metal clamps in the middle ages was the prime cause of its final dismemberment.

The temple was the usual Doric peripteral hexastyle, 60m by 22m, with 6 stuccoed poros columns at the ends and 15 on the sides. Both pronaos and opisthodomos had 2 columns between antae. The architrave was decorated with shields captured from the Persians at Plataea (E side) and from the Gauls (W and S sides). Some of the spouts and marble tiles have been discovered, but not a fragment of the pediments described by Pausanias. Earthquakes and systematic spoliation have left practically nothing of the sekos, so that we know nothing with certainty about the arrangement of the *Adyton*, or inner shrine. This was an underground chamber, in which were the *Omphalos* and the *Oracular Chasm*.

To the W of the temple are the foundations of a Roman building (Pl. XX), in which was found the statue of Antinous, now in the museum.—From the SW angle of the temple we may descend past the *House of the Pythia* (?; Pl. XXIX) to the S walk (Pl. 25). In the SE corner was probably the *Offering of the Messenians of Naupaktos* (Pl. XXIII), erected to commemorate their victory at Sphakteria. Below the temple ramp was the monument of Aemilius Paullus (Pl. 26).

The Sacred Way was protected above the Temple of Apollo by a retaining wall, called the *Ischegaon*, constructed c 355 BC of reused material from the Alkmaeonid temple. This was examined by the French School during the 1950–57 excavations. At the NW angle of the terrace was the *Offering of Polyzalos*, which was buried in some catastrophe (? 373 BC) and from which the celebrated Charioteer was recovered. Adjoining on the W is the *Lion Hunt of Alexander the Great* (Pl. 42), a large rectangular exedra of dressed stones.

An epigram on the back wall has established the identity of this exedra with the monument described by Pliny and Plutarch. It was dedicated in 320 BC by Krateros, who had saved the life of Alexander the Great during a lion-hunt near Susa. A bronze group by Lysippos and Leochares represented the incident (comp. also the mosaic at Pella).

We mount a Roman staircase to the *Theatre, one of the best preserved in Greece, built in the 4C BC, and restored by Eumenes II in 159 and by the Romans. The Cavea was contained in a parallelogram 50m broad. The N and W sides of the *Analemma*, or supporting wall, coincide with the line of the peribolos. The 35 tiers of seats were divided into two uneven sections by a paved *Diazoma* or landing (23 in the lower section and 7 in the upper). The seats were of white marble from Parnassos. The *Orchestra* was paved with polygonal slabs and measured 18m across. It was surrounded by an enclosed conduit. The front of the *Stage* (Pl. 43) was adorned with a frieze in relief depicting the Labours of Herakles (now in the museum). There is a fine *View of the sanctuary from the top of the theatre (596m).

Between the stage buildings and the Alexander exedra a pathway runs E above the Ischegaon, passing a semicircular exedra (Pl. 41). Beyond is the *Monument of the Thessalians* (Pl. 40), a rectangular exedra, dedicated by Daochos II of Pharsala, who as hieromnemon represented Thessaly in 336–332 at the Amphictyonic League, over which he presided. On a plinth 12m long (now in the Museum) stood statues of his house; the inscriptions remain in situ and five of the statues are in the museum. Beyond is the ruined *Temenos of Neoptolemos* (Pl. 39), beneath which have been excavated remains of a primitive village of the Mycenaean period that gradually became superseded as the cult grew in importance. In front is a long base attributed to the Corcyraeans.

Somewhere NE of the theatre was the *Fountain of Kassotis* (595m), the water of which descended into the Adyton. This was an artificial reservoir fed by the *Delphousa* (now *Kerna*), a spring which rises from a rock 70m N. The Pythia drank the waters of this spring before prophesying. Two stages of the *Kerna Fountain*, one Classical, the other Archaic, have been uncovered between the theatre and the stadium. Farther E of the theatre was the *Lesche of the Knidians* (Pl. 45). This was a club-house (used also for ritual dining) dedicated by the Knidians c 450 BC. The building formed a rectangle 18·9m by 9·8m, with a door in the middle of the S side. The walls, of unburnt brick, rested on a socle of poros. The wooden roof was held in place by 8 wooden pillars. The club was adorned by Polygnotos with paintings described in detail by Pausanias.

A path winds up from the diazoma of the theatre to (5 minutes) the **Stadium**. This was situated in the highest part of the ancient city (645m). The N side is hewn out of the rock. The S side was artificially supported, and recent excavations now afford a fine view of the massive supporting blocks of Classical masonry (5C BC). Four pillars re-

main of the Roman *Triumphal Arch* which decorated the SE entrance
of the final form given it by Herodes Atticus. The *Track* was then
established at 600 Roman feet (177m). Both starting-point (*Aphesis*)
and finishing post (*Terma*) had stone sills with posts separating the 17
or 18 runners.—The N long side had 12 tiers of seats; 13 staircases
divided it into 12 rectangular blocks. A rectangular tribune, on which
are benches with backs, was the stand of the *Proedria* or presidents of
the games. The W end of the *Sphendone* had the conventional semicircular shape (unlike the Stadia at Olympia and at Epidauros). Here
were 6 tiers of seats divided by 3 staircases into 4 *Cunei*. The S long
side had only 6 tiers of seats. There was accommodation for 7000
spectators.

Above the Stadium, to the W, on the slopes of Mt Ayios Ilias (700m), the *Fortress
of Philomelos*, the sole fortification of Delphi, was built in 355 BC as a defence
against the Lokrians of Amphissa. The hill again saw fighting in the Communist
civil war.—To the S of the fortress are threshing-floors and tombs. Here was the
West Necropolis. Sepulchral relics of every age, from the Mycenaean to the
Byzantine, have been found in this region. The *Chapel of Ay. Ilias*, on the road
between the Sanctuary and the village, stands on a rectangular platform partly
built of ancient masonry. This was the site of the *Synedrion* or place of assembly
built by Hadrian for the Amphictyonic League. The spot was called *Pylaea*. The
name was afterwards given to a suburb which came into existence here in Roman
times.—Above the chapel is an interesting *Tomb* and, N of the tomb, is the *House
of the French School*. Below this is a sepulchral crypt.—Just S is the Museum.

The *** *Museum**, rebuilt in 1959–61 and splendidly arranged, is especially rich in Archaic sculpture from the site; the free-standing work
may be compared with that in the Acropolis museum, while the relief
sculpture ranks with the Aegina marbles in Munich.

TERRACE: Sarcophagus of Meleager, discovered by Capodistrias;
large panelled mosaic (5C AD) depicting animals and birds.—We enter, and ascend the stair (right) to the LANDING (R. 1), where stands the
Omphalos, a sculptured stone found in the S wall of the Temple of
Apollo and anciently believed to mark the point where the eagles of
Zeus met at the centre of the known world. Cauldron on marble stand
(7C; restored). The poor frieze of the Labours of Herakles (1C AD) on
the left wall is from the proscenium of the theatre.

ROOM 2 (HALL OF THE BRONZE SHIELDS). On the walls, heavy bronze shields of Cretan or Hittite style. Small bronze Kouros (Daedalic; c
650 BC); Griffins.

ROOM 3. Two *Kouroi, erected to commemorate Cleobis and Biton,
who were called to heaven by the Gods while asleep in the Heraion of
Argos as a reward for yoking themselves to their mother's chariot; the
statues, which are mentioned by Herodotus, mark the transition between the Daedalic and true Archaic styles (? 582 BC). Bronze statuette of Apollo (c 530 BC). Five metopes from the TREASURY OF
SIKYON (second quarter of 6C BC). These are Sikyonian work, in yellow limestone, very carefully executed but in poor condition.

Left to right: 1. *The Dioscuri and the Argo*. Castor and Pollux, on horseback,
appear on the right and left of the ship; in the midst of the warriors in the Argo is
Orpheus.—2. *Europa and the Bull*.—3. *The Dioscuri and Idas, Son of Aphareus
on a Cattle-Lifting Raid in Arcadia*. Castor is leading, followed by Idas and Pollux
(Lynkeus, brother of Idas, is not shown). The raiders fell out after their expedition
and all, except the immortal Pollux, were killed.—4. *Calydonian Boar*. Under its
belly is the silhouette of a wounded hound.—5. *Flight of Helle on the Ram with
the Golden Fleece*.

In ROOM 4 are displayed the relics recovered in fragments in 1939 from
an apothetes, or sacred dump, in front of the Stoa of the Athenians
Archaic *Bull (6C BC) of silver sheets, originally attached by silver

nails to a copper frame; hooves, horns, and other gold-plated parts are better preserved. •Head of a seated male chryselephantine statue with elements of the gold decoration of the garments, notably two plates with repoussé animal motifs in differing styles (6C BC). Another ivory head with its golden diadem. Forearm of a chryselephantine statue. Miniature friezes in ivory from a throne or casket. Ivory statuette of a god with a tame lion (7C BC). Bronzes: Athletes (early 5C BC); censer held up by an exquisite female figure (c 460 BC).

DELPHI MUSEUM

ROOM 5. HALL OF THE SIPHNIAN TREASURY. Displayed are the East Pediment, much of the • •Frieze, a caryatid with polos capital, and part of the doorway with admirable lotus and palmette decoration. In addition the hall contains the winged •Sphinx of the Naxians (Ionic work of 570–560B.C.), and another caryatid head with polos, of unknown provenance, once thought to have belonged to the Treasury of Knidos.

The *East Pediment* represents the dispute between Herakles and Apollo over the Delphic tripod.—The *Frieze*, in a mature Archaic style, foreshadows in its rhythmic quality that of the Parthenon nearly a century later. The horses are especially spirited and the fallen corpse almost natural in position. The four sides have no narrative continuity: the *E Side*, below the pediment, depicts in two panels an Assembly of Gods (supporters of Troy to the left of Zeus, of Greece to the right) who watch Homeric heroes fighting over the body of Patroclus. The *N Side* shows nine groups of Gods in battle with the Giants, grouped round three chariots. The names were painted at the bottom of the composition after the manner of ancient vases. The chariot of Cybele and the death of Ephialtes are well preserved. The *S and W Sides* (believed to be by a different sculptor) are fragmentary.

ROOM 6 contains 24 surviving metopes (some very fragmentary) out of 30, from the ATHENIAN TREASURY. Good authorities place these stylistically (moulding of stomach muscles) in the days of Kleisthenes (510–500 BC) or earlier, but the expressive •Heads and fluidity of the figures have been thought to confirm Pausanias' contention that the treasury was dedicated after Marathon. The metopes represent the Labours of Herakles (N and W sides), the Exploits of Theseus (S side) and the Battle of the Amazons (E side). Note especially Herakles and the Arcadian Stag, Theseus and the Bull of Marathon.

In ROOMS 7 and 8 are grouped pedimental statuary from the ARCHAIC TEMPLE OF APOLLO. All the figures have unfinished backs, with tenons and mortises to fix them to the tympanum. Some traces of colour survive. Lion's head spouts; Nike acroterion, and other fragments; inscriptions. Small bronze of a walking cow.

The Inscriptions concern the history of the temple: lists of subscribers to its rebuilding; re-dedication; repairs by the Emp. Domitian (AD 84); also, with musical notation, Hymns to Apollo composed in the 2C BC.

ROOM 9. Grave stelai; bronze kalpis (early 4C); circular altar with reliefs, found in the Tholos.—In ROOM 10 are Metopes and other fragments from the Tholos.

ROOM 11 contains sculpture of the 4C BC. Left to right: Fragment of pillar.—Three colossal Dancing Girls, grouped round a column representing an acanthus stalk, probably a monumental support (9m high) for a tripod; the figures were possibly Thyiads, who celebrated feasts in honour of Dionysos.—Five *Statues from the votive offering of Daochos of Thessaly, celebrating the victory of his master Philip in 336 BC at Chaironeia. This family monument of nine statues reproduced in marble a group in bronze at Pharsala, of which part at least was by Lysippos. The group, identified from the surviving inscription of the plinth, forms a genealogical succession of 7 generations from the 6C BC. The best-preserved figures are those representative of Agias, great-grandfather of the dedicator (depicted as an athlete), who had not only won an Olympic wreath, but had five victories at the Nemean, three at the Pythian, and five at the Isthmian Games; and Agelaos, his young brother, who won a track event at Delphi.—Statue of a Philosopher.

ROOM 12, the HALL OF THE CHARIOTEER contains the famous *Charioteer and the few other surviving fragments of the Auriga of Polyzalos, of which it was part. The figure was discovered in 1896 where it had fallen when the remainder was crushed during the earthquake of 373 BC. The rider, dressed in a long tunic (xystis), is represented life-size. On his head is a victor's fillet. He holds the reins in his right hand. From this calm and formal pose we may infer that he is performing his lap of honour. Taken out of its context, the figure is at first sight less than satisfactory. The disproportion of the body, often criticised, may have been a deliberate attempt to counter optical distortion when seen from below. Similarly the eyes, of magnesium and onyx, wonderfully preserved, are not symmetrical. The work, one of the few great surviving bronzes of the 5C, dates from c 475 and was dedicated by a Sicilian prince to commemorate a chariot victory in the Pythian Games in 478 or 474 BC. The sculptor may have been Pythagoras of Samos, who was in exile at this time at Rhegion.

ROOM 13. Small *Bronzes and pottery (case of excellent fragments); *Antinous, in polished Parian marble, particularly good of its genre, with an expression of gentle melancholy; Head, probably of Titus Q. Flaminius, victor of Cynoscephalae (197 BC); Head of an unknown philosopher, expressive (Hellenistic); Young girl laughing, reminiscent of the arktoi found at Brauron.

Excursions from Delphi

To the Sybaris Cave and the Gorge of the Pleistos. This excursion takes 3½–4 hours there and back, or 2½ hours if the visit to the gorge is omitted. A new earth road descends from the main road E of Marmaria. The path descends in zigzags, crosses some retaining walls, and reaches an irrigation ditch at the bottom of the gorge. Thence it ascends for c 100m, passes some caves, crosses the stream, passes near a waterfall which works a fulling mill, and ends (1 hour) at a deep well-like hole in the rock full of water in winter. This is called *Zaleska* and was in antiquity the *Spring of Sybaris*. It is dangerous to approach the well over the chaos of slippery rocks that surround it.

The *Cave of Sybaris* is a large cavern in a deep ravine on the hillside beyond the Pleistos. This is known also as *Krypsana* ('Hiding Place') or *Asketario* ('Hermitage', after a hermit who is said to have lived in it). It was used as a refuge by the people of Kastri during the War of Independence.—From the cavern we descend again to the torrent as far as an irrigation ditch, which we follow for

150m; then we turn right to reach a path which ascends in ½ hour to the little *Monastery of the Panayia*. On the right are the ruins of a Chapel of the Redeemer.

We may descend to the Pleistos (1½ hours more), passing the spring of *Kephalovrysi*, which turns some mills, and by the *Chapels of Ayios Vasilios, Ayios Ioannis* and other chapels, near an ancient well and a sacred wood.

To the Corycian Cave. With a car the cave is more easily reached from Kalívia, above Arákhova, by a marked track (or ¾-hour walk).

From Delphi the site fence now blocks the ancient rock-cut path starting above the stadium; the modern mule-path swings out in wider zigzags to the W and is reached direct from the village. In c 1 hour we reach the top of the **Phaedriades**, known today as *Elafókastro* (1225m). The path continues on the *Plateau of Livadhi*, used as a pasturage by ancient and modern shepherds alike, as far as the conspicuous watering troughs. Here we turn right (E) and cross the low ridge. On the E slope a broad path will be found at the entrance to the forest, leading down the valley (this is marked with red arrows and signs). These are not easy to follow near two small tarns, where we make for the gap between two hills. From this gap a rough path climbs in zig-zags. 2½ hours. We reach (1299m) the low arched entrance to the **Corycian Cave**, now called *Sarantavli* ('Forty Rooms'). This cave, which Pausanias thought the finest he had seen (X, 32, 2), was sacred to Pan and the Nymphs (inscriptions). Above it the Dionysiac orgies were celebrated by the Thyiades (Aeschylus, *Eumenides* 22). When the Persians were marching on Delphi, the inhabitants took refuge in the Corycian Cave (Hdt. VIII, 36); it was again used as a refuge during the War of Independence and on other occasions. Within a faint light reveals the pink and green walls of the cave, and the stalactites and stalagmites. Excavations of the French School in 1970 showed the periods of use to be Neolithic, late-Mycenaean, and 6–4C.

Ascent to Parnassos, see Rte 45.

V THESSALY

Thessaly, one of the most fertile areas of Greece and, in summer, one of the hottest places in Europe, consists of a vast plain surrounded on all sides by mountains. On the N the Kamvounian Mts separate it from Macedonia; on the W is the Pindos range beyond which is Epirus; to the E Olympos, Ossa, and Pelion bar the way to its sea coast on the Gulf of Salonika; to the S. Othrys divides it from Aitolia and from Phthiotis and Phocis. In antiquity Thessaly included also the long narrow valley of the Spercheios between Othrys and Mt Oiti, in which is the city of Lamia. In the SE the peninsula of Magnesia extends beyond Pelion almost to Euboea, and the Northern Sporades, with the sea encroaching into the Gulf of Volos. Mountain passes give access to Thessaly from outside.

In the Tertiary epoch the whole plain was under water. It is nowadays drained by the Peneios, which rises in the Pindos and, receiving important tributaries, flows through the Vale of Tempe into the Gulf of Salonika. The surrounding mountains are covered with forests of pine, oak, and beech; the plain yields corn, rice, tobacco, and fruit. Unfortunately agricultural labour is so scarce that much of the land is uncultivated. The horses of Thessaly have always been famous; Thessalian cavalry helped the Athenians in the Peloponnesian War. Cattle and sheep thrive on its pastures. In the mountains bears, wolves, and wild boar still roam but are seldom seen; in the plain the fauna include hares, herons, cranes, storks, and wildfowl.

The population includes Albanians and Vlachs, some of whom are still nomadic shepherds. The province has three large towns, Larissa, its political centre, Volos, its chief port, and Trikkala. Thessaly is traversed from S to N by the main line of the Greek State Railway, with branches to Volos and Trikkala; the principal towns are linked by good roads with frequent bus services. The archaeological interest of Thessaly is mainly prehistoric. Rural life in the villages is hardly affected by modern changes.

From a very early date Thessaly was divided into four districts or tetrarchies, ar organisation which subsisted up to the time of the Peloponnesian War. The divisions were *Hestaeotis* (region of Trikkala), in the NW; *Thessaliotis* (including Pharsalos, now Farsala), in the SW; *Pelasgiotis* (Larissa), in the E and NE, in which was Skotoussa, the original home of the Dodona oracle; and *Phthiotis* (Othrys), in the SE, which included the Homeric city of Phthia and was the country of Deukalion and of Achilles and his Myrmidons. There were also four secondary divisions: *Magnesia*, covering the peninsula of that name (Rte 49); *Dolopia*, S of Thessaliotis, inhabited by the ancient race of the Dolopians who fought before Troy; *Oetaea*, in the upper valley of the Spercheios (now part of Phthiotis and Phocis); and *Malis*, a district on the shores of the Maliac Gulf (Gulf of Lamia), which extended as far as Thermopylae.

For some time after the conquest Thessaly was governed by kings who claimed descent from Herakles. Later the kingship was abolished and the government in the separate cities became oligarchic, with power concentrated in the hands of a few great families descended from the kings. The most powerful of these were the *Aleuadai*, who ruled at Larissa, and their kinsmen the *Skopadai*, whose seat was at Krannon (c 24km SW of Larissa). Pausanias reminds us (VII, 10, 2) that the Aleuadai betrayed Thessaly to the Persians in 480 BC. The general attitude of these northern oligarchs was never cordial to the rest of Greece, although, says Thucydides (IV, 78), the common people of Thessaly liked the Athenians. As time went on, the rulers formed themselves into a kind of confederation. Each of the four main divisions remained politically independent but, to guard against the contingency of war, a chief magistrate was elected under the name of *Tagos* (Ταγός), who had supreme command. He was generally one of the Aleuadai.

Other cities of importance in antiquity besides Larissa and Krannon were Pharsalos and Pherai. About 374 BC Jason, tyrant of Pherai, was elected Tagos. His rule and that of his successor Alexander (died 357) was so unbearably harsh that the Thessalians solicited aid from the Thebans and threw off their yoke. Twenty years later, Philip of Macedon, similarly invited, annexed the whole country to his own dominions. In 275 Pyrrhus, king of Epirus, after his adventures in Italy, made himself master of Thessaly and Macedonia. In 197, the Romans took Thessaly under their protection, as part of a Roman province (comp. Strabo, XVII). Larissa soon became the political and religious capital of the reorganised confederation, which was surrounded by a number of minor leagues.

In the imperial era Thessaly was united to Macedonia, but in the reign of Diocletian it became a separate province.

In the 12C, after a succession of invaders, Thessaly became the centre of a Bulgar-Vlach kingdom known as *Great Wallachia*. The Turks conquered the country in 1389 and held it for five centuries. The Congress of Berlin (1878) assigned to Greece Thessaly and the District of Arta (Rte 53); three years later Turkey ceded to Greece the whole of Thessaly S of the Peneios. Greece retained her new acquisition despite the disastrous war of 1897, and after the war of 1912–13 she obtained the remaining area of Thessaly.

47 Central Thessaly

A. Lamía and the Valley of the Spercheíos

LAMIA (Λαμία, Hotels C, D), the chief town of the nome of Fthiotis and the seat of an archbishop, is a lively but undistinguished town of 41,667 inhab., lying below two wooded hills. It is a market centre for cotton, cereals, and garden produce. A characteristic sight is the stork's nests on the roofs.

History. *Lamia* is remembered for the Lamian War (323–322 BC) in which the Athenians attempted to free themselves from Macedonian domination. Leosthenes seized Thermopylae and shut up Antipater, the Macedonian viceroy, in Lamia. After Leosthenes had been killed in a sortie, the command passed to Antiphilos. A Macedonian relief force freed Antipater, and Antiphilos was defeated at Krannon. A stronghold in the middle ages, Lamia was known to the Franks as *Gipton* and to the Catalans as *El Cito*, whence perhaps the Turkish name *Zitouni*. Since 1961 Lamia has had 'sister town' links with Dover, Delaware.

Round the central PLATEÍA ELEVTHERÍAS are grouped the Nomarkhia, the Cathedral, and several hotels. Odhós Dhiákou leads to *Platéa Dhiákou*, adorned with a characteristic statue of Athanasios Dhiakos, a local patriot. Hence a street ascends in steps the hill of Ayios Loukas (restaurant). Just to the E of Plateia Elevtherias is the shaded PLATEÍA LAOÚ (good taverna), where the waters of the Gorgopotamos gush from a fountain. Dominating the town on the NE is the **Kastro**, a castle of the Catalan Duchy of Neopatras (1319–93). Traces of Middle and Late Bronze Age occupation and a Protogeometric tomb have been found in recent years. The walls stand on Classical foundations and show masonry of many later epochs (incl. Roman; Catalan; Turkish battlements). They command a fine view both to E and W. There is a road up to the main gate.

BUSES from Plateia Laou to *Almiros* and *Volos* (twice daily); to *Pelasgia* (6 times); to *Dhomokos* (8 times); and *Farsala* (5 times). Opposite corner to *Larissa* (5 times), *Trikkala* (4), *Kardhitsa* (4), and *Kozani* (3); also to *Kastoria* (daily).

FROM LAMIA TO KARPENISI, good road, 82km (51 miles). The road runs W with the railway to (8km) *Lianokládhi Station*, junction for Lamia, on the main Athens–Salonika line. We cross the railway and gradually ascend in the lush broad valley of the Spercheios. The huge mass of Mt Oiti looms on our left as we continue through the village of (14·5km) *Lianokládhi*. Excavation of a mound by the Ipati turn has revealed a M.H. Apsidal house.

At the far end of the village a road diverges left across the river to **Loutrá Ipátis** (Λουτρά Υπάτης; 3km; Hotels A, B, C, D, E), a thermal establishment whose waters (25·5°C) are good for skin diseases and bronchial infections. The branch road continues to (5 m) **Ipáti**, the ancient *Hypata* and the *Neo-Patras* of the Franks and Catalans, finely situated on the N slope of Mt Oiti. In antiquity it was the capital of the Aenianes, a tribe which migrated S from Ossa. During the Lamian War it was the centre of the military operations of the confederate Greeks. Some ancient masonry can be seen in the Catalan castle. In the 13C it was the capital of the dominions of John Doukas who with help from Athens here defeated the forces of Michael VIII Palaiologos in 1275. In 1318 it became the second capital of Alfonso's Catalan duchy 'of Athens and Neo-Patras'. The town was taken by the Turks in 1393 and made the seat of a pasha. Here were born Leo the Mathematician (c 800) and St. Athanasios the Meteorite (1305–83). The inhabitants cultivate tobacco and weave linen. Ipáti is the starting-point for the ascent of *Mt Oiti* (Οίτη) legendary scene of the death of Herakles, whose summit (Pírgos; 2153m) may be climbed from the Trapeza refuge of the Greek Alpine Club (3½ hrs from Ipáti). The descent from the refuge may be made in 4 hrs to *Pavlianí*, c 8km W of Brallos (Rte 44A).

23km *Kastrí* takes name from a ruined fortress with square towers.— 30km *Varibóbi* has readopted the name of *Makrakómi*, a town known to Livy, the ruins of which stand on the hill to the NE of the little market-town (2374 inhab.). Beyond the Spercheios we see *Sperkheiás* (2607 inhab.), to the E of which, on the left bank of the tributary Inakhos, is *Ayios Sóstis*, site of ancient *Sosthenis*, mentioned by Ptolemy. About 5km to the N of Makrakómi are the Baths of *Platístomon* (Λουτρά Πλατυστόμου, Hotels C, D), the waters of which are recommended in cases of dyspepsia, anaemia, disorders of the stomach, and spinal complaints. Another road climbs N to Smókovon (comp. Rte 47C).

Beyond Makrakómi another road diverges across the river to *Palaiovrákha* on the N slope of Mt Goulinás (1466m; view). Between this village and its neighbour Pterí (or Fteri) are some remains of ancient *Spercheiai*.—The vegetaion becomes increasingly temperate as the valley narrows to a gorge. Above (47·5km) *Ayios Yeoryios* the slopes become increasingly wooded and the climb gradually steeper. The valley divides. Just beyond (52km) *Khani Panétsou* in the Dipotoma valley by-roads lead NW to *Merkádha*, *Mávrilon*, and *Ayía Triás* (34km), a beautiful mountain village which upheld a tradition of learning in Turkish times. We climb out of the valley by continuous turns to (60km) *Timfristós* (841km), known for its cherries. The road now zigzags across the spruce-clad saddle between Pikrovouni (1503m; N) and Kokkalia (1721m; S). As we reach the road-summit (c 1430m), on the watershed of the Southern Pindos and the boundary between Phthiotis and Eurytania, there is a fine view of the peak of Mt Timfristós. Along the summit ridge a difficult road runs S to Krikéllo (18km) and *Dhómnista* (26km; Hotel B). Our road winds down to *Ayios Nikólaos* (left; 1km) in the enclosed valley of the Karpenisiotis. Beyond the Miríki turn, a track leads (right) to the *Refuge of Dhiavolótopos* (1840m; 40 beds; 2 hrs walk from Karpenisi) on **Mt Timfristos**, or *Veloukhi*, the summit (2315m) of which towers above the road.

82km **Karpenísi** (Καρπενίσι; Hotels B, C, D, E) is the chief and only sizeable place (pop. 5100) of Evritania, by population the smallest nome of mainland Greece. The town was captured by Communist rebels in January 1949 and held for 18 days. Its houses occupy both slopes of a torrent that descends to a small plain, wholly enclosed by mountains and dominated on the N by the peaks of Timfristos. At present somewhat bleak and without charm, the town is undergoing increasing industrial development. One road leads S to *Méga Khorió* (15km; Hotel D) on the N slope of *Mt Kalliakoúdha (2100m)*. Its companion village, *Mikró Khorió*, was overwhelmed on 13 January 1963 by a landslide while most of the 336 inhab. were at a church festival in another village.

From Karpenisi to *Agrinión*, see Rte 54.

B. From Lamía to Lárissa via Fársala

ROAD, (114km) 71 miles, part of the traditional S–N route through Greece, which has been only partly superseded by the new highway to Salonika via the coast. 35km *Dhomokós*.—68km *Fársala*.—114km **Lárissa**. Bus several times daily in 3–3½ hrs.

RAILWAY (from Lianokládhi), 127km (79 miles) in 2–2½ hrs, part of the main line from Athens to Salonika. From Lianokládhi the railway climbs at a gradient of 1 in 50 for nearly 36km to surmount the barrier of Mt Othrys; its course lies W of the road. There is a succession of bridges, then follow 27 short tunnels as the line climbs out of the Spercheios valley. It reaches the summit-level (585m) to the E of Mt Mokhlouka (892m), then descends, crossing the W end of the drained Lake Xynias.—43·5 *Angeías*; we accompany the river Sofadhitikos through a gap in the hills.—Beyond (61km) *Thavmakós* (comp. below) the kastro of Dhomokós may be seen. The railway then accompanies the road in the plain to *Néon Monastírion* (see below).— 85km **Palaiofársalos** is the most important junction in Thessaly; branch lines run E to Volos and W to Trikkala

and Kalambaka (Rte 50). Farsala is c 13km E. The line
surmounts a low ridge.—101·5km *Dhoxará*.—109·5km
Krannón; the ruins of the ancient city are 10km W.—127km
Lárissa.

We quit Lamia by Odhos Ipsilándi. The road skirts the E side of Mt
Profitis Ilias, soon joining the by-pass, and begins the gradual ascent
of the *Furka Pass* (850m), the main route through the brown W foothills
of Mt Othrys. There are fine views to the left over the Spercheios to Mt
Oiti. On the curving descent is (16km) the *Khani Dragoman Agà*, now
a taverna. We cross the level cultivated plain formed by the draining of
Lake Xynias. Some walls of ancient *Xyniai* survive near its S limit (S of
the modern village, 3km W of our road). On the banks, near the village
of *Ombriakí*, two Neolithic settlements have been identified. We pass
chromium mine workings and surmount another ridge.

35km **Dhomokós** (Δομοκός; pop. 1735), chief town of an eparchy
and seat of a bishop, is picturesquely situated 1km above the road
(left) on a rocky hill (520m). Its railway station, in the plain to the N,
keeps the ancient name, *Thaumakoi*. Some Classical masonry can be
seen built into various house on the hill.

The town, which commanded the defile of Koile, was so called because of the
astonishment (thauma) of the traveller from the S who had climbed over rugged
hills and had suddenly been confronted with the vast plain of Thessaly. Thaumakoi was vainly besieged by Philip V in 198 BC and was taken by Acilius Glabrio in
191. During the Greco-Turkish war of 1897 Dhomokos was the last stage in the
retreat of the Greek army under Constantine I (17 May). The advance of the
Turks, who reached the Furka pass two days later, was halted only by the intervention of the Powers.

The abrupt descent affords a fine *View of the Thessalian Plain, in
which we continue N.—The road to Trikkala (Rte 47C) and Ioannina
diverges at (60km) *Néon Monastírion*. On a hill (right) some well-
preserved walls (known as Yinaikókastro) remain to locate ancient
Proerna; its Temple of Demeter has been recognised in the village.—
After *Vrisiá* we pass between two isolated hills, Plake (left) and Griva
(right). Beyond the turning to Stavros is a restaurant.—68·5km **Fársala**
(Φάρσαλα; Hotels D, E), four-fifths destroyed in the earthquake of
1954, has nothing of interest save its past history and is mainly noted
for its 'halva' sweetmeat. Its bishopric was suppressed in 1900 and
incorporated in the see of Larissa, but with 7094 inhab., it is still the
largest place in its eparchy. It has a station, 3km N, on the railway from
Volos to Trikkala. The ridge of Fetih-Djami, SW of the town, has been
occupied since Neolithic times.

The *Battle of Pharsalus* (9 August, 48 BC), which took place in the plain to the W,
decided the issue between Pompey and Caesar and the fate of the Roman world.
Pompey, trusting to his overwhelming superiority in cavalry, led by Labienus,
planned to turn Caesar's right wing and fall upon his rear. Labienus' cavalry
charge was put to flight, panic spread through Pompey's army, and Pompey
himself fled with an escort of only four men. His army lost 15,000 and the
remainder surrendered next day. Yves Béquignon (B.C.H. 1960) concludes that
the battle took place on the left bank of the Enipeus.

We cross the Volos–Trikkala railway and the Enipeus, an important
tributary of the Peneios, on a five-arched bridge.—82km *Khalkiádhes*.
Here a by-road leads right to *Ano Skotoússa*, to the E of which are
some remains of ancient *Skotoussa*, the supposed original home of the
Dodona oracle.

Above to the N and E rise the mountains of Khalkodónion or Kara Dagh, anciently called Kynos Kephalai or Cynoscephalae ('dogs' heads') and famous for two

battles. The *First Battle of Cynoscephalae*, in 364 BC, was between Alexander of Pherai and the combined forces of Thessalians and Thebans. Alexander was defeated but the Theban general Pelopidas was killed. The *Second Battle of Cynoscephalae*, in 197, irreparably weakened the power of Macedonia. The Romans under Flaminius totally defeated Philip V of Macedon, the issue being decided by an elephant charge. An uneasy period followed, ending in the battle of Pydna and complete Macedonian dependence upon Rome.

92km *Záppion*. The road continues in the plain through agricultural land, passing the Xenia motel on the way into (114km) **Lárissa**, see Rte 48.

C. From Lamía to Kardhítsa and Tríkkala

ROAD, 118km. (73 miles). 56km *Néon Monastírion*.—70km *Sofádhes*.—92km **Kardhítsa**.—118km **Tríkkala**.

To (56km) *Néon Monastírion,* see Rte 47B. We branch left and run NW through the Thessalian plain, crossing torrents and streams from the Pindos on our left.—70km *Sofádhes* (Σοφάδες; Hotel E) an agricultural centre (5009 inhab.) on the Thessalian railway, is by-passed to the W. A by-road leads (left) in 8km to the village of *Philiá where an important pan-Thessalian sanctuary of Itonian Athena was located in 1963. Excavations yielded Geometric and Archaic bronzes, amber and ivory objects, Hellenistic inscriptions, and architectural remains of Hellenistic and Roman times. Mycenaean and Early Christian material has also been found. On a prominent hill (183m) to the N, near the hamlet of Pírgos (3km), are some remains identified by an inscription found at Mataranga (comp. below) as ancient *Kierion*, a place Stephanus of Byzantium equated with Thessalian *Arne*.—We pass (left) remains of an old bridge and (right) conical mounds. At (84km) *Ayios Theódhoros* we join the road from Larissa just W of Mataránga.

92km KARDHÍTSA (Kardhítsa; Hotels C, E), the capital of its nome, is an uninteresting town of 27,291 inhab., laid out on a rectilinear plan in Turkish times. It has no ancient associations. An important market-town attracting custom from the Thessalian plain and from the mountainous Agrafa region, it trades in tobacco, cereals, cotton, silk, and cattle, and is served by the Thessalian railway. Its buildings are liberally adorned with storks' nests. There is a pleasant park. Recently methane gas has been discovered in the vicinity. Kardhítsa was the birthplace of Gen. Nikolaos Plastiras (1883–1953), leader of the revolution of 1922.

BUSES hourly to *Trikkala*; 5 times daily to *Larissa*; and to surrounding villages.

From Kardhitsa a road runs SW to (10km) *Mitrópolis*, where a group of Hellenistic tombs were recently found, then ascends to the hydroelectric LAKE OF MEG-DOVA at (26km) *Koróni*. This is formed by the **Tavropos Barrage** on a tributary of the Acheloos. After serving electrical generators, the water provides irrigation in the plain and finally discharges into the Peneios.—About 8km along this road, in the foothills of Pindos, are the ruins of ancient **Metropolis**, a civic-centre made up of several towns, including Ithome (see below). It formed, with Trikke, Pelinnaion, and Gomphoi, a fortified rectangle protecting the approach to the Thessalian plain. Within the enclosing walls, circular in plan, is the citadel. Metropolis was captured in 191 BC by Flaminius and occupied by Caesar before the battle of Pharsalus. To the S of the modern village (comp. above) a Mycenean tholos tomb was discovered in 1958. Above, on the mountainside (1151m), are the little fortresses of *Voúnesi* and *Portitsa*.

About 34km SE of Kardhitsa (bus in summer) is **Smókovo Spa** (Λουτρά Σμοκόβου; Hotels B, C, D, E), with alkaline sulphur springs (38·9–40°C), efficacious for nervous, rheumatic, catarrhal, and skin complaints. The spa is beautifully situated at an altitude of 450m in a shady ravine and is an excursion centre. Thence a secondary road continues a serpentine course through *Rendína*, with a fine old monastery (frescoes of 1662), to join the Lamia–Karpenisi road at Makrakómi (p. 417).

Another road runs W from Kardhitsa in company with the railway to (11km) *Fanário*, a village of 1033 inhab., situated on the W side of a ricky hill called 'the Beacon' (*Φανάρι*). A Hellenic wall and a Byzantine fortress mark the site of 'rugged *Ithome*' of the Iliad, one of the towns incorporated in Metropolis (comp. above). It was 'a heap of stones' in Strabo's day.

From Kardhitsa to *Larissa*, see Rte 50.

The broad level road drives NW. The local inhabitants may be seen in the fields wearing bright shades of red, and many fine horses graze. Prominent to the W is the castle at Ithome (comp. above).—108km *Agnanteró* has a local festival on 27 August. We cross the Peneios.

118km (73 miles) **TRÍKKALA** (Τρίκαλα; Hotels B, C, D), the third largest town in Thessaly, with 40,857 inhab., is attractively situated on both banks of the Lethaios (locally Trikkalinos), some distance from its confluence with the Peneios, at the end of a low ridge (Mt Khasia) projecting from the N limit of the Thessalian plain. The town is the capital of the nome of Trikkala and seat of an archbishop. Its population is increased in winter by the influx of Vlach shepherds driven from their mountains by the inclement weather. It has an important market in cereals, rice, silk, cotton, tobacco, and livestock.

Buses (KTEL 17 Trikkálon) from Plat. Kitriláki to *Larissa* (frequently), to *Athens*, and to local destinations; (KTEL 16 Kardhítsis) from Od. Amalías to *Kardhitsa* and to *Kalambaka*.

Tourist Police/Police in Od. Kapodistríou.

History. Trikkala is the *Trikke* of Homer, the domain of Podaleiros and Machaon, the two sons of Asklepios, 'cunning leeches' who led the Trikkeans to the Trojan War ('Iliad', II, 729). It was credited with the earliest of all the temples to Asklepios and in later times had a medical school of repute. Trikke was one of the four cities of Hestaiotis forming a defensive quadrilateral (comp. above). The plain of Trikke produced the finest of the renowned Thessalian horses, the features of which are reproduced in the frieze of the Parthenon. The name *Trikkala* first appears in the 12C. Under the Turks Trikkala was the chief town of Thessaly despite periodical uprisings such as that of Dionysios 'the Skylosophos', its bishop. After the battle for Athens in 1945, Trikkala became one of the communist guerrilla strongholds.

The road from Kardhitsa passes, close to Ayios Konstandinos, the **Kursum Cami**, a mosque built by Sinan Pasha in 1550, with a fine soaring dome supported on four slender columns. It is destined as a museum. The river Lethaios divides the town. On its banks are numerous cafés. The Plateía Ríga Ferraíou on the S bank is connected by bridges with the Plateía Kitriláki and the large central PLATEÍA AMERIKÁNON, both opening on the N bank. Odhós Vasiléos Konstandínos leads W to the **Frourion**, a Byzantine fortress on Hellenistic foundations, where the lower ward has a Tourist Pavilion (view) and the great keep (no adm.) a castellated clock tower. To the NW are some remains of the *Asklepieion* (?), partly excavated by the Greek Archaeological Service in 1912. The *Bazar*, to the E of the Frourion, is a picturesque quarter of old Turko-Greek houses. The principal churches lie in this quarter.

A pleasant EXCURSION may be made to Gomphoi and the Porta Panayia in the foothills of the Pindos to the SW. We pass the railway station and drive SW across the plain.—7km *Piyí*.—10·5km *Ligariá* stands above the Portaïkos, a torrent that often floods the plain.—At 12km an unpaved road leads to *Gómfoi* (1·5km), a village on a hill overlooking the Pamisos, 5km W of *Lazarína*. Ancient **Gomphoi**, of considerable importance by reason of its domination of the chief pass from Thessaly into Epirus, was one of the four strongholds forming a square (comp. above). It was fortified by Philip II. In the civil war it supported, to its cost, Pompey against Caesar. On its site the Byzantines founded the city of *Episkope*. Many ancient blocks are incorporated in the houses of the village.—We now see ahead the Stená tis Pórtas with, right, half-way up the mountain, the great monastery of Dousiko (see below).—19km *Píli* (1852 inhab.) stands at the entrance to the *Stenatis Pórtas*, a beautiful defile through which the Portaïkos emerges from the Pindos. The PORTA PANAYIA, a charming church across the river (bridge) and 1·5km upstream, was founded in 1283. The narthex is later. Within, the mosaic figures of Christ and of the Virgin are striking. On the marble ikonostasis the figure of Christ is on the left, a reversal of customary Orthodox iconography.—A rough road leads (right) from the village across the bridge and up to the MONASTERY OF DOUSIKO (5·5km; women not admitted), known locally as *Ai Vessáris*, which stands at 762m above its village on the opposite slope amid chestnuts and limes. It was founded in 1515 by the Blessed Bessarion (later Abp of Larissa), and completed in 1556 by his son. The monastery is on the grand scale with 336 cells, a library of importance and an imposing church having a carved wooden ikonostasis of 1767.—Up the defile, 2·5km beyond Píli, stands an attractive single-arched *Bridge* built in 1518 by the Blessed Bessarion; a pebble mosaic decorates the rock face on the far side.—20km. We cross the river.—At 22·5km the asphalt ends and a difficult route into Epirus continues through wonderful scenery via (34km) *Eláti*, high in a valley on the W side of *Kerketion* (Kóziaka; comp. Rte 51). Higher up to the right is the *Khatzípetros Refuge* (1250m) from which the summit (1900m) may be climbed.—48km *Pertoúli*, cold even in August at nearly 1220m beyond the watershed, has a forestry station of Salonika University.— 58km *Neraïdhokhóri* stands above the infant Acheloös, down which remote tracks and paths descend to mountain villages to N and W. The three villages mentioned all have inns.

From Trikkala to *Kalambaka* and the *Meteora*, see Rte 51.

48 Lárissa and its Environs

LÁRISSA, or *Lárisa* (Λάρισα), the chief town of its nome and capital of the province of Thessaly, with 102,048 inhab., is an important road centre, the headquarters of the Greek First Army, and the seat (since the 7C) of the Metropolitan 'Bishop of the Second Thessaly and Exarch of All Hellas'. Situated in the middle of the Thessalian plain on the right bank of the Peneios, with its spacious squares and busy streets it has more the air of a city than anywhere else in central Greece. Its long history is scarcely apparent, though some vestiges of the Turkish enceinte still survive to the S of the town. The quality of local ouzo, halva, and ice cream is noted. The bicycle, unusually in Greece, is here a conspicuous feature and the presence of storks on the roofs adds a bizarre touch to the townscape.

Airport, just E of the town; 4 flights per week to Athens.—OFFICE at Papanastasíou 70 and Koumoundhoúrou.

Railway Station, 1·25km S of the centre, for the main Athens–Salonika line, and for Volos.

Hotels A, B, C, D.

Zakharoplasteia and Cafés in the main square and in the Alkazar park.

Post Office, Od. Papanastasíou.—O.T.E. CENTRE, Od. Filellínon.

Information, etc. N.T.O.G. Koumoundhoúrou; TOURIST POLICÉ Papanastasíou; *Olympic Airways*, Papanastasíou/Koumoundhoúrou.

Buses (stations, see plan). To *Athens* (occasionally); to *Volos* (frequently); to *Trikkala* (frequently), also to *Ioannina* (daily); to *Tirnavos* and *Elasson* (frequently); to *Kozani* (regularly), also to *Karditsa* (regularly); to *Farsala* (regularly) from Od. Irakliou (Plat. Riga Ferraiou).—S.E.K. COACHES from the main square to *Athens* and to *Salonika*.

History. The name *Larissa*, meaning 'citadel', is of pre-Hellenic origin, and a settlement seems to have existed on the site from the earliest times. Palaeolithic remains were discovered in 1960 on the W outskirts. An early ruler, Aleuas, who claimed descent from Herakles, founded the powerful family of the Aleuadai. The dynasty attracted to their court the poet Pindar, the sophist Gorgias, and the physician Hippocrates, the last two of whom died at Larissa. In 480 BC the Aleuadai supported Xerxes; four years later the Spartans attacked them unsuccessfully. At the end of the 5C BC their power was weakened by a democratic revolt and by the rise of the tyrants of Pherai, the most formidable of whom was Jason. The last Aleuadai injudiciously invited the aid of Philip of Macedon, who annexed Larissa and the whole of Thessaly. After the second battle of Cynoscephalae (197) the Romans made Larissa the capital of the reorganised Thessalian confederation. In 171 Perseus, king of Macedon, defeated the Romans near Larissa. Pompey passed through the city on his flight after the battle of Parsalus.

Achilleios, Bp and patron saint of Larissa, was present at the Council of Nicaea (325) and by the 5C the city had metropolitan rank. Larissa fell to the Bulgars in 985. Byzantine rule was restored, and, though the Normans laid siege to the town in 1096, survived till the Frankish occupation of the 4th Crusade, when Thessaly fell to Boniface of Montferrat. Theodore Angelos drove out the Franks and Michael II, his nephew, ruled Thessaly from Arta. Michael's illegitimate son, John Doukas, defied the emperors and his half-brother in Epirus alike. After his death in 1289, his son John II remained the ward and vassal of Guy de la Roche until 1308, when he threw in his lot with Byzantium in time to rid his territories of the Catalan Grand Company, who passed through on their way S. In 1318 John II died without an heir and Thessaly, invaded from all sides, was quarrelled over until Andronikos III restored uneasy Byzantine rule. By bloodless conquest Thessaly fell in 1348 to Stephen Dušan, who installed its conqueror Gregory Preljub, as 'Caesar' in Trikkala. After Dušan's death another period of anarchy in 1355–59 ended when Symeon Uroš established himself as 'Emperor'. His son, John Uroš, turned monk and the Serbs became little more than Byzantine vassals. By 1393 Bayezid's Turks were encamped on the Spercheios and Thessaly remained Turkish until 1881. The Turks renamed Larissa *Yenişehir* ('new town') in contradistinction to the 'old town', of Krannon. It was the headquarters of Mehmed IV during the siege of Candia in 1669 and its military garrison inhibited the participation of Thessaly in the War of Independence. Larissa did not, however, succeed Trikkala as the Turkish capital of Thessaly, until 1870.

The centre of Larissa is a huge square with several names, shaded by limes and orange trees and lively with cafés, patisseries, and cinemas. From its NW corner Vasilissis Sofias, where in 1968 was located the late-Hellenistic *Theatre*, leads shortly to the low hill, once the Acropolis of the ancient city, now crowned by a *Clock Tower* (To Rolóï). Farther NE is the Byzantine *Frourion*. To the W are the unfinished new *Cathedral* and some vestiges of a Classical *Temple*, overlooking the new bridge which replaced a medieval bridge of 12 arches across the Peneios. Beyond, along the river, extends the *Alkazár*, a fine shady park (cafés), a favourite promenade in summer.

Returning by Odhos Venizelou, we pass between the *Philharmonic Hall* and the covered *Market*. Opposite a small public garden is a *Mosque* with a conspicuous minaret. Here is housed the **Archaeological Museum**, containing Thessalian antiquities from the nome of Larissa. In the single hall are displayed a menhir from Soufli tumulus (Middle Bronze Age); Archaic temple fragments and funerary stelai from Larissa; later sculpture, displaying the characteristics typical of Thessalian workmanship; late-Imperial stelai depicting mounted warriors (the Greco-Roman antecedents in art of the Byzantine portrayal of St. George). Important are the early prehistoric finds (in cases) from the valley of the Peneios, dating from the Palacolithic epoch to the Neolithic.

The mound (*Magoula*) *of Gremmou*, near Dhendrá, 10·5km from Larissa off the Kozani road to the left, represents the site of Homeric *Argyssa*, though the principal antiquities dug from the mound since 1955 by the German Institute have belonged to the Neolithic era.

A road leads SW to (c 24km) the ruins of **Krannon**, once one of the foremost cities of Thessaly and the seat of the *Skopadai*, kinsmen of the Aleuadai, whose wealth was proverbial. The poet Simonides (556–467 BC), who beat Aeschylus in a competition for the best elegy on the fallen at Marathon, lived for a time at Krannon under the patronage of the Skopadai. At Krannon, in 322 BC, Antipater, the Macedonian regent, defeated the confederate Greeks and so put a stop to the Lamian War. Excavations of the Greek Archaeological Society have laid bare the ruins of a *Temple of Asklepios*, by the side of which flowed and still flows an ancient stream, the waters of which warmed the wine with which it was mixed. Here in 1960 were discovered two tholos tombs of the 5C BC, showing a remarkable survival in Thessaly of a Mycenean form. The Turks called Krannon *Eskişehir* ('Old Town' or 'Old Larissa'), by way of contrast to the 'New Town' of Larissa (see above). 5km SE of Krannon, excavations at two cemetery sites in the vicinity of the village of *Ay. Yioryios* produced rich finds including weapons and huge Thessalian fibulae of c 650–550 BC.

From Larissa an asphalt road runs NE via Omorfokhórion to (20km) *Sikoúri*, continuing (unpaved) to *Spiliá* (786m), 8km farther on, departure point for the mountain refuge (3 hrs) on *Mt Ossa* (comp. below). A group of Mycenean tholos tombs was identified in 1969 near the village.

FROM LARISSA TO AYIA, 39km (24¾ miles), bus. We take the Volos road E across the plain, and at 6·5km branch left.—At (16km) *Elevthérion*, a rough by-road goes off left for *Marmarianí* (6·5km) where many tholos tombs were examined in 1903 and there are scanty remains of ancient Lakereia. We pass into the Dhotion Plain.—At 18km to the S of the road, after the turning for *Neokhóri*, a hill *Palaíkastro* has remains of an extensive building complex of the 5C BC. About 1km ENE of this site a fine built tomb of the 5 and 4C was found in 1972.— 39km **Ayiá** (Hotels E; F/A), chief place (3454 inhab.) of an eparchy, is situated on the S slopes of Ossa above the gorge dividing Ossa from Pelion, and c 11km from the sea. It has a 16C monastery with frescoes of 1721. Guides may be hired for expeditions on **Mt Ossa**, or *Kissavos* (1978m), a bold isolated mountain commanding a magnificent *View. Mules can be taken almost to the summit, from which Mt Athos and, in clear weather, the Turkish coast may be seen. The Giants, in their war with the Gods, are fabled to have piled Pelion on Ossa in order to reach the summit of Olympos. The W slopes of Ossa provided Verde antico and Atrax marble (serpentine) for the buildings of ancient Rome.

To the NW of Ayia (7km) is *Melívia*, occupying the site of ancient *Meliboias*, native place of Philoktetes.—The royal estate of *Polidhéndhri* (c 16km SE) was donated by King Paul to the State in 1962 as a training school for Greek farmers.

From Larissa to *Farsala*, see Rte 47B; to *Volos*, see Rte 50; to *Tirnavos* and *Elasson*, see Rte 58; to the *Vale of Tempe*, see Rte 57; to *Trikkala* and *Meteora*, see Rtes 50 & 51.

49 Magnesía

A. From Lamía to Vólos

ROAD, 111km (69 miles), of which 82km by National Highway (toll).—51km (32 miles). Exit for *Glifá* car ferry.— 86km (54 miles). Exit for *Vólos.*—88km (55 miles) *Mikrothívai* and 93km (58 miles) *Néa Ankhíalos* (**Phthiotic Thebes**).—111km. **Vólos.**—Buses from Plateía Laoú twice daily to Almirós and Vólos, 6 times to Pelasyía.

We quit Lamia on the E and in 4km join the National Highway. At *Megálo Vrísi*, beyond the turn to the national road and 4km from Lamia, is a prehistoric mound site which may be Homeric *Alos*. 16km *Stilís* (Στυλίς; exit), the port of Lamia, by coasting steamer. It occupies the site of Thessalian *Phaleron* and its pop. 4690 derive their livelihood from olive culture.—Just beyond *Karavómilos* (Hotel C), at 26km we see (left) *Akhinós*, backed by a flat-topped hill (chapel) bearing remains, perhaps to be identified with the *Echinos* referred to in the 'Lysistrata'.—30·5km. Exit for *Rákhes* and *Pelasyía* (Πελασγία); about 1½ hrs N on foot from Pelasyia (buses from Lamia and Volos) are the remains of *Larissa Kremaste*.—36km. Parking area by the channel (Dhiavlos Oreon), across which is *Mt Likhás*, the W promontory of Euboea (comp. Rte 42).—40km Toll Gate.—51km (32 miles) Exit: roads to Pelasyia (17km; comp. above), and to *Glifá* (11km; car ferry to Ayiókambos in Euboea, comp. Rte 42).

Here we may make a seaward detour (c 10km farther), passing just inland of *Akhilleo*, a popular bathing-place, to *Ftelió* (officially Pteliós), a pleasant village lying inland of the site of Homeric *Pteleon*, marked perhaps by a medieval tower on a height nearer the sea (Mycenean tombs to the NW).—Passing *Soúrpi* (Σούρπη), a nesting-place of storks, we may rejoin the National Highway by the ruins of ancient Halos (comp. below).

If we stay on the old road, Hellenistic *Halos* lies to the right, its acropolis on a hill to the left. The site, which has been surveyed but not excavated, was probably founded in the Hellenistic period. The town was laid out on a grid plan and surrounded by a wall with numerous towers. The small acropolis (subsequently crowned by a Byzantine fortress) was connected to the town by similar walls which ran down the hillside in a V-shape, from the summit to the NW and SW corners of the town defences. The fortifications and the absence of public buildings (though there was an agora) suggest that Halos was a military foundation. At the time of its construction, the site was closer to the sea and effectively dominated the passage between Mt Othrys and the Pagasitic Gulf.

The *Mont Xinias* (10km W) dates from the 17C, when it moved down from a higher site, where there are ruins of the 5–13C.—**Almirós**, 6·5km beyond Halos, is the capital of an eparchy, with pop. 6143 and a small museum. It has an hourly bus connection (in 45 min) with Volos. Benjamin of Tudela remarks on the presence of numerous Italian and Jewish merchants at Almiros, and the Emp. Alexios III in 1199 granted trading concessions here to the Venetians.

63km Toll Gate. To our right is *Mt Khlomon* (893m) which guards the Trikkeri Strait (Dhiavlos Trikeriou), the landlocked entrance to the gulf of Volos, scene in 480 BC of the first encounter between the Greek and Persian fleets (comp. Rte 42).—70km (44 miles). Exit for Halos and Almiros, see above.—76·5km Xirias bridge, followed by the return spur from Almiros.—At 87km we take the Volos exit, quitting the Highway which continues N to join near Velestinon (c 16km on) the line of the old Volos–Larissa road (Rte 50).

We are now following the old road.—88km (55 miles) *Mikrothívai* stands below the flat hill of **Phthiotic Thebes**, which is ringed by ruined classical walls with 40 towers and has remains of a temple of Athena, a theatre, and a stoa; the walls may be seen from the road (two fields' lengths away) about a mile beyond Mikrothívai. Finds are in the Volos museum.—93km (58 miles) **Néa Ankhíalos**, a village (3646 inhab.) by the sea, founded by refugees in 1906, and occupying the site to which Phthiotic Thebes moved in Early Christian times below the acropolis of ancient *Pyrasos*, its port. This is one of the most important Early Christian/Early Byzantine sites in Greece. In five large areas of excavation (three of them along the main road) five important basilicas (A, B, G (the basilica of Archbishop Peter), D, and 'Martyrios') have been excavated, as well as the two predecessors of Basilica G which underlie that building. They range in date from mid 4C to mid 6C AD and the site was abandoned about 620. Fine mosaics and architectural fragments have been found, some of which may be seen in the small *Museum* which lies within the site enclosure to the left of the road. A rich baptistery has recently been investigated near Basilica G. Also on the site are two bathing establishments, sections of a roadway and other houses and public buildings.

The road now follows the pretty coast above little bays backed by olive-clad hills. From the summit of the last rise there is a wide panorama over the Gulf, then a fine view down to Volos, with Mt Pelion behind. The sanctuary of *Amphanai* (right) was located by the German Institute in 1972. In the plain we pass the sites of Pagasai and Demetrias (comp. below) and enter (111km) **Volos**.

B. Vólos and its Environs

VÓLOS (Βόλος), a bustling town of 71,378 inhab., capital of its eparchy and of the nome of Magnesia and constituting a deme still officially called Pagasai, is the seat of an archbishop (Metropolitan of Demetrias) and the chief port of Thessaly. Its harbour dates from 1912, but some form of maritime town has existed hereabouts from the remotest antiquity. It is the main channel of Thessalian exports: cereals, garden produce, cotton, silk, olive-oil, skins, sugar, and soap. With its mills, tanneries, and refineries, it rivalled the industrial potential of Piraeus until stricken by two disastrous earthquakes in 1954 and 1955. The recent start of a rail and road ferry to Syria has given new impetus to a large industrial area on the Larissa road. The town provides no monument of interest; but its attractive site between Mt Pelion and the Gulf and the quality of its hotels and restaurants make it the pleasantest base in Central Greece, and its museum should on no account be missed.

Hotels. B, C, D, E; many on or near quay.

Restaurants. Many on quay.

Post Office, Pávlou Melá.—O.T.E. CENTRE, Iólkon/Sokrátons.—TOURIST OFFICE, near the harbour.—TOURIST POLICE, ELPA Larissis 2/ Alexánduras 217.

Buses from KTEL Larissa to *Athens*, regularly; to *Larissa*, frequently; to *Velestino*, regularly; to *Almiros*, frequently; to *Pelasyia*, daily; to *Loutra Aidipsou*, daily, via Arkitsa. From KTEL 29 Magnesias to *Portaria* and *Makrinitsa*, frequently; to most other villages on *Pelion*, 2–3 times daily; to *Lekhonia*, etc.

Steamers from Town Quay to the *Northern Sporades, Euboea*

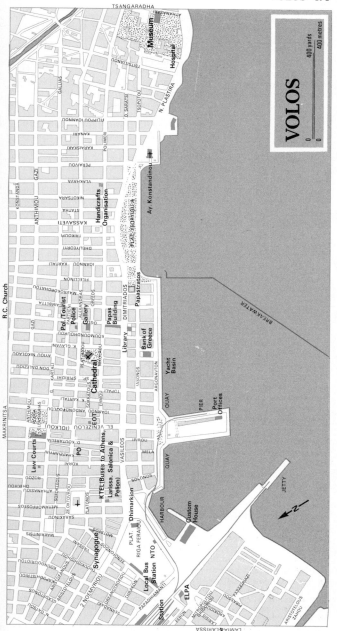

VOLOS

400 yards
400 metres

Near the Railway Station at the NW end of the town, the PLATEÍA RÍGA FERRAIOU, a huge triangle behind the *Dhimarkhíon*, borders the picturesque *Fishing Harbour*. Hence Odhós Vasiléos Konstandínou, or Dhimitriádhos, the uninspiring main street, runs through the chequerboard town parallel to the waterfront. The bustling quayside leads to the open space, the social centre of the town, which fronts the *Landing Stage* (whence boats sail for the Sporades). Here a model of the Argo forms a graceful monument to the past. The quay is continued S for nearly a mile by the ARGONÁVTON, a splendid esplanade (venue of the volta).

The ***Museum**, at the SE extremity of the town, was founded in 1909 by Alexis Athanasakis and, rebuilt after the earthquakes, was reopened in 1961. Its collection of c 300 painted stelai is unique.

VESTIBULE. (Theochares Room). A changing exhibition of finds from recent rescue excavations (various periods) in the area controlled from the Museum, together with a map of sites investigated in recent years. A 4C sarcophagus from Velestino has a reconstructed burial.

ROOM A, to the right: *Painted Grave Stelai* from Demetrias (Hellenistic); Mycenaean vases and bead jewellery from various Thessalian sites; Mycenaean and Protogeometric finds from the palace of Iolkos. Geometric pottery from Thessalian sites. In doorway, Head of a youth from Meliboia (reminiscent of the Kritian Boy).

ROOM B. Walls: relief grave stelai from Phalanna, Larissa, Pherai and Gonnoi (5C BC); votive reliefs from other sites (4C). In cases: Bronze votives from the sanctuary of Itonian Athena at Philia; Geometric bronzes from Thessalian sites; Palaeolithic flints and bone implements from Larissa, Sesklo and sites in the Peneus valley; prepottery Neolithic tools (7th mill. BC), including a bone and flint saw.

ROOM G has excellent new displays illustrating various aspects of life in the Neolithic period: architecture, agriculture, stock rearing, implement technology, manufacture of pottery, jewellery and figurines; spinning and weaving, etc. There is also a reconstructed section through a Neolithic site demonstrating the Neolithic sequence with appropriate pottery and artefacts.

ROOM D (left of vestibule): Painted grave stelai are further displayed; good model of site of Demetrias and Pagasai. In the centre, good male torso in marble (? Roman copy of original of the 5C BC). In cases: Vases and figurines of Archaic to Hellenistic date; Hellenistic glass vases (tomb offerings) and gold jewellery.

ROOM E (beyond). Offerings from various graves; drawings of tombs and graves; fine case of gold jewellery.

ROOM Z. An excellent display of reconstructed burials of all periods from Mycenaean to Classical with the skeletons and grave offerings in place (in some cases, also stelai). Here also are the later stelai from Demetrias.

The site of ancient **Iolkos**, also within the periphery of the town, lies to the right of the Larisa road between the railway and a dried-up river bed, perhaps the ancient Anauros. The site was firmly identified in 1956 by the Greek Archaeological Service (D. Theokaris) and occupies a mount Ayii Theodhori), 9m high and measuring c 412m × 320m, partly surrounded by a medieval wall. Until expropriation of modern property is completed' the greater part of the area cannot be explored.

Iolkos, famous in legend as the place whence the Argonauts set forth in quest of the Golden Fleece, had a flourishing existence in Early, Middle, and Late Helladic times, and probably continuity of occupation down the ages. With other towns it was depopulated by Demetrios Poliorketes and its inhabitants moved to Demetrias. Excavations since 1958 have shown the existence of two Myceraean palaces which it is tempting to ascribe respectively to King Pelias, uncle of Jason (c 1400 BC) and to Eumelos and Alcestis (palace destroyed by fire c 1200 BC).

A stiff climb (bus) may be made to ANO VOLOS, the medieval town, with houses built on the sides of steep hills rising to 793m. One of the houses has frescoes (1912) by Theophilos. The church of the Metamorfosis on the hill of Episkopi has a 16C ikon.

Excursions from Volos

The ruins of the cities that preceded Volos are of considerable archaeological importance. The places described below are within easy reach of the town, and each of the excursions can be made in a day or half-day, though they are not recommended to the casual visitor.

I. TO PAGASAI AND DEMETRIAS. The adjacent remains of the two cities lie c 3km S of Volos and can be reached in 10 minutes by car or bus, in ½ hr on foot, or in ½ hr by hired boat from Volos quay. We take the Almiros road to the SW (Rte 49A). This goes through the middle of ancient **Demetrias** (bus stop by track leading to Theatre) and then passes between **Pagasai** and a pleasant beach (taverna). The site was first explored in 1920–23 and excavations since 1961 by Prof. Milojčić (German Institute) have resulted in a definitive survey. An important Hellenistic complex—a palace or fort—has been investigated as well as various later (Byzantine) buildings. On the ground there is at present little to see as much of the area is fenced. On the promontory to the S is the important prehistoric site of Pevkákia.

Pagasai was the port of Iolkos and afterwards of Pherai. The port gave its name to the Pagasitikos Kolpos (Gulf of Volos). The Argo was, by the traditional story, built at Pagasai, which had a famous oracle and an altar of Apollo mentioned by Hesiod. It flourished in the 5C BC under the wing of Pherai. It was captured by Philip II of Macedon who separated it from Pherai and incorporated it in Magnesia. When Demetrios Poliorketes founded *Demetrias* just to the N, Pagasai became a dependency of the new city. Demetrias was a favourite resort of its founder and his descendants. It was the base of Philip V but tamely surrendered to the domination of Rome in 196. After the battle of Pydna (168) its fortifications were razed. The great towers of the Hellenistic ramparts were hastily strengthened in c 50 BC with outer lines. Concealed in the stone plinths of these were discovered the painted stelai now in the museum at Volos. These had come from neighbouring cemeteries. In the Byzantine epoch it was joined to the see of Thessaly. Invading Saracens sacked the town in 902.—Off the coast here in 1275 the Euboean Franks were utterly defeated by the forces of Michael VIII Palaiologos.

II. TO DHIMÍNI AND SESKLO, 6·5km and 18·5km W of Volos by road. The two sites lie 2 hours' walk apart to the S of the main Larissa road (Rte 50). A bus may be taken to either. Though of great importance to archaeologists, the sites are not very illuminating to the layman (a visit to Volos museum first is recommended).—We take the Larissa road and then, still in the outskirts of Volos, an asphalted road (left; signposted) to the village of *Dhimíni* (Διμήνιον). At the beginning of the village a track (right; sign) leads to the hill crowned by pre-historic remains of the 4th millennium BC that have given the name 'Dimini' to a culture of the period known more generally as Neolithic B.—To reach **Sésklo** (Σέσκλο) by road we follow the Larissa road for 10·5km, then turn left over a rogh railway crossing. Beyond, a tarmac road continues S towards the village, but after 3km a further left turn (small sign in Greek) brings us in c 1km to the Acropolis which has given name to a culture of the Neolithic A period; its presence has since been found widely in Thessaly and also elsewhere in Greece.

The hill has remains of a large palace with prodromos, megaron having a square hearth, and opisthodomos. Further excavations since 1962, however, have revealed remains of a very much remoter era (? 7th millennium BC). The site is fenced, but a partial view can be had from outside if it is shut.—About ¾ hr away is the ruined 'Palaiokastro' which may be *Aisonia*, the city of Jason's father.

C. Mount Pélion

**Mount Pélion (Πήλιον; 1651m), or *Pílion Oros*, the long mountain range that occupies the greater part of the peninsula enclosing the Pagasitic Gulf, forms one of the most delightful regions of all Greece. Its climate, cool in summer but mild in winter, with abundant streams from the upper slopes, encourages a lush vegetation scarcely found elsewhere on the Greek mainland. It is famed for its fruit, exports chestnuts, and produces attar of roses. From its slopes the sea is rarely hidden from view. The delightful villages, well-watered and shady, have timber-framed houses with balconies; stone-paved mule paths wind between their gardens. The churches are low and wide and have an exo-narthex supported on wooden pillars, which often extends from the N and S sides of the nave in the form of a pentise.

The ancients envisaged the Giants piling Pelion on Ossa in the war with the Gods. Pelion was the home of Chiron, wisest of the Centaurs, who taught Achilles the art of music and looked after Jason in his childhood. Here the gods celebrated the nuptials of Peleus and his unwilling bridge Thetis. The trees of the mountain supplied timber for the Argo.

I. TO PORTARIA AND ZAGORA, 47km (29 miles), bus to Zagora twice daily; to Portaria and Makrinitsa 10–11 times daily. We pass (4km) *Ano Volos* (comp. above), climbing steadily. The road winds steeply to (14km) **Portariá** (Πορταριά; a beautiful summer resort 769 inhab.) with a magnificent plane-tree and spring in its square. It has excellent cheese and unresinated red wine. The small *Church* (1273) has frescoes of 1581. Portariá is the starting-point for the 3½-hr climb to *Pliasidhi* (1548m), one of the main heights of Pelion.

A by-road diverges round the Megarevma ravine to **Makrinítsa** (Μακρυνίτσα; 2km; Hotels A, E), a delightful village of 546 inhabitants. Old mansions have been made guest houses by the NTOG. The picturesque little Plateia has a huge hollow plane-tree, a sculptured marble *Fountain*, a small *Church* with apsidal sculptural decoration, and a fine view. Higher up is the formerly monastic church of the *Panayia* (18C) with Greek inscriptions and Roman and Byzantine carvings built into the walls. A small chapel, with a school below, has frescoes. A street name commemorates Charles Ogle (1851–78), special correspondent of 'The Times', who was killed here (it is said in cold blood by order of the Turkish commander) while reporting on a fight between local insurgents and the Turks.

From Portariá the road continues to climb in zigzags, then runs along a high ledge affording enormous views over the Gulf.—25km *Khánia* (1158m; Hotels B, C, E), amid beech woods, stands at the head of the pass with a wide panorama in either direction. It has a chair-lift to Pliasidhi. Under the radar-capped crests of Pelion, we descend a tremendous valley through chestnuts, oaks, and planes, joining the road from Tsangaradha (see below) just over a mile short of (47km)

Zagorá (Ζαγορά; 488m; Rooms), a large community (2675 inhab.) of four hamlets on the E slope, facing the Aegean. In the plateia is the church of *Ayios Yeóryios* a typical Pelionic construction with an 18C ikonostasis. The countryside around is famed for the variety of its fruit (plums, damsons, pears, peaches, fraises de bois, etc.) and its good red wine.

Below Zagora on the coast is *Khorevtó* (7km), with a fine sandy beach, from which motor-boat excursions may be made.

II. TO MELIES AND TSANGARADHA, 55km (34 miles), buses daily to Tsangarádha, continuing to Makirrákhi; also to Miliés. We quit Volos to the SE, passing cement works and oil refineries, and skirt the Pagastic Gulf.

On the outskirts of Volos, the road passes a prominent hill (left) on which is the site of *Góritsa*. The settlement, above the sea, and probably of the 4C BC is laid out on a strict grid plan and surrounded by a fortification wall with towers. There was a cemetery outside the W gate. The quarries from which the building stone was hewn have been located in the vicinity.

8km *Agriá* (3997 inhab.; Hotels D, E; F/A) is served by town buses.— 10km *Káto Lekhónia* is the terminus of a bus service (frequent).— 12km *Ano Lekhónia* (tavernas). We pass through orchards.—At (19km) *Kalá Nerá* (Hotels B, C, D, E; F/A) diverges the road to **Miliés** (8km), birth-place of Anthimos Gazi (1764–1828), who raised the Thessalian revolt in 1821. A charming village, it is a good base for walks in the Magnesian peninsula.—Just beyond (22km) *Korópi* we turn inland, leaving (right) a by-road to *Afissós* (Hotels B, C, D, E; F/A), a small seaside resort on the Gulf. The road climbs; the view is at first obstructed by olive-groves, then, as we reach the pass above (27km) *Afétai*, or *Niáou*, there is a fine *View over the whole Gulf. We leave on our right the road to *Argalastí* (11km); Hotels B, E; F/A), chief town (1577 inhab.) of Southern Pelion.

Beyond (36km) *Niokhóri* we join a by-road from Miliés. We cross a deep valley and get out first sight of the Aegean.—45·5km *Lambinoú*. The road winds vertiginously in and out of the deep clefts that fissure the E face of Pelion; the *View extends to the island of Skiathos.— 55km **Tsangarádha** (Τσαγκαράδα; Hotels A, B, C, E), verdantly situated amid oak and plane forests at 472m, enjoys superb views down to the sea. A road (7km) descends to the superb beach at *Milopótamos*.

III. FROM TSANGARADHA TO ZAGORA, 23½km (14½ miles), one of the most beautiful roads in Greece, a splendid day's *Walk in spring or autumn. The road runs fairly level at c 1600 ft on the slopes, which are clad with oak forests and plane-trees.—6km *Moúresi*.—At (12km) *Kossós*, a pretty village, the church of Ayia Marina has frescoes and a pentise 'cloister'. *Ayios Ioánnis* (Hotels B, C, D, E), its bathing-place, lies below (7km by road).—17km *Makirrákhi*, another pleasant hamlet. We join the road from Portariá (comp. above).—23km *Zagorá*.

50   From Vólos to Lárissa and Tríkkala

ROAD, 122km (76 miles), asphalted and mainly level. 19km
(12 miles) *Velestíno*.—61km (38 miles) *Lárissa*.—122km
Tríkkala. By bus a change is necessary in Larissa.

STATE RAILWAY to *Lárissa*, 60km (37 miles) in ¾/a hr;
through railcars to Athens.

THE THESSALIAN RAILWAY from Volos to *Tríkkala* (and
Kalambáka), via Palaiofársalos, 164km (102 miles), follows
the road to (19km) *Velestínon* (comp. below). It then turns S
to cross two low passes round the E and S slopes of
Khalkodhonion.—31km *Aerinón* stands c 5km N of Phthiotic
Thebes (Rte 49) and just N of the National Highway.—
44km *Rigaíon*. About 3km SE of the station are *Erétria*,
with chromium mines and a mineral railway, and, on a hill
(509m), the ruins of *Eretria of Phthiotis*, a prehistoric site
with a fortified acropolis. This Eretria, according to Strabo,
was one of the cities under the sway of Achilles.—At
(69km) *Fársala* the line crosses the Lamia–Larissa road (Rte
47B).—79km *Palaiofársalos*, junction for the main Athens–
Salonika line, is near the village òf *Stavrós*. The line now
follows roughly the course of the Lamia–Kardhitsa–Tríkkala
road (Rte 47C).—98km *Sofádhes*.—113·5km *Kardhitsa*.—
125·5km *Fanári*.—*143km Tríkkala*. To (164km) *Kalambáka*,
see Rte 51.

We quit Volos, passing over the railway, and in the next mile or so
leave on our left roads to Almiros and Lamia (Rte 49A) and to Dhimini
(Rte 49B). We follow the railway, ascending the *Defile of Pilav-Tepe*
(137m), named ('heap of rice') after a conical tomb of the Hellenic age
(left) opened in 1899. On the way up we cross the line of the Karla
Tunnel (see below) and see below us the expanding Volos industrial
zone. Just beyond (10km) *Latomeíon Station*, which serves neighbouring quarries, we leave on our left the by-road to Sesklo (Rte
49B).—19km **Velestíno** (Βελεστίνον) is a railway junction of some
importance where the line to Tríkkala (comp. above) parts company
with the branch to Larissa. By the station a by-road leads left for the
town (3164 inhab.), pleasantly situated amid gardens and fountains in
a ravine of Khalkodhónion (p. 419). It was the birthplace of the revolutionary poet Rigas Feraios (1757–98), who was executed by the
Turks in Belgrade for working towards a Balkan confederacy. Rich
prehistoric remains (Middle and Late Bronze Age) have been found
beneath the modern village.

Velestinon occupies the site of **Pherai**, at one time one of the great cities of
Thessaly; its port was Pagasai. Pherai was the legendary home of Admetus,
whose wife Alcestis sacrificed her life for him, in a story that inspired a celebrated
tragedy of Euripides and an opera by Gluck. In the 4C BC the rulers of Pherai
tried to dominate the whole of Thessaly and to interfere in the Greek world
generally. The most notorious were Jason, elected Tagus of Thessaly in 374 and
assassinated in 370, his successor Alexander who, defeated by the Theban general Pelopidas, died in 357, and Lykophron II, driven out in 352 by Philip of
Macedon. Antiochus the Great (223–187) took Pherai in 191, but it was almost
immediately recaptured by M. Acilius Glabrio.—Some archaeological explorations were made by the Greek Archaeological Service in 1920 and 1923, and
again, in collaboration with the French School, in 1925–26.
   The primitive city was built on a hill about 1km SE of the historic city, on which
the town of Velestinon was built. The *Acropolis* is on a trapezoidal plateau to the
N of the Vlach quarter; here are the remains of the Larissan Gate and of a temple
of Hercules. The city proper extended to the SW; near the church of the Panayia
are traces of the walls. Walls and towers uncovered on the hill of Ay. Athanasios
show that this too was within the enceinte. Pherai was noted for two fountains,

Hypereia and *Messeis*. The former is in the centre of Velestinon; the basin and conduit are covered with tiles.—On the Larissa road was uncovered a Doric *Temple of Zeus Thaulios*, rebuilt in the 14C with columns from an earlier temple, which in turn covered an ancient cemetery. A Hellenistic stoa, at least 49m long, was found in 1983. Archaic bronzes were removed to Athens and Geometric pottery to Volos.

We now have a choice of roads, almost equidistant. The faster National Highway runs slightly above the W of the plain, with views across it (toll after 24km). We describe the more interesting old road.— 23km *Rizómilos*. To the right was the large marshy LAKE KARLA, the ancient *Boibeïs*, one 24km long and 8km wide with a depth of 4–6m. Controlled and drained by a tunnel (comp. above) inaugurated in 1961, which takes surplus water to the Pagasitic Gulf, the lake is now a mere fraction of its former size and cannot be seen from the road. On the reclaimed and irrigated land experiments are being made with various crops, including cotton.

The ruins of several ancient cities are on the original shores: on the E is *Boibe*; on the NW *Armenion* (comp. below); on the SE is *Glaphyrai*, where there are foundations of a temple. The seaward side is fringed by *Mavrovouni* (1087m) and the saddle that connects it with Pelion.

32km *Armenió*. The site of Homeric *Armenion* is said to lie a little farther W at Kokkinés, and the huge Mycenean circuit of walls on the hill of Petra, overlooking the lake (right), is equated with *Kerkinion*. The plain is dotted with mounds showing prehistoric occupation. The modern villages lie mainly to the E. The range of Olympos rises ahead.—61km **Larissa** (Rte 48) may be by-passed.

Beyond Larissa the road runs W through the plain, which is interrupted ahead by isolated moderate hills culminating in MT DOBROUTSI, the ancient *Titanos* (767m). At (79km) *Koutsókheron* the village fountain has been hewn from a large Doric column drum. To our right, one behind the other, are the twin heights above *Goúnitsa* between which, through the impressive *Defile of Kalamaki*, the Peneios emerges into the plain.

About 1 hour SW of Koutsókheron, on a spur of Mt Dobroútsi, is the *Palaiókastro* of *Aléfaka*, the wreck of a Byzantine fortress built on ancient foundations. The ancient remains belong to *Atrax*, once inhabited by the warlike Perrhaebi. One of the city gates, flanked by a fine piece of polygonal wall, survives in part. A number of gravestones and inscriptions from the site are in the Larissa Museum.

Beyond the village we cross the winding Peneios above its entry into the defile. A by-road (right), affording a view into the defile, leads in 11km to Dhamasion (see Rte 58).—At (86km) *Pineiás* road and river pass between Dobroútsi and the abrupt spur of *Zárkos* (684m), the vertical W scarp of which looms over the village of *Zárkos*, 3km N of our road. Here was an ancient city, possibly *Phayttos* or *Pharkadon*, which in the Middle Ages became the seat of the Bp of Gardiki (comp. below).—At 94km, between modern *Farkadhón* (to the N) and the confluence of the Peneios with its most important tributary, the Enipeus (to the S), a road diverges S to Kardhitsa (28km).

The Kardhitsa road crosses the Peneios and its affluents. It follows the course of an old Turkish stone road, the fine bridges of which, mostly abandoned, survive on its W side. Just S of (8km) *Vlokhós* we pass through a line of hills surmounted by ancient citadels, the identity of which is in doubt. That rising prominently above the road (right) may be *Peirsia*; farther right Kastro of Kourtíki may be *Limnaion*; to the left is *Pétrino* (? *Phakion*).—10·5km *Palamá* (pop. 5448).—At 20km) *Ayios Theodhoros* we join a more direct but less interesting road from Larissa and the Lamia–Kardhitsa road (Rte 47C).

100km Crossroads. To the right, *Neokhóri* (3km), to the NW of which,
in the foothills of Andikhasia, are some remains of Thessalian
Oichalia.—Just before (110km) *Petróporos* we pass below the hill of
Palaiogardiki (right), the summit of which commands a fine view of the
plain of Tríkkala. Near by, the abandoned Byzantine town of *Gardiki*,
which gave title to a bishop (see above), has a ruined church (Ayia
Paraskevi), and occupies the site of *Pelinnaion*, of which there survive
fragmentary walls, with gates and towers. Pelinnaion was one of four
strongholds forming a defensive quadrilateral.—122km **Tríkkala**, see
Rte 47C.

51 The Metéora and the Central Píndos

The visit to the Metéora can hardly occupy less than half a day even if confined to
the three principal monasteries with the use of a car between them. It is inadvisa-
ble to allow less than a full day for the journey thence to Ioannina, though
Metsovo can be reached in a long afternoon's drive (c 3¾ hours).

A. From Tríkkala to Kalambáka. Metéora

ROAD to Kalambáka, 21km (13 miles); bus in ½ hr,
continuing to (23km) *Kastráki* for the Metéora (through
service from Larissa regularly). The tour of the monasteries
may be effected by asphalted road, 21km round from
Kalambaka; on foot the ancient stone paths are shorter but
often steep.

RAILWAY to Kalambáka, 22km in 40 minutes, 6 times daily;
through trains from Volos, via Farsala and Kardhitsa (comp.
Rte 50).

We quit Tríkkala by the Castle and turn NW. The road, lined with
poplars, drives straight across the plain, accompanied by the railway.
To the W rise the steep slopes of *Kerkétion*, a long range running N
and S and having its highest point (1900m) near its S end (ascent, see
Rte 47). On an isolated foothill, W of our road (near the village of
Peristéra), are some ruins to be identified with ancient *Pialeia.*

23km **Kalambáka** (Καλαμπάκα; Hotels A, C, E), an attractive little
town of 5692 inhab., spreads fanwise on the green slopes at the foot
of the Meteora rocks near the point where the Peneios emerges from
the Pindos gorges.

History. Kalambáka is the *Aiginion* of antiquity, a town of the Tymphaei stated
by Livy to have been impregnable. Here Caesar joined Cnaeus Domitius before
marching on Pharsalus. The Byzantines called the town *Stagoi*, perhaps a corruption of εἰς τοὺς Ἁγίους, and they established here a bishopric in the 10C; the see is
now at Tríkkala. In 1854 a force of Greeks captured and temporarily held
Kalambáka against the Turks.

The CATHEDRAL, dedicated to the Dormition of the Virgin, bears an
inscription ascribing its foundation to Manuel I Comnenos (mid-12C)
The chrysobull of Andronikos III painted on the N wall of the narthex
concerns the privileges of the diocese not the building of the church.
The present edifice, an aisled basilica, stands on even earlier founda-

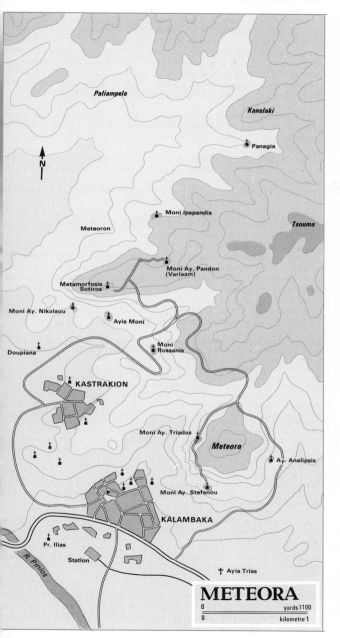

Paliampela

Kanalaki

Panagia

N

Moni Ipapandis

Meteoron

Tsouma

Moni Ay. Pandon
(Varlaam)

Metamorfosis
Sotiros

Moni Ay. Nikolaou

Ayia Moni

Doupiana

Moni
Rossanis

KASTRAKION

Moni Ay. Triados

Meteora

Ay. Analipsis

Moni Ay. Stefanou

KALAMBAKA

Pr. Ilias

Station

R. Pinios

† Ayia Trias

METEORA

0   yards 1100

0   kilometre 1

tions; some mosaics remain beneath the sanctuary floor. The Synthronon in the apse as well as the *Ciborium* and centrally placed Ambo probably belonged to the earlier building. There are several layers of paintings. From the 12C decoration have survived some frescoes on the N wall of the diaconikon. The remaining frescoes were painted by Cretan artists after a reconstruction in 1573, when the narthex and cloisters were added.—The church of *Ayios Ioannis Prodromos* (11–14C) is constructed of Roman materials.

A ROAD from the town centre leads round the W end of the colossal mass of rock that looms over Kalambáka. Beyond the by-road to Kastráki (1278 inhab.) we enter the weird valley of the Metéora. The foot-path is shorter.

The **'METÉORA** (Τὰ Μετέωρα) comprise a series of monastic buildings perched on a cluster of detached precipitous rocks. These are composed of a stratified conglomerate of iron-grey colour scarred by erosion of wind and streaked by centuries of rainwater. 'They rise' (in the words of Dr Henry Holland who visited them in 1812) 'from the comparatively flat surface of the valley; a group of isolated masses cones, and pillars of rock, of great height, and for the most part so perpendicular in their ascent, that each one of their numerous fronts seems to the eye as a vast wall, formed rather by the art of man, than by the more varied and irregular workings of nature. In the deep and winding recesses which form the intervals between these lofty pinnacles, the thick foliage of trees gives a shade and colouring, which while they enhance the contrast, do not diminish the effect of the great masses of naked rock impending above.' Awe-inspiring in the most favourable conditions, the landscape in lowering weather or by the light of the full moon is daunting in the extreme.

History. The earliest monastic community here, the 'Thebaid of Stagoi' a Doupiani developed before 1336 among the hermits who earlier sought in the caves religious isolation and a secure retreat from the turbulent times. Their Protaton, or communal church, is located by a small chapel (comp. below) on old foundations. Before the end of the century this skete and its protos had been eclipsed by the Meteoron, which, with other communities, was encouraged and endowed by the Orthodox Serbian conquerors of Thessaly. During the Turkish conquest the monasteries became an asylum for refugees. At its greatest extent the community numbered 13 monasteries, all coenobite, and c 20 smaller settlements, flourishing under Abbot Bessarion in the time of Suleiman the Magnificent, deriving revenues from estates on the Danube granted by the voivodes of Wallachia. The Patriarch Jeremias I (1522–45) raised several of them to the rank of imperial stavropegion. They declined in the 18C, and were already a decaying curiosity to early-19C travellers. They lost their independence to the Bp of Trikkala in 1899. The motor road that now makes the visit a commonplace of tourism has shattered the solitude and isolation. There are now only some ten monks, largely occupied in receiving visitors, and some twenty nuns. However continuing religious occupation seems assured by the Church's policy of a period of monastic service for its priests.

Access was intentionally difficult, being made either by a series of vertical wooden ladders of vertiginous length (20–40m), which could be retracted a night or in emergency, or in a net drawn up by rope and windlass to specially built towers, overhanging the abyss. The old methods, uncomfortable at best and often perilous, gave way in the 1920s to steps cut on the orders of Polykarpos, Bp of Trikkala, though the rope and windlass is still occasionally used for taking in provisions. The monasteries may be visited daily 8–12, 3–6, but the Gt Metéora is closed on Wednesdays. There is now no guest-house. ·

Beyond the Kastraki turn the road bends right. On the left stands the Doúpiani Chapel (comp. above), rebuilt in 1861. The 'Broad Rock (left), on which is seen the Great Meteoron, rises above several lesser pillars: the cleft rock of the *Prodromos* whose scanty ruins, already deserted in 1745, are now inaccessible; on a higher rock *Ayios Nikó-laos tou Anapavsá* (c 1388), partly repaired in 1960 when its frescoes, by Theophanes the Cretan (1527), were restored; and the inaccessible *Ayía Moní*, dangerously perched on its slender pinnacle in 1614 and ruined in an earthquake in 1858. We leave Rousanou to the right, take the left fork, pass Barlaam (left), and arrive at the **Great Metéoron**, or coenobitic *Monastery of the Transfiguration*, the largest and loftiest of the monasteries, built on the Platys Lithos ('Broad Rock'; 534m).

The Great Meteoron was founded by St. Athanasios as the poor community of the Theotokos Meteoritissa. Its privileges were guaranteed in 1362 by the Serbian Emp. Symeon Uroš and under the guidance of John Uroš, his son, who retired here c 1373 as the monk Ioasaph, it became a rich monastic house. Euthymios, Patriarch of Constantinople (1410–16), made it independent of local jurisdiction, but its head was not officially granted the title of Abbot (hegoumenos) until c 1482.

The *Katholikon* was reconstructed at his own expense by Ioasaph in 1387–88. His apse and sanctuary, decorated with painting in 1497–98, form the E extension of the existing church, which was enlarged after an earthquake in 1544. It is a Greek cross in square with a dome set on a drum. The paintings are in good preservation. The *Refectory* (1557), on the N side of the church, has a vaulted roof set on five pillars.

From the SE corner of the monastery (or from the path in the ravine towards Barlaam) there is a striking view of the neighbouring rock. Here among the vultures' nests can be descried two painted ikons and broken lengths of the ladders that once gave access to *Hypselotéra*, highest of the monasteries and dedicated to the 'Highest in the Heavens' ('Υψηλοτέρα τῶν Οὐρανῶν'). This convent was founded c 1390 and disappeared in the 17C, possibly owing to the peril of the ascent.
About 30 minutes N of the Broad Rock is the seldom-visited *Hypapantí*, derelict but still accessible, in a huge cavern. It merits a visit for its brightly painted frescoes and gilded ikonostasis. The inaccessible *Ayios Dhimítrios* stands on top of a nearby rock. It was destroyed by Turkish gunfire in 1809 after having served as headquarters of a local klephtic band.

The monastery of *Barlaam* is approached by bridge from the road. The windlass and rope in the *Tower* (erected in 1536) were much used for materials in 1961–63 when the refectory was reconstructed as a *Museum* for the monastic treasures. The founders in 1517, Nektarios and Theophanes Asparas of Ioannina, reoccupied a site where a 14C anchorite named Barlaam had built a church dedicated to the Three Hierarchs. This they restored and it survives (repaired and frescoed in 1627–37) as a side chapel of the present *Katholikon* erected in 1542–44. This is a good example of the late-Byzantine style with a carved and gilded ikonostasis and frescoes by Frangos Kastellanos and George of Thebes (in the narthex; 1566).
We return to the main fork. **Rousánou**, a small monastery compactly set on a lower hill, is approached by bridges built in 1868. It was founded before 1545 by Maximos and Ioasaph of Ioannina, but by 1614 had decayed to such an extent that it was made subject to Barlaam. It has recently been reoccupied by a convent of nuns. The *Church*, with an octagonal dome, is a smaller version of that of Barlaam, with frescoes of 1560.
Ayía Triádha, the monastery of the Holy Trinity, situated on an isolated pillar between two ravines, is entered by 130 steps partly in a tunnel through the rock. Off the passage leading into the courtyard a round chapel carved out of the rock was dedicated to St. John the Baptist in 1682. The little *Church* of 1476, ornamented in brick and tile, was not improved by the addition in 1684 of a large and ugly narthex.

The conventual buildings are in an attractive half-timbered style with a pretty garden.

The **Moní Ayíou Stefánou**, or nunnery of St. Stephen, though the farthest away by road, is the only monastery visible from Kalambaka. It is easy of access since its solitary pinnacle is joined directly to the Kuklióli hill by a bridge. The convent was founded c 1400 by Antonios Cantacuzene (probably a son of Nikephoros II of Epirus), whose portrait in the *Parecclesion* (the original Katholikon) was defaced by Communist rebels in 1949. The *New Katholikon*, rebuilt in 1798, is dedicated to the martyr Charalambos, whose head is the monastery's chief relic.

B. From (Tríkkala) Kalambáka to Ioánnina

ROAD, 152km (94½ miles). To (21km) **Kalambáka**, see above.— 80·5km *Katára Pass*.—93km **Métsovo** (2km S).— 152km **Ioánnina**. Buses daily. This is a mountain road of spectacular grandeur, crossing the highest pass in Greece open to motor traffic. In winter this route is closed by snow; even in early summer the snow-line must be crossed. The road is unsurfaced near the summit and there is some danger of landslides, so that the state of the road and the weather conditions should, if possible, be ascertained before leaving. The crossing should be attempted only in full daylight by drivers with experience of mountain roads.

The Píndos, or *Pindus Mountains*, an offshoot of the Dinaric Alps and an integral part of the backbone of Greece, runs from N to S and separates Epirus from Thessaly. From its S end a branch, under the name of OTHRYS, starting from Mt Veluchi (Tymphrestos), runs E to the Gulf of Volos and bounds the Thessalian plain on the S. The highest of the range's many peaks rise to the E and SE of Ioannina: these include *Kakarditsa* (2320m), *Peristeri* (2295m) and *Kataphidi* (2393m). Farther S the range divides: the W branch, culminating in *Tsournata* (2168m), is separated by the valley of the Agrapha from the E branch, the *Agrapha Mountains* (*Dolopia* in antiquity). In classical times the highest peak was called *Lakmon*, a name transferred to Mt Zygos (1555m), a peak to the E of Peristeri. The mountain sides are thickly wooded with trees of beech, oak and pine to within a short distance of the bare crests. Five important rivers have their source in the Pindos: the *Arakhthos*, flowing S through Epirus into the Gulf of Arta; the *Akheloös*, through Epirus, Akarnania, and Aitolia into the Ionian Sea; the *Aoös*, through Epirus and Albania into Adriatic; the *Aliakmon* and the *Pinios* into the Gulf of Salonika. In many parts of the range the rivers find their way down through deep valleys or gorges. Wolves and wild boar are still common in places; brown bears survive, and, in smaller numbers, the lynx. Of the larger birds Egyptian and Griffon vultures greatly outnumber the Golden Eagle.

Most journeys in the Pindos other than by the Katara Pass or by the Karpenisi–Frangista route in the S (Rte 54) still need the planning and equipment for a mountain expedition (comp. the trek led in 1963 by Sir John Hunt: *Geog. Jnl*, September 1964).

From Tríkkala to (21km) **Kalambáka**, see above. The Metsovo road leads W past the Xenia motel and ascends the valley of the Peneios in company with the abandoned earthworks of a railway (to Kozani; comp. Rte 58), begun by a Belgian company before 1939.—(At (31km) *Khani Mourgane* the road to Grevena (Rte 62) diverges to the right. We cross the Peneios by a Bailey bridge. A by-road goes off (left) across a bridge of 11 arches to *Kastaniá* (18km) and *Amáranton* (21km) in a side valley to the S. Our road now makes height on the slopes of the flat-topped *Mt Orthovoúni* (1106m).—At (47km) *Orthovoúni* (680m) the peaks of *Notia*, usually snow-covered, are prominent to the SW, while the ranges ahead fill the horizon in a seemingly level circle. The road continues at the higher level along the S slopes of *Krátsovon* (1565m). Beyond (55km) *Trigón*, steep descent. Just after (57km) a Petrol Station, we pass below *Pévki* (right). Panayia is seen far ahead.—64km *Koridhallós* stands to the E of a pass into an isolated valley of the Khasia range.—We cross a mountain torrent to (68km) *Koutsofianí*, a hamlet above the large village of *Panayía* which dominates the junction of the valleys. We now climb sharply in zigzags towards the main watershed between Khásia (right) and Notiá (left). Turning to *Malakási* (6km, left). The holm-oak gives place to pine and beech.—6km *Kámbos tou Dhespóti* (Restaurant; petrol) at a height of 1300m.

We mount to (80·5km) the **Pass of Katára** (1707m; refuge). Just before the summit splendid view in both directions. The road winds round the head of the W valley, keeping nearly level for some distance. After a mile or two in disappointingly bleak and enclosed surroundings, sudden superb *View of Metsovo backed by a gigantic range of snow-clad peaks. The road makes a great loop, descending amid slopes clothed in fir, beech, and box, affording views of peaks in every direction. Turning to *Vovoúsa* (right; 35·5km), an isolated village in the Valiakalda range.—At 93km we leave the main road at a saw-mill and in 2km reach Metsovo.

Métsovo (Μέτσοβο; Hotels A, B, C, E) has the status of deme and eparchy though little more than a large mountain village, having 2705 inhab., many of them Vlachs. The attractive houses are built in terraces on the steep side of a mountain separated from Mt Zygos (1555m) by two deep ravines. The town is divided by the chasm of the Metsovitikos into two parts—the 'Prosilio' (exposed to the sun) and the 'Anilio' (away from the sun)—which are connected by a bridge. All the five great rivers in the Pindos have their sources near Metsovo. The views on all sides are wonderful and the air exhilarating. The woollen rugs and local embroidered textiles are very attractive. The *MUSEUM (*Mouseío Laïkís Tékhnis*; visit guided), a beautiful display of the handicrafts of the region, occupies the restored 'arkhontikó' of Baron Michael Tositsa (1885–1950).

In the 17C Turkish vizier, in disgrace with his sultan, sought asylum at Métsovo and was kindly treated. Later returning to favour at court, he repaid the generosity of his hosts when, in 1669, the town was granted special privileges, giving it virtual independence which lasted to the time of Ali Pasha. Many rich Christian families took refuge at Metsovo, which has since had a reputation for its philanthropists, among them George Averoff (1815–99). The monastery of Ayios Nikolaos has frescoes by Eustathios (1702).

BUSES daily to *Athens*, via *Tríkkala* or via *Ioannina*; to *Salonika*, to *Ioannina*.

Above Metsovo we emerge high above the Metsovitikos, longest affluent of the Arachthos, in a wild landscape of sandstone. The road here is subject to falls of rock. We descend the rugged N side of the gorge, across which, above the gentler forest-clad S slopes, tower the outlying crags and central mass of *Peristéri* (2295m).—At (104km) *Votonósi*, where Tsolakoglou (first Quisling prime minister of Greece) signed an armistice with the Germans in 1941, the vegetation becomes less alpine; judas-trees, walnuts, etc. are seen again. We descend to the swift-flowing river. A by-road to Peristéri crosses the river by a Turkish pack-horse bridge. The road rises higher as the river drops below into a wild boulder-strewn gorge, while Peristéri rises to view again on the left.

We get a splendid *View down the widening river while we climb round the S side of Mt Dhemati. Across the river on Mt Gradhetsi, above *Mirkrá Gótista*, is the highest fortified enceinte of antiquity (3C BC) yet found in Greece (1562m). Ahead rises the streaked, forbidding *Mitsikeli* range (1809m) as we descend to (126km) *Baldoúmas* (café; petrol) and cross the tributary Zagoritikos on a Bailey-bridge. The road now ascends in serpentine loops over the S part of Mitsikeli, affording retrospective *Vistas of range upon range of the Pindos.— 137km *Mázia* occupies the saddle between Mitsikeli and Dhriskos. From the summit a broad well-engineered road descends, with views across Lake Pamvotis.—139km The Monastery *Panayía Dourahán* is reputed to have been founded in 1434 by Dourahan Pasha as a thanks offering to the Virgin for protecting his night ride across the frozen lake.—145km *Stroúni* is a starting-point for climbing Mitsikeli (Refuge 2½ hrs above the village). We descend to (152km) **Ioánnina** (Rte 52).

VI NORTH-WESTERN GREECE

pirus or *Ípiros* ('Ήπειρος; "The Mainland" '), the NW province of
Greece, is separated from Albania by an artificial frontier, and from
Thessaly by the Pindus range. On the S it is washed by the Gulf of Arta
and on the W by the Ionian Sea, with the island of Corfú lying opposite
the frontier between Greece and Albania. The mountainous character
of the interior and the scarcity of communications have always isolated Epirus, whose inhabitants were only partly Hellenic. The few
Greek colonies were confined to the coast and to the low-lying region
of the S. The province, the most humid in Greece, is well wooded and
yields a little corn; it has long been famous for its flocks and pasturage
and for its breed of Molossian dogs. Its principal rivers are the Arta
(Arachthos), the Kalamas (Thyamis), and the Mavropotamos
(Acheron). Epirus is divided into four nomes: Ioannina, Preveza, Arta,
and Thesprotia. The largest towns are Ioannina and Arta, both well
inland, the Preveza, on the coast. The main roads are now better than
most maps suggest. In antiquity the oracle of Dodona was renowned

as the oldest in Greece.

History. Of the 14 tribes inhabiting Epirus, the chief were the Chaones, the Thesproti and the Molossi, which gave their names to the three main divisions of the country. Each tribe was governed by its own prince. The Molossians, who claimed descent from Neoptolemos (Pyrrhus), son of Achilles, later took over the whole country as kings of Epirus. The most famous of these kings was Pyrrhus (318–272 BC). In 286 he invaded Macedonia, of which he became king for a brief period. In 280 he accepted the invitation of the Tarentines to join them in their war against Rome. After his victory at Heraclea, he came within 24 miles of Rome. A second Pyrrhic victory, at Asculum (Apulum), in 279, exhausted both sides. After adventures in Sicily helping the Greeks against the Carthaginians Pyrrhus returned to Italy in 276; his defeat near Beneventum in the following year obliged him to leave Italy for good. But he did not remain idle. In 273 he again invaded Macedonia, becoming king for the second time, again for a short period Afterwards he turned against Sparta and Argos, where he was ignominiously killed. After his death the kingship of Epirus was abolished, and the country divided between three generals. In the Macedonian wars, Epirus joined the Macedonians, went over to the Romans (198), and then turned against them (170). After the defeat at Pydna in 168 of Perseus, the last king of Macedon, 7 towns in Epirus were destroyed and 150,000 of the inhabitants enslaved, and the country became a Roman province.

In the Middle Ages Epirus was constantly invaded. After the division of the Byzantine empire the country was divided into *New Epirus*, with Dyrrachium (Durazzo), and *Old Epirus*, with Acarnania. After the capture of Constantinople by the Crusaders in 1204, a despotate of Epirus was set up. The first despot Michael I, made Ioannina his capital. A later despot, Theodore Angelus, seized the Latin kingdom of Thessalonika in 1223. The dynasty expired at the end of the 13C. In 1318–35 Epirus with Cephalonia came under the domination of the Orsini, returned briefly to Byzantium, fell to the Serbs (1348–86), and returned to Cephalonia under the Tocci. The Turks captured Ioannina in 1431. In the 15C and 16C the Venetians occupied several strong points in the country. Epirus took no part in the War of Independence In 1881 the District of Arta was freed from Turkish domination. During the Second Balkan War the Greek army took Ioannina (February 1913), and occupied all the north of Epirus; but much of this liberated territory was subsequently given to Albania. In the Second World War the Greek army threw back the invading Italians in 1940 and, until the German intervention, reoccupied Northern Epirus.

Aitolía and Akarnanía (Αιτωλακαρναία), together form the most westerly nome of Central Greece, lying between Epirus and the Gulf of Patras. **Aitolía**, on the E, is divided from Akarnania by the river Acheloös. Its W half, lying between the Acheloos and the Evenos, was anciently called *Old Aetolia* and included the city of Kalydon, mythologically famous for the boar hunt. *New Aetolia* or *Aitolia Epikteto* ('Acquired Aetolia') extended to the E from the Evenos to the country of the Ozolian Locrians. The interior of Aitolia is roadless, wild and mountainous, with numerous peaks exceeding 1800m, and is accessible only to determined travellers.

Aetolia, originally inhabited by the Curetes, derives its name from Aetolos, son of Endymion, who fled hither after having killed Apis. The five cities of Old Aetolia all took part in the Trojan War. The three tribes living in New Aetolia were barbarous, ate raw flesh, and spoke an unintelligible dialect (Thuc. III, 94). Loosely connected by a religious tie, they had a common temple at the sanctuary of Thermon. After the battle of Chaironeia (338 BC), they formed the Aetolian League which, at the beginning of the 3C BC, was strong enough to frustrate the invading armies of the Gaul Brennus. Before the expansion of the rival Achaean League under Aratos, the Aetolians reached the zenith of their power. They acquired or dominated Locris, Phocis, central Akarnania, and Boeotia, as well as numerous cities in the Peloponnesus. In the ruinous War of the Leagues (219–21 BC), Philip V of Macedon, with the Achaeans as allies, invaded Aetolia. In 211 the Aetolians allied themselves with Rome, and in 197 they helped the Romans to win the battle of Cynoscephalae. Later they joined Antiochus the Great against the Romans, and in the peace of 188 their federation was virtually dissolved. In 31, after the battle of Actium, Octavian (Augustus) completed the depopulation caused by centuries of warfare by transferring most of the inhabitants to his new ity of Nikopolis, on the Epirus side of the Ambracian Gulf. In the War of Independence the Aetolians defeated the Turks at Karpenisi, and Mesolongi endured three sieges.

Akarnanía has the sea on three sides. It is bounded on the N by the Ambracian Gulf; on its W coast it is joined by a causeway to the island of Levkas, and has two other Ionian Islands—Ithaca and Cephalonia—and numerous islets to the S. A mountain range (over 1500m) occupies most of the eparchy of Xiromeros between Astakós, on the S coast, and Vónitsa, on the Ambracian Gulf.

The Akarnanians emerged from obscurity at the beginning of the Peloponnesian War (431 BC). Like the Aetolians, they were uncivilised, living by piracy and robbery, and like them they formed their towns into a league, which first met at Stratos, their chief town. South and central Aetolia are entirely agricultural, but the cultivation is not intensive. Currants are grown near Mesolongi, olives round Aitoliko, and tobacco near Agrinion. The mountain eparchies depend upon the produce of the forests; Xeromeros, in Akarnania, exports valonia, the acorn of the *Quercus aegilops*, used for tanning.

52 From Igoumenítsa to Ioánnina, Párga and Préveza

A. To Ioánnina (and Dodóna)

ROAD 101km (63 miles), a fine modern *Highway through rugged mountainous country. Buses of KTEL 21 regularly.

Igoumenítsa (Hotels B, C, D, E; F/A), the port of call on the Greek mainland of car ferries from Brindisi and Otranto and the terminus of a local ferry (6–10 times daily; comp. Rte 56) from Corfu, was an insignificant village until, in 1936, it became the seat of the nomarch of Thesprotia. Rebuilt on the ruins left by the occupying troops in 1944, it is now a flourishing transit town (5879 inhab.) with a pleasant sea front.

Through the formerly marshy plain to the N the Kalamas, the ancient Thyamis, winds its way to the channel separating Corfù from the mainland. A barrage (1962) at the exit of the last defile now controls irrigation, and experiments are being made in rice growing. The small hills which rise above the marsh are considered by some authorities to represent the ancient *Sybota Islands*, near which a naval battle was fought in 433 BC between the Corinthians and Corcyraeans (Thuc. I, 45). Their name is now held by a group of islands between Igoumenitsa and Parga to the S.
From Igoumenitsa to *Preveza*, see Rte 52B, 52C: to *Parga*, see Rte 52C.

Climbing out of Igoumenitsa, the Ioannina road enters a level valley enclosed by rugged mountains.—9km Turning to Filiátes and Sayiádha.

This road runs out towards the Albanian frontier and military restrictions may be encountered. The road is unpaved to Elaia, then asphalt.—1km We cross the Kalamas (military check at the bridge).—3km *Elaia* (the road from Elaia back to the main road near Neraídha, marked as good on many maps, is very rough).—9km *Filiátes* (Filiátes; 220m) is a lively market town. The former Turkish population dwindled in the plague of 1821 and the town was repopulated by Christian refugees. A cheese factory was built in 1963–65 by United Nations Association volunteers. *Yeroméri*, near by, has a monastery founded in 1285.—14km Turning

to *Plaísion* (5km), a decayed old town with a 17C church, which in the 19C had
flourishing tanneries. It was the birthplace of Kyra Vasiliki, consort of Ali Pasha.
Besieged by Albanians in 1908–13 and looted and burnt in 1943, it now has only a
third of its former population.—23km *Sayiádha*, rebuilt on the coast after the hill
town was destroyed in 1940–41, has a jetty opposite Corfù. The old ruins can be
seen high above the road.

The main road turns S to cross a spur and descends again to the river,
which here makes a wide loop through a gorge to the N. We follow the
right bank below steep hills; the villages lie across the river. The
precipitous W ranges of the Pindus rise ahead. The Paramithiá road
(see Rte 52B) diverges 1km before (23km). *Menína* (officially
Neráïdha). Our road rises continuously amid scrub, passing a turning
to the 16C *Moní Pagánion*. Beyond (38·5km) *Plakotí*, it zigzags sharply
up to 610m while the river threads another ravine. In the local collection of antiquities at *Polídhroso* (10km further) is the first complete
Etruscan 'jockey-cap' helmet to be found in Greece, perhaps brought
to the area by a veteran of the wars of Pyrrhos. The view opens out
ahead (café) as we descend by continuous turns to rejoin the river at
(52km) *Vrosína*, where an old packhorse bridge (left) crosses a tributary.
We cross the Tyrias and undulate through cultivated hills.—At
(69·5km) *Soulópoulo* we cross another affluent of the Kalamas and
climb out of the river basin through countryside patterned by stone
walls.—Just beyond (80km) *Klimatiá* a poor road diverges N to **Zítsa**
(6·5km; 680m), a picturesque little town (966 inhab.) locally renowned
for its somewhat sweet wine. Its prosperity in Turkish times is attested
by its stone houses and paved streets. The monasteries of *Profitis Ilias*
and *tou Pateron* (14C), fired with nationalist zeal in 1778 by Kosmas
Aitolou, fostered Greek schools. Byron sings the charms of the view in
'Childe Harold' (II, xlviii).
   86km Turning for *Rodhotópi* (5km) with slight remains of ancient
Passaron, a Molossian town which survived into Roman times. The site
of its Sanctuary of Zeus Areios was identified by inscriptions in 1954.—
At 92·5km we join the Kónitsa road in the upland plain N of Ioannina.
Beyond the airport, at the N end of the lake, the Métsovo road (Rte
51B) comes in from the left.
   101km (63 miles) **IOÁNNINA** (Τά Ιωάθθιθα), a deme (44,829
inhab.) of the eparchy of Dodona, is the capital of the nome of
Ioánnina, the seat of the Government-General of Epirus and of an
archbishop, and an army headquarters. It occupies a rocky promontory jutting into lake Pambotis oppsite the foot of the precitous Mt
Mitsikeli. The busy and friendly town lies at 475m in the midst of a
plain divided between pasture and the cultivation of cereals and
tobacco. Local industries include the manufacture of filigree silver
jewellery. To the E and SE of the town rise the highest peaks of the
Pindus. In summer the temperature is oppressive; winters are long
and cold.

Airport, with twice daily service to Athens via Agrinion, also twice weekly to
Salonika. *Olympic Airways* in upper, main square, Mégaro Kourtío.

Hotels B, C, D.

Post Office and *O.T.E.*, Od. 28 Oktovríou.—INFORMATION BUREAU (N.T.O)
Od. Nap. Zérva.—*Tourist Police*, opposite P.O.

Buses from opp. Clock Tower (KTEL 13 Agrinion) regularly to *Arta*, continuing
sometimes to *Agrinion*, *Mesolongi*, and *Patras*; from the Froúrion (KTEL 20) to
Athens, etc.; from KTEL 21, 4 Zosimádhou, to *Perama*, *Igoumenitsa*, *Konitsa*
etc.; from Ay. Marúnis (times not very convenient) to *Dodona*.

History. *Ioannina* is first documented in 1020 and may have taken name and site from a monastery of St John the Baptist. Taken by Bohemond, eldest son of Robert Guiscard, in the 11C, it was visited in 160 by Benjamin of Tudela. Ioannina dates its importance, however, from the influx of refugees in 1205 from Constantinople and the Morea and its consequent fortification by Michael I Angelos. An archbishopric was established here between 1284 and 1307. In 1345 Ioannina was captured by the Serb Stefan Dušan, proclaimed in the following year Emperor of Serbia and Greece. In 1431 it surrendered to the army of the Sultan Murad II. In 1618, after an abortive rising led by Dionysos Skylosophos', the fanatical Bp of Trikkala, the Christians were expelled from the citadel and their churches destroyed. Nevertheless, upon in 1666 found the town rich and populous. Its zenith was reached under *Ali Pasha* (Born in 1741 at the Albanian village of Tepelini), a brilliant, resourceful, and vindictive adventurer who alternately bought and served the Sultan of Turkey. Having assisted the Turks in their war of 1787 against Austria, he was made Pasha of Trikkala in 788, in which year he seized Ioannina, then a town of 35,000 inhabitants, and made it his headquarters. In 1797 he allied himself with Napoleon, but the next year he took Preveza from the French. In 1803 he subdued the Suliots. After 1807 his dependence on the Porte was merely nominal. Byron visited Ioannina in 1809, while Col. W.M. Leake, the great topographer of Greece, was British resident, and Henry Holland was Ali Pasha's doctor. In 1817 Ali entered into an alliance with the British, who gave him Parga. At length the Sultan decided to eliminate this daring rebel. He was captured at Ioannina after a siege, and executed there in 1822. Two years before his death, besieged by Ismail Pasha, he had set fire to the town. The Congress of Berlin (1878) assigned Epirus to Greece, but it remained in Turkish hands for over 5 more years. On 21 February 1913, the Greek army entered Ioannina.

Ioannina was long famous for its *Schools*, founded by Michael Phi-anthropinos (1682–1758), Leondat Giouma (1675–1725), and Mele-os (1690), later Bp of Athens and a noted historian and geographer. They were all destroyed in the fire of 1820.

The social life of Ioannina centres on Odhos Yeoryíou tóu Prótou which connects PLATEÍA PÍRROU, a beautiful belvedere laid out in front of the *Municipal Offices* (*View of Mitsikeli), and the KENTRIKÍ PLATEÍA with its clock tower (*To Rolói*) farther down the hill. Commanding the central square is the *Merarkhia* (army HQ) in front of which the Colours are ceremonially lowered each evening. Behind, the museum and gardens occupy the levelled upper esplanade of the Kastro, which once sheltered the Christian quarter of *Litharitsa*, its walls were demolished by Ali Pasha and the material used to build his palace and outer fortifications of the town. The N part of the castle has been restored as a café-restaurant.

The *Museum*, opened 1970, has five halls, of which the first is the most important. HALL A (right), cases arranged chronologically from right to left. Case 1. Stone tools from Cambridge Univ. excavations in Paleolithic caves at Asprokhalikó and Kastrítsa; Cases 2 & 3. Neolithic and Bronze Age finds, chiefly from L.H. IIIB–C cist graves (swords, daggers); Case 4. Protogeometric vases from the region of Agrinion.—Cases 5–9, finds from the cemeteries of Vitsa, ranging from 9C Geometric to late-Classical; notable are the small stylised Geometric horse (case 7) and a fine bronze kylix (case 9); two superb bronze beaked Pitchers (in central cases) are especially attractive with their marbled patina.—Case 10. Vases and terracotta figurines of Persephone from the Nekyomanteion of Ephyra (see Rte 52C), also the windlass mechanism.—In Case 11 note the finger ring of crystal with a sculptured bull, also elaborate gold earrings, from Ambracia; gilded bronze plaque depicting Klytemnestra and Orestes, small but exquisite.—Case 12. Finds from many sites including heads of Goddesses.

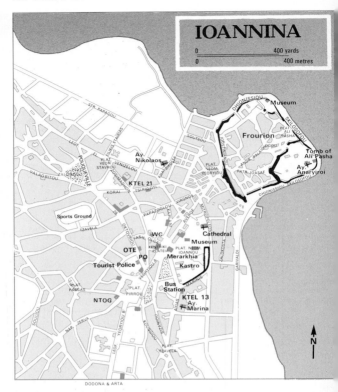

Table cases 13 & 14. Epirote coins. Some of the large bronze *Vessels from the Votonosi discovered in 1939 are displayed in Case 15, while Cases 16–20 and VIII–XI contain *Votive bronzes (eagle warriors, boy with dove, lion) and oracular tablets of lead from Dodona.

In the CORRIDOR are inscriptions from Dodona, Ionic capitals from Kassope, and grave goods from Mikhalitsi (model cart from a child burial).—HALL B. Marble sculptures from Mikhalitsi include female heads and an elaborate sarcophagus.—Beyond HALLS C & E, with 19–20C paintings, HALL D shows fine Frankish-Byzantine *Capitals from a church at Gliki and hoards of Venetian coins.

Odhos Avérof, lined with silversmiths, descends directly to the **Frourion**, the fortress of the Despots, restored in 1815 by Ali Pasha as his headquarters. The *Walls*, though impressive, preserve very little Byzantine work. The landward side was protected by the 'Khandáki', a moat (now filled in) joining the two little landing places (comp. below) and crossed by three wooden bridges. Towards the NW is the former *Turkish Library*, restored in 1973. Enclosed by a wall in the NW corner, overlooking the lake, is the picturesque *Cami of Aslan Pasha, a conventual foundation of 1618. An implausible tradition places here the rape and murder in 1801 of Kyra Phrosyne and her 17 companions. The mosque, which continued in use until 1928, now houses the crowded **Municipal Museum**. On the way up are cannon and piles of balls. Note the recesses for shoes in the vestibule. The Mosque has a well-proportioned dome. Striking among the exhibits are the Epirote costumes and adornments of the 18–19C.

The *Minaret* (when accessible) affords a superb *View of the lake and the surrounding mountains. We look down (SE) on the inner citadel of *Its-Kalé* (military; adm. sometimes granted) with the *Fetihie Cami*, or Victory Mosque, a circular *Tower*, the *Tomb of Ali Pasha*, and the restored *Palace* (officers' mess) where the 'Lion of Ioannina' entertained Byron and Hobhouse in October 1809.

The shady Leofóros Dhionissíou Skilosófou runs by the lakeside beneath the walls. In the cliff is the cave where the Skylosophos was caught and flayed alive in 1611. From the Skála Psarádhika, with its quaint fishing boats, we may reach the **Cathedral** (Ayios Athanasios), rebuilt in 1820, with ornate carved woodwork and the tomb of a local patriot of 1828. We may continue S below the Kastro to a charming disused *Mosque*, its truncated minaret the haunt of storks, whence the picturesque Odhos Koungiou ascends to Plateia Pirrou (comp. above).

The **Lake of Ioannina**, or *Limni Pambotis*, is fed by torrents from the precipices of Mitsikeli and discharges its waters into swallow-holes. It is 10–11km long, averages 3km across, and ranges in depth from 9–20km, with shallow reedy shores. After very wet weather it may form one with the Lapsista marsh to the N. The local boats are similar in design to those on Lake Kastoria. A boat (hourly) plies to the ISLAND (Taverna; crayfish and eels) in the lake, on which are numerous monasteries very prettily situated amid trees and flowers. We first visit the *Monastery of the Prodhromos* (St. John the Baptist), to the E of the little island village. Its most ancient parts (13C) are the katholikon and the E aisle. It was restored in the 16C, the 18C frescoes in the 19C.—In the 16C *Monastéry of Pantaleímon*, near by, Ali Pasha was killed on 17 January 1822; the bullet marks on the floor witness to his assassination. The katholikon is in the form of a basilica. There is a small *Museum* of prints and costumes. The *Monastery of Ayios Nikólaos Spanós*, or Philanthropiní, on a rocky height to the N of the village, was built in the 13C and rebuilt in the 16C. It has a katholikon with decorated doors and 16C frescoes.

In the *Apse*, Communion of Saints. In the nave vault, the Almighty and the Evangelists; on the walls, Life of Jesus. *Narthex*: In the vault, Annunciation; N side, the five founders of the monastery kneeling before St. Nicholas; above, Head of Christ; NW corner, Portraits of Greek philosophers.

The *Monastery of Ayios Nikólaos Dhílios*, or Stratigopoúlou, is the oldest (11C). It lies to the E of the Monastery of Spanos. In the katholikon, Fresco (restored in 16C); Judas returning his pieces of silver. In the Narthex, Lives of the Virgin and St. Nicholas, Last Judgment.—To the S the *Monastery of Ayios Eleoúses* takes name from a 15C ikon brought here from the kastro. The katholikon (before 1584) has 18C frescoes.

At the N end of the lake, on the way to *Pérama* (4km; bus) is an isolated hill in which are a spectacular series of *Caverns, discovered by accident when places of refuge were being sought in the Second World War. Their stalagmites and stalactites are admirably lit by electricity and well worth a visit; parties are taken through the ½-mile of galleries by guides (8–sunset).

At the S end of the lake, on the hill of *Kastritsa*, near an old monastery, is the site of ancient *Tekmona*. Below this, palaeolithic remains were dug in 1966 by the British School. Kastritsa (c 8km) is reached by taking the W lakeshore road out of Ioannina, branching left for Katsiká, then left again for Dhrosokhóri (rough road).

The EXCURSION TO DODONA should on no account be missed. ROAD (asphalted), 22km (13½ miles), infrequent bus. We take the Arta road, passing the Xenia Hotel and an artillery barracks, and run level through tobacco fields with distant views (left) of the Pindus.—At 8km we turn right and wind over a ridge (fine retrospective views of the lake and the Pindos) into the enclosed valley of Tsarkovitsa at the foot of MT TOMAROS, the long ridge of which rises from the N end (1332m) to two peaks at the S (Mt Olitsikas; 1974m).

The road ends by the *Tourist Pavilion* at the entrance to (22km) the ruins of **Dodóna**, beautifully sited facing Mt Tómaros amid fresh and smiling scenery. The modern village of *Dhodhóni* (Δωδόνη) stands a little farther W.

The Oracle of Zeus at Dodona, regarded as Pelasgic, was reputedly the oldest in Greece. 'Wintry Dodona' is mentioned in both Iliad and Odyssey. Strabo says that the oracle was moved from Skotoussa, in Thessaly, in obedience to the command of Apollo, but Herodotus tells of the arrival of a dove from Egyptian Thebes. Homer assumes that the servers were men, called them *selloi*, prophets of Zeus, who did not wash their feet and slept on the ground. In the time of Plato, however, the divine message was given by priestesses in a state of inspired frenzy. According to Herodotus the oracle spoke in the rustling of leaves in the sacred oaks in sounds made by beating a copper vessel with a whip. The Molossian word 'peleiae' seems to have meant both doves and old women; there are trees but no oaks in the vicinity today and the main sound is the tinkling of sheep bells.

The site was identified in 1873 by Constantin Karapanos, who discovered a number of bronze objects now in the museum at Athens. More scientific excavations have been undertaken by the Greek Archaeological Service since 1952 and some judicious restoration made.

We enter along the axis of the *Stadium*, of which part of the Sphendone has been uncovered. The seating rises on the N side on a bank thrown up against the w retaining wall of the theatre at the end of the 3C BC. The superb *Theatre* was judiciously restored in 1960–63 for use at the annual festival of drama. Constructed originally in the time of Pyrrhus (297–272 BC), it was destroyed by the Aetolians in 219 BC and rebuilt shortly afterwards by Philip V out of the spoils taken from

Thermon. It suffered at the hands of the Romans in 168–167 BC and was converted into an arena about the time of Augustus when the lowest seating was replaced by a protective wall (comp. below).

The SKENE is built in good isodomic masonry. The outer *Façade* consisted of a stoa of 13 octagonal columns. An *Arch* admitted to the centre of the stage. Double *Gateways*, with Ionic half-columns, lead into either parodos, whence we reach the *Orchestra*. The fine drainage channel in the shape of a horseshoe is well-preserved.

The CAVEA is partly recessed in the side of the Acropolis hill and partly supported by massive retaining walls of excellent rusticated ashlar masonry up to 21m high, buttressed by towers. It is divided by two diazomata, the three resulting banks of seats having 21 (reduced later to 15; comp. above), 16, and 21 rows (the lower two banks restored to position). Ten stairways divided the lower banks into 9 kerkides, while the topmost bank has 18 wedges. Two broad staircases added later against the façade lead up to the upper diazoma, while a *Ceremonial Entrance* from the direction of the Acropolis opens into the topmost gallery; here cuttings show where a gate fitted. The back retaining wall is largely whole though some wall slabs of the gallery have fallen forward.

Behind the theatre a well-preserved *Gate* leads into the ACROPOLIS. The surrounding wall, 3–4·5m wide, is now less than 3m high. The enclosure is roughly quadrilateral with towers on three sides. The fabric is of various periods with Hellenistic predominating.

A path descends to the terrace, E of the theatre, site of the **Sanctuary**. Only foundations subsist. The large hypostyle hall is shown by inscribed decrees and an inscribed altar to be the *Bouleuterion* of the Epirot confederacy built by Pyrrhus. To the S of the bouleuterion, a rectangular building of c 200 BC, destroyed in 169, was probably the *Prytaneion* or else a hostel for important officers of the Epirot League. Beyond, to the E, is a small, rectangular *Temple of Aphrodite*. The TEMENOS OF ZEUS NAIOS, of *Hiera Oikia*, is a complex ruin in which four stages of growth can be differentiated. At first worship centred upon the sacred oak-tree; fragments of votive tripods of the 8C BC have been recovered. A stone temple was not built until the 4C, consisting merely of cella and pronaos. This and the oak were then surrounded by a peribolos wall. The wall was replaced in the time of Pyrrhus by an enclosure of Ionic colonnades facing inwards on three sides with a blind wall on the E next the tree. After the burning of the sacred groves in 219 BC the temple was enlarged with an Ionic portico and an adyton, and the peribolos rebuilt with an Ionic propylon.

Beyond are two successive versions of a *Temple of Dione*, and a *Sanctuary of Herakles*. These are overlain by an Early Christian *Basilica*, which incorporates an honorific decree of 180 BC. Dodona sent a bishop to the Council of Ephesos in AD 431, but the basilica is probably of Justinianic date.

FROM IOANNINA TO THE VIKOS GORGE, road c 80·5km, a comfortable half-day excursion by car. The Konitsa road (see below) is followed to (19km) *Kariés*. Beyond the village a by-road (signposted Vitsa) diverges right, climbing the slope of Mitsikeli with wide views over the main road. It soon turns E, running level through a gap into the Zagoria, an upland forested valley extending SE. Below Asprángeloi and again at a further junction we bear left, following signs for Monodhéndri.—36km *Vitsa*, an old stone-built village, commands wide views of forest-clad mountains. Some indeterminate excavations (left; finds in Ioannina) are passed just before (40km) *Monodhéndri* (1090m). A difficult cobbled road through the village square leads in ½ mile to the deserted monastery of *Ayía Paraskeví* (1412), perched high on a sheer cliff above the **Vikos Gorge (Farángi Víkou)**. The cells and frescoed chapel have been restored and vertiginous paths with perilous bridges lead on to caves and hermits' cells. In the lush gorge the river Voïdhomati runs NW to Vikos; the beautiful region would repay exploration (strong walking boots and provisions needed). In the lower part of the gorge, on the right bank of the river and near the monastery of Ay. Anaryroi, excavation of a palaeolithic rock shelter began in 1981.

FROM IOANNINA TO KONITSA AND NEAPOLIS (Kozani or Kastoria). ROAD, 174km (108 miles); some discretion needed in view of proximity of Albanian frontier. Leaving the Metsovo road to the right and that to Igoumenitsa on the left, our road runs N across the marshy plain of Lapsista at the foot of Mitsikeli.—17km *Asfáka* stands on the E shore of the seasonal *Lake Miradhia*.—At (19km) *Kariés*, by-road (right) to the Vikos Gorge (see above).—33km *Memorial to the Fallen* of 1940–41 and Museum at the junction of the by-road to the monastery of *Vélla* (2·5km SW). Vella takes its name from a ruined Byzantine town near by; its bishopric was merged with that of Ioannina in 1842.—34km *Kalpáki* (600m; Inn; police post), a road junction of great strategic importance, commands the chief route into Greece from Albania. Here, on 1–14 November 1940, the Greek army fought a stubborn defensive battle against the Italian invaders; their counter-offensive threw the Italians back over the Albanian frontier.

Here diverges a road now effectively serving only the eparchy of Pogonion, but once leading to Argyrokastro (Gjinokastrë in Albania). *Dhelvinákion* (22km), with 884 inhab., has superseded *Pogoniani* as chief town of the region. The archbishopric of Pogoniani, perhaps found by Constantine IV Pogonatos (668–685) and dissolved in 1863, may originally have had its seat at *Molyvdhosképastis* (best reached from Konitsa; see below), where the monastery of Koimisis Theotókou dates from his reign and was restored by Andronikos Comnenus c 1183. The frescoes were restored in 1521 and there is 14C woodwork.

The main road makes a steep ascent with views of Mt Gaméla (right), the several rugged peaks of which rise to 2480m.—After the junction below (28 miles) *Yeroplátanos*, the road descends in loops to the Voïdhomati, crosses the river below the Vikos Gorge (comp. above), and runs through an upland plain growing melons. At *Merópi* (8km NW of Yeroplátanos) and *Palaiópirgos*, were excavated in 1979– 81 two tumuli (of many) with cist tombs and finds from the 11–4C BC, as well as part of the prehistoric settlement.

64·5km **Kónitsa** commands the road from a hillside above the colossal gorge through which the Aoos emerges from the Pindos. To the NE towers *Smolikas* (2579m), highest peak of the Pindos; to the S, Gamela (see above). The town (2849 inhab.), seat of an eparchy and birthplace of the mother of Ali Pasha, was conquered by the Turks of Murad II in 1440. The Greeks entered the town on 24 February 1913. It remains a typical mountain market centre. From 24 December 1947 to 15 January 1948 its garrison withstood violent attacks of the communist Gen. Markos, who intended to make it his capital. The church of the *Kokkini Panayia* has frescoes.—From Konitsa a road leads W towards the frontier (19km), where the Aoos below its confluence with the Voïdhomati becomes the Vijosë (Viosa) as it flows through Albania into the Adriatic above Valona. The river is crossed by two ancient bridges, *Bourazani* and *Mertzani*, near Molyvdhosképastos (comp. above).

From Konitsa a broad new road climbs sharply out of the Aoos Valley, then winds amid the W foothills of Smolikas. It descends to the Sarandáporos and follows its left bank upstream. At 89km the river is crossed.—Beyond (95km) *Pirsóyianni*, which is by-passed, a tributary is bridged at the confluence, and the road gradually bears E. We cross the boundary into the nome of Kastoria and quit the river for another tributary.—Beyond (119km) *Eptakhórion* a steady climb passes a spring and picnic site to a summit of 1443km at the boundary of the nome of Kozani. Here is a wide view of the S.—135·5km *Pendálofos* (1060m), a picturesque mountain village with stone houses that formed the headquarters of the British Mission to the Greek Resistance in the Second World War. The road zigzags down to the gorge of the Pramoritsu, or Koutsomilia, then gradually climbs into more open upland. Beyond (150km) *Morfí* it drops down again to the Koutsomilia, crossing the torrent to climb a long windswept ridge with extensive retrospective views near (158km) the Omali turn.—164·5km *Tsotilion* (840m; Hotel D), with one of the first colleges founded during the Turkish domination. The road descends to (174km) *Neápolis*, whence to Kastoria or Kozani, see Rte 62.

From Ioannina to *Metsovo* and into Thessaly, see Rte 51B.

B. To Préveza via Paramithiá

ROAD, 112km (69½ miles), asphalt to (58km) *Glikí*, then
alternating with good gravel.

For the first 24km we follow the Ioannina road (Rte 52A), then turn
right. The road crosses a ridge.—34km (21 miles) **Paramithiá**
(Παραμυθιά; Hotels D, E), a large village (pop. 2468), picturesquely
scattered on the slopes below the W scarp of Mt Korillas, is the chief
place of the eparchy of Suli. Its name, which means 'consolation', is
variously derived. It was called by the Turks *Aij Donat Kalessi* and by
the Venetians *Castel San Donato*, names again variously derived as a
corruption of the ancient *Aidonati* or after the 4C Donatos, Bp of
Euroia. In the 18C Paramithiá was the capital of one of the three
sanjaks of Epirus. About 10 minutes above the town is the ruined
Venetian *Kastro*, built on Hellenic foundations. The town was temporarily held by British forces in 1941. At *Velianí*, 6·5km SE, remains of a
7C basilica may mark the see of the Bp of Photike.—We now continue
in the enclosed valley of the Kokkitos below the steep scarps of
Paramithiás.—At (40km) *Prodhrómio* a rich Macedonian warrior burial
in a cist beneath a mound was found in 1979. Finds included a fine
bronze hydria used as the ash urn, gilded wreaths and iron weapons
and armour. Here a bad road diverges (right) to *Mórfion* (see below).—
58km *Glikí* (Γλυκή), on the Akherontos, is possibly the site of *Euroia*;
there are remains of a church of the Despotate, supposed to be the
burial place of Bp Donatos.

The Akherontos, the mystic *Acheron* of mythology, was the river of the nether
world. It comes down from the mountains of Suli and flows through a deep and
gloomy ravine with precipitous sides, suggesting the terrors of Hades. At Glikí it
enters the wide plain of Phanari, where it traverses meres and swamps, never
wholly dry even in summer, which were known to the ancients as the
Acherousian Lake. The river flows past Ephyra (comp. below) and enters the sea
at *Ammoudhia* on the Bay of Fanari, S of Parga.
    A track leads through the gorge, and after 1 hour turns N and enters by a
narrow pass into the region of Suli. The scenery is grand and impressive.—1½
hours. The **Castle of Suli** stands on an isolated hill near the ruined village of the
same name, 366m above the Acheron. It was one of the strongholds of the Suliots,
a tribe of Christian Epirots, mustering about 4000 fighting men and women.
Their territory, like Montenegro farther N, was a centre of stubborn resistance to
the Moslems. From 1790 they were at war with Ali Pasha until 1803, when at
great cost he captured their principal fastnesses, and they retired to the Ionian
Islands. At the outbreak of the War of Independence most of the Suliots returned
to the mainland where they again engaged the Turks. Among them was Markos
Botsaris, defender of Mesolongi. In 1823 Great Britain negotiated their capitula-
tion on favourable terms and they all emigrated to Cephalonia.—A road has been
planned to link the area with Ioannina.

We descend to (69km) *Skepastón*, beyond which we immediately join
Rte 52C.—112km **Préveza**, see Rte 53B.

C. To Párga and Préveza

ROAD, 99km (61½ miles).—28km *Margaríti.*—38km
Mórfion, for **Párga** (12km).—52km *Kastrí,* for *Ephyra.*—
56km *Skepastón.*—99km *Préveza.* This excellent scenic
road through rich agricultural country with tidy villages
provides the shortest direct route (using the ferries at
Preveza and Rion) from Igoumenitsa to Athens (476·5km;
bus in 9 hours).

The road skirts the S side of Igoumenitsa bay. At *Ladhokhóri* (3km),
near the sea, was found in 1975 a Late Roman mausoleum of brick and
stone construction with four fine sculptured marble sarcophagi (now
in the Ioannina Museum). A courtyard house was associated with the
Mausoleum.—At 12km is *Platariá,* with a good beach. We turn inland
up a broad valley between mountain ranges, then descend through
low hills on to a dyke road across marshes.—28km (17½ miles)
Margaríti, (Rest.) despite its size (850 inhab.) controls a tiny eparchy of
a few neighbouring villages. The relics of its more important past
under Venetians and Turks disappeared when the town was fired
during military occupation in 1944, though remains of two fortresses
crown neighbouring heights.—38km (24 miles) *Mórfion* stands at the
junction of the road (right) to *Parga* (12km). From this road also Ephyra
(see below) can be reached more directly.

PÁRGA (Hotels B, C, D; F/A), a clean and picturesque little seaside
town (1693 inhab.) backed by slopes of orange and olive groves,
stands opposite the island of Paxos, 19km distant. The town spreads
across the neck of a rocky headland, crowned by a *Frourion* of Norman
origin (its keep is adorned with the Lion of St. Mark). The tiny bay has
rocks and islets and many cafés along the waterfront. The larger bay of
Khrissoyiali (Hotel B), a mile to the W, has a superb sweep of beach,
partly occupied by the Club Méditerranée. Tourist development is so
far within bounds.

Parga was already important in the 14C. In 1401 it came under the protection of
the Venetians, who dominated it until 1797, except for brief intervals in 1452–54
and after 1701 when it fell into Turkish hands. It fell to the French, who left a small
fort on the densely wooded islet of the Panayia, enjoyed a brief existence in 1800–
07 as an independent state under the aegis of Russia, then at the Treaty of Tilsit
passed again to the French. Ali Pasha bought it from the British who had replaced
the French in 1814. He drove out its people who sought refuge in the Ionian Is.
Some of them later returned, but thenceforward to 1913 Parga was subject to
Turkey, when it became Greek.—Constantine Kanaris, the admiral of the War of
Independence, was born here in 1790.

For Preveza, we bear left at Mórfion and cross a ridge to the valley of
the Acheron, with cotton fields.—52km *Kastrí* occupies the site of
Pandosia whose Classical walls are still imposing. Immediately before
the Acheron crossing a turning (right; signposted) leads in 5km by a
dyke-road to *Mesopótamo.* Here (road right in village), on a rocky hill
above the confluence of the Kokytos with the Acheron
(Periphlegethon), are the *Remains of the **Nekyomanteion of Ephyra**,
oracle of the dead and sanctuary of Persephone and Hades. From the
site the extent of the ancient Acherousian Lake is obvious; the river
(comp. above) flows on to the sea through willows and poplars. The
Acropolis of *Ephyra* rises to the N.

The Nekyomanteion is an astonishing construction with labyrinthine corridors and windowless rooms, both above and below ground.
The remains, impressively complete in plan with standing arches, are
in excellent polygonal masonry, Hellenistic in date, and were ruined

by fire in 168 BC. The core of the complex is a unit with exceptionally thick walls consisting of an undivided central corridor, with three rooms off either side. There was evidence of offerings of grain and liquids (? honey), as well as the sacrifice of animals. Two terracotta busts of Persephone were also found here. The arrangements and purpose of the complex recall Homer's description (Od. x, 512) of the visit of Odysseus to the House of Hades and his sacrifice to the spirits of the dead. Remains of a bronze windlass suggest that mechanical trickery may have been employed, after a preparation involving disorientation techniques and hallucinatory drugs, in inducing satisfactory spiritual visitation.

The coast road to the SW of Mesopótamo leads to *Ríza* (22km). 2km to the S of the village, above the small port of *Akrolíthia* were found in 1980 the substantial remains of a *Roman nymphaeum* of the 3C AD, called locally *Frangoekkissiá*. The main chamber (of three) has four entrances and six semicircular niches. It may have been in the grounds of a private estate. The road continues SW to join the new coast road (below).

56km We join Rte 52B just below *Skepaston*. The road now climbs steeply, then winds S through a long valley.—At 75·5km a road (signposted Zalonga) climbs (left to the village) of *Kamarína* (officially *Zálongon* after its mountain), continuing as a dirt road to a footpath (5·5km; left; small sign) leading in 3 minutes to **Kassope**. On a plateau facing S these ruins of the 4C BC were discovered in 1951–55; excavations were resumed in 1976. The city was laid out early in the 4C BC on the Hippodamian system and protected by a polygonal wall. It was burned by the Romans in 167 BC and abandoned when Nikopolis was founded.

The Souliot Women at Zalonga. Engraving

Investigations have concentrated on the area round the *Agora*. This is bounded on the N by a *Stoa* with octagonal Doric columns. It has some unusual terracotta antefixes (eagles and thunderbolts; eagles and Ganymedes). A row of bases in front and to the E were originally occupied by statues of deceased citizens dedicated to the city and the Gods. The building, of the 3C, is underlain by a predecessor. On the W side of the agora was a paved rectangular area bordered by orthostats, beyond which passes one of the N–S streets, which was roofed at this point to form a kind of stoa. On the other side of the street, a rectangular building still under study (possibly a *Prytaneion*) is centred round a small courtyard which had a Doric portico. To the E of the agora is a small *Odeion*. Immediately behind the N stoa are the remains of a *Katagogeion* (hostel) consisting of rooms (each with a table and hearth) around a court, which had a peristyle of octagonal Doric

KASSOPE

0 metres   100   200

Odeion
North Stoa
Katagogeion
Prytaneion (?)
Theatre

columns and an entrance porch on to the street to the W. To the N of the katagogeion a number of houses have been excavated. Most consist of rooms round a
small court and were built in the Classical period, though often altered subsequently. Farther NW are the *Theatre* and a 'Macedonian' *Chamber Tomb*.

The road climbs a further 500m to the *Monastery of Zalonga*, where
the Suliot mountaineers took refuge when attacked by Ali Pasha. Sixty
women escaped with their children to the summit, whence, after performing their traditional dance, they threw themselves over the precipice. This act is commemorated by a huge sculpture above the
monastery (footpath).

Beyond (80km) *Arkhángelos* we emerge on the Bay of Gomares joining a new coastal road, on which (3km N) is *Kastrosikiá* (Hotels B, C).—
At 90km the ruins of *Nikopolis* lie to the left.—99km **Preveza**, see
below.

53 From Ioánnina to Arta and Préveza

A. To Arta

ROAD, 78km (48½ miles), well engineered section of the
main highway to Athens. BUSES (KTEL 13) regularly,
continuing usually to Agrinion and Patras.

From Ioannina to (8km) the Dodona turn, see Rte 52. The road continues straight and level with views of the scarred heights of Mt
Tómaros (right). A causeway carries the highway across a marsh-
lake. We ascend between *Bizáni* (left) and *Manolássa* (right), two
heights known as battlefields in 1913.—22km *Kháni Avgóu* stands on
a col (629m), with highest point on the route. The walls of *Pirtelia* are
visible on the isolated hill (right) as we descend to the cultivated upper
valley of the *Louros*. The road has been realined; on the old loop is
(31km) *Kháni Emín Agá*, a police post with a small museum illustrating the campaign of 1912–13; a memorial, opposite marks the site of
Constantine's headquarters during the siege of Ioannina.
  We pass the principal springs that feed the infant Louros.—33km
Khánia Teróvou (Restaurants). At the entrance to the Louros `Gorge
the road crosses to the right bank. The river, shaded by great planes,
flows between *Xerovoúni* (1614m), the long range of mountains to the
E and *Zarkorákhi* (1332m; to the W). Here and there are remains of
fortifications ancient and modern.—40km *Potamiá (Platanakia
Rest.)*.—Near (42km) *Kleísoura*, the narrowest point and the nome
boundary, we traverse a tunnel.
  The valley broadens and bamboo is grown. Soon after Kerasóna it
narrows again, becoming craggy.—56km *Ayios Yeóryios*, with an
ornamented church, appears 1km left on a hill. Just before its turning
is (right) the *Asprokhalikó* cave which in 1965 proved to contain the
first large stratified deposits of Middle and Upper Palaeolithic date
found in Greece. The site was further investigated in 1981. We reach
the artificial lake formed by the LOUROS DAM. Immediately beyond
(right) is the entrance to a rock-cut conduit, part of a *Roman Aqueduct*
that fed Nikopolis, over 64km away. Some spectacular arches can be

seen by the Ay. Yeoryios road (comp. above). About 1·5km farther down (left) is a hydro-electric station. We pass (right) the *Paidopolis Zirou*, an orphanage of the Royal Foundation.—65km *Filippiás* (Φιλιππίας; 3279 inhab.) has an excavated 13C church in the *Monastery of the Pantánassa*, some of whose architectural elements were probably brought from Nikopolis.

A rough by-road crosses the river to *Kambí* (5km), continuing amid the S foothills of Xerovouni to *Kastrí* (16km; bus daily), the ruins of a classical town destroyed in 167 BC (rough path in 10 minutes).

About 3km farther on, by an orangeade factory, we leave the road to Preveza (Rte 53B), turn left across the Louros, and traverse the orange-groves of the Ambracian plain. At the approach to the Arakhthos a road enters on the right from *Salaóra* (18km; with fish hatcheries) on the Ambracian Gulf. Crossing the Arakhthos to enter Arta, we see (left) a Turkish packhorse *Bridge: the legend according to which the mason built his wife into the foundations to strengthen the bridge is enshrined in a song that has currency with other Balkan peoples.

78km (48½ miles) **ARTA** (Hotels B, C, E), pleasantly situated in a loop of the Arakhthos, is a friendly town (18,283 inhab.) interspersed with orange groves. Remains are coming to light of its ancient past as *Ambracia*, capital of Pyrrhus, king of Epirus, and it retains reminders of its period of greatness as the seat of the Despotate of Epirus.

History. Ambracia was colonised by Corinth c 625 BC and had a grid plan as early as the 5C BC. Pausanias found only ruins. After the fall of Constantinople and of the Morea to the Franks, Michael I Angelos, with the approval of the exiled Emp. Alexios III, set up the autonomous Despotate of Epirus at Arta, or Narte. Here Euphrosyne, Alexios' empress, died in exile. The town fell to the Turks in 1449, but soon passed to the Venetians. The French held it for two years after the Treaty of Campoformio (1797), but, after a period of subjection to Ali Pasha of Ioannina, it fell again under direct Turkish rule in 1822–1912. Hoca Ishak Efendi (1774–1834), the accomplished linguist who first introduced western science into Turkish education, was born at Arta.

The FROURION, a 13C castle occupied by the Xenia Hotel, commands the bend of the river. The restored outer walls, with reused classical blocks, afford pleasant views northward to Xerovouni. Some scanty remains of a Classical *Temple* survive near the river bank. To the SW off Od. Pírrhou is *Ayios Vasílios*, a small 14C church with the elaborate brick and tile decoration characteristic of the area. Farther on is *Ayia Theodhora*, properly the church of St. George the Martyr, a conventual church where Theodora, consort of Michael II, took the veil and ended her days. The domed narthex, perhaps added in her lifetime, has outstanding brick and tile decoration; within stands a reconstruction of Theodora's tomb (excavated in 1873), originally erected by Nikephoros I, her son. The fine capitals are said to derive from Nikopolis.

Odhos Pirrhou continues SW. Below a narrow street (50m left) in 1976 was found the *Bouleuterion*. Farther on (right) are the foundations of a large Doric *Temple* of the early 5C BC, uncovered in 1964–69. Its tiles were stamped AMBP. Sections of the ancient town wall (c 500 BC) have been located on Odd. Porfiríou Mitropolítou and Rógon. The busy PLATEÍA KILKÍS, the main square with the bus station, has several restaurants. Beyond is the larger PLATEÍA SKOUFÁ S dominated by the former metropolitan church of **Panayia Parigoritissa**, a huge square edifice crowned by six domes, erected in 1282–89 by Nikephoros and John, sons of Michael II. The gloomy interior has a certain majesty; the curious sub-structure of the central dome, borne on antique columns on a primitive cantilever principle, cannot be as unsound as it appears. The mosaics of the Pantocrator and the prophets in the dome (cleaned) belong to the original decoration.

By the river to the S of the town is the *Káto Panayía*, a nunnery founded by Michael II whose monogram can be traced on the S wall of the church. It shelters 20 orphaned girls who weave blankets and carpets (for sale). The Church incorporates prophyry columns perhaps from a Syrian Temple of Aphrodite (classical foundation blocks visible in the terrace). The exterior walls are adorned with bands of cable and meander patterns with decorative motifs worked in red tile. The frescoes within are mainly of the 18C; fragments in the apse date from the 13C.

Among the monasteries for which the region is noted we may visit the *Moní Vlakhérnai* (NE of the town), transformed into a convent of nuns by Theodore Angelos c 1225, not many years after its foundation. The church was embellished by Michael II. Fragments of the original marble templon are built into the narthex doorway. Within are two marble tombs, believed from their fragmentary inscriptions to belong to Michael II and to two of his sons.—*Ayios Dhimitrios Katsoúri* (5km SW of Arta), the chapel of a Patriarchal monastery, was built in the 10C and altered in the 13C. The frescoes are assigned to the late 12/early 13C. The nearby church of *Ayios Nikólaos tis Rodhiás* (12-13C) also retains frescoes of the early 13C. Two unusual scenes are preserved in the W corner bays—the three Hebrews in the Fiery Furnace and the Seven Sleepers of Ephesus.—The *Panayía tou Bryóni*, on the Amfilokhia road, was enlarged with a transept and dome during the Patriarchate of Germanos II, perhaps at the time of his visit to Epirus in 1238.—The monastery at *Péta* (c 5km) E) has a 17C epitaphios from the Morea and a monument of 1821.

B. To Préveza

ROAD, 108km (67 miles), following the Arta road to (65km) *Filippiás* (comp. above), then branching right.—100km **Nikópolis—108km Préveza**. BUSES several times daily.

From Ioannina to (68km) the Fix orangeade factory, see above. The Preveza road turns SW and runs roughly parallel with the lower reaches of the Loúros. Just beyond (71·5km) *Néa Kerasoús* we see (left; easiest access from village side on old road), on a low hill, the extensive ruins of **Rogon**, or *Rogous* (ancient BOUCHETION), protected by a marshy loop of the river. An excellent polygonal enceinte encloses a medieval citadel, built on ashlar foundations (end 5C BC, then three subsequent phases of alteration and reconstruction before it was abandoned after 31 BC), with a church (defaced frescoes). The place gave its name to a medieval see.—At (79km) *Stefáni* at the S end of the Thesprotiká range, we join a road from *Thesprotikó* (10km N), a deme of pop. 2005.—Beyond (83km) *Loúros* (Rfmts.), a large village (pop. 1744), the road runs straight and level in the lush plain irrigated by the Loúros.—At (95km) *Mikhalítsi*, off the road to the right, tombs of the 4C BC have been explored. The peninsula narrows to an isthmus. On the E is a marshy lagoon, the haunt of herons and other wildfowl.

The road passes through the extensive and overgrown site of **Nikopolis**, the city founded by Augustus after his victory at Actium. To the W is the Bay of Gomares where he had concentrated his forces before the battle.

History. In commemoration of his victory, Octavian (Augustus) raised the status of Patrai to that of Roman colony and founded the new *Colonia* of *Nikopolis* ('victory city') on his camp site. To populate the new city, he resettled the inhabitants of most of the towns of Aetolia and Akarnania, including Kalydon, Ambracia, and Amphilochian Argos. It was made a member of the Amphictyonic League and to it were transferred the Actian games. St. Paul spent a winter (? 64) at 'Nicopolis of Macedonia', where he wrote his Epistle to Titus. By AD 67 the city was the capital of an Epirot province. The philosopher Epictetus (c 60–140) had a school here, and the city was the reputed birthplace of Pope St. Eleutherios (175–189). Thriving in the time of Strabo, it was plundered by Alaric, Genseric, and Totila. Justinian rebuilt its defences, reducing their compass. At the coming of the Slavs, the Byzantines removed the seat of the theme to Naupaktos and Nikopolis decayed. Here, in 1795, John Sibthorp, the English botanist, fell ill and returned to die in Bath.—The Greek Archaeological Service has excavated at intervals since 1913.

Parts of the site are very overgrown and the visit arduous. The **Theatre** is prominent to the right of the road. The walls of the proscenium still

NIKOPOLIS

0   400 metres

PARGA

Monument

Smyrtoula

Theatre

Stadium

Kafenion

ARTA

Aqueduct

Baths

Kafenion

City Walls

Basilica C

Great Gate

Odeum

Alkison

Gate

Museum

Doumetios

N

City Walls

PREVEZA

stand, and the auditorium rises to the upper portico, its niches and
arcades the haunt of storks. In several places may be seen the holes in
which the poles for the velarium, or awning, were fixed. The line of the
cunei can be distinguished though the stone seats have mostly
vanished.

A dirt road to the left skirts the side of the *Stadium*, which unusually in Greece
was rounded at both ends like those of Asia Minor; it leads in 450m to the village
of *Smyrtoula*, above which are the remains of the commemorative MONUMENT
erected by Augustus after the battle of Actium on the site where his tent had been

pitched. A massive podium of masonry is preserved in whose face are cuttings, shaped like enormous bassviols, in which the prows of ships must have been attached. The monument was of the Corinthian order. Numerous fragments of a frieze with a Latin inscription commemorating the victory are lying about. It is beautifully carved in letters a foot high. One fragment bears the letters TUNO, indicating that the monument was dedicated to Neptune.

The road runs S, meeting the road from Parga (Rte 52C) near some ruined *Baths*, then enters the Byzantine enceinte. To the left are the excavated remains of the BASILICA OF ALKYSON, a double-aisled church with tripartite transept, founded by Bp Alkyson (died 516). Two heads in mosaic survive from its Christian decoration. Just beyond the basilica a track leads (right) through a fine *Gate* in Justinian's ***Walls**, here extending for c 500m in a good state of preservation. The path may be followed past the Augustan *Odeion*, restored for use in the annual festival of ancient drama (Aug), to the *Great Gate* in the *City Walls* of the Augustan age. Some remains of the *Aqueduct* that supplied the city with water from the Louros survive to the N as well as part of the *Nymphaeum* in which it terminated.

Continuing along the main road we come to the **Museum**, opened in 1972. On the walls of the Lobby are inscribed stelai bases and gravestones. Two rooms display statues, sarcophagi, Roman portraits (notably Agrippa, Augustus's general at Actium, and Faustina the Younger, wife of Marcus Aurelius) and capitals; in the centre of the first room, grave *Lion (3C BC); in the second, huge cylindrical base with Amazonomachia reliefs (reused as the ambo of the Alkyson basilica); large glass cinerary urn; rings and lamps.—In the field near by (phylax will guide) is the **Basilica of Doumetios**, or *Basilica A*, dated from its fine floor mosaics to the second quarter of the 6C. Adjacent is the palace of the archbishops of Epirus Vetus who had their seat here.—Near the S wall is the smaller *Basilica Γ* and, outside the walls, *Basilica Δ* with a peacock mosaic floor.

108km (67 miles) **Préveza** Πρέβεζα; Hotels B, C, D, E), the unprepossessing chief town (12,662 inhab.) of a small nome, stands on the N shore of the shallow strait, here only 1km wide, through which the waters of the Ambracian Gulf reach the sea. The waterside esplanade is a favourite evening promenade. A car ferry crosses the strait (halfhourly).—There is an airport with a daily connection with Athens (TERMINAL at Spiliádhou and Balinoú).

Preveza occupies the site of ancient Berenikia, founded c 290 BC by Pyrrhus in honour of his mother-in-law Berenice, queen of Ptolemy Soter. The town was occupied by the Venetians in 1499. Ceded to the Turks by the Treaty of Carlowitz (1699), it was retaken in 1717. In 1797 it passed, with the Ionian Is., to the French, but the next year it was retaken by Ali Pasha in the name of the Sultan of Turkey and remained in Turkish hands until it fell to the Greek army in 1912. In 1881–1912 the Greco-Turkish frontier ran through the strait.

On the S side of the strait is the sandy promontory of **Aktion** (Latin, *Actium*), sharper in outline than that of Preveza and almost closing the entrance to the Gulf. At the naval BATTLE OF ACTIUM, on 2 September 31 BC, Agrippa, Octavian's commander, with a smaller but more manoevrable fleet, routed the combined navies of Antony and Cleopatra. The royal leaders deserted the army they had massed for an invasion in Italy, and it surrendered a week later. Ships sunk in the battle have been located beneath the sea and archaeological investigation is planned. By the ferry landing-place stands a Venetian fort. On the promontory, 1km N, are scanty remains of the *Temple of Apollo Aktios*.

A temple, under the protection of neighbouring Anaktorion, existed here in the 5C BC. From it came two kouroi now in the Louvre. Gymnastic games and horse races were held. After his victory at Actium, Augustus rebuilt the temple and consecrated in special boathouses examples of the vessels captured in the battle. The festival he transferred to his new city of Nikopolis, adding naval and musical events. The '*Actia*', held every five years and declared sacred, thus took rank with the four great Hellenis games.

To *Levkas*, and to *Amfilokhia*, see Rte 54.

54   From Arta to Mesolóngi

ROAD, 123km (76½ miles), traversing the varied countryside of Aitolia and Akarnania with its characteristic lakes and lagoons and impressive monuments. The road, already good, is still being widened and realined, with bypasses of main towns. 43km *Amfilokhia.*—72·5km *Strátos.*—85km (53 miles) **Agrínion**, for *Thérmon.*—114km *Aitolikó*, for *Oíniadai.*—119km *Plévron.*—123km Mesolóngi. Bus either direct or by changing at Agrinion, regularly.

We quit Arta and turn SE through orange-groves.—12km *Kombóti* (1·5km left; pop. 1882) was the native town of Nik. Skoufa, one of the founders of the Philike Hetaireia. As we approach the Ambracian Gulf the road rises on the oak-clad slope of *Makrinóros*, a long mountain ridge parallel to the shore. The pass *en corniche* thus formed, sometimes called the 'Thermopylae of Western Greece', was guarded in antiquity by a string of forts. At its summit is Kastro Palaiokoulia, defended during the War of Independence by the Greek captain Iskos.—18km *Menídhi* marks the N end of the pass; 27·5km *Anoixiátikon*, the S end.—Just beyond (34km) *Kríkelo* we see (left) the little church of Ayios Ioannis, behind which (road signposted) rise the insignificant remains of *Amphilochian Argos*, a town of some importance in the Peloponnesian War.—43km **Amfilokhía** (Αμφιλοχία; Hotels C, D) is situated at the head of the Gulf of Karvasará, the farthest inland reach of the Ambracian Gulf. The town (pop. 4343) was founded by Ali Pasha as a military station; its former name, *Karvasarás*, is supposed to be a corruption of 'caravanserai'. On the hill (189m) above are some remains of an ancient town with long walls, perhaps to be identified with *Limnaia*.

FROM AMFILOKHIA TO LEVKAS, 59km (37 miles). The road follows the S verge of the Ambracian Gulf, often away from the shore amid marsh, cotton fields, or low hills. To the left Mt Bergandi rises to 1428m; *Thýrion* (Museum with Classical and Roman material, including inscriptions, from ancient *Thyreion*), on its N slope, has adopted the ancient name of a place where Cicero, sailing along the Akarnanian coast, spent two hours at the house of his friend Xenomanes.— 38km (23 miles) **Vónitsa** (Hotesl C, D, E), chief town of the eparchy of Vónitsa and Xiromeros, has a small port below a Venetian citadel of 1676. An asphalt road runs W from Vónitsa to the Aktion–Preveza ferry (12km), passing after 5km, near the shore, the conspicuous hill- top ruins of *Anaktorion*, a Corinthian colony of 630 BC. To the SW of Vónitsa, a minor road passes through *Pálairos* (22km) to *Mítikas* (42km) where there are the substantial remains of an Early Christian basilica dedicated to St. Sophia. The unfinished road continues S to Astakos (see below).—Our road bears SW. Coming in to (49km) *Ayios Nikólaos* we meet another road from Aktion (10km) and beyond the village cross the outlet of the marsh-lake Voulkariá to the Ionian Sea. We see (left) the *Castle of Grivas*, dating from the War of Independence, then cross a long causeway which brings us to the

Frankish Kastro Santa Maura (comp. Rte 56), guarding a gap between the main-land and the island of Levkas. The strait is crossed by chain ferry (free), whence another causeway carries the road into (59·5km) *Levkas* (see Rte 56).

We cross a low saddle behind the town between two ranges of hills.—49km *Stános*, on the W slope, overlooks the N arm of *Lake Ambrakia*, which we cross on a causeway, continuing along the E shore.—64km Poor by-road (right) to *Astakós* (41km), with pop. 2624, formerly *Dragomestre*, coastal base of Sir Richard Church's operations in Western Greece in 1828. A little beyond the turning we see in the distance *Lake Ozeros* (right).

72·5km *Strátos* (Στράτος), a melancholy village (left) stands in the centre of the *Ruins of **Stratos**, the ancient capital and largest city of Akarnania. The walls, dating from before 429 BC and particularly well preserved, stand on a low bluff commanding the broad Acheloös. A folk-dancing festival is held annually in September.

History. The site was occupied in early times but *Stratos* first achieved importance in the 5C BC. During the Peloponnesian War Knemos of Sparta besieged it vainly in 429 BC and in 426 Eurylochos passed below its walls without daring to attack. Agesilaos failed to take it in 391, but it passed to Kassander in 314, and in 263, when Akarnania was partitioned, fell to the Aitolians. After the dissolution of the Aitolian League (188), the Romans held it against Philip V and Perseus of Macedon, but before our era began it had lost all importance. The site was explored by the French School in 1892, 1910–11, and 1924.

The *Walls* embrace four parallel N–S ridges with their three intervening depressions. A transverse N–S wall divides the city into two parts. With the exception of the *Theatre* (still buried), most of the public buildings seem to have been in the W sector. In the centre of the S wall, to the right of the track to the village, is the MAIN GATE, with a defensive interior court. The remains of the *Agora* are scanty. Thence we may follow the central wall up past the ancient quarries to the *Acropolis*, seemingly a fortified rather than a religious place. Curiously placed athwart a projecting section of the W wall is the Doric TEMPLE OF ZEUS, built on a platform c 70m from E to W. Peripteral, with 6 columns by 11, and somewhat larger than the Athenian Hephaisteion, it dates from the 4C, probably after 338 BC. An Ionic colonnade surrounded the cella on three sides. The stylobate and parts of the cella walls survive.

The road passes within the E wall of Stratos, then turns to cross the ACHELOOS BARRAGE (Φράγμα Αχελώου). The former bridge is 5km upstream. The *Acheloös*, or *Aspropotamos*, is the longest river (217km) in Greece. Rising in the Pindus, it forms the boundary between Aitolia and Akarnania, and falls into the sea opposite the Echinades Is. Since 1960 the river has been harnessed to provide power (comp. below) and irrigation. A by-pass to the W avoids Agrinion.

85km (53 miles) **Agrínion** (Αγρίνιον; Hotels B, C, D, E), a lively town of 34,328 inhab., is the capital of the eparchy of Trikhonidhos and the largest place in the nome. It is a tobacco-growing centre, linked by air services with Athens and Ioannina, and a starting-point for the visit to Thermon. It was almost completely rebuilt after an earthquake in 1887. There is a small archaeological *Museum*. The site of *Ancient Agrinion* has been located above the village of *Megáli Khóra*, 4km NW of the town.

FROM AGRINION TO THERMON, 32km, infrequent bus. A tarred road branches right from the Karpenisi road (comp. below) and traverses the agricultural villages along the N shore of *Lake Trikhonis*. *Mt Vlokhos* (610m; left) affords a wonderful view. At (11km) *Paravóla* are some remains of ancient *Boukation* (Classical and 4C with Byzantine towers).—We run along the shore, then climb in turns above orange groves to *Myrtiá*, where is a monastery of 1491.—29km *Ayía Sofía* is a long pretty village with gushing streams; its Byzantine church incorporates blocks from a **Temple of Aphrodite**.—32km *Kefalovrísi*, (Hotels D), officially *Thermon*, has a charming rural square with country inns and restaurants, reminiscent of Mt Pelion. Just over 1km S at 'Palaio Bazari' are the remains of ancient **Thermon**, the spiritual centre of the Aitolians, who here held their elections of magistrates at an annual festival.

The festival was the occasion also for a great fair and for athletic games. Thermon became a Pan-Aitolian sanctuary centred on the temple of Apollo Thermios. Some 2000 of the statues collected here were destroyed by Philip V of Macedon when he sacked the place in 218 BC. The Greek Archaeological Service excavated the ruins in 1898–1916.

The SANCTUARY, with its E side against Mt Mega Lakkos, was surrounded by a rectangular peribolos protected by towers dating from the 3C BC. The largest of three temples, near the N wall, is the *Temple of Apollo Thermios* (6C BC), a narrow peripteral building with five columns at the ends and 15 at the sides. A row of columns down the centre divided the building lengthwise; some column-drums remain in place. The walls may have been made of sun-dried brick. The entablature was of decorated wood; the frieze and acroteria of painted terracotta. At a lower level (not clearly visible) are the foundations of a temple of the Geometric period built with an apsidal peristyle. To the N, and at a still lower level are houses of a prehistoric village, one of them particularly large and well-built with an apsidal end. To the S is a *Fountain*, still operating, with three spouts, and beyond three *Stoas* locate the agora. Notable in the *Museum* are Archaic terracotta metopes and decorative fragments from the Temple, Middle Bronze Age pottery, part of a Mycenaean helmet, and a fine pair of bronze horses mounted on a single base (Geometric).

The return to Agrinion may be made by the S shore of the lake, making a round

Thermon, Temple of Apollo. Reconstruction of section of wooden entablature with painted terracotta metopes, antefixes, etc. (c 630 BC)

of c 72·5km; or, by another poor road (infrequent bus), *Navpaktos* (Rte 55) may be reached.

FROM AGRINION TO KARPENISI, 116km (72½ miles) in course of improvement; a tough but impressive drive over a series of ridges of the Southern Pindus with climbs up to 1219m. Bus once daily. The road winds NE in the foothills of *Panaitolikón*.—Beyond (24km) *Kelanítis* we climb in earnest to reach a saddle affording the first view of Lake Kremaston.—40km *Ayios Vlásios* (1158m), a scattered mountain village (restaurant). We descend and just after (47km) *Khoúni* pass a tarred road to *Kremastá* (6·5km, left), standing just below the confluence of the Acheloös with its two greatest tributaries. Here a great dam, 172m high, and a hydro-electric power station have been constructed by an American company.—51km Fork left for **Lake Kremaston**, the largest artificial lake in Greece, which drowned several villages, rebuilt on the slopes above. The main road veers E to cross an arm of the lake by a new bridge and regains the line of the former road (which made use of a ferry crossing) near (63km) *Ayios Yeóryios*. We zigzag high above the valley to (75·5km) *Frangísta* (Φραγκίστα). The road suddenly reaches a small plane-shaded opening with springs, grass, and a café.—We climb steeply to 1067m, then descend to cross the Megdova by (92km) the *Markopoulos Bridge* (Restaurant). The road climbs again through firs

to a col (c 1220m) in the W outliers of Timfristós, then descends.—117km
Karpenisi, and thence to Lamia, see Rte 47A.

Quitting Agrinion we turn S. The route runs straight across the irrigated plain dividing Lakes Trikhonis (left; comp. above) and Lysimakhia (right), crosses the canal linking the two lakes, joins the road
coming from the S shore of Lake Trikhonis, then follows the SE shore
of *Lake Lysimakhia* before turning S into the hills.—102km
Frangouléika lies in the pretty valley that leads into the *Stená tis
Kleisoúras*, a long cleft in the sandstone, in which stands the monastery of Ayios Eleousas. At the exit, pleasant prospect of the Aitolikó
lagoon.—108km Turning (right) to *Angelókastro* (16km) where there
are remains of a Byzantine fortress (13C). The coastal plain is planted
with olives. The realigned road runs well above the older road (and
eventually by-passes Mesolongi).—114km Turning to *Aitolikó* (7km)
and (14·5km farther) **Oiniadai**.

 Aitolikó (Αιτωλικόν), a medieval refuge-town of 4368 inhab.,
stands on an island between its lagoon and the larger seaward Lagoon
of Mesolongi, and is joined to the mainland at either end by fine stone
bridges. The 15C church of the *Panayia* has wall paintings. William
Martin, an English deserter seaman, was one of the 600 who here
successfully defied Omer Vrioni's siege in 1823.

From Aitolikó an asphalt road runs W in very flat arable country. We leave on the
right a road to Astakos (46km; see above), pass through *Neokhóri* (3262 inhab.),
cross the Acheloös by a new bridge, and reach *Katokhí* (2774 inhab.) with a
ruined medieval tower. In the village we ignore the more important road on our
right and beyond the village the road divides (no signpost): either branch (gravel)

leads in c 1·5km to the ruins of **Oiniadai**, that to the right approaching the harbour side, that to the left the Acropolis, a rocky wooded hill known as *Trikardho Kástro*. The city, explored by the American School in 1901, is heavily overgrown and a wary eye should be kept for snakes and hornets as well as for the dogs of the local vlachs. On all sides, except the S, it is surrounded by the marshes of Lezini, the ancient Lake Melita. On the S a plain slopes down to the Acheloös. The well-preserved *Fortifications follow the irregular hill.

Oiniadai, though unhealthily situated and inaccessible in winter, was strategically important as the key to S Akarnania. It was taken after a siege in 455 BC by exiled Messenians established at Naupaktos, and attacked in vain by Pericles in

PLEURON

0   100 metres

after F.Noac

453. Demosthenes in 424 forced it to join the Athenian alliance. It fell to the Aitolians in 336 and, without bloodshed, to Philip V in 219. The Romans captured it eight years later and handed it over to the Aitolian League. The town was restored to the Akarnanians in 189.

We enter, near a cottage, by the E wall. The closely jointed polygonal masonry is of the 6C. To the S are the main *Gate*, one of many with arched openings, a feature unusual in Greek architecture, and the *Acropolis*. In the other direction are the remains of a small *Theatre* having 27 rows of seats; inscriptions on the lowest three rows record the freeing of slaves and date the building (late 3C BC). Farther N are remarkable vestiges of the *Docks* reconstructed by Philip V. Here are a buttressed quay, porticoes surrounding a basin hewn in the rock, berths with traces of the rings to which the ships were moored, and their slipways. To the SW of the port are some remains of *Baths* of Greek construction.

Beyond Aitolikó the road continues through rice fields. To the right are salt flats.—119km Ancient **Pleuron** (Plévron) is conspicuous from the main road but difficult of access owing to a water pipeline and culverts. The two lower hills of Petrovouni and Gyphtokastro have some Archaic remains of an enceinte that probably represents *Old Pleuron*, the city of the Curetes destroyed by Demetrios II, son of Antigonus Gonatas, in 234 BC. An arduous path ascends to the enceinte of ashlar masonry (Kastro Irinio) the *New Pleuron* built soon afterwards. The splendid WALLS, the most remarkable antiquity in Aitolia, have 36 towers and 7 gates; the circuit is almost complete and stands in places to fifteen courses of Hellenistic masonry.

Within are the ruins of a *Theatre*, perhaps the smallest in Greece. The stage, with the proscenium, backed on to the city wall; a small doorway led through the orchestra to a square tower. In a hollow to the SE is a *Cistern, 31m × 20m, with a depth of 4m, divided into five rectangular basins by four partition walls pierced by triangular openings. Near the E wall is the *Agora*, a rectangular terrace 145m long. It is crowded with the debris of buildings; among them is a portico 60·5m × 10m, with enclosing walls still standing to a height of c 0·6m. There are also exedrae and pedestals. On a hill to the N is the site of the *Acropolis*, which had square towers. Below the terrace the hill sinks rapidly E towards the city walls. At the foot of the depression is a fine gateway 1·7m wide, 2·7m high and 2m thick. The lintel is formed of two large horizontal blocks; in it and in the stone of the threshold are seen the holes for the gatepost.

At *Finikiá*, on the slopes below the acropolis, are the substantial remains of a three-aisled Early Christian basilica.

123km (76½ miles) **MESOLÓNGI** (Μεσολόγγιον; Hotels B, D, E; F/A), or *Missolonghi*, with 10,164 inhab., is the capital of the nome of Aitolia and Akarnania, and the seat of a bishop. The town is, by repute, more familiar to the English-speaking world than many others in Greece of greater importance, for here Lord Byron (born 1788) died of fever on 19 April 1824, after ten months of incessant activity in the cause of Greek independence. Mesolongi, now by-passed by the main highway, is situated on the E shore of a vast lagoon (Limnothalassa) partly given over to fish hatcheries and the haunt of many water-birds. This has always been too shallow to allow the approach of vessels of any size, and a long causeway extends S to deep water at *Tourlídha*. The local sailing boats have affinities with the Egyptian felucca and the nets are unusual. Drainage and reclamation work is hastening the disappearance of the fishing community and their characteristic reed huts built on piles. In the local cafés the 'mezès' are varied and good.

History. *Mesolongi* was the W centre of resistance against the Turks in the War of Independence, and had to endure three sieges. In 1822 it was defended by Mavrogordato against a force of 10,000 led by Omer Vrioni and Reshid Pasha. In 1823 its commander was the Suliot, Markos Botsaris. In January 1824 Lord Byron came to Mesolongi and inspired the defenders with his enthusiasm; he died the following April before the beginning of the final siege. In April 1825 Reshid Pasha appeared before the town with 15,000 troops. The defenders numbered only 5000. Hampered by furious sorties and by a lack of supplies, Reshid Pasha could make no headway for six months. Then Ibrahim Pasha, with 10,000 Egyp-

Capture of Mesolóngi, engraving

tians, advanced to his aid from the Peloponnese. After fluctuating struggles for the islands in the lagoon, the enemy closed round the devoted town. At the end of their resources after 12 months of siege, almost the whole population determined to break out. Their attempt (the 'Exodos') was made on the night of 22/23 April 1826. Though they managed to get clear of the town, they were frustrated by the treachery of a Bulgarian deserter, who had forewarned the besiegers. The fugitives, imagining themselves safe, were ambushed by 1000 Albanians on the slopes of Mt Zygos. Out of the 9000 who left Mesolongi—soldiers and civilians—only 1800 made good their escape to Amphissa. Meanwhile those who had stayed behind fired their magazines, overwhelming themselves and their enemies in a common destruction.—In 1828 the Turks surrendered Mesolongi without firing a shot.

The town is entered through the Venetian walls by the 'Gate of the Sortie', rebuilt by King Otho to protect the hastily repaired earthen rampart through which the exodos mas made. Within the gate (right) is a pleasant garden with the *Heroön* (adm. free) commemorating the heroes of the town's three sieges. A large central tumulus contains the bodies of unnamed defenders; to the right is the tomb of Botsaris, and between the two, a statue of Byron erected in 1881, beneath which is the poet's heart. The centre of the town is the PLATEÍA BOTSARI, where the *Dhimarkhíon* houses the Museum of the Revolution, with Byron relics and several dramatic pictures of the war. Odhos Trikoupis leads W and at its end Odhos Levidou brings us to a small square where a *Memorial Garden* occupies the site of the house in which Byron died: the house was destroyed in the Second World War. Continuing round a school we reach the causeway, with a bust of the poet Kostis Palamas and the reconstructed base of the historic *Windmill* blown up by Christos Kapsalis on 11 April 1826.

55   From Mesolóngi to Athens

A. Via Ríon

ROAD to 41km (25½ miles) *Andírrion*, whence by ferry to *Ríon*; from Rion to *Athens* (211km), see Rtes 38, 24. Bus regularly in 5½ hrs; also from Mesolongi to Patras.

The road runs E towards the dark mass of Varásova. To the right are seen the mountains that rise behind Patras.—5km Turning (left) to *Ayios Simeon*, the monastery where the people of Mesolongi made their last stand after the 'exodos' in 1826.—At 8·5km a track (left; signposted) leads in a few minutes to ancient **Kalydon**, celebrated in the heroic age as the home of Oeneus and his sons Tydeus and Meleager. On the neighbouring slopes, culminating at Mt Zygos (950m), took place the hunt of the Kalydonian boar. Though Strabo couples Kalydon with Pleuron as an ornament to Greece, it was historically insignificant. The city received its death blow when Augustus transferred its inhabitants to Nikopolis and most of the public treasures to Patras.

To the right of our path are some remains of a *Heroön*, comprising a number of rooms grouped round a peristyle court with a well and cistern. Under the main room is a sepulchral chamber. The path continues to a farmhouse standing just outside the West Gate (foundations) of the ancient town. A natural spur extends SW for c 350m, commanding the plain and the gulf. Here stood the **Sanctuary of Artemis Laphria**, excavated by Danish archaeologists in 1925–32. A massive foundation platform locates the 4C *Temple*, erected on a terrace supported by 6C retaining walls. Remains of metopes were recovered from earlier temples of c 570 and c 620 BC.

We cross the Evinos. The road passes inland of *Mt Varásova* (916m), the ancient Mt Chalkis, by a low pass to emerge *en corniche* above the Gulf of Patras on the barren flanks of *Klókova* (Taphiassos; 1041m). The *Views across the gulf comprise Patras itself and the mountains behind as far as the long crest of Erymanthos.—At (32km) *Ríza* we descend to the narrow coastal plain. Palaiokastro Mamakou (left) may be ancient *Makynia*. The torrents crossing the Patras-Rion road are conspicuous across the water.—At 38km our road diverges right to **Andírrion** (Αντίρριον), where the ferry to *Rion* (Rte 38) across the Little Dardanelles' provides the shortest approach from NW Greece to **Athens** (211km from Rion; comp. Rtes 38, 24).

Andírrion, like Rion, has a picturesque medieval fortress. It is known as the Castle of Roumeli.

B. Via Delphí

ROAD, 348km (216 miles), mountainous with splendid
scenery, but arduous driving between Navpaktos and
Amfissa.—54km **Návpaktos**.—116km *Lidhoríki*.—161km
Amfissa. Thence, via (183·5km) **Delphí** to *Athens*, see Rte
45. BUSES daily from Navpaktos to *Amfissa* in 4 hrs; also
daily from Amfissa to *Delphí*; several times daily from
Delphi to *Athens* (poor connections).

From Mesolóngi to (37·5km) the *Andirrion* turning, see Rte 55A.
Beyond Andirrion the road runs a field's length from the sea, and for a
brief period affords a long view right down the Gulf of Corinth.

48km (30 miles) **Návpaktos** (Ναύπακτος; Hotels B, C, D) is a charming little town (9012 inhab.) with a good beach. The picturesque,
mainly Venetian, *Castle*, from which ramparts descend to enclose the
little *Harbour*, recalls its medieval past when it was known in the
West as *Lepanto*. The plateia, shaded by jacaranda trees, looks across
the Gulf to Mt Panakhaïkon.

Here in 1571 the Turkish admiral fitted out before the decisive *Battle of Lepanto*,
fought in fact off the Echinades. The allied fleet, under Don John of Austria,
natural son of the Emp. Charles V, included contingents from Venice, Genoa, the
Papal States, Spain, Sicily, and Naples. The Turks were assisted by the Bey of
Alexandria and the Bey of Algiers. The result was the overwhelming victory of
Christendom, and the Moslem sea-power suffered a blow from which it never
recovered. The young Cervantes, creator of 'Don Quixote', here lost the use of his
left hand.

Ancient *Naupaktos*, a town of the Ozolian Locrians, was taken in 455 by the
Athenians. Here they established a colony of Messenians, who had been dispossessed by their Spartan conquerors. The place played an important part in the
Peloponnesian War; it was successfully defended in 429 by Phormion and in 426
by Demosthenes against the Spartans, and became a base for the Sicilian
expedition.

A by-road (buses daily) leads inland to (48km) *Thermon*, see Rte 54.

Quitting Navpaktos, we cross the *Mornos* near its mouth on a five-
span bridge. A by-road goes up the W side of its valley to Paliokhoráki
(9km); higher up it flows through a gorge; our road will cross it twice
more still higher up its course.—At (58km) *Kastráki* a by-road leads
(right) to *Evpálion* and *Monastiráki* (6·5km), a pretty place on the coast
where Herodotus located ancient *Erythrai*. The way continues
through rolling hills interspersed with orchards and little streams,
climbing gradually. Prominent on a bluff, to the right as we climb, is a
radar station commanding the Rion strait. The mountains behind
Patras become very prominent beyond the Gulf.—74km *Kardhára* lies
hidden (left) off the road. We reach a col with splendid retrospective
views of the Gulf, and descend to (76·5km) *Goumaíoi* (or Filothei).—
78km. Turning (left) for the *Varnákova Monastery* (5km), a Byzantine
foundation rebuilt by Capodistrias in 1831. Our road turns N, crosses a
second col, then follows a ledge high up the mountainside above a
side valley of the Mornos. During the gradual descent to the main river
the horizon becomes increasingly filled with peaks, those to the N
barren, those to the E clothed with forests.—87km. We cross the Mornos, here narrow and swift, at its confluence with a Loufolóreko, entering the valley of the tributary in order to cross it.

A by-road continues up the valley to *Terpsithéa* (13km). Off it (left), at (5km)
Limnitsa, tracks lead into the mountains to *Khrísovo* and *Katafíyio*, once refuges
from the Turks.

We climb high above the N bank of the Mornos. The slopes opposite are cultivated in terraces by scattered smallholders; above extend dark pine forests. We descend again almost to river level to cross a side stream. The valley becomes broader with views ahead towards Mt Giona (2509m).—101km Turning to *Krokíli* (11km), native village of Yiannis Makriyiannis, a hero of the 1821 revolt. At (108·5km) the turning to *Pendayioí* (18km) we get an extensive view to the N up the Kókkino valley towards the Vardhousia Mts (2437m). We cross the Kókkino and leave a by-road to *Dhiakópion* (7km) on our left. Our road skirts a conical hill with the remains of *Kállion* (ancient *Kallipolis*). The site was excavated in intensive campaigns from 1976 by the Greek Archaeological Service and the French School in advance of flooding for creation of the Mornos barrage. Remains are of the Hellenistic to Late Roman periods and include the city wall, houses, public buildings and the Roman cemetery. The site suffered destruction by the Gauls in 279 BC. Below is (113km) the *Mornos Tourist Pavilion*. Next to an old packhorse bridge we cross the Mornos for the last time and turn S into the valley of the Velá. Higher up, the Mornos is being dammed to provide water for Athens. About 1·5km farther on we pass a stone-arched bridge of an older road.

116km **Lidhoríki** (559m; Hotel E), a pleasant mountain village with 790 inhab., is the chief market centre of Doris, one of the two eparchies of Phocis. It was known to the Catalans as *Ledorix*, and was one of the three strong-points of the county of Salona. We continue S in the shallow and comparatively populous valley of the Velá, passing Palaiokastro, an ancient site.—127km. Roads branch (left) to *Malandrinó* and (right) to *Amigdaliá*. Beyond this turn some classical walling is visible (left). We climb amid scrub to the road summit (850m), passing, near the top, the monastery of *Panayía tis Koutsouriótissas*. We pass (right) a tarred road to Eratiní (with, after 3km, a track to Ayioi Pándes), and then a road, mostly unpaved, to Galaxídhi (comp. Rte 55C).

Our road bears NE. Ahead and right rises the range of Parnassos as we descend to (143km) *Vounikhóra* (761m). Beyond the village the *View opens out to the right affording a glimpse of the Bay of Galaxidhi with Khriso and Delphi lying on the Parnassian slopes.—From (152km) *Ayía Evthímia* (460m) tracks descend to Galaxídhi and Itéa. The landscape mellows suddenly as we come into full view of the olive groves which fill the valley, at the head of which stands Amfissa. We descend by turns on the flank of Mt Kokinari to (161km) **Amfissa**, whence via (183·5km) **Delphi** to (347·5km) **Athens**, see Rte 45.

C. Via Galaxídhi

ROAD, 312km (195 miles), new highway to Itéa along the Gulf of Corinth, thence joining Delphi–Levadhia road.

To (48km) *Návpaktos*, see Rte 55B. Just E of the town the ways part by the Mornos. The new road (right), crossing the river nearer its mouth, soon approaches the coast, which it then follows most of the way. There are few villages, the place-names being derived from beaches or isolated churches.—65km *Káto Marathiás*. Farther on a cluster of hamlets faces the I. of Trizonia.—84km (52½ miles) *Ayios Nikólaos* is linked 3 times daily by car ferry with Aigion (1 hr ; Rte 38).—92km *Paralía Tolofónos* (Hotel B) and (95km) *Eratiní* (Hotel D) are served by a minor road while the main road passes to landward. Eratiní stands on the bay of *Vitrinitsa* where in 1675 died Sir Giles Eastcourt, one of the first recorded Englishmen to visit Greece. The site of ancient *Tolophon*, with a well-preserved enceinte, lies near (104·5km) *Ayioi Pándes*.

The road now skirts the sheltered inner bays of the W side of the Gulf of Itea.—114km (71¾ miles) **Galaxídhi** (Γαλαξίδι; Hotels B, C, D), a well-built old seafaring town with inhabitants in absentia, is picturesquely situated on a wooded bay with a fine view of Parnassos. The church of the *Metamorphosis* was reputedly rebuilt by Michael II Angelos in gratitude for his recovery from an illness; it has an exceptionally good altar screen. There is a small maritime museum. The town has sections of ancient wall, which belonged perhaps to ancient *Chaleion*.

The coast is scarred with quarries and mines, bauxite being loaded by cableway and tip direct into ships. The little Bay of Salona, site of Salona's medieval port, now *Ormos Itéas*, was also the scene of Frank Abney Hastings' exploit with the steamship 'Karteria' against the Turks in 1827.

133km **Itéa** (Hotels B, C), with 4438 inhab., the modern harbour of Amfissa, stands round a headland at the head of the Gulf. It is a fresh and pleasant small resort, busy at intervals with cruise ships disembarking their excursions to Delphi.

From (135km) *Kírra* Delphi can be reached by hilly mule-path. French excavations have shown ancient *Kirrha* to have flourished in Early and Middle Helladic times, though it is best known for its part in the First Sacred War.

Recent excavations have revealed part of a Classical harbour-front building and some remains of the harbour itself can be made out beneath the sea. There is a Frankish tower on the sea front, mainly constructed of reused Classical blocks. This (rather than Galaxidhi, as usually supposed) may have been the port of medieval Salona (Amphissa).

Those with robust vehicles and a head for heights may essay the narrow precipitous zigzag that climbs 610m up the face of Koútsouras and across its saddle to (155km) *Dhesfína*. The road continues in an enclosed valley.—At (159km) the large *Moní Timíou Prodhrómou*, it divides. The right branch makes a steep descent to Andikira (11km, Rte 45), while the left branch crosses another ridge to (168km) *Dhistomo*. Hence to (195km) **Levadhia** and via Thebes to (314km) **Athens**, see Rte 45.

56 The Ionian Islands

The **IONIAN ISLANDS**, known also as the *Eptanisa*, from the seven principal islands, lie in the Ionian Sea mainly along the W coast of Greece. The 'seven islands', from N to S, are *Corfú* (off the coast of Albania and Epirus); *Paxoi* (off the coast of Epirus); *Levkas* (off Akarnania); *Ithaka*, *Cephalonia*, and *Zante* (at the entrance to the Gulf of Corinth); and *Kithira* (to the S of the Vátika Peninsula in the Peloponnese). The smaller islands include the group of the Othonian Islands—*Fano*, *Merlera*, and *Samothraki*—to the NW of Corfú; *Andipaxoi*, S of Paxoi; *Meganisi* and *Kalamos*, between Levkas and the mainland of Akarnania; the *Echinadhes* lying E of Ithaka near the mouth of the Acheloös; and *Andikithira*, S of Kithira. A claim by Pal herston at the time of the 'Don Pacifico' incident in 1848 that the islets f Sapienza and Cervi, off Messenia, formed part of the Ionian Islands vas not sustained. The grouping of the islands is a largely artificial onception of medieval and 19C politics. The group, excluding Kithira now administered from Piraeus), still remains nominally an administrative region, divided into four nomes, but the frequency of communication between each nome and Athens is greater than between the omes. The islands are here treated together because of the interest to ritish travellers of their tenure by Britain in 1815–64 as a protectorate.

The largest of the islands is Cephalonia, which also has the highest nountain, but by far the most important is Corfú, with the most populous city. The scenery combines the lush greenness of the English ountryside (together with a rainfall spread through the year) with the haracteristic Greek seascape. The high hedges that line the roads are lso unusual in Greece. The total population of the four nomes is 82,651.

Climate and Season. The climate of the Ionian Islands is generally temperate, but ubject to sudden changes. Their winter is rather rainy and their summer rather oo hot, but in spring and autumn they are enchanting. The average temperature anges from 6·7°–32·8°C (44°–91°F); the annual average of rainy days is as high as 00. The *Scirocco*, which blows from the SE, is most depressing and disagreeale. Frost is rare, and snow seldom falls except on the tops of the hills. Squalls *borasche*) are frequent. Earthquakes, especially in Zante, Levkas, and Cephaloia are not uncommon.

History. The name Ionian is not easily explained; Herodotus in his account of the onian peoples does not refer to the *Ionian Islands* as such. In the Homeric age a naritime people, under the generic name of *Kephallenians*, inhabited the islands t the mouth of the Gulf of Corinth. **Ulysses** or *Odysseus*, King of Ithaca, was the pic personification of this naval realm, which comprised the islands (or cities) of *haca, Doulichion, Same*, and *Zakynthos*, as well as the islets (Od. IX, 21 ff). At ne 'extreme end of the earth' was *Scheria* (? Corcyra or Corfù), where dwelt the riendly Phaeaceans. Since classical times authorities have not been agreed as to ne modern equivalents. The traditional school identifies Ithaca with Ithaka, ame with Same in Cephalonia, and Zakynthos with Zante; but, echoing the erplexity of the ancients, it is hazy about Doulichion. Strabo (X, 2) insists that it vas one of the Echinades. Others place it at Pale, in Cephalonia. The revolutionary views of Dörpfeld, put forward in detail in 1927, that Levkas is ancient thaka, modern Ithaka ancient Same, and Cephalonia ancient Doulichion, have ot received general support; though the theory removes the problem of the lentification of Doulichion (which, since it sent 40 ships to Troy as against 12 rom the other three cities, must have been larger than the Echinades), it poses ther problems, equally insoluble. Samuel Butler reminds us that we ought not to ook for the accuracy of a guidebook in a narrative that tells us of a monster with ix heads and three rows of teeth in each; and, remembering that the whole egion is particularly prone to seismic disturbances, we must perhaps be resgned to the geographical mysteries of the Odyssey. A thorough archaeological xploration of Cephalonia may one day clarify its position in the Mycenaean vorld and provide new answers. Some lively views have recently been put forvard by experienced yachtsmen on the Homeric topography of this area.

After the age of Homer the islands ceased for centuries to have any common ond of union. At the outbreak of the Peloponnesian War (431 BC) Corcyra, Cephallenia, and Zakynthos were allies of Athens, and Leucas (Levkas) of Spara. Both the Corcyreans and the Leucadians provided fleets for their respective eaders.

Towards the end of the 3C BC the islands became Roman. In AD 890 the yzantine emperor Leo the Philosopher (886–911) formed all seven into one rovince; and in this condition they belonged to the Eastern Empire after the isintegration of Italy. In the decline of the Empire they were again divided up, nd various Latin princes owned the different islands. They are heard of occasionally in the struggles between the Greek emperors and the Western crusaders. hey were desolated by the ravages of corsairs, Christian as well as Mohammean. After many vicissitudes, the inhabitants of Corfù placed themselves, in 386, under the sovereignty of Venice, the state which was more than any other influence the destinies of the islands. During the next two centuries Venice obtained control of most of the other Ionian Islands; but two of them remained independent much longer. Levkas was annexed in 1684. Kythera not till 1717.

The rule of the Venetians, much less severe than in the Archipelago, embodied some of the principles of Machiavelli. The more prominent citizens, instead of being imprisoned or executed, were ennobled. Frequent intermarriages made for a close assimilation of races, and the ascendency of the more cultured partner helped to consolidate the domination of Venice. Education was discouraged and Ionian youths were granted the privilege of purchasing degrees at Italian universities without having to pass examinations. Italian became the official language and the Roman Catholic religion was established. The humbler classes who formed the great bulk of the population, remained faithful to the Greek tongue and to the Orthodox Church.

On the fall of Venice in 1797, the Treaty of Campo Formio transferred the Ionian Islands to the French Republic, and they were occupied by a small French garrison. The French soldiers were driven out in 1798 by a combined Russian and Turkish force. By the provisions of the Treaty of 21 March 1800, between the Tsar, and the Sultan, the Ionian Islands were formed into a separate state, with the high-sounding title of the *Septinsular Republic*. The republic was under the protectorate first of the Porte, later of Russia. This period of quasi-independence (1800–07) proved to be little better than a reign of terror. Within two years all seven islands had risen against their general government and each separate island against its local authorities. Horrors, resembling those of the Corcyrean factions described by Thucydides (III, 81) were of daily occurrence. In 1802, on the change of masters, the principal Ionians sent an envoy to the Tsar, imploring his interference, and as a result the Russian plenipotentiary, Count Mocenigo, a native of Zante, which had become particularly notorious for the number of its assassinations, was empowered to proclaim new forms of administration.

But in 1807, by the Treaty of Tilsit, the islands were given back to France, and incorporated in the province of Illyria. In 1809 Great Britain came on the scene General Oswald took Cephalonia, Ithaka, Zante, and Kythera that year, and Levkas in 1810. Paxos was reduced in 1814 and after the fall of Napoleon Corfú was surrendered by its French defender, at the command of Louis XVIII, to Sir James Campbell. The Treaty of Paris (1815) made the Ionian Islands an independent state under the protection of the British crown.

Sir Thomas Maitland (1759?–1824) was first Lord High Commissioner. A constitution was drawn up at his direction, and adopted by the Ionian Constituent Assembly in 1817. The administration at Corfú comprised the Lord High Commissioner, the Senate of six members, and the Assembly. The Senate and the Assembly of 42 deputies were ciphers, for the Lord High Commissioner, had the right of veto on all their acts, charge of foreign relations, and the immediate control of the police and health departments. He was represented in each of the other six islands by a British Resident, with local functions similar to his own.

Maitland was not slow to make use of his dictatorial powers and soon acquired the nickname 'King Tom'. Despte the defects of the colonial system, the next thirty years gave the Ionian Islands an era of peace and prosperity unparalleled on the mainland. The administration of justice became impartial. Direct taxation was practically abolished and the revenue, raised chiefly by import and export duties, was freed from peculation. Trade and agriculture were encouraged; educational establishments (including even a short-lived university at Corfú) were founded; and excellent roads, unknown in Greece since Roman times, were built as well as harbours, quays, and aqueducts. The Greek Church was restored.

Nationalist feeling soon overrode material considerations. The islanders, who had at first welcomed the British particularly resented the measures taken to enforce their neutrality in the Greek struggle for independence. The achievement by Greece in 1830 of her immediate aims increased the discontent with foreign rule. A powerful opposition, headed by Andreas Mustoxidi, agitated for union with Greece. In 1858, Gladstone was sent on a special commission and for a few days exercised the functions of Lord High Commissioner. He vainly attempted to meet the situation by proposing a number of reforms. As late as 1862 he declared that it would be a 'crime against the safety of Europe' to give up the islands.

On the change of dynasty in Greece, however, Great Britain voluntarily ceded all rights over the Ionian Islands by the Treaty of London signed in 1864; at the same time their union with Greece was formally recognised. Edward Lear made a tour in 1863, drawing his 'Views in the Seven Ionian Islands'.

A. Corfú (Kérkira)

Approaches BY AIR. From *Athens*, 4 times daily in c 50 minutes. From *London* direct several times a week.

BY SEA. CAR FERRY from *Igoumenítsa*, many times daily in 1½ hr; from *Pátras*, several times a week via *Sámi* in 10 hrs; buses from Athens connect at both ports. Through buses from Athens via Rion and Igoumenitsa.

Corfú is a port-of-call also (several times daily in summer; several times weekly in winter) of international CAR FERRY services, Patras–Brindisi, Corinth–Brindisi, Patras–Ancona (break of journey at Corfu—no extra charge—must be notified before embarkation); and it is visited by innumerable cruise ships. Passengers without an international ticket travelling between two Greek ports can do so only by Greek shipping lines.

CORFÚ, in Greek **Kérkira** (Κέρκυρα), is the best known and most beautiful of the Ionian Islands. With a length of 64km and an extreme breadth in the N of nearly 32km, it is in area the second largest of the seven islands, but its population (pop. 36,901) is much greater than that of the more spacious Cephalonia. Its capital is likewise the most important and populous town in the group. The most northerly of the Ionian Islands, situated less than 3km off the N Epirot coast of Albania, and the nearest Greek land to Italy, Corfu has a natural importance as the gateway between East and West. Until the Balkan Wars of 1912–13 extended the Greek frontier, it had long been a Christian outpost on the very verge of Turkish territory.

The land, especially in the long S peninsula, is well-watered and fertile. Cypress, fig, orange, and lemon trees are found in magnificent profusion, but above all the olive, which here unpruned almost attains the size and dignity of a forest tree. About four million grow in the island, providing a large output of oil. Cactus is common. Vineyards abound, producing good white wine (unresinated) and a rather sweet heavy red wine with a short life. Apples and pears are grown and, more important, tomatoes. The broad N section is crossed by a range of hills from W to E, culminating in Pantokrator (914m). In the S a lesser range is topped by Mt Ayioi Dhéka (567m), a conspicuous landmark.

The effects of the long Venetian domination are still apparent. Italian, once the official language, and strongly tinged with the Venetian dialect, is still quite commonly spoken and understood. The place-names are bi-lingual, with a preference for the Italian form. Among the legacies of British rule are cricket and ginger beer. A local specialty is the *kum-kwat*, the crystallised miniature Japanese orange. Except in Corfu town, hotels are mostly closed in winter.

History. The name *Corfu* is an Italian corruption of Koryphó, a Byzantine name derived from the two peaks (Κορυφαί) on which the citadel of the chief town is built. The ancient name *Corcyra* appears first in Herodotus. About 734 BC (traditional date, not yet confirmed by pottery found) a colony was planted here by the Corinthians, which soon became rich and powerful enough to found colonies of its own. Corinth soon became jealous and apprehensive, and c 664 BC a battle was fought between their respective fleets, the first Greek sea-fight on record. The Corcyreans took no part in the Persian wars. In 432 BC they invoked the help of Athens against the Corinthians. The consequent engagement off the Sybota Is., between the Corcyreans and their mother-city, precipitated the Peloponnesian War. During this struggle the power and importance of Corcyra was irretrievably squandered in the calamitous feuds between the oligarchic and democratic parties. The victory of the democrats in 425 BC was signalised by atrocities. Corcyra was chosen by the Athenians for the final review of their fleet in 415 BC on the eve of the Sicilian expedition.

Though Corcyra never recovered her former importance, the island was by 37? BC, according to Xenophon, in a wonderful state of fertility and opulence. After a succession of masters, it became Roman in 229 BC. Here Octavian assembled hi fleet before the battle of Actium, and hither came at various times Tibullus, Cato and Cicero. In AD 67 Corcyra was visited, while on his way to Greece, by Nero who, according to Suetonius, sang and danced before the altar of Zeus a Kassiope.

During the Crusades, the geographical position of Corfu again brought it into prominence. Robert Guiscard seized the island in 1081 during his wars with the Eastern Empire. Richard I of England landed here on his return from the Holy Land in 1193, on his way to Ragusa and unexpected captivity. Passing from the Venetians to the Genoese and back again (1204–14), Corfu came under Epiru until 1267, then under the Angevins of Naples. Towards the end it suffered greatly at the hands of pirates. In 1386, the inhabitants invoked the aid of Venice under whose sovereignty they remained until her downfall in 1797. Venice made Corfu her principal arsenal in Greece and surrounded the town with extensive fortifications, which set at defiance the whole power of the Ottomans in 1537 and 1570, and, above all, in the celebrated siege of 1716, remarkable as the last grea attempt of the Turks to extend their conquests in Christendom. In this siege the personal efforts of the High Admiral of the Ottoman Empire were frustrated by the skill and daring of Marshal Schulenburg, a soldier of fortune from Saxony.

Soppoto. Battle between Venetians and Turks, 1670. Engraving

The subsequent history of Corfu is largely that of the Ionian Islands as a whol (see above). Count John Capodistrias, the first President of independent Greece was a Corfiot. In 1915–16 the island was used as a base for the reorganisation o the Serbian army after its disastrous retreat, until its transfer to the Salonika fron In Aug 1923, in consequence of the murder of Gen. Tellini, the Italian president o the Greco-Albanian Boundary Commission, Italy bombarded Corfu, and subse quently occupied the island, together with Paxos, Antipaxos, Merlera, and Samo thraki, until 27 Sept, when the incident was closed by the payment of an indemnit of 50 million lire. As a result, however, Corfu remained a 'frontier region' wit special restrictions from 1924 to 1961. In the Second World War the island wa occupied in 1941–43 without much unpleasantness by the Italians and later b the Germans. There followed ten days of bombardment and fighting (13–23 Sep before the city was reduced by the Germans. During this time a quarter of th town was destroyed, including the seat of the Ionian parliament, the magnificen old library of the former university with 70,000 volumes, and 14 churches with their paintings of the Ionian school. In the international channel NE of Corfu on 22 Oct 1946 two British destroyers hit an uncharted Albanian minefield, deliberately laid, losing 45 men.

Corfu has a tradition of musical performance dating from 1733. Edward Lear (1812–88), author of the 'Book of Nonsense', lived for some time at Corfu while painting and writing about Greece.

The town of **Corfú** or *Kérkira* (Κέρκυρα), situated on an irregular peninsula about the middle of the E coast, just S of the islet of *Vido*, is the capital of the island and the largest town in the Ionian Islands. Including the suburbs of *Mandouki* to the W and *Garitsa* and *Sarokko* to the S, now all contiguous, it has 35,561 inhabitants. Destined by the Venetians to become the headquarters of their Greek possessions, it was strongly fortified, and their fortresses arrest the attention of every new arrival. As a busy port-of-call for steamers plying between Brindisi and Piraeus, for cruise ships, and for naval vessels, it is a favourite resort of visitors. The old town has narrow streets and tall houses, having formerly been enclosed by walls. During the British occupation it was given a good water supply and extended towards the site of the ancient city to the S. The grave damage, caused by the fighting in 1943 between Italians and Germans and worsened in 1944 by Anglo-American bombing, left scars which are slowly disappearing.

Airport, just beyond the suburb of Sarokko. TERMINAL, Kapodhistríou 20.

Hotels A, B, C, D, E.

Tavernas near Mon Repos beach, near the Achilleion, at Kanoni, at Perana, etc.

Post Office (Pl. 6), Leof. Alexándras 26.—O.T.E. CENTRE (Pl. 6), Od. Mántzaros.

Informaton Offices N.T.O.G., opp. Municipal Theatre; TOURIST POLICE, Arseníou 31.

Buses from the Spianádha (Pl. 3) to *Mon Repos* and *Kanoni*; from Plat Theotóki (Sarokko; Pl. 6) to *Dasia, Ipsos*; to the *Achilleion*, etc.; from the Néon Froúrion (Pl. 2) to *Kassiopi*, etc.

Motor-Boats in summer, from below the Spianadha to *Dasia* (out morning; return aft. and early evening).

Amusements. CASINO at the Achilleion, 5½ miles S; TENNIS CLUB (Pl. 7); DANCING at Club Mediterranée camps, tickets from Town Office; BATHING (nearest) at Mon Repos beach (Pl. 16).—CONCERTS in the Bandstand on Sundays.

The modern HARBOUR extends along the NW edge of the city, from the Adriatic steamer berths to the W (Pl. 1) to the drive-on quay of the Igoumenitsa car ferry to the E (Pl. 2). From the *Custom House* (Pl. 2) we follow the quay E beneath the untidy lower slopes of the **Néon Froúrion** (Fortezza Nuova), built in 1577–88 by the Venetians. The fortress, having served the French, was given its superstructure by the British and only ceased to be a military post after 1864. Until the Second World War it was used by a police school; during the war its casemates sheltered the Corfiots from air raids; the barrack-block is now occupied by a naval detachment. The bastions, picturesquely overgrown by fig trees and wild flowers, may be explored (closed at midday) from the E side entrance. The W wall above the dry moat has two large Lions of St. Mark.

We reach the sun-drenched PLATEIA YEORYIOU B', with its judas-trees, where even the horses of the hired carriages wear hats. The *Porta Spilia* (16C), incorporated in a later edifice, admits to the main street through the heart of the town (comp. below). From the SE corner another narrow passage passes the Nea Yorki hotel and leads by stepped streets (skalinadhes) into the Kambielo (Campiello) quarter

CORFU

0   300 yards
0   300 metres

4

Byzantine Museum
(Antivouniotissa)
Police
Archbishop's
Palace
AKRA AY. NIKOLAOS
Nomarkhia
Corfu Club
Baths
athedral
Mus.of Asiatic Art
Old Palace
piridon/OU SPIRIDONOS
Panayia Mandrakina
Ionian Bank
Mandraki
Panayia
Ay.
Ioannis
ion VOULGAREOS
RC Cath.
Spianadha
of Greece
DOUSMANI
Schulenburg
Statue
Palaion Frourion
Law
Courts SPARCHOU
Old Fortress
ruins
(Sound & Light
MOUSTOXIDOU
Folk Dances)
KAPODHISTRIOU
St George
ment
8
Maitland Rotunda
Brit. Vice.
Restaurant
Con.
(Ionian Academy)
AKADIMIAS
Nautical Club

Museum

SILEOS KONSTANTINOU

uglas Obelisk

11

12

GARITSA BAY

15

16

VASSILEOS KONSTANTINOU

ALKIVIADOU DARI

Anemomilos

N

y. Iason & Sosipatros   for continuation see inset   Beach where constricted alleys (kantounia) wind through high tenements; here are an attractive Venetian well-head of 1699 and the church of *Panayía Kremastí* and the *Pantokrátor* both with good altar-screens.

In fine weather it is better to follow the sea road, flanked by handsome houses along the line of the old walls, and enjoying good views of the mainland. As we round the point we pass the *Archbishop's Palace*, the former *Nomarkhia* (1835), on the site of Capodistrias' birthplace, and the *Corfu Literary Society*. The point affords also a view of the citadel.

The **Royal Palace** (Pl. 3), a large classical building constructed of Malta stone, has an elegant Doric portico of 32 columns, set forward and linking two gates (of St. Michael and St. George) in the form of triumphal arches; beyond these the portico curves forward to lateral pavilions. Above the cornice are sculptured seven medallions with the emblems of the Ionian islands. In front stands a bronze statue, by Prosellenti, of Sir Frederic Adam, who organised the water-supply of Corfu.

The palace was designed by Col. (later General Sir George) Whitmore in 1819 to serve as treasury of the newly created Order of St. Michael and St. George, and as residence for the Lord High Commissioner. A legislative assembly was incorporated. In 1864 the building was handed intact to the King of the Hellenes; it served as a royal residence but fell into disrepair after 1913. After some damage by billeted refugees in the Civil War, the High Commissioner's private apartments were restored for the Greek government for use as a museum, while in 1954, at the instance of Sir Charles Peake, then British ambassador in Athens, the state rooms were restored as a memorial to the British connection with Corfu.

The State Rooms (no adm. at present) comprise the *Throne Room*, meetingplace of the Ionian senate, with the original throne and full-length portraits of High Commissioners; the *Rotunda*, or ballroom, with ceiling motif of the badge of the Order and the original floor; and the *Dining Room*. One wing houses a collection of Chinese and Japanese porcelain and bronzes, presented by Greg. Manos, a former Greek ambassador in the Far East, while in another room are floor mosaics from the Christian Basilica (comp. below); and Ikons by Hieremias Palladhes (16C), Yeoryios Kortezas, Emmanuel Tzanes, and Mikhail Dhamaskinos.

The *Esplanade** (Pl. 3, 7), or *Spianadha*, a huge open space separating the citadel from the town, served the Venetians as parade and exercise ground. It is divided by a central avenue. The N half of the Esplanade, known as the Plateia, in front of the Palace, forms the 'field' on which in July are played the traditional cricket matches between two local clubs and visiting teams from Britain and Malta. Its former gravel surface has given place to turf but a matting wicket is still used. On the W it is bounded by the 'LISTON', an imposing arcaded row of tall houses designed during the French occupation in 1807–14 in imitation of the Rue de Rivoli; here are many popular cafés. On the grass-sown S half of the Esplanade (The Spianadha proper) rise a bandstand (*Palko*) and an elegant Ionic *Rotunda* in memory of Sir Thomas Maitland, first Lord High Commissioner (1815–23). At the S end the former Ionian Academy (now a school) faces the Nautical Club whose 'eights' row offshore.

On the central avenue stands a *Statue of Marshal Schulenburg*, erected by the Venetians in his lifetime just after the siege of 1716. Executed by Ant. Corradini in Carrara marble, it was removed here from the citadel by the British. To the N the glacis of the citadel is occupied by exotic gardens, containing a statue of the eccentric Philhellene Lord Guilford (1769–1828), founder of the Ionian Academy. Beyond on the wall stands the chapel of *Panayía Mandrakína* (1700). A bridge flanked by cannon of 1684 crosses the 16C moat, where (left) motor-boats may be hired and (right) the local children usually swim. The **Pálaion Froúrion** (Fortezza Vecchia), or *Citadel* (open daily, subject to some restrictions; no cameras), occupies a promontory with two heights, first heard of as '*Korypho*' in 968, which remained through the Middle Ages the fortified township. The heights are crowned by the 'Castel di Terra' with a semaphore and lighthouse, and the 'Castel de Mar', a Byzantine foundation, formerly the powder magazine. Explosions in the 18C destroyed most earlier work, but the W bastions are substantially as built in 1558 by Savorgnani and Martinengo. Below to the S is the former *Garrison Church* of St. George, with a Doric portico, built by the British (1830). On the N side are the buildings of the *Military Academy*, which with some ancient Venetian barracks overlook the little harbour of *Mandraki*. On the seaward point once stood a temple of Hera Akraia.

The landward fortress, reached by a curving tunnel, affords a magnificent *View, depending for its greatest effect on its gorgeous colouring. To the E extends the long mountainous coastline of Albania and Epirus. To the W the island rises above and beyond the town.

Leoforos Kapodhistríou runs along the W side of the Esplanade behind the Liston. Near its N end are two museums, *The Museum of Byzantine and Post-Byzantine Art* in the churches of Antivouniótissa (Od. Arseníou), and the *Museum of Asiatic Art*. The latter is opposite the church of **Ayios Spiridon**, erected in 1589–96. The early-18C ceiling paintings of Panayotis Doxaras were tastelessly refurbished in the 19C. The marble iconostasis (1864; by the Austrian Maurs) takes the form of a complete church façade. Adm. And. Pisani's lamp, near the pulpit, dates from 1711.

Spiridon, Bp of Cyprus, suffered during the persecution of Diocletian and was a member of the Council of Nicaea in 325. His body was brought to Corfu in 1489 and is preserved in a richly-ornamented silver *Sarcophagus* (1867; Viennese) to the right of the high altar. Four times a year (11 August; first Sunday in Nov; Palm Sunday; Saturday in Holy Week) the remains are carried in solemn procession round parts of the town and esplanade. The routes and rites are different and commemorate miraculous deliverances, respectively from the Turks in 1716, from plague in 1673, from plague in 1630, and from famine (? before 1553). So popular is the saint that nearly half the boys in the island are named after him.

We turn left into Od. Filarmoníkis, with its animated vegetable market, and soon meet OD. NIKIFÓROU THEOTÓKI, the main pedestrian street since Venetian times, which runs through the town from the Liston to the Old Port. Beyond it we cross, farther on, Od. Voulgaréos, the narrow arcaded street that channels traffic from the Esplanade towards Sarokko. On the corner stands the *Dhimarkhíon*, built in 1663 as a Venetian loggia; converted (1720) into the Teatro San Giacomo, it became in 1903 the town hall. A mutilated relief of 1691 in the E façade commemorates Morosini's victories. N.C. Mantzaros (1795–1874), who here directed the opera, is best remembered as composer of the Greek national anthem. In the square, to the S, stands the elegant façade (1658) of the *Latin Cathedral* (St. James), remarkably unadorned for Italian work of this period; the church, made a roofless shell in 1943, has been restored. The former Archbishop's Palace (1754; later, Law Courts), opposite, is still in ruins.

In the quarter within the ramparts farther S, the former *Ionian Parliament*, removed here from the palace in 1855, was given after 1869 to the British community as their Anglican church; bombed in the war, it was repaired in 1961 to house a small art gallery.

Leofóros Yeoryíou Theotóki runs SW towards the PLATEÍ A THEOTÓ KI, the centre of the modern quarter that has evolved from the former suburb of Sarokko (San Rocco). We pass on the way the site of the *Municipal Theatre* of 1902, ruined in 1944. It was the HQ of the Serbian army in 1915–16 and here in 1918 was proclaimed the new country of Yugoslavia. A new theatre was designed in 1963 by P. Sakellarios to replace it.

To the W (1km) of the Plateía Theotóki in the convent church of *Platitéra* (Pl. 5) are the tombs of Count John Capodistrias and of Photios Tzavellas (1774–1811), the Suliot klepht, and there are paintings by Clotzas (Last Judgment) and Poulakis (Revelation of St. John).—From Sarokko Leof. Alexandhras runs down to the Bay of Garitsa.

From the Spianadha Leofóros Vasiléos Konstandínou skirts the Bay of Garitsa. Beyond the Corfù Palace Hotel we come to the ***Museum** (Pl. 11). Beneath the colonnade (A): Inscribed state bases.—GROUND FLOOR HALL (B), Sculpture, mostly Roman copies of Greek originals.

FIRST FLOOR. On the *Landing* (Δ), left, huge Pithos (6C BC); tomb monuments from the Garitsa cemetery; vigorous lion-head spouts from the Classical temple of Mon Repos; early Doric capital, with abacus bearing an Archaic inscription; funerary stele with boustrophedon inscription in Homeric hexameters honouring Arniada, a Corcyraean general who died in battle on the Arachthos in Epirus (6C BC); (case 1) pottery (7–6C) from tombs.—CORRIDOR ROOM (E): left of door (case 2), Prehistoric finds from Sidhari, Ermones, and Aphiona; right of door (case 3), Archaic finds from Garitsa cemetery; along the wall, arranged chronologically, finds from the Hieron at Kerousádhes, from Ródha, and from N Epirus, as well as from Garitsa: notably Corinthian and Laconian pottery, terracotta antefixes from the Temple at Ródha (5C BC), and (case 8) inscribed bronze decrees appointing consuls (4C BC; transferred here from the National Museum in 1967); (case 9) Head of Aphrodite (c 300 BC; Praxitelean school); large Protocorinthian olpe decorated with four bands of animals; bronze komast carrying a rhyton (part of a lebes; 570 BC).

HALL OF THE GORGON (Z). *Pediment (restored) of the Archaic Temple of Artemis (590–580 BC): the central Gorgon is flanked by hybrid 'panthers', the whole composition stiff, formalised, but not lacking in grandeur. Other architectonic fragments of the same temple include triglyphs and metopes, the terracotta sima and antefixes, and those in Parian marble with which they were replaced c 520 BC.— NORTH HALL (H). Head of a Corinthian kouros, in Naxian marble. Bronze figures of men and beasts, sculptured terracotta roof tiles, Gorgon's head, lion spout, all from a large temple (of Hera?) excavated in the grounds of Mon Repos in 1962–67. Part of a smaller pediment from Figareto with horizontal figures. Lead plate showing the profile of a frieze. Painted *Sima from a smaller building, reminiscent of the temple fragments at Thermon (p. 461). *Lion of Menekrates, probably the crowning ornament of his tomb; discovered in 1843 (though not on the tomb), its date is disputed between 625 and 550 BC. Terracotta votive figurines from the Small Hieron of Artemis, near Kanoni. Archaic torso of the type of the Kassel Apollo; head of Menander, good copy of an original by Kephisodotos and Timarchos; head of an unknown philosopher (Roman copy of an original c 300 BC).

An *Obelisk* to Sir Howard Douglas (died 1841) stands at the seaward end of Leofóros Alexándras, where a road leads towards a hill crowned by the prison. Here during the demolition of the Venetian fort

0   5 miles
0   8 kms

Perouládhes · ○
Ag Stefanos ○   Sidári
Avlióti   Astrákeri
AKR.
AYIA AIKATERINI
Maghouládhes ○   **Karousádhes**
Kavvadhádhes ○   Kavalloúrion   Ródha
Velonádhes   Loútsai
Rakhtádhes ○   Agrafoí
Ay. Pandeleímon
Ay. Dhoúloi   **Epískepsis**
Agrós ○   Nimfaí ○   Perithia   ○ Kassiópi
Páyoi ○   Kastellánoi   Striñilas
Makrádhes ○   Skriperón   Zigós   Spartílas
Lákones ○   Dhoukádhes   ○ Sokrákion   Kouloúra
Palaiokastrítsa ○   **Áno Korakiána**   Kentroma
Gardeládhes ○   Nissákion
Liapádhes   Pirgí
○ Ípsos
○ Káto Korakiána
Yiannádhes ○   ○ Dassia
○ Gouviá
AKR.   ○ Kondokálion
AYIAS
YEORYIOS   MIRTIOTISSA
✝   Ay. Nikólaos   ○ Afrá   **Potamós**
Pélekas ○   Alepoú
Kanálion   **KÉRKIRA**
Varipatádhes ○   **(CORFÙ)**
Sinarádhes
○ **Kinopiástai**
Ay. Dhéka ○   **Gastoúrion**
Káto   ACHILLEION
Garoúna   ○ Benítsai
Pentation ○
Ano Pavliána
○ Strongilí
Áyios Matthaíos ○
Vranganiotika ○   ○ Messonghi
Khlomatianá
Korissia   ○ **Khlomós**
○ Korakádhes
Aryirádhes
Perivólion   Ay. Ioánnis
Ringládhes
Vitaládhes   **Levkímmi**
AKR.
LEVKIMMI
Kritiká ○
Palaiokhórion ○
Dragotiná ○   ○ Kávos
AKR.
ASPROKAVOS

CORFU
ISLAND

of San Salvatore in 1843 was discovered an extensive necropolis. The huge circular *Tomb of Menekrates* (in the garden of the police station) (? 7C BC) was supposedly crowned by the lion in the museum. Menekrates, according to the inscription, was drowned.

The *English Cemetery*, on the N side of the Prison, has interesting memorials both civil and military. Here are buried the dead from H.M.S. 'Saumarez' and 'Volagé' (1946).

The pleasant *Promenade, backed with gardens, skirts the suburb of *Garitsa*, or Kastradhes, and curves to the left. Keeping straight on in the district called *Anemómilos*, we reach the Byzantine church of *Ayíon Iásonos kai Sosípatros*. This is an inscribed-domed cross church of the two-column type with a dome on an octagonal drum. It has bands of Cufic decoration and incorporates three ancient monolithic columns. There is an early 11C fresco of St. Arsenius on the E wall of the narthex. SS. Jason and Sosipater, according to tradition the disciples of St. Paul from Tarsus and Iconium, were the first preachers of christianity in Corcyra and Sosipater was here martyred under Caligula. Two 15C tombs beneath the screen are sometimes optimistically shown as those of the saints.

Here we are within the bounds of '**Palaiópolis**' or ancient **Corcyra**, which occupied the peninsular between the bay of Garitsa (anc. *Alkinoös*) and the lagoon of Khalikiopoulo (anc. Hyllaian Harbour). The ancient city was sacked by the Goths in the 6C and later abandoned. The later Greeks and Venetians used it as a quarry in the erection of the modern town of Corfu. A large tower, forming the SE extremity of the harbour of Alkinoös was excavated in 1965 beside the church of Ay. Athanasios.

About 5 minutes farther on is the entrance to the royal villa of **Mon Repos** (no adm.), laid out for Sir Frederic Adam in 1824 and successively the summer residence of British Lord High Commissioners and Greek kings. Here in 1921 was born Prince Philip, Duke of Edinburgh. Opposite the gates is the gutted Palaiopolis church of *Ayía Kérkyra*, where an inscription recording its foundation by Bp Jovian before 450 and reused elements of a Doric temple have survived successive destructions in the 11C by the Saracens, in 1537 by the Turks, and in 1940. A Venetian lion of a 17C rebuilding also survives.

The Basilica, which succeeded a semicircular building of the 2–1C (itself on foundations of a 6C temple), had double aisles and an exo-narthex and was comparable with Ayios Dhimitrios at Salonika. After its sack by the Goths, it was reconstructed with single aisles using old materials.

A path to the right leads to further remains of the ancient lower city. Just W of the monastery of Ayioi Theódhoroi are vestiges of the Archaic *Altar* and *Temple of Artemis*, from which came the pediments in the museum. The building was peripteral with 8 columns by 17. Another hundred yards to the W is the ruined chapel of *Nerándzika* built over a section of the ancient city *Walls*; these can be traced to the shore of the lagoon.

TO ANALIPSIS AND KANONI. The road (followed by a bus) continues S to the village of *Análipsis* (1km farther), on the site of the acropolis of the old city. Here are the meagre remains of the 6C Doric 'Kardhaki' temple and of a fountain (used in Venetian times and for watering British ships). The larger Archaic temple of the 7C, which was

Corfu: Temple of Artemis, E front. Top: Gorgon pediment.
Bottom: restoration of terracotta and painted decoration

replaced (c 400 BC) by a Classical building (comp. above) on the same
site, lies within the grounds of Mon Repos to the N. Passing the Corfu
Hilton we come to (4km) **Kanóni** (Hotels A, C), a semi-circular terrace,
fashioned as a gun position by the French and called by the British
'One-gun Battery'. It commands a celebrated *View across the former
entrance to the Hyllaian harbour. In the foreground are two little islets,
each bearing a monastery. A causeway (reached by a steep path)
leads to *Vlakhérnai*, gleaming white beneath its red roofs, from which
small boats cross to PONDIKONÍSI (*Mouse Island*) where the monastery
peeps from a thick clump of cypresses (pilgrimage to the disappointing 19C chapel on 6 Aug). It was the inspiration of Arnold Boecklin's
'Isle of the Dead', and is one of two claimants to be the ship of Odysseus turned to stone by Poseidon.

The Hyllaian harbour, once guarded by moles and a chain, is now cut off by a
causeway across which (on foot only) we may reach Perama (see below).

Excursions on the Island

I. TO THE ACHILLEION AND BENITSES, a round of 24km, asphalt road.
We quit Plateía Theotóki on the SW, pass the airport (Pl. 13) and skirt
the lagoon of Khalikiopoulos. At 5km *Vrióni* we leave on our left the
road for Perama and Benitses (by which we shall return), continuing
by the inland road. At 6·5km we leave, on our right, a road for *Ayioi
Dhéka* (3km), starting point for the ascent in 1½ hr of the mountain of
the same name (1860ft; *View).—8·5km *Gastoúri* (Hotels B, C) just
beyond which, on the summit of a wooded eminence overlooking the
sea and the town of Corfu, stands the **Achilleíon**, built in 1890–91 by
the Italian architect Cardilo for the empress Elisabeth of Austria. After
her assassination it was bought by Kaiser Wilhelm II, who spent every
spring here in 1908–14. It passed to the Greek government as enemy
property and in Dec 1962 was leased to Baron von Richthoven as a
casino for roulette and chemin-de-fer. The villa, dedicated to Achilles, favourite hero of the empress, is set in an Italian landscape garden,
liberally ornamented with statuary, of Homeric subjects and proportions but mediocre inspiration. The Dying Achilles, by Herter (1884),
should however be noted. The mansion, a curious pastiche within of
Teutonic fin-de-siècle neo-Classicism, has been restored. The
ground floor includes a *Museum* of mementoes of its former owners,
including fine portraits of the Emp. Elisabeth by Winterhalter and the
saddle-throne from which Wilhelm II dictated despatches.

The best view is obtained from the neighbouring hill of Ayia Kiriaki. Near by is a
French Military Cemetery (225 graves) of the First World War, when the Achilleion became an allied naval hospital.

Our road drops by steep bends to join the coastal road (comp. above)
halfway between Perama and (12km) **Benítses** (Hotels A, B, C, D, E; F/
A), a pretty fishing village with a small beach. Amid an orange grove,
on private land, are some remains of Roman villa baths with mosaic
pavements. Continuation to the S, see below. The return to Corfu is
made by the *Coastal road. We turn back, leave on our left the road to
the Achilleion by which we came, and pass its ruined private
landing-place.—16km *Pérama* (Hotels A, B, C, E; F/A). About 1km
farther on, a promontory (Restaurants) commands views of Pontikonisi
(comp. above) and Mon Repos. We rejoin the road on which we started
out.—24km *Corfú*.

II. TO PALAIOKASTRITSA, 25km (15½ miles). This road also starts at
Plateia Theotoki and after 1km divides (left to Pelekas, see below). We

pass the monastery of Platitera (comp. p. 477) and bear left, rejoining the coast some way outside the town. To the right we see *Lazaretto*, an islet offshore, formerly the quarantine station. We skirt the sheltered roadstead of Gouviá, where some French ships evaded pursuit by Nelson. The bay has large hotels, camping sites, a yacht marina, and a youth hostel.—8km *Kondokáli* (Hotels A, C, D; F/A) lies at its S end. On the shore is a roofless Venetian Arsenal, or galley repair shed, of 1716.—Beyond (9km) *Gouviá* (Hotels A, B, C, D; F/A), we quit the coast road (continuation, see below) and turn inland.—14·5km Turning (signposted XOPIA) to Skriperón and, via the col of Ayios Pandeleimon (*View), to *Sidhári* (35·5km from Corfu), where Early Neolithic pottery was unearthed in 1965, and *Perouládhes* (38·5km) at the NW corner of the island. The road is tarred to *Sidhari*, good gravel beyond. Both places have beaches, and good sandy coves can be reached on foot between the two.

Offshore, 11km NW, are three islands (*Epikoússa*, *Othonoí*, and *Mathráki*), with 569 inhabitants between them, constituting the final limit of Greek sovereignty in the NW.

22km By-road for *Lákones* (2km) which commands a lovely panorama of Palaiokastritsa and its surroundings; here the classical student can assess the merits of locating on the coast below the site of Homeric *Scheria*, with the twin ports of the Phaeacians and the gardens of Alkinoös. From Lakones a mule-path climbs to *Angelókastro*, a castle already existing in 1272 when it is referred to in the Neapolitan Angevin archives as Castrum Sancti Angeli. This commands an even finer view, including the citadel of Corfu. We descend to the delightful *Bay of **Palaiokastritsa** (Παλαιοκαστρίτσα; Hotels A, B, C, D, E; tavernas, good lobsters). The road continues to the gates of the monastery, attractively sited on a promontory (92m; view) with terraced gardens. Though founded in 1228, it now has little that dates before the 18C.

III. TO PANTOKRATOR AND KASSIOPI. To (9km) Gouviá, see above. We continue by the coast road, surmount a wooded promontory, and descend to the shore of a beautiful bay.—At (13km) *Dasiá* (Hotels A, B, C, D; F/A) is the huge camp of the Club Méditerranée and other camping-sites. To the left a by-road leads to the *Castello Mimbelli*, a hotel occupying a 19C castle in a Venetian Gothic style that once belonged to George II of the Hellenes.—At 13km a turn (left) leads in 1km to the village of *Káto Korakianá*, where the small wood-roofed chapel of *Ay. Nikólaos* dates from the 17C, though the E part of the N wall is assigned to the 11C. Frescoes of this period are now in the Corfu Museum.—14·5km **Ípsos** (Hotels B, C, D; F/A).—16km *Píryi* (Πύργι; Hotels C, D; F/A). *Ayios Márkos* (1·25km) has a church (Ay. Merkourios) of 1075 with contemporary frescoes in Cappadocian style, and another (Pantokrator), above the village, with good wall paintings of 1576. The road divides.

The asphalted left branch mounts to *Spartíla* (8km farther), whence an unpaved, steep and rocky road leads to the *Pantokrátor* monastery (18·5km), built in 1347 on *Mt Pantokrator* (906m), or *Monte San Salvatore*, the highest point of the island. The summit is spoilt by a radio mast, but the *View is superb. In clear weather the coast of Italy is just visible above the horizon to the NW. To the E are the Acroceraunian Mountains, the castle and plain of Butrinto, with its river and two lakes, the villages extending far into the interior of Albania. To the S the city and whole island of Corfu are stretched out like a map with Paxoi and Levkas in the distance.

The right branch continues along the NE coast with views across the strait to Albania.—19km *Barbáti* beach is seen below (right).—22·5km *Nisáki* (Hotel A; F/A, to the E).—37km **Kassiópi**, a charming fishing village, preserves its ancient name and a large Angevin *Castle*, the haunt of owls. The church may occupy the site of the Temple of Zeus visited by Nero. It was rebuilt after 1537 and enlarged in 1590 by successive Venetian admirals. Note the ikon Panayia Cassiopitra by Th. Poulakis (c 1670) and 17C frescoes. A broad new road continues W to (53km) *Ródha* (Hotels B, C, E; F/A), site of another temple (5C BC) explored in 1938 by John Papadimitriou.

IV. THE S OF THE ISLAND. From (12km) Benitses (see above) a road continues S along the coast to (20km) *Moraḯtika* (Hotels A, B, C, E), with fine sands. The road turns inland near the huge Mesongi Beach hotel (510 R) to pass down the middle of the long peninsula. A path leads (right) to *Gardhíki* (3km) with remains of a Byzantine castle and of Upper Palaeolithic occupation.—27km *Vranganiótika*. To the right lies Lake Korission.—35km *Argirádhes* (pop. 977).—44km *Levkímmi*, a decayed town (pop. 2012), is the centre of a group of villages, of which (31 miles) *Kávos*, near the SE tip of the island, has an attractive beach.

From Corfu a road runs W to (13km) *Pélekas* (beach; buses), an attractive cluster of colour-washed houses with a famous belvedere furnished by the Kaiser. Winding by-roads (buses regularly) lead N to *Glifádha* (beach; regular buses; Hotels A, B). The Glifádha bus passes through the villages of *Ermones* (Hotel A), occupied in the Neolithic and Bronze Ages, and *Váthos*. From the latter can be reached (half-hour walk) the convent of *Mirtidhiótissa*, near a pleasant beach. The road continues to the summit of Ayios Yeorgios (392m).

Between the Gouviá road and the Pélekas road, a third runs out, via Potamos, to **The Village**, a reconstruction by the Bouas family of a complete community, with church, museum of bygones, local crafts and a good restaurant. The buildings, constructed with old materials, form a living replica of the Venetian era in Corfu.
  Near Ermones is the *Corfu Golf Club*.

B. Páxoi

APPROACHES. From Corfù, daily ferry in 4 hours (this leaves Paxoi in the morning, returning in the afternoon). From Patras and Parga in summer, inquiry should be made locally.

Páxos, more correctly **Páxoi** (1286 inhab.), the smallest of the seven chief Ionian Islands, is 8km long and only 3km broad. It is situated 14·5km S of Corfu and 13km W of the coast of Epirus off Parga. The island produces little else than olives, almonds, and vines. The highest point is not more than 180m above the sea. Its farm houses and churches are particularly attractive. The principal village is an attractive cluster of Venetian houses at *Gáïo* (1km S; Hotel B) on the E side. The harbour is curiously formed by a small rocky islet crowned with a fort, and sheltering a little creek which can be entered at both ends. It is a sailing centre in the summer. A road (8km; bus) links Gáïo with *Lákka*, the second little harbour at the N end of the island.

Immediately S of Paxoi, and separated from it by a narrow channel, is the rocky islet of ANDÍPAXOI, inhabited by a few shepherds and fishermen and cultivated for garden produce and wine by the Paxians. It is visited by sportsmen in the season for shooting migratory quail, and has good bathing-beaches, also on the E coast.

C. Lévkas

Approaches. BY ROAD and chain ferry from Akarnania, see
Rte 54.

LÉVKAS (Λεύκας), more often spoken of in the accusative form and
pronounced *Lefkádha*, is an island separated at its NE corner from the
mainland of Akarnania by a shallow lagoon and a narrow strait,
through which runs the Levkas Ship Canal. The name of the island is
derived from the white cliff at its southern tip. The island has a length
of 32km and its breadth varies between 8 and 13km; with minor attendant islets, it forms a nome of 21,863 inhabitants. The centre of the
island is occupied by a range of limestone mountains, culminating in
Mt Elati (1082m). The most populous and wooded district is that
opposite the mainland, where the valleys, running down to the sea,
are sprinkled with small villages. The island exports oil, wine, and salt,
of which a considerable quantity is obtained by evaporation in the
lagoon.

The Topography of the NE end of the island is peculiar. A long narrow sandy spit
(the *Yiro*) runs out from the N coast, sweeping E towards the mainland which it
virtually joins in an area of marshes. This spit encloses a shallow lagoon which
surrounds the modern town of Levkas on three sides and extends S between the
island and the mainland. Much of the lagoon is only 0·6–1·5m deep, and to the S
there are islands and sandbanks.
    The evidence of ancient writers suggests that in antiquity Leukas was joined to
the mainland by an isthmus, probably across the narrow strait to the SE of the
modern town and roughly opposite Ancient Leucas (comp. below). But if, as is
also believed, a canal was cut by the Corinthian colonists in the 7C BC, then
Thucydides (III, 81) implies that it was silted up by 427 BC when the Peloponnesians 'transported their ships over the Leucadian isthmus'. The canal was restored, probably about the time of Augustus, and a stone bridge, of which some
remains are still visible near Fort Constantine (comp. below), was built from the
ancient city of Rouga, on the Akarnanian coast. In the middle ages one of the
Latin princes built a fort on the Yiro, midway between Levkas and the mainland
and on the landward side of the channel that breaches it. This fort, which
acquired the name of FORT SANTA MAURA, from a chapel within its walls so
called, gave an alternative name to the whole island. It was remodelled by the
Turks, who connected it with Levkas by an aqueduct of 260 arches, serving also
as a causeway, 1190m long, which divided the lagoon into two. The aqueduct
was shattered by earthquake of 1704 but survived as a dangerous causeway till
1825 (ruins in lagoon N of existing road causeway). The Venetians maintained
the canal and the Venetian governor lived initially in the fort, while the town,
then called *Amaxikhi*, that developed into modern Levkas grew up at the nearest
point on the island.
    During the protectorate of Russia *Fort Alexander* and *Fort Constantine*, a few
hundred metres N of it on the Akarnanian shore, were built to guard the S
approach channel. A little farther S are the remains of a medieval fort. The
Anglo-Ionian government constructed a harbour on the spit of sand flanking Fort
Santa Maura and protected by a mole ending in a lighthouse. In 1905 the Greek
government built the existing LEVKAS SHIP CANAL from Fort Santa Maura
southwards past Forts Alexander and Constantine. Its length is 5km and it is kept
dredged to a depth of c 4·5m.

History. *Leucas* was colonised by the Corinthians in 640 BC, about a century
after Corcyra. The Leucadians had three ships at the Battle of Salamis, and they
sided with Sparta in the Peloponnesian War. The island was devastated by the
Corcyraens in 436 BC and by the Athenians ten years later. In the war between
Rome and Philip of Macedon, the Akarnanians, who had made Leucas their
capital in 230 BC, rejected the Roman alliance, and were reduced after a gallant
defence vividly described by Livy (XXXIII, 17). Leucas continued to be important
under the Romans, its bishop being one of the fathers at the Council of Nicaea in

AD 325. The island passed in the 13C to Giovanni Orsini as the dowry of his wife Maria, daughter of Nikephoros Comnenus, Bp of Epirus. The Turks seized it in 1479. Thenceforward the island was alternately Turkish and Venetian until 1718, when it was formally ceded to Venice. It suffered four bad earthquakes in the 18C, when it shared the political fortunes of the other Ionian Islands. Levkas was captured from the French in 1810 by a force under Gen. Oswald that included Richard Church, Hudson Lowe, and Kolokotronis.

Native to Levkas are the writers Aristoteles Valaoritis (1824–79), and Angelos Sikelianos (1884–1951). Here also was born, of an Irish army surgeon and a Kytheran mother, Lafcadio Hearn (1850–1904) who ended his life (as Yakumo Koizumi) a citizen of Japan.

Lévkas (Hotels B, C, E), the capital (6415 inhab.), directly approached by the causeway, was badly damaged by earthquakes in 1867 and 1948 and takes character from the light and temporary nature of its upper stories. The Cathedral (*Pantokrator*) of 1684 has the tomb of Valaoritis. A little *Museum* (ikons and antiquities) is housed below the Library (weekday mornings, free). The ceiling paintings of *Ayios Mínas* are by Nicolas Doxaras (died 1761), and *Ayios Dhimítrios* has paintings attributed to Panayiotis Doxaras (died 1729). The causeway, affording glimpses in the water (left) of its Turkish predecessor (comp. above), and followed (right) by the modern deep water canal, leads to the chain ferry. Beyond stands the *Castle of Santa Maura* (adm. free), erected by Orsini in 1300. It passed to Walter de Brienne in 1331 and from the Angevins to the Tocco family after 1362, but the present structure is largely due to Venetian and Turkish repairs.

A good view of the town, with the lagoon, causeway, and canal, may be had from the Convent of *Faneroméni*, high up the hill immediately W of the town (3km; road signposted Tsoukaládhes, where it peters out).

TOUR OF THE ISLAND, 80km (50 miles), bus. Roads are being improved, but asphalt will be found only in stretches. Elsewhere conditions vary between indifferent and bad, but those not minding dust and a rough ride may make a round tour of this attractive and still peaceful island. We bear inland, then soon fork left for the E coast. On a hill to the right is the site of ancient *Leucas*, where traces of walls remain amid the modern terracing. We reach the shore in sight of Forts Alexander and Constantine, with the medieval Fort of St. George, on the opposing shore (comp. above).—16km *Nídhri* (reached also by caique from Levkas), a port-of-call for yachts, stands opposite the islet of *Madhoúri*, the retreat of A. Valaoritis. On the peninsular of Ayia Kiriaki, across the landlocked bay of Vlikho (5 minutes by boat), is the house in which lived Wilhelm Dörpfeld (1853–1940) during his long excavations when trying to prove that Levkas, not Ithaki, is the island described as Ithaka by Homer. His tomb is 200m from the house. He uncovered Early Bronze Age circular tombs in the plain of Nidhri.—22km *Vlikhó*, off which lies the island of *Skórpios*, property of the late Aristotle Onassis. The village churches in the S part of the island have 17C and 18C frescoes.—40km *Vasilikí* is a pretty fishing village on a deep bay backed by a fertile plain.

A track leads S along the rocky peninsular to *Ayios Nikólaos Níras*, at the end of a bad road down the W coast. Cape *Dukáto* (8km; lighthouse), the ancient *Leukatas*, the point to the S, is the precipitous white cliff (60m), which gives the island its name. A few fragments and sherds mark the once famous Temple of Apollo. The place is well-known from the sea by many passing travellers but rarely visited. Here Childe Harold 'saw the evening star above Leucadia's far-projecting rock of woe''. The rock was the scene in antiquity of leaps or dives into the sea (katapontismos), performed as a trial, a sacrifice, or a cure for unrequited love. The leap was successfully performed in the time of Strabo and of Cicero by having live birds attached to the victim (or performer) and rescue boats handy. Sappho is supposed to have leaped to her death here.

From Vasiliki we may turn N and return to the W side of the island (poor road), via (47km) *Ayios Pétros* and (51·5km) *Komelion*.

D. Ithaka and Cephalonia

Approaches. CAR FERRY daily from Patras to Cephalonia (Sámi), in c 4 hours continuing (c 1½ hours) to Ithaka; also less frequently between Sami and Corfu. Other ferry services connect Cephalonia (Ayía Evfímia) with Ithaka and Astakós (Mainland), Cephalonia (Argostóli) with Zákynthos, Cephalonia (Póros) with Killíni (Peloponnese).—AIR service to Cephalonia from Athens in ¾ hour (airport 6·5km S of Argostoli); sometimes from Cephalonia to Zakynthos.

ITHAKA, in Greek **Itháki** (Ιθάκη), with an area of 114 sq. km, makes up for being the second smallest of the seven islands by its fame in the Homeric epic. 27km long and 6·5km wide at its broadest part, it is divided into two unequal peninsulas by a narrow isthmus and everywhere rises in rugged hills, which reach their highest point in the N peninsula. Ithaka is separated from Cephalonia by the Ithaka Channel, a deep strait hardly 4km across at its narrowest. Its N extremity, Cape Marmakas, is 11km from the S coast of Levkas. To the NE lie the islets of Arkoudhi and Atokos. The island's 3648 inhabitants, with 522 more on Kalamos and Kastos, near the Akarnanian coast to the NE, are administered as an eparchy of the nome of Kefallinia.

The bold and barren outline of the mountains and cliffs is impressive. There is hardly any level ground. The coasts are indented by numerous small harbours and creeks, the λιμένες πάνορμοι of the Odyssey (XIII, 195). Exceptions to the general barrenness are seen in the cultivated declivities of the ridges and in little valleys, where olive and almond trees grow; the upper slopes are clothed with vineyards or with evergreen copses of myrtle, cypress, arbutus, mastic, oleander, and all the aromatic shrubs of the Levant. Here and there among the rocks are little green patches, gay with wild flowers.

The inhabitants, who enjoy a high reputation for hospitality, are industrious and make the best of their scanty soil, tilling their minute holdings. Ithakan wine is reputed the best in the Ionian Islands and the roast hare is noted. The Ithakans have always been first-rate mariners and the depopulation of the island is partly due to their roving disposition. English spoken on the island may have been acquired in Australia or South Africa.

History. Few architectural remains have so far been discovered to confirm the topography of the Odyssey, though Geometric tripods have come to light in circumstances very suggestive of Homer. After the heroic period the island retired into obscurity. By 1504 it was practically depopulated owing to the depredations of corsairs and to the furious wars between Turks and Christians. The Venetians resettled on it Ionians from neighbouring islands.

Vathy (Hotels B, E), like the island officially called *Itháki*, the chief town (2037 inhab.), lies in the S peninsula at the end of a deep inlet (Bay of Vathy) opening from the *Gulf of Mólo*, which almost separates the island into two halves. The town, which dates only from the 16C, is beautifully situated, extending in one narrow strip of white houses round the S extremity of the horseshoe deep (βαθύς) from which it takes its name. Comparatively large ships can moor close to the doors of their owners. In the harbour is a chapel, once the *Lazaretto*. The majority of the town has been repaired or rebuilt since 1953. The carved wooden screen in the *Cathedral* is worth a visit. The rebuilt Museum was opened in 1965. Within, owing to the efforts of Miss Sylvia Benton who salvaged the pieces from the earthquake ruins and supervised their mending, are nearly 1000 vases (mainly 8–6C) found by the British School in two shrines at Aetos. The house of Odysseus Androutsos was ruined. An old Venetian town once stood below the cliffs high above the present town.

EXCURSIONS (cars can be hired; a guide is advisable).

I. GROTTO OF THE NYMPHS. About 2·5km W of Vathy is the little *Bay of Dhexiá*, perhaps the harbour of *Phorkys*, in which the sleeping Odysseus was deposited by the Phaeacians. At 192m, c ¾ hour S of the bay and marked by a copse of cypresses, a stalactite cave, known as *Marmarospiliá*, is equated with the *Grotto of the Nymphs* (Od. XIII, 103). A narrow entrance only 1·8m high leads to a cavern 15m across. At the S end there is an opening in the roof, presumably cut to carry off the smoke of the sacrificial fires, 17m above the floor.

II. THE S END OF THE ISLAND. A track runs S from Vathy through a fertile vally to a col, c 5km from the town. Hence by a cliff path (left) in 15 minutes we may reach the spring of Perapigádhi (67m). This is identified with Homer's *Fountain of Arethusa*, where the swine of Eumaios were watered. The peasants call the neighbouring cliff *Korax* (Raven rock). On the plateau of *Marathiá* to the S may have been located the pigsties of Eumaios. A path leads down in 40 minutes to the Bay of *Ayios Andréas*, where Odysseus landed on his return from Pylos in order to avoid the ambush laid for him by the suitors of Penelope.

III. TO ALALKOMENAI AND PISAETOS. The road passes the Bay of Dhexia (comp. above) and at 4km divides. To the left we climb to the chapel of (6·5km) *Ayios Yeóryios* (130m). Here on the sides and summit (20 minutes) of the rocky hill of Aëtós (381m), which rises from the narrow isthmus connecting the two parts of the island, are situated the remains of **Alalkomenai**, known to the locals as *Kástro tou Odysséos* and wrongly identified by Schliemann in 1878 as the site of the Homeric capital. The walls, of polygonal masonry, date from c 700 BC. The view is magnificent. On the slopes the British School uncovered remains of an Archaic temple and a large dump of vases of Geometric and Archaic Corinthian ware. Eagles nest on the heights.— 7km *Pisaëtós*, a creek, has a pleasant pebble beach.

FROM VATHY TO STAVROS. The road coincides to 4km with that to *Pisaetos* (comp. above). We keep right and cross the isthmus with the Gulf of *Mólo* on our right. Ahead rises *Mt Nírito* (806m) round which at 12km, the road divides. Formerly called Anoyi, the mountain has taken the ancient name, the 'Neritos ardua saxis' of Virgil and Νῆριτοϛ εἰνοσίφυλλον of Homer, though its barren slopes (if correctly identified) must since have been greatly disforested. The circuitous route on the E side passes the monastery of *Katharón* (556m) affording a *View over the Gulf of Vathy, and the village of *Anoyí*. The better road along the W flank above the Ithaka Channel passes above *Ayios Ioánnis*, a bathing place served by a lower by-road.—14·5km *Levkí* (160m).— 18km **Stavrós** is the focal point (364 inhab.) of the villages in the N part of the island, with a restaurant, an unexpectedly Americanised café, and a regular morning taxi service to Vathy (return in the afternoon).

A path descends SW in 20 minutes to the bay of *Pólis*, the name of which recalls the Homeric capital. On its NW shore opens a Cave-sanctuary (*Spílio Louízou*), explored in 1930 by the British School. It yielded pottery of all periods from Mycenaean to Roman, and 12 Geometric tripods (Il. XIII). A late ex-voto inscribed ΕΥΧΗΝ ΟΔΥΣΣΕΙ ('my vow to Odysseus') suggests that Odysseus was the object of a local hero-cult. About 1km N of Stavros is the Kastro on the hill of **Pelikáta**. Excavations of the British School revealed the ruins of a small settlement of the early Bronze Age which flourished to Mycenaean times. Apart from a few Hellenic and Hellenistic tombs, the site was not again occupied until the Venetian period. Part of a circuit wall, which ran just below the flat summit, is preserved with part of a paved road alongside. A small *Museum*, restored in 1957, contains materials from the site and from Polis, including the tripods (comp. above), also other local finds, rescued undamaged in 1953.

Beyond Pelikata we may visit the chapel of *Ayios Athanásios* near the ruins of a tower of the 6C BC, a spot popularly called the *School of Homer*. Near *Exógi* (to the NW) is the spring of Melanídhro.
From Stavrós the road descends E to *Fríkes*, to the N of which is a camp of the Club Mediterranée, and *Kióni* (6·5km), attractively sited above the E coast.

CEPHALONIA, in modern Greek **Kefallinía** (Κεφαλληνία), in Italian *Cefalonia*, with 27,649 inhab., is the largest in area of the Ionian Islands. Separated from Ithaka by the Ithaka Channel, it lies between Levkas and Zante, exactly opposite the entrance of the Gulf of Patras. Of very irregular shape the island is rugged and mountainous. A lofty ridge runs from NW to SE, the foothills covering almost the whole island. The chief summit is the highest point of the Ionian Islands. Cephalonia is divided into three eparchies, which together with that of Ithaka, form the nome of Kefallinia. The population has halved in the 20C and is still falling. The *airport* (Olýmpic Airways office in Argostoli) has a daily connectioin with Athens and some international charters.

The soil is fertile but not at all well watered, there being few constantly flowing streams; and the landscape lacks the luxuriance of Corfu and Zante. Characteristic features of the fine scenery are the noble forests of a local fir-tree (*abies Cephalonensis*) which give the mountain slopes their sombre look; the currant vineyards; and the olive groves. Perfumes are made from the flowers and pines, and there are excellent local wines. About one-sixth of the land belongs to the convents.

History. There were four cities in ancient Kephallenia: *Pale, Kranioi, Same*, and *Pronnoi*. Herodotus mentions that 200 citizens of Pale fought at Plataea. The Athenians, without fighting, gained over the Kephallenians at the outbreak of the Peloponnesian War. In the Roman wars in Greece the island was reduced (189 BC); according to Strabo, C. Antonius possessed the whole island as his private estate. It was afterwards given to the Athenians by Hadrian. In the Middle Ages it was taken from the Normans of Sicily by Robert Guiscard, who died on the island in 1085. Subsequent masters were the Pisans (1099); Margaritone of Brindisi (1185), succeeded by the Orsini (1194) and the Tocchi (1323); the Turks (1485); the Venetians (1500); and the French (1797). A member of the short-lived Septinsular Republic, it was taken in 1809 by the British, who held it with the other Ionian Islands until 1864. *Sir Chas. Napier*, Resident in 1822–30, built roads and did much else for the island. After his day, in 1848, a rising of the inhabitants was checked at the entrance to the town of Argostoli by a section of a British company under a sergeant. The following year another insurrection was as speedily suppressed.
In 1943 the occupying Italian force, comprising 9000 troops of the Alpine 'Acqui' Division, not only refused to cooperate with or surrender to the Germans, but for seven days fought them for possession of the island. Three thousand were forced to surrender and during three ensuing days were shot in cold blood (it is said on Hitler's personal order). Only 34 survived by shamming death. The bodies were taken in 1953 to a cemetery in Bari. Much of the island was destroyed by earthquake in 1953.

The majority of visitors (except those arriving by air) land at **Sámi** (Hotels C, D, E), a pleasant modern anchorage (935 inhab.) on the deep bay that indents the E coast opposite Ithaka. Here Don John of Austria anchored his fleet before Lepanto. On the two hills of Ayioi Fanéntes and Palaiókastro, above the town, are some remains of ancient **Same**, the island's capital in antiquity, ringed by cyclopean and polygonal walling; a walk of c ½ hour is necessary to reach the remains, but, from the harbour, part of the wall can be seen against the skyline. At the back of the town, c 200m from the harbour, is a Roman building with a mosaic. Sami is in an area of speliological interest (comp. below).

FROM SAMI TO ARGOSTOLI, 23km (15 miles), asphalt road, bus. On the outskirts of the town is a turning (right) to the N of the island. Near Vlakháta 2·5km along this road is (left) the remarkable semi-underground *Lake Melissani* (adm. includes short boat trip). An artificial tunnel leads to a small lake of clear turquoise and indigo water; a boat takes the visitor to an inner cavern.—2km Turning (left) form Póros (24km; Hotels B, C, E) and the SE of the island.—3·5km The *Cave of Drogaráti* (small charge for adm.) a large, electrically lit, stalagmitic cavern, lies 500m right of the road.—The road now winds up through maquis to the AGRAPIDIAES PASS (549m). Near the top a road leads (left) to *Mt Ainos*, climbing first to a radar station on the N crest, then continuing to a television station on the summit (1619m).— 16km Col, with fine view down to Argostóli and across the gulf.

A tarred road descends (left) to a small plain in which lies *Frangáta*. This village and *Valsamáta*, its neighbour, were built after the earthquake with funds subscribed from Britain. About 2km beyond Frangáta is the convent of *Ayios Yerásimos* (closed 1–3), with the venerated silver sarcophagus of St. Gerasimos, the patron saint of the island, who founded an order of women in 1554 and was beatified in 1622.

As we descend, in the distance (left) the walls of Ancient Kranioi (see below) can be seen following a low ridge.—21km Immediately below the road in a cleft is *Ayía Varvára*, a little cave chapel. We pass turnings (left) round the Lagoon of Koutavos (see below) and (right) to Assos and the N end of the island (see below), then cross a causeway to reach (24km) *Argostóli*.

Argostóli (Αργοστόλιον; Hotels B, C, D), the capital (6788 inhab.), seat of the nomarch and of an archbishop, has been completely rebuilt since the earthquake of 1953. The *Archaeological Museum* contains a good collection of miscellaneous prehistoric finds; Middle Helladic from Kokkolata, Mycenaean from Masakarata, etc, also terracotta revetments from a Doric temple at Miniá (early 6C BC) and a good bronze head of the 3C AD. The excellent *Public Library* preserves the Venetian archives and has a *Museum* of local interest. The town is delightfully situated some way up the gulf of Argostoli in an inlet so shallow that a causeway and bridge 640m long have been thrown across it to shorten the road in from the E. The bridge, with its many arches, was built by the British military commander in 1813. The circuit of the shallow *Lagoon of Koutavos*, thus cut off, makes a pleasant walk (5km) and may include a visit to the ruins of *Kranioi*, on a double hill above the modern waterworks. Parts of the ancient walls, nearly 5km round, are well preserved, with a section beside the road, and a shrine of Demeter and Kore has been identified by an inscribed statue base. It probably consisted of a small Doric temple and functioned from the 6C to the late Hellenistic period. The cult was closely associated with a nearby spring. There is little to be seen. (The site may also be reached from the Argostoli–Sami road by a track above Ayia Varvara.) On the E side of the bay, along the Assos road to the N of the causeway, is a *British Cemetery* (key with cottage just before, right).

Another short excursion may be made to the tip of *Lássis* (Hotels A, C, E), the peninsula on which Argostóli stands. 2·5km N of the town are the marine katavothrai, where the sea pours endlessly into subterranean tunnels. A team of Austrian scientists has shown that the water reappears at Melissani (comp. above). The flow was used in the 19C to drive mills. It was interrupted by the earthquake but a mill has been put into order again. On the headland of Ay. Theodori a lighthouse ('Sapper' Doric of 1820, rebuilt) commands the entire gulf. We may continue round Telegraph Hill and return (left) to the town, or go on S to the well-known beaches of *Makrí Yialós* and *Platí Yialós* (Hotel A), with organised facilities for bathing.

A longer excursion (c 26km) to the S of Argostóli, using minor but tarred roads, comprises several places of interest. We leave by the W shore of Koutavos.— 6·5km *Kástro*, a village on the site of *San Giorgio*, the medieval and Venetian capital of the island, which clustered round the 13C CASTLE OF ST. GEORGE. This is perched on an isolated hill, surrounded by considerable remains of houses, churches, and of a convent. The remains of the citadel include a drawbridge, the enceinte, churches, and barracks. The town, which once had 15,000 inhab., was destroyed by an earthquake in 1636 and abandoned for Argostoli in 1757. The *View comprises the peninsula of Paliki on the W, Mt Ainos, and the island of Zante. We turn SW.—8km The necropolis of *Masarakáta*, excavated by Kavvadias, yielded 83 Mycenaean tombs, one of the tholos type. Another necropolis at Kokkoláta, nearer Argostoli, has pre-Mycenaean tombs.—At (10km) *Metaxáta* the house occupied by Lord Byron in 1823–24 was wrecked in 1953 but a plaque on the gate opposite commemorates his still-flourishing ivy. Near here have been found graves of the Classical period. We may return via LIVATHO, the richest agricultural district of the island. At *Lakíthra* (rebuilt by French subscriptions) are antique grain silos hewn from the rock. The model village of *Kourkoumeláta*, built after 1953 by Andreas Vergotis, whose body lies in its cemetery, has the look of a prosperous city suburb. Returning N towards the coast we pass *Miniá* and, by the shore, the *Airport*.

A ferry crosses the gulf several times daily in ½ hour to **Lixoúri** (Λειξούριον; Hotels C; F/A), the second town (2842 inhab.) of the island, situated on the isolated peninsula of *Paliki* (by poor road 31km). It is served also by steamer services from Patras and Zante, and occasionally from Piraeus. Here were born Elias Meniates (1669–1714), patriotic writer, and Andreas Lascaratos (1811–1901), satirist and anti-clerical pamphleteer. There is a folklore museum. The ancient city of *Pale* was situated close to the sea, c 1·5km N of Lixouri, which was probably built in great part from its ruins. Little now remains of the city which once successfully resisted Macedonia, and Lixouri itself has suffered ruin in 1867 and 1953.

The SE end of the island, reached by roads passing either flank of Mt Ainos, is thickly sown with hamlets, of which the principal is *Skála*. Here foundations have been found of an Archaic temple (6C BC). Beneath the ruined church of Ayios Athanásios has been excavated an extensive Roman villa of the 2C AD, of which the second room was early converted to Christian use. Mosaics with metrical inscriptions naming Krateros as the artist include an apotropaic representation of

Phthonos (Envy being devoured by wild beasts).—At *Markópoulo*, to the SW, a strange (? migratory) phenomenon occurs c 6–15 August when small harmless snakes invade the church.

FROM ARGOSTOLI TO FISKARDO, 53km, arduous road, bus daily. From Argostoli it is 29km (from Sami 16km) to a road-junction (Sinióri) in the valley that lies between the main part of the island and Mt Kalón in the northern PENINSULA OF ERISSOS. On the W side of this peninsula, 10km farther N, **Assos** (restaurant) occupies the most beautiful situation on the island. The ruined Venetian *Castle* (1595) stands on a peninsula headland commanding two anchorages. The cottages and vineyards within the large enclosure are attractive, while the picturesque village on the isthmus below relieves the stern grandeur of the sea and mountains. The main road runs on to **Fiskárdo** (Hotel B), near the N end of the island, probably the ancient Panormos. The place takes name from Robert Guiscard, who died here in 1085. One of the few places to suffer no earthquake damage, Fiskárdo still has houses typical of the island before the disaster. The curious *Church* (ruined) on the headland to the NE has twin W towers of Norman type, but nothing is known of its history. There is also a small lighthouse, possibly Venetian. Much of the tiny village is owned by rich expatriates. The ferry from Sami to Paxos and Corfu calls once a week.

E. Zánte

Approaches. Car ferry, regularly from Killíni (Rte 40) in 1½ hours; through bus from Athens via Patras. Car-drivers should obtain a priority ticket for the return from the agent in Zákinthos.— BY AIR from Athens daily in 1 hour.—TERMINAL at Róma 16.

Zánte, officially styled by its ancient name of **Zákynthos** (Ζάκυνθος), in modern transliteration *Zákinthos*, is the southernmost of the four central Ionian Islands. It lies 21km W of the Peloponnesian coast, and is separated from it by the deep Channel of Zante. It is 40km long and 19km broad (458 sq. km). The beauty and fertility of Zakynthos and the picturesque situation of its capital on the margin of its semicircular bay have been celebrated in all ages, from Theocritus onwards. Pliny and Strabo describe the richness of its woods and harvests, though Herodotus, who had visited the island, remembers only the pitch wells (IV, 195). The Homeric epithet 'woody' is no longer apposite, as its woods have been mostly replaced by currant vines and olives, the mainstays of the export trade. The potency of its wine merits mention by English travellers as early as 1517. Mandolato is a local brand of nougat.

The island abounds in gardens, and in spring and autumn is carpeted with fragrant wild flowers, whence the Venetian jingle 'Zante, fior di Levante'. In the W of this volcanic island the land is barren and mountainous (*Mount Yíri*, 756m); the fertile E half has no height greater than *Mount Skopos* (485m). The island has suffered from periodic earthquakes, one of the worst having occurred in 1820. Those of 1840 and 1893 were less severe, but that of 1953 wrecked the island.

As in Corfu and Cephalonia, there are many Roman Catholic families in Zante, chiefly of Italian origin. A large proportion of its inhabitants are descended from settlers brought by the Venetians from the Peloponnese (comp. Ithaka), from Christians who emigrated from Cyprus and Crete when those islands were conquered by the Turks, and from younger branches of noble Italian families.

History. Homer, both in the Iliad and in the Odyssey, calls the island by the name it still officially bears, though Pliny (IV, 54) affirms that it was in the earliest time called *Hyrie*. An ancient tradition quoted by Strabo ascribed to the Zakynthians the foundation of Saguntum in Spain.

According to Thucydides (II, 66), Zakynthos was colonised by Achaeans from the Peloponnese. Herodotus (VI, 70) relates how Demaratos, the exiled King of Sparta, who had taken refuge in Zakynthos, was hospitably sheltered by the inhabitants from the wrath of the pursuing Lacedaemonians and escaped thence to Persia. Not long before the Peloponnesian War the island was reduced by the Athenian general Tolmides. An ally of Athens during that war, it appears to have been subsequently dependent on Sparta. Later it belonged to Philip III of Macedon (Polybius V, 4). During the second Punic War it was occupied by the Romans. It was afterwards restored to Philip, whose deputy Hierocles of Agrigentum sold it to the Achaeans. It again became Roman in 191 BC.

The part played by Zante since has been insignificant. It was ravaged by the Vandals (in 474), Saracens, and Normans, and depopulated by the Turks (in 1479). It was Venetian from 1489 to 1797. Kolokotronis took refuge in Zante in 1805. Richard Church conducted the landing of a small British force in 1809. During the War of Independence some of the chief families of Zante and Cephalonia distinguished themselves by their efforts on behalf of the national cause, despite official discouragement. Lord Byron, whose enthusiasm for the Greek cause had assured the success of two loans floated in London, banked the first instalment of £40,000 in Zante. Frank Abney Hastings died on Zante in 1828 of tetanus as a result of a wrist wound received the week before at Aitoliko.

Zante was the birthplace of Ugo Foscolo (1778–1827), whose Ionian nationality is generally merged in his Italian reputation; of Andreas Kalvos (died 1867), the poet, whose remains were returned to his native island in 1960 from Lincolnshire where he lived with his English wife; and of Solomos (1798–1857), the Greek national poet, who, inspired by Dante, forged Demotic Greek into a poetic idiom. Andreas Vesalius (1514–64), the founder of modern anatomy, was ship-wrecked off Zante and died on the island, while returning from a pilgrimage to Jerusalem enforced on him by the Inquisition for an experiment in human dissection.

Zákynthos (Hotels B, C, D, E; F/A; also at Argási, 4km S, see below), the capital (9764 inhab.) of the island nome, faces Loutra Killini on the Peloponnesian coast. The town, which is the seat of an archbishop, stretches along its bay for 2·5km, but extends in depth only at one point, uphill to the castle. It has been almost completely rebuilt since the earthquake of 1953 in the attractive arcaded style for which it was celebrated. A few of the old streets survive. There are two museums. In Plateia Solomos is a small *Museum of Byzantine Art* mainly retrieved from wrecked churches; the local carving of various ikonostaseis is notable; here also is a sculptured relief by Thorvaldsen from a monument (1820) to Maitland. This museum also contains a fine collection of post-Byzantine icons. The *Solomos Museum*, in St. Mark's Square a little inland, is installed above the Mausoleum of the two poets, Solomos and Kalvos. The site of Ugo Foscolo's house is now a small garden with a marble monument. Among the reconstructed churches worth a visit are *Ayios Nikólaos tou Mólou* (on the quay), and the *Kyría ton Angélon*, beyond the Xenia Hotel. At the N end of the town is a *British Cemetery*.

Towards the S end of the town, the *Panayía Faneroméni*, before 1953 the finest church, has been rebuilt. In *Ayios Dhionísios*, farther on, are the relics of the local St. Dionysios (died 1622), the island's patron, brought back in 1716 from the Strophades, also frescoes by Cozzari, a local pupil of Tiepolo. Both churches have conspicuous campanili.

The ruins of the Venetian **Kastro** (107m) occupy the flat top of the hill above the town. The *View comprises the W coast of Greece from the Mesolongi lagoon to Navarino Bay, backed by the lofty mountains of Akarnania, Aitolia, Arcadia, and Messenia. On the headland across the Channel of **Zante** rises Chlemoutsi (Rte 40). To the W extend enormous currant vineyards.

MT SKOPOS (485m), so called from a rock on the top resembling a sentry, may be ascended in 2½ hours. John Dallam, the English organ-builder, with two companions, climbed it on Easter Sunday 1599 while on the way to deliver an organ to Mehmet III as a gift from Elizabeth I. The road SE along the shore is followed for 3km whence a path mounts to the right passing the Panayia Skopiotissa. The most striking feature of the view from the top is the gloomy peak of Ainos in Kephalonia rising abruptly from the sea.—Farther SE the road runs very prettily via *Argasi* (Hotels B, C, E) to (11km) *Vasilikó* (Hotels C, D) beyond which is *Cape Yeraki*, with quarries of sandstone.

EXCURSIONS FROM ZAKYNTHOS. A. TO THE NORTH, 61km, asphalt. We round the S of the Kastro hill, then bear NW through currant vineyards to (15km) *Katastári*, the island's largest village (1091 inhab.), at the N end of the plain. Here there is a turn to the saltpan and beach of *Alikés* (2·5km, right; Hotels C, D). The road winds up with views across to Cephalonia, passes below the *Moní Ayios Ioánni Pródhromos* (16–17C), with a good icon by Th. Poulakis, then turns W across a cultivated plateau.—28km Road (right) to *Volímes* (5km) whence there is a 10km walk to Skinari lighthouse at the N tip of the island, with another 16C monastery to visit on the way. 30km Road (right) to *Anafonítria*, where the monastery has a medieval tower and wall-paintings and the reputed cell of St. Dionysíos.—The road turns S through *Maríes* and a series of upland villages often out of sight of the sea. Beyond (46km) *Ayios Nikólaos* the road winds down with views of the plain, the airport, and the Bay of Lagana.—At (56km) *Makhairádo* the church has a splendid interior with a fine carved iconostasis.—61km *Zákinthos*.

B. TO THE SOUTH-WEST, 20·5km, asphalt. We leave the town by the Lithakiá road.—3km Turning to the Airport. We pass a succession of roads leading to *Laganá* (Hotels B, C,D), a beach c 6·5km long with restaurants (crowded at summer week-ends).—At 16km we branch left and in 1km reach the shore of the Bay of Kerí, where are curious pitch springs (Píssa tou Keríou), a natural phenomenon known to Herodotus and Pliny, and used then as now for caulking ships. One may be seen at the base of the jetty.—20·5km *Kerí* has a 17C church and a beach with small cafés.

Over 48km to the S of Zante lie the remote **Strophades**, visited only 2 or 3 times per year by caique from Zante. On the larage island stands a Byzantine fortress-monastery, once rich and populous until it succombed to Saracen attack; it has a handful of monks, and in 1624–1716 guarded the relics of St. Dionysios of Zante. The only other inhabitants keep the lighthouse on the N point. The island is a breeding-place of shearwaters; in April wild doves on their migratory passage are decimated by hunters. The smaller island takes its name of *Artonísi* from a native species of gull.

VII NORTHERN GREECE

The provinces of Macedonia and Thrace, northernmost of modern Greece, are relatively recent acquisitions. Macedonia has been under Greek sovereignty since 1912, Thrace since 1920. Unknown before the First World War except to experienced Balkan travellers, and little visited as late as 1950, the region has great natural beauty and interest; it is now easily accessible, and increasingly fostering tourism, though remoter parts can still be remarkably primitive. The province of **Macedonia** (2,121,953 inhab.) is only part of the large but ill-defined area to which the name of Macedonia has been given since classical times; much of it is now within the territory of bordering states. The Greek province is shaped like a gigantic capital L, on its side, with the short arm extending N from the Thessalian border and the long arm bounding the Aegean Sea on the N, as far as its junction with Thrace. This part of Macedonia is relatively narrow, varying in width from c 45–95km, with Yugoslavia and Bulgaria beyond the frontier. On the W Macedonia marches with Albania. In the S Mount Olympos rises on the Thessalian border and extends into both provinces. To the W of Olympos the Kamvounian Mountains divide Macedonia from Thessaly.

Macedonia is divided politically into thirteen nomes and one autonomous region. These are: Florina; Kastoria; Grevena; Kozani; Emathia; Pella; Salonika; Pieria; Chalcidice; Kilkis; Serres; Drama; Kavalla; and the Ayion Oros (Athos). The regional capital is Salonika, second city of Greece and seat of the Minister for Northern Greece. Among the dozen most populous centres in the country are also Kavalla, Serres, and Drama. Of the great cities of ancient Macedonia that have no modern counterpart we may mention Pella, Pydna, Potidaia, Olynthos, Philippi, and Amphipolis.

Thrace, or *Western Thrace* (Dhitikí Thráki), as it is called to distinguish it from the region regained by Turkey, is the NE province of Greece. Extending from the Nestos to the Evros, which forms the frontier with Turkey it has a population of 345,220. The interior is largely covered by the Rhodopé Mountains, which rise to 2278m and lie mainly in

Bulgaria. The province is divided politically into the nomes of Xanth
Rhodhopi, with the chief town, Komotini; and Evros. Western Thrac
was part of the Ottoman Empire before the Balkan Wars of 1912–1.
The Treaty of Bucharest (1913) gave it to Bulgaria, but in 1920, afte
the Treaty of Neuilly (1919) it became Greek. From 1920 until the wa
of 1922 with Turkey, Eastern Thrace also was under Greek rule.

The original Thracians were Indo-European but not Hellenic; they came from th
Carpathian region, and had fair or red hair and grey eyes. They spoke a languag
so far undeciphered. The whole area beyond the Strymon seems hardly to hav
been reached by the Bronze Age, and the ethnic and historical affinities of Thrac
are with Bulgaria and Turkey rather than with Greece (comp. below).

The climate of the northern provinces is Balkan rather than Mediter
ranean, with extreme temperatures in summer and winter and a cons
derable rainfall. Their topography has few affinities with that of sou
thern Greece. The coastline is little indented and safe anchorages ar
scarce. The larger rivers are perennial. The mountains are for the mo
part covered with dense forest or scrub. The interior is mountainou
the W regions being traversed from N to S by part of the mountai
backbone of Greece. The ranges are divided at intervals by valley
through which flow five important rivers. From W to E these are th
Aliakmon (Bistritsa), the Axios (Vardar), the Strymon (Struma), mark
ing the E frontier of classical Macedonia, the Nestos (Mesta), markin
the modern boundary between Macedonia and Thrace, and the Evr
(Maritsa), dividing Western from Eastern Thrace. Mountain lakes ar
numerous on and near the NW frontiers and the formations of a
additional forty by means of barrages is contemplated; the shallowe
marsh-lakes formed in the plains are slowly disappearing with th
harnessing of the rivers. A noteworthy geographical feature of Mace
donia is the Chalcidice Peninsula, with its three prongs—Cassandr
Longos, and Athos—projecting boldly into the Aegean and helping t
form the Gulf of Salonika (ancient Thermaic Gulf) on one side and th
Gulf of Orphani (Strymonic Gulf) on the other. Off the boundary wit
Thrace is the island of Thasos.

The argillaceous planes have not been cultivated to the extent th
might have been expected; but this is largely due to the chequere
history of the provinces. Important products are tobacco, rice, bean
sesame, and poppy seed; fruit and a wide variety of vegetables ar
grown in increasing quantity, and a sugar-beet industry, started i
1960, has proved highly successful. Manufactures include wine, cl
th, macaroni, and soap. More important are the hydro-electric sch
mes in construction, and the development of Ptolemaïs as an industri
area: fertilisers are manufactured on an increased scale. Though ric
in minerals (copper, chrome, gold, iron, lead, molybdenum, silve
magnesite, asbestos), Macdeonian mines are not yet fully exploite
There is trade in timber, livestock, skins, furs, and wool. In Thrac
sunflowers are grown for their seed oil.

During the long Middle Ages the population of Macedonia becam
very mixed. Slavs, chiefly Bulgarian, with a strong admixture of Bo
nian and Serbian elements, and Turks were predominant inland wh
le the coast from the Aliakmon to the Strymon including the Chalc
dice trident was mainly Greek. A profound change was caused by th
provisions of the Treaty of Lausanne (1923), whereby 348,000 Mo
lems living in Macedonia were exchanged for 538,600 Greeks fro
Asia Minor. As a result of the events of the Second World War and th
Civil Wars the greater part of the Slav population retired or was exile
across the neighbouring frontiers. In Thrace, however, the Turkis

population was not exchanged after 1922 but allowed to remain (as Greeks were allowed to remain in Constantinople). This fact gives to the province a special flavour, Turkish villages alternating with Greek; here Greeks and Turks still live together, yet separately, as they did all over the Ottoman Empire until 1922. The Moslem minority comprises two-sevenths of the population; they enjoy full Greek citizenship and freedom of worship in their mosques. The N provinces are still suffering depopulation by emigration, in recent years to Western Germany, Australia, and Canada.

The northern provinces are still rich in the variety of their flora and fauna, though excessive local hunting is rapidly exterminating many unique species, just as constant grazing of domestic goats is destroying many rare plants. The formation of national parks is still under consideration. Lions, which (according to Herodotus) troubled Xerxes in Macedonia, seem not to have survived into our era, and though the brown bear is protected on the Bulgarian side of the Rhodope Mountains, its appearance in Greece seems to be limited to the Pindus near the Albanian frontier. The jackal is still seen, wild cat and wild boar inhabit Pindus, and wolves are not unknown. Roe deer and wild goat are much depleted since the war. Many of the larger European birds may be seen: vultures, hawks, and the golden eagle in the mountain regions, and storks, herons, cormorants, pelicans, and occasionally flamingoes in the coastal plains and marshes. Of the many reptiles, only two snakes are harmful: one, the adder, is common. The harmless lizards grow to a surprising size. Tortoises abound. The insect life is rich.

Communications now compare favourably with those elsewhere in Greece. The railways remain slow by reason of the terrain they traverse, but the main roads are mostly asphalted. The highway linking Yugoslavia with Turkey, which traverses the entire region, has been completely renewed. For much of its length in Greece it follows the course of the **Via Egnatia** (or Egnatia Odhos), the great military road between the Adriatic and Byzantium, systematised by the Romans in the 2C BC to form, together with the Via Appia, a direct link from Rome via Brundusium with the East. Parts of it undoubtedly date from Macedonian times, at least the reign of Philip II. It had two branches starting from Apollonia (Avlona) and Dyrrachium (Durazzo), passed Lychidnus (near Lake Ochrida), Herakleia-Lynkestis (Bitolj), Edhessa, Pella, Thessalonica, Amphipolis, and Philippi. Neapolis (Kavalla) was the E terminus until the conquest of Thrace in AD 46, ships being taken thence for the Troad. Later the road was extended through Thrace by Akontisma and Trajanopolis, to end at Byzantium (Istanbul). Its name may derive from its builder but not from Gnatia in Apulia. Augustus founded colonies along its route; Nero installed inns; Trajan repaired it in AD 107–112 (adding on the Italian side the Via Trajana as an alternative to the Via Appia). Milestones found on its route as far apart as Ochrid, Amphipolis, and Akontisma bear witness to repairs by Caracalla in 216–217. An epitaph discovered near the site of Ad Duodecimum, a staging post 12 Roman miles W of Philippi, commemorates C. Lavus Faustus 'institor tabernas'. From the 4C AD the Via Egnatia lost importance to the N route via Sirmium, Belgrade, Naissus (Niš), Serdica (Sofia), Philippopolis (Plovdiv), and Hadrianopolis (Edirne), as Milan replaced Rome as the starting-point.—Good modern hotels are to be found in the larger towns, at recently exploited seaside resorts, and at some archaeological sites and beauty spots; elsewhere accommodation is still limited.

History. Archaeological research has suggested that in the earliest times Macedonia had affinities with the NW; its short late-Neolithic culture (c 2600 BC) stemming from the Danube. In Macedonia the Early and Middle Bronze Age (2500–1700) had Anatolian or Northern origins, and Aegean influences are felt only briefly in the Mycenaean period, soon cut short by the so-called 'Lausitz incursions' an Iron Age migration from Central Europe, of which the 'Dorian invasion' was part. These people from the Hungarian plains swept all before their iron swords, passing onward to the S. A return wave from Thessaly founded the historical state of Macedonia about the 8C BC.

The problem of whether Macedonians were Greeks has been endlessly debated from the time of Herodotus to the present day, usually to the accompaniment of political polemics. Some Greek tribes probably settled in the S part of Macedonia. According to one tradition their leaders were the three sons of the Heraclid Temenos, who had fled from Argos. The youngest of the three, Perdikkas, is said to have founded the Macedonian monarchy and to have made his capital at Aigai, in Emathia. Another tradition makes an earlier Heraclid, Karanos, the founder of the dynasty and Perdikkas only the fourth of the line. It seems reasonably certain that by the 7C BC a kingdom was established at Aigai, from which the whole region was subdued and unified. Hence the poetic name of Emathia for the whole of Macedonia. The Greek settlers intermarried with the aborigines and spoke a dialect akin to the Doric, but with many barbarous words and forms; so much so that the Macedonians were never regarded as genuine Hellenes, though seldom actually called Barbarians. After the 6C BC Greek influence increasingly filtered N from Thasos.

From written record little is known of Macedonia until the reign of Amyntas I (c 540–505), under whom it was virtually a satrapy of Persia. His son Alexander I (died c 455 BC) was a secret philhellene despite the fact that he accompanied Xerxes on his invasion to Greece. He later extended his kingdom to the Strymon. The reign of Perdikkas II (454–414), coinciding with the period of Athenian expansion, is characterised by scheming but not very able vacillation between Athens and her enemies. Archelaus (413–399) was a patron of Greek art and literature and established cordial relations with Greece, which remained friendly until the advent of Philip II (359–336). That king, intent on universal conquest, began by seizing various Greek cities on the Macedonian coast, such as Amphipolis, Pydna, Potidaea, Methone, and Olynthos. The well-meaning but misdirected efforts of Demosthenes (comp. the Philippic and Olynthiac orations) to rouse the Athenians against the danger from Philip met with little response. The Athenians were not really aroused until Philip, invited by the Amphictyonic League (see Delphi), marched through the pass of Thermopylae on the pretext of punishing the Locrians of Amphissa. Through the influence of Demosthenes, the Athenians allied themselves with the Thebans, but the allies were defeated at Chaironeia in 338 and the independence of the Greek city states was lost. A congress held at Corinth after the victory decided on war against Persia; but, in the midst of his preparations, Philip was murdered. He was succeeded by his son Alexander the Great (336–323), who was destined to fulfil the ambition of world conquest that Philip had cherished.

On Alexander's death there was general upheaval. His regent in Macedonia, Antipater, won the Lamian War against the Greeks with the victory of Krannon. Antipater's son Cassander, who had been deprived by his father of the succession to the regency, proclaimed himself king of Macedonia in 306 and, after the battle of Ipsos (301), secured the possession of Macedonia and Greece. On his death in 297, his son Philip IV held the throne for a few months. In 294 Demetrios Poliorketes, son of Antigonus the One-Eyed, one of Alexander's generals who had become king of Asia and had been killed at Ipsos, was acknowledged king of Macedonia; but in 286 he was deserted by his own troops, who offered the throne to Pyrrhus, king of Epirus. Two years later Pyrrhus had to hand over Macedonia to Lysimachus, another of Alexander's generals, who had made himself king of Thrace in 306. In 277 Antigonus Gonatas, son of Demetrios Poliorketes, obtained the throne of Macedonia, though Pyrrhus contested it again in 273. Demetrios II (239–229), son of Antigonus Gonatas, and Antigonus Doson (229–220) tried to win the mastery over Greece. Now came the period of the three Macedonian Wars (214–205, 200–194, and 171–168), and of the last Macedonian kings. Philip V (220–179) was defeated by the Romans at Kynoskephalai in 197, and his son Perseus (178–168) at Pydna in 168. After Pydna Macedonia was divided into four republics with capitals at Thessalonica, Pella, Pelagonia (Herakleia Lynkestis), and Amphipolis. This arrangement did not last long, for in 148 Macedonia became a Roman province. In 27 BC, as a senatorial province, Macedonia was separated from Achaia, and extended N to the Danube, E to the Hebros (Evros), and S and SW to include Thessaly and Epirus. After the Roman subjugation of Thrace in AD 46, Macedonia, no longer a frontier province, recovered some of its prosperity, attracting the missionary zeal of St. Paul.

The Goths invaded Macedonia in AD 252. In 289 Diocletian altered the province's boundaries by taking away Thessaly and Epirus. Constantine created the diocese of Macedonia, which took in Thessaly, Epirus, and Crete, the province becoming one of the first to receive the epithet 'Salutaris'. The Byzantine centuries saw incursions by Goths (378), Huns (434), Ostrogoths (478), Bulgars (500), Slavs (527), Huns again (540), and Goths again (558). In the 7C the Serbs reached the gates of Thessalonica. The 9C was marked by the invasions of Bulgars and Saracens who, at the beginning of the 10C, seized Thessalonica. In

1014 Macedonia came under the rule of Byzantium. In 1185 William of Sicily sacked Thessalonica. After the capture of Constantinople in 1204 by the army of the Fourth Crusade, the Latin kingdom of Thessalonica was given to Boniface of Montferrat; but his successor was expelled in 1223 by Theodore Angelus, despot of Epirus, who called himself Emperor of Thessalonica. He was defeated in 1230 by the Bulgarian Tsar Ivan Asen II, who incorporated N and central Macedonia into the second Bulgarian or Bulgar-Vlach Empire, the remainder being absorbed in the Nicaean (Byzantine) Empire in 1246. On the extinction of the direct line of the house of Asen, the power of Bulgaria declined, and NW Macedonia again came under the despotate of Epirus. In the 14C Macedonia fell under the domination of the Serbs. Stefan Dušan (1331–55) conquered all Macedonia except Thessalonica, as well as Thessaly, Epirus, and part of Bulgaria. In 1364 Murad I, sultan of Turkey, routed the united Serbs, Hungarians, and Vlachs on the banks of the Maritsa and by 1375 the whole of the Balkan peninsula, with Macedonia, came under Turkish domination. The invasion of Timur (Tamerlane) reversed the trend of expansion. After the battle of Ankara in 1402, in which the Turks under Bayezid I were totally defeated, Timur reinstated the various principalities that had been suppressed, including the Christian ones in E Europe. Under Murad II the Turks defeated the Christians at Varna in 1444 and established Ottoman domination in E Europe. This survived till the Balkan Wars of 1912–13.

In 1900–08 the so-called 'Macedonian Struggle' took place, when armed bands (Greek 'andartes', Bulgarian 'comitajis', and Serb 'chetniks') contended for supremacy in various mountain regions. Greek Macedonia became a reality in 1912 (comp. below). The Treaty of Bucharest (1913) fixed the Mesta as the frontier with Bulgaria, which retained its seaboard on the Aegean until the end of the First World War. The treaties of St. Germain (1919), of Neuilly (1919, and of Sèvres (1920) attempted to solve the problem of Macedonia. For several years until the war with Turkey in 1922 the whole of Thrace passed to Greece. The Treaty of Lausanne (1923) gave back Eastern Thrace to Turkey. In the Second World War Macedonia served in 1940 as the base for the successful Greek campaign against the Italians, but fell within a week to the German onslaught in 1941 (comp. below).

Campaigns. BALKAN WARS. In October 1912 the Balkan League (Bulgaria, Serbia, and Greece) rose against the Turks.

By the end of the month the Bulgarians had defeated the main Ottoman armies in Thrace, and the Serbs were in possession of the whole of old Serbia and most of Albania. The Greeks, under Crown Prince Constantine, advanced through the most difficult passes of Olympus, captured Elassona, defeated Hassim Tahsim Pasha at Servidje (Servia), and occupied Verria and Vodena (Edhessa), while the Turks retreated on Salonika and Monastir (Bitolj). On 1 Nov the Greeks won a victory at Yenidje Vardar (Yiannitsa) on 8 Nov (6 Oct O.S.; St. Demetrius' Day) George I led his troops into Salonika. In Epirus a small column had captured Preveza and was besieging Ioannina.

An armistice was signed, but the Congress of London, meeting on 16 Dec, had no result except to show that the Bulgarians had not abated their claims to Macedonia and were intriguing against Serbia. On 6 March Ioannina surrendered; three weeks later the Bulgarians, assisted by the Serbs, took Adrianople. Meanwhile, the Greek Navy, under Adm. Koundhouriotis, controlled the Aegean; Lesbos, Chios, and Samos were captured.

The First Balkan War ended with the Treaty of London (30 May 1913), and all territory West of the line Enos–Midia was ceded to the Balkan League as a whole. A Graeco-Serb treaty was ratified on 1 June after the Bulgarians had tried and failed to expel the Greek forces from the Mount Pangaion district to the east of the Struma mouth. Towards the end of June the Greeks were attacked by the 2nd Bulgarian Army under Gen. Ivanof on a wide front and lost Gevgeli. On 2 July the Greeks, their infantry attacking with dash and supported by mountain guns, recaptured the town; next day Lachanas was captured by bayonet assault. On 6 July they took the store-town of Doiran. Retreating to Strumnitsa and the Rupel Pass, the Bulgarians committed atrocities at Serres and Sidhirokastron Demirhisar). By the end of the month the Greeks had reached the Kresne Pass, the Rumanians were threatening Sofia and the Bulgarians had lost.

In the spring of 1916, during the FIRST WORLD WAR, the Bulgarians invaded Macedonia. In the previous autumn the Allies had landed an expeditionary force at Salonika, where Venizelos established a provisional Government. Until final victory in 1918 the inadequately equipped Allies (British, French, and Greek) could do no more than hold in check Austrians, Germans, and Bulgars on an almost static line along the N frontier and the Struma. The main battle areas were in the Monastir Gap and round Doiran, but malaria and dysentery accounted for a great part of the casualties.

SECOND WORLD WAR. The Axis attack on Greece followed immediately upon the indefinite postponement of the invasion of Britain in favour of a drive for the Middle East. Mussolini, acting prematurely, and without Hitler's knowledge delivered on 28 Oct 1940, an ultimatum to Gen. Metaxás demanding the passage of Italian forces, which provoked a terse ʾΟχι in reply. After the Italian attack Greek forces soon moved forward from W Macedonia into Albania, inflicting great losses on the Italians. British air units moved to Greece, but Greece, afraid of provoking German intervention, declined the aid of British land forces until February when it was obvious that such intervention was not only inevitable but imminent. The wavering attitude of Yugoslavia and the possible effects, both on Greek morale and Turkish participation, of withdrawing from E Macedonia, had prevented any political decision being reached on which line should be defended. The available British force, commanded by Gen. Sir Maitland Wilson, consisted of the 1st British Armoured Brigade Group (Brig. H.V.S. Charrington), the New Zealand Division (Maj.-Gen. Sir Bernard Freyberg, V.C.), and the 6th Australian Division (Maj.-Gen. Sir Iven Mackey). The Australians were still arriving when the Germans invaded.

At 5.45 on the Sunday morning of 6 April German forces in overwhelming strength were launched simultaneously against Yugoslavia and Greece. On 7 April, the Bulgarian Army occupied Alexandroupolis and Komotini, and Von List's 12th Army crossed the frontier at Doiran and Gevgeli. The Greek hope of holding the Metaxás Line in E Macedonia was at once shown to be militarily impossible, but since the commanders in Albania could not be persuaded to give up their gains and retreat before the Italians, it was decided, against the judgment of the British commander, to try and hold the 'Aliakmon Line' (Kaimaktsalan–Vermion–Olympos). Salonika fell on the morning of 9 April and a small British armoured force held the Vevi pass for three days while Greek troops withdrew from northern frontier positions. The New Zealand brigades dug in athwart the Servia pass, the Petra pass, and the gap between Olympos and the sea. The collapse of Yugoslavia and a swift enemy advance in the NW from Kastoria to Grevena, driving towards the Meteora, cut off the Greek army in Albania and threatened to turn the Aliakmon Line even before preparations were complete. The 9th Panzer Div. reached the Aliakmon on 14 April and a fighting withdrawal and disengagement was ordered to Thermopylae. The Servia pass was held until 17 April when German troops were already penetrating the Vale of Tempe; rearguard actions were then fought in Tempe and at Elasson and the New Zealand forces were extricated through the Larissa bottleneck by 19 April. In Athens Greek surrender and British evacuation were already under consideration and the campaign turned into a race for the southern beaches.

The Civil Wars of 1946–49 were waged with ideological intensity from beyond the Greek frontiers, the aim being Communist domination rather than acquisition of territory. Many civilians, particularly children, were kidnapped from frontier areas for indoctrination in Albania or Yugoslav Macedonia and though the bitterness has slowly healed and military control on movement has now been relaxed, depopulation is still characteristic of the NW frontier region.

57 From (Athens) Lárissa to Salónika. Mount Olympos

ROAD, 154km (96 miles). This forms part of the main highway from Athens to Salonika (c 504km), which by-passes Larissa to the E; on the section through the Vale of Tempe a toll is levied.—27km *Vale o Témpe.*—51km *Pandeleímon.*—67·5km Turning to *Litókhoron* (5km) for the ascent of Mt Olympos.—87km **Kateríni.**—120km *Aiyínion.*—

185km **Salónika**.—BUSES several times daily; through service from Athens by Pullman in 9 hours.

RAILWAY, 171km (106 miles), the main State Rly line from Athens (510km), regular trains daily in c 2½ hours (fast through trains from Athens in c 8 hours; sleeping-cars on night trains).—*Plati* (133·5km from Larissa), where the line is a few kms N of the road, is the junction for Veroia, etc. (Rte 61).

AIR SERVICE (Olympic Airways) from Athens to Salonika regularly in 50 minutes. The route passes over Parnes and across the Euripos near Chalkis. Mt Dhirfis is seen on the right. As the aircraft passes over the strait separating Skiathos and Skopelos, the striking coastline of Magnesia and the Gulf of Volos are well seen. During the flight up the Thermaic Gulf, Pilion, Ossa, and Olympos appear successively to the left, while reaching out on the right are the three prongs of Chalkidiki, Kassandra in the foreground, Sithonia behind, and in the far distance Athos, the Holy Mountain.

Larissa, see Rte 48. We quit the town by the museum and join the by-pass. The road passes the first of the refineries for the sugar industry started in 1960, and runs parallel to the railway. Ahead (left) we see the Olympos range, while the great cone of Ossa rises to the right above brown stony foothills (comp. Rte 48). We cross a flat cultivated plain, the bed of the classical *Nessonis*, one of the lakes by the recession of the flood that once covered the Thessalian plain.—14km *Girtónis Station* (Restaurant).—27km Turnings to *Tirnavós* (left; 33km) and *Ambelákia* (right; 3km).

On the *Tirnavós* road, we reach (3km) the site of ancient **Gonnos** (or Gonnoi) which lies 2km to the S of the modern village of *Gónnoi*. The remains are on a group of low hills to the right of the road. Gonnos was important throughout antiquity because it is situated to control both the W end of the Tempe pass and a N–S route over the E shoulder of Mt Olympos. There are signs that the site was occupied from prehistoric to Roman times but it seems to have been of particular importance in the Macedonian period.

The focus of settlement in the Archaic period was on the NE hill where the remains of a *circuit wall* can be made out. An apsidal *Temple of Athena* was built in Archaic times and reconstructed in the 4 or 3C BC. The city wall was extended in the Hellenistic period to take in the other two hills. There were twelve *towers* at the SW where there is also a *gate*; a second lying to the SW, on flatter ground where the line of the wall has almost disappeared. The *Agora* has been conjecturally located on the lower slopes of the NE hill. A *Temple of Artemis*, identified from inscriptions, is near the SW gate and a *Temple of Asklepios* (Late Roman or Hellenistic) some 300m E of the walls. To the NW of the acropolis are the remains of a channel which apparently brought water from a spring on the mountain.

Ambelákia, beautifully sited amid oaks on Mt Kissavos, derives name from its vineyards. It was already known for its cotton and silk in the 17C, and became in 1780 the centre of a 'joint partnership' of spinners and dyers of red yarn, claimed as the world's first working 'co-operative', with branch offices as far away as London. The town was ruined in 1811 by the bravos of Ali Pasha, but the *Mansion of George Schwarz* (its president) and that of his brother, Demetrios, attest their prosperity; their rococo painted interiors have been splendidly restored. The village is now a summer resort (600m).

At (29km) *Témbi*, formerly Baba, starts the toll road; the railway is seen across the river.

The **Vale of Tempe*, in Greek just *Témbi* (Τὰ Τέμπη), is a glen of surpassing beauty between Olympos and Ossa through which the Peneios, Thessaly's principal river, flows to the sea. The glen, called *Lykostoma* ('Wolf's Mouth') in the Middle Ages, is 10km long and only 27–50m wide; it is the most practicable way out of the Thessalian plain to the NE. It was formed in the Quaternary Epoch by a convulsion that rent the mountains and, by providing the Larissan Lake with an outlet to the sea, allowed the Thessalian plain to emerge. The Thessalians,

according to Herodotus (VII, 129), attributed the convulsion to Posei
don, the god of storms and earthquakes. This violent topographica
distortion finds an echo in the legends of the War of the Gods an
Giants (Gigantomachia).

The attraction of the glen is one of contrast. The stern, almost ver
tical cliffs, scarred by winter torrents and only partly clothed with iv
and other climbing plants, are offset by the peaceful river scener
below. The swift and turbid Peneios is overshadowed on either side b
plane-trees and willows. The banks are fringed with lentisk, *agnu
castus*, terebinth, and laurel.

Tempe, whose praises are sung by innumerable Roman and other poets, was
centre of the worship of Apollo. The god, having killed the serpent Python
purified himself in the waters of the Peneios, and cut a branch of laurel which h
replanted by the Castalian Fountain at Delphi. In memory of this event, ever
eight years a mission of well-born youths was sent from Delphi to Tempe, t
bring back cuttings of the sacred laurel. The Vale of Tempe was one of the
gateways to the interior of Greece, but it could be turned by a narrow track to th
N via the Forest of Kallipeuke and the town of Gonnoi and by passes through th
Olympos massif. In 480 BC a force of 10,000 Greeks occupied Tempe, to deny it
passage to the Persians, However, hearing that Xerxes was already turning thei
position by the inland roads, they withdrew to Thermopylae, abandonin
Thessaly to the invader. Herodotus (VII, 128, 173) tells us that the Persians cam
over the shoulder of Olympos and down on Gonnoi (as did the Germans in 1941)
In 168 BC the Romans entered Thessaly by way of Gonnoi, but they established
military post in the Vale of Tempe.

Beyond the *Spring of Venus* we reach the Wolf's Mouth (see above)
On a rocky hillock (right) stand the ruins of the medieval *Kástro ti
Oraiás* (Castle 'of Oria', really 'of the beautiful maiden'), linked with
local legend and popular song; at the foot of the rock are the remains o
an ancient fortress. At *Ayía Paraskeví* a graceful suspension bridg
(for foot passengers only) crosses the river; it leads to a chapel an
grotto on the opposite bank. The sea appears ahead.—36·5km Th
Spring of Daphne provides a cool and refreshing retreat.

A by-road continues on the right bank to *Omólion* (3km), which in ancient time
had a Temple of Poseidon Petraios; a tomb near the river produced an exquisit
hoard of Classical jewellery in 1961 (now in Larissa museum). Protogeometri
tombs have yielded iron, bronze, and gold objects.—13km *Stómion* (Hotels E; F
A), formerly Tsagezi, is a peaceful seaside resort, with thermal springs, below th
steepest face of Ossa.

We cross the river and the railway (37km *Station for Pirgetós*) and
with the mouths of the Pinios (fish hatcheries) on the right, thread th
last low foothills of Kato Olympos. *Aigáni*, a post on the Turkis
frontier of 1881–1912, can be seen on the hills c 3km left. Soon after
wards We pass the *Spring of Diana*—52km (32½ miles
Pandeleímon, on the site of the ancient *Herakleia Platamona*, guard
the narrows between Kato Olympos and the sea. Here is the splendi
*CASTLE OF PLATAMÓNA, built by Crusaders in 1204–22 to comman
the entrance to the Thermaic Gulf. It was taken by Theodore Angelo
in 1218 when the Lombard followers of Roland Piche fell from th
walls 'like birds from their nest'. Near by is a sandy beach, with tw
camp-sites. The *Spring of the Muses* is (left) between the Xenia an
the castle. Northwards is spreading coastal holiday development. W
pass out of the toll road.—At (58km) *Skála Leptokariás* (Hotels B, C, D
is the beginning of a bad road (comp. below) through the Olympo
massif via *Leptokariá* to Elasson. To the left, row upon row of peak
rise to the crest of Olympos, usually snow-capped or shrouded i
cloud.—63·5km *Pláka Litokhórou* (Hotels B).—70·5km *Limí*

Litokhórou, with the railway station of Litókhoron; the town (comp. below) is seen to the left.

The coastal plain broadens into the strip known to the ancients as PIERIA, birthplace of the Muses. Just beyond the station we cross the tiny Baphyras, a stream made navigable by the Macedonians to serve Dion, the site of which lies 6·5km NW (signposted from the main road).

We cross the Mavroneri, the *Aison* of Plutarch (comp. below), and skirt (87km) **Kateríni** (Hotels C, E), a market town of 38,016 inhab., that commands a wonderful view of Olympos. Its *Paralía* (Hotels B, C, D, E; F/A) lies 7km E on the Thermaic Gulf.—To Elasson, see below.

Ancient Dion may also be approached from Kateríni. An asphalt road (16km; bus) runs S to the modern village (also known as *Malathriá*). Just before the name sign of the village, in a fenced enclosure (right) can be seen the dromos and impressive façade of a Macedonian tomb. The site of Dion, a little to the SW of the village, is entered from the South Gate.

Dion rose to prominence under Archelaus (413–399), who built a temple to Zeus, a stadium for festival games, a theatre (to which Euripides contributed plays), and an enceinte wall. In Macedonian times the place was a troop concentration centre rather than a city. Here Philip II celebrated his triumph after the capture of Olynthos, and here Alexander sacrificed before invading Persia. With Dodona, the city was laid waste by the Aitolians in 220 BC, Philip V taking revenge in 218 by destroying Thermon. Dion was quickly rebuilt, for Philip made it his base before Kynoskephalai as did Perseus his before the Third Macedonian War. After the Battle of Pydna (comp. below) the Romans established here the *Colonia Julia Diensis*. The town had a bishop in AD 346. It was sacked by Alaric and seems not to have recovered. Explorations undertaken in 1928–31 by Salonika University were renewed in 1962. The line of the walls has been traced but the remains appear to be later than the time of Archelaus. The Roman town measured c 500m by 460.

A relatively small part of the main site is accessible to the visitor but it contains interesting and important remains. The line of the fortifications which defines the limits of the city is clear, the most intensively excavated sections being at the SW and E. Visitors are advised to purchase the useful leaflet with a plan of the site and details of the Museum.

Opposite the entrance to the site, we cross the line of the city wall and step onto the main *S–N Street*, part of the original 4C layout but paved with large blocks in the Roman period. The row of buildings immediately to the left are *storerooms* and *workshops* of the 3 and 4C AD, though the large squared blocks of earlier Hellenistic structures can be seen beneath their floors. Farther on (left) an impressive *Roman façade* has relief sculpture consisting of alternating shields and cuirasses. A side road leads off (right) and then a second, opposite which we turn left off the main street. A side street (left; dead end) has remains of *private houses* of the 2 and 3C AD. Beyond these we turn left between the W side of the same complex and the remains (farther W) of an *Early Christian basilica*, whose predecessor on the same site had a mosaic floor. Climbing the bank (right) we can look down into the E apse and the aisle of the building. The narthex lay beyond. Architectural fragments from the buildings can be seen. Continuing W, we reach the *town wall*, of which a substantial section can be observed. The original structure (4C) was mainly of large squared blocks; the later (Roman and Early Christian) repairs can be easily distinguished. There are projecting square towers. Returning a few metres, we see (right) the remains of a substantial Roman bath building (Severan period), whose

DION
Central Area

0 metres   50   100

Macedonian Tomb

Fortification wall

Christian Basilica

Greek theatre

Basilica

Baths

Private houses

Odeion

Roman theatre

Workshops

Sanctuary of Asklepios

Entrance

MAIN STREET

Sanctuary of Demeter

Sanctuary of Isis

N

hypocaust system is its most immediately obvious feature. It was finel
appointed. The bases of some of the columns which adorned the inte
rior can be seen. Statues of the god Asklepios and his family (now i
the Museum) were found here and the building may thus have bee
part of a larger therapeutic complex. This view is perhaps supporte
by the existence close by to the E of an *Odeion*, which can be reache
by a path along the S side of the baths.

We are now close to the entrance, opposite which, on the other sid
of the road, are the remains of a *Sanctuary of Demeter*. Some finds ar
as early as the 5C. The oldest architectural elements are two rectangu
lar 'megarons' of large square blocks which can be easily made ou

among the rather confusing structures of the later layout. To the S of this is a small *Temple of Asklepios*.

Returning to the road, we turn right (E), cross the stream and reach (right) the *Sanctuary of Isis*, a large complex of Hellenistic origin. It is best viewed from the E side. A central passage leads to an altar. Behind this is a façade of four columns and a flight of steps, at the top of which lay the *Temple of Isis* in her guise of Goddess of Birth. To the S and N of the main temple are *smaller temples* to Isis (as Goddess of Fortune) and to Aphrodite Hypolimpidia (i.e. below Olympos). Copies of some of the votive statues, and of the cult state of Isis as Goddess of Fortune have been set up in the positions of the originals.

Returning to the cart track which leads S opposite the site car park, we may visit the overgrown remains of the Hellenistic *theatre* and a large Roman *odeion*. The former is easily visible as a large semicircular artificial bank to the right of the track. Part of the orchestra and lower rows of seats are visible. To the NE, at the edge of a wood is the 2C AD Roman *odeion*, similar to that in the main site but on a larger scale.

In the village is the excellent new *Museum with finds from Dion and other sites in the vicinity. It is most attractively laid out and has a particularly good collection of Hellenistic and Roman material.

GROUND FLOOR. The finds from the different structures are colour-coded. *Blue*: Statues from the Baths, including Dionysos, the family of Asklepios, other portraits. *Yellow*: The Sanctuary of Isis—including the cult statues of Isis (as Fortune) and Aphrodite Hypolimpidia, as well as other votive sculptures. *Green*: The Sanctuary of Demeter—heads of Demeter and Aphrodite, altar of Aphrodite, case of votive offerings. *Red*: Finds from other sanctuaries. *Blue*: Finds from the cemeteries of Dion, including ivory heads and human and animal limbs from Macedonian tombs, various grave goods. *Red*: Architectural members and other finds from the Early Christian basilicas. *Orange*: Other objects of stone, coins.

UPPER FLOOR. Finds from Pieria (*yellow*) and Olympos (*green*), the former including many grave stelai, a two-zone relief of country scenes, bronze votives (in case) from a rural shrine near *Ritini*. *Red*: interesting display illustrating daily life at Dion on the basis of domestic and other objects.

At (99km; 62 miles) *Kítros* (1882 inhab.; 1km W of the road), a custom recalling Aristophanes survives, when, on 8 January (St. Domenica), the women take control of the village, ejecting the men from the cafés; similar events occur at *Kolindhrós* (3693 inhab.; c 16km NW). At *Alikí*, 3km E of Kítros, are the largest salt works in Greece. They surround the *Touzla Marsh* which corresponds to the ancient harbour of **Pydna**. Though some terraces have been observed and pottery found, there is nothing here to see but a pleasant beach (tavernas and rooms). Hammond places the Greek city on the kastro of Makriyialós much farther N, and Macedonian and Roman Pydna, transferred by Archelaus away from the sea, at Alónia, NW of Kitros. This was the place which gave name to the famous battle of 168 BC.

When Lucius Aemilius Paullus took command of the Roman forces in 168, Perseus, the last king of Macedon, held an impregnable position SE of Dion. By a feigned attempt to turn the Macedonian position, the Roman general induced Perseus to retire to a point 11km S of Pydna, near the Aison (comp. above), where the decisive Battle of Pydna took place between 38,000 Romans and 43,000 Macedonians. At first the Macedonian spearmen (in the centre) carried all before them; but their close order was broken in their headlong drive over the uneven ground. Then the Roman legions counter-attacked the Macedonian centre, while the two Roman wings threw themselves upon the Macedonian right wing. The Romans finally broke through the formidable phalanx. Some 20,000 Macedonians were killed and 11,000 captured; their king, who fled to Samothrace, was taken later and ended his lift as a state-prisoner in Italy.

111km *Palaión Elevtherokhórion* (Hotels C). Hereabouts was located ancient *Methone*, founded, according to Plutarch, from Eretria. The town was used on several occasions by the Athenians as a base against the Macedonians, and Philip II lost an eye besieging it.

The old road (30·5km longer) continues via *Aiyínion* (4436 inhab.) to join the Verria road at *Alexándreia*, see Rte 61.

The main highway branches right across the Pedhias Kampania, crossing the Aliakmon and the Axios near their mouths, and joins the Verria road in the outskirts of (155km) **Salonika**.

Mount Olympos

OLYMPOS (Ολυμπος; in modern Greek *Ólimbos*), the highest mountain range in Greece, the traditional abode of the Gods, rises on the N limit of Thessaly and falls away into Macedonia. The massif soars to 2917m and wears a crown of snow from early Autumn to the end of April. On the seaward E side is a line of vast precipices cleft by tree-filled ravines. To the S the main range is separated by a depression from *Káto Ólimbos*, or LOW OLYMPOS, a region of wooded hills rising to 1587m *Metamórfosis*. It is easy of access from *Kariá* on the Elasson-Leptokariá road (see below). To the N rises HIGH OLYMPOS, with the highest peaks grouped round the centre of the massif in the form of an amphitheatre enclosing the deep Mavrolongos valley. Oak, chestnut, beech, and plane trees flourish at the lower elevations; higher up pine forests reach almost to the snow line. The principal summits are in three groups. To the S are *Serai* (2704m), *Kaloyeros* (2701m), and *Palaiomanastri* (2815m). The central group comprises *Skolio* (2911m), from which fine precipices fall into the Tigania glen; *Skala* (2865m); *Mytikas* ('the needle'), highest of all (2917m; the Pantheon more broken; and *Stafani*, the 'Throne of Zeus' (2909m), a majestic curve of limestone arête. Then, separated from the central group by the Col of Porta (2682m) come *Toumba* (2784m) and *Profitis Ilie* (2787m), an easy shale-covered peak on the top of which is a tiny chapel, which used to be visited once a year by monks; hence an arête called *Petróstrounga* descends towards the valley of the Varkos.

This range is the most famous with the name of Olympos, though there are mountains of that name in Euboea, Elis, Laconia, and Arcadia; also in Cyprus and in Asia Minor. In Greek mythology Olympos was the residence of the gods whose life of pleasure was there imagined in human terms unencumbered with moral philosophy. Hesiod incorrectly reports Olympos as 'never struck by the wind or touched by snow'. Lions seem to have survived in the country about Olympos down to Classical times (Herod. VII, 126; Paus. VI, 5, 5). Evidence of a Sanctuary of Zeus of the Hellenistic period involving animal sacrifices was found in 1965.

The sultan Mehmet IV is said to have attempted the highest peak without success in 1669, and in 1780 a French naval officer, G.S. Sonnini, reached Ayie Dhionisios. Leake in 1806 and Pouqueville in 1810 toured the lower area. After 1821 it became a notorious haunt of nationalist bands and bandits. Heinrich Barth, in the wake of the medieval church builders, climbed Profitis Ilias in 1862 and in 1904 Tvigic, the Serbian geographer, did some geological work on the slopes, but the difficulty of the approach and the insecurity of the region deterred all but the keenest. As late as 1910 Edward Richter, on his third attempt at the climb, was captured and held to ransom by bandits after his escorting gendarme had been killed. In 1912 the territory passed from Turkey to Greece and the following year two philhellene Swiss artists, Daniel Baud-Bovy and Freder-

Boissonas, with Chr. Kakalos, a local guide, climbed the Throne of Zeus and Mytikas. In 1921 an official mission of two Swiss topographers, Marcel Kurz and Hans Bickel completed the exploration of the range and mapped it. A large international party explored the summits in 1927, and since the Greek Alpine Club established a shelter in 1931 the mountain has been explored by increasing numbers (508 in 1959). Col. John Hunt here held mountain training courses in 1945, and since 1961 the Greek Army has had a ski school on the slopes.

A. BY CAR FROM LARISSA. From Larissa to (61km) *Elasson* and (70km) *Mikró Elevtherokhórion*, see Rte 58. Here we turn right and shortly, at (75·5km) *Kallithéa*, the road divides; the left branch passes through the picturesque *Stená Pétras* between Olympos and Pieria to Katerini (131km). We take the right branch. Beyond (84km) *Olimbiáda* a military road (18km long) branches left through *Spármos* to *Refuge B* (Vrissópoulos) below the Army Ski-Training Centre, which was moved here from Mt Vermion in 1961. The old road continues E under High Olympos to (99km) *Kariá*. Low Olympos rises to the right. The road passes below (116km) *Leptokariá* to join the Salonika highway at (120km) *Skala Leptokariás* (comp. above), whence it is a further 58km to *Larissa*.

B. THE ASCENT FROM LITÓKHORON. **Litókhoron** (Hotels D), a pleasant well-watered town of 6109 inhab. connected with its railway station (8km) by bus, stands nearly 305m up on the E flank of Olympos. Its people have long had a reputation as mariners and were prominent in the abortive uprising of 1878. The place developed in the 1920s as a health resort for the tubercular. Notwithstanding the provision of a military road up Olympos from the W (comp. above), Litokhoron is the principal centre for climbing in the Olympos massif. Here from the office of the Greek Alpine Club (E.O.Σ.) information may be obtained, guides hired, and the keys of refuges borrowed. There are fixed charges for guides climbing, mules, and food.

The ascent (arduous rather than difficult for mountaineers) is made in two days, the night being spent at a refuge. July and August are the best months.

ROUTE 1 (red marks). The dusty road (practicable for vehicles to the springs; 18km; see below) ascends NW passing the lower monastery of Ayios Dhionísios (the '*Metókhi*') and climbs steadily up the slopes of *Stavrós* (950m) where there is abundant water.—1½ hours. Hut (refuge D) of the Alpine Club of Thessaloniki (1000m). We wind along the N side of the *Mavrolongos Valley* shaded with pines, in which flows the Enippéas.—2½ hours. We see below us the ruined Monastery of *Ayios Dhionisios* a building of c 1500 visited by Sonnini in 1780, blown up by the Turks in 1828, but rebuilt before 1856. It was destroyed in 1943 by the Germans, who believed it to be used by guerrillas. The ruins may be reached in 20 minutes by a path across a declivity, but we continue almost level on the main path (following the red marks).—At (3½ hours) *Prióna* (c 1006m), a primitive settlement of goat-herds with lean-to shelters, the springs of the Enippeas afford the last running water.

From this point the route rises fairly steeply amid thick beech woods in a region rich in botanic interest. We climb almost to the head of the Mavrolongos to reach (7 hours) the **Katafíyio Spílios Agapitós** (2100m; 60 beds; rain-water reservoir), the A refuge of the Greek Alpine Club, on a spur facing E towards the sea. The refuge can now be reached also from the Ski School of the Greek Army (comp. above). From the refuge the climb to one or other summit takes c 2½ hours; the vegetation gives out after c 1 hour. The mountain is usually shrouded in cloud at the mid-day hours in hot weather. The red marks continue to the summit of Mytikas.

ROUTE 2 (blue marks) diverges right a little beyond the Monastery.—5 hours. *Petróstrounga* (2254m). Here are a spring (Strangos) and, lower down, a cave.—8 hours. *Profítis Ilias*, with the King Paul Refuge (C; 18 beds) and a chapel. The traverse of the high summits from *Proftis Ilias* should be undertaken only by experienced mountaineers.

An alternative starting point for ascents is *Kokkinopló*, a village (site of ancient *Pythion*), 18km from Elasson on the Katerini road (comp. above).

58 From Lárissa to Kozáni and Bitolj

ROAD, 246km (154 miles), one of the two international routes between Greece and Yugoslavia. We leave Larissa by the Pinios bridge.—17km **Tirnavós**. Thence up the Titarissios basin.—61km **Elassón**.—117·5km **Sérvia**. We cross the Aliakmon.—145·5km **Kozáni** (turn right in the town).—174·5km *Ptolemaïs*.—207·5km *Vévi*.—233km **Níki** (frontier post9.—248km **Bitolj** (Monastir).—
BUSES to *Elassón*, frequently in 1½ hours; to *Kozáni*, regularly in 4 hours. From Kozani to *Ptolemaïs* frequently; to *Flórina* regularly.

RAILWAY from Kozani to Bitolj, 120km, daily in 5 hours (change at Amíndaion).

We cross the Pinios and pass an Agricultural School of the Royal National Foundation.—5km *Yiánnouli*. The straight road runs NW across the plain.—17km **Tirnavós** (Τυρναβός; Hotel D) on the farther bank of the Titaríssios, is the chief town (10,965 inhab.) of an eparchy and a centre of ouzo production and of textile industries.—The road turns SW to enter the narrow gap between two hills, Tepes (left) and Kladhares (right), through which the Titaríssios emerges to the Thessalian plain. A ruined tower guards the entrance. Before 1912 the Greco-Turkish frontier followed the ridge (which is crossed farther E by an older road to Elassón, 19km shorter, in the *Pass of Melouna*; 540m, view). We follow the river.

The **Titaríssios** has various other names, owing to uncertainty as to which affluent constitutes the main stream. In antiquity it was also called **Europos**, and today it is known as *Xeriás*, *Voulgára*, and *Sarandáporos*. The 'lovely Titaríssios', as Homer calls it (Il. II, 748) drains both Kato Olympos and the Kamvounia range, but its longest stream rises on Mt Titaros. In the Tertiary epoch the river fed the Larissan lake; it now joins the Pinios a few miles W of the Vale of Tempe.

29km *Dhamásion*, reached by ford, lies on the other bank in the narrows. A ruined fortress crowning an isolated stony hill to the N of the village is the *Mylas* that resisted the Macedonians in 1717 BC. The beautiful vale gradually broadens and the sandy river flows between thickly wooded banks.—45km *Doméniko* was identified by Leake with *Chyretiai* on the evidence of an inscription. *Verdhikoussa* (1100m) 13km W on the slopes of Antikhasia, with 2174 inhab., has abundant springs.—The road makes a long curving ascent away from the river undulating through sheep pastures to the twin villages of (55km) *Galanóvrisi* (left) and *Stefanóvouno*.

62km (38 miles) **Elassón** (Ελασσών; Hotels D) stands at the mouth o a short gorge, through which flows the Elassonítikos. The town (6527 inhab.) has an annual fair on 20 August.

Elasson occupies the site of the 'white *Oloosson*' of Homer (Il. II, 739); its epithe derived no doubt from the limestone rocks in the neighbourhood. Chief town o the warlike Perrhaebi, it existed from the Bronze Age, but declined after the 5C BC. It was made the Turkish base in 1897, and its capture by Greek forces in 191 opened the way N.

A fine Byzantine *Bridge* spans the river. On a steep rock overlooking the gorge (footpath or motor road) is the *Panayía Olimpiótissa*, a monastery with a Byzantine church resembling that of the Holy Apostles at Salonika. It has cushion capitals and a carved wooden door o

1296. Two classical tombstones are built into the gate. A little *Museum*, in a half-ruined mosque on the river bank, contains other relics of the past (police will locate key).

About 4km E of Elasson is **Tsarítsani** (pop. 2234), a village founded, it is said, by a colony of Bulgarians in the 10C. Later the Slavs were replaced by Greeks, who preserved a kind of independence under the Turks. they manufactured silk and cotton, and practised agriculture, but their prosperity vanished with the plague of 1813.—About ¾ hour SE of the village is the *Monastery of St. Athanasius*; about 1½ hours E on a W outlier of Kato Olympos is the *Monastery of Valétsiko* ('The Child'), founded by the Bulgarians, with a legend of a royal child miraculously healed.

We cross the Elassonítikos on a bridge (Restaurant) c 2·5km N of the town. The road winds over a hill (330m) used as a defensive position by the Turks in 1912.—At (70km) *Mikró Elevtherokhórion* a road to Katerini and Olympos (Rte 57) diverges right. We cross several arms of the Sarandáporos ('Forty fords'), an affluent of the Titaríssos, mounting higher in the rolling country that characterises its upper course. Away to the E towers Mt Olympos. To the SW of the village of *Vouvála* (3km W of our road) are ruins of ancient *Azoros*.—The road ascends towards the Kamvoúnia range and Títaros, which together form a natural barrier between Thessaly and Macedonia. It veers W from its former line.

The difficult old road (now abandoned) passed through the STENÁ SARANDAPÓROU, or *Defile of Boloustana*, a natural cleft that opens between the two ranges. In the defile King Perseus is said by Livy to have stationed 10,000 men to deny its passage to the Romans; Hassim Tahsim Pasha failed to defend it against Prince Constantine's assault in 1912.

The new road bears W past *Sarandáporon* to thread a gap in the Kamvounian range S of Mt Dhovrás. Metaxás is seen to the right on its S slope.—108·5km *Polírrhakhon*. A steep descent takes the road through the jagged cleft of STENÁ PÓRTAS into the Aliakmon valley where the line of the old road is rejoined. In the gap two roads (see below) branch left; we turn right in the plain below the vertical cliffs of *Mt Borsána* (885m).

The **Aliakmon** rises in the Pindus on the Albanian frontier and flows for 175km entirely in Greek territory. Its upper course (comp. Rte 62) lies in gentle valleys, but in most of its middle reaches it threads narrow gorges, except for a few miles near Servia where its valley widens into a plain. This has been submerged since 1973 by the building of the Aliakmon Barrage some 16km downstream. Neolithic and Early Bronze Age settlements in the valley were investigated in 1971–73. Some finds from a mound excavated in 1931 by W.A. Heurtley are in Salonika museum. The mound was re-explored in 1971–73 before submersion and dated to c 4930–4650 BC. In its middle course the river is nowhere followed by a road, nor is it served with any continuity by tracks. In medieval times it was probably navigable to a point near Veroia; today its flat lower reaches are controlled by the Vavares Barrage (Rte 61). The mountains commanding the valley on the S provide a natural defence line against invaders from the N, which can, however, be turned by the easy pass between Grevena and Kalambaka.

In the Stena Portas two roads branch SW. The poor higher road winds through hilly country to the SE of the river. In a glen below (18km) *Mikróvalton* is the Panayía Stanoú (or Zidhaníou), a monastery founded in the 16C and rebuilt after destruction by the Turks in 1854.—20km *Tranóvalton*.—Beyond (25km) *Lazarádhes* bridle paths continue in 3 hours round the steep N side of *Vounása*, the highest peak (1615m) of the Kamvounia range, or over its E spur, to Dheskáti (Hotels D, E; comp. Rte 62). On the left bank of the Aliakmon, beneath Vounása (2 hours from Lazarádhes), is the Monastery of *Osios Nikánoros Závorda*, where in 1959 was discovered a complete 13C MS of the dictionary of the Patriarch Photios (c 820–891), previously known only by an incomplete copy in Cambridge. It incorporates quotations from lost classics. The buildings date from 1534. Frescoes of the Raising of Lazarus, the Entry into Jerusalem, and the Crucifixion are thought from their similarity to those of Barlaam (Meteora) to be by Frangos Kastellanos.

The new lower road provides an alternative route to Kozani (c 10km longer). It turns SW in the valley to *Rímnion* on the lakeside. Here it is carried across the lake by causeway and bridge to *Aianí*, whose several churches are decorated with 15–16C mural paintings. Here eight cist tombs have yielded grave goods of the 9C BC.

117km (73 miles) **Sérvia** (Σέρβια; 453m) a town of 3369 inhab., commands the only major route S from the Aliakmon valley. It is situated 6·5m from the river, between two sharp rocks and dominated by a Byzantine *Fortress*, which occupies a high hill behind the town. Within the Kastro is the ruined church of *Ayios Theodhoros*.

Servia derives its name from a colony of Serbs, settled here in the 7C by Heraclius as a buffer to other invaders. By the 10C it was in the hands of the Bulgarians, who defended it valiantly but in vain against Basil II. In the 13C it was a frontier stronghold, and it has suffered in many wars. It was bombed on 14 April 1941, and occupied the following day by the Germans. The New Zealand 4th Brigade held a line behind the town from Kastanea to Rimnion until 17 April. Thirty German volunteers worked for a year in 1960–61 to make good war damage.— Some remains at *Palaiográtsano*, on the N slope of Piéria 11km NE of Servia, probably represent the ancient *Phylakai*. At *Velvendós*, in the valley below (by-road from Servia), was born Stamatios Kleanthes (1802–62), the architect.

The Aliakmon hydro-electric lake is crossed by the longest bridge in Greece. Beyond the bridge a private road of the Electricity Authority (ΔΕΗ) branches NE in 16km to the Aliakmon Barrage (Frágma Aliákmonos). Above the road junction on the SW spur of *Patsoúra* is a fortress of uncertain date. We climb gradually. To the right is a series of isolated small hills (Skopós; Rte 62). Kozani can be by-passed to the E.

145km (90½ miles) **KOZÁNI** (Κοζάνη), though no longer astride the main Athens–Salonika road, remains the nodal point of communication between Macedonia and Epirus and the most important strategic centre for NW Greece. It is a clean and invigorating town (30,994 inhab.) with winding streets; the old houses are well kept, and many attractive timber-framed cottages are set off by walled gardens and cobbled courts. The capital of a nome and the seat of a metropolitan, it was a centre of Greek culture during the Turkish occupation. The inhabitants, who are notably good-looking, make textiles and agricultural tools.

Airport (see above) with daily service to Athens.—BOOKING OFFICE, Vasiléos Yioryíou and Dhragoúmi.

Railway Station, 1·25km S of centre; 3 good trains daily to Salonika in c 4 hours.

Hotels B, C, D.

Buses from Odhos Makedhonomákhon, just off main square, hourly to *Salonika* and to *Ptolemaïs*; 6 times daily to *Larissa* and to *Grevena*; 4 times daily to *Siatista*, to *Kastoria*, and to *Florina*; 3 times daily to *Servia* and to *Veroia*; twice daily to *Athens*; daily to *Kalambaka* and *Ioannina*.

Kozani was entered on 14 April 1941, by the 9th Panzer Division. As a centre of royalist sympathies, it was much harried by left-wing bands in 1944– 45.

The centre of the town is the verdant PLATEÍA NÍKIS, with a tall clock-tower of 1855, whence all the principal roads of Western Macedonia radiate. *Ayios Nikólaos*, the metropolitan church, is a low, wide building of 1664–1721 lit by two lanterns. Built mainly of wood, it has ornate stalls and iconostasis, and a W gallery on pillars. The frescoes are blackened with age. The *Museum* contains finds from a wide area and the *Library* has valuable 16C MSS. On a hill NW of the town, the park in front of the picturesque *Metamórfosis tou Sotíros* commands a good view of the town and over the plain of the Aliakmon to Sérvia.

From Kozani to *Salonika* and to *Kastoria*, see Rte 62.

From Kozani the road leads N.—142·5km *Koíla*. We join the railway and skirt the W side of Sarigkiol (see Rte 62), with low hills on our left.—157km *Kómanos*.—162km *Proástion* lies (left) in the *Stená Kománou*, a low 'pass' in which is situated the huge Ptolemaḯs thermo-electric station, opened in 1959 and later linked with the Yugoslav grid.—167km **Ptolemaḯs** (Hotels C, D), a growing town (pop. 22,109) on an upland plain, has become, since the exploitation of its lignite mines, an important industrial centre, producing low-grade coal, sulphuric acid, and nitrate fertilisers. It is the chief town of the eparchy of Eordaia.—Near (172km) *Perdhíkkas* a dam will provide further power. Here two elephants' tusks and stone tools have been found in a context which is probably Upper Pliocene.—At (185km) the *Mnemeía Pesónton Crossroads*, with a memorial to the fallen of the Balkan Wars, we cross the road from Kastoria to Amindaion (Rte 63).
    188km *Xinó Neró* (2km left) has mineral waters. We keep company with the railway (gradient 1 in 40) in the gentle curving *Stená Kirli Derven*, crossing the line at (195km) *Kleidíon Station*. The pass was held for three days against the Germans in 1941 while railway installations were destroyed at Amindaion. We by-pass (198km) *Vévi* (Rte 63A) and leave the old Florina road on our left. Joining the course of the Via Egnatia, our road crosses an upland plain, watered by the Gieléska, leaves the new road via Florina on the left, and continues to (224km) **Níki** (*Tourist Pavilion*) where the Greco-Yugoslav frontier is marked by no natural barrier (the so-called 'Monastir Gap').—It is now more generally approached via Florina (comp. Rte 63). The road continues between the Peristeri Mountains (W) and the marshy Tserna to (238km) **Bitolj** (Hotel C), or *Monastir*, a Yugoslav provincial capital, the ancient *Herakleia Lynkestis* (site above main road to left).

59   Salónika

SALÓNIKA, in Greek **Thessaloníki** (Θεσσαλονίκη), the Biblical *Thessalonica*, with 406,413 inhab., is the second city of Greece and the natural centre of communication with her Balkan neighbours. It is the residence of the Minister for Northern Greece, capital of the nome of Salonika, and a university city. Boasting a church of Apostolic foundation, it remains the seat of an Orthodox metropolitan and of a Roman Catholic bishop. In addition to being the headquarters of a Greek army corps, it has served as Advanced HQ (SE Europe) of NATO, with an armoured division. The city rises from the Bay of Salonika in the form of an amphitheatre on the slopes of Mt Khortiatis. Its citadel, the battlemented walls, and the huddled hillside houses of the upper town give to Salonika an appearance which remains characteristic despite its rapid transformation, since the devastating fire of 1917, into a modern city. Its monuments have re-emerged from the sordid but picturesque slums that hid them; though somewhat over-restored (and having no individual rival to the great churches of Ravenna), they are surpassed as an illustration of ten centuries of Byzantine architecture only by those of Istanbul. Outside the walls the huge grounds of the annual International Fair divide the old town from the new. Local industries are growing (fertilisers and animal foods, agricultural machinery, etc) and oil and sugar are refined. This is having an effect on the harbour, long rendered idle by the competition of Piraeus, and a few passenger shipping links have recently been restarted. The climate of Salonika runs to extremes: the winters are often severe, when the city is swept by the Vardarats, or Vardar wind from the NW; the summers can be oppressive.

Streets at right angles to the sea are number from the seaward end; those parallel to the sea from Axios Sq. (NW). Plan refs. refer to central plan.

Airport at *Mikrá*, 11·25km SE, with international services from London, Germany, etc.; also frequent domestic service to Athens; daily to Herakleion, Lemnos, Lesbos; less frequently to Ioannina, Rhodes, Skiathros; connecting buses from corner of Komnínon and Vas. Konstandínou (Pl. 14).

Hotels, A, B, C, D, E. Mostly near Egnatías or between it and the waterfront.

YOUTH HOSTEL, 42 Od. Príngipos Nikoláou (Pl. 12).—*Camping Sites* at Néa Kríni (comp. below).

Restaurants. *Olympos-Naousa*, Strátis, 5 and 27 Vas. Konstandínou; *Averof*, 17 Singroú; *Clochard*, *Riva*, Proxénou Koromilá; *Payiantes*, Mitropóleos; *Nea Ilyssia*, 17 Leóndos Sóifou; *Perdika*, 40 Vas. Sofías; *Ivi*, *Kairon*, 63 and 54 Tsimiskí.

Post Office, 23 Tsimiskí; Branch Office near the White Tower.—O.T.E. CENTRE, 55 *Vas. Iraklíou*.—TOURIST POLICE, 10 Egnatías (Plat. Metaxá).—ALIENS OFFICE, 25 Tsimiskí (W end).

Information Offices. *N.T.O.*, 8 Od. Aristotélous; *E.L.P.A.*, Vasilíssis Olgas/Aigaíon; *Olympic Airways*, Komnínon.

Buses. LOCAL SERVICES (KTEL 54): 1 (from the Rly. Stn.) and 2–7 traverse Tsimiskí or Vas. Konstandínou and Vasilíssis Olgas; 4 terminates at *Mikró Karavoúrnou*. 22, 23, and 24 serve Venizelou and terminate by the Ramparts in the upper town. To the *Agricultural School*, *Ayia Trias*, etc., from 23 Karólou Dil (Pl. 15); to *Asvestokhorion* from 22 Singroú.—COUNTRY BUSES from Plat Dikastiríon or near by.—**Long-distance Buses** leave from various streets off the NW end of Odhos Egnatías: to *Veroia* and *Naousa* (KTEL 25 Imathias) from 26 Oktovríou, 10; to *Kilkis* from 22 Afrodhítis; to *Edessa*, to *Kozani*, to *Kastoria*, and to *Florina* from Anayenníseos 42; to *Serres*, to *Nea Apollonia* and *Stavros*, and to *Katerini* from Yiorg, Ivánof 59; to *Evzóni* from Odysseós; to *Kavalla* from Langádha 59; to *Langadha (KTEL 39 Thessalonikis) from 10 Frángon; to Ierissos* and *Khalkidiki* from Karakási 68; to *Ioannina (KTEL 20) from* Chr. Pípsou *19 to Athens* from Monastirioí 67.—O.S.E. 'PULLMAN' COACHES to *Athens* from the Railway Station.

Motor Launches in summer from quay (near White Tower) to *Aretsou*, *Peraia*, *Ayia Trias*, etc.—**Taxis** *are painted blue and white.*

Consulates. *British Cons.-General*, 39 Leof. Vas. Konstandínou; *American Consulate*, 59 Leof. Vas. Konstandínou; *Yugoslav Consulate*, 98 Vassilíssis Olgas.—BRITISH COUNCIL, 3 Leof. Vas. Konstandínou.

Banks. *Bank of Greece*, 12 Tsimiskí; *National*, *Ionian and Popular*, 3 and 7 Franklin Roosevelt; *Commercial*, 21 Ionos Dhragoúmi.

Clubs and Learned Organisations. *Inspectorate of Classical Antiquities* at the Museum; of *Byzantine Antiquities*, 114 Megálou Alexándrou; *Institute of Macedonian Studies*, opposite White Tower; *Greek Alpine Club*, 14 Venizélou.

Booksellers. *Molho*, 10 Tsimiskí; *P. Zakharopoúlou*, 23 Tsimiskí; *Kaufmann*, 10 Aristotélous.

Theatres. *Vasilikon* (Royal), *Stratou* (Tekhnis), *Parkou* (Théâtre de l'atelíer) *Makedhonikon Spoudhon*, all near the White Tower.

Baths (Loutra). *Olympia*; Nadir, Aristotélous; *Paradeisos* (old-fashioned), Egnatías.—PUBLIC LAVATORIES in Plat. Aristotélous and by the White Tower.

Sports Centre between the University and the Kaftándzoglou Stadium.—TENNIS CLUB, *Astir*, Kíprou.

Festivals. *International Fair* in September. *St. Demetrius* (26 October; religious processions) to *Okhi Day* (28 October; military parade) is a three-day holiday.

Churches are open to visitors 8–1.30 & 3.30–8.

History. The unimportant ancient town of *Therme* was incorporated with twenty-five others in 316 BC by Kassander and given the name of *Thessalonikeia* (in Strabo's spelling) after his wife, who was half-sister to Alexander the Great. It must soon have been fortified, for Antigonus Gonatas retired on it after his defeat in 274 by Pyrrhus, king of Epirus. In 146, when Macedonia became a Roman province, Thessalonica was made its capital. Its geographical position at the head of the gulf favoured its development, which was accelerated by the building of the Via Egnatia. Cicero spent part of his exile in 58 at Thessalonica; Pompey took refuge here in 49 from Caesar. Literary visitors included the Greek satirist Lucian and the historian Polyaenus. The city's support of Antony and Octavian before the Battle of Philippi assisted its fortunes. In AD 49–50 St. Paul preached at Thessalonica, where he antagonised some of the Jews, who attacked the house in which he had been staying. His two letters to the church he founded here have come down to us as the Epistles to the Thessalonians; he revisited the city in 56. Thessalonica repelled repeated attacks by the Goths in the 3C. Galerius, who succeeded to the E half of the Roman Empire on the retirement of Diocletian, dwelt in the city, where the persecution he instigated claimed as a victim St. Demetrius, afterwards patron saint of the city. Constantine mustered his fleet here before his successful campaign against Licinius in 324. Under Theodosius the Great (379–395) Thessalonica became the seat of the prefecture of Illyricum, a metropolitan see, and the base of the Emperor's operations against the Goths. Here Theodosius himself, severely ill, was converted to Christianity and afterwards issued the Edict of Thessalonica (380), reversing Julian's toleration of pagan gods and condemning the Arian heresy held at Constantinople. In 390, after Botheric the Goth, military commander of the city, had been lynched for failing to control his soldier's outrages, Theodosius invited the populace to a special performance in the circus and there had c 7000 of them massacred. For this crime he was made to do penance by St. Ambrose, Bishop of Milan.

Favoured by Justinian, Thessalonica rose to become the second city of the Byzantine Empire. Having endured further invasions of the Goths, and resisted five sieges by Avars and Slavs, it remained an enclave in Slav dominions until Justinian II's expedition of 689, and seems to have returned to direct Byzantine administration as a theme only after Stauricius' offensive c 783. SS. Cyril (died 869) and Methodius (died 885) the brothers who converted the Slavs to Christianity were natives of Thessalonica.

Thessalonica was stormed by the Saracens (led by the Greek renegade Leo of Tripoli) in 904, when 22,000 of its inhabitants were sold into slavery. It served Basil II as base against the Bulgars, who besieged it without success in 1041. When in 1185 the army and fleet of William II of Sicily, commanded by Tancred, captured the city, the celebrated Homeric scholar Eustathios, then Abp. of Thessalonica, left a detailed account of its barbarous sack. At the end of the Fourth Crusade, the city became the capital of the Latin kingdom of Thessalonica under Boniface of Montferrat (1204). Kalojan of Bulgaria was killed here in 1207 while attacking the walls, and Henry of Flanders died in the city in 1216, poisoned perhaps on the eve of marching against Theodore Angelus, despot of Epirus. Thessalonica fell to Epirus in 1222 (Theodore proclaiming himself Emperor), while the rest of Macedonia came under the sway of Ivan Asen II of Bulgaria; but in 1246 John Vatatzes reappropriated both to the Byzantine empire of Nicaea. In the 14C possession of Thessalonica was the recognised first goal of every usurper with his eyes on the Imperial throne. The Catalan Grand Company besieged the city unsuccessfully in 1308. Michael IX died here in 1320 and hence in 1328 his son Andronikos III launched his successful campaign against his grandfather. The same century witnesses the religious struggles of the Hesychasts, or Quietists, and the insurrection of the Zealots, a 'people's party' who murdered the nobles in 1342. The short period of reform before they were crushed coincided with the artistic Golden Age of the city. During a long period of anarchy Thessalonica fell to the Ottoman Turks in 1387 and again in 1394, but in 1403, after the Mongol Timur had crushed Bayezid I at Ankara, it was restored to the Byzantines. In 1423 Andronikos Palaeologus, son of the Emp. Manuel II, despairing of keeping back the Turks, placed Thessalonica under Venetian protection. However in 1430 Murad II stormed, sacked, and occupied the already depopulated city. Some churches were transformed into mosques.

The population was suddenly increased by the influx of 20,000 Jews banished from Spain by the Edict of the Alhambra (1492). They absorbed the Bavarian Jews who had arrived twenty years earlier. By the middle of the 16C they constituted the major part of the population, and had formed a small autonomous community speaking Ladino, a form of Castilian, which they wrote in Hebrew characters. Towards the end of the century the Greeks returned in some strength. The city suffered from fires in 1545 and 1617 and from the Jewish schism of 1659 when the sect of Donmeh broke away. In 1821, at the outbreak of the Greek War of Independence, a sympathetic movement at Salonika was savagely suppressed. During the 19C the Turks made a show of reforms; the Greeks improved their schools; the Jews increased their influence. In 1876 the French and German consuls were murdered by the mob; Pierre Loti, arriving in the frigate 'Couronne' in time to see the assassins hanged, found in Salonika's romantically squalid alleys the original of his 'Aziyadé'. In 1888 the railway link was forged with the rest of Europe, and in 1897–1903 a new harbour constructed.

Salonika (known to the Turks as *Selaïnik*) became a centre of intrigue against the misrule of Abdul Hamid. Here in 1906 was formed the Turkish Committee of Union and Progress (Ittihat ve Terakki Cemiyeti), which secretly organised the Macedonian revolt of 1908. In 1909 Abdul Hamid was deposed and exiled to Salonika. In the First Balkan War the Greek Army made a triumphal entry into Salonika on 8 November (26 October O.S.), 1912, and the city was ceded to Greece by the Treaty of Bucharest (1913). King George I was assassinated in Salonika on 18 March 1913. During the First World War the Entente landed an expeditionary force at Salonika on 12 October 1915, and here Venizelos set up his provisional government of National Defence. The railway link with Athens via Larissa was completed the following year. In the Second World War, German tanks, advancing down the Vardar, entered the city on 9 Apr 1941, three days after the start of the campaign, after Canadian engineers had destroyed installations during the night. During the occupation most of Salonika's Jewish population (c 60,000) was deported to Poland, never to return.

The city was damaged by fires in 1890, 1898, and 1910, at which time it still had oil street lamps. Fire devastated the city on 5 Aug 1917, rendering 70,000 homeless, and the shanty town of refugees was swollen in 1923 by the exchange of population with Turkey. Replanning of the centre was put in hand in 1925–35, but the greatest transformation occurred after 1950. Since then Salonika has become a modern city, though the higher part of the city still retains some of the old atmosphere. In June 1978 severe earthquakes caused casualties and disruption. The early churches suffered worst and the old-established Mediterranean Palace hotel was wrecked, but serious damage to recent buildings was not widespread.

A. The Centre of the City

Despite many changes made since the fire of 1917, the ancient chessboard plan remains a feature of the town. The principal thoroughfares run roughly parallel to the sea. Ayiou Dhimitríou, Egnatías, and Tsimiskí effectively dividing the old city into four belts. The EGNATIA ODHOS extends from the Axios Gate in the NW to the Kassandreia Gate in the SE (though the actual gates are no more).

The street occupies an ancient course and, since it was spanned by two triumphal arches, was long assumed to represent the famous Via Egnatia. It is now supposed, however, on the evidence of milestones, that the Egnatian Way entered from Pella by the Axios Gate but left again by the Letaia Gate, also on the NW, without passing through the city, rather as its successor does today.

Halfway along on the upper side opens the PLATEÍA DIKASTIRÍON (Pl. 10), a vast square cleared by the fire of 1917. It served as the bus terminal until, in 1962, new courts were proposed. Immediate finds led to the identification of the Imperial Roman FORUM, and systematic excavations were begun by the Greek Archaeological Service under Ph. Petsas. The *Odeion* and two stoas bounding the forum have been unearthed, and a long double *Cryptoporticus* explored. The courts have been abandoned and the area will remain the central square of Salonika. The lower part has been attractively planted with gardens. At the W corner stands the **Panayía Khalkéon**, founded (as an inscription on the marble lintel of the W entrance tells) in 1028 by Christophoros of Lombardy, and restored in 1934. The church contains an almost complete cycle of frescoes belonging to the original decoration and must have been painted very soon after the construction of the building. The name *Our Lady 'of the Coppersmiths'* recalls the time from 1430 to 1912 when it served the Turkish smiths as a mosque (the Kazancilar-Cami). The brick church has the form of a Greek cross-in-square, extended to the E by three apses and to the W by a narthex. The central dome, with a straight cornice, is mounted on a lofty octagonal drum, and the arms of the cross have triangular pediments, which give a markedly angular appearance to the whole. On the façade, however, brick half-columns support deep round arches and the cornices of the two W domes follow the rounded lines of the windows in the Athenian manner. The contrast suggests a later date for the upper stage of the narthex although the fresco of the Last Judgment inside is placed in the 11C. Within, the dome is supported by four marble columns. Contemporary frescoes in the dome (Ascension), round the drum, and in the apse, seem to derive from the mosaics of Ayia Sophia (see below). On the opposite corner the picturesque * *Çifte Hamam*, a Turkish bath-house erected by Sultan Murad II in 1444, survives in use as the *Loutra Paradeisos*. It preserves its original dedicatory inscription. Beneath are remains of late Roman buildings.

Off the Egnatia Odhos, in Odhós Ayías Sofías (left), is the **Panayía Akheiropoíetos** (Pl. 11), one of the earliest Christian buildings still in use. It was probably dedicated to the Virgin soon after Her recognition by the Third Oecumenical Council (Ephesus, 431 AD) as Theotókos (Mother of God) and completed c 470.

It took its name (Αχειροποίητος: 'Made without hands') at some time after the 12C from a celebrated ikon supposed to have been miraculously painted. A later popular name, *Ayía Paraskeví* (Good Friday), is said to come from a mistranslation of the Turkish name Eski Djuma, meaning 'old place of worship' (Djuma also meaning Friday since that was the Moslem day of worship). The church was converted into a mosque in 1430, not without detriment to its fabric. It was restored in 1910 but suffered further deterioration in 1923 when refugees were billeted in it. Reconsecrated, it has again been restored.

The church is a basilica of Syrian type with nave and two aisles. The atrium and exo-narthex have disappeared. The narthex opens into the nave by a 'trivilon' (τρίβηλον), a triple opening formed by two columns and closed by curtains. The arcades are formed by monolithic columns with 'Theodosian' capitals; the mosaics on the soffits, depicting birds, fruit, and flowers, show Alexandrian influence. Frescoes of c 1225 have survived in the S aisle, above the arcade between it and the nave. Eighteen of the Forty Martyrs remain, depicted either in bust in medallions or as full-length figures. Near the S chapel (the former baptistery) are some brick walls of a Roman house and below the S aisle have been unearthed two layers of Roman mosaic flooring.

Farther E is *Ayios Pandeleímonos*, a pretty church with a central dome and a domed narthex, first mentioned in 1169 as a dependency of the Rossikon (Mt Athos). The cloister which surrounded it on three sides disappeared during its Turkish period as the *Issakié Mescid Cami*. It was transformed (c 1500) by Kadi Ishak Çelebi, whose magnificent mosque is still the central feature of Bitolj. Damage in 1978 was severe.

Farther on, the realigned Egnatía Odhós passes to the right of the **Arch of Galerius** (Pl. 12), beneath which the road in its narrower days made a slight angle. The great triumphal arch, erected to commemorate the emperor's victories over the Persians in AD 297, was shown by the excavations of E. Dyggve, the Danish archaeologist, in 1939 to have formed part of a larger design, which included a Palace, Hippodrome, and Mausoleum. There survives of the arch part of its W half; the entire E half has disappeared. Two further piers to the SE carried a similar span, forming a double gate crowned by a central dome. The springers of the transverse arches can be seen above the cornice of the reliefs. Beneath them ran a lateral way, extended to the NE by a porticoed avenue leading to the rotunda (see below). The structure is of brick throughout, the piers being faced with *Reliefs in stone, in four zones separated by bands of sculptured garlands, and crowned by a cyma and cornice.

S PIER E side. In the *Scene of Sacrifice* on the second zone from the bottom, Diocletian, Augustus of the East (left), in the imperial purple, and Galerius (right), his son-in-law, and Caesar, in military uniform, celebrate the latter's victories. The altar is decorated with reliefs of Jupiter and Hercules, of whom respectively they claimed to be the reincarnation. The scene below represents the surrender of an Eastern town; those above, prisoners begging for clemency, and (top) Galerius addressing his troops. In the adjacent reliefs beneath the main arch, above a row of victories, Galerius is seen (top to bottom) riding in his chariot between two towns which receive him and bid him farewell; fighting on horseback (crowned by an eagle on the sculptured band); receiving the surrender of Mesopotamia and Armenia.—On the N PIER the various scenes of combat, some with elephants, are less well preserved.

The line of the Roman avenue (comp. above), leads to **Ayios Yeóryios** (Pl. 12), the oldest as well as the most conspicuous intact monument in Salonika, with the only surviving minaret. The *Rotunda*, built of brick on the same axis as the triumphal arch, was probably erected in the lifetime of Galerius to serve as his mausoleum. The brick dome is protected by a low-pitched timber roof borne on the outer walls, one of the first known examples of this practice in Europe. After having served as church and mosque, the building is now preserved as an ancient monument (closed by earthquake damage).

Having died in Serdica (Sofia), Galerius was buried in near-by Romulianum, his birthplace, since Licinius would not permit his body to be moved to Thessalonica. The rotunda was transformed into a church before 400, when the SE recess was converted into an arch and the sanctuary constructed; the main entrance was moved from the SW to the NW, and a narthex added. At the same time an ambulatory (now destroyed) was added round the outside and the recesses in the original wall opened into it. Some time after the 10C the upper part of the sanctuary fell and the dome was repaired. The buttresses date from this time. This is possibly the church known in the Middle Ages as the *Asomaton*, or Archangels, which gave its name to the quarter and its gate. For some time in the 15C the Asomaton served as the Metropolitan church of the Greeks. In 1591, the year of the Hegira 999 (when the end of the world was expected) the rotunda was turned into the *Mosque of Sinan Pasha*; later it was renamed after Hortaci Suleïman Effendi; his tomb (19C) stands in the courtyard (SE side). The elegant stelai surrounding the church date from the time of Mahmoud II (1807–39).

INTERIOR (closed at present). The marble stoup at the entrance is supported by columns of green Thessalian marble. The circular wall, 6m thick, has eight barrel-vaulted recesses. Over each recess is an arched window; above and between these are small lunettes; the dome is c 24m across. *Mosaics, Hellenistic in feeling and dating from the end of the 4C, decorate the dome and recesses. Eight compositions round the dome represent elaborate architectural façades with saints in prayer. Their vestments are varied and their features individual; all were martyred in the East, the majority under Diocletian. Of the middle zone, which probably represented the Apostles, only some sandalled feet survive. The central figure of Christ is lost, though some heads remain of the attendant angels. In the recesses (that to the SE restored in 1885) medallions with birds and fruit are displayed on a gold ground. In the apse which, like the bema and the ambulatory (now destroyed), was added to the original building upon its conversion into a church, four truncated columns (of a ciborium?) show the original floor level. There are some badly preserved frescoes showing the Ascension which have been assigned to the second half of the 9C. Sculptural fragments and other Christian evidences have been gathered together in the building and a fine *Mosaic of St. Andrew has been remounted.

Seaward of the Arch of Galerius, Od. Goúnari leads to PLATEÍA NAVARÍNOU, a large square formed by the excavations since 1970 in the **Palace of Galerius** (Pl. 16). A deep area is surrounded by a low wall so that the remains can be seen from various vantage points. Most impressive is an octagonal building, richly decorated within, perhaps the throne room.

A short walk NW takes us to **Ayía Sophía** (Pl. 11), conspicuously situated in a garden, planted with palms and Mediterranean pine, that occupies the site of its former atrium. The main façade closes the end of Odhos Ermoú. The heavy exterior was not improved by the loss of the elegant Turkish portico, ruined by an Italian air raid in 1941, and the structure suffered severely in 1978.

The date of Ayia Sophia (the church of the Holy Wisdom) is disputed. Its imperfect pendentives and the style of its masonry led some scholars to think it older than its Justinianean namesake in Constantinople. More likely the building represents a transitional form between the domed basilica and the domed cruciform church and should be dated to the early 8C, perhaps to the reign of Leo III the Isaurian (717–40). It remained to the Christians until 1585 when it was transformed into a mosque by Raktoub Ibrahim Pasha. Damaged by fire in 1890, it was reconstructed in 1907–10 and restored to Christian worship in 1912. The Greeks used its minaret (since demolished) for a machine gun post in 1913 while subduing the Bulgarian garrison which had barricaded itself in a school nearby.

The spacious INTERIOR remains impressive despite being shored up with extensive wooden scaffolding. The drum, borne on pendentives, on which the dome rests, is a square with rounded corners rather than a circle. The dome, 10m in diameter, is decorated with mosaics of the Ascension. In the centre, in a circular medallion supported by two angels, the Almighty is seated on a rainbow throne; in the drum are the Virgin with an angel on either side, and figures of the Apostles divided by trees. Below the angels is a Greek inscription in four lines from Acts I, 11 (Ye men of Galilee, why stand ye gazing up into heaven?). The mosaics are now attributed to the 9C or 10C. In the apse are monograms of Constantine VI and of the Empress Irene, and the Virgin enthroned. The presence can be traced of an earlier mosaic of the cross, which during the iconoclastic period accompanied the liturgical inscription now interrupted by the Virgins feet; the existing mosaics, therefore, are dated to 785–97. In the arches of the W wall of the narthex, part of the original fresco decoration of the 11C remains. Fragments of full-length male and female saints can be distinguished, with busts of saints below them.

To the SE, across the road, is the entrance to a subterranean chapel, dedicated to St. John the Baptist, that connects with the crypt of a Roman nymphaeum.— Excavations to the E of the church in 1961 laid bare part of a basilica of the 4C AD adorned with mosaics and frescoes.

From the S side of the church Odhós Skholeíon Exadháktilon leads past a large school to the principal shopping street of the city, still known by its Byzantine name of TSIMISKI' (Pl. 14, 15). Its previous alternative name of Megalou Alexandrou has now been transferred elsewhere. To the S in Od. Ay. Sofías stands *Ayios Gregóris Palamá*, built in 1912–13 to serve as the cathedral. Here is re-interred the body of Abp Gregory Palamas (c 1295–1359), champion of the Hesychasts. The Tsimiskí crosses Odhós Karólou Dil, which honours Charles Diehl (1859–1944), the French Byzantist, and Odhós Aristotélous (see below). On the left is the *Post Office*. Just beyond, on the right, the picturesque remains of the *Iaoudi Hamam* form part of a market. To the W is Eleftherias Square. We now turn up the lively ODHÓS ELEF-THERÍOU VENIZÉLOU, with fashion shops. At its crossing with the Egnatía Odhós (lined to the W with hotels) a cinema occupies the former *Hamza Beg Cami*, founded in 1468, enlarged before 1592 and partly rebuilt after a fire in 1620. It is the largest mosque on Greek soil. Behind rises the *Dhimarkhíon*. Venizelou St mounts to the *Dioikitírion* (Pl. 6), administrative centre of the Ministy of Northern Greece, which continues on the same site as the Turkish Konak. The square before its façade is laid out as a memorial to Prince Nicolas, first military governor of Macedonia (1912). Odhós Ayíou Dhimitríou follows an ancient course.

  Ayios Dhimítrios (Pl. 6), a double-aisled basilica of the 5C, with transepts flanking the apse and projecting farther E, is the largest church in Greece. The building was reduced to a shell by the fire of 1917,

Roman period
5th century
7th century
Later

0   20 metres

AYIOS DHIMITRIOS

though the main arcades stood and the sanctuary survived to roof
level. It was reconstructed in 1926–48, where possible with surviving
materials, more or less as it had been before the fire, save that the open
timber roof has been replaced by one of reinforced concrete.

History. Local tradition makes St. Demetrius a native of Thessalonica, though
Sirmium, near Mitrovitsa, also claims him. He was martyred at the command of
Galerius. The saint, as the city's guardian, defended it against enemy attacks. His
tomb exuded a sacred oil with miraculous powers of healing. His cult fostered the

opposition of Thessalonica to the 14C iconoclastic movement. A fair, of considerable importance in the Middle Ages, accompanied his festal days (20–26 October). Immediately after the edict of toleration the Christians built a small church on the site of the martyrdom. In AD 412–13 Leontius, prefect of Illyricum, miraculously healed of paralysis, founded 'between the ruins of the Roman bath and the Stadium', a large church which was damaged by fire in the reign of Heraklius (c 629–34) and shortly afterwards rebuilt by Abp John with the addition of the E transepts. The plan seems to have remained unaltered despite later repairs. Here in 688 the Emp. Justinian II celebrated his success against the Slavs. The church was pillaged in 1430 but left to the Christians until 1491 when, in the reign of Bayezid II (as shown by an inscription formerly above the W door), it became the Kasimiye Cami. Between 1907 and 1912, when it was returned to Christian use, its wonderful mosaics were rediscovered, only to be largely destroyed in the fire of 1917. The rebuilding was achieved by architects Zachos (died 1938) and Thanopoulos under the supervision of Ephor S. Pelekanides.

A cruciform appearance is given to the exterior by the transept roofs, which break the line of the aisles although they do not form a true crossing with the nave. Outside the W front, which is flanked by two low towers, stands the great *Phiale*, a canopied immersion font. The usual entrance is by the S door. The spacious **Interior**, 43m long, has been impressively restored, though the upper surfaces have only whitewashed plaster in place of the destroyed revetment of polychrome marble (traces above the arcade). The NAVE, 12m wide and ending in an apse, is flanked by double aisles, with round arches supported by columns of green, red, and white marble. The ancient shafts (some renewed) must have been replacements from elsewhere after the first fire for they have pedestals of uneven height. The carved *Capitals with their imposts repay detailed attention; many are Theodosian. The ancient marble revetment has been renewed on the piers, and the floor repaved in Thessalian marble.

At the W end are a curious wall painting with a unicorn and a calendar of movable feasts for 1474–93. On the N side is the marble tomb (1481) of Osios Loukas Spantounis, of Florentine workmanship most unusual in Greece. A domed chamber at the NW corner, survives from a Roman building and probably held the tomb of St. Demetrius; it is poorly frescoed. At the entrance is a damaged mosaic of the saint.

On the floor of the nave remains of a hexagonal base mark the site of the silver ciborium of St. Demetrius, burnt in 581. The great polygonal *Choros* is a noteworthy copy. On the first pier of the S arcade a fresco depicts Abp Palamas with the blessed Ioasaph (presumably John VI Cantacuzenos who took the habit under that name). The *Iconastasis* and the furnishings are replicas of Byzantine work in fretted marble, the *Ambo* to the left, the *Cathedra* to the right. On the pier behind the throne, fresco of Osios Loukas (died 953). To the right and left of the iconostasis survive five *Mosaics, three contemporary with Leo's rebuilding. Right Pier. St. Demetrius and the builders of the church, presumably the prefect Leontius and Abp John, defender of the city in 617–619; St. Sergius sumptuously attired as captain of the Imperial guard (a later work); St. Demetrius with a deacon (discovered when a masking Turkish wall was removed). Left Pier. St. Demetrius with two children; Virgin and (?) St. Theodore (its date is still disputed).

In the outer S aisle are frescoes of the Saint and of the miraculous defeat of a Barbarian invasion. At the SE corner stands the dark little *Chapel of St. Euthymios*, with frescoes of 1303.

The CRYPT, brought to light by the fire, is entered from the S transept. Here have been identified the *Martyrion* of the saint (early 4C), an adaptation perhaps of part of the *Roman Bath* in which St. Demetrius was traditionally imprisoned. Beneath its apse was found a small cruciform reliquary-crypt containing a phial of blood-soaked earth. Parts of a fountain from a fish pond described by Abp Eustathios (died 1193) were also discovered. A stretch of paved Roman *Street* shows that the martyrion was above the ground level at that time.

To the NW of the church Byzantine walls, fragments of columns, and Hebrew tombstones lie in disorder. To the N rise two domes of a Turkish bath. The trifoliate church of **Profítis Ilías** (Pl. 6), which served the 14C *Néa Moní*, occupies the site of a Byzantine palace, as its Turkish name (*Eski Séraï Camisi*) suggests. Converted to the Moslem rite of Fethi Murad, it was disfigured by massive external buttresses, the removal of which has revealed its fine brick decoration. The square narthex, with an upper story supported on pillars, is characteristic of the monastic Katholikon (much damaged mosaics and medieval graffiti.) Internally the church needed such thorough restoration that its only original features are the four columns supporting the dome and fragmentary mosaics in the small window embrasures of the drum.

B. The Sea Front and the Eastern Quarter

From the centre Odhos Aristotelous, a broad flower-planted avenue, crosses Odhos Ermou and the Tsimiski and descends to the sea. At the seaward end is the British Consulate-General. LEOFÓ ROS VASILÉOS KONSTANDI'NOU (Pl. 14), a quayside esplanade with noted restaurants, replaces the 10C seaward rampart demolished in 1866–74. To the right it leads to PLATEÍA ELEFTHERÍAS, centre of banking, and to the *Harbour*.

The original port, constructed by Constantine the Great, was silted up in the Middle Ages. A new harbour was fashioned by a French company in the late 19C and in 1911 Salonika was the third port of Turkey. The competition of Piraeus and the through railway to Athens killed its passenger services and after the Second World War its commerce was virtually non-existent. Since 1960 new Macedonian industries have improved traffic to the extent that a new quay was begun in 1962. A Free Zone encourages Yugoslav use of the port.

We turn left along the promenade. On the shore at the far end (1km), set amid trees, is the famous *White Tower* (Pl. 16), or *Lefkós Pírgos* (Λευκός Πύργος), 32m high, which marked the S angle of the ramparts. Built c 1430 either by the Venetians or the Turks, it served in the 18–19C as a prison for the Janissaries. Their massacre in 1826 at the order of Mahmoud II gained for it the name of Bloody Tower, forgotten since the application of whitewash. The central chambers now form the headquarters of the four Sea Scout groups of Salonika and the summit affords a fine view of the city.

Grouped opposite the Tower, at the corners of Leoforos Vasilíssis Sofías (Rte 59C), are the *Officers' Club* and the *Society for Macedonian Studies* (Εταιρεία Μακεδονικών Σπουδών), with the adjacent *State Theatre* (1961), and by the sea the *National Theatre*. Beyond, a *Park* divides the old town from its huge E extension. An avenue leads (left) to the entrance of the Fair (see below).

Along the foreshore a broad ESPLANADE was laid out in 1961–62 on reclaimed land. This promenade, flanked by gardens, extends S to (4km) the new *Yacht Basin*. Beyond is the *Villa Allatini*, where the banished Abdul Hamid II, sultan of Turkey, lived in 1909–12; it is now a military hospital.—5·5km **Mikró Karavoúrnou**; on the point stands the *Kiverneion*, or Government House, a splendid Ionic building in white marble, which successfully adapts a pure class-

ical style to modern use. A military encampment prevents access to the prominent *Tumulus* opposite.—Beyond the point are *Arétsou* (Hotel C, a popular seaside resort with tavernas, N.T.O.G. beach, and yacht marina, and *Néa Kríni* (camping sites). Both afford a fine view across the gulf to Mt Olympos.

LEOFÓROS VASILÉOS YEORYÍOU TOU PRÓTOU continues E to its crossing with Odhos Ayías Triádhos, on the corner of which a marble bust commemorates the assassination here in 1913 of George I. The road continues as LEOFÓROS VASILÍSSIS ÓLGAS (comp. below), off which (left) is the *Yeni Cami*, a large mosque which housed the archaeological museum in 1917–62. No. 68 houses the MUSEUM OF POPULAR ART (adm. free), with traditional costumes of N Greece. Leofóros Stratoú leads back along the N side of the park past the Army Headquarters to the permanent site of the **International Fair**. The commercial fair, held in the Middle Ages as part of the festivities of St. Demetrius (October), was revived in 1926.

Inland, beyond the fair, rises the University (p. 518) and farther to the NE a new *Sports Centre*, with a covered *Swimming Pool*, and the *Kaftándzoglou Stadium*, erected from a bequest of Lysimachos Kaftandzoglou (1870–1937), the diplomat, and opened in 1960 by King Paul.

Across the road from the Fair entrance stands the *Archaeological **Museum**, opened in 1963. In front of the building are two fine sarcophagi. In the entrance hall are available some useful books and minor publications about material in the museum and sites in the vicinity.

The museum takes the form of an inner and an outer series of rooms laid out round a court. The inner rooms (access from hall opposite entrance) house finds from *Sindhos* (comp. below). We begin with the outer series. It should be noted that little of the Classical and Byzantine material is at present (1986) on display.

OUTER ROOMS: R. 1 (to left of entrance) contains Neolithic to Iron Age finds from sites in Macedonia, with a map showing their location. Included is material from current British School excavations at *Assiros Toumba*, N of Salonika. Under a glass case is the outline body of a girl with grave goods and jewellery, as found near Verroia (12–10C BC). R. 2 (up steps from vestibule). Ionic capital and other fragments from a temple at Thermi (end 6C BC). A small head, which may be part of the frieze, is just inside R. 3; also sculptures of various periods. R. 4. Portrait head of a man from a grave relief of mid 1C, and other Hellenistic works.

ROOM 5, a long hall, partially arranged as a Roman courtyard with a central floor mosaic and wall mosaics, all from a villa in Salonika. The floor mosaics depict three legends: Dionysos and Ariadne at Naxos; Zeus and Ganymede; Apollo and Daphne (?). The wall mosaic of three spirited horses (right) is attractive. Statuary includes a powerful Atlas, from the Agora of Salonika (1C BC); a dignified bust of Dionysos, from Drama; three headless Muses (late Roman copies of Hellenistic originals). Against the right-hand wall is a marble arch with rich relief decoration, part of the Palace of Galerius in Salonika (early 4C AD), discovered in 1957; on the left is shown Thessalonica personified; on the right, a portrait of the emperor; on the sides Pan and a dancer. Beside are two engaged capitals with figures. Cases against the wall contain fine glass objects mainly from excavations on the site of new University buildings; also Hellenistic pottery including a mould-made 'Megarian' bowl with scenes in relief of the Trojan War.—R. 6. Portrait statues and heads, mainly of 1C AD, with two fine figures of Augustus and (headless) possibly Claudius.—R. 7. Later portrait heads: Girl, with pendant ear-rings, her fashionably dressed hair and petulant expression realistically caught; other fine female heads; statue of the Emp. Hadrian (?); *Bronze head of a man (the Emp. Gallienus ?) from Riakia (Pieria).—R. 8. By the wall are two fine busts of a man and a woman (late 4C AD). In a case is Byzantine pottery.

From R. 7 a door to the left of the entrance leads via a corridor to a spectacular exhibition of finds from the *Royal Tombs of Verghina (see Rte 61) and other rich Late Classical and Hellenistic material. The corridor has photographs and a model of the site. Amongst the spectacular objects on display are a ceremonial shield of intricate workmanship, a gold wreath, gorytus and casket, ivory figures of the Macedonian Royal Family, armour and metal vessels—all from the Tomb of Philip II. Also to be noted are a gold medallion with the head of Philip and the famous Dherveni crater (4C), a bronze vessel with appliqué statuettes and silver ornamentation. A further gallery beyond the Verghina room is at present closed.

Returning to the vestibule we enter the INNER ROOMS which are occupied by a modern display of finds from the rich Late Archaic/Early Classical cemetery discovered in 1980 in the NW suburb of *Síndhos*. Of the 121 graves excavated, objects from 36 are displayed. The tombs varied greatly in quantity of grave goods. Some had only a few vases; the contents of others (e.g. Tomb 67) occupy several showcases. The finds include gold funerary masks, silver vessels, gold and silver jewellery, bronze vessels, weapons and armour (helmets with gold trimmings). Also model furniture in iron, and carts (one exceptionally fine, with three terracotta mules, from Tomb 59). These probably reflect the expected activities on the deceased in the next world. There are many clay figurines and fine vases.

On the far corner stands YMCA Headquarters, behind which the *Municipal Library* (open 8–1, 4–8) faces on to the beginning of the Tsimiski.

C. Tour of the Ramparts

The Byzantine *Ramparts* seem to have taken their present course in the reign of Theodosius (AD 379–395). Whether this perpetuates an enceinte of Kassander is uncertain, but here and there well-laid courses of Hellenistic masonry remain. Their 4C length are c 8 kilometres, about half of which survives, with upwards of 40 towers, almost all square, spaced very irregularly at distances varying between 7·6m and 128m. The construction consists largely of rubble with courses of brick, though in places it is entirely of brick, sometimes with rows of brick arches to give added strength. This device (which enables the wall to remain standing even if the base is sapped) was not again revived in Europe until the 12–13C. Inscriptions survive from a number of rebuildings. The walls stand to a height of 7·6–15·2m, though the upper courses are largely 14C or 15C work with restorations. In places 3·7–5·5m from the wall, can be traced an outwork (proteichisma) designed to deny access to enemy battering rams. All the major gates have now disappeared.

From the White Tower we take LEOFÓROS VASILÍSSIS SOFÍAS (Pl. 16). The ancient ramparts, here almost completely vanished, followed the line of the next street to the W. The Plateía Kalamarías occupies the site of the Kassandreia Gate on the Egnatía Odhós, one of four gates in the E wall. It is known by an inscription to have been repaired by Abp Eusebius in the 6C. To the left we catch a glimpse of the Arch of Galerius. Odhós Panepistimíou continues NE alongside gardens in which short sections of the wall are preserved. To the right extends the site.

The **Aristotelian University of Salonika** (Pl. 12), founded in 1925 and removed here in the following year to the building, the former *Turkish Military Academy*, that faces the road. The university now occupies a huge precinct covering much of the former Jewish cemetery, systematically desecrated by the Germans in 1943. Among the more striking new buildings are the circular *Meteorological Observatory* and the huge *Polytechnic School*. The *Library* contains 300,000 books. Passing between the *Chemical Faculty* and the *Central Hospital* we bear left across a square where Odhós Ayíou Dhimitríou once threaded the walls by the Gate of the Archangels.

A little to the N a red house in Odhós Apostólou Pávlou (next to the Turkish Consulate) is the *Birthplace of Mustafa Kemal* (Atatürk; 1881–1938), first President of Turkey. A plaque was placed here in 1933. Kemal, the son of a government clerk, spent his childhood in the city and attended the Military Cadet School. In 1907–11 he was posted to the Turkish Third Army (then in Salonika), and took part in the march to Constantinople that overthrew Abdul Hamid.— Near by is the 14C church of *Ayios Nikólaos Orfanós* where the contemporary frescoes were successfully cleaned in 1963.

From the road to the left of the *Evangelistria Cemetery* the first lane (left) leads shortly to the walls, here partly hidden by popular occupation. We may follow the cobbled Odhós Athinas inside them or, better, the path outside, parallel to a new road that ascends past the grounds of the *Municipal Hospital* (Pl. 4). Here the walls become continuous with sections remaining to the battlements. Part of an inscription, 9m long in brick, high up on the *Hormisdas Tower* reads τείχεσιν αρρήκτοις εΟρμίσδας ξετέλεσε τήνδε πόλιν (by indestructible walls Hormisdas completely fortified this town). Hormisdas the Younger held various offices in Salonika and Constantinople under Theodosius. The *Chain Tower* (Gingirli Koule), so called from the heavy stringcourse half way up, is a circular keep of the 15C, contemporary with the White Tower, and probably replaced a corner tower destroyed in 1430. To the left of its modern steps some regular masonry appears to be of classical date. We may pass inside the circuit through a gap in the wall or continue round the outside of the Acropolis.

The **Acropolis** still retains the greater part of its wall, though on the E side it is largely Turkish. The long section facing N is of greater interest. We may enter from within the city (see below), or from outside, beyond the Chain Tower, by the *Gate of Anna Palaeologus*, first opened in 1355 by the widow of Andronikos III. It preserves a Byzantine inscription. The triangle here, where the Acropolis wall meets the city wall, probably is to be identified with the *Trigonion* where the storming Turks gained entry in 1430. Within the Acropolis unremarkable suburban villas climb haphazard to the *Eptapirghion* (Yedi Koule), a fortress with seven towers, that crowns the summit. The massive central tower bears an Arabic inscription recording its construction in 1431 by Sungur Çauş Bey. The stronghold still serves as a prison (no adm.). Outside the Acropolis the barren countryside extends to the walls; in the cold winter of 1961 jackals were seen on the fringes of the city.

Odhós Eptapirghíou follows the excellently preserved *South Wall* of the Acropolis, which is also of the main circuit of the city. Steps mount to the top, where the walk within the inner and outer parapets, accessible for c 100m, commands the Acropolis; hence in 1345 the enraged mob hurled the nobles on to stakes below. The original towers face towards the Acropolis which, more vulnerable to an expected assault from the landward, might be invested first. In the 14C when the likelier danger had proven to be from the sea, four shallow towers were added on the seaward side. The second one bears

the device of Andronikos II Palaeologus. A small secret *Postern* su:
vives between the second and third. A modern gate has been opene
towards the W end, nearly opposite which stands the *Moni Vlataío*
(or Vlatadhon; Pl. 3), a monastery which takes name from its foundatio
in the 14C by the Cretan brothers Vlatades. Since the church is ded
cated to the Transfiguration, they were probably Hesychasts. Largel
rebuilt in 1801, the church (originally on the plan of Ayia Ekaterin
preserves original frescoes in the bema and in the paracclesion to th
right. The monastic buildings will house a Patriarchal Academy
Patristic Studies. Farther along Odhós Eptapirghíou, the wall is part
hidden by old houses.

A lane leads (left) to **Osios David** (Pl. 2), a tiny church probably dating from th
late 5C, though its foundation is attributed by tradition to Theodora, daughter
Galerius. In medieval times it served the Moni Latómou. Its plan, an inscribe
cross of Syrian type and unusually early date, was mutilated when it became
mosque. In 1921 beneath plaster in the apse was discovered a *Mosaic, contem
porary with the church, of Christ, depicted beardless, between Ezekiel an
Habakkuk. It appears to interpret the visions of Ezekiel I and II in the spirit of th
New Testament, for the two prophets can also represent SS. Paul and Peter. La
12C frescoes of exceptional quality were recently discovered in the S vault. The
show the Baptism, Nativity and Presentation.

We may pass outside the walls again by the *Eski Delik*, an ancie
gate, later blocked, then reopened by the Turks. The N walls follo
the rugged natural contour. The two abrupt angles of the salient W
the gate are exceptionally furnished with polygonal towers, one with
postern. Just beyond the second is the triangular *Tower of Manu
Palaeologus* (c 1230), on which (6m up) can be seen an inscription
four lines coupling his name with that of George Apokaukos, probabl
governor of the city. The ramparts facing NE and N, pierced by th
Turkish *Yeni Delik* (New Gate), incorporate numerous vestiges of He
lenistic masonry and one section of Roman construction. A little di
tance from the wall is **Ayía Ekateríni** (Pl. 5), a pretty church of simila
plan to the Dhodeka Apostoloi (see below) without a narthex. Th
outer walk has arcades, closed externally with glass, and surmounte
by a wavy cornice. The church dates from the late 13C; the contempo
rary paintings were much spoiled during its time as the *Yakob Pash
Cami* after 1510.

The extreme NW corner of the ramparts is furnished with mo
frequent towers and protected by an outwork. The *Letaia Gate*, with
hexagonal barbican, has been reduced to ruin in this century; the
remains some pseudo-isodomic masonry incorporating reused class
ical blocks. A few metres inside the gate is the ***Dhódheka Apóstol**
(Pl. 5), the least restored and perhaps the most charming of Salonika
churches. Founded by the Patriarch Niphou (1312–15), it was
monastic church until its conversion to the Mohammedan rite as th
Soouk Sou Cami. The E end has richly patterned brickwork. Roun
three sides of the central cross-in-square runs an outer aisle havin
four corner domes. The narthex has an arcaded façade. The inne
dome is borne on four columns with capitals from an earlier edific
The wall paintings, extensive but damaged, include a Tree of Jesse
the S aisle. The four barrel vaults that support the drum have livel
mosaics. S Vault. Nativity, with a bucolic shepherd and soulful an
mals; the handmaiden Salome prepares a bath; the midwife tests th
temperature of the water, while the Child apprehensively turns awa
The Transfiguration is powerfully composed.

Just below are the *Loutrá Phoenix* with an attractive dome.

We descend Odhós Irínis, where an animated fruit market largely masks the wall, to PLATEÍA METAXÁ (Pl. 9), or Axíou, the busy W entrance to the city. A *Statue of Constantine*, liberator of Salonika, occupies the site of the sculptured Golden Gate of the Flavian epoch, described and drawn by 19C travellers, but since totally demolished.

Here converge the two principal routes into the city. To the N in Odhós Langadhá stands a fine *Memorial* (1962) to the 50,000 Salonikan Jews who perished in the gas chambers of Auschwitz. The monument, a monolithic block of Pentelic marble, was designed by the Italian architect, Manfredo Portino.—To the NW Odhos Monastiríou leads shortly to the *Railway Station*.

From the square, Odhós Frángon follows the line of the early Byzantine walls, fragments of which survive in the derelict *Top Hane*, the Turkish fort and arsenal, and near the Roman Catholic Church. Between here and the modern harbour lay the classical port, silted up in the Middle Ages. Here now extends an interesting quarter of Turkish warehouses, threaded by streets paved with lava.

In the nearer suburbs of Salonika there are two British Military Cemeteries of the First World War. The *Zeitenlik* or *Lembet Road Cemetery*, off the W side of the Serres road, contains 1648 British graves; the *Monastir Road Indian Cemetery*, km from the centre beyond the station; commemorates 520 fallen. Other cemeteries are situated at Mikra (see below; 1900 burials) and near Khortiatis (see below; 586 graves).

D. Excursions from Salonika

. TO AYIA TRIAS AND THE THERMAIC GULF. Road 29km (18 miles), bus in summer; also by motor-boat. We leave the city by the long Leofóros Megálou Alexándrou (once briefly renamed after John Kennedy) which, behind the waterfront esplanade, takes eastbound traffic (return by the older Leof. Vasilíssis Olgas, parallel inland). Soon a turning goes off left for *Pilaía* (12,015 inhab.) and *Panórama* (see below); between the two is *Anatolia College*, an American school for boys and girls. It was founded (as a boys' school) in 1886 in Asia Minor and removed to Salonika after the First World War.—The main road keeps inland of Aretsou and continues through lengthening ribbon development.—At 7km a road leads left (1km) to the *American Farm School* (Amerikániki Yeoryikí Skholí), founded in 1903 by John Henry House in order to introduce modern methods into Greece (c 800 students; visit on application to the Director). We pass the *Army Staff College* and just touch the shore.—10km The Northern HQ of the Hellenic Air Force stands where the road to Poliyiros diverges left (Rte 64A).—11km Turning (right) for the Airport; beside the road is the very prominent *Tsairi Toumba*. Other mounds can be seen as we skirt the airport.—At 16km the road to Nea Moudhiana and Kassandra bears left.—We continue past turns to *Peraía* (Hotels B, C), with a relay station of the American radio, and *Néoi Epivátai*, both popular beach resorts.—23km (14½ miles) **Ayía Triás** (Hotels B, C) has a large camp site and bathing beach of the N.T.O.G., and a Youth Hostel.—Beyond Ayía Triás is a turn (unpaved) for *Angelokhóri*, a centre of tomato and cucumber growing; before the village a track leads (right) to Cape Megálo Karabournoú, site of ancient *Dinaion*. The main road continues to (29km) *Néa Mikhanióna*, a busy small fishing town on the open gulf, with many shaded restaurants just above the long beach.

II. Mount Khortiátis (1201m) rises to the E of Salonika, and separates the Gulf of Salonika from Lake Langadha (Koronia). The summit is in a prohibited zone, but a height of 672m may be reached by road. The approach road quits the N suburbs of Salonika and rises to (9km) Asvestokhórion (Hotel B), a popular summer resort (270m; 2602 inhab.) on the W slope of Profitis Ilias (768m).—14km Near quarries roads descend (right) to Panorama (see below) and, soon after (left) to Ayios Vasílios on the Via Egnatia by the lake (Rte 66).—We pass the remains of an aqueduct and reach (18km) Khortiátis, facing NW on wooded slopes. Thence the road climbs a further 5km to the prohibited zone, affording a fine view over Salonika; there is also a signposted path from Khortiatis to (1¾ hours) a refuge of the Alpine Club.—We may return by taking the S turn at the quarries to reach first Nea Panorama (with the option of bearing left and descending via Thermi, Rte 64), then **Panórama** (Hotel C) just above Anatolia College (comp. above).

III. FROM SALONIKA TO GHEVGELI. Road, 82km (51 miles) and railway (79km in 2 hours). This is the main highway into Yugoslavia and the main railway route to Belgrade by the plain and valley of the Axios (Vardar). To (23km) Yefira, see Rte 60. The road turns N and follows the left bank of the Axios. The river is largely controlled by irrigation and anti-flood works. From Yefira to the border the old road through the villages and the National Highway run parallel. From (39km) Kastanás the railway runs between the roads. To the E are the American drainage works that reduced the former Lake Amatovon. At (53km) Limnótopos, we cross one of the sluices.—60km Polýkastron (Hotels C, D), formerly Karasouli, has an international Military Cemetery with British graves. A large ammunition dump here was blown up in a German air raid in April 1917. The village is at the SW end of Lake Ardzan, also drained, on the N shore of which the Iron Age site of Chauchitsa (Tsaoutsitza) was excavated by the British School in 1921. The railway now crosses to the W of roads and river to follow the Vardar through the Stena Tsingane Derven, a defile 10km long at the E foot of Païkon (with molybdenum mines in the foothills), to the frontier station of Idhoméni. The roads remain E of the isolated Mt Skhóli (354km), passing (69km) Mikró Dhásos, to (74km) **Evzóni** (Hotels B, D, E), beyond which is the frontier post, still on the left bank of the river. The Vardar is crossed on Yugoslav soil.—82km **Ghevgeli** (Motel).

60 From Salónika to Edhessa

ROAD, Via Egnatia, 89km (55 miles), straight and level with a good surface; dual carriageway to Khalkídhon; bus hourly.—RAILWAY, see Rte 61.

We quit Salonika by the Plateía Axíou (Pl. 9) and the Railway Station, at first following the international line to Yugoslavia through industrial suburbs.—At (7km) *Dhiavatá*, road to Kilkis (37km, right). We cross the Serres railway and pass a memorial to French soldiers killed in the First World War. As we cross (11km) the Gallikos, from whose sandy bed small quantities of gold are extracted, the prehistoric mound of *Gradhembórion* can be seen to the N. A road branches left to Síndhos and into the central Pedhias Kampanias (comp. Rte 61).

At (7km) **Síndhos** important cemeteries of late 6–early 5C were discovered in the course of construction work in 1980. The burials which were in stone cists, stone or clay sarcophagi or simple pits, probably belong to the nearby settlement mound of *Néa Ankhíalos*, which is perhaps to be identified with the ancient town of *Chalastra*. Potters' kilns were constructed over the cemetery area in the 4C. For the spectacular finds see description of Thessaloniki Museum.—11km *Pírgos*, another candidate for Chalastra, was on the coast in Classical times. Between Síndhos and Pírgos, Xerxes' fleet lay, waiting for the army to catch up.—15km *Néa Málgara*, a huge refugee settlement amid rice-fields on the right bank of the Axios, is built on land reclaimed since ancient times.—25km *Klidhíon* may represent ancient *Haloros*, where, following preclassical boundaries, the nome of Imathia pushes a narrow tongue to the sea.

14km A large flat mound to the left is called *Trapezoeidés*.—We cross over the National Highway to the frontier (comp. above) and over the railway to Yugoslavia.—24·5km *Yéfira* (right; Motel C), at the junction of the old road to Yugoslavia (spur to the Highway), is (as its name indicates) where the Axios was bridged before its diversion to its modern bed. A prehistoric table-mound and classical finds prove the antiquity of the site; here in 1912 was signed the agreement surrendering Salonika to Greece. About 1·5km farther on irrigation canals carry water from the *Axios River Barrage* (1954–58), situated 3km N of the road (earth approach-road on top of dyke). We cross the Axios by a girder bridge (guard posts; traffic lights) of 14 spans, built by British sappers (228 Army Field Company) in 1945 (plaque, left at bridge entrance).

The **Axios**, or *Vardar*, the largest river in Macedonia, rises deep in Yugoslavia and flows for only 80·5km through Greece from the 'Iron Gates' to the sea. Before the flood and reclamation works, instituted by Venizelos in 1925, gave the river its present bed, the area was largely malarial marshes. Further irrigation works, jointly controlling the Axios and Aliakmon, undertaken in 1953–63 by C. Karamanlis, will bring the greater part under cultivation.

31km (19 miles) *Khalkidhón* (3036 inhab.; Restaurants) grew up after 1923 round the old timber-framed han at the junction where the Via Egnatia and the Veroia road, also of Roman origin or earlier, divided to pass Lake Loudhias. We follow the Via Egnatia. About 1·5km farther on a road diverges to Idomeni. To the S extends a fertile plain, drained by the Loudhias, an artificial river that perpetuates the name of the classical LAKE LOUDHIAS (later Lake Yiannitsa), drained in 1927–36. At an earlier era this was connected with the sea (comp. below). A series of

funeral mounds, to the left of the road, marks the edge of the lake.—
38km (23½ miles) *Pélla* (2272 inhab.).

PÉLLA (Πέλλα), capital of Macedonia at the height of its greatness
and birthplace of Alexander the Great, was formerly connected by a
shallow navigable lagoon with the Thermaic Gulf. Chance finds in
1957 located the exact site of the city, estimated to have occupied 3·8
sq. km; and excavations by Prof. Makaronas and Ph. Petsas in 1957–68
uncovered the celebrated mosaics of c 300 BC which are the principal
artistic attraction of the place so far. The last few years have seen
spectacular further progress in investigation, under Mrs M. Karamanoli-Siganidhou, but much is not yet laid out for visiting.

An earlier settlement called *Bounomeia* by Stephanus Byzantius may have lain to
the S, where prehistoric sherds have come to light. *Pella* is mentioned by Herodotus and has yielded coins from the mid-5C BC. The Macedonian capital was
transferred from Aigai to Pella by Archelaus (413–399 BC), whose artistic entour-
age included the painter Zeuxis, the poet Agathon, who died at the court in 400
and Euripides, who died here in 406. At Pella were born Philip II in 382 and
Alexander the Great in 356. The city flourished especially under Antigonus
Gonatas. It fell to Aemilius Paulus after the Battle of Pydna, and from 148 BC lost
importance to Thessalonica. At one time the Romans called it *Diocletianopolis*; its
site may then have been moved to the W.

The most spectacular finds have come from the N part of three rectangular blocks, cut across by the main road. The richest of the houses
occupying the whole of 'Block 1' immediately behind the 'apotheke'

s the **House of the Lion Hunt**, a building of the late 4C BC, 50m wide
nd more than 90m long, having three open courts running N and S.
Three of its dozen rooms were decorated with mosaics now in the
museum. Fragments of painted plaster, bronze bosses from the doors,
nd terracotta antefixes show it to have been a splendid edifice, and its
tamped roof tiles suggest that it had an official function. The building
s bordered by broad streets lined with clay water-pipes and stone
ewers. Much of the central peristyle (six columns square) has been
e-erected and the great patterned pebble mosaics of the main rooms
estored.

Block 5 (two blocks to the W) has yielded a further range of mosaics.
The Rape of Helen (Pl. D) and Stag Hunt (Pl. E), originally lifted, had
een restored to position.

The extensive *agora* lies to the NE of the main site, and W of the road leading up
o the modern village of Pella. It occupied five insulae of the town grid and over
0,000 sq. metres. The large square was surrounded by Doric porticoes, with
hops, workshops (potters, coroplasts) etc. behind. On the N side was a *Temple
f Aphrodite and Cybele*. The main street of the town traversed the agora, with a
monumental gateway at the E.
To the NW is a *Sanctuary of Demeter and Kore*, circular, with an altar at the
entre: this is still being excavated.
On the *Acropolis* which occupied a hill to the W of the modern village, some
istance to the N of the fenced site, a large and important complex, almost
ertainly a palace, is being investigated. It is hard to identify it with the *Palace of
rchelaos*, painted by Zeuxis, where Alexander was born in 356 BC, since it
eems only to have been built about that time (and substantially altered in the
llowing century). It consists of two large square units side by side. The E had
ooms round the court and was probably residential; the W only colonnades. The
wo elements are linked by a monumental façade and entrance which had a
alcony of Doric columns.
Other houses, and sections of the defences, have been located 200m to the S of
e Museum. No trace has yet been found of the theatre where the Bacchae of
uripides received its first performance in c 408 BC.

Among the finds displayed in the *Museum* are the superb *Mosaics
rom Blocks 1 and 5. The life-size figures are fashioned with natural
ebbles of various colours; special features are outlined with strips of
ead or clay. The eyes (all missing) were probably semi-precious sto-
es. The positions from which the mosaics came are indicated on the
lan. Lion Hunt (Pl. C), perhaps the rescue of Alexander himself by
rateros near Susa; Dionysos on a leopard's back (Pl. B); Griffin
ttacking a deer (Pl. A); Amazonomachia (Pl. F).

ROOM 1. Griffin and deer mosaic. Restored wall painting from a
ouse (architectural motifs). Sculpture, including a head of Alexander
e Great, a fine seated female figure and a marble dog (460–50 BC)
rom a cemetery. Inlaid table. Architectural fragments, antefixes and
oof tiles (inscribed).

ROOM 2. Lion Hunt and Dionysos mosaics. Grave stelai. Marble
Hellenistic statuette of horseman; marble measure for liquid. Archi-
ectural fragments.

ROOM 3. Case with fine Hellenistic 'West Slope' style vases from a
vell in the agora. Silver coins. Gold jewellery. Remarkable series of
Hellenistic and Early Roman terracotta figures and, in some cases, the
noulds from which they were made, from coroplast's workshop in the
gora; including representations of Athena with a horned helmet.
Marble figure of Hekate. Pottery and small finds.

o the S of the road, rising above the drained marsh, is a small green mound,
riginally the late-Helladic settlement of *Phacos*. On it was later built a fortified
easury that served the Macedonian kings and is described by Livy.

39·5km *Néa Pélla* (right) is a refugee settlement. By the road are th
so-called *Baths of Alexander*, a Hellenistic fountain, repaired by th
Romans; here probably Aemilius Paulus pitched camp and a Roma
settlement developed.—48km (29¾ miles) **Yiannitsá** (Γιαννιτσά
or Γενιτσά; Hotel C), seat of an eparchy and the largest town (21,08
inhab.) in the nome of Pella, lies to the right of the road. As *Yenicey*
Vardar it was a holy place of the Turks. In an ill-used mosque are th
tombs of the Evrenos family (14–15C), descendants of the conqueror c
Macedonia. A bronze *Monument* by the road commemorates the Batt
le of Yiannitsa (1912), which ensured the liberation of Salonika. Th
battle actually took place at (53km) *Melíssi*, where the Turks fiercel
contested the crossing of the Balítsa.—56km *Kariótissa*. To the N,
10km away, *Meterizi* (1597m), the third highest peak of the *Páïko*
Mts, rises abruptly from the plain. Mt Páïkon itself (behind right) i
1649m. We cross two of the large flood canals that channel to th
Aliakmon the waters of the Vodas, the Moglenitsa, and countless
mountain streams from Vermion that once inundated the plain
Edhessa and its waterfalls are seen ahead.—We meet the railway fror
Veroia at (73km) *Skídhra* (Hotels C, E), a fruit grading and cannin
centre (4319 inhab.). The road from Veroia (see below) is joined at th
S end of the bridge spanning the Vodas.—75km *Mavrovoúnio*
stands on the N bank. Orchards of peaches and pears extend along th
road. Beyond (83km) *Rizárion* the valley becomes lush as we agai
cross the copious streams of the Vodas below Edhessa's falls. A shor
steep hill mounts to the ridge.

89km (55¾ miles) **EDHESSA** (Hotels B, D, E) is beautifull
situated above a steep bluff, facing SE, over which the waters of th
Edhesseos fall into the Salonikan plain. The town itself occupies
semi-circular plateau (350m), backed by the foothills of Mt Vermior
Through it flow numerous cascades which gave it its Slav name c
Vodena (The Waters). Capital of the nome of Pella and seat of a metro
politan, the town (16,054 inhab.) is a favourite summer resort. Its com
manding situation on the Via Egnatia has always given it strategi
importance. Its industries include the manufacture of carpets, and it i
a prominent trading and agricultural centre. The view from the tow:
takes in the Pindos on the W, Olympos to the SE, and the height
beyond Salonika to the E.

History. Until the discoveries in 1977 at Vergina, *Edessa* was thought to be th
site of ancient Aigai, a belief the local inhabitants are disinclined to relinquish.
was a flourishing place in antiquity. During the temporary Bulgarian occupatio
it was called *Vodena*. In October 1912 the Greek army entered the town. It wa
re-occupied by Bulgarians in the Second World War.

The numerous streams that score the town unite on the E to fall i
cascades. To see them, we go to the cemetery and then turn right at th
chapel. Thence a path leads direct to the *Falls*. The drop is 24m, afte
which the water descends steeply to the plain. The cliffs are covere
with luxuriant vegetation, including vines, pomegranates, figs, an
nut-trees. There are said to be crayfish in the waters. The volume c
the cascades is diminished by hydroelectric works. Under the falls is
cave with stalactites. Odhós Makedhonomákhon has attractive ol
houses. From the terrace near the *Archbishop's Palace*, farther to th
right, there is a splendid *View*, with the attractive *Monastery c
Kaisarianá* in the foreground. The church of *Koímisis tis Panayías*, now
the archiepiscopal chapel, incorporates antique columns, probabl
from a temple on the site and has a good ikonostasis. Traces of th
city's medieval walls can be seen in the lane descending to the right

At the N end of the town is a fine single-span *Bridge*, of Roman or Byzantine date, which carried the Via Egnatia. Some Roman inscriptions and 5C mosaics found in 1963 are stored in an attractive 15C mosque, behind the Clock Tower.

The ancient circuit of the lower city was traced in 1968 in the Longos' area below the falls. The recent excavations (free; Phylax on site) near Ayía Triádha should not be missed. They are reached by taking the Salonika road for 5km and, at a sharp bend, turning left down a by-road. The site has a remarkable stretch of wall incorporating a cave shrine; a gate leads to a paved main street having an Ionic colonnade (inscriptions).—The road continues to the hydroelectric works (no adm.) but a right fork leads to the foot of the falls. By the huge pipe are remains of a marble Byzantine Church.

From Edhessa a road leads N, followed by a bus (6 times daily) to (24km) **Aridhaía** (Hotels B, C, D, E), or *Ardhéa*, seat with 4205 inhab. of the eparchy of *Almopías*, in a low well-watered plain hemmed in by the magnificent crests of the Vóras range that form the Yugoslav frontier. Here are grown pimentos, tobacco, and silk. The French built a Decauville railway from Skidhra to serve the area in the First World War; this survived as a passenger line until 1935.—A road goes on W to *Loutrá Aridhaías* (11km), a large hydropathic establishment in a pretty glen with plane trees shading the tumbling waters.

To *Naousa* and *Veroia*, see Rte 61.

61   From Salónika to Véroia (and Edhessa)

ROAD, 75km (46½ miles), leaving the Via Egnatia (Rte 60) at (30·5km) *Khalkidhón*, and continuing, flat and monotonous, to (75km) **Véroia**. BUS every ½ hour.

RAILWAY, 69km (43 miles), 6–8 trains daily in c 70 minutes; the line branches from the Athens line at (19km) *Platí* and runs 1·5–5km S of the road most of the way to (69km) *Véroia*. Beyond Veroia the railway continues N via Naousa to (111km) *Edhessa*.

From Salonika to 30·5km *Khalkidhón*, see Rte 60. The road traverses the PEDHIAS KAMPANIAS, an exposed plain of exceptional flatness, that extends to the Gulf of Salonika; it was once a lagoon into which both the Axios and Aliakmon drained, and as late as classical times was navigable nearly to Pella. The settlement of *Adhendron* ('without trees'), on the railway (left), is aptly named. We cross the *Loudhias*, an artificial river created in 1925 (comp. Rte 60), and enter the ancient district of *Emathia*, a monotonous country populated by herds of buffalo and goats, which gives name to the modern nome.—43·5km Turning for *Platí* (3km left), an important railway junction (comp. above; 2088 inhab.) with a sugar refinery.—At 49km the old road to Athens forks left through *Alexándreia* (Hotels D, E), or *Yídha*, a sprawling agricultural town (pop. 10,543).—66km We cross the sluice by which the waters of the Vodas are diverted to the Aliakmon. At *Néa Nikomídhia*, 4km N, a neolithic settlement was laid bare in 1961–64 by a combined team from the British and American Schools. Radio-carbon tests have given a date of c 6200 BC, by far the earliest Neolithic known on the Greek mainland though Palaeolithic sites have since been located in Epirus. Houses of two periods were found, arranged round a central structure which yielded female idols and serpentine axes. The settlement was fortified.—At (72km) we pass close to *Véroia Station* (right), leave the Vergina road (see below) to the left, join that from Edhessa, and enter Véroia from the North.

75km (46½ miles) **VÉROIA** (Βέροια), anciently Βέρροια, the *Berea* of the New Testament, and nowadays pronounced Vérria, is the capital of the nome of Imathia and the seat of a metropolitan. Situated on a travertine terrace (188m) near the E foot of Mt Vermion, it serves as a base for skiers. Water from the Tripotamos, a tributary of the Aliakmon, runs through the streets. Cloth handicrafts are worked from hemp and flax spun locally, and the town (pop. 37,087) has a market (Tuesday) for peaches and apples from the district. Its appearance is changing rapidly from ramshackle vernacular to undistinguished modernity.

Hotels C, D.

Post Office, Leof. Mitropóleos.

Buses to *Vergina*, also to *Naousa* and *Edhessa* (regularly) from Ayios Antónios; to *Salonika* and to *Kozani* (frequently) from the Plateia Orologíou.

History. *Beroea* emerges at the end of the 5C as the second city of Emathia, known from an inscription to have been dedicated to Herakles Kynagidas. It was the first Macedonian city to surrender after the Roman victory of Pydna in 168 BC. Pompey here spent the winter of 49–48 BC. St. Paul and Silas, having experienced trouble at Thessalonika, withdrew to Beroea, where the Jews, more noble than those of Thessalonika, searched the scriptures daily (Acts XVII, 10–12). At an early date Beroea became a bishopric. When Diocletian reorganised the Roman colonial empire, he made Beroea one of the two capitals of Macedonia. About the end of the 10C it endured the Bulgar invasions, and in the 14C was occupied by the Serbs. The Turks, who called the town *Karaferiye*, established here a military colony.

At the top of the hill at the entrance to the town remnants of the ramparts survive. A *Tower*, of pseudo-isodomic construction resembling the Letaia Gate at Salonika has been dated to the 3C AD; among reused blocks are incorporated grave reliefs and shield metopes. Odhos Venizelou leads straight down to the centre, but it is pleasanter to take the broad road to the left. This curves round to form an esplanade where ramparts once overlooked the plain. Here the **Museum** stands in a garden lined with inscribed tombstones from Roman and later times. Displayed within are Geometric brooches, breast ornaments and weapons from tombs at Vergina and Levkadhia; Neolithic finds from Nea Nikomidhia; Roman portraits and sculptural fragments found in Veroia; also a stele (2C BC) inscribed with the rules of the Gymnasion; and the painted roof from the destroyed church of Ayii Fotini.

Farther on the garden suburb of ELIÁ has a belvedere and tourist pavilion. The broad Leoforos Ilias runs up to meet Venizelou at the centre of the town. Hence Mitropoleos rises gently past a Byzantine church and the modern Cathedral (re-used capitals in the narthex) to the Plateia Orologiou, site of the Kastro, now partly occupied by law courts. Behind the Hawaii Restaurant by the side of a mosque and minaret is the so-called *Bema* (a fanciful reconstruction of 1961) from which St. Paul is said to have preached. From the W corner of the square the narrow Odhos Kentrikos leads N to the *Old Metropoli* (closed and decaying), with Early Christian columns and a minaret opposite which stands the *Plane tree* from which the Turks hanged Abp Kallimachos in 1436. Beyond the remnants of the old lower town

The numerous churches of wattle and timber construction were the most unusual feature of the lower town. Built during the Turkish domination, they were sited inconspicuously behind houses and their appearance disguised. Formerly they were hard to find. Most of the ramshackle old houses have recently been replaced by modern blocks and the churches revealed. They have been over restored but (though supposedly open at museum hours) are usually locked.

THE PRINCIPAL EXCURSIONS are to Mt Vermion and to the Macedonian tombs at Vergina and Levkadhia.

Royal and noble *Macedonian Tombs*, subterranean like those of Mycenae, were splendid structures, built of local poros stone, with a vaulted roof. Smaller tombs have a pediment or a simply sculptured cornice. Later and grander examples take the form of the classical temple having a complete façade with columns, entablature, the pediment. The doors were generally of marble and hung on metal hinges. The chamber within was furnished with marble couches or thrones; its walls were usually plastered and painted. The façade may also be frescoed. Some twenty or more tombs have so far been excavated in Macedonia, of which the most important and accessible are those near Veroia.

The road to Vergina (11km; bus 8 times daily) quits Véroia near the Tourist Pavilion, passing Lofos Vikellis, with the birthplace of the writer Konstantinos Vikelas (1808–86). The house is preserved.—5km Ayía Varvára has a spring and a café. The Piéria Mts stand out ahead. We descend to the *Aliakmon Barrage*, a graceful concrete structure, 320m long, whose 19 piers carry the road across the river. The curved approach on the N side was made necessary by the discovery during construction of a *Temple Tomb* (visible left; no adm.) of the 3C BC. The outer doorway has triglyphs, the inner doorway is white with a yellow moulding. The interior is plastered and painted in bands, white below, black and red above. At the end of the bridge we turn left.

11km **Vergína** (Βεργίνα), a refugee village of 1923, named after a legendary queen of Beroia, replaces a city that existed from the beginning of the Iron Age to Classical times. This is now considered with some certainty to have been *Aigai*, which Perdikkas, founder of the Macedonian monarchy, made his capital.

The residence of the kings until the seat of government was transferred to Pella, it remained the national sanctuary and the royal burial-place. Here Philip II was assassinated in 336 BC. A tradition that the Macedonian dynasty would perish as soon as one of the kings was buried elsewhere was given point by the chaos that followed the burial of Alexander the Great in Asia. The place was pillaged by Gaulish mercenaries left to guard it by Pyrrhus in 274/3 BC.

The **Great Tumulus** (not accessible to visitors) which, until its excavation, covered the smaller mound overlying the **Royal Tombs**, may well have been ordered by Antigonos Gonatas to protect his own tomb and cover the damage by the Gauls. Broken tombstones from their destruction were found in the fill. Of the four tombs covered by the smaller mound, two are of particular interest. One (otherwise looted of its contents) has fine wall paintings including a remarkable scene of the Rape of Persephone by Hades. Greatest interest has however attached to the other, unlooted and with a hunting scene over the façade, which most authorities now consider to be the burial place of Philip II. Within were found two marble sarcophagi containing burial caskets of gold, and all the panoply of royal burial: purple and gold cloth (now finely restored) shrouding the bones, gold wreaths, sceptre, miniature ivory portraits from a throne or bier (apparently representing members of the Macedonian Royal Family), armour, weapons, a ceremonial shield with exquisite decoration, and silver and bronze vessels. The **Finds** are on display in Salonika. Apart from the archaeological dating and the general character of the contents, a remarkable reconstruction of the features of the male occupant of the tomb, using forensic methods (J.H.S. 1984), has indicated a horrific eye wound such as Philip is known to have suffered in his lifetime.

*Vergina. Tomb painting of the Rape of Persephone by
Hades*

The inaccessibillity of the tombs with their fine architecture and wall painting
can be countered by perusal of the excellently illustrated book *Vergina: th*
Royal Tombs by the excavator, M. Andronikos. Other Macedonian tombs hav
recently been discovered in the vicinity of the Great Tumulus.

The so-called PALACE OF PALATITSA (named after the old village t
the NE at its first discovery in 1861 by a French expedition) is situate
on a low hill to the SE marked by a large oak-tree. Excavations of th
Greek Archaeological Service in 1937–40 were resumed in 1954–61
The building, roughly 90m square, dates probably from the reign o
Antigonus Gonatas and was destroyed by fire. The N side, where th
lower courses of the outer wall are well preserved, is littered wit
poros drums and capitals. A triple *Propylaia* leads through the E win
to a central *Peristyle* of pilasters (16 by 16) having double engage
columns. On the S side is a *Mosaic Floor* finely executed in polych
rome pebbles. Below the Palace and 100m to the N a small 4C theatr
was discovered in 1982. The location of this in relation to the palac
closely accords with the account of the assassination of Philip which

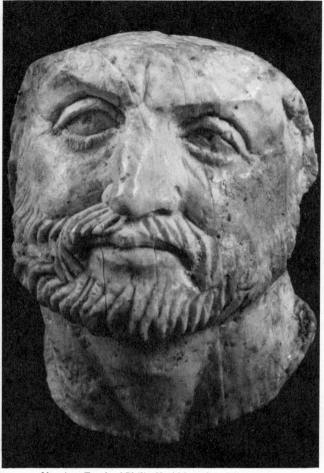

Vergina, Tomb of Philip II of Macedon. Miniature ivory head of Philip

took place in the theatre of Aigai in 336.—Between the palace and the village extends a vast tumulus CEMETERY of the Early Iron Age (10–7C BC) excavated by Prof. M. Andronikos in 1952–61. Of the hundreds of mounds, many were disturbed in Hellenistic times, but intact burials have yielded iron swords, bronze ornaments (including a triple double-axe amulet), Lausitz ware, and Protogeometric pottery. We descend the right side of a ravine to the *Tomb of Vergina, a Macedonian temple tomb with an Ionic façade closed by two pairs of marble doors. Within, a marble *Throne, 1·8m high, with a footstool, has arms supported by carved sphinxes and a back with painted decoration.— Another tomb of this type has been found to the E of Palatitsa.

Vergina. Reconstruction of the Tomb of Philip

FROM VEROIA TO EDHESSA, 47km (29 miles). From Ay. Antonios the
road leads N across the Tripotamos, then follows the railway.—13km
Náousa Station lies off the road (right). The flourishing town (19,383
inhab.) of **Náousa** (*Kioski Restaurant*, good; bus from the station)
stands 6·5km W on a travertine terrace between two tributaries of the
Arapitsa, one of which falls near by in a cascade. The town is
renowned for its full red wine, its peaches, and its silk. Naousa is a
corruption of *Nea Augousta* and has been known to the Turks as
Agustos; it occupies an ancient site, perhaps that of *Mieza* (but comp
below). The town was destroyed in 1821 and again suffered in 1944–
48 but its narrow streets remain on an old plan. In its carnival masked
dancers with scimitars symbolise the oppression of the Janissaries.
Near the modern church of *Ayía Paraskeví* a fine park looks out over
the plain and there is small military museum. The wooden Ayios
Dhimítrios is built over an ancient edifice.

At (14km) *Kopanós* an important cemetery (4C to Hellenistic) was
discovered in 1977. The settlement with which it is to be associated

may lie beneath the modern village.—16km **Levkádhia**, a hamlet W of the road, has given name to three Macedonian tombs, lying near the main road before we reach the village turn. The discovery of a building with mosaics S of the village and another on a hill near the Arapitsa suggest that Levkadhia was a place of some importance, perhaps the ancient *Mieza* where Aristotle taught. The tombs are usually locked and it is necessary to locate the phylax to have them opened. Signposted (right, on a by-road crossing the railway) is the 'Great Tomb', protected by a concrete hangar (sometimes closed). This is the largest *TEMPLE TOMB so far unearthed.

On the *Façade* two outer pilasters and four Doric fluted columns support an entablature with painted metopes and triglyphs and a frieze in bas-relief depicting a battle between Macedonians and Persians. A second (Ionic) story, rising above the vault, has seven false doors surmounted by a pediment (of which only fragments survive). Two life-size frescoes in vivid colours represent (left) the deceased with Hermes Psychopompos and (right) Aiakos and Rhadamanthys, the judges of the Underworld. An ante-chamber leads to a square barrel-vaulted *Chamber* with painted panels between engaged pilasters. Rows of nails remain *in situ* where presumably garlands were hung. The tomb is dated to the beginning of the 3C BC.

Beside the main road, 200m farther N, is the '*Kinch*' *Tomb*, and 300m beyond this (left; signposted) is a much smaller vaulted *Lyson Kallikles Tomb* of the early 2C BC, plain without, which held the urn burials of three related families. Their names are inscribed on the niches inside, and the walls are painted with garlands and decorative panels. Another tomb found in 1971 has good paintings and ivory sculptures.

At (32km) *Skídhra* (see Rte 60) we join the Via Egnatia.—47km *Edhessa*.

Mt Vermion (2027m) is the most densely forested mountain in Greece, with beech, oak, chestnut, pine, hazel, whitethorn, cornel-cherry, and evergreen maquis, in which dwell roedeer, red deer, and wild pig. It is approached from Veroia (farther, but newer road) or from Naousa, whence a steep road mounts to (18km) *Seli* (Refuge, 18 beds), a village (1420m) on the NE slope. Here winter sports are held from mid January to mid March (Greek ski championship in late February). Chair lifts rise to the ski slopes. In late spring and summer the mountain affords delightful walks.

62 From Salónika to Kozáni and Kastoriá

ROAD, 221km (137 miles). To (30·5km) *Khalkidhón*, see Rte 60; thence to (75km) **Véroia**, see Rte 61. Beyond Veroia broad road through magnificent mountain scenery. 92km *Kastanéa*.—135km **Kozáni**, thence through relatively flat upland country.—155km *Siátista* turning.—178·5km *Neápolis*.—209km *Argos Orestikón*.—220·5km **Kastoriá**. BUS frequently to Kozani; regularly from Kozani to Kastoria.

RAILWAY to *Kozáni* (222km), 4 through trains daily in 4–5 hours. The line follows the road to (69km) *Véroia* (see Rte 61), then turns N to (111km) *Edhessa* (comp. Rte 61), whence it runs W following the road described in Rte 63 to (162km) *Amíndaion*. Here the line divides, the S branch following Rte 58 to *Kozáni*.

From Salonika to (30·5km) *Khalkidhón*, see Rte 60; thence to (75km) **Véroia**, see Rte 61. Beyond Véroia the road winds up past army depots, a reservoir, with a hydro-electric station, and a restaurant with trout pools.—80km *Tripótamos*. Orchards clothe the rolling hills as we climb into the Tripotamos valley, which divides the outlying spur of

Máti Poulioú (left; 1238m) from the main Vermion range.—84km
Yeoryíanoi. A turning (left) crosses a ridge to *Lefkópetra* (5km), but
scanty remains of an ancient temple are hardly worth the diversion.
The road clings to a shelf on the N side of the narrowing valley, which
is beautifully clothed with oak and beech woods.—89km Spring.—
92km **Kastanéa** is magnificently situated up the hillside (902m) amid
orchards of apples and nuts. Above the village stands the *Monastery
of Panayía Soúmela*, built by refugees who brought with them (c 1930)
from the Soumela monastery in Pontus an ikon of the Virgin attributed
to St. Luke. It is a scene of pilgrimage on 15 August.—As we cross the
shoulder of Máti Poulioú, from a height of 1081m there bursts a tremendous * *View into the Aliakmon Valley; the river, just over 3km
away, is more than 914m below. Beyond it the jagged heights of *Piéria*

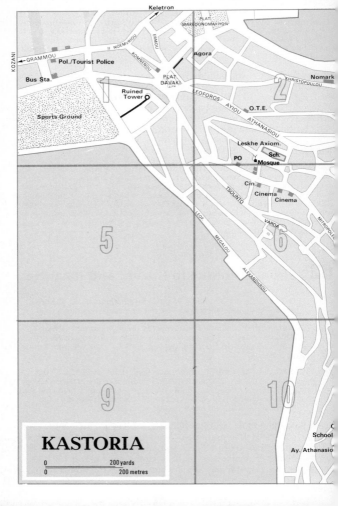

tower to 2190m.—We continue to climb and from the steep turns obtain a retrospective view towards Kastanéa before turning away from the Aliakmon to reach (100km) the road summit (1359m) on *Diavasis Kadovas*, a S ridge of Vermion.—From (101·5km) *Zoödhókhos Piyí* (1359m; Restaurant), which takes name from a small church built above a spring, Mt Olympos is seen to the E behind Pieria. We descend by a spectacular ladder and vertiginous curves.—At (108·5km) *Polímilos*, with water mills, we enter a gentle upland valley with the *Skopós Hills* to the S; the villages lie off the road on their slopes. To the right extends a level plain, where the former *Sarigkiol* ('Yellow Marsh') has been drained.—113km *Voskokhório*. Here a small Christian basilica (? early 6C) came to light in 1935; At *Akríni* (11km right) another, with delightful animal mosaics, was uncovered in 1959.—

The road descends gently with long straight stretches to (127km) *Dhrépanon*. Joining the railway from the N (Rte 58) and the road from Larissa, it enters (135km) **Kozáni**.

Kozani and thence to *Larissa* and to the Yugoslav frontier (*Nikī*), see Rte 58; to *Grevena*, see below.

Beyond Kozani the road maintains a fairly constant level just below 610m all the way to Kastoria, keeping company to *Siátista* with an unfinished railway planned to link *Kozani* with *Kalambaka*.—141km *Vaterón*. A flat-bottomed pass opens between the *Voúrinos* and *Askion* ranges, which extend to N and S.—155km *Khani Bára*. Turning for Siátista (right; 3km).

Siátista (Hotel C) seems to have been settled in the 16C and to have become a caravan centre of merchants trading with Vienna. In the 18C as *Sisechte* it was noted for its wines, tanneries and for industry, but after 1821 it gradually declined. Since its vineyards were destroyed by phylloxera in 1928–35, it has reverted to the fur trade. The town (5702 inhab.), consisting of the two districts of *Khora* and *Yeraneia*, is (like Kastoria) noted for its 18C houses, timber-framed with jutting balconies and gabled roofs. The *Poulikos Mansion*, with an elaborately panelled and frescoed interior, was restored in 1962. The church of *Ayios Dhimítrios*, was founded in 1647, was rebuilt after a fire in 1910; *Ayía Paraskeví* dates from 1677. The *Manousákis Library*, left to the town by the 19C scholar, contains local archaeological finds.

158·5km A *Restaurant* stands at the parting of the ways to Kastoria and Grevena.

FROM THE SIATISTA FORK TO GREVENA AND KALAMBAKA. Road, 98km, mixed asphalt and gravel; bus from Kozani 6 times daily to Grevena, once to Kalambaka. We turn S and cross the Aliakmon. The road continues sinuous and undulating below the foothills of the Pindus W of the river.—Beyond (16km) *Vatólakkos* we enter the valley of the Greveniotikos.—28km **Grevená** (601m; Hotels C, D) is the chief town (7433 inhab.) of a mainly agricultural nome that corresponds roughly to the ancient district of *Elimeiotis*. It has a school of forestry. The town, at the confluence of two branches of the Greveniotikos, is the focal point of numerous mountain tracks. It was a centre of Greek learning in the Middle Ages and the headquarters of the Armatoles, an irregular militia of Byzantine times, kept up by the Turks, from whose ranks arose the patriotic brigand, or klepht. A comparable situation arose in 1944–49 with the German retreat, when ELAS supporters fought the established government. We descend into the curious eroded grey gorge of the Venetikos, which we cross; visible are the remains of two previous bridges. We now climb again into wooded uplands with views towards the Aliakmon.—60km Road to Dheskati and Elasson (see Rte 58).—71km *Ayiófillon* is on the low watershed that divides the Aliakmon basin from that of the Pinios. By-road (left) to Deskati (comp. above).—At 88km near the Meteora, we join the road from Ioannina (Rte 51B).—98km *Kalambaka*.

We turn NW into upland country, drained by the upper Aliakmon, where hamlets are frequent.—165km *Midhrókastron*. Far to the W is seen the distant *Smolikas* (comp. below), usually snow capped.—168km *Kalonérion* heralds, as its name suggests, a greener and more fertile countryside. We cross the Aliakmon and its tributaries by a series of Bailey bridges.—178·5km *Neápolis* (pop. 1872; Hotel C), makes cheese.

The Kastoria road recrosses the Aliakmon and winds amid slopes clad with oak.—195km *Vogatsikón*, a pretty small town on seven low wooded hills, below the bluish-grey mountain (1361m) of the same name, is situated above a gorge. The road runs along the hillside above the beautiful valley.—Beyond (201km) *Kostarázion* where there is a military garrison, a concrete bridge crosses the emissary from Lake Kastoria that feeds the Aliakmon.—We bypass (209km) *Árgos Orestikón*, an important garrison town (pop. 5979) with a military airfield on an ancient site. It is noted for the manufacture of 'flokkates' and 'kilimia', varieties of woollen carpet. The road surmounts a low rise and descends to (215km) *Dhispílion* (Hotel B), on Lake Kastoria, meeting the road from Edhessa (Rte 63). Kastoria is seen across an arm of the lake. We pass a large military cemetery.

Lake Kastoria (*Limni Kastorias*), or *Lake Orestias*, 620m above sea level, and measuring c 6·5km long by 5km wide, is almost divided into two by the peninsula on the neck of which the town is built. The lake, which varies in depth from 7·5m to 15m, is fished for carp, tench, and eels. In summer the waters are hot, turbid, and often covered with a green film, and frogs keep up an incessant chorus; in winter the lake is often frozen. Birds abound and adders are not uncommon round the shores. Traces of a prehistoric lake dwelling were found on the S shore in 1940. The circuit (road, 32km, almost at lake level) can be made by car comfortably within an hour; it is interesting mainly for the surrounding mountains and for the apple orchards at the N end.

221km (137 miles) **KASTORIÁ** (Καστοριά), the seat of a metropolitan and capital of a nome, is delightfully situated on the isthmus of a peninsula reaching into the lake from its W shore. Many of its 17,133 inhabitants are occupied in the fur trade, being especially skilled in matching and joining rejected pieces of mink imported from abroad. Their large houses, many of the 17–18C ('arkhontiká'), with workshops on the ground floor, are scattered amid trees and approached by narrow cobbled ways of the Turkish period when the town was known as *Kesriye*. Storks nest on the roofs. Of the 72 churches for which the town was noted, fifty-four survive; seven of the Byzantine period and about thirty others of medieval date were scheduled in 1924 as ancient monuments. With one exception the Kastorian churches are basilican, the earliest having two low aisles while the later ones are without. The naves are barrel-vaulted. Exteriors are either decorated with crude patternwork (including chi-rho symbols) in tile, or plastered and frescoed. Most churches are kept locked. Keys are either at nearby houses or with the phylax and enquiry must be made. There is a *Folk Museum* in the old town. The town is subject to sudden winds and changes of temperature.

Airport. 10km SE with daily service to/from Athens.

Hotels, A, B, C, D, E.—**Restaurants** near the Káto Agorá.

Post Office, Mitropóleos; O.T.E. CENTRE, 19 Ay. Athanasíou.—TOURIST POLICE, 25 Grammón.—OLYMPIC AIRWAYS OFFICE, Megálou Alexándrou 15; daily service to Athens.—*Banks* in the lower town.

Buses frequently to *Argos Orestikon*; regularly to *Kozani*; daily to *Amindaion*; also to *Salonika*, via *Edhessa* (and once via *Kozani*); daily to *Florina*; to *Athens*, etc.

Carnival at Epiphany (6–8 January); Anniversary celebration of liberation from the Turks, 11 November.

History. The ancient *Keletron*, mentioned by Livy (xxxi, 40), probably occupied the hill Vigla above the shoreward suburb. It was captured in 200 BC after a siege by the Roman consul, P. Sulpicius Galba. Removed to the present site, the town was renamed *Justinianopolis*, according to the contemporary Procopius, after its refounder, but soon called *Kastoria* after the beavers that haunted the lake. The town was occupied by the Bulgars of Tsar Samuel in 990–1018 until freed by Basil II. It was surprised and captured in 1083 by Robert Guiscard from an English garrison of 300 men. Bohemond spent Christmas 1096 here, having crossed the Pindus by a route of his own. Disputed in the 12C between the despots of Epirus and emperors of Nicaea, Kastoria enjoyed a period of prosperity under Michael Paleologus. The town continued to thrive under the Serbs who held it in 1331–80. After five years of Albanian rule, it fell to the Turks in 1385 who remained its masters until 1912. A colony of Jews continued its trade with Vienna and Constantinople, and its fur industry has flourished for 500 years. It was the Greco-American base for the final campaign against rebels of the Grammos and Vitsi Mts in the severe winter of 1949.

The *Bus Terminal* (Pl. 1) marks the entrance to the town. Some remains of the Byzantine *Ramparts* that guarded the neck of the isthmus can be seen from Plateía Dhaváki which is named after a hero of 1940 (statue). Odhós Mitropóleos, the main street of the town, runs SE past the Post Office. Steps on the left mount past the little *Taxiárkhis* (Pl. 7) by the Gymnasion to the *Panayía Koubelídhiki*, an 11C triconchial church with a high central drum. Its frescoes date from the 13–16C. Farther along, off the triangular Plateía Omónoias, is *Ayios Nikólaos Kasnitsis* (Pl. 6), a single-chamber wood-roofed chapel with a semicircular apse. The late 12C frescoes are in a bad state of preservation but include a large number of images from the Orthodox Festival cycle. N of the door leading to the nave is depicted the donor of the church, Nikephoros Kasnitzi the Magistros, accompanied by an inscription. S of the door is his wife, Anne.

The left fork goes on to the Plateía Pávlou Melá. The *Taxiarkhai of the Metropolis* (Pl. 11) is a small three-aisled basilica containing remnants of 10C frescoes in the diakonikon and prothesis. The remainder of the interior frescoes (1359) were executed by the monk Daniel and include the Dormition of the Virgin at the W end of the nave. The external frescoes represent 15C persons buried in the church and a 13C Virgin and Child over the door. In the narthex is Melas' tomb. Beyond the ornate 19C Cathedral, with its detached belfry, is *Ayios Athanásios* (Pl. 10; key at No. 27, to the left), built in 1384–85 by Stoias and Theodore Musaki, members of the ruling Albanian family. In the contemporary frescoes the saints are depicted in Byzantine princely or military costume; above are scenes of the Life and Passion of Christ.

We return to Omonoia Square and take the right fork. *Odhos Mandakasi*, a pretty lane, to the right, descends, to the unspoilt *Karíaki* quarter near the S shore. Here three excellent examples of *Arkhontiká* lie to the SE of *Ayioi Anáryiri* (Pl. 11), an over-restored church with an unusual W gallery; its screen, carved and gilded, has panels of topographical scenes. The lakeside avenue leads to Ayios Ioánnis Theólogos, (Pl. 12) whence we follow the principal motor road through the town. *Ayioi Apóstoloi* (Pl. 12) was frescoed by Onouphrios in 1545. Of the group of churches just to the N (Pl. 8) *Ayios Nikólaos by Ay. Thomás* has been restored since it was hit by an Italian bomb in the Second World War; the frescoes date from 1663. *Ayios Stéfanos*, an 11C basilica with a tall nave and a clumsy barrel vault, to the NE, has a hexagonal apse and 12–14C frescoes and iconostasis. In the adjacent *Ayios Yeóryios* (rebuilt under the Turks) the Normans assembled to give themselves up to the Emp. Alexis in 1085. *Ayioi Anáryiroi Varlaam* (Pl. 4), a small but very high three-aisled, barrel-vaulted and wood-roofed basilica with a semicircular apse, is the oldest church in Kastoria. It contains fragments of early 11C frescoes in the narthex (Constantine, a donor; SS. Constantine and Helen; SS. Basil and Nicholas). The remainder of the frescoes were executed by two different painters and are assigned to the late 12C. The scene of Jesus and Nathaniel is one rarely depicted in Byzantine art. Its screen is also decorated.—*Ayios Stéfanos* is a small high and narrow barrel-vaulted basilica with a semi-hexagonal apse containing some poorly preserved frescoes from the 10C in the narthex and in the W part of the nave. The remainder have been assigned to the late 12C.

Below the Xenia Du Lac (Pl. 7) in a garden overlooking the lake, stands a statue of Athanasios Khristopoulos (1772–1847), a native poet. Odhós Ayíou Athanasíou returns to the Plateía Dhaváki, whence we skirt the *Byzantine Wall* to the Káto Agorá. The covered market faces the PLATEÍA MAKEDHONOMÁKHON (Pl. 2), laid out to celebrate Gen.

James Van Fleet, head of the US Military Mission to the Greek Army (1948–50). At the little quay, with a fish market, can be seen the curious wooden boats peculiar to the lake, their primitive pattern unchanged, perhaps, since the earliest times.

The lakeside walk is recommended for the *Views of the surrounding mountains. We leave the town on the NE and follow the Leoforos Stratigou Athanasiou Sougaridhou. This leads in c 1 hour to the *Moni Panayía Mavriótissa*, which is a one-aisled wood-roofed church with a semicircular apse. The frescoes from the original decoration of the building which are on the E and S walls of the nave and on the E wall of the narthex, as well as part of its exterior wall, are assigned to the early 13C. They have an interesting miniature quality. The two headless figures in the upper register to the left of the Tree of Jesse on the exterior of the S wall are variously identified as the Emperor Alexius (1081–1118) and his son John II, or as Michael VIII (1259–82) with his brother John Palaeologus. On its SE side is attached the chapel of *Ayios Ioánnis Theólogos* in which there are 16C frescoes. The return (slightly longer) can be made by continuing round the rocky peninsula to the SE corner of the town.

At *Omorphoklissiá*, formerly *Gallista*, 19km SW of Kastoriá, is the church of Ayios Yeóryios, restored in 1955. A small rectangular edifice, built in the 11C, it was extended under Andronikos II (inscription). In the exo-narthex survive vigorous frescoes of seven saints from the beginning of the 14C, as well as an old wooden statue of St. George.

63   From Kastoriá to Edhessa

A. Via the Stená Kleísouras (Amíndaion)

ROAD, 125·5km (78 miles), crossing (30km) the *Kleisoura Pass*, steep and tricky on the W side, narrow and unsurfaced on the E.—61km (38 miles) *Mnemeía Pesónton Crossroads* (4km W of *Amíndaion*; the km posts on this road show distance from Amindaion). We turn left on to the main Kozani–Niki road (Rte 58).—69km *Kirli Derven Pass* (easy).—At (75km) *Vévi*, join the road from Florina (Rte 63B).—122·5km **Edhessa**.—BUSES daily in 3½ hours continuing to Salonika; to *Amíndaion* also daily (different times).

We quit Kastoria by the Kozani road (Rte 62) and bear left at (5·5km) *Dhispílion*, skirting the marshy confines of the lake. The road ascends the valley of the little Xeropotamos. Just short of (23km) *Vassileiás*, we climb out of the valley of the E by a zigzag (retrospective *Views of Lake Kastoria), and the road becomes narrow and mountainous. Beyond (26km) *Vérga*, a grim alpine village, the hills are eroded by water-courses. Falls of rock may be encountered. The *Stena Kleísouras* is a steep and isolated saddle between Mt Vérbista (at the S end of the Vernon range) and Mt Moríki (The N extension of Askion).—30km The summit (1180m) is marked by a stone arch. *Kleísoura*, where the church of Ayios Dhimítrios has a carved wooden templon of the 15C, stands a little higher to the right. The view into the Aspropotamos plain to the E is not beautiful. The descent, less abrupt, follows the slopes of Vérbista, but as we enter the nome of Florina the road deteriorates. *Varikón* (reached via Kleisoura) is seen in a deep valley below.—A low saddle takes the road into the Mesikantítsa valley. The summit of Mt Vítsi, scene of much fighting in 1947–49, is seen to the left, while ahead the horizon is closed by the Vóras range, an enormous vista of mountains rising to 2438m on the Yugoslav frontier, 40km away.—39km *Lékhovon* enjoys cool springs on the oak-clad slope of Vérbista. A monument to Vanghelis (died 1904), leader of a nationalist band, stands by the road near the village of *Aspróyia* (left).—47km *Sklíthron*. The road, still shut in by hills, runs straight and level in the Stara valley to (53km) *Aetós*, from which a plain growing corn extends SE towards Perdikkas.—61km *Mnemeia Pesonton Crossroads* (Rte 58).

Ahead the road continues to **Amíndaion** (3·5km), a railway junction (3205 inhab.) and headquarters of an armoured group, that reputedly takes name from one of Alexander's generals. It is better known by its former name, *Sorovits*, for the battle fought here on 22–24 October 1912. In 1941 the railway was blown up before the advancing Germans by British irregular troops led by the author Peter Fleming. The local red wine has merit. A prehistoric cemetery (222 tombs) yielded valuable finds in 1900. Amindaion may be the *Cellis* of the itineraries.— The road continues beside the railway along the shore of the little Lake Petron to (11km) *Ayios Pandeleímon* on Lake Vegoritis. The railway follows the W shore of the lake to join the road just beyond *Ayios Spiridón* (comp. below).

We turn left on to the Ptolemaïs–Niki road (Rte 58), leaving it again (right) after c 13km for (75km) *Vévi*, where we join the road from Florina. Thence to (126km) **Edhessa**, see below.

B. Via Flórina

ROAD, 136km (85 miles), hilly and winding, passing within 9·5km of the Albanian frontier. (There are no apparent restrictions on the main road, but on by-roads travellers may find police posts where they are discouraged from proceeding.) Gravel to (35·5km) *Trígounon*, then asphalt.—65km **Flórina**.—88km *Vévi*.—137km **Edhessa**.—BUS daily to Florina; also from Florina to Edhessa, regularly.

RAILWAY from Florina to Edhessa (Salonika), 85km in 2 hours, three times daily (from Amindaion, 50km in 70 minutes, six times). The branch from Florina joins the line from Bitolj (Rte 58) at *Mesonísion* in the plan N of the road, passes S. of Vevi and traverses the Kirli Derven pass (Rte 58) to *Amíndaion*. Thence it skirts Lake Vegoritis, passing through *Arníssa*.

From Kastoria we take the lakeshore road N and quickly turn away left on gravel surface. We climb into bare hills and get a good retrospective view of Kastoria and its lake. Surmounting a ridge, the road descends to the oak-forested upper valley of the Aliakmon, which is crossed by Bailey bridge. In the river bed are stone breakwaters.— 19km *Gávros Police Post*, and, immediately before it, road (right) for *Melás* (15km), formerly *Státistan tou Korestíon*, where the patriot Pavlos Melas was killed by the Turks in 1904.—At 25km we cross the river again by a memorial of the civil war (1948–49) and, soon after, leave on our left the road to *Koritsa* (Korçë; 56km) in Albania (the frontier is closed).—At 29km we pass (right of road) a bust of Christos Kota, a champion of Macedonian Hellenism, burnt alive by the Bulgarians; the near-by village is named after him.—The road, now asphalted, rises in the fertile small valley of the principal affluent of the Aliakmon, here called the Livadhopótamos.—Just beyond (35·5km) *Trígounon* is a Police Post, where a road (left), signposted to *Laimós* (19km), climbs to a saddle overlooking the **Prespa Lakes**. *Megáli*

Préspa is shared between Albania, Yugoslavia, and Greece; *Mikré Préspa* between Albania and Greece only.—The road improves.— 38·5km *Andartikón*. We continue to climb amid fine beech forests to (48km) the summit of the *Pisodhérion Pass* (1498m; inn) between the Varnoús (Peristéri) and Vérnon ranges. Here there is another Police Post. We descend, with a splendid vista down the wooded Lerínska valley to Florina and the plain beyond.

65km (40½ miles) **Flórina** (Φλώρινα; 660m; Hotels B, C, D), with 12,562 inhab., is the capital of the nome of Florina. It has an important Agricultural School and a small Zoo. Near the entrance to the town is a statue of Kota (comp. above). Old Turkish houses, picturesque but mostly derelict, line the river. The church of *Ayios Yeóryios*, pleasantly situated outside the town, affords a view over the plain. Excavations on *Ay. Kharálambos*, a hill to the S, in 1931–34, uncovered the remains of a town built by Philip II (c 352 BC) and burnt in 48 BC in the campaign that ended at Pharsala. This is not *Herakleia Lynkestis*, now surely placed by inscription at Bitolj. The finds are housed in a new *Museum* near the railway station. To the W of the town, at *Pétres*, excavation began in 1982 of a Hellenistic town. Some of the pottery and terracottas found were imported from Pella.

Florina was a coveted objective of the guerilla rebels of the Civil War. They failed to take it in May 1947, and their assault on it using 4000 men and artillery, defeated in February 1949, was their last major effort.

We take the Salonika road E across the Monastir plain. The road crosses the railway to Yugoslavia, then at 78·5km briefly joins the course of the ancient Via Egnatia which comes in on the left from Bitolj (Rte 58). The ancient road probably turned S through the Kirli Derven pass (Rte 58) to Amindaion and crossed the valley now flooded by Lake Vegoritis to rejoin the modern road near Arnissa.—At 84km beside an unusual memorial (1917) from the Drina Division to their Serbian brothers, we fork left.—88km *Vévi* (Βεύη). The road traverses an upland plateau in a stony, desolate landscape. Ahead rise the massive outlying peaks of VÓRAS; behind the nearest (Piperitsa, 1996m) towers the snow-clad *Kaimaktsalán* (2524m).—97·5km *Kélla* (960m) is a stone-built town (877 inhab.) reminiscent of the Scottish highlands; just beyond we have a view (right) down to Lake Petron. The winding road undulates amid scrub covered hills. At a second summit level of 960m on the boundary between the nomes of Florina and Edhessa, sudden *View across the N end of Lake Vegoritis to Arnissa. After an enclosed descent we join the gorge of a torrent that feeds the lake at Ayios Spiridón and descend to the lakeside.

Lake Vegoritis (540m), or *Ostrovo*, is 19km long from N to S; its greatest width is 8km. In places it is 49m deep. It is well stocked with fish, lake-trout having been successfully introduced from Switzerland in 1958. Off Arnissa, towards the N, is an island on which are the remains of a mosque which local tradition claims was once in the centre of a village now submerged. The level of the lake, which was formerly liable to periodic flooding, is controlled by an underground outflow that feeds the Vodas. In ancient times its area was considerably less.

113km Crossroads; Panayítsa lies 4km N, *Árnissa* 2·5km right on the lake, where there is a trout hatchery. The main road passes behind the town, while the railway hugs the shore. Together they thread the almost level STENA EDHESSIS, joining the canalised *Vodas*, or Edhesseos, near its emergence from the marsh lake that feeds it.—At (134km) *Ágras* a hydroelectric station was opened in 1954; further works to harness the waters may diminish the famous Edhessa falls. Here is buried Tellos Agapinos, who fought under the name of Kapetan Agras in the Macedonian struggle and was killed while on a mission under truce to the Bulgarians in 1907. The valley broadens and becomes lush as we descend. The railway, seen intermittently across the river between its seven tunnels, crosses a viaduct.—136km (85 miles) **Edhessa**, see Rte 60.

64   Chalcidicé and Mount Athos

The peninsula of **Chalcidice**, in Greek **Khalkidhikí** (Χαλκιδική), received its name from the number of colonies planted there by the city of Khalkis in Euboea. Geographically it is the most prominent feature of Macedonia, projecting into the Aegean between the Gulf of Salonika on the W and the Gulf of Orfani on the E. It branches into three smaller peninsulas: Kassandra (anciently Pallene), Sithonia or Longos, and Athos (Akte). The Gulf of Kassandra (Toronaios Kolpos) separates Kassandra and Sithonia, and the Singitic Gulf comes between Sithonia and Athos. Other than in the W, along the S coastal plain, and in Kassandra, the interior is wooded and mountainous, the highest point Mt Athos, rising to 2033m. On the landward side the limit of Chalcidice is marked by the lakes E of Salonika, though the nome boundary runs a few miles S of them. Administratively the region is divided into the nome of KHALKIDHIKÍ, which comprises the greater part of the peninsula, and AYION OROS, coterminous with the territory of Athos, which has an autonomous constitution. The inhabitants are mainly engaged in agriculture, though the mines are important and tourism is playing a rapidly increasing role. Many kilometres of new road across the centre of the peninsula, with offshoots southwards into Kassandra and Sithonia, have recently been built to foster tourist holiday development of the coastal areas. The coasts in the remote past supported flourishing cities, some of them, notably Olynthos, of more than local importance. Finds from the many archaeological sites are in the Salonika and Poliyiros museums.

A. From Salónika to Ouranópolis

ROAD, 143km (89 miles), asphalt.—BUS at least twice daily.

From Salonika to (10km) the Ay. Trias turn, see Rte 59D. We bear left and pass, soon afterwards, a turning (left) to *Thérmi*, a small place bearing the name of the predecessor of Salonika. The road runs in a cultivated plain dotted with factories.—19km *Loutrá Thérmis*, a small spa with hot springs.—25km *Vasiliká* (Tavernas). The village stands (right) on a by-road to *Sourotí*, 5km SW, with mineral waters. The plain changes to a wide valley as we cross the nome boundary and we climb along the N side.—31km Crossroads, with (left; 3km) the *Moní Ayía Anastasía Pharmakolítria*, founded c 888 by Theophano, wife of Leo VI the Philosopher.—39·5km *Galátista*, a mining centre (2128 inhab.), occupying the site of ancient *Anthemous*, was the scene of a Communist massacre in 1945.—48km *Ayios Pródromos* stands in pleasant upland country.—At 56km the road divides. To Poliyros, see Rte 64D.

The road now climbs round the slopes of *Mt Kholomón* (1165m) amid chestnut woods, rising to 1006m on a ridge just below the summit before descending to (86km) *Arnaía* (Hotel E), beautiful centre (2244 inhab.) of a fruit and wine-growing region.—At (91km) *Palaiokhórion*, a good road runs S to the equally delightfully situated *Megáli Panayía* (8km) beyond which a bad road descends to the Singhitikos Gulf at *Pirgadhíkia* (27·5km). Another poor road diverges left at 96km to *Olympias Bay* (19km; Hotels C, D), the ancient *Kapros Limen*, on the Strymonic Gulf, and thence along the shore NW to Stavrós (Rte 66).

At (99km) *Stáyira* (Tourist Pavilion) a modern statue of Aristotle stands amid the ruins of a Byzantine fortress. In the village a Byzantine hall church has been restored. The remains of ancient *Stageira*, birthplace of Aristotle, lie on the by-road to Stratónion, see below. This, or (100km) *Stratoniki*, represents the ancient Stratonike. In the hills to the S, gold and silver were mined in the 16C; probably the same mines provided the coinage of Akanthos in antiquity. Today iron and magnesite are worked. New forests have been planted on the coastal slopes.—113km By-road to *Stratónion* (1km left).

129km (80 miles) **Ierissós** (Hotels D, E) is a straggling fishing village (2632 inhab.) on the shore of the bay of the same name. The ruined medieval watch-tower outside the village to the NW has Hellenic foundations, and reused marbles. Ancient also are the remains of a mole still affording shelter to local boats. These vestiges of antiquity mark the site of *Akanthos*, passed through by Xerxes and seized by Brasidas in his Macedonian campaign. Akanthos was founded from Andros. Its large Archaic, Classical and Hellenistic cemetery is by the shore, with tombs in the sand, some of which (4C) are cremations carried out in a clay-lined grave, the clay being fired in the process to create a kind of terracotta coffin. A part has been excavated and finds are in Poliyiros museum.—The road continues to (133·5km) *Néa Rhódha* (Xerxes Restaurant), on the N shore, and to the landing stage of (136km) *Tripití*, on the S shore of the vale of *Provlaka*, as the narrowest part of the isthmus is called. The name is a contraction of Proaulax, the **Canal** (αὔλαξ).

In 480 BC, aware of the disaster that had befallen Mardonius eleven years before, when he lost 300 ships and 20,000 men trying to round the promontory of Athos, Xerxes ordered a canal across the isthmus for the passage of his invasion fleet. The citizens of Akanthos awarded heroic honours to Artakhaies, who died while in charge of its cutting and was given a state funeral by Xerxes. The canal was dug in a hollow between low banks past the town of *Sane* (long since vanished). Several artificial mounds and substructions of walls can be traced along its course. Its width seems to have been 12–15m, and it is nearly filled up with soil. The isthmus is estimated to have risen 14m since the canal was cut.

Beyond Tripiti, with views towards the islet of *Amouliani*, we pass a Hotel (A) and reach (143km) *Ouranópolis* (Hotels A, B, D, E; Tavernas), known also as *Prosfori*, and from its tower as *Pirgos*. The fishing village (647 inhab.) built by refugees in 1922, has adopted the name of a lost town founded by Alexarchos, son of Antipater, in 316 BC though it is as likely to be ancient Dion. The inhabitants make knotted rugs to Byzantine patterns, a 'tradition' started by an Australian (Mrs J.N. Loch) in 1928. Beyond lies the territory of the Holy Mountain.

B. Mount Athos

The wild, roadless, and picturesque peninsula of **ATHOS** or AYION OROS ('Holy Mountain'), anciently known also as *Akte*, easternmost of the three prongs of Chalcidice, is connected to the mainland by a low isthmus only 2·5km across (see above). The length of the peninsula is c 50km and its breadth varies between 5 and 10km. The area of the nome of Ayion Oros is 339 sq. km. The population, exclusively male, is given by the 1971 census as 1732, though the last monograph on Athos puts the figure at '1163 of which only 518 are housed in monasteries, the remainder in dependencies'. Our figures which include lay brethren are mainly from a Greek source of 1976. The ground rises abruptly from the isthmus to 91m and for the first dozen miles maintains a level of about 180m, for the most part beautifully wooded. Beyond the land becomes mountainous, rising immediately S of *Kariaí*, the administrative capital, to 610m; hence a rugged broken country, covered with dark forests, extends to the foot of *Mt Athos* (2033m), a cone of white limestone which rises in solitary magnificence from the sea. The jackal is still common.

The Holy Community, a kind of monastic republic (see below), is composed of 20 monasteries, of which 17 are Greek, one (Roussikon) Russian, one (Zografos) Bulgarian, and one (Khiliandarion) Serb. There is also a Roumanian retreat, but the number of hermitages and cells has dwindled steadily along with the number of monks throughout the century, though the last few years have seen a revival of interest in the monastic life amongst the younger generation and a number of new novices have entered the orders. Divorced from distracting modernity, unaffected by hurry (the Julian Calendar, 13 days behind the rest of Europe, is still in use, and the day divided into Byzantine hours of variable length with sunset as 12 o'clock), the Holy Mountain affords to the devout a glimpse of life wholly dedicated to God, to the weary a welcome, if temporary, retreat from the world, and to the lover of nature and medieval art a treasury of beauty. That visitors are, in a sense, a contradiction of the reason for the community's existence should not be lost sight of by the traveller.

Formalities. The visitor, who must be male and (unless a theological student) over 21 years of age, must apply through his consul to the Foreign Ministry in Athens or to the Minister for Northern Greece in Salonika for a permit to visit Athos (fee). A letter of introduction from the Metropolitan of Athens or the Archbishop of Salonika is an additional advantage, and members of the clergy should have a written permit from the patriarchate of Constantinople. The documents must be presented immediately upon arrival to the Nomarch at Kariai, who will issue a residence permit (*diamonitirion*), which has to be presented at each convent visited (take care to recover it when leaving). Members of conducted groups avoid personal formalities. A special permit is needed for photography. Filming and tape-recording are forbidden.

Mules are hired for the journey to the first convent, which will arrange for transport to the next, and so on. The gates of the monasteries are open only during the daytime. It is considered presumptuous to ride up to the gates; one should dismount and approach on foot. The visitor will everywhere be received with kindness and simple courtesy, lodged (for a maximum of four days), and entertained with fish, vegetables, rice dressed in various ways, cheese, sweetmeats, fruits, and very fair wine made on the mountain. He should not expect meat, which few of the monks ever taste. On 159 days in the year they have but one meal and then eggs, cheese, wine, fish, milk, and oil are forbidden; on the other days they are allowed only two meals. The visitor's contribution to monastic funds on leaving should be at least commensurate with the hospitality he has received. Supplementary rations and a supply of insecticide may not come amiss.

Organised tours of the Holy Mountain (advertised as 'strenuous and austere') are arranged by Inter-Church Travel and other organisations; by this means the traveller is enabled to see more historical and artistic treasures than he could on his own, while inevitably substituting for the atmosphere of remote and timeless dedication something of the restless urgency of modern tourism. A better spiritual understanding of the unique nature of Athos is gained by a solitary stay in one or two monasteries.

Approaches. BY SEA either from *Ierissós* by caique down the E coast to Vatopedhi (uncertain owing to frequent rough seas), or by the regular motor-boat service from *Ouranópolis* down the W coast to Dhaphní. There are two buses daily in summer from Salonika to the ports (comp. above). The morning bus connects three times weekly with the late-morning boat from Ouranópolis. At Vatopedhi mules may be hired for Kariai. From Dhaphni a motor-road to Kariai (bus in 1 hour) was constructed in 1962 for the millenary celebrations.—BY LAND Kariai may be reached on foot or muleback in c 6 hours though this approach may lead to administrative difficulties.

History. Strabo, echoing Herodotus, says that Pelasgi from Lemnos came to the peninsula, where they founded five cities; Kleonai, Olophyxos, Akrothoon, Dion, and Thyssos. Colonies were also planted here by Eretria. On the isthmus stood the towns of Akanthos and Sane. Of all these only Akanthos is known by any remains. In 480 BC Xerxes dug his canal (see above), and in the time of Alexander the Great Deinokrates, architect of the Temple of Diana at Ephesus, proposed to fashion Mt Athos into a gigantic statue of the world-conqueror.

The fame of Athos rests entirely on its medieval monasteries. Legends of foundation by the Virgin herself, by St. Helena, or by one or other Roman emperor of the 4C or 5C, often supported by documents forged in the 18C, seem to have been tacitly abandoned with the official celebration in 1963 of the 1000th anniversary of the founding of the monastic community. It is likely that anchorites lived on the mountain at an earlier time, fugitives, perhaps, from iconoclastic persecution in 726–842; Peter the Athonite, the most famous of the early monks, is supposed to have lived for 50 years in a cave. Existing *lavras* (λαύρα, cloister or monk's cell) were organised by Athanasios the Athonite, friend and counsellor of the Emp. Nikephoros Phokas, the first historical benefactor of the Holy Mountain. He founded the monastery of the Great Lavra (963 or 961) and instituted the strict rule of the Abbot Theodore. Thereafter foundations multiplied under the protection of the emperors (especially Alexius I Comnenus, who placed them under imperial jurisdiction), until they reached the number of 40, with, it is said, 1000 monks in each. Andronikos II relinquished his authority to the Patriarch in 1312. The incursions of the Latins, Catalans (1307), Serbs (1346), and Turks caused the abandonment of a few outlying sites, but the importance of Mt Athos was not impaired. It reached its zenith in the 15C, after which a period of decadence set in, followed by reinvigorating reforms. After the fall of Constantinople in 1453 the monks kept on good terms with the sultans, one of whom, Selim I, paid a state visit to the peninsula. Thanks to this political dexterity, the Holy Mountain remained the spiritual centre of orthodoxy. It built its own schools, one of which, that of Vatopedhi, had a famous headmaster, Eugene Bulgaris (1753–59). At the beginning of the War of Independence the community joined the insurgents, but sank defeated under the Turkish yoke.

Despite its seclusion, Mt Athos has always attracted the attention, not always disinterested, of the outside world. The Vatican has frequently, but without success, tried to exercise some influence. Russia was dominant here from 1830 to 1890. In 1912 the peninsula was occupied by Greek troops, and the Treaty of London (1913) proclaimed its independence and neutrality. During the First World War the Allies sent in a detachment and a cultural mission. In 1926 Mt Athos was formed into a theocratic republic under the suzerainty of Greece. During the Second World War a German antiquarian expedition visited the Holy Mountain.

Organisation. By a decree of 16 September 1926 the peninsula forms part of Greece but enjoys administrative autonomy, while in church matters it depends on the Oecumenical Patriarch. All monks, of whatever race, become Greek subjects on retiring to Mt Athos; no heterodox or schismatics are admitted. Women are excluded. The Hellenic Republic is represented by a governor having the rank of nomarch, answerable to the Ministry for Foreign Affairs, and by a police force. The administrative autonomy is centred in the Synod, or Holy Council (*Hiera Synaxis*), with its seat at Kariaí, comprising 20 deputies (*Antiprósopoi*), one from each convent. The deputies are elected annually in January; and four of them, appointed in rotation, form the *Epistasia*, having executive powers. One of the four takes precedence as the First of Athos (Ο πρῶτος τοῦ Ἀθωνος). The Holy

Council exercises also financial and judicial authority.

The 20 convents are divided into two categories; *Coenobite* (κοινοβιακαί; 'living in common') and *Idiorrhythmic* (ιδιόρρυθμοι; 'eccentric', 'going their own way'). In the eleven coenobite convents all members are clothed alike, pool their resources, and live on the same meagre fare in the common hall or refectory (*Trápeza*). The monks of the nine idiorrhythmic convents enjoy a milder rule. They live apart from their fellows, though their convents may have refectories, and they have no property in common. Each monk provides his own clothes and obtains his food from his own resources. All of them attend services for at least 8 out of the 24 hours. These include Mass (*Leitourgía*), Vespers (*Hesperinón*), Compline (*Apódheipnon*), and Nocturnal Office (*Nykterninón*) which may on occasion last throughout the night and even exceptionally for 24 hours.—As well as the convents, there are *Anchorites*, who live apart in cells, some of them well-nigh inaccessible; *Sarabaites*, groups of two or three hermits living in hermitages or small houses; and *Gyrovakes*, mendicant and vagabond monks. The small retreats and cells have various names, such as *Sketai* (σκῆται) *Kellia*, *Kathísmata*, etc.

Each convent is administered by an abbot (*Hegoúmenos*), elected for life or for a definite period, assisted by two or three coadjutors (*Epítropoi*) and by a Council (*Synaxis*) of Elders (*Proistámenoi*). There is also a class of inferior monks (*Paramikroí*), who do manual labour. The monk begins as a novice (*Dhókimos*, or *Rasophóros*, from the name of his black gown). In the next three years he becomes Crusader (*Stavrophóros*) or *Mikróschema* (wearer of short coat); then *Megalóschema* (wearer of long coat; this coat has elaborate symbolic embroidery). All the monks are bearded and wear their hair long, either hanging down or tucked into a bonnet known as a *skouphía*; their normal dress is the *zostikon*, a black gown with a leathern girdle.

Among the oldest and most strictly observed of the rules is that of Constantine Monomachus (1060), which forbids access to 'every woman, every female animal, every child, eunuch, and smooth-faced person'. This rule, relaxed in 1345, was confirmed in 1575, 1753, and 1780, and is still officially in force, save that it is no longer incumbent upon a visitor to be bearded. She-cats and hens are however now openly tolerated; some pig-breeding is indulged in; and the ban on young boys is not always strictly enforced.

The coenobitic monastery resembles 'a compound of the walled town and the galleried inn' (Sherrard), having usually the form of a rectangle and being guarded by towers. The entrance is through a door at one of the four corners. The principal building in the middle of the enclosure, is the *Katholikón*, or communal church, cruciform with double narthex and several cupolas. Between the church and one of the short walls is the *Phiále*, a canopied stoup containing holy water. Built into the short wall beyond is the apsidal *Trápeza* (refectory), with an ambo from which a monk reads during meals, and, near the seat of the hegoumenos, a platter for the consecrated bread. Against the opposite short wall is the *Archontaría*, or guest-chamber. The monks' cells, adorned with porticoes and balconies, line the long walls.

Art. Though many treasures, particularly classical manuscripts, have been pillaged, burnt, neglected, or sold in the past, Athos is still rich in minor works of art. Little except charters and chrysobuls survive from the earliest times, but the archives (now jealously guarded) of Grand Lavra, Vatopedhi, and Iveron, and the library of Vatopedhi, are of the first importance. Reliquaries, chalices, and illuminated MSS survive in quantity. In the major arts of architecture and painting, if there is not much of the first rank, there is sufficient of interest and merit to give a comprehensive picture of the late-Byzantine scene. The principal features in which Athonite churches diverge from general Byzantine practice are the apsidal ends to the transepts and the double narthex, divided into *lete* and *mesonyktikon*, often flanked by side chapels. Two schools of painting are represented. The *Macedonian School* skilfully adapts painting to architectural media. Its protagonists are Manual Panselinos (early 14C), and his contemporaries. The *Cretan School*, affected by the art of Italy and S Germany, was founded c 1535 by Theophanes and continued by Frangos Kastellanos of Thebes. Some discoloured frescoes have been repainted from time to time.

Orthodox decoration, intended to illustrate Church doctrine, has become traditional and stereotyped. The Katholikon of Docheiariou is a complete example. In the top of the dome is the Almighty in glory, surrounded by the Virgin, John the Baptist, prophets, and angels. In the three apses and behind the ikonostasis are paintings illustrating the life of the saint commemorated. In the dome of the central apse are the Madonna and Child, with Christ below. In the left apse, Death and Resurrection of the Saviour, with Old Testament figures; in the right

MT ATHOS

apse, Christ and the Trinity, and similar figures. Above the altar, the Risen Christ. In the nave and choir are depicted the great church festivals, arranged in four parallel zones. In the narthex the cupolas glorify Christ; on the walls are Church councils, lives of the martyrs, and the Last Judgment. In the refectory (e.g. at Lavra) the subject of the frescoes is food. There may be local variations of the traditional style.—There are few ikons of importance.

The visitor arriving by sea at Daphne (Dhafní) takes the attractive road (bus) to Kariaí which at first runs close to the sea and then turns inland to the NE. After ½ hour it passes the idiorrhythmic convent of **Xeropotámou** (40 monks), pleasantly situated c 140m above the sea. It derives its name from a seasonal torrent. By forged documents the convent acquired in the 18C a 'traditional' foundation by Pulcheria, empress in 450–457. Its first genuine mention is in the 10C; it received privileges from Michael VIII in 1275 after an earthquake the previous year, and the Sultan Selim I (or, more probably, Selim II) rescued it from a period of decay. The earliest of the present buildings dates from 1763, when also the paintings in the katholikon were executed. Two ancient reliefs are built into the W wall of the court; the 'Roman' inscriptions are 18C forgeries and the two busts on the clock-tower (said to be St. Paul of Athos and Pulcheria) are of the 15C. The chief treasures are a piece of the Cross (30cm long) and the so-called *Paten of St. Pulcheria, depicting the Virgin at prayer standing adored by two angels with censers; in the first band is a procession of angels; in the second, the Apostles prostrate in worship. The paten was made in the 15C; the mounting showing the inscription, with the name, is an 18C addition. From the guest-chamber there is a fine view.

To St. Pantaleimon and other W coast monasteries, see below.

Farther on is the coenobite convent (50 monks) of **Koutloumousíou**, situated in the most fertile part of the peninsula, amid gardens, vineyards, olive plantations, and cornfields. This convent is first documented in 1169. It takes name from the princely Seljuk family of Kutlumush, of which its convert founder was a member. Bad fires in 1857 and 1870 wrought havoc with all but the *Katholikon*, rebuilt before 1540, and the arcaded E range, which dates from 1767. The frescoes of the katholikon have been repainted. There is a fine view of Kariaí from the monastery.—2 hours *Kariaí*.

Kariaí or *Karyes* (Κάρυαι; post and telegraph office; telephone) is the capital of Mt Athos; hence its other names of *Prótaton* ('Foremost') and *Mese* ('Middle'). It is a little town surrounded by vineyards and gardens, with a few shops kept by monks and lay brothers. Its monastery was reputedly founded by Constantine and destroyed by Julian the Apostate. The restored basilican Church of the **Protaton**, the oldest on Mt Athos, dates from the 10C. Various additions since 1508 were stripped away in 1955–57. The *Ikonostasis dates from 1607. In the *Chapel of St. John the Baptist* are *Frescoes of the Nativity and of the Presentation in the Temple attributed to Manuel Panselinos (early 14C) and considered the finest in the peninsula; others, of a later date, are of admirable freshness and delicacy. There are also silver filigree crosses and a wonder-working ikon. The *Council House* has a chamber in which the 20 deputies deliberate sitting on divans. Each of the deputies has a lodge at Kariaí to accommodate himself and younger monks of his convent attending the school here. Visitors to any of the lodges are hospitably received. The *Athonite School for Novices* was established in 1950 for 60 boys.

The hazel (λεπτοκάρυα) from which the town derives its name, is common. Hazel nuts are exported.

FROM KARIAÍ TO VATOPEDHI, 3 hours. The track, passing the huge ruinous Russian church of *St. Andrew*, goes N.—**Vatopédhi** (Βατοπέδιον),
one of the largest on Mt Athos and the most modern (with electric
light, telephone, and motor-boats, and keeping European time), is an
idiorrhythmic convent with 50 monks. The monastery, which somewhat resembles a country mansion, is built round a huge triangular
court in a charming pastoral setting overlooking a little bay, with a
highly picturesque harbour. The SE wing was destroyed by fire in
February 1966.

Foundation traditions tell of Constantine as well as of Theodosius, the miraculous
rescue of whose son Arcadius from the sea by the Virgin is supposedly commemorated by the name Vatopaidion (βατός, bramble, and παιδίον, child). The story
tells of the boy being placed under a bramble for the hermits to find. The name is
more likely Vatopedhion (bramble-*ground*). The historical founders are Athanasius, Nicholas, and Antony from Adrianople (late 10C). The Emp. John VI Cantacuzenus retired here in 1355 under the name Ioasaph. The monastery was a
cenobion in 1573–1661.

Most of the attractive buildings are of the 17C or later. The
KATHOLIKON (Annunciation), is an 11C basilica adapted to the plan of
a Greek cross. It has a massive detached belfry and a double narthex.
The 15C bronze doors, from St. Sophia, Salonika, have panels in relief
depicting the Annunciation. Over the second door is an 11C mosaic of
Intercession (δέηβις): centre, Christ in glory; at the sides, the Virgin
and John the Baptist. The inner doors, inlaid with ivory are dated 1567.
The impressive interior, which has a polygonal apse, is decorated with
frescoes of the Macedonian school (1312), restored in 1789 and 1819.
Porphyry columns support the dome. In the *Chapel of St. Demetrius*
(N) are ikons of St. Peter and St. Paul (16C), in a beautiful frame; of the
Holy Conductress, in a 13–14C frame, with reliefs of Christian
festivals; of St. Anne; and of the Crucifixion (13C) in a 14C metal
frame. The ikonostasis is a fine work of art. The *Chapel of the Holy
Girdle* contains a good Nativity. The ˙Cup of Manuel Paleologos
(early 15C) is made of a block of jasper 25·5cm across, on a silver base
decorated with enamel; the engraved handles are in the shape of
dragons. There are some fine crosses with silver-gilt ornamentation.
The most notable relic, the 'Girdle of the Virgin', was given to the
monastery by Lazar I of Serbia (1372–89).

The *Library* contains 8000 volumes. Especially noteworthy are an Octateuch
(first eight books of the Bible); a psalter (No. 610), autographed by Constantine
IX Monomachos (1042–54); an evangelistary (No. 735), and a MS of Ptolemy's
Geographia, with which are 17 chapters of Strabo's *Geography*, the *Periplus* of
Hadrian, and 42 maps in colour. Two fragments of frescoes were discovered in
the Library, the first representing only the heads of the Apostles Peter and Paul.
They are attributed to the painters commissioned by Stephen Nemanja and his
son (c 1197–98) to decorate the Refectory.
  The monks' walk is an attractive promenade.—Not far from the convent are the
ruins of the *Athonite Academy*, founded in 1749 with the aid of the learned
Eugene Bulgaris of Corfù, but destroyed in the same century. Some arches of its
aqueduct survive.

FROM VATOPEDHI TO ESPHIGMENOU, 2½ hours. The convent of
Esphigménou (coenobite; 40 monks) stands on the edge of the sea, at
the mouth of a torrent in a little narrow valley (whence probably its
name: ἐσφιγμένος, compressed). First mentioned in a document of
1034, it was restored in the 14C, but plundered by pirates in 1533.
Except for short periods of revival, it lay abandoned till the end of the

Athos, Vatopedhi. Decoration from the 13C bronze door

18C. Its possession of the cave of the hermit Antony of Kiev (983–1073) assured it Russian support, but, though it was restored in the 19C, it has never been of the first importance. The *Church* (1808–11), overpoweringly ornate, has an ikonostasis carved with figures of Adam and ve. It has a portable mosaic ikon of Christ (12C) and (in the library) an 1C Menologion (calendar).

About 1 hour away by track is **Khiliandhárion** (31 monks; all Slavs), n idiorrhythmic Serbian convent, northernmost of the monasteries on he E side of the peninsula. It is situated nearly a mile from the sea, in a ale watered by a torrent, and surrounded by thickly wooded hills. Its ame is said to be derived from its having originally been built for 1000 nonks (Χίλιοι ἄνδρες). It was founded in 1197 by the Serbian prince tefan Nemanja and his son Sava, and rebuilt in 1299 by Stefan Milu- in, who eventually retired, after his abdication, to Vatopedhi. Only he Katholikon was undamaged by a fire in 1722, and the cell of St. ava was destroyed by another in 1961. The convent has electric nstallations (disused) and a tractor, gifts from Yugoslavia. The court as a double arcade. The *Katholikon* (1293), built of brick of different olours arranged in patterns, has a richly decorated narthex of c 1380. t contains frescoes of the 13–14C, restored in 1863–64 by artists of ialatista following the original style, a marble mosaic pavement 12C), and the cenotaph of Stefan Nemanja (the Monk Simeon). The ttle *Chapel of the Ascension* was decorated in 1302. The *Liti* is a ectangular hall in front of the church in which prayers are said on aturdays. The *Refectory* has frescoes on its walls. Noteworthy are a osaic ikon of the Virgin and Child (13–14C), another of the Panagia richerousa ('with three hands'; 14C), an altar cloth of 1399, with hrist standing between two angels blessing St. Basil and St. John hrysostom.

he *Library* contains interesting MSS in Slavonic tongues. In the *Muniment oom* of the library are four *Ikons depicting archangels from the ikonostasis resented by Stefan Dušan, charters and deeds of gift from Byzantine emperors nd princes of Serbia and Bulgaria, as well as firmans promising protection and rivileges from successive sultans and viziers.—The surrounding countryside ffords delightful walks and the shore good bathing:

he northernmost part of the peninsula consists of hills intersected by deep alleys, down which torrents flow to the sea, the shore of which is indented with ttle bays. The hills are covered with the fragrant and feathery Isthmian pine, nd with every variety of shrub and flower. The foliage of the N and S is blended i great variety, the olive with the oak, and the orange with the pine.

ROM VATOPEDHI TO IVIRON, 4 hours or by infrequent caique. The ath runs SE and S, close to the E coast of the peninsula. After 2½ ours we reach **Pantokrátor** (20 monks), an idiorrhythmic convent ounded c 1357–63 by Alexios the Stratopedarch and John the Primi- erius, whose inscribed tombs have been found in the narthex. The valls, repaired in 1536, have a massive tower. It is built on a sea- vashed rock above a small cove and affords a fine view of Stavroni- ita. The old Katholikon has been often renovated (fragmentary 14C escoes). The library has interesting 11C MSS.—An hour later we ome to another idiorrhythmic convent, that of *Stavronikita* (25 10nks), perhaps founded in 1153 but refounded in 1542 by the 'atriarch Jeremiah of Constantinople. The monastery, with its mas- ive tower, crowns a precipitous rock at the edge of the sea. The *atholikon* has frescoes of 1546 executed by monks. It has a mosaic kon of St. Nicholas and a psalter of the 12C.—After another hour we rrive at **Ivíron** (Monastery of the Iberians), also idiorrhythmic, with 0 monks (Greeks, Russians, Roumanians, and Georgians). It was ounded n 979 or 986 by three Iberians or Georgians under charter om Basil II the Bulgar-Slayer. Badly damaged by fire in 1865, it is a welter of buildings in an enclosed valley near the sea. The entrance opens into a vast court surrounded by heterogeneous buildings. In the middle is the *Katholikon*, with a pavement that dates from the foundation. In a little chapel (1680–83) adjoining is the miraculous 10C ikon of the Panagia Portaítissa which, found by one of the Georgians in the sea, enabled him to walk upon it. The *Library* is rich in MSS, particularly of the gospels including one the gift of Peter the Great. The Treasury (seldom shown) has a carved cross of 1607, another of carved wood (Raising of Lazarus), and remarkable vestments, including an embroidered tunic said to have belonged to the Emperor John Tsimiskis.

Athos, Iviron Monastery. Christ Pantocrator in the dome of the church

Near the convent is a former asylum for the mentally afflicted and lepers (good beach nearby).—A road leads direct from Iviron to Kariai (1½ hours).

FROM IVIRON TO THE GRAND LAVRA, 6½ hours. The path runs SE along the coast to the end of the peninsula. After 1½ hours amid green meadows we reach the idiorrhythmic convent of **Philothéou** (35 monks), supposedly founded in the 9C by three monks of Olympus Arsenius, Denys, and Philotheos), but first mentioned in the 12C. It numbered Stephan Dušan among its benefactors. The convent was rebuilt after a fire in 1781. Round its church are workshops where the monks employ themselves in wood carving. There is a fine view hence of the convents of Stavronikita and Pantokrator. About ½ hour farther on through rich and fertile country, or 40 minutes direct from Iviron, is the coenobite convent of **Karakállou**, situated in hazel woods 460m). It was founded in the 15C by Peter Raresch IV of Moldavia and dedicated to SS. Peter and Paul by one John Karakallos. The convent, which has 30 monks, was restored in 1548. The mountainside falls abruptly to the sea and the view over the Aegean embraces Samot-race, Imbros, and Tenedos.

Some 4 hours from Karakállou we reach the ***Grand Lavra** (Η Μονή τῆς Μεγίστης Λαύρας), an idiorrhythmic convent, with 250 monks, including Russians, Rumanians, and Bulgarians (lavra means cloister or monk's cell). The largest and perhaps the finest of all, partly because (alone of the 20) it has never suffered from fire, it is comparatively simple in plan, without the multiplicity of buildings characterising some of the others. It was founded in the time of Nikephoros Phokas (963–64) by Athanasius of Trebizond. Resembling a fortified village, with a fine 10C *Tower*, it stands on a gently sloping spur 152m) overlooking a little harbour guarded by a fort. The entrance is by a long, winding and vaulted passage, with several massive iron gates. In the court are two ancient cypresses, said to have been planted at the foundation. The *Phiale*, erected in 1635, incorporates Byzantine relief panels between eight Turkish stalactite capitals. Paintings within the dome represent the Baptism of Christ. Below is an antique porphyry basin with a sculptured bronze fountain. The *Katholikon*, completed in 1004, which externally resembles a domed basilica, consists of a triconchal Greek cross extended to the W and flanked by parecclesia in the form of two smaller cross-in-square churches. A hideous exo-narthex of 1814 now abuts the three W fronts, occupying the site of St. Athanasius's cell. Painted baroque doors of the Turkish period lead into the church, which was frescoed all over by Theophanes the Cretan in 1535–60. Representations of Nikephoros Phokas and his nephew, John I Tzimisces, benefactors of the church, dominate the nave. In the right paracclesia is the *Tomb of St. Athanasius*. To the left the *Chapel of St. Nicholas* has frescoes by Kastellanos. The cruciform *Refectory*, built by Gennadios, Abp of Serres in 1512, has ***Frescoes by Theophanes the Cretan**. Within the apse, Last Supper. Side walls (in three bands): below, SS. Athanasius, Euthymus, and Gregory Palamas; middle, scenes of martyrdom; above, illustration of the hymn Αγιον ἐστύ. To the S, Life of St. Solitarius, Council of Nicaea, scenes in the life of the Virgin. To the N, Death of a just man, scens in the life of St. John. To the E, Last Judgment centre, Second Coming; left, Paradise; right, Hell). The *Chapel of the Trinity* (*Ayia Trias*) has an ikonostasis of the 15–16C.

The treasures include the ikon of Koukouzelissa (12C), reliquary of Nicephoros Phokas (11C or earlier), and an enamelled ikon said to be that of John Tzinitzas

(12C).—The *Library* has 5000 volumes and 2250 MSS, including a Bible of Nicephoros Phokas, set with precious stones; two leaves (from Galatians and 2 Corinthians) of the 6C 'Codex Euthalianus' are preserved.

Directly above the Grand Lavra rises the peak of **Mount Athos** (2033m), with its white cone and its precipices, in striking contrast to the dark foliage of the ridges below. The ascent can be made in one day from the convent via Kerassiá (see below; start in the early morning, return in the evening). It was climbed in 5 hours from Néa Skíti by Sir John Hunt in 1948. On the summit is the little *Chapel of the Transfiguration*, in which a service is held annually (on 6 August). The peak was one of the stations of the fire-beacons that carried Agamemnon's signal to Klytemnestra (Aesch. *Agam.* 284). The * *VIEW all round is unsurpassed, embracing the whole N Aegean.

FROM THE GRAND LAVRA TO DHAFNI, 10 hours, not counting halts. This itinerary follows the contour of the peninsula, rounding its extremity and going up the W coast. Hereabouts are numerous hermit's cells (σκῆται), many of them almost inaccessible.—2 hours *Kerassiá* is the principal halting-place (accommodation) and the closest point for the ascent of the Mountain (see above). A short distance away, on the coast, is *Kafsokalívia*, a colony of painters and wood carvers who live in small groups.—3¾ hours *St. Anne's*, a retreat where 157 monks live in separate houses, clings in terraces to a steep mountainside. Here is a shrine with a relic of St. Anne.

About 5 hours from the Grand Lavra, the coenobite convent of **Ayíou Pávlou** (125 monks) is beautifully situated in an angle of stupendous cliff above a boulder-strewn torrent. Founded in the 11C by Serbs and Bulgars, it gets its name, not from the Apostle, but from a son of the Emp. Maurice, one of its chief benefactors. After a period of desertion, the buildings were renewed wing by wing in the 19–20C; the Katholikon of 1447 was replaced in 1844–50. The library was lost in a fire in 1905. The *Chapel of St. George* has good frescoes in the Cretan style, dated 1423 but probably of the 16C: figures of saints and Apostles and, in the narthex, the Virgin as the source of life (Ζωοδόχος πηγή).—A difficult path leads hence in ¾ hour to the coenobite convent of **Dionysíou** (40 monks) founded in 1375 by Alexios III Emperor of Trebizond at the instance of Dionysios, brother of Theodosius, Abp of Trebizond. The convent stands on a precipitous rock where a bleak gorge reaches the sea; it is approached from its little landing-stage by 420 steps. The huge *Tower* was built in 1520 and Peter IV Raresch of Moldavia restored the buildings (1547) after a fire in 1535. The *Katholikon* has frescoes of 1547 by Zorzis (Cretan school). In the refectory is a Last Judgment (1603). There are the silver reliquary of St Niphon and (in the library) a superb chrysobul and c 600 MSS.—About 1 hour farther, just above the sea and shut in by rocky cliffs, is the compact and attractive **Gregoríou** (coenobite, with 36 monks) founded c 1395 and rebuilt after a fire in 1762–83. Its Katholikon has paintings of 1779.—About 1 hour farther on is the coenobite convent of **Simonópetra**, picturesquely situated over 305m up on a rock isolated on all sides save the NE, where a bridge of three superimposed arches joins it to the cliff. Its buildings, reconstructed on the old foundations in 1893–1902, with funds form Czar Nicholas II, are supported by heavy beams overhanging the precipice, recalling architecturally the Potala at Lhasa in Tibet. The view is magnificent.

The convent was founded in 1257 by St. Simon and favoured by the Serbian Emp. John Ugleš. Fires took their usual toll in 1580 and 1625, and Turkish occupation

Athos. Etching (1887) of Simonópetra

n 1821–30, while the library and much else was destroyed in 1891. The convent
as 32 monks.—From Simonopetra Daphne is 2 hours walk.

OTHER CONVENTS ON THE WEST COAST. From Xeropotamos a path
eads NW in ½ hour to **St. Pantaleímon** or **Roussikón**, a huge coe-
obite convent once supporting 1500 Russian monks (now 20). It was
ounded in 1169 in an earlier abandoned building, burnt down by the

Catalan Company in 1309, but reendowed by Andronikos II two years
later. It was occupied for about eighty years after 1735 by Greek
monks, but rebuilt in 1812–14 in an exotic Russian style. It was swept
by fire in 1968 when the assembly hall was destroyed. Above its scattered barrack-like blocks on the waterfront rise many towers and
domes surmounted by golden crosses. It has a soapstone paten with a
representation of the Virgin and Child, and an illuminated MS of S
Gregory of Nazianzen. The singing of its Russian choirs was famous.
At the monastery are some architectural and sculptural fragments
from the temple of Zeus Ammon at Kallithea on the Kassandra
peninsula.—About 1 hour farther, at the edge of the sea, is the coenobite convent of **Xenophóndos** (70 monks), founded at the end of the
10C by the monk Xenophon. The *Old Katholikon* has frescoes of the
school of the Cretan Theophanes while the *New Katholikon* (1837) has
two fine 14C mosaic panels of saints. In the refectory is a good Last
Judgment.—Half an hour farther on, standing 46m above the sea, is
the idiorrhythmic convent of **Docheiaríou**, with 25 monks, architecturally one of the most charming. It was founded at the beginning of the
10C by Euthymios, who had been Receiver (δοχειάρης) of the Grand
Lavra. The *Katholikon* is one of the finest on Mt Athos; its frescoes, by
an unknown artist of the Cretan school (1568) embody the traditional
style of decoration in all its completeness. Count Alexander IV of
Moldavia and his countess Roxandra are depicted as founders. The
convent has an interesting ikon, an epitaphios of 1605, and 11–12
MSS.—The path now leads through wooded country to (1 hour
farther) the little coenobite convent of **Konstamonítou** (21 monks),
hidden in a deep defile. It was founded, according to the most probable account, in the 11C by someone from Kastamon, but tradition
has altered the medieval spelling from Kastamonitou to accord with a
legendary foundation by Constans, son of Constantine the Great. Its
buildings are all of the 19C.—Finally, after another ½ hour, midway
between the coasts we reach **Zográphou**, a coenobite convent of 1
Bulgarian monks founded by Slav nobles from Ochrid at the end of the
10C. The two churches date from 1764 and 1801 but the rest were
largely rebuilt in 1860–96 in an ugly style.

Its miraculous ikon of St. George (Italian style, 15C) is said to have come from
Palestine without human aid, in the same way as the House of the Virgin at Loreto
(see 'Blue Guide Northern Italy'). The monks declare that it was painted by
divine will and not by man; hence the dedication to the Zographos or Painter.
There is a small hole near the eyes of the painting made by an unbelieving bishop
from Constantinope, who (it is said) inserted his finger in derision and could not
withdraw it, so that it had to be cut off.
    The ride from Zografou across the peninsula to Khiliandhari is one of the finest
on the Holy Mountain.

C. Olynthos and Kassándra

ROAD TO PALIOURI, 119km (72 miles), fast highway to Néa Moudhaniá. 42km *Néa Kallikráteia.*—67·5km *Néa Moudhaniá*, for **Olynthos** (8km).—72·5km *Potidaía.*—92km *Kallithéa.*—119km **Palioúri**.

ˈrom Salonika we take the road past the airport and at 16km diverge ʈeft. The road passes through an open region of well-tended fields and kirts (42km) *Néa Kallikrátia* (the site of an ancient settlement) on the ʑea, only to turn inland again.—51·5km *Elaiokhória*. The Petrálona ꞈavern (5km left), where a Neanderthal skull came to light in 1960 ɳnd a full skeleton in 1976, may have been occupied in 500,000 BC.— 5·5km *Néa Tríglia*.—67·5km *Néa Moudhaniá* (pop. 4142; Hotel C) ꞈas a small harbour. We skirt the town and reach a vast crossroads ʋith traffic lights.

The road to the left runs through a flat cultivated plain across the ʋase of the Gulf of Kassandra into Sithonia, joining Rte 64D at Paralía ˈerakína (16km). We may diverge along this road to visit ancient Ɂlynthos, turning left after 5·5km by a mound, and at the beginning of ꞈhe modern village (1·5km farther) taking a signed track (right) for ɳnother 1km and fording the Retsinikia. The site of **Olynthos** (fenced; ꞈhylax; free) occupies twin flat-topped mounds running N and S, ꞈverlooking the Retsinikia. In the 5C and 4C BC it was the most impor-ɳnt of the Greek cities in this part of the Macedonian coast.

ˈeolithic dwellings occupied the S spur of the hill in the early 3rd millennium BC. ꞈhe Bronze Age settlement was at Ayios Mamas (see below), but c 800 BC the S ꞈill was reoccupied by a Macedonian tribe. It was settled by Bottiaians in the 7C. ꞈerxes here requisitioned troops and ships in 480 BC (Herod, VII, 122); meditat-ɳg rebellion in the following year, it was burnt by Artabazus and the site given to ꞈe Chalcidians. Their city paid tribute to Athens until, in 432, Perdikkas II of ꞈacedon moved many inhabitants of neighbouring Chalcidian towns into Olyn-ꞈos and it became the head of the Chalcidian League. The population grew to c ɀ0,000 inhabitants, and the town spread to the N hill. It maintained its independ-ɳnce except for a short period of submission to Sparta (379 BC). After first siding ʋith Macedon, Olynthos was reconciled to Athens by Demosthenes, who in his Ɂlynthiac Orations, urged his countrymen to support the Olynthians against ꞈhilip. In 348, however, Philip took and destroyed Olynthos so thoroughly as to ꭓxcite the comment of Demosthenes that a visitor to the place would never realise ꞈhat there had been a city there (Phil. 3, 117). A Byzantine church later occupied ꞈart of the site.

ꞈhe classical city was built on the Hippodamian system with insulae of ꞈniform area, measuring 300 by 120 Greek feet. Its excavation by the ꞈmerican School in 1928–34 provided a knowledge of Greek town-ꞈlanning and domestic building comparable with that gained by ꞈoman scholars from Pompeii. Sculptural and architectural frag-ꞈents, exactly dated by the historic destruction, clarified the relation-ꞈhip between Classical and Hellenistic styles. Its pebble mosaics ꞈconservation in progress), forerunners of those at Pella, have been ꞈovered over; some mosaics have been uncovered for display but ꞈhese are not easy to find without help from the phylax and the site ꞈtherwise offers little to the layman. There are numerous open ꞈisterns.

ꞈeturning to Nea Moudhaniá, we continue S and traverse the narrow ꞈsthmus that joins Kassandra to the mainland; here in 1960 road-ꞈuilders unearthed a tomb containing a laurel wreath of the 3C BC, ꞈhe first gold object found in the area. To the right, beyond the shallow canal cut across the isthmus in 1937 lies (72·5km) *Néa Potidaía* and its generally unremarkable remains, though a Classical cemetery, discovered nearby in 1974, included the graves of Athenian cleruchs.

Potidaia, a Dorian colony founded c 600 BC from Corinth, soon minted its own coins. After Salamis the strongly fortified port led the Chalcidian revolt against the Persian lines of communication, resisting a siege by Artabazus. It became a member of the Delian Confederacy. Its revolt from Athens in 432 BC was one of the immediate causes of the Peloponnesian War (Thuc. I, 56). The city was subdued in 429 after a siege of two years; in the campaign Socrates saved the life of Alcibiades while serving as a hoplite. Potidaia remained an Athenian cleruchy until 404 when it passed to the Chalcidians. Recovered by Athens in 363–356, it fell to Philip of Macedon who gave it to the Olynthians. After destruction in the Olynthian War, the place was refounded by Kassander as *Kassandreia*, and became the most prosperous city in Macedonia. It repulsed the Roman fleet in the Third Macedonian War (171–168). It was destroyed by the Huns.

The peninsula of **Kassandra**, the ancient *Pallene*, is the most fertile of the three prongs of Chalkidike. Before the War of Independence it contained a population of cattle-and sheep-farmers. When news arrived in 1821 of the revolt of the Greeks in the S, the people of Kassandra decided at first to join in but, finding themselves unprepared, tried to back out. It was too late. The Pasha of Salonika, entering the peninsula, put all the inhabitants to the sword and razed all their houses. Kassandra was left untenanted for two years and only in the last few years has anything been done to restore its former prosperity.

From Nea Potidaia the road follows the E side of the peninsula. *San* (Hotels A, B), 11km down the W coast, was probably the site of a Euboean colonial settlement. 84km *Néa Fókaia* has a prominent medieval watch-tower.—88·5km *Áfitos* marks the site of ancient *Aphytis*, where in 380 BC Agesipolis of Sparta died of fever while campaigning against Olynthos. A sanctuary of Zeus Ammon (4C BC with an associated Sanctuary of the Nymphs and Dionysos (Xen. Hell. 5, 3, 13) were found and excavated in 1969–71 (finds in Poliyiros museum).—At (92km) *Kallithéa* (Hotels A, B, C, D), the road divides to form a circuit of 76km round the peninsula.

The pleasant E coast road continues close to the shore through wooded hamlets.—5km *Kriopiyí* (Hotels A, B, E) has an N.T.O.G. camp site.—10km *Khaniótis*. By the sea, 3km short of (29km) **Palioúr** (Hotels B, E) is a Xenia hotel (B) and a large N.T.O.G. camp site. To the SE the peninsula ends in Cape Kalogriá, the ancient *Kanastraion*.

From Palioúri the road turns inland through *Ayía Paraskeví* to the W coast at (40km) *Loutrá* with hot springs.—At (47km) *Néa Skióni* (Hotels D), chance finds in 1956 included coins and walls, relics presumably of *Skione*, once the chief town of Pallene.—Farther on is *Kalándra* (Hotel A), the site of ancient *Mende*, noted for its wine and as the birthplace of the sculptor Paionios. At *Válta* some pottery of the 6C BC came to light in 1956; here or on Cape Poseidon to the SW may have lain ancient Kassandreia. The road recrosses the peninsula through (72·5km) *Kassándra*, properly Kassandreia, an unattractive little town (2062 inhab.), to (76·5km) *Kallithéa*.

D. Políyiros and Sithonía

ROAD to *Nikítas* 104km (65 miles), with, beyond, a circuit of 111km (69½ miles).

From Salonika to (56km) the Palaiókastro turn, see Rte 64A. We bear ₅ through the village (533m), situated amid oak-woods, and wind through shaly hills.—65km (40½ miles) **Políyiros** (Πολύγυρος; ₁35m), the chief town (pop. 4075) of Khalkidhiki and seat of the Bp of ₁assandra. The ARCHAEOLOGICAL MUSEUM is to the right at the ₑnetrance to the town. Opened in 1970, it houses finds from all over ₁halcidice. Of particular interest are those from the sanctuary of ₁mmon Zeus at Aphytis and a head of Dionysos from the associated ₁anctuary; early black-figure idols from Olynthos; and a Late Archaic ₁lazomenian larnax. Three silver coins displayed were found in the ₁and of a skeleton at Akanthos.

Beyond Poliyiros the road winds down through rounded hills, ₁asses large quarries, and reaches (81km) the coast at a T-junction. ₁he road to the right leads past Ancient Olynthos (8km; see above) ₁nd joins Rte 64C at Néa Moudhaniá. We turn left. 85km *Psakoúdhia* ₁Hotel B). The site of ancient *Sermyle* is to be sought on the coast S of ₁rmília or Vatopédhi, inland villages served by by-roads (left).— ₁8km *Metamórfosis* (right; Hotel D; F/A). Beyond a camp site we ₑach (104·5km) *Nikítas* (1797 inhab.) at the base of the Sithonia ₁eninsula. About 1·5km farther on the road divides.

₁ith its trees, sharp hills, and rocks, **Sithonia** is more attractive than Kassandra ₁nd still unspoilt though a coast road encircles the peninsula. The right branch ₁llows the W coast with occasional accessible but deserted coves.—17km *Néos ₁larmarás* is a pleasant village with good seaside restaurants (Panos). Beyond ₁xtend the estates (c 18 sq. km) of John C. Carras, run as a model farm to produce ₁lives, citrus fruits, almonds, and excellent wines for **Porto Carras** (Hotels A, B), a ₁illage expressly built in a modern Mediterranean idiom as a resort for 3000 ₁uests and 1800 permanent residents. It has full sporting and cultural facilities, ₁cluding a theatre for 4500 spectators, and a yacht marina. Its two vast hotels are ₁lly open. Fine scenery with sandy coves and beaches extend below the wooded ₁opes of Melítonas (494m).—42km *Toróni* has cheap rooms and a good beach. A ₁mall fishing fleet works from *Pórto Koufó*, at the S end of which are extensive ₁uins of ancient *Torone*, presently being excavated by a joint Greek-Australian ₑam. The site was occupied from prehistoric times to the 17 or 18C AD. Visible ₑmains are of extensive fortifications, some probably Classical in date with ₁uch later rebuilding, and a number of Early Christian basilicas, especially that ₁ Ayios Athanássios, next to the road to Porto Koufo which has well-preserved ₑscoes and mosaics.—The peninsula ends in Cape Dhrepanon, the ancient ₁errhis Promontory.

The road climbs over a spur with splendid views down towards (54km) ₁alamítsa. Beyond (62km) the turning to *Sikéa*, seen 2km left in a bowl of hills, ₁e road runs nearer sea level.—62km *Sárti* is a pleasant little place with seaside ₑstaurants. The road runs *en corniche* with fine *Views up and down the coast ₁d across to Mt Athos.—At (106·5km) *rmos Panayías*, a tiny rock-strewn bay, a settlement of the 6C AD has come to ₁ght with a basilican church. As we turn across the peninsula towards Nikitas, a ₁ad branches right to *Ayios Nikólaos* (4km), whence a poor road continues to ₁rgadhákia (16km).

65 From Salónika to Sérres

A. By road via Lakhanás

ROAD 95km (59 miles), the shortest route, coinciding for the first
90km with the main road to Bulgaria. Hilly winding road through
varied upland country; careful driving necessary. In 1916 this was
the main supply road for the right wing of the allied army and was
remade by British engineers.—Buses hourly in 2¾ hours.

We quit Salonika by its dreary N suburbs. The busy highway carrie
traffic for Lakhanás, Nigrita, and Kavalla through a gap (290m) in th
Khortiatis range that shuts in the town to N and E.—11km *Dhervé*
(signs to 'Macedonian Tomb' and 'Ancient Cemetery'). Burial moune
of the 4C BC covering cist graves were explored here in 1962; the
yielded iron weapons, a pair of gilt bronze greaves, a uniqu
embossed krater of gilt bronze, vases of silver and alabaster, and th
burnt remains of a papyrus roll (4C BC), all now in Salonika Museun
To the right diverges first the Kavalla road (Rte 66), then that to Nigri
(see below), and c 1·5km farther on we leave on our left a road to Kilk
(Rte 65C). We cross a cultivated plain. By the side of the road a
(18·5km) a spring and (20km; left) the *Toúmba Assiros*, a promine
mound, excavated by the British School from 1975 and found to hav
been occupied probably continuously from c 2000 BC to c 800 BC. Th
former Turkish name of (22·5km) *Ássiros* (right of road) was Giove
nak. We begin the long climb into the foothills of the *Krousia M*
(Turkish: Beşik Dağ), the ancient Dysoron, which separate the Axi(
basin from the Strymon. From the ridges fine views of the pla
take in Lakes Koronia and Volvi and the heights of Khalkidh
ki. Beyond (35km) *Dorkás* (Taverna) we cross a declivity with pine cl
slopes. At the top of the next rise, by-road (right) to *Vertískos* (8kn
which gives its name to the mountains to the SE. The road undulates
(45km) *Xilópolis* at the head of another wooded valley.

52km (32 miles) **Lakhanás** was the farthest point reached by th
Bulgarians in 1913. We pass first a *Memorial* of the bayonet charg
that checked their advance, with a small *Museum*; then, at the road
summit level (623m), 1km W of the village a *British Military Cemeter*
in which are buried 270 soldiers who died on this front in 1916–17. Th
panorama extends to the Kerkini or Beles Mts (2032m; comp. belov
on the Bulgarian frontier.—55km *Evangelístria* stands on an irregula
spur projecting into the Strymon plain.—59·5km *Kefalokhórion* ha
wayside tavernas.

The **Strymon**, or *Struma* (250km long), called by the Turks Kara-Su, rises in th
Bulgarian mountains, enters Greece through the Rupel Pass, and flows general
SE through a broad and fertile plain enclosed by parallel chains of mountains. I
upper reaches have been dammed to form a new lake (comp. Rte 65C). Its lov
course has been controlled and the former *Lake Achinos*, anciently calle
Prasias, drained. At the SE end of the lake lay the city of *Myrkinos*, founded c 5
by Histiaias. The river empties into the Kolpos Orfanou or Strymonic Gulf. At on

ime it formed the boundary between Macedonia and Thrace. In the First World War the river demarcated the static front line until the break-out of July 1918.

We descend gradually amid scrubby hills.—71·5km *Kalókastron*, where in 1917 Stanley Casson recognised Byzantine walls and the remains of a Roman town, looks out from a low ridge towards Serres. To the left of the road is the *Struma Military Cemetery*, established in 1916 by the 40th Casualty Clearing Station; it contains the graves of 932 officers and men of the British, Indian, and Maltese forces who died on the Strymon front.—At 76·5km we cross the artificially embanked Strymon by a long bridge.—81km *Provatás* (1510 inhab.) produces ouzo. *Monokklissiá* (2·5km S) is notorious for its practices of 8 January (comp. Rte 57), when the women confine the men to domestic chores while they revel in street and tavern. The inhabitants brought the custom from E Thrace in 1922; it may derive from the Dionysiac rites of ancient Thrace. Crossing the Belitsa, a tributary of the Strymon, and the railway, we pass (90km) the road to *Sidhirókastro* (19km; see below) and Bulgaria.

After Sidhirokastro, the road (Europabus twice weekly to Sofia in 8 hours) and railway (daily to Sofia in 9 hours from Salonika) to Bulgaria follow the river through the formidable RUPEL PASS, guarded by the conspicuous *Rupel Fort*.—0km *Koúla* and (43·5km) *Kuláta* are the frontier posts, beyond which the Bulgarian highway continues in the Struma valley.—153km **Sofia**.

We pass the huge Kolokotronis Barracks and enter (95km) Sérres. **Sérres** or *Sérrai* (Σέρραι; Hotels B, C, D) is the capital of its nome and one of the most important commercial cities (45,213 inhab.) in Macedonia. Situated at a low elevation (50m) at the foot of mountainous country (to the NE), it overlooks the fertile plain to the SW through which the Strymon flows some 24km away. Serres is a pleasant town, with wide streets, surrounded by abundant woods and luxuriant gardens. It has a covered swimming-pool.

History. *Siris*, or *Serrhai*, was already chief town of its district in the time of Herodotus; in its plain Xerxes left the sacred mares of the Chariot of the Sun. It became the seat of a bishop and later of a metropolitan, and played a strategic role throughout the Middle Ages. It was ravaged in 1195–96 by the Bulgarians who defeated a Byzantine army and took prisoner Isaac Comnenus, the sebastorator. In 1205 the marauding Vlach, Johannica, besieged Serres; Hugues de Coligny was killed and the surrendered Frankish garrison slaughtered; Boniface de Montferrat, hastening from the Morea, recaptured and refortified the town. It resisted the attacks of Cantacuzenus but fell in 1345 to Dušan, who here promulgated his legal code (1354). Helen, his widow, retired here under the religious name of Elizabeth. Though Manuel recaptured Sérres for the Byzantines in 1371, it attracted the attention of the Ottoman Turks the following year and in 1383 fell decisively into the hands of Lala Shahin. It remained Turkish (as *Siruz*) until 1913, when it was seized by the Bulgarians who set it on fire in their retreat. On 29 June the town celebrates its freedom from the Bulgarians.

The town, almost entirely rebuilt since the Bulgarian incendiarism, is best seen from the ruined 14C *Kastro* (Rfmts) that crowns the round wooded hill to the N. To the NE is a pretty cypress-planted *Cemetery*; to the NW an ancient *Aqueduct* spans a gully. Immediately below lay the Christian quarter (Varoch), where two Byzantine churches have been completely restored since 1951. The *Old Metropolis*, dedicated to SS. Theodore, is a large aisled basilica of the 11C, rather too high for its length, with a pretty domed chapel at one corner. In the apse is a

huge mosaic of the Last Supper, still splendid in its decay. The neigh
bouring *Ayios Nikólaos* an attractive cross-in-square, has an exonar
thex wider than the building. Its octagonal drum and small domes ar
ornamented with brick decoration. Two decayed *Mosques*, pictures
que if unimportant, show where the former Turkish quarter lay. In th
central square, opposite the Dhimarkhion, is a huge edifice with si
domes which has seen Moslem and Christian worship in turn and i
now an archaeological store.

Oinoússa, an attractive village with an old church, stands (6km E) at the mouth
the Kazil Tsai valley, in which there are asbestos mines. Higher up the valle
(12km), in a cool wooded site, is the *Moní Timíou Prodhrómou* (1275), with th
tombs of the founders and of Gennadios II Scholarios (died 1472), first Patriarch
Byzantium under the Turks, and wall paintings.
From Sérres a steep but beautiful mountain road crosses the pass between th
Vrontous Mts and Menoikion to (48km) *Káto Nevrokópion* (Rte 68).

FROM SÉRRES TO DRAMA, 70km (43¾ miles), asphalt, bus. The roa
keeps to higher ground 1·5–5km N of the railway, affording super
views of the mountain chains that ring the Strymon valley and th
Drama plain.—10km Near the village of *Toúmba* (right) has bee
located a large Neolithic settlement with Karanovo-type pottery.
29km *Néa Zíkhni* (259m) is the seat (2726 inhab.) of the small eparch
of Phyllis.—At (33km) *Mesorrákhi* (189m) diverges the road to Amph
polis (Rte 66). Through the broad valley of the Angitis, for a sho
distance, road, river, and railway run close together, before the roa
climbs to (50km) *Alistráti* (261m), a village of 2622 inhab., once th
seat of a bishop, on the easternmost spur of Menoikion. The descer
commands a view N to the Falakron range across the Drama plain. *
56km we cross the Angitis and see (right) the Sitagroí tumulus exca
vated by the British School in 1968–69 (finds in Philippi museum).
59·5km *Sitagroí*.—At 67km we join a road from Kato Nevrokopion.
70·5km **Drama** (Rte 68).

B. By road via Nigríta

Though this road is narrower and slightly longer, it has less traffic
and the more varied scenery.

Leaving the Lakhanás road (see above) at (11km) *Dhervéni*, we turn N
passing (16km) between the *Saratse Toumba*, a Bronze and Iron Ag
tumulus, and the derelict *Perivolákion Station*, once the terminus
the Stavros Military Railway (comp. Rte 66).—19km **Langadhá**
(Hotels B, D), the seat of an eparchy, with 5890 inhab., has alkalin
warm springs (2·5km SE). Here the Anastenaria, a ritual fire-walkin
ceremony, takes place on the feast of SS. Constantine and Helen (2
May).

Tradition asserts that c 1250 in the Thracian village of Kosti, the church of S
Constantine caught fire. The sacred ikons were heard groaning in the flame
whereupon certain villagers dashed into the fire and rescued them without su
fering harm. The ikons have been handed down by the families concerned fro
one generation to the next and the descendants honour their saints each year l
walking barefoot on fire in a state of ecstasy carrying the ikons. The walkers a
called Anastenarides from their imitative groaning (αναστενάζω). In 1914, whe
their territory was transferred from Turkish to Bulgarian rule, they fled with th
ikons to Ayia Eleni (Serres), Mavrolefki (Drama), Meliki, and Langadhas, wher
until 1948, their rituals were held in secret owing to opposition from the Gre
Orthodox Church. Clerical objections in 1960 caused the ceremonies to be he

that year only in Ayia Eleni. The orgiastic dance to drum and lyre with attendant chorus, together with the sacrifice of a bull decked with garlands, suggests an origin far earlier than the 13C, and the ceremony probably survives, shorn of attendant excesses, from the pre-Christian worship of Dionysos.

The road climbs into the wooded foothills of *Mt Vertískos*, passing close beneath the steep S side of Kharvata (1103m). The chief town of the S slopes is (49km) *Sokhós*.—We skirt an upland plain with the marshy *Vromolimnai* ('stinking lakes'), a once notorious breeding-place of malaria; the Greek army began draining them in 1961. The road climbs the W spur of Mt Kerdhilion and makes a devious descent. To the NE extends the area once occupied by Lake Prasias (comp. above), the extent of which is betrayed by the prehistoric mounds that lined its shores.—81km **Nigríta**, a town of 6531 inhab. and the seat of the eparch of *Visaltia*, overlooks the Strymon valley. It is a centre for tobacco. The Bulgarians took the town in April 1913 and destroyed it on retiring two months later.

At *Dimitrítsi*, 13km NW, the Greek general Branas defeated the retreating Normans in 1185, putting an end to their expedition.

Crossing a long bridge over the Strymon, we enter (100km) **Serres** from the S past the Railway Station.

C. By Railway via Sidhirókastro

RAILWAY, 162km (101 miles), 6 trains daily in 2¾–6 hours. This is part of the through route to Turkey (see Rte 69B). Between Salónika and Sérres the line makes a wide detour to the N via (42km) *Kilkís*, (97km) *Rodhópolis*, and (130·5km) *Sidhirókastro*, so that the distance covered is much greater than by road.

The roads that follow the course of the railway are mainly poor and local. From Salonika the best road to *Kilkís* (48km) branches left from the Sérres road (comp. Rte 65A), though from the direction of Edhessa it is better to turn up the Gallikos at Dhiavéta, following the railway. From Kilkís its continuation crosses the Krousia Mts to (88·5km) *Rodhópolis*. By road Sidhirokastro is better reached from the Lakhanas road (comp. Rte 65A) or visited from Sérres.

The line runs NW but after 8km diverges from that to Ghevgheli and Central Europe.—Before (22km) *Filadhelfianá* we cross from the left to the right bank of the Gallikos.—30km *Gallikós*.—42km *Kilkís Station* (198m) is situated on the Salonika–Kilkis road by the village of *Kristóni*, 5km SW of the town. Just SW of the station is *Sarigöl Military Cemetery*, with the graves of 659 British soldiers who died here in 1917–18 of wounds received in the attacks of the Bulgarian defence of Doiran. **Kilkís** (Hotels C, E), capital of the nome of the same name, with 11,148 inhab., was the scene of the defeat on 21 June 1913 of a Bulgarian attempt on Salonika. To the S of the town a conspicuous monument crowns a wooded hill and a museum records the battle. The town's former name was *Avrathisari*. A small *Museum*, by the Nomarkhia at the far end of the town, houses the archaic kouros found at Evropós in the Axios Valley and bronzes from an Iron Age grave at Chauchitsa.

We cross the road from Kilkis to Doïráni at (52km) *Metallikón*. An inscribed base for statues at Hadrian and Sabina erected by the city of *Bragylae*, found in 1952, gives for the first time the ancient name of the place. The railway descends the Ayák, or Doiránis, to the shore of

Lake Doiran.—71km *Doiráni Station* is now separated by the Yugoslav frontier from the town whose name it bears. **Lake Doiran** (10km by 6·5km), well stocked with fish, is shared between Greece and Yugoslavia. It formed part of the Vardar-Doiran front in various actions of the First World War.

On 'Colonial Hill' above the station (1·5km S) is the *British Salonika Force Campaign Memorial*, an obelisk, 12m high, guarded by two carved couchant lions, with panels bearing the names of 2160 fallen who have no known grave. In the *Doiran Military Cemetery*, adjoining to the E, lie 1300 dead (875 British).

The railway-line follows the SE shore, then bears NE across the foothills of the KERKINI MOUNTAINS. Parallel, to the N, runs the main range, whose steep crest, rising in *Demir Kapon* to 2032m, forms the inhospitable frontier with Bulgaria; it is better known by the Slav name of *Belasica*.—Beyond (87km) *Kastanoússa* in the narrow *Tepé* pass (270m), the views become extensive on all sides.—97km **Rodhópolis** is the centre of the alpine area. The railway now veers E through marshy country watered by the Koumoulis.—Beyond (111km) *Mandráki* we enter the valley of the Strymon, which to the S has been transformed into *Lake Kerkinis* by a dam.—120km *Viróneia*, a Greek headquarters during the war of 1913. Between here and the right bank of the Strymon were the silver mines of the Macedonian kings.—At 128km the line crosses the Strymon on a long bridge near its emergence from the Rupel Pass, then turns SE, leaving the line to Sofia (opened 1965).—133·5km *Sidhirókastro Town Station*, 4km S of the town.

Sidhirókastro ('Iron Castle'; Hotels C, D, E; cafés in the Plateia), a town of 6157 inhab., capital of the eparchy of Sintike, is picturesquely situated at the foot of a hill on which is a medieval Kastro. The town is better remembered by its Turkish name Demir Hisar and is improbably to be identified with the ancient *Herakleia Sintike*. It is watered by the Chrysovitikos, a tributary of the Strymon. The town carries on a brisk transit trade. The church of *Ayios Dhimítrios* incorporates the pedimental façade of a Macedonian tomb as its templon. On a hill to the E is a monastery cut out of the rock. Road to Serres, see Rte 65A.

We traverse a bare region given over to cotton cultivation. Beyond (145·5km) *Skotoúsa* we reach the broad valley of the Strymon.— 162km (101 miles) **Sérres**. The station lies c 2·5km from the town centre.

66   From Salónika to Kaválla

ROAD, 166km (103 miles), in good condition throughout, on the course of the Via Egnatia to (101·5km) *Amphípolis*. Buses frequently

At 101km, beyond the Strymon bridge, a new road diverges to follow the coast and reach *Kaválla* (176km) via *Néa Péramos*. This route is 10km farther than the older road. It is much faster to Nea Peramos but much slower thereafter where road improvements still have a long way to go. At 126km there is a turning (left) to *Loutrá Elevthéron* (Hotels C, D, E), a summer resort, near the mouth of the pretty Marmara, with hot springs. Just beyond the 130km post there is a Byzantine fort with well-preserved tower, on a cliff top immediately to the right of the road.

We quit Salonika as in Rte 65, and at (10km) *Dherveni* leave the Serres road on our left.—Beyond (13km) *Layiná*, with a spring, the road was paralleled by a railway (now derelict but visible a field's width left) of 60cm gauge, built by the Allies in 1916–17 from Sarakli (now

Perivolákion; Rte 65B), just N of (16·5km) *Kavallárion*, to Stavrós (see below). We approach LAKE KORONIA, 14·5km long but nowhere more than 6m deep, which is of great ornithological interest. Near the W end of the lake a typical mound gives evidence of prehistoric occupation.—24km *Ayios Vasílios*. To the right rises Mt Khortiátis with its prominent observatory and radar station; we cross a series of torrent beds.—38km *Langadhíkia*. We run above the S shore of the much prettier LAKE VOLVI (19km long) enclosed on its N side by the Volves hills or *Mt Besikíon* (658m).—At (51km) *Loutrá Vólvis* (Hotel C) are the hot sulphur springs of *Néa Apollonía* (2·5km), a local spa. Beyond the Kotza Potamos and a tumulus (right), (59km) *Apollonía* preserves the name of a station on the Via Egnatia, perhaps founded by Chalcidians c 432 BC on land given them by Perdikkas II of Macedon, and mentioned in the Acts of the Apostles (xvii, 1). The Roman character of the road remains. We pass several brick kilns.—71km *Rendína*, also with hot springs, lies at the E end of the lake at the mouth of the *Stena Rendinas*, a pretty ravine sometimes called the 'Macedonian Tempe', which we traverse to the sea. Here stood *Arethousa*, where the 'Tomb of Euripides' became known to Roman travellers as a staging post. On the right rises the hillock with remains of a school whose foundation is attributed to Aristotle; opposite is the hot spring where Alexander the Great used to bathe when a student. A little farther on a cave (left) faces the by-road to *Stavrós* (3·5km right; Hotels C, E), a small bathing resort (2259 inhab.) and roadstead.

We reach the sea at the head of the STRYMONIC GULF (formerly the *Gulf of Orfani*), one of the two great inlets bordering the Chalcidice peninsula. The foothills of *Mt Kerdhilion* (1091m) approach close to the sea.—83km *Asproválta* (Hotels D; F/A) has a fine sandy beach and an N.T.O.G. camp site; the coast for the next 16km is undergoing development.—At (98km) *Néa Kerdhíllia* a by-road runs inland to *Aïdonokhóri*, perhaps ancient Tragilos, where remains of a Heroön have been dug and a shrine of Leda and Aphrodite, with finds going back to the 6C BC. Finds show this to have antedated Amphipolis.

Just after the turn the *Lion of Amphipolis* guards the long bridge over the Strymon. The colossal animal, reassembled from fragments in 1936–37, has been mounted on a pedestal built on the ancient foundation with blocks of the 2C BC dredged from the Strymon, where they may have been reused in a medieval dam. Originally the lion may have honoured Laomedon, the sailor of Mytilene who later became governor of Syria. Beyond the bridge, amid low hills (left), are the scattered remains of ancient **Amphipolis**; the site is well worth the short diversion up the Drama road (1km farther on). From the road the outline of the acropolis walls can be seen. The city was built on a commanding eminence (154m) above the E bank of the Strymon, just below its egress from Lake Achinos (now drained), c 5km from the sea. A loop of the river flowed round the W half of the city walls.

The place, which belonged to the Edonians of Thrace, was originally called *Ennea Hodoi* ('Nine Ways'), for which reason, according to Herodotus (VII, 114), Xerxes on crossings its bridges buried alive nine local boys and nine girls. It was colonised as *Amphipolis* by the Athenians in 437 BC after an abortive attempt 28 years earlier. Deriving its wealth from the gold mines of Mt Pangaion, Amphipolis was one of their most important N possessions: hence the consternation when it surrendered to the Spartan Brasidas in 424. The historian (and general) Thucydides saved its port of *Eion*, at the mouth of the Strymon, but, for failing to save Amphipolis as well, he was exiled for 20 years by his countrymen (Thuc. IV, 104–6; V, 26). In 421 the Athenians made an unsuccessful attempt to retake the city; in the cavalry battle both Kleon, the Athenian demagogue and general, and his opponent Brasidas were killed. Amphipolis was seized by Philip II of Macedon in 358. After the battle of Pydna (168) it became the capital of one of the four republics provisionally set up by the Romans. St. Paul passed through Amphipolis on his way to Thessalonica ('Acts', XVII, 1). The city was a station on the Via Egnatia and the seat of a bishop in the Early Christian period. Excavations have been made since 1956 by the Greek Archaeological Service. Visitors with limited time should go directly to the recently exposed walls (see below).

The Drama road climbs, and soon (left) there is a small sign in Greek (*Macedonian Tomb*). Two tombs lie on the hill right of the road: one had been plundered, but the other yielded precious articles now in Kávalla museum. Further up the road, another sign (left) indicates ancient walls and, a short climb above the road, further sections of the defences can be seen. Substantial remains of a Classical gymnasium have recently been discovered in this vicinity (ask directions). After another 300m is the turning (left) for the modern village. On the hill opposite the turn is a Hellenistic cemetery of rock-cut tombs. In the village, the church contains a relief of Totoes, the Thracian equivalent of Hypnos. Signs leads the visitor through the village and up the hill to the main archaeological area, on the acropolis of the ancient city (phylax in attendance for much of the day). The principal remains so far excavated are not of the Classical period but of five churches of the 5 and 6C AD, four basilical and one with a hexagonal internal layout. Some of the mosaics (including fine and varied representations of birds) can be seen, protected by wooden shelters; others remain semi-permanently covered. A short distance further up the track are the remains of a Roman house, again under a shelter to protect its mosaics. It has a paved courtyard with a well in addition to mosaic floors and an apsidal room which originally had painted plaster decoration. Beside the house and not yet fully investigated is a building with statue dedications in front.—100m below these structures, down a track, is a remarkable Hellenistic house (covered) with fine painted decoration employing architectural motifs of the kind which formed the basis for the First Pompeian style. A *Shrine of Clio* borders a deep ravine to the SE.

Beyond the village turn, the next turning left from the Drama road leads in 400m to a derelict railway station below a ruined Byzantine tower, which once bore an inscription stating that it was built in 1367 for the monastery of the Pantocrator on Mt Athos. Here and farther on three long sections of the *CITY WALLS stand in places to a height of 7m. These have now been proved by soundings at 64 places to form a circuit of nearly 7km with an inner acropolis wall of 2km. Built in fine coursed masonry, with towers, gates, sluices for flood waters resembling archery embrasures, and walkways, the walls extend to guard a crossing of the Strymon. Farther on (500m), within a fenced enclosure are further sections of the wall and the interesting fossilised wooden piles of the *Ancient Bridge*. If the site is closed, these can be adequately viewed from the track which runs alongside the river.

FROM AMPHIPOLIS TO DRAMA, 53km, new road. After 8km the road divides, the older road (left) running N to join the Serres–Drama road (30km; Rte 65A) at Mesorrákhi.—The right branch runs in upland country with views W across the Strymon plain and with the mass of Pangaion to the E.—20km *Rhodholívos* (2954 inhab.) is the most populous village of the eparchy of *Phyllis*. Neolithic dwellings and remains of a Temple of Diana have been unearthed here.—25km *Próti* (1771 inhab.)—53km *Drama*, see Rte 68.

As we continue towards Kávalla, the silted up harbour of *Eion*, with the walls (10–14C) of Byzantine Khrysoupolis beside it, is visible to the right between the road and the sea. Below (111km) Boúrnali, an isolated little hill, the road turns inland, while another (opposite) leads in 500m to the fine beach and summer resort of *Toúzla*.

A by-road skirts the hill to (2km) *Orfánion*, the village that gives its name to the gulf; the prominent walls (not yet archaeologically explored) are Turkish and perhaps Byzantine.—Near (8km) *Kariani*, Gaïdhourókastro may represent the site of *Galepsos*, where Perseus of Macedon touched in his headlong flight to Samothrace after his defeat at Pydna (Livy, 44–5). At the sea the road joins the new coastal highway to Kavalla (comp. above).

We enter the beautiful valley between Mt Pangaion on the N and Mt Símvolon on the S, following the ancient road taken by Xerxes in 480 BC; by Roman times the Via Egnatia had been diverted round the N of Pangaion in order to pass through both Amphipolis and Philippi.— 123km *Podhokhórion*, which has a three-aisled Early Christian basilica, excavated in 1973, is connected by road with Karianí (see above). The villages are mostly to the left of the road on the S slopes of Pangaion, where, near *Kiría*, a shrine of the rider-hero (Ήρως Αὐλωνείτης has been located.—143km Turning (asphalt) for Néa Péramos (13km), affording an alternative coastal run into Kávalla (comp. below).—146·5km **Elevtheroúpolis** or *Pravion*, a flourishing town of 4411 inhab., mainly engaged in tobacco culture, is the capital of the eparchy of Pangaios and the seat of a bishop. It is the usual base for the ascent of Mt Pangaion.

TOUR AND ASCENT OF **MOUNT PANGAION**. A road (64·5km, mostly unpaved; bus daily to Mesolakkia) traverses the bare N side of the mountain, rejoining the main road near Bournali (see above).—6·5km *Andifílippoi*. *Palaiokhórion* lies in a valley to the left.—15Km. **Nikisianí** nestles in a broader valley 3km to the left. Traces of ancient gold workings have been observed. Hereabouts, according to some authorities, was *Skaptesyle*, where Thucydides had an estate incorporating gold mines, to which he retired in exile after the fiasco at Amphipolis. Here he collected materials for his history and here he died. Other scholars place the estate near Stavros or near Khrisoupolis. A large *Tumulus*, 1km right of the road, was excavated in 1959–60 by D. Lazarides, when six shaft graves yielded vessels and coins (4C BC) now in Kávalla museum.—29km *Kormísta*. For the ascent of Pangaion, see below.—42km *Rodhólivos* stands on the Drama–Amphipolis road comp. above).

Mules may be hired at Kormista for the ascent of the mountain. **Mount Pangaion** was celebrated for its oracle of Dionysos, for the roses that grew on its slopes, and for the gold and silver mines in its neighbourhood. Here the Maenads tore Orpheus to pieces for comparing Apollo with Dionysos. The higher slopes are of crystalline white marble so the metal deposits must have been lower down. Its riches attracted the cupidity of the ancient world and led to constant strife between neighbouring states until Philip II of Macedon gained control.

A climb of 2 hours brings us to the **Monastery of the Ikosifoiníssis** (Μονή τῆς Εἰκοσιφοινίσσης), beautifully situated 753m up in the midst of plane woods. The monks welcome visitors (donation expected). The monastery is said to have been founded in the time of Sozon, metropolitan of Philippi (443–54) but is probably not earlier than the 10C. It suffered much under the Turks, notably in 1823, when it was charged with having sheltered partisans in the War of Independence. The *Katholikon*, a fine Byzantine edifice restored in 1954, has good modern frescoes. The library is rich in treasures, including a MS Gospel on vellum (1378), with a cover inlaid with precious stones.

The ascent is generally made early in the morning in order to see the sunrise. The route up is via the *Cavern of Asketótrypo*, past a secondary summit (1705m) to the highest peak, *Pilaf Tepe* (1958m). Above the tree line the path commands the whole Strymon valley.

At 159km we join the road from Drama (Rte 68) and wind up through the gap in the barrier ridge that separates Kávalla from its hinterland; the old Turkish paved road is clearly seen below (right). From the summit (210m), with a sanatorium, a large Tourist Pavilion and post office, and the *Monastery of St. Silas*, we get a superb sudden *View of the Bay of Kávalla, with the town framed between the hills and the sea; in the middle distance is the island of Thasos, and on a clear day Samothrace and even the Dardanelles can be seen. The road zigzags down to the town.

166km (103 miles) **KAVÁLLA** (Καβάλα), beautifully situated at the head of its bay and best seen from the sea, rises in a shallow amphitheatre on outlying slopes of Mandra Kari, one of the chain of hills that link Mt Simvilon with the Lekanis massif. The old citadel occupies a rocky promontory jutting into the sea. The second largest city (56,375

inhab.) of Macedonia, it is the chief town of the small nome of Kavalla
the seat since 1924 of the metropolitan of Philippi, Neapolis, and Tha
sos, and the headquarters of an army corps. Kavalla is the exporting
centre of Macedonian tobacco. It is the best base for visiting Philippi
and the main embarkation point for the island of Thasos.

Airport. At Khrisóupolis (30km SE) with two flights per day to Athens. Bus from
TERMINAL on quayside, Paraliakí Leofóros 8.

Hotels A, B, C, D, E; many in Venizélou and Erithróu Starroú.

Restaurants of good quality in the centre and by the old harbour.

Post Offices (Pl. 3), Omonías and Khrisostómou Metropolítou 8.—O.T.E. CEN
TRE (Pl. 7), Megálou Alexándrou/Melá.

N.T.O.G. office at Plateía Eleftheriás (very good). TOURIST POLICE/POLICE
Omonías 119.

Buses for local destinations from Plat. Karaóli Dhimitríou; long-distance Bu
Station at the quayside. Frequent services to all main towns in Macedonia an
Thrace.

Ferry frequently to Prinos (Thasos); occasionally to Limenaria. Other steame
connections to Samothrace, Limnos, Lesbos, Chios, Kimi (Evvia), Ayios Konstan
dinos, Piraeus.—**Air Service** twice daily to Athens direct; terminal on quayside
(Pl. 6).

Ancient Drama Festival in August at Philippi and Thasos.

History. Kavalla occupies the site of *Neapolis*, the port of Philippi and apparently
of its predecessor, and is said to have been a colony of Thasos. At the time of the
Battle of Philippi the fleet of Brutus was stationed here. Neapolis was the usual
port of disembarkation for travellers to Europe from the Levant. St. Paul landed
here on his way to Philippi ('Acts', xvi, 11). In the Byzantine era the town seems to
have adopted the name of *Christoupolis*. The burning of the town by the Nor
mans on their march towards Constantinople in 1185 is recorded by an inscrip
tion from the kastro wall. Here Ramon Muntaner and the Catalan Grand Com
pany landed from Gallipoli (1306) at the start of their march to Athens. Kavall
was Turkish until 1912, since when it has suffered three Bulgarian occupations in
1912–13, 1916–18, and 1942–44. Here was born Mehmet Ali (1769–1849), the son
of an Albanian farmer, who became pasha of Egypt and founder of the dynasty
that ended with King Fuad II in 1953.

The business centre of the city occupies a depression to shoreward of
the citadel, the accident of which necessitated the *Kamares Aqueduc*
(Pl. 8) which forms the town's most prominent feature. Built in a style
that derives ultimately from Roman models, this fine structure on three
tiers of arches appears to date from the reign of Suleiman the Magnifi
cent (1520–66), and carried water to the citadel. Odhós Ellenikís Dhi
mokratías, to the N, and neighbouring streets retain some old Turkish
houses and shops, but these are fast disappearing. From PLATEÍA
NIKITÁRA, below the aqueduct, Odhós Omonías runs NW to become
the main shopping street. It passes across the landward end of the long
PLATEÍA ELEVTHERÍAS (Pl. 7), which extends to the inner harbour
This is a small artificial basin within the large *Harbour*, formed by
the construction of two long moles since the war. Extensive land re
clamation has provided a new seafront to the W (comp. below).

To the E, on the promontory, the OLD CITADEL is surrounded by
well-preserved Byzantine walls, restored after an earthquake in 920
(inscription) and again in the 16C; ancient blocks of stone are incorpo
rated in them. The attractive multi-domed *Imaret* (Pl. 11), an almshou
se for 300 softas, was founded by Mehmet Ali after his native town had
unwisely rejected the alternative suggestion of a harbour. The semi
nary was endowed with the revenues of Thasos, and membership
brought free pilaf and exemption from military service; it was known
locally as Tembel-Haneh, the lazy man's home. The most interesting

monument in the city, it is in a melancholy state of decay.

Excavations by Ephor Lazarides in 1959–61, N of the Imaret, uncovered the peribolos of a *Sanctuary of the Parthenos* (6C BC); the pottery found included examples from all over the Aegean (see below).

In the Seraidaris Garden is *Mehmet Ali's Birthplace* (Pl. 15), a pleasant Turkish house with good panelling, admirably cared for by the Egyptian government until 1961 and since by the Greek authorities (ring for caretaker). Below are the stable and kitchen; above, the harem and the pasha's quarters. In the little square, beyond, is a lively equestrian *Statue of Ali* in bronze, by Dimitriades, below which a *Belvedere* affords a view towards Thasos. The rocks on the E side of the peninsula afford excellent swimming to the locals. The ruined Byzantine *Kastro* (Pl. 12) that crowns the promontory is submerged on the E flank of the hill by old houses (mosque, baths, etc); the central keep is approached from the E side and its walls afford a fine view of the harbour.

From Plateía Elevtherías, Odhós Khrisostómou Smírnis (Venizélou) leads W past the *Public Garden* (Pl. 6), then passes between tall *Warehouses*, where tobacco is graded and stored. These formerly backed directly on the shore. Kavalla once had 200 of them. Just to the right is the *Cathedral* (Pl. 1), with a marble iconostasis of many compartments.

In gardens at the W end of the sea front stands the **Archaeological Museum**. Built in 1965 it comprises two ground-floor rooms linked by a wide corridor, an upstairs room, and courtyards. Exhibits are labelled in English.

GROUND FLOOR. The ENTRANCE HALL has Hellenistic and Roman sculpture from Amphipolis. ROOM I contains some Early Christian and Byzantine sculpture and architectural fragments from Neapolis (Kavalla). Finds from the Kavalla Sanctuary of Parthenos (6–5C BC), including Ionic capitals, figurines, a votive naïskos in the form of a treasury, and pottery (both local and imported). Along the CORRIDOR, with a large map showing ancient sites in Eastern Macedonia, are displayed Late Neolithic and Early Bronze Age finds, mainly from Dikili Tach, though the best finds from this site are in the Philippi museum. Also a collection of sculpture including, at the far end, a Metope (5C BC) from Aïdonokhóri (anc. Tragilos), showing a fight between two hoplites.

ROOM II, finds from the cemetery at Amphipolis: polychrome glass; gold wreaths and diadems, and *Jewellery; coloured busts of goddesses; grave stelai (one painted); figurines; and pottery, clearly from a local workshop, as yet undiscovered. At the end of the room: partial reconstruction of a double funeral chamber (3C BC) with paintings; its stele stands to the left. Nearby are gold and other articles (male and female) from the same tomb, including a polished silver mirror in a folding case and a man's ring bearing the picture of a youth.

The FIRST FLOOR ROOM (access from entrance hall) houses finds of Archaic–Roman date, mostly from colonial foundations in the area (Abdera, Oisyme, Galepsos, Tragilos). Most of the extensive explanatory material relating to the colonies is in Greek, but some of the labels are in English. Material from Abdera includes the Dolphin mosaic from a Hellenistic house, a painted Clazomenian sarcophagus from the earliest period of settlement, architectural terracottas and terracotta figurines from a sanctuary. From Nikisiani, pottery, polychrome figurines, silverware and coins of Philip II (gold staters) and Alexander the Great. From Drama, a lamp and chain in the form of a slave (2C

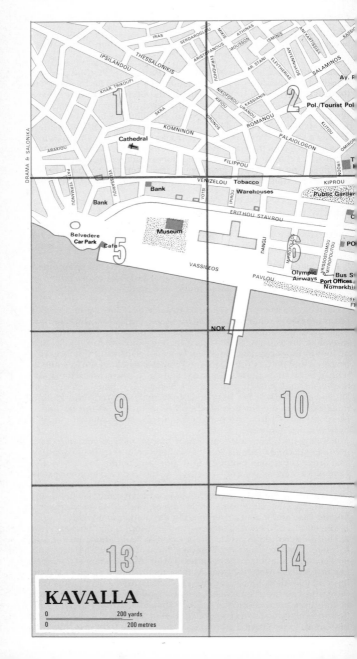

KAVALLA

0   200 yards

0   200 metres

AD). From Aïdonokhori (Tragilos), a massive painted larnax (3C BC) and votives from a sanctuary of Aphrodite and Leda.—In the COURTYARD are various marbles and inscriptions.

A coast road runs W from Kavalla to *Néa Péramos* (20km), where it joins the fast new road from Amphipolis (see Rte 66, introduction).—At (4km) *Kalamítsa* (Hotel B), site of ancient *Antisara*, of which a 4C Asklepieion and an earlier wall have come to light, is the pleasant Batis beach; farther on a fine N.T.O.G. beach (Restaurant) and camp site, and the Tosca Beach (select and not cheap) backed by its Hotel, A). The road continues past beaches and coves to (16km) *Iraklitsa* and (20km) Néa Péramos, a small resort. To the right of the track leading S from the village is the acropolis of ancient *Oisyme*; finds from its cemetery by the shore are in Kavalla museum. On the hill, on the opposite side of the track, is the fortress of the Byzantine city of *Anactoroupolis*.

67 Thásos

CAR FERRY from Kaválla regularly to Prinó harbour; less regularly to Límen. Also from Keramoti (Rte 69A) frequently to Limen.—The island deserves more than a day trip, Limen itself meriting at least a whole day's exploration.

Thásos, the northernmost of the islands of the Archipelago, is of volcanic origin, mountainous, and of great natural beauty. Situated close to the mainland, its nearest point is only 10km from the mouth of the Nestos, and it thus faces the boundary between Macedonia and Thrace. Politically the island forms an eparchy of the Macedonian nome of Kavalla. Its area is 399 sq. km; almost circular in shape, it has a length from N to S of c 24km and a width of c 19km. Its highest point is *Mt Hypsarion* (1142m), nearly in the centre. The mountainsides are covered with forests, pines, planes, and chestnut trees predominating; the timber has always been in demand for shipbuilding.

The population of 13,111 is distributed btween the capital and ten other villages, of which the most modern is *Limenária*, on the SW coast, where zinc workings are exploited. In the coastal areas tobacco and olives are cultivated. A road encircles the island: otherwise the only means of communication is by mule track. There is good water in the island. The marble quarries of Thasos have always been famous; the gold mines earned in antiquity for the island the epithet of 'golden'. Minerals worked today include silver, antimony, and zinc.

History. The tradition of an early Phoenician occupation, recounted by Herodotus (VI, 47), is not confirmed by excavation, though the Parian colonists of c 710–680 BC seem to have had commerce with Tyre. The Parians, among whom was the poet Archilochos, excused their annexation of the island by calling it the command of Herakles, and the Phoenician myth probably dates from the time of Theogenes (mid-5C), the boxer-politician who claimed Herakles as his father. The colonists prospered by exploiting the Thasian gold mines and later took control of Skaptesyle on the mainland. Their zenith of prosperity was in the 6C BC. Early in the 5C Histiaios, tyrant of Miletus, unsuccessfully besieged the island. In the Persian wars, despite the famous walls of their city, the Thasians submitted tamely to the invader. A dispute with Athens about the mainland mines led to the reduction of the island in 463, but in 446 Thasos seems to have taken over again the mineral wealth of Galepsos. From Thasos in 424 Thucydides set out on his unsuccessful attempt to break the Spartan siege of Amphipolis. Lysander massacred its Athenian partisans in 404, but Thasos again allied with Athens in 389 and became a permanent member of the second Athenian league. About 340 the island was seized by Philip II and it remained Macedonian until the Romans arrived in 196 BC. During this period it developed a flourishing export of wine, and Thasian merchants carried on the trade between Thrace and Southern Greece. Under the Empire Thasian marble and oil enjoyed an international reputation. The medieval history of Thasos is obscure; the capital was removed to the interior because of pirates. Before passing under Turkish domination in 1455, the island was a fief of the Genoese Gattilusi. In 1760 it was given by Mahmud II to the family of Mehmet Ali, and became in consequence in 1813–1920 a quasi-independent appanage of Egypt, having its own president. In 1770–74 it was occupied by a Russian fleet which made great inroads into its timber. In October 1912 it was occupied by the Greek army, in 1916 by the Allies, and in 1941 by the Bulgars.

Thasos was the birthplace of Polygnotos, the painter, of the rhapsodist Stesimbrotos, and of Theogenes, son of Timoxenos, who is said by Pausanias to have carried off no fewer than 1400 athletic crowns. The physician Hippocrates lived for three years in Thasos, whose climatic variations he recorded. Excavations since 1910 have been undertaken by the French School, which publishes an excellent detailed guide.

The island capital is **Límen** ('The Harbour'; Hotels B, C, D, E; F/A), or **Thásos**, on the N coast, on the site of the ancient city of Thasos. As well as being the administrative headquarters with 2300 inhab. Limen is the seat of a bishop and popular as a summer holiday centre with Greeks and Yugoslavs.

*TOUR OF THE WALLS, 2 hours. The earliest circuit was demolished by order of Darius (492–1), the second by Kimon (464–3); the existing wall, on the old foundations throughout, dates mainly from a reconstruction in 412–411 BC. Two styles of masonry, polygonal and ashlar, can be distinguished. From the modern landing-place at Limen we first visit the ancient *Naval Harbour*, which, although silted up, still shelters small caiques. The two moles, once protected by walls forming a marine extension of the enceinte, have been raised to the level of the water, in which can be seen the foundations of a large round tower at the angle of the S mole.

From this harbour a path, following the line of the walls, leads N. We soon reach two ancient gateways which afforded access to the shore between the two harbours. Each gate is adorned with an Archaic bas-relief, contemporary with the date of the circumvallation (494 BC), after which they have been called the *Chariot Gate* and the *Gate of Semele-Thyone*. The first relief represents Artemis in her chariot, the horses of which are held by Hermes; the second is a mutilated group of Hermes and the Graces.

Inland of the gate an ancient quarter has been uncovered by removing most of the Roman remains to show the growth of the town between the 8C and 5C BC.

The path ascends gradually inland (E) and we see, submerged in the sea, the remains of the moles of the *Commercial Harbour*. The constructions on the promontory are of medieval date. *Thasopoúla*, the small island to the N, now inhabited only by birds and snakes, has slight ancient and medieval remains. The path, now bears S along the walls, here of admirable polygonal blocks, to a wood of holm oaks, amid which (below right) is the cavea of the *Greek Theatre*. The remains were tidied up in 1957 to show the surviving architectural members of the 4C BC, recovered from the late remodelling of the orchestra (by the Romans for wild beast shows).

We continue to climb, following the scarp (the wall here has been destroyed) to the **Acropolis**, a ridge with three summits. The first is known by inscriptions to have held a *Sanctuary of Pythian Apollo* (the god who told the Parians to colonise Thasos). The existing remains except for parts of the foundations are of the *Genoese Citadel*, dating partly from a reconstruction by Tedisio Zaccaria (c 1310) and in part from the Gattulisi era. At the S angle is the guard-room, built of ancient materials; near by, in the outer wall, is an elegant relief of a

Acropolis

Temple

Artem

Theatre

Dionysion

Dimitriadis
Quarter

Poseidonion

Gate

Chariot Gate

Harbour

HARBO

Sanctuary

THASOS

0   150 metres

funeral feast (5C or 4C BC).—The wall now runs SW through remains of a medieval village to a high terrace of fine construction on which are the foundations (all that survives) of the 5C *Temple of Athena*, identified in 1958 by the discovery of sherds dedicated to Athena Poliouchos. The path now descends to a little col where there is a rock-hewn *Sanctuary of Pan*, with a worn Hellenistic bas-relief of the god piping to his goats. Just beyond this a high rock forming the third summit ·commands an extensive *View of Samothrace and the mainland.

We descend steeply to the SW by a secret *Stairway* hewn from the rock in the 6C BC, until we regain the line of the walls. Having passed a tower, we note a large stone on which is carved an *Apotropaion*, two enormous eyes to protect the enceinte from the Evil Eye. Just before reaching a sharp bend in the wall to the W, we come to the *Gate of Parmenon*, with its lintel still in place; near by is a block signed with the name of the craftsman: 'Parmenon made me'. We pass through the gate and descend. On reaching level ground we turn away from the town to see the *Gate of Silenus*, an unusual oblique postern, with a colossal mutilated *Bas-relief of Silenus holding a kantharos; below is a niche for votive offerings. The sculpture, which is of Ionian workmanship and unique for its style and size, survives from the earliest circuit. Beyond a tower with embrasures is the *Gate of Dionysos and Herakles*. An archaic inscription still in place records that these two gods were the patron divinities of Thasos. The relief of the archer Herakles is in Istanbul; that of Dionysos is missing. We go on to the *Gate of Zeus and Hera*, which has 5C bas-reliefs in the Archaic manner: before the seated Hera stands Iris; before Zeus, Hermes. A few metres away, in the midst of olive trees through which we glimpse the sea, is the fine Roman *Sarcophagus of Poliades*. The line of the walls continues NW, crossing the village square (see below) to reach the harbour.

THE LOWER TOWN, 1 hour. A few yards E of the two gates near the naval harbour (see above) is a group of ruins, the chief of which is the *Sanctuary of Poseidon* entered by a path between gardens. This is a large quadrangular terrace with the remains of a circular and a square altar. At the gate of the sanctuary are two bases with inscriptions (beginning of 4C); a little in front, almost intact, is the *Monumental Altar to Hera Epilimenia* (Protectress of Harbours), which had an inscription (now in the Museum) reciting the sacred law forbidding the sacrifice of she-goats.—To the S is the *Sanctuary of Dionysos*, a triangular temenos, re-explored in 1957–58, and covered again except for the remains of a 3C choregic monument. On its semicircular base are engraved the names of victors in a theatrical competition; the categories in which they competed were represented by statues; the statue of comedy is in the museum together with the colossal head of Dionysos from the centrepiece of the group.

The **Agora** (entered from the square by the Museum) is bordered by porticoes. Its layout has been clarified by judicious restoration of the foundations since 1955. The place was entered from the harbour by *Propylaia* in the NW corner, and from the town side by several passageways which led into the *South West Stoa*, a Doric colonnade of 33 columns (1C AD). In the S angle of the square is a monumental *Altar*. The *South East Stoa*, also of the 1C AD, had 31 columns of which three have been re-erected at the E end. This fronted a long hypostyle gallery, entered by four doors; the wall which they pierced still stands to a height of 1·8m. Beneath the E end is the base of a *Monument of Glaukos* (7C BC). In the centre of the Agora the excavators have unearthed a *Heroön of Lucius Caesar* and another of *Theogenes*; and in the N angle a *Sanctuary of Zeus Agoraios* surrounded by a balustrade, later interrupted by a *Tholos* (3– 2C BC). On the NE side, next to the Propylaia, is a building with projecting wings (c 330 BC), similar to the Stoa of Zeus at Athens; this survived to the 5C AD when it gave place to a Christian *Basilica*.

Outside the E angle is the unexplained flagged *Passage of the Theoria* (c 470 BC) from which came reliefs now in the Louvre, and inscriptions with lists of magistrates (in the museum). Farther to the E is the *Artemision*; ex-voto objects dedicated to Artemis have been recovered dating from 7C BC. The Hellenistic sanctuary had a square temenos, traced in 1959, though most of its statuary was carried off to Istanbul in 1909.

The **Museum** is generally opened on request by the caretaker. In the CENTRAL HALL (I). Colossal Kriophoros (early 6C; unfinished), found in the acropolis wall; Head of Pegasus, part of the architectural decoration of the Herakleion; Torso of a kouros, found in the sea off Cape Pachys; Funerary stele (late 6C); painted terracotta plaques and heads, including a frieze of riders; Head of Silenus (c 525 BC); Kouros of the school of Pythagoras from the Herakleion; Head of a horse from the same (c 460 BC), much less archaic in style.—ROOM II (behind) contains finds from the Temple of Artemis, including a bronze statuette of the goddess and an exquisite lion's head in ivory (6C BC); boustrophedon funerary inscription of Glaukos, son of Leptine, of Paros (companion of Archilochos); fine silver coins; Archaic pottery.—In the small R. III off the main hall: beautiful Attic kylix, shining as new.—ROOM IV (front). Architectonic fragments; metope carved between triglyphs in one piece; statues of Dionysos and Comedy; inscriptions.—ROOM V (opposite): Two heads, school of Skopas; Relief decoration of an altar to Cybele (2C AD); head of young Dionysos (3C BC); Aphrodite on a dolphin with Eros clinging to its tail; reliefs; beautiful but mutilated reclining youth; Roman imperial *Heads, among them a negroid head and portraits of Claudius, Julius Caesar, and Lucius Caesar.

Outside the S corner of the Agora a paved street, uncovered for 50m, leads SW, passing a well-preserved *Exedra* (1C AD), the remains of an *Odeion* (left), and the so-called *Court of 100 Flagstones*. Continuing, we reach the remains of the *Triumphal Arch of Caracalla*, identified by its inscription, and the **Herakleion**, or *Sanctuary of Herakles*.

The monumental entrance to the sanctuary was a Propylon, with a staircase, leading to the COURT. On the N side is an *Ionic Temple*, a peripteral edifice with 6 by 8 columns surrounding a single chamber (early 5C). In front of it is a ruinous *Altar*. To the S, partly covered by the modern road leading to the Silenus Gate, is a building divided into rooms, which incorporated or replaced a 6C Temple in polygonal masonry. In the S corner is a *Triangular Court*, which had a circular monument.—Farther to the S an empty site marks the *Monument of Thersilochos* (excavated in 1913 and filled in again).

In the village square are a few fragments of an Early Christian *Basilica* (?6C), probably ruined in 904 when Leo of Tripoli occupied the island. To the E of the apse is a mosaic belonging to a building of the age of Hadrian; the caretaker of the museum will remove the protective cover.

An asphalt road leads in 35 minutes past a classical cemetery to *Makri Ammos* (Hotel A, summer only), a pleasant beach with two small tavernas.

An easy excursion may be made to two delightful inland villages. The road rises through pine-woods, and, crossing a ridge, emerges on a ledge (*View of the beautiful bay of Potamiá.—5km *Panayía* (Hotels B, D, E) has a square with two gushing fountains, shaded by plane-trees.—6·5km *Potamiá*, slightly larger, with steep stone streets and old Turkish houses, is a starting-point for the ascent of Ipsarion (Hypsarion; 1142m) in 2–3 hours.

The road, now part of the island round (92km), continues down the E coast. The island abounds in unexcavated Hellenic and medieval remains (an account of which in J.H.S., vol. 29, 1909 is supplemented in B.C.H., 1930). On *Cape Pirgos*, in the NE, are some remains of an ancient lighthouse inscribed as his own tomb and memorial by one Akeratos. Vestiges of ancient *Koinyra* may be found farther S. At *Alikí* are ancient marble quarries, an Archaic sanctuary, and two excavated basilican churches. The best preserved of many Hellenic TOWERS is near *Thimoniá*, the greatest concentration of them near *Astrís*; they were probably for defence against pirates. Beyond Astris the road passes the Theologos turn before reaching (54km) *Limenariá* (Hotels C, D, E), a centre (1448 inhab.) of cadmium mining. *Theológos*, in the Dipotamos valley below the S slope of Ipsarion, was the medieval capital. The house of Mehmet Ali's youth survives. Remains of a castle (*Kouphókastro*) crown a hill to the south-east.

From Limenaria the road follows the W coast passing many small pensions and camping places amid the pines.—*Órmos Prínou*, incorrectly but more usually called *Prinó* (Hotels B, C, D, E), is c 16km short of Limen (bus).

68   From Kaválla to Philíppi and Dráma

ROAD, 37km (23 miles), passing (15km) *Philíppi*. Frequent bus (20-minute ride to Philippi).

We quit Kavalla by the Salonika road (Rte 66) and beyond the coastal range take the right fork. The road passes the airfield of Kavalla.—8km *Dáton*, a village on the edge of the marshy plain of Philippi (left), bears the name held by the district even before the foundation of Philippi. The ensuing straightness of the modern road (Restaurant at 12km) is deceptive, for the Roman road ran farther E. On it, 1km before it rejoins our course at the approach to Philippi, is the *Khan of Dikili Tach*, where a monument erected by a Roman officer, C. Vibius, has Latin inscriptions on each face. Opposite, on the S side of the Roman road, is a hill where the French School has unearthed an important prehistoric settlement. Its Neolithic and Early Bronze Age pottery is dated to the period of the foundation of Troy. Finds are in the Philippi and Kavalla museums. Where the two roads meet, ancient stone fragments strewn about the tobacco fields show that a large suburb extended to the E of Philippi.

15km **Philíppi** guarded the narrow gap between hill and marsh through which the Via Egnatia has to pass. The highway formed the *decumanus* of the city and the modern road, on the selfsame course, passes through the excavations; the bus stops at the entrances. To the left, farther on, is the larger archaeological area with the forum of the Roman city and, opposite (i.e. on the same side of the road as the theatre), Basilica A. The Museum is further on, to the right. Bus travellers should disembark at the forum; those with cars may be best advised to park below the Museum rather than in the large car park. To the right, at the beginning of the ruins is the theatre, with a large car park and tourist pavilion for the festival. Dominating the plain, the Greek acropolis with its prominent medieval towers occupies the last outcrop of the Lekanis range which extends E to the Nestos. In general visible remains are Roman or Early Christian.

History. The ancient town of *Krenides* ('Fountains'), colonised by Thasos in the 6C BC but lost to local tribes, was refounded in 361 BC by Thasians led by the exiled Athenian Kallistratos, only to be taken over in 356 by Philip II of Macedon, who renamed it *Philippi* after himself. The place was of little importance until the establishment of the Via Egnatia as a military road. After the momentous battle of 42 BC (see below), the city was refounded with veterans of the battle by Octavian and from 27 BC bore the name *Colonia Julia Augusta Philippensis*. Philippi was the first stage on the journey westwards from its port, Neapolis (Kavalla). In AD 49 St. Paul, having sailed from the Troad to Neapolis, spent some time at Philippi, where he first preached the gospel in Europe and where, with Silas, he was cast into prison ('Acts', xvi, 9–40). Six years later St. Paul again visited Philippi ('Acts', xx, 6). From his prison in Rome in 64, or possibly earlier from Ephesus, he wrote his Epistle to the Philippians, for whom he seems to have had a special affection. Christianity throve at Philippi, which had a large basilica as early as the 5C. It was occupied by the Goths in 473. It gave the title to a Byzantine metropolitan and (though the city was deserted by c 950) remained his seat until, in 1619, the see, renamed 'Philippi and Drama' was transferred to Drama. Since 1924 the title has passed to the Metropolitan residing at Kavalla.—The site has been excavated by the French School (1920–24 and since 1927).

Battle of Philippi. Following the assassination of Julius Caesar in 44 BC, the republicans Brutus and Cassius made for the East. By the time Antony and Octavian, great-nephew of Julius, had temporarily assuaged their own rivalry by the device of the triumvirate (43), Brutus, who had seized Macedonia, and Cassius, who had secured Syria, were in control of all the Roman provinces E of the

Adriatic, and commanded 19 legions and numerous cavalry. Leaving Lepidus behind to rule Italy, Antony and Octavian, with an equivalent force, marched against Brutus and Cassius. The armies met in the plain of Philippi in October 42. The republicans were encamped to the W of the town athwart the main road (where traces of their field works have been noted). In the ensuing two battles Brutus and Cassius made the same mistakes as Pompey had at Pharsalus. Having command of the sea at Neapolis and shorter communications, their obvious policy was to exhaust the enemy by avoiding action. A hazardous frontal attack by Antony forced a pitched battle, and muddled generalship contributed to the defeat of Cassius, who committed suicide. Brutus, who had been victorious over Octavian, was three weeks later forced against his better judgment to fight again in the same place, where the legions of the Triumvirate were executing a dangerous infiltration between his troops and the marsh. The outcome was disastrous and Brutus, too, killed himself. The poet Horace fought on the republican side and joined in the 'headlong rout, his poor shield ingloriously left behind' ('Odes', II, 7).

The FORUM, a paved rectangle 99m by 50m, had uniform porticoes on three sides approached by steps. The plan is quite clear, though the remains do not stand much above the foundations. On the N side monumental *Fountains* flanked a *Tribune* and monuments to citizens and emperors; the decumanus passed along and above its rear wall (remains parallel with and below the modern road), leaving a view towards the Acropolis. The rear walls of all four sides make an enclosing rectangle, and this replanning of the general ensemble can be dated by inscriptions to the reign of Marcus Aurelius. At the NE and NW angles stood two *Temples*; on the E side a *Library*. The S side replaced houses of the Augustan period.

To the S of the forum rise the conspicuous remains of the 'DIREKLER' (Turkish: 'Pillars') or **Basilica B**, one of the failures that marked the slow transition from the true basilica to the cruciform church with dome. The 6C architect attempted to cover the E end of a basilica with a brick cupola. The E wall collapsed under the weight before the altar or synthronon could be assembled, so that the sanctuary was never dedicated. The W end, still standing in 837 when the invading Bulgars carved an inscription in it, fell in turn, leaving only the narthex to be converted into a small church in the 10C by the addition of an apse made out of reused materials. The pillars, formed of reused antique blocks, have interesting capitals with acanthus-leaf decoration. The central arch of the W wall shows the springing of the narthex vault. Chunks of the fallen dome survive and a fine *Capital. The Bulgarian inscription was removed in 1943. Two contemporary annexes to the N from the *Baptistery*; two to the S, designed perhaps as the diakonikon, probably constituted the sanctuary itself after the collapse of the chancel.

The remains, particularly interesting to students of architecture, are exhaustively discussed by Paul Lemerle in 'Philippes et la Macédoine oriental à l'époque chrétienne et byzantine' (1945). To make way for the basilica a covered market and the greater part of a *Palaestra* were levelled; much of the material went into the church. The most interesting part surviving (below the SE corner) is a monumental *Public Latrine*, almost perfectly preserved, which is approached by a descending flight of steps and a double portal. Many of the 50 marble seats are still in place.—Farther over are *Roman Baths*, built c AD 250 and destroyed by fire soon afterwards (mosaics destroyed by the Bulgarians in 1941–45).

Excavations by Prof. Pelekanides since 1960 E of the Forum (the area is fenced off but the remains can be seen from the road) uncovered remains of an octagonal **Church**, comparable in size and plan with San Vitale at Ravenna, except that the octagon is inscribed in a square. Excavation is complete and publication in progress. It had an inner colonnade of 20 columns on seven sides with a marble screen closing the bema on the eighth. The church was approached from the Via Egnatia by a great gate (perhaps that described by Eusebius). On the N side it had a *Baptistery* communicating with *Baths*. Beneath the octagon a Macedonian tomb has yielded gold finds (at present in Kavalla, but possibly to be returned): the massive stone at the entrance is still in position. More recent excavation has shown that there was an earlier octagonal structure on the site and that a 4C basilican church dedicated to St. Paul preceded that, in turn. S of the octagonal building is the *Bishopric*.

On the N side of the road is **Basilica A**, erected c 500 on a prepared terrace. It was probably ruined in an earthquake in the same century, then used as a quarry. Its plan was recovered before 1939 and its N walls stand to a considerable height.

The terrace is reached by Propylaea and a broad *Stairway* (to the left of the modern entrance). Half-way up on the right was a *Crypt* of Roman date, taken by the 5C to be the prison of St. Paul and later frescoed with scenes from his life and crowned by a chapel. On the terrace the foundations of a Hellenistic temple were converted into a *Cistern*. A huge paved *Atrium*, having a W façade with fountains and three porticoes, extended E to the CHURCH, which is entered by three doors. The *Narthex* gave access at the N end to a separate *Baptistery* (well preserved, with mosaic floor) and by three openings to the church itself. This is an aisled basilica with E transepts and semi-circular apse, comparable in size with Ayios Demetrios at Salonika. Within can be traced the position of an *Ambo* and the *Screen*. The E wall, unusually, had two doors.—Farther W, close to the museum, a third basilica was located in 1963.

The MUSEUM is above the road to the W of the entrances to the Forum and Basilica A. Outside are Early Christian mosaics from a country house at Piyes tis Voiranis near Bournabasi; also architectural fragments from Philippi. Within, most of the exhibits (except those from the British excavations at Sitagroi!) are labelled in English as well as Greek. In the vestibule are finds from the French School's Neolithic site at Dikili Tach. The main ground floor room contains Early Christian material from Philippi: fine capitals and other architectural members, many with sculptural decoration; also a mosaic, inscriptions and a case with coins from excavations in the octagonal church.—An alcove at the far end has finds from Sitagroi.—The upstairs room (closed for rearrangement, July 1986) has chiefly Roman finds from the site. At the far end are Nike figures and an Athena from a temple in the Forum. Restored drawings show their original position on the building (acroteria). A case of finds from Roman tombs includes glass and pottery. A small group of earlier items has a fragmentary inscription of a plan for the city of Philippi by Alexander the Great.

From the museum a path ascends to the ACROPOLIS (311m) with its three massive medieval towers built on the ruins of the Macedonian walls. The climb is recommended more for the view of the forum, the octagonal church, the battlefield, and the plain than for the remains, though the hill is remarkable also for the variety of its insect life (butterflies, dragonflies, etc.). On the way up are some Christian evidences, carved in the rock, and the ruins of a *Sanctuary of Egyptian Deities* (Isis, Serapis, Harpocrates), comprising a terrace of substructions of various buildings.

Returning to the basilica and continuing E round the base of the rocks, we encounter a series of *Rock Sanctuaries*. Farther on are numerous lengthy Latin inscriptions (2–3C) recording benefactors of a religious college, dedicated to Silvanus. There are also scores of reliefs cut in the rock (extending above the theatre), mainly dedicated to Bendis, the Thracian equivalent of Artemis. We descend to the

Theatre, built against the slope of the hill, which dates back to the foundation of Philippi. Of the original building there survives some well-built masonry of the analemma and parodoi. In the Roman era (2C AD) the theatre was remodelled; the orchestra was paved, the paradoi vaulted. Remains of the Roman *Frons Scenae* show it to have resembled the type of Asia Minor, with its rubble wall pierced by five doors. The Roman stage disappeared in the last alterations (3C) into an arena. To this period belong three bas-reliefs of Nemesis, Mars, and Victory, found in the W parodos. Recent excavations have shown that the cavea had an upper tier, probably added during the Roman period. Visible are the lateral passageway dividing lower tier from upper, the front wall of the upper tier, with draining vents, the rubble foundations for the seating and the vaulted substructure. The building remained virtually whole till the 16C. The seating of the cavea was restored in 1957–59 to allow the staging of dramatic performances.

To regain the road, we follow the Byzantine enceinte, which was built on the top of the 4C walls. Although ruinous, its line can be traced along the slope of the Acropolis and for most of its course in the plain. It is equipped with towers and redans. No trace remains of the arch which early travellers describe as bestriding the road.

We by-pass (24·5km) *Dhoxáto* (114m), a deme of 3389 inhab., engaged in tobacco cultivation. We join the road from Paranestion (comp. below) on a low plateau and cross the railway. The isolated *Korílovo* (623m) stands out on the right, while *Bóz Dág* (2231m), the summit of the Falakron range, towers to the N.

37km (23 miles) **Dráma** (Δράμα; 105m, Hotels B, C, D), a thriving town of 36,109 inhab., is the capital of the nome of Dráma, the seat of a metropolitan, and the headquarters of an army corps. It is ringed but not overshadowed to the N by the heights of Falakron, and commands the 'golden plain', the tobacco from which provides its livelihood. The town has a *Tobacco Research Station*, but the processing of timber affords a secondary occupation. Though it holds no particular interest for the tourist, its large shaded squares and restaurants make it a pleasant place to pause.

History. *Dráma* is thought to occupy the site of an Edonian town called *Drabeskos* by Thucydides (I, 100), where the Athenians in 465 BC were cut to pieces in their first and unsuccessful attempt to colonise Amphipolis. The Edonians, a Thracian people who dwelt between the Strymon and the Nestos, were notorious for their orgiastic worship of Dionysos. Drama was of some importance in the late-Byzantine era. Boniface de Montferrat fortified the town in 1205 and her in 1317 died Irène de Montferrat, second wife of Andronikos II. The Turks occupied it in c 1371. Briefly in the 14C Dráma (previously in the see of Philippi) was raised to the status of metropolitan see, only to be incorporated with Serres. In 1619 the see of Philippi (which already included Kavalla) was removed to Dráma, the metropolitan taking the dual title 'Philippi and Drama'. In 1924 this see was divided, the title of Philippi passing to the new see at Kavalla.

FROM DRÁMA TO XANTHI BY THE INLAND ROAD, 88·5km (55 miles), asphalt except for c 1·5km near the Plovdiv turn. We quit the town by the Kavalla road (Rte 68), but turn left at (5km) *Khoristí*, and follow the course of the railway all the way to Stavroúpolis.—Beyond (16km) *Nikifóros*, a centre of tobacco cultivation, are remains of an aqueduct. The road traverses rugged country with wild mountain views all round as we cross the watershed between the Angistis and the Nestos. Just before (36km) *Paranéstion*, the railway crosses the Nestos by Bailey bridge to the left of the road bridge. Keeping to the left bank, we follow the river valley to the SE, passing through the most attractive country of the route.

The **Nestos**, or *Mesta*, rises in the Rhodope Mts in Bulgaria and divides Macedonia geographically from Thrace, though the modern nome boundaries rather reflect local convenience. Under the Treaty of Bucharest (1913), the river formed the frontier with Bulgaria, which for two or three years enjoyed an Aegean seaboard extending from the Mesta to Dedeagatch and beyond. Above Paranesion the river is enclosed in inaccessible gorges that rival in wildness that between Stavroupolis and Toxotai, and the whole of its basin N to the Bulgarian frontier is hemmed in by the Rhodope chain, the rolling heights of which, swathed in beech forests, constitute much of the nome of Drama. The area, which has a good climate and fertile soil, has not found favour with Anatolian Greeks, and since 1923 has remained practically uninhabited. The lower course of the Nestos lies through the alluvial plain of Chrysopolis.

At (61km) *Stavroúpolis* (Hotel E), a deme of 1316 inhab., in the fairest part of the Nestos valley, a kafenion in the attractive little plateia has an interesting collection of bygones. To the SE, reached from the station by minor road (turn after 3km towards Komniná, then take signposted motorable track left for 1·5km), is a remarkable vaulted tomb, excavated in 1953. The chamber is 3m square and the vaulted dromos 4·9m long. The tomb was constructed in local marbles with paintings done directly on to the marble surface (a technique unusual in Macedonia). Within are two handsome marble funerary couches.—From Stavroúpolis the road turns E, climbing through a low pass to the N of Akhlat Tsal (1401m).—At (80km) the junction of two predominantly Moslem valleys we meet the road from Plovdiv, guarded by police-post.—88·5km **Xánthi**, see Rte 69.

FROM DRAMA TO KATO NEVROKOPION, 45km. The Road at first goes NW as far as (24km) *Prosotáni* (pop. 3716), the ancient Pyrsopolis, which it leaves on the left. It then turns N into the Falakron Mts, climbing the *Stena Granitou*, a defile between Mavro Longos (1404m) and Vothlitsi (1201m). The valley broadens and divides, the main road following the W opening in thick woods (the right branch goes on to the Bartiseva refuge from which Boz Dag is climbed).—From (33km) *Granitis* (793m) we descend into an intensely cultivated flat depression, where (45km) *Káto Nevrokópion* guards the road to the Bulgarian frontier (no crossing), 11km to the N.—To the E of this road, between Dráma and the frontier, live the nomadic Sarakatzanai who wear a picturesque costume.

From Drama to *Serres* see Rte 65A.

69   From Salónika to Alexandroúpolis and the Turkish Frontier (Istanbul)

A. By road

ROAD, 735km (457 miles), of international standard all the way. To (166km) **Kaválla**, see Rte 66.—222km **Xánthi**.—290km **Komotiní**.—355km **Alexandroúpolis**.—388·5km **Ardhánion**. Here the main highway into Turkey diverges via Ipsala and Keşan (**Istanbul**, 264km; *Gallipoli–Çanakkale* ferry, 162·5km, for **Izmir**).—454km **Dhidhimótikhon**.—494km *Kastenéai (frontier)*.—*504km* **Edirne**, whence 232km to *Istanbul* (BUS from Xánthi).

From Salonika to (166km) **Kaválla**, see Rte 66. We quit Kaválla by its E suburbs, passing a huge stadium. Beyond (176km) *Néa Karváli*, where scanty remains of a large enceinte have been equated with ancient Akontisma, we turn away from the coast and at 183·5km pass (right) a square (?) Roman fort.—187km *Pondolívadhon* is to become an industrial dependency of Kaválla. An ancient site (right) may be *Pistyros*, a point of Xerxes' march mentioned by Herodotus. To the left indented foothills of the *Lakanis Mts* (home of the Edoni) rise to 1298m; to the right the flat Pedhias Khrisoupoleos extends to the Nestos.—191km *Gravoúna*.

About 1·5km beyond the village a by-road runs S to (4km) **Khrisoúpolis** (Χρυσούπολις), seat (7119 inhab.) of the eparchy of Nestos and in Byzantine times a town of some importance on the high road. It was known to the Turks as Sari Saban, meaning Yellow Plain. 3km SW of Khrisoúpolis is the Airport which, although officially described as 'Kavalla' is almost equidistant between Kaválla and Xánthi.—18·5km **Keramoti** (Hotels D, E; Campsite; Taverna) is linked by frequent car-ferry with Thasos, 5km offshore. The successful culture of oysters was started in 1959 in the little inlet on which the harbour stands, and the bird life is varied.

The villages lie off the road in the foothills to the left.—203km *Kríni* has a small medieval fortress.—206km *Parádheisos*, a prettily terraced village (cafés), overlooks the tree-grown banks of the Nestos. The river is crossed by a barrage which controls the irrigation of the whole delta. The Via Egnatia appears to have crossed the river nearer its mouth. To the right of the road, towards the river, are some scattered remains of Byzantine *Topeiros*, including a three-aisled Middle Byzantine church. We join the railway (comp. p. 581), and enter Thrace.—210km *Toxótai* (left), with a minaret, and *Tímbano*, with wooden balconies, are typical villages of the S slope of Akhlat Tsal (left), where Turkish growers still produce the prized Xanthíyaka, the finest quality of Turkish tobacco. The picturesque irregularity of these villages with their gardens and decaying mosques is emphasised by neighbouring Greek refugee settlements, planned in rigid lines with churches in the functional style of the 1920s. A huge sugar factory epitomises a more recent agricultural direction.

222km (138 miles) **Xánthi** (Ξάνθη; Hotels B, C, D, E), seat of a metropolitan and the prosperous capital (31,541) of the nome of Rhodopis, stands at the opening of the narrow upper valley of the Esketze, the ancient Kosintos. The main road by-passes the town which, however should not be missed. The main attraction is the beautiful traditional houses of *Old Xánthi* (Ξάνθη) which cluster on the hillside to the N of the modern town and below the Byzantine *Kastro* (sections of fortifications visible), which was built to defend the defile from Bulgar incursions. There is a *Folk Museum* (Λαογραφικό Μουσείο; open evenings and Sunday mornings) in Od. Antíka, containing local costumes, traditional implements, etc. The *Cathedral* has a collection of icons manuscripts and church plate. On the higher slopes are some monasteries, one of which, the *Moní Megíston Taxiárchon*, houses the *Ecclesiastical College of Xánthi*. Byzantine *Xanthea* grew up below the Kastro. Under the Turks a mere summer resort, Xánthi has, since the coming of the railway, superseded Yenije (comp. below) as the centre of the fine tobacco growing area. A brand of cigarettes (kiretsiler), obtainable only locally, is much prized. The lower town has been considerably rebuilt in recent years, but apart from sections of Byzantine structures, there are some delightful streets of old low buildings with small shopes, cafés, etc.—The new **airport** at Khrisoupolis (comp. above) serves Xánthi, as well as Kaválla, and buses connect with the flights, starting from the Olympic Airways office at Michael Vógdhou 6a.

FROM XANTHI TO ABDERA, 26km (16 miles) bus. From the Porto Lagos road (see below) we take the right fork at (8km) *Vaféika*.—11km *Yeniséa*, long the centre of the tobacco trade and the local Turkish capital (Yenije), has declined in importance. Continuing beyond the modern village of (19km) *Ávdhira*, we reach the sea at (27·5km) *Ayios Pandeleimon*. Just before reaching the sea, there is a sign (left) to the *Archaeological Site* and the road leads in a few metres to the remains of ancient **Abdera** (Άβδηρα), (a city traditionally founded by Herakles on the spot where Abderos was killed by Diomede's horses, but in fact colonised c 656 BC from Klazomenai. Refounded c 500 BC by refugees from a Persian occupation of Teos (SW of Smyrna), it became a prominent member of the Delian League and famous for the beauty of its coinage. Democritus, the 5C philosopher who expounded an atomic theory, Protagoras (c 481–411), the first of the Sophists, and Anaxarchos, the counsellor of Alexander the Great, were all born here, but despite the celebrity of its school of philosophy, the inhabitants generally were proverbial for their dullness. Hippocrates and Juvenal inveigh against its sickly air. Abdera shared the fortunes of Macedonia and, despite a sack in 170 BC by an over-zealous general, remained nominally free of Rome down to Imperial times, when the city apparently succumbed to its climate. The site continued important in the Early Christian and Byzantine periods when a fortress (**Polystylon**) was built on the Classical acropolis. Roads connected Polystylon with Xanthea and Peritheorion. It is known to have been the seat of a bishop in the 9C.

Systematic excavations began in 1950 directed by D. Lazarides for the Greek Archaeological Service. The nature of the site is probably best appreciated by climbing first the track immediately opposite the gate to the fenced site, which leads in a few metres to the acropolis of Polystylon. The first conspicuous monument is a small single-aisled *church* of the 12C, with the remains of a contemporary *cemetery* beside it. Below are good sections of the *defences*, the Byzantine built over the Classical, with the masonry of the two periods clearly distinguishable. A square *tower* of the Classical system is preserved. Within the wall some parts of a *bath building* with hypocaust can be made out. In the sea beyond, within the lines of the modern breakwater, can be seen the scattered remnants of the ancient *harbour* mole. On the highest point of the promontory, its position indicated from below by a triangulation block, is a fine three-aisled Early Christian *basilica* of c 600, with an octagonal *baptistery* at the NW.—From this point, the broader extent of the Greek and Roman city can be best surveyed. It lay in a depression N and E of the acropolis. The wall circuit, almost 5·5km in total, has been fully traced. The acropolis is in the SW corner, though its Archaic predecessor may have been on the high ground to the NW. The whole of the valley seems to have been settled and the E limit, as defined by the wall, extended to a second (smaller) harbour out of our sight beyond the furthest visible promontory. (This can be reached, if desired, by following the dirt road beyond the archaeological site.)

We may now descend and enter the gate to the main site. The most impressive remains soon confront us. To the right is a Roman *bath* building and, beyond, the *city wall*. Past the path are Late Roman *houses*. A large square structure was a *forward tower*, into which Roman burials (fragments of sarcophagi visible) were later inserted. N of this is the *gateway* to the city, protected by two square *towers*. The wall (and towers) in fine masonry belong, in origin, to the Classical period, but the wall itself underwent many later repairs and differences in constructional style are evident here and there. The main structure has an inner and an outer face, with rubble filling. Within the gate, the remains are less impressive. They belong almost exclusively to *blocks of houses* of the Hellenistic and Roman periods, sometimes with Classical buildings shown to underly them, as in the first units visible, where a paved Roman floor is at the top and Classical remains at the bottom of the excavated sequence. In general the house remains are disappointing to the visitor, though it is possible to make out paved courts with wells and drainage channels, column bases, threshold blocks, the outlines of rooms, etc. The town was laid out on a

grid system from the 4C, with several houses in blocks of uniform size.
At the far NE of the site are buildings which included a *coroplast's
workshop*. Beyond this, and best reached by a branch off the dirt road
which encircles the site, is the *theatre*, of whose remains there is little
to be seen.

At *Dhiomídhia* (6km S of Xánthi) there is an important prehistoric
(especially Late Neolithic) settlement on the hill *Tepés* to the N of the
village.

The road to Plovdiv in Bulgaria is closed at the frontier. A permit is
required to go beyond (8km) the Stavroupolis fork, and there is little of
interest between there and (49km) the frontier post.

From Xánthi there is a choice of two routes: the main road leading SE
to Lagos on the coast or the Via Egnatia, which, although here a
secondary road, is an adequate and rather more interesting alternative for the the the antiquary; it is also c 10km shorter.

FROM XANTHI TO KOMOTINI BY THE VIA EGNATIA, 48km (30 miles)

The road strikes due E, followed by the railway (Rte 69B). About 1·5km beyond *Amaxádhes*, a track (right) leads in 5km to the best-preserved part of *Anastasioupolis* (Byzantine *Peritheorion*).

The town was a station on the Via Egnatia, probably taking its name from Anastasius I (491–518): it lies on the N shore of Lake Vistonis. After destruction in the early 13C, it was rebuilt and renamed under Andronicus III (1328–41). At the edge of the lake, among trees, is a fenced archaeological area. The site is very overgrown but the spectacular remains make the effort involved worthwhile. Preserved nearly to its original height is the *S Gate* of the city, which gave onto the harbour (marble plaques to each side have monograms of the Palaiologues). Also to be seen here are a tower and sections of the fortification wall. Most of the wall circuit can be traced and different periods of construction distinguished.
    Returning to the main road, there is a further sign to Anastasioupolis after 3km. Here the road passes through a section of walling which also served as an aqueduct and dates to the time of Justinian. The archaeological area can also be reached via this track (c 30 minutes on foot; the track is blocked to vehicles at the railway line).

Beyond (28km) *Iasmós*, we cross (32km) the *River Kompsátos*. Just beyond the bridge (signs) a rough path leads in 5 minutes to a delightful medieval bridge with two arches, a central pier and the original surface partly preserved. There appears to have been no parapet. Returning to the main road we soon pass (left) the fenced remains of a Byzantine church and shortly (33km) enter *Políanthos* which has a Byzantine castle and, to the N, at *Kedík Kazín*, the remains of a Hellenistic fort. A Hellenistic cemetery has also been excavated in the vicinity. Before (39km) the turn (left) to *Sóstis*, there is a sign to *Keraséa* (left; 10km), a hill village, where there is a Byzantine cemetery and a recently excavated 11C Byzantine church (one-aisled) with an *opus sectile* marble floor. On the main road a sign (right) to Prehistoric Settlement can be safely ignored: there is nothing to see.

An alternative and rather more pleasant route into Komotiní (13km) is to turn into Sóstis and proceed via (5km) *Mískhos*, with an attractive silver-capped minaret.

42km Track (left; signposted; rough but passable) to the site of medieval *Mosynopolis*, the limit of Norman penetration in 1185. Originally Porsula, the town was granted city rank by Diocletian with the name *Maximianopolis*, and sent a metropolitan to the Council of Ephesus. Geoffroy de Villehardouin, a chronicler of the 4th Crusade, accepted it as his fief. The best-preserved section of the walls, with square and round towers, is by the track after 1km, but other remains can be seen over a wide area. Inscriptions and architectural fragments from the site are in the Komotiní Museum. (The track continues 2·5km farther to join the alternative route to Komotiní just beyond Miskhos—comp. above.)
    Returning to the asphalt road, there are signs to *Paradhími*, known for its prehistoric tomb (finds in Kaválla and Komotiní Museums).—At 44km we join the main road, (comp. below).
    The main road leaves Xánthi to the SE, crossing the railway. The well-watered country to the right grows excellent tobacco.—At (230km) *Vaféïka*, by-road (right; see above) to Abdera. Between Vaféïka and *Koutsoú* (at c 4km) an extensive Hellenistic and Roman site was discovered to the S of the main road in 1973. There are also remains of the Classical period.—248km (154 miles) **Pórto Lagos**, the port of Komotiní, stands on a tongue of land separating the Vistonian Gulf from Lake Vistonis. The remains of a Byzantine basilica of the 10C lie right of the road (sign) just beyond the town. The church is an early example of the inscribed-cross type and was built over the remains of an Early Christian structure. The church stands within a

fortified Byzantine settlement. Remains of the defences are particularly evident towards the sea, where they include a tower. They can be
seen also on the other side of the road. The place still has a bishop.
Worth a glance are the old Genoese fort and an attractive church.
Beyond the channel through which the lake drains into the sea, the
road is carried on a causeway with a marshy lagoon on the right. Fish
and eels are caught in great numbers and the area is celebrated for the
variety of its water-birds. The eels are almost exclusively exported
live in tanks to Germany and Central Europe. The fish traps can be
visited.

A low hill rising to the SE (off the by-road to Fanári) may be the site of ancient
Dikaia. Graves have been excavated (1977). Near the village is an N.T.O.G.
camp site.—Some ruins, identified with *Stryme*, once famed for its wine, were
explored by Salonika University (1957–59) on the remote coast c 16km farther E.
A city wall was traced with houses, which yielded a hoard of Maroneian tetradrachms of the 4C BC.

At 278·5km is *Messoúni* airport. We join the direct road from Xánthi
(see above) between Paradhimi and Maximianoupolis, then cross the
Akmar.—289km (180 miles) **Komotiní** (Κομοτηνή; Hotels B, C, E)
a garrison town only 22·5km from the Bulgarian frontier, and the
capital of Greek Thrace, has pleasant broad streets and squares. It is a
flourishing market centre (34,051 inhab.) for tobacco, cattle, hides
and agricultural goods (annual livestock fair in Holy Week). About
half of the inhabitants are Turks, who know the town as *Gümülcüne*
and many are Bulgarian speaking (Pomaks). Here are the University
of Thrace and a Moslem secondary college. The city is linked by bus
with Istanbul. An Olympic Airways bus connects with one flight a day
from Alexandroúpolis (Komotini terminal at Vasiléos Yioryíou 2).
The seasonal Boukloutza on which Komotiní stands has been diverted
since the town was flooded in 1960. The walls of a Byzantine fortress
are to our left on entering the town. The *Archaeological Museum*
opened in 1976, on the S side of the inner ring road (Od. N. Zoídhou)
houses finds from the whole of Thrace. The objects are attractively
displayed and it should not be missed. Outside is a fine Roman sarcophagus with garlands and bucrania. Within, outstanding is the unique
gold imperial *Bust of Marcus Aurelius found at Plotinoupolis. Also
displayed are a remarkable phallic altar; a Clazomenian sarcophagus
from Abdera and fine objects from graves at the same site; Archaic
pottery and a grave stele from Dikaia (part formerly in Athens); interesting votive plaques from the Sanctuary of Demeter at Mesembria
finds from the Paradhimi tomb and tombs at Ardhanion and Orestiadha
honorific decrees from Doriskos and Maroneia (4C BC); also from
Maroneia, an inscribed marble block (3C) with impressions of feet and
a fine relief of a Thracian rider (4C); case of Greek, Roman and
Byzantine coins; ground plans of Stryme, Mesembria and Maroneia.

N of Komotiní, an asphalt road leads towards *Nimféa* (15km). After 5km the road
enters an attractively wooded area, with unobtrusive amenitites for picnicking.
An unsurfaced road diverges (right) to *Pandhrósos*. The main road continues to
climb and (3km) beyond the Pandhrósos turn) reaches the impressive Byzantine
fort of *Kalés tis Nimféas* with splendid views over the plain of Komotini. Access to
Nimfea itself is restricted by the military.
   The principal archaeological sites of this region, the ancient KIKONES, lie to
the SE of Komotiní on the coast. They are cut off from the hinterland by barren
limestone hills scored by ravines and torrents. A road (bus from Komotiní) crosses
the railway and the Filiouri to (18km) *Xilayaní* and to (31·5km) *Marónia* (pleasant
square and cafés). Thence the road descends, with occasional signs to antiquities, through the middle of the ancient site, to the coast (4km).
   The site of **Maroneia** was a city of importance from Homeric times to the

Genoese period. The Classical site of the 4–3 BC occupied an enormous area, the wall circuit being 10·5km in extent, running from the sheer-faced acropolis of Ay. Athanásios above the village down to the coast (Ayios Charálambos). The extensive ruins, visited by Reinach in 1880, when the walls were still up to 12m high, have been partially explored since 1973 and investigations continue. The area is thickly wooded and, although several interesting features can be easily approached by roads and tracks, a full exploration of the remains requires time, determination and a knowledge of the literature (in particular D. Lazarides, Maroneia kai Orthagoria, Athens, 1972, in Greek.

We follow the road down from the village to the *Theatre* and *Sanctuary* (IEPO), reached by a dirt track in 0·5km and 1·3km respectively. The theatre (right) which has been recently reinvestigated was a Hellenistic construction, altered in Roman times. Some of the seating survives, part of the stage building (re-using material from earlier buildings) and the foundation for the proskenion columns, with a number of architectural elements. The seating was provided with a protective barrier (thorakion) in the Roman period for contests involving wild animals. The theatre was built across the ravine and was protected from damage by storm water by an enormous built drainage channel which can be seen to have passed beneath. 200m NE of the theatre is a substantial section of walling with towers. The foundations of the sanctuary complex (probably dedicated to Dionysos), farther on, can be made out. The main temple had a pronaos and cella (with hearth or base for cult statue) and ancillary structures but the surviving remains are hardly worth more than a glance.

Returning to the main road, a short distance further down (left) is the most accessible part of the city wall, with two square towers. The wall in general is 2·3–3m thick and has square or round towers at irregular intervals; more frequent on flat ground. A sign to 'Mosaic' can be ignored since it is covered and the house remains are uninformative. 300m farther down the road (no sign) the Byzantine fortifications have been partly cleared and are impressive. They were constructed on an earlier (Classical) system which protected the harbour. We reach a parking space above the harbour. In an enclosure immediately to the right are the well-preserved remains of a double monumental gateway with three openings in each face, possibly Hadrianic and the entrance to the agora. Farther right (200m) excavations are in progress. Left from the car park, beside a restaurant, are the fenced remains of a Byzantine church.

The acropolis of *Ayios Yióryios* (3km NE) has walling and was used in prehistoric and probably archaic times.

294km Turning (left) to *Gratíni* (Γρατύνη; 13km), with by-road to *Páterma* (17·5km).

After leaving the main road, we reach (7km) a turning (left) to Iámpoli (ΙΑΜΠΟΛΗ; small sign; road unsurfaced, rough in places but passable). After Iámpoli (9km) the road continues to the poor Turkish village of Páterma (17·5km) which depends for its livelihood on tobacco cultivation. Beyond Paterma (2km) a track leads off (left), just beyond a roadside well (right) to the fenced remains of a one-aisled Byzantine church of the 11–12C. Returning to the road and continuing, we reach (3km from the village) a fine three-arched medieval bridge, carrying its narrow track across the river. The wooded surroundings are delightful.

Gratíni (Byzantine *Gratianos*) is reached by ignoring the Iámpoli turn and continuing along the asphalt road. The pleasant village lies at the foot of a steep hill (20–30 minute climb; path overgrown in places) crowned by the ruinous remains of a Byzantine fortress of the Palaeologue period. A fine Byzantine cistern (with some modern repair) is still in use and accessible, by the little chapel on the summit. Just off the village square, in a neglected plot, is a subterranean funerary chapel of the 13C.

302·5km *Aratos* has an attractive minaret.—At (306·5km) *Arísivi*, to the left of the road are six arches of a Roman bridge that carried the Via Egnatia over the Filiouri. The road turns SW at (317km) *Sápai*, a pleasant town of 2510 inhab., where the fez and the veil linger on. From here there is a road to *Arrianá*, 3km to the N of which, at the *R. Filiouri*, is a Roman bath of the 2C AD and a Late Roman cemetery.—Beyond (323·5km) *Vélkion* we cross a stream and the railway by a double bridge (1961) and climb amid scrub-covered hills noted for quail, woodcock, and snipe.—339km By-road to Mesembria (Mesimvría).

The road passes through *Dhíkella* (1·5km), whence an unsurfaced but adequate track continues to the site of **Mesembria** (Mesimvría) (8km). The town was a Samothracian colony of the late 7C and is mentioned by Herodotus. It is sometimes called 'Aegean' Mesembria to distinguish from another site of the same name on the Euxine.

The most conspicuous part of the site (fenced) is an unusual *fortified settlement* which occupies only the SW corner of the whole walled area which included an *acropolis* to the N. The defensive circuit can be traced at many points on the ground but is most easily appreciated in the area of the fortified settlement against which it is built. The E part of the fortifications of the city (which have *three* N–S arms) may belong to the first period of settlement, with an acropolis at that time on the E hill.

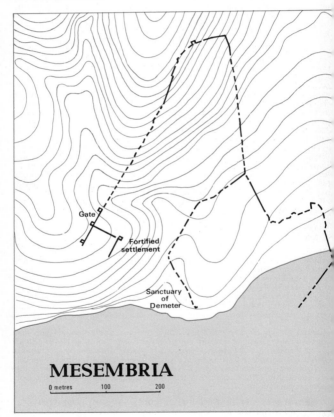

MESEMBRIA

0 metres   100   200

The fortified settlement (so-called because it seems to represent a 'town within a town') can be best surveyed from the top of the large tower (20m beyond the site plan, which gives a good idea of the line of the walls and is useful for orientation) which lies at the NE corner of the fort, projecting beyond both its E and N walls. The thickness of the walls can be clearly discerned, as can the fact that the earlier buildings excavated outside the limits of the fort (N) and partly underlying its walls are on a different alignment from those within. The fort therefore belongs to a secondary phase of the life of the settlement. Within the complex small one-and-

wo-room units (workshops?) lie against the W and part of the N walls. The
uildings are laid on the Hippodamian system, with *streets* on an orthoganal
rid—three running E–W and two N–S. In the centre are house blocks and
gainst the W wall two *houses*. The rooms of that at the NE corner (below the
ower) can be easily distinguished, with court, threshold block, etc. Three diffe-
ent phases of construction have been noted between the 5C and 2C BC. Most of
ne visible remains belong to the second of these, though evidence for the diffe-
ent periods can be seen here and there, with underlying walls on different
lignments and layered surfaces to the streets. A large building in the centre of
ne site may be a public building of some kind.

The city *fortifications* are best seen at the W side, where there are three towers.
he second (from the S) bears inscriptions, the third (beyond the fortified settle-
nent) guards a *gate* into the town with two marble steps and an unusual circular
assage in its N side. The masonry of the walls is in a variety of styles, often of fine
quality.

Returning to the site entrance and proceeding a few metres in the direction of
Ohikella, the S section of the central leg of the wall crosses the road and can be
raced to a tower above the sea. A structure (three-roomed, but not easy to
dentify) of fine large blocks which abuts on the wall c 20m inland from the tower
s the 4C *Sanctuary of Demeter* from which came an inscribed base and the fine
otive plaques which are in the Komotiní Museum. An extensive cemetery has
een found to the W. The site as a whole is still being investigated.

There is a good beach and a fine view W to the mountain spur that hides
Maroneia (path; 3½ hours).

The road descends to the coast amongst the dense vineyards of
343km) *Mákri*, built on the site of a Byzantine settlement. Sections of
he fortification walls can be seen and three churches have recently
een investigated in or near the village.—349km *Néa Khilí* (Hotels C,
)).

355km (220½ miles) **ALEXANDROÚPOLIS** (Αλεξανδρούπολις,
ften written abbreviated to Αλεξ/πολις), the pleasant chief town
34,535 inhab.) of the nome of Evrou, was known to the Turks as
Dedeagaç. It was renamed after King Alexander in 1919. With air
ervices to Athens and Salonika, a station on the Salonika–Istanbul
ailway, and a sea connection with Samothrace, it is the best centre
rom which to explore Thrace. It is noted for its fish; caviare and muss-
ls are specialities.

Airport, 6·5km E, with services to Athens about 3 times daily.—AIR TERMINAL
n sea front E of lighthouse, Colétti and Ellis 8.

Railway Station, E of centre of town.

Hotels A, B, C, D, E; F/A.

Restaurants. *Panellinion*, near the hotels; also near the Dhimarkhíon and near
he lighthouse.

Post Office on the sea front W of the Harbour.—TOURIST POLICE, Od.
Karaïskáki.

Buses to *Xanthi*, *Kavalla*, and *Salonika* daily; to *Dhidhimotikhon* and *Orestias*, 7
imes daily; to *Makri*, 5 times daily.

Steamer to Piraeus (weekly) via Samothrace and Lemnos.—**Caique service** to
Samothrace daily in summer.

Wine Festival in July–September.

he Turkish name (Dede-ağaç; Tree of the holy man) derives from a colony of

dervishes established in the 15C. The place remained a fishing village unti
reached in 1872 by the railway from Edirne, after which it rapidly usurped th
importance of Ainos. The Greek archbishopric was transferred in 1889. Ancien
Zone is placed hereabouts.

The main road, parallel with the sea, forms the principal boulevard c
the town, Od. Dhimokratías (formerly, and still on several signs, Leof
Vasiléos Yiorgíou B), venue of the 'volta' which necessitates the even
ing diversion of traffic. On the shore facing the large artificial harbou
is a conspicuous lighthouse, to the W of which a broad promenade ha
been laid out above the beach. The huge modern cathedral farthe
inland is prominent from the sea. There is an archaeological collectio
in the *Old Dhimarkhíon* (Town Hall) in Plateía Polyteknhíou (als
called Eleftherías; good restaurant), reached via Od. Kípro
(ΚΥΠΡΟΥ) the entrance unsigned and well-concealed in an arcad
with sculpture from the area and finds from the Sanctuary of Demete
at Mesembria, also plans of the Sanctuary of the Great Gods o
Samothrace.

Beyond Alexandroupolis road and railway continue E togethei
passing the airport.—368·5km We cross the Tsáï. On the far bank wa
the Roman and Byzantine staging-post of **Trajanopolis**, which suc
ceeded *Doriskos* (see below). It was the scene in 161 under Marcu
Aurelius of the spectacular miracles of St. Glyceria, a Roman maidei
later martyred in the Propontis. After a long period as a Metropolita
see, the town seems to have been ruined in the wars of 1205 and los
importance to Demotika; the see was removed c 1353 to Peritheorior
To the left of the road is a magnificently preserved *Hána* or staging
post built for use in the 14 and 15C when the town itself had gone int
decline. The adjacent thermal springs are efficacious against kidne
ailments. The hills visible to the S are across the Turkish frontier.–
379km. Turning (right) for ancient *Doriskos*, a Persian fortress tow
established in 512 BC by Darius I, where Xerxes numbered his armie
in 480 (modern scholarship suggests that Herodotus' inflated figure
be reduced to 200,000). Some remains (not so far identified as earlie
than 4C BC) stand on the flat-topped hill of Sarayia (c 1·5km left
overlooking the railway. The by-road goes on into the Evros delt
(comp. below; permit necessary).—382·5km *Férai* (Φέραι), wit
4917 inhab., was known to the Turks as Farecik. A turn (right; sig
'Byzantine Temple') doubles back into the town. In the angle is
picturesque water gate. In the centre of the town, at the highest poin
is the church of *Ayía Sophía*, Katholikon of the monastery of th
Theotokos Cosmosoteira, built by Isaac Comnenus in 1152. It is of th
domed-inscribed cross plan. The interesting frescoes (in need c
cleaning), much defaced by the Turks, are of the same date. There ar
fine carved capitals. The monastery was provided with defences, part
of which are visible: in the 14C it became a fortified civilia
settlement.—At (388.5km) *Ardhánion*, we quit the main highway t
Turkey which follows the ancient course of the Via Egnatia, crossin
the Evros by a long bridge (1962) to *Ipsala* (11km; anc. Kypsela), th
Turkish frontier town.

The ancient *Kypsela*, greatest city of the Thracians, lost importance by the 4C B(
and in Livy's time was only a fort. Returning towards Thessalonika from hi
meeting here with Henry of Flanders in 1207, Boniface of Montferrat was inter
cepted and decapitated by a Bulgarian ambush.
  The **Evros** (Εβρος anc. *Hebros*; Turk., Meriçi; Bulg., Maritza), of which w

have periodic glimpses, rises in Bulgaria S of Sofia and, after a course of c 500km, enters the Aegean opposite the island of Samothrace through a delta 11km wide. Since 1923 its lower course through the flat Thracian plain has formed the boundary between Greece and Turkey, save where the suburbs of Edirne make a Turkish enclave W of the river. It is navigable for small boats as far as Edirne, below which it is crossed by bridges only at Pithion and Ipsala. Its waters abound in fish and water fowl; rare geese and eagles may be seen. Round its twin mouths, noted by Strabo, are several swamps and lakes, of which the largest is Gala-Gölu, the ancient *Stentoris* of Herodotus, on the Turkish side. Some way SW of this lake is the town of Enos, familiar to diplomats as one end of the Enos–Midia line and the ancient *Ainos*, the foundation of which Virgil ascribes to Aeneas.— The river has given its name to the nome of EVROU whose capital is Alexandroupolis. The hill slopes that rise in the W of the province to 914m are clothed with oak forests; cereals, vines and tobacco are cultivated in the plain.

397·5km *Provatón* is a local communication centre, with (2km beyond the village) a memorial of Gen. Asimakópoulos.—421km *Souflí* (Σουφλί; Hotels C, D, E) is a pleasant town (5043 inhab.), engaged in the cultivation of vines and silk worms. It has old timber-framed houses, the best of which are up the hill to the left of the main road. One of these, the *Arkhontikó Kourtídhi*, contains the interesting *Folk Museum*. The house itself is a fine example of a traditional upper-class family house (arkhontiko) with rooms opening off a large *saloni* upstairs, workrooms on the ground floor and a summer kitchen and other utility rooms off the courtyard. The ground floor has a display of equipment and illustrative material to demonstrate the process of silk production (the original function of this part of the house). Upstairs are examples of local costumes and silk items. The side rooms contain memorabilia of the original owner, a restored kitchen, etc. In the church of *Ayios Yiórgios* is a fine 18C carved iconostasis.—At (432km) *Mándhra* we meet a by-road that descends a wooded valley from Mikrón Déreion (22·5km NW), a group of villages near the Bulgarian frontier.

454km (282 miles) **Dhidhimótikhon** (Διδυμότειχον; Hotels B, D; *Taverna* in Odhos Venizelou; *Cafés* and *Nat. Bank* in the Plateia; *Public Lavatory* facing the Dhimarkhion), a market town (8374 inhab.) of Turkish timber-framed houses, clusters round an abrupt hill overlooking the Erithropotamos or Kizil Remma. An inscription, found in 1937, identifies the site with *Plotinoupolis*, founded by Trajan in honour of his wife, Plotina.

History. The fortress-town of *Demotika* played an important part in Byzantine history. In 1189 during the *Third Crusade* Frederick Barbarossa held the town hostage while negotiating with the Emp. Isaac II Angelos. Hither the wounded Michael IX fled after his defeat by the Catalan Grand Company at Aprus (1305), and here in 1341 John VI Cantacuzene had himself proclaimed emperor. The town fell to the Turks in 1361 and Murad I made it his capital for four years before transferring to Adrianople; his son Bayezid was born here. Charles XII of Sweden lay at Demotika in 1713–14, a virtual prisoner of Ahmed III, to whose dominions he had fled after the Battle of Poltava.

To the right, as we cross the bridge, is the sheer-sided hill of *Ayía Pétra* crowned by an aerial mast. This was the core of Roman *Plotinopoulis*. Recent excavations, mainly on the NE flank, have revealed little of interest for the casual visitor, though we must recall the fine gold bust from here in the Komotiní Museum. The road climbs into the town. In the Plateia (off the main road to the left) is a large square mosque with a pyramidal roof. It was begun by Murad I and completed by his son, Bayezid. It has a fine interior (wooden ceiling, calligraphic inscriptions) and the minaret has two fretted balconies. The town has other interesting Ottoman buildings (including hamams) which have recently been studied.

A short distance above the Plateia, in a fine old house, is the outstanding *Folk Museum (open regularly in the evenings and at most other times by request), begun by a co-operative of local schoolmasters in the 1970s and supported by the local authority. It is well laid out and organised. Particularly interesting are items in the BASEMENT connected with agricultural, domestic and industrial activities (threshing sledges, liquor still, dyeing equipment, ironworker's furnace). On the GROUND FLOOR is a large range of material, including women's costumes from various parts of Thrace. Amongst the domestic items are wooden flasks and vessels. The FIRST FLOOR has more costumes (including men's), furniture, a prisoner's stone ball, reconstructed kitchen, etc. The SECOND FLOOR (not yet completed) has equipment related to the production of wool, and weaving (vertical and horizontal looms).

Above the Folk Museum are the walls of the **Kastro**, much of the interior of which is occupied by post-Byzantine buildings, including the cathedral of *Ayios Athanásios*. The most impressive section of walling is to the left, as we ascend (view across to Plotinopoulis, comp. above). Passing into the settlement with its delightful old houses, we reach the cathedral, a 19C structure on Byzantine foundations. Beside it are the conspicuous though partial remains of an arched Byzantine building, probably a *Hana* (hostel). Below is a rock-cut cavern, popularly supposed to have been the prison of Charles XII. Another close approach to the fortifications may be made by ascending Od. Ermou (EPMOY), a narrow street c 100m N of our original point of entry into the Kastro. At first concrete, this soon reverts to its ancient surface and climbs the N face of the fortifications. The walls afford a good view of the *Evros*; there is a military post on the summit.

On the far side of Dhidhimotiko, a fork (right; asphalt, deteriorated in places) off the main road leads to (10km) *Petrádhes*, (16km) *Pithion* and rejoins the highway at (23km) *Thoúrion*. From Petradhes, a frontier village, a road runs to (11km farther) Uzunköprü in Turkey.

At **Píthion** (Byzantine *Empythion*), well seen on a low hill above the Evros as the road begins to descend towards the village are the outstanding remains of a *Byzantine Fort* of the 13C, used by John Cantacuzenus as a headquarters. The central tower is preserved to a height of two storeys and probably had a third. The interior architecture (arches, brick vaults, stairways) is impressive and it was probably a partly domestic establishment. Linked to this by a section of wall with a fine gateway is a smaller tower, probably exclusively military in character. Other sections of the defences survive close by and part of the outer system can be seen in the village.

Another road leads W up the Erithropotamos valley to (31km) *Zóni*, on the Bulgarian frontier, whence it continues via (48km) *Filákion* and down the right bank of the Arda to (62km) *Kastanéai* (see below). From Zoni an old Ottoman road (now in Bulgarian territory) traverses the mountains to Komotiní (107km). These roads are generally subject to military control and permit on both sides of the frontier.

The highway continues N, rejoining the railway (which makes a wide loop to the E through Pithion) at (464km) *Thoúrion*.—At (475km) *Orestiás* (Hotels C, D), seat of an eparchy (12,685 inhab.) and the only refugee settlement in the North to be founded as a town, sugar is refined. The minarets of Edirne can be seen in the distance (right) from the road into (494km) **Kastanéai** (Custom House).

The small triangle of Greek soil lying between the Arda and the Evros is served by a road from Kastaneai and by railway to *Orménion*, its principal village.

503km (313 miles) **EDIRNE**, formerly *Adrianople*, both names being successive corruptions of *Hadrianopolis*, a city which has lost its former importance, stands beyond the frontier. Refounded by Hadrian in AD 125 from *Uscudama*, chief town of the Bessi, it remained a strategic stronghold until the decline of the Ottoman Empire. The period of its zenith in 1367–1458 as the Ottoman capital left many fine buildings though the later Selimiye Cami by Sinan is its masterpiece. It remains the market town of the area.

B. By Railway

RAILWAY to *Alexandroúpolis*, 442km (274 miles), two trains daily in 7½–8¾ hours and Píthion, 555km (344 miles) in 10–11½ hours, one (the daily through train from Piraeus to Istanbul) continuing via Uzunköprü to 834km (518 miles) *Istanbul* in 35 hours from Athens.— To *Sérres*, see Rte 65; to *Dráma*, 5 trains daily in 4–7 hours. One extra train daily between Drama and Alexandrouplis (in c 4¾ hours) and two from Alexandroupolis to *Píthion* (2½ hours), continuing to *Edirne* (3½ hours) and *Orménion* (4 hours); or to *Dhíkaia* and *Svilengrad*.

The railway was designed in Turkish times as a strategic route and built by a French company in 1892–95. It was deliberately laid at least 19km from the coast so as to be beyond the range of naval bombardment, and at the two ports where for convenience it approached the coast (Dedeagatch and Salonika) was provided with inland by-passes (now abandoned). The section E from Alexandroupolis dates from 1869–72.

From Salonika to (162km) *Serres*, see Rte 65. The railway now follows the N limit of the former Lake Prasias, winding across the plain. The landscape is peppered with tumuli. Many of the settlements were established after 1923 as refugee colonies. For some distance the only interest is provided by the changing perspective of the Menoikion range to the N and the more distant views, to the S, of Kerdhilion. Between (187km) *Tholós* and (194km) *Mirrínis*, where the line crosses the Amphipolis road, a branch line (no passenger service) diverges to Tzagezi. We keep company with the Serres–Drama road through the Angitis valley, and beyond (206km) *Angístis*, where a fine but looted Macedonian tomb near the station was excavated in 1972, thread the *Tasliki Stena*, the narrow gorge by which the river forces its way out of the Drama plain between Menoikion and Pangaion. We cross the 'golden plain' of Drama, extensively cultivated with tobacco.—232km (144 miles) **Dráma**, see Rte 68; the station lies 1km S of the centre. Beyond Drama the line runs E, followed closely as far as Stavroúpolis by a secondary road described in Rte 68. We ascend the valley of the Xeropotamos (maximum gradient 1 in 40) to reach, at (257·5km) *Plataniás*, the watershed (322m) between the Angitis and the Nestos. The line descends equally steeply the Stena Korpilón and at (269km) *Paranéstion* crosses the Nestos and follows it.—Beyond (292km) *Stavroúpolis* it threads a spectacular defile passing through numerous tunnels.—At (312·5km) *Toxótai* we cross the Kavalla–Xanthi road.— 327km **Xánthi**, see Rte 69A. Beyond Xanthi the line runs E, following the low ground to the S of the Via Egnatia. The railway passes SW of (373·5km) **Komotiní** (Rte 69A), the station of which is 2·5km from the centre. For a while the railway keeps well S of the road to Alexandroúpolis, then, at (405·5km) *Méstis*, just S of Vélkion, crosses it at right angles, continuing E to a summit of 278m and (420km) *Kírki* in the valley of the little Iren. The hills to the N have tin and silver mines. The railway descends the stream to (441km) **Alexandroúpolis**

(Rte 69A).

Hence to (539km) *Dhidhimótikhon* the line is never more than 3km E of the road (see Rte 69A); in places they run together.—553·5km **Píthion** (Πύθιον), on a loop to the E of the road, is an important frontier where the Hellenic and Turkish State Railways meet. The little town occupies the site of an ancient fortified city with an acropolis (see Rte 69A). To the SE the line crosses into Turkey.—563km *Uzunköprü.*—833·5km **Istanbul**.

The W branch from Pithion, which once linked with the international line from Turkey into Bulgaria, is now virtually defunct since the Turks have built a new connecting line entirely on their own territory.

70   Samothrace and Lémnos

These two islands, which geographically form part of the Eastern Sporades (Rte 74), are described here as they are more easily reached from the Thracian coast.

A. Samothrace

Motor caique from Alexandroupolis (34km in 5 hours) daily in summer, twice or 3 times weekly in winter. The island is also visited by occasional steamer services which tend to change each year.— Hotels B, C. E.

The island of **Samothráki** (Σαμοθράκη, in English *Samothrace*, lies some 32km SW of Alexandroupolis and almost equidistant from the Gallipoli peninsula. The surrounding sea, swept by the prevailing N winds, is usually rough and stormy, making access difficult. There is only one anchorage. Save for a narrow coastal plain in the N and a region of rolling hills to the SW, the island, elliptical in shape and only 176 sq. km in area, consists of eroded granite mountains, rising in Mt Fengari to 1600m. Wild goats roam the mountainsides. Winters are hard, with heavy rains and thick snow. The island enjoys copious springs, and in classical times was probably much more fertile. Fruit is abundant. Politically the island belongs to Thrace as an eparchy of the nome of Evros. More than one third of the population (2871 inhab.) is concentrated in Khora.

History. In the Neolithic and Bronze Ages Samothrace was occupied by people of Thracian stock. From 'the topmost peak of wooded Samothrace' Poseidon watched the fighting on the plains of Troy (Iliad, xiii, 12), a city supposedly founded from the island though in fact more likely founded from Lemnos (comp. below). The non-Greek Thracian language and religion survived the arrival of Greek colonists c 700 and in cult ritual to the 1C BC. Archaeological evidence contradicts the classical tradition that the colonists were earlier and came from Samos; Strabo indeed suggests that the Samians invented the story for their own glory. The colonists' dialect has been shown by inscription to have been Aeolian rather than Ionian, and probably derived from Lesbos or the Troad. In the 6C Samothrace had a silver coinage, the city reached its greatest extent, and colonies were established on the mainland. The Samothracian navy was represented at Salamis. In the 5C her power declined, though the fame of her cult increased until the island became the chief centre of religious life in the N Aegean. At the Sanctuary of the Great Gods Herodotus and King Lysander of Sparta were initiated. Aristophanes and Plato refer to its Mysteries. Here Philip of Macedon met and fell in love with his wife Olympias of Epirus, mother of Alexander the Great. The Macedonian dynasty continued to adorn the sanctuary until their downfall. Though the presence of the sanctuary assured the independence of the city, the island was used as a naval base by the Second Athenian League, by King Lysimachos of Thrace, and by the Ptolemies, Seleucids, and Macedonians in turn.

After the Battle of Pydna, Perseus, the last king of Macedon, sought refuge in the island, only to be taken prisoner by the Romans. Aristarchus (fl. 155–143 BC), editor of Homer, was a native. In 84 BC the sanctuary was pillaged by Corsairs, but soon revived under Roman patronage. The legend that Dardanos the legendary founder of Troy, had come from Samothrace and that his descendant, Aeneas, had brought the cult to Rome, gave Samothrace a particular interest to the Romans. Varro and Piso (father-in-law of Julius Caesar) were initiates. The island, a natural port of call between the Troad and Neapolis, saw St. Paul on his way to Philippi. Hadrian visited Samothrace and though an earthquake c AD 200 began its decline, the ancient religion survived to the 4C. In 1419 the island was visited by Buondelmonte, and in 1444, when it had passed into the hands of the Genoese Gattilusi, princes of Enos and Samothrace, by Cyriacus of Ancona. It was taken by the Turks in 1457, passed to Greece after the First World War, and suffered a Bulgarian occupation in 1941–44.

The landing-place of *Kamariótissa*, on the W coast, is close to the promontory of Akrotiri. The church of the *Panayia Kamariotissa* is on the site of an early Christian basilica of which some architectural fragments may be seen. In the craggy fold of the mountains above is the village of *Khóra*, or Samothrace, with 941 inhab. and a medieval castle. On the N coast, reached by road from Kamariótissa, is the ancient *Palaiópolis*, marked on the W by a grove of plane-trees and the Tourist Hotel (comp. above). The ancient city, now a confusion of rocks and wild olive trees, occupies the shoulder of Ayios Yeóryios, a ridge extending N towards the sea from the central massif of Fengari. From the Acropolis on the ridge the colossal *City Wall*, archaic (polygonal) and Hellenistic, runs W across a ravine and takes in a smaller hill before reaching the shore by a small chapel. Two ruined medieval *Towers*, built of antique materials by Palamede Gattilusio in 1444, command the sea, beneath which lie remains of the harbour mole and of a Byzantine church. Between the ancient city and the Xenia Hotel a river descends to the sea. The torrents that feed it bound the **Sanctuary of the Great Gods**. A path leads past the museum (see below) to the site.

The religion of the Great Gods was a pre-Greek Chthonic cult. The Great Gods comprised the Great Mother of Axieros (related to Cybele and later identified with Demeter), an ithyphallic fertility god called Kadmilos (later identified with Hermes), the powerful Kabeiroi (Dardanos and Aetion), twin demons later fused with the Dioskouroi, and Axiokersos and Axiokersa (Hades and Persephone). In later times Hekate, Aphrodite, and Kadmos and Harmonia were added by assimilation or confusion. Ancient writers fought shy of saying much about the Kabeiroi, whose wrath was considered implacable. They were Anatolian in origin and, save at Thebes, hardly known in mainland Greece. Towards the end of the Archaic period Samothrace overtook Lemnos in importance as their principal place of worship.

The sanctuary had an extra-territorial character, apparently independent of the city-state that adjoined it, since at festivals this sent envoys like any other polis. Initiation into the mysteries, which was not essential for attendance at the sanctuary (unlike Eleusis), was open to anyone, regardless of nationality, sex, age, or social status. Initiation could be obtained at any time, and its two degrees (myesis and epoptia) could be taken without interval. A moral standard seems to have been required for the higher degree (which was not obligatory but, rather, exceptional) and some form of confession and absolution preceded it. Ceremonies apparently took place by torchlight.

The early sanctuary, approached from the W, occupied the promontory between the E and central torrents. A sacrificial area of the 7C BC underlies the Temenos, and utilitarian structures were added piecemeal in the 5C and early 4C. The temple area was lavishly renewed in marble by the Ptolemies. A new access from the town side was provided by Ptolemy II Philadelphus, after which the site was extended to a typically Hellenistic planned design on the promontory between the central and W streams.

SAMOTHRACE

0   50 metres

Excavations were begun in 1863 by Champoiseau, French consul at Adrianople, who discovered the famous Victory now in the Louvre in Paris. A French mission mapped the site in 1866. Austrian expeditions, directed by A. Conze in 1873 and 1875, uncovered the Ptolemaion; its marbles were divided between Austria and Turkey, but only a few of those shipped to Gallipoli arrived at Istanbul. A Swedish team worked on the site in 1923–25. In 1938 systematic exploration was begun by the Institute of Fine Arts, New York University, under Karl Lehmann and Phyllis Williams Lehmann and continues at present under James R. McCredie. Guide in English to the Excavations and Museum, by the excavators.

To the left of the path, the **Anaktoron** (Pl. A) served as a hall of initiation into the Mysteries (myesis). Built of good polygonal masonry the present building dates to early Imperial times, but its design is nearly identical to its predecessors of the 4C and 3C BC. Its walls still stand in places to a height of 3·6m. The interior (27m by 11·5m), reached by three doors, from the W terrace, was divided by a partition into a main hall and an inner sanctum (on the N). This was guarded by bronze statues and marked by a warning stele. Limestone bases show where a wooden grandstand occupied the E and part of the N wall of the hall. In the centre was a circular wooden platform; in the SE corner a libation pit.—Built on to the S end of the Anaktoron was a *Sacristy* (Pl. B; Iera Oikia), dating to the 3C or 4C AD, which replaces an early Imperial Building. Here, it seems, the novice was vested and hither he returned to receive a document certifying his initiation.

The *Rotunda* (Pl. C), the largest circular building known in Greek architecture (more than 20m across), was dedicated to the Great Gods by Queen Arsinoe between 289 and 281 BC, whence its appellation **Arsinoeion**. Numerous marbles that survived the destroying earthquake have been arranged to show the structure of the building. A marble wall, crowned by a beautiful marble stringcourse, was surmounted by a gallery of pilasters supporting a Doric entablature. Within, the gallery had Corinthian half-columns with an Ionic cornice.

In the interior of the rotunda are some walls of the *Orthostate Structure*, the early 4C predecessor of the Anaktoron.

Farther S (Pl. x; reached from the path) a *Sacred Rock* of blue-green porphyry has a yellow tufa pavement from which libations were poured.

The **Temenos** (Pl. D) is a rectangular precinct, open to the sky; surviving courses of masonry represent only the foundations of its latest state in the 4C BC. It was entered on the NE side by an Ionic *Propylon* of Thasian marble, of which many fragments can be seen both here and in the museum. Within the precinct probably stood a famous statue of Aphrodite and Pothos by Skopas. Abutting is an artificial terrace with a good view towards the sea.

To the S are the imposing remains of the **Hieron** (Pl. E; the Sanctuary), a Doric edifice used for the Epopteia, or higher initiation ceremonies. Begun in the last quarter of the 4C BC, it was not finished until c 170 years later and was extensively restored in the 3C AD. The limestone foundations are complete and most of the euthynteria in Thasian marble still in situ. The *Façade* consisted of a double porch of 14 columns standing before antae; five columns and one architrave block were re-erected in 1956 and the steps restored with modern blocks. The capital on the corner column was returned from Vienna, where the pedimental statues still remain.

A marble ceiling beam is preserved in the pronaos. The marble floor has disappeared, leaving the limestone under-pavement exposed. The spectators' benches on either side date from the Roman restoration, as does the marble floor of the apse. Here foundations of limestone blocks and irregular fieldstones (5C and 6C BC respectively) show that the building had precursors.—Outside the foundations, on the E side, two sacred stones flank a torch-holder; here it is conjectured the hierophant heard the candidate's confession before admission.

Along the W side of the Hieron were two buildings. That to the N, dubbed the *Hall of Votive Gifts* (Pl F), took the form of a rectangular stoa with a Doric limestone colonnade of 6 columns between antae. Built c 540 BC, it survived with minor repairs for close on a thousand years. Adjacent, to the S, is the better-preserved substructure of the *Altar Court* (Pl. G), a hypaethral enclosure entered through a colonnade, the unequal spacing of whose columns is indicated by the surviving drums. Fragments of the architrave bear a dedicatory inscription by (?) Arrhidaios, half-brother of Alexander the Great.

The outline of the *Theatre* (Pl. H) is recognisable though all but two of its seats of white limestone and red porphyry vanished in 1927–37. The river is channelled under the orchestra in a late-Roman concrete culvert (restored).

A path winds up to the WESTERN HILL. The N part of this is occupied by the so-called '*Ruinenviereck*' (Pl. L), a medieval structure probably a fortification, built entirely of antique material from the sanctuary. Along the ridge above the theatre was a *Stoa*. Its foundations (Pl. J), 90m long, laid bare by the Austrian expedition, were examined in 1963–64. Hundreds of blocks with elements of Doric and Ionic orders from outer and inner colonnades survive. It was probably of the early 3C BC. Farther on is the *Nike Monument* with the foundations of the precinct or building in which the statue stood. There was a shallow upper and a deep lower basin; in places the clay pipelines that fed and drained it can be traced.

The Parian marble 'Winged Victory', that formed the centrepiece of the monument, was removed to Paris in 1863 and the ship's prow on which it stands in 1891. The right hand, recovered in 1950, is on permanent loan to the Louvre.

The path leads across the river and over the hill where the crowded *South Necropolis* (6C BC–2C AD) was excavated in 1957 to the E ravine, beyond which stood the **Ptolemaion** (Pl. K), a monumental gateway to the sanctuary, dedicated to the Great Gods by Ptolemy II Philadelphus. The sub-structure is pierced by a barrel-vaulted tunnel through which at that time the river was channelled. The foundations carried an Ionic portico on the E and a Corinthian portico on the W. The Austrians carried off many decorative elements of its two pediments; other blocks lie in the ravine. Abutments for a wooden bridge (with a span of c 18m) that crossed the river after its course had been altered by an earthquake can still be seen. Immediately opposite are a flagged circular Area and a later Doric structure dedicated by Philip and Alexander, successors to Alexander the Great.

The **Museum** is arranged as an aid to the understanding of the site. In HALL A typical sections of each building have been reconstructed from available fragments, though these are not necessarily in their original juxtaposition. Also in this room are two Stelai, from the Anaktoron and the Hieron, prohibiting entry to the uninitiated.—HALL B is devoted to SCULPTURE. Fragments from the Propylon of the Temenos (c 340 BC): monolithic Ionic column of Thasian marble; necking with anthemion ornament and fragmentary capital; portions of the frieze of over 80 dancing maidens and musicians, probably depicting the wedding of Kadmos and Harmonia (in deliberately archaistic style). Two figures retrieved from the central river bed of the sanctuary, probably parts of a pedimental group (c 460–450 BC): Bust of the blind seer Teiresias, which owing to a misidentification by Cyriac of Ancona became a model for Renaissance portraits of Aristotle; the eyes were recut in the 19C when the bust was used as an ikon on a house in Khora. Headless statue of (?) Persephone.

Case 1 contains religious and votive objects, including iron finger rings (one of the outward signs of initiation commented upon by Pliny); *Case* 2, coins and stamped roof tiles; in *Case* 3 are small architectural fragments; water-spouts, antefixes, mouldings, sections of floor, ceiling, etc. *Case* 4 displays sculptural pieces (4C BC–1C AD), including a marble portrait head of Queen Arsinoe III; bronze statuette of Herakles; fragments in high relief representing Centaurs.

HALL C. Acroterial Victory from the Hieron (c 130 BC), reconstituted in 1950 from fragments buried after the statue fell in the earthquake c AD 200. Cases on the right side of the hall contain finds from the Sanctuary (the pottery reflects its long histroy and the cosmopolitan origins of its pilgrims); those on the left side objects from tombs round the city. *Case* 2. Bronze decorations from the Propylon of the Temenos; votive gifts, including fragments of an iron chain-mail cuirass of the 3C BC (? Gaulish La Tène workmanship). *Case* 3. Local ware of the 7C BC. *Case* 10. Terracotta statuette of a young winged god (3C BC) from the S necropolis; fine blown glassware; complete contents of a Roman tomb chamber of AD 135; terracotta figurine of a girl (early 1C BC). *Case* 11. Stele of c 400 BC with an inscription in Greek characters but in an undeciphered (presumably Thracian) language. Further inscriptions, set up in the courtyard, include lists of initiates, dedications, etc.—HALL D. Grave goods, pottery, and jewellery from the cemeteries.

ASCENT OF MT SAOS, 5–6 hours from *Khora,* or (preferable) in 4 hours from *Therma,* a place on the N coast with hot sulphur springs, 2 hours E of Palaeopolis. **Mount Saos**, *Saoce or Fengári* (1560m) was the peak from which Poseidon gazed upon the plains of Troy; the modern traveller can do the same. The *View is all-embracing. N to W, the coast of Thrace and Macedonia as far as the Chalkidike peninsula and Mt Athos, with the island of Thasos in between; S, the islands of Imbros and Lemnos; E, the Dardanelles, the plain of Troy, and Mt Ida in the far distance.

B. Lémnos

Approaches. BY AIR, from Athens twice daily, in 45 minutes; also twice weekly in c 40 minutes from Salonika; less frequently to Lesbos.—TERMINAL, Od. N. Gavofallídhi, Mýrina.

BY SEA. Connections once or twice weekly with Piraeus, Kimi (Evvia), Ayios Konstandinos, Kavalla, Alexandroupolis, Lesbos, Samothrace, Ayios Evstratios.

The island of **Lemnos** (Λήμνος; *Límnos*) is situated in the middle of the N Aegean, midway between Mt Athos and Asia Minor. Intervening on the Asian side are the Turkish islands of Imbros and Tenedos. To the N rises Samothrace; to the SE is Lesbos, to the nome of which Lemnos belongs, together with the islet of Ayios Evstratios which lies due S. Lemnos, with a population of 16,017 and an area of 453 sq. km, is almost bisected by two deep inlets of the sea—the Gulf of Moudhros in the S and the Bay of Pournia in the N—the isthmus between them being only 3km across. Valerius Flaccus ('Argonautica', II, 431) calls the island 'tenuis Lemnos', though the W half is rugged and hilly, rising in the NW corner to 430m. The bare plains of the E yield small quantities of cereals, sesame, cotton, and tobacco. Numerous hot springs attest to the island's volcanic origin.

History. According to Homer the inhabitants of Lemnos were of Thracian stock; Herodotus and Thucydides, however, call them Pelasgi or Tirrheni (the same Tyrrhenian pirates the Dionysos transformed into dolphins). This may well represent two stages of pre-Greek history. Recent archaeological evidence shows that Lemnos had the most advanced Neolithic civilisation in the Aegean, and a Bronze Age culture of Minoan–Mycenaean type, connected with Troy and Lesbos, which continued without a sharp break into the Geometric period. In the 8–6C the island seems to have had contact with the Greeks, though it is certain from inscriptions that before the 6C the inhabitants were not Greek; their language is undeciphered and their burial customs show affinities with Villanovan (Etruscan) burials in Italy. The island is said by Polybius to have borne the more ancient name of *Aithaleia*, it possibly took the name Lemnos from a goddess identifiable with the Great Mother. The principal cults, however, were those of Hephaistos (said to have been thrown down to Lemnos from Olympos for intervening in a quarrel between Zeus and Hera, his parents) and of the Kabiroi.

Among many legends is that of the curse of Aphrodite upon the Lemnians for impugning her virtue. This alienated the men from their wives, who murdered their husbands. Only king Thoas escaped, saved by his daughter Hypsipyle. When the Argonauts put in at Lemnos, some of their number stayed behind to marry the Lemnian widows, becoming by them the fathers of the Minyans. The Minyans were driven out by the Pelasgians to Elis Tryphilia in the Peloponnesos. Homer tells of Philoktetes, the most celebrated archer of the Trojan War, who spent ten years on Lemnos with a wounded foot. The proverbial expression 'Lemnian deeds' for atrocities is attributed by Herodotus (VI, 138) to an episode in the Persian Wars. The Lemnians carried off some Athenian women from Brauron. The children of this enterprise looked down on their Lemnian half-brothers, whereupon the Lemnians slaughtered both them and their Athenian mothers.

Lemnos fell to Persia c 513 BC and changed hands more than once before the end of the Persian wars. Here Hippias is said to have died after Marathon. From 477 BC the island formed part of the Delian League, and later received cleruchies from Athens (they dedicated the famous Lemnian Athena of Pheidias on the Acropolis of Athens). Lemnian troops fought for Athens at Sphakteria (425) at Amphipolis (422) and at Syracuse (413). Save for brief periods of domination by Sparta (404–393), by the Macedonians, and by the Seleucid Antiochus the Great, Lemnos remained under Athenian influence to the time of Septimius Severus. The island was twice visited (AD 162 and 165) by Dioskorides. In the 2C and 3C the Lemnian Philostratus family achieved fame in Rome as sophists. The island was plundered by the Heruli and later passed to Byzantium. It had a bishop in the 4C and became a metropolitan see in the reign of Leo VI. In 924 the Saracens under Leo of Tripoli were defeated by a Byzantine fleet off the island. Venetian merchants settled in the 11C and 12C, establishing soveriegnty after 1204 under the Navigaiosa grand dukes. In the 13–15C the island was disputed between Venetians, Genoese, and Byzantines, and after 1462 between Venetians and Turks. John of Selymbria spent some years in exile here after 1344 and Gregory Palamas took refuge here in 1349. After 1670 the Turks in their turn used it as a place of exile for disgraced notables. Orloff's Russians occupied the island in the war of 1770, only to be driven out by Hassan Bey. Lemnos became Greek for a few months in 1829 before being exchanged with the Turks for Euboea. It fell to Greece in 1912, and was the British base for the Gallipoli campaign. Its connection with Turkey ended by treaty in 1920.

The island capital and chief port *Mírina* or **Kastron** (Hotels B, C, D; F/ A) is situated on the W coast. The verdant town (3744 inhab.) is the seat of the Metropolitan of Lemnos. Its two good anchorages are divided by a rocky promontory on which, in commanding position, stood the ancient *Myrina*. The conspicuous Turkish walls rise on ancient foundations; houses and streets can be traced; and inscriptions attest a sanctuary to Artemis. The MUSEUM is arranged for the purposes of study and labelled in Greek and Italian. Finds from Hephaisteia and Poliochni are well displayed in ten rooms.

Two roads lead towards Mudros, the inland one to the N passing near a *Bath-House*, built by Hassan Bey. The shorter way, more southerly, which touches the coast, passes *Kondiá*, to the SE of which, at *Vriókastron* and *Trochaliá*, are some Bronze Age remains. The roads join at *Livadhokhórion* and continue to **Moúdhros**, or *Mudros*.

The *Gulf of Mudros* one of the best natural harbours in the Aegean, became the base, in the First World War, of the Mediterranean Expeditionary Force. Hence Sir Ian Hamilton launched his attack on the Dardanelles (25 April 1915). In the same harbour the armistice with Turkey was concluded on 30 October 1918 on board H.M.S. 'Agamemnon'.—*East Mudros Military Cemetery*, to the NE of the town, with c 900 British Commonwealth dead, contains also a French memorial, though the French graves were removed in 1922. At *Portianós*, on the W side of the inner harbour, lie a further 350 dead of the Gallipoli campaign.

The most important archaeological remains of Lemnos are at **Polióchni** on the E coast below Cape Voroskópos (anc. *Droskopos*). This presumably represents the Homeric 'Lemnos'. Excavations in 1931–36, by Alessandro della Seta of the Italian School, uncovered four superposed settlements, the latest an unfortified town of the Late Bronze Age (c 1500–1000 BC). Beneath lay a city of the Copper Age (pre-Mycenaean and probably earlier than Troy VI), and beneath that again remains of two Neolithic cities. The later of these was equipped with stone baths, the earliest found in the Aegean. The *Town Walls* (c 2000 BC), with towers and gates, stand in places to a height of 5m. The city seems to have been destroyed by an earthquake. The main street and a number of houses were explored. The earliest city (4th millennium BC) is believed to be more ancient that Troy I.

A third road runs from Mudros to the NE tip of the island. *Kómi*, between Mudros and Kondopoúlion, is known from an inscription to have had a sanctuary of Herakles, but only slight Byzantine remains are visible today. The *Bay of Pournia*, to the N of the road, has yielded several sites to the excavator's spade. The medieval castle of KOKKINO, or *Kotchinos*, rose to importance with the decline of Hephaistia (see below). Here in 1442 the Empress of Constantine XI Palaeologus died in childbirth while under siege by the Turks; the castle was successfully defended by the Venetians against the Turks in 1476. Between the castle and the village of *Repanidhion* lay *Mosychlos*, famous in antiquity and in the Middle Ages for Lemnian Earth, a red bole containing a large percentage of silica, used as a tonic and astringent medicine. It was extracted on only one day in the year (latterly 6 August) to the accompaniment of religious ceremonies and exported (anciently under the seal of Artemis; 'terra sigillata') right up to the 19C.—The hamlet of *Palaiópolis*, on a rocky peninsula above the sea, occupies the site of **Hephaistia** (Ηφαστία), in Classical times the principal city of Lemnos, paying the larger tribute to Athens. It had pre-Greek origins. It became seat of a Byzantine bishop, fell to the Venetians in 1204, and c 1395 was wrecked by a landslide and abandoned. Excavations in 1926–30 and 1937–39 by the Italian School uncovered a necropolis (8C BC) and a sanctuary destroyed in the last years of the 6C BC. Hellenistic material, including potters' kilns, has been found in recent excavations. The local pottery carries Minoan–Mycenaean traditions into the Geometric period; imported ware proves a lively trade with Macedonia, Corinth, and Athens. Among traces of later Greek occupation are a *Theatre*, remodelled in Roman times, and Byzantine churches.—On the opposite side of the bay (at *Khlóï*) is the **Kabeirion**, excavated in 1937–39 by the Italian School. The sanctuary goes back to the Pelasgian epoch, when it had precedence over that of Samothrace. It occupies two level tracts divided by a rocky spur. Archaic foundations have been ascribed to an *Anaktoron*, a *Telesterion*, and a *Stoa*. The N level is occupied by a huge edifice, probably the Hellenistic *Telesterion*, with a façade of 12 Doric columns. Among many inscriptions listing officials of the cult was found a letter from Philip V requesting initiation as epoptes.—*Cape Hermaeon*, on the NE coast, was, according to Aeschylus, one of the series of hills on which fire-beacons were lit at the instance of Agamemnon to signal to his wife Klytemnestra at Mycenae the fall of Troy (*Agamemnon*, 283), possibly an anachronism suggested by a similar system used in the opposite direction by Xerxes during the invasion of Greece (?).

Submarine research in 1960 in the *Charos Reef*, 16km offshore, located blocks of marble belonging to an Archaic Temple of Apollo that once stood in the ancient town of *Chryse*. One of the prehistoric centres of the island, Chryse is mentioned by Herodotus as having been engulfed by the sea as the result of an earthquake. Here (according to the Iliad) died Philoktetes, the exiled Achaean general.

About 32km S of Lemnos is the small island of **Ayios Evstrátios** or **Aistrates** (17 sq. miles) used periodically as a deportation settlement for political offenders. Its highest point is Mt Semadhi (296km). Small quantities of iron, coal, and oil are found. The island village, *Ayios Evstrátios*, lies on the NW coast. The site of the ancient city, on a hill between two streams, shows traces of Mycenaean, Greek, Roman, and Byzantine occupation. Nowadays the island is dry and waterless and food is scarce. The beaches are unattractive.

VIII ISLANDS OF THE AEGEAN

The **Aegean Sea** is bounded on the N by Macedonia and Thrace, on the W by the mainland of Greece, on the E by Asia Minor and on the S by Crete. Ancient writers divided it into the *Thracian Sea*, in the N; the *Myrtoan Sea*, in the SW, so called after Myrtos, an obscure island off the coast of Argolis; the *Ikarian Sea*, in the E, named after the island of Ikaria; and the *Cretan Sea*, in the S. The derivation of the word Aegean (Αιγαίον) is uncertain; it may be from αιγίς, in its secondary meaning of squall, in reference to the sudden gales that affect the area. The Byzantines and Venetians calls it the *Archipelago*, and the Turks, the *White Sea*.

In the centre of the Aegean are the **Cyclades** (Κυκλάδες), a group of islands forming a rough circle (κύκλος) round Delos. In antiquity only twelve or fifteen islands were regarded as belonging to the Cyclades (Strabo, X), and they depended on Delos. Today some thirty islands and islets are comprised within the nome of the Cyclades (*Kikládhon*), with its capital at Ermoúpolis (Syros). This political division, which includes Delos and the S Sporades, as well as the Cyclades proper, is divided into eight eparchies and has over 88,000 inhabitants. The **Sporades** are three island groups 'scattered' in the Aegean, to the N, S, and E of the Cyclades. The Southern Sporades are described with Delos and the Cyclades in the first three routes of this section; the Eastern Sporades, excluding the Dodecanese, in the remaining route. The Northern Sporades are described for convenience in Rte 43; the Dodecanese are described in a separate section (IX) and Amorgos with them; Crete, which partly closes the Aegean on the S, occupies a separate volume.

The **Aegean islands** are the peaks of a submerged plateau now 90–200m below the surface and bounded by deeps of 600–900m. In the N they are formed of limestone, gneiss, schist, and marble; in the S of volcanic rock, lava, basalt, and trachyte. The highest point is in the island of Naxos. These mountainous and largely arid islands have lost their once luxuriant forests, but the larger ones produce olives, figs, and vines. The wines of Santorini and Naxos are renowned. The marble of Paros and Tinos is famed. Milos has long been noted for obsidian. Iron is found in Serifos, Kithnos, and Andros. The limpid air and the equable climate are a great attraction and the heat of summer is alleviated by the periodic N winds (Tramontana; anc. Boreas) and later by the more predictable Etesian winds (Meltémi), which, blowing also from the N, prevail from early July to mid-September, sometimes reaching gusts of great violence.

The little seaside villages, with their clean white houses and their sparkling streets paved with marble, vary widely in atmosphere from island to island as the temperament of the islanders varies with the resources of the islands. They often contrast markedly with the villages inland, where terraced cultivation is a feature of the landscape. Windmills, another characteristic feature, usually have a dozen sails of canvas furled to tiny triangles. The inhabitants, partly Roman Catholic, claim a purer Greek strain than those of the mainland: they have, perhaps, been more influenced in the past by contact with the Italian peninsula and less by contact with the Turks. They are hospitable to strangers.

The islands are increasingly tending to diverge into two categories: those 'earmarked for tourist development' on which for half the year modern, mainly characterless, hotels and souvenir shops superimpose an alien sophistication, but give some sort of prosperity; and those where the slow rhythm of island life continues, free from the stresses of modern technology but equally free from its benefits. Tiny 'unspoilt' islands subject to increasing depopulation do without mains electricity, hot water, the international telephone, and wide choices of food; they may have days without transport and be two islands away from medical aid. Visitors should remember that it is pointless to opt for the simple life and then be irked by its simplicity. The larger islands are in fact better able to absorb tourists without losing their individuality.

COMMUNICATIONS. Most of the islands may be reached by regular steamer services (increasingly being replaced by vehicle ferries), which serve the islands in groups, travelling outward one day and returning in inverse order next day. Two of the Cycladic routes make the return voyage in the day every day with a common port-of-call in Syros and on some days Mykonos provides a further interchange point between the Cyclades and the Dodecanese. Apart from this, to reach an island on a different round it is usually necessary to return to Piraeus. Services are most frequent on Monday and Saturday, least frequent on Tuesday and Sunday. Those outlined in the route headings were those in force in summer 1986; they are less frequent in winter and subject to change. Sailing times should always be checked on day of sailing (tel. 143, in Athens). The Eastern Sporades and several of the Cyclades are individually linked by air with Athens.

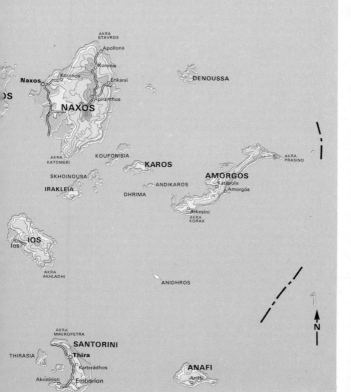

THE CYCLADES

0	25 miles
0	40 kilometres

IKARIA

AKRA PAPAS

AKRA EVROS

Mikonos
MIKONOS

DILOS

OS

AKRA STAVROS

Apollona

Koronis

Naxos

Koronos

Enkarai

NAXOS

Apiranthos

DENOUSSA

AKRA PRASINO

AKRA KATOMERI

KOUFONISIA

KAROS

AMORGOS

Katapola

Amorgós

SKHOINOUSA

ANDIKAROS

IRAKLEIA

DHRIMA

Arkesini

AKRA KORAX

IOS

Ios

AKRA AKHLADHI

ANIDHROS

N

AKRA MAVROPETRA

SANTORINI

Thira

THIRASIA

Karterádhos

ANAFI

Akrotírion

Emborión

Anáfi

CRUISE SHIPS operating from Piraeus usually combine the most popular islands into a round trip of 5–7 days, calling nearly always at Mykonos, Delos, Rhodes, Heraklion (Crete), and Santorin. Additional calls may be made at Patmos and Kos. More ambitious rounds include Istanbul, Troy, Izmir, Ephesos, and Halicarnassos in Turkey.

Travellers who wish to go from island to island according to their fancy must hire a caique, an expensive and often arduous business, or a yacht, which (though not less expensive) is more easily arranged. Details of the many yacht brokers in Athens and Piraeus may be had from the Greek Yacht Brokers and Consultants Association, 25 Loukianoú, Athens. Of the 81 Greek harbours and anchorages now equipped with facilities for servicing of yachts, some 25 are in the Aegean island area. The Aegean is an uncertain and capricious sea and should be sailed only by yachtsmen of experience; excellent pilots may be found among the sailors of Mykonos, Skyros, and Milos.

History. At some remote period the Cyclades were populated by Carians. Thucydides tells us that (I, 4) King Minos conquered the Cyclades and expelled the Carians. Herodotus (I, 171) says that in ancient times the Carians, who went by the name of Leleges, were subjects of Minos and served in the ships of his navy; and that, long after the time of Minos, they were driven from the islands by Ionians and Dorians and settled on the mainland of Asia Minor.

So far there have been relatively few discoveries of the Neolithic Age in the Cyclades. They enjoyed a flourishing Bronze Age civilisation which had affinites at first with Crete and later with Mycenae. For ease of reference, the Cycladic Bronze Age has been divided into the Early, Middle and Late Cycladic, each division being subdivided into three. These nine periods, roughly corresponding to those into which Sir Arthur Evans divided the Minoan civilisation in Crete, cover c fifteen centuries from 2600 to 1100 BC. Perhaps the most important single evidence of the spread of Cycladic civilisation is the volcanic mineral obsidian. The principal though not the only place in the Aegean where obsidian is found is Melos, which abounds in it. This mineral was of great importance before the discovery of copper and bronze and even for some time after they had come into use. The prehistoric trade in obsidian from Melos was considerable, and it has been found in Crete and other Aegean islands, on the mainland of Greece, in Thessaly, and on the coast of Asia Minor. This dispersal proved the early existence of sea communications even before the discovery of the 'Libyan' fresco in Thera, where civilisation seems to have been on a par with Crete.

Before the end of the Early Cycladic Period people lived in houses often grouped in villages. Some of the pottery had elaborate designs of spirals and glaze paint was introduced. Melos made pottery with white designs on a dark ground, inspired by Early Minoan examples. Model boats of lead prove not only the use of this metal but the commonplace of navigation. Primitive marble figurines were imported into Crete. In the Middle Cycladic Period there was considerable progress. The second city at Phylakope had larger and better-built houses, and it was protected by a wall. Pottery designs showed a naturalistic tendency, flowers and animals being freely represented. During this period Middle Minoan pottery of the best style was imported into Melos, and Melian vases imitated the Cretan polychrome designs on a black ground (Kamares ware). Contemporary Melian vases have been found in the Temple Repositories at Knosses. Intercourse with the mainland is proved by the discovery in Melos of Minyan ware of the Middle Helladic Period. Before the end of the Middle Cycladic Period (c 1600 BC) the Cyclades appear to have been completely under the domination of Crete, thus confirming the tradition that they were conquered by Minos (comp. above). This view is borne out by the fact that in Melos there was a script resembling and probably derived from the Minoan, and by the discovery on Thera of Middle Minoan vases imported from Crete. The Flying Fish fresco found in the Palace at Phylakope and the frescoes on Thera may have been the work of Cretan artists. Cycladic pottery imitating Cretan and small objects in bronze, ivory, and stone show that the culture of the islands was now a reflection of the Minoan. After the volcanic explosion of Thera the influence of the mainland became stronger and Mycenaean imports rivalled Minoan. At the end of the 15C, when the centre of Aegean civilisation passed from Knossos to Mycenae, both native pottery and imported ware declined in quality. As the use of metal spread, the demand for Melian obsidian fell off and the island's fortunes waned. In the third period of Late Cycladic the imports from Crete stopped altogether and the only source of supply was the mainland. At the end of this phase the culture shaded off into that of the Protogeometric Period.

In the 10C and 9C Ionians colonised the islands and Delos became the religious centre of the Greek world. The islands were overrun by the Persians in the invasion of 490 BC. In 478/7 they were included in the Delian League and so imperceptibly became incorporated in the Athenian Empire. They remained tributary to Athens till 404, after which they had a few years of independence. In 378 they joined the Second Athenian League and again came under the influence of Athens. In the Social War (357–355) they revolted, only to become subject to Macedon. In 308 they passed to Antigonus, who founded the League of Islanders; then to the Ptolemies who, vanquished at Andros in 228, were supplanted by the Macedonian, Antigonus Doson. He was succeeded by Philip V. After Philip's defeat at Cynoscephalae in 197, the Cyclades passed to the Rhodians, and later to the Romans. Temporarily conquered by Mithridates in 88, they were returned to Rome. They were abandoned by the Eastern Empire to the raids of the Goths, Saracens, and Slavs.

In 1204 the islands were given by the Crusaders to Venice, who handed them over to adventurers as hereditary fiefs of the Republic. The result was twenty small vassal states. Members of the Ghizi family held Tenos, Mykonos, Skyros, Skopelos, Skiathos, and Astypalaea, as well as parts of Keos and Seriphos, of which the Giustianini and Michieti had the remainder. The Sanudi held Naxos and Paros, and many smaller islands, and called themselves dukes of Naxos; the Navigajosi aspired to the title of grand dukes of Lemnos; the Venieri were marquesses of Cerigo (Kythera); the Viari had Cerigotto; the Barozzi, Santorini (Thera); the Dandoli, Andros; the Quirini, Amorgos; and the Foscoli, Anaphe. Most of these island dynasties were suppressed by the Turks after the fall of Constantinople in 1453; but some survived for another century. Among them were the dukes of Naxos, who had almost from the start broken with Venice and gone over to her enemies. In 1210 Marco Sanudi, first Duke of Naxos, took an oath of fealty to the Latin emperor Henry of Flanders and, as a reward, was made feudal superior of the other Aegean barons, with the grandiose title of Duke of the Archipelago and Sovereign of the Dodecanese.

Early in the 17C the islands were ransacked by English adventurers looking for antiquities. Admiral Sir Kenelm Digby acted as the agent of Charles I, who is said to have amassed 400 pieces of sculpture. The rival collection of the Duke of Buckingham was enriched by the efforts of Sir Thomas Roe, ambassador to the Porte. More successful than either was the Rev. William Petty, chaplain to the second Earl of Arundel (1580–1646), whose daring adventures in the pursuit of the antique became a byword. The famous Parian Chronicle was one of his prizes. Lord Arundel is regarded as the founder of classical archaeology in England; his collection of ancient sculptures was presented in 1667 to the University of Oxford by his grandson Henry Howard, afterwards sixth Duke of Norfolk. It is now in the Ashmolean Museum, Oxford.

The Civil War brought these archaeological forays to an end. In the month that Naseby was fought (June 1645) the Turks invaded Crete. During the 24 years of the Candian War the islands were alternately occupied by Turks and Venetians. On its termination in 1669 the Archipelago enjoyed a century of comparative peace, broken by the outbreak in 1770 of war between Turkey and Russia. The Russian fleet spent the winter of 1770–71 at Paros and annexed eighteen of the Cyclades to the Russian Empire. The Russian domination lasted however, for only four or five years. Thereafter no event of importance disturbed the tranquility of the islands till the Revolution of 1821.

In both world wars the Aegean was tragically prominent. In 1915, during the first, the natural harbour of Moudros, on the island of Lemnos, was made the Allied base, and the island of Imbros the GHQ of the ill-fated Dardanelles Expedition. In the Second World War the Germans had for a time air and local naval superiority which enabled them to occupy Crete after Greece had been overrun and, later, to thwart the British landings at Kos and Leros.

71   Northern Cyclades

A. Sýros

STEAMER from Piraeus, 127km in 3½–5½ hours at least twice
daily, continuing either via Tínos to Mýkonos, or via Páros to Náxos.
Additional services continue to Sámos; also to Ios, Santoríni, Síkinos,
and Folégandros; less frequently to some other islands.

From Rafína, regular service via Andros, Tinos and Mikonos in 3–5 hours.
  NOTE: Syros is a main centre of Aegean (and especially Cycladic) see communications; it is often possible to travel from one island to another via Syros when
there are no direct services.

Síros (Σύρος, more usually in English spelled **SYROS** or **Syra**), situated
in the centre of the Cyclades, owes its development to its port and its
manufactures. The island, 22·5km long with a maximum width of 9km,
is pleasant but not spectacular and no longer deserves the eulogy of
Homer, who calls it rich in herds ánd flocks and having plenty of wine
and corn. It does, however, produce barley, wine, oil, figs, and green
vegetables. Syros is the nursery of Roman Catholicism in Greece;
about half the population of its capital and nearly all the inhabitants outside it are Catholic.

  Ermoúpolis (Hotels A, B, C, E; restaurants on the quay), capital of
the island and of the nome of the Cyclades, is situated on the E coast. The clean town, with well-built 19C mansions adorned
with wrought-iron balconies, has 13,876 inhab., two-thirds of the
island population. It is the seat of a Greek archbishop and of a Roman
Catholic bishop. The older quarters are built on two conical hills, that
to the S, crowned by the RC cathedral, being the medieval *Ano Siros*,
still a separate deme of 1689 inhabitants. The hill of Vrontadho, to the
N, is the Orthodox quarter. The port is the traffic centre of the Cyclades, with steamer services to many islands and the possibility of caiques to others.

History. Nothing survives of the ancient city of *Syria*. In the Middle Ages the
inhabitants, in fear of pirates, withdrew from their seaside town to a lofty hill
about 1·5km inland, where they built Ano (Upper) or Old Syros. This became the
quarter of the Roman Catholics, descendants of the Genoese and Venetian
settlers who, during the Turkish rule after 1566, were under the protection of the
King of France. The inhabitants took no active part in the War of Greek Independence, but took refugees from Psara and Chios, who founded Ermoupolis. The
port became the coal-bunkering station for packet ships of the E Mediterranean
and the chief port of Greece, but declined when oil-burning became general to
its present role as mercantile junction of the Aegean. Syros is one of the most
highly industrialised towns in Gréece, with cotton mills and tanneries.

Protected by the Asses' Isle (Gaidhouronisi) and by a long breakwater,
and bounded on the S by the old *Lazareta*, or quarantine station, the
port is generally crowded with cargo ships laid up or under repair. It
has a hydraulic slip capable of lifting large vessels. Round the outer
harbour are ironworks and tanneries. The lower town is built round
the inner or *Commercial Harbour*. To the left, behind the waterfront, is
the conspicuous belfry of the church of the *Koimisis*.

  The *Quay*, bustling and animated, is lined with cafés, tavernas, and
shops selling loukoumi (Turkish delight), and farther W enlivened by
caiques and fish markets. Odhos Ermou, or Od. Khiou (the fruit and
grocery market) farther on, lead to PLATEÍA MIAOÚLIS, the town cen-

tre. This dignified square, paved with marble and shaded by trees, contains a bandstand and an obelisk to Andreas Miaoulis (1768–1835), the admiral and patriot. It is dominated by the *Town Hall*, an elegant building of c 1870, and round the square are grouped arcaded cafés, clubs, and the Public Library. Behind this is the Apollo Theatre. In the side street to the left of the Town Hall, below the *Clock Tower*, is the entrance to the small *Museum*. Here three rooms contain prehistoric antiquities from Paros, casual finds from Syros (including a phallic idol similar to those on Delos), and a small relief of a boar hunt from Amorgos. To the W is the Orthodox *Cathedral* (Metamorfóseos), with the tomb of Anthimos Gazis (1758–1828), the Thessalian patriot.

Hence, partly by 800 steps (stiff climb; c 1 hour), Odhós Omírou passes between the French *École des Frères* (right) and *St. Sebastian* (left), and mounts to **Ano Síros** (180m), which may be reached by bus or taxi via the fashionable quarter of *Neapolis*. Halfway up is the French *Hospital*, served by sisters of mercy. In the upper town are many Catholic churches and the cathedral of St. George, *Ayíou Nikoláou* of the Orthodox faith, and tier upon tier of whitewashed houses. Next to Ayios Yeóryios and shaded by pepper-trees is the *British Military Cemetery* where lie 108 British and other dead from the Aegean Is., more than half of whom were drowned when the transport ship 'Arcadian' was torpedoed on its way from Salonika to Alexandria on 15 April 1917. Ano Siros was the birthplace of Markos Vamvakaris who achieved fame as a singer of *rebetika*, the Greek equivalent (in content, if not style) of the American blues. The view of the port and of neighbouring islands is striking.—Another splendid viewpoint is the church of the *Anastasis* on the hill of *Vrontado*.

The favourite summer evening promenade is the E wall of the commercial harbour.—In the Vaporia quarter, with its elegant villas, is the church of *Ayios Nikólaos*, adorned with a blue dome, and higher up the *Tríon Ierárkhon* and its orphanage. A road leads N from the first along the cliffs in 30 minutes to *Ayios Dhimítrios*, a fair example of modern 'Byzantine' style (1936).

Kíni (11km) on the W shore and *Galessás* (11km), farther S on the slopes above the coast, are pleasant villages served by buses (from Custom House). A frequent service plies on the asphalted road via (3·5km) *Mánna* to **Poseidonía** (Hotels B, C); and *Fínikas* (Φοίνικας), situated a mile apart on an inlet of the SW coast. They bear the names of the two cities ruled, according to the Odyssey, by Ktesios, father of Eumaeus the swineherd (Od. xv, 406); minor finds have been unearthed in both places. Poseidonía, better known by its popular name *Dellagrázia* (Ντελλαγράτσια), is the favourite summer resort of the islanders, with attractive villas and small tavernas. Beyond Manna a by-road leads S to *Vári* (10km; Hotels C, D), a developing resort on a pretty bay, whence Dellagrazia may be pleasantly reached on foot in 2 hours round the S coast.

The N quarter of the island, rising in Mt Pirgos to 450m, is accessible only on foot or muleback. Here is the so-called *Cave of Pherekydes*, recalling the teacher of Pythagoras (fl. c 544 BC). Farther N near *Khalandrianí* tombs of the Cycladic era, excavated by the Greek Archaeological Service, yielded vases and other finds. At *Kastrí*, a sheer and isolated hill beyond Chalandriani, is an impressive refuge settlement of the late 3rd millenium BC with fortifications and towers (at least 2 hours walk from Ermoupolis; seek directions).

B. Andros and Tínos

FERRIES, at least once a day, leave Rafína (50 minutes from Athens by frequent bus; comp. Rte 21) for *Gávrion* (2½ hours), the main harbour of **Andros**, regularly continuing to *Tínos* (6 hours) and sometimes to Síros (6½ hours).

Tinos is better served by daily boats from Piraeus direct (5 hours) or via Siros (5½ hours).

ANDROS (9020 inhab.), or *Ándhros* (Ανδρος), the northernmost and one of the largest of the Cyclades, is 34km long and 13km wide with an area of 303 sq. km. It is separated from Euboea by the dangerous Doro Passage and from Tinos by a strait only 335m wide. The well-wooded island produces figs, oranges, lemons, oil, silk, and wine. Andros was sacred to Dionysos and there was a tradition that during the festival of the god a fountain in his sanctuary flowed with wine. It has little antiquarian interest and is not much visited by foreigners. Apart from a short 'season' (July–August), when the island is thronged with Athenian holiday-makers, Andros is a good choice for a restful stay. Characteristic of the island are the stone field-walls, which are given rhythm and visual interest by triangular orthostats set at intervals, and the medieval dovecotes, square towers ornamented in patterned tilework. The latter are also found on Tinos, and seem to have marked a Venetian craze for dove-keeping combined with the competitive mania for tower building which swept Italy (comp. Bologna, San Gimignano, etc.).

History. The island is said to have been settled by Andreus, a general of Rhadamanthos of Crete, and later colonised by Ionians. Andros joined the fleet of Xerxes in 480 BC, for which Themistokles attempted to impose a heavy fine on the islanders; on their refusal to pay, he laid siege unsuccessfully to their city (Herod. viii, 111). Later Andros became subject to Athens and then to Macedon. In 200 BC the Romans captured it and handed it over to Attalos I of Pergamon. In the Byzantine era it suffered from piratical raids. From 1207 the Dandoli held it under Venice as a hereditary fief. It was seized by the Turks in 1556 and ceded to Greece after the War of Independence.

The steamers call first at *Gávrion* (Hotels B, C), an unprepossessing village on a sheltered bay (sandy beach to the NW), from which the connecting bus plies to the capital (1¾ hours).

About ¾ hour inland at Ay. Pétros is a fine round *Hellenic Tower*, of five floors, c 20m high. It is built on a base of large stone 4m high and has an inner hall 5·5m in diameter with a corbelled dome pierced by lunettes. A shaft dug into the wall above the entrance gave access by means of ladders to the upper stories, served also by a winding staircase. In the walls are windows with stone shields and loopholes.

8km *Batsí* (Μπάτσιον; Hotels B, C, D), a seaside village farther along the coast, is attractively grouped round its little harbour, the steamers' other port-of-call. The road rises steadily along the S slope of Mt Petalon (994km), the central culmination of the island, with views toward the unimportant island of *Gyáros*. We pass above (16km) *Palaiópolis*, whose scattered habitations drop amid steep cultivated terraces to a wide bay. Near the shore remains (wall, gateway, mole) of the ancient city of *Andros* have been identified, but are scarcely worth the effort entailed in locating them. The road divides, the right branch continuing to *Kórthion* (16km); Hotel C), a small landing-place on a deep bay near the SE corner of the island.

On the promontory of *Zagorá*, c 2·5km beyond the fork, an important Late Geometric settlement was excavated by the University of Sydney in 1967–69 and subsequently. The neck of the sheer promontory is closed by a fortification wall. Within are the remains of blocks of houses and a small freestanding Temple which apparently continued in use after the site was abandoned. Finds from the site are in the museum in Andros (comp. below).

Our road turns inland on the slopes of Pétalon to run high above the beautiful valley of *Mesaria*, which divides the island into two unequal parts. The villages multiply, fig-trees abound, and the countryside is dotted with dovecotes.—24km *Ménites*. A stiff climb of 1 hour in the direction of Phállika (SE) leads to the *Moní Panakhrántou* supposed to have been visited by Nikephoros Phokas.—27km *Mesariá* has a Byzantine church (1158). We descend through *Lámira* to (32km) the 'Khora' or chieftown.

The town of **Andros** (Hotels B, C), seat of a bishop with 1631 inhab., is situated on the E coast and subject to cool winds even in summer. It occupies a low eminence between two exposed beaches and extends picturesquely along the rocky tongue of land that juts out between them. The poor anchorage is on the N side. The main street (no motors), paved in marble and overhung by little balconies, descends past the *Post Office* (within is a large-scale map of the island) to the little *Plateia Kaïrs* overlooking the sandy S beach. Off the Plateia is a small museum devoted to the sculptures of Michael Tombros (1889–1970). Beyond it continues along the spine of the promontory in the *Kato Kastro* past the Metropolis and the little maritime *Museum* in the windswept Plateia Riva. Here a modern bronze to the Unknown Sailor faces the eroded ruins of a Venetian castle, built on a detached outcrop of rock joined by a narrow bridge.

The new *Archaeological Museum* (good guidebook to the Zagora finds available in English) houses material from all over the island, including Palaiopolis, but the most prominent displays are of material from the Late Geometric settlement at Zagora. After an introductory section, these rooms illustrate (successively) Architecture (the fortification wall and domestic); Coarse Pottery; Fine Pottery; Personal and Household Objects; The Temple; The Cemetery. There is also a collection of ancient sculpture in the primary school (Dhimotikó Skholío).

On the slopes, 3km NW, stands *Apoíkia* (Hotels C) with mineral springs, the water of which is celebrated throughout Greece. The road passes the medieval tower of Montelos.

TINOS (Τήνος), lying between Andros and Mykonos and NE of Syros, is 27·5km long and 12km wide. The port and capital lies on the S coast; there is also an anchorage at Panormos on the N coast. Elsewhere the island rises abruptly from the sea, especially in the NE where Mt Tsiknia attains 713m. In the centre it is peppered with white villages, compactly built on the hillsides. Their characteristic churches have an Italianate look with many-storied open-worked belfries, attractive W façades and lateral arcades. Conspicuous also in the green and pleasant landscape are the medieval dovecotes (comp. Andros). Tiny terraces are intensely cultivated with vines, figs, and vegetables. The wine of Tinos, famous in antiquity, is still esteemed, both the retsina and the sweet unresinated vintage. The Tinians are skilful workers in marble.

History. The island was anciently called *Ophiousa*, as it was said to abound in snakes; for the same reason the name *Tenos* may derive from the Phoenician word tenok. A celebrated temple was dedicated to Poseidon who was credited with sending storks to exterminate the snakes. In 480 BC the Tenians were forced to serve in the fleet of Xerxes against Greece, but one of their ships deserted to the Greeks before the battle of Salamis with news of the Persian intentions. For this service the name of Tenos was inscribed on the Tripod of Delphi (Hdt. VIII, 82). Tenos was captured by the Venetians under Andrea Ghisi in 1207. It withstood assaults for over 500 years, not falling to the Turks till 1714. The long Venetian domination made Tenos the most Catholic of the Cyclades. In the War of Greek Independence, while the Orthodox inhabitants took an active part, the Catholics held aloof. Today they have their own bishop and their churches, convents, and schools. The Ursulines have a noteworthy girls' school at Loutra (see below). In 1822 the discovery of a wonder-working ikon of the Virgin made Tenos into a place of pilgrimage. On 15 Austust 1940, before the port of Tenos, during the celebration of the Feast of the Assumption (see below), the Greek cruiser *Helle* was torpedoed by a submarine of unknown nationality, on the eve of the outbreak of the war between Greece and Italy.

Tinos (Hotels B, C, D, E), the capital, is an attractive town of 3879 inhab., with houses of dazzling whiteness, dominated by the great pilgrims' church. The cheerful waterfront abounds with hotels, restaurants, and cafés, which, while modest, are of a standard to encourage a stay. A broad avenue leads in 5 minutes to the church of PANAYIA EVANGHELÍSTRIA (Our Lady of Good Tidings), which, with its conventual buildings, forms a picturesque group. The white marble, of which it is built, includes reused material from the Temple of Apollo at Delos, as well as local and Parian stone. A gateway with an ogee arch, preceded by a floor of pebble mosaic, admits to the great *Court*, shaded by trees and surrounded by porticoes. A monumental staircase mounts to the *Church*, where, surrounded by innumerable gold and silver ex-votos, is displayed the celebrated ikon discovered in 1822. Twice a year, on the feasts of the Annunciation (25 March) and of the Assumption (15 August), thousands of halt and sick pilgrims from all over Greece flock hither in hope of a cure.

On the right of the descent from the church is the **Museum**, built in 1969 in the island's dovecote style. It contains a colossal pithos of the 7C BC with five bands of frieze figures in relief; another (2·5m high) with geometric designs; sculpture of various periods; and a sundial attributed to Andronikos Kyrrhestes. In a room above are modern paintings and sculpture. A group of Late Roman buildings was excavated to the NW of the church precinct in 1973.

At *Kiónia*, ½ hour W along the shore, just before the Tinos Beach hotel, is a *Sanctuary of Poseidon and Amphitrite*, first dug by Belgian archaeologists in 1900. Since 1975 the French School have established the limits of the sanctuary, founded in the 4C and destroyed in the mid-1C, and exposed foundations of a portico 170m long.

Excursions. Buses from the quay to most of the island villages.

1. TO XOMBOURGO AND KOMI. The road runs N to (6·5km) *Tripótamos*, where we turn left, then right (leaving the Isternia road) to skirt the W side of **Xómbourgo**, a hill (565m) crowned by the ruins of a Venetian castle commanding a fine *View of the Cyclades. The ascent (1½ hours) is best started from (13km) *Xynará*, where the catholic archbishop resides. Below the Kastro lie the remains of the ancient city of *Tenos*, which flourished from the 8C to the 4C. Excavations in 1958–59 uncovered parts of the fortification wall (7C BC), a huge public building, and a Geometric temple. At (17km) *Loutrá* in a beautiful situation, is the girls' school run by Ursuline nuns. The road continues to (17km) *Kóm.* and (19km) *Kalloní*, whence a rough descent may be made to the N coast at the shallow bay of *Kolimvíthras*.

2. TO ISTERNIA AND PANORMOS, 35km (21¾ miles), the most attractive excursion but poor road. We take the left fork at Tripotamos (comp. above) and run along the S flank of the hills with views seaward to Syros.—14km *Kardhianí.—* At (25km) *Istérnia* the church has a dome incorporating pottery tiles.—30km *Pánormos*, locally called *Pirgos*, the largest village (352 inhab.) on the island, has celebrated quarries of white, black, and green marble. The old grammar school built by Capodistrias in 1830, houses a School of Fine Arts. Below the village, at

Ayía Thékla was recently discovered the first certain tholos tomb to be found in the Cyclades. Its construction does not match the fine ashlar masonry of some of those on the mainland but it is clearly a tomb of this well-known Mycenaean type. It was used in the 14 and 13C BC.—35km *Ormos Panórmou*, its small harbour, has a fine beach.

3. *Moní Kekhrovouvíou*, with eighty nuns, is reached by bus in 30 minutes on the road to Falatádhos to the NE of Tinos.

C. Mýkonos and Délos

STEAMERS from Piraeus 2–4 times daily in 5½–7½ hours. The return journey is made in the afternoon or overnight. A round trip (allowing a view of Tinos and Mykonos) can be made in a long day.—From Tinos twice daily in c 1 hour. From Syros in c 3 hours.—There are occasional connections to the Rhodes and the Dodecanese by steamer and smaller craft make summer trips to Naxos, Paros, etc.

BY AIR. Many flights a day in 50 minutes; also daily to Crete, Thera, Rhodes; less frequently to Samos, Chios; also international charters.

Míkonos, more familiarly in English **MYKONOS**, is a rocky island of 60 sq. km producing manganese and a little barley, wine, and figs. Four-fifths of the 4850 inhabitants live in or around the capital, which, from being solely the point of departure for Delos, has developed into the most popular tourist centre of the Cyclades, welcoming cruise ships daily.

History. In antiquity the island had two cities, *Mykonos*, on the W coast, and *Panormos*, on the N coast. Strabo notes that baldness was prevalent here so that bald men were sometimes called Mykonians. The Persian commander Datis touched at Mykonos in 490 BC on his way to Greece. After the Persian wars the island became an Athenian colony. In the middle ages it belonged to the dukes of Naxos and later was incorporated in the Venetian province of Tenos. In 1822, under the leadership of the heroine Manto Mavrogeneous, the islanders repulsed an attack by the Turks. Mykonos now forms part of the eparchy of Syros.

The town and port of **Mykonos** (Hotels A, B, C, D, E) is situated on the W coast on the site of the ancient city, a curving bay ending in a low promontory and backed by an amphitheatre of hills. Its small churches and chapels, and its glittering white houses, with their arcades and marble staircases, give it a special charm, and its narrow lanes see-mingly inexhaustable scope for losing one's way (a deliberate defence against pirates). The less attractive ESPLANADE, lined with cafés, is a favourite promenade and the pelican, which has become in the last two decades the mascot of the island, a constant curiosity. In summer artists from all countries frequent the *Skholí Kalón Tekhnón*, a branch of the Athens school of fine art. The locally woven linens are colourful.

Of the many little churches erected from the proceeds of fishing and piracy, the *Paraportianí*, near the quay, is typically picturesque. Near by is the *Local Museum* with a floor of black Tinos marble and pygones from demolished houses. The Metropolis and the Roman Catholic church, bearing the Ghizi escutcheon, are on the way to the promontory where three celebrated windmills catch the wind in their small triangular sails. Below them picturesque houses rise straight from the sea.

At the other end of the bay, beyond the Leto hotel, the *Archaeological Museum* contains important finds from the necropolis of Rheneia, used in 425 BC during the purification of Delos. Notable are a statue of Herakles in Parian marble; cinerary urns, ossuaries in lead, and a quantity of pottery from all parts of the Aegean found on Delos. Of unusual interest is a fine 7C *Pithos (found in Mykonos in 1961; restored) showing relief scenes of the Trojan horse and the massacre at Troy.

To N and S of the town paths lead to several beaches in 20–40 minutes; *Ayios Stéfanos* has a bungalow hotel (Hotels B, C, D), the farther ones, reached by bus, afford better bathing.

Excursions. These are of minor interest but may be combined with visits to more distant beaches. Boats may be hired in the harbour and taxis (fixed charges displayed) from the square.
1. *Garden of Rapháki*, ¾ hour E. This garden, with its fine trees, was bequeathed by the patriot sailor Sourmales, who ran the blockade of Crete in 1862.—2. *Mt Ayios Ilías*, 2 hours N on mule-back. This hill (364m), the highest point of the island, is supposed to be the *Dimastos* of Pliny. The return may be made via the sandy bay of *Pánormos*. At Palaiókastro, near by, the ruined medieval castle of *Darga* occupies the site of the ancient city of Panormos.—3. *Lenós*, 1 hour SE, has the remains of a round Hellenic tower and of a gatehouse.—4. *Tourliani*, or Ano Merá, 4km E, has a convent. On the sea beyond is *Kalafáti Beach* (Hotel B). About 1·5km out to see is the islet of *Dhragonísi*, with remarkable caves haunted by seals, and crumbling cliffs.

FROM MYKONOS TO DELOS, caique c 8.30–9, returning from 12. The crossing (c ½ hour) is often choppy and cold; in rough weather (not infrequent when the N wind blows) it cannot be made. On leaving Mykonos we pass the islets of Ayios Yeoryios and Kavouronisi and head for Cape Kako, the N point of Delos. On a clear day Tinos stands up grey and black to starboard with the Panayia Evanghelistria white above the town and the villages prominent below Xombourgo. Syros is seen for a time ahead (beyond Rheneia) and, far to port, Paros. The cloud effects above the islands are often enchanting. We double Cape Kako and enter the strait separating Delos from Rhenia.

The island of **DELOS** (Δήλος), or Lesser Dhílos (η Μικρή Δήλος), is 5.5km long and 1.2km wide, and has an area of only 5 sq. km. It is separated from Rheneia or Greater Dhílos by a channel 900m wide running from N to S. Two rocky islets, Little Rhevmataria and Great Rhevmataria (ancient Isle of Hecate), rise from the middle of the channel. The W coast is indented by three small havens—the Bay of Skardhana; the Little Harbour, the ancient Sacred Harbour, adjoined by the ancient Commercial Harbour; and the Bay of Phourne. On the other side of the island, on the NE coast, is the anchorage of Gourna, used by caiques in rough weather. The interior of the island is sharply undulating, reaching a height of 113m in the bare conical Mt Kynthos. To the SW is the dry gorge of the Inopos.

Delos, though the smallest of the Cyclades, was once the political and religious centre of the Aegean, with a teeming population. Birthplace of Apollo and Artemis, it boasted an oracle second only to that of Delphi and a famous temple of Apollo, raised by the common contribution of the Greek states. Today it is virtually uninhabited except by members of the French School and their staff, whose houses and offices are clustered near the ruins of the Sanctuary of Apollo. The unremitting exertions of the French School, begun in 1873 and still in progress, have revealed a complex of buildings that bear comparison with those of Delphi and Olympia. The archaeologists have unearthed the great Panhellenic Sanctuary and the area of the Sacred Lake; the maritime and commercial city, with its docks, harbours, and warehouses; and finally a town of the 3C BC, the streets of which invite comparison with those of Pompeii. The **Ruins extend for over 1km; to explore the site thoroughly more than one visit is necessary. There is a

Tourist Pavilion (Hotel B) on the site with a restaurant and bar; it has only four rooms but camping is permitted.

History. *Delos* was anciently called *Ortygia*, or Quail Island. The remains of a prehistoric settlement on the top of Mt Kynthos prove that Delos was inhabited at the end of the 3rd millennium BC. From a very early period it was a religious centre and a busy port. The Ionians who colonised the Cyclades in the 10–9C brought to Delos the cult of Leto, who here was said to have given birth to Artemis and Apollo. By the 7C the sacred island, under the protection of Naxos, became the headquarters of a league of Aegean Ionians, who held a great festival, the *Delia* (see below) in honour of Apollo, celebrated in the Homeric Hymn. The Athenians took advantage of their kinship with the Ionians to enter the league, of which they became the ruling spirit. They sent religious embassies annually to Delos (see below) and purified the sanctuary on more than one occasion. The first purification was by Peisistratos in 543 BC. Polykrates, tyrant of Samos (died 522 BC), having conquered the Cyclades, attached Rheneia to Delos with chains and dedicated the larger island to Apollo.

In 490 BC, the Delians fled from their island to Tenos, but the Persian commander Datis, who had sent his fleet to Rheneia, left Delos inviolate. Delos was the centre of the *Delian* or *First 'Athenian' Confederacy*, the maritime league founded in 478 BC under the leadership of Athens, and its treasury was established in the island until its transference to Athens in 454.

In 426 the Athenians ordered a second purification of Delos. They removed to Rhenia all the coffins of the dead which were in Delos and passed a decree that thenceforward no one should die or give birth in the sacred island, and that all who were near the time of either should be carried across to Rheneia. After the purification the Athenians restored the Delian Festival, which had lapsed in the course of years (see below) and instituted the Delian Games. In 422 the Athenians banished the remaining Delians on the pretext that they were impure and unworthy of the sacred island. Later, however, at the bidding of the Delphic oracle, they let the Delians return. Athenian overseers called *Amphictiones* administered the temple, with the nominal concurrence of the Delians. Plutarch tells us that in 417 Nikias, head of the Athenian embassy, disembarked in Rheneia and crossed to Delos in procession on a temporary wooden bridge that he had brought with him.

After the defeat of Athens at Aegospotami in 404, Delos appealed to Sparta and from 401 to 394 enjoyed a short independence until the Athenians regained possession. In 378 they instituted the *Second Athenian Confederacy*, notably different from the first, as it was purely defensive and not an instrument of imperialism. The Delians were not satisfied, as only two years later they attempted to regain control of the sanctuary, and the Athenians had to reassert their authority.

By 315 BC the command of the Aegean had passed to Egypt. Delos, again independent, became the centre of an island confederacy, and entered on the most prosperous period of its history. Rich offerings flowed into the sanctuary. Honours decreed to foreign benefactors attest to the variety and importance of the island's diplomatic and commercial relations. From the mass of contemporary inscriptions that have survived we may obtain a detailed picture of the temple administration and of the island economy. Delos was a democracy with an archon, a senate and an assembly. The care of the sanctuary was in the hands of four *Hieropes* elected annually, each of whom combined the office of priest and administrator.

By 250 BC the first Romans had settled in Delos, and Roman merchants soon predominated over other foreign immigrants. In 166 the Roman senate allowed the Athenians to reoccupy the island and in order to counterbalance the commercial power of Rhodes made Delos into a free port. The Delians were expelled, never to return and the island became a cleruchy under the control of an Athenian *Epimeletes*. The Romans, however, remained the true masters of the island. In 146 the importers of Corinth moved from their devastated city to Delos. Strabo says that the great religious festival was now in essence a trade fair on a heroic scale, and reminds us that Delos acquired the grim reputation of being the slave-market of Greece, as many as 10,000 slaves changing hands in a single day. The sanctuary continued to attract its devotees, but it was trade that filled the island coffers. An association of Italian merchants, with the backing of Rome, was formed under the title of *Hermaists*, and made itself prominent. Commercial houses and syndicates of merchants from Tyre, Beyrout, Alexandria, and elsewhere formed trade associations. The town was embellished with monuments of every kind.

In 88 BC, during the First Mithridatic War, in which Athens had supported Mithridates and Delos repudiated Athens in favour of Rome, Menophanes, a general of Mithridates, descended on the island. He killed natives and foreigners alike, enslaved the women and children, seized the sanctuary treasure, looted the merchandise, and razed the city to the ground. Regained the following year by Sulla, Delos was returned to the Athenians and partly rebuilt with Roman aid. In 69 the island was sacked by Athenodoros. About 66 BC the Roman legate Triarius built a wall round the city to protect it from further piratical attacks. But its day was done. In the 2C AD we find Pausanias observing that, were the temple guard withdrawn, Delos would be uninhabited. Philostratus (3C) says that the Athenians put the island up for sale but there were no offers. The emperor Julian is said to have consulted the Delian oracle. Ravaged by successive masters of the Cyclades—barbarians, pirates, Knights of St. John of Jerusalem; used as a marble quarry by Venetians and Turks, and even by the inhabitants of Mykonos and Tenos; the sacred island sank into insignificance.

In the 17C Sir Kenelm Digby removed marbles from Delos for the collection of Charles I.

The Delian Festivals. Festivals called *Delia* in honour of Apollo and Artemis and their mother Leto were celebrated in Delos from remote antiquity. The Athenians took part, sending ambassadors called *Deliastae* and later *Theoroi*. The sacred vessel, called *Theoris*, in which they sailed, was said to be the one which Theseus had sent after his adventures in Crete. In the course of time the ancient festival ceased to be held, and it was not till 426 BC that the Athenians revived it (see above). They not only restored the *Delia* but instituted the Delian Games. Festival and games were held every four years. In virtue of their leadership of the Delian Confederacy, the Athenians took the most prominent part in the ceremonies. Though the islanders shared in providing choruses and victims for the sacrifices, the leader *Architheoros*, was an Athenian. On arrival in the island, the embassy from Athens marched in procession to the temple, singing the *Prosodion*, the hymn recounting the story of Leto and the birth of the divine twins, and intoning chants in honour of Apollo. The procession then made a solemn tour of the sanctuary. After that, the victims were sacrificed, and the games began. The games comprised athletic sports, horse-racing, and musical contests. The *Geranos*, or sacred dance, was performed before the altar of Apollo. Proceedings ended with theatrical plays and banquets.— The *Lesser Delia* were simpler but an annual festival. For this the Athenians sent the Theoris every year to Delos. Before embarking, they offered sacrifice in the Delion at Marathon, to ensure a happy voyage. During the absence of the sacred vessel, the city of Athens was purified and it was forbidden to execute criminals.

Plan. The numbered references on our plan correspond with those in the definitive Guide of the French School, though not every building is described in our text.

I. Harbour Area

We disembark at a mole (made of debris removed during the excavations) at a point between the Sacred Harbour (left) and the Commercial Harbour (right). If we have come ashore at Gourna, the rough-weather landing-place on the NE coast, we take a path across the island to the Sacred Harbour, past the Stadium, the Gymnasium, and the Museum. The **Sacred Harbour**, which by the 2C BC was also used as a commercial port, was protected on the N by a breakwater of granite blocks, 150m long built in Archaic times. Most of its remains are underwater and the harbour is sanded up. From the 2C BC the *Commercial Harbour* extended S for c 800m being divided by moles into five basins. Some mooring stones are visible.

At the base of the modern mole is an open space called the **Agora of the Competialists** (Pl. 2), which divides the maritime and residential quarters to the S (see below) from the Sanctuary to the N. The Competialists were the heads of associations of freedmen and slaves who celebrated annually the Roman festivals of the Lares Compitales, gods of the crossroads. In the centre are parts of a circular shrine, and a larger square base, both offerings of the Hermaists to Hermes and his mother Maia. They probably also built c 150 BC the *Ionic Naiskos* (left) before which stands a marble offertory box, adorned with a relief of two snakes.

We turn left into a paved road, 13·8m wide, known as the DROMOS, or *Sacred Way*. It is lined with exedrae and statue bases, notably, at its commencement (right), that of an equestrian statue of Epigenes of Teos, a general of Attalos I of Pergamon (241–197 BC). On the seaward side are the remains of the **Stoa of Philip** (Pl. 3), dedicated to Apollo by Philip V of Macedon, who was master of the Cyclades until his defeat at Kynoskephalai in 197 BC. The dedicatory inscription on the architrave is clearly seen. The stoa in grey marble, 71·3m by 11m, had sixteen Doric columns, fluted on the upper part only, of which one remains standing. The building was doubled on the W some thirty years later by a stoa with 25 columns that faced the sea. To the right of the Sacred Way is the so-called *South Stoa* (Pl. 4), built in the 3C BC.

A passage through this portico led into the **Agora of the Delians** (Pl. 84), which before the three stoas were built had direct access to the shore. It is bounded N and E by an angled 2C portico, over which is an Ionic storey, and S by another portico (3C), set obliquely. A white mosaic survives from the Imperial epoch when Roman baths were installed here.—To the S and E of the Agora are the ruins of houses; one of them has been called the *House of Kerdon*, from a sepulchral stele now in the Museum. Near the SE corner of the Agora, at a crossroads, is the *Shrine of Tritopator*, ancestor of the Attic family of Pyrrhakides. This is a little circular enclosure, with an opening to the NW. Behind it, reached by a few steps, are the ruins of the BASILICA OF ST. QUIRICUS (Pl. 86), a 5C Byzantine apsidal church.

II. The Hieron of Apollo

At the end of the Dromos in a little square (right) are a small sanctuary, and the marble *Exedra of Soteles*. Three marble steps lead up to the *South-West Propylaia* (Pl. 5), erected in the mid-2C BC by the Athenians to form the main entrance to the sanctuary of Apollo. It had three doorways and four Doric columns. A statue of Hermes was erected in front of its predecessor in 341 BC. We enter the **Hieron of Apollo**, a huge precinct enclosing temples, altars, votive offerings, and remains from a thousand years of worship. Within we see on the right the *Oikos of the Naxians* (Pl. 6), a 7–6C building with a central colonnade. It replaced a Geometric structure and may take its orientation from 'Building Γ' (Pl. 7), the most ancient temple (perhaps of Mycenaean date), respected throughout antiquity; the remains of this lie 5·5m E. Against the N wall of the Oikos is the rectangular base of the colossal *Statue of Apollo* (Pl. 9), made of Naxian marble. It bears the celebrated inscription in Archaic letters (7C BC) 'I am of the same marble, statue and pedestal'; a 4C dedication 'The Naxians to Apollo'; and numerous graffiti of Venetian and 17C travellers.

The god was represented as a kouros in characteristic Archaic posture, nude, standing, with hands on thighs; he wore a metal belt. Plutarch relates that Nikias, sent in 417 BC from Athens in charge of the sacred embassy brought with him a bronze palm-tree among the votive offerings (the base of which survives; comp. below). A gust of wind blew over the palm-tree, which carried with it the statue of Apollo. It was then probably re-erected in the present position. Two fragments of the statue that the Venetians tried in vain to remove (part of the trunk and part of the thighs) are now behind the Temple of Artemis (see below); a hand is in the museum; part of a foot is in the British Museum.

On the right of the Sacred Way are three important temples. The first is the **'Great' Temple of Apollo** (pl. 13), begun at the time of the foundation of the Delian Confederacy in 477 BC. Construction languished after the transfer to Athens of the treasury in 454, and was not resumed until the 3C BC. Erected on a high base of granite blocks, and approached by steps of Delian marble, it was a Doric hexastyle peripteral edifice (29·6m by 13·4m) having thirteen columns at the sides. The columns were fluted only at the base and at the neck of the capitals. The metopes were plain and the architrave was decorated with palm leaves and lion-mask spouts placed above each triglyph. The cella had pronaos and opisthodomos.

Adjoining is the *Temple of the Athenians* (Pl. 12), a Doric amphiprostyle building of 425–417 BC with six columns in front. It measures 17·8m by 11·4m, and had a *Prodromos* with four columns in antis. In the *Cella* were the statues, probably chryselephantine, which gave the temple its alternative name of 'House of the Seven'. They were placed on a semicircular pedestal of Eleusinian marble, the base of which has been reconstituted behind the temple. The roof sloped to a ridge presumably to accommodate the Archaic statue of Apollo, by the Naxian sculptors Tektaios and Angelion, previously in the Porinos. Fragments of the corner acroteria are now in the Museum.

The third temple, in poros and dating from the 6C, is the **Porinos Naos** (Pl. 11) of the inscriptions. It is 15·7m long and 10m wide. Here was originally deposited the treasure of the Delian Confederacy.

In front, on the Sacred Way, a long base bears a 3C inscription in honour of Philetairos, first King of Pergamon (280–263 BC). An adjacent base has a Doric frieze with roses and bullheads alternating with metopes.—The buildings arranged in an arc to the N have been given the name of *Treasuries* on the analogy with similar structures at Olympia and Delphi. Beneath this group are remains of a Mycenaean settlement.

To the W of the Sacred Way, in a paved square, is the angled *Stoa of the Naxians* (Pl. 36). In its SW corner are the granite foundations, with a cylindrical hollow in the middle, of the *Bronze Palm-Tree* (see above) dedicated by Nikias. On one of the fragments (replaced) of the lower marble course of the monument can be read the name of Nikias, beginning the dedicatory inscription. Near by have been set up some courses of a column on which was a statue of Antiochus the Great (223–187 BC).—To the NW of the column are two late 6C houses (Pl. 43, 44) called the *Hieropoion* and the *Oikos of Andros*.—To the N of the houses, near a portico, three of whose columns have been replaced, is a *Temple* (Pl. 42) preceded by a colonnade, perhaps the *Keraton* built by the Athenians. Portions of its sculptured frieze have been set up on a neighbouring wall. Close by are the foundations of an apsidal building (Pl. 39) which may have enclosed an altar.

The **Artemision** or *Sanctuary of Artemis*, farther N, is bounded by Ionic porticoes on the E and N. To the left is a semicircular platform hewn in the rock, which seems to have been a cult object from the Late Helladic II period, perhaps the *Sema* or tomb of the two Hyperborean maidens who brought the first offerings to Apollo. The Ionic *Temple of Artemis* (Pl. 46), on a high granite base, was rebuilt c 179 BC on the site of an Archaic predecessor, itself orientated to a Mycenaean forerunner. Behind it are two fragments of the kouros (comp. above) abandoned here by 17C collectors. Many statues of Artemis have been found here (now in the museum), including that dedicated by Nikandre now in Athens.

To the E and S of the Apollo temples was an open space bounded by an Archaic building with a central colonnade, perhaps the *Bouleuterion*, and the *Prytaneion*, where a votive herm has been re-erected. Farther E is the '**Monument of the Bulls**' (Pl. 24), a misnomer derived from its decoration. It is an oblong building, 67m long and 3·8m wide, of Hellenistic date and unusual design, which had a granite peribolos. The foundations, all that remains, are in gneiss and granite. A Pronaos, at the S end, led into a long gallery with a hollow floor placed over a partitioned framework and surrounded by a pavement 46cm above it. It probably housed a trireme dedicated after a naval victory, perhaps by Demetrios Poliorketes, and is therefore to be identified with the *Neorion* named in inscriptions. A cella at the N end has a trapezoidal base or altar.

The Hieron is bounded on the E by a late enceinte wall (Pl. 26), with an entrance gateway (Pl. 27) through which we may quickly reach the Museum (see below). Just outside the gate vestiges of a small *Sanctuary of Dionysos* are characterised by several choregic monuments in the form of a huge phallus with Dionysiac reliefs on the pedestal, one erected by Karystos c 300 BC.

Extending westwards to form the N boundary of the Hieron is the **Stoa of Antigonus** (Pl. 29), dedicated, according to its mutilated inscription, by a king of Macedon, son of Demetrios (supposedly, therefore, by Antigonus Gonatas). The portico, 124m long, has two longitudinal galleries with a salient wing at either end. On the S side were 47 columns; within were 19. The triglyphs of the frieze are decorated with bulls' heads. In the E wing a statue of C. Billienus has been replaced on its base. In front of the stoa are two parallel lines of statue bases, including the *Base of the Progones*, on which stood some 20 statues of the ancestors, real and mythical, of Gonatas. This may have been modelled on the Monument of the Eponymous Heroes in the Agora at Athens.

Near by in a circular abaton (Pl. 32) is a Mycenaean ossuary, comprising small chamber tombs, reached by a dromos, in which were found skeletons and Mycenaean and earlier vases. This may be the *Theke*, where Arge and Opis, two of the Hyperborean maidens, were buried and where some curious sacrificial rites were performed (according to Herodotus) by the women of the island.—In the street outside the Hieron, behind the stoa, is the *Minoe Fountain* of the inscriptions. Farther on, adjoining the S end of the Stoa of Antigonus, is an *Oikos* (Pl. 47) of 402–394 BC. The gap beyond was a passage admitting to the Hieron, beyond which are some remains of the *Ekklesiasterion* (Pl. 47), several times enlarged, and of a 5C edifice comprising two hypostyle halls with a peristyle court between, doubtfully identified as the *Thesmophorion* (Pl. 48).

II. Region of the Sacred Lake

The **Agora of Theophrastos** (Pl. 49; often muddy), raised on an embankment and dating from c 166 BC, is named after the Epimelete Theophrastos, whose statue-base survives. Antoher base commemorates L. Cornelius Sulla. To the N is the little *Sanctuary of Poseidon Nauklarios*, identified by an inscription on its 4C altar. Adjacent is a large hypostyle hall (Pl. 50), which resembles in form the Telesterion at Eleusis and has been given the name '**Stoa of Poseidon**'; it seems, however, to have been built c 208 BC as an exchange or merchants' hall. The original inscription 'The Delians to Apollo' was altered in 166 BC to read 'The Athenians to Apollo'. Doric and Ionic columns, forty-four in number, supported a roof sloping to a ridge with a central lantern. The S side comprised an open Doric colonnade.

Returning E past the phylax's house we see the foundations of the *Dodekatheon* (Pl. 51), a small hexastyle Doric temple of the 4C BC, dedicated to the Twelve Gods. Turning left we have (right) the remains of a small *Temple of Leto* (Pl. 53) of the 6C, and (left) a granite

← N →

Stadium

Xystos

Gymnasium

Archegesion

Museum

Granite Palaestra

67

69

64

68

29

27

65

Sacred Lake

52

H

32

19

18

17

16

House of Comedians

61

57

53

35

51

47

46

Lion Terrace

60

50

48

44

49

DELOS

0 — 100 metres

Mt. Kynthos

Sanctuary

Sanctuaries of Foreign Gods

103

Grotto

100

Heraion

98

House of the Dolphins

95

House of the Masks

90   91 97   93

House of Hermes

113

Theatre Quarter

Theatre

8

Aphrodision

84

115

SACRED WAY

4

3

2

ed our

Maritime Quarter

building with a double court. The ground floor was divided into small rooms, perhaps sculptors' workshops, while above was an assembly room. A ruined Doric *Propylon* leads to the **Agora of the Italians**, a huge open court, 101m by 69m, surrounded by a Doric peristyle of white marble columns on red bases with an Ionic colonnaded gallery above.

The Agora was built by Italian residents of Delos; the peristyle by individuals or trade groups known as Hermaists (see above). Begun c 110 BC, it was repaired after Mithridates' sack, but abandoned before 50 BC. On the inner side is a series of cells or exedrae containing votive monuments, statues, and mosaics. Noteworthy cells on the W side are those of *L. Orbius*, *O. Cluvius*, and *C. Ofellius*, the last with a fine nude statue by the Athenian sculptors Dionysios and Timarchides, now lying overturned by its base; the cell of P. Satricanius, on the N side has a good mosaic. In a cell on the E side was found a statue of a fighting Gaul. Outside, on the E, S, and W sides, are lines of shops opening into the street.

The avenue leading N are bordered on the left by the **Terrace of the Lions**. Here at least nine lions in Naxian marble of the 7C BC guarded the sacred area. Five remain *in situ*; at least one more, removed in the 17C, adorns the Arsenal at Venice. The lean animals are represented 'sejant', that is, sitting on their haunches with their front legs upright, and face the Sacred Lake.

The **Sacred Lake**, dry since 1926, is an oval depression surrounded by a modern wall, which represents its extent in Hellenistic times. This is the lake called 'The Hoop' (Τροχοειδής) of which Herodotus was reminded when describing the Sacred Lake of Sais in Egypt (II, 170). In it were kept the sacred swans and geese of Apollo. The marshy ground that extended to the S before the construction of the Agora of the Italians was probably part of the domain of Leto. This lake, possibly formed by an overflow of the Inopos which, a little to the N, fell into the Bay of Skardhana, was closely associated with the cult of Apollo. A palmtree has been planted in the centre in memory of the sacred palm to which Leto clung when giving birth to Apollo (comp. *Odyssey* IV).

Beyond the Lion Terrace a street ascends to the **Institution of the Poseidoniasts of Berytos** (Pl. 57), an association of Syrian shipowners and merchants from Beirut, who worshipped Baal, a god they identified with Poseidon.

The vestibule leads into a court bounded W by a portico into which opened four chapels. One of these, later than the others, was dedicated to the goddess Roma and contains her statue. On the E side a colonnade leads to peristyle court, with a cistern. To the W of this court is another court, with a mosaic pavement, which was probably used as a meeting-place. To the S were reception rooms and, in the basement below them, a series of shops. Statues found in this building included the 'Slipper-slapper' group of Aphrodite and Pan.

Beyond the Institution a road runs N–S alongside four houses bearing apotropaic symbols. To the N the **House of the Comedians** was excavated, with the adjacent two houses, in 1964. It had an unusual peristyle of two stories, Doric and Ionic, in marble.

To the W, situated on the promontory overlooking the Bay of Skardhana, is *Hill House* (Pl. 60), well-preserved but unremarkable.

Returning along the N flank of the Institution in the direction of the Sacred Lake, we reach the **House of the Diadumenos** (Pl. 61), so called from the discovery here of a replica of the celebrated statue of Polykleitos. The house had an elaborate water-supply system. Turning E and leaving on the left a Hellenistic altar, we next enter the *Lake House* (Pl. 64), which occupies a trapezoidal island with doors on streets to E and W. On the other side of the farther street is the *Granite Palaestra* (Pl. 66), built partly of granite blocks some time after 166 BC. In the middle of this building is a large cistern of four compartments, with a poros roof; it is surrounded by a Doric peristyle. To the N was a granite colonnade.—To the E is a granite retaining wall, between which and the city wall, is the *Well of the Maltese*, the only known well in Delos before the excavations. Adjoining is the *Lake Palaestra*, ruined when the city wall was built.

The **City Wall** (Pl. 69), called also the *Wall of Triarius*, was built by the Roman legate Triarius c 66 BC to protect Delos from the attacks of the pirate Athenodoros. It was partly built over houses and shops which were demolished and filled with rubble to form a foundation. The S part of the wall was demolished in 1925–26. It skirted the E side of the Sacred Lake and of the Agora of the Italians. On a bastion of the wall, a little to the S, was found a small *Prostyle Temple* (Pl. 68), with four columns, open to the E and with an altar in front.

Hence the *Tourist Pavilion* and the *Museum* are conveniently reached.

Enthusiasts who wish to explore farther to the NE will come shortly to the *Archegesion* (Pl. 74), sacred to the worship of Apollo in the guise of the legendary king Anios. The latest part of the structure dates from the 6C BC. Farther on are the square Ionic peristyle of the *Gymnasium*, and the *Stadium*, both built before the *Xystos* (covered track) was added (c 200 BC) between them. Beyond the Stadium is a cluster of ancient houses and near the E shore the remains of a *Synagogue*.

IV. The Museum

The **Museum** contains most of the finds from the island except the finest sculpture which is in Athens. Although closed at present, it is likely to reopen shortly and a description of its previous layout is retained here as a general guide, in spite of the likelihood of rearrangement. In the CENTRAL HALL, kouroi and korai of the 6C; in the centre, Triangular Base, in white marble, one of its corners decorated with a ram's head, the other two with gorgon masks. This base carried a statue of Apollo by the Naxian sculptor Eutychartides (end of 7C BC). Archaic Sphinx from Naxos, replaced on its capital. Archaistic Bas-Relief in marble, depicting a procession of four gods.—To the left, by the wall, two marble Stelai from the Temple of Good Fortune; in each of them was set a bronze relief. The surviving one, replaced, shows Artemis, with a torch in each hand, lighting the fire of an altar; the satyrs on either side indicated a connection with the cult of Dionysos.
FIRST ROOM TO THE LEFT. In the centre, Fragments of paintings, mainly from the Stadium quarter, which decorated the houses and domestic altars. To the right, on a bench, two Heads of Gauls.—Seated statue of Dionysos; two statues of actors dressed as Silenus, one of them with a wine-skin and a tambourine; Roman portrait-statues; statue of pensive Muses and of Artemis with a hind. Sepulchral relief of a seated woman holding a leaf-shaped fan.—To the left, Fragments of corner Acroteria (Victories) and of the ridge of the Temple of the Athenians showing Boreas carrying off Orithyia and Aurora with Kephalos. Colossal Head; numerous Herms.—In front, Sepulchral Steles, including that of Kerdon, representing him falling off a ship. Two kneeling Satyrs wearing shorts made of ivy-leaves, from an altar of Dionysos. Relief of a coiled Serpent with bearded head above a platform covered with drapery; personification of the Agathodaemon. Above, Omphalos surrounded by a coiled serpent.
SECOND ROOM TO THE LEFT. In glass cases, from the left. Objects from the Sanctuary of Apollo. Figurines, terracottas and vases. The vases include examples of Corinthian, Attic, and Cycladic ware; among them, 152. Aryballos, 546. Lekythos. Numerous perfume bottles; Orientalising Geometric vases mainly from the Sanctuary; Hellenistic vases and figurines found in various houses. —In the middle of the room are articles of furniture.
THE ROOMS TO THE RIGHT contain sculpture fragments and inscriptions.

V. The Theatre Quarter and Mt Kynthos

From the Museum we return towards our starting point and turn S into the **Ancient Town**. Here is the quarter where Delos is comparable with Pompeii. In sharp contrast with the spacious sanctuaries and public buildings, the crowded residential area, with twisting narrow streets, huddles behind the shore establishments on rising ground. With the increase of population it spread right up to the sanctuaries.

The **Delian House** of the Hellenistic and Roman period had its rooms grouped round a central courtyard which was reached from the street by a corridor. Richer homes had a peristyle round the court, with marble columns, and the walls plastered and painted. The court had a mosaic floor serving as an impluvium, beneath which a cistern stored rainwater. The RHODIAN PERISTYLE is also found on Delos; a large hall fronted by a taller colonnade occupied one side, and one or two storeys of rooms the others.

The ROAD OF THE THEATRE, paved and drained, ascends between houses and shops giving directly on to the street. Here and there niches show that the street was lit by lamps. To the right is a house with a stove and built-in basins, probably a *Dyer's Workshop*. A small passage and steps lead up past a dolphin mosaic covering a cistern to the *House of Cleopatra*. The marble colonnade has been restored and in the courtyard stand two elegant statues representing Cleopatra and Dioscourides, the Athenian owners (2C BC). On the opposite side of the road is the *House of Dionysos*, where part of the staircase to an upper floor remains. In one room the rough plaster has graffiti (triremes, horseman, etc.), perhaps done by the plasterers before they added the surface layer for the painted marbling. The courtyard contains a mosaic in opus vermiculatum of Dionysos, wreathed in ivy leaves and holding a thyrsos, mounted on a panther wreathed in vines. Farther along, the *House of the Trident*, one of the largest on the island, has a 'Rhodian' peristyle and an elegant well-head. The mosaics are simple but striking, and include an anchor with a dolphin and a trident with a ribbon tied in a bow.

Prof. Lalemand has pointed out the resemblance between this design and the trademarks on amphorae found in a sunken ship off Marseille, and suggests that the house belonged to the Delian wine-merchant who owned the ship. Another mosaic depicts a Panathenaic amphora suggesting that a member of the household had won a victory in a chariot-race.

We come to the **Theatre**, built in the early 3C BC to hold c 5500 spectators. It is surrounded by a fine analemma of local marble but the theatron is ruinous except for the lower tiers. The *Orchestra* has been restored. The *Skene* had engaged Doric columns and was flanked by Paraskenia, each having two higher columns. From the highest point of the theatre, 17m above the orchestra, there is a fine *View over the excavations and the shore.

To the W is a huge *Dexamene* (Pl. 115), or cistern, of nine compartments, which collected water from the theatre and partly supplied the town. Near by is the great foundation which supported the Altar of Dionysos, with, behind it, remains of a little *Temple of Apollo* in antis, dated by an inscription to 110–109 BC. Two adjacent temenoi were dedicated to Artemis-Hekate (W) and Dionysos, Hermes and Pan (E).

Abutting the theatre on the SE is a building known as the '*Hotel*' (Pl 113). It had three stories and a large cistern, from which it is conjectured to have put up visitors to the festival. The **House of the Masks** (Pl. 112) is notable for its *Mosaic pavements with designs inspired by the cult of Dionysos or directly by the drama. It may have been used as a hostel by visiting troupes of actors. The walls were plastered and painted to represent marble. One mosaic has comic and satyric masks

The best known depicts Dionysos seated on a panther. The god holds the thyrsos and a tambourine; the detail shows even the whiskers of the animal.—The *House of the Dolphins*, across the street, is named from another fine mosaic (Erotes on dolphins) signed by the artist.

An ancient path ascends **Mt Kynthos** (112m) which commands a wonderful view of the Cyclades. The height furnished a surname for both Apollo and Artemis, who must have been worshipped here in the 7C BC. The site has yielded remains of Cycladic dwellings of the 3rd millennium, but it was abandoned for long periods and became an important sanctuary only in 281–267 BC when existing buildings were rebuilt and the peribolos constructed. On the flattened summit stood the *Sanctuary of Kynthian Zeus and Athena*; here niches for votive offerings, statue bases, and a dedicatory mosaic were found. The little distyle vestibule of 208 BC was replaced in 94 BC by a marble propylon.

Near by, on the S summit, are the remains of a little *Sanctuary of Zeus Hypsistos* and other gods.—To the E, on a barely accessible terrace (58m) has been excavated a *Sanctuary of Artemis Locheia*, with the foundations of a temple having a doorway in the middle of the long S side.—On the way down to the N (traces of an ancient road) are the ruins of several other sanctuaries.

We descend by the Sacred Way, pausing to look at the **Grotto of Herakles** which is roofed to a peak with inclined slabs of granite in a Cyclopean fashion reminiscent of the Sybil's Cave at Cumae, though probably of Hellenistic date. On a platform outside stands a circular marble altar of the Hellenistic period, while within is the pedestal that bore a statue of the hero. Farther down is a sanctuary attributed by the Athenians to Agatha Tyche (good fortune), in reality the *Philadelpheion* (Pl. 103) dedicated to the cult of Arsinoë, sister and wife of Ptolemy II Philadelphos, who was defied after her death in 270 BC. We reach the terrace of the Heraion.

The **Heraion** is firmly identified by the dedication to Hera of vases and terracotta figurines found beneath the imposing marble *Altar* of the S. The *Temple*, of the early 5C, was also of marble and had a Pronaos of two columns in antis. It replaced a 7C edifice in poros of which foundations are visible below the later pavement.

Below to the left extend the *Sanctuaries of the Foreign Gods*, which occupy a long terrace; the S section is reserved for Egyptian, the N for Syrian divinities. Against the granite retaining wall of the Heraion terrace is the E portico of an enclosure having in the centre an *Avenue* bordered by alternating little sphinxes and massive altars. To the N is **Serapeion C** (Pl. 100), the most important of the three Egyptian sanctuaries at Delos. The main entrance was on the S side. Serapis had powers of healing and of foretelling the future.

The paved court was bounded on the S and partly on the W by an angular Ionic portico. To the N is the little *Temple of Serapis* (first half of 2C BC), revealing careful construction. We note a course of bluish marble and, behind, a poros wall coated with stucco. To the E, on a higher level, is the marble façade of the *Temple of Isis*. At the end of the cella is a statue of the goddess, on a rocky bench serving as a base. In front of the temple, lower down, is a *Perfume Altar*, the upper part of which is decorated in front with four slabs of marble in the form of horns.

From the Sanctuary Court we approach the great **Sanctuary of the Syrian Gods** (Pl. 98), whose cult started c 128 BC. Here were worshipped Adad and Atargatis, introduced from Bambyke-Hierapolis, and after ten years regularised under an Athenian high priest. Atargatis was then identified with Holy Aphrodite and the worst orgiastic rites of the fertility cult abandoned. The *Theatre* (400–500 spectators) in which its rites were performed was protected from view by walls which surrounded the precinct. This was entered by a portal with Ionic columns. Sacred fish were kept in a tank in the sanctuary.

From the S end of the terrace a long flight of steps descends to the bed of the **Inopos**, a torrent only a few hundred metres long which even in ancient times must have had a long dry season. It flowed from a source on Mt Kynthos past the Sacred Lake into the Bay of Skardhana, and is mentioned in the Homeric Hymn. The Delians imagined that its waters came from the Nile, an association perhaps endorsed by the resemblance of the local lizards to baby crocodiles. A *Reservoir* (Pl. 97) in white marble, provided with a staircase, sluice-gates, and outlet channnels, collected the waters. Today terrapins inhabit it.

On the farther bank, S of the reservoir, are the ruins of the **Samothrakeion** (Pl. 93), dedicated to the Kabeiroi, built on two terraces. The upper level bore a *Temple* of the 4C BC with a Doric portico, and the lower level a circular shrine (2C BC) for the reception of offerings to the Chthonic divinities, together with a monument to Mithridates (120–63 BC) having two Ionic columns and a frieze of medallions depicting his generals and allies.

Turning N we enter a street running between the Reservoir (left) and a row of shops. Between two of the shops is an alley, with a bench (left) carved with dedicatory inscriptions to Serapis, Isis, and Anubis. At the end of the alley is a staircase leading to the ruins of **Serapeion B**. The court of this sanctuary is bounded on the E by a covered portico, under which is a rectangular crypt. The little *Temple*, placed in the NW corner of the court, faces S.

The street bears left in front of the *House of the Inopos* (Pl. 95). Beyond the reservoir, on our left, are the *Shrine of the Nymphs of Pyrrhakides*, a little circular building, and **Serapeion A** (Pl. 91), the oldest sanctuary of Serapis on the island. Its temple stands on a stepped basement in a paved court; under its cella is a rectangular crypt, reached by a staircase and supplied with water by a conduit. Descending the ancient road we pass the **House of Hermes** with three storeys built against the hill. The colonnades of the ground and first floors have been restored. Here were found a number of Herms. Farther on is a small *Temple of Aphrodite*, built of irregular marble blocks in the 4C BC. We pass behind it and descend to the Agora of the Competialists (Pl. 2).

VI. The Maritime Quarter

Along the seashore, S of the landing-place, a series of *Magazines* or *Warehouses* have their backs to the Theatre Quarter. They opened on to a quay bordering one of the four basins of the Commercial Harbour.—Continuing S, we cross the line of the City Wall (comp. above), which here ran down to the sea, and reach a second group of Magazines.

There was no communication between these warehouses and the Theatre Quarter behind them, an indication that the trade of Delos was essentially a transit trade between E and W. Island blocks, divided by streets running parallel to the sea or at right angles to it, each had a central court surrounded by large structures used as bonded warehouses. A typical example is the *Magazine of the Columns*. The building adjoining it has a fine marble basin in a vestibule.

About 800m farther S is the **Bay of Phourne**, sheltered from the N winds by a rocky promontory on which are the ruins of a *Sanctuary of Asklepios*, with three buildings in line. The northernmost is a prostyle Doric temple with four columns, measuring c 15m by c 6m. Beyond it is a large hall of granite with a door on its E side; and finally the Propylaia to the sanctuary, paved in white marble.

Rhéneia, or **Greater Delos**, now uninhabited, on the W side of the Channel of Delos, is 10km long and has a maximum width of c 4km. It is almost divided into two by a narrow isthmus about its middle. It has a ruined *Lazaret* for ships in quarantine bound for Syros, with an anchorage facing Delos (25 minutes by caique). That part of the shore which faces the Rhevmataria islets (10 minutes from the Sacred Harbour) was reserved as a birthplace for pregnant, and as a necropolis for dying Delians expelled from their island by the Athenians. Rhéneia was the landfall of Nikias in 417 BC, when he crossed in state to Delos on the bridge that he had brought with him. The island town was on the W coast, facing Syros.

In the area for expectant and dying Delians are a series of tombs, circular sepulchral altars and sarcophagi with holes for the insertion of steles, and numerous ruined little houses, probably for the reception of the evicted people.

In the village of *Herakleion* a sanctuary was discovered, with a well and a portico.—Opposite Great Rhevmataria, on the seashore below the chapel of *Ayía Kiriakí*, is the **Necropolis**, discovered in 1898, in which the Athenians during the purification of 426 BC, places the coffins exhumed from Delos. This is a walled enclosure c 65m square, divided into small rectangular sections. It contained a mass of human bones and vase fragments of every period down to the 5C.—A little to the S, in the small bay of *Porto Generale*, is a curious Greek columbarium. This is a rectangular vault, reached by a staircase, and containing on either side two tiers of niches for coffins, closed by stone slabs.

72 Western Cyclades

Despite its proximity to Attica, this is the least visited group of the Aegean islands.

A. Kéa

STEAMER daily from *Lávrion* (comp. Rte 17) in 2 hours; some services also by FERRY from *Rafína* (Rte 22), sometimes continuing to *Kíthnos*.

KÉA, the ancient **Keos**, locally known as *Tziá* (1198 inhab.), is the nearest of the Cyclades to Attica, being only 21km from Cape Sounion and 64·5km from Piraeus. Oval in shape, 19km long from N to S and 10km wide, the island which has a hilly interior rises to 568m. It is well watered (hence its early name of *Hydroussa*) and has always been one of the most fertile of the Cyclades (comp. Virgil, 'Georgics', I, 14). The eparchy of Kea includes the islands of Kithnos, Serifos, and Makronisos.

History. At an early date *Keos* was populated by Ionians. Kean ships fought on the Greek side at Artemision and Salamis (Hdt. VIII, 1, 46). The island had four cities; Ioulis, with its port Koressia, Karthaia, and Poiëessa. Ioulis was the birthplace of the lyric poets Simonides (556–468) and Bacchylides (481–431), of the sophist Prodikos, of the physician Erasistratos, and of the peripatetic philosopher Ariston. The Keans, unlike the Chians, were noted for their modesty and sobriety: hence the adage οὐ Χῖος ἀλλὰ Κεῖος (Aristophanes, Ran. 970).

Landing is made at **Livádhi** (Hotels B, C), officially *Korissía*, pleasantly situated amid trees on the bay of Ayios Nikolaos in the NW of the island. Ancient *Koressia* occupied a site a little to the W, with a temple of Apollo Sminthios, from which the kouros in the National Museum was recovered in 1930. About 1·5km E round the bay is *Vourkári*, a fishing hamlet which attracts summer visitors.

Opposite, on the pretty promontory of *Ayía Iríni*, are the remains of an important prehistoric settlement excavated in the 1960s and 1970s by a team from the University of Cincinatti under the late J.L. Caskey. Several volumes of the final publication have now appeared and an excellent short guidebook is available. Most of the building remains that can be seen belong to *houses* of the early Late Bronze Age (the largest complex, to the S of the site, is called 'House A'). Nearby can be seen the *gateway* into the settlement and, close to that, a long, narrow free-standing building which was a *Temple* and yielded fine large terracotta figures in a Minoan style. In the N part of the site, some finely built houses of regularly laid thin slabs belong to the Early Bronze Age. Two sets of *fortifications* can be seen. The inner (only a short section visible) is Middle Bronze Age in date and has horseshoe-shaped towers. The outer belongs to the end of the same period and is more substantial. A *spring chamber* beyond the defences was reached by a covered passage. The site is one of the most important in the Cyclades, especially for demonstrating interconnections between these islands, on the one hand, and Crete and the Greek Mainland, on the other. The site came under strong Minoan influence from c 1600 BC. It was wrecked by an earthquake c 1450 BC by which time Mainland features are equally prominent. Subsequently the town was rebuilt but less intensively occupied. Although it was abandoned as a settlement during the 11C, the Temple seems to have remained in continuous use until later antiquity. Amongst later finds are a 5C dedication inscribed to Dionysos.

An earth road continues NE to the delightful bay of (5km) *Otziás*, then turns E to (10km) the monastery of *Panayía Kastrianí* (18C; rooms).

A road (bus) climbs to the depopulated town of **Khóra** (Hotels B, E), the island capital with 568 inhab., on a hill (349m) once occupied by the ancient city of *Ioulis*. The *Kastro* of Domenico Michelli (1210), demolished in 1865, incorporated material from a Temple of Apollo situated on its acropolis. A small *Museum* displays antiquities from the island and particularly finds from Ayia Irini. About 15 minutes E of the town is a colossal *Lion* carved out of the rock, 6m long and 2·7m high—rude but vigorous piece of sculpture.

The extensive ruins of ancient *Poiëessa* (Ποιήεσσα) on the W coast may be reached in c 2 hours from Khora, via *Astra* and *Káto Meriá*. The bays of *Písses* and *Koúndhouros* (Hotel B), to the S, afford good bathing and the interior of the island is generally attractive. The return may be made via the ruined monastery of *Ayía Marína*, built around a Hellenic ·Tower, probably the finest of its kind in Greece. It is c 7·5m square, and built of rectangular blocks of schist, admirably joined without mortar. There are three storeys supported by stone joists.

On the opposite coast, c 1½ hours SE of Káto Meriá is *Póles*, where the ruins of ancient *Karthaia* include a Doric Temple of Apollo and two other buildings, one of them conjectured to have been the choregic school of Simonides. Considerable remains of the enceinte wall can be traced.

B. From Piraeus to Mílos

STEAMER, daily, calling at *Kíthnos, Sérifos, Sífnos*, and *Kímolos*. Serifos and Sifnos are served by every boat, Kithnos and Kimolos less frequently. There are usually weekly connections to Syros and to Santorini (comp. Rte 73).

AIR SERVICE, twice daily to Milos.

KÍTHNOS (Κύθνος), separated from Keos by a strait 8km wide, owes its alternative name *Thermia* to its hot springs. A low-lying island with an area of 75 sq. km, it has a steadily declining population. Since 1940, when the iron mines went bankrupt, the Thermiots (684 inhab.), all but a handful of whom are divided between two villages, have made a precarious living by farming, fishing, and latterly fruit-growing.

Kythnos supplied two ships to the Greek fleet at Salamis. It was a member of the Delian Confederacy and became tributary to Athens. After the death of Nero in AD 68, an imposter claiming to be the emperor was driven ashore at Kythnos in a storm; he was seized and put to death by Calpurnius Asprenas, the proconsul of Galba. Pliny notes that the island produced excellent cheese; it still does, other products being barley, wine, figs, and almonds. Copper was apparently mined and worked on the island in the Early Bronze Age.

According to the weather the boat puts in at Loutrá on the NE coast or at Mérikhas on the W. The tiny harbour of **Loutrá** (Hotel C) has warm iron-bearing springs which cover the ground with a reddish despsit. The Turks used them for bathing and King Otho built a *Hydro* for invalid visitors. One spring (37° C) is used for drinking; another is hot (52°). The waters are used in the cure of eczema, gout, sciatica, and nervous complaints.—On Cape Kephalos (154m), the NE point of the island (45-minute walk), stands the *Kástro tou Kataképhalou*, the medieval citadel, abandoned c 1650; the ruins include towers, monasteries, and the Byzantine church of Our Lady of Compassion with wall-paintings.—The site of ancient Kythnos has been located at *Rigókastro* in the NW of the island.

A road leads from Loutrá to (4km) **Kíthnos**, known also as *Messariá* or just *Khóra*, the little capital (631 inhab.), where several churches have ikons by Skordili (c 1700). *Ayía Sába* (1613) bears the arms of Ant. Gozzadini, a descendant of the Italian medieval governors. The road continues S to (8·5km) *Síllaka*, officially Dhriopís (Δριόπις), the other village (701 inhab.) and former capital. Near by is Katafíki, the best known of the island's many caves.—A longer return (14km) may be made to Khora via the hamlets of *Mérikhas* (Hotel C) and *Episkopí*, each on a sheltered inlet of the W coast.

On a headland of the SE coast (1 hour by mule from Dhriopis) stands the *Panayía tis Kanálas*, a monastery with a holy ikon of St. Luke.

SÉRIFOS

SÉRIFOS (Σέριφος), a small rocky island (65 sq. km), with 1133 inhab., lies almost equidistant between Kithnos and Sifnos and c 13km from either. Lighters land passengers at *Livádhi* (Hotels B, C, E), the hot little land-locked harbour from which the road rises through market gardens to (1·5km) **Khóra** (409 inhab.), a white village built precipitously on a commanding spur. Accommodation must be found in private houses. *Psilí Ammos*, 20 minutes walk to the NE, is the best sandy beach.—A road runs W across the island to (6·5km) *Megálo Khorió*, said to be the site of ancient *Seriphos*; in 1880–1912 it was the centre of a mining district, with outlets to the sea at *Megálo Livádhi* and Koutalá on the SW coast. A little iron ore is still shipped.

On ancient Seriphos Perseus and Danaë were washed ashore, and here later Perseus turned King Polydeuces to stone with Medusa's head. The Roman emperors used the island as a place of exile for political prisoners.

A path from Khora leads NE in 1 hour to *Kallítsos*, a pretty village, and (15 minutes more) to *Moní Taxiárkhon*, an interesting building of late medieval date. The return can be made in 1 hour via *Galaní*, farther W.—*Panayía*, to the NW of Khora, is called after its 10C church.

SÍFNOS

SÍFNOS (Σίφνος), situated 19km SE of Sérifos, is a fertile island with a delightful climate and an abundance of excellent water. The interior is mountainous, with Mt Profitís Ilías rising to 680m. Much of the countryside is terraced for the production of olives, grapes, citrus and other fruits, almonds and vegetables, and for the grazing of animals. The island is dotted with monasteries and churches, local tradition claiming 365 in all—one for each day of the year.

In pre-Classical times Siphnos was famous for its gold and silver mines, which Herodotus says made the Siphnians the wealthiest of the islanders by the late 6C BC. When the mineral deposits were exhausted in the Classical period the deceitfulness, greed and poverty of the people became a byword, and Pausanias relates a characteristic tale to the effect that the mines were flooded by Apollo after the Siphnians had attempted to renege on their customary annual tithe to Delphi. Numerous ancient mines are to be seen on the island, most notably at the peninsular of Ay. Sóstis on the NE coast. Also of interest are the remains of nearly 50 circular towers located at strategic points throughout the island, and dating from the Classical and Hellenistic periods.

The ship berths between high cliffs in the bay of *Komáres* (new hotels in construction) on the more rugged W coast. Atop the slopes on the N side are two monasteries, the larger being that of Ay. Simeón. A bus ascends under the cliffs of Profitís Ilías on the S to (5·5km) *Apollónia* (Hotels B, C,), the island capital (920 inhab.). Its flat-roofed white houses rise in an amphitheatre on three terraced hills. At *Stavrí*, the town's principal quarter and main square, are a library and folklore museum built in 1967. In the N quarter of Péra Yitoniá are the house of the poet Kleánthis Triandháfillos (or Rabagás) (1849–89) and the church of *Panayiá Yeraniofóra*, where the external figure of St. George was restored in 1767. The foundations on which this church was constructed may well be those of a 7C BC temple to Apollo. The frescoed church of *Sotíra* has a carved wooden ikonostasis.

About 1·5km to the N is *Artemóna* (820 inhab.; Hotel B), the second village of Sifnos. It is believed Artemona's main church, *Panayía Kókhi* was built on the site of an ancient temple to Artemis. From this village there are central paths (surfaced road under construction) to the N of the island and the small settlement on the bay of *Khersónisos*.

SE from Apollonia, through the village of *Exámbela*, roads run to the bays of *Fáros* (6·5km) and *Platí Yialós* (9·5km; Hotel B), both excellent bathing places with sandy beaches. Below Apollonia to the E lies the hamlet of *Káto Petáli* (1·5km) on the road leading to *Kástro* (a further 1·5km), a delightful but decaying medieval village on the E coast, occupying the site of **Ancient Siphnos**. Part of the 14C wall built by the Venetian Corogna family survives, and there are many old churches, also a *Museum* (comp. below). On the way to Kástro, to the S, is the nunnery of *Khrisostómou*—built in 1550, it was adorned by the Bavarians and used as a school from 1834–44. On the SW coast is the charming bay of *Vathí*, best reached by boat, but also accessible by foot along pathways from Plati Yialos (60 minutes) and Exambela (90 minutes).

Three ancient acropolis sites have been identified on the island. To the S of Apollona paths lead past Mt Ay. Andréas (427m), on the summit of which is a walled settlement inhabited from the third millenium BC, excavated on behalf of the Greek Archaeological Service in the 1970s. The visible sections of the fortifications are of the Mycenaean and Geometric periods. At *Kástro* (Ancient *Siphnos*) on the E coast sections of white marble walling of the 6C BC were discovered in the 1930s by the British School, along with foundations of houses of the Geometric period and the site of a temple of the 7C BC, the votive deposit of which has been unearthed. Most of the archaeological artefacts from the island have been collected in a small but interesting museum in Kástro. A third acropolis is situated at the church of *Ay. Nikitas*, some 5km N of Artemóna. The site has not been excavated, but the walls probably date to the Archaic period.

KÍMOLOS (Κίμωλος), an island barely 8km across with 787 inhab., lies between Sifnos and Milos, from which it is separated by a strait only 1km wide. Pliny says that it was once called *Echinousa*, from echinus, a sea-urchin; it owed its Italian name, *Argentiera*, to the silver mines formerly worked here. The island has long been noted for its Fullers' earth, used in the preparation of cloth and in barbers' shops in Athens (Aristophanes, *Ran.*, 713). Kimolos was incorporated by Marco Sanudi into the duchy of Naxos; it later became a notorious pirates' nest. Its olive trees were felled by the Venetians during the Turkish wars and it is now barren, but given colour by the variety of its rocks.

Kímolos, the only village, crowns a hill 1km from *Psáthi*, its harbour, which is on the SE coast (landing by lighter). The little houses open on to an inner court. The church of the *Evanghelistria* dates from 1614. *Prássa*, 15 minutes N by boat, has radioactive springs. On the W coast *Palaiókastro*, on a steep rock 396m high, has remains of strong fortifications.—Excavations in 1937 on the islet of *Ayios Andréas*, off the SW shore, revealed remains of an ancient settlement which, with its *Necropolis* (on the mainland opposite) lasted from Mycenaean to Early Christian times.

The barely inhabited islet of *Políaigos* lies off the SE extremity of Kímolos.

MÍLOS (Μῆλος), or *Melos*, the SW outpost of the Cyclades, with 8287 inhab., is divided almost into two by an arm of the sea forming a spacious natural harbour, the entrance to which is on the N. The coast is much indented. The island has an area of 153 sq. km and is roughly 21km long by 13km wide. Mt Profitis Ilias (751m) rises to the SW of the gulf, but the rest of the island is arid low hills, much gashed by mines and quarries. The volcanic nature of the soil is expressed in the hot springs, the mines of sulphur and alum, and the obsidian that gave the island its importance in prehistoric times. Bensonite, barium, perlite and kaolin are also mined. Drilling to examine the possibilities of exploiting geothermal energy has taken place recently. Melos was the first island to yield detailed information about the sequence of occupation in the Cyclades in the Bronze Age, through the key site of Phylakope. From the island came also the famous Venus di Milo, now in the Louvre in Paris. The eparchy of Milos includes the islands of Sifnos, Kimolos, Sikinos and Folegandros. Tourist facilities are concentrated in Adhamas, though rooms are also available in Plaka and Pollonia. There is a small airstrip with two or three connections a day to Athens.

History. *Melos* was a centre of the Bronze Age civilisation that flourished in the Cyclades contemporaneously with, and at first independently of, the Minoan civilisation of Crete. Before the end of the Middle Cycladic Period (c 1600 BC) Melos, with the rest of the Cyclades, seems to have been absorbed in the Cretan empire associated with King Minos. When the sceptre passed from Knossos to Mycenae, the Cretan colonial possessions passed also. After the Dorian invasion (c 1100 BC) Melos was colonised by Dorian Lacedaemonians. In the Peloponnesian War it declared itself neutral, but, provoked by Athens, it inclined towards Sparta. Athens, having command of the sea, determined to coerce the Melians into submission (416 BC). Before taking action, the Athenians sent envoys to Melos. Thucydides has preserved in his 'Melian dialogue' (V, 85–111) the gist of the speeches made on either side. The Melians declined the Athenian terms and the Athenians besieged their city. After several months the Melians surrendered unconditionally. The Athenians killed all the males of military age, enslaved the women and children, and repopulated the island with 500 Athenian colonists. In the middle ages the island was under the Franks. During the Turkish domination (here very lightly felt) and afterwards, the Melians acquired and kept a reputation for intrepid seamanship which they still enjoy. Here in 1628 Sir Kenelm Digby began his memoirs. From Melos in the 1680s a party under Abp Georgirenes migrated to London where they built the first Greek church there on a site assigned to them by James, duke of York. The memory of this survives in 'Greek Street', Soho. During the First World War the island was an Allied naval base.

The port of Mílos is *Adhamas* (commonly *Adhámata*; Hotels B, C, Rooms), founded on the E side of the harbour by Cretan refugees fleeing Turkish reprisals in 1912. Their ikons can be seen in the small and attractive church of *Ayía Triádha*. Both this and the church of Christ and the Virgin (with prominent clock tower) at the highest point of the town have pebble mosaics; the latter also has a fine painted iconstasis. On the shore to the W of the town stands a small monument to French soldiers and sailors who died on Milos in 1897.

A winding road ascends NW, through the lower villages of *Triovásalos* and *Karódhromos* (leaving *Tripití* to the W and *Plákes* to the E), to (3·5km) **Pláka**, officially *Milos* (735 inhab.), the island capital, constructed in a defensive position about 1800 as a protection against piratical raids.

The village can also be reached by a path from the N side of Adhamata which skirts the obsidian quarry of Sta Nýchia above the village and later joins the old roadway, stone-paved in part, to ascend to *Tripiti* (pleasant cafeneion with small terrace overlooking valley), just below Plaka. Between Tripiti and Plaka, a long ridge (*Piryiántes*) was the acropolis of the ancient site, which occupies the slopes below Tripiti down to the ancient harbour (now the pretty fishing hamlet of *Klíma*). A road down from Tripiti gives access to the most important parts of the site. To the SW are extensive and impressive Early Christian *catacombs*. The long narrow entrance leads into a low-pitched room, beyond which run tunnels, lined with tombs, some with the remains of frescoes. N of the catacombs are good sections of the *city wall* (other parts traceable over a wide area)—part with fine polygonal masonry adjoining a round bastion of regularly coursed stonework. The Venus di Milo was discovering close by in what seems to have been the *gymnasium*, whose running track was laid out on the flat ground immediately below. Farther on is the *theatre*, probably Roman, excavated in 1917 and somewhat restored. Its situation is impressive and the view may have distracted attention from the performances. Nearby is an Early Christian baptistery. To the NW (paths) is a prominent low conical hill crowned by a small church of Profitis Ilias. On the flat ground to the E of this may have been the ancient *agora*. The remains of a substantial building, perhaps a Roman temple, can be seen.

We may ascend to Plaka by paths from Profitis Ilias (more sections of the city wall visible). The village is attractive with its typically Cycladic houses and narrow alleyways. The church, dedicated to the Virgin and built in 1810 of materials brought from the abandoned Zefiria (comp. below), is finely situated to the N, with a terrace at the top of a sheer cliff (view to Andímilos; pleasant at sunset). There is a small *Folk Museum* close by which includes some interesting relics of the pilots (telescopes, etc.) for which the island was at one time famous. To the E is the small catholic church of the *Rosaria*, with a memorial to Louis Brest, the French consul on Melos who removed the Venus to France. Above the village rises the *Kástro* (980m) whose Frankish remains enclose the beautiful 13C church of *Thalassítra*. The antiquities were much destroyed by German gun emplacements in the Second World War. From the summit there are excellent and extensive views, much to be recommended both for themselves and for appreciating the complex geography of the island.

On the lower edge of Plaka a small Neo-classical building (formerly a school) has been restored (1984) and contains the *Archaeological Museum*. The vestibule and room to the right have sculpture and inscriptions from Classical and Roman Melos; the room across the vestibule Archaic, Classical and Roman material (pottery, etc.) mainly from tombs; the room to the left important finds (mainly pottery) from the 1911 excavation season at Phylakope (finds from the main campaign are in the National Archaeological Museum in Athens).

A road leads E to the N coast (occasional buses to Pollónia, starting from Adhamas) and (7km) the ruinous site of **Phylakope**, excavated by the British School in 1896–99 and 1911. The remains of three successive Bronze Age cities were discovered. The *First City* dates from the Early Cycladic period; the *Second* is Middle Cycladic; the *Third* had two main phases, in the first of which strong Minoan influence is evident in the pottery and frescoes (including that of Flying Fish, in Athens), while in the second Mycenaean is dominant. This latter is reflected in the construction of a Mainland-style *palace* with megaron which can be recognised on the N side of the site, by the sea, by its massive threshold block, now broken. It was preceded by another large building, in which fragments of a Linear A tablet were found, possibly the administrative centre in the 'Minoan' stage. During renewed work in 1974–77, a *Mycenaean shrine* (LH IIIA–C) yielded many finds including a tiny gold mask and a terracotta cult figure probably of Mainland manufacture. The shrine can be seen close to the city wall, to the right of the path leading from the main road into the site. There were two elements, East and West, with a paved court between containing a stone bench and ceremonial standing stone. The *city wall* is also well preserved to the W end of the town. —Interesting also are the natural hexagonal basalt pillars, originating from the Glaronisia (see below).—The road continues to (10km) *Pollónia* (Rooms; restaurant), an attractive fishing village facing the island of *Kímolos* (daily caique).

To the NW (boat from Pollonia) are the curious volcanic islets known as the *Glaronísia* (Gull Is.). They have remarkable caves and crystalline rocks.

From Adhamas, a road runs SE along the shore. After 3km there is a by-road (left) past the electricity works to (1km) *Zefiría*, the capital of the island from the 8C to 1793, when the survivors of an epidemic moved to the Plaka area. The village is still known locally as *Khóra* (the term for an island capital) and all the major church festivals are celebrated there. The double church (to Christ and the Virgin) is delightful. Many architectural fragments from the once prosperous village, which had numerous churches and monasteries, can be seen in the fields around.

From Zefiría a rough road (ask for directions) leads W (4km farther) to the beautiful shingle beach of *Palaiochóra* backed by multicoloured rocks.

Immediately beyond the Zefiría fork, by the coast road, small rings of bubbles can be seen a few metres out to sea. These mark the eruptions of hot springs. The road passes salt pans, the airstrip, and continues through *Próvata* to the pleasant monastery of *Ayía Marína* (formerly rich). Before Ayía Marína a road leads W to the deserted but intact monastery of *Ayíos Ioánnis Sidherianós*. Beyond here the roads serve mines and quarries in the S and W of the island (*Khálakas*) where there is virtually no permanent settlement.

To the NW of Milos is the uninhabited islet of *Andímilos*, a reserve for a rare species of chamois.

73 Southern Cyclades and Southern Sporades

STEAMER, direct or via Syros, 2–3 times daily to *Páros* and *Náxos*, continuing at least once daily to *Ios* and *Santorini* (*Thíra*) and returning in reverse order. Twice weekly the boat calls at *Síkinos* and *Folégandros*, and once weekly at *Anáfi*. Santorini can also be reached once a week from Milos by a boat that continues to Rhodes and Crete, and once weekly from Paros on the way to Herakleion. Amorgós, the most easterly of the S Sporades included in the nome of the Cyclades is served by steamers to the Dodecanese and is described with them; comp. Rte 75.

A regular local service connects Naxos with Amorgos, via Irakliá, Schoinoússa, Ano Koufoníssi and (sometimes) Donoússa. Other routes (including to Mikonos) are worked in the summer by small steamers.

BY AIR. To *Paros* several times daily in 45 minutes; connections to Crete and Rhodes. To *Thira* three times daily in 40 minutes; connections to Crete and Rhodes; also international charters.

PÁROS (ΠΑΡΟΣ), one of the most attractive of the Cyclades, with 8516 inhab., has an area of 166 sq. km and is oval in shape. The interior is almost entirely taken up by *Mt Profítis Ilías* (771m), on the slopes of which are the famous marble quarries. The mountain slopes evenly down to the maritime plain which surrounds it on every side. Barley and wheat are grown and the red wine is full and palatable, but there are few trees. Sheep, oxen, goats, and asses are numerous. Paros was the birthplace of the lyric poet Archilochos (fl. 714–676 BC), inventor of Iambic verse. The island had a bishop before 431; the present joint see with Naxos dates from 1683.

History. Paros was colonised by Ionians. In the 7C it sent a colony to Thasos, the poet Archilochos accompanying the expedition (comp. Rte 67). In 490 BC Paros sent a trireme with the Persian fleet. After Marathon Miltiades led a retaliatory expedition against the island but failed to take it, receiving an injury that, becoming gangrenous, proved fatal (Hdt. vi, 133). After the defeat of Xerxes, in 480, Paros became subject to Athens.

In the Middle Ages Paros formed part of the duchy of Naxos until 1389. In 1537 it passed to the Turks, who held it until the War of Greek Independence. In the early 17C the 'Parian Chronicle' was discovered in the island by Wm Petty, chaplain to the Earl of Arundel. This is a chronological account of the principal events in Greek history (biased on the side of art rather than politics), from Kekrops (traditional date 1582 BC) to the archonship of Diognetos (264 BC). The greater part of this inscription is in the Ashmolean Museum at Oxford. Hugues Creveliers, the original of Byron's 'Corsair' operated from Paros in the 1670s (he was eventually blown up in his flagship by an offended servant). The Russian fleet spent the winter of 1770–71 at Paros.—Excavations on the island have been the care of the German School.

Backed by distant hills beyond the coastal plain **Paroikía** (Hotels B, C, D, E), or *Paros*, the capital (2716 inhab.), lies on the W coast. The town extends along the shore in a restful horizontal fashion, the line of its white flat-roofed houses broken only by the blue domes of churches. The ship moors alongside a small mole.

The **Panayía 'Ekatontapilianí'**, traditionally the cathedral church of Our Lady 'with a hundred doors', a corruption probably of *Katapolianí* ('below the town'), was greatly altered externally, some may think not for the better, by its restoration in 1960–63 under Prof. Orlandos from Venetian Baroque to a primitive Byzantine style. The church had needed attention since the earthquake of 1733. Said to have been founded by St. Helena, mother of Constantine, while she was on her

PAROS CATHEDRAL

0   10 metres

Ay. Nikolaos

Diakonikon

Baptistery

way to the Holy Land in search of the True Cross, it occupies the site of a secular Roman edifice of c 300 (mosaics of the Labours of Hercules). Altered in the 10C after an earthquake, it has the form of a Greek cross, sombre and impressive, with an unusual triforium and a dome borne on pendentives. The apse is flanked by 'parekklisia', of which one at any rate antedates the main building, for *Ayios Nikolaos* (left) dates at least from the time of Justinian I; it has Doric column shafts and a marble ikonostasis of 1611. The *Baptistery*, off the S transept, has a sunken immersion font, cruciform in plan.—In the *Archaeological Museum* (near the Gymnasion) are a winged victory of the school of Skopas, an inscription relating to Archilochos, and part of the 'Parian Chronicle'.

The narrow main street, or the parallel shore promenade, leads to a hillock, crowned by the ruined Venetian *Castle* built in 1260 with material from a Temple of Demeter. The temple site is occupied by the church of *Ayíou Konstandínou*. Near the school a bust commemorates Panayiotis Kallierou (1861–1937), the Pestalozzi of Greece, who taught here for 30 years. Farther on, the hill of Ayía Anna, with windmills affords a pleasant sea view.

To the S of Paroikia, just beyond the Xenia hotel, are a *Grotto of the Nymphs* and, on the terrace of a small hill (left), some remains of an *Asklepieion*. Farther S are the site of the *Pytheion* and the *Moní Khristós Dhásous*, attractively surrounded by trees. The road, not very interesting, continues with views of Andíparos to the villages at the S end of the island. Near (10km) *Piskopianá* the Grávari estate is known as *Petaloúdhes* from the migratory butterflies seen there (comp. Rhodes).

TO NÁOUSSA, 10·5km (6½ miles), bús. The road leads NE past the park. At 2km Track (right; c 3km) to the *Monastíri Zoödhókhos Piyí Longobárdhas* (women not admitted) with a library and wall-paintings. At the next fork we bear left and cross the little Helytas, c 180m beyond which we see (left) the excavated remains of a 7C basilican church on the site of the *Heroön of Archilochos* (4C BC). There are vestiges of a *Sanctuary of Delian Apollo* on the hill called Kastro to our left. Fragments of the cult statue and base have been collected and partly reassembled in the museum. The road passes small churches to the right and left in a pleasant valley between rolling green hills.

On a concealed plateau on top of unpromising cliffs at the head of *Náoussa Bay* (W) is the important Late Bronze Age site of *Koukounariés*, still in the course of excavation by Dr D. Schilardhi. The settlement, which is defended both by its situation and a strong wall, was burnt down by invaders in the early 12C BC. It was reoccupied and rebuilt in the 8C BC, to which period apparently belongs the foundation of a Temple of Athena, recently discovered on the SE slopes.—10·5km *Náoussa* (Hotels B, C, D, E; F/A), a pretty fishing village with 1229 inhab., has a small caique harbour, interesting churches, and a half- submerged Venetian fortress. Harbour installations are submerged in the bay, as are a number of wrecks including one Russian wreck of the late 18C. Remains of an early Geometric fortified site lie on Oikonomos headland to the E.

To reach the famous **Parian Marble Quarries**, we take the Náoussa road and fork right beyond the park up the Helytas valley. On the other side of the valley (left) rises Profitis Ilias with a Cave of Eileithyia and a sanctuary of Aphrodite. We continue to (5km) *Maráthi*. The quarries (sign) lie some way beyond the main track to the deserted monastery of Ayios Mínas. The numerous excavations are underground. The largest is 100m long and nearly 9m wide with a chamber on either side of the central passage. The marks of the wedges used by the ancient quarrymen are visible everywhere; also to be seen is a sculptured tablet. The quarries had lain idle for centuries until 1844 when marble was required for the tomb of Napoleon. The road goes on to (17km) *Márpissa* (Hotels B, C, E; F/A) and other E coast resorts.

The 635 inhab. of **Andíparos** (Αντίπαρος; Hotels C, D) are served by a daily mail boat from Paroikia (1½ hours). The island, now separated from Paros by the 'Fourteen-foot Channel'; was joined to it in prehistoric times. Its ancient name was *Oliaros*. The principal attraction is the stalactite *Cavern* at the S end of the island (excursions in summer from Paroikia).

In 1964–65 excavations by the British School on the islet of *Saliagós* (between Paros and Andiparos) uncovered a Neolithic site, the first to be excavated in the

Cyclades. Stone building foundations, obsidian arrow-heads, a 'fiddle' idol, and a marble figurine of a fertility cult were found, the relics of a sheep-farming people of the 4th millennium BC.—On *Dhespotikó*, an islet to the W of Andiparos, the *Prepesinthos* of ancient times, early Cycladic cist-graves were explored in 1960 by the Greek Archaeological Service.

NÁXOS (Νάξος), the largest and most beautiful of the Cyclades, made an indelible impression on the youthful Byron. The island, 30km long and 19km wide, forms a complete eparchy. The interior of Naxos is traversed by a mountain range, rising to 1004m in Mt Zévs, or Zas, the highest summit in the Cyclades. Other peaks are Kóronos (1000m) in the N island, and Fanári (930m) between it and Zas. The island is divided by fertile and well-watered valleys. Groves of olive, orange, lemon, pomegranate, and fig trees abound, and fruit, oil, corn, and wine are exported. Local wine can be good, the honey is excellent, and the cheeses varied. Citron, a local liqueur, is distilled from leaves. Emery is found in abundance. The marble of Naxos, scarcely inferior to that of Paros, was anciently much used for statuary. The 14,037 inhabitants are Orthodox except for a few Roman Catholic descendants of medieval Venetian settlers, who have their own archbishop (of Naxos-with-Tinos). There are a number of little-known small Byzantine churches (see AJA, 1968).

Naxos (Hotels B, C, D, E; F/A), the *Chora*, with 3735 inhab., perpetuates the site of the ancient and medieval capitals on the W coast. The Mycenaean settlement has been shown by recent excavations to have been at Grotta, just to the N, where a large site near the orthodox cathedral (*Mitrópolis*), still under excavation, has produced an apparently continuous sequence of use from the Mycenaean to Roman periods, with features including a Mycenaean wall and Geometric ritual structure. Much of the modern development on the outskirts is unappealing but the narrow lanes and small shops of the old 'agora' off the small coastal plateia) are attractive, though the people are in general less spontaneously friendly than is usual in the Cyclades. The island has become very popular with tourists in recent years, though most visitors stay in the Chora, where the hotels are concentrated and it is not hard to find quieter places elsewhere. There are bus tours of the island in the summer and cars, scooters and bicycles can be rented.

History. *Naxos* is perhaps best known in myth as the place where Theseus deserted Ariadne on his way back to Athens from Crete, a story celebrated in one of the most accomplished poems of Catullus and an opera by Richard Strauss. Herodotus says that the Naxians were Ionians of Athenian stock. In 501 BC Naxian exiles, living in Miletus, enlisted Persian aid against the island's ruler. The failure of the Persian expedition precipitated the Ionian revolt (Hdt. v, 30). The Persians sacked the island in 490. The Naxiots sent four ships to join the Greek fleet at Salamis, and in 471 were the first of the allied states to come under the dominion of Athens. At the battle of Naxos in 376 BC the Athenians routed a Lacedaemonian fleet. In 1207 Naxos was seized by Marco Sanudi, who founded a Venetian duchy. Breaking with Venice, he put himself under the protection of Henry of Flanders, the Latin emperor, and was rewarded in 1210 with the titles of Duke of the Archipelago and Sovereign of the Dodecanese, making him feudal superior of the other Aegean barons. His house, and the succeeding dynasty of the Crispi, ruled over much of the Cyclades for 360 years. Naxos fell to the Turks in 1566 but became a seat of Greek learning. In 1770–74 it was occupied by the Russians.

On the quay is a statue, erected in 1963, of Petros Protopapadhakis (1858–1922), the politician, a native of Apíranthos. A causeway crosses to the islet of *Palatia* where the huge doorway of the *Temple of Apollo* stands on a partially restored stylobate amid remnants of shattered columns. The temple may date from the days of Lygdamis, tyrant c 530 BC. The harbour mole, rebuilt by Marco Sanudi, corresponds with an ancient breakwater.

The walls of the town have mostly disappeared. From the little square, lanes climb to the outer enceinte of the **Kastro**, within which are picturesque houses of Venetian character, many bearing coats of arms. The *Panayía Theosképastos* preserves a remarkable 14C ikon of the Crucifixion. The Latin *Cathedral*, founded in the 13C, is paved with heraldic tombstones, many still claiming titles centuries after the Duchy of the Archipelago had fallen to the Turks. It has a (recently cleaned) 10C icon of the Virgin and Child, a unique example of a full-length representation in its period. Near by is the building which until recently was the French Ursuline convent and a house, at one time a school at which Nikos Kazantzakis was a pupil for 2 years, now the *Museum*. It contains Cycladic idols and bead jewellery; Mycenaean pottery, including fragments of a large pithos decorated in relief with chariots and riders (note the Homeric figure-of-eight shields), from sites within the town, from tombs on Aplomata and from Kamini and Koufonisi; small Classical torsos and sculptures, fragmentary kouroi from Sangri, and a Roman mosaic.

Excursions. TO ENGARES (8km). Just outside the town to the N rises the hill of *Aplómata*, with Mycenaean chamber-tombs (on the very edge of the cliff) and a memorial to a local resistance hero of 1944. Here was the ancient fort of *Delion*, where occurred the events in the Naxo-Milesian war, related by Plutarch. The *Moní Khrisostómou*, above, was built about the same time by Bp Anthimou. We turn inland to (8km) *Mitriá* in the fruit-growing Engarés valley. From Mitria, a road runs NE to the Melanes area. The main road (very rough) continues on or near the E coast to the beautiful *Faneroméni* monastery (1606) and Apollona (comp. below).

TO APIRANTHOS, (28km). The main road of the island leads SE across the fertile plane of *Livadhi*. At 2km we leave on our left a road to *Mélanes* (9km) and the quarries of *Flerió* (12km) where two unfinished Kouroi of the 7C lie abandoned.—5km *Galanádho*, just beyond which is the fine *Bellónia Pírgos* (tower house) with a double church, orthodox on one side, Catholic on the other. To the right of the road is a cluster of villages, of which *Trípodhes* (also *Vívlos*) is the most important. An hour's walk from it towards the sea are towers of various periods.—8km We reach a col, from which a mule-path descends (left) to *Ayios Mámas* (9C), once the cathedral of Naxos.—8km *Sangrí*, which we leave on our right, has many relics of the Middle Ages in its vicinity (towers, churches, monasteries), together with (at *Yíroulas*, a 30-minute walk SW) the site of ancient *Aulonos*, where a temple of Demeter and Kore has been superseded by a Byzantine church.

About 3km N of Sangrí, opposite the tower of *Vaséon*, the small single-aisled chapel of *Ay. Artémios* has aniconic frescoes of the 9C. Beyond Sangri there is a turn (right) for *Ayiassós* (10km; beach, restaurant, rooms). After a short distance, on the hillside to the left (Mt Profitis Ilias) is visible the abandoned monastery of the *Kaloritissa* (locally *Kalorítsa*) which has a *Cave Church of the Nativity* with some aniconic frescoes of the 9C and two later layers from the early 10C and 12/13C.

We enter the olive-growing plain of *Tragaías*, of which **Khalkí** is the principal village in a group. Its Byzantine churches have wall-paintings; of the Venetian tower-houses the Pírgos Frangopoúlou is the most striking; in the area are the ruins of Epáno Kástro, built by Marco Sanudi II (1244–63).

In *Khalkí* the domed church of *Protóthronos* (9–10C) has fragments of an early basilica in the apse, where there is also a stone synthronon. An inscribed marble lintel built into the wall was probably taken from the *templon* of the church. The legible part records the date 1052 and the names of the donors, the bishop Leo and the protospatharios Nicetas. Beneath the dome frescoes, the remains of a similar composition were exposed, probably part of the first (10C) decoration. These were detached and are now housed in the Ducal palace in the town of Naxos. Assigned to the restoration before 1083 is the existing dome decoration—the Deesis in the conch in the apse, the S vault and the surviving frescoes in the NW corner of the church, i.e. the compartment of the narthex, organised as a separate parekklesion in the 11C.

Near Khalki is *Ay. Yióryios Diassorítis* (11C), with three layers of frescoes, those of the 11/12C recently restored. Also near the village is the *Panayía Dhamiótissa*, of free-standing cross type with a dome. The frescoes are dated to the 12/13C and include the Crucifixion and the Dormition of the Virgin. On the road from Khalkí to *Moní* is the *Panayía Dhrosianí* in which some fragments of pre-iconoclastic decoration have recently been exposed in the N apse and dome. 13C frescoes have been removed.

At *Tsikalarió*, just below, there is a Geometric site.—19km *Filóti*, the island's largest village (1474 inhab.), a former Frankish fief, stands on the N flank of Zas (1003m), the highest point of the Cyclades.—28km **Apíranthos** (Απείρανθος; post office), called locally *Aperáthou*, an attractive village (882 inhab.), was rebuilt by the Sommaripa and Crispi in the 14C on an ancient site.

Just outside Apeiranthos is the church of *Ay. Yióryios*, with, attached to the NW corner, *Ay. Pakhómios* with its twin apsidal recesses. The inscription of 1253/54 on the templon of Ay. Yioryios probably relates to the frescoes of both churches. Also near the village is the three-aisled basilica of *Ay. Ioánnis Theólogos* with remains of three layers of frescoes. The earliest are assigned to the 10C, while the major part of the decoration dates from the beginning of the 11C and the 12C.— To the SE of Apeiranthos is the interesting church of *Ay. Kyriakí* which contains some of the earliest aniconic decoration in Greece, dated to the 9C. Some remains of a later decoration can be seen in the S aisle.

Buses (via Apeiranthos) serve the villages in the N of the island, notably (13km) *Koronís* (548 inhab.) centre for the rich emery quarries (to the E), which are linked by aerial ropeway with a bay on the E coast; and (21km) *Komiakí*, a pretty village, and (21km) *Apóllona*, on the NE coast. Here there is a colossal *Kouros*, broken, unfinished and showing the working methods.

The Hellenistic *Tower of Kheimárrou* in the SE (due S of Zas) can be reached in 3½ hours on foot from Filoti or by a very rough road. It stands to 45 courses of masonry.

The four islets to the E and SE of Naxos (but in the eparchy of Thera) are served by steamers once or twice a week and a local service from Naxos (variable). *Donoússa*, or Denoussa, has a Geometric fortified settlement explored in 1969–72. In a bay off the island on 9–10 August 1914 S.M.S. 'Goeben' and 'Breslau' coaled during their successful escape to Constantinople.

IOS or **Nio** (119 sq. km), lying E of Sikinos (see below) and between Paros (N) and Santorin (S), belongs to the eparchy of Thera. As the name implies, this beautiful little island was Ionian. An apochryphal Life of Homer relates that, during a voyage from Samos to Athens, the poet was driven ashore on Ios, died there and was buried on the seashore. Ios was a fief of the Venetian Pisani, but was captured by the Turks in 1537. The hilly interior has twin peaks—Pirgos (722m) and Megalo Vouno (714m). The island yields corn, dairy produce, and oil. The oak forests of Ios were once a considerable source of wealth. Landing is made by small boat to *Ormos Iou* (Hotels B, C, D, E), an excellent harbour, on the W coast, with a good beach (Yialós) near by and a better one in Milopótamos bay to the S. The island capital, **Ios** (1362 inhab.), lies 1km inland near the site of the ancient city. Ios is remarkable for the large number of its attractive chapels, said to amount to 400; *Ayía Ekateríni* incorporates fragments of classical sculpture. Behind the town windmills grind the corn. The ruined *Palaiókastro*, built by the Crispi in the 15C, stands on a commanding height 2½ hours E. At the N tip of the island (2 hours walk) is the creek of *Plakotós*, where the Dutch traveller Paasch van Krienen claimed to have discovered the tomb of Homer in 1770; all he did was to open some prehistoric graves. At the S end of the island is the sandy bay of *Manganári* (Hotel B).

THÍRA (Θήρα), or **SANTORÍNI** (Σαντορίνη), is the most important of the southern Sporades and the most southerly of the islands included in the nome of the Cyclades. It owes its alternative name to its patron, St. Irene of Salonika, who died here in exile in 304; officially it has readopted the ancient name *Thera*. The island, one of the great natural curiosities of Greece, is a huge volcano, the centre of which disappeared in a terrific explosion in prehistoric times. Today it has the form of a crescent of area 75 sq. km, the horns projecting westward, with an intrusion of the sea now forming a roadstead where once the crater rose. In the middle of this lagoon, which is 208 fathoms (380m) deep, are the Kaimeni ('Burnt') Islands still actively volcanic. On its NW side the island of *Therasia* partly continues the circular outline. Between its S coast and the S horn of Thira is an opening of the sea, in the middle of which is the tiny islet of Aspronisi.

The inner (W) side of the crescent of Thira has weirdly shaped precipitous cliffs up to 305m high. Thence, to the E, the ground, covered with lava and pumice, slopes down gradually to the sea, the surface being interrupted by conical hillocks and by a few hills, the highest being Megalos Ayios Ilias (566m), Mikros Ayios Ilias (337m), and Mesa Vouno (338m), all in the SE, and Megalo Vouno (333m) in the N. On the volcanic soil only vines and tomatoes are cultivated, but an experiment is being made with growing pistachios. The potent Santorini wine has a great reputation. The mining of pumice ash is the island's main industry. Apart from one or two wells, the island is waterless, and rainwater is collected in cisterns. The light is famous for its intensity. The ships call first at *Oía* at the NW horn of the island, where disembarkation is by motor-boat.—By air the island can be reached directly from Athens twice daily in 55 minutes.

Geology. The island, originally a volcano of marble and metamorphic schist with its main crater in the middle of what is now the roadstead, has from earliest times changed its shape as the result of eruptions. One, analogous to that of Krakatoa in 1889 and placed c 1500 BC, caused the middle of the island to sink, so that a circular depression 10km wide came into being, into which the sea poured. In the SW, the islet of Aspronisi is the only surviving land remnant. In 236 BC another eruption separated *Therasia* from the NW of Thera. In 196 BC, the islet of *Hiera* or *Old Kaimeni* made its appearance. In AD 46 another islet, *Thia* appeared and vanished. In 1570 the S coast of Thera, with the port of Eleusis, collapsed beneath the sea. Three years later *Mikra Kaimeni* appeared, and in 1711–12 *Nea* or *Great Kaimeni*. In January 1866 there began a violent eruption that lasted two years, observed by Fouqué, the French geologist and archaeologist. This eruption produced the George I Volcano, in the S of Great Kaimeni, and the islet of *Aphtoessa*, which disappeared in 1868. Another eruption began in July 1925, and lasted till May 1926; this joined Mikra and Nea Kaimeni. Further disturbances occurred in 1928. An earthquake in July 1956 caused great damage; over half the buildings on the W coast were destroyed.

History. *Thera*, anciently known as *Kalliste* ('most beautiful') was populated before 2000 BC and its colonists are said to have founded the African city of Cyrene. The great eruption that transformed its shape and which, together with the preceding earthquakes, destroyed its settlements may have been the catastrophe that overwhelmed the Cretan palaces but there are many chronological problems still unsolved. Thera has been suggested as the site of Metropolis, the destroyed capital of the lost 'continent' of Atlantis. In legend it was colonised by Cadmus who had stopped at the island during his search for Europa. In the

THERA

0   50 metres

Heron of Theras

Sanctuary of Egyptian Gods

Byzantine Church

Basilistai House

Cisterns

Sacred Way

Tomb

Sanctuary of Apollo Karneios

Theatre

Stoa Basilike

South Agora

Mithraeum

Temple of Dionysos

North Agora

Ptolemaic Garrison Buildings

Platys Tolchos

Baths

Chapel

Heroon

for continuation see above

at same scale

Baths

Grotto

Gymnasium of the Epheboi

for continuation see below

Peloponnesian War Thera and Melos were the only two of the Cyclades that declined alliance with Athens, but Thera escaped the fate of Melos. It was eventually, however, absorbed in the Athenian empire. The Ptolemies made the island into a naval base. In 1207–1335 it was held by the Barotsi as a fief of the Sanudo, and was thereafter included (till 1537) in the duchy of Naxos. The ancient city of Thera was situated in the SE of the island; the medieval capital *Skoros* to the NW of the modern capital. The island has been used in the present century as a place of exile for political prisoners. Vampires were once said to be especially prevalent in Thera.

Excavation. In 1869 the French School discovered on the S coast of Therasia the ruins of a prehistoric city overwhelmed by the great eruption of c 1600 BC and covered with pumice thrown up by it. This discovery proved that Thera, like Melos, was a centre of Cycladic civilisation.—In 1896–1903 the German archaeologist Baron Hiller von Gärtringen excavated the ruins of Thera city; the neighbouring necropolis is still being excavated.—In 1867 the French started investigations near Akrotiri; current excavations on this site were begun in 1967.

In favourable weather ships berth at *Ormos Athiniós*, a tiny haven beneath towering volcanic cliffs on the inner side of the crescent; a bus and taxis take passengers to Firá, the island's capital. In unfavourable weather, ships anchor offshore below Firá, whose dazzling white houses and domes extend along the clifftop nearly 210m above. Motorboats take passengers to *Skala Fira*, whence Firá is reached by mule up a steep, zigzagging, paved track. Most cruise ships use Skala Fira. Transport on the island is by bus (infrequent), taxi, or mule (not necessarily cheaper than taxi).

Firá, officially *Thíra* (1573 inhab.; Hotels A, C, D, E) has an Orthodox and a Roman Catholic cathedral, French schools, and a Dominican convent. From the terraces there is a magnificent view of the Kaimeni islets and Thirasia. The damage of 1956 has been made good with modern variations in new materials on the traditional barrel-vaulted style of building. At the Orthodox Cathedral is a Byzantine Museum. Immediately to the S of the town are the pumice mines, with shiploading chutes. In the N part of the town, near the RC Cathedral, is a school founded by Queen Frederika where local girls are trained in carpet weaving. Near by is a small factory making spectacle frames. Just below is the *Museum*, founded in 1902 and moved to the present new building in 1970. (Another museum is projected near the Orthodox Cathedral to house all prehistoric material. The Classical exhibits will remain in the present building.)

VESTIBULE. L.M. 1A jars from the French excavations at Akrotiri in 1867; case of Early Cycladic figurines and small objects from the pumice mines; vases from recent excavations at Akrotiri.—L-SHAPED HALL. In the long arm: Geometric and Archaic finds, mainly pottery; 'Santorini Vases'. On a pedestal is an outstanding 7C Archaic *Vessel, with relief decoration including a pelican and charioteers with Pegasus. Four Archaic kouroi; statuette of a woman combing her hair. In the shorter arm: pottery (6C and later), including three intact Attic black-figure vases; case of small figurines and animals; Hellenistic and Roman sculpture, continued in the SMALL ROOM, beyond, and in the COURTYARD. Here are also inscriptions, Archaic to Roman.—BASEMENT. Late Roman and Early Christian glass, lamps, etc.

FROM FIRA TO AYIOS ILIAS AND ANCIENT THERA. By taxi direct to Ayios Ilías and on to Ancient Thera. By bus to Pírgos, thence on foot to Ayios Ilías (45 minutes) and Ancient Thera (30 minutes more); or by bus (mornings) to Kamári, thence on foot with a steep climb to c 4km up the road to the ruins. By mule, c 3 hours, with visit to Ay. Ilías.

ROAD, 12km (7½ miles). We run SE through vineyards. 5km Turning (left) to *Monólithos*, a conspicuous isolated outcrop by the shore which has produced traces of Mycenaean occupation in the 13C BC, the first attested on the island after the volcanic catastrophe of the 15C BC.—Soon after a road forks right to *Pírgos*, with picturesque old houses and a Venetian fort. Hence a road ascends to the top of *Megálos Ayios Ilías*, the highest point on the island (566m). The *View is magnificent, extending to the mountains of Crete. On the summit are a radar station and a small monastery of 1711, with a museum of ikons, MSS, and vestments.—Our road continues SE, passing *Episkopí* (right), a Byzantine church of 11C; there are two chapels, at one time used simultaneously by the Orthodox and RC faiths.—Beyond *Kamári* (Hotels C, D, E; F/A), with its black beach, we climb in steep zigzags to (12km) the *Selládha*, the high saddle where the road ends. A short way up a path (left) is the entrance to the ancient city.

Before entering the ruins we may see near the top of the road the Classical and Archaic cemeteries, being excavated; also, left of the road, a section of ancient paved road. Below the Selládha, to the SW, is the Geometric necropolis; here were found some of the famous 'Santorini Vases'; fine pottery and bronze tripods continue to come to light.

Ancient Thera, covering an area 800m long from NW to SE and 140m wide, occupies a rocky spine of Mesa Vouno and was built on a terrace supported by massive foundations. In the Byzantine era it was surrounded by a wall. The main street, crossed by numerous side streets, ran along its entire length.

Archaic tombs show that *Thera* was in existence before the 9C BC. The ruins, however, largely date from the time of the Ptolemies (300–145 BC), who made Thera into an advanced naval base from which they could control the Aegean, and from the Byzantine era. The port of Thera, *Oia*, was situated at Kamári at the foot of Mesa Vouno.

From the entrance gate the path leads up to the tiny chapel of *Ayios Stéfanos*. This was built over the ruins of the Byzantine *Basilica of the Archangel Michael* (4C or 5C). About 200m farther on we come to the *Temenos of Artemidoros of Perge* (right), an admiral of the Ptolemies. The enclosure, with a black lava floor, has an Altar of Concord and, in relief on the wall, the Eagle of Zeus, the Lion of Apollo Stephanephoros, the Medallion of Artemidoros, and the Dolphin of Poseidon. We reach a narrow stepped road leading up to the Ptolemaic Garrison buildings, with the *Gymnasium* and the *Governor's Palace*. Back from these towards the N is a little grotto converted into a Chapel of Christ, and N again, the *Votive Niche of Demeter and Kore*, with a throne carved out of the rock, at the entrance to a large cave called Pitaros.

The main street enters the **Agora**, 110m long by 16·5–30m wide and divided into two. The N part, with a row of shops, overlooks the *Platys Teichos* ('broad wall'), a fine quadrangular bastion of unknown purpose. Beyond (right) are the *Altar of Ptolemy Philometer* and the terrace of the *Temple of Dionysos*. The S part of the Agora is bordered by the STOA BASILIKE, or *Royal Portico* (40m by 10m) with an interior Doric colonnade and rows of columns against the walls. It was probably founded by one of the Ptolemies. The roof was restored in the time of Trajan, and further alterations were made in AD 150. Above and behind it are four blocks of Hellenistic houses, decorated with mosaics and provided with cisterns and lavatories. Each block stands in a little square. One of the houses has a wall-medallion in relief bearing a phallus inscribed 'To my friends'. Beyond the Agora are (right) *Roman Baths*, complete with well, wood oven, and water conduits, and (left) the *theatre*.

A track leads up W past the *Basilistai House*, or Residence of Ptolemaios the Benefactor, to the ruins of Byzantine churches (earlier the Temple of Pythian Apollo). Just beyond is the *Sanctuary of the Egyptian Deities* (Isis, Anubis, Serapis) with small niches carved in the rock.

We descend towards the promontory, following the SACRED WAY past the small *Temple of Ptolemy III* and the *Column of Artemis*, partly engaged in the rock, to the Temple of Apollo Karneios. This dates from the 6C BC and occupies a rectangle 32m by 10m. The gate, on the SW, opens into a square court with a cistern. On the E side is a room; on the W are the paved *Pronaos* and the *Cella*, flanked on the SW side by two little rooms with walls and doors intact.—On the W side of the temple are the foundations of the *Heroön of Theras*, the eponymous coloniser from Sparta. Below, to the N, is the *Chapel of the Annunciation*, near which are remains of a Heroön and a Rotunda.

We reach next the **Terrace of the Festivals**, with a fine view across the beach of Perissa to the promontory of Akrotíri. This terrace, dating from the 6C BC, has impressive retaining walls in two styles (best seen from below at the end of the promontory) and it overlooks further Roman Baths.

This terrace was the religious centre of the oldest Dorian cults. On it were celebrated the *Gymnopaediai*, dances of nude boys in honour of Apollo Karneios. Scratched on the rocks are names of the gods inscribed by the faithful, and of favourite dancers, with erotic appreciations by their admirers. Some of these graffiti are as early as the 7C BC.

At the extreme S of the City is the **Gymnasium of the Epheboi**, with a spacious court and many more graffiti, including numerous outlines of feet. Off the court are a staircase, a rotunda, and numerous rooms; and, in the N corner, the Grotto of *Hermes and Hercules*, the gods of the epheboi.

On foot or by mule, instead of returning the same way, we may descend from the Selládha to (½ hour) *Períssa* (Hotels D, E) on the coast (buses to Firá in summer). A white church, built in the 19C as a result of the miraculous vision of a peasant, occupies the site of a Byzantine basilica. The flying buttresses were added after an earthquake. In the S corner are the foundations of a circular *Heroön* converted in the 1C AD into the tomb of a certain Herasikleia.—We turn inland.—4km **Emboreió** (Hotels C, D), or *Nimporio*, a village of 1039 inhab., situated on the foothills of Mesa Vouno, has a regular bus to Fira. In the cemetery is a statue of Polyhymnia surrounded by a wall. Beyond Emboreion, beside the road (right), is the chapel of *Ayios Nikólaos Marmarinós*, converted from a marble *Temple of Thea Basilica* (the Mother of the Gods) of the 3C BC (note the coffered ceiling). Near the S tip of the island (30 minutes S of Emboreion) are some remains of ancient *Eleusinos*.—We pass the turning (left) for Akrotíri (see below) and, following the road N, passing Pirgos (right), reach (16km) Firá.

FROM FIRA TO AKROTIRI, 12km to the village (bus daily), thence 1km to the site; taxi to the site. The road runs high above the bay, passing turnings (right) to Ormos Athiniós and (left) to Pírgos and Períssa.—12km (7½ miles) **Akrotíri** (207 inhab.) has a ruined medieval castle. At the entrance to the village a road leads left in 1km to the excavations, begun in 1967 by the late Prof. Sp. Marinatos (who died at work here in 1974) and continued under Prof. C. Doumas. The site may be compared with Herculaneum, alike for the similarity of complete burial beneath layers of pumice by a great eruption, and for the magnitude of the discoveries.

The *site is in a ravine below the village, the roofs which cover the remains being about level with the ground surface at the sides. The visitor follows a marked route round the remains. Although Akrotíri has produced an enormous number of outstanding finds (especially

AKROTIRI

0 metres

Sector Alpha

N

House of the Ladies

West House

SQUARE

Sector Delta

ROAD

Xeste 2

Sector Gamma

Sector Beta

Xeste 3

Xeste 4

Entrance

he frescoes), these can at present only be viewed in Athens (National Archaeological Museum), though a new Museum is planned for the sland to house them. The attraction of the site is its architecture, the best-preserved of any prehistoric settlement in the Aegean and, in some cases, surviving up to the third storey. The buildings date to L.M. A (later 16C BC). There is no regular plan: the town being composed of house-blocks and independent 'villas', divided by narrow streets. Some of the construction is of simple rubble masonry but some of the villas are magnificently built of fine ashlar masonry. Noteworthy are the slab paving of some of the upper stories and the threshold, lintel and jamb blocks of intact doors and windows. A few finds have been left *in situ*—millstones for grinding grain and large storage vessesl (in the N part of the site).

FROM FIRA TO OIA, 13km, bus or taxi. By mule or on foot in c 2½ hours. As far as Foinikiá the road runs inland of the path. The path leaves Fira on the N and follows the cliffs through white hamlets.—½ hour Merovígli (taverna), a village on a height; its name Ημεροβίγλι means Watch Tower'. On the left is a promontory (304m) bearing the ruins of Skaros, the medieval capital of the island, with a castle of the Crispi.—The path continues to skirt the shore as far as (1 hour) a track fork on the slopes of *Megalo Vouno* (333m). The turning to the right leads in ½ hour to Cape Koloumbos, on the NE coast, near which some rock-hewn tombs have been discovered.—Keeping left, we reach (1¾ hours) the hamlet of Foinikiá, near here joining the road.—2½ hours Oia (360 inhab.), the official but incorrect name adopted by Apáno Meriá; for ancient Oia see above. The village was ruined by the 1956 earthquake. Below the village, to the S is the little port of *Ayios Nikólaos*, facing the island Thirasia (boats available).

Thirasía, once part of the island of Thera before the great prehistoric eruption, is now an island c 5km long and 2·5km wide. It has a land-ing-place at *Manolás*, in the middle of the E coast. The ancient city of Therasia was in the N of the island. In the S, between Capes Kimina and Tripiti, are pumice ash quarries, which supplied much of the material for building the banks of the Suez Canal. In these quarries a Middle-Late Cycladic settlement was accidentally discovered in 1869. Nothing remains to be seen.

EXCURSION TO NEA (GREAT) KAIMENE. A motor-boat from Skála Firá crosses in 20 minutes to the island. From the landing stage a walk across cinder leads in 30 minutes to the Metaxá Crater where gases and hot vapours issue from issures.

Anaphe (Ανάφη), or *Anáfi*, is a small island (37·5 sq. km) to the E of Santorini, to which politically it belongs. It was celebrated in legend as having been raised out of the sea by Apollo as a refuge for the Argonauts when overwhelmed by a storm. Landing is made at *Ayios Nikólaos* in the centre of the S shore. Anáfi, or Khóra (285 inhab.), the only village, lies 15 minutes inland. Paths lead E to (80 minutes) Katelimátsa, where there are ancient ruins, and on to (100 minutes) the attractive monastery of the *Kalamiótissa*, site of a temple of Apollo of which there are remains. Other traces of ancient habitation can be seen to the N of Katelimátsa, at Castélli (20-minute walk). Many antiquities were removed by the Russians in 1770–74 to St. Petersburg.

Síkinos and Folégandros lie between Ios and Milos and belong to the eparchy of Milos. **Síkinos** (Σίκινος; 37·5 sq. km; 290 inhab.) is said to have once been called *Oinoe* ('Wine I') from the fertility of its vines. The S coast is rocky and barren, but elsewhere the island produces vine, figs, and wheat. The Skala at *Aloprónoia*, on the SE coast, is exposed and often inaccessible. About 1 hour inland, in the middle of the island, is the village capital, called *Kástro* or *Khóra*, at the foot of a rock crowned by a fortified monastery (Zoödhókhos Piyí), now ruinous. To the SW (1¾ hours), at *Episkopí*, stands a Heroön, or temple-tomb (3C AD), converted in the (?) 7C into the church of Koimisis Theotokou, and remodelled after earthquake damage shortly before 1673. At the NE tip of the island (1½ hours from Kastro) is *Palaiókastro* with ruins of another ancient sanctuary.

Folégandros (Φολέγανδρος) is one of the smallest of the Cyclades (35 sq. km; 567 inhab.). From *Karavostásis*, the harbour, a narrow road leads in 40 minutes to the pretty Khóra (248 inhab.), with a medieval portion called *Kástro*. The ancient city crowned the hill above. The beautiful church of *Panayía* stands on a headland to the N. *Apáno Meriá* (312 inhab.), a scattered village, lies 1 hour to the NW of Khora; from the windmills on the way a wide view embraces Sifnos and Kimolos and the coast of Crete.

74   The Eastern Sporades

The **Eastern Sporades** lie off the coast of Asia Minor. Imbros and Tenedos belong to Turkey; most of the remainder, which extend S to the Dodecanese, are under Greek sovereignty. Samothrace and Lemnos, the most northerly, are described for convenience with Thrace (from which they are most easily accessible; see Rte 70). The islands generally are more fertile and greener than the Cyclades, and if they have been less exploited for relics of antiquity, they had till recently preserved more of the customs and traditions of the more immediate past.

A. Ikaría and Sámos

STEAMERS from Piraeus ply daily (direct or via Paros or Syros), to Ikaría (in 8½–11 hours) and to Sámos (Vathý in 9½–15 hours; Karlóvasi in 12–17 hours), where arrival may be very early in the morning. At Ikaria the usual port-of-call is Ayios Kírikos, but some steamers call regularly at Evdhilos. Samos is also connected weekly with Khios, Lemnos, and Salonika, and with the Dodecanese.— Occasional connections to Kuşadasi on the Turkish mainland.

BY AIR several times daily in 45 minutes. The air-field lies between Pithagórion and the Heraíon.—TERMINAL, Kanári and Smírnis.

Ikaría (Ικαρία), a delightful, green, well-watered island with many scattered hamlets among the orchards and vineyards, is noted for its honey, as well as its radioactive hot springs. With *Foúrnoi* it forms an eparchy (8885 inhab.) of the nome of Samos. The name, possibly deriving from the Phoenician 'ikor' in reference to an abundance of fish, attracted to itself a legendary past in which Ikaros and Daedalus figure prominently (a modern sculpture based on the myth adorns the harbour mole at Ayios Kírikos). In antiquity the island had other names, notably *Doliche*. The S coast rises to a ridge (*Atheras*), the highest point of which (1880m), SW of the capital, was known to the ancients as Pramnos or Drakanon.

The little capital, *Ayios Kírikos* (Hotels B, C, E; Rooms) with 1880 inhab., lies on the SE shore. Neighbouring to the E is **Thérma** (Hotels B, C, D, summer only), the principal spa, whose name and fame were similar in antiquity. Some Roman remains can be seen. An unidentified Archaic acropolis and Classical tombs have been noted at *Katafíyion* c 6·5km E. Remains of *Drakanon*, another Classical town, lie near Fáro at the E end of the island. Most impressive here is the circular *Tower of the 3C. Some finds are on show in the Gymnasion of Ayios Kírikos.

40km from Ayios Kirikos (daily buses; impressive views) is the pretty village of *Evdhilos* (Εὐδηλος; Hotels B, E; Rooms), in the middle of the N coast, which can be used as a base for the W half of the island. At *Kámbos* (3km W), with a small *Museum*, are the remains of ancient *Oinoe*. The Byzantine town on this site readopted the name of Doliche, and left the ruins called 'Palatia', which incorporate a Roman odeion (visible), and the attractive 11C church of Ayía Iríni.

Farther W (11km) is *Armenistís* (Rooms) with good beaches and beyond (4km), reached by a poor road, the beautifully situated sanctuary of *Artemis Tauropolos* at *Na*. The stone of the temple and various other buildings has been mostly fed to the lime kilns. The site, lying opposite Mykonos and on the direct route from Ionia to Delos, was the starting point for processions to the Delian sanctuary.—Inland the most interesting excursion is to the *Kástro tis Nikariás* a small fort of the 10C. This is best reached via the village of *Steli* (occasional bus; 1 hour on foot from Evdhilos, with a further hour or more for the ascent, which involves a steep climb).

Foúrni consists of a small group of islands, of which only two are inhabited. The daily caique (weather often rough) calls first at the smaller of these, *Thýmaina*. By the harbour of the village of Fourni (Rooms), the largest island, are the substantial remains of a Hellenistic (and Roman) fortified town. Inscriptions can be seen carved on the rocks. At *Khrissomiliá* (c 10km N, best reached by boat), a prettily situated village, are the remains of an ancient building of marble (a temple or tower) with a Byzantine church built above.

SÁMOS

SÁMOS (Σάμος) lies closest of all Greek islands to the coast of Asia Minor, to which it was connected in prehistoric times, being separated from Cape Mykale by a strait c 3km wide. A range of mountains (a continuation of the mainland chain) runs through the island from E to W, rising to peaks at Karvouni or Ampelos (1140m) in the centre and Kerkis (1445m) in the extreme W. Samos, with an area of 492 sq. km supports 31,634 inhabitants. The N coast, on which lies the capital Vathy (in the bay of the same name) is precipitous and rocky, while the S coast opens on little plains and beaches admirably suited for bathing. The island is thickly wooded and abounds in springs and winter torrents. At all times it has been known for its fertility, which gave rise to many of the names by which it was known in antiquity (Anthemousa, Phyllas, Dryousa, etc.), and which led Menander to claim it could produce even birds' milk (Strabo xiv). The main products are wine (the Samian Moschato, a sweet red wine, is widely exported and has a high reputation), tobacco, shipbuilding timber, and olive oil. The mean winter temperature is warmer than that of Athens.

History. That *Samos* was inhabited at least as early as the 3rd millennium BC is proved by neolithic finds at Pithagorion. The island's name is said to derive from a Phoenician word meaning 'high'. Pelasgians introduced the cult of Hera, and the Classical writers endowed the island with an eponymous hero, son of an Argonaut colonist. Later Samos was settled by Ionians. In the 8C or 7C Samos came into the possession of territory on the opposing mainland, which gave rise to continual boundary disputes with Priene. About 650 BC the Samian Kolaios voyaged through the Pillars of Hercules and returned with wealth that soon become proverbial. After the overthrow of the tyrant Demoteles during the 6C Samos was ruled by a landed aristocracy (the Geomoroi).

About 540, Polycrates and his brothers Pantagnotus and Syloson became tyrants (it is possible that the dynasty was established earlier by their father Aeaces). Polycrates soon ousted his brothers and ruled alone, bringing Samos to the height of its prosperity. He built up a great naval force, annexed many of the neighbouring islands and concluded alliances with Cyrene and with Amasis of Egypt. His court attracted many eminent artists and poets, among them Anacreon of Teos, and Polycrates was responsible for what Herodotus describes as the three greatest works to be seen in any Greek land—the aqueduct constructed by Eupalinos, the mole of the harbour, and the temple of Hera (the largest known to Herodotus) built by the architects Rhoikos and Theodoros. During this century, Samos founded many colonies, especially in the Propontis, and as far afield as Zancle in Sicily. In 522 BC Polycrates was tricked and captured by the Persian satrap Orontes and crucified on the mainland opposite.

Syloson, Polycrates' borther, now became tyrant with Persian support, although anti-Persian feeling in the island led to Samian participation in the Ionian revolt against Persia. In the battle of Lade however, in 494, the Samian fleet deserted to the Persians. Samos fought on the Persian side at Salamis, but finally turned against Xerxes at the battle of Mycale. In 479–440, Samos was an independent member of the Athenian League, contributing ships instead of tribute. Following a revolt, Samos was crushed by Pericles after a nine-month siege—a feat which received favourable comparison with the capture of Troy. A democratic régime was installed, though in 424–412 this was overthrown by the oligarchs. The island was faithful to Athens during the Peloponnesian War, and was captured by the Spartan Lysander in 404 BC. In 394 BC the Athenian admiral Konon recaptured Samos, which seceded from Athens in 390. The Athenians recaptured the island in 365 and replaced the entire native population with colonists. The Samians returned from exile only in 321 BC as the result of an edict of Alexander the Great, put into effect after his death by his regent Perdikkas. In the same year Antigonus Monophthalmus gained control of Ionia, and probably of Samos which he certainly controlled some time before 306. After his death Samos fell to Lysimachus of Thrace, and when he was defeated and killed in the battle of Corupedion in 281, passed under the influence of the Ptolemies of Egypt who used the island as a naval base. Later in the century Kallikrates of Samos became Ptolemy's admiral, a position amounting to viceroy of the sea. Ptolemaic control of the island lasted until 197 BC, with a short interruption in 259–246 when Samos came under the rule of Antiochus II. After a brief occupation by Philip V of Macedon, Samos came under the influence of the Pergamene dynasts, and became part of the Roman province of Asia in 129 BC. The works of art of the city and sanctuary were plundered by Verres in 82 BC and further suffered from pirates' raids between c 70–67 BC. It recovered somewhat under the proconsulship of Cicero in 62 BC, but was plundered again by Antony, who with Cleopatra visited the island in 39 BC. Relations between Augustus and Samos were more friendly—he restored the island's autonomy (19 BC), preserved until AD 70 when Vespasian removed it. Augustus also restored many works of art to Samos.

In the Byzantine era Samos belonged to the eparchy of the Cyclades. It was from here that Nikephoros Phokas embarked on his expedition against Crete in 960. This period marks the rapid decline of Samos. After the invasion of the Turks in 1453 it was depopulated until the 17C, when it was re-occupied and ruled by an archbishop. Samos was occupied by the Russians in 1772–74. In 1821 the island played a leading part in the uprising and proved such a valient adversary that 'to go to Samos' became the proverbial expression used by the Turks to mean certain death. The Samians won a series of victories, but the island was restored to the Turks at the end of the war. They were, however, accorded special privileges amounting to autonomy. They were governed by a Greek prince, the first being Stephanos Bogaridas (1834–59). In 1912 the Turkish fleet at Vathy was bombarded by two Italian warships, and Samos was reunited with Greece. In 1943 Samos was temporarily occupied by the British, and heavily bombarded by the Germans, who later seized it. After the war it was plagued by partisans.

Vathý (Βαθύ; Hotels B, C, E; F/A), the capital of the island, consists of the port of **Samos** (or *Limín Vathéos*), with 5575 inhab., situated in a deep bay on the N coast, and the attractive suburb of *Ano Vathí* (2160 inhab.) on a hill to the S of the bay. This affords a wonderful view of the port itself, the bay, and the coast of Asia Minor. The town dates from the 19C when it was named *Stephanoupolis* after the first autonomous governor. The best local bathing is to be found in sandy coves c 5–8km W.

The *Museum* (expected soon to reopen) lies behind the Public Garden, next to the Town Hall and the Post Office. Housed in it are outstanding finds mostly of the 6C BC from the ancient city of Samos and the Heraion. These include sculptures (among which are the three remaining statues of the Archaic group by Geneleos) and grave reliefs, votive bronzes, with a large collection of griffin-heads; pottery and ivories; and inscriptions. The centrepiece is now likely to be an enormous kouros (5m tall), the body discovered in the Heraion sanctuary in 1980, the face in 1984. The figure is inscribed as a dedication and dates to 570/60 BC. There is much fine miniature sculpture in various materials (including wood).

SHORTER EXCURSIONS. The monastery of Zoödókhos Piyí, founded in 1756 on the hill Pabaidhóni, is 7km from Vathy to the E. It is noted for its wood-carving, its hospitality, and for the spectacular view it affords of the strait of Mykale. A visit to Ayía Zóni (1695), another monastery, in the plain of Vlamari, c 3km from Vathy, can easily be combined in the excursion.

A visit may be paid to the lighthouse of Kótsikas c 5km N of Vathy at the mouth of the bay (fine view).

About 2·5km S of the town, off the Pithagorion road (see below) by-roads lead to Palaiókastro (6km from Vathy) and to (12km) the Strait of Mykale (Stenon Kouzantazi) close by the bathing-beach of Psilí Ammos.

Regular STEAMER excursion weekly to Patmos; Caiques to Kuşadasi, the Turkish port opposite Samos which is close to the ruins of Ephesos.

THE PRINCIPAL EXCURSIONS on the island are to ancient Samos and the Heraion and to Karlovasi. By car they can be combined into a round TOUR OF THE ISLAND, 85km (53 miles), in a day.

TAXIS for hire (legally fixed prices displayed in Plateia); BUSES daily to Karlovasi, either direct or via Pithagorion but inconveniently timed; frequently to Pithagorion, either by the main road or via Mytilini and Khora.

The road leads S over a ridge affording a splendid view of the Strait of Mykale and of the islands of the Dodecanese. The modern town of (14km) **Pithagório** (Πυθαγόρειον; Hotels A, B, C, D, E) lies on the S coast of the island. Formerly called Tigáni, it was given its present name in 1955 in honour of Pythagoras. It has 1360 inhabitants and occupies the site of **Ancient Samos**. A small Museum contains sculptures, among them an Archaic statue of Aiakes; Archaic grave stelai bearing anthemia; Hellenistic grave reliefs; and Roman remains. A new museum is planned to house these objects, together with a further collection (inaccessible to the public) now in the Kastro of Logothetes.

The Castle of Logothetes, built in 1824, and the church of the Transfiguration occupy the hill to the W of the harbour which is shown by the discovery of neolithic pottery to have been the site of the prehistoric town of Astypalaia, later incorporated into the town of Samos.

The mole of the harbour is built on the foundations of the ancient mole of the era of Polycrates, described by Herodotus (3, 60) as one of the greatest works of any Greek land. There are three miles of good pebble and sand beaches to the W.

A short way out of the town on the main road to Vathy a track branches (left) to the traces of the ancient Theatre. Here the path divides, the right branch leading to the small monastery of Panayía Spilianí which hides the mouth of a series of underground caves and cisterns used as a place of refuge during the Turkish occupation and during more recent wars. The left branch continues to the Eupalineion (Evpalínion), or *Tunnel of Eupalinos*, completed during the tyranny of Polycrates in 524 BC.

The tunnel may have been started during the tyranny of Aiakes and probably took fifteen years to complete. It was hewn through the mountain, under the direction of Eupalinos of Megara, its architect, from the N side (outside the walls) to a point within the walls, working being begun from both ends. Besides assuring the water supply during time of siege, the tunnel provided an escape route in emergency. It was so used by Maeandrius during Darius' attack. The visitor needs a torch. A low and narrow entrance from a small white building gives place in the tunnel proper to a ledge beside the deep water channel.

Beyond the tunnel we may continue W to reach the *City Wall*. This wall runs spectacularly up the side of the mountain, turns E along the top and returns towards the sea at a point E of the Panayía Spilianí. Its whole extent of 7km with 35 towers has been traced. It is excellently preserved at the top, and the views over Mykale and over the inland plain are superb.

FROM PITHAGORION TO THE HERAION, 8km asphalt; taxi, no convenient return bus. From the Khora road we take the left fork, pass the airfield on our left and at 6km again take the left fork.

The **Heraion**, or *Sanctuary of Hera*, lies on the coast at a place called *Kolonna* after the one surviving column of the great temple. It is close by the torrent Imbrasos, which is said to have seen the birth of Hera, and is a few minutes' walk on the Pithagorion side of its small village, frequented as a bathing resort. Few Greek sanctuaries can boast a history of such length that can be traced in such detail.

Excavations undertaken by the German Archaeological Institute in 1910–14, 1925–39, and since 1952 have revealed that the history of the site begins in the Bronze Age. Among buildings uncovered is a tholos tomb of the late-Mycenaean period. The continuous history of the sanctuary during the next centuries is attested by two temples earlier than the first great temple. The early 8C structure was developed into the first true Greek temple by the addition of a peristyle (7 × 17); after its descruction c 670 BC, it was replaced by another (6 × 18 columns). During the 6C the sanctuary was widely extended, activity beginning probably a generation before Polycrates and being continued by him. To this period belongs the great temple. Further buildings belong to the Hellenistic and Roman periods and include a Christian basilica of the 5C AD.

The first GREAT TEMPLE was built about the middle of the 6C by the celebrated Samian artist Rhoikos, in association (according to some authorities) with the architect Theodoros. Herodotus claims it was the largest temple of its day. Built in the Ionic order, 97·5m long by 49m wide, it was a dipteron, having 8 columns by 20 (rectangle on Plan). This temple was destroyed by fire c 525 BC and many of its parts, notably the column-bases were reused in a larger replacement. The second temple (Pl. 1), probably begun under Polycrates, extended farther to the W; the *Pronaos*, on the E, had three rows of eight columns, while the *Opisthodomos*, on the W, had three rows of nine. Its construction suspended at the death of Polycrates, was resumed during the early 5C and again in the 3C but was never completed. A single column, itself incomplete, stands at the present time.

The complex of buildings immediately to the E includes an *Altar* (Pl. 2), a late building having butresses (Pl. 3), a small *Bath* (Pl. 4), a peripteral *Temple* (Pl. 5) belonging to the Roman era, a second Roman *Temple* (Pl. 6), dating from the 2C AD, and a *Basilica* of the Early Christian era. All that remains of the last today is the N aisle with the foundations of the nave, and the apse (Pl. 7). To the S lies the base (Pl. 8) on which stood statues of the orator Cicero and his brother Quintus. Beyond this group, to the E, is the large *Altar* (Pl. 9) which is said to have been erected by Rhoikos. This was constructed on the site of a cult area of the 2nd millennium BC above a more recent altar which had been restored in the Geometric period.

To the N of this group of buildings lies another complex of constructions dating from various periods. These include two small *Temples* in antis (Pl. 10, 11), the second of which overlies a peripteral temple, and

HERAION (Samos)

0   50 metres

N

a third Temple (Pl. 12) of late date. To the W of this group are the foundations of a circular building (Pl. 13), and farther to the W an Archaic *Stoa* (Pl. 14). A number of members of the temple of Rhoikos were found beneath this stoa, where they were buried after the fire, thus proving it to belong to the late Archaic period. Between this stoa and the great temple is a *Stoa* (Pl. 15) of the Hellenistic period.

In the extreme E area of the site have been uncovered the foundations of a number of buildings, including treasuries, temples, and administrative offices. Also, four wells were discovered here full of vases dating from the Geometric period to the 7C. A late-Mycenaean wall and the remains of several Mycenaean buildings were also found in this area.

About 1·5km W of the site and 10 minutes walk from the village is the *Pírgos Sarakíni*, a tower dating from the Turkish occupation (late 16C).

Our round tour continues by the right fork (comp. below) to (22km) *Khóra* (1100 inhab.), before 1821 the island capital, then winds across the rugged centre of the island.—35km *Pírgos* (724 inhab.; Hotel D).—51km (31¾ miles) **Karlóvasi** (Καρλόβασι; Hotels B, D) is a small port (4752 inhab.) on the N coast (2 hours from Vathy), at which all boats to and from Piraeus call. An Olympic Airways bus service connects with one flight a day from the main airport. The area inland of the town is rich in vines which contribute to the reputation of the Samian wines. From Karlovasi the visitor can make many walks on *Mt Kerkis*, from the summit of which a magnificent view of the Aegean and the neighbouring islands may be obtained. Hence too the villages of *Léka*, *Kastanéa*, and *Marathókambos* (Hotels B, D) may be visited, the last offering a splendid view of the S coast of the island.

The road from Karlovasi to Vathy skirts the coast all the way, offering spectacular views of the rocky coastline. Beyond the huge plane-tree of *Ayios Dhimítrios*, it runs high along the cliffs.—64·5km *Ayios Konstandínos* is a fishing hamlet. Just beyond is a Tourist Pavilion (*Ta Plantanákia*) and a branch road through woods to Manolátes in an area growing cherries and nuts.—69km Turning to *Vourliótes*, a centre of vine-growing, from which may be visited the monastery of *Vrondianí*, the oldest on the island, founded in 1566. Tombs of the 3–

4C AD were discovered here in 1961.—75km *Kokkárion* (Hotels B, C, D, E) has a small harbour. Hence we approach Vathy along the W side of its gulf through *Malagari*, a region of many pine-trees.—85km (52 miles) *Vathy*.

B. Chíos

APPROACHES. BY AIR from Athens at least twice daily in 1 hour, occasional connections with Mykonos, Samos and Lesbos.

STEAMERS daily from Piraeus to Chios direct in 9–11 hours (overnight; very early arrival), continuing to Lesbos (comp. also Rte 74C), and occasionally Salonika.

CHÍOS or **Khíos** (Χίος, famed for its fertility and with a delightful climate, lies 64·5km NW of Samos and 56km S of Lesbos. A strait only 8km across separates it from the peninsula of Karaburnu in Asia Minor. With Psará and some dependent islets it forms a nome of 49,865 inhabitants. Chios, 48km long and with a width varying from 13 to 24km, deserves Homer's epithet Παιπαλόεσσα (craggy). The island is traversed from N to S by a mountain range, culminating in Mt Pelinaion, or Profitis Ilias (1297m), in the N. The volcanic origin of the island is proved by the frequency of earthquakes, some of which have been catastrophic. There are numerous springs but no rivers and the cultivation of the eastern plains is dependent upon irrigation. Chios is the chief source of mastic, a resin of the lentisk tree, once used in making picture-varnish, but now almost entirely in the flavouring of a favourite Levantine liqueur and in the manufacture of chewing-gum. The villages where the tree is 'milked' are called Mastikhokhória. Lemons, oranges, and tangerines are exported; olives and almonds are grown. Chian wine, famous in antiquity, is produced on the NW coast. The Chians of the Classical era were overfond of it, according to Aristophanes, who contrasted them with the sober inhabitants of Keos (comp. Rte 72A).

History. According to some authorities the name Chios is of Phoenician origin and means mastic. That the island was occupied in the Neolithic and Bronze Ages has been proved by excavation (see below). Whoever may have been the earliest settlers, Chios was by tradition colonised by the Ionians. Neleus and Androklos, younger sons of Kodros, King of Athens, after a dispute about the succession to the throne, crossed the Aegean in search of a new home 140 years after the fall of Troy. They settled on the W coast of Asia Minor between the rivers Hermus and Maeander and in Chios and Samos, the two islands off this coastal strip. In historical times we find twelve cities united into the IONIC CONFEDERACY. These cities were, from N to S Phokaea, Erythrae, Klazomenae, on the Gulf of Smyrna (Izmir), the city and island of Chios, Teos, Lebedos, Kolophon, Ephesus, the city and island of Samos, Priene, Myus, and Miletus. Smyrna, which was situated in this district but was of Aeolic origin, was added c 700 BC to the confederacy. Its common sanctuary was the Panionion, on the promontory of Mykale, opposite Samos; here was held the *Panionia*, or great national assembly of the confederacy.

These cities soon attained a high degree of civilised prosperity. In them, as nowhere else in the Greek world save at Athens, the arts and literature throve exuberantly. Out of the lengthy list of artists and authors after Homer (claimed as a native of Chios) we may mention the philosophers Thales of Miletus, one of the Seven Sages, and Pythagoras of Samos, the poet Anacreon of Teos, and the painters Apelles of Kolophon, Zeuxis of Herakleia (Miletus), and Parrhasius of Ephesus. Other natives of Chios were the tragic poet Ion, the historian Theopompos (born c 378 BC), and the sophist Theocritus (4C BC). The chief cities of Ionia had an international reputation, which endured into our era, and they occupied a special place in the early history of Christianity: witness the Acts of the Apostles, the Epistles of St. Paul to the Ephesians, and the Revelation of St. John to the Seven Churches of Asia, two of which were Ephesus and Smyrna.

In the 6C and 5C BC Chios had a celebrated school of sculpture. One of its artisans, Glaucus (fl. 490 BC), invented the art of soldering metals. Chios was the first Greek city to engage in the slave trade, later so profitable in Delos. Towards the end of the 5C the Chians had more domestic slaves than any other Greek state except Sparta.

The Ionians were first conquered by Croesus, king of Lydia (reigned 560–546), and then in 545 by Harpagus, a general of Cyrus, king of Persia. In 499 BC, instigated by the wayward Aristagoras, Governor of Miletus, the Ionians revolted against Persian domination. Aristagoras canvassed help for the rebels from Athens and Eretria. Athens sent twenty ships 'the beginning of mischief both to the Greeks and to the barbarians' (Herod, V, 97). At the Battle of Lade in 494, the Greek fleet was worsted, despite the valour of the Chiot Squadron, and Miletus sacked.

In 477, after the defeat of the Persian invasions, Chios joined the Delian Confederacy and remained a member till 412. Thucydides says (III, 10) that Chios and Lesbos were the only free allies of Athens, the remainder being subordinate in lesser or greater degree. In 412 Chios revolted agains Athens. Though she was joined by other Ionian cities, including Miletus, Teos, and Mytilene, the Athenians defeated the Chiots and ravaged their country. In 378 Chios joined the Second Athenian Confederacy; in 354 she revolted again and her independence was recognised. In 333 the island was captured by a general of Alexander the Great. In the 3C BC Chios joined in alliance with Aetolia. Later, as an ally of Rome, she took part in the war with Antiochus. Her wealth excited the cupidity of the legionaries and the island was pillaged by Verres and by the forces of Mithridates. In 86 BC, after its recapture by Sulla, it regained its independence, which was at first respected by the Roman emperors. After the earthquake of 17 BC Tiberius contributed towards its rehabilitation. Vespasian incorporated it in the province of the Islands.

From now on the history of the island becomes obscure. St. Paul 'sailed over against Chios on his way to Miletus' (Acts XX, 15). A Christian church was established in the island. In the 8C it was ravaged by Saracens. Occupied by Zachas, a pirate chief, it was freed in 1092 by Alexander Comnenus. In 1172 it was captured by Doge Vital Michialli; and in 1204, occupied by Venetians. They were replaced in 1261 by the Genoese. There followed incursions of Franks, Catalans, and Turks. By the middle of the 14C, however, Genoese domination was secure under the aegis of the Giustianini. In 1344 they formed a kind of chartered company, the *Maona*, which administered the island and was responsible for its defence. Chios again became prosperous. As early as 1513 a consul for the English was appointed to look after the affairs of the Levant Company who were engaged in trading cloth for wine. In 1566 the Turks under Piali Pasha captured the island. Thereafter, until 1821, despite several risings, it enjoyed under the Turks a measure of semi-independence. At the beginning of the War of Greek Independence in 1821 the Samians induced the Chians to join them in the revolt. In 1822 the Turks inflicted dreadful vengeance. They massacred 25,000 and enslaved 47,000. Only the mastic towns were spared. In the same year the Greek admiral Kanaris avenged his compatriots by destroying with fireships the Turkish flagship, with its commander Kara Ali; but his was a hollow victory. Those Chiots who had escaped the massacre had fled abroad. The more fortunate of the Chian refugees later made a name for themselves as merchants in London (the Rallis brothers), Liverpool, Manchester, Paris, Marseilles, Leghorn, Palermo, Odessa, Alexandria, and India. Chios never fully recovered from the events of 1822. The earthquake of 1881 did great damage; over 3500 of the islanders perished. In 1912 the island was liberated by the Greek fleet. Many of the best-known shipping families are Chiot.—From Chios came Leo Allatius (1586–1669), scholar and librarian of the Vatican.

Khíos, or *Khóra*, the capital of the island and a seaport with 24,070 inhab., is situated in the middle of the E coast, facing Asia Minor, and is known to the Turks as *Sakiz*. It occupies the site of the ancient city. The town lies within a fertile coastal strip; behind are wooded hills, with the bare mountains of the interior beyond.

Airport, 4km S.—TERMINAL, Prokimaía.

Hotels B, C, D.

Post Office, behind quay, near S end.

Buses from Od. F. de Coúlans to most villages.

Ferry daily to Çeşme in 1 hour (May–October); weekly in winter.

The *Harbour* is smaller than in antiquity, as landward building has encroached upon it. From it we quickly reach *Plateia Vounaki*, the town centre, laid out on the W with gardens containing a statue of Kanaris, by Tombros, and vestiges of a 16C church. On the opposite side of the square is a former Turkish mosque, converted into a small *Byzantine Museum* (at present closed). The collection comprises Byzantine frescoes and ecclesiastical objects; also some post-Byzantine items including a copy of Delacroix's famous canvas of 1824 (original in the Louvre). To the N rises the ruined 14C **Froúrio** which commanded the harbour. There survive a few towers, gates, and case-mates, some bearing the arms of the Giustianini. Within is the old Turkish quarter, established in the 16C over the ruins of Genoese houses, and the marble tomb of Kara Ali.

The *Gymnasion* dates from 1792. The *Library* was founded in 1817 by Adhamantios Koraï (1748–1833), the great scholar, who bequeathed to it his own collections, including works on Egypt given to him by Napoleon. It was further enriched in 1962 by the collections of Dr Philip Argenti, well known in London as scholar and philatelist. Above the library is a small ethnological and costume museum and the picture gallery of the Argenti family.

The *Archaeological Museum* is in the S of the town (Od. Michaélon). It contains finds from excavations on the island, including Emborio, Fana and Ayio Gala (comp. below); also a large collection of inscriptions, including a letter to the people of Chios from Alexander the Great; architectural fragments from the Temple of Apollo of Fana.

Though swamped by modern building, scanty remains of walls and of a theatre may be traced on a hill to the N of the town. Outside the town (N) are the *Tabákika* behind which are remains of an Early Christian basilica, and an imposing *Leper Hospital* founded in the 16C. Also outside the town is another Early Christian basilica, *Ay. Isidhóros*.

EXCURSION TO NEA MONI, 14km, asphalt (bus on Thursday; daily as far as Kariés then 8km mountain walk). The convent of **·Néa Moní** was founded between 1042 and 1054 by the Emp. Constantine IX Monomachos after the discovery by a peasant of the miraculous ikon. The 11C church, which has a marble pavement, was badly damaged in the earthquake of 1881, when the main dome fell, but has been restored. The contemporary *Mosaics* include a Dormition of the Virgin, Raising of Lazarus, a Deposition from the Cross, the only known mosaic example in Greece, etc. There is a small ecclesiastical museum.

TO ANÁVATOS (bus on Thursday morning, returning in afternoon; 1 hour, across mountains to NW). Perched high on a rocky elevation, this evocative Byzantine village now has a tiny population of old people. The grey, tower-like houses are well preserved and the church on the acropolis has been renovated. In 1822 hundreds of the inhabitants were massacred by the Turks.

TO KARDHAMILA, 28km N, asphalt. The road (signposted) quits Plateia Vounaki, passing (right) a bronze *Memorial to the Unknown Sailor* by Apartis.—4km *Vrontádhos*, a town of 4300 inhab., struggles along the coast. On its N outskirts is the Stone of Homer, or *Dhaskalópetra*, an enormous block of dressed stone on a spur, probably a country shrine connected with the cult of Rhea or Cybele.—7km (right; on a promontory) Tomb of Yianni Psychares (1932), son-in-law of Renan.—Beyond (10km) the little bay of *Milínka*, with a spring, the road zigzags up, then descends again to the sea. View across to the five Oinoussai Is. (see below).—16km *Langádha*, a fishing village (simple restaurants).—The road passes the Plain of Delphinion. In antiquity the city of *Delphinion* was a strong point with more than one harbour. The Athenians fortified it in 412. The site of the harbours was explored by the British School in 1954.—28km **Kardhámila** (Καρδάμηλα; Hotel B) is made up of the picturesque upper town (717 inhab.) and *Mármaro* (1131 inhab.), especially noted for the skill and daring of its sailors. Nagós and Vlikhádha, on the shore to the N, are noted for their beaches and tavernas (excellent fish and local fruit).

TO VOLISSOS, 40km NW, asphalt. We leave Khora by the Kardhamila road, but diverge left after a mile. The road climbs round Mt Aipos.—9km *Memorial* to the fallen of 1912.—18·5km *Ayios Isidhoros*. The view opens out over the W coast to Psará.—40km (25 miles) *Volissós* was once the home of the Homeridai, a clan that claimed descent from Homer. The so-called Castle of Belisarius was probably built by the Genoese. Beyond Volissos the road continues W to the *Moní Ayías Markéllas*, named after a local 16C saint.

At the NW of the island, reached from Volissos, is the site of *Ayio Gála*, excavated by the British School in 1938. There are two caves, the upper containing two Byzantine churches and remains of a Neolithic settlement, the lower more Neolithic finds. The caves are shortly to be opened to the public.

TO PIRGI AND MESTA, 35km (22 miles), asphalt to Pirgí. We leave by the inland southern road, passing a turning (right) for *Lithí*, a fishing village on the W coast, birthplace of the philanthropist, Andreas Singros.—8km We skirt (right) *Váviloi* a village with a church frescoed in 1963 by a Hawaiian artist; beyond Vaviloi is *Sklaviá* (2km) with Byzantine and medieval remains, and, farther N, the *Panayía tis Krínis*, a church of 1287.—10km Small col, with two windmills. Ahead (left) on its hill can be seen *Naós tis Sikeliás*, a church of the 13C with characteristic tile ornament.—20km *Armólia*, with turning (left) for Kalamotí (see below). Soon after is a kastro on a hill (right).— 23·5km Road (left) to Emborio (3m; see below).—25km **Pirgí** (Πύργιον), a medieval fortress *Town of 1204 inhab., is the most interesting and attractive place on Khios, with churches and houses having curious sgraffito decoration. Good examples surround the main square, off one side of which is the tiny church of *Ayioi Apóstoloi*, with 12C frescoes. The narrow streets have many round-roofed houses, and arches span the streets as a protection against earthquakes. Today Pirgí is the principal mastic town.—31·5km *Olímboi*; turning (left) for Kato Fana (see below).—35·5km *Mestá*, formerly the principal mastic centre, has ramparts and tortuous streets; some of the women still wear traditional costume.

At **Emborió** on a promontory of the SE coast, an Early Bronze Age settlement was unearthed near and at sea-level, which had four stages of existence and was destroyed in a great fire. It has been equated with *Leukonion*, a rival to Troy. The town survived the fire and in the Middle and Late Bronze Ages and spread up the hill, later crowned by a late-Roman fortress which was ruined c AD 660. A Greek city of the 8–6C BC was discovered on the higher hill (Profitis Ilias), N of the harbour. Traces of fifty houses were revealed, as well as a megaron and a temple of Athena. Nearer the harbour an Archaic temple (6C) was discovered, replaced in the 5C by a Classical building; both were used in the 6C AD as quarries for the building of a Christian basilica. The only visible remains are of the megaron and Temple of Athena on Profitis Ilias (a steep climb), and an Early Christian baptistery S of the harbour. A votive deposit yielded a kylix signed by the potter Nikesermos, now in the Chios museum.—The black pebble beach offers good bathing. Underwater exploration brought to light numerous amphorae not only of Chian origin but also from Attica, Rhodes, Kos, and Thasos, an indication of the extent and importance of the wine trade to Chios.

At *Káto Faná* some ruins of a Temple of Apollo (late 6C) mark the site of ancient *Phanai*, which existed as early as the 9C. Both this site and Emborió were excavated by the British School in 1951–54.

The return to Khóra may be made by branching right at Armolia through *Kalamóti*, then continuing N along the road closer to the coast (asphalt except for 3km). We pass *Ayios Mínas* (c 1590), where in 1822 the Turks massacred 3000 Chiots (ossuary), then cross the Kambos plain, a rich citrus-growing area, with (right) *Kondári*, where the liberators disembarked in 1912. The *Kámbos* region is worth visiting, with its old Genoese houses, one of which, a beautiful mansion in gardens, has become a taverna.

Off the NE coast of Chios, in the strait separating it from Asia Minor, are the five small *Oinoussai Is.* (daily boat from Khora, usually not returning same day; inn; post office; good bathing). The inhabitants (975) are renowned sailors and fishermen and have produced some leading shipowners. the Navtikó Gymnásio is the only nautical boarding school of Greece.—In the bay of Çeşme in 1770 a Roman squadron destroyed a huge Turkish fleet.

About 19km W of the NW coast of Chios lies the island of **Psará** (Ψαρά; Hotel A; Rooms), whose inhabitants won renown in the war of Greek Independence. It is reached by caique three times weekly from Volissos and three times from Chios town. Rocky and mountainous it has an area of 41·5sq. km and a population of 487, all, save a few monks, in one town. At *Arkhontikí* in 1962 Mycenaean tombs of the 13C BC were uncovered together with traces of a settlement. The monastery of the *Panayía* is 10km N of the main village.

After the fall of Constantinople in 1453 the islanders fled to Chios, whence some of their descendants returned to mingle with refugees from Euboea and Thessaly. In the Russo-Turkish war Psarian ships harried the Turks. The Psarians escaped reprisals because the Turkish governor was prevented from landing by bad weather, and after the Treaty of Kutchuk Kainardji achieved a certain protection and prosperity by sailing under the Russian flag. Psara was the birthplace of Konstantinos Kanaris (1785–1877) and many other noted sailors. In the war that began in 1821, Psara (with Hydra and Spetsai) was among the first to revolt, Psara in particular causing the Turks great annoyance. In 1823 the Psarians raided the coast of Asia Minor. In revenge the Turks under Hosref Pasha attacked the island from Mytilene in June 1824. Influx of refugees from Chios, Lesbos, and Smyrna had swollen the population to 20,000. The Turks silenced the batteries of Kanalos on the N side of the island, and stormed the island with 14,000 Janissaries. The islanders blew up their own powder magazines at Ftelia and Palaiokastro, and only 3000 souls escaped the subsequent massacre by the Turks. Ruined houses, a simple white memorial (1956), and six famous lines of Solomos bear witness to the event. The refugees fled to Monemvasia and later founded Néa Psará in Euboea. In 1844 Psara was given special electoral privileges, but the island has never recovered.

C. Lésbos

APPROACHES. BY AIR: from Athens at least three times daily in 45 minutes; less frequent connections with Lemnos, Rhodes, Samos, Salonika.

FERRIES from Piraeus daily overnight via Khios. Occasional connections with Lemnos and Salonika to the N, and Samos and Rhodes to the S. .

Caique service daily in summer round the island; occasionally from Mólivos, via Mitilíni, to *Ayvalik* on the Turkish mainland (c 56km to Pergamon).

LÉSBOS (Λέσβος, in modern pronunciation *Lésvos*; more generally called **Mitilíni** after its capital) is after Crete and Euboea the largest of the Aegean islands, with a maximum length of 70km, a width extending to 45km, and an area of 1632 sq. km. It lies close to Asia Minor, its NE coast facing the Gulf of Edremit (Adramyti), and is 301km from Athens. To the N is Lemnos and to the S Khios. Oval in shape, Lesbos is deeply indented by two arms of the sea: the Gulf of Kalloni in the S and the Gulf of Yera in the SE. The interior is mountainous, fertile with dense olive plantations in the E, bare in the W, where much of its former vegetation has been petrified in a remarkable manner. The climate is temperate, with mild winters and cool summers, especially at Molivos, where the temperature tends to drop heavily at night; in

Mytilene it is usually warmer and sometimes humid. The island is subject to earthquakes and there are numerous hot springs. The population (88,603 inhab.), still diminishing by emigration, is mainly occupied in producing the olives and olive-oil for which the island has long been celebrated; there are over 100 refineries. The vineyards also are productive though less famed than they were in antiquity. The chief manufacture is soap; there are also tanneries and textile mills, and in the W tobacco is cultivated. The roads were built during the Turkish occupation by an English engineer. The island's fauna include the rare star shrew, called locally 'blind mice', and a species of salamander. Notable also are the herds of horses that graze round the Gulf of Kalloni, connected perhaps with the ancient horse-breeding traditions of the Troad. Though there is little of great archaeological importance, the cultural associations, both ancient and modern, and beautiful scenery and beaches of the island are increasingly attracting visitors.

History. Its geographical situation and its many harbours made *Lesbos* a centre for trade and communications from the earliest times and it is only recently that the division between Greece and Turkey has, by severing its connections with Asia Minor, frustrated its natural role as an intermediary between the mainland and the Aegean. Prehistoric remains indicating occupation from c 3300 BC until destruction by fire at the end of the Mycenaean period relate closely to those at ancient Troy. According to Homer, Lesbos, siding with Troy, was invaded by both Achilles and Odysseus. The inhabitants were probably Pelasgian, but in the 10C BC the island and the mainland opposite were colonised by Aeolians under the leadership of the Penthelides, the last of whom was murdered in 659 BC. A struggle developed between Methymna and Mytilene for the leadership of the island, and although Mytilene won and has remained the capital, a tradition of independent resistance was fostered in the W part of the island, which was to recur at critical moments. Lesbos was governed oligarchically with increasing chaos until Pittacus, one of the Seven Sages (589–579), calmed the island and as Aesymnetes (dictator) gave it its period of greatest prosperity and cultural importance. A large fleet and wide mercantile interests (especially in Egypt) were combined with a high standard of education and a comparative freedom for women, two traditions still noticeable today. Terpander, the father of Greek music, and Arion, who invented dithyrambic poetry, had already made Lesbos famous in the 7C, but it was with Alcaeus and Sappho, both aristocrats and enemies of Pittacus, that the island reached its cultural climax. In 527 Lesbos fell under Persian domination and was not freed until 479, when it joined the Athenian League.

In 428 soon after the Peloponnesian War started, Mytilene tried to break away with Spartan help, but the plan was betrayed by Methymna to Athens. The Mytileneans were severely punished (Thuc. III, 36–50). This was the dramatic occasion when a second galley with a reprieve was sent after the first had left with orders for wholesale massacre, and arrived in time. In 405 Lesbos fell to the Spartans and thereafter changed hands frequently, being ruled by Persia, Macedonia, and the Ptolemies until Mithridates occupied it (in 88–79 BC) only to be ousted by the Romans. According to Suetonius, Julius Caesar 'won his spurs' during the Roman storming of Mytilene. It was much favoured by Pompey. St. Paul, on his way back to Jerusalem from Greece (c AD 52), spent a night at Mytilene before passing by Chios and Samos. By the 5C Lesbos had many fine basilicas.

As a Byzantine dominion, the island was used as a place of exile, notably for the Empress Irene in 809. It suffered Saracen invasions in 821, 881, and 1055, which prompted the inhabitants to quit the coast for the mountains. In 1085 it fell to Tzachas, the Seljuk conqueror of Izmir, although Alexius Comnenus retook the island which remained under Byzantine control until 1128, when it passed for a time to the Venetians. In 1204 Lesbos became part of the Latin empire, but fell to the Greeks of Nicaea in 1247. At the end of the 13C it was devastated by Catalan mercenaries and in 1334 Dom. Cataneo made an attempt on it. In 1354 it was given to Francesco Gattelusio, a Genoese adventurer who had helped John Paleologus regain the Byzantine throne, as a dowry for John's sister Maria, who married Francesco; the island then enjoyed a century's untroubled prosperity under the Gattelusi who established an important trading principality in the N

Aegean. Lesbos fell to the Turks in 1462 and, despite attempts to free it by Orsano Giustiniano in 1464, by Pesaro in 1499, and by a Franco-Rhodian fleet in 1501, remained under Turkish domination till 1912, though enjoying considerable privileges and prosperity in the 19C (despite a revolt in 1821). Large numbers of refugees from Asia Minor were absorbed after 1912. In 1941–44 the island was occupied by German forces.

The chief town, near the SE corner of the island, is **Mytilene** (Μυτιλήνη), pronounced *Mitilíni*, capital of the nome of Lesbos, which includes the islands of Lemnos and Ayios Evstratios. It is the seat of a metropolitan. The modern town (24,115 inhab.) is spread over the slopes overlooking the harbour and the isthmus that joins to the mainland the wooded promontory on which the kastro stands. Still retaining much of its Levantine flavour, Mytilene is a bustling entrepôt port without particular interest and need not long detain the visitor from an exploration of the island.

Airport, 10km S of the town.—TERMINAL, Kavétsou 44.

Hotels, A, B, C, E, F/A.

Post and Telegraph Offices in town.

Market Buses from near S quay (once daily to most villages).

In antiquity the castle hill, with the Classical town, was separated from the mainland by a channel joining the N and S ports. Later the city overflowed from the island and the channel was crossed by marble bridges, one of which was found on the main N–S street in recent salvage work. According to Vitruvius the new town was built on the Hippodamian (grid) plan, a fact he deplored since the streets caught the full blast of the N and S winds. Modern work in the town has yet to confirm this. Mytilene was a favourite place with the Julio-Claudian emperors and more dedications to them have been found than in any other Greek imperial city.

The ancient S port has become the main *Harbour* with the boat agencies distributed along the N and E quay, the hotels, restaurants, cafés, and town theatre on the W quay, with the main shopping street or Agora running parallel behind to the N harbour. An old harbour master's office has been turned into a folk museum at the N end. By the Italianate church of Ayios Therapón is a fine new *Byzantine museum* housing a good collection of well displayed icons.

There is a new museum under construction on the road up to the castle. Beyond the old museum at the foot of the pines planted in the First World War is an E.O.T. beach. One can now drive around the edge of the peninsula to the N harbour whose ancient remains are visible under water. In this *Epáno Skála* area are visible here and there through salvage excavations various ancient buildings, including a fine archaic apsidal structure behind the mental hospital and some Roman houses (now being excavated by the Canadian Institute) in front.

The **Kastro**, which affords a fine view over the town and across to Turkey, was constructed (according to a Latin inscription above the W gate) by the Gattelusi in 1374 on the site of a Byzantine castle. The Turks added towers for artillery and outer walls and a dry moat, as well as fortifications running down to the N harbour. They also built a medresse, or theological college, which is still well preserved inside the upper bailey and numerous other structures, now in ruins, inside the castle. Excavations in the upper bailey in 1985 revealed a Hellenistic altar and nearly a thousand votive terracotta figurines.

The main entrance is on the S side through an inner and outer gate, whence we pass through the upper bailey to the Gattelusi innermost stronghold, a keep-like arrangement of high walls and massive towers originally surrounded by a dry ditch. Built into the gate tower are the arms of the Gattelusi with the Paleologue eagle, scales and the monogram of the imperial family (other such heraldic devices are to be seen throughout the castle) as well as reused Roman funerary reliefs of gladiators and wild beast fighters. In the SE corner of the upper bailey are extensive crypts.

The ancient *Theatre* lies on the side of a hill at the W edge of town amid pine trees (clearly visible some 2km from the Kastro). Excavations have revealed at various times this century the orchestra, the stage and some seating as well as clearing the collapsed vomitoria. Some restoration in 1968 stabilised the theatre in its Roman form, when it had been converted for gladiatorial combat and wild beast fights by building a high wall around the orchestra. The Roman general Pompey is said to have used the theatre at Mytilene as his model for the first stone-built theatre in Rome in 55 BC although the two structures in no way resemble each other.

To the N of the theatre above Ayia Kyriaki cemetery are remains of the city *Walls* in polygonal masonry of the 5C BC, which ran from the N breakwater of the N port (Maloeis) to the S end of the S port, encompassing all the theatre hill. Lower down was the site of a late-Roman *Villa*, where were found the Khorafa mosaics (4C), depicting scenes from the comedies of Menander.

To the S of Mytilene a road runs along the coastal plain.—At (4km) *Vareiá* a track leads inland to *Akrotíri* (1·5km), where there is a museum of paintings by Theophilos and the Teriade Gallery of Modern Art. Just to the S of (6km) *Neápolis* are remains of the early-Christian basilica of Argala. Beyond the airport and (10km) *Krátigos* the road, no longer asphalted, continues round Cape Argilios at the SE corner of the island. At 20km a lane branches left to Cape Ermouyenis (1km) at the entrance to the gulf of Yera (chapel, café, and beach); keeping right, we reach (22km) the site of the Early Christian basilica of Loutra with a mosaic—25km *Loutrá* is an old thermal station. Hence an asphalt road returns to Mytilene (8·5km) over a saddle of Mt Amali, affording superb views both E and W, or (if we keep left) another descends to Skála Loutrón and Koundhouroudhiá on an inlet of the gulf of Yera, across which a regular passenger ferry plies to Pérama (see below).—For the N outskirts of Mytilene, see below.

TO YERA AND PLOMARI, 41km (25½ miles). The island's (asphalted) main road runs W from Mytilene and crosses a low ridge. Soon after reaching the shore of the Gulf of Yera we pass the hot springs of (9km) *Thérmai Yéras* (below the road, left, down a short unsignposted track). About 1·5km farther on Pelasgic walls can be found on a steep hill.— At 12km we turn off to the left through a region thickly populated in antiquity. Soon after a river bridge and before the big olive refinery at (14km) *Dípi* (Ντίπι) are some remains of an ancient harbour (partly submerged).—Near (15km) *Káto Trítos* (1km right) are ruins of ancient houses. We cross a ridge and descend to (23km) *Palaiókipos*, with an underground church (Taxiárkhon).—From (25km) *Pappádhos* (Hotel E) a road leads (right; 1·5km) to *Mesagró* and the remains of the medieval Castle of Yera. At the far end of Pappadhos are turnings to Pérama (1·5km) and to Skópelos (1km right).

Pérama, with a tannery and oil refineries, stands on the Gulf of Yera, near the site of ancient *Hiera*, said by Pliny to have been destoyed by earthquake. *Skópelos* (2107 inhab.) has catacombs (Lagoúmis tis Ayías Magdhalínis) and a Turkish fountain.

Our road winds across the E shoulder of Mt Olympos, then descends through a narrow valley to Ayios Isidoros on the shore.—41km **Plomári** (Πλωμάρι; Hotel C), a centre (3503 inhab.) created as *Bilmar* in the 19C when the inland villagers returned to the S coast, is now the second town in size of the island, famed for its ouzo, with a small port. Hence a poor road leads N to *Megalokhóri* (8·5km) and through chestnut forests round the slopes of Olympos to Ayiassos (see below).

TO AYIASSOS AND POLIKHNITOS, 45km (28 miles). We follow the main road W (see above), pass the turn to Plomári, then after another mile turn left.—Just beyond (15km) *Keramía*, turning (left; 1·5km) for *Ippeion* (ruins of ancient houses near by).—22km Fork left for Ayiassos (4km).

Ayiassós (Αγιασός; Hotel B), a shaded and well-watered hill-town of 3294 inhab., stands on a by-road under Mt Olympos (966m). It is noted for weaving and pottery. The monastery of the *Koimíseos tis Theotókou*, of Byzantine foundation, has a good collection of ikons and a big festival on 14–15 Aug. On *Kastelli*, a pine-clad hill to the NW are strong walls of a medieval castle. The remains of *Penthile*, 4km S on the Plomari road, now ploughed out, are fabled to date from the Aeolic migration.

The major road continues W through beautiful pine woods with views of Mt Olympos to (40km) *Vasiliká*, supposed place of exile of the Empress Irene.—43km *Lisvórion* has thermal springs.—45km *Polikhnítos* (Πολυχνίτος; Hotel E), a little town (3342 inhab.) with hot saline springs. A road goes through the town W to *Skála Polikhnítou* and the salt flats on the Gulf of Kalloni; another road (left) goes S to *Vríssa* (5km; Hotel E), with a Genoese tower near by, and down to *Vaterá* (8km), a long beach with cafés ending to the W in Cape Phokas, site of a Temple of Dionysos and probably of the ancient city of *Brisa*, earlier known as *Lyrnessos*.

FROM MYTILENE TO ·MANDAMADHOS (and Molivos), 37·5km (23 miles). Coast road asphalted to Makriyialos Bay, then unsurfaced inland. The road runs NW.—At (4km) *Koúrtzes* the hot baths (Thermakiás) date from Roman times. About 1km farther on a road branches (left) to *Mória* (1·5km), a village, W of which stand several impressive arches of a Roman aqueduct that brought water to Mytilene.—8km *Pámfilla*. We cross the base of a small promontory.— 10km *Pirgoi Thermís*, 17C Turkish towers, just beyond which a track leads (left) to the *Panayía Tourlotí*, a Byzantine church of the 15C or earlier.—12·5km **Loutrá Thermís** (Hotels B, E, on the sea). We arrive opposite the *Sarlitza Hotel* (E), immediately left of the entrance to which are the baths. The therapeutic qualities of the hot saline and chalybeate springs (49°C) were recommended by Claudius Galen. By the modern spring is the site of an ancient temple to Artemis and an adjoining complex of baths.

The prehistoric site of **Thermi**, to the E of the road, was excavated in 1929–33 by the British School under Miss Winifred Lamb. It was first occupied at the beginning of the Bronze Age (c 2750 BC) evidently by colonists from the Troad since there is a close resemblance between the black pottery found here and that of Troy I. Cycladic influences then began to outweigh those from Asia Minor and c 2000 BC the city was depopulated, despite the construction of considerable fortifications. The site was reoccupied c 1400 until its destruction by fire some 200 years later (by Greek armies in the Trojan War?).

Beyond (16·5km) *Mistegná*, where are traces of ancient *Aigeiros*, a by-road ascends (left) to *Néai Kidhoníai* with a ruined medieval castle.—25km *Vatíka* (cafés) has a good beach.—32km *Aspropótamos* lies to the right of the road, on the Bay of Makriyialos. We turn inland to (37km) *Mandamádhos* (Hotel E) a village (1395 inhab.) set amid low hills, where the church of the Taxiárkhon, 800m N, possesses a remarkable black ikon of St. Michael, carved in wood and smelling of spring flowers. At a festival soon after Easter bulls are sacrificed and eaten, a rite suggestive of a pagan origin (comp. below).

The dirt road continues to (43km) *Kápi*, where it divides to pass either side of Mt Lepedimnos (969m). To the S a passable road leads via (52km) *Ipsilométopo*, where (30 minutes S) an Early Christian basilica of c 550, with columns, mosaic, and tombs, was excavated in 1925 (Greek Archaeological Service), to (55·5km) *Stipsi* (Στύψη) and then joins the main Kalloni-Petra road (comp. below).—On the N road is (45km) *Klió*, whence a track leads down to the Gulf of Tsonia (good beach; cafés); a wooded hill in this area bears remains of a fort, perhaps the historic castle of *Ayios Theódhoros*, where Giustiniano encountered the Turks in 1464. A very difficult road continues W of *Klió* to (49km) *Sikamiá*, the beautiful little port of which (reached by track; 4km right) is known locally as 'Little Egypt' because of its warmth in winter.—52km *Argennós*.—62km (38½ miles) *Mólivos* (comp. below).

FROM MYTILENE TO KALLONI AND MOLIVOS, 62km (38½ miles), by the main (asphalt) road. To the Plomari and Ayiassos turns, see above. Keeping to the right we cross pine-wooded hills.—30km Kakadhélli bridge, N of which, at a locality called *Mésa*, are remains of an Ionic pseudo-dipteral temple of Aphrodite (8 by 14 columns).—We reach the *Gulf of Kalloni* at (33km) the turning (left; 3km) for ancient *Pyrra*, or Pyrrha, set in a little valley. The remains of an earlier Pyrra (destroyed by earthquake c 231 BC) are believed to have been located some 8km SW beneath the gulf. Near the first site has been excavated the Early Christian basilica of 'Akhladeris'. The by-road continues to *Vasiliká* on the Ayiassos-Polikhnitos road—The main Kalloni road now skirts salt-flats.—36km Turning (right; asphalted) to Ayía Paraskeví.

About 1km up this turning some vestiges of ancient *Gerna* are marked by a chapel.—3km *Ayía Paraskeví*, a large village (2470 inhab.) is noted for its festival of St. Charalambos soon after Easter. A bull sacrifice is followed by an equestrian parade and races.

There are many attractive excursions in the district. About 45 minutes E is the Early Christian basilica of *Khalinádhos*, built in the 6C on the Syriac plan; columns and capitals have been restored to place and other columns have been observed in a chapel on the hill of Tsikniá overlooking the Kalloni-Molivos road. About the same distance NW on the road to Stipsi is the *Packhorse Bridge*, built by the Gattelusi, with a fine arch across the two affluents of the Tsiknias; 5km W of Ayia Paraskevi on a track which leads to the main Kalloni-Petra road, near *Klopédhi*, ruins of two archaic temples, one to Apollo Napaios, yielded numerous Aeolian capitals of the 6C BC now in the Archaeological museum at Mytilene.

We cross the Tsikniás.—39·5km *Arísvi*; vestiges of ancient *Arisbe*, ruined by earthquake in 321 BC, can be reached by track to the right; on its acropolis are remains of the Byzantine castle of Kalloni, rebuilt by the Turks but abandoned in 1757.—40km **Kalloní** (Καλλόνη; Hotel; F/A; 1553 inhab.) stands at an important crossroads. Its *Skala*, 2km S on the gulf, is the centre of the sardine-fishing and a good red wine is also locally produced.

We turn N, leaving the Antissa road (see below), and shortly pass the track to (15 minutes, left) the Byzantine *Moní Myrsiniótissas*, with the tomb of Bp. Ignatius (d. 1568); the nuns do embroidery. We climb out of the Plain of Kalloni, meet at 49km the road from Stipsi (comp. above) and, topping a rise, descend to **Pétra** (Hotel C) on the NW coast. It is notable for the church of the *Panayía Glykofiloússa* (1747) built on top of a high rock near the fine beach. The 16C church of *Ayios Nikólaos* is frescoed; festival 15 Aug. The road meets the shore at *Khiliopigádha*, supposedly the landfall of Achilles.

62km (38½ miles) **Mólivos** (Hotels A, B; *Rest. Kokhili, Neon*; tourist office by the bus stop) has officially resumed its ancient name **Methymna** (Μέθυμνα), pronounced Míthimna, a word of pre-Greek derivation. Picturesque tower-houses face S over a small fishing harbour and a long beach. On a steep hill above the maze of narrow stepped streets, a Genoese *Castle* of the Gattelusi dominates the town and commands a fine view N across the strait to Cape Baba in Turkey. Remains of polygonal walls (8C BC), of an Archaic temple, and of a Roman aqueduct are visible.

Methymna, the second city of Lesbos, was the birthplace of the poet Arion (fl. 625 BC) and the historian Hellanicus (c 496–411 BC). The celebrated Lesbian wine grew in the neighbourhood. The city refused to join the great Lesbian revolt (428 BC); in 406 it was sacked by the Spartans.

Along the coast, 3km E, is *Eftaloús*, with radioactive springs and good bathing. From this his native village Kleanthes Michaelides, the 19C short-story writer who died in Hull, took his pen name Argyris Eftaliotis.

THE W PART OF THE ISLAND is best approached from Kalloni (see above). We bear left outside Kalloni.—5km The monastery of *Leimónos* (left), built in 1523 by St. Ignatius, metropolitan of Methymna, has a museum and library with 450 MSS, including an 8C evangelistery; festival 14 Oct. On 'Tyrannídha' hill (690m), to the right of the road, took place the Turkish last stand in 1912 (memorial). The terrain is rough and volcanic. As we climb there are fine retrospective views over the Gulf of Kalloni and its salt pans.—9km Col; we descend above the little plain of *Fília*. The road passes just above (16km) *Skalokhóri* (religious festival on 23 Aug). From here a track leads down to the coast near ancient Antissa (see below). Soon after we see the NW coast.—25km *Vadhoússa*.—30km (right; just below the road) the Byzantine *Perivóli* monastery (1590, restored 1962) has good frescoes of the Second Coming.—32km Turning to *Gavathá* (right) with a fine beach (cafés).—34km *Andissa* (1280 inhab.; Hotel E).

The remains of ancient **Antissa** (comp. above) lie on the coast near a ruined Genoese castle. The ancient acropolis was excavated by the British School in 1931; its life extended from the Bronze Age until the Romans destroyed it for harbouring the Macedonian admiral Antinora in 168 BC.

Beyond modern Antissa the road divides. The left branch turns S to Eressos (see below). The right branch continues W, passing (40km) a stepped pathway (left) up to the Ipsilon monastery on Mt Ordimnos (view). Just beyond is a track (left) signposted to the Petrified Forest (comp. below).—52km *Sígri* (Σίγρι; Hotel B; Village G.H.), lies at the W end of the island. The red-roofed village has a small Turkish castle of 1757 on a low rocky promontory and a fine beach. The region of Sigri is famous for the *Petrified Forest* (Απολιθομένο Δάσος), well seen on the rough track that leads SE to Eressos. This unique phenomenon was caused by various trees (mainly conifers and sequoia) being buried in volcanic ash (when is not certain) and then petrified by the action of hot waters containing silicic acid and iron pyrites.

49km **Eressós** (Ερεσός), known to the Turks as *Herse*, has 1392 inhab. and a local archaeological museum with sculpture and mosaics. The modern inhabitants, as in many other villages, migrate down to the coastal plain in summer, where (3km S) *Skála Eressoú* (Hotel C) occupies the site of *Ancient Eressos*, birthplace of Sappho and of the philosopher Theophrastos (d. 287 BC). The village lies at the E end of a long beach underneath a rocky acropolis (Vigla) on the E side of which are to be seen the remains of a Byzantine-Genoese castle, some Roman cisterns, and a fine example of Archaic polygonal walling. In the village are the ruins of a large 5C basilica of St. Andrew with mosaics; along the beach by the mouth of the Khalandras, remains of a similar basilica of Aphendélli (also 5C) in the Syriac style.

To the SE of Lesbos, near the Asiatic shore, are the three islets of *Arginusae*, off which in 406 BC the Athenians won a naval victory over the Lacedaemonians. The Spartan admiral Kallikratidas was killed and 70 of his ships sunk or captured. The Athenians lost 25 ships and were prevented by the weather from rescuing the crews. For this omission eight of the Athenian commanders in the battle were recalled to Athens, tried, and six of them executed. This drastic action was a major factor in the Athenian annihilation at Aegospotami.

IX THE DODECANESE

The **DODECANESE** (Δωδεκάνησα; 'Twelve Islands') are politically a group of islands, lying in the SE Aegean, off the coast of Asia Minor, of which they are geographically a part. Their name is a misnomer, for 14 islands have independent local government status and a few of their dependent islets are inhabited. The nome is divided into four eparchies: that of Kalymnos includes also Patmos, Lipsos, Leros, and Astypalaia; that of Karpathos includes Kasos; that of Kos includes Nisiros; and that of Rhodes includes Telos, Syme, Chalki, and Megisti, the last lying some way to the E of Rhodes. They are strictly the SE continuation of the Eastern Sporades, and are sometimes rather confusingly called Southern Sporades. Their total population is about 145,000.

The somewhat misleading term Dodecanese for this group is of relatively recent date. It came into use in 1908, when 12 'privileged' islands of the Eastern Aegean, excluding Rhodes, Kos, and Lipsos, but including an intruder, Ikaria (see Rte 74), united in protest against the deprivation by Turkey of the special privileges that they had enjoyed since the 16C under Suleiman the Magnificent (1495–1566). In the course of years the term has come to include the island of Rhodes and other islands not on the list of 1908: so much so that Rhodes is now regarded as the chief of the Dodecanese and its city is their capital.

During the Italo-Turkish war of 1911–12 the islands were seized by

Italy and were retained by her as a pledge for the fulfilment of the first Treaty of Lausanne (1912). After the First World War the Treaty of Sévres (1920) gave the islands to Italy but, by an agreement between Italy and Greece, they were all to be passed on to Greece. This agreement was repudiated by Italy after the disastrous Greek campaign of 1922. The second Treaty of Lausanne (1923) gave the Dodecanese to Italy. In 1944–45 the islands were occupied as opportunity occurred and put under British Military Administration. On 7 March 1947 they were officially united to Greece. By far the largest of the islands is Rhodes.

Approaches. By Air from Athens to *Rhodes*, 3–5 times daily in 55 minutes; also in summer from Herakleion daily. To *Kos* daily in 50 minutes.—Rhodes and Kos are also served in summer by direct flights (mainly charter) from some European countries.—For *other connections*, see under Rhodes and Kos.

By Sea. From Piraeus the departure is usually made in the afternoon, and the voyage takes 19–27 hours according to route and ports of call. There are c 10 services weekly. They may be divided into those taking the long S route (Rte 75B), twice weekly, calling at either Ios or Folegandros, Thira, Ayios Nikolaos and Siteia in Crete, *Kásos*, *Kárpathos*, and *Khalkí*; and those which take the N route (Rte 75A). These in general call at Mykonos or *Pátmos* (sometimes both), *Léros*, *Kálymnos*, and *Kos* (also, infrequently, at *Nísyros*, *Tílos*, and *Sými*). One service weekly substitutes for Patmos and Leros *Amorgós* and *Astipálaia*. Many of the services carry cars.

From Salonika a steamer does a weekly round via the Eastern Sporades and Ikaria to Patmos, Leros, Kalymnos, Kos, and Rhodes and return.

A local steamer (once weekly) connects all the W Dodecanese in a round voyage from Rhodes.—Kastellorizo, see Rte 76.

The Dodecanese enjoy special exemptions from customs duties and returning visitors must clear customs before leaving even for destinations in Greece.

75 From Piraeus to Rhodes

A. The Northern Route

STEAMERS from Piraeus, see above; also some other services; small steamer occasionally from Naxos.

The alternative route, via the Cyclades, calls at Amorgós and Astipálaia.

AMORGÓS (Αμοργός), the most easterly of the Cyclades, and part of the eparchy of Thira, is a narrow island, 18km long, extending from SW to NE, with 1722 inhabitants. It has three mountain peaks: Krikelas (780m) in the NE, Profitis Ilias (735m) in the centre, and Korax (576m) in the SW. Krikelas lost its forest in 1835 in a fire that lasted three weeks. The cliffs on the S coast are scenically magnificent. In antiquity there were three cities, Aigiale, Minoa, and Arkesine, all situated on the N coast. Amorgos was the home of Semonides (fl. 664 BC), who came here from Samos. The local waters were the scene of the decisive defeat of the Athenian fleet in the Lamian War, from which Athenian naval power never recovered.

The landing-place is *Katápola* (Rooms), on the W coast, about the middle of the island. On a hill above it are the considerable remains of *Minoa*, including a gymnasium, a stadium, and a temple of Apollo, excavated by the French School in 1888. Renewed excavations in the last few years (Prof. L. Marangou) have considerably added to knowledge of the site, discoveries including a Hellenistic distyle temple and, on the summit, a Geometric enclosure wall and traces of prehistoric occupation. A track leads in 50 minutes to **Amorgós** (361m), or *Khóra* (Rooms), the pleasant little capital. About ½ hour NE of Khora, at the base of a precipitous rock, is the celebrated *Khozoviótissa*, or Convent of the Presentation of the Virgin, founded by the Emp. Alexis Comnenus. It contains an ikon of the Virgin 'miraculously' conveyed hither from Cyprus.

About 3 hours SW of Khora, at *Sto Khorió*, is a well-preserved Hellenic tower, from which a path leads in 1 hour to the scanty ruins of *Arkesine*.—If we go N from Khora, we reach in 3 hours (or boat from Katápola) *Aigiáli* (234 inhab.; Hotel C), near which is the church of *Exokhorianí*, incorporating a temple of Athena. Near here was found in 1906 a tablet on which were inscribed 134 verses relating to the laws of Amorgós (now in the Epigraphical Museum in Athens).—At the NE extremity of Amorgós are the ruins of *Aegiale*, best visited by sailing-boat from Katápola. The tombs excavated here have yielded pottery and other objects dating from the Early Cycladic period.

ASTIPÁLAIA (Αστυπάλαια; the accent is impartially placed on any of the last three syllables, and in local dialect the name becomes *Astropaliá*), the westernmost of the Dodecanese, is said to be the only Aegean island without snakes. It lies 40km SE of Amorgos and about the same distance W of Kos. By the Venetians in the Middle Ages and again during the later Italian occupation it was called *Stampália*. The island consists of two peninsulas connected by a long slender isthmus and has a length of 18km. The coastline is much indented and has high cliffs. The hilly interior rises to 506m on the W peninsula and to 335m on the E. The women's traditional costumes are of great variety and elaboration. The long Venetian occupation has left its mark on the dialect and outlook of the inhabitants, who number 1034.

History. The island, which had some importance in antiquity, was called Ichthyoessa from its abundance of fish and the 'Table of the Gods' because of its flowers and its fertility—today not much in evidence. After a Mycenaean period, it received colonists from Epidauros. The most colourful Astipalaian was the strong-man Kleomedes, who killed his opponent Ikkos of Epidauros in a boxing match during the 71st Olympiad and was disqualified. He returned mad with rage and grief to Astipalaia and pulled down the local school about its children's ears, killing them all. The Romans used the island bays in their operations against Aegean pirates. From 1207 to 1522 Astipalaia was ruled by the Venetian family of Quirini, who introduced settlers from Mykonos and Tinos. In 1522 it fell to the Turks who slightly altered its name to Ustrupalia. Except during the Cretan War (1648–68) and during 1821–28, they held it until 1912, when it became the first of the Dodecanese to be occupied by the Italians and the springboard of their expedition to Rhodes.

The port of *Periyialó* (Hotel D), situated on the W side of the Bay of Maltesana, virtually forms one commune with the island capital **Kastéllo** (80m), named after its Venetian castle. The streets of the town are steep and narrow and many of the houses have wooden balconies. The **Castle**, built by John Quirini in the 13C, has its entrance on the W. Over the vaulted entrance, which bears the Quirini arms, is the restored Church of the *Madonna of the Castle*; on the outer wall of the apse the Quirini arms are repeated. On one occasion the defenders of the castle are said to have repelled assailants who were milling round the gate by throwing down on to them beehives full of previously maddened bees. The interior of the castle is a complex of narrow lanes, dilapidated houses and covered passage-ways, among which is another church, *St. George's.*

Of the many attractive seaside hamlets, linked by dirt roads or mule paths, the prettiest is Livádhi, just SW of the town.

The steamers on the more direct services leave Cape Sounion to port, and round the S point of Kea (light-house) close inshore. Kithnos is seen to starboard and Siros, farther on, to port.

PÁTMOS (Πάτμος), where St. John the Divine received his Revelation, is the northernmost of the Dodecanese. Though its area is only 39 sq. km, a most irregular shape gives the island a long coastline with many little bays. Its three sections are joined by two narrow isthmuses, of which that nearest the centre forms the focal point of the island. Here was the ancient city, here is the modern port, Skala, dominated from the S by Patmos Town and its fortified monastic crag. The rocky and volcanic soil is moderately hilly, rising to 270m. The climate is healthy, but the arid soil yields only a small quantity of cereals, vegetables, and wine, not sufficient for the needs of the 2500 inhabitants. Sponge-fishing used to be the main occupation but is now defunct. The water is brackish.

History. *Patmos* receives passing mention by Thucydides, Strabo, and Pliny. The first inhabitants were Mycenaeans, then Dorians, who later received Ionian colonists. The Romans made it a place of exile for political prisoners. Here, in AD 95, during the reign of Domitian, was banished St. John the Divine, by tradition identified with the Apostle John, though the identification has been disputed. For centuries the island was deserted owing to incursions of Saracen pirates. In 1088, the blessed Christodoulos, a Bithynian abbot, obtained permission from Alexis I Comnenus to found a monastery at Patmos in honour of St. John. The island was captured by the Venetians in 1207. In 1461 Pope Pius II took both island and monastery under his protection. The Turks captured Patmos in 1537, and exacted from the monks an annual tribute. In 1669 the island received Venetian refugees from Candia (Crete).

Landing is made at **Skála** (Hotels B, C, D; F/A), the commercial centre (1352 inhab.) of the island, situated in a sheltered bay that opens to the E. The animated Plateia, with arcaded buildings in the Italian colonial style, opens directly from the quay. Near by on the shore is a pleasant church with twin domes. A motor-road (2km; taxis) has all but superseded the ancient paved mule-path (20 minutes) to Patmos Town. On the ascent there are fine *Views of the surrounding islands and rocks. Half-way up are the new buildings of the *Theological College*, founded in 1669 and attended by students from all Greece, and the CONVENT OF THE APOCALYPSE (Μονή της Αποκαλύψεως), a cell of the monastery. Here are three small churches, and the *Cave of St. Anne*, where by tradition St. John dictated the Revelation to his disciple Prochoros.

Pátmos, or *Khóra* (748 inhab.), has pleasant 16–17C houses spread round the foot of the monastery, 152m above the sea. The fortified *Monastery of St. John*, founded in 1088 by the Blessed Christodoulos, has the appearance of a great polygonal castle, with towers and battlements. It is visited by the faithful on 21 May, the saint's day, and celebrates Easter week with some pomp. An excellent illustrated guide is available in English. To the left, as we enter by the fortified gate, is the tomb of Gregory of Kos, Bp of Dhidhimotikon (d. 1693). The *Entrance Court*, built in 1698, is attractive. Its E side forms the exonarthex of the church, which incorporates elements from an earlier chapel and perhaps from a Temple of Artemis. Between the arches hangs a huge wooden simantron.

We enter the CHURCH by the right-hand door, which admits to the

Founder's Chapel; his marble sarcophagus is surmounted by a reliquary covered with repoussé scenes in silver-gilt (1796). We pass into the *Narthex* by a low doorway having an ancient lintel and a medieval door, and thence into the church proper, a Greek cross-in-square. The floor, of grey and white marble, dates back to the foundation. The Ikonostasis (1820) is heavy and ornate, and some of the furniture has inlaid work in a Saracen style. Above the door of the Outer Treasury is an ikon on a gold ground, signed by Emmanuel Tzanes (1674). The 12C *Chapel of the Theotokos*, to the S, contains near-contemporary *Frescoes, brought to light in 1958, when later paintings were stripped away. Behind the altar, the Holy Trinity, represented as three angels being given hospitality by Abraham; below, the Virgin, flanked by the archangels, Michael and Gabriel, wearing Byzantine imperial robes.

Leaving by the S door, we find ourselves in the *Inner Courtyard*, from which opens the *Refectory*, a modified 11C edifice equipped with long stone tables. The walls have remains of late 12C frescoes, executed in two phases. They represent scenes of Christ's Passion, his miracles, an illustration of Psalm 102, etc.—A stair leads up to the *LIBRARY (c 2000 printed books) in which are displayed a selection from the collection of 890 MSS. The greatest treasure, since the 9C Plato codex was removed in 1803 (now in Oxford), is 33 leaves of the *Codex Porphyrius*, comprising most of St. Mark's gospel. The greater part of the book (182 ff) is in Leningrad. It was written in the early 6C on purple vellum, in uncials of silver and the holy names in gold. Important textually also are an 8C Book of Job, with commentaries drawn from 19 scholars; and the Discourses of St. Gregory, written in 941 in Calabria. This is one of the works listed in 1201 in a surviving Catalogue of the Library. Some exquisite illumination in the Byzantine tradition can be seen in various Gospels and Cartularies (12–14C). Also displayed are charters and deeds from the *Monastic Archives* (13,000 documents), including the foundation chrysobul of Alexis Comnenus.

The *TREASURY, the most important monastic collection in Greece outside Mt Athos, contains embroidered stoles (15–18C); ikons, notably a miniature mosaic framed in silver of St. Nicholas (11C) and a celebrated St. Theodore (13C); church furniture, including a handsome chalice of 1679, a superb crozier (1677) with gold relief decoration and pale blue enamel work, ornamented with diamonds; benediction crosses in wooden filigree; pendant model ships (16C) in enamelled silver set with precious stones, worn by the wives of rich ship-owners. The windows command a fine view of Skala and the W roof terrace the finest *Panorama of the greater part of the Aegean.

Some vestiges of *Ancient Patmos* crown the hill *Kastelli* behind Skala to the NW.—Launches depart at frequent intervals in July–Aug for various beaches, of which *Grikou* (Hotels B, D; F/A) lies to the SE; *Kámbos* (taverna) to the NE (25 minutes); and *Lampí*, bright with coloured stones, on the N coast.

Arkoí, to the NE of Patmos and N of Lipsoi, is a dependent islet with under 68 inhabitants.

Lípsoi (Λείψοι), situated E of Patmos and N of Leros and surrounded by numerous islets, is one of the smallest of the Dodecanese with an area of 15·5 sq. km. Its outline is irregular and indented, especially on the SE coast, in which is the little harbour. The only centre of population is the village (574 inhab.) of *Lipsoi* (Hotel D) above the harbour. A little food is produced; fishing has some importance.

LÉROS (Λέρος), like Patmos, consists of three peninsulas joined by two isthmuses, its irregular shape being caused by deep indentations of the sea. The largest of these, affording safe anchorage, are the Bay of Alinda on the E coast, on which is the island capital, and the bays of Gourna and Porto Lago, on the W coast. The island is well wooded and its hills accessible by Italian military roads. The fertile valleys in the centre yield olives, figs, carobs, tobacco, fruit, and wine.—The airport (office in Platanos) has a daily service to Athens, less frequently to Kos.

History. Leros and Kalymnos are believed to have been the Kalydnian Isles mentioned by Homer. Leros is said to have been colonised by Miletus. The inhabitants had a reputation for being unprincipled. The island was famed for its honey and for a Temple of Artemis, associated with the story of Meleager and his sisters. Leros shared the medieval history of its neighbours. In 1916 the Royal Navy set up a base at Porto Lago, which was greatly developed by the Italians after 1923. Here on 3 Feb 1926 Adm. de Pinedo ended his pioneer flight from Australia. In the Second World War British forces temporarily occupied Leros. In more recent times of political stress it has known internee camps.

Island Customs. During the Carnival men and women compose satirical verses which children, in the garb of monks, recite at parties given in houses where a marriage has taken place during the previous year. This custom seems to derive from the ceremonies in honour of Dionysos at Eleusis. A peculiarity of local law is that all real property passes in the female line, with the result that virtually all the houses and landed property belong to women.

The ship enters Porto Lago bay (comp. above) and landing is made at **Lakkí** (Hotels B, C, D, E), with 2469 inhabitants and a prominent mental asylum. An asphalt road mounts to (3km) **Plátanos** which, with *Ayía Marína* (Hotels, B, C, E), its other port on the Bay of Alinda, 3km NE, forms the capital, with 2462 inhabitants. The houses rise on the hillside below the *Kastro*, which is situated on a height inaccessible from the E and precipitous on the other sides. The castle, originally Byzantine, was rebuilt by the Knights of St. John. A cross on the hillside marks the *British Military Cemetery*, where lie the casualties of the battle in November 1943.

From Platanos a road leads round the bay to the summer resort of *Alinda*, while a mule path descends to *Pantéli*, a beach 500m SE of the castle.

Leros is surrounded by numerous islets. About 19km E is *Pharmáko*, or Pharmakousa, where Julius Caesar, returning from his notorious sojourn in Bithynia, was captured by pirates and detained for 38 days until his ransom arrived; he later caught and crucified his captors.

KÁLYMNOS (Κάλυμνος) lies immediately S of Leros and W of the Asiatic peninsula of Bodrum (Halicarnassus). The island is approximately rectangular in shape, with a peninsular extension to the NW separated by a channel of only 2·5km from Leros. Its greatest length is 21km and its width 13km, giving an area of 109 sq. km. The surface is mountainous and barren, except in the valleys. A range extending along the peninsula joins the northernmost of three transverse ranges in the main part of the island. The central range is the highest, with Mt Profitis Ilias (686m); it is continued on the W by the hills of the islet of Telendos. These three ranges are separated by two fertile valleys, that of Vathy between the N and the central range, and that of Pothia and Brosta between the central and S range. The coastline is much indented, with precipitous cliffs and small coves. The population of 14,457 is mainly concentrated in the island capital *Pothiá*. The chief industry now as in ancient times is the fishing and marketing of sponges. The produce includes figs, oranges, olives, grapes, and cereals. Kalymnos was famed for its honey, which rivalled that of Attica.

History. Kalymnos is believed to be one of the Kalydnian Isles of the Homeric

Catalogue of Ships, the other being Leros. The earliest inhabitants were Mycenaeans; later the island was colonised by Dorians from the Argolid. In antiquity its fortunes tended to follow those of Kos, and in the Middle Ages it underwent the usual Venetian, Rhodian, and Turkish periods. It was most actively opposed to Italian rule, using blue and white paint everywhere to simulate the Greek national colours, and in 1935 rioting against an attempt to suppress Greek in schools and to set up an autocephalous Church of the Dodecanese. In the Second World War most of the Kalymnians took refuge in the Asiatic peninsula opposite the island, whence they dispersed to various places, including Gaza in Israel.

The capital **Pothiá** (Hotels B, C) or *Kálymnos*, is also the chief port and the industrial and commercial centre of the island, a town (10,118 inhab.) comparable in size with Ermoupolis in Syra. It is situated at the head of a bay of the S coast. Lively in autumn and winter when the sponge-divers are home, it is less gay after Easter-tide when they depart *en masse* for the North African coast. To the SE of the town, which holds little interest for visitors, is a small thermal establishment. There is a small *Archaeological Museum*.

A motor-boat may be taken in 35 minutes to the *Cave of Kefalás*, near the SW promontory of the island. The cave (adm. fee) was explored in 1961 and discovered to have been a sanctuary of Olympian Zeus.

A road (bus; cars for hire at Pothia) leads up the fertile and beautiful valley. Soon after leaving the town, we pass on the left a hill with three disused windmills on its slopes and on its summit a ruined *Castle of the Knights*, with a little church and rock-cut Mycenaean tombs.—3km *Khorió* (2611 inhab.) is the former capital of Kalymnos, built below a *Castle* which served as a refuge in the Middle Ages. Farther on the valley narrows.—Near (4km) *Dhámos* we pass a ruined church, of which only the apse remains, near which are the remains of a Temple of Apollo and a theatre.—The road now bears SW and descends.— 5·5km *Pánormos* (Hotels C, D), on the W coast, and *Mirtées* (Hotels B, C, D), 1·5km farther on, are summer resorts.

To the N, close to the shore, is the islet of **Télendos**, with ancient remains the most important being Roman and Early Christian (baths, basilica), and the ruins of the *Monastery of Ayios Vasíleios*, dominated by a medieval castle. Since the Middle Ages the coastline has receded; for about a mile from the shore the remains of medieval houses can be seen under water.

FROM POTHIA TO VATHY, poor coast-road. Just beyond the entrance to the inlet is seen the mouth of the *Grotto of Daskaleios*, the most considerable of the caves in the island. It is accessible only from the sea and difficult to reach. Immediately inside is a chamber 25m long, from which opens on the right another chamber, at a lower level, with stalactites and stalagmites and a cavity full of brackish water. Here many prehistoric objects were found, ranging from the Neolithic to the Bronze Age.—At the head of the inlet we reach the district of **Vathý**, comprising three villages, *Rhína*, the little port, *Plátanos*, named after a huge plane tree, and *Metókhi*, farther inland. 100m N of the harbour are the remains of an Early Christian basilica, with a small church of *Ayía Iríni* built over the NE corner. At *Ayios Pandeleímon*, to the N of Vathy, is an ancient settlement with an Early Christian basilica (*Palaiopanayía*). There is another basilica 500m to the N.—The VALLEY OF VATHY is the most delectable part of the island, its luxuriant vegetation thriving on the volcanic and well-watered soil. At its mouth are orange and tangerine orchards and occasional olive groves; farther inland are figs and vineyards. The barrenness of the enclosing hills is in sharp contrast to the fertility of the valley. It is rich in antiquities. At Rhina is a rock-hewn throne; near Platanos are cyclopean walls and a little chapel in an enclosure of Hellenic walls.

Between Kalymnos and Kos is the islet of *Pserimós* (10 sq. km), with a monastery and a hundred inhabitants.

The island of **KOS** (Κώς), or *Cos* (20,350 inhab.) is the second most visited of the Dodecanese, though, with an area of 282 sq. km, it is only one-fifth the size of Rhodes. It is a long narrow island, with a length of 45km from NE to SW, and a width varying from 11 to 1·5km, its narrowest part being the isthmus leading to the Peninsula of Kephalos at its SW end. It is situated at the entrance to the deeply indented Gulf of Kos, the Ceramic Gulf of antiquity, between the Asiatic Peninsula of Bodrum (Halicarnassus) on the N, from which it is separated by only 5km, and the Peninsula of Knidos on the S, which is 16km away. A long mountain chain runs near the S of the island from Cape Phoka, at its E end, to the neighbourhood of Pylae, in the centre. Its highest point is Mt Oromedhon or Dhikaios (847m), gently sloping on the N, precipitous on the S. In the NW there is a plateau, whence the ground slopes towards the sea. The Peninsula of Kephalos is moderately hilly, with Mt Latra rising to 428m, the hills sloping down to Cape Krikelos, the southernmost point of the island. The coastline is scarcely indented, and there is only one real harbour, Mandraki, at the city and port of Kos, which is situated at the NE end of the island. The inhabitants are mainly engaged in agriculture. Kos produces an abundance of juicy grapes, as well as fine water melons and oil, cereals, vegetables and tobacco. Among local wines are Glafkos (white) and Apellis (red).

The island is better watered than any other of the Dodecanese. It is especially rich in warm and tepid ferruginous springs celebrated even before the time of Hippocrates, the greatest physician of antiquity, who was born at Kos c 460 BC and is said to have died in 357 at the age of 104. Another native was the poet Philetas, a contemporary of Ptolemy II Philadelphos (285–247 BC). The bucolic poet Theocritus, born at Syracuse c 310 BC, lived for a time in Kos as a disciple of Philetas. His 7th Idyll has a Coan setting. The painter Apelles, whose Aphrodite Anadyomene adorned the Asklepieion, is claimed as a native of Kos, though he may have been born in Ionia at Kolophon or Ephesus. He flourished in the time of Alexander the Great (336–323 BC).

History. The island has had several names. Thucydides and Strabo called it *Kos Meropis*, Pliny *Nymphaea*, and Stephanos of Byzantium *Karis*. In the Middle Ages it was known as *Lango*, perhaps because of its length, and later as *Stanchio*, a corruption of 'stin Ko', whence the Turkish *Istanköy*. Kos was inhabited in Neolithic times, as is proved by discoveries in the Cave of Aspropetro, near Kephalos. It was colonised by Carians and, in the Homeric Age, by Dorians from Epidauros. In the Persian wars it was under the sway of Artemisia, queen of Caria, and so fought on the losing side. Kos was at first a member of the Dorian hexapolis and of little importance. Its city (later remembered as Astypalaia, 'old city') was situated in the SW of the island and was destroyed by the Lacedaemonians in the Peloponnesian War. The new city of Kos was founded in 366 BC and rapidly prospered to become one of the greatest maritime centres of the Aegean. Its sanctuary of Asklepios and school of medicine made it famous all over the ancient world. The city was adorned with a plethora of artistic monuments. Its wines and silks had a great reputation; the light silk dresses called *Coae vestes* were well known to the Romans for their transparency.

Kos was occupied by Alexander the Great in 336 BC, and on his death in 323 passed to the Ptolemies. Ptolemy II Philadelphos was born in the island in 309. Cleopatra is said to have used the island as a store for some of her treasures. Later Kos was allied to Rome before becoming part of the pro-consular Province of Asia. In the Byzantine era Kos was the seat of a bishop and many Early Christian basilicas (5–6C) have been uncovered. In the 11C Kos was ravaged by Saracens. Later it passed to the Genoese, becoming in 1304 a fief of the Zaccharia family. Two years later it was ceded to the Knights of St. John, who did not take possession till 1315. The Knights made it into a strong-point. It was attacked by the Turks in 1457 and 1477, and fell to them, with Rhodes, in 1522. Hadji Ali Haseki, voivode and tyrant of Athens, was finally exiled to Kos and there on 23 Dec 1795 beheaded. In 1912, after nearly four centuries of Turkish domination, it was occupied by the Italians in the course of their war with Turkey. In the Second World War British forces temporarily occupied the island until driven out by the Germans.

The city of **Kos** is situated in a plain at the NE end of the island, just S of the Kos Channel (here at its narrowest; 5km), which separates it from the Anatolian coast. Despite undistinguished modern buildings it is a pleasant town with tidy open streets, resplendent gardens and orchards, and extensive Classical and Roman remains. The climate is somewhat relaxing but there are numerous springs. Of the 11,851 inhabitants, about half are Muslims and most of the remainder of the Orthodox faith. Kos has some importance as a trading port, and has given name in English to a variety of lettuce introduced from its shores.

Airport, 26km W near Andimákhia; daily services to Athens in 50 minutes, to Rhodes in 45 minutes; Leros, occasionally, in 15 minutes; also to Frankfurt, and (by charter) elsewhere. *Terminal* at Leofóros Vasiléos Pávlou 22.

Hotels, A, B, C, D, E; F/A.—**Restaurants** on the waterfront.

Tourist Police. **Police** on Aktí Miaoúli, near Castle.—**Post Office**, Meropídhos/Xánthou.—OTE CENTRE, 8 Víronos.

Bus Station, Kleopátras/Pisándrou.—BICYCLES for hire by the hour.

Admission to *Museum, Castle*, and *Roman House* at standard museum hours; to the *Asklepieion* at standard site hours.

History. There is a settlement of the Minoan and Mycenaean periods beneath the modern town of Kos and a number of Mycenaean tombs have been discovered to the SW as well as Protogeometric and Geometric graves within its walls. The ancient city, founded in 366 BC, had a perimeter of c 4km. Devastated by earthquakes c 5 BC, in AD 142, and again in 469, it was virtually destroyed in 554. The old materials were largely reused in each new rebuilding and later pillaged for the medieval defences. The CITY OF THE KNIGHTS, bounded by an enceinte, erected in 1391–96 to counter the menace of Bayezid, occupied only the agora and harbour quarter of the old city. Vestiges remain opposite the castle, whence the course of the wall may be traced to the SW tower (see below). The Schlegelholz Bastion, adorned with arms of the bailiff and of Grand Master Heredia, survives at the SE corner; within the walls remain three small Byzantine chapels and a house bearing the arms of Bailiff Francesco Sans (1514). Archaeological explorations, begun in 1900 by Rudolf Herzog, were undertaken after 1928 by Luciano Lorenzi of the Italian School, and given impetus by the havoc caused on 23 April 1933 by a severe earthquake. The most important digs were in 1935–43. Many of the mosaics recovered were removed to adorn the castle in Rhodes.

The picturesque harbour of *Mandraki* has the same name as its counterpart in Rhodes. It is well equipped as a yacht station. Opposite the landing-place the former *Palace of the Regent*, by F. di Fausto (1928), houses the Town Hall, Custom House, and Port Offices. We turn left and mount to the terreplein of the castle, now PLATEIA PLATANOU. In the centre grows the so-called *Plane-tree of Hippocrates*, a gigantic tree with a trunk 14m in diameter and branches propped up by antique marble fragments. Inevitably tradition insists that Hippocrates taught under its shade, though it is not more than 500 years old. To the right stands the *Mosque of Gazi Hassan Pasha*, or *of the Loggia*, a three-storeyed building of 1786, entered on the first floor by a graceful staircase with a double portico or loggia. An elegant *Minaret* stands at the corner. Beneath the tree a *Fountain* has for basin an antique sarcophagus. A little grove shades the cemetery.

From the terreplein a stone bridge leads across the outer moat (now a palm-shaded avenue) to the **Castle of the Knights**, the city's principal monument. The fortress has two enceintes, one within the other. We enter by a drawbridge and a gateway in the S curtain wall of the outer enceinte. Above the gate are a Hellenic frieze and the quartered arms of Amboise and the Order.

The original castle, roughly rectangular in plan, was begun in 1450 by the Venetian Fantino Guerini, governor of Kos (1436–53), and completed in 1478 by the Genoese Edoardo de Carmadino (governor 1471–95). After the unsuccessful Turkish assault of 1480, an outer enceinte was begun in 1495 by Grand Master Pierre d'Aubusson and completed in 1514 by G.M. Fabrizio Del Carretto. In its construction Italian architects and craftsmen were employed. Both enceintes incorporate masonry from the Asklepieion and other ancient Greek buildings. There is a deep fosse between the two lines of walls.

A passageway leads to the S terrace, from which a flight of steps gives access to the *Antiquarium*, containing Coan marbles, inscriptions, sculptural fragments, sepulchral monuments, and a number of fine knightly escutcheons carved in marble. One of the inscriptions commemorates the physician Xenophon, who helped to poison the Emp. Claudius (Tacitus, 'Annals', xii, 67, 2).

The heavy cylindrical *Bastion Del Carretto*, at the SW angle of the Outer Enceinte, resembles the bastion of the same name in the walls of Rhodes. The corresponding *North-East Tower*, which projects somewhat, commands a good view over the sea towards Anatolia. The NW tower, or *Tower of Aubusson*, overlooking the harbour, is polygonal. It bears the arms of Aubusson quartered with those of the Order, and an Italian inscription of 1503.

From the terrace we descend a staircase to the left of the Antiquarium and reach a horseshoe ravelin in front of the Inner Enceinte. On its right is the entrance. All four angles of the Inner Enceinte have cylindrical towers, with battlements and embrasures, and appropriate escutcheons. The inner curtain wall is similarly adorned. On the *Inner South-West Tower* are the fleurs-de-lis of France.

We turn S again and enter the partially walled area of the Chora, or city of the Knights (comp. above), excavated since the earthquake of 1933 to show Roman levels of the AGORA AND HARBOUR QUARTER.

The N sector of the excavations lay outside the Hellenistic city walls. From E to W may be distinguished a Hellenistic sanctuary, orientated to the N; next, a *Stoa* (4–3C), of which 8 columns with acanthus capitals have been re-erected. These were recovered from the foundations of the *Harbour Basilica*, built on the remains of the Stoa in the 5C AD. Its ruins lie immediately S of the Mosque of the Loggia. Farther W are scanty but extensive vestiges of the *Sanctuary of the Port Quarter*, probably an Aphrodision. The S sector of the area represents the N extremity of the ancient city proper, which is divided by a broad road running N–S. To the E are insulae of houses and shops. To the W lies the **Agora**, just within the Knights' W gate, which bore through the Middle Ages the name 'Porta tou Forou'. A fine stretch of rusticated ashlar masonry marks its E boundary and some columns have been re-erected.

We quit the site by the gate leading to PLATEIA ELEFTHERIAS, the main square of the town. The **Museum** contains sculpture of the Hellenistic and Roman periods, notably a small Aphrodite and Eros, figures of Diana of Ephesus, and a statue of Hippocrates. Across the square is the 18C *Defterdar Mosque*. Odhos Vas. Pavlou leads to another area of excavations in which are a large *Roman House* (rebuilt by the Italians to protect its many mosaics) and the *Central Baths*. Hence we may turn right to visit the **Odeion**, approached by an avenue of cypresses; of its 14 rows of marble seats, seven are original. The near-by church of *Ayios Ioánnis Pródhromos* is the baptistery of the largest Early Christian church of Kos.

Opposite are the *WESTERN EXCAVATIONS, a huge L-shaped area below the Acropolis, a low hill crowned by a minaret. A section of the *Decumanus Maximus* is exposed with the houses on its N side, many of which retain mosaics (3C AD) and frescoes. The large *House of the Europa Mosaic* is the best preserved, and yielded many complete statues. The *Cardo*, beautifully paved and recalling the streets of Pompeii, leads N. To the left are extensive *Roman Baths*. The calidarium is well preserved; the frigidarium was transformed into a Christian *Basilica* at a later date. The marble immersion font and much of the mosaic door survives of the baptistery, the marble doorway of which has been re-erected. Farther W the colonnade of the *Xystos* of a Hellenistic gymnasium (2C BC) has been restored. To the right of the road, beyond a row of antique taverns, stands the restored *Forica* of the Baths, a sumptuous latrine built round a peristyle court. Beyond, a shelter protects a large mosaic showing gladiatorial scenes.

A flight of steps by the Forica leads up to the Acropolis, whence the picturesque Odhos Apellou, an old street of the Turkish quarter, returns NE. Farther NW are some remains of the *Stadium*, principally the curious aphesis, or starting-gate.

THE PRINCIPAL EXCURSION is to the Asklepieion, 4km by road. We take the Kephalos road and, beyond the town, fork left.—3km *Ghermí*, or Khermetes, a Muslim village, officially *Platánion*. By an avenue of cypresses we approach the **Asklepieíon**, or *Sanctuary of Asklepios*. It occupies the site of a grove sacred to Apollo Kyparessios, mentioned in the 4C, but it was not built until after the death of Hippocrates (357 BC) and dates from the Hellenistic period.

The sanctuary was one of the main seats of the Asklepiadai, supposed descendants of Asklepios, who were a hereditary close order of priests, jealous guardians of the secrets of medicine. The technique of healing differed from that at Epidauros and elsewhere, where cures were effected by suggestion. At Kos, as is revealed by inscriptions, patients underwent positive treatment at the hands of physicians on lines laid down by Hippocrates. Herondas in his fourth mime describes a sacrifice at the Asklepieion. The sanctuary had the right of asylum. It throve in the days of the Ptolemies and later under Nero. The rich court physician Xenophon (see above), on his return to Kos, lavished on the sanctuary the statues he had amassed in Rome. Even in the late-Imperial period great baths were built.

In the 6C AD all was overwhelmed, either by an earthquake or in 554 when Anatolian hordes ravaged the island. The Knights of St. John used the ruins as a quarry. A local antiquary, G.E. Zaraphtis, identified the site; in 1902 the German Herzog began systematic excavation, and the work was completed by the Italians with their customary extensive restoration. An International School of Medicine is planned near by.

We pass (left) remains of *Roman Baths* (1C AD), where the hypocaust and plunge bath are well preserved, and ascend to the LOWER TERRACE of the sanctuary. This was surrounded on three sides by porticoes. On the fourth side was a retaining wall of massive proportions, part of which survives. Near the middle of the wall are a fountain, which still plays, the staircase leading to the Middle Terrace, and several reservoirs fed by conduits from ferruginous and sulphurous springs and drawn upon by invalids taking the cure. Between the reservoirs and the staircase are the remains of a small *Temple*, with the pedestal of a statue of Nero as Asklepios (the inscription records its dedication by the physician Xenophon). On this terrace were probably held the Asklepian Festivals, which, on the evidence of inscriptions, included athletic games and other contests.

ASKLEPIEION (Kos)

0 _____ 40 metres

Temple

Temple

Temple

Altar

Baths

We ascend to the MIDDLE TERRACE. On the right is an Ionic *Temple in Antis*, dating from the late 4C or early 3C BC, and so the oldest temple in the Sanctuary. The capitals, of painted marble, are exceptionally fine; the rest of the building was in white or black marble. In the floor of the cella was a coffer of marble slabs for the reception of votive offerings. The temple was adorned with paintings by Apelles, including the celebrated Aphrodite Anadyomene, removed by Augustus to Rome. Behind the temple is a *Roman House* on a Greek foundation, probably the priest's dwelling. In front of the temple, to the left, is the *Great Altar*, similar to that at Pergamon; it is in the form of the Greek letter Π, with a central staircase. Its ceiling, partly surviving, was coffered; between the columns of the portico were statues of Asklepios, Hygieia, and members of their family, attributed to the sons of Praxiteles. To the left of the altar is a *Roman Temple*, orientated aslant. It is a peripteral Ionic building, with half-fluted columns and a magnificent entablature with floral decoration, part of which remains. In the wall at the end of the terrace is a *Monumental Staircase*, to the left of which is an *Exedra*, with niches for statues.

The UPPER TERRACE occupies the site of the Sacred Wood. On it is the great Doric **Temple of Asklepios**. This is peripteral, with six columns by eleven. It stands on a base of three carved steps, the lowest of which is of black marble. The well-preserved *Pronaos* is in antis; its threshold is a black limestone monolith. In it was installed in the Christian era a chapel of the *Panayía tou Társou*, the altar of which survives. Three sides of the terrace were lined with porticoes, on which houses were later built.

From the Upper Terrace there is a magnificent *View. Below is the town of Kos, with its harbour, surrounded by gardens and orchards. In the distance, across the sea, are the Peninsula of Knidos to the SE, the deeply indented Gulf of Kos to the E, the Promontory of Bodrum (Halicarnassus) to the NE, and the islands of Pserimos and Kalymnos to the NW.

The Asklepieion is situated near the foot of **Mt Oromedon**, the highest peak of which is *Dhikaíos* (847m). The mountain has many springs, one of which, ¾ hour distant, supplies the town of Kos with water by means of an aqueduct. This is the ancient *Vourina*, the Sacred Spring of Theocritus. It is enclosed in a domed building approached by a corridor. Another fountain has the name of *Kokkineró*, or 'Red Water'.

FROM KOS TO KEFALOS, road, 43·5km, traversing the island lengthwise. We leave on the left the turning for the Asklepieion, which we see on our left 1km farther on, with Mt Dhikaíos behind it. To the right, reaching to the sea, extends an agricultural plain. At (9km) *Zipári*, which had an early basilica dedicated to St. Paul (mosaics and early font) a road leads left for *Asfendiou* (3km; 244m), on the slopes of Dhikaíos, where a Byzantine basilica and a small temple of Demeter and Kore were explored by the Italians. Dhikaíos can be ascended in 1 hour.—On the left is the mountain ridge forming the backbone of the island; on the right, over the sea, are the islands of Pserimos and Kalymnos. We pass a ruined Roman aqueduct. From (15km) *Pili* (1816 inhab.) a mule-track leads to **Old Pylai** (4km), a ruined village dominated by a hill (320m) on which are the remains of a concentric Byzantine *Castle*. Within the lowest enceinte is the church of the *Purification of the B.V.M.*, incorporating ancient masonry and decorated with well-preserved 14C frescoes.

From Pilí a winding road descends to *Kardhámaina* (Hotels A, B, C, D, E), on the S coast, where pottery and tomato-juice are made. There are remains of a Hellenistic theatre and of an Early Christian basilica (Ayía Theótis). It has an infrequent caique service to Nisyros.

After passing a large windmill, the road rises to a plateau and begins to descend.—At (25km) **Andimákhia** (128m), a straggling village of 1460 inhab., is the airport of Kos. A track leads left in 3km to the battlemented *Castle of Antimachia* (144m), dating from the time of the Knights. It is triangular in plan and has a drawbridge in front of its only gate, which bears the quartered arms of Amboise and of the Order. Inside are ruins of houses, cisterns, and two churches.

As we proceed, we obtain a view of the curving end of the island, dominated by Mt Latra (428m), and known as the Peninsula of Kephalos. The road, unsurfaced beyond the airport, gradually descends to cross a stream and then rises steeply to a bare plain, where the island contracts into an isthmus only 1·5km across. The road approaches the N coast and then descends to (34km) the shore of the Bay of Kamares, on the S coast. In the bay is the picturesque *St. Nicholas Rock*. The ruins of two Christian basilicas are exposed. The ancient capital city of *Astypalaia* was in the neighbourhood, but its exact location is unknown.—43·5km **Képhalos** (106m; 1976 inhab.; Hotels B, C, D, E) dominates the Bay of Kamares. On a neighbouring height is a ruined *Castle*. About 20 minutes S are the remains of a Hellenistic Doric *Temple* in antis; its stylobate and some column drums remain. About 10 minutes farther are another Temple in antis and a *Theatre*. The rock-hewn *Cave of Aspripetra*, farther SE, has yielded Neolithic objects.

Nísyros (Νίσυρος), a small pentagonal island of 41·5 sq. km, is an extinct volcano, whose hot sulphurous springs have been celebrated since antiquity. The population of 984 souls is divided among four places linked by one road, 8km long. *Mandráki* (650 inhab.), on the N coast, has a ruined castle of the Knights and a subterranean church; its little spa (*Loutrá*) is 1·5km to the E. Farther on is *Páloi*, a fishing hamlet, with more baths. The other villages, *Emboriós*, and *Nikiá* (prettier of the two with an extraordinary view), are on the rim of the central depression, which is 4km across. The central cone, within, rises to 692m.—In summer there are daily excursions from Kos (boat 2¾ hours and bus).

Tílos (Τήλος), lying between Nisyros on the N and Khalki on the S, is accurately described by Strabo as long, high, and narrow. The Italians, reviving a medieval name of uncertain origin, called it *Piscopi*. Apart from a coastal plain in the N, the interior is hilly, rising in the NW to 654m. Most of the 301 inhabitants are engaged in agriculture. The women wear traditional costume. The rugged coastline is indented with bays. *Livádhia*, the island landing-place, on a bay of the NE coast, is connected with *Mikró Khorió*, a hamlet just below a central saddle, by a dirt road c 1·5km long. The road continues N to (7km) *Megálo Khorió*, which through the ages has been the island capital. There are remains of Archaic-Classical walls; the church of the Archangel Michael is on the foundations of a Greek temple of the Acropolis; and the whole site is crowned by a ruined castle of the Knights built of ancient masonry and incorporating a Classical gateway.

Syme (Σύμη), or *Sími*, is situated at the mouth of the Doridis Gulf, between two Asiatic peninsulas—that of Knidos on the N and that of Dorakis on the S. It is only 10km from the latter, which was called Cynossema Promontory in antiquity. The island is 24km N of Rhodes, across the Strait of Marmara, and there is a daily connection. Of irregular shape, it has an area of 67 sq. km. The arid interior is hilly, but the once deficient water supply is now augmented by a solar still. The coasts have high cliffs and are difficult of access, but there are inlets in which small ships can find shelter. Except in the fertile valley of Pedhi and Panaidhakia and on the plateaux, the soil is allergic to cultivation. The climate is mild except in the height of summer, when the temperature may exceed 38°C. The population (23,000 in 1912; 6300 in 1937), much reduced by emigration, is 2273, all but a few in the capital. Small quantities of cereals, wine, olives, honey and tobacco are produced. The main industry is sponge-fishing. Symian divers are the ablest in the Aegean; they recovered the Ephebos of Antikythera. Their ships pass by inheritance in the male line, houses in the female line with the dowry.

History. The Homeric Catalogue of Ships records a contribution of three vessels from Syme to the Trojan expedition. Later Syme was colonised by the Carians, who abandoned it during a drought. In 411 BC the Lacedaemonians, after a successful engagement off Knidos with an Athenian naval detachment, set up a trophy on Syme. This action led to the revolt of Rhodes from the Athenian Confederacy. The islanders have always been renowned shipbuilders. They built fast skiffs for the Knights of St. John and were employed in the same capacity by the Turks, under whom they enjoyed numerous privileges and extensive estates on the mainland. Much of their timber was used up during the War of

Independence.

The town of **Syme** (Hotels A), in the N of the island, is divided into *Yialós*, on its bay, and *Khorió*, above. Most of the inhabitants live in the upper town, where there is a small *Museum*. On a height above the town is a *Castle of the Knights*, partly built of blocks from the walls of the ancient Acropolis which once surrounded the hill. Over the entrance gate are the arms of Aubusson quartered with those of the Order (1507). Inside the castle are the *Church of the Panayía*, and the remains of a Temple of Athena. Below the houses of Upper Syme is the ancient Greek necropolis.

The *Bay of Emborió*, 2·5km NW of lower Syme, once the island's commercial harbour, is now a summer resort.—In the *Bay of Pédhi*, 2·5km E, is an isolated village normally occupied by farm labourers and fishermen and frequented by summer visitors. In the vicinity are Greek and Roman remains.

The *Monastery of St. Michael Panormítis* (motor-boat in 1¾ hours), is situated on the Bay of Panormitis at the S extremity of the island. It was built in the 18C, and used as a staging camp in 1945 for refugees returning from Turkey. The church has fine frescoes and an ikon of St. Michael. The sanctuary contains offerings from Symians all over the world. The chief festival, on 7–9 Nov, attracts pilgrims from far and wide. In the church is a magnificent ikonostatis by Mastro Diaco Tagliaduro of Kos.

B. The Southern Route

STEAMERS, see above. By this route a visit to the Dodecanese can be conveniently combined with a tour of Crete.

BY AIR, Occasional connections between Rhodes–Karpathos–Kasos–Siteia (most frequent are between Rhodes and Karpathos).

Kásos (Κάσος) is the most southerly of the Dodecanese. It lies c 48km E of Zakro in Crete, across the Kasos Channel, and is separated from Karpathos by a channel of 11km. The island, elliptical in shape and with an area of 49 sq. km, has an overall length of 18km with precipitous and inaccessible coasts, save on the NW side where the few villages are scattered. The sea is often rough. The hilly interior rises in Mt Priona to 549m. The population (1184) has been greatly reduced by emigration, in the past particularly to Egypt. More than 5000 Kasiots are said to have helped build the Suez Canal.

Kasos is mentioned in the Homeric Catalogue of Ships. It was made subject to the Venetian family of Cornaro in 1306, when they acquired Karpathos, and was lost to the Turks only in 1537. In 1824 the Egyptians ravaged the island, an event remembered as 'the Holocaust' by the Kasiots, and for some years afterwards the island was deserted.

Emborió (Hotels C), the port, midway along the N coast, lies just E of the capital, *Frí* (Φρύ), an abbreviated form of *Othrys*. It has many abandoned houses and is uninteresting save for the fine view of Karpathos to the E. Inland is *Póli*, the former capital, on the site of the acropolis of the ancient city.

KÁRPATHOS (Κάρπαθος), better known by its medieval name *Scarpanto*, is the chief of the group midway between Crete and Rhodes. Long and narrow, it is 48km from end to end with a maximum width of 11km and has about the same area as Kos. The coastline is steep but little indented: there are bays, but only the Bay of Tristoma at the N end affords much protection from the prevailing winds. A mountain range traverses the island from N to S, rising to Mt Profitis Ilias (1014m) and Mt Kalolimni (Lastros; 1120m), the twin peaks in the centre which virtually divide the island in two, isolating one part from the other. The long N section, covered with stunted pine trees on the E and bare on the W, is sparsely populated, preserves many ancient customs, and has few springs; the more populous S section (known as 'European' Karpathos) is well watered and its valleys are productive. The 5833 inhabitants are mostly engaged in agriculture and pasture. There are said to be more Karpathiots in Piraeus than in Scarpanto. A great concourse of emigré islanders assembled in 1966 to discuss the island's future economy.

History. In antiquity, as officially today, the island was called *Karpathos*, though Homer has it as Krapathos. Its medieval name of *Scarpanto* was revived by the Italians and is still in common use. The Turks called it *Kerpe*. Despite its size, Karpathos has had an uneventful existence. The Latin Empire gave it in fief to the Genoese Andrea and Lodovico Moresco. In 1306 it was acquired by the Venetian family of Cornaro, who yielded it to the Turks in 1538. In 1835 Sultan Mahmoud II gave it certain financial privileges.

The chief port and 'capital' is **Pigádhia** (Hotels C, E; F/A), or *Kárpathos*, a modern town (1266 inhab.) on the wide sandy bay of *Vrónti* in the SE of the island. Gardens and olive-groves fringe it on the NW. The rocky citadel to the E is the site of Classical *Potidaion* and equally of a Minoan settlement (tombs near by). Minoan and Mycenaean remains (chiefly tombs) have been found at various points on the island.

TOUR OF THE S PART OF THE ISLAND, 34·5km (21½ miles). The road leads NW to (7km) **Apéri** (149m), the former capital (407 inhab.), divided into two by a stream. It is the seat of the Metropolitan of Karpathos and Kasos. The streets are steep and narrow, many of them in steps.—The road ascends SW to (9km) *Voládha* (450m), with a castle on a prominent hill.—11km *Othos* (399m), starting-point of the overland route to the N half of the island (comp. below).—14km *Pilés* (399m), with pleasant gardens, looks towards the W coast, to which we descend and turn S.—19km *Finíki* is a little fishing harbour in a fertile region growing citrus fruits and vegetables. At the S end of the same bay is (22km) *Arkássa*, a picturesque village, with fruit orchards. It has remains of a 5C Byzantine Church (Ayía Anastasía), the mosaic pavement of which is in Rhodes museum. On a steep-sided promontory to the SW are some remains of Classical *Arkaseia*.—A road, less good, climbs inland to (28km) *Menetés*, a village served by bus (20 minutes) from (34·5km) Pigádhia (comp. above).

The centre of the island is reached by a mule-track from Othos (comp. above) round the W side of Mt Kalolimni.—14km *Mesokhorió* is built on a precipitous rock on the W coast. Here a stream gushes out of the pavement of a church. In the environs are the church of *Ayía Irini*, with frescoes, and many Byzantine ruins. On the islet of *Sókastro*, close inshore, is a ruined Frankish castle. From Mesokhorio a mule-track leads across the island to *Spóa* (351m) above the little E coast harbour of Ayios Nikólaos. From Spóa, where the pine forests are bent double by the wind, a mule-path goes along the mountain crest in 6 hours to Olimbos (see below).

The N part of the island is reached more easily (in 2 hours) by hired launch from Pigadhia though there is now an indifferent road. Landing is made at *Dhiafáni* on the NE coast, whence a mule-path ascends to (9km) **Ólimbos** (331 inhab.), perched on the flank of Profitis Ilias, overlooking the W coast. On the slopes of the mountain are more than 40 windmills. Olimbos is supposed to be the oldest settlement in Karpathos. The inhabitants wear traditional costume, not merely on special occasions, but for everyday use. Their dialect retains many ancient Doric words. The well-built houses are in three sections and have handsome doors with wooden locks and keys said to be of a pattern dating back to Homeric times. The Byzantine village church has some frescoes. In the vicinity are the remains of an ancient temple.—About 3 hours N is *Trístoma*, with a landing-place on a relatively sheltered bay. A headland about half-way to Trístoma is taken as the site of *Brykous*.

Immediately N of Karpathos and separated by a channel only 27m wide is the islet of *Sariá* (10·5 sq. km), inhabited in summer only by shepherds. On it are the ruins of a Byzantine church.

The island of **Khalkí** (Χαλκή), the ancient *Chalke* and medieval *Charki*, lies 16km W of Rhodes. The bare and hilly interior culminates in Mt Merovigli (596m). There are no springs and few wells. The population (334 inhab.) has been greatly reduced by emigration. The landing-place *Nimboreió*, or Skala, at the NE corner of the island, is served by daily boat from Kameiros Skala. A mule-path climbs inland in 30 minutes to the village of *Khorió* (274m), now virtually abandoned. Its church is partly built of Hellenic materials. One mile inland, on top of a bare hill, formerly a Greek acropolis, is the Castle of the Knights, built on Greek foundations and incorporating much ancient masonry. Inside is the church of Ayios Nikólaos, with late Byzantine frescoes.

76   Rhodes

The island of **RHODES** (Ρόδος), in Greek *Rhódhos*, with 84,300 inhab., is separated from the SW coast of Asia Minor by the Strait of Marmara, about 11km wide. By far the largest of the Dodecanese with an area of 1398·5 sq. km, Rhodes is diamond-shaped, 77km long from N to S and with a maximum width of 35·5km. It is traversed from N to S by a range of hills rising from either end towards the W centre, where Mt Ataviros shoots up to 1215m. The other summits do not exceed 823m. Much of the island is very fertile, with a wide variety of plants and trees; vegetation grows to some of the mountain-tops. There are oranges, lemons, figs, pears, pistachio and olives. Broom, myrtle, heath, spurge and laurel grow in profusion, as well as aromatic plants such as lavender, sage, marjoram and styrax. The rock-rose is so exuberant that Rhodes is often called the 'Island of Roses'. The fauna include deer (reintroduced by the Italians), foxes, hares, badgers, martens, and hedgehogs; partridges, vultures, jackdaws, and jays. In antiquity the island was infested with snakes (its name may derive from 'erod' a Phoenician word for snake), and farmers still wear leather boots to the knee as protection against a small species which is poisonous. The larger snakes are harmless. Some of the lizards are large: the 'Rhodes dragon' (*Agama stellio*) grows to 35·5cm. There are so many butterflies that Rhodes has been called 'Butterfly Island'.

The climate of Rhodes resembles that of eastern Sicily. The temperature varies from 10°C in winter to 30–32°C in summer. The winds are constant and occasionally violent, though the E side of the island is usually sheltered. Their force is put to use in the numerous windmills that are a feature of the landscape. The year is equally divided into a dry season, from April to the end of October, and a wet season, from November to the end of March. The best months for a visit are April–May and September–October. From spring to autumn the island is crowded with tourists from every country in Europe and hotel accommodation is at a premium.

**RHODES
ISLAND**

RHODES
(Rodhos)

Kremasti
Asgourou
Koskinoú
Paradhísion
Triánda
IALYSOS
Maritsá
Faliraki
Kallithéa
Soroní
Fánai
Kalavárda
Afándou
KAMEIROS
Sálakos
M. TSAMBIKAS
*Profítis
Ilias*
Apóllona
Arkhángelos
Malón
ALIMNIA
PHARAKLOS
Haráki
Émbonas
Atáviros
C. Ay. Isidhoros
Kálathos
Láerma
Líndos
LINDOS
Sánai
Monólithos
CASTLE
Vátion
Apolakkiá
Arnítha
Mesanagrós
C. Laharia
Kattaviá

N

| 0 | | 5 miles |
| 0 | | 8 kilometres |

History. In antiquity the island was called *Aithrea, Ophioussa* (from its snakes), *Telchinia* and several other names. The name of *Rhodes* is of uncertain etymology, but is probably not derived (as so often stated) from the Greek word for rose, ῥόδον. In one of his Odes, Pindar tells us of the birth of Rhodes, offspring of the love of Helios, the Sun God, for the nymph Rhoda. In the prehistoric era the island shared the culture of Crete and later of Mycenae. Homer mentions three cities in Rhodes—Lindos, Ialysos, and Kameiros ('Iliad', II, 656). These three cities, with Kos, Knidos, and Halicarnassus, formed the Dorian hexapolis in the SW corner of Asia Minor.

The three Dorian cities of Rhodes attained a high degree of prosperity, with trade routes throughout the Mediterranean, and founded colonies in the neighbouring islands and on the coasts of Asia Minor and Europe. In the 6C BC they were governed by tyrants. Having submitted to the Persians in 490, in 478 the Rhodians joined the Delian Confederacy as subject-allies of Athens, but in 411, late in the Peloponnesian War, they revolted in favour of Sparta. In 408 the three cities united to found the capital *City of Rhodes*, which they populated with their own citizens. This was planned by Hippodamos of Miletus, the most famous architect of his age.

The new city, whose planning Strabo praises extravagantly, immediately became prominent. At first it had an oligarchic government and in 396 it submitted to Sparta. Later its citizens acquired a democratic constitution and went over to the Athenians, whom they helped, in conjunction with the Persian fleet, to defeat the Spartans at the battle of Knidos (394). In 378 Rhodes joined the Second Athenian Confederacy, but in 357 she revolted again, this time at the instigation of Mausolus, king of Caria, who placed a Carian garrison in the island. As allies of Persia the Rhodians gave help to the city of Tyre when it was besieged by Alexander the Great. In 332 they had to suffer a Macedonian garrison, which they expelled after the death of Alexander. In the wars that followed, they allied themselves with Ptolemy I, who assisted them in 305 when their city was besieged by Demetrios Poliorketes. When, after a year, Demetrios was compelled to raise the siege, he was so impressed by the defenders' valour that he left them his siege artillery, from the sale of which they defrayed the cost of the Colossus. The Rhodians accorded divine honours to Ptolemy as their saviour: hence his name Soter.

Soon afterwards with heightened prestige, Rhodes attained the zenith of her prosperity. Her port became the centre of trade between Italy, Greece and Macedonia, and Asia and Africa. She became the first naval Power in the Aegean, with ships well built, efficiently manned and skilfully manoeuvred. Her currency was everywhere accepted. Rhodian law, the earliest code of marine law, was universally esteemed: Augustus adopted it as a model, an example followed by Justinian, and its provisions are still quoted today. With a population of 60,000–80,000, the city was lavishly equipped and adorned and began its artistic golden age. The devastation wrought by the great earthquake of 222 BC inspired an international programme of aid in money and talent. Even as late as the 1C AD, when the city had been despoiled of most of its treasures, Pliny counted no fewer than 2000 statues, many of them colossal. The Rhodians were enthusiastic admirers of athletics, music, and oratory. The orator Aeschines (389–314 BC), after his discomfiture at the hands of Demosthenes, founded at Rhodes a school of rhetoric, which was later to be attended by famous Romans, including Cato, Cicero, Julius Caesar, and Lucretius. Apollonius (fl. 222–181 BC), a native of Alexandria, taught rhetoric at Rhodes with so much success that the Rhodians awarded him the cognomen Rhodius.

By the 2C BC the Rhodians were allies of Rome. Their help against Philip V of Macedon, which led to his defeat at Cynoscephalae in 197, gained them the Cyclades, and the participation of their fleet in the war against Antiochus the Great, king of Syria, won them in 188 BC the former Syrian possession of S Caria, where they had from an early period made numerous settlements. The Rhodian espousal of the cause of Perseus brought swift Roman retribution. After Pydna Rhodes had to surrender her possessions on the mainland of Asia Minor and, in 166, found her trade injured when the Romans declared Delos a free port. In the Mithridatic wars Rhodes recovered the favour of Rome. Mithridates unsuccessfully besieged the city. Sulla restored to Rhodes her lost Asiatic possessions. In the civil war Rhodes sided with Julius Caesar and suffered in consequence at the hands of Cassius, who plundered the city in 43 BC and destroyed or captured the Rhodian fleet. This was a fatal blow to the naval power of Rhodes.

Augustus accorded to Rhodes the title of Allied City. Vespasian (emperor AD 70–79) incorporated it in the empire. Reattached to the province of Asia, it became under Diocletian (284–305) capital of the province of the Islands. It was visited by St. Paul during his second or third journey (Acts, xxi, 1) and it had a bishop at a very early date. In the 4C the bishops of Rhodes were granted the title of Metropolitan, with jurisdiction over 12 of the dioceses of the Archipelago. In the 9C the Rhodians deserted the Roman church. In 1274, however, we find the Metropolitan of Rhodes attending the Council of Lyons and a signatory of the short-lived reunion of the Eastern and Latin churches.

After the division of the Empire in 395, Rhodes naturally became part of the Eastern Empire and followed its destiny. From 654 it was frequently pillaged and for a time occupied by the Saracens. In 1082 Alexander Comnenus gave the Venetians important privileges in the island. In the Crusades Christian ships used the ports of Rhodes as a convenient stopping-place. During the Fourth Crusade, which established the Latin empire of Constantinople, the Greek Governor of Rhodes, Leo Gavalas, declared the independence of the island. Later the Genoese obtained control of it and in 1306 received as refugees the Knights of St. John of Jerusalem. The refugees soon became the masters of Rhodes.

The *Knights of St. John of Jerusalem*, otherwise Knights of Rhodes and later Knights of Malta, were originally *Hospitallers*, charitable brotherhoods founded for the care in hospital of the poor and sick. They originated c 1048 in a hospital which merchants of Amalfi had built in Jerusalem for pilgrims to the Holy Sepulchre. Their first rector, Gerard, formed them into a strictly constituted religious body subject to the jurisdiction of the Patriarch of Jerusalem. The Order soon became predominantly military and the Hospitallers were sworn to defend the Holy Sepulchre to the last drop of their blood and to make war on infidels wherever met. In 1191, after Saladin had captured Jerusalem, they retired to Acre. Bitter rivalry arose between them and the Knights Templars, ending in hostilities in which the Templars got the upper hand. Clinging to Acre, the Hospitallers were driven out in 1291 after a terrible siege, and they sailed to Cyprus. In 1306 they fled from Cyprus to Rhodes. Having in vain demanded from the emperor the fief of Rhodes, they took it by force in 1309, after a two years' siege.

The brethren were divided into three classes—knights, chaplains, and serving brothers or fighting squires who followed the knights into action. In the 12C the Order was divided into seven 'Tongues' or Languages—Provence, Auvergne, France, Italy, Spain (later subdivided into Aragon and Castile), England and Germany. Each 'Tongue' had a Bailiff, and the Bailiffs, under the presidency of the Grand Master, elected for life by the Knights, formed the chapter of the Order. The modern British Order of St. John of Jerusalem, founded in 1827, may be regarded as a revival of the 'Language' of England.

Having conquered Rhodes, the Knights of St. John built a powerful fleet which protected the island's trade. Pope Clement V assigned to them part of the property of the Templars who had been suppressed in 1312. For two centuries the Knights of St. John defied the Turks. For his assistance to the Knights during the siege of 1313, Amadeus V, count of Savoy, was rewarded by a grant of the arms of the Order with a collar bearing the letters F.E.R.T. (Fortitudo ejus Rhodum tenuit). The Knights took part in the capture and later in the defence of Smyrna, and withstood two great sieges—in 1444 by the Sultan of Egypt, and in 1480 by Mehmet II, at which time their infantry general ('turcopolier') was an Englishman, John Kendal. At last, in June 1522 Suleiman I, having captured Belgrade, attacked Rhodes with a force said to have numbered 100,000 men. The Knights mustered only 650, with the addition of 200 Genoese sailors, 50 Venetians, 400 Cretans and 600 of the inhabitants. Pope Adrian VI vainly implored the Christian princes to come to their aid. The Turks had the city blockaded by sea. They eventually secured the heights above it and thence shelled the fortifications. Several times the besieged repaired the breaches in the walls, but their numbers daily diminished. They had spent their strength and traitors had infiltrated into their ranks. In December the Turks made another and final breach in the walls. The Knights capitulated on honourable terms. On 1 January 1523, the Grand Master, Villiers de l'Isle Adam, with 180 surviving brethren, left the island. They first retired to Candia (Herakleion), Crete, and in 1530 to Malta.

After their departure the churches were converted into mosques. Not till 1660 were the Fathers of the Mission able to return to Rhodes and administer to the Christian slaves. In 1719 they were placed under the protection of the Apostolic Prefecture of Constantinople. In 1873 French Franciscan Sisters established schools and in 1889 the Brothers of the Christian Doctrine founded the College of St. John. In 1877 the island was created an apostolic prefecture.

In 1912, during their war with Turkey, the Italians captured Rhodes after a short siege. In the latter part of the Second World War the Germans took over from the Italians. In 1945 the island was freed by British and Greek commandos, and in 1947 it was officially awarded to Greece.

Rhodian Art. Rhodian artefacts of the 2nd millenium BC show marked influences of Crete and Mycenae. No palaces have been discovered, but chamber tombs have yielded sepulchral furniture, notably pottery, women's ornaments, and weapons. The vases are of pinkish yellow, with marine and floral decoration and imported although they have some peculiarities of design. The women's ornaments include articles of glass paste (Mycenaean), gold jewellery engraved with the burin, filigree work, precious stones and incised scarabs. Among the weapons are bronze swords and daggers.

As elsewhere in the Aegean, the Mycenaean Age was succeeded by the Geometric and Orientalising Periods (1100–650 BC). The excavations at Lindos, Ialysos, Kameiros, and Vrulia have given rich yields of pottery. Rhodian vases of the 7C and 6C decorated with animal figures, including goats and fugitive hares, palm, and vine leaves, and geometric designs (roses, circles, and swastikas). With the native ware are found vases from Corinth, Attica, Cyprus, and the Orient. The votive clay and porcelain statuettes, scarabs, and engraved stones found in the Temple of Athena at Lindos and at Ialysos are of Phoenician origin.

The foundation in 408 BC of the city of Rhodes brought an influx of famous artists. Lysippos of Sikyon, the sculptor attached to the court of Alexander the Great, produced at Rhodes his famous Chariot of the Sun. Under the influence of Lysippos was founded the *School of Rhodes*, which flourished for three centuries and of which Pliny gives an account. Leaders of the school included Protogenes, the painter from Caria who lived in poverty until acclaimed by Apelles, Chares of Lindos, creator of the Colossus of Rhodes, and Bryaxis, responsible for at least five statues of note. These were followed by a host of other artists, both native and immigrant, of whom little is known save their names, many of which appear on statue bases uncovered on the Acropolis of Lindos. The sculptors, from Chares downwards, worked chiefly in bronze. We know something about Philiskos, author of a group of the Muses, which was carried off to Rome, perhaps by Crassus, and placed in the Porticus of Octavia. Inspired by Lysippos, Philiskos was especially skilled in the treatment of drapery. Heliodoros of Rhodes produced a group of Pan and Olympus, now believed to be in the Museum at Naples.

The loss of her independence did not halt the artistic activity of Rhodes. One of her sculptors made a Colossus 12m high, dedicated to the Roman people and placed in the Temple of Athena Polias and Zeus Polieos on the Acropolis of Rhodes. There followed Boïthos of Chalcedon, and Apollonios and Tauriskos of Tralles, who made a group of Dirce which was found in the Baths of Caracalla in Rome and is now at Naples. Pliny mentions Aristonidas, who executed a statue of Atamos bewailing the death of his son Learchos. The group of Menelaus and Patroclus, a fragment of which is now in Rome under the name of Pasquino, came from Rhodes. Best known of all is the Laocoön, found in 1506 in the Golden House of Nero in Rome; this group was produced in the 1C BC by the Rhodian sculptors Agesander, Polydorus, and Athenodorus. After the creation of this masterpiece Rhodian art declined.—Such ancient monuments as remain in the island prove that in the Hellenistic age the Doric style prevailed.

The Byzantine era contributed little of note that has survived. With the arrival of the Knights of St. John the art of Rhodes becomes westernised. The Grand Masters, most of whom came from France or from Spain, naturally favoured the style of their native countries, and French or Spanish Gothic predominated. We may distinguish two periods: from 1309 to 1480, and from 1480 to 1522. In the earlier period the Knights depended on local labour unfamiliar with the Gothic style, and the work was heavy and maladroit, with intrusive Byzantine elements. In the second period, which was inspired by d'Aubusson (1476–1503), one of the most eminent of the Grand Masters, we see the hand of the Western craftsman. The Gothic character of the work remains, but the forms are more harmonious, the execution more accurate, and the decoration natural or cleverly stylised. Towards the end of the period a few Renaissance motives were introduced, alleviating the severity of the monastic Gothic. These included marble cornices to doors and windows, elaborate escutcheons, and inscriptions carved in superb Latin characters. Here and there are forms deriving from Sicily and southern Italy.

The walls of Rhodes, with their succession of towers, bastions, lunettes, ravelins, and barbicans, are a magnificent example of military architecture of the 14C, 15C, and 16C. The inscriptions and escutcheons that adorn the walls enable us to follow the history of their development. Up to the time of the siege of 1480 the emphasis was on the architectural aspect; later building and modification relied less on the architect than on the engineer. Many Italian engineers were employed on the work.

Gothic influences persisted into the Turkish period, which added little but an Oriental veneer, some elegant minarets and fountains, and the introduction of pottery from Anatolia. The brief Italian period left a mixed legacy of bombastic architecture, over-restoration, and well-engineered roads.

The **City of Rhodes** (40,392 inhab.), situated at the N end of the island, today consists of two distinct parts. The *Old City*, hemmed in by walls built by the Knights, is clustered round the Central or Commercial Harbour, and is itself divided into two. In the NW is a walled enclosure called the *Castle of the Knights* or *Collachium*. The rest of the city is known as the *Chora*. The *New Town*, built since the Italian occupation of 1912, and consisting largely of hotels, extends to the N of the Old City as far as the N extremity of the island, and westwards to the foot of the Acropolis of ancient Rhodes. It includes two quarters of the Greek city, Marasi and Neochori. On its E side is Mandraki, the second and smaller harbour of Rhodes, generally used by yachts and caiques calling at the island. The gardens of Rhodes are noted for their oleanders, bougainvilleas, and hibiscus. The city has suffered greatly from earthquakes. That of 225 BC overthrew the Colossus. Others occurred in AD 157, 515, 1364, 1481, 1851, and 1863. Of the ancient city few traces remain, though much of its street plan has been plotted under the present town. One side of its tourist appeal is represented by the existence of a golf course and casino.

Airport, 16km SW. Several services a day to Athens; daily (in summer) to Herakleion and Paros; less frequently to Salonika, Lesbos, Thera, Kos, Siteia, Karpathos, Kasos, Kastellorizo.

Hotels L, A, B, C, D, E, F/A.

Post Office (Pl. 7), opposite the cathedral. **O.T.E.**, 25 Martíou.—OLYMPIC AIRWAYS, 9 Ieroú Lókhou.

Tourist Police, Od. Eth. Dhodhekanissíon; N.T.O.G., Makaríou.

Buses from Od. Papágou, behind the Agora to the island villages to the W, *Lindos* etc.; from Od. Avérof to villages in the E of the island. Also Excursions to *Lindos, Kameiros*, etc.

The MODERN CITY is laid out along the waterfront of **Mandráki** (Pl. 7), the northern of the two natural harbours, now equipped as a yacht anchorage. The harbour entrance is guarded by two bronze deer (that to seaward replacing the former Italian she-wolf). On the mole protecting the E side of the basin stand three windmills and Fort St. Nicholas, a cylindrical tower dating from 1464–67, topped by a lighthouse (view).

The word Mandraki, used elsewhere in the area for small enclosed harbours, means a small sheepfold. The alternative name *Harbour of the Galleys*, is a misnomer; Mandraki was always secondary to the equally misnamed Commercial Harbour, and under the Knights was occupied by small boat builders. Here probably stood the **Colossus of Rhodes**, a bronze statue of Helios, the Sun-god, set up by Chares of Lindos c 290 BC and considered one of the seven wonders of the world. Its erection was financed by the sale of the siege artillery that Demetrios Poliorketes had presented to the city at the end of his unsuccessful siege (305–304 BC). It was 60 cubits (c 27m) high. Helios, the protector of the city of Rhodes, was represented with his head framed in sunrays and dressed in a chlamys; in his right hand he held a torch, which served as a beacon to mariners. The tradition that the statue bestrode the harbour entrance and that ships passed beneath it is without foundation. The earthquakes of 225 BC overthrew the statue. For eight centuries its huge fragments lay undisturbed, respected by the superstitious reverence of the Rhodians. At last, in 653 Saracen corsairs collected them and brought them to Tyre. There they were sold to Jewish merchants of Emesa, who carried them away on 900 camels to be melted down and resold.

The public buildings lining the waterfront all date from the Italian occupation and were designed in various monumental styles by Florestano di Fausto. Dominating the harbour mouth is the square campanile of the **Cathedral** (Pl. 7), or *Church of the Evangelist*, built in

1925 on the model of the church of St. John in the Old City, destroyed in 1856. The *Fountain* outside the W end is a copy of the 13C Fontana Grande at Viterbo; the main *Post Office* stands opposite. Linked to the Cathedral is the *Nomarkhía*, or Prefecture, formerly the Governor's Palace, the most considerable monument of the Italian period, built in a Venetian Gothic style. Its picturesque arcaded façade, with marble decoration, closing the seaward side of the Plateia, is set off by the severity of the *Dhimarkhíon* and the *Theatre*. To the N is a popular public beach (fee).

Beyond the Theatre rises the elegant minaret of the *Mosque of Murad Reis* (Pl. 3). In front stands a circular turbeh enclosing the tomb of Murad Reis, admiral of the Turkish fleet during the siege of Rhodes. In the cemetery flanking the mosque are the tombs of many noble Turks who died in exile in Rhodes, including a Shah of Persia and a prince of the Crimea. Farther on, beyond the Hotel des Roses (1927), the road follows the shore to *Akrotiri Ammou* (Sandy Point), the N extremity of the island. Here the HYDROBIOLOGICAL INSTITUTE (Pl. 2) houses a remarkable collection of preserved marine creatures caught in local waters (sharks, sun-fish, manta, sword-fish, etc.) and an *Aquarium* unusually rich in octopods, molluscs, crustacea, etc.

The W shore, overlooked by many hotels, is still freely accessible.

Returning S along Mandraki, here fronted by gardens, we pass in succession the *Law Courts*, a popular café under a neo-Gothic loggia, and the *Bank of Greece*. Contrasting with their golden stone is the flat whiteness of the NEA AGORA (Pl. 7), a huge polygonal market in a Turkish style, which is the focal-point of the modern town. Beneath the N wall of the medieval city extends the *Garden of the Deer*, ablaze with sub-tropical flowers.

We enter the * *Old City** by the *New Gate*, or *Gate of Liberty*, opened in 1924, and enter the Plateía Sými or Arsenal Square. We are now in the **Collachium**, or *Castle of the Knights*, the preserve of the Knights of St. John, divided from the remainder of the city by an inner wall. In it are the Palace of the Grand Masters and the 'Inns' or residences of the 'Tongues' (see above). In Arsenal Square, which communicates with the commercial harbour (see below) by Arsenal Gate, are the remains, discovered in 1922, of a *Temple of Aphrodite* (Pl. 11) dating from the 3C BC. They include foundations, bases, and shafts of columns, and fragments of the entablature. To the right is the *Municipal Gallery*, while behind the temple is the INN OF THE TONGUE OF AUVERGNE (Pl. 11), a 15C building restored in 1919, the side of which overlooks the attractive Plateía Argirokástrou. In the centre of this square a Byzantine font serves as fountain; the heaps of cannon-balls were amassed during the siege of 1522. On the right the Institute of History and Archaeology (with the ephorate of antiquities) occupies the *Palace of the Armeria*, built in the 14C under Roger de Pinsot and used as the first hospital of the Order. Also in this square is the *Museum of Decorative Arts* (Mon, Wed, Fri, 9–1). We pass beneath an arch. Beyond (left) is the 13C Byzantine *Church of St. Mary* which became the first Cathedral of the Knights. After 1522 the Turks converted it into a mosque called *Enderoum*, and it now serves as a *Byzantine Museum*.

In the courtyard of the building opposite is an amusing modern mosaic of black and white pebbles in a style that has survived unchanged in Rhodes from Byzantine times.

Leaving on our right the Street of the Knights (see below) we enter Hospital Square. Here on the left is the INN OF THE TONGUE OF ENGLAND (3; Pl. 11), built in 1482, despoiled and almost destroyed in 1850, rebuilt on the original plan by Colonel Sir Vivian Gabriel, and repaired by the British in 1949. Opposite stands the **Hospital of the Knights** (Pl. 11), begun in 1440 over the remains of a Roman building and completed in 1481–89. During the War of Greek Independence the Turks used it for their sick and wounded, but later degraded it into barracks. It was skilfully restored under Amedeo Maiuri in 1913–18. Bomb damage sustained on the S side in the Second World War has again been made good. The FAÇADE, set forward from the plain E wall above, consists of eight deep arches of unadorned severity. Seven, surmounted by a wall relieved by two string-courses lead into open magazines, while the one to the right of centre shelters the main gateway and supports a projecting apsidal chapel (comp. below). By skilful use of vertical moulding this arrangement is given the appearance of a gate-tower. The *Portal* is decorated with a rope design. The original door of cypress was presented by Sultan Mahmoud to Louis-Philippe in 1836 and now reposes at Versailles.

Since 1916 the building has housed the *Archaeological Museum*. The GREAT COURT is enclosed by a double portico, of which the lower storey is vaulted. Beneath the lower colonnade are various fragments; in the centre crouches a marble lion (1C BC); in the corners are cannon balls and catapult shot. An outside stair leads to the upper gallery where are ranged funerary stelai and altar-bases. The entire E wing is occupied by the INFIRMARY WARD, a rectangular hall divided lengthways by an arcade borne on seven columns; its ogee arches support a ceiling of cypress-wood.

The ward held 32 beds with brocaded canopies, and the patients ate from silver plate. Two surgeons were on duty at all times. The dark cubicles that open from the hall have been variously explained as confessionals, isolation wards, and wardrobes.

Beneath a flamboyant arch in the long wall opens the vaulted exedra, with three Gothic windows, that projects above the main gate. This held an altar where mass was said daily. Round the walls of the hall are ranged *Memorials* of the Knights from the destroyed church of St. John. Notable are a classical marble sarcophagus used in 1355 as the tomb of Grand Master Pierre de Corneillan (lid in the Cluny Museum, Paris; copy here) and tomb-slabs of Thomas Newport (1502), of Nicholas de Montmirel (1511), commandant of the Hospital, of Tomaso Provena (1499), and of Fernando de Heredia (1493). Heraldic devices include the royal arms of England.

Beyond the Infirmary Ward is a Small Hall (at present temporarily closed), with reliefs on the walls, once the refectory for the hospital staff, and beyond this three rooms of **Sculpture**. *First Room*: Head of Helios; head of Menander (after Praxiteles). *Second Room*: small headless Nymph, seated on a rock; bearded Dionysos (Hellenistic); Zeus; Asklepios and Hygieia (2C AD); *Aphrodite of Rhodes, kneeling and separating the strands of her hair, after emerging from the waves (1C BC). *Third Room*: Head of Bacchus, in porphyry; stooping Nymph (headless) where the vertical folds of the himation emphasise the soft round form of the body; the famous *Aphrodite 'Thalassia' of the 3C BC, also called Venus Pudica, found in the sea off Sandy Point.

Still at first-floor level we enter a garden that overlooks the *Little Court*, excavated in 1907, with a 6C mosaic pavement from Arkassa in Karpathos.

Key to numbers in Old Town

3. Inn of England
4. Inn of Italy
5. Inn of France
6. 'Palace of Zizim'
7. Inn of Spain
8. Chapel of France
9. Inn of Provence
10. Loggia
11. Artillery Gate
12. St Anthony's Gate

Aquarium

KASSOU

LEROU

AKTI KALINNIOU

KONSTA

S Maria

PTHENOS AMALIAS

AKTI MIAOULI

APOLLONIOU RODIO

DILVERAKI

KALIGA

IKOSTOKTO

OKTOVRIOU

ALEXANDROU

DIAKOU

FANOURAKI

MOEAT

AKTI KANARI

ΤΣΑΛΔΑΡΙ

MAKRIOU

Therm

PAPALOUKA

VENIZELOU

Orphanage

S
(Hot

VORIOU IPIROU

RIGA FEREOU

Temple of Zeus

Bastic
St G

Acropolis

DIAGORIDON

AY. IOANNOU

Bar

Theatre

Temple of Apollo

Ancient Stadium

IRAKLIOU

RHODES

0	400 yards
0	400 metres

We cross to two further rooms. In the first, funerary stele of young Timarista taking her last farewell of Crito, her mother, a work of the 5C BC; Crito's hair was recut after damage in antiquity. In the second, two headless Kouroi (6C BC) found at Kamiros, but which appear to come from Paros and Naxos; two fragmentary heads; sculptured perirrhantirion stand of the 7C BC.—We return to the gallery to visit its surrounding rooms (not always open): on the first side three containing pottery from excavations at Kamiros and Ialysos; then three interlinked rooms containing jewellery from Mycenaean tombs in Ialysos, and a hoard of 75 silver coins from Kremasti; on the last side, four rooms which include pottery from Ialysos.

Leaving the museum we turn left from Hospital Square to ascend the cobbled *Street of the Knights (Odhos Ipoton; Pl. 11), the main thoroughfare of the Collachium which it traverses from E to W, rising towards the Palace. Its noble buildings, plentifully adorned with coats-of-arms, were restored with care and accuracy in 1913–16, so that the street provides a faithful picture of late medieval architecture, though the overall effect is perhaps too tidy to evoke the full spirit of the Middle Ages.

The knightly houses and inns follow the same general pattern, having two storeys with a flat ornamental façade and a terrace roof. Vaulted store-houses, or stables (?), occupied the lower floor while the upper storey was reached by an open stair and gallery from a central court. The rounded arches, the horizontal emphasis given by string-courses, and the large square windows suggest that the Renaissance was already affecting even a military order of medieval chivalry.

On our left is the N façade of the Hospital (see below) with a good portal at the far end. Opposite is the *Inn of the Tongue of Italy* (4; Pl. 11) rebuilt in 1519 when Del Carretto was Grand Master. Beyond a house bearing the arms of de l'Isle Adam quartered with those of his mother (d. 1462) is the *INN OF THE TONGUE OF FRANCE (5; Pl. 11), architecturally the most harmonious building in the street. It was built in 1492–1509, disfigured by the Turks, and carefully restored at the expense of Maurice Bompard, French ambassador to the Porte. The escutcheons include that of Pierre d'Aubusson (Grand Master 1476–1503). The crocodile gargoyles recall the legend of Gozon (comp. below). The building opposite, with an Aragonese portal and an attractive garden court, bears the Spanish arms of Villaraguts. Next to it is a charming building with an upper floor in the Turkish style.

In a side street (right) is the so-called *Palace of Zizim* (6; Pl. 11), pretender brother of Bayezid II, given asylum here for a short time in 1482 before being conveyed to France.

Farther on (right) the small *Chapel of the Tongue of France* (8; Pl. 11) bears a statue of the Virgin and Child and the lilies of France. The adjacent *Chaplain's House*, dated by the arms of Béranger (Grand Master 1365–74) on the façade, is occupied by the Italian consulate. An arch spans the road. Two buildings, to the left of the street, before and beyond the arch, constitute the *Inn of the Tongue of Spain* (7; Pl. 11); the first (Aragon and Castile) dates from the mid-15C, the second from c 50 years later. The *Inn of the Tongue of Provence* (9; Pl. 11) of 1518, to the right, has an elegant portal surmounted by four coats-of-arms set in a cross-shaped niche.

At the top of the street we enter Citadel Square beneath the *Loggia of St. Peter* (10; Pl. 11), a modern reconstruction of a portico of unknown purpose. Already in ruins before the explosion of 1856, it used to join the entrance-court of the Palace to the *Conventual Church of St.*

John which lay parallel to the palace. A fragment of wall is all that remains of the church, and a Turkish school now occupies the site.

Built in a plain 14C style, more or less faithfully copied in the church on Mandraki, it contained the tombs of the Knights. After 1522 it was turned into a mosque. In 1856 it was destroyed when lightning struck the minaret and exploded beneath it a forgotten underground cache of gunpowder, killing c 800 people.

On the N side of the square in the highest part of the Collachium stands the **Palace of the Grand Masters** (Pl. 11; charge for adm.; weekdays, summer 9.30–1, 3.30–7, winter 9.30–1, 2.30–5; Sun and hol. from 10; closed Tues), rebuilt in 1939–43 from old drawings of the original 14C building.

Son et Lumière in English, French, German, and Swedish (entrance from municipal garden outside the walls).—The tour of the walls (see below) begins from the main entrance of the Palace.

The Palace stands on the site of an ancient temple of Apollo. Begun soon after the arrival in Rhodes of the Knights, and completed at the end of the 14C, it was a superb building on a rectangular plan, 79m by 75m, and was in effect an independent fortress designed with underground store-rooms to withstand a siege. It served in time of peace as the residence of the Grand Master and the place of assembly of the Order. Repaired after the earthquake of 1481, it suffered little damage in the siege of 1522. The Turks turned it into a prison. It was badly damaged by the earthquake of 1851 and the remains were further shattered by the explosion of 1856. Some of the material was used by the Turks to build a military hospital (since razed) in the grounds. The Italians, intending to use it as a summer residence for Victor Emmanuel III and Mussolini, rebuilt the exterior as far as possible in the old style, but redesigned the interior for modern occupation, including central heating, disguised lifts, and electric chandeliers. The preparations were barely completed when Italy relinquished the island.

The *Courtyard* is decorated with Roman statuary. The **Interior** achieves grandeur though sometimes at the expense of taste. The spacious halls have timber ceilings supported on Roman and Byzantine columns and are paved in coloured marbles or with vast antique *Mosaics brought from Kos. Some are lit by alabaster windows. The furniture, of many styles and periods, includes good Renaissance woodwork from Italian churches. The windows afford charming views of the city and sea. The garden contains sarcophagi of Masters, and a bronze she-wolf of Rome that once adorned the E mole of Mandraki.

At the W end of the square we pass through the Collachium wall by a double arch to Plateía Kleovoúlou, a long tree-lined 'piazza' with small shops and cafés. To the right an arch and a shaded walk (comp. below) lead to the Amboise Gate and then over the moats (deer in the outer moat) out to the new town. We turn left towards the ugly *Clock Tower*, which replaced a 15C tower (overthrown in 1851) at the SW corner of the Collachium. A few yards farther on Odhós Apolloníon leads (right) to the *Kurmale Medresses* (Pl. 11; 'College of the Date-Palm'), called locally *St. George's*, a derelict Turkish adaptation of a Byzantine conventual church. The dome, set on a drum of 21 blind arches, preserves its ancient tiles.

The **Mosque of Suleiman** (Pl. 11), erected soon after 1522 on the site of a Church of the Apostles and rebuilt in 1808, is preceded by the customary court with a fountain. It has a double portico, a portal in a Venetian Renaissance style, and an elegant minaret with a double balcony. Opposite is the *Turkish Library* (1793) with illuminated 15–16C Koran. Hence we descend ODHÓS SOKRÁTOUS, the former *Bazar*, whose balconied houses, open shops and coffee-houses still preserve a Turkish atmosphere. Beyond the *Mosque of Aga* (Pl. 11), curiously raised on wooden pillars, we reach Plateía Ippokrátous. Here the

Municipal library and Island Archives occupy the so-called *Palace of the Castellan* (Pl. 12), a square building of 1507 bearing the arms of Amboise. It was probably the commercial court of the Knights and was restored by the Italians after use as a mosque (above) and a fish-market (below). The upper hall, supported by an arcaded loggia, is reached by an external stair and a sculptured marble portal; the windows are delicately moulded. To the E of Od. Pithagóra, the long street that runs S towards the Koskinou Gate, lies the former Jewish quarter, once noted for its animation compared with the Turkish streets.

Odhós Aristotélous continues E past houses with Turkish wooden balconies to *Martyrs' Square*, damaged in the Second World War. A fountain adorned with bronze sea-horses, stands in front of the mis-named *Admiralty* (Pl. 16), whose inscriptions in Latin and Greek suggest that it was the palace of either the Orthodox metropolitan or the Latin archbishop. Odhós Pindhárou passes (right) the ruins of the Gothic church of Our Lady of the Bourg, now split in two by a road with an arched exit to the waterfront, and ends before the *Hospice of St. Catherine* (Pl. 16), founded by Fra Domenico d'Alemagna in 1392 to shelter Italian pilgrims travelling to the Holy Land; it was enlarged in 1516. At the NE corner of the town is the small church of Ayios Phanoúrios, beyond which, on the ramparts (left) stood the church of *Our Lady of Victory* (Pl. 12), built to commemorate the heroic defence of this rampart in 1480 and destroyed c 1522. To the left *St. Catherine's Gate* leads to the **Commercial Harbour**, the larger of the two harbours of Rhodes.

This, the 'Grand Harbour', was protected by two moles, defended with artillery, between which was stretched a chain. The N mole bore the *Tower of Naillac*, a key-point during the siege, but overthrown in 1863 (reconstruction planned); that to the E, separating the harbour from the Bay of Akandia and once adorned with 15 windmills, has been enlarged to form the modern quay where inter-island steamers moor. The defences round the harbour consist of a high curtain-wall with a *Marine Gate* (1478; sometimes by confusion called St. Catherine's Gate, see above) that recalls the Fort St. André at Villeneuve-lès-Avignon in Provence; it figured prominently in the film 'Guns of Navarone'. Following the wall we may re-enter the old city by the *Arsenal Gate*, or reach Mandraki by traversing the NE salient by the *Bastion of St. Paul*.

The interest of the old city has by no means been exhausted, and visitors staying in the city may explore the confined alleys that thread its S sector at their leisure. The small houses and occasional churches, the unexpected archways and courtyards, and the mosques (for the most part derelict and stripped) present a colourful mixture of medieval and eastern styles.

We may begin in the SE with two former churches, the *Ilk Mihrab Cami*, whose name marks it as the first shrine at which Allah was worshipped in 1522, and the neighbouring *Dolapli Mescidi*, or Oratory of the Well; both are decorated with frescoes. Farther W, beyond a characteristic windmill, is the *Redjeb Pasha Cami* (1588), the most notable mosque built by the Turks on Rhodes, with Persian faience decoration. The *Peial ad Din Mescid* has returned to the Greek rite; the frescoes were restored by the Italians in 1938.

Grouped near the centre of the town are the **Ibrahim Pasha Cami**, a spacious mosque of 1531, whose plane-tree is said to have provided a place of execution for the Turks, the ruined *Demirli Cami*, once a Gothic church, and the disused *Kavakli Mescidi*, a small Byzantine church provided with a minaret. In the square of the *Mustapha Cami* are the *Turkish Baths* (1765, rebuilt), whence the Mosque of Suleiman (see above) may be regained via the disused *Takkeci Cami* (once the Greek church of Ay. Sotira). In the SW corner of the town is the *Abdul Djelil Mescid*, a medieval church with cable ornament and vaulting, damaged in the Second World War.

Tour of the Walls

No visitor should omit the tour of the walls, which is conducted on Mon and Sat at 4, in winter 3 from the courtyard of the Palace (see above). A complete circuit takes 1½ hours—generally the guided tour ends at the Italian Tower, reached in ¾ hour. From the top a good defender's view is obtained; a visitor who has already seen the harbour defences is well advised to return (mostly by shaded walks) along the outside of the same section to obtain an attacker's view.

The ***Walls of Rhodes**, a masterpiece of 15–16C military architecture, are well preserved throughout their extent of 4km, having successfully withstood the siege of 1480 and for a long time that of 1522. They bear 151 escutcheons of Grand Masters and knights.

In places the walls have ancient or Byzantine foundation blocks, but little is known of the Byzantine enceinte save that it resisted the Knights for three years. The remaining towers probably date in part from before 1330, as does the moat. Reconstruction began under Grand Masters Heredia (1377–96) and de Naillac (1396–1421), who built a massive tower on the N mole of the main harbour. In 1437–71 the walls were rebuilt to incorporate a number of detached towers. After the siege of 1480 and the earthquake of 1481, Pierre d'Aubusson (1476–1503) began a systematic and thoroughgoing reconstruction; the curtain-walls were thickened, parapets widened, the gates reduced in number from five to three and made more difficult of access, and the ditches doubled in width. The work was completed by del Carretto (1513–21), with the technical help of Italian architects. In 1522 Villiers de l'Isle Adam, again with Italian help, organised the final defences. In 1465 the enceinte had been divided into eight sectors, each allotted to one of the 'Tongues', and this arrangement was in force at the time of the final siege.

The fortifications, strongest on the landward side, comprise a continuous vertical or scarped wall, on which is a platform or walk, 13·7m wide, also continuous, protected by battlements and embrasures sited for firing in any direction. In many sectors there is also a lower walk. This circumvallation is surrounded by an external fosse, 32–46m wide and 15–20m deep, provided with scarp and counterscarp.

We quit Citadel Square by the *Artillery Gate* and *St. Anthony's Gate* and cross the dry moats of the Palace to reach the wide parapet above the **Gate of Amboise** (1512). A bridge of three arches spans the outer moat. The main gate, which bears the arms of the Order and of Amboise, opens below us between massive cylindrical towers. In the thickness of the wall the vaulted road makes an S-bend, then passes beneath a second gate, over an inner moat, and through a third gate to a *Terreplein*, now a shaded avenue (comp. above). This was exposed to fire on all sides and still separated from the Palace and the town by a third moat with further bridges and gates.

We follow to the S the short sector of the TONGUE OF GERMANY, the least numerous defensive group. On the left we see Suleiman Square, the Clock Tower, and the mosques of Hurmale and of Suleiman. The *Bastion of St. George* has a relief of St. George on the original square tower, with the arms of Pope Martin V, of the Order, and of Grand Master Antonio Fluvian (1421–37). A polygonal bulwark was added later, and in 1496 the roadway through it was closed when the final bastion was erected. The next sector is that of the TONGUE OF AUVERGNE, ending at the circular *Tower of Spain*.

Beyond the tower is the sector of the TONGUE OF ARAGON, one of the most picturesque, which bears SE and then S. From it there is a comprehensive view, taking in the mosques of Suleiman, of Mustapha, of Ibrahim Pasha, and of Redjeb Pasha, the Tower of the Windmills, the Commercial Harbour, the Tower of St. Nicholas, the port of Mandraki, the new town and the coast of Anatolia. The ravelin was completed in 1522 which did not prevent the Turks in December making here the breach that enabled them to capture the city.

The *Tower of St. Mary* bears a relief of the Virgin and Child and an inscription dated 1441. Round the tower in 1487 a great polygonal bastion was added for the protection of the *Gate of St. Athan* by d'Aubusson; later he closed the gate. Reopened for a sortie in 1522, it was closed again by Suleiman in 1531 and remained so until 1922. The wall turns E to one of its most striking sectors, that of the TONGUE OF ENGLAND. Along it we see numerous windmills, one of them, all white, being predominant. The *Gate of Koskinou*, or Gate of St. John, shows clearly the difference between early and later military architecture. The earlier wall has a square tower with small embrasures and battlements, while the additions of c 1480 take the form of a huge bastion of horseshoe plan with ravelins and embrasures for larger artillery. Its defence was shared between the Tongues of England and PROVENCE, whose sector follows a zigzag line marked by three towers.

The large *Bastion del Carretto*, or of Italy, is a blend of an older tower and a semicircular bastion of 1515, 50m in diameter and of three storeys. The sector skirting the Bay of Akandia, fronted by a ravelin, was defended by the TONGUE OF ITALY. Nearing the mole on which is the Tower of the Windmills the wall makes a right-angled turn to the left. Just beyond the tower is the Gate of St. Catherine. The new sector, that of the TONGUE OF CASTILE, skirts the Commercial Harbour (described above). Half-way is the picturesque *Marine Gate*, with large guardrooms. Beyond it the wall coincides for a time with the E wall of the Collachium. Beyond a square tower with a chapel (frescoes), the *Arnaldo Gate* leads into Hospital Square. Passing *Arsenal Gate* we arrive at the *Gate of St. Paul*, where the wall runs both W and E along the mole. This is commanded by a tower and protected without by a low triangular curtain with a parapet. At a late period the defence of the Naillac mole was allotted to the Captain of the Port.

From the Gate of St. Paul to the Gate of Amboise (where we began) is the sector of the TONGUE OF FRANCE. This runs in a general E–W direction, passing above the Gate of Liberty. At the circular *Tower of St. Peter*, which bears a figure of St. Peter and the arms of Pope Pius II, the wall turns abruptly S and then again W. Skirting the Palace of the Grand Master, we gain Citadel Square.

TO THE ACROPOLIS, 20 minutes. We take Odhós Ethnárkhou (Arkhiepiskópou) Makaríou and pass the Soleil Hotel, in the grounds of which excavations (1960) revealed a cellar containing more than 100 intact amphorae, possibly buried in the earthquake of 227–226 BC. From Leofóros Vasilíssis Fredheríkis we take the right fork, whence Odhos Diagorídhon (right) rises towards Mt *Ayios Stefanos* (111m), a ridge called also *Mt Smith* after Adm. Sir Sidney Smith (1764–1840), who occupied a house here in 1802 while keeping watch on the French fleet. The **Acropolis**, identified in 1916 and partly excavated in 1924–29, occupies its gentle E slope. Amid olive groves (left) are a *Stadium* (restored) and a small *Theatre*, of unusual square plan (only the orchestra and three seats are original work). A massive retaining wall supports a higher terrace where the stylobate of a *Temple of Pythian Apollo* bears three corner columns tastelessly fabricated from fragments. A small fountain-house, below, has a plaster-lined cistern and feed channel with draw-basin behind. At the N end of the ridge is the site of a *Temple of Athena Polias*, marked now only by some foundations and a few column drums. Odhos Voríou Ipírou winds back down into the town.

Excursions in the Island

ROAD CONDITIONS. The road down the W coast to Ancient Kamiros and then inland almost to Embona is asphalted. On the E coast there is asphalt to Lindos and Lardhos. The unpaved roads, however, are generally much superior to those on the mainland. To those who enjoy leisurely motoring through sparsely inhabited country with varying scenery, the island offers a reasonable network of roads leading to Kattavia in the S and linking the two coasts. Below are described only excursions to places of particular interest.

TO RHODINI, 3km S on the Lindos road. This is a pleasant ancient park, where, it is said, was once the School of Rhetoric of Aeschines. The park, frequented by peacocks, is shaded by plane-trees and has a stream and ponds. There are remains of a Roman aqueduct, and about 20 minutes' walk SW is the so-called *Tomb of the Ptolemies*, a Hellenistic rock tomb with a decorated façade (restored 1924).

TO IALYSOS AND MT PHILAREMOS, 15km SW. From the Nea Agora we take any road leading W and on reaching the sea turn left and follow Leofóros Triándon, the coast road, past the huge Rodos Palace (L) and a succession of other hotels.—3km Turning (left) to *Malpasós*. On the right of this road is the *Cave of the Dragon* with a cypress in front. The legend concerning the dragon said to have been killed here by Dieudonné de Gozon, a Provençal knight who later became Grand Master (1346–53), was convincingly exploded by F.W. Hasluck ('BSA', Vol. XX).—5km *Ixia* (Hotels L, A, B, C; F/A).—9km *Triánda* (Hotels A, B, C; F/A), with 7212 inhabitants, has an interesting little church. A good road rises to the left to (15km) *Mt Phileremos*, an isolated wooded hill (267m) whose level summit (*View) was the site of **Iálysos**, one of the three ancient cities of Rhodes. The strategic value of this hill, dominating the plain, has been recognised from Phoenician times; John Cantacuzene was besieged here by the Genoese in 1248, and hence Suleiman directed the siege of Rhodes in 1522. It was contended in 1943 between the Germans and Italians. Of the classical Acropolis there remain the foundations of a 3C *Temple of Athena Ialysia*. Later remains include some ruins of a Byzantine church. Imposing, though over-restored in 1931 and given a new tower, is the Knights' church of *Our Lady of Phileremos*, with Catholic (left) and Orthodox altars. Above is the restored *Monastery*, from which a path leads N to a ruined castle of the Knights. Lower down are a *Fountain* of the 4C BC, reconstructed in 1926, and the *Necropolis* where c 500 tombs have been excavated in Late Mycenaean, Geometric, Archaic, and Classical cemeteries.

TO KALLITHEA, 10·5 km. From Arsenal Gate we follow the shore road, then, by a large cemetery (left), turn left over a bridge. Soon after, we see (right) the caves of the Hellenistic and Roman necropolis (1C BC–1C AD).—6·5km *Rení Koskinoú* (Hotels A, B, E).—10·5km *Kallithéa* (Hotel A), a strange hydropathic establishment comprising mock-Moorish buildings, gardens, and grottoes, all placed amid the natural shore rocks. The waters are recommended for various internal ailments.

FROM RHODES TO LINDOS, 55km (35 miles), bus 5 times daily, also excursion coaches daily.—3km *Rhodhiní* (see above). The road passes through varied scenery of hills interspersed with fertile plains and orange groves. White cubic houses and date palms give the villages a Saharan appearance.—13km *Faliráki* (Hotels A–E; F/A). Several roads lead down to beaches.—21km *Afándou* (Hotels A, B, D, E; F/A), the first 'Saharan' village (3723 inhab.). Near by is a U.S. transmitter that broadcasts the 'Voice of America'. To the SE, near the coast, is *Katholikí*, where the church has elements from Classical times.— 26km. Immediately after a river bridge, turning (right) to *Eleoússa*, passing (3km) the *Eptá Piyés*, seven springs which form a little lake in a gorge of pine-trees.—Our road now threads a narrow gap with *Mt Tsambika* (326m) to the left. *Moní Tsambíkas* (signposted) has an ancient tree in the courtyard and a good carved screen in the church.— We cross a ridge (233m) and descend to *Arkhángelos* (Αρχάγγελος), another village (4164 inhabitants) of African appearance, dominated by a Castle. Near by the church of Ayioi Theodhoroi (1377) has wall paintings. The road turns inland, then descends steeply to a fertile valley with nut and orange groves.—38·5km *Malóna*, from which a road (5km) descends to the coast and a promontory where stands the *Castle of Pharaklos*, one of the strongest built by the Knights. It is well seen from our road as we continue S.—Just beyond (50km) *Kálathos* the road divides, the right branch continuing to the S of the island. We turn left; from the top of a low but rocky pass we gain a sudden *View of Lindos as we descend to the village.

*Líndos (Λίνδος), now a village of 661 inhab., was the chief of the three cities before the foundation of Rhodes, and in the Middle Ages was the most important place in the island after Rhodes itself. Its delightful situation, with a beautiful beach (Hotels A; F/A; restaurants), its old houses and trafficless streets, and its superb acropolis give it a charm altogether unique.

History. The site was occupied in the 3rd millennium and a temple to Athena existed from at least the 10C BC. Thanks to a geographical position between two harbours it became the most important of the three ancient cities of Rhodes. Colonists from Lindos founded Parthenopea (forerunner of Naples) and Gela, in Sicily, during the 7C. In the 6C Lindos was governed by tyrants, the most celebrated of whom was Kleoboulos (fl. 580 BC), one of the 'Seven Sages', who had a weakness for setting and solving riddles. After the foundation of the city of Rhodes, Lindos remained the religious centre of the island. St. Paul is said to have landed at Lindos on his way to Rome. In the Byzantine era the acropolis was turned into a fortress, which the Knights of St. John made into the headquarters of a castellany, with twelve knights and a Greek garrison. In 1317 Grand Master Foulques de Villaret took refuge in the castle after the Knights had deposed him. The Turks continued to use the acropolis as a fortress. In 1902–14 and in 1952 a Danish mission excavated the acropolis, but the restorations were done by the Italians before 1938.

DOMESTIC ARCHITECTURE. In Lindos there are numerous 15C houses built in a style derived from the Gothic of the Knights with Byzantine and Oriental decoration. They have a gatehouse, a courtyard with staircase, and the main building, usually with doorways and windows elaborately carved with rope designs, doves, roses, etc. The floors are paved in black and white pebble mosaic. The reception room usually contains Lindos ware, either medieval or in modern reproduction. The ceilings are often painted.

LINDOS POTTERY. There is a story, without foundation, that in the 14C a Grand Master captured a Levantine ship in which some Persian potters were travelling, and that he forced the potters to work for him at Lindos: this is supposed to have been the origin of the Lindos dishes. Manufacture of the ware is supposed to have stopped after the Turkish occupation. In fact there were no native potteries, and all the dishes and vases came from the mainland of Asia Minor. Instead, however, of the stylised Persian decoration, the Lindos ware had floral motives, such as tulips, carnations, hyacinths, and roses in bud or in bloom, with a green background picked out in red. Since the Second World War very attractive copies of this ware have been made in Rhodes itself.

At the W end of the village is the small PLATEIA, shaded by mulberry trees, with an old fountain and two restaurants. Here, or in the road (left) towards the beach, may be found parking space. Near the Plateia donkeys may be hired for the Acropolis. In the village most of the streets are only just wide enough to take a donkey with panniers. We follow the arrows for the Acropolis, leaving on our left the Church of the Panayia (see below), and running the gauntlet of many souvenir shops. The path climbs steeply.

The **Acropolis** occupies a triangular outcrop of rock (116m) accessible only from the N side. From below it presents the aspect of a huge medieval *CASTLE remodelled and enlarged by the Knights from an earlier stronghold. Passing under the outer gate we come to a terrace, where hewn out of the rock, is an exedra with a *Relief, 4·6m long and 5·5m high, of the stern of a ship, with its lateral rudder and the helmsman's seat; the deck served as the base of a statue of a priest of Poseidon called Hagesandros (inscription). To the right of the relief are the remains of the ancient *Sacred Way*. A long staircase leads to the main gate by which we enter a vaulted passage. Above (spiral stair) is a medieval chamber, which formed part of the *Governor's Palace*. Within the battlemented enceinte is the ruined Byzantine chapel of *St. John*.

The SANCTUARY OF ATHENA LINDIA occupies the greater part of the area to the S, which is strewn with bases of statues inscribed with the names of local artists. From a huge double-winged Stoa (added c 208 BC) a monumental staircase leads to a higher terrace with foundations of the *Propylaea* built after 407 BC. The small *Temple* (23m by 7·5m) beyond, stands at the edge of the cliff near the S point of the Acropolis. The existing remains, including the W wall of the cella, date from a rebuilding after a fire in 348 BC. They overlook the smaller rock-girt harbour associated by tradition with the supposed visit of St.·Paul. The SE end of the Stoa affords a splendid *View of the *Great Harbour*, with the two islets at its entrance and the promontory beyond.

THE VILLAGE. Descending from the Acropolis and entering the village, we pass (right) the *House of Phaedra Moschorídes*, with a doorway of 1642. We may now quit the main street and explore the maze of unspoilt streets to the S, with their many old houses, courtyards, and staircases. Particular houses are not necessarily marked nor easily identified, but worth seeking out are the *House of Ioánnis Krékas*, for its wooden ceiling, and the *House of Papás Konstandínos*, the most elaborately decorated of the Lindos houses. Its gatehouse has an ogival doorway and the courtyard an elegant staircase, while the main façade is pierced by ogival and rectangular windows. At the S end of the village we see (left) an ancient wall of well-made limestone blocks, part of the peribolos of a *Temple* of the 2–1C BC. Alongside, set in the hill, is the *Theatre*. Its cavea is divided into two by a landing and into five cunei by four staircases; some 27 steps remain. Returning towards the Plateia we may visit the church of the *Panayía*, bearing the dates 1484–90 but probably earlier. It has the form of a Latin cross, with an octagonal drum and cupola. The interior has frescoes executed in 1779 by Gregory of Syme (restored 1927) and the floor is of black and white sea pebbles.

On the promontory of Ayios Aemilianós, near the NE end of the Great Harbour, is the so called *Tomb of Kleoboulos*, a pre-Hellenic cylindrical structure formed of square blocks of masonry, recalling the Lelego-Carian tombs on the mainland. The sepulchral chamber is approached by a dromos. In the Middle Ages the tomb was converted into the church of St. Aemilianos.

FROM RHODES TO KAMEIROS (36km; bus daily) AND MONOLITHOS (c 80km). This excursion may be combined with that to Ialysos (comp. above). Beyond (9km) Trianda we continue along the coast with views across the sea to the coast of Turkey.—12km *Kremasti* (Κρεμαστή; 3119 inhab.) is noted for its annual festival held on 14–23 Aug, which, like those of antiquity, combines religious ceremonies (here centred on a miraculous ikon of the Virgin) with athletic games, music, and dancing. To the S (2km) is *Maritsés*, the airport of Rhodes. Beyond, close to the shore, was found a collection of amphorae of the 2C BC, nearly all with the craftsman's name and mark, stacked and awaiting shipment.—At 18km, just after a long ford, is a turning (left) to the wooded area of Kalamon with a Cattle Breeding Station and an Agricultural School. Beyond a Boy Scout village extends the VALLEY OF BUTTERFLIES (*Petaloúdhes*). The myriad butterflies, best seen in July–August, are attracted by the thick growth of storax with its pungent scent.—The main road continues through fig orchards and past numerous wind pumps. On the outskirts of (30km) *Kalavárdha*, we bear right along the coast.

34km Turning (left, signposted) to **Kámeiros** (1km), the third of the ancient cities of Rhodes, called 'chalky' by Homer. It was rediscovered in 1859 after centuries of oblivion and excavated in 1929. The extensive REMAINS, undisturbed in the Middle Ages, occupy a gentle slope overlooking the sea. The city had neither fortifications nor acropolis. We come first to an imposing *Temenos*, or court, of the 3C BC, with scanty remains of a Doric temple, beyond which rises the main street of the town. Here a number of houses have come to light including one with a peristyle court. Above, the *Agora* consists of a long row of shops bordered by a Doric *Stoa* (3C) of which 6 columns with their entablature have been well restored. It covered a 6–5C *Cistern* made redundant by a new system of wells, a row of which may be seen behind. A few traces remain among the trees higher up of a peripteral *Temple of Athena*.

Leaving Kameiros, we may either continue along the coast road or return to the Kalavardha fork and take the asphalted inland road.

THE COAST ROAD. We pass the ruins of *Kretinae*, a city said to have been founded by Althaemenes from Crete.—42km *Mandrikó*.—45km *Kámeiros Skála*. About 6·5km out to sea is a group of islets, of which the largest is *Alímnia* (8 sq. km), with a ruined castle of Greek origin, rebuilt by the Knights. To the SW of Alimnia is Khalki.—Near (51·5km) *Kritínia* is **Kastéllos**, an important castle of the Knights, perched on a rock (130m) and dominating the sea. Probably built in 1480, it is on three levels, each assigned to a different Grand Master. It is ruinous on the precipitous NE side (*View). We turn inland.—61km *Embóna* (435m), a village growing wine and tobacco, is the starting-point for the ascent of *Mt Ataviros*, the highest mountain in the island (1215m).

The ascent takes 2 hours, and the descent about the same time. The mountain is bare of vegetation and has no springs. From the summit the whole of the island of Rhodes can be seen. On it are the scanty remains of the *Temple of Zeus Atabyros*, said to have been built by Althaemenes, founder of Kretinae (see above). It is certainly one of the oldest temples in Rhodes. It was adapted in the Byzantine era into the Church of St. John the Baptist. The site was excavated in 1927 but the cella could not be found. About 100m NE are the remains of a stoa or propylaeum. Votive offerings found on the site and now in the Rhodes Museum include bronze, lead, and terracotta statuettes of oxen, goats, and other domestic animals.

About 1km farther on we rejoin the inland road.

THE INLAND ROAD. From the Kalavardha fork we ascend the lower slopes of Mt Profitis Ilias and at 45km reach a road leading to the left up the mountainside.

This well-engineered but steep and winding road ascends continually, with fine retrospective views of the sea. It soon enters the Wood of the Prophet, luxuriant thanks to a local superstition that the prophet will slay anyone cutting down a tree. The trees are mainly pines, including umbrella pines and cypresses. 6·5km Hotels (A), in a wonderful situation 701m above the sea. The hotels are appropriately named ('Stag' and 'Doe') because of the number of deer in the neighbourhood. A path leads to the summit of Mt Prophet Elias (799m).—The road continues to Eleoúsa and the E coast.

Just short of (52km) *Embona* (comp. above) we meet the coast road. We now make a wide sweep round the foothills of Ataviros, on the E side of which is the *Monastery of Artamíti* (380m).—We continue through sparsely inhabited hills to (c 80·5km) *Siána* (443m). A steep track, ending in a dangerous descent, leads to the *Castle of Monolithos*, situated on the top of a precipitous rock called *Monopetra* (236m) and accessible only by a single path. Inside it are two cisterns and the modernised church of *Ayios Pantaléonos*, with another edifice beside it. There is a magnificent *View over the sea towards Khalki and another landwards of Mt Akramytes.—14km S of Monolithos is *Arnitha*, where an Early Christian complex has been excavated at *Ayía Iríni*.

Kastellórizo

STEAMER ('Panormítis') from Rhodes, twice weekly in 6–8 hours.

BY AIR. Occasional connections with Rhodes.

Kastellórizo, officially *Megísti*, the Italian *Castelrosso*, once celebrated for its medieval castle, belongs to the Dodecanese on ethnological rather than geographical grounds, for it is in the E Mediterranean rather than the Aegean. It is 116km E of Rhodes. Largest of a miniature archipelago lying close to the coast of Lycia, Asia Minor, it is a small triangular island 6·5km long by 3km wide, with an area of 9 sq. km and thus the smallest of the 14 islands of the Dodecanese. Of its 11 dependent islets only two, *Rhó* and *Strongilí*, are inhabited—by lighthouse-keepers. The coastline is precipitous and inaccessible save on the E side, where it forms a bay on which is the only centre of population. The interior is hilly. Cape Ayios Stefanos, at the N end of the island, is only 2·5km from the Anatolian coast. The inhabitants depend on tanks of rainwater collected during the winter rains. The chalky soil yields only olives, grapes, and vegetables in insignificant quantities.

The 222 inhabitants are mainly concentrated in the little port and village of *Kastellórizo*, or *Megísti*, on the E coast. Many thousands of Castellorizans, however, live abroad, and the island is largely supported by the remittances of its emigrants who retire here when their fortunes have been made. The port of Kastellorizo provides the only safe shelter on or near the Asiatic coast between Makri and Beirut, and the island's caiques do a lively transit trade.

History. In antiquity the island was called *Megiste*, that is, the largest of the small archipelago. Another name for it appears to have been *Kisthene*. The Turks called it *Meis*. In 1306 it was occupied by the Knights of St. John, who strengthened the existing castle and used it as a place of detention for recalcitrant knights. The island was captured in 1440 by Djemal ed Din, Sultan of Egypt, who destroyed the castle. In 1450 Alfonso I of Aragon, king of Naples, reconquered the island and rebuilt the castle. Kastellorizo remained in possession of Naples, except for short intervals, until it was captured in 1512 by the Turks. It was temporarily occupied by the Venetians in 1570 and again in 1659, when the castle was again destroyed. From 1828 to 1833 it was held by the Greeks. During the First World War it was bombarded from the Anatolian coast. Since 1920 it has shared the fortunes of the Dodecanese.

Steamer passengers land at *Mandráki*, the port of the island capital **Kastellorizo**. The Plateia is the centre of the small town. From it ascend narrow lanes, in which are houses with characteristic wooden balconies, and windows of Anatolian type. In another square is the modern church of Ayios Yeóryios and, near it, the *Cathedral* of SS. Constantine and Helena. The cathedral is divided into nave and aisles by monolithic granite columns from the Temple of Apollo at Patára, in Lycia; the columns support ogival arches. From the end of this square is a good view of Mandraki and the Anatolian coast.—From a small square near Mandraki we may take the Street of the Knights, which follows the line of the promontory guarding the harbour. Leaving the street, we turn right into a steep and partly stepped path, which leads to the *Lycian Tomb*. This is cut out of the rock and has a Doric façade and a rectangular interior. Many similar but less elaborate tombs are to be found on the Anatolian coast opposite (see below).—Higher up are the ruins of the **Castle of the Knights**. This was built by Juan Fernando Heredia, 8th Grand Master of the Knights of St. John. Its vicissitudes up to its second destruction are noted above. There survive parts of the curtain wall, and of three towers. A Doric inscription found on the site proves that a fort existed here in classical times.

A path on the right of the harbour leads to the *Palaiókastro*, on the top of Mt Viglo (270m). This is an ancient Greek stronghold built on a rectangular plan (81m by 61m). Inside are numerous cisterns and an ancient tower of squared blocks. To the E are the remains of propylaea, with a Doric inscription of the 3C or 2C BC on which is recorded the name Megiste and its dependence on Rhodes. There is a good view of the town and of the Anatolian coast.

TO THE BLUE GROTTO, 3 hours by boat. This is the most attractive excursion in the island; the best time for a visit is late afternoon. Leaving the harbour, we bear SE and follow the inaccessible coast until we come to a slight curvature of the coastline, in which is the narrow mouth of the grotto. The *•Blue Grotto, locally known as Phokeale* ('Refuge of Seals'), recalls the Blue Grotto of Capri, but it is more extensive. Its length is 40–46m, its breadth 24–30m, and its height 20–24m. As at Capri, the gorgeous colouring is said to be caused by the reflection and refraction of the sun's rays through the water. The roof on the left side has collapsed, the debris forming a little island. At the end of the cave, on the right, is another grotto.

On the Anatolian coast, opposite Kastellorizo, is the town of *Kaç (Antiphilo)*, with a Roman theatre, numerous Lycian tombs and other ancient remains.

INDEX

Ancient names are printed in CAPITALS; personal names in *italics*.

Key page to Map numbers

Toll Highway	
Main Road	
Secondary Road	
Other Road	
Railway	
Sites	general ◇ castle ☐ temple ▥ monastery ⚲
Nome Boundary	
International Boundary	

Explanation of contour

2500
2000
1600
1000
600
200
100
0

Heights in metres

14

BULGARIA

Podkova

Skalotí

Dhipótama
Melívoia
Médhousa

Melitaina
Nimfa

Perivlepton
Kariófiton
Oraíon
Ekhínos

olikarpon
Paranéstion
Dhafnón

R

Makriplávi
Pteléa
Stavroúpolis
Kekhrókambos
Xánthi
Séleron
Iasmos
Sóstis
MOSYNOS
Karidhia

Plataniá
Lekáni
Kromnikón
KOMOTINI
Kósmion

aní
Nikifóros
Toxótai
ANASTASIOUPOLIS
Amvrosia
Méga
Dhoukáton

oristí
hoxáton
Skopós
Dhialékton
Khionístra
Yenisaía
Koutsón
Sálpi
Glikonérion
Xi

Áyios
Athanásios
Kremastí
Lágos
PERITHEORION

Zigós
Gravoúsa
Khrisoúpolis
Ávdhira

Krinídhes
Néa Karváli
Ávaton
ABDERA

ACONTISMA
Eratinón
Zilóti

KAVÁLLA
NEAPOLIS
Khrisokhóri
Néa Kariá

Elevtheroúpolis
Keramotí

Néa Péramos
THASOPOULA

DISYME
AKRA
VRASIDHAS

Rakhónion
Thásos

Príno
Panayía

Kalirrákhi
Potamiá

Maríais

Limenária
Áno Theológos

PANAYIA
AKRA SALONIKOS

SIDHERITIS
AKRA
PLÁKA

AKRA
MOURTZEFLÓS
Pláka

Sardaí
Atsikí
Panayía

MYRINA
Repanídhion

Kástron
Tsimándhria
Moúdhros

Thános
Kamínia

AKRA
VATOPEDHION

ion
AKRA
AYIA IRINI

ros
Kariaí
LEMNOS

Dháfni

ATHOS
AKRA
AKRÁTHOS

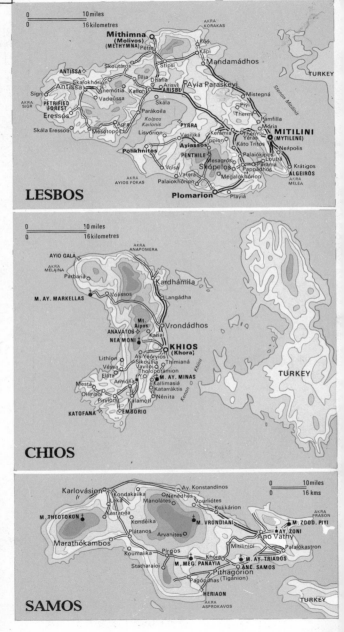